6/01

ENCYCLOPEDIA OF
EUROPEAN SOCIAL HISTORY

EDITORIAL BOARD

ENCYCLOPEDIA OF
EUROPEAN SOCIAL HISTORY

FROM 1350 TO 2000

VOLUME 1

Peter N. Stearns

Editor in Chief

Charles Scribner's Sons

an imprint of the Gale Group

Detroit • New York • San Francisco • London • Boston • Woodbridge, CT

Copyright © 2001

Charles Scribner's Sons
An imprint of the Gale Group
1633 Broadway
New York, New York 10019

1 3 5 7 9 11 13 15 17 19   20 18 16 14 12 10 8 6 4 2

Printed in United States of America

Library of Congress Cataloging-in-Publication Data
Encyclopedia of European social history from 1350 to 2000 / Peter N. Stearns, editor-in-chief.
    p.   cm.
    Includes bibliographical references and index.
    ISBN 0-684-80582-0 (set : alk. paper) — ISBN 0-684-80577-4 (vol. 1)—ISBN
0-684-80578-2 (vol. 2) — ISBN 0-684-80579-0 (vol. 3) — ISBN 0-684-80580-4 (vol. 4)
— ISBN 0-684-80581-2 (vol. 5) — ISBN 0-684-80645-2 (vol. 6)
    1. Europe—Social conditions—Encyclopedias.   2. Europe—Social life and
customs—Encyclopedias.   3. Social history—Encyclopedias.   I. Stearns, Peter N.
HN373 .E63 2000
306'.094'03—dc21
                                                                00-046376

The paper used in this publication meets the requirements of ANSI/NISO Z39.48–1992 (Permanence of Paper).

EDITORIAL AND PRODUCTION STAFF

Managing Editor
STEPHEN WAGLEY

Assistant Managing Editor
ANNA GROJEC

Manuscript Editors
JONATHAN ARETAKIS   JOHN BARCLAY   SYLVIA CANNIZZARO
GUY CUNNINGHAM   JESSICA HORNIK EVANS   MARY FLOWER
JUANITA GALUSKA   JEANNE F. KAPLAN   INGRID STERNER

Illustration Editors
NINA WHITNEY   LIBBY TAFT   CAROLE FROHLICH

Proofreaders
GRETCHEN GORDON   CAROL HOLMES   EVANGELINE LEGONES   LAURA SPECHT PATCHKOFSKY

Designers
LISA CHOVNICK   PAMELA GALBREATH

Compositor
IMPRESSIONS BOOK AND JOURNAL SERVICES, INC.

Cartographer
DONALD S. FRAZIER, FRAZIER EDUCATIONAL RESOURCES

Chronology
GREG GOODALE

Indexer
KATHARYN DUNHAM, ParaGraphs

Production Manager
EVI SEOUD

Publisher
KAREN DAY

CONTENTS

CONTENTS

CONTENTS

ix

CONTENTS

CONTENTS

CONTENTS

ALPHABETICAL TABLE OF CONTENTS

MAPS

❧❧

VOLUME 5

INTRODUCTION

Social history as a field developed in Europe. It is hardly surprising that some of the most striking discoveries and analyses in social history developed in application to the European past. French scholars first articulated some of the basic premises of the field in the early part of the twentieth century. Since then not only French but also German, Italian, and British social historians have pioneered in theoretical and methodological approaches, even as they have been increasingly joined by researchers elsewhere. Marxist contributions from eastern Europe have also played a significant role in social history's unfolding, particularly in relation to topics such as class structure. Correspondingly, social history has gained unusual stature in the discipline of history more generally in many European countries, though not without some contests—particularly in the field of teaching—about what purposes historical knowledge should serve.

European social history has often joined fruitfully with other disciplines, such as sociology, which are sometimes friendlier to historical inquiry than their counterparts in other regions. Dutch sociologists and English anthropologists have contributed important social history work. Finally, imaginative investigations of European social history, including such distinctive events as the formation of the world's first industrial proletariat, have attracted scholars from many places besides Europe itself, as the European experience becomes something of a seedbed for sociohistorical formulations more generally.

Wide agreement exists on what social history is as a particular approach to research concerning the past. Social historians explore changes and continuities in the experience of ordinary people. They pursue this focus on two assumptions: first, that groups of ordinary people have meaningful histories that help us better understand both past and present; and, second, that ordinary people often play a major, if unsung, role in causing key developments and are not simply acted upon. Further, for ordinary people and for more elite sectors, social historians probe a wide variety of behaviors and beliefs, not just political actions or great ideas. They argue that the past is formed by connections among behaviors, from family life to leisure to attitudes toward the state, and that we better understand current social concerns, such as crime or health practices, if we see how they have emerged from history. The effects of dealing with ordinary people and the sources of information available about them and of widening the facets of social life open to inquiry have generated an explosion of historical information and topics. Specialists in European social history may thus focus on kinship, sexuality, adolescence, sports, or rural protest— the range is staggering, as is the usable history now available.

While remaining true to its basic principles, social history has continued to evolve since its effective origins as an explicit field in the 1920s and 1930s. Changes have involved the use of new or revived theories. They have included varying degrees of interest in quantification. Intense concern for statistical probes, in the 1970s, has given way more recently to greater attention to cultural evidence and to links with anthropological approaches to deeply held values and rituals. Intense interest in the working class and the peasantry has persisted, but attention has been directed to other topics including gender (first, women's history and, more recently, constructions of masculinity) and age groupings from childhood to old age. Facets of behavior have expanded to include ambitious investigation of the history of the senses, of gestures, and of humor. The evolution of social history transcends Europe, of course, but many key new developments, including new topics, are often first sketched in application to European patterns.

The definition of social history and its continued dynamism must include an ongoing tension between this field and some other types of historical inquiry. Social historians often reconsider familiar historical periodization, for example. The forces that shape developments such as the Renaissance, for example, may apply more to formal politics and intellectual life than to social structures or popular beliefs and behaviors. At least conventional periodization must be tested for its applicability to social history concerns. While social historians deal with chronology and certainly with change, they typically focus less on precise dates and events, more on shifts in larger patterns such as birthrates and beliefs about women's roles. Approaches to the causes of change may alter. Despite some early definitions that argued that social history is "history with the politics left out," the role of the state remains a key topic in European social history. But social historians do not assume that the state is the source of all major historical developments or that what the state intends to do, in forging a new law or a new activity, is what actually happens, given the importance of popular reactions in reshaping day-to-day activities. The rise of social history has downgraded certain topics for historical inquiry; diplomatic history is far less lively, as a field in European history, than was the case in the 1950s. But social history has also recast certain traditional fields, leading to new efforts to explore military behavior in light of conditions of ordinary soldiers, for example, or interest in examining the actual dissemination of ideas as part of a "new" intellectual history. Here too, social historians dealing with Europe have often played a leading role in bringing about larger redefinitions.

The richness of European social history continues to develop despite some obvious difficulties in applying the characteristic methods and topics to the Continent. Social historians frequently face challenges in uncovering sources, particularly for the centuries before modern times. Some parts of Europe—Scandinavia, for example, because of the record keeping of local Lutheran churches in the seventeenth and eighteenth centuries—have better records for studying literacy and demographic behavior than others. But problems of place go beyond differential qualities of evidence. For many topics, Europe is simply not a particularly good unit, and since social historians remain wedded to specific data deriving from place, they face some real barriers to Europe-wide generalizations. Family forms, for instance, vary significantly from one region to the next; some places have typically emphasized extended family units, others have been more commonly nuclear. Trends have sometimes moved in opposite directions: notoriously, eastern Europe was tightening its manorial system in the seventeenth and eighteenth centuries, just as western Europe was largely abolishing serfdom.

As a result of these kinds of these kinds of complexities, few social historians have tackled Europe as a whole, though there are important individual efforts, particularly concerning certain aspects of popular culture and popular unrest. But if Europe is not usually a logical empirical unit, what is? Europe in modern times developed a network of nation-states, and many social historians simply use this unit as a matter of convenience; where the state causes social patterns, more than convenience may be involved. But social historians may be edgy about national histories, because they too often assume coherences that should in fact be tested. Hence, some social historians deliberately look at larger regions, like the Mediterranean, or more commonly at small regions whose geography and traditions most actively shape ordinary life. Given Europe's regional diversity, comparison is also a key methodology, and while social historians have been slow to pick up its challenge, important work has compared gender patterns or labor relations across regional and national boundaries.

A final place-related issue involves Europe's position in the world. European history has often been treated in considerable isolation, particularly after the Middle Ages when European dependence on ideas imported from Islam and the Byzantine Empire declined. European social history, focused on ordinary people and activities, might enhance the tendency to look at European patterns in isolation. Recent work, however, has partially reemphasized Europe's place in the wider world. European social patterns have often been influenced by beliefs, styles, and economic relationships involving many other areas. Correspondingly, social issues arising in Europe often spilled over to have wider impacts, including emigration to other parts of the world, imperialism, and other movements. Social historians have helped develop a new sense of Europe's wider international ties.

This Encyclopedia builds on several generations of social historical work involving Europe. It calls attention to social history dimensions for major places and periods. By discussing such topics as the relationships between state and society, the "new" military and labor history, and changes in technology and capitalism, the Encyclopedia relates sociohistorical findings to more familiar topics. The bulk of the Encyclopedia is given over, however, to examinations of central sociohistorical concerns, both groups and facets of social behavior. Sections thus bring together discussions of family history, gender, health and illness, population trends, social structure, childrearing and age relations, the body and emotions—these and other themes encompassing the range of knowledge that has developed since World War II. The opening section comprises a set of essays that explore major issues of theory and method that can be linked to more explicit topics such as social mobility or sexuality.

Essays in the Encyclopedia deal with Europe from the fourteenth and fifteenth centuries to the present. European society was hardly new at the end of the Middle Ages, but changes in family structures (the rise of the "European-style" family in some areas), the beginnings of a more commercial economy with attendant changes in class structure, and cultural shifts associated with the Renaissance and with religious change helped set a number of new social trends in motion. In addition to explicit discussions of periodization, topical essays devote careful attention to the major periods—the breaks in direction and causes of change—relevant to specific subjects such as crime or recreation. Topical essays also take into account the crucial issues of regional diversity, such as the extent to which various parts of Europe (south, east, northwest, and so on) and sometimes different nations need to be differentiated and compared, and the extent to which they can be subsumed under larger patterns.

European social history is a work in progress. Debates persist. Comparative work for many subjects is still in its infancy. New topics continue to emerge, along with new uses of source material and novel connections between the social history approach and other kinds of history, cultural analysis, and social science. The Encyclopedia emphasizes what is already known, but it also supports the further quest.

Encyclopedia of European Social History contains 209 articles arranged in twenty-three topical sections. The articles were contributed by nearly 170 scholars from twenty-nine American states, four Canadian provinces, nine European countries, and Australia. Each article is followed by cross-references to related articles and each article includes a bibliography. To aid the reader of this thematically arranged encyclopedia, an alphabetical table of contents appears in the frontmatter of each volume. A comprehensive index is included in volume 6.

The illustrations were chosen by the Scribner staff, which was also responsible for the captions. The chronology was prepared by Greg Goodale of George Mason University and the Scribner staff. Biographies of nearly three hundred figures important in social history—historical figures, monarchs and government officials, contemporary interpreters of society, and social historians—in volume 6 are taken from publications of the Gale Group, available in the Gale Biography Resource Center and adapted for the Encyclopedia. Sincere thanks are due to Stephen Wagley, who coordinated and motivated this project with uncommon skill.

Peter N. Stearns
1 October 2000

CHRONOLOGY

The chronology is arranged by decade; the first section covers the first half of the fourteenth century. Most decades include a summary of general trends, a selection of notable events year by year, and important rulers and government officials. Some decades beginning in the late nineteenth century include notable publications and achievements in the study of social history.

1300–1350

Albigensian heresy is suppressed in France and Italy; Montaillou in southern France is one of the last strongholds. Growth of trade fairs, the largest of which are held in Lyon, Bruges, Antwerp, and Geneva. Italians develop shipping insurance to protect against loses that result from rough seas, pirates, highwaymen, and other hazards. Black Death kills approximately 25 million Europeans between 1346 and 1352; most regions experience two centuries of labor shortages and do not return to preplague populations until the mid-sixteenth century.

Popes begin residence in Avignon (1305). Beginning of Hundred Years' War (1337). Artisans briefly seize control of Nürnberg's government (1348). Giovanni Boccaccio sets his *Decameron* (1348–1353) in the plague years.

1350s

The concept of a public health commission evolves in Venice in order to combat further visitations of the plague. Travel accounts including John of Mandeville's are evidence of continuing curiosity of Europeans about geography even as exploration slows due to collapse of the Mongol Empire.

English Parliament passes the Statute of Laborers fixing wages in response to demand for scarce labor resulting from the plague (1351). Ottoman Empire expands into Europe (1353). Paris merchants briefly seize power from a weak monarch as rural peasants rise against the French nobility (Jacquerie of 1358).

1360s

Revolts against monarchs and nobles result from increased power of laborers during the decades following the Black Death. Rebellion of laboring classes in Ypres (Low Countries; 1366). Wool workers and other laborers in Florence, having established unions (1345), strike and attempt a revolution; they fail (1368). Brethren of the Free Spirit, Beghards, Beguines, and Konrad Schmid's flagellant movement in central Holy Roman Empire.

1370s

Working class rebellions continue throughout Europe. Playing cards are introduced into Europe. John Wycliffe criticizes papal authority and church's sacramental doctrine, defends England's decision to end payments to the pope, who is financing France's military campaigns against England during the Hundred Years' War.

Charterhouse, first English public school is established (1371). Dancing at festivals turns into mass manias in Aix, Cologne, and Metz (1372). Pope Gregory XI leaves Avignon and reestablishes the papacy in Rome (1377). Western Schism begins upon Gregory's death as competing popes are elected (1378); Urban VI remains in Rome, Clement VII settles in Avignon. Revolutionary governments in Florence (Ciompi, or wool-carders, revolt, 1378–1382) and Ghent (Low Countries; 1379–1382)

1380s

Nürnberg and Bruges (Low Countries) pay midwives out of city funds to assist poor women. Rapid European conquests by Ottoman Empire in the Balkans begin.

Riots occur in Strasbourg, Paris, and southern France over the imposition of new taxes (1380). Wat Tyler leads peasant revolt in England (1381) to protest the Statute of Laborers and high poll taxes; he is supported by followers of Wycliffe who preach egalitarianism and millenarianism. Nicole Oresme opposes astronomy and magic in *De divinatione* (1382).

1390s

Humanist scholarship and the revival of interest in classic Greek and Roman authors begins in Italy. Witchcraft trials are held in Boltinger (Switzerland).

University of Bologna awards a medical degree to a woman (1390). *Le menagier de Paris*, French handbook of household management (c. 1393). Wycliffites, now called "Lollards," petition English Parliament to reform the Church by rejecting corruption, clerical misbehavior, transubstantiation, and auricular confession (1395).

1400s

Persecution of Lollards and other heretics in England. English Parliament prohibits the making of gold or silver by alchemy. Eustache Deschamps' *Demonstrations contre sortilege* (Demonstrations against sorcery) argues against contacting the dead. Christine de Pisan's *Livre de la cité des dames* (Book of the city of ladies; 1404–1405). University of Paris counts 10,000 students in 1406, nearly 20,000 by 1490. Bethlehem (Bedlam) Hospital in London becomes an asylum for the mentally disabled (1402). Similar asylum is founded in Valladolid, Spain (1409).

1410s

Teachings of John Wycliffe influence John Hus, advocate for church reform in Bohemia; Hus is executed at the Council of Constance (1415). Hus's followers in Bohemia break from the Roman church and lift restrictions on serfs. After Emperor Wenceslaus IV dies (1419), they war with church and Empire. The war is partly based on nationalist antipathy toward Germans who have migrated into Bohemia. Western Schism ends with the election of Martin V (1417). Prince Henry of Portugal establishes a school of navigation at Sagres (1419).

1420s

Thomas à Kempis's *De imitatione Christi (On the Imitation of Christ)* extols the virtues of humility and is rapidly adapted by French, English, Polish, and other translators. In Bohemia Taborites break from the Hussites to form egalitarian millennialist movement. In Würzberg (Germany), labor shortages and wage discrepancies result in the employment of more women than men in building trades during the next century.

Joan of Arc leads military campaign against England. *Catasto*, a form of income tax, is imposed in Florence (1427), the accounting for which indicates that 4.74 people live in the average rural household, while 3.91 people live in the average urban household.

1430s

Scotland and Florence require their citizens to conform to dress codes appropriate to class (sumptuary laws); England and German and Spanish towns adopt similar ordinances. Consumption of alcohol after dark is prohibited in Scotland (1430). Peasant revolts occur in Worms (Germany; 1431), Saxony, Silesia, the Rhineland, Brandenburg (1432), Norway, Sweden (1434), and Hungary (1437). Medici family dominates government in Florence that is favorable to learning and the arts. Utraquists (Hussites who wished to receive communion in both kinds, bread and wine) reconciled with the Catholic Church (1436). Reconciliation of Roman and Orthodox churches at the Council of Florence (1439).

1440s

Portuguese explorers sailing down the west coast of Africa make contact with black Africans; by 1448, 800 Africans are enslaved and living in Portugal. European explorations will lead to further questioning of Christianity and Europe's centrality. Johan Gutenberg begins the development of a printing press; printing presses are introduced into much of Western Europe by the end of the century; initial output is mainly religious texts. Peasant revolt in Denmark (1441).

1450s

Hundred Years' War concludes as France reconquers its territory from the English, except Calais. Gutenberg prints Vulgate Bible.

Jack Cade's peasant revolt in England demands egalitarian reforms and forces the repeal of Statutes of Laborers (1450). Ottoman Turks capture Constantinople (1453). Siena enacts legislation to encourage marriages by denying bachelors employment in government positions (1454). Government of Florence pays dowries for poor women. Women demand and receive restrictions on unlicensed silk weavers in Cologne (1456). Salzburg (Austria) peasants revolt against the Empire as a result of a tax imposed on cattle; revolt spreads to Styria, Carinthia, and Carniola (1458).

1460s

Sforza family comes to power in Milan, beginning competition with Florence for cultural supremacy in Italy.

Franciscans institute an interest-free loan program, the *monte di pietà,* for the poor (1463). Bowling is banned in England (1465), football and golf in Scotland (1467) as part of new elites' attacks on popular culture. Catholics, in power again in Bohemia, return peasants to serfdom. The Church of the Moravian Brethren is founded (1457); its adherents will reject the authority of the Catholic Church in 1467.

1470s

Physicians begin to categorize epidemics scientifically as opposed to calling all outbreaks "the plague." Attacks occur in Spain against Jews who had recently been converted to Christianity.

Hans Bohm, preaching egalitarianism and millenarianism and demanding social justice and religious reform, leads a peasant agitation in Würzburg (Germany; 1470). Typhus appears in Europe (1477). The Spanish inquisition is placed under both clerical and state authority by the pope (1478).

Isabella, queen of Castile (1474–1504). Ferdinand II, king of Aragon (1479–1516) and, as Ferdinand V, king of Castile (1474–1504).

1480s

In Florence, 28 percent of boys receive education from formal schools. Spanish inquisition assumes authority to rule on heresy, apostasy, sorcery, sodomy, polygamy, and blasphemy. Cities in Aragon attempt to block inquisitors from entering their walls; rural peasants join inquisitors and the monarchy in demanding the cities yield.

Papal bull warns against dangers of witchcraft (1484). Women in France are prohibited from employment as surgeons (1485). *Malleus Maleficarum* (Hammer of witches; 1486). Bartolomeu Dias rounds the Cape of Good Hope (1488).

1490s

Syphilis appears in Europe. Antonio de Nebrija, *Gramática de la lengua catellana* (1492). Spain conquers Granada from last Muslim rulers in Iberian Peninsula (1492). Spain expels Jews (1492). Christopher Columbus sails west, lands in Western Hemisphere (1492). Bundschuh, organized peasant movement, revolts in Alsace and southern Germany (1493). French under Charles VIII invade Italy. Girolamo Savonarola, Dominican friar and church reformer, dominates government of Florence (1494–1498). Poland restricts movement of serfs (1496 and 1501). Pawnshop opens in Nürnberg (1498).

1500s

Population growth in western Europe; populations of Spain, Naples, and Sicily will double in sixteenth century; population of London will increase from 40,000 to 200,000. 154 European cities have more than 10,000 inhabitants. Some city governments begin to buy food stocks for emergencies. Florence has seventy-three charitable organizations; England has 460 hospitals. In England, serfs constitute only 1 percent of the total population.

Pedro Alvares Cabral lands in Brazil (1500). In Speyer (Germany) antifeudal peasant revolt occurs (1502). Beginning in 1505, the newspaper *Zeitungen* is sporadically published. Nürnberg licenses prostitutes to counter unlicensed houses of prostitution (1508). Erasmus, *The Praise of Folly* (1509).

Henry VIII, king of England (1509–1547).

1510s

The bishop of London orders midwives to be licensed to practice. Women are permitted to practice surgery throughout England. Attempt to introduce the inquisition to Naples fails in the face of popular opposition. Tens of thousands of peasants successfully, though briefly, revolt in Styria and Carinthia (Austria) against feudalism. Publishing spreads rapidly in Germany as a result of religious controversies and the decline of publishing in Italy. 150 books are published in Germany (1518), 990 will be published in 1524. The City of Cracow opens a library for the public.

Peasants in Bern canton revolt during Carnival (1513). Hungarian peasants revolt against the Holy Roman Empire (1514). Fifth Lateran Council (1512–1517) allows the Franciscans to charge interest in their pawnshops. Erasmus publishes New Testament in Greek (1516). Martin Luther posts Ninety-five Theses (1517). Erasmus, *Colloquies* (1518).

Francis I, king of France (1515–1547). Charles V, Holy Roman Emperor (1519–1558) and king of Spain as Charles I (1519–1556).

1520s

Communeros revolt in Spain (1519–21). Martin Luther's address to German nobles; he is excommunicated by the pope (1520). He affirms the authority of ecumenical councils over the pope and publishes a German translation of the Bible (1522–1534). Peasants demand egalitarianism and religious reform during the German Peasants' War (1524–1525). The Swedish Diet of Vesteres, at which miners and peasants are represented, adopts Lutheranism (1527). Henry VIII of England applies to the pope for an annulment (1527). Imperial army sacks Rome (1527). Venice imposes censorship on its printers (1527).

1530s

Castiglione's *Book of the Courtier* (1528) becomes popular throughout Europe as a guide to proper elite manners. Plague, famine, and war have reduced Rome's population to 40,000; by 1600, its population will be 105,000. Radical Refomers (Anabaptists) gain adherents from Switzerland to the Dutch provinces and assume power in Münster and Lübeck. In Münster they are suppressed by allied Catholics and Lutherans (1534–1535). Act of Supremacy separates English church from Roman church (1534). Prussia restricts movement of serfs (1538). France institutes a public lottery (1539). The most popular books in France are the Bible, *The Imitation of Christ,* and *Gargantua* by François Rabelais.

1540s

Spain's Bolivian mines flood Europe with silver, causing economic instability. By 1542, Italian bankers are charging a 26 percent interest rate against Spain.

Society of Jesus (Jesuits) is sanctioned by the pope (1540). Nicolaus Copernicus, *De revolutionibus orbium coelestium* (On the revolution of the heavenly spheres; 1543). Council of Trent begins its meetings (1545–1563). The Pitaud rebellion seizes Limoges (France), demanding "public freedom and public repose" (1548). Ket's Catholic Rebellion in England, a response to religious conflict and the overabundance of labor; Ket briefly establishes a commune in Norwich (1549). Jesuits open their first school in Messina, Sicily (1549).

Edward VI, king of England (1547–1553). Henry III, king of France (1547–1559). Catherine de Médicis, queen of France (1547–1589).

1550s

Plans to divert sewers into the Seine River are thwarted because half of all Parisians drink from it. Bridewell Hospital creates a workhouse for London's poor. Consumerism is reflected by the popularity of earrings in France, the existence of nineteen sugar refineries in Antwerp, the introduction of tobacco to Spain, and the licensing of alehouses in England.

Hamburg merchants create a stock exchange (1558). France prohibits abortion (1556). The Papal *Index Librorum Prohibitum* (Index of forbidden books) is instituted (1559).

Mary I, queen of England (1553–1558). Philip II, king of Spain (1556–1599). Elizabeth I, queen of England (1558–1603).

1560s

In Poland, 12 percent of boys attend school. London's Merchant Tailor's school designs a curriculum to provide similar education for girls and boys. Toledo counts 50,000 textile laborers. Martin Guerre is tried and executed in Languedoc (see Natalie Z. Davis's *Return of Martin Guerre*). Scotland burns 8,000 witches between 1560 and 1600. Johan Wier condemns the idea of witchcraft and is sent into hiding by severe criticism. Iced cream is introduced in Italy.

Beginning of Wars of Religion in France (1562). England enacts a law for poor relief (1563). England is involved in slave trading and piracy. A Papal Bull is issued against bullfighting (1567); it is ignored in Spain, where many fear prohibiting the popular pastime would lead to riots.

James VI, king of Scotland (1567–1625) and king of England as James I (1603–1625).

1570s

In Norwich (England), 80 percent of girls aged 6 to 12 work, while only 33 percent of boys do; another 33 percent of boys are in school. Dice and stage plays are popular in England; permanent theaters are constructed in London.

Christian naval victory at Lepanto (1571). Strikes against a new Spanish tax occur in the Netherlands (1571). England legalizes credit sales of necessities (1572). Thousands of French Huguenots are killed during the St. Bartholomew's Day Massacre (1572). In Germany, the braziers' guild imposes a 92-hour workweek (1573). Confederation of Warsaw grants freedom of religion to all sects (1573).

Rudolf II, Holy Roman Emperor (1576–1612).

1580s

Russia restricts movement of serfs, a result of labor surpluses. Jesuits establish Sunday schools for child laborers in the Netherlands. Compulsory and universal education is instituted in Württemberg. Puritan sects break from the Church of England. Potatoes, eggplant, tomatoes, and coffee are introduced in England, where prices for all goods double over next sixty years, while wages increase by only 20 percent (price revolution). The Catholic Jean Bodin and the Protestant King James VI of Scotland reaffirm the evils of witch magic, while astrology is condemned by the Spanish inquisition and Pope Sixtus V.

Pope Gregory XIII decrees new calendar (1582). Spanish Armada sails against England (1588). 100,000 Parisians stage a march against the Huguenots (1589).

Henry IV, king of France (1589–1610).

1590s

Amsterdam's population grows from 75,000 (1590) to 300,000 (1620). Artisans in Amsterdam develop magnifying lenses, resulting in the production of telescopes and microscopes that will prove the heliocentric system and discover microscopic life. Spain experiences famine, plague, and labor shortages (1599–1600). Theaters in England are ordered closed on Thursdays to avoid competition with bull baiting. New poor laws create workhouses throughout England.

Wars of Religion in France end with conversion to Catholicism of Henry IV, first Bourbon king (1594). After Jesuits are briefly expelled, the Edict of Nantes compels religious toleration in France (1598). The second inquisition trial of Menocchio results in his execution (1599–1600; see Carlo Ginzberg's *Cheese and the Worms*).

1600s

Spain's population declines while England's doubles during the seventeenth century. Ursulines advance the education of girls in Catholic Europe. In England, approximately 10 percent of women are literate. The regular use of knives and forks is introduced to England and France from Italy. France begins an ambitious road building program; peasants are forced to build roads without pay through the corvée. Tulips become a popular consumer good in the Netherlands.

German brothels are shut down for health reasons (1601). The English Cotswald games, a festival of rural sports, begin (1604), lasting until 1852. Peasants led by Ivan Bolotnikov revolt in Russia (1606–1607). Galileo constructs refracting telescope to observe the heavens (1609).

James I, king of England (1603–1625) and king of Scotland as James VI (1567–1625).

1610s

The growth of Jesuit influence over education is reflected by their 372 colleges (1615); by 1700, they will manage 769 colleges and 24 universities. In England, tobacco and alcohol are denounced; football is prohibited.

Bohemian towns revolt against the Empire (1609–1620). Religious and nationalist revolts in Russia expel Polish armies (1610–1611). Millenarian, egalitarian, and charismatic sects emerge in England. During an Estates General in France the third estate attacks the taille (headtax; 1614). Pope forbids Galileo to defend Copernican system (1616). Dutch Republic and Saxe-Weimar implement compulsory education (1618–1619). Beginning of Thirty Years' War (1618–1648).

Louis XIII, king of France (1610–1643).

1620s

In Spain, a book is published detailing a method of communication for individuals who are mute (1620). In the Netherlands Jan Baptista von Helmont uses magnetism to "cure" disease; he is tried by an ecclesiastic court for denying the cures are the workings of God (1621). Cardinal Richelieu becomes chief minister of king of France (1624). Publication of William Harvey's tract on the circulation of blood (1628) and successful blood transfusion. A plague kills approximately 1 million in Italy (1629–1631).

Charles I, king of England (1625–1649).

1630s

Advertising appears in Paris. Due to the availability of sugar, lemonade becomes popular in France. Tobacco sales in France are restricted to medicinal needs. Hotel Dieu Paris trains midwives.

Galileo, *Dialogo sopra i due massimi sistemi del mondo* (1633). Trial of Galileo before inquisition (1633). Theophraste Renaudot establishes a free medical clinic for Paris's poor (1635). King Charles I permits Englishmen to watch and participate in sports on Sundays (1636); Puritans condemn this and all festivals. Opera house is built in Venice (1637). Tulip market crashes, causing economic hardship in the Netherlands (1637). Antitax uprising in Perigord (1637–1641) establishes communes and briefly captures town of Bergerac.

1640s

Jansenism grows in opposition to Jesuits in France. Scotland bans scores of holidays.

English Civil War (1641–1649) ends in establishment of Commonwealth dominated by religious Dissenters (non-Anglicans), many of whom advocate universal suffrage, egalitarianism, and millenarianism. Neapolitans briefly remove the Spanish governor from power and rescind taxes during the Mansaniello Revolt (1647). Treaty of Westphalia ends Thirty Years' War (1648); Germany's population has fallen by one-third due to the war, famine, plague, and emigration; nobles appropriate "deserted" lands. Shabbetai Tzevi proclaims himself the Jewish Messiah (1648), gaining adherents throughout Europe. Fronde of the Parlement opposes royal government in France (1648–1649). Cossacks and Tartars revolt against Poland transferring the Ukraine to Russia (1648–1656). Russia places new restrictions on movement of serfs (1649). Execution of King Charles I of England (1649).

Louis XIV, king of France (1643–1715).

1650s

Commonwealth in England. Jews are allowed to immigrate to England. London's first coffeehouse opens; by 1700, 3,000 coffeehouses will have been established there. In England, introduction of postage stamps places the burden of paying on the sender; the penny post leads to stagecoaches and public intercity travel; hackney coaches, an early form of public transportation, had been introduced in the 1620s.

Second Fronde in France (1650–1653). A court in Cambridge punishes two preachers because they are women (1653). Picture book for children is published in Nürnberg (1654). James Harrington, *Commonwealth of Oceana* (1656).

Oliver Cromwell, lord protector of England (1653–1658).

1660s

France reduces festival days from fifty-five to twenty-one. Jean-Baptiste Colbert attempts to control arts, crafts, and industry in France. Cities throughout Europe in this period increase in size because of emigration from the countryside; urban mortality rates remain higher than urban birthrates.

Restoration of English monarchy with restrictions (1660). Amsterdam has sixty sugar refineries (1661). Omnibus service (*carosse à cinq sols*) estab-

lished in Paris (1662). Two-thirds of Englishmen migrate from their home parishes; many to London where the plague of 1665 and the Great Fire of 1666 kill tens of thousands. Salamanca University's student enrollment falls from 7,800 to 2,076 in 1700. Shabbetai Tzevi lands in Constantinople, converts to Islam (1666).

Charles II, king of England and Scotland (1660–1685).

1670s

Plagues in central Europe kill hundreds of thousands. Minute hands appear on watches. Peasant revolts occur in Bordeaux and Brittany over taxes and food shortages. Salons and participation by women in intellectual pursuits increasing among the upper classes in France.

Stenka Razin leads Cossacks and peasants in a rebellion along the Don and Volga Rivers in Russia (1670–1671). Craftsmen and factory workers in Amsterdam, Haarlem, and Leiden go on strike (1672). A fashion magazine appears in Paris (1672). François Poullain de La Barre in *De l'egalite des sexes* advocates equality for women, particularly in education (1673). Antoni van Leeuwenhoek develops microscope (1674). Laborers in England riot against modern looms (1675). Leeuwenhoek observes spermatozoa (1677).

1680s

Street lighting is introduced in London. The pressure cooker is invented in London, leading to better food preservation.

French court settles in Versailles (1682). Turks besiege Vienna and are repulsed (1683); Austrians begin advance against Ottoman Empire in the Balkans. Peasants in England revolt against a new tax on gin, forcing the government to withdraw the tax; 537,000 gallons of gin are distilled (1684). In France, Louis XIV revokes the Edict of Nantes (1685); French and Savoyan Huguenots, Jews, and Waldensians are expelled or forcibly converted. Tottenham High Cross girls' school near London reforms its curriculum to include natural sciences, astronomy, and geography (1687). Isaac Newton, *Principia mathematica* (1687). Last execution of a religious heretic in Poland (1689). Act of Toleration in England (1689).

Peter I (the Great), emperor of Russia (1682–1725). James II, king of England and Scotland (1685–1688). William III (1689–1702) and Mary II (1689–1694), king and queen of England, Scotland, and Ireland.

1690s

English societies to improve manners, combat drunkenness, and fight immorality are established. Press censorship largely ends in England. Sweden and France follow (1766, 1796). Brandenburg, Anhalt-Dessau, and Russia require men to enter military service. Peter the Great imposes a tax on beards to raise money and requires that European fashions be worn.

A stream-driven pump is devised in France (1690). Bank of England established (1694). Scotland and France institute universal compulsory education for boys and girls (1696 and 1698). English manufactured goods exports rise from a value of 3,873,000 pounds (1699–1701) to 8,487,000 pounds (1772–1774). Over 100 fairy tales are published in France between 1690 and 1710.

1700s

English, Portuguese, French, and others ship approximately 6 million African slaves to the Americas during the eighteenth century. European grain production doubles or triples between 1700 and 1900. Aristocratic birthrates begin to fall. Physicians begin assisting normal births, replacing midwives. City of Berlin taxes unmarried women. In France, the average marrying age for women rises from 22 to 26.5 years by 1789. Denmark abolishes serfdom. Russia extends serfdom to industrial work; peasants revolt. Convicts are sent to Siberia. Mass opposition in France temporarily forces the government to withdraw plans for new taxes.

Peter the Great founds St. Petersburg, Russia (1703); 40,000 men are compelled to drain St. Petersburg's bogs. Epidemics kill approximately 1 million people in central Europe (1709–1711).

Frederick I, first king of Prussia (1701–1713). Anne, queen of Great Britain and Ireland (1702–1714).

1710s

Britain's periodical circulation reaches 44,000 per week.

English textile workers strike against looms (1710). A steam engine pumps water out of mines near Wolverhampton, England (1712). Executions for witchcraft end in England, Prussia, France, and Scotland (1712–1722). Bernard Mandeville, *The Fable of the Bees* (1714). Lady Montagu innoculates her son against smallpox while in the Ottoman Empire (1717);

the practice spreads slowly in Europe. Prussia mandates school attendance (1717) and frees serfs on crown lands (1718).

George I, king of Great Britain and Ireland (1714–1727). Louis XV, king of France (1715–1774).

1720s

In England, approximately 25 percent of women are literate. Expansion of Freemasonry in Great Britain and Europe. The average Englishman consumes one ounce of tea per month (by the 1820s this figure is one ounce of tea per week). Consumption of sugar doubles in England between the 1720s and the 1820s; between 1700 and 1787 European sugar imports rise from 57,000 tons to 286,000 tons. Enclosure laws affect approximately 50 percent of agricultural lands in England; peasants and yeomen resist enclosure.

French authorities capture Cartouche and his 500 highwaymen (1721). Women lead a revolt against bakers in Paris (1725). *Gay's Fables* (1726) is a popular book for English children. Quakers advocate the abolition of slavery (1727).

George II, king of Great Britain and Ireland (1727–1760).

1730s

Brown rats spread throughout Europe, reducing the incidence of plagues; the house cat is an increasingly valued pet. Pet ownership in general is popular among the middle class. Russian peasants are responsible for the soul tax, recruiting levies, and *corvées* (required labor). French peasants lose one-third of their income in taxes and *banalités* (required labor) and must spend twelve to fifteen days a year repairing roads. Two centuries after English replaced Latin in religious ceremonies of the Church of England, English replaces Latin in court proceedings.

France prohibits barbers from performing surgery, setting a trend toward professionalization (1731). A women earns a degree at the University of Bologna (1732). Invention of flying shuttle (1733), part of growth of technological changes that lead to accelerated domestic production in Britain. England's Parliament imposes high duties to discourage gin consumption (1736). John Wesley begins open-field preaching (1739).

Anna Ivanovna, empress of Russia (1730–1740).

1740s

Anti-Semitic pogroms occur in Russia. In Prussia, freedom of worship and the press is granted. Expansion of factories in England, requiring twelve to fourteen hours of work per day, six days a week and beginning the separation of work from home life. Cotton factories are built in Birmingham and Wolverhampton, and an iron rolling mill opens (1740s–1755).

First conference of Methodists (1744). In London, a clinic opens for treating sexually transmitted diseases (1747).

Frederick II (the Great), king of Prussia (1740–1786). Maria Theresa, Holy Roman Empress (1740–1780). Elizabeth Petrovna, empress of Russia (1741–1762).

1750s

Mortality rates fall rapidly leading to a doubling or tripling of populations of Russia, England, and Spain over the next century.

Voltaire in Prussia (1750–1753). Portugal restrains the activities of its Inquisition (1751). Jews are legally permitted to naturalize in Britain after 1753. University of Moscow founded (1755). Seven Years' War (1756–1763). A chocolate factory opens in Germany (1756). High rates of poverty and illegitimacy are reflected by the 15,000 children abandoned to the London Hospital (1756–60). A women earns a degree at the University of Halle (1754). Portugal expels Jesuits (1759).

1760s

Freedom of the press granted in Sweden.

Jean-Jacques Rousseau's *Émile* (1762) advocates children be taught "naturally." Rousseau's *Du contrat social* (1762). A woman becomes editor of the *Reading Mercury* (1762). Paris prohibits smallpox vaccinations (1763). Norwegians revolt against Danish taxation (1765). France expels Jesuits (1764). Cesare Beccaria, *Dei delitti et delle pene* (1764) espouses penal reform. Residents of Saragossa (Spain) revolt and sack their city (1766). Vienna's Prater Park is opened to all citizens (1766). Spain expels Jesuits (1769). Day care is provided in Alsace (1769).

George III, king of Great Britain and Ireland (1760–1820). Catherine II (the Great), empress of Russia (1762–1796). Joseph II, Holy Roman Emperor (1765–1790).

1770s

Major plague in eastern Europe.

Pope Clement XIV suppresses Society of Jesus (1773); the closing of Jesuit schools disrupts education across Europe. Pugachev's Russian peasant revolt nearly succeeds (1773–1775). The industrial revolution advances in England where a spinning mill is built, a national hatters union forms, a court rules that slavery in the homeland is illegal, and Lancashire laborers destroy factories (1779). 18,000 spectators attend a English cricket match (1772). Savoy abolishes serfdom (1771); France abolishes provincial parliaments (1771). Price riots and "the Flour Wars" occur in Rouen, Reims, Dijon, Versailles, Paris, and Pontoise. Johann Pestalozzi founds an orphan school in Zurich advancing Rousseauean educational reforms and the kindergarten concept (1774). There are 77 hospital beds for Brussels' 70,000 inhabitants (1776). F. A. Mesmer expelled from Paris (1778).

Louis XVI, king of France (1775–1792).

1780s

In France, 40,000 children are abandoned every year of this decade. After Britain's loss of thirteen North American colonies, Parliament begins to enact political reforms, a process that ends because of the French Revolution.

Last execution of a witch occurs in Switzerland (1782). Revolt by disenfranchised Genevans briefly creates a representative government (1782). Thirteen British colonies in North America become independent as "United States" (1783). A school for the blind is established in Paris (1784). An English court rules that foxhunting cannot constitute trespass (1786). United States adopts constitution (1787–1788). Edict of Toleration for Protestants in France (1787). Britain begins transporting convicts to Australia (1788). Jeremy Bentham, *Introduction to the Principles of Morals and Legislation* (1789).

French Revolution begins as Louis XVI convokes Estates General; oath of the Tennis Court; fall of the Bastille; National Assembly abolishes feudal institutions; Great Fear in countryside (1789).

1790s

Continuation of French Revolution: republic established (1792); King Louis XVI executed (1793); Reign of Terror (1793–1794). Half of France's agricultural lands become peasant owned. Economic confusion and famine result in food riots; armed resistance to Revolution in the Vendée. French Revolutionary wars (1792–1802).

France grants liberty to Protestants and Jews (1790). France legalizes divorce (1792). Denmark abolishes slave trade (1792). France abolishes slave trade and slavery (1794). Freedom of the press granted in France (1796). Illegitimacy rates reach 15 to 20 percent in western Europe partly as a result of urbanization. Combination Acts (1799, 1800) in Britain curb the ability of labor to organize. Paris Zoo opens (1793). Condorcet, *Esquisse d'un tableau historique des progrès de l'esprit humaine* (1795). Thomas Malthus, *An Essay on the Principle of Population* (1798).

Francis II, last Holy Roman Emperor (1795–1806), and, as Francis II, first emperor of Austria (1804–1835).

1800s

360 cities have over 10,000 inhabitants. Accurate censuses reveal the populations (in millions) of Britain and Ireland, 15.6; France, 28; Germany, 27; Italy, 17–18. Population of London is 864,000; population of Paris is 547,756. Europe's annual population growth rate will be 7.6 percent during the nineteenth century.

In France, domination of Napoleon (to 1815). Concordat between France and the papacy restores Catholic Church (1802). Napoleonic Code codifies French civil law (1804). Napoleonic Wars (1802–1815). Spain's Latin American colonies take advantage of the situation and stage successful wars of independence (to 1820s)

Robert Owen creates a utopian factory town in New Lanark, Scotland (1800). Philippe Pinel, *Traité sur l'aliénation mentale ou la manie* (1801). Serbs revolt against the Ottoman Empire (1804–1813). Emancipation of serfs in Prussia (1807). Britain abolishes slave trade (1808).

Alexander I, emperor of Russia (1801–1825).

1810s

Continuation of Napoleonic Wars (to 1815). Restoration and reaction throughout Europe following defeat of Napoleon. Scottish mill workers are 69 percent female; 46 percent are under age eighteen. Transportation improvements include the rapid spread of macadamized roads, public omnibuses, steamship service (1819–1840s).

Canneries are built in London and Paris (1810 and 1811). Luddites destroy machines in Nottingham and Yorkshire (1811). Regency Act in Great Britain (1811). Friederich Ludwig John establishes a gymnastic society in Berlin (1811). Prussia emancipates Jews (1812). One-fifth of Tuscans and one-third of Florentines require public assistance (1812); 35 percent of poor families here are headed by a single mother; *monte di pieta* (loan office and pawnshop) provides hundreds of thousands of small loans. First European steamship, Henry Bell's *Comet* (1812). Labor strikes in England (1818–1819) culminate in the Peterloo Massacre at Manchester; reforms improving conditions and establishing a twelve-hour workday are passed by Parliament. First crossing of Atlantic Ocean by a steamship, *Savannah* (1819).

1820s

Revolution in Spain reinstates the mostly liberal 1812 constitution, though it prohibits freedom of worship. Francis Place educates Britain's laboring classes about contraceptives.

200,000 Greeks die seeking independence from the Ottoman Empire (1821–1829). Britain's Parliament passes liberal reform legislation, including laws criminalizing the abuse of domestic animals, allowing labor to organize, and permitting Catholics to hold public office (1822–1828). First steam-powered passenger railway, the Stockton-Darlington Railway, in England (1825). Anthelme Brillat-Savarin, *La physiologie du goût* (1825). F. W. A. Froebel, *The Education of Man* (1826). Peasant revolts begin in Russia (1826); sporadic revolts to 1860s. Saint-Simon, *L'exposition de la doctrine de Saint-Simon* (1828–1830). Improvement of London's public safety is reflected by purification of water supply and the consolidation of its police forces (1829).

Nicholas I, emperor of Russia (1825–1855).

1830s

52,000,000 Europeans emigrate from the Old World between 1830 and 1920. Birmingham's death rate rises from 14.6 to 27.2 per thousand (1831–1844) reflecting squalid urban conditions.

German pig iron production increases 10,000 percent between 1835–1839 and 1910–1913. Revolutions in Switzerland, France, Belgium, Hesse-Cassel, Hanover, and Saxony. In Modena, Parma, Bologna, Ancona (Italy), and Poland, revolutions fail, but establish nationalism as a force.

Auguste Comte, *Cours de philosophie positive* (1830). Britain expands suffrage (though not to the working class or women) and weakens expensive poor laws (1832–1834). First railway on the Continent, between Budweis, Bohemia, and Linz, Austria (1832).

England requires birth registration (1837). Chartist movement in Britain (1838–1848), partly in protest against weakening of poor laws. The juvenile workday is restricted to ten hours in Prussia (1839). Britain abolishes slavery (1833).

Victoria, queen of the United Kingdom (1837–1901).

1840s

Across Europe, 3 to 5 percent of children attend secondary schools. 200,000 laborers are employed operating Britain's railroads. Manorialism abolished throughout central Europe.

Royal botanical gardens (Kew Gardens) near London opened to the public (1841). Edwin Chadwick's *Report on the Sanitary Condition of the Labouring Population of Great Britain* (1842). Silesian weavers revolt against modern machinery (1844); Silesian peasants must work 177 days a year to fulfill feudal obligations. The alarm clock is invented in France (1847). Great famine in Ireland (1847–1854); Ireland's population falls from 8,175,000 in 1841 to 5,100,000 by 1881; famines throughout Europe produce hundreds of food riots. Austria-Hungary emancipates serfs (1848). 21,000 Norwegians join the Thrane labor movement (1848–1852).

Revolutions of 1848; liberal-nationalist revolutions throughout Europe are briefly successful in Germany, Belgium, France, Italy, and Austria-Hungary; suppressed in Spain, Britain, and Russia. Marx and Engels, *Communist Manifesto* (1848).

Francis Joseph I, emperor of Austria (1848–1916).

1850s

France institutes an old-age pension system (1850). Henry Charles Harrod buys a grocery store in London and begins selling consumer goods (1850). London hosts the Great Exhibition, leading to future world fairs and international trade fairs (1851). Peasants in southern France revolt (1851). Napoleon III establishes second French Empire (1851). Joseph-Arthur de Gobineau, *Essai sur l'inégalité des races humaines* (1854–1855). Britain permits civil divorces without the restriction of requiring parliamentary approval (1857). Jews are permitted to become members of Britain's Parliament (1858). Apparitions of the Virgin Mary in Lourdes, France, give rise to major Catholic pilgrimage site (1858). Charles Darwin, *The Origin of Species* (1859).

Alexander I, emperor of Russia (1855–1881).

1860s

Daily weather forecasts, a subway line, an association of football clubs, and a stoplight appear in London while debtors' prisons are abolished. In Paris, a bicycle factory opens and bicycle races are staged. Newly established department stores in England and France suggest that consumerism continues to grow.

Russia emancipates serfs (1861). Jean-Martin Charcot begins his association with Salpêtrière hospital, Paris (1862). Ferdinand Lasselle founds first workers' party in Germany (1863). World's first underground urban railway opens in London (1863). Romania emancipates serfs (1864). Pope Pius IX condemns liberalism, socialism, and rationalism in the *Syllabus of Errors* (1864). First International Workingmen's Association founded (1864). Switzerland's Nestlé introduces baby formula (1866). First French socialist party founded (1867–1868). Karl Marx, *Das Kapital*, volume 1 (1867). École Pratique des Hautes Études founded in Paris (1868).

William I, king of Prussia (1861–1888).

Thorold Rogers, *History of Agriculture and Prices in England* (1866–1902).

1870s

Censuses determine the population (in millions) of Britain and Ireland, 31.5; France, 36.1; Germany, 41; Italy, 26.8. Labor unions are legalized in France.

Married Women's Property Act in Britain (1870). Franco-Prussian War (1870–1871). Communes challenge the defeated French government in Paris, Lyon, and Marseille (1871). Beginning of *Kulturkampf* in Germany (1871). Germany expels Roman Catholic religious orders and mandates that marriage be a civil ceremony. Britain introduces the secret ballot for voting (1872). Public transportation carries 1.4 million passengers in Prague (1874); 50 million will use Prague's public transportation in 1910. German Socialist Labor Party founded (1875). First telephone exchange in London (1879).

William I of Prussia becomes first emperor of Germany (1871–1888).

J. R. Green, *A Short History of the English People* (1874).

1880s

Between 1881 and 1901, Italy's population increases from 29.3 to 33.4 million even as 2.2 million emigrate. London's population is 3.3 million; population of Paris is 1.2 million.

Pogroms (attacks on Jews) in Russia through the 1880s. France reinstates freedom of the press, permits divorce, and mandates education for girls. The telephone, vending machines, electricity, and typewriters are rapidly introduced throughout Europe.

Aletta Jacobs opens a birth control clinic in the Netherlands (1882). Second Married Women's Property Act in Britain (1882). Germany establishes a national health insurance program (1883) and is followed by Austria (1888). Fabian Society founded in Britain (1884). End of *Kulturkampf* in Germany (1887). Louis Pasteur becomes director of Institut Pasteur, Paris (1888–1895). John Dunlop manufactures first bicycles with pneumatic tires (1888). Emmeline Pankhurst founds Women's Franchise League (1889). Second International Workingmen's Association (coalition of socialists parties) founded (1889). Germany establishes compulsory old-age pension system (1889). The bra is invented in Paris, replacing corsets (1889).

Alexander III, emperor of Russia (1881–1894). William II, emperor of Germany (1888–1918).

English Historical Review founded (1886).

1890s

In Denmark, one-third of women over age 15 work outside the home; half work as servants, one-sixth work in industry, figures that are echoed throughout Europe.

Infant welfare clinics established in Barcelona (1890). Switzerland introduces a national social insurance program (1890). Leo XIII, *Rerum novarum,* encyclical on condition of workers (1893). Dreyfus affair in France (1894–1899). Sigmund Freud and Josef Breuer, *Studien über Hysterie* (1895). London School of Economics founded (1895). In France, an audience pays to see a motion picture, *La sortie des ouvriers de l'usine Lumière* (Workers leaving the Lumière factory, 1895). Athens hosts the first modern Olympic games (1896); 250 athletes from fourteen nations participate. Lifebuoy soap, advertised as preventing body odor, appears in London (1897). Sigmund Freud, *Die Traumdeutung* (On the interpretation of dreams, 1899).

Nicholas II, emperor of Russia (1894–1917).

Émile Durkheim, *De la division du travail social* (1893). Sidney and Beatrice Webb, *The History of Trade Unionism* (1894). Émile Durkheim, *Les règles de la méthode sociologique* (1895). Émile Durkheim, *Le suicide* (1897). Sidney and Beatrice Webb, *Industrial Democracy* (1897).

1900s

The presence of fish and chip vendors in England is responsible for increased protein consumption among the working class.

Paris Métro begins operation (1900). Guglielmo Marconi transmits first transatlantic radio broadcast (1901). Emmeline Pankhurst founds Women's Social and Political Union (1903). First Tour de France bicycle race (1903). University of Manchester founded (1903). Strikes in the Netherlands and Milan end violently (1903, 1904). Russo-Japanese War (1904–1905). Peasant revolts, anti-Jewish pogroms, and riots after Russia's military defeat by Japan force the tsar to institute liberal reforms (1902–1905). France ends the official status of the Catholic Church (1904). Revolution of 1905 in Russia. France establishes voluntary unemployment insurance (1905). Finland grants women's suffrage (1906). Young Turk revolt in Turkey (1908). Sigmund Freud and others found Vienna Psycho-Analytical Society (1908).

Edward VII, king of the United Kingdom (1901–1910).

Revue de synthèse historique founded (1900). Max Weber, *Die protestantische Ethik und der Geist des Kapitalismus* (1905–1906). Sidney and Beatrice Webb, *English Local Government* (1906–1909).

1910s

Sigmund Freud, *Über Psychoanalyse* (1910). Britain establishes national health insurance, unemployment insurance, and old-age insurance programs (1911). Italy (1912) and Norway (1913) grant women's suffrage. Balkan Wars (1912–1913). University of Frankfurt founded (1914).

World War I (1914–1918), with heavy casualties and civilian deaths from military operations, famine, influenza, and revolutions. After military reverses, Russia plunges into revolution and civil war (1917–1921). Breakup of German, Austrian, Ottoman, and Russian empires; independence of Finland, Estonia, Latvia, Lithuania, Poland, Czechoslovakia, Hungary, and Yugoslavia.

Germany establishes eight-hour workday (1918). Membership of the Confederazione Italiano del Lavoro grows from 250,000 to 2,200,000 (1918–1920). Women gain the right to practice law in Portugal, England, Italy, and Germany (1918–1920). Third International founded (1919).

John and Barbara Hammond, *The Village Laborer* (1911). Émile Durkheim, *Les formes élémentaires de la vie religieuse* (1912). Lucien Febvre, *Philippe II et la Franche-Comté* (1912). R. H. Tawney, *The Agrar-*

ian Problem in the Sixteenth Century (1912). G. D. H. Cole, *The World of Labour* (1913). John and Barbara Hammond, *The Town Laborer* (1917). Alice Clark, *The Working Life of Women in the Seventeenth Century* (1919). John and Barbara Hammond, *The Skilled Laborer* (1919).

1920s

Radio stations established throughout Europe.

Establishment of Irish Free State (1922). Great Britain and Austria institute unemployment insurance (1920). France's anti-abortion law carries the death penalty (1920). 3,747 divorces are granted in Great Britain (1920); 39,000 in Germany (1921). 173,000 German children are born out of wedlock; in France, 65,000; in Italy, 49,000 (1921). German trade union membership is 9,193,000; British trade union membership is 4,369,000 (1923). Eight million man-days are lost in Britain due to strikes (1924).

Fascists come to power in Italy (1922). Italy revokes right to strike and women's suffrage, and criminalizes abortion (1925–1930). France establishes compulsory old-age and sickness insurance programs (1925). Collectivization of Soviet agriculture, which results in massive famines (1928–1932).

R. H. Tawney, *The Acquisitive Society* (1921). Marc Bloch, *Les rois thaumaturges* (1924). Georges Lefebvre, *Les paysans du Nord* (1924). G. D. H. Cole, *Short History of the British Working-Class Movement* (1925–1927). Economic History Society founded in Britain (1926). Dorothy George, *London Life in the Eighteenth Century* (1926); R. H. Tawney, *Religion and the Rise of Capitalism* (1926). *Economic History Review* founded (1927). Lucien Febvre, *Martin Luther* (1928). Bloch and Febvre found *Annales d'histoire économique et sociale* (1929).

1930s

Worldwide economic depression leads to massive unemployment; 5,660,000 in Germany (1931), 2,800,000 in Great Britain (1932). Economic conditions, anti-Semitism, and a reaction against modernist decadence elevate the Nazis to power in Germany (1933); they persecute Jews, suppress labor unions, and protect the environment. Nazis institute Nuremberg Laws in Germany (1935). Regular television broadcasts in Germany (1935). British Broadcasting Corporation begins television service (1936). Fascists assume power in Eastern Europe and in Spain, the latter after a three year civil war (1936–1939). France nationalizes arms factories (1937) beginning a nationalization trend that

will continue in Western Europe after World War II. Germany's economic recovery is reflected by its 350 movie theaters and 12,000 periodicals (1938). In the Soviet Union, Stalin's reign of terror results in millions executed or internally exiled and enslaved. Beginning of World War II (1939).

Ivy Pinchbeck, *Women Workers and the Industrial Revolution* (1930). Marc Bloch, *Les caractères originaux de l'histoire rurale française* (1931). R. H. Tawney, *Equality* (1931). Georges Lefebvre, *La grande peur* (1932). Hans Rosenberg, *Die Weltwirtschaftkrisis von 1857–1859* (1934). G. D. H. Cole and Raymond Postgate, *The Common People* (1938). A. L. Morton, *A People's History of England* (1938). Marc Bloch, *La société féodale* (1939–1940). Norbert Elias, *Über den Prozess der Zivilisation* (1939).

1940s

World War II (1939–1945). Nazis kill over 7,000,000, mostly Jews and Gypsies, in concentration camps (1941–1945).

Population (in millions) Britain, 46; France, 40; Germany, 66; Italy, 47 (1946). United States' Marshall Plan bolsters the economies of European countries in response to increased Soviet influence over Eastern Europe; where the "Iron Curtain" falls (1945–1949). Decolonization begins as Great Britain, France, and the Netherlands cede independence to Asian states (1946–1948). The Netherlands, Belgium, and Luxembourg form a customs union, "Benelux" (1948). Britain establishes National Health Service (1948).

Lucien Febvre, *Le problème de l'incroyance au XVIe siècle* (1942). G. M. Trevelyan, *English Social History* (1944). Marc Bloch shot by Germans (1944). Sixième Section of École des Hautes Études founded in Paris (1945). *Annales d'histoire économique et sociale* changes name to *Annales: Économies, Sociétés, Civilisations* (1946). British Communist Party Historians' Group founded (1946). Fernand Braudel, *La Méditerranée et le monde méditerranéen à l'époque de Philippe II* (1949). Maurice Dobb, *Studies in the Development of Capitalism* (1946).

1950s

European Coal and Steel Community is established by Germany, Italy, France, and Benelux (1951) as a limited trade union; it grows in terms of commodities covered and participating nations until it becomes the European Union. Strikes in Poland and Hungary against Stalinism result in suppression by the Soviet Union; Soviet Union invades Hungary (1956). Decolonization continues: between 1956 and 1964, most of European colonies in Africa become independent; 9,000,000 immigrate from the colonies to European nations between 1958 and 1974) creating large minority populations in France, Great Britain, and Italy.

Past and Present founded (1952). G. D. H. Cole, *History of Socialist Thought* (1953–1960). Huguette Chaunu and Pierre Chaunu, *Seville et l'Atlantique* (1955–1959). George Ewart Evans, *Ask the Fellows That Cut the Hay* (1956). Dona Torr, *Tom Mann and His Times* (1956). Arbeitskreis für moderne Sozialgeschichte founded at Heidelberg, Germany (1957). John Saville, *Rural Depopulation in England and Wales* (1957). Henri-Jean Martin, *L'aparition du livre* (1958). Hans Rosenberg, *Bureaucracy, Aristocracy, and Autocracy* (1958). Albert Soboul, *Les sans-culottes parisiens de l'An II* (1958). Raymond Williams, *Culture and Society* (1958). Asa Briggs, *Chartist Studies* (1959). Eric Hobsbawm, *Primitive Rebels* (1959). George Rudé, *The Crowd in the French Revolution* (1959).

1960s

Foreign immigration continues, particularly in Germany where large numbers of Turks are invited to immigrate in order to fill vacant low-wage jobs. Televisions and automobiles become popular consumer goods and by 1970 Western Europeans will have 200 of each per thousand people. Legal restrictions on homosexuality ease.

Belgian doctors strike against a national health insurance law (1964). Popular protests in Czechoslovakia voice displeasure with neo-Stalinism; Soviet Union crushes the "Prague Spring" (1968). In France massive demonstrations by students and workers (1968). France permits contraception (1968).

Philippe Ariès, *L'enfant et la vie familiale sous l'ancien régime* (1960). Rudolf Braun, *Industrialisierung und Volksleben* (1960). Asa Briggs, *Essays in Labour History* (1960). Pierre Goubert, *Beauvais et le Beauvaisis* (1960). Michel Foucault, *Folie et déraison* (1961). Robert Mandrou, *Introduction à la France moderne* (1961). Raymond Williams, *The Long Revolution* (1961). Richard Cobb, *Les armées révolutionaires* (1962). Eric Hobsbawm, *The Age of Revolution* (1962). Asa Briggs, *Victorian Cities* (1963). E. P. Thompson, *The Making of the English Working Class* (1963). Eric Hobsbawm, *Labouring Men* (1964). George Rudé, *The Crowd in History* (1964). Charles Tilly, *The Vendée* (1964). Rudolf Braun, *Sozialer und kultureller Wandel in einem industriellen Landesgebiet* (1965). Richard Cobb, *Terreur et subsistances* (1965). François Furet, ed., *Livre et société dans la France du 18e siècle* (1965–1970). Peter Laslett, *The World We Have Lost* (1965). Jan Vansina, *Oral Tradition* (1965). Center for the Study of Social History founded at University of Warwick (1965). Michel Foucault, *Les mots et les choses* (1966). Emmanuel Le Roy Ladurie, *Les paysans de Languedoc* (1966). Emmanuel Le Roy Ladurie, *L'histoire du climat depuis l'an 1000* (1967). Hans Rosenberg, *Grosse Depression und Bismarckzeit* (1967). Michel Foucault, *L'archéologie du savoir* (1969). Eric Hobsbawm, *Industry and Empire* (1968). Richard Cobb, *A Second Identity* (1969). Norbert Elias, *Die höfische Gesellschaft* (1969). Eric Hobsbawm, *Bandits* (1969). Harold Perkin, *The Origins of Modern English Society* (1969). Hans Rosenberg, *Probleme der Sozialgeschichte* (1969).

1970s

Soviet Union's rapid economic growth ends and a decline begins. Economic malaise prompts the European community to continue its expansion adding Britain, Ireland, and Greece; it begins negotiations with Spain and Portugal.

Switzerland grants women's suffrage (1971). Britain is paralyzed by postal and coal strikes (1971, 1972). Arab oil embargo forces drastic energy conservation measures throughout Europe (1973). End of fascist regime Portugal (1974–1975). End of Franco regime in Spain (1975). Both countries grant women's suffrage and disengage from their African colonies (1975–1976). France legalizes abortion (1975). In Italy, women gain the right to sue for paternity (1975). Italy legalizes abortion (1977). Spain permits contraception (1978).

Maurice Agulhon, *The Republic in the Village* (1970). Richard Cobb, *Police and the People* (1970). First National Women's Liberation Conference in Britain (1970). Gareth Stedman Jones, *Outcast London* (1971). Keith Thomas, *Religion and the Decline of Magic* (1971). Richard Cobb, *Reactions to the French Revolution* (1972). *Dictionary of Labour Biography* (1972–). Sheila Rowbotham, *Women, Resistance, and Revolution* (1972). H. J. Dyos and Michael Wolff, eds., *The Victorian City* (1973). Sheila Rowbotham, *Hidden from History* and *Women's Consciousness, Man's World* (1973). Perry Anderson, *Passages from Antiquity to Feudalism* and *Lineages of the Absolutist State* (1974). Immanuel Wallerstein, *The Modern World System* (1974). Richard Cobb, *Paris and Its Provinces* (1975). Michel Foucault, *Surveiller et punir* (1975). Eric Hobsbawm, *The Age of Capital* (1975). Emmanuel Le Roy Ladurie, *Montaillou* (1975). E. P. Thompson, *Whigs and Hunters* (1975). Charles Tilly, ed., *The Formation of the National States in Western Europe* (1975). Michel Foucault, *Histoire de la sexualité* (1976–1984). Edward Shorter, *The Making of the Modern Family* (1976). Jacques LeGoff, *Pour un autre moyen age* (1977). Lawrence Stone, *The Family, Sex, and Marriage in England* (1977). Louise Tilly and Joan W. Scott, *Women, Work, and Family* (1978). Fernand Braudel, *Capitalisme et civilisation* (1979). Emmanuel Le Roy Ladurie, *Le carnaval de Romans* (1979).

1980s

Frustration with established parties grows in Western Europe. Massive antinuclear demonstrations and environmental concerns give rise to Green (environmental) parties while concerns over immigration and unemployment give rise to right-wing parties. Right-wing extremism is intertwined with skinheads, young, disaffected men, many of whom participate in football rowdyism and violent attacks on foreigners and individuals with disabilities. Solidarity labor union challenges the Polish communist government.

Spain permits abortion (1985). Glasnost and perestroika reforms liberalize Soviet communist regime (1985–1991). Soviet control in Eastern Europe slackens and communists are forced out of power in Poland, Czechoslovakia, Hungary, Romania, and East Germany (1989–1991).

Jacques LeGoff, *La naissance du Purgatoire* (1981). Lawrence Stone, *The Past and the Present* (1981). E. A.

Wrigley and Roger S. Schofield, *The Population History of England and Wales, 1541–1871* (1981). Gareth Stedman Jones, *Languages of Class* (1983). Keith Thomas, *Man and the Natural World* (1983). Michel Vovelle, *Idéologies et mentalités* (1982). Joan W. Scott, "Gender: A Useful Category of Historical Analysis" (1986). Eric Hobsbawm, *The Age of Empire* (1987).

1990s

Estimated population (in millions) of Britain, 58.6; France, 58; Germany, 84; Italy, 57.5.

Eastern Europe struggles to overcome the legacy of communism; after years of declining growth, economies slowly improve though Russia's remains stagnant, partly due to corruption and organized crime. Some eastern European nations join the European Union. In western Europe, the spread of personal computers and the Internet revolutionizes consumerism, tourism, and other economic sectors. The economy experiences a long expansion though unemployment rates remain stubbornly high. European nations participate in international conflicts including wars in the former Yugoslavia. Biotechnology promises to extend human life spans and the quality of life. Europeans demonstrate against genetically altered foods.

EuroDisney amusement park opens near Paris (1992). Mad-cow disease ravages British herds (1995–1998). European Union adopts common currency (euro) and abolishes customs barriers (1999).

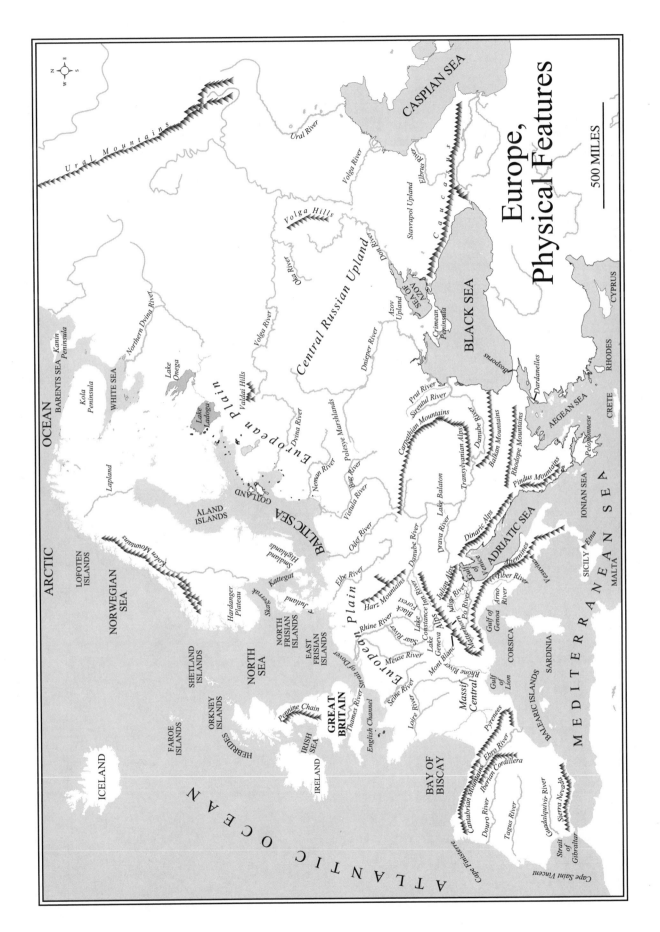

Europe,
Physical Features

500 MILES

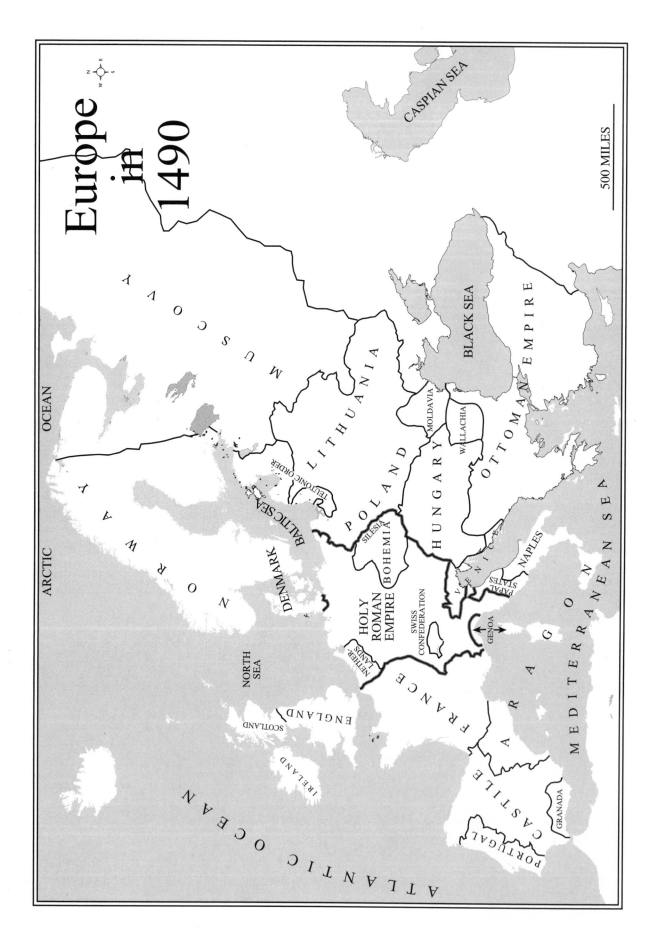

Europe in 1490

N E / W S

500 MILES

CASPIAN SEA

ARCTIC OCEAN

MUSCOVY

NORWAY

LITHUANIA

TEUTONIC ORDER

BALTIC SEA

DENMARK

POLAND

SILESIA

BOHEMIA

HOLY ROMAN EMPIRE

SWISS CONFEDERATION

NETHER- LANDS

FRANCE

HUNGARY

MOLDAVIA

WALLACHIA

BLACK SEA

OTTOMAN EMPIRE

VENICE

PAPAL STATES

NAPLES

GENOA

ARAGON

MEDITERRANEAN SEA

NORTH SEA

SCOTLAND

IRELAND

ENGLAND

CASTILE

PORTUGAL

GRANADA

ATLANTIC OCEAN

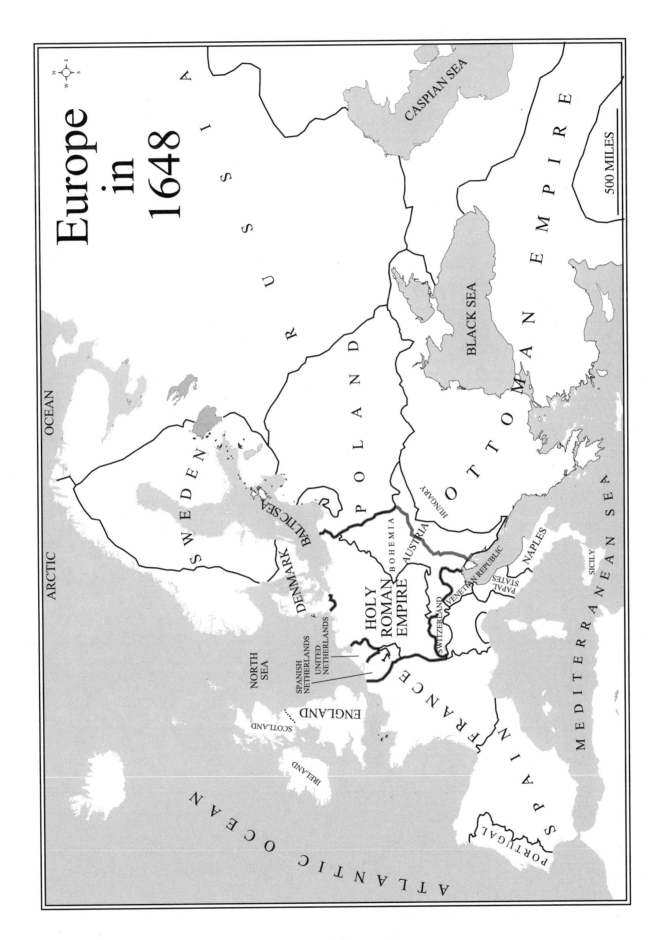

Europe in 1648

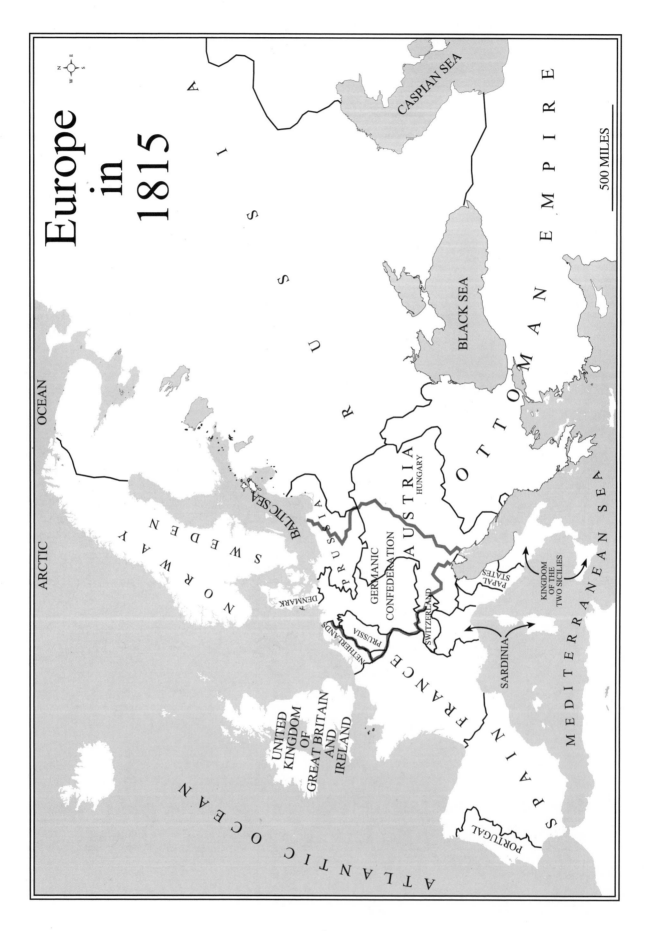

Europe
in
1815

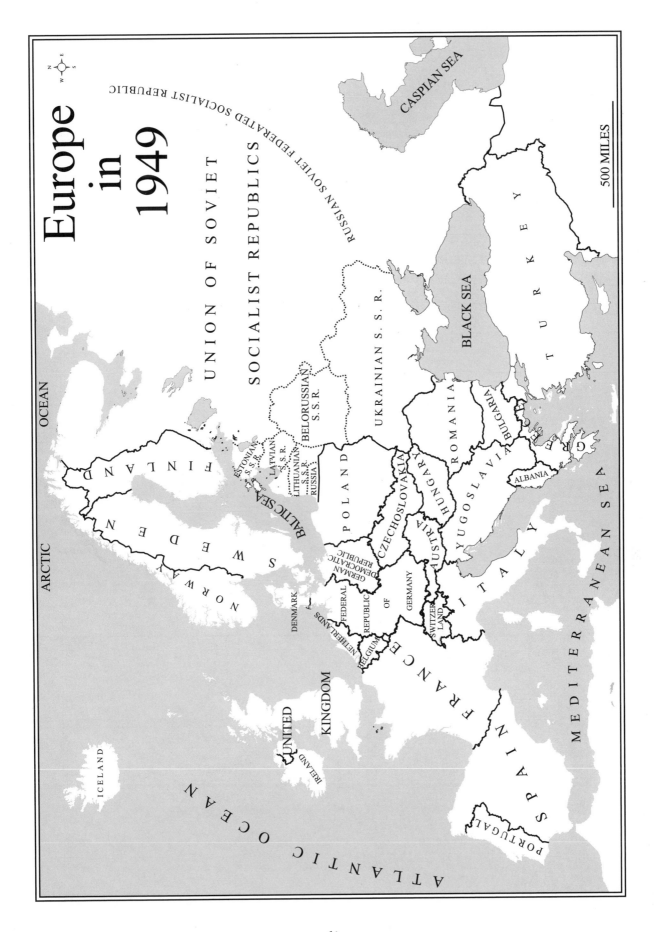

Europe
in
1949

COMMON ABBREVIATIONS USED IN THIS WORK

A.D.	*Anno Domini,* in the year of the Lord
AESC	*Annales: Économies, Sociétés, Civilisations*
ASSR	Autonomous Soviet Socialist Republic
b.	born
B.C.	before Christ
B.C.E.	before the common era (= B.C.)
c.	*circa,* about, approximately
C.E.	common era (= A.D.)
cf.	*confer,* compare
chap.	chapter
CP	Communist Party
d.	died
diss.	dissertation
ed.	editor (pl., eds.), edition
e.g.	*exempli gratia,* for example
et al.	*et alii,* and others
etc.	*et cetera,* and so forth
EU	European Union
f.	and following (pl., ff.)
fl.	*floruit,* flourished
GDP	gross domestic product
GDR	German Democratic Republic (East Germany)
GNP	gross national product
HRE	Holy Roman Empire, Holy Roman Emperor
ibid.	*ibididem,* in the same place (as the one immediately preceding)

i.e.	*id est,* that is
IMF	International Monetary Fund
MS.	manuscript (pl. MSS.)
n.	note
n.d.	no date
no.	number (pl., nos.)
n.p.	no place
n.s.	new series
N.S.	new style, according to the Gregorian calendar
OECD	Organization for Economic Cooperation and Development
O.S.	old style, according to the Julian calendar
p.	page (pl., pp.)
pt.	part
rev.	revised
S.	*san, sanctus, santo,* male saint
ser.	series
SP	Socialist Party
SS.	saints
SSR	Soviet Socialist Republic
Sta.	*sancta, santa,* female saint
supp.	supplement
USSR	Union of Soviet Socialist Republics
vol.	volume
WTO	World Trade Organization
?	uncertain, possibly, perhaps

ENCYCLOPEDIA OF
EUROPEAN SOCIAL HISTORY

Section 1

METHODS AND
THEORETICAL APPROACHES

THE GENERATIONS OF SOCIAL HISTORY

Geoff Eley

As a recognized specialism, social history is still young—dating in most countries only from the 1960s. Of course, as a dimension of historical writing, social history has always been there. The classics of historiography may all be read for their social content. During the later nineteenth century, most European countries produced some indications of what "social history" might be in universities, by private individuals, and in alternative institutional settings like labor movements, where socialist parties quickly developed an interest in the archives of their own emergence. Specifically social histories were rarely produced inside the newly established academic discipline of history as such. The dominance of nationalist paradigms meant that statecraft and diplomacy, wars, armies, empire, high politics, biography, administration, law, and other state-focused themes occupied the agenda of teaching and scholarship to the virtual exclusion of anything else.

GERMANY AND BRITAIN: SOCIAL HISTORY OUTSIDE THE HISTORICAL PROFESSION

In Germany the new national state of 1871 wholly ruled the professional historian's imagination. Bismarck's role as the architect of German unification and the related processes of state-building inspired histories organized around statecraft, military history, and constitutional law, first under Leopold von Ranke (1795–1886) and his contemporary Johann Gustav Droysen (1808–1884), and then under Heinrich von Treitschke (1834–1896). Other contemporaries, such as Karl Marx (1818–1883) and Jacob Burckhardt (1818–1897), had no presence in this official Imperial German context. Karl Lamprecht (1856–1915) opened his work toward the social sciences, psychology, art history, and the study of culture, precipitating the *Methodenstreit* (conflict over methodology) in 1891, but without shifting the protocols of the discipline. Likewise, leading economists of the historical

school such as Gustav von Schmoller (1838–1917), or sociologists like Max Weber (1864–1920), produced historical work of enormous importance, but again from outside the historical profession per se.

A similar narrative applied to Britain, where a liberal cohort—Henry Thomas Buckle (1821–1862), James Bryce (1838–1922), Edward Augustus Freeman (1823–1892), John Robert Seeley (1834–1895), and others—celebrated the English political tradition, reinforced by Lord Acton (1834–1902), who founded the *English Historical Review* (1886) and conceived the *Cambridge Modern History.* Otherwise, pre-1914 British historiography's achievements were in the medieval and Tudor-Stuart periods, in religious history, landholding, and law. Bryce set the tone when inaugurating the *English Historical Review:* "It seems better to regard history as the record of human action. . . . States and Politics will therefore be the chief parts of its subject, because the acts of nations . . . have usually been more important than the acts of private citizens." Seeley concurred: "History is not concerned with individuals except in their capacity as members of a state" (quoted in Wilson, "Critical Portrait," pp. 11, 9).

After 1918 openings occurred toward social history in Britain and Germany, partly with the founding of new universities less hidebound with tradition, such as the London School of Economics (1895), Manchester (1903), and Frankfurt (1914), partly as academic history consolidated itself as a discipline. In Britain the specialism of economic history helped, generating large empirical funds for later social historians to use, managed analytically by the grand narratives of the industrial revolution and the rise of national economies. The founding of the Economic History Society (1926) and its *Economic History Review* (1927) encouraged the practical equivalent of the German historical school of economists before 1914. R. H. Tawney (1880–1962) laid the foundations of early modern social history in a series of works—*The Agrarian Problem in the Sixteenth Century* (1912), *Tudor Economic Documents* (edited with Eileen Power; 1924), *Religion and the Rise of Capitalism* (1926),

Business and Politics under James I (1958), and his famous monographic article, "The Rise of the Gentry" (1941). "Tawney's century" (1540–1640) was constructed with comparative knowledge and theoretical vision. *Land and Labour in China* (1932) was another of his works. In this broader framing of social and economic processes, *Religion and the Rise of Capitalism* was the analogue to Max Weber's *The Protestant Ethic and the Spirit of Capitalism* (1904–1905).

The main early impulse toward social history was a left-wing interest in the social consequences of industrialization. Like Weber, Tawney was politically engaged. A Christian Socialist, Labour Party parliamentary candidate, advocate of the Workers' Educational Association, and public intellectual (especially via *The Acquisitive Society* [1921] and *Equality* [1931]), he practiced ethical commitment in his scholarly no less than in his political work. Sometimes such work occurred inside the universities, notably at the London School of Economics under Beatrice (1858–1943) and Sidney Webb (1859–1947), and political theorist Harold Laski (1893–1950), as well as Tawney. It reflected high-minded identification with what the Webbs called the "inevitability of gradualness"— the electoral rise of the Labour Party, but still more the triumph of an administrative ideal of rational taxation, social provision, and public goods. The Webbs' great works—the nine-volume history, *English Local Government from the Revolution to the Municipal Corporations Act* (1906–1929), plus *The History of Trade Unionism* (1894) and *Industrial Democracy* (1897)— adumbrated the terrain of a fully professionalized social history in the 1950s and 1960s.

The Webbs were linked to the Labour Party through the Fabian Society's networks, peaking in the LSE's contribution to public policy, social administration, and the post-1945 architecture of the welfare state. Equally salient for social history's genealogies was the Guild Socialist G. D. H. Cole (1889–1959), teaching at Oxford from the 1920s, in the Chair of Social and Political Theory from 1945. The radical liberal journalists and writers John (1872–1949) and Barbara Hammond (1873–1961), also should be mentioned. Their trilogy, *The Village Labourer, 1760–1832* (1911), *The Town Labourer, 1760–1832* (1917), and *The Skilled Labourer, 1760–1832* (1919), presented an epic account of the human costs of industrialization beyond the administrative vision of the Webbs. Their precursor was the radical Liberal parliamentarian and economic historian J. E. T. Rogers (1823–1890), who countered the dominant constitutional history of his day with the seven-volume *History of Agriculture and Prices in England* (1866–1902), which—like much pioneering economic history from

GEORGE DOUGLAS HOWARD COLE
(1889–1959)

G. D. H. Cole taught successively philosophy, economics, and social and political theory at the University of Oxford, and emerged between his first book, *The World of Labour; A Discussion of the Present and Future of Trade Unionism* (1913), and the 1920s as a leading British socialist intellectual. His ideas of Guild Socialism were shaped by the labor unrest of 1910–1914 and World War I, and informed his many histories of socialism, trade unionism, and industrial democracy, extending from *A Short History of the British Working Class Movement 1789–1925* (originally three volumes, 1925–1927), to the multivolume *History of Socialist Thought* (1953–1960). His coauthored *The Common People, 1746–1938* (1938) with Raymond Postgate remained the best general account of British social history "from below" in the 1960s. *Essays in Labour History, 1886–1923* (1960), edited by Asa Briggs and John Saville, which brought together Britain's best practitioners of the field of the time, was a memorial to Cole.

Marx to Tawney—assembled rich materials for the social history of the laboring poor.

A true pioneer for such work was Rogers's younger Oxford contemporary, John Richard Green (1837–1883), who left the Anglican clergy to become a historian in 1869. Eschewing the classical liberal celebration of a limited English constitutionalism, soon to be translated onto imperial ground by J. R. Seeley's *Expansion of England* (1884), Green's inspiration was a popular story of democratic self-government, realized in his *Short History of the English People* (1874). He rejected "the details of foreign wars and diplomacies, the personal adventures of kings and nobles, the pomp of courts, [and] the intrigues of favourites" in favor of the episodes of "that constitutional, intellectual, and social advance, in which we read the history of the nation itself." The *Short History* counterposed the "English people" to the "English kings [and] English conquests," or to "drum and trumpet" history. It established a line of popular history outside the universities, running through the Hammonds, and the Irish histories of Green's wife Alice

Stopford Green (1847–1929), to *A People's History of England* (1938) by the Communist Arthur Leslie Morton (1903–), which drew inspiration from the antifascist campaigns for a popular front. Like Cole's work in labor history, and Tawney's in the sixteenth and seventeenth centuries, this bridged directly to social history post-1945 in its concern with ordinary people, with the broader impact of social and economic forces like industrialization, and with its political engagement.

THE INCLUSIVENESS OF DEMOCRACY: THE IMPORTANCE OF DEMOCRATIC POLITICAL CULTURE TO THE ORIGINS OF SOCIAL HISTORY

Social history began in political contexts effaced by subsequent professionalization. Women in particular disappeared from the historiographical record. One exception was Eileen Power (1889–1940), at the London School of Economics from 1921, whose works ranged from *Medieval English Nunneries c. 1275 to 1535* (1922) and *The Wool Trade in English Medieval History* (1941) to the popular *Medieval People* (1924). More typical was Alice Clark (1874–1934), who attended the LSE as a mature student, pioneered the study of women's work before the industrial revolution in *Working Life of Women in the Seventeenth Century* (1919), and then left academic life for social activism. Clark destabilized the progressivist account of industrialization by showing its narrowing effects on women's work and the household economy, in ways that "startle in their modernity" (Sutton, "Radical Liberalism," p. 36). Dorothy George's *London Life in the Eighteenth Century* (1925), Ivy Pinchbeck's *Women Workers and the Industrial Revolution, 1750–1850* (1930), and the contributions of Beatrice Webb and Barbara Hammond in their famous partnerships all retain their pioneering status. As Billie Melman shows in "Gender, History, and Memory," this reflected both women's social and educational advance and the political conflicts needed to attain it. By 1921, 91 percent of the British Historical Association were women, and 64 percent of the 204 historical works published between 1900 and 1930 by women born between 1875 and 1900 were in social and economic history. This work was linked to political activism, through Fabianism, the Labour Party, and feminist suffrage politics before 1914.

The importance of left-wing politics—identification with the common people—to early social history was even clearer in Germany. The foundations were firmer, through German sociology's pioneering

HANS ROSENBERG (1904–1988)

Hans Rosenberg's career became paradigmatic for the West German social history of the 1970s. His approach mirrored that of his contemporary Eckart Kehr—passing from the liberal history of ideas (in Rosenberg's earliest publications in the 1930s), through concern with deep structural continuities of the German past, to a model of the socioeconomic determinations of political life. His classic *Bureaucracy, Aristocracy, and Autocracy: The Prussian Experience, 1660–1815* (original German edition, 1958) was followed by influential essays on the Junkers, *Probleme der deutschen Sozialgeschichte* (1969), and a social explanation of Bismarckian politics by cycles of the economy, *Grosse Depression und Bismarckzeit: Wirtschaftsablauf, Gesellschaft und Politik in Mitteleuropa* (1967). Each work had a long gestation, going back to an essay of the 1940s. His conception of economic conjunctures and their founding importance for politics was first explored in *Die Weltwirtschaftskrisis von 1857–1859* (1934). As he said in *Bureaucracy, Aristocracy, and Autocracy,* his work "approaches political, institutional, and ideological changes in terms of social history, and it does not reduce social history to an appendix of economic history" (p. viii).

achievements before 1914 and in the Weimar Republic, the labor movement's institutional strengths, and the intellectual dynamism in Weimar culture. The works of Gustav Mayer (1871–1948), the Engels biographer (1934), remain classics, especially his essay "Die Trennung der proletarischen von der bürgerlichen Demokratie in Deutschland 1863–70" (1911). Mayer's career was blocked by nationalists at Berlin University in 1917. He was appointed to a position in the department of the history of democracy, socialism, and political parties under the changed conditions in 1922, and entered exile in Britain in 1933. Weimar democracy was a limited hiatus between pre-1918's exclusionary conservatism and Nazism after 1933, in which space briefly opened for alternatives to the nationalist state-focused historiography established post-1871.

One dissenting nexus surrounded Eckart Kehr (1902–1933), who died while visiting the United

States. His *Battleship Building and Party Politics in Germany 1894–1901* (1930) drew heavily on the social theory of Marx and Weber and related politics to socioeconomic structures, reinforced by a series of essays (later collected as *Economic Interest, Militarism, and Foreign Policy* [1965]). Kehr's associate Hans Rosenberg (1904–1988) also fled the Third Reich for the United States in 1936, eventually returning to Germany in 1970. They and others were rediscovered by West German social historians in the 1960s, and reinstated as the precursors of a long-interrupted tradition.

Just as vital in the 1920s was the flowering of German sociology, with a cohort of young exiles after 1933. Hans Speier (1905–) studied with Emil Lederer (1882–1939) and Karl Mannheim (1893–1947) in Heidelberg, worked at a Berlin publishing house, had links to the German Social Democratic Party's Labor Education department and the city's social services, and was married to a municipal pediatrician. His book on white collar workers, translated as *German White-Collar Workers and the Rise of Hitler* (1986), went unpublished until 1977. Speier taught at the New School for Social Research in New York, joined by his former teacher Lederer, whose studies of white collar workers went back to 1912. Hans Gerth (1908–1978), whose 1935 study of Enlightenment intelligentsia was eventually republished in 1976, went to the University of Wisconsin, and introduced Max Weber's works into English, while his coeditor of the famous selections *From Max Weber* (1948), C. Wright Mills, spread Speier's influence via his own classic *White Collar: The American Middle Classes* (1951). Like the work of Kehr, Rosenberg, and other dissenting historians, this critical sociology was recovered by West German advocates of social science history in the 1970s. It traveled back to its country of origin via the post-1945 traditions of U.S. social science.

Until 1933 German and British historiographies developed roughly in parallel. In neither society were university history departments open to social history, with its connotations of popularization and political dissent. German conditions were better, given the extra supports for marxism and progressivism in the labor movement. But the disaster of Nazism in 1933–1945 scattered the progressive potentials into an Anglo-American diaspora, including younger generations yet to enter the profession, such as Eric Hobsbawm (1917–), Sidney Pollard (1925–), and Francis L. Carsten (1911–1998). With the conservative restoration of academic history after 1945, social history made little progress in West Germany before the 1970s. In Britain, by contrast, the foundations were being assembled. The democratic patriotism of World War II then moved some historians away from the narrower state-focused work dominant in the profession.

Similar trajectories occurred elsewhere in Europe too. The potentials for social history coalesced in the initiatives of reform-minded sociologists, or in the internalist histories of labor movements, but with little imprint on academic history, where state-centered perspectives stayed supreme. This was true in central Europe (Austria, Czechoslovakia), the Low Countries, and Scandinavia, as well as Germany and Britain. Sweden, with half a century of virtually uninterrupted social democratic government from the 1930s, was a classic case. The progressivist public culture brought together converging traditions of historical work, sustaining the social history departures of the 1960s—on the one hand, the pioneering investigations of reform-driven social expertise (in demography, family policy, public health, and so on); and on the other hand, the popular institutional histories of the labor movement.

Elsewhere, the shoots were destroyed by fascism and dictatorship (Hungary 1920–1944, Italy 1922–1945, Portugal 1926–1974, Spain 1939–1975, most of eastern Europe from the mid-1920s and early 1930s), by Nazi occupation in World War II, or by Stalinization of Eastern Europe after 1948. Some national historiographies were disastrously hit. In Poland the signs were vigorous after 1918, with new universities, new chairs of history, new journals, and a general refounding of intellectual life under the republic. Beyond the older military, constitutional, and legal historiography, freshly endowed with resources under the new state, Polish historical studies saw the establishment of economic history by Jan Rutkowski (1886–1949) and Franciszek Bujak (1875–1953), new explorations in cultural history, and the first moves to specifically social history (as elsewhere, in medieval and early modern studies of landholding and religion). As such, Polish historiography showed similar potential to Germany and Britain. But Nazism obliterated these, by the most brutal wartime deprivations, destruction of libraries and archives, erasure of prewar institutional life, and the physical liquidation of the intelligentsia, including the profession of historians. After 1945 institutional supports were recreated remarkably fast by reestablishing the universities and founding research institutes, only to be compromised once again by Stalinization. This reemphasized democracy's importance for social history in both the political changes of 1918 and the longer-run influence of labor movements and other progressive factors of intellectual life.

THE *ANNALES* PARADIGM IN FRENCH HISTORY: THE SOCIAL SCIENCE MODEL

One case of social history's institutionalization inside academic history was France, where key interwar departures established unbroken lines of continuity down to the 1970s. Certain underlying conditions enabled this to happen. One was the well-known centralization of political culture, higher education, and the administrative state in France, where access to central resources, the levers of intellectual patronage and prestige, and the metropolitan matrix of knowledge production in Paris gave the academic elite far more power to set the terms of discussion than in the more dispersed intellectual cultures of Britain, Germany, and elsewhere. From early in the twentieth century, the École Pratique des Hautes Études (founded 1868) dominated scholarly research, and the new sixth section dealing with the social sciences after 1947 quickly overshadowed the older fourth section responsible for history and philology.

The French Revolution's place in the country's political life was inherently encouraging to social history, given popular insurrection and the presence of the masses in 1789–1793. From Albert Mathiez (1874–1932) to Georges Lefebvre (1874–1959) and Albert Soboul (1914–1982), the Revolution sustained a strong line of social-historical research lacking in Britain until Christopher Hill revived study of the English Revolution in the 1950s. Lefebvre, in *Les paysans du Nord pendant la Révolution francaise* (1924) and *The Great Fear of 1789: Rural Panic in Revolutionary France* (original French edition, 1932), and Soboul, in *The Parisian Sans-Culottes and the French Revolution, 1793–4* (original French edition, 1958), produced innovative and inspiring classics of social history. Ernest Labrousse (1895–1988) pioneered the quantitative study of economic fluctuations. He situated 1789 in an economic conjuncture, for which the history of prices and wages, bad harvests, and unemployment gave the key (*La crise de l'économie francaise à la fin de l'Ancien Régime et au début de la Révolution* [1944]). His general model (comparing 1789, 1830, and 1848) worked upward from price movements and the structural problems of the economy, through the wider ramifications of social crisis, and finally to the mishandling of the consequences by government.

As in Britain and Germany, an early impulse to social history came from economic history or sociology, but with greater resonance among historians. For *The Great Fear*, which concerns peasant uprisings in the first phase of the French Revolution, Lefebvre read the crowd theories of Gustav Le Bon, the social theory

of Émile Durkheim, and the ideas of Maurice Halbwachs about collective memory. The influence of the economist François Simiand (1873–1935) was key. In 1903 he disparaged traditional *histoire événementielle* (history of events), and attacked the historians' three "idols of the tribe"—politics, the individual, and chronology. Simiand's essay appeared in a new journal, *Revue de synthèse historique,* founded in 1900 by the philosopher of history Henri Berr (1863–1954), which opened a dialogue with social science. Among Berr's younger supporters were Lucien Febvre (1878–1956) and Marc Bloch (1866–1944), who joined the *Revue* in 1907 and 1912 respectively.

Febvre's dissertation, *Philippe II et la Franche-Comté* (1912), was palpably indifferent to military and diplomatic events. He located Philip II's policies in the geography, social structure, religious life, and social changes of the region, stressing conflicts between absolutism and provincial privileges, nobles and bourgeois, Catholics and Protestants. He inverted the usual precedence, which viewed great events from the perspective of rulers and treated regional histories as effects. Region became the indispensable structural context, for which geography, economics, and demography were all required. Appointed to Strasbourg University in 1920, Febvre met Bloch, who rejected traditional political history under Durkheim's influence before the war. In 1924 Bloch published *The Royal Touch,* which deals with the popular belief that kings have the ability to heal the skin disease scrofula by the power of touch, and its relationship to conceptions of English and French kingship. This remarkable study freed historical perspective from simple narrative time, reattaching it to longer frames of structural duration. It practiced comparison. It also stressed *mentalité,* or the collective understanding and religious psychology of the time, as against the contemporary "common-sense" question of whether the king's touch actually healed or not.

These twin themes—structural history (as against political history or the "history of events"), and history of mentalities (as against the history of formal ideas)—gave unity to the Febvre-Bloch collaboration. In his later works Febvre switched to studying the mental climate specific to the sixteenth century, in *Martin Luther: A Destiny* (original French edition, 1928), and especially *The Problem of Unbelief in the Sixteenth Century: The Religion of Rabelais* (original French edition, 1947). Bloch, conversely, shifted from the archaeology of mind-sets to the archaeology of structures in *French Rural History: An Essay on Its Basic Characteristics* (original French edition, 1931), and *Feudal Society* (original French edition, 1939–1940). With his holistic account of feudalism, combining analysis of the "mental structures" of the age with its socioeconomic relations for a picture of the whole environment, Bloch departed radically from prevailing work. He insisted on comparison, making Europe, not the nation, the entity of study. He exchanged conventional chronologies (like reigns of kings) for epochal time, or the longue durée. He shifted attention from military service (the dominant approach to feudalism) to the social history of agriculture and relationships on the land. He moved away from the history of the law, landholding, kingship, and the origins of states in the narrow institutional sense. All these moves came to characterize "structural history."

In 1929 Bloch and Febvre made their interests into a program with a journal, *Annales d'histoire économique et sociale.* The journal quickly acquired prestige, as Febvre and Bloch moved from Strasbourg to Paris. But it was after 1945, with the founding of the sixth section for the social sciences of the École Pratique des Hautes Études, with Febvre as president, that *Annales* really took off, tragically boosted by Bloch's execution by the Germans in June 1944 for his role in the Resistance. His indictment of French historiography's narrowness now merged into enthusiasm for a new start, denouncing the rottenness of the old elites, who capitulated in 1940 and collaborated with the Nazis under Vichy. The change of name to *Annales: économies, sociétés, civilisations* (1946) signified this enhanced vision. The sixth section also placed history at the center of the new interdisciplinary regime, in a leadership among the social sciences unique in the Western world. Sociology, geography, and economics were key influences for Bloch and Febvre, now joined by structural anthropology and linguistics, including Claude Lévi-Strauss (1908–), Roland Barthes (1915–1980), and Pierre Bourdieu (1930–). The term *histoire totale* (total history) now became identified with *Annales.*

Febvre's assistant was Fernand Braudel (1902–1985), his heir as president of the sixth section (1956–1972) and director of *Annales* (1957–1969). Braudel's career was framed by two monuments of scholarship—*The Mediterranean and the Mediterranean World in the Age of Philip II* (original French edition, 1949), researched in the 1930s, and the three-volume *Civilization and Capitalism, 15th–18th Century* (original French edition, 1979). In these great works Braudel schematized the complex practice of his mentors, distinguishing three temporalities or levels of analysis that functioned as a materialist grand design, shrinking great men and big events into the sovereign causalities of economics, population, and environment. Braudel's causal logic moved upward from the structural history of the longue durée (land-

ANNALES, 1950–1970

Attempts to replicate Braudel's *Mediterranean* included the twelve-volume *Seville et l'Atlantique (1504–1650)* (1955–1959) by Pierre Chaunu (1923–), and the three-volume *La Catalogne dans l'Espagne moderne. Recherches sur les fondements économiques des structures nationales* (1962) of Pierre Vilar (1906–). With Pierre Goubert (1915–) and Emmanuel Le Roy Ladurie (1929–), demography then surpassed price series and economic cycles as the main technical concern, in *Beauvais et le Beauvasis de 1600 à 1730: Contribution de l'histoire sociale de la France du XVIIe siècle,* two volumes (1960), and *The Peasants of Languedoc,* two volumes (original French edition, 1966) respectively. A collective project managed by Francois Furet (1927–1998) on *Livre et société dans la France du XVIIIe siècle* (1965–1970) applied quantification to patterns of ancien régime intellectual life, extending literacy into the statistical study of book production, reception, the sociology of the reading public and the provincial academies, content analysis, and so forth. It corresponded to Febvre's last work, prepared for publication by Henri Jean Martin, *The Coming of the Book: The Impact of Printing 1450–1800* (original French edition, 1958). Robert Mandrou (1921–1984) cleaved more to "historical psychology," dissecting the "mental climate of an age" in various works, including *An Introduction to Modern France: An Essay in Historical Psychology* (original French edition, 1961), and *Magistrats et sorciers en France au XVIIe siècle, une analyse de psychologie historique* (1968). The independent scholar Philippe Ariès (1914–1984) pioneered cultural histories of the early modern era converging with *Annales.* His *Centuries of Childhood* (1960) was one of the most influential works of history in this early postwar time.

scape, climate, demography, deep patterns of economic life, long-run norms and habits, the reproduction of social structures, the stabilities of popular understanding, the repetitions of everyday life), through the medium-term changes of conjunctures (where the rise and fall of economies, social systems, and states became visible), to the faster moving narrative time of *l'histoire événementielle* (human-made events, the familiar military, diplomatic, and political histories *Annales* wanted to supplant). In this thinking, the "deeper level" of structure imposed "upper limits" on human possibilities for a particular civilization, and determined the pace and extent of change. This was the historian's appropriate concern, from which "events" were a diversion.

Braudel's rendering of *Annales* ideals realized the goal of Green's *Short History of the English People*—the dethroning of kings—but divested of all progressivist or "whiggish" narrative design. This uplifting quality was exchanged for a very different model of progress, rendering the world knowable through social science (economics, demography, geography, anthropology, and quantitative techniques). *Annales* history became counterposed to the historiography of the French Revolution, where progressivism and the great event remained alive and well. *Mentalité* solidified into an implicit master category of structure. Braudel's project was imposingly schematic. His works were ordered into a reified hierarchy of materialist determinations, locating "real" significance in the structural and conjunctural levels, and reducing the third level to the most conventional and unanalytic recitation of events. Reciprocity of determination—so challenging in Bloch's work on feudalism—disappeared. Major dramas of the early modern age such as religious conflict startled by their absence. But Braudel's magnum opus on the Mediterranean had few parallels in the sheer grandiosity of its knowledge and design.

In social history's comparative emergence, *Annales* had a vital institution-building role, with (uniquely in Europe) long continuity going back to the 1920s, establishing both protocols of historical method and understanding, and a cumulative tradition of collective discussion, research, training, and publication. Interdisciplinary cohabitation with the social sciences was essential, with history (again uniquely) at the center. Quantification was hard-wired into this intellectual culture: "from a scientific point of view, the only social history is quantitative history," in one characteristically dogmatic statement (François Furet and Adeline Daumard in 1959, quoted by Iggers, *New Directions,* p. 66). As it emerged into the 1960s, these were the hallmarks—history as a social science, quantitative methodology, long-run analyses of prices, trade and population, structural history, a materialist model of causation. Certain key terms—longue durée, *mentalité,* and of course *histoire totale*—passed into historians' currency elsewhere.

Under Braudel *Annales* became a magnet for "new" history in France. Until the 1970s, it was mainly known in English for Bloch's *Feudal Society* (translated 1961), although Philippe Ariès's maverick history of childhood also appeared in English (1962).

Its influence extended into Italy, Belgium, and eastern Europe, especially Poland, where many connections developed. *Annales* also opened dialogues with historians in the Soviet Union.

BRITISH MARXIST HISTORIANS: POPULIST SOCIAL HISTORY AFTER WORLD WAR II

National historiographies move on varying times, with the dynamics of intellectual cultures and traditions, institutional pressures, and local debates, as well as the external exigences of national politics and contemporary events. While Germany experienced the catastrophe of Nazism, severing the shoots of historiographical growth, and France enjoyed institutional continuities around French Revolutionary studies and *Annales,* Britain experienced modest sedimentations of social-historical work. George Macaulay Trevelyan (1876–1962), Cambridge Regius Professor of Modern History from 1927, maintained the popularizing tradition with his classic *English Social History: A Survey of Six Centuries, Chaucer to Queen Victoria* (1942), and also trained John Harold Plumb (1911–), a major influence on British social history between the 1950s and 1970s. In the 1950s a wider archipelago of activity appeared—with the economic historians Hrothgar John Habakkuk (1915–), Max Hartwell (1921–), and Peter Matthias at Oxford; George Kitson Clark (1900–1975) and Henry Pelling (1918–) at Cambridge; A. E. Musson (1920–) and Harold Perkin at Manchester; Arthur J. Taylor and Asa Briggs (1921–) at Leeds; F. M. L. Thompson in London. Asa Briggs was especially influential, through his early research on Birmingham and more general works like *Victorian Cities* (1963), and in the pathbreaking local research edited in *Chartist Studies* (1959) and *Essays in Labour History* (1960). Perkin occupied the first university post in social history (Manchester, 1951), took up the first professorial chair (Lancaster, 1967), and published the key general history, *The Origins of Modern English Society, 1780–1880* (1969).

Thus Britain saw the gradual accrual of a scholarly tradition, borne by an array of economic historians, pioneers like Briggs, the social policy nexus at the London School of Economics, and the networks of labor history (solidified by the Society for the Study of Labour History and its bulletin in 1960). The Communist Party Historians' Group (1946–1957) had disproportionate impact in social history's great 1960s expansion. Its members came to the Communist Party (CPGB) via antifascism, and most left in the crisis of communism in 1956, which ended the

Group's existence. Very few taught at the center of British university life (at Oxbridge or London). Some were not historians by discipline, like the older Maurice Dobb (1900–1976), the Cambridge economist, whose *Studies in the Development of Capitalism* (1946) focused an important discussion. Others had positions in adult education.

These British marxist historians included Eric Hobsbawm (1917–), Christopher Hill (1910–), Victor Kiernan (1913–), Rodney Hilton (1916–), George Rudé (1910–1993), John Saville (1916–), Dorothy Thompson (1923–), Raphael Samuel (1938–1996), and E. P. Thompson (1924–1993). Their collective discussions shaped the contours of social history in Britain, with international resonance comparable to *Annales*. University history departments gave them few supports. Rudé and E. P. Thompson secured academic appointments only in the 1960s, Rudé by traveling to Australia. The main impulse came from politics, a powerful sense of history's pedagogy, and broader identification with democratic values and popular history. A leading mentor was the nonacademic CPGB intellectual, journalist, and Marx scholar, Dona Torr (1883–1957), author of *Tom Mann and his Times* (1936), to whom the Group paid tribute in *Democracy and the Labour Movement* (1954), edited by John Saville.

The Group aimed for a social history of Britain to contest official accounts, inspired by A. L. Morton's *A People's History of England* (1938). Some members specialized in British history per se—Hilton on the English peasantry, Hill on the English Revolution, Saville on labor history, Dorothy Thompson on Chartism. Others displayed extraordinary international range. Hobsbawm's interests embraced British labor history, European popular movements, and Latin American peasantries, plus the study of nationalism and his unparalleled general histories, from *The Age of Revolution, 1789–1848* (1962), through *The Age of Capital, 1848–1875* (1975), and *The Age of Empire, 1875–1914* (1987), to *The Age of Extremes, 1914–1991* (1994). Kiernan was another remarkable generalist, covering aspects of imperialism, early modern state formation, and history of the aristocratic duel, as well as British relations with China and the 1854 Spanish Revolution. Rudé was a leading historian of the French Revolution and popular protest, with *The Crowd in the French Revolution* (1959), *The Crowd in History* (1964), and his collaboration with Hobsbawm, *Captain Swing* (1969). Two others were British historians with huge international influence—Raphael Samuel as the moving genius behind the History Workshop movement and its journal; and E. P. Thompson through his great works, *The Making of the English Working Class* (1963),

Whigs and Hunters: The Origin of the Black Act (1975), and *Customs in Common* (1991).

This British marxist historiography was embedded in specifically British concerns. Several voices spoke the languages of English history exclusively—Hill, Hilton, Saville, the Thompsons. The broader tradition was intensely focused on national themes, as in E. P. Thompson's famous "The Peculiarities of the English" (1965) and first book, *William Morris, Romantic to Revolutionary* (1955), or the cognate works of Raymond Williams (1921–1988), *Culture and Society* (1958) and *The Long Revolution* (1961). British concerns were strongest in two areas. The Group decisively shaped labor history, in Hobsbawm's foundational essays in *Labouring Men* (1964), Saville's influence (institutionalized in the multivolume *Dictionary of Labour Biography* from 1972), and after 1960 in the Labour History Society. Labor history in Britain was linked to specific questions about the presumed failure of the labor movement to follow Marx's development model. It also shaped the history of capitalist industrialization in Britain, most notably through the standard of living controversy between Hobsbawm and Hartwell in 1957–1963 over whether industrialists had improved or degraded living standards of the working population. Saville's *Rural Depopulation in England and Wales, 1851–1951* (1957) was a counterpoint to the mainstream accounts of G. E. Mingay, *English Landed Society in the Eighteenth Century* (1963), and F. M. L. Thompson, *English Landed Society in the Nineteenth Century* (1963). Several classics addressed this question, from E. P. Thompson's *The Making of the English Working Class*, and Hobsbawm and Rudé's *Captain Swing*, to Hobsbawm's general British economic history, *Industry and Empire: From 1750 to the Present Day* (1968).

In other ways, the marxist historians were the opposite of parochial. Rudé worked with Lefebvre and Soboul; Kiernan practiced an eclectic version of global history; Hobsbawm maintained wide connections with Europe and Latin America; Thomas Hodgkin (1910–1982) and Basil Davidson (1914–) vitally influenced African history, again from the margins in adult education and journalism. Hobsbawm interacted with Braudel and other *Annalistes,* and with Labrousse, Lefebvre, and Soboul. Internationally, Hobsbawm and Rudé transformed study of social protest in preindustrial societies. Rudé deconstructed older stereotypes of "the mob," using the French Revolution and eighteenth-century riots in England and France to analyze the rhythms, organization, and motives behind collective action, specifying a sociology of the "faces in the crowd." Hobsbawm analyzed the transformations in popular consciousness accompanying capital-

RICHARD COBB (1917–1996)

Richard Cobb was a contemporary of the British marxist historians, and trained under Georges Lefebvre with George Rudé and Albert Soboul. He taught in Aberystwyth, Manchester, and Leeds (1953–1962) before moving to Oxford. He exercised legendary influence in the 1960s as an inspiringly original social historian, with a penchant for reckless bohemianism. His *Les Armées révolutionnaires: Instrument de la Terreur dans les départements, avril 1793 (floréal An II)*, two volume (1962, translated as *The People's Armies*, 1987) was followed by *Terreur et Subsistances, 1793–1795* (1965), *A Second Identity: Essays on France and French History* (1969), and *The Police and the People: French Popular Protest, 1789–1820* (1970). In Leeds he was a friend of E. P. Thompson, whose article "Moral Economy" began as an intended collaboration with Cobb on grain riots. If social history implied identification with the common people, Cobb was one of its most charismatic practitioners. Traumatized by 1968, he shed this stance. The later works— *Reactions to the French Revolution* (1972), *Paris and its Provinces, 1792–1802* (1975), and a string of mainly personal writings—became ever more idiosyncratic and suffered as a result. But he re-created the world of the 1790s with remarkable eloquence, knew the archives like the back of his hand, and inspired a generation of French Revolutionary specialists—Colin Lucas, Peter Jones, Gwynne Lewis, Olwen Hufton, Alan Forrest, Martyn Lyons, William Scott, Richard Andrews, Colin Jones, Geoffrey Ellis, and others.

ist industrialization—in studies of Luddism and pre–trade-union labor protest; in *Primitive Rebels* (1959) and *Bandits* (1969), concerning "archaic" protests in agrarian societies (social banditry, millenarianism, mafia); and in work on peasants and peasant movements in Latin America. He pioneered the conversations of history and anthropology, and redefined politics in societies without democratic constitutions or a developed parliamentary system.

The Communist Party Historians' Group's biggest step was the new journal, *Past and Present* (a "Journal of Scientific History"), launched in 1952 to preserve dialogue with non-marxist historians when the Cold War was otherwise closing it down. The editor and instigator was the ancient history historian John Morris (1913–1977), joined by Hobsbawm, Hill, Hilton, Dobb, and the archaeologist Vere Gordon Childe (1892–1957), who were all marxists, plus a group of distinguished non-marxists, including ancient history historian A. H. M. (Hugo) Jones (1904–1970), Czech historian R. R. Betts, Tudor-Stuart historian D. B. Quinn (1909–), and generalist Geoffrey Barraclough (1908–1984). From the start, contacts with Europe were good, including eastern Europe (with early articles by the Soviet historians Boris Porshnev and E. A. Kosminskii, and the Czechoslovaks J. V. Polisensky and Arnost Klima), and France (not only Lefebvre and Soboul, but also *Annales*). In 1958 the board was broadened to lessen the marxist dominance, with early modernists Lawrence Stone (1919–) and John Elliott (1930–), medievalist Trevor Aston (1925–1986), archaeologist S. S. Frere (1918–), and the sociologists Norman Birnbaum and Peter Worsley. The subtitle changed to a "Journal of Historical Studies."

In its first twenty years, *Past and Present* made vital contributions to the rise of social history. One was internationalism, for it brought European work into English, aided by its editors' political networks, direct exchanges with France, and the 1950 International Historical Congress in Paris and its new social history section. Secondly, like *Annales*, it urged comparative study of societies within an overall frame of arguments about historical change, posed at the level of European or global movements and systems. This commitment, which crystallized from the agenda of the Communist Party Historians' Group, recurred in the annual conference themes from 1957—early modern revolutions, the general crisis of the seventeenth century, origins of industrialization, war and society 1300–1600, science and religion, colonialism and nationalism. Thirdly, it opened interdisciplinary conversations with sociologists and anthropologists, encouraged by marxist acceptance of the indivisibility of knowledge, again paralleling *Annales*. Fourthly, social history went together with economics, whether via the *Annaliste* master category of structures, or via marxism and the materialist theory of history. Academically, where social history was disengaged from the "manners and morals" mode of popularizing, or projects of "people's history," it was coupled to economic history, as in departments of economic and social history created in some British universities in the 1960s.

"Social history" meant understanding the dynamics of whole societies. It was the ambition to connect political events to underlying social forces. In 1947–1950 the Communist Party Historians' Group focused on the transition from feudalism to capitalism and associated questions (rise of absolutism, bourgeois revolution, agrarian problems, the Reformation). Hobsbawm's two-part article on "The Crisis of the Seventeenth Century" (1954) then prompted the salient discussion of *Past and Present's* first decade, collected as *Crisis in Europe, 1560–1660* (1965), edited by Trevor Aston. This debate energized historians of France, Spain, Sweden, Germany, Bohemia, Russia, Ireland, and early modern Europe generally, as well as historians of Britain. It connected the seventeenth-century political upheavals to forms of economic crisis graspable in Europeanwide terms, in "the last phase of the general transition from a feudal to a capitalist economy" (Aston, *Crisis,* p. 5). It built a case for studying religious conflict in social terms. It grasped the nettle of conceptualizing the histories of societies as a whole, with profound implications for their future historiographies, as in John Elliott's treatment of "The Decline of Spain" (1961). It reemphasized the convergence between *Past and Present* and *Annales,* for Hobsbawm relied on work sponsored by Braudel. One key essay by Pierre Vilar ("The Age of Don Quixote") was not translated until much later, in 1971. Above all, the debate demonstrated the "comparative method."

PROLIFERATION AND GROWTH: THE BOOM YEARS, THE 1960s TO THE 1980s

Annales and *Past and Present* laid the cumulative foundations for social history's rise in the 1960s. *Past and Present's* main strength remained medieval and early modern, where its international influence became sovereign. By 1987 only five of thirty-three titles in the *Past and Present Publications* series (Cambridge University Press) fell after the French Revolution. *Annales* also consolidated its influence, partly from Braudel's post-1962 base at the Maison des Sciences de l'Homme. Work was systematically translated, beginning with Braudel's *Mediterranean* (1972) and *Capitalism and Material Life, 1400–1600* (original French edition, 1973), plus Peter Burke's edition of articles, *Economy and Society in Early Modern Europe* (1972). Traian Stoianovich's *French Historical Method: The Annales Paradigm* (1976) gave a systematic guide, and in 1978 Immanuel Wallerstein founded the Fernand Braudel Center in Binghamton and its journal, *Review.* This further institutionalization, and concurrent transplanting to the United States, continued with Lawrence Stone's founding of the Shelby Cullom Davis Center at Princeton University (1969), which with J. H. Elliott's presence at

the Institute of Advanced Study became a transatlantic outpost of *Past and Present.*

By 1971, when Hobsbawm published his stock-taking survey, "From Social History to the History of Society," social history had already taken off, and the next decade saw a remarkable diffusion—with conferences, international networks, new journals, and special societies (like the British Social History Society, 1976). This was inseparable from events in the world at large. The big 1960s expansion of Western higher education created a brief buoyancy of funding for scholarly history on a freshly professionalized basis. The political ferment radicalized new generations of students toward new kinds of history, pushing on the discipline's boundaries in vital ways.

The best index was the launching of new journals. Anticipating and shaping these trends was *Comparative Studies in Society and History,* founded in 1958 by the medievalist Sylvia Thrupp, in a program of comparative social science. It was followed in the United States by *Journal of Social History* (1967–), *Journal of Interdisciplinary History* (1970–), *Radical History Review* (1973–), and *Social Science History* (1976–). In Britain there were *Social History* and *History Workshop Journal* (both 1976–), plus *Journal of Peasant Studies* (1973–), and *Journal of Historical Geography* (1975–) beyond the discipline. The West German *Geschichte und Gesellschaft* was launched in 1975. Existing specialisms like labor history broadened their charge, turning from institutional histories of socialism and trade unions, and associated studies of working conditions, industrial relations, and strikes, to social histories of the working class. This was true of the British *Bulletin of the Labour History Society,* whose conferences reflected the new ambitions. The same applied to the U.S. Study Group for European Labor and Working-Class History formed in December 1971, whose newsletter became *International Labor and Working Class History.* In West Germany *Archiv für Sozialgeschichte,* a yearbook of socialist history (1961–), transformed itself in the early 1970s into a hefty annual of current social-historical research.

The influence of social science. Social history's arrival was borne by interdisciplinarity, which meant dependence on social science. In the United States, a one-sided dialogue continued between sociology and history, as a succession of Social Science Research Council Reports (1946, 1954, 1963) expounded the virtues of theory for historians. Programmatic publications appeared, including *Sociology and History: Methods* (1968) edited by Seymour Martin Lipset and Richard Hofstadter, and Robert F. Berkhofer Jr.'s *A Behavioral Approach to Historical Analysis* (1969). In

France, by contrast, the sixth section's structure already placed history at the heart of interdisciplinary work, now reinforced by Braudel's Maison des Sciences de l'Homme. In Britain the relationship was more pragmatic. Marxism had lost self-confidence after the crisis of Stalinism in 1956, and *Past and Present* turned to dialogue with non-marxist sociology and anthropology, where sociologist Philip Abrams (1933–1981) and anthropologist Jack Goody were especially active. Hobsbawm's *Primitive Rebels* was conceived in a running conversation with Meyer Fortes, Max Gluckman (1911–1975), and other social anthropologists.

This first phase of interdisciplinarity saw the ascendancy of U.S. behavioral science, guided by modernization theory. *Comparative Studies in Society and History* held the vanguard place, followed by *Journal of International History, Journal of Social History,* and then *Social Science History* in the Social Science History Association. Other new journals, such as *Politics & Society* (1970–) and *Theory and Society* (1974–), published articles by sociologists and political scientists writing historically. The turning to sociology was eclectic, as historians sought to "learn" theory from their colleagues. The most self-conscious borrowings involved methodology rather than theory per se, with sophisticated quantification in demography, family history, mobility studies, migration, urban history, and more. An extreme version of such dependency developed in West Germany in the 1970s. The destructive effects of Nazism left an exceptionally conservative historiography commanding the 1950s, and despite the efforts of Werner Conze (1910–1986) and his *Arbeitskreis für moderne Sozialgeschichte* (formed in Heidelberg, 1957), little work in social history occurred before the 1960s. Without strong indigenous supports, Hans Ulrich Wehler (1931–), Jürgen Kocka (1941–), and others turned directly to U.S. social sciences, as well as to Max Weber. Their new journal *Geschichte und Gesellschaft* was the result.

One boom area for social science was family history, pioneered in Peter Laslett's *The World We Have Lost* (1965). Demanding a new "social structural history" embracing whole societies and the "structural function of the family in the pre-industrial world," Laslett headed the Cambridge Population Group with evangelical zeal. But aside from extreme methodological sophistication, Laslett's main achievement became his "null hypothesis" for the nuclear family's continuity across industrialization, laying to rest the myth of progressive nucleation. Demographic historians became masters of falsification, dismantling ungrounded claims in dialogue with contemporary sociology (as in Michael Anderson's *The Family in Nineteenth-Century Lancashire* [1971], a response to Neil J. Smelser's *Social Change in the Industrial Revolution* [1959]). But their ability to retheorize social change beyond the technics of the immediate debates was far less. From the foundational conference of 1969, bringing twenty-two international scholars to Cambridge (Peter Laslett, ed., *Household and Family in Past Time* [1972]), to the apogee of the Cambridge Group's achievement, in E. A. Wrigley and Roger S. Schofield, *The Population History of England, 1541–1871* (1981), the broader implications were unclear. The strongest explanatory program for demographic history remained *Annales,* where population was the prime mover of social change, notably in Emmanuel Le Roy Ladurie's *The Peasants of Languedoc* (original French edition, 1966). Ironically (given Laslett's default cautions), the first two general histories of the family in the 1970s, Edward Shorter's *The Making of the Modern Family* (1976), and Lawrence Stone's *The Family, Sex, and Marriage in England 1500–1800* (1977), presented bold teleologies of modernization, expressed in Stone's "rise of affective individualism."

Family history was integrated more successfully in studies of "protoindustrialization," using work by Franklin Mendels ("Proto-Industrialization: The First Phase of the Industrialization Process," in *Journal of Economic History,* 1972) and the Swiss historian Rudolf Braun's *Industrialization and Everyday Life* (original German edition, 1960) and *Sozialer und kultureller Wandel in einem ländlichen Industriegebiet* (1965). The pioneering book was Peter Kriedte, Hans Medick, and Jürgen Schlumbohm, *Industrialization Before Industrialization: Rural Industry in the Genesis of Capitalism* (original German edition, 1977), which reconnected family and demography to capitalism and production in a social history of industrialization. This continued through Charles Tilly's studies of proletarianization, and David Levine's *Family Formations in an Age of Nascent Capitalism* (1977), and *Reproducing Families: The Political Economy of English Population History* (1987). In German-speaking Europe, Michael Mitterauer and Reinhard Sieder, *The European Family: Patriarchy to Partnership from the Middle Ages to the Present* (original German edition, 1977), laid out a similar program, as did essays by Karin Hausen and Heidi Rosenbaum in the inaugural issue of *Geschichte und Gesellschaft.* Nonmaterialist aspects of family life remained neglected by comparison. David Hunt's *Parents and Children in History: The Psychology of Family Life in Early Modern France* (1970) seemed an idiosyncratic exception. On the other hand, Eli Zaretsky's *Capitalism, the Family, and Personal Life* (1976) explored territory feminist historians were about to map.

This story of social history's takeoff in the 1960s, sustained by social science, was replicated in other subfields. In 1971 Hobsbawm listed six of these: demography and kinship; urban studies; class formation; "mentalities" or "culture" in the anthropological sense; social transformations like industrialization or "modernization"; and social movements and social protest. Urban history was a good microcosm. Distinctive to the English-speaking world, it was forged in Britain by H. J. Dyos (1921–1978). Building on Leicester University's tradition of local history and studies of local government going back to the Webbs, Dyos formed the Urban History Group (1962–1963), whose newsletter was institutionalized as the *Urban History Yearbook* in 1974, becoming the journal *Urban History* in 1992. Dyos was a tireless proselytizer, combining social science rigor with eclectic thematics, from the city's political economy and spatial organization, through the social histories of the built environment, land sales, mass transit, labor markets, slum dwelling, and suburbanization, to urban images and representations. The two-volume showcase, *The Victorian City: Images and Realities* (1973), coedited with Michael Wolff, defined urbanization as a site where social scientists, humanists, and historians could meet. The memorial for Dyos, *The Pursuit of Urban History* (1983), edited by Derek Fraser and Anthony Sutcliffe, confirmed this transdisciplinary potential. The urban community study became the vehicle for studying class formation. Elsewhere (as in Sweden and West Germany in the 1970s), the subfield was slower and more narrowly convened around social science.

History of youth and childhood was also invented by social historians in the 1960s. Impetus came from historians of population and family, especially among early modernists. Most exciting were the deconstructive implications, turning the basic categories of the human life-course into historical creations, with childhood as an artifact of the specifically modern era. Philippe Ariès's *Centuries of Childhood* (original French edition, 1960) was key. Interest also focused on youth subcultures inspired by 1968 in freely cross-disciplinary ways—partly at the Birmingham Centre for Contemporary Cultural Studies, partly in radical criminology and the sociology of deviance. Such work intersected with new social histories of crime, doubly moved by the positivist excitements of social science methodology (measuring change, establishing patterns, specifying causal relations) and populist identification with "history from below." The British marxist historians—Rudé's studies of the crowd, Thompson's *The Making of the English Working Class,* Hobsbawm in general—also provided inspiration. As so often, Hobsbawm's writings—on primitive rebel-

THE IMPACT OF CHARLES TILLY (1929–)

Charles Tilly was trained in sociology at Harvard (Ph.D. 1958), and taught for many years with a joint appointment in sociology and history at the University of Michigan, before moving to the New School for Social Research in 1984. His many books and essays across a wide variety of subjects, concentrating on nineteenth-century France and Britain, made him the preeminent sociologist and social historian of collective action in the 1960s and 1970s. He stood for quantitative and collaborative research on the grand scale, specifying the bases and rationality of collective action in relation to the impact of capitalism (including its demographic aspects) and the growth of national states. His impact on social historians trained in the United States since the 1960s was enormous, including William H. Sewell Jr. and Joan W. Scott, whose *Structure and Mobility: The Men and Women of Marseilles, 1829–1970* (1985) and *The Glassworkers of Carmaux* (1974) directly reflected the social science ascendancy of social history's growth in the 1960s. The wider cohort included Tilly's students at the University of Michigan, such as Michael Hanagan, author of *The Logic of Solidarity: Artisans and Industrial Workers in Three French Towns, 1871–1914* (1980), and Ronald Aminzade, author of *Class, Politics, and Early Industrial Capitalism: A Study of Mid-Nineteenth Century Toulouse, France* (1981). Another line of influence passed from Lynn Hunt, author of *Revolution and Urban Politics in Provincial France: Troyes and Reims, 1786–1790* (1978), to Ted W. Margadant, author of *Urban Rivalries in the French Revolution* (1992), which attempts to do for the towns what Tilly had done for the countryside in *The Vendée.*

lion, social banditry, social criminality—had defined the basic terrain.

In the 1960s identifying with the people and learning from social science (the doubled genealogies of social history, in British marxism and *Annales*) were not in serious tension. Charles Tilly's *The Vendée* (1964) was an exciting model of archivally grounded historical sociology, connecting political allegiance to socioeconomic patterns in the French Revolution. One strand of Tilly's later work concerned capitalism and state-making, from *The Formation of the National*

States in Western Europe (1975) to *Coercion, Capital, and European States,* A.D. 990–1990 (1990). A cognate interest concerned demographic studies of proletarianization, in *Historical Studies of Changing Fertility* (1978) and in many essays. But Tilly was best known for his sociology of collective action. This required longitudinal research, with big resources, large teams, and huge machineries of quantitative production. After *Strikes in France, 1830–1968* (with Edward Shorter, 1974), and *The Rebellious Century, 1830–1930* (with Louise and Richard Tilly, 1975), Tilly produced *The Contentious French* (1986), and *Popular Contention in Great Britain, 1758–1834* (1995). These were quantitative histories of changing "repertoires of contention" and the rise of modern mass politics, in an argument summarized in "How Protest Modernized in France" (1972), and "Britain Creates the Social Movement" (1982). Tilly's corpus included a programmatic textbook, *From Mobilization to Revolution* (1978), and the macroanalytical *European Revolutions, 1492–1992* (1993), rejoining collective action to capitalism and state-making.

The populist tradition: E. P. Thompson and his impact.

Tilly prodigiously historicized theories of social change—as in *Big Structures, Large Processes, Huge Comparisons* (1984). The main alternative to social science history came from E. P. Thompson, whose *The Making of the English Working Class* (1963) inspired several generations of social historians. His work advanced an eloquent counter-narrative to gradualist versions of British history as the triumphant march of parliamentary evolution, grounding the latter in violence, inequality, and exploitation instead: "I am seeking to rescue the poor stockinger, the Luddite cropper, the 'obsolete' handloom weaver, the 'utopian' artisan, and even the deluded follower of Joanna Southcott, from the enormous condescension of posterity" (p. 12). *The Making* was also an antireductionist manifesto—attacking narrowly based economic history, overdeterministic marxism, and static theories of class. For Thompson, class was dynamic, eventuating through history—a relationship and a process, a common consciousness of capitalist exploitation and state repression, graspable through culture. Through *The Making* the move from labor's institutional study to social histories of working people gained huge momentum, embracing work, housing, nutrition, leisure and sport, drinking, crime, religion, magic and superstition, education, song, literature, childhood, courtship, sexuality, death, and more.

Thompson wrote his great work outside the academy, working in adult education in Leeds, as a Communist (until 1956), New Left activist, and pub-

lic polemicist. He created the Centre for the Study of Social History at Warwick University in 1965, directing it until 1972, when he resigned. Beyond the networks of labor history and *Past and Present,* Thompson's *The Making* was loudly attacked. But it energized younger generations. It also inspired the reviving marxisms so central to the developing social history wave.

Thompson's impact helped two initiatives on the margins to form. One was the Social History Group at Oxford (1965–1974), including the marxist author of *Outcast London* (1971), Gareth Stedman Jones (1942–); the historian of Spanish anarchism, Joaquin Romero Maura (1940–); the historian of Nazism, Tim Mason (1940–1990); and especially Raphael Samuel (1934–1996), a schoolboy member of the Communist Party Historians' Group, who taught at Ruskin, the Oxford trade union college, from 1961. Samuel's annual History Workshops became a vital engine of social history, starting modestly, but soon mushrooming into an international event. The first thirteen Workshops met at Ruskin (1967–1979), before migrating around Britain. They inspired a series of pamphlets (twelve, 1970–1974) and books (over thirty, 1975–1990), a local movement, public interventions (in the debate on national curriculum, 1983–1990), and *History Workshop Journal.*

The second movement was women's history. Originally via tense contention with History Workshop and older mentors like Hobsbawm and Thompson, pioneers like Sheila Rowbotham (1943–) drew important support from both. Future leaders of women's history emerged from History Workshop's milieu, including Anna Davin (1940–), Sally Alexander (1943–), and Catherine Hall (1945–). Rowbotham's early works—*Women, Resistance and Revolution* (1972), *Hidden from History* (1973), *Woman's Consciousness, Man's World* (1973)—became markers of the future field. The first National Women's Liberation Conference (Ruskin, 1970) originated as a women's history meeting, and History Workshop 7 (1973) concerned "Women in History." These political contexts, like earlier twentieth-century moments and the Communist Party Historians' Group, shaped social history's emergence.

In the 1960s Thompson moved back in time. His social history of property crimes and the law in eighteenth-century political order, *Whigs and Hunters* (1975), and the work of his Warwick students in *Albion's Fatal Tree* (edited by Douglas Hay, 1975), explored customary culture's transformations under capitalism. Two essays, "Time, Work-Discipline, and Industrial Capitalism" (1967) and "The Moral Economy of the English Crowd in the Eighteenth Century" (1971), appeared in *Past and Present* (whose board Thompson joined in 1969), and a third on "Rough Music" in *Annales* (1972). Two others followed in *Journal of Social History* (1974) and *Social History* (1978), plus a famous lecture on "The Sale of Wives." Gathered in *Customs in Common* (1991), this work transformed perceptions of transition to industrial capitalism, dismantling the industrial revolution's gross causality. *Albion's Fatal Tree* made crime and punishment "central to unlocking the meanings of eighteenth-century social history" (p. 13), and a host of work now confirmed this claim, signaled by three collections of essays: J. S. Cockburn (ed.), *Crime in England, 1550–1800* (1977); V. A. C. Gatrell, Bruce Lenman, and Geoffrey Parker (eds.), *Crime and the Law* (1980); and John Brewer and John Styles (eds.), *An Ungovernable People: The English and their Law in the Seventeenth and Eighteenth Centuries* (1980).

Thompson's influence was international. *The Making* shaped North American, African, and South Asian agendas, no less than it did studies of class formation in Britain and Europe. His eighteenth-century essays had equal resonance, especially "The Moral Economy" (the object of a retrospective international conference in Birmingham, 1992). The 1970s internationalized social history through conferences, journals, and translation. Thompson, Hobsbawm, Tilly, and others joined a series of round tables on social history organized by the Maison des Sciences l'Homme, convening scholars from France, Italy, West Germany, and elsewhere.

Large areas even of the historiographies of Britain and France could not be included here. In France Maurice Agulhon explored the forms of political culture and working-class sociability in the first half of the nineteenth century, especially *The Republic in the Village: The People of the Var from the French Revolution to the Second Republic* (original French edition, 1970). The social history of the nineteenth-century French peasantry has been extraordinarily rich, a gold mine for the politics of the countryside. The proliferating social historiographies of West Germany in the 1970s might have been presented, likewise those in Italy, Scandinavia, and parts of eastern Europe. The historiographies of Wales, Scotland, and Ireland experienced exciting renaissance after the 1970s, and the intellectual cultures of smaller nationalities offered fertile territory for historiographical innovation.

Social history's heyday was the 1970s to late 1980s. Greater self-confidence bridled against social science leadership, and the new journals—*Social History* and *History Workshop Journal* in Britain, *Radical History Review* and the short-lived *Marxist Perspectives* (1978–1980) in the United States—reflected these

tensions. The later 1970s saw several stocktaking essays—by Elizabeth Fox-Genovese and Eugene Genovese (1976), Gareth Stedman Jones (1976), Lawrence Stone (1977 and 1979), Tony Judt (1979), and Geoff Eley and Keith Nield (1980). Social historians emerged from the tutelage of the social science paradigms so appealing ten years before. A new generation was claiming its institutional space, flying the banner of a restlessly aggrandizing social history. This social history was more secure in its own autonomies, impatient with the authorizing function of social science. It professed an unproblematic materialism, often inspired by a marxist revival, open to other social theories, and confident of its own pedagogy. It was never a unitary phenomenon. But some notion of social determination, conceptualized on the ground of material life, aspiring to "society as a whole," delivered a common framework. Hobsbawm's 1971 essay, "From Social History to the History of Society," much cited, translated, and reprinted, provided the characteristic argumentation.

DISPERSAL: SOCIAL HISTORY, FEMINIST THEORY, AND "CULTURAL TURN"

From the later 1980s social history lost its primacy as the acknowledged source of innovation, while the "new cultural history" became the main interdisciplinary site instead. An eclectic and anthropologically oriented cultural analysis took its cue from the American anthropologist Clifford Geertz (1926–) and early modernist Natalie Zemon Davis (1928–), as well as from Thompson. It continued via an antireductionist British marxism, exemplified by Raymond Williams, the Birmingham Centre for Contemporary Cultural Studies, and sociologist Stuart Hall (1932–). It was further extended by the reception of Michel Foucault (1926–1984), whose philosophical works *The Order of Things* (original French edition, 1966) and *The Archaeology of Knowledge* (original French edition, 1969), and highly original treatments of madhouses (1961), hospitals (1963), and prisons (1975), were systematically translated in the 1970s, as were the three volumes of his *History of Sexuality* (original French edition, 1976–1984), and various editions of essays and interviews. Finally, feminist theory became unavoidable for social historians in the 1980s, whereas women's history had been more easily compartmentalized and kept at bay before.

The changes may be variously tracked. Between his 1960s polemics and essays of the mid-1970s, Gareth Stedman Jones stood for a "non-empiricist" and "theoretically informed history," which was material-

CRIME, PUNISHMENT, AND FOUCAULT

Histories of crime and punishment were an important barometer of changes in social history. During the 1970s, social history of crime, law, and imprisonment burgeoned in one of the most popular areas, British history ranging from the sixteenth to the nineteenth centuries, affording an excellent handle on questions of social and political order. Important examples were the products of E. P. Thompson's time at the Warwick Center for Social History—*Whigs and Hunters* and *Albion's Fatal Tree* (both 1975)—and Michael Ignatieff's *A Just Measure of Pain: The Penitentiary in the Industrial Revolution 1750–1850* (1978). Anthologies edited by J. S. Cockburn (1977); V. A. C. Gatrell, Bruce Lenman, and Geoffrey Parker (1980); and John Brewer and John Styles (1980) indicated the scale of activity. Then, from the late 1970s historians were reading Michel Foucault. The next major anthology, edited by Stanley Cohen and Andrew Scull, *Social Control and the State: Historical and Comparative Essays* (1983), already revealed Foucault's impact, with two essays (by Ignatieff and David Ingleby) dealing directly with his ideas. During the 1980s, work on prisons, hospitals, asylums and other places of confinement, social policy and public health; and all forms of governmentality became permeated by Foucault's arguments about power, knowledge, and "regimes of truth." Lynn Hunt's emblematic anthology on *The New Cultural History* (1989) marked this shift, with an essay by Patricia O'Brien on "Michel Foucault's History of Culture." By the 1990s, authors prominent in the 1970s discussions were taking a strong cultural turn, with superb results—from Peter Linebaugh's *The London Hanged: Crime and Civil Society in the Eighteenth Century* (1991), through V. A. C. Gatrell's *The Hanging Tree: Execution and the English People, 1770–1868* (1994), to Richard J. Evans's gargantuan *Rituals of Retribution: Capital Punishment in Germany 1600–1987* (1996). Foucault was not essential to the new directions taken by these authors—for instance, an excellent sampling of German work edited by Richard J. Evans, *The German Underworld: Deviants and Outcasts in German History* (1988), revealed little of Foucault's explicit presence. But it became impossible to imagine the field without him.

ist in social history's common understandings of the time. His *Outcast London* (1971) seemed a worthy successor to its British marxist precursors. Then, in *Languages of Class: Studies in English Working Class History, 1832–1982* (1983), he proposed a linguistic analysis that left the familiar ground of social historians behind. This was followed in 1986 by Joan W. Scott's *American Historical Review* article, "Gender: A Useful Category of Historical Analysis," reprinted in her *Gender and the Politics of History* (1988), which presented more elaborate poststructuralist propositions. By questioning the assumptions around which social analysis was ordered, Foucauldian "discourse" theory destabilized social history's recently acquired self-confidence. Social history became one site of epistemological uncertainty in the humanities and social sciences. Leading voices were questioning social history's underlying materialism, including the determinative coherence of the category of "the social" itself.

Feminism was key to this turmoil. In social historians' earlier advocacy—from *Annales* and *Past and Present* through Hobsbawm's 1971 essay to the later 1970s—women's history played no part. When the latter's pioneering works appeared, they were consigned to a discrete subfield, conceptualized via "separate spheres" or subsumed into the history of the family, a pattern only partly broken by syntheses like Louise Tilly and Joan W. Scott's *Women, Work, and Family* (1978). Only the turning from women's history to gender, as the historical construction of sexual difference, made feminist work impossible to ignore. Much social history still continued unaware. Ira Katznelson and Aristide R. Zolberg (eds.), *Working-Class Formation: Nineteenth-Century Patterns in Western Europe and the United States* (1986), was a telling example. But cumulative studies of gender and work, and gendered critiques of the welfare state, paralleled Scott's theoretical intervention, and by the 1990s social history was examining its gendered suppositions. Works by Sonya O. Rose, *Limited Livelihoods: Gender and Class in Nineteenth-Century England* (1992), Anna Clark, *The Struggle for the Breeches: Gender and the Making of the British Working Class* (1995), and Kathleen Canning, *Languages of Labor and Gender: Female*

Factory Work in Germany, 1850–1914 (1996), set a new standard in this respect, reinforced by the new journals—not just *History Workshop Journal, Social History,* and *Radical History Review,* but also those in women's studies, including *Feminist Studies* (1972–), *Signs* (1975–), *Feminist Review* (1979–), and the newer *Gender and History* (1989–), *Journal of Women's History* (1989–), and *Journal of the History of Sexuality* (1990–).

By 1990 some historians were speaking the language of "cultural constructionism." The impact of deconstructive literary theory and British cultural studies was also felt, mediated extensively by feminism. As "race" pervaded social anxieties and political exchange, it also joined gender as a central category of historical analysis, strengthened by postcolonial studies. Empire returned to the domestic history of European metropolitan societies, initially via anthropology, literary criticism, and cultural studies, exemplified in the work of Ann Stoler, Ann McClintock, or Paul Gilroy. Historians gradually responded in kind, mainly by route of gender. Catherine Hall's work, moving from the classically social-historical *Family Fortunes: Men and Women of the English Middle Class, 1780–1850* (with Leonore Davidoff, 1987) to more recent essays on the "racing" of empire, was especially important. In the future, works like Mrinalini Sinha, *Colonial Masculinity: The 'Manly Englishman' and the 'Effeminate Bengali' in the Late Nineteenth Century* (1995), Antionette Burton, *Burdens of History: British Feminists, Indian Women, and Imperial Culture, 1865–1915* (1994), and Laura Tabili, *We Ask for British Justice: Workers and Racial Difference in Late Imperial Britain* (1994), can only increase.

Not all such works took the "linguistic turn" or disavowed a social analytic. But social history was now enhanced by attention to language and cultural histories of representation. The result was a mobile "culturalism," not indifferent to social analysis or contextualizing, but far more drawn to the domain of meaning than before. This eased a rapprochement with intellectual history. It pulled history toward literary theory, linguistic analysis, history of art, studies of film and other visual media, reflexive anthropology, and theories of cultural representation. This threw open the agenda of possible histories. Another range of new journals made the point, all interdisciplinary (or perhaps a-disciplinary), and all containing historical work, whether the authors were formally historians or not—*Critical Inquiry* (1974–), *Social Text* (1979–), *Representations* (1983–), *Cultural Critique* (1985–), *Cultural Studies* (1987–), *New Formations* (1987–). An important programmatic volume was edited by Lynn Hunt, *The New Cultural History* (1989).

Hunt herself migrated from a previous identity. Having begun as a Tilly-influenced urban historian of the French Revolution, she emerged with the wholly culturalist *Family Romance of the French Revolution* (1992), and two related anthologies, *Eroticism and the Body Politic* (1991) and *The Invention of Pornography: Obscenity and the Origins of Modernity, 1500–1800* (1993). This became a familiar pattern, contrasting W. H. Sewell's *Work and Revolution* (1980) to his *Structure and Mobility: The Men and Women of Marseilles, 1820–1870* (1985, but begun many years before), and Scott's *Gender and the Politics of History* (1988) to her *Glassworkers of Carmaux* (1974). Social histories addressed in Judith R. Walkowitz's *Prostitution and Victorian Society: Women, Class, and the State* (1980), shaped by the *History Workshop Journal* milieu, were now revisited in her *City of Dreadful Delight: Narratives of Sexual Danger in Late-Victorian London* (1992), using the new post-Foucauldian and poststructuralist analytic.

The pattern was repeated many times. In German history feminism was again key, especially for work on Nazism, where studies of societal racialization became overdetermined by gender-historical perspectives, beginning with the benchmark volume, *When Biology Became Destiny: Women in Weimar and Nazi Germany,* edited by Renate Bridenthal, Atina Grossman, and Marion Kaplan, (1984), and continuing through Gisela Bock's *Zwangssterilisation im Nationalsozialismus: Studien zur Rassenpolitik und Frauenpolitik* (1986). In the 1990s gender history, explicitly uniting social and cultural perspectives, transformed the German field. Poststructuralist perspectives also entered discussions of the Holocaust via Saul Friedländer (ed.), *Probing the Limits of Representation: Nazism and the "Final Solution"* (1992), just as the social histories of Nazi genocide were being intensively addressed. In the field at large, Rudy Koshar's *Germany's Transient Pasts: Preservation and National Memory in the Twentieth Century* (1998) brilliantly demonstrated the value of a poststructuralist analytic, enriching social history rather than superseding it—all the more eloquently given Koshar's earlier *Social Life, Local Politics, and Nazism: Marburg, 1880–1935* (1986), conceived under Charles Tilly's direction.

These departures scarcely lacked controversy, particularly in labor history, with demographic history the main materialist redoubt. In German history Canning's work (combining gender theory with a critical poststructuralist approach) set the pace. In French history, Sewell and Scott shaped discussion, valuably mapped in Lenard R. Berlanstein's anthology, *Rethinking Labor History: Essays on Discourse and Class Analysis* (1993), and further stimulated by Jacques

GERMAN WOMEN'S HISTORY

Women's history moved to the center of the most innovative work in German history during the 1980s, mirroring social history's main trends. Beginning with institutional studies of early feminism in books by Richard J. Evans (1976 and 1979) and Jean H. Quataert (1979), research moved quickly to women's social experience in work, the family, public health, charity, and so on. Ute Frevert delivered the first general account, *Women in German History: From Bourgeois Emancipation to Sexual Liberation* (original German edition, 1986), while anthologies edited by Karin Hausen (1983), John C. Fout (1984), Ruth-Ellen B. Joeres and Mary Jo Maynes (1986), and Renate Bridenthal, Atina Grossmann, and Marion Kaplan (1984) surveyed the emerging activity. The last of these, *When Biology Became Destiny: Women in Weimar and Nazi Germany*, proved especially influential, building on early essays from 1976 by Renate Bridenthal and Claudia Koonz ("Beyond *Kinder, Küche, Kirche*: Weimar Women in Politics and Work") and Tim Mason ("Women in Nazi Germany"). Claudia Koonz's *Mothers in the Fatherland: Women, the Family, and Nazi Politics* (1987) was a major intervention on the Third Reich, joining Gisela Bock's *Zwangssterilisation im Nationalsozial*ismus: Studien zur Rassenpolitik und Frauenpolitik (1986), and the earlier works by Dörte Winkler, *Frauenarbeit im "Dritten Reich"* (1977), and Jill Stephenson, *Women in Nazi Society* (1975) and *The Nazi Organisation of Women* (1981). Important books followed on Nazi marital policies (Gabriele Czarnowski, 1991), the *Bund Deutscher Mädel* (Dagmar Reese, 1989), Nazi treatment of lesbianism (Claudia Schoppmann, 1991), women's work (Carola Sachse, 1987 and 1990), and Nazi family policy (Lisa Pine, 1997). Atina Grossmann contributed field-defining essays on the "new woman" in the Weimar Republic and a study of the movement for birth control and abortion reform, *Reforming Sex* (1995), joining Cornelie Usborne's *The Politics of the Body in Weimar Germany: Women's Reproductive Rights and Duties* (1992). In earlier periods, Isabel V. Hull's *Sexuality, State, and Civil Society in Germany, 1700–1815* (1996), and Dagmar Herzog's *Intimacy and Exclusion: Religious Politics in Pre-Revolutionary Baden* (1996) also shifted the German field's overall agenda, as did Kathleen Canning's *Languages of Labor and Gender: Female Factory Work in Germany, 1850–1914* (1996) for the later nineteenth century.

Rancière's *The Nights of Labor: The Worker's Dream in Nineteenth-Century France* (original French edition, 1981). In British history debates were fierce, as prominent figures moved polemically away from social history altogether. Patrick Joyce traveled from *Work, Society, and Politics: The Culture of the Factory in Later Victorian England* (1980), through the broadened culturalism of *Visions of the People: Industrial England and the Question of Class, 1848–1914* (1991), to a theoretically rationalized intellectual history in *Democratic Subjects: The Self and the Social in Nineteenth-Century England* (1994), a trajectory also followed by Stedman Jones. Other new work, like Robert Gray's *The Factory Question and Industrial England, 1830–1860* (1996), Anna Clark's *Struggle for the Breeches* (1995), or Sonya Rose's *Limited Livelihoods* (1992), negotiated the tensions between classical and poststructuralist approaches more creatively.

This new cultural history picked up the threads from Febvre and Bloch in *Annales*'s founding years. Lynn Hunt's new interest, "in the ways that people collectively imagine—that is, think unconsciously about—the operation of power, and the ways in which this imagination shapes and is in turn shaped by political and social processes" (*Family Romance*, p. 8), recalled the history of *mentalité*. Some *Annalistes* themselves took a cultural turn. In 1975 Le Roy Ladurie published *Montaillou: The Promised Land of Error*, a study of medieval heresy, followed by *Carnival in Romans* (original French edition, 1979), exchanging the longue durée's epochal sweep for microhistorical snapshots of an intense event. A relative outsider to *Annales*, Michel Vovelle (1933–), in *Ideologies and Mentalities* (original French edition, 1982), took a more extensive approach, freeing cultural history from population's and the economy's structural hold and giving it a broader anthropological and psychological read. Jacques Le Goff (1924–), director of the École from 1972 to 1977, explored the perceptions and interior logics of the medieval world view, including

19

ORAL HISTORY

Oral history became a vital tool of the social historian, drawing on work by the Africanist Jan Vansina, *Oral Tradition: A Study in Historical Methodology* (1965), community history projects, and a variety of literary and folklorist traditions, institutionalized via the British-based journal *Oral History* (1973–). The unquestioned pioneer was a nonacademic historian, George Ewart Evans (1909–1987), whose democratic commitment to the history of ''ordinary people'' produced a remarkable series of books, from *Ask the Fellows Who Cut the Hay* (1956) to *Spoken History* (1987). Paul Thompson (1935–) shaped oral history as an international field, with an early handbook, *The Voice of the Past: Oral History* (1978), and the first international conference (Essex University, 1979), editing the proceedings as *Our Common History: The Transformation of Europe* (1982). In the 1980s history workshop movements in Britain and West Germany inspired a boom of popular and scholarly activity, as did the Swedish writer Sven Lindqvist's *Dig Where You Stand* (1978), which built on Scandinavian traditions of eth-

nology going back to the 1930s. Lutz Niethammer pioneered oral history in West Germany, presiding over studies of popular experience in the Ruhr between Nazism and the 1960s (1986) and in the GDR (1991), and editing the basic handbook, *Lebenserfahrung und kollektives Gedächtnis. Die Praxis der Oral History* (1980). In Italy oral history also began outside the academy (in the work of Gianni Bosio, Danilo Montaldi, Cesare Bermani, Rocco Scotellaro) in popular politics. In Luisa Passerini's, *Fascism in Popular Memory: The Cultural Experience of the Turin Working Class* (original Italian edition, 1984), and Alessandro Portelli's two volumes, *The Death of Luigi Trastulli and Other Stories: Form and Meaning in Oral History* (1991) and *The Battle of Valle Giulia: Oral History and the Art of Dialogue* (1997), Italian work addressed the dialectics of memory and forgetting. Here oral history connected to a huge preoccupation of the 1990s with history and memory, best approached via Patrick Hutton, *History as an Art of Memory* (1993), and the journal *History and Memory* (1989–).

Time, Work and Culture in the Middle Ages (original French edition, 1977) and *The Birth of Purgatory* (original French edition, 1981). Among the next generation, Roger Chartier's (1945–) work on print cultures broadened into *The Cultural Origins of the French Revolution* (original French edition, 1990) and the more general *Cultural History: Between Practices and Representations* (1988).

Yet *Annales* lost its distinctive place. For the 1970s the history of *mentalité* was a panacea for many social historians elsewhere. It seemed an alternative to high-cultural and canonical intellectual history, promising access to popular and everyday cultures, and inviting quantitative and anthropological methods. Above all, it was moved by the drive for "total history." But while the conference that launched *Review* (1978) was still celebratory, a few years later some searching critiques appeared—in *Past and Present* (Stuart Clark, 1983), *American Historical Review* (Samuel Kinser, 1981), *Social History* (Michael Gismondi, 1985), *History and Theory* (Patrick Hutton, 1981), and *Journal*

of Modern History (in debates by Chartier, Robert Darnton, Dominick LaCapra, and James Fernandez, 1985–1988). These exposed the fuzzy determinisms in Braudel's and Le Roy Ladurie's work. While none of the *Annales* achievements were gainsaid, their primacy shrank back into a wider international discussion. Historians' treatments of culture moved on, either beyond the old early modern heartland, or to the new ground of linguistic history and cultural studies, where the dynamism came from feminists, popular culture specialists, and intellectual historians, unmoved by the *Annales* paradigm, or directly critical of it. Literary texts, such as Peter Stallybrass and Allon White's *The Politics and Poetics of Transgression* (1986), an imaginative use of the Soviet cultural theorist Mikhail Bakhtin, became more influential. While Chartier's influence continued to grow, the triumphal codification of the *Annales* achievement in *La Nouvelle Histoire* (1978), edited by Chartier with Le Goff and Jacques Revel, started to resemble an epitaph.

GERMANY AND THE "HISTORY OF EVERYDAY LIFE"

West Germany in the 1980s was a fascinating case of creative acceleration. The historiographical deficits perpetrated by Nazism were compensated by adopting U.S. social science in the 1970s—by Jürgen Kocka and Hans Ulrich Wehler for the nineteenth century, Hans Mommsen (1930–) and Martin Broszat (1926–1989) for the twentieth, eclipsing the influence of Werner Conze, who had protected a place for social history in the earlier time. This social science history institutionalized a high level of methodological and theoretical sophistication, for which Wehler's multi-volume *Deutsche Gesellschaftsgeschichte* (1987, 1995) was a continuing monument. But a new movement emerged to the left, unhappy with macrostructural analysis, and urging a more interpretive approach to ordinary people's lives instead. By exploring social history in its subjective and experiential dimensions, the elusive connections between politics and culture could be concretely addressed. The "insides" of the "structures, processes, and patterns" of social analysis could be found. This "history from below" entailed "decentralizing" the approach by carefully constructed historical "miniatures" ("microhistory"). It involved a critique of the optimistic teleologies of modernization driving the social science approach. This new movement took the name *Alltagsgeschichte* (history of everyday life). Its main architects were Alf Lüdtke (1943–), Hans Medick (1939–), and Lutz Niethammer (1939–).

Alltagsgeschichte drew from the British marxist and *Annales* traditions via round tables in Göttingen and Paris in 1978–1982, which produced two volumes, Robert Berdahl et al., *Klassen und Kultur: Sozialanthropologische Perspektiven in der Geschichtsschreibung* (1982), and Hans Medick and David Warren Sabean (eds.), *Interest and Emotion: Essays on the Study of Family and Kinship* (1984). Pierre Bourdieu, the German philosopher Ernst Bloch (1885–1977), E. P. Thompson, and British anthropology were all influences. The turn to "ethnological ways of knowing" was a common theme. These perspectives were opposed by social science historians, confining *Alltagsgeschichte* to the margins of the West German profession. Like social history's other innovations, it drew sustenance from a political movement, coinciding with the peace movement and the Greens, based in public sector pedagogies in museums, exhibitions, schools, adult education, city cultural offices, local publishing, and self-organized local research. A history workshop movement ("barefoot historians") was inspired by its British precursor, stressing oral history,

popular memory, and public issues of dealing with the Nazi past. By 1990 the height had passed, but two new journals were launched, *WerkstattGeschichte* (1992–) and *Historische Anthropologie. Kultur, Gesellschaft, Alltag* (1993–), now rivaling *Geschichte und Gesellschaft* as a site of creative social-historical work.

Alltagsgeschichte took various emphases. One was early modern, in the work of Medick and David Sabean (1939–). Medick worked first on early modern political thought, but retooled for a village study of protoindustrialization, talking with the Cambridge Population Group and social anthropologists, E. P. Thompson, *Annalistes,* and others. His *Weben und Überleben in Laichingen 1650–1900. Lokalgeschichte als allgemeine Geschichte* (1996), was conceived as a "total history," combining approaches too often kept apart—quantitative and qualitative, structural history and anthropologies of meaning, history of the family and history of politics, the study of the case (microhistory) and analysis of societal processes of change. The program was laid out in Kriedte, Medick, and Schlumbohm, *Industrialization Before Industrialization* (1977). Sabean's companion study, *Property, Production, and Family in Neckarhausen, 1700–1870* (1990), was a similar tour de force. Superficially, these works emulated the longitudinal community study of Franco-British demography. But the interpretive ethnographies made the difference, exemplified in Sabean's earlier *Power in the Blood: Popular Culture and Village Discourse in Early Modern Germany* (1984). A key text was Medick's article " 'Missionaries in the Rowboat'? Ethnological Ways of Knowing as a Challenge to Social History" (1984), now reprinted several times.

Alf Lüdtke also worked within local parameters of quotidian life, moving from the practices of early nineteenth-century state violence (*Police and State in 19th Century Prussia,* [original German edition, 1982]) to the ambiguities of working-class culture in its everyday expressions, from *Kaiserreich* to the German Democratic Republic (GDR). In *Eigen-Sinn. Fabrikalltag, Arbeitererfahrungen und Politik vom Kaiserreich bis in den Faschismus* (1993), Lüdtke pursued the ambivalencies of working-class survival under successive political regimes, through all the modalities of recognition, self-assertiveness, adjustment, and conformity. Lutz Niethammer moved from studies of denazification after 1945, through the social history of housing before 1914, to a collective project on popular experience in the Ruhr, the three-volume *Lebensgeschichte und Sozialkultur im Ruhrgebiet 1930 bis 1960* (1983–1985), based partly on oral history. This was followed by a similar study of industrial life in the GDR (with Alexander von Plato and Dorothee Wierling), *Die*

COMMUNITY STUDIES

Availability of local records (parish registers and their equivalents) and sophisticated demographic methods (like family reconstitution and census analysis) made village studies the classic setting for historical demography. While technically sophisticated, the resulting work could be indifferent to specificities of culture and place, encouraging much potential polarization between social science historians and "qualitative" ones. Social historians at the Max Planck Institute for History in Göttingen used the framework of protoindustrialization to transcend this division, beginning with Peter Kriedte, Hans Medick, and Jürgen Sclumbohm, *Industrialization Before Industrialization* (1977). David Sabean complemented his intensely technical *Property, Production, and Family in Neckarhausen, 1700–1870* (1990) with the imaginatively culturalist *Power in the Blood: Popular Culture and Village Discourse in Early Modern Germany* (1984), a richness also achieved by Medick in his companion study of Laichingen (1996) and the associated essays. Likewise, Thomas Sokoll's *Household and Family among the Poor:*

The Case of Two Essex Communities in the Late Eighteenth and Early Nineteenth Centuries (1993) was accompanied by advocacy of historical anthropology, as in his essay for Thomas Mergel and Thomas Welskopp (eds.), *Geschichte zwischen Kultur und Gesellschaft: Beiträge zur Theoriedebatte* (1997). *Annales* treated social and cultural analysis as discrete projects, whether in Le Roy Ladurie's books, *Montaillou* (1975) and *Carnival in Romans* (1979), as against the *Peasants of Langedoc* (1966), or in Braudel's schematic separation of his three levels. British early modern studies more successfully integrated the two, as in Keith Wrightson and David Levine, *Poverty and Piety in an English Village: Terling, 1525–1700* (1979); Keith Wrightson, *The Making of an Industrial Society: Whickham, 1560–1765* (1991); and Barry Reay, *Microhistories: Demography, Society and Culture in Rural England, 1800–1930* (1996). The journal *Continuity and Change: A Journal of Social Structure, Law and Demography in Past Societies* (1986–) encouraged this dialogue across "quantitative and qualitative" work.

volkseigene Erfahrung. Eine Archäologie des Lebens in der Industrieprovinz der DDR (1991), conducted in the final years of Communist rule. *Alltagsgeschichte* was anthologized in Alf Lüdtke (ed.), *The History of Everyday Life: Reconstructing Historical Experience and Ways of Life* (1995). Among monographs, Thomas Lindenberger's *Strassenpolitik: Zur Sozialgeschichte der öffentlichen Ordnung in Berlin 1900 bis 1914* (1995) especially stood out.

PRESENT TENSE: SOCIAL HISTORY IN THE TWENTY-FIRST CENTURY

As the year 2000 approached, social history had acquired impressive diversity. It had moved from the pioneering qualities of the 1960s, through a period of exuberant growth and aspiring hegemony, to uncertainty and flux in the 1980s, and finally to the eclectic indeterminacy of the 1990s and later. For a while, social historians threatened to separate into camps, as convinced materialists and structuralists faced culturalists and "linguistic turners" across a hardening polemical divide. Such theoretical and epistemological

polarities were repeated across the humanities and social sciences, with varying connections to wider political debates. By the later 1990s, however, much of the passion had cooled.

All the forms of work established during the 1960s and 1970s continued in great profusion, from the technical specialisms of family and population history, to the social histories of class formation, and all the subfields described above, plus others barely mentioned, like the social history of religion, or the growth area of consumption. The huge proliferation of women's history, and its rethinking via gender, stimulated many creative departures, not least in histories of masculinity and histories of the body. Other fields emerged more prominently for concentrated cross-national research, including most notably social histories of the bourgeoisie.

What disappeared, or had at least gone into recession, was the totalizing ambition—writing the history of whole societies in some integral and holistic way. Part of this was still alive. All phenomena (a policy, an institution, an ideology, an event) might still be placed in social context, or read for their social

THE RUSSIAN REVOLUTION

The Soviet field revealed social history's development in a microcosm. In Britain Edward Hallett Carr (1892–1982) provided an imposing framework with his multivolume *History of Soviet Russia* (1954–1978), while at Birmingham University Robert W. Davies (1925–) pioneered socioeconomic history of the Stalin years. Moshe Lewin (1921–) reached Birmingham from Vilna via the USSR, Israel, and Paris (where he studied with Braudel), moving later to the United States, with a string of influential books, from *Russian Peasants and Soviet Power: A Study of Collectivization* (1966) to *The Making of the Soviet System* (1985). Another ex-citizen of Vilna, Teodor Shanin, contributed *The Awkward Class: Political Sociology of Peasantry in a Developing Society, Russia 1910–1925* (1972). In the United States Leopold Haimson, author of a key two-part article, "The Problem of Social Stability in Urban Russia, 1905–1917" (1964–1965), inspired historians of the working class, who by the 1980s had energized the field. Reginald E. Zelnik mapped early industrialization through *Labor and Society in Tsarist Russia: The Factory Workers of St. Petersburg, 1855–1870* (1971) and *Law and Disorder on the Narova River: The Kreenholm Strike of 1872* (1995). William G. Rosenberg clarified 1917 itself in *Strikes and Revolution in Russia, 1917* (1989), with Diane P. Koenker. Ronald Grigor Suny shaped the general agenda with his "Toward a Social History of the October Revolution" (1983). A fourth figure, Sheila Fitzpatrick, took a more social science approach to the Stalin period. The advance of society-centered approaches against the Soviet field's traditional state-centered emphasis threatened to obscure questions of Stalinist rule, but Lewin, Rosenberg, Suny, and others kept them in view. Questions of political order were addressed in Fitzpatrick's *Everyday Stalinism. Ordinary Life in Extraordinary Times: Soviet Russia in the 1930s* (1999); those of class formation in Lewis Siegelbaum and Ronald Grigor Suny's conference volume, *Making Workers Soviet: Power, Class, and Identity* (1994); and Soviet societal transformation in Stephen Kotkin's *Magnetic Mountain: Stalinism as a Civilization* (1995).

meanings. But the stronger view, subjecting all facets of human existence to social determinations, was now harder to maintain. "Society," as a confident materialist projection of social totality, had become much harder to find. Coherence was no longer derived as easily from the economy, or from the functional needs of the social system and its central values (or from some other ordering principle, like the mode of production and its social relations), because the antireductionist pressure of contemporary social and cultural theory had ruled this out. This was very empowering. As the hold of the economy became loosened, and with it the determinative power of the social structure and its causal claims, the imaginative and epistemological space for other kinds of analysis grew. The rich multiplication of new cultural histories was the result.

But there were also costs. The founding inspiration for much social history was a series of grand debates concerning the general crisis of the seventeenth century, the nature of revolutions, the connection between popular revolts and early modern state formation, the rise of absolutism, and so on. For a while, this impetus carried over. In the mid-1970s, Robert Brenner's major article in *Past and Present* (1976) provoked a wide-ranging debate over agrarian class structure and the origins of capitalism. Rodney Hilton reedited the debate between Maurice Dobb, Paul Sweezy, and others during the 1950s over *The Transition from Feudalism to Capitalism* (1976). Perry Anderson published his two volumes, *Passages from Antiquity to Feudalism* and *Lineages of the Absolutist State* (both 1974). Immanuel Wallerstein (a self-avowed Braudelian) published the first volume of *The Modern World-System* (1974). Charles Tilly edited *The Formation of National States in Western Europe* (1975). Combinations of modernization theory and neo-Braudelian vision inspired other attempts to capture the structural transition to the modern world, as in the works of Keith Thomas (1933–), *Religion and the Decline of Magic: Studies in Popular Beliefs in Sixteenth and Seventeenth-Century England* (1971) and *Man and the Natural World: Changing Attitudes in England, 1500–1800* (1983).

Among social historians (by contrast with historical sociologists), this ambition seemed to have

HISTORY AFTER THE "LINGUISTIC TURN"

After Gareth Stedman Jones's *Languages of Class: Studies in English Working Class History, 1832–1982* (1983) and Joan Scott's poststructuralist challenge in *Gender and the Politics of History* (1988), social historians experienced a crisis of direction. Stedman Jones and Scott were identified with the breakthrough to social history in the 1960s and 1970s, including a marxist stress on the axiomatic priority of social explanation, but they now advocated forms of linguistic analysis and the primacy of discourse, which denied the former materialism. Debates occurred in many of the leading journals, including *American Historical Review* (1987, 1989), *Journal of Modern History* (1985–1988), *International Labor and Working Class History* (1987), *Past and Present* (1991–1992), and *Social History* (1992–1996), through which "postmodernism" became a catchall term for a variety of culturalist influences, from Foucault, poststructuralism, and literary deconstruction to cultural studies, postcolonialism, and forms of feminist theory. Many social historians accused postmodernists of apostasy—of abandoning social history's calling, or retreating into playfulness, and even rejecting the historian's normal rules of evidence. Self-described postmodernists such as Patrick Joyce accused

their critics of clinging to obsolete concepts and approaches, especially materialist conceptions of class. For a while debates became extremely embittered, and in western Europe historians dismissed the linguistic turn as a specifically U.S. preoccupation. However, the more extreme polemics, such as Bryan D. Palmer's *Descent into Discourse: The Reification of Language and the Writing of Social History* (1990), seemed to subside, leaving imaginative combinations of social and cultural history in place, including Kathleen Canning's *Languages of Labor and Gender: Female Factory Work in Germany, 1850–1914* (1996), Rudy Koshar's *Germany's Transient Pasts: Preservation and National Memory in the Twentieth Century* (1998), and Leora Auslander's *Taste and Power: Furnishing Modern France* (1996). The debates were presented in Keith Jenkins (ed.), *The Postmodern History Reader* (1997), and a journal, *Rethinking History: The Journal of Theory and Practice* (1997–). Robert F. Berkhofer Jr.'s sympathetic exegesis, *Beyond the Great Story: History as Text and Discourse* (1995), contrasted poignantly with his earlier *A Behavioral Approach to Historical Analysis* (1969), a manifesto for social science perspectives at the inception of social history's contemporary emergence.

gone. Hobsbawm—with his four *Age* volumes and *Nations and Nationalism since 1870* (1990)—remained an exception. In that sense, the power of forward motion, so energizing in the 1960s and 1970s, borne by what seemed the unlimited capacity of social explanation, had certainly departed. That amorphously aggrandizing desire for primacy in the discipline was replaced by a more eclectic repertoire of approaches and themes, for which the new cultural history and its very different kinds of interdisciplinarity became the key. The boundaries between different kinds of history became extraordinarily more blurred. Many

social historians continued to reproduce the distinctive (and legitimate) autonomies of their work, methodologically and topically. But many others were moving increasingly freely across the old distinctions of the social, the cultural, the political, the intellectual, and so on, allowing new hybridities to arise. The openness in these directions was the greatest single change in the stance of social historians in the 1980s and 1990s, and showed every sign of continuing. A continued willingness to participate in the conditions of its own disappearance may be the greatest mark of social history's success.

See also other articles in this section.

BIBLIOGRAPHY

General

Burke, Peter, ed. *New Perspectives on Historical Writing.* Cambridge, U.K., 1991.

Hobsbawm, Eric. "From Social History to the History of Society." In his *On History*. New York, 1997. Pages 71–93.

Iggers, Georg G. *Historiography in the Twentieth Century: From Scientific Objectivity to the Postmodern Challenge.* Hanover, N.H., 1997.

Iggers, Georg G. *New Directions in European Historiography.* Middletown, Conn., 1975.

Iggers, Georg G., ed. *The Social History of Politics: Critical Perspectives in West German Historical Writing since 1945.* New York, 1986.

Jones, Gareth Stedman. "History: The Poverty of Empiricism." In *Ideology in Social Science: Readings in Critical Social Theory.* Edited by Robin Blackburn. London, 1972. Pages 96–115.

Lloyd, Christopher. *Explanation in Social History.* Oxford, 1986.

McLennan, Gregor. *Marxism and the Methodologies of History.* London, 1981.

Melman, Billie. "Gender, History and Memory: The Invention of Women's Past in the Nineteenth and Early Twentieth Centuries." *History and Memory* 5 (1993): 5–41.

Perkin, Harold J. "Social History." In *Approaches to History: A Symposium.* Edited by H. P. R. Finberg. London, 1962. Pages 51–82.

Sutton, David. "Radical Liberalism, Fabianism, and Social History." In *Making Histories: Studies in History-Writing and Politics.* Edited by Richard Johnson, Gregor McLennan, Bill Schwarz, and David Sutton. London, 1982. Pages 15–43.

Wehler, Hans Ulrich. "Historiography in Germany Today." In *Observations on "The Spiritual Situation of the Age": Contemporary German Perspectives.* Edited by Jürgen Habermas. Cambridge, Mass., 1984. Pages 221–259.

Wilson, Adrian. "A Critical Portrait of Social History." In *Rethinking Social History: English Society 1570–1920 and its Interpretation.* Edited by Adrian Wilson. Manchester, U.K., and New York, 1993. Pages 1–58.

Zunz, Olivier, ed. *Reliving the Past: The Worlds of Social History.* Chapel Hill, N.C., 1985.

The Annales Paradigm

Burguière, André. "The Fate of the History of Mentalities in the *Annales*." *Comparative Studies in Society and History* 24 (July 1982): 424–437.

Burke, Peter. *The French Historical Revolution: The Annales School, 1929–1989.* Stanford, Calif., 1990.

Clark, Stuart. "French Historians and Early Modern Culture." *Past and Present* 100 (August 1983): 62–99.

Davis, Natalie Zemon. "Women and the World of the *Annales*." *History Workshop Journal* 33 (Spring 1992): 121–137.

Dosse, François. *New History in France: The Triumph of the Annales.* Translated by Peter V. Conroy. Urbana, Ill., and Chicago, 1994. Translation of *L'histoire en miettes: des "Annales" à la nouvelle histoire.*

Fink, Carole. *Marc Bloch: A Life in History.* Cambridge, U.K., 1989.

Gismondi, Michael. " 'The Gift of Theory': A Critique of the *histoire des mentalités*." *Social History* 10 (May 1985): 211–230.

Hutton, Patrick. "The History of Mentalities: The New Map of Cultural History." *History and Theory* 20 (1981): 413–423.

Kinser, Samuel. "Annaliste Paradigm? The Geohistorical Structure of Fernand Braudel." *American Historical Review* 86 (February 1981): 63–105.

Renouvin, Pierre. "Ernest Labrousse." In *Historians of Modern Europe.* Edited by Hans A. Schmitt. Baton Rouge, La., 1971.

Vilar, Pierre. "Marxist History, a History in the Making: Towards a Dialogue with Althusser." *New Left Review* 80 (July-August 1973): 65–106.

Marxist Historiography

Cobb, Richard. "Georges Lefebvre." In his *A Second Identity: Essays on France and French History.* Oxford, 1969. Pages 84–100.

Dworkin, Dennis. *Cultural Marxism in Postwar Britain: History, the New Left, and the Origins of Cultural Studies.* Durham, N.C., 1997.

Hill, Christopher, Rodney Hilton, and Eric Hobsbawm. "*Past and Present:* Origins and Early Years." *Past and Present* 100 (August 1983): 3–14.

Hobsbawm, Eric. "The Historians' Group of the Communist Party." In *Rebels and Their Causes: Essays in Honour of A. L. Morton.* Edited by Maurice Cornforth. Atlantic Highlands, N.J., 1979. Pages 21–47.

Kaye, Harvey J. *The British Marxist Historians: An Introductory Analysis.* Cambridge, U.K., 1984.

Kaye, Harvey J., and Keith McClelland, eds. *E. P. Thompson: Critical Perspectives.* Cambridge, U.K., and Philadelphia, 1990.

Le Goff, Jacques. "*Past and Present:* Later History." *Past and Present* 100 (August 1983): 14–28.

Samuel, Raphael. "British Marxist Historians, 1880–1980." *New Left Review* 120 (March-April 1980): 21–96.

Schwarz, Bill. " 'The People' in History: The Communist Party Historians' Group, 1946–56." In *Making Histories: Studies in History-Writing and Politics.* Edited by Richard Johnson, Gregor McLennan, Bill Schwarz, and David Sutton. London, 1982. Pages 44–95.

Social Science History

Abbott, Andrew. "History and Sociology: The Lost Synthesis." *Social Science History* 15 (1991): 201–238.

Abrams, Philip. *Historical Sociology.* Ithaca, N.Y., 1982.

Anderson, Michael. "Sociological History and the Working-Class Family: Smelser Revisited." *Social History* 1 (October 1976): 317–334.

Burke, Peter. *History and Social Theory.* Cambridge, U.K., 1992.

Calhoun, Craig. "The Rise and Domestication of Historical Sociology." In *The Historic Turn in the Human Sciences.* Edited by Terrence J. McDonald. Ann Arbor, Mich., 1996. Pages 305–338.

Landes, David, and Charles Tilly, eds. *History as Social Science.* Englewood Cliffs, N.J., 1971.

McDonald, Terrence J. "What We Talk about When We Talk about History: The Conversations of History and Sociology." In *The Historic Turn in the Human Sciences.* Edited by Terrence J. McDonald. Ann Arbor, Mich., 1996. Pages 91–118.

Skocpol, Theda, ed. *Vision and Method in Historical Sociology.* New York, 1984.

Skocpol, Theda, and Margaret R. Somers. "The Uses of Comparative History in Macrosocial Inquiry." *Comparative Studies in Society and History* 22 (1980): 174–197.

Smith, Dennis. *The Rise of Historical Sociology.* Cambridge, U.K., 1991.

Somers, Margaret R. "Where Is Sociology after the Historic Turn? Knowledge Cultures, Narrativity, and Historical Epistemologies." In *The Historic Turn in the Human Sciences.* Edited by Terrence J. McDonald. Ann Arbor, Mich., 1996. Pages 53–89.

Tilly, Charles. *As Sociology Meets History.* New York, 1981.

Proliferation and Growth

Aston, Trevor H., and Christopher H. E. Philpin, eds. *The Brenner Debate: Agrarian Class Structure and Economic Development in Pre-Industrial Europe.* Cambridge, U.K., 1985.

Baker, Alan R. H., and Derek Gregory, eds. *Explorations in Historical Geography: Interpretive Essays.* Cambridge, U.K., 1984.

Evans, Neil. "Writing the Social History of Modern Wales: Approaches, Achievements and Problems." *Social History* 17 (October 1992): 479–492.

Hendrick, Harry. "The History of Childhood and Youth." *Social History* 9 (January 1984): 87–96.

Johansen, Hans. "Trends in Modern and Early Modern Social History Writing in Denmark after 1970." *Social History* 8 (October 1983): 375–381.

Price, Richard. "The Labour Process and Labour History," and Patrick Joyce, "Labour, Capital, and Compromise: A Response to Richard Price." *Social History* 8 (January 1983): 57–75; and 9 (January 1984): 67–76. Further exchange between Price and Joyce can be found in *Social History* 9 (May 1984): 217–231.

Samuel, Raphael, ed. *People's History and Socialist Theory.* London, 1981.

Scott, Joan W. "The History of the Family as an Affective Unit." *Social History* 4 (October 1979): 509–516.

Strath, Bo. "Recent Development in Swedish Social History of the Period since 1800." *Social History* 9 (January 1984): 77–85.

Wilson, Stephen. "Death and the Social Historians: Some Recent Books in French and English." *Social History* 5 (October 1980): 435–452.

Women, Men, and Gender

Alexander, Sally. *Becoming a Woman and Other Essays in 19th and 20th Century Feminist History.* New York, 1995.

Bennett, Judith M. "Feminism and History." *Gender and History* 1 (1989): Pages 251–272.

Frader, Laura L., and Sonya O. Rose, eds. *Gender and Class in Modern Europe.* Ithaca, N.Y., 1996.

Riley, Denise. *"Am I That Name?": Feminism and the Category of "Women" in History.* London, 1988.

Rowbotham, Sheila. *Dreams and Dilemmas: Collected Writings.* London, 1983.

Scott, Joan W. *Gender and the Politics of History.* New York, 1988.

Steedman, Carolyn Kay. *Landscape for a Good Woman: A Story of Two Lives.* New Brunswick, N.J., 1987.

The Cultural Turn

Bennett, Tony. *The Birth of the Museum: History, Theory, Politics.* London, 1995.

Castro-Klaren, Sara. "Literacy, Conquest, and Interpretation: Breaking New Ground on the Records of the Past." *Social History* 23 (May 1998): 133–145.

Chartier, Roger. *On the Edge of the Cliff: History, Language, and Practices.* Baltimore, 1997.

Crew, David. "Who's Afraid of Cultural Studies? Taking a 'Cultural Turn' in German History." In *A User's Guide to German Cultural Studies.* Edited by Scott Denham, Irene Kacandes, and Jonathan Petropoulos. Ann Arbor, Mich., 1997. Pages 45–61.

De Grazia, Victoria, with Ellen Furlough, eds. *The Sex of Things: Gender and Consumption in Historical Perspective.* Berkeley, 1996.

Gilroy, Paul. *The Black Atlantic: Modernity and Double Consciousness.* Cambridge, Mass., 1993.

Hall, Catherine. "Politics, Post-Structuralism and Feminist History." *Gender and History* 3 (Summer 1991): 204–210.

Lüdtke, Alf, ed. *The History of Everyday Life: Reconstructing Historical Experiences and Ways of Life.* Translated by William Templer. Princeton, N.J., 1995. Translation of *Alltagsgeschichte.*

Steinberg, Marc W. "Culturally Speaking: Finding a Commons between Post-Structuralism and the Thompsonian Perspective." *Social History:* 21 (May 1996): 193–214.

Disagreements

Appleby, Joyce, Lynn Hunt, and Margaret Jacob. *Telling the Truth about History.* New York, 1994.

Berkhofer, Robert F., Jr. *Beyond the Great Story: History as Text and Discourse.* Cambridge, Mass., 1995.

Canning, Kathleen. "Feminist Theory after the Linguistic Turn: Historicizing Discourse and Experience." *Signs* 19 (1994): 368–404.

Chartier, Roger. "Texts, Symbols, and Frenchness." *Journal of Modern History* 57 (1985): 682–695.

Cohen, Ralph, and Michael S. Roth, eds. *History and—: Histories within the Human Sciences.* Charlottesville, Va., 1995.

Darnton, Robert. "The Symbolic Element in History." *Journal of Modern History* 58 (1986): 218–234.

Dirks, Nicholas B., Geoff Eley, and Sherry B. Ortner, eds. *Culture/Power/History: A Reader in Contemporary Social Theory.* Princeton, N.J., 1994.

Domanska, Ewa, ed. *Encounters: Philosophy of History after Postmodernism.* Charlottsville, Va., 1998.

Eley, Geoff. "Is All the World a Text? From Social History to the History of Society Two Decades Later." In *The Historic Turn in the Human Sciences.* Edited by Terrence J. McDonald. Ann Arbor, Mich., 1996. Pages 193–243.

Eley, Geoff. "Problems with Culture: German History after the Linguistic Turn." *Central European History* 31 (1998): 197–227.

Fernandez, James. "Historians Tell Tales: Of Cartesian Cats and Gallic Cockfights." *Journal of Modern History* 60 (1988): 113–127.

Harlan, David. "Intellectual History and the Return of Literature." *American Historical Review* 94 (1989): 581–609.

Jenkins, Keith, ed. *The Postmodern History Reader.* London, 1995.

Jones, Gareth Stedman. "Anglo-Marxism, Neo-Marxism, and the Discursive Approach to History." In *Was bleibt von marxistischen Perspektiven in der Geschichtsforschung?* Edited by Alf Lüdtke. Göttingen, Germany, 1997. Pages 151–209.

Jones, Gareth Stedman. "From Historical Sociology to Theoretical History." *British Journal of Sociology* 27 (1976): 295–305.

Joyce, Patrick. "The End of Social History?" *Social History* 20 (January 1995): 73–91.

Joyce, Patrick. "The Return of History: Postmodernism and the Politics of Academic History in Britain." *Past and Present* 158 (February 1998): 207–235.

Katznelson, Ira. "The 'Bourgeois' Dimension: A Provocation about Institutions, Politics, and the Future of Labor History." *International Labor and Working Class History* 46 (Fall 1994): 7–32.

Kirk, Neville. "In Defence of Class: A Critique of Recent Revisionist Writing upon the Nineteenth-Century English Working Class." *International Review of Social History* 32 (1987): 2–47.

Kirk, Neville. " 'Traditional' Working-Class Culture and 'the Rise of Labour': Some Preliminary Questions and Observations." *Social History* 16 (May 1991): 203–216.

LaCapra, Dominick. "Chartier, Darnton, and the Great Symbol Massacre." *Journal of Modern History* 60 (1988): 95–112.

Mayfield, David, and Susan Thorne. "Social History and its Discontents: Gareth Stedman Jones and the Politics of Language." *Social History* 17 (1992): 165–188.

Palmer, Bryan D. *Descent into Discourse: The Reification of Language and the Writing of Social History.* Philadelphia, 1990.

Toews, John E. "Intellectual History after the Linguistic Turn: The Autonomy of Meaning and the Irreducibility of Experience." *American Historical Review* 92 (1987): 879–907.

THE SOURCES OF SOCIAL HISTORY

Mary Lindemann

Social historians exploit a variety of archival, manuscript, literary, and nonwritten sources. Indeed almost every historical source is grist for the social historical mill, thus a survey of the sources of social history must always be incomplete. Enterprising social historians over the decades have unearthed many new documentary treasures and devised novel ways of using old sources. This brief survey concentrates, therefore, only on the most common ways social historians have employed sources.

QUALITATIVE AND QUANTITATIVE SOURCES

An old but still functional distinction is that separating quantitative and qualitative information. Social historians who use principally quantitative materials apply the methods of the social sciences, in particular sociology, political science, statistics, and demography, to history, thereby writing social science history. Quantitative sources are generally those that allow historians to count or those that historians can analyze statistically. Historians who mine them work with large collections of data, frequently laboring in teams and using computers to correlate, aggregate, and evaluate the data accumulated. Many historians focus on discerning broad structural shifts and documenting secular, that is, century-long, changes. Their sources are habitually those generated by governments, for instance, censuses and tax lists, as well as parish records, price and wage data, hospital ledgers, and property deeds. These historians practice what they like to characterize as "history from the bottom up" and "history with the politics left out." Such scholars—as, for instance, Emmanuel Le Roy Ladurie on the peasants of Languedoc, Georges Duby on medieval rural life, and David Herlihy and Christiane Klapisch-Zuber on Tuscans and their families—have typically dealt with masses of people and are concerned mostly with uncovering the structural forces affecting or even determining people's lives.

One type of social history prefers what might be called qualitative sources, those that are either not quantifiable or that do not lend themselves easily or readily to quantification. Such were the sources of the "old" social history and of the narrative history that related the stories of entire peoples or whole groups. These authors usually based their judgments on the evidence in elite writings, novels, and other prose forms. Thomas Babington Macaulay's splendid, multivolumed *History of England from the Accession of James II* (1849–1861) and Jules Michelet's *The People* (1846) are classic examples.

Those historians who instead looked for the hidden mainsprings of history and searched for broader structures criticized "older" histories as impressionistic. Whether these dissenters were historians working in the *Annales* paradigm or were those driven by "grand social theories," that is, the metahistorical narratives proposed by Karl Marx, Max Weber, Émile Durkheim, Ferdinand Tönnies, and Georg Simmel, they accepted the existence and action of major determinant processes in history and rejected analyses based on the influences of "great men" and "great ideas." This caused a turn to quantifiable sources as well as a search for what the *Annales* historian Fernand Braudel called the *longue durée* (long time frame). These scholars typically evinced a passionate curiosity about people, including peasants, women, the poor, transients, and heretics, often neglected by old-fashioned historians and traditional histories that highlighted political, intellectual, and diplomatic matters. In addition some, again like Braudel, suggested that the methods of geography and geology and their sources, such as measuring tree rings to determine climatic change or, as Georges Duby and others attempted, a minute analysis of field patterns to determine modifications in agricultural practices, had to be brought to bear on the historical experience.

The search for structures that lay deeply embedded in the society required attention to large sets of data. Some of these sources had been employed previously. Economic historians, for example, had estimated long-term adjustments in prices and wages and located movements in standards of living. Still, not everyone was satisfied with detecting and examining structures. Others were displeased with the fastidious and sometimes boring or clumsy prose style quantifiers preferred. These scholars called for a return to narrative as Lawrence Stone proposed in *The Past and the Present* (1981).

Moreover macrohistorical movements or grand structures seemed to rob people of their agency in shaping history and denied them their own choices in life. Structural history has an unfortunate tendency to place people in socioeconomic "boxes," where their actions were constrained if not dictated by huge impersonal forces that they could not perceive, control, or evade. Individual agency was lost, as was the political part of human experience. In reaction, some historians insisted, for instance, that knowing the sizes of families or households—understanding perhaps that one family type, described by John Hajnal, had persisted since the late Middle Ages—revealed little about what "went on" in those units. High levels of infant mortality might be interpreted as demonstrating that families invested hardly anything either materially or emotionally into very young children and that little true affection existed in families produced by marriages arranged by parents who based their decisions primarily on economic considerations. To discuss feelings and emotions, historians consulted other sources, including "ego-documents," court rolls, administrative records, diaries, letters, and prescriptive literature like advice manuals.

Of course the division between quantitative "lumpers" on the one hand and qualitative "feelers" on the other is artificial, as is the split between those who supposedly look only for structures and those who prefer to stress the ability of individuals to manipulate their own situations. Rarely do "pure" types of any exist. Quantitative historians often turn to qualitative sources if only for illustrations. Historians who prefer qualitative or anecdotal materials always have been plagued by nagging questions of typicality, and few ignore the possibilities of counting when and where they can. Many historians have gracefully combined the two types of sources to great benefit, as, for instance, Stone did in his works on the aristocracy and on family, sex, and marriage in early modern England. It is also important that some sources, especially court records, have been used extensively both qualitatively and quantitatively in social history writing. Moreover, in the late twentieth century a renewed desire to return politics to the social historical agenda, a "linguistic turn" that emphasizes the methods of textual and literary criticism, the rise of a "new" cultural history, and microhistory, encouraged historians to cast their source nets more widely and to adopt unfamiliar ways of exploring old standbys, such as wills, fiction, and court cases.

Besides the rough quantitative-qualitative split discussed above, sources can be further divided into four broad categories:

1. sources produced by government or administrative agencies, broadly defined;
2. nongovernmental sources or those created by private groups and individuals, including businesses;
3. researcher-generated sources, including interviews and oral histories; and
4. nonwritten sources and artifacts.

Many of these are deposited in archives and libraries, but they may also remain in private hands. Artifacts may not be "deposited" in any real sense at all, although of course archives, museums, and private collections preserve large numbers of artifacts. The first two categories have proven the richest sources for social historical studies.

GOVERNMENTAL SOURCES

The governing process at local, national, and international levels begets a range of sources and vast quantities of material suitable for historical inquiries. Archives maintained by government agencies house the bulk of these records. Although some scholars have criticized such sources for revealing only the perspective of elites, almost all historians plow these fertile fields. Despite frequent and extensive use by researchers over decades, their riches are far from depleted. While the variety of these documents is immense, social historians have most regularly and thoroughly mined tax rolls and censuses; criminal, civil, and ecclesiastical court cases; notarial records, especially wills; parish registers; property accounts; guild and union records; and police files. Obviously other sources that some might consider purely political or even diplomatic, such as the records of city councils or the military, can also yield vital information for the social historian. Indeed the social historian who probes issues of state and society, for example, ignores at his or her peril the actions of governing bodies, such as city councils and parliaments, or the inner workings of political parties as they discussed and molded social, welfare, economic, and cultural policies.

Historians and demographers who investigate population movements regularly use tax rolls, censuses, and parish registers to amass information about the movement of peoples and to collect raw data for calculations of mortality, morbidity, nuptiality, and fertility. In the history of governance, however, the census is a relatively recent phenomenon. At least theoretically censuses make a comprehensive accounting of a specified population. The word "census" is of Latin origin, and the Romans took what they called censuses principally for computing tax burdens and for purposes of military conscription. Modern censuses, those meant to include all or almost all of the members of a given population, date from the eighteenth century and only became a normal and usual function of government in the nineteenth century. The U.S. census, for instance, began in 1790. Its purpose was explicitly political, that is, to calculate seats in the House of Representatives. Some European states had initiated censuses earlier, but they were rarely inclusive. Social historians and demographers use censuses to determine the movement of people; the composition of a population; employment patterns; the relative wealth and poverty of a population and its segments; racial and ethnic makeups; standards of living; settlement patterns; and types of housing.

Despite the wealth of facts they contain, censuses have proven less useful for historians and demographers in determining mortality, morbidity, marriage, and birthrates. In the nineteenth century most states mandated civil registers of births, marriages, deaths, and in some cases disease occurrences. The registration of the last pertained mostly to infectious or contagious diseases, especially to sexually transmitted ones. Civil records deliver to medical historians meaningful information about diseases, but they also permit scholars to develop perspectives on vital statistics and compare them synchronically and diachronically. Governments generally prepare aggregate data and publish it in printed volumes of statistics; in digitalized and machine-readable forms; on CD-ROMs; and on the Internet. These aggregations then serve as sources, rendering to researchers an abundance of analyzable material. Such database collections have also been compiled for earlier times.

Scholars doing demographic, population, and family reconstruction studies for periods before censuses and civil registers were introduced normally consult parish registers. Raw data for the quantitative analysis of the size and the health of populations first were generated in the sixteenth century, when some Protestant parishes began keeping track of births and deaths by recording christenings and burials as well as weddings. The Council of Trent (1545–1563) mandated that Catholic parishes record similar occurrences. Even before such specialized registers existed, the bills of mortality began recording deaths from plague in Milan in 1452. The most famous of these bills date from the great plague of London in the mid 1660s. Historians of the family have often used such sources to reconstruct families and households. Louis Henry pioneered the method of family reconstruction in the 1950s to study fertility among French women. Subsequently family reconstruction re-created entire parishes and whole villages, as demonstrated in Arthur Imhof's *Die verlorenen Welten* (1984) and David Sabean's two volumes on the Württemberg village of Neckarhausen (1990, 1998). The application of statistical packages and computer programs has facilitated and accelerated the task of family reconstruction.

Tax rolls, known as *cadastres* in the medieval and early modern periods, and tax records, including property, income, excise, and sales, furnish equally sustaining nourishment for knowledge-hungry social and economic historians. Historians who plot shifting patterns of wealth occasionally employ extremely sophisticated statistical techniques to discover and evaluate the rise or fall of real wages and to determine relative standards of living. They often work comparatively, linking societies chronologically, geographically, or both. The assemblage of prosopographies or collective biographies relies heavily on tax rolls as well as on censuses, parish registers, and wills. Real estate records and property plans, urban and rural, function in a like manner, allowing historians to determine patterns of landholding and uses and alterations in them over time.

Social historians have exploited court records, particularly criminal records, extensively and creatively and to many different purposes. Historians who ascertained secular developments in crime, for example, the striking decline in personal offenses and the equally striking rise in property crime after the Middle Ages, turned to court records, both secular and ecclesiastical. For the early modern period these documents are far more likely to exist for towns than for rural areas. Some cities possess enviable series of unbroken records. Amsterdam's, for example, run from the late sixteenth century through the early nineteenth century. These records have yielded valuable information on issues far removed from crime by revealing the lives of those who left little other evidence. Criminal acts frequently occasioned extensive, probing investigations that produced dossiers rich in details. In these records historians often recover the voices of those who otherwise would have remained mute. Court cases have permitted social historians to construct sophisticated studies of prostitution, such as that of Lotte van de Pol for Amsterdam, and equally fascinating treatments of other aspects of everyday life in major urban centers. The deliberations and decisions of ecclesiastical courts disclose the dimensions of religious dissent of course but also broader morals, common attitudes, and daily routines. Historians have made astonishing discoveries in the annals of the various Catholic inquisitions. Heavily exploited in quantitative terms to trace, for instance, the numbers and characters of the persecutions of heretics, such documents also have been useful in building microhistories.

Microhistory arose as a reaction to a prevalent trend in social history, that is, the practice of studying large groups by evaluating masses of material and seeking to define overarching structures. Historians who practice the abductive method of microhistory turn instead to examining a few extraordinarily revealing documents, often those that record unique or sensational events, such as the incidents of early modern cannibalism studied by Edward Muir. These scholars seek to reinsert individuals and historical agency into history by revealing the contours of European popular culture. The most famous examples of a successful microhistorical approach are Carlo Ginzburg's story of a heretic miller in *The Cheese and the Worms* (1980) and Natalie Zemon Davis's brilliantly retold tale of *The Return of Martin Guerre* (1983).

Police files function in many of the same ways as court records. Police records per se developed when governments began to recast police forces as executory agencies and created policemen in the nineteenth century. Police records reveal much about those people society defined as criminals, yet their utility far exceeds that objective. Police agents also infiltrated trade unions and kept a watch on other groups considered suspicious or deemed deviant. Therefore much knowledge about early unions, such as the Trade Unions Congress (TUC) or the seemingly innocuous friendly societies in Britain, derives from police reports filed on groups and individuals.

Notarial records are of inestimable worth in reconstructing everyday lives. Notaries were legally empowered to compose, witness, and certify the validity of documents and to take depositions. In addition they drew up wills and marriage agreements. Their archives are voluminous but usually poorly indexed and thus cumbersome to consult. Notarial records, especially wills, have helped count and calculate wealth and family arrangements; document trends in religious beliefs, as Michel Vovelle traced the progress of dechristianization; prove affective relationships within families; follow the movement of property and goods among kin; and analyze the role of gender in familial and business relationships. The possibilities for the historical exploitation of notarial records are by no means exhausted by this list. Late twentieth-century studies used notarial records to

observe the dynamics of migrant communities in early modern Europe.

Finally, the records of guilds and unions can be included among administrative or governmental sources. Unions differ from guilds in that they represent laborers rather than all the members of a particular craft. A new phenomenon in the nineteenth century, labor unions generally kept their own records, which, along with the accounts of political parties, sometimes were placed in government safekeeping. At the end of the twentieth century many unions and political parties maintained their own archives distinct from government collections. Guilds (and unions, too, to some extent) were multifunctional organizations that exercised cultural, philanthropic, and religious functions as well as economic ones. Their records not only reveal details about economic structures and production methods but also trace religious, social, and cultural trends among nonelite groups. Those interested in the history of industrialization and the rise of free-trade practices have used guild materials and in particular disputes among apprentices, journeymen, and masters to follow subtle shifts in the business world, especially during periods of economic upheaval, depression, or boom. These records have been equally useful in documenting the early history of consumerism. The right to produce new commodities, such as umbrellas in the seventeenth century or porcelain in the eighteenth century, had to be negotiated among the various craft guilds. But guilds also formed defenses against new entrepreneurs, like the porcelain manufacturer Josiah Wedgwood, who worked outside the craft system.

NONGOVERNMENTAL SOURCES

Historians generally seek the more or less official records described above in archives and libraries, yet nongovernmental material frequently reposes in archives and libraries as well. Personal papers, memoirs, business records, and clipping files or scrapbooks are often deposited for preservation in archives even though they properly belong to the category of private and personal records. Newspapers, magazines, prescriptive literature, and fictional works are found more frequently in libraries than in archives, although many archives house extensive runs of newspapers.

Social historians have quarried newspapers for a multitude of reasons. Obviously newspapers, a novelty of the eighteenth century, help determine what happened. Yet the definition of "what happened" differs for the social historian as compared to the diplomatic or political historian. The social historian might be more interested in articles on society and culture or in advertisements and letters to the editor than in so-called hard news. Of course newspapers reported on political issues that bore on social history directly or indirectly, for example, parliamentary debates on the implementation of social insurance schemes or old-age pensions. Other historians have looked at advertisements to document, for instance, the rise of a consumer culture, the proliferation of goods and services, the growth of pharmaceutical and patent medicine businesses, and a burgeoning book trade. The rise of the penny press has much to say about changing tastes among the reading public and about rates of literacy. The history of fashion, too, can be pursued in newspaper columns. Few social historical topics cannot but be enriched by a thorough survey of contemporary newspapers and magazines.

An early type of what might be called a general-interest magazine that lacked pictures and advertising was the moral weekly that appeared in manuscript in the seventeenth century and in print in the next century. Journals, like Joseph Addison and Richard Steele's *Spectator* (1711–1712), the most famous and the most widely imitated of the many moral weeklies, had literary pretensions. But more important for the purposes of the social historian, they also critiqued conventional morals and society. Akin to the moral weeklies but more practical in content, the publications of the many "beneficial" and "purposeful" organizations of the mid- to late eighteenth century were explicit attempts to stimulate improvements in agriculture, business, and commerce as well as manners and morals. Titles like *The Patriot* (*Der Patriot*) in Hamburg (1721–1723) were generally moral in tone and content. But the *Deliberations* (*Verhandlungen und Schriften*) of the Patriotic Society founded later in Hamburg (1765) focused on practical proposals for the best ways to relieve the poor, raise silkworms, or build and maintain urban hospitals. In the Netherlands *The Merchant* (*De Koopman*) discussed economic morality and proper commercial behavior in the 1760s but also detailed schemes for reawakening a flagging commerce and animating declining industries in the republic.

Journals shade over into another source that social historians have exploited quite lavishly and sometimes slavishly, prescriptive literature. This literature includes all publications that prescribe behavior, like catechisms, sermons, advice manuals, and articles in newspapers and journals, for instance, women's magazines. Prescriptive literature touches on practically every topic of concern to social historians. For example, women received advice on household management, on style, on "getting and keeping a man," on sex, on the proper expression of emotions, and on the choice of a career. Newly enthroned experts, such as physicians, addressed a plentitude of advice literature to parents about how to raise their children. Easy to find and use, such material provides a surfeit of information on social standards and behavioral expectations. Prescriptive literature is, however, less serviceable in determining what people actually did than in determining what they were instructed to do. Thus advice literature may produce a false picture of reality unless combined with other sources.

Social historians once used novels, poems, plays, and other forms of fiction as illustrative material or as contemporary "witnesses" of their times. These sources fell out of fashion as the new social history, with its tendency to emphasize masses or large groups of people and nonliterate persons or nonelites, took firm hold. In the early twenty-first century, however, under the impact of the new cultural history and after the "linguistic turn," social historians returned to belles lettres, reading them as texts, often deconstructing them into their component parts, pinpointing where concepts and phrases originated, and identifying the extent to which they represented a cultural heritage that linked popular and elite cultures. Immensely influential both as a theoretical work and as an example, Mikhail Bakhtin's study of François Rabelais identified a culture of the grotesque that elites and nonelites shared.

Not only governments and organizations such as guilds assembled and maintained documentary collections. Various other organizations, voluntary, philanthropic, and mutual benefit, for instance, preserved their records as well. Moreover personal papers and "ego-documents" are indispensable aids if sometimes also lucky finds for historians in general and for the social historian in particular. Many social historians have expressed considerable skepticism about the value of government-generated sources for writing an informed and reliable history from the bottom up and therefore search for more personal and immediate materials in less-known and less-frequented archives.

Commercial records are invaluable in composing economic and business histories and in investigating the lives of laborers through personnel records. Historians have emphasized the utility of such sources in constructing collective biographies (or prosopographies, the technical term for early modern collective biographies) of several social classes or status groups. Yet much there is worthy of the attention of anyone interested in the development of business cultures or the involvement of business in matters of welfare and social insurance or for scholars studying patterns of production and consumerism.

A number of private groups, such as philanthropic and eleemosynary societies, for example, the Coram Foundling Hospital in London, clubs, ladies' charitable circles, suffragette groups, friendly societies, benevolent associations, and international leagues like the YMCA and YWCA, construct, staff, and maintain their own collections. Such sources form the nucleus for institutional histories but expedite or make possible other kinds of historical inquiries as well. Benevolent societies can reveal much about laborers' quotidian experiences, for example. An investigation of clubs might demonstrate how networks of sociability evolved and contributed to the creation of a public sphere, such as that postulated by Jürgen Habermas, or reveal the social and philanthropic activities that women dominated.

A wide range of what might be called nondeposited sources is also available. To some extent these include things that have not been identified as sources or whose existence is unknown to the historical community. Some ingenuity is required. Michael B. Miller, for instance, found and catalogued many of the business records of the Parisian *grand magasin* (department store), the Bon Marché, stored in the building, and he marshalled them into a history of marketing, consumerism, and bourgeois culture in late nineteenth-century France. Poking around in old edifices, attics, barns, and outbuildings has produced unsuspected cornucopias. Serendipity is not to be scorned; some of the most mesmerizing historical finds have been accidental. Judith Brown's lively account of a lesbian nun in seventeenth-century Italy (*Immodest Acts: The Life of a Lesbian Nun in Renaissance Italy*, 1986) rested on just such a fortuitous discovery. Historians sometimes judge it expedient to advertise in national or local newspapers or in more specialized journals to locate previously unsuspected caches. The diligent prying of historians has brought to light casebooks of physicians, surgeons, and midwives; bundles of letters and diaries; and annotated almanacs that had been left to molder away in attics or basements.

In the late twentieth century historians paid increasing attention to what Dutch and German scholars call "ego-documents." These are not traditional biographies or autobiographies but rather the writings of ordinary people, often those living on the edge of respectable society, who never intended to publish their manuscripts. The term sometimes is expanded to include contemporary narratives written about such people. A good example of such a contemporary account is F. L. Kersteman's *De bredasche heldinne* (The heroine from Breda, 1751). A number of these have been uncovered, edited, and published and have aided social historians in lifting individuals out of the maelstrom of history by endowing ordinary lives with agency, dignity, and texture. Admittedly these documents have clarified the actions and thoughts of the idiosyncratic and the marginal more than those of the average person. Nonetheless, such works are equally precious for comprehending the choices ordinary people made and understanding why they embarked on their courses of action. Ego-documents have demonstrated how the rigid categories constructed by historians preoccupied with studying large groups and big structures might be less confining in practice and how even the *menu peuple* (lesser folk) exercised volition.

RESEARCHER-GENERATED SOURCES

Not all scholars, however, look at sources held in archives, libraries, or private hands. Many social historical documents are generated by researchers themselves. Interviews, oral histories, and photographs are excellent examples of common researcher-generated materials. Another such source might be the databases historians have built up from raw numbers that are evaluated either by the researchers or by others for further, often different forms of historical analysis.

Interviews and oral histories seem for the most part restricted to recent historical events and circumstances where the subjects are still alive and talking. Oral historians have sought ways to recover the lineaments of ordinary lives, probing aspects of sexuality and emotions, for example, that written records might fail to reveal or even conceal. Historians studying nonliterate societies employ anthropological techniques to reclaim knowledge about groups that left behind few or no written traces. While it is true that sometimes the oral recitation of legends, epics, and tales permits the historian to delve far back in history using sophisticated methods of recovery and regression, most oral histories focus on those who articulate their own stories. Not all oral histories or interviews, for that matter, are primarily researcher-generated. Oral history projects, the most famous of which is the American Federal Writer's Project of the 1930s that chronicled the memories of former slaves, assemble teams of interviewers to collect oral histories on tape, as interview notes, or from questionnaires. The tapes or transcripts are then deposited in archives and made available to others, who often use them for purposes entirely distinct from those the original collectors envisioned.

Another example of a generated source is the database. Databases are usually compilations of statistical materials or raw data that can be quantified. The material is arranged to make it easy or easier to search and retrieve information. Large-scale projects, such as demographic studies extending over centuries or investigations of family size and composition, require enormous databases. Examples include the Demographic Database in Umeå, Sweden, an outstanding source for the study of mortality, morbidity, and fertility trends; and the database built by the Cambridge (England) Group for the History of Population and Social Structure for analyzing small groups, such as the household and the family, over time.

NONWRITTEN SOURCES AND ARTIFACTS

Photographs are another form of evidence that is sometimes researcher-generated but that, like artifacts, is not written. Most archives and libraries have large photographic and iconographic collections of photographs and other pictorial material, such as paintings, drawings, posters, lithographs, woodcuts, medals, and icons. Social historians have used iconography for a wide variety of purposes. While many historians are content to employ pictures as illustrations, others have used them more subtly and creatively in forging their arguments. There depictions become evidence and proof. Caroline Bynum's study of female saints, *Holy Feast and Holy Fast* (1987), uses iconography portraying holy women and Christ figures to link physicality and medieval religiosity. Robert Scribner's *For the Sake of Simple Folk* (1981) made woodcuts an integral part of his portrayal of the faith of "simple folk" during the Reformation. Photographs have provided analytical material for many modern historical studies on family life, street culture, industrialization, technology, and the commercialization of leisure among others. Other nonwritten sources—moving pictures, films, advertisements, playbills, and fashions—can be employed similarly, although all require the mastery of techniques peculiar to the specific medium. Pictures are no more transparent than other media.

Maps and collections of maps are less integral to most social historical inquiries, although zoning maps, street plans, and field divisions have been effective in discussions of housing configurations, the construction of community, local patterns of sociability, agricultural change, and even the structuring of patronage-clientage axes in neighborhoods. Medical historians have deployed maps to demonstrate the relationships between diseases and socioeconomic factors, such as poverty.

Other nonwritten sources fall into the category of artifacts. While artifacts may be found in libraries and archives, they are just as often not. Museums, especially those devoted to representations of everyday life, provide information for historians who study material culture as well as urban and rural lifestyles. Furniture; conveyances, such as carriages, automobiles, and airplanes; household items, such as dishes and cooking utensils; clothing; and even knickknacks illuminate the physical conditions of life among a range of social groups or classes.

Architecture, too, is important. Open-air museums contain real buildings or replicas that represent the types of housing people inhabited and often exhibit the physical layout of villages and neighborhoods. When older sections of cities and villages still exist, these living museums are critically important for giving historians a viscerally real sense of place. Nothing conveys the feel of a medieval city better than a stroll down one of its serpentine streets. The vistas of Georges-Eugène Haussmann's Paris convey the culture of the European belle epoque, as do the paintings of Edgar Degas and Henri de Toulouse-Lautrec. In the last two decades of the twentieth century cultural historians "read" monuments, memorials, and hallowed sites for their historical content in efforts to construct histories of memory and commemoration. Likewise the concepts of display, representation, and self-fashioning have required historians to interpret statues and paintings as well as texts for information on how, for instance, regal figures like Louis XIV devised their special images of kingship and exerted authority.

The intriguing subject of social space and its construction leads historians to look at the layout of roads and places, especially where public spectacles such as executions and fireworks were staged, and to seek information on how class, status, and gender determined the allocation of space. Historians have also investigated the political implications of public spaces and performances, among them Lynn Hunt in her study of class and culture in the French Revolution and Mona Ozouf in her investigation of revolutionary festivals.

This brief survey of the sources of social history by no means exhausts the topic. Rather, it merely highlights the fact that almost no document is without its use for social history. Social historians have been and will continue to be imaginative in their application of sources and unflagging in their attempts to unearth new ones.

Social history once was termed the history of the "inarticulate." In fact, through discovery of new sources and innovative uses of familiar ones, social historians have advanced a host of topics previously considered unresearchable. Consequently the field has moved from areas with abundant records, such as protests, to cover a much wider range of topics and groups, many of which have gaps in data. For instance, it is hard to document how children experienced childhood, or to pinpoint the frequency of adulterous behaviors, though qualitative evidence of divorce cases provides clues. The discovery of new sources and the clever exploitation of older ones have allowed social history to remain fresh and innovative and have reduced the sense that some areas of life will be forever veiled to the historical gaze.

See also **Printing and Publishing** *(volume 5); and other articles in this section.*

BIBLIOGRAPHY

Bakhtin, Mikhail. *Rabelais and His World.* Translated by Helene Iswolsky. Cambridge, Mass., 1968.

Braudel, Fernand. *La Méditerranée et le monde méditerranéen à l'époque de Philippe II.* 2 vols. Paris, 1949.

Brown, Judith C. *Immodest Acts: The Life of a Lesbian Nun in Renaissance Italy.* New York, 1986

Bynum, Caroline Walker. *Holy Feast and Holy Fast: The Religious Significance of Food to Medieval Women.* Berkeley, Calif., 1987.

Davis, Natalie Zemon. *The Return of Martin Guerre.* Cambridge, Mass., 1983.

Duby, Georges. *Rural Economy and Country Life in the Medieval West.* Translated by Cynthia Postan. Columbia, S.C., 1968.

Ginzburg, Carlo. *The Cheese and the Worms: The Cosmos of a Sixteenth-Century Miller.* London, 1980.

Habermas, Jürgen. *The Structural Transformation of the Public Sphere: An Inquiry into a Category of Bourgeois Society.* Translated by Thomas Burger with Frederick Lawrence. Cambridge, Mass., 1989.

Hajnal, John. "European Marriage Patterns in Perspective." In *Population in History.* Edited by D. V. Glass and D. E. C. Eversley. Chicago, 1965. Pages 101–143.

Hajnal, John. "Two Kinds of Preindustrial Household Formation System." *Population Development Review* 8, no. 3 (1982): 449–494.

Herlihy, David, and Christiane Klapisch-Zuber. *Tuscans and Their Families: A Study of the Florentine Catasto of 1427.* New Haven, Conn., 1985.

Hunt, Lynn. *Politics, Culture, and Class in the French Revolution.* Berkeley, Calif., 1984.

Hunt, Lynn, ed. *The New Cultural History.* Berkeley, Calif., 1989.

Imhof, Arthur E. *Die gewonnenen Jahre: Von der Zunahme unserer Lebensspanne seit dreihundert Jahren, oder von der Notwendigkeit einer neuen Einstellung zu Leben und Sterben.* Munich, 1981.

Imhof, Arthur E. *Die verlorenen Welten: Alltagsbewältigung durch unsere Vorfahren, und weshalb wir uns heute so schwer damit tun.* Munich, 1984.

Laslett, Peter, with Richard Wall, eds. *Household and Family in Past Time.* Cambridge, U.K., 1972.

Le Roy Ladurie, Emmanuel. *The French Peasantry, 1450–1600.* Translated by Alan Sheridan. Berkeley, Calif., 1987.

Macaulay, Thomas Babington. *The History of England from the Accession of James II.* 5 vols. London, 1849–1861.

Michelet, Jules. *The People.* Translated by G. H. Smith, F.G.S. New York and Philadelphia, 1846.

Miller, Michael B. *The Bon Marché: Bourgeois Culture and the Department Store, 1869–1920.* Princeton, N.J., 1981.

Muir, Edward. "The Cannibals of Renaissance Italy." *Syracuse Scholar* 5, no. 3 (Fall 1984): 5–14.

Ozouf, Mona. *Festivals and the French Revolution.* Translated by Alan Sheridan. Cambridge, Mass., 1988.

Pol, Lotte C. van de. *Het Amsterdams hoerdom: Prostitutie in de zeventiende en achtiende eeuw.* Amsterdam, 1996.

Sabean, David Warren. *Kinship in Neckarhausen, 1700–1780.* Cambridge, U.K., and New York, 1998.

Sabean, David Warren. *Property, Production, and Family in Neckarhausen, 1700–1870.* Cambridge, U.K., and New York, 1990.

Stone, Lawrence. *The Crisis of the Aristocracy, 1558–1641.* Oxford, 1965.

Stone, Lawrence. *Family, Sex, and Marriage in England 1500–1800.* New York, 1977.

Stone, Lawrence. *The Past and the Present.* Boston, 1981.

Vovelle, Michel. *Piété baroque et déchristianisation en Provence au XVIIIe siècle: Les attitudes devant la mort d'après les clauses des testaments.* Paris, 1973.

THE ANNALES PARADIGM

Peter Burke

The phrase "the Annales Paradigm," coined by the American historian Traian Stoianovitch in 1976, implies that the French journal currently entitled *Annales: histoire et sciences sociales* (but long known as *Annales: Économies, sociétés, civilisations)*, offered or offers a model for a revolution in historical writing along the lines of the scientific revolutions whose structure was studied by Thomas Kuhn. To speak of a single model or paradigm, rather than a set of different paradigms, is something of a simplification. To identify a single journal or even the movement associated with it with the series of innovations described as "the new history" (*la nouvelle histoire*) is something of an exaggeration. All the same, the editors of the journal (which was founded in 1929 under the title *Annales d'histoire économique et sociale* and has continued to publish important studies of social history in the wide sense of that fluid term) have always encouraged their readers to experiment with new approaches.

THE FOUNDERS

The founders of the journal, Lucien Febvre (1878–1956) and Marc Bloch (1886–1944), colleagues at the University of Strasbourg after World War I, were also collaborators in the project of reforming, if not revolutionizing historical writing in France and elsewhere. Their goal was a broader, "more human" history that would be less concerned with narrating political events and describing institutions. The new history would be problem oriented rather than story oriented. It would be particularly concerned with the analysis of economic and social structures and trends.

The new historians, as Febvre and Bloch envisaged them, would be consciously interdisciplinary, drawing ideas and methods from geography, psychology, sociology, social anthropology, linguistics, and so on. The editorial in the first issue of *Annales* (as it is generally known) amounted to a declaration of war on the artificial divisions between history and the social sciences and between the medieval and modern periods. "The walls are so high that they often impede the view." The editorial committee included a geographer, an economist, a sociologist, and a specialist in political science, and contributors were encouraged to write economic or social history in the broad sense of those terms. From the start, *Annales* was no ordinary journal but the flagship of a movement.

To understand the aims of Febvre, the senior partner and the movement's charismatic leader (one is tempted to say "prophet"), and Bloch, his more moderate and constructive colleague, it is necessary to look at what they themselves had produced before the foundation of the journal. Febvre, a specialist on the early modern period, had written his doctoral thesis on his native province of Franche-Comté in the age of its ruler Philip II. He had worked on the French Renaissance but was best known for two interests, the history of religion and historical geography, on which he had published a lively textbook, *La terre et l'évolution humaine* (*The Earth and Human Evolution;* 1922), arguing strongly against the determinism particularly associated at that time with the German geographer Friedrich Ratzel (1844–1904). As for religion, Febvre had published studies of the Reformation and Counter-Reformation in Franche-Comté, a biography of Martin Luther (1928), and in 1929 itself, a typically aggressive and path-breaking article on the origins of the Reformation in France, castigating his colleagues for practicing a hidebound ecclesiastical history focused on institutions rather than what he advocated, a history of religion informed by social history and psychology.

Bloch, on the other hand, was a historian of the Middle Ages. Like Febvre, by 1929 he had produced two rather different kinds of history. He was best known as an economic historian specializing on the problem of serfdom and working more generally on French rural history—on which he would publish a major monograph in 1931. However, he was also the author of a remarkable study in what would later be known as "the history of collective mentalities," a book about the long-lasting belief in the healing pow-

Marc Bloch. ©HARLINGUE-VIOLLET

The publication of the first issue of *Annales* in 1929 was an important event in the history of historical thought, but the books and articles already mentioned suggest that Bloch and Febvre had begun their intellectual innovations much earlier. Nor were they completely isolated in their critique of the historical establishment of their time or in their attempt to renew historical studies. Economic historians in Germany, Britain, and elsewhere were rebelling against the traditional dominance of political history. A senior colleague who was something of a model as well as a friend to both of them was Pirenne, whom they had invited to edit the new journal. Another was the Frenchman Henri Berr (1863–1954), a historical entrepreneur whose editorship of the interdisciplinary *Revue de synthèse historique,* as well as of a series of book-length studies entitled *Évolution de l'humanité* (The evolution of humanity) gave Febvre, Bloch, and other historians of their persuasion the opportunity to make their ideas known to a wider public than that of their students and colleagues.

Among the books published in Berr's series, two especially deserve a mention here. Bloch's *La société féodale* (*Feudal Society*; 2 vols., 1939–1940) is an unusually original work of synthesis. It moves away from the traditional legal conception of feudalism, in terms of land tenure on condition of military service, toward what would later be described as a "total history" of a type of society dominated by warriors, which came into existence as a response to invasion. It was a history of social structures and collective attitudes (or "historical psychology") as well as economic and political institutions. Febvre, who reviewed the book, found it a little too sociological for his taste in the sense that it privileged structures over individuals. Febvre's own contribution to the series, planned in the 1920s but published only in 1942, was *Le problème de l'incroyance au XVIe siècle: La religion de Rabelais* (*The Problem of Unbelief in the Sixteenth Century: The Religion of Rabelais*). The book focused on a single individual in order to explore the problem of the limits to thought in a particular period of history. In this study, reacting with his usual vehemence against an earlier interpretation, Febvre argued that Rabelais was not an unbeliever. He could not have been an atheist because, according to Febvre, atheism was literally unthinkable at this time. There was no place for this idea in the mental structures of Rabelais and his contemporaries, or as Febvre preferred to say, in their *outillage mental,* which he understood in terms of the "pre-logical thought" that had been described by his former teacher, the philosopher Lucien Lévy-Bruhl (1857–1939).

ers of the kings of France and England, *Les rois thaumaturges* (*The Royal Touch*; 1924). Bloch too had recently published an important article on historical method, "A Contribution towards a Comparative History of European Societies" (1928).

Annales d'histoire économique et sociale was an appropriate title for the journal in the 1930s. Economic history predominated, making the journal a French equivalent of the German, *Vierteljahrsschrift für Sozial und Wirtschaftsgeschichte* (founded in 1903), with which it deliberately competed, and the British *Economic History Review.* However, "economic history" was understood by the *Annales* group in a wide sense of the term, as two classic articles in the first volume show: one by the Belgian historian Henri Pirenne (1862–1935) on the culture of medieval merchants, and the other by Georges Lefebvre (1874–1959) on the French Revolution as an event in agrarian history. In any case, the editors intended from the start to cultivate what they called "the almost virgin territory of social history." In the 1930s they singled out three themes for particular attention: urban history, the family, and the comparative study of nobilities.

Je voudrais essayer de fixer par écrit
certaines idées sur la Méthodologie historique
...
se sont développées dans mon esprit
depuis quelque temps et, mais affectent
encore une forme ... et flottante et
des contours vagues —

L'histoire n'a pas d'existence
scientifique — Le progrès capital des
sciences de la vie organique a été
d'écarter cette notion d'"histoire" — Du
jour où on ... au lieu d'"hist naturelle"
n a dit "biologie" du jour où on a
cessé de décrire pour expliquer et classer

Bloch's *Meditations*. Marc Bloch wrote his *Meditations on History* in 1906.

THE SECOND GENERATION

World War II was a watershed in the history of the *Annales* movement. Bloch was shot by the Germans in 1944, while Febvre effectively became part of the establishment after 1945, as a member of the Institut de France, French delegate to UNESCO, and founder of the Centre des Recherches Historiques (1949) at what was then the École Pratique des Hautes Études. Aged sixty-seven in 1945, Febvre gradually left the direction of both the journal and the movement to his intellectual "son," Fernand Braudel (1902–1985).

Braudel, who was already working on his doctoral thesis in the 1930s, was among the early contributors to *Annales*. Drafted in prisoner-of-war camps in Lübeck and Mainz, and defended as a thesis in 1947, *La Méditerranée et le monde méditerranéen à l'époque de Philippe II* (*The Mediterranean and the Mediterranean World in the Age of Philip II*; 1949) is viewed as one of the most important products of the *Annales* movement, as well as one of the most outstanding and original historical studies published in

the twentieth century. The change of title, encouraged by Febvre, from "Philip II and the Mediterranean" to "The Mediterranean and Philip II," was extremely significant. To the surprise of its early readers, this large volume began with some three hundred pages of historical geography, moving on to a description of economic, political, and social structures and trends (notably refeudalization and the "bankruptcy of the bourgeoisie"). Only in the third and final section did Braudel offer a relatively conventional account of the major events of Philip II's long reign.

The division of the volume into these three sections was justified in the preface by what might be called Braudel's historical sociology of time. In the first place, he distinguished what he called "unconscious history" or "the long term" *(la longue durée)*, from the relatively superficial short term, the time of events and experience *(histoire événementielle)*, which he described in one of his most famous phrases as "surface disturbances, crests of foam that the tides of history carry on their strong backs." Within the long term, Braudel went on to distinguish the time of social structures, changing gradually over the centuries, from geo-historical time, profoundest and slowest of all, which was measured in millennia.

Braudel's ideas about time became paradigmatic, at least in certain circles in France, especially after their elaboration in one of his most important articles, "Histoire et sciences sociales: La longue durée" ("History and the Social Sciences: the Long-Term;"1958; Trans. in Baudel, 1980). The effect of these ideas can be seen in a series of French doctoral theses, beginning with those of Pierre Chaunu (b. 1923) on Spain's transatlantic trade (1955–1960) and Pierre Goubert (b. 1915) on the Beauvais region (1960). These theses were generally divided into two parts, under the headings "structures" and "trends" *(la conjoncture)*.

This adaptation of Braudel, which virtually eliminated the events to which he had devoted the third part of his own dissertation, owed a good deal to the example and teaching of his older colleague, Ernest Labrousse (1895–1986). A Marxist, Labrousse had published two important studies in economic history in 1933 and 1944, at a time when Braudel was virtually unknown. He later turned to social history, including that of the nineteenth-century bourgeoisie, and became a kind of "grey eminence" of the *Annales* movement, a major influence not only on young historians working for their *doctorat d'État*—among them Maurice Agulhon (b. 1926), Pierre Chaunu, François Furet (1927–1997), Pierre Goubert, and Emmanuel Le Roy Ladurie (b. 1929)—but also on Braudel himself, whose increasing interest in quantitative history (most visible in the second edition of his *Mediterranean,* published in 1966) owed much to Labrousse's example.

The young historians mentioned above formed the second generation of the *Annales* group, together with the medievalist Georges Duby (1919–1997), the agricultural historian Jean Meuvret (1909–1971), best known for his emphasis on the recurrent "subsistence crises" of the old regime, and, on the edge of the group, the Marxist historian of Spain, Pierre Vilar. Duby, Goubert, and Le Roy Ladurie established the pattern of regional histories of the Maconnais, the Beauvaisis, Languedoc, Provence, Savoy, Brittany, and so on. Their studies began with geographical structures and ended with economic and social trends, which were usually studied over a century or more. They wrote what the French call "serial history" *(l'histoire sérielle)* and distinguished phases of expansion ("A-phases," as the French economist François Simiand called them) from phases of contraction ("B-phases"). The trends this group of historians analyzed were social as well as economic. Indeed, one hallmark of the new generation was the interest it showed in a new subdiscipline, historical demography, virtually founded by Louis Henry (b.1911) and established at the Institut National des Études Démographiques but involving historians from the very beginning.

As for Braudel, his second major work, *Civilisation matérielle et capitalisme* (*Capitalism and Material Life 1400–1800*; 1967), originally commissioned by Febvre, was a highly original work of synthesis, joining economic to social history in the study of material culture and everyday life as well as placing pre-industrial Europe in comparative context by its frequent references to the Americas, China, and Japan. Braudel, ably seconded by Clément Heller, and partially supported by American funding, also reorganized historical research at the École des Hautes Études en Sciences Sociales (EHESS), and created and controlled an interdisciplinary Maison des Sciences de l'Homme.

THE THIRD GENERATION

In 1968, when Braudel was sixty-six and expected, if not exactly ready, to retire, the students of Paris went onto the streets. "The events" *(les événements),* as they were known, had their repercussions even on event-despising structural history. Braudel decided that the committee running *Annales* required new blood, and brought in Marc Ferro (b. 1924) and Jacques Revel (b. 1942). In the longer term, looking back from the end of the century, the movement of 1968, with its

Fernand Braudel. ©ROGER-VIOLLET

slogan "the imagination in power," now appears to be related to a major shift of emphasis in *Annales* history (as in historical writing elsewhere), the so-called "cultural turn."

In France this turn had two successive phases. First was the attempt to apply quantitative methods to the study of the "third level"—as Chaunu called it in a memorable article published in Braudel's *Festschrift* in 1973—or what Marxists call the "superstructure," in other words, the realm of culture and ideas, viewed as less "fundamental" than economic and social structures. What Chaunu preached, Michel Vovelle practiced in his *Piété baroque et déchristianisation en Provence au 18e siècle* (Baroque piety and de-Christianization in Provence in the 18th century; 1973), a study of attitudes toward death and the afterlife based on the analysis of some thirty thousand wills, comparing and contrasting the attitudes of rich and poor, townspeople and country people, males and females, and so on. The historical sociology of religion practiced by Gabriel Le Bras (1891–1970), a former colleague of Febvre's at Strasbourg, is a still earlier example of the serial history of culture, based on the statistics of confessions, communions, and vocations to the priesthood, which the Church itself compiled. A similar approach was followed in studies of literacy in France based essentially on the evidence of signatures and published in book form as *Lire et écrire* (*Reading and Writing*; 1977) by François Furet and Jacques Ozouf.

Attempts to write the history of mentalities in a quantitative style reached their culmination, or their extreme, outside the *Annales* group in the so-called "Laboratory of Lexicometry," which counted the occurrences of keywords in newspapers and other texts during the French Revolution. However, the revival of the history of mentalities or the historical psychology of Bloch and Febvre came to be associated with the second phase of the cultural turn, the reaction against quantitative methods. On the margin of the *Annales* group, the amateur historian Philippe Ariès (1914–1982), despite his training as a demographer, became increasingly interested in cultural variations in attitudes toward childhood and death. Alphonse Dupront (1905–1990), who like Labrousse supervised many doctorates and so exercised considerable influence on the next generation, studied the history of religion as a form of historical psychology, concerning himself in particular with crusades and pilgrimage and with viewing these phenomena over the *longue durée*. Georges Duby, turning away from his earlier work on agrarian history, examined the idea of the three estates of the realm as part of the history of the collective imagination in the Middle Ages. Jacques Le Goff (b. 1924) made a similar study of the development of the idea of purgatory.

Like Duby, Le Roy Ladurie turned from the study of agriculture to the study of culture in his best-selling *Montaillou village occitan* (1975), in which he used Inquisition records to reconstruct the mental as well as the material world of some peasants in the south of France at the beginning of the fourteenth century. The book owes its fame and its many translations to the author's gift for bringing some forgotten individuals back to life, but it is important for other reasons as well. Like Febvre, Bloch, and Braudel, Le Roy Ladurie draws frequently on the ideas of scholars working in other disciplines, from the peasant studies of Alexander Chayanov and Teodor Shanin to the social anthropology of Edmund Leach and Pierre Bourdieu. *Montaillou* is also one of the most famous examples of what would be known a little later as "microhistory," the attempt at the historical reconstruction of a small community, in this case on the basis of Inquisition records that had long been known and utilized by historians of heresy but had never been employed as the basis of a community study.

The return of the history of mentalities and the reaction against economic and social determinism of the 1970s and 1980s went with a rediscovery of politics and to a lesser extent with a rehabilitation of the history of events so strongly rejected in earlier phases of the *Annales* movement. Marc Ferro, for some years the secretary to the committee directing the journal, was at the same time a historian of the Russian Revolution and World War I. Le Roy Ladurie worked on the court of Louis XIV and the politics of the regency. Maurice Agulhon concentrated on the nineteenth century, examining political history at the village level and analyzing the political meaning of "Marianne," the personification of France.

As for events, even Braudel believed that they were worthy of study as evidence for the history of structures, and Duby, who wrote a book on changing perceptions of the thirteenth-century Battle of Bouvines, followed him in this respect. Vovelle and Furet, who studied not only the old regime but also the French Revolution, took events still more seriously. Breaking both with tradition and his Communist past, Furet reinterpreted the Revolution in a controversial essay, not in social but in cultural terms, viewing it as a change that took place at the level of political culture and even of discourse.

Later developments in the movement are illustrated by the work of Roger Chartier (b. 1945), and Bernard Lepetit (1948–1996). Chartier approached cultural history, more especially the history of reading, as a history of practices and representations. In so doing he was indebted not only to the *Annales* tradition of the history of mentalities and the "book history" of Henri-Jean Martin (b. 1924; whose mentor was Lucien Febvre), but also to the social theory of Michel de Certeau and the new approach to bibliography developed by the New Zealand scholar Don Mackenzie. Lepetit was equally innovative. Making his name with a study of French towns, which awoke an interest in transport networks and urban systems, Lepetit went on to study social structures as networks of individuals in a manner reminiscent of the sociologists Luc Boltanski and Bruno Latour.

The change in *Annales*'s subtitle from "Économies, sociétés, civilisations," to "Histoire, sciences sociales" in 1994 may be interpreted as an attempt to return to the origins of the movement. In similar fashion, over the long term the historian of *Annales* may detect a circular tour from the stress on agency (especially in the work of Febvre) to an emphasis on structure (in Bloch, and still more in Braudel) to the rediscovery of agency by Lepetit and others. Through all these changes, the *Annales* group maintained a distinct identity, thanks in part to the journal, and in part to the concentration of historians following the paradigm in one institution, the École des Hautes Études en Sciences Sociales, where they have the opportunity for daily contact with workers in neighboring disciplines such as anthropology and sociology.

THE RECEPTION OF *ANNALES*

It would be a mistake to identify French historical writing since 1929 with the *Annales* movement, however warm its reception has been in some quarters in France. The paradigm has always had its critics, from Charles Seignobos (1854–1942), against whose approach both Febvre and Bloch liked to define themselves, to Henri Coutau-Bégarie and François Dosse (b. 1950), who launched attacks in the 1980s on what they described as "the new history phenomenon" or the "fragmentation" of history.

The interest in the *Annales* outside France owes a great deal to the perception of the movement as offering some kind of "third way" of writing social and cultural history between Marxism on one side, with its emphasis on the economy, and traditional political history, in the style of the German, Leopold von Ranke (1795–1886), on the other. However, the reception of the French paradigm and of the historians who contributed to it varied a great deal in both timing and temperature according to local interests and traditions. In Poland, for example, the movement was received with enthusiasm almost from the start by historians such as Jan Rutkowski (1886–1948). Later, when Poland was ruled by the Communist Party, it was precisely the difference between the *Annales* paradigm and Marxism that made the former so appealing. In Spain, on the other hand, the interest in the work of Bloch, Febvre, and, above all, Braudel, on the part of Jaime Vicens Vives (1910–1960) and his followers was associated with crypto-Marxism and with opposition to the Franco regime.

In Britain and the United States, as in Germany (where historians were long committed to the primacy of the political), the interest in *Annales* flowered relatively late. In Britain, it was above all the left-wing historians associated with *Past and Present,* notably Eric Hobsbawm and Lawrence Stone, who expressed sympathy for the French paradigm from the 1950s onward (Marc Bloch had long been appreciated by medievalists, but more, perhaps, for his substantive conclusions than for his innovations in approach or method).

In the United States in the 1970s, sympathizers with the movement, especially the work of Braudel, ranged from the world historian William McNeill to the Marxist economic historian Immanuel Wallerstein. In a kind of intellectual leapfrog, Wallerstein learned from Braudel, while Braudel derived ideas from Wallerstein. It was Braudel, for example, who first used the term "world economy" (*économie-monde*) in 1949, but it was Wallerstein who analyzed this economy as a system of three interrelated parts, a "core," a "periphery," and a "semiperiphery."

Another important distinction to make when speaking of the reception of *Annales* is between the periods studied by different groups of historians. The concentration of leading *Annales* historians, especially Febvre and Braudel, on the early modern period has meant that specialists on the sixteenth and seventeenth centuries have always been unusually interested in the French paradigm. Again, thanks to Bloch and Pirenne, medievalists were interested in the movement from the first and in the age of Duby and Le Goff they continued to find it inspiring. The Russian scholar Aaron Gurevich is a good example of a scholar who developed his own ideas in dialogue with the French.

On the other hand, relatively few members of the *Annales* group have written about the nineteenth and twentieth centuries. The principal exceptions to this rule are Agulhon, Ferro, and Alain Corbin, who is close to the group in his concern to explore new territories, such as the lure of the sea and the history of smell and sound, even if he is not part of the *Annales* network. Conversely, foreign historians of the nineteenth and twentieth centuries appear to be relatively little aware of the *Annales* paradigms. When they are aware of these paradigms, like Henk Wesseling, a Dutch scholar specializing on colonialism, these historians are often critical of the dismissal of the history of events, considering it inappropriate, if not completely misguided, for the period in which they are interested.

In the last few years, one of the most important channels of diffusion of the *Annales* paradigm has been via the multivolume collective histories of private life and of women, edited by Ariès, Duby, and Michelle Perrot. These histories appeal to ordinary readers as well as professional historians, they have been translated into a number of languages, and they have inspired similar projects on a national scale (for example in Brazil). At the same time as this diffusion, however, we have seen a proliferation of alternative paradigms for social and cultural history. Innovation is no longer identified with Paris. For their part, French historians associated with the journal remain open to ideas from abroad. For example, when the English classical scholar Geoffrey Lloyd published his *Demystifying Mentalities* (1990), criticizing some features of *l'histoire des mentalités collectives,* it was welcomed by the leading *Annales* historian Jacques Revel and was quickly translated into French. The "cultural turn" of the last generation of historians developed in France, the United States, and elsewhere, in part independently and in part as a result of two-way exchange rather than one-way influence.

Although the founders of *Annales* emphasized interdisciplinary cooperation, the impact of the French paradigm on the social sciences is relatively recent. Even in the age of Braudel, who debated with Claude Lévi-Strauss and the sociologist Georges Gurvitch, the intellectual traffic was mainly in one direction. Michel Foucault surely learned something important from the historians associated with *Annales*—from the history of collective mentalities for example—but he did not acknowledge this in public. Indeed, he was a severe critic of what he perceived as the exaggerated empiricism of the historians. In the 1980s and 1990s, however, the situation changed.

In the English-speaking world, for example, scholars inspired by the *Annales* paradigm—or at any rate, by part of it—included the sociologist Charles Tilly, the social anthropologist Marshall Sahlins, the developmental psychologist Jerome Bruner, the geographer Alan Pred, and the archaeologist Ian Hodder. Bruner, for example, was attracted by the idea of "mentality," and Hodder by serial history and the long term, while Sahlins was concerned with the interplay between events and structures (starting out from Braudel but going beyond him). Terms such as *mentalité, conjoncture,* and *longue durée,* whether they are translated or left in the original French, whether they are quoted with approval or disapproval, are no longer confined to the vocabulary of historians.

As might have been expected, it is not always the same part of the paradigm, or the same paradigm, that appeals to different scholars, and the relative importance of (say) the econometric and the mentalities approaches is not easy to assess. In similar fashion, it is difficult to measure the historical importance of the journal itself compared with that of the monographs by leading historians associated with it. On this point, two suggestions spring to mind, one chronological and the other geographical. It is likely that the journal performed an indispensable function in building an intellectual tradition in the early years of the movement. However, it is probable that *Annales* gradually lost this function to exemplary works such as *The Mediterranean* or *Montaillou.* As for the geography of influence, it may well be the journal that has made the greatest impact within France itself. Outside France, on the other hand, the *Annales* "school" is widely identified with the monographs, some of them translated into six or more languages.

The placing of the term "school" in quotation marks is more than a whim or a sign of indecision. The hesitancy reveals a recurrent tendency in the history of intellectual movements, the fact that its followers sooner or later diverge from the ideas and ideals of its founders (hence Marx was not a Marxist, Luther was not a Lutheran, and so on). In the case of the *Annales* movement, one might argue that the intellectual distance between the generations has been unusually great. Braudel was close to Febvre in many respects, but his geographical determinism is in striking contrast to Febvre's voluntarism, his emphasis on the capacity of humans to use their environment for their own purposes rather than letting it shape them. In similar fashion, the so-called "third generation" of *Annales,* with their cultural turn, rejected Braudel in their historical practice while continuing to respect him. That these major intellectual shifts should have taken place with relatively few personal conflicts suggests that the movement has been characterized by a style of leadership that is pragmatic rather than dogmatic. However authoritarian Febvre and Braudel may have seemed on occasion, they generally allowed their followers the freedom to diverge. The lack of a climate of orthodoxy helps explain the truly remarkable capacity for self-renewal that the group demonstrated.

See also **The Population of Europe: Modern Demographic Patterns** *(volume 2);* **The Early Modern Period** *(in this volume); and other articles in this section.*

BIBLIOGRAPHY

Bintliff, John, ed. *The Annales School and Archaeology.* Leicester, U.K., 1991.

Braudel, Fernand. *On History.* Translated by Sarah Matthews. Chicago, 1980.

Burke, Peter. *The French Historical Revolution: The "Annales" School, 1929–89.* Cambridge, U.K., 1990.

Chartier, Roger. *Cultural History between Practices and Representations.* Translated by Lydia G. Cochrane. Cambridge, U.K., 1988.

Chaunu, Pierre. "Un nouveau champ pour l'histoire sérielle: Le quantitatif au troisième niveau." In *Mélanges Braudel.* Toulouse, France, 1973. Pages 216–230.

Clark, Stuart. "The *Annales* Historians." In *The Return of Grand Theory.* Edited by Quentin Skinner. Cambridge, U.K., 1985. Pages 177–198.

Coutau-Bégarie, Henri. *Le phénomène nouvelle histoire.* Paris, 1983.

Davis, Natalie Z. "Women and the World of the *Annales.*" *History Workshop Journal* 33 (1992): 121–137.

Dosse, François. *The New History in France: The Triumph of the Annales.* Translated by Peter V. Conroy Jr. Urbana, Ill., 1994.

Fink, Carole. *Marc Bloch: A Life in History.* Cambridge, U.K., 1989.

Hunt, Lynn. "French History in the Last Twenty Years: The Rise and Fall of the *Annales* Paradigm." *Journal of Contemporary History* 21 (1986): 209–224.

Raphael, Lutz. *Die Erben von Bloch und Febvre: Annales-Geschichtschreibung und nouvelle histoire in Frankreich, 1945–80.* Stuttgart, Germany, 1994.

Stoianovich, Traian. *French Historical Method: The Annales Paradigm.* Ithaca, N.Y., 1976.

MARXISM AND RADICAL HISTORY

Bryan D. Palmer

Marxism was born in European history. Karl Marx and Friedrich Engels elaborated the materialist concept of history out of engagements with German philosophy, French socialism, and British political economy. In the mid–nineteenth century historical materialism—the radical contention that the production and exchange of things necessary to the support of human life, the process through which wealth was created and distributed, was the root cause of social change and the political revolutions of the eighteenth century—stood much of the interpretation of the European past, embedded in Hegelian idealism, on its head. For Marx and Engels the mode of production was the motor of historical process. Its movement was impossible to understand outside of the necessary frictions and periodic clashes of a society divided into irreconcilable classes, primarily the new social strata, the bourgeois and the proletarian. From the time of its birth marxism was inexplicable outside of the transformations associated with the rise of capitalism, a social formation defined by an accumulative regime driven forward by the extraction of surplus associated with the wage system and production for profit. Capitalism and its histories of class formation and struggle figured centrally in marxist histories, although the materialist concept of history also was applied fruitfully to precapitalist modes of production, as evident in G. E. M. De Ste. Croix's challengingly imaginative and elaborately researched *The Class Struggle in the Ancient Greek World* (1981).

THE ORIGINS OF MARXIST HISTORY

The first marxist histories accentuated different analytic features of historical materialism. In his historical writings on France, for instance, Marx presented scathing indictments of the personnel of bourgeois power, exposing the contradictory nature of capitalist "progress" and of those, such as Napoleon Bonaparte, who would be called upon to lead its march. Such social histories were conscious assaults on the hypoc-

risies of bourgeois rule and parodies of the democratic order. Fueled by a partisan analysis relentless in its use of oppositional language, Marx meant to convey to all concerned the powerful class divisions at work in historical process. Marx also commented on the failures of proletarian organization in the Paris Commune, while Engels reached back into the German experience to outline the social upheavals of the German peasant wars. In their later works of political economy, Marx and Engels were equally passionate but less attuned to the place of political rule or the mobilization of class resistance. These histories, such as Marx's *Capital* (volume 1, 1867), outlined capital's original accumulations (by means of dispossessing a landed peasantry, divorcing small artisan producers from the means of production, and pillaging new colonial conquests) and its relentless appetite for surplus (manifested in extending the length of the working day, suppressing working-class collectivity, elaborating ever more intricate divisions of labor, and charting new technological innovation).

These and many other writings formed the theoretical foundation on which marxist histories rested for the next century and more. Within what might be called "the classical tradition," marxist histories were produced by intellectuals whose primary commitment was to the revolutionary movement. Their historical writing, seldom far removed from theoretical questions, was often a direct attempt to explore historical themes originally addressed by Marx or Engels. Thus Karl Kautsky, one of a small contingent developing the materialist concept of history in the late nineteenth century, produced a study of religion, *The Origin of Christianity* (1923), a staple of marxist critique in this period. Kautsky attempted to situate European and American agriculture in an 1899 publication, *The Agrarian Question*. His *Communism in Central Europe in the Time of the Reformation* (1897) returned directly to Engels's concern with the German peasant uprisings of the sixteenth century, as did Belfort Bax's *The Peasants War in Germany, 1525–1526* (1899). Early writing on the Paris Commune included Lissagaray's

History of the Commune of 1871 (1886), translated from the French by Marx's daughter Eleanor Marx Aveling.

With the increasing importance of revolutionary activity, most especially in Russia and culminating in the October Revolution of 1917, marxist histories intersected directly with the perceived needs and understood accomplishments of proletarian insurrection. Vladimir Ilyich Lenin's *The Development of Capitalism in Russia* (1899) was a massive study of the rural economy. An investigation of the tsarist countryside, the book aimed to outline how varied modes of production coexisted to produce a specific historically contextualized social formation and to develop from this research strategic directions for a workers' revolution in a setting of "combined and uneven capitalist development." This theme also set the stage for Leon Trotsky's magisterial three-volume narrative *The History of the Russian Revolution* (1932), probably historical materialism's most elegantly executed chronology of class revolt in the first fifty years of marxist historical production. Trotsky's text was preceded by Louise Bryant's memoir *Six Red Months in Russia* (1918) and John Reed's more chronologically focused and journalistically inclined *Ten Days That Shook the World* (1919).

The revolutionary movement stimulated marxist research and bore rich fruit in the pre–World War I period. Subjects barely touched upon by the founders of historical materialism emerged out of the new global capitalism orchestrated by monopoly and threateningly powerful imperialist rivalries. Rudolf Hilferding's *Finance Capital* (1910) and Otto Bauer's *The Nationalities Question and Social Democracy* (1907) were both published, like Lenin's book, before their authors reached the age of thirty. They prefigured the concerns of Rosa Luxemburg, whose writings addressed the new regime of capital accumulation and accentuated the role of colonies. Luxemburg's politics breathed a vibrant internationalism and a particular resistance to national parochialism.

But troubling signs as well showed up on the marxist horizon in 1914. The fracturing of the Second International, the working-class organization of marxism at the time of World War I, suggested the powerful challenges to orthodoxy that emerged in this period, detailed in the French marxist Georges Haupt's *Socialism and the Great War: The Collapse of the Second International* (1972) and in Carl Schorske's *German Social Democracy, 1905–1917: The Development of the Great Schism* (1955). The Russian Revolution failed to spread to the advanced capitalist economies of the West, and the ground receptive to Stalinist containments was being tilled. One seed was the rise of the

international Left Opposition, grouped around Trotsky and later organized in the Fourth International. The scant serious historical self-reflection on marxist theory and history produced in these years, such as Trotsky's *The Revolution Betrayed: What Is the Soviet Union and Where Is It Going?* (1937), emanated from this dissident quarter. The Stalinist Comintern of the interwar years was notable for its mechanical practices and routinization of theory. As Perry Anderson argued in *Considerations on Western Marxism* (1976), the interwar years and beyond largely saw the relinquishment of historical, economic, and political themes in marxist intellectual production and the replacement of marxist activists at the writing center of historical materialism by university-based scholars of the left. The center of gravity of continental European marxism, in Anderson's metaphor, turned toward philosophy. Certainly the major marxist thought in this period was cultivated among a layer of what Luxemburg and Kautsky dubbed *Kathedersozialisten,* professorial socialists. From György Lukács to Jean-Paul Sartre, class consciousness was written about more as an aesthetic possibility than as a combative historical process.

Nevertheless, some marxist histories produced in the post-1920 period continued to conjoin the social and the political within a grounding in economic life. Much of this writing was produced by Communist Party (CP) intellectuals, among them the Russian émigré turned English journalist Theodore Rothstein, who wrote *From Chartism to Labourism* (1929), an important early account of the history of the British working-class movement. Something of a combination of Henry Mayhew, Charles Booth, and Engels, Jürgen Kuczynski authored a multivolume set of short histories of labor conditions in Germany, France, and Great Britain that prefigured, in its range of concerns and attention to periodization, the later approach of Eric J. Hobsbawm. But perhaps the most important marxist history in these interwar years was sustained by two British CP figures, Maurice Dobb and Dona Torr. Dobb returned to the themes of *Capital* in his *Studies in the Development of Capitalism* (1947). Torr, in a series of largely party-circulated and often inaccessible publications, many of which were short educational or agitational pieces, stimulated interest and concern about the working class and its movements among a cohort of historians whose formative political years were spent in the struggles for colonial independence, the popular front organizations and cultural milieu of the late 1930s, the battle to defeat fascism both politically and militarily, and the postwar campaigns for peace and nuclear disarmament.

The Marx Family. Karl Marx with his daughters Jenny, Eleanor, and Laura, and Friedrich Engels, c. 1860. ©STOCK MONTAGE

THE HISTORIANS GROUP

From the mid-century nursery of marxist history's perhaps most celebrated collectivity, the Communist Party of Great Britain (CPGB) Historians Group, emerged a contingent of historians later known simply as "the British Marxists." Among others, Christopher Hill, Rodney Hilton, Victor Kiernan, Eric J. Hobsbawm, Edward P. Thompson, Dorothy Thompson, John Saville, and a precocious Raphael Samuel, the future founder of *History Workshop Journal,* literally were schooled in historical research in this informal but highly influential CPGB Historians Group. With economic history as the base, this contingent produced an eclectically rich superstructure of social histories. Individuals associated with this CP historiography of the 1940s and 1950s eventually dominated entire fields of social history and left their interpretive mark on generations of scholarship.

Hill's first book, *Lenin and the Russian Revolution* (1947), marked his communist commitments but was distanced from his actual area of academic specialization. He rewrote the social, intellectual, cultural, and political history of seventeenth-century England and its varied revolutions, both actual and threatening. Ensconced in the Oxford of All Souls College and Balliol, Hill did much to give marxist history impeccable academic credentials. Relishing the historical moment when his fellow citizens repudiated monarchy and actually took the head of a king, Hill was indefatigable in poring over the sources of his period. He was perhaps at his creative best in the company of the precursors of marxist revolt, the Levellers, Diggers, and Ranters, who confirmed for Hill that class resistance was more of a factor in preindustrial capitalist England than many had acknowledged. In *The World Turned Upside Down: Radical Ideas during the English Revolution* (1972), Hill explored the imaginative ideas of social transformation that germinated in the first third of the seventeenth century and were released into public debate in the two decades following the revolution of property of 1640. Over the course of more than fifty years of writing, Hill produced a massive body of research on subjects as varied as images of the Antichrist, John Milton, radical pirates, Oliver Cromwell, the place of the church and various dissident sects, and the socioeconomic shift from Reformation to industrial revolution. Even those not enamored of marxism, such as Lawrence Stone, acknowledged that "the age of Puritan revolution" was regarded by the mid-1960s as "Hill's half-century" and that Hill was one of a few historians who had managed thoroughly to dominate a field.

E. P. Thompson's impact was different but no less significant. Thompson, whose training was originally more in literature than in history, entered the academic world in ways distinctly different from Hill's entry. The unfortunate climate of tightening anticommunism in post-1948 Britain ensured that a younger Thompson did not get the foothold in university life that Hill had established in the late 1930s and the 1940s. Working in adult education, Thompson was active in the post–World War II politics of communism, especially the peace movement of the early 1950s, and later in the 1950s he was decisively antagonistic to the CP hierarchy. Along with Saville, whose work focused on the economic history, institutions, and biography of nineteenth-century labor, Thompson led many historians out of the CP and into the beginnings of the New Left. Their shift preceded developments in the United States by a number of years and had a more disciplined relationship to marxism than the American campus-led upheavals of the mid-

1960s. Thompson and Saville became the editors of the *New Reasoner,* an early journal of socialist humanism that published a number of importantly suggestive forays into the social history of nineteenth-century England.

At precisely this time Thompson wrote his first major book, *William Morris: Romantic to Revolutionary* (1955), a pioneering and detailed exploration of Morris's marxism and the beginnings of organized socialist agitation in England in the 1880s. Thompson was also at work on *The Making of the English Working Class* (1964), which was originally conceived as an adult education primer on the history of the labor movement from 1790 to 1945. Led into the sources and complexities of class formation in England, he never got past the period leading up to Chartism, the subject on which his wife, Dorothy Thompson, wrote *The Chartists* (1984). His conceptualization of class as more than a static category of historical place, mechanically called into being by the dispossession of landed labor and the rise of the steam-powered factory, grew directly out of Thompson's understanding of Stalinism's distortions, both political and intellectual. His book was an engaged attempt to write working-class people and their consciousness of themselves, their aspirations, and their needs back into the history of the industrial revolution. Mainstream economic historians argued that historical progress was marked by rising standards of living measured out in calculations of the "mythical average" diet, wage rate, and housing stock. Certain marxist circles saw proletarianization as a "lawed" process in which working for wages necessarily produced a realization of the need for a working-class revolution directed by the vanguard party. Contradicting those positions, Thompson offered a rich tapestry of crowds and challenging ideas, midnight marches and purposeful machine breaking, radical artisans and the atrocities of child labor.

The fulcrum on which this presentation of experience's diversity balanced was resistance to the new amalgam of state power and the impersonal ordering of laboring life in the mills, factories, mines, and sweated outwork of early-nineteenth-century England. Thompson regarded the accomplishments of England's first workers as a "heroic culture." Polemical and passionate, he humanized history, and his tone was often irreverent and defiant of academic convention, stamping *The Making of the English Working Class* as perhaps the most influential radical social history produced in the last half of the twentieth century. Indeed a Thompsonian sensibility to class formation became an understood position within labor history by the 1970s and 1980s, and few histories of the working class in any national context written in the last two decades of the century did not engage with Thompson in some way.

Thompson next branched out in many directions, but most importantly for social history he produced a series of controversial, stimulating, and broadly researched essays on time and work discipline, the bread riot, and folkloric customs, such as charivari, or rough music, and the wife sale. Their completion was delayed by Thompson's physically exacting immersion in the campaign for nuclear disarmament in the late 1970s and 1980s. Eventually published in *Customs in Common* (1991), these studies refocused attention on the layered meanings of plebeian life in preindustrial capitalist settings. At pains to read the recorded histories of common experience against their often class-biased grain, Thompson discovered reservoirs of adaptation and forms of resistance that previous historians, including himself, had dismissed because they were reported with the nonchalance, even hostility, of "superior" classes. Thus the wife sale was less a brutal and misogynist practice of the degraded patriarchy of the lower classes, as depicted in Thomas Hardy's novel *The Mayor of Casterbridge* (1886) and countless folkloric accounts, than it was a reciprocal recognition of the breakdown of a domestic union in an epoch that allowed the poor no access to divorce. If it bore the trappings of a patriarchal order, it nevertheless sustained mutual decision making and goodwill among laboring people that were statements of the human resources those people brought to the changing conditions of their times. Thompson indeed moved away from marxism as he finished his studies of eighteenth-century plebeian cultures. In his imaginative account of William Blake, commenced in the 1960s but not published until 1993, at which point Thompson was dying, he confessed that, while he thought himself a "Muggletonian marxist" in 1968, he had subsequently come to have less certainty about both halves of this coupling. His writing nevertheless sustained sensibilities and attachments, especially to the radical resistance to the abuses of property's power, that were not unrelated to the origins of Thompson's histories in communist scholarship in the late 1940s and early 1950s.

Thompson's strengths as a historian were never in the realm of economic history, which he felt others in the Historians Group were more capable of developing. In pushing his studies back in time from the industrial revolution and the 1790s to the earlier eighteenth century and before, Thompson addressed popular culture during the transition from feudalism to capitalism. Marxist historians, led by Rodney Hilton, had in fact pioneered important studies of this tran-

sition, stimulating one of the most significant interpretive debates in the social and economic history of Europe. In Marx's writing the transition from feudalism to capitalism was posed ambivalently, placing accents first on the corrosive influence of mercantile activity and later on changing relations of production. Precisely because of that ambivalence, marxist histories debated the origins of capitalism, forcing mainstream historiography onto the terrain of marxist analysis. In the 1950s, in the first phase of this exchange, Paul Sweezy and Maurice Dobb adopted, respectively, the exchange and property-production positions. Their contentions led to series of essays in the American academic marxist journal, *Science and Society*, as well as a pivotal statement in the British publication *Past and Present*, a forum less tied to the Communist Party and more open to marxist-liberal dialogue.

THE TRANSITION DEBATE

The transition debate revived in the 1970s, witnessing significant marxist and nonmarxist interchange. Perry Anderson's *Lineages of the Absolutist State* (1974), which addressed state formation at the interface of Dobb, Sweezy, and an eclectic reading of nonmarxist historiography, prefaced this analytic cross-fertilization. But the critical challenge to marxist understandings of the transition came, by the 1970s, from neo-Malthusian scholarship that placed increasing emphasis on the demographically driven factors that influenced capitalism's emergence out of feudalism. Important reflections of that scholarship emerged in marxist social histories of family formation, of which the most compelling and elegant example in English was the two-volume statement by Wally Seccombe, *A Millennium of Family Change: Feudalism to Capitalism in Northwestern Europe* (1992) and *Weathering the Storm: Working-Class Families from the Industrial Revolution to the Fertility Decline* (1993). In two highly influential articles responding to the new debate, Robert Brenner put forth, with panache and analytic sweep, a resolutely marxist presentation of agrarian class structure in preindustrial Europe, taking a critical approach to what he called neo-Smithian marxism. Brenner in turn stimulated responses from many quarters. Originally published in *Past and Present* between 1976 and 1982, they were collected by T. H. Aston and C. H. E. Philpin in *The Brenner Debate* (1985). Brenner became associated with a structural appreciation of the class and property relations school of marxist history in terms of this debate over the relationship of feudalism's dissolution and capitalism's rise. Ironically he later explored the mercantile and political sides of precapitalist experience in his powerfully detailed *Merchants and Revolution: Commercial Change, Political Confict, and London's Overseas Traders, 1550–1653* (1993).

Like Brenner, Hobsbawm produced wide-ranging marxist histories difficult to pigeonhole. One of his earliest writings was an analytic tour de force of direct relevance to the transition debate. In a two-part *Past and Present* (1954) article that attempted to address the crisis of the seventeenth century, Hobsbawm explored why the industrial revolution did not proceed directly from the contradictions of sixteenth-century feudalism but stalled for a century, albeit in ways that provided the primitive accumulations necessary for capital's future explosive growth. A cosmopolitan intellect who, unlike most other communist historians, did not break from the CPGB in 1956, Hobsbawm was at home in many countries. His work was driven by an internationalism and a range that established him as an authority on bandits and primitive rebels, peasant revolts, the labor aristocracy, the new unionism of the late nineteenth century, and virtually all aspects of the histories of socialism. In his later years he turned increasingly to the production of sweeping syntheses of European and world history that gave comprehensive accounts of the modern world from the eighteenth century forward. Two collections of essays, *Labouring Men* (1964) and *Workers: Worlds of Labor* (1984), comprise something of a guidebook to the concerns of the social history of the working class as it developed from the 1960s to the 1980s. A fine critic and connoisseur of jazz as well as a regular commentator on public events, Hobsbawm was marxist history's Renaissance man.

Indeed the range of the British Marxist historians was striking. Kiernan wrote histories of imperialism and orientalism and treatments of Shakespeare and the romantics. Marxist historians, unlike their mainstream counterparts, rarely confined themselves to a resolutely narrow area of specialization. (Hill was something of an exception.) No other national culture produced a body of marxist historians of comparable range and depth. Hobsbawm, for instance, collaborated with George Rudé, whose histories of crowds and popular revolt in eighteenth- and nineteenth-century France and England linked him to the impressive marxist historians of the French Revolution, headed by Albert Soboul.

DEBATES ON THE FRENCH REVOLUTION

The class content of the world's most decisive bourgeois revolution, the French transformation unleashed with the events of 1789, had long been a staple of radical socialist thought. François-Alphonse Aulard, Jean-Joseph Jaurès, and Albert Mathiez wrote histories of the economic determinations of this broadly social revolution, and Georges Lefebvre's important studies, including *The Coming of the French Revolution, 1789* (1947) and *The Great Fear of 1789* (1973), were illustrative of the social histories of the popular classes that began seriously in the 1940s and 1950s. As a chronicler of the urban *menu peuple* (petty people), Soboul wrote first of the Parisian sansculottes and eventually offered a comprehensive two-volume study, *The French Revolution, 1787–1799* (1974). Soboul and others in France rarely moved out of the focused appreciation of their specific subject matter. The detailed researches of Lefebvre and Soboul stimulated an evocative historical narrative that meshed well with national pride, producing the irony of a marxist interpretation of a bourgeois revolution attaining the status, for a time, of an "official" history within a bourgeois society.

Of course other marxist histories existed in France. Among them were some internationally acclaimed works of labor history, including studies by two influential women scholars, Rolande Trempé's *Les mineurs de Carmaux* (1971) and Michelle Perrot's *Workers on Strike: France, 1871–1890* (1987); studies of popular iconography, such as Maurice Agulhon's *Marianne into Battle: Republican Imagery and Symbolism in France, 1789–1880* (1981); and rich tapestries of local experience, of which John Merriman's *The Red City: Limoges and the French Nineteenth Century* (1985), is a prime example. But if French marxists produced invaluable and influential works, their interpretive marxist eggs were generally concentrated in one basket. When new trends of historiography challenged the social analysis of the French Revolution, it was relatively easy for a focused mainstream criticism to appear successful in breaking the lot. In the 1980s and 1990s a revived antimarxist historiography of the French Revolution largely displaced the class-based analysis associated with Soboul. The British Marxists have been somewhat more resilient precisely because their collective and collaborative work has been wide-ranging.

MARXIST AND NATIONAL HISTORIOGRAPHY

Soviet and Chinese historiography in this period was largely formulaic and made few breakthroughs of an innovative sort in the realm of European social history. Because its purpose was to serve the Marxist-Leninist state, it tended to be polemical in nature, railing against inaccuracies and misinterpretations that routinely appeared in Western historical writing. On the whole marxist historians in the postrevolutionary states produced official Marxist-Leninist histories that served well the orthodoxies of the Communist Party. As a consequence social histories like those generated by the dissident communists in Great Britain did not appear in China or the Soviet Union, and accounts of the Russian Revolution, of necessity reproducing a specific Stalinist version of historical process, never broke out of mechanical molds. Among the most useful products were anthologies of documents, such as Y. V. Kovalev's *An Anthology of Chartist Literature* (1956). In a rare synthetic statement by an East German historian, Andreas Dorpalen presented an analytic sweep across centuries of the central European past in *German History in Marxist Perspective: The East German Approach* (1985).

Useful social histories of specific countries and the major left-wing upheavals associated with them are abundant. For Austria the divergent approaches to the history of socialism characteristic of the 1950s, when political history was more in vogue, and the 1990s, when social history's ascendance was a decade old, are evident in two texts: Joseph Buttinger's *In the Twilight of Socialism: A History of the Revolutionary Socialists of Austria* (1953) and Helmut Gruber's *Red Vienna: Experiment in Working-Class Culture, 1919–1934* (1991). The history of European socialism is the subject of Donald Sassoon's massive study, *One Hundred Years of Socialism: The West European Left in the Twentieth Century* (1996). Specific episodic struggles, such as the Spanish Civil War, have also received extensive treatment. Pierre Broué and Émile Témime's *The Revolution and the Civil War in Spain* (1972), a Marxist-Trotskyist overview, is heavily institutional and political in its treatment, while Burnett Bolloten's *The Spanish Civil War: Revolution and Counterrevolution* (1991) is unparalleled in its detail. The most succinct marxist account of the events in Spain in the 1930s, Felix Morrow's *Revolution and Counter-Revolution in Spain* (1936) is a product of Trotskyist perspectives. In her appreciation of gender, anarchism, and popular culture, Temma Kaplan, in *Anarchists of Andalusia, 1868–1903* (1977) and *Red City, Blue Period: Social Movements in Picasso's Barcelona* (1992), captures something of the concerns of social history in the 1980s and 1990s by giving attention to women, the representational realm, and sociopolitical mobilizations of resistance.

CLASS ANALYSIS AND GENDER

Kaplan's gendered approach exposed the long-standing presence of what Claire LaVigna called in her title "The Marxist Ambivalence toward Women" (1978). While the "woman question" was indeed addressed in marxist histories and movements, it was subordinate to more class-based priorities, as suggested in Barbara Taylor's exploration of the importance of gender in early utopian socialism and the demise of its centrality with the rise of the "scientific" school associated with Marx and Engels. But marxist explorations of the woman question seldom moved much beyond Engels's *The Origins of the Family, Private Property, and the State* (1884), which is overly reliant on the nonmarxist anthropology of Lewis H. Morgan. Not until so-called second wave feminism, one sustaining feature of which was the broad-ranging marxist approach in Simone de Beauvoir's pathbreaking *The Second Sex* (1949), did a revived socialist feminism produce histories sensitive to the complexities of women's experiences. Sheila Rowbotham was a major voice in this undertaking. Her *A Century of Women: The History of Women in Britain and the United States in the Twentieth Century* (1997) is a detailed look at women's place in twentieth-century Britain and the United States, a history of inequality in the political, economic, and social realms that produced struggles for the vote, equal pay, and reproductive rights.

THE IMPACT OF MARXISM ON SOCIAL HISTORY

Marxism's intersection with social history thus has been wide-ranging and highly influential, if at times constricting in what it seemed able to address. It has nevertheless actually charted particular spheres of study, such as important realms of the debate over the nature and meaning of the transition from feudalism to capitalism. In other areas, most obviously labor history but also particular chronological periods and topics, such as the English revolutions of the seventeenth century or the French Revolution of the late eighteenth century, marxist histories achieved, for a time at least, interpretive hegemony. The concerns of marxist histories always have been a fusion of the economic, the political, and the sociocultural. Hill, for example, believed that all history was intellectual history, but this did not prevent him from writing on matters that blurred distinctions between the material and the cultural, a crossover that produced or at least illuminated the social. It is inconceivable that European social history from the Renaissance to the modern period could have developed historiographically without the insights of marxist perspectives.

Equally important, marxist approaches highlighted for all historians—conservatives, radicals, feminists, and liberals—significant themes in the historical process. Those themes include the relationships of economic life and social being; the appreciation of large-scale socioeconomic transformation and the making of class, gender, and national-ethnic identities; and the importance of "totality" in historical process and the reciprocity of mercantile, landed, protoindustrial, and capitalist relations in the emergence of the modern world. Indeed marxist histories stimulated and enlivened social history, assuring it a measure of intellectual tenacity by forcing reconsiderations and new appreciations of large issues. State formation, the subject of a stimulating synthetic statement by Philip Corrigan and Derek Sayer that bridged the medieval and the modern, is one such area that marxist approaches have reinvigorated. It is impossible to think of social history in the 1990s, for instance, without acknowledging the weight of Thompson's *The Making of the English Working Class,* not so much because of the persuasiveness of its research and argument, which have been contested, but rather because of its tone, vision, and sensibilities. This feel for a new kind of history, which became the enduring attraction of "the social," was not the monopoly of the marxists, but they contributed mightily toward it. Consequently marxist histories affected the changing balance of historical thought as much as they grew out of the material circumstances and internal debates, polemics, and ruptures of the marxist movement itself.

The marxist movement was never a monolith, and sociopolitical and intellectual histories of marxism in the European past mark an evolution of uncommon diversity. The major early political studies of the marxist First and Second Internationals, including A. Müller Lehning's *The International Association, 1855–1859: A Contribution to the Preliminary History of the First International* (1938) and James Joll's *The Second International, 1889–1914* (1974), were later complemented by national surveys and specific accounts of particular countries in restricted chronological periods, many written by nonmarxists. Among these Tony Judt's *Marxism and the French Left: Studies in Labour and Politics in France, 1830–1981* (1986) is notable for its breadth, and Gerald H. Meaker's *The Revolutionary Left in Spain, 1914–1923* (1974) sets the stage well for an appreciation of the momentous conflicts of the civil war of the 1930s. The Italian communist experience proved fertile ground for a marxist engagement with the national question, especially acute in a country economically, socially, culturally, and politically fractured. The "southern ques-

tion" preoccupied major marxist thinkers, such as Antonio Labriola and Antonio Gramsci.

Germany's unique politics of Nazism stimulated significant marxist engagements, such as those of Tim Mason, in which social histories of class intersect with the politics of a disturbing defeat of the left and open out into histories of class acquiescence and subterranean resistance. British communism's eclectic origins in religious dissent, the autodidact Labour Colleges, the meeting of Lib-Lab consciousness, Fabianism, trade unionism, and the mythological power of the Russian Revolution have been appreciated by marxist historians, such as Raphael Samuel and Stuart Macintyre, while marxist explorations of various aspects of the Labour Party have sustained important intellectual engagements. The peculiarities of Scandinavian socialism have generated equal interest. In the nation-states won to marxism out of the dissolutions of World War II and through the contradictory "liberations" of Joseph Stalin's Red Army, marxism as a social movement was suffocated at its potential birth, leaving it deformed and awaiting its overthrowers, the most illustrious of whom would appear, to Western eyes, to be Lech Walesa and Poland's labor movement Solidarność (Solidarity).

No unity congeals this ongoing relation of social change and the dissenting tradition, but it is impossible to consider European history without addressing the marxist presence. No sooner had communism fallen in 1989, with marxism proclaimed dead and history and ideology supposedly at their end, than marxist ideas and movements began to reemerge out of the seeming wasteland of Stalinist decay. At the beginning of the twenty-first century, marxist thought and communist political organizations were down but certainly not out. The ills of capitalism—increasing economic inequality and its manifold oppressions and destabilizing violence—remained very much in evidence, especially in the new, wildly erratic, and wartorn frontier of acquisitive individualism's market economies, Russia and its former eastern European satellites.

Marxist histories, as the site of new understandings of the social and as the lived experience of mobilizations attempting to transform society and politics, have greatly influenced European history. Their intellectual, cultural, economic, and social meanings have been profound, and, although their future at the turn of the century was perhaps more clouded than at any time in the previous hundred years, they have remained a force to reckon with.

See also **Capitalism and Commercialization; Communism** *(volume 2);* **Social Class; Working Classes; Collective Action; Revolutions; Labor History: Strikes and Unions** *(volume 3).*

BIBLIOGRAPHY

Abendroth, Wolfgang. *A Short History of the European Working Class.* Translated by Nicholas Jacobs and Brian Trench. London, 1972.

Abraham, David. *The Collapse of the Weimar Republic: Political Economy and Crisis.* Princeton, N.J., 1981.

Agulhon, Maurice. *Marianne into Battle: Republican Imagery and Symbolism in France, 1789–1880.* Cambridge, U.K., 1981.

Alexander, Robert J. *International Trotskyism, 1929–1985: A Documented Analysis of the Movement.* Durham, N.C., 1991.

Amyot, Grant. *The Italian Communist Party: The Crisis of the Popular Front Strategy.* London, 1981.

Anderson, Perry. *Arguments within English Marxism.* London, 1980.

Anderson, Perry. *Considerations on Western Marxism.* London, 1976.

Anderson, Perry. *The Lineages of the Absolutist State.* London, 1974.

Aston, T. H., and C. H. E. Philpin, eds. *The Brenner Debate: Agrarian Class Structure and Economic Development in Pre-Industrial Europe.* Cambridge, U.K., 1985.

Bax, Belfort. *The Peasants War in Germany, 1525–1526.* London, 1899.

Beauvoir, Simone de. *Le deuxième sexe.* Paris, 1949. First American edition, *The Second Sex.* Translated by H. M. Parshley. New York, 1953.

Bettelheim, Charles. *Class Struggles in the USSR.* Translated by Brian Pearce. 2 vols. New York, 1976.

Bolloten, Burnett. *The Spanish Civil War: Revolution and Counterrevolution.* Chapel Hill, N.C., 1991.

Brenner, Robert. *Merchants and Revolution: Commercial Change, Political Conflict, and London's Overseas Traders, 1550–1653.* Princeton, N.J., 1993.

Broué, Pierre, and Émile Témime. *The Revolution and the Civil War in Spain.* Translated by Tony White. Cambridge, Mass., 1972.

Bryant, Louise. *Six Red Months in Russia.* New York, 1918.

Buttinger, Joseph. *In the Twilight of Socialism: A History of the Revolutionary Socialists of Austria.* Translated by E. B. Ashton. New York, 1953.

Carr, E. H. *The Bolshevik Revolution, 1917–1923.* 3 vols. Harmondsworth, U.K., 1966.

Claudín, Fernando. *The Communist Movement: From Comintern to Cominform.* Translated by Brian Pearce and Francis MacDonagh. Harmondsworth, U.K., 1975.

Corrigan, Philip, and Derek Sayer. *The Great Arch: English State Formation as Cultural Revolution.* Oxford, 1985.

Degras, Jane, ed. *The Communist International, 1919–1943.* 4 vols. London, 1971.

De Ste. Croix, G. E. M. *The Class Struggle in the Ancient Greek World.* Ithaca, N.Y., 1981.

Dobb, Maurice Herbert. *Studies in the Development of Capitalism.* New York, 1947.

Dorpalen, Andreas. *German History in Marxist Perspective: The East German Approach.* Detroit, Mich., 1985.

Engels, Frederick. *The Origin of the Family, Private Property, and the State, in Light of the Researches of Lewis H. Morgan.* 1884. Reprint, New York, 1942.

Frank, Pierre. *The Fourth International: The Long March of the Trotskyists.* Translated by Ruth Schein. London, 1979.

Gramsci, Antonio. *Selections from the Prison Notebooks of Antonio Gramsci.* Edited and translated by Quinton Hoare and Geoffrey Nowell Smith. London, 1971.

Gruber, Helmut. *Red Vienna: Experiment in Working-Class Culture, 1919–1934.* New York, 1991.

Hill, Christopher. *The Collected Essays of Christopher Hill.* 3 vols. Amherst, Mass., 1985–1986.

Hill, Christopher. *Lenin and the Russian Revolution.* 1947. Reprint, Harmondsworth, U.K., 1971.

Hill, Christopher. *The World Turned Upside Down: Radical Ideas during the English Revolution.* New York, 1972.

Hobsbawm, E. J. *Age of Extremes: The Short Twentieth Century, 1914–1991.* London, 1994.

Hobsbawm, E. J. *Labouring Men: Studies in the History of Labour.* London, 1964.

Hobsbawm, E. J. *Revolutionaries.* London, 1973.

Hobsbawm, E. J. *Workers: Worlds of Labor.* New York: Pantheon, 1984.

Hobsbawm, E. J., and George Rudé. *Captain Swing.* New York, 1968.

Joll, James. *The Second International, 1889–1914.* London, 1974.

Judt, Tony. *Marxism and the French Left: Studies in Labour and Politics in France, 1830–1981.* Oxford, 1986.

Kaplan, Temma. *Anarchists of Andalusia, 1868–1903.* Princeton, N.J., 1977.

Kaplan, Temma. *Red City, Blue Period: Social Movements in Picasso's Barcelona.* Berkeley, Calif., 1992.

Kautsky, Karl. *Communism in Central Europe in the Time of the Reformation.* London, 1897.

Kiernan, V. G. *Marxism and Imperialism.* London, 1974.

Kovalev, Y. V., ed. *An Anthology of Chartist Literature.* London, 1956.

Kuczynski, Jürgen. *The Rise of the Working Class.* Translated by C. T. A. Ray. New York, 1967.

LaVigna, Claire. "The Marxist Ambivalence toward Women: Between Socialism and Feminism in the Italian Socialist Party." In *Socialist Women: European Socialist Feminism in the Nineteenth and Early Twentieth Centuries.* Edited by Marilyn J. Boxer and Jean H. Quataert. New York, 1978. Pages 146–181.

Lefebvre, Georges. *The Coming of the French Revolution, 1789.* Translated by R. R. Palmer. Princeton, N.J., 1947.

Lefebvre, Georges. *The Great Fear of 1789.* Translated by Joan White. London, 1973.

Lehning, A. Müller. *The International Association, 1855–1859: A Contribution to the Preliminary History of the First International.* Leiden, Netherlands, 1938.

Lenin, V. I. *The Development of Capitalism in Russia.* 1899. Reprint, Moscow, 1964.

Lissagaray. *History of the Commune of 1871.* Translated by Eleanor Marx Aveling. London, 1886.

Marx, Karl. *Capital.* Edited by Frederic Engels. Translated by Ernest Untermann. 3 vols. Chicago, 1909.

Marx, Karl, and Frederick Engels. *Selected Works: Karl Marx and Frederick Engels.* Moscow, 1969–1970.

Mason, Tim. "Labour in the Third Reich, 1933–1939." *Past and Present* 33 (April 1966): 121–141.

Mason, Tim. *Nazism, Fascism, and the Working Class.* Edited by Jane Caplan. Cambridge, U.K., 1995.

Meaker, Gerald H. *The Revolutionary Left in Spain, 1914–1923.* Stanford, Calif., 1974.

Merriman, John M. *The Red City: Limoges and the French Nineteenth Century.* New York, 1985.

Mitchell, Harvey, and Peter N. Stearns. *Workers and Protest: The European Labor Movement, the Working Classes, and the Origins of Social Democracy, 1890– 1914.* Itasca, Ill., 1971.

Morrow, Felix. *Revolution and Counter-Revolution in Spain.* 1936. Reprint, New York, 1974.

Panitch, Leo. *Social Democracy and Industrial Militancy: The Labour Party, the Trade Unions, and Incomes Policy, 1945–1974.* Cambridge, U.K., 1976.

Panitch, Leo. *Working-Class Politics in Crisis: Essays on Labour and the State.* London, 1986.

Perrot, Michelle. *Workers on Strike: France, 1871–1890.* Translated by Chris Turner. New York, 1987.

Reed, John. *Ten Days That Shook the World.* New York, 1919.

Rowbotham, Sheila. *A Century of Women: The History of Women in Britain and the United States in the Twentieth Century.* London, 1997.

Rudé, George F. E. *The Crowd in the French Revolution.* Oxford, 1959.

Sassoon, Donald. *One Hundred Years of Socialism: The West European Left in the Twentieth Century.* New York, 1996.

Seccombe, Wally. *A Millennium of Family Change: Feudalism to Capitalism in Northwestern Europe.* London, 1992.

Seccombe, Wally. *Weathering the Storm: Working-Class Families from the Industrial Revolution to the Fertility Decline.* London, 1993.

Schorske, Carl E. *German Social Democracy, 1905–1917: The Development of the Great Schism.* 1955. Reprint, New York, 1970.

Soboul, Albert. *The French Revolution, 1787–1799.* Translated by Alan Forrest and Colin Jones. London, 1974.

Soboul, Albert. *The Parisian Sans-culottes and the French Revolution, 1793–1794.* Translated by Gwynne Lewis. Oxford, 1964.

Taylor, Barbara. *Eve and the New Jerusalem: Socialism and Feminism in the Nineteenth Century.* London, 1983.

Thompson, Dorothy. *The Chartists: Popular Politics in the Industrial Revolution.* New York, 1984.

Thompson, E. P. *Customs in Common.* London: Merlin, 1991.

Thompson, E. P. *The Making of the English Working Class.* New York, 1964.

Thompson, E. P. *The Poverty of Theory and Other Essays.* New York, 1978.

Thompson, E. P. *William Morris: Romantic to Revolutionary.* 1955. Reprint, New York, 1977.

Thompson, E. P. *Witness against the Beast: William Blake and the Moral Law.* New York, 1993.

Trempé, Rolande. *Les mineurs de Carmaux, 1848–1914.* 2 vols. Paris, 1971.

Trotsky, Leon. *The History of the Russian Revolution.* Translated by Max Eastman. 3 vols. New York, 1932.

Trotsky, Leon. *The Revolution Betrayed: What Is the Soviet Union and Where Is It Going?* Translated by Max Eastman. Garden City, N.Y., 1937.

INTERDISCIPLINARY CONTACTS AND INFLUENCES

Louise A. Tilly

Contacts and influences between history and other disciplines are not new. Nineteenth-century economics was frequently historical, as the work of Karl Marx shows; Max Weber, Émile Durkheim, and Marx, the classical sociological theorists, likewise found their problems in historical change; and political theory took as two of its central concerns how forms of government evolve or modify and how war or natural disasters may change opportunities for states. In short, shared subject matter has a long history. What is different in the interdisciplinary studies that came to the fore starting at the end of the nineteenth century is a self-conscious borrowing of methods and theories, which could only occur once methods were formalized.

Economics, demography, and statistics (and less so, sociology and political science) had developed both more theory and more formal methods by the end of the nineteenth century than had history. In the same period some historians had begun to conceive of history itself as a science. Its central method was finding reliable sources of information and verifying the authenticity of sources by their closeness to the actors, places, and times of the events, institutions, and persons being studied. In Germany, Leopold von Ranke was central to this development; in France, Charles Seignobos. Both of these scholars, as well as the major English historians, defined history as a verifiably objective description of political facts (events and the development of governmental institutions in particular) isolated from their economic and social context. There was also a local history more concerned with small-scale events such as the origins of towns and cities, local government, agriculture, trade, and religion, but it developed apart from academic history and was dismissed as nonscientific and naive. "Social" history, such as it was, focused on daily life, material culture, manners, and morals.

THE PATHS TOWARD INTERDISCIPLINARY HISTORY

Influenced by Émile Durkheim and his followers' effort to apply the principles of the natural sciences to social facts, the French economist François Simiand challenged the Seignobos school in 1903, attacking the "idols" of history: acceptance of periodization without consideration of its significance and focus on politics and powerful persons rather than on nonpolitical or apolitical groups, institutions, or phenomena. Simiand urged that historians adopt more scientific methods, rigorously defining their problems, collecting and measuring data, analyzing temporal change and spatial correlations, and studying causality rather than chronology. Simiand's own monographs, on wages and social change and economic cycles "*à longue période*" (both published in 1932), were strictly quantitative, joining the established economic history of prices and wages, but much more ambitious in coverage and periodization. By this time the *Annales d'histoire économique et sociale,* founded by Marc Bloch and Lucien Febvre with the help of Henri Berr in 1929, was three years old.

Bloch and Febvre also urged the end of the disciplinary schism between students of past time and those of contemporary societies and economies among historians, economists, and sociologists. They called for a flow of methods and interpretive perspectives among scholars. Their prescription for breaking down barriers and surmounting schism was not methodological or theoretical discussion but exemplary practice ("*par le fait*"). The *Annales* would welcome and publish research in many fields and specialties, research unified by a commitment to impartiality. In their own scholarly research and writing, and in the journal, Bloch and Febvre practiced what they preached— Bloch borrowing from economics, geography, and sociology, and Febvre more commonly from social psychology and what later came to be called *mentalités.* Under their direction, the *Annales* gave little attention to the continuing theoretical debate about history as science, focusing instead on comparisons among social groups and interdisciplinary borrowings.

In the post–World War II period, the influence of Ernest Labrousse (whose first book, *Esquisse du mouvement des prix et des revenus en France au XVIIIe siècle* had come out in 1933) and Fernand Braudel grew. The latter, whose encyclopedic survey of the Mediterranean over the *longue durée* and conceptualization of total history were admired but seldom emulated on the same scale, became editor of *Annales.* In the course of the 1950s, Labrousse began to send his doctoral students to regional archives to study the social and economic structure of France before and after the Revolution (1700–1850), thus incorporating Braudel's evocation of the long period with his own quantitative approach. The apprentice historians of the Sixth Section (history) of the École des Hautes Études en Sciences Sociales, where Braudel taught, also incorporated the *Annales* approach, drawing on human geography (the study of human interaction with the physical environment), reconstructing price and wage series, and incorporating rapidly developing demographic history in their densely documented regional studies from the 1960s onward. Demographic history had become more sophisticated statistically through Louis Henry's development of family reconstitution—a method that could demonstrate changes in patterns of birth, death, and marriage for periods before vital statistics registration or censuses. Family reconstitution revolutionized knowledge of Old Regime demography and became a component of the regional and local studies of French social historians.

In English history, interdisciplinary approaches (other than economic history, which was well established by the beginning of the twentieth century) arrived by at least two paths. One was exemplified by the formation of a new journal, *Past and Present,* in early 1952. Its board of editors, which included several important Marxist historians, avowed that it would not shirk controversy. Echoing Karl Marx's words from the *Eighteenth Brumaire of Louis Bonaparte,* the editors wrote in the first issue, "Men are active and conscious makers of history, not merely its passive victims." They also objected to the indiscriminate borrowing of ideas from social science, specifically "the structural-functional approach as developed in contemporary sociology." Their goal was to "widen the somewhat narrow horizon of traditional historical studies among the English-speaking public" and to follow the historical example of Bloch and Febvre, eschewing "methodological articles and theoretical dissertations" and making their point "by example and fact." In the 1960s the initial Marxist perspective became less evident; in its place a variety of interdisciplinary approaches became customary.

The other English path to interdisciplinarity had been laid out earlier by Lewis Namier, who pioneered the interdisciplinary method of prosopography, or collective biography, a protostatistical approach. Through such an analysis, one could discover variation along group characteristics like age, social class or status, family connections, origins of wealth, or political patronage. Interested in heighteenth-century politics, Namier chose to look closely at the House of Commons, "that invaluable microcosmic picture of England." He gathered biographical detail about the men elected to the Parliament of 1761, their constituencies, and their political sponsors, as well as mentions in parliamentary or private records of other political figures great and small, and analyzed his data by simple statistical methods, mostly cross-tabulations. The information he generated about patronage and connections cast light on the politics of the government and Parliament in the period following the election.

In 1965 Lawrence Stone published his massive prosopographic study of members of the peerage in the sixteenth and early seventeenth centuries, drawing on private archives that had recently been made available to historians. As a result his evidence was much richer than Namier's. His goal was first to "describe the total environment of an *élite,* material and economic, ideological and cultural, educational and moral; and [second] . . . to chart the course of a crisis in the affairs of this *élite* that was to have a profound effect upon the evolution of English political institutions" (Stone, 1965, pp. 7–8). The crisis, of course, was the rising importance of the House of Commons in politics and the temporary eclipse of the peerage in the period of revolution and Commonwealth. The Restoration and Glorious Revolution restored the standing of the peerage, but its political influence was tempered by those events, with long-term consequences for the English political system and class structure.

Also in England by the 1960s, scholars interested in demography, such as E. A. Wrigley, Peter Laslett, and Roger Schofield—leaders of what became the Cambridge Group for the History of Population and Social Structure—began family reconstitution methods like the French, which showed that in the seventeenth and eighteenth centuries typical households were small, consisting of a nuclear family and perhaps servants and including three generations or more distant kin less often than had been believed. They also found a surprisingly high degree of geographic mobility, especially of young people, including children, who moved to become servants or apprentices.

Much of the "new social history" of the 1960s and 1970s drew its inspiration from sociology and other social sciences, but not all of it was friendly to interdisciplinarity. E. P. Thompson's *Making of the English Working Class* (1963) became one of the classics of modern social history and a model for labor and social historians over the ensuing decades. But despite its innovation in seeking out new sources for English working-class history such as police records (cautiously utilized) and popular religious literature, *The Making* is less explicitly interdisciplinary in its approach than the studies already described. Indeed, Thompson's preface contains an irritable attack (echoing that of *Past and Present*'s editors) on sociology and specifically on the sociologist Neil Smelser's study of cotton textile industrialization and family relations. Nevertheless, Thompson's affectionate exposition of the ways of life of various groups of workers can be seen as a kind of retrospective ethnography, and in later writings he acknowledged the relationship of anthropology to his work.

In the United States, economic historians such as Robert Fogel and Albert Fishlow, questioning the importance of railroads in American economic development, had begun to use computers to perform complex statistical analyses on historical data assembled from business and local government records. Political historians such as Lee Benson and Allan Bogue collected local electoral records and ecological data and analyzed them with the help of computers, and William O. Aydelotte began a similar project with British parliamentary voting records. American historians of Europe adopted the interdisciplinary methods of studying social structure, patterns of population change, economic conditions, and associational politics (parties, elections, labor unions, social movements, and reform). Questions about colonial demography and family life were explored by John Demos and Philip Greven. And Stephan Thernstrom pursued distinctively American questions about nineteenth-century social mobility with the help of computer-analyzed nominal census data. By 1966 the *Times Literary Supplement* could devote the larger part of three issues to "New Ways in History," highlighting the advances of interdisciplinary approaches. Interdisciplinary collaboration was promoted by the strong historical interests of many European sociologists, such as British researchers dealing with family sociology, which facilitated interaction beyond uses of quantitative methods.

Interdisciplinary work was not always welcomed by the established journals of the time, however. Rather, its publication depended on newer journals. *Comparative Studies in Society and History,* the first United States journal of interdisciplinary history, had been founded by the economic historian Sylvia Thrupp in 1958. As suggested by its title, the journal's chief focus was comparisons, not interdisciplinarity, but as the title also indicates, both cross-sectional and temporal comparisons drawing on history and social science fields like sociology and anthropology were envisioned by the editorial board, which included scholars in both those fields as well as historians. In 1967 the *Journal of Social History* was launched by Peter Stearns. The journal has been eclectic and open, and as definitions of social history have become more inclusive, new methods and subjects have been incorporated.

Interdisciplinary history received its name in 1970, when the *Journal of Interdisciplinary History* began publication. (The *International Encyclopedia of the Social Sciences* [1968] discussed comparative method and studies but had no entry in its index for "interdisciplinary" method, theory, or studies.) The concept of interdisciplinarity had earlier been integral in teaching and research programs in area studies and American studies, but in the late 1960s and the 1970s it proliferated in black or African American studies, women's studies, religious studies, and numerous similar new programs. The declared intent of the founding editors (both historians and social scientists) of the journal was to be "catholic both conceptually and geographically," yet to "guard against faddishness, the all-too-easy appropriation of inappropriate techniques . . . ; the confusion of technical mastery with the effective use of such mastery; . . . the temptations of jargon," and so on (Rotberg and Rabb, 1970, pp. 4–5). The American journals devoted to the newly interdisciplinary history quickly found a place on historians' reading lists.

A group of historians and political scientists who specialized in United States history took the initiative to convene other interdisciplinary scholars to found the Social Science History Association in 1974 and its journal, *Social Science History,* the first issue of which was published in fall 1976. The purpose of the organization, the editors of its journal wrote, was to improve "the quality of historical explanation by encouraging the selective use and adaptation in teaching and in research of relevant theories and methods from the social science disciplines." They also welcomed historical comparisons, and declared their "total commitment to . . . systematic contact and interchange of ideas between kindred spirits in history and in the social sciences" ("Editors' Foreword," 1976, pp. i–ii). The organization, which began with a strong tilt within its leadership toward United States quantitative political history, encouraged wide participation in governance, including planning the program of the yearly conference. Over the years, the disciplinary distribution of the leadership and members has shifted away from American politics to a much more eclectic mix of interests. The association has drawn wide participation from European scholars, dealing with topics like demography and crime, and from researchers concerned with European topics.

A DECADE OF INTERDISCIPLINARY HISTORY AND A LOOK INTO THE FUTURE

In 1980 (its tenth anniversary), the *Journal of Interdisciplinary History* convened a conference, "The New History: The 1980s and Beyond"; articles reporting on the various subfields appeared in two issues (vol. 12, nos. 1 and 2, summer and autumn 1981). Overall, the articles on specific fields reflect a decline in interest in and use of quantitative methods in political and family history, but a reaffirmation of the importance of political history; continued confidence in the value of quantitative methods for periods in which qualitative evidence is scarce (medieval history and population history); a call for greater development of psychohistory; a flight from the most technically sophisticated type of econometric history, and new efforts to bring economic history closer to historians' concern with the diversity of human behavior; strong interest in anthropology and history but no consensus about possible approaches to interdisciplinary historical anthropological studies; linkage of concepts of "the construction by human beings of meaning" (formerly the concern of intellectual historians) with other histories and anthropology; and an understanding of science and its history as an aspect of culture.

The journal's coeditor Theodore K. Rabb concluded in "Towards the Future" that as a form of knowledge, history had lost its coherence, but that had been so for some time. What historians could agree upon, he continued, was that materialist concerns had shrunk compared to the previous decade and that there are different paths to meaning. Nevertheless, historians share standards for judging the quality of a historical work.

EXEMPLARY WORKS IN INTERDISCIPLINARY HISTORY TO THE EARLY 1980s

Some of the major works that were produced up to the early 1980s in interdisciplinary European history may be classified into three categories: major efforts to answer very large, basic questions in interdisciplinary ways that give the authors the opportunity to claim a place as the most general and powerful combination of disciplines; collaborations at the borders between social science and history, in which social science middle-level theories and methods are borrowed

with results that better address questions in both disciplines; and confrontations between history and social science disciplines, in which differences in perspective produce a dynamic tension that permits new insights. The last of these will not be discussed because it occurs less often in research projects than in teaching courses that aspire to interdisciplinarity.

Candidates for the first category, the imperialist claims of major works to be the do-all, end-all interdisciplinary combination, are relatively rare. *Time on the Cross* (1974), Robert Fogel and Stanley Engerman's effort to answer many of the long-standing major questions about slavery in the American South, is a good example. The two volumes (one describing the findings, the second a technical exposition of methods and quantitative measures) were the result of an immense effort to collect, code, and analyze data from plantation and government records. Their provocative findings aroused controversy among both economic historians and southern historians, who challenged the results in book reviews, articles, and two volumes of collected essays. Similar claims for methodological superiority and definitive answers were made for behavioralist theories in political science and structural-functionalist sociology; most of the authors of these types of studies were social scientists, political scientists, and sociologists who tended to feature theoretical discussion, rather than historians. Robert Berkhofer's proposal in *A Behavioral Approach to Historical Analysis* (1969) that historians adopt behavioral theories and the methods developed to study human behavior in social science (psychology, sociology, and anthropology) was read by historians, but its recommendations were seldom adopted.

Studies in the second category are all from social history, which has been characterized by a concern with ordinary people in the past, or "history from below," as Peter Stearns put it. Its basic method has been collective "biography," the assembling of standardized descriptions of individuals into a set—like the pioneering English prosopographies—which can be analyzed for variation and commonalities. The units to be analyzed are not necessarily individuals; they may be events like strikes, groups like families, or categories like occupations. The earliest works in interdisciplinary family history, such as *The World We Have Lost* (1965), were demographically informed but offered little demographic analysis. In that study, Peter Laslett reminded his readers of some common misconceptions of the demography of the period, such as that youthful marriage was common (it was limited to the upper classes), and emphasized the fragility of life for young and old because of frequent epidemics. Laslett also edited the volume *Household and Family in Past Time: Comparative Studies in the Size and Structure of the Domestic Group* (1972), which reported comparative studies of household size (based on census-type listings mostly from Europe). A chapter by the anthropologist Jack Goody raised a gentle warning based on his fieldwork in West Africa: notions in the past and in other cultures of a "household" were not necessarily equivalent to the later census concept of those eating and sleeping under the same roof. Others pointed out as well that the composition of the household would vary with the age of the head and of its members. Indeed, studies designed to investigate the questions raised by Goody later undercut the simple picture based on census-type listings.

David Levine's comparative study of three English villages from 1600 to 1851, *Family Formations in an Age of Nascent Capitalism* (1977), based on family reconstitution for the earlier part of the period, discovered changes in demographic behavior such as an earlier age of marriage and higher fertility in one village when its economic base was transformed from agriculture to nonmechanized framework knitting. The other villages experienced less economic change and were characterized by correspondingly less modification in family formation and fertility. There, youths who could find no work in their native village migrated to find work.

The sociologist Michael Anderson's study of industrialized England, *Family Structure in Nineteenth-Century Lancashire* (1971), examined the household economics of textile worker households in a small city during the twin processes of industrialization and rural to urban migration as an application of sociological exchange theory. Anderson traced the relationship between structural constraints and family relations. Although he used nominal census lists as his source, Anderson examined the internal dynamics of families, not simply their structure. He chose a historical moment in which families were experiencing far-reaching change in life both at home and work, so that the context would be part of the problem. He concluded that continuity marked rural families' experience of industrial factory work. Newly industrial households cooperated in migration, job finding, and pooling income. Tamara Hareven's *Family Time and Industrial Time: The Relationship between the Family and Work in a New England Industrial Community* (1982) added oral history to the kinds of economic and demographic structural evidence used by Levine and Anderson. Her work borrowed methods from anthropology as well.

Another large category of early interdisciplinary studies examined productive work and workers and their politics in the past. E. J. Hobsbawm and George

Captain Swing. Protest against mechanical harvesting machines and high bread prices swept through the English countryside in 1833, encouraged by letters signed "Captain Swing." British print, 1830s. ©THE BRITISH MUSEUM

Rudé, well-known historians of labor and protest, collaborated in *Captain Swing* (1968), a study of the English agricultural laborers' protest of 1830, drawing on an epidemiological model. They drew on geography as well to map the process by which protest spread among farm laborers and then to workers in rural manufacturing. Joan Scott's *Glassworkers of Carmaux: French Craftsmen and Political Action in a Nineteenth-Century City* (1974) combined Marxist theory with social science methods, studying demographic change through family reconstitution, which indicated increased putting down of roots by glassworkers' households at the end of the nineteenth century, as the men's earlier customary craft migration was ended by changing technology and organization of work in the glass industry. Settling in Carmaux, glassworkers modified their forms of organization and of collective action, mounting a successful strike.

INTERDISCIPLINARY HISTORY, 1980 TO THE PRESENT

The post-1980 period was characterized by four changes in interdisciplinary history: the emergence and rapid development of new subjects for investigation, in particular women's history, which itself was quickly supplemented by studies of gender; fewer purely materialist and structural interpretations and the rise of cultural ones, either supplementing the former or replacing them; a shift in the disciplines to which historians turned for methods and theory from demography, sociology, and economics to to cultural anthropology, literary criticism, linguistics, and philosophy, in particular regarding questions about power and the construction of meaning; and vigorous and proliferating debate about historical method and theory.

A work in the prosopographic tradition of social history is Bonnie G. Smith's *Ladies of the Leisure Class: The Bourgeoises of Northern France in the Nineteenth Century* (1981), which also exemplifies an ethnographic approach. Smith portrayed the ideology of spheres as the sociocultural framework for bourgeois women's lives. Over the course of the century, these women came to be concerned almost exclusively with the family and home; these institutions shaped their values and behavior. Nancy Hewitt demonstrated, in *Women's Activism and Social Change: Rochester, New York, 1822–1872* (1984), also a prosopographic study, that there were cultural (religious) and subtle class differences even among middle-class women. Following up on calls for attention to gender (the social construction of sex), historians of working-class women looked at cooperation and rivalries between men and women workers at home and at work. Patricia A. Cooper's *Once a Cigar Maker: Men, Women, and Work Culture in American Cigar Factories* (1987) exemplifies this approach. Cooper distinguished between male work culture, which stressed autonomy, manliness, and control over the work process, and women's more isolated identity, often burdened as well with their obligations at home. As conditions of work changed, so too did women's identity, as they became conscious of common interests with men workers.

Parallel developments occurred in English women's history, exemplified by a major study, Leonore Davidoff and Catherine Hall's *Family Fortunes: Men and Women of the English Middle Class, 1780–1850* (1987), which ambitiously addressed not only gender relations but class formation. Focusing on family, Davidoff and Hall were alert to gender differences, showing how ambitious men were embedded in familial (usually female) support as they built careers and rose in the world. However, over the time period studied, the authors noted that because of women's disadvantaged position vis-à-vis accumulating capital and political participation, their world shrank to the domestic sphere exclusively. Davidoff and Hall also

examined middle-class women's roles as writers of popular fiction in prescribing the ideology of spheres and as church members in passing down religious values in the family. Gay Gullickson's *Spinners and Weavers of Auffay: Rural Industry and the Sexual Division of Labor in a French Village, 1750–1850* (1986) reconstructed families in order to understand the household division of labor by sex and explored the way of life of the village. All of these historians of gender combined social-structural investigations of the social history type and gender analysis, which drew more on anthropological, cultural, and philosophical concepts.

In "Gender: A Useful Category for Historical Analysis" (1986), Joan Scott made a case for abandoning social history altogether, at least insofar as it rests upon the analysis of social-structurally defined categories of historical populations. For her, gender as an analytical category centered on meaning, power, and agency: "Gender is a constitutive element of social relationships based on perceived differences between the sexes, and gender is a primary way of signifying relations of power" (Scott, 1986, p. 1067). She called for "a genuine historicization and deconstruction of the terms of sexual difference . . . analyzing in context the way binary opposition operates, reversing and displacing its hierarchical construction, rather than accepting it as real or self-evident or in the nature of things" (pp. 1065–1066). Of the studies that have been published following Scott's prescriptions, one which made a particularly seamless argument combining a structural framework and cultural analysis is Kathleen Canning's *Languages of Labor and Gender: Female Factory Work in Germany, 1850–1914* (1996). Canning's presentation of evidence about the organization of work and how women were represented by their employers—in the way that they were disciplined, the hierarchies of skill and wages—and by philanthropic institutions effectively supported her argument.

Examples of combined methodologies can of course be found outside women's and gender history as well. William H. Sewell Jr.'s *Work and Revolution in France: The Language of Labor from the Old Regime to 1848* (1980), for example, combined an interpretive narrative account of the changing institutional framework around artisanal production in Old Regime, revolutionary, and nineteenth-century France with an anthropologically informed study of the language with which French workers discussed their work and themselves.

Growing use of anthropology showed also in a variety of projects dealing with early modern European social history, where anthropological models for studying rituals and phenomena such as witchcraft were widely deployed. By the 1980s and 1990s, this interdisciplinary activity extended to the use of cultural studies theories and models, for modern as well as early modern social-cultural history. These developments both reflected and furthered the "cultural turn" in European social history.

Alf Lüdtke, Hans Medick, and David Sabean, who worked together at the Max Planck Institute for History in Göttingen, Germany, individually and together drew on similar concepts from anthropology. Although all three had written history strongly influenced by sociological theory, Medick and Sabean had become interested in the cultural context of family history and demography by the late 1970s and 1980s. The chapters in their coedited volume, *Interest and Emotion: Essays on the Study of Family and Kinship* (1984), combined structural and anthropological cultural approaches in different ways. Sabean also published three monographic works that continued the combined approach: *Power in the Blood: Popular Culture and Village Discourse in Early Modern Germany* (1984), *Property, Production, and Family in Neckarhausen* (1990), and *Kinship in Neckarhausen, 1700–1870* (1998). The first of these studies was the one most fully influenced by cultural approaches, while the second was rather more structural but still concerned with discourse and social relationships, and the last used formal procedures borrowed from the anthropology of kinship but generalized in its final chapters about relationships between kinship and gender.

Medick too published a village monograph, *Weben und Überleben in Laichingen 1650–1900: Lokalgeschichte als Allgemeine Geschichte* (1996), but he and Lüdtke rejected to a greater extent than had Sabean the social-structuralism of much German social history. In a sometimes angry debate with Jürgen Kocka and Hans-Ulrich Wehler, the senior German academic exponents of structuralist, often quantitative social history, Medick and Lüdtke became advocates for *Alltagsgeschichte* (history of everyday life), which draws heavily on cultural anthropology. The debate has swirled around sensitive topics like the history of ordinary people in the Nazi period, but the essays in the one translated collection (edited by Lüdtke) of the group's work, *The History of Everyday Life: Reconstructing Historical Experiences and Ways of Life* (1995), strongly resembled what in the United States might

be called politically left sociocultural history. The topic was ordinary people's lives, but the framework was explicitly political. (The essays also have a good deal in common with articles published in the English *History Workshop Journal,* founded in 1976 with the subtitle "A Journal of Socialist Historians," later modified to "Socialist and Feminist Historians." *History Workshop* has not been discussed here because it has not been consciously interdisciplinary, nor have article authors usually drawn self-consciously on social science or other disciplines.)

The fourth characteristic of post-1980s interdisciplinary historical scholarship is the proliferation of articles and books discussing theory and method. One book may stand in for the long list of titles— *The Historic Turn in the Human Sciences* (1996), edited by Terrence J. McDonald. Although the title of this collection of essays reversed the turn of history to interdisciplinarity since the 1960s, the individual chapters by historians looked in both directions. To the degree that there was consensus among the authors, they detected (or recommended) a turning away among both historians and social scientists from scientistic approaches. Illustrative of this point of view is the chapter by William H. Sewell Jr., "Three Temporalities: Toward an Eventful Sociology." The three temporalities described here were teleological temporality (exemplified by Immanuel Wallerstein's world system analysis), Charles Tilly's temporal frame of the "master processes of history" (capitalist development and state formation), and Theda Skocpol's "experimental temporality" (comparison of cases as a "natural experiment"). To these failed efforts Sewell opposed "eventful temporality," which he illustrated by discussing works by two younger sociologists, Mark Traugott and Howard Kimeldorf, in which chronological explanatory narrative, contingency, and the recognition that "all social processes are path dependent" avoided the pitfalls of teleology. Sewell noted in his conclusion that both Wallerstein and Tilly had taken steps in this direction.

Sewell's theoretical essay points to a potential for bringing sociology and history closer together again, but the work he advocated may seem too much like description for most sociologists to accept. What is needed now is greater experimentation with different epistemological approaches that fulfill Bloch and Febvre's goal of writing history "*par le fait.*"

See also **Social Class; Collective Action** *(volume 3);* **Gender History; Kinship** *(volume 4); and other articles in this section.*

BIBLIOGRAPHY

Anderson, Michael. *Family Structure in Nineteenth-Century Lancashire.* Cambridge, U.K., 1971.

Aydelotte, William O., ed. *The History of Parliamentary Behavior.* Princeton, N.J., 1977.

Benson, Lee. *The Concept of Jacksonian Democracy: New York as a Text Case.* New York, 1964.

Berkhofer, Robert F., Jr. *A Behavioral Approach to Historical Analysis.* New York, 1969.

Bogue, Allan G. *From Prairie to Corn Belt: Farming on the Illinois and Iowa Prairies in the Nineteenth Century.* Chicago, 1963.

Braudel, Fernand. *The Mediterranean and the Mediterranean Work in the Age of Philip II.* Translated by Siân Reynolds. 2 vols. Rev. ed. Berkeley, Calif., 1995.

Canning, Kathleen. *Languages of Labor and Gender: Female Factory Work in Germany, 1850–1914.* Ithaca, N.Y., 1996.

Cooper, Patricia A. *Once a Cigar Maker: Men, Women, and Work Culture in American Cigar Factories.* Urbana, Ill., 1987.

Davidoff, Leonore, and Catherine Hall. *Family Fortunes: Men and Women of the English Middle Class, 1780–1850.* London, 1987.

"Editors' Foreword." *Social Science History* 1 (1976): i–ii.

Fishlow, Albert. *American Railroads and the Transformation of the Antebellum Economy.* Cambridge, Mass., 1965.

Fogel, Robert William. *Railroads and American Economic Growth: Essays in Econometric History.* Baltimore, 1964.

Fogel, Robert William, and Stanley L. Engerman. *Time on the Cross: The Economics of Negro Slavery.* Boston, 1974.

Gullickson, Gay L. *Spinners and Weavers of Auffay: Rural Industry and the Sexual Division of Labor in a French Village, 1750–1850.* Cambridge, U.K., 1986.

Hareven, Tamara K. *Family Time and Industrial Time: The Relationship between the Family and Work in a New England Industrial Community.* Cambridge, U.K., 1982.

Hewitt, Nancy A. *Women's Activism and Social Change: Rochester, New York, 1822–1872.* Ithaca, N.Y., 1984.

Hobsbawm, E. J., and George Rudé. *Captain Swing.* New York, 1968.

Labrousse, Ernest. *Esquisse du mouvement des prix et des revenus en France au XVIIIe siècle.* Paris, 1933.

Langlois, Charles Victor, and Charles Seignobos. *Introduction aux études historiques.* Paris, 1992.

Laslett, Peter. *The World We Have Lost.* New York, 1965.

Laslett, Peter, ed. *Household and Family in Past Time: Comparative Studies in the Size and Structure of the Domestic Group over the Last Three Centuries in England, France, Serbia, Japan, and Colonial North America, with Further Materials from Western Europe.* Cambridge, U.K., 1972.

Levine, David. *Family Formations in an Age of Nascent Capitalism.* New York, 1977.

Lüdtke, Alf, ed. *The History of Everyday Life: Reconstructing Historical Experiences and Ways of Life.* Translated by William Templer. Princeton, N.J., 1995.

McDonald, Terrence J., ed. *The Historic Turn in the Human Sciences.* Ann Arbor, Mich., 1996.

Medick, Hans. *Weben und Überleben in Laichingen 1650–1900: Lokalgeschichte als Allgemeine Geschichte.* Göttingen, Germany, 1996.

Medick, Hans, and David Sabean, eds. *Interest and Emotion: Essays on the Study of Family and Kinship.* Cambridge, U.K., 1984.

Namier, Sir Lewis Bernstein. *England in the Age of the American Revolution.* 2d ed. London, 1961.

Ranke, Leopold von. *The Theory and Practice of History.* Edited with an introduction by Georg G. Iggers and Konrad von Moltke. New translations by Wilma A. Iggers and Konrad von Moltke. New York, 1983.

Rotberg, Robert I., and Theodore K. Rabb. "Interdisciplinary History." *Journal of Interdisciplinary History* 1 (1970): 3–5.

Sabean, David. *Kinship in Neckarhausen, 1700–1870.* Cambridge, U.K., 1998.

Sabean, David. *Power in the Blood: Popular Culture and Village Discourse in Early Modern Germany.* Cambridge, U.K., 1984.

Sabean, David. *Property, Production, and Family in Neckarhausen 1700–1870.* Cambridge, U.K., 1990.

Scott, Joan W. "Gender: A Useful Category for Historical Analysis." *American Historical Review* 91 (1986):1053–1075.

Scott, Joan W. *Glassworkers of Carmaux: French Craftsmen and Political Action in a Nineteenth-Century City.* Cambridge, Mass., 1974.

Sewell, William H., Jr. *Work and Revolution in France: The Language of Labor from the Old Regime to 1848.* Cambridge, U.K., 1980.

Simiand, François. "Méthode historique et science sociale." *Annales: Économies, Sociétés, Civilisations* 15 (1960): 83–119. Originally published in *Revue de synthèse historique,* 1903.

Smelser, Neil. *Social Change in the Industrial Revolution: An Application of Theory to the British Cotton Industry.* Chicago, 1959.

Smith, Bonnie G. *Ladies of the Leisure Class: The Bourgeoises of Northern France in the Nineteenth Century.* Princeton, N.J., 1981.

Stone, Lawrence. *The Crisis of the Aristocracy, 1558–1641.* Oxford, 1965.

Thernstrom, Stephan. *Poverty and Progress: Social Mobility in a Nineteenth-Century City.* Cambridge, Mass., 1964.

Thompson, E. P. *The Making of the English Working Class.* London, 1963.

CLIOMETRICS AND QUANTIFICATION

Michael P. Hanagan

"Cliometrics," a term invented by economic historians, refers to the use of social science approaches in the study of history. "Quantification" refers to techniques for rendering historical sources machine readable and to the application of statistical analysis to historical data; it is commonly used in cliometrics. History was one of the last fields affected by the cliometrics and quantifying revolution, inspired by the spread of logical empiricism, that swept the social sciences in the post–World War II period. The use of statistical techniques in the social sciences acquired considerable momentum in economics in the 1940s and in sociology and political science in the 1950s and 1960s. In the 1960s many student radicals were suspicious of cliometrics and quantification, but others sought to turn the tools of established scholars against them. These cliometricians and historical quantifiers argued that the systematic study of classes and popular groups necessarily depended upon numbers and research designs as opposed to information about elites that could be culled from memoirs and contemporary writings.

Embraced by some younger radicals and some established historical scholars, cliometrics and quantification flourished in the 1960s and 1970s but have come under increasing attack by cultural and postmodernist historians; the eclipse of logical empiricism among social scientists reinforced the postmodernist attack. Despite the development of new and more powerful statistical techniques and the heightened access to these techniques that resulted from the spread of personal computers and the development of statistical software, the expansion of cliometrics and quantification methods has slowed. The 1980s and 1990s witnessed a decline in the standing of cliometrics and quantification but, paradoxically, also witnessed the appearance of some of the most outstanding and important products of these methods and approaches.

SOCIAL SCIENCE ROOTS OF CLIOMETRICS

Cliometrics was largely a product of the 1960s and it emerged most powerfully in the United States, but important historians in almost every European country were influenced by or shared its perspective. At the time, the dominant methodological approach within the social sciences was the logical empiricism of Karl Popper (1902–1994) and Carl Gustav Hempel (1905–). Their approach emphasized the separation of theory and observation. According to Popper and Hempel, theories proposed universal natural laws generating testable statements about events. Empirical investigation confirmed these statements and thus corroborated the theory or disconfirmed them and falsified the theory.

True to its empiricist roots, logical empiricism was very little interested in causation. To say that "x causes y" was to say: (1) that x preceded y, (2) that x and y were highly correlated, and (3) that there was some plausible story explaining why x might produce y. Logical empiricists were not particularly concerned with the actual mechanisms connecting x and y and remained satisfied with very general explanations of the causal factors at work. For example, social scientists might investigate whether a father's economic status or a child's educational attainment better predicted the child's occupational level, and they would see their work as addressing the question of whether family influence or intelligence was more important in explaining success. Very little attention was paid to the actual processes connecting job applicants to job markets.

The logical empiricist approach to the social sciences rapidly gained ground during the immediate post–World War II period, the era of the cold war when social scientists sought to develop social policies in response to a perceived communist threat and to the social and economic problems caused by colonial revolution and decolonization. The development of what was called modernization theory in the social sciences in the United States focused on problems of industrializing and "modernizing" less-developed nations and on reconstructing a devastated Europe. In the United States, the application of statistical techniques to economics and psychology in the 1940s and 1950s, followed by sociology and political science in the 1950s and 1960s, pointed the way for social-science–oriented historians. Among the most important developments within the social sciences, particularly sociology, was the elaboration of powerful statistical techniques taught in courses required for graduate students. Far and away the most important of these formal methods was regression analysis and related techniques, more formally known as the general linear model (GLM). In simplest terms, GLM measures to what extent a straight-line relationship exists between two variables such that a given change in variable x corresponds to a consistently proportional change in variable y.

While always important in the social sciences, measurement played an especially important role in the logical empiricist understanding of science, for it was essential to verification. The statistical techniques that social scientists developed fitted well their conceptions of proof—the individualist assumptions of these techniques also reflected scholars' concepts of the social world. In the 1960s great strides were made in developing GLM as a technique for comparing the variation of one or more different factors, independent variables, with the variation in another factor, the dependent variable. While GLM was indeed a powerful tool of statistical analysis and every student learned by rote its basic constraints, the analytical significance of these constraints was seldom discussed in any detail, probably because the individualistic assumptions of the statistical method so easily coincided with those of the dominant theories. One of these assumptions was "case-wise independence," the condition that what happens in one case does not influence what happens in any other. For example, a GLM analysis of the role of a child's educational level in explaining occupational level assumes that education exerts its influence separately and individually on each child. But one of the most basic understandings about the character of job markets, that they can constitute niches filled by groups who hire their own, violates the assumption of case-wise independence when each applicant is treated as an individual. The idea that clusters of individuals exert influence—that Ivy Leaguers hire Ivy Leaguers or Italian contractors hire Italian laborers—the basic argument of network analysis, presents special difficulties for GLM. The spread of personal computers made GLM analysis widely accessible. The rapid development of statistical packages such as the Statistical Package for the Social Sciences (SPSS) made advanced statistical analysis accessible to a wide audience, and the adoption of interactive statistical programs for personal computers greatly increased the number of potential users. A characteristic feature of SPSS was that it was best adopted for dealing with "attributive data," that is, with individual cases, each of which possessed distinctive characteristics—precisely the kind of data best suited for GLM. In the 1960s, GLM analysis of several thousands of cases often required access to computers and computer programs only available in a few dozen universities in the United States. By the 1980s the same analyses could be carried out at home on a personal computer and later via the Internet.

In the early 1980s cliometrics and quantification advanced rapidly in part due to the application and development of powerful new statistical techniques, the nonlinear probability models, known as "logit" and "probit" models. The introduction of nonlinear probability models greatly facilitated the application of familiar statistical techniques to entire new categories of data. While GLM techniques had some very desirable statistical properties and were widely available and easily interpretable, they were most effective when both the "dependent variable," what was to be explained, and the "independent variables," the explanatory factors, were expressed in continuous interval measures rather than in qualitative categories. GLM techniques could often produce statistically reliable estimates when using, for instance, years of education or father's social status to predict adult income, but often yielded serious misestimates when used to explain, for example, how religion or marital status related to political party affiliation. New techniques replaced estimates of linear relations between dependent and independent variables with estimates of the probability of nonlinear relations. Thus, analyses of relationships among individual units of data were extended to a very large body of questions of great importance to historians and social scientists.

One of the reasons that it is important to distinguish between quantification, the application of statistical methods to historical data, and cliometrics, the application of social science research designs to historical analysis, is that different types of statistical analyses appealed to different groups. Analytical statistics that included GLM and probability models was often used by cliometricians, while non-cliometric quantifiers often favored descriptive statistics. GLM and nonlinear probability models were favored by cliometricians who emphasized the need to clearly define and measure both dependent and independent variables and who often used sampling techniques and measures of strength and reliability. Non–social-science quantifiers were for their part most interested in descriptive statistics—the world of means, modes and averages—that made it possible for scholars to quickly summarize some phenomenon that interested them which might then be integrated into more traditional historical analyses. Computers enabled these scholars to deal with amounts of data undreamt of by previous scholars, but much of this work involved creating series of tables that compared one variable with others but did not search for complex relationships among explanatory variables and generally did not employ sampling techniques.

Relying heavily on quantification, the cliometric movement spread among historians in various specialties, who turned to their neighboring social science in search of useful techniques and research strategies. The wholesale borrowing of statistical methods and research designs from adjacent disciplines was a characteristic feature of the period. Political historians often turned to political science to learn techniques of analyzing voting, while social historians usually resorted to sociology and historical demography. During the 1960s, when population control was an important theme of public discussion, interest naturally arose in the causes and timing of population increase. Historical demographers not only addressed recognized social problems, but also confronted problems of missing data endemic to the historical profession. Unable to use the survey methods available to contemporary students of population, they were forced to develop a historical methodology. The development of historical demography clearly reflected different national approaches to historical analysis. French historical demographers influenced by Louis Henry remained largely descriptive, exploring the dynamics of fertility change in peasant villages. In contrast, the Princeton Fertility Project reflected the social scientific approach dominant in the United States. Princeton historical demographers were devoted adherents of modernization theory and sought to use demographic change to map the spread of modern social attitudes across Europe.

CRITIQUES AND NEW DIRECTIONS IN CLIOMETRICS

By the late 1970s, cliometrics came under attack from historians, but this was only part of a larger, general critique of social science methods and theoretical underpinnings. One of the most common criticisms was the failure of social science theory to account for agency. For social scientists including cliometricians,

it was alleged, variables and not human beings caused social phenomena. Of course the disappointing results of many of the larger cliometric projects, such as the Princeton historical fertility study, only reinforced the conviction that little was to be gained by large-scale interdisciplinary projects. Some leading advocates of social science history, for example Lawrence Stone, recanted and called for a return to narrative history. Many other historians became preoccupied with human agency and turned to cultural analysis and interpretive methods as a way of getting at human purposes. At the extreme, the French philosopher and historian Jacques Rancière rejected all historical generalization as a kind of authoritarian restriction on individual action. Most historians responded to this controversy by returning to traditional topics and methods.

Attacks on logical empiricism in cliometrics were not solely the weapons of opponents of social science history. Among those interested in applying social sciences to history, the leading methodological critics of logical empiricism were "realists." Realists concentrated on the identification of explanatory mechanisms underlying social phenomena and maintained that the social sciences should not assume the burden of all-embracing explanation and search for a unifying causal analysis behind all social phenomena. Understanding the different causal forces at work was the major preoccupation of realist social scientists who argued that various models could often be usefully combined to present a more comprehensive explanation. Although there are many varieties, realist explanations tend to emphasize the study of processes rather than stable relationships or steady states. They emphasize the study of causal mechanisms and their variety tended to make precise measurement less important than it was for logical empiricists. Many social scientists turned to structured comparisons of two or a few cases. Prominent historical sociologists such as Theda Skocpol emerged who did not use quantitative methods.

Within the social sciences, realists and others have sought to develop techniques for measurement that enable them to uncover mechanisms rather than concentrating simply on measures of association. A major critique of GLM and the individualist explanations of social phenomena developed among those cliometricians and quantifiers who were involved in network analysis, sometimes styled a "relational realism." A lot of the inspiration for the development of network analysis came from the United Kingdom, where scholars such as Elizabeth Bott had underscored the importance of networks in social analysis. The development of formal methods in network analysis, however, occurred largely in the United States, where

THE PRINCETON FERTILITY PROJECT

The study of historical demography was one of the most important areas in which American social science approaches influenced European researchers. Beginning in 1963 in Princeton, the demographer Ansley J. Coale assembled a Europeanwide research team to study the "demographic transition" one of the basic paradigms of modernization theory. Coale developed basic indices to measure trends in marriage and marital fertility and non-marital fertility from standard census material and Princeton demographers used these indices to measure fertility in major European administrative units such as French departments, Belgian arrondissements, and German administrative areas. The often used GLM to analyze the relationship between the decline in European fertility in the modern era and other regional characteristics such as secularization, industrialization, and literacy. Between 1971 and 1986, the Princeton European Fertility Project issued a series of volumes that reported on demographic change within most European nations including an overall survey of its findings published in 1986 and co-edited by Coale and Susan Cotts Watkins.

The Princeton project produced no clear answers but it did lead to a new understanding of the problems that needed to be explained. One of the established doctrines of historical demography, the "demographic transition," was revealed as a myth. Long presented as an empirical description, the theory claimed that declining mortality initially promoted rapid population growth. Individual families only slowly distinguished a permanent mortality decline from normal short-term fluctuations and, initially, most families would continue their so-called "natural fertility" in the expectation that infant and child mortality would continue to keep population stationary or only very slowly increasing. As more children survived, however, and families found themselves strapped to support an unexpectedly large number of maturing children in an increasingly competitive environment, families would abandon traditional conceptions and turn to some form of birth control. Eventually, a new demographic equilibrium was attained based on decreased mortality and fertility. Unfortunately, the systematic comparison of European mortality and fertility figures showed no evidence that mortality declines preceded fertility declines. Sometimes mortality declines preceded fertility declines, but in other periods the relationship was reversed.

The Princeton group did discover a series of sudden, sharp declines in fertility that set in during the late nineteenth century in most of Europe (during the late eighteenth century in France) that proved to be lasting; once fertility had declined precipitously it never again reached previous heights. Princeton historical demographers tended to argue that the rapid decline in birthrates corresponded to the spread of modern attitudes, but they never managed to provide reliable indicators of modernization and fertility change. Persuasive explanations of the rapid fertility decline in the late nineteenth and early twentieth centuries were not, however, forthcoming from Princeton.

In many ways the Princeton project revealed the strengths and weaknesses of logical empiricist social science approaches. The project was a relatively large-scale effort involving a variety of talented scholars over decades. It developed sophisticated measurement techniques that remain of considerable value. Yet the belief that the administrative divisions of European states provided relatively homogenous units in which the spread of modern attitudes from individual to individual could be traced proved illusory. With only a few exceptions, Princeton historical demographers made little effort to explore what was going on within departments, arrondissements, and other administrative areas. They did not examine how the presence of a military garrison with large numbers of unmarried males or a textile town with large numbers of single women, side by side with rural communities of small-holding peasants, might influence their findings, much less look at what was happening to selected households or individual families. When they carried out micro-studies of small units, they focused narrowly on such demographic factors as breastfeeding rather than looking at the larger cultural, social, and economic context. Coale and his collaborators were convinced that the spread of modern attitudes led to fertility control. Despite their blinkered conceptions, it is a tribute to their commitment to empirical investigation that, in the end, they admitted that their findings were largely negative.

Disappointment with the results of the Princeton project as well as the collapse of a number of other similar research efforts led to a disillusionment with quantitative social science approaches to history.

Harrison White and his students, such as Marc Granovetter, played a pivotal role in developing network analysis as method. The Toronto sociologist Barry Wellman is also an eloquent advocate. John F. Padgett and Christopher K. Ansell's use of network theory to analyze the Medici rise to power in fifteenth-century Florence presaged a new approach to historical sociology. Network analysts collected "relational data" concerning ties and connections that linked individuals to larger units and could not be reduced to individual properties. Techniques such as GLM and non-linear probability models were of only limited value for analyzing relational data. Network analysts had to develop their own techniques for identifying and comparing networks and for measuring their distance, direction, and density.

Peter S. Bearman's work on the English Civil War, *Relations into Rhetorics,* presents important examples of the application of network methodology, statistical methods, and theories to historical analysis. In a study that focuses on Norfolk County between 1540 and 1640, Bearman challenges the established "revisionist" orthodoxy in the study of the English Civil War, which rejects class categories or indeed almost any variety of general categories as simply too general, obscuring the complexity of interests and allegiances on all sides in these social conflicts. The revisionists emphasize instead a host of more prosaic interests—intrigues at court, the war plans of the 1620s, plain economic interest, the pressure of local and country politics, the scramble for office.

Bearman shows how network concepts can effectively respond to such objections. He concedes that "categorical" terms such as "class," "aristocrat," or "merchant" are too large and embracing for the detailed analysis of concrete events. Belonging to a category such as a class does not, as Bearman reminds us, imply a self-conscious identity or even necessarily a typical set of behaviors. Just because the entire population of a modern country can be divided into class categories does not tell us whether any important section of the population identifies itself as a class or acts in a class manner. Instead of using "categories" to analyze collective action, he proposes to use "networks" seen as the "structure of tangible social relations in which persons are embedded." In contrast with such abstractions as categories, networks are real associations of people; they may be centered on kinship ties, religion, economic interests, patronage, or other relations, and they may take a variety of forms from hierarchical to egalitarian. Categorical social terms only make sense in terms of collective action when they can validly be applied to existing social networks, Bearman argues. Without being embodied in real so-

cial relations, individuals who comprise social categories can have only very limited opportunities to engage in collective action.

Bearman's study of Norfolk County between 1540 and 1640 reveals the impressive potential in such analysis. Concentrating on elite networks within Norfolk over four approximately twenty-five-year periods, Bearman looks at the state-formation process from the local level. He shows that the state was as much drawn into local affairs by the local power vacuum as by any wish of its own to assert predominance in local affairs. Bearman suggests that the progress of proletarianization and class formation was responsible for dissolving local kin-group solidarities. Gradually, in the first half of the seventeenth century, the consolidation of landholdings and the growing convergence of economic processes made the powerful less interested in drawing on kinship ties and more inclined to participate in national politics.

But the collapse of kinship ties in the county of Norfolk preceded the integration of elites into the monarchical system. By means of appointment to parish jobs, local elites could link themselves to powerful protectors at the national level. As a result, over the period, the basis for appointment to a clerical position changed. Unfortunately for the Crown, it did not have a consistent policy in place or the resources to accommodate these potential entrants on the political scene. In the early period, appointments had been made with a view to extorting church property from the candidate as a condition for appointment; in the later period, appointments were based on the candidate's religious convictions. Religious rhetoric provided the bases for acquiring standing in national politics, acquiring allies, and winning protection at the national level.

The accomplishments of Bearman's book are methodological as well as substantive. Some of his most important conclusions are derived from his use of block modeling, a statistical technique until recently relatively little used by historical researchers, to identify and define networks. Indeed, in the historical study of seventeenth century England, issues of network have come to the fore. In many ways Bearman's use of block modeling underscores the point that our choice of methods must flow from our arguments and the logic of our underlying analyses. As historians turn more to the study of real social relations embodied in networks, they will very likely find formal methods of network analysis more productive and rewarding than GLM.

While interest in cliometrics has declined greatly over the last two decades, nevertheless, under the influence of realist approaches to the social sciences, the

1990s have produced some of the most significant works employing both a sophisticated use of statistics and social science method of any time since the 1960s. These works include John Markoff's analyses of the French *cahiers de doléances* and the relationship between agrarian violence and state legislation, the remarkable study of postwar Italian strikes by Roberto Franzosi, the study of English riots by John Bohstedt, the study of English crowd protest by Charles Tilly, and the examination of the origins of the German welfare state by George Steinmetz. One of the characteristic features of these works is their movement between aggregate data analysis and microanalysis of cases whose significance is underlined by the findings of aggregate analysis. Research projects have been designed to accommodate specific historical contexts, and the integration between historical research and formal methods has become more intimate.

These recent works often combine the analysis of aggregate evidence that defines larger patterns with cases studies that explore causal forces. John Bohstedt's examination of the English food riots between 1790 and 1810 employs a research design that allows him to identify and to use the best evidentiary sources that he could locate in order to construct a persuasive general argument. His studies incorporate macro and micro levels of analyses in a structured way. First, the study outlines large-scale arguments that are then compared against aggregate evidence. A look at the patterns found in the aggregate analysis serves to focus attention on the behavior of microunits such as market towns and open field villages. Next, case studies of various towns and political movements, selected according to the patterns found in the aggregate evidence are used to reinforce and to extend the original arguments. The ability to move systematically between arguments on the macro and micro levels depends both on research design and on willingness to use primary sources.

Bohstedt's study looks at the way in which communities influenced food riots in the era of the Napoleonic Wars, and his strong research design, geared toward effective use of primary sources safeguards against the tendency to allow established models to dictate the course of research. Scholars such as E. P. Thompson have suggested that food riots were a response to the intrusion of commercialism in a preindustrial "moral economy," while others have argued that high corn prices produced discontent. Bohstedt's presentation of data from contemporary newspapers and Home Office files supplemented by a systematic examination of the geographic incidence of food riots by county shows that neither relationship provides much explanatory power. Although hard-pressed by high prices and commercialism, neither the agrarian countryside nor London produced many food riots; however, such riots were endemic in regions dominated by small market towns, and some well-known riots occurred in emerging industrial cities.

Bohstedt's macro-evidence allows him to identify some important variations whose significance he pursues in detail at the micro level, examining two cases from areas where food riots did occur. He argues that community structure was fundamental to the character of riots. In areas with many small market towns such as Devonshire, the food riot was a bargaining process used as a popular protest against town-dwelling merchants that often persuaded farmers to lower the price of grain. But looking at the growth of large cities in Lancashire such as Manchester, he found that a Devonshire-type food riot was impossible there. No single marketplace existed, and rioters who lacked personal contact with merchants and landlord were unable to win concessions. In Manchester, the food riot was regarded as a disorderly protest and repressed. In the largely rural counties of England and Wales populated by village dwellers, the "food riot" was also impossible. The riot was a direct challenge to farmers who could easily retaliate against protesters familiar to them.

What is most remarkable about recent research in cliometrics has been the combination of a variety of approaches to history, both quantitative (or social scientific) and narrative, in a systematic way. Quantitative methods have been used to identify larger patterns and cases studies used to explore causal relationships within the patterns identified by quantitative analysis. Thus, the sharp dichotomy between quantitative and qualitative analysis so prevalent in the debates of the 1960s and 1970s has been rendered largely obsolete. The quality of recent works in cliometric history and the importance of their findings surely argues that they will not remain permanently out of Clio's favor.

QUANTIFICATION

While cliometrics made great progress in the 1950s and 1960s, the turn to quantification was still broader and more inclusive. A variety of historical investigators turned to quantitative methods as the only way to use important historical records. Many quantitative historical investigators did not necessarily see themselves as "testing" social science propositions but as seeking to understand a particular historical phenomenon such as the European fertility decline. They viewed themselves as pursuing traditional historical goals and using quantitative methods only because the natures of their sources required it. In the 1960s and 1970s a sharp and clear distinction existed between cliometricians who used social science methods and quantification and those historians who used quantification but rejected logical-empiricist social-science methods. In the 1980s and 1990s, as social science oriented historians abandoned logical empiricism and many quantitative historians became more analytical, the distinction became less clear.

Inspired by the pioneering work of the economic historian François Simiand, French scholars were often in the forefront of the preparation and use of quantitative measures. The efforts of Ernest Labrousse to relate changes in the price of bread to eighteenth-century social protest depended on the gathering of both long and short term data on historical price fluctuations. Georges Lefebvre's work on the French Revolution was based on the systematic analysis of tax records. At the same time, the work of the most prestigious member of the *Annales* school, Fernand Braudel, relied heavily on comparative statistical material; all his life, Braudel remained a voracious consumer of statistical data. The efforts to define long-term patterns in history seemed to require the assembling of statistical documentation. Emmanuel Le Roy Ladurie's classic work on the peasants of Languedoc depended on property records, and Yves Lequin's magisterial study of the working class of the Lyonnais was based on census material and demographic methods.

One of the most important European developments in this regard was the process of "family reconstitution" originated by Louis Henry in France in the 1950s. Essentially, Henry used parish registers of births, deaths, and marriages to "reconstitute" the population of French villages over relatively long periods of time and to derive basic estimates of fertility and mortality. Most of the efforts of Henry and his collaborators focused on small villages because researchers spent a great deal of time per family in preparing their estimates and also because migration posed serious problems; the presence of large numbers of single individuals or migrant married couples could lead to serious exaggerations. Small villages, it was assumed, would have less of these than larger communities.

Family reconstitution was the foundation of one of the most important historically oriented quantitative research projects of the 1960s and 1970s, the Cambridge Group for the History of Population and Social Structure. Some of the most prominent members of the group were Peter Laslett, R. S. Schofield, Richard Wall, and E. A. Wrigley. Unlike many research projects oriented towards quantitative research, the Cambridge group was fortunate to find in Peter Laslett not only a sophisticated demographer but a gifted popular exponent of quantitative historical research. In the English-speaking world his book, *The World We Have Lost,* remains a classic defense of social history and the quantitative methods on which it was based. That it has so few rivals in its field helps explain the relative decline of quantitative history. Quantitative historians employed techniques that were not readily understandable to most historians, much less the wider reading public. Too often, the temptation to employ pretentious jargon proved irresistible and ultimately brought discredit on the entire field.

While the Cambridge group generated considerable attention and produced important works on family structure, nonmarital fertility, and social structure, its single most important product was E. A. Wrigley and Roger Schofield's attempt to estimate English population trends between 1541 and 1871, and the efforts of the Institut National des Études Démographiques (INED) to estimate French population trends in the past. The great contribution of the Wrigley and Schofield book was to entirely reframe the question of fertility change. Instead of presuming a "natural fertility" that had remained almost constant right up to the fertility decline of the nineteenth century, Wrigley and Schofield showed long periods of fertility decline followed by periods of fertility increase. Their work seemed to rule out the possibility that fertility decline could be uniquely linked to modernity, and it drew attention to long-term processes of historical change.

Another area in which quantitative history made great strides in the 1960s and 1970s and continued to make important strides in the 1980s and 1990s was in the study of popular politics. One of the interesting developments in this field was that as their statistical methods became more sophisticated, students of collective action began to move in the same direction as network theorists, away from general universal explanations and towards locating theoretically interesting relationships within precisely historical contexts. In this area quantitative historians often benefited from the work of historical sociologists such as Charles Tilly or, later, Sidney Tarrow but often addressed their studies to fellow historians concerned with more single-mindedly historical issues. This work on collective action challenges the seemingly invincible conviction of many historians that quantitative analysis is necessarily biased in favor of the status quo or established ideas. Studies such as the recent work of John Markoff show that quantitative analysis can be a powerful critical tool.

John Markoff's study of protest and agrarian revolution, *The Abolition of Feudalism,* represents a most important contribution to this literature, challenging central assumptions of revisionist historiography and proposing an important new perspective on the French Revolution. Belying revisionist claims that bourgeois and noble had grown alike in the years before 1789, he demonstrates substantial differences in approach to economic and social problems on the part of different elites; class differences remained important and were to prove crucial over the course of the revolution. More important than this concession to orthodoxy, however, is Markoff's exploration of the dialogic relationship between politicians and protesters between 1789 and 1794. Due credit is given to the anti-feudal discourse of the National Assembly in giving direction to agrarian protest, but the rooting up of the feudal regime only began with such sloganeering; waves of peasant protests in 1790 and 1793 successfully pressured legislators to make good on their promises. Older historiography showed peasant protest as the mobilization of preexisting agrarian interests. Markoff analyzes how peasant interests reconfigured themselves to take advantage of the political opportunities opened to them by the revolutionary legislature. His is a grand study of revolutionary process.

But Markoff's study is also remarkable in its attention to language and its analysis of the reforms that different groups proposed. Its power rests on the exploitation of three major sources using quantitative methods. The first, a major scholarly accomplishment, is the machine-readable sample of the *cahiers de doléances* assembled by Markoff in collaboration with Gilbert Shapiro and others at the University of Pittsburgh. These *cahiers* were reports from more than forty thousand meetings of noblemen, clergymen, and the Third Estate held in the spring of 1789 throughout France. They provide a view of what some important groups demanded on the eve of a revolution. The second important source assembled by Markoff is a collection of some 4,700 rural-centered protests between the summer of 1788 and 1793, allowing a comparison of protestors' demands with the list of reforms articulated in 1789 to see how they evolved over time. Third is the data collected by Jean Nicolas and Guy Lemarchand on rural protest between 1661 and 1789, which enabled Markoff to compare patterns of pre-revolutionary and revolutionary agrarian protest.

Unlike previous work on the *cahiers,* Markoff's study compares the demands articulated by each estate as well as the work of the parish assemblies. Nobles emphasized civil liberties and seldom used the language of hierarchy and divine entitlement, but rather stressed that their seignorial rights were a form of property and tended to portray the nobility as a body of equals rather than an ordered hierarchy. As a body,

the Third Estate called for the abolition of status privileges and market impediments. It condemned the nobility's monopoly of military commissions, the heavy tax on noble land sold to commoners and the nobles' privileged legal access as well as seignorial monopolies, their right to tolls and the *corvée*. Focusing on the demands of village assemblies, a subset of the Third Estate's demands reveal that peasants did not frame their demands in the discourse beloved of intellectual historians; without denouncing "feudalism," they reveal systematic hostility to clerical and seignorial privilege. With regard to the clergy, they opposed the tithe, particularly its variability and accrual to tithe-holders, as well as charges for the major rituals of peasant life. With respect to nobility, they demanded the abolition of privileged dovecotes, rabbit warrens and fishponds, hunting rights, and such periodic dues as well as the end of monopolies, particularly oven and milling monopolies, although they were willing to see some reform of seignorial courts. Interestingly, peasants were not happy about taxes, but except for such indirect taxes as the salt taxes and town duties, they called for reform rather than abolition. Evidently, after centuries of defying state taxation, peasant communities had come to accept the state's right to tax, albeit in a more just form.

The most exciting and truly revolutionary aspect of Markoff's work is his examination of the evolution of peasants' demands and legislative responses during the years of revolution itself, revealing a dialogic relationship between peasant protestors and legislators, in which politicians responded to protest and in so doing also shaped its character. Revolutionary legislators responded to outbreaks of peasant rebellion by increasingly radical agrarian legislation. In turn, peasants learned that legislators were willing to grant them concessions in some areas and not in others.

This study is even more interesting concerning the seignorial regime itself. While peasants may not have possessed a generalized vocabulary for describing the landed regime, they still had a relatively coherent view of what they wanted changed and abolished that amounted to a thoroughgoing reform. Markoff sides with those who portray the celebrated "abolition of the feudal system" on the night of 4 August 1789 as propaganda for mild reforms that took back almost as much as they gave. Yet Markoff shows that the adoption of antifeudal rhetoric by legislators was to have important costs in excess of its intended mild reforms, for it pointed out a direction for discontented peasants. Subsequent waves of peasant unrest would lead to legislation in March 1790, August 1792, and July 1793 that cumulatively abolished feudalism root and branch.

Markoff's work represents a major challenge to all efforts to portray the French Revolution as having relatively feeble social consequences or as devoid of genuinely social conflict. The strength of his argument depends on his use of extremely large bodies of evidence, in his case principally the *cahiers,* which can hardly be exploited in any other way than by sample and by statistical analysis. Indeed, Markoff demonstrates the extremely misleading character of many uses of the *cahiers* based on selective and narrow readings of very small sections. Although Markoff uses quantification and a clever research design, his major task is to evaluate existing historical analyses of the French Revolution rather than to test or fashion a general theory of social revolution or political mobilization. By the 1990s both a sociologist such as John Markoff and a historian such as John Bohstedt employed sophisticated research designs and quantitative methods to address essentially historical questions. The distinction between cliometrics and quantification, so clear at the beginning of our period, was eroding as social scientists acquired a new respect for historicity and historians paid more attention to research design and sophisticated quantitative methods.

By the 1990s quantitative techniques were often consigned to a niche within the historical profession. Demographic historians, family historians, and econometric economic historians continued to play an important role within their fields but had relatively little influence on adjacent areas of study. Econometric economic history embraced the individualist assumptions of traditional economics and tended to establish itself in economics departments. While some of the most rigorous justifications for cliometrics and quantification disappeared with the ebb of logical empiricism, new approaches to the social sciences developed, such as relational realism, that still employed sophisticated research designs and formal methods. New approaches to social science method eliminated many of the dichotomies that had divided social scientists from historians in the 1960s and 1970s. The Markoff study reminds us of the many existing historical sources that can only be fully exploited with quantitative methods. Tempered in adversity, a new cliometrics and quantification emerged in the 1980s and 1990s. More rooted in historical analysis, capable of moving between micro and macro history, they focused not simply on the analysis of individual properties, but also on the study of relations.

See also **Modernization; The Population of Europe: Early Modern Demographic Patterns; The Population of Europe: The Demographic Transition and After** *(volume 2); and other articles in this section.*

BIBLIOGRAPHY

Cliometrics

Abbott, Andrew. "From Causes to Events, Notes on Narrative Positivism." *Sociological Methods and Research* 20 (1992): 428–455.

Abbott, Andrew. "Transcending General Linear Reality." *Sociological Theory* 6 (Autumn 1988): 169–186.

Bearman, Peter S. *Relations into Rhetorics: Local Elite Social Structure in Norfolk, England, 1540–1640.* New Brunswick, N.J., 1993.

Bhaskar, Roy. *Reclaiming Reality: A Critical Introduction to Contemporary Philosophy.* London, 1989.

Bohstedt, John. *Riots and Community Politics in England and Wales, 1790–1810.* Cambridge, Mass., 1983.

Bott, Elizabeth. *Family and Social Network: Roles, Norms, and External Relationships in Ordinary Urban Families.* London, 1957.

Callincos, Alex. *Making History: Agency, Structure, and Change in Social Theory.* Ithaca, N.Y., 1988.

Coale, Ansley J., and Susan Cotts Watkins., eds. *The Decline of Fertility in Europe: The Revised Proceedings of a Conference on the Princeton European Fertility Project.* Princeton, N.J., 1986.

Fogel, Robert William, and G. R. Elton, *Which Road to the Past? Two Views of History.* New Haven, Conn., 1983.

Franzosi, Roberto. *The Puzzle of Strikes: Class and State Strategies in Postwar Italy.* Cambridge, U.K., 1995.

Granovetter, Mark. "The Strength of Weak Ties: A Network Theory Revisited." In Peter Marsden and Nan Lin, eds. *Social Networks and Social Structure.* Beverly Hills, Calif., 1982. Pages 105–130.

Griffin, Larry J., and Marcel van der Linden. eds. *New Methods for Social History.* Cambridge, U.K., and New York, 1999.

Knodel, John E. *The Decline of Fertility in Germany, 1871–1939.* Princeton, N.J., 1974.

Lesthaeghe, Ron J. *The Decline of Belgian Fertility, 1800–1970.* Princeton, N.J., 1977.

Livi-Bacci, Massimo. *A History of Italian Fertility during the Last Two Centuries.* Princeton, N.J., 1977.

Lloyd, Christopher. *Explanation in Social History.* Oxford, 1986.

Lowen, Rebecca S. *Creating the Cold War University: The Transformation of Stanford.* Berkeley, Calif., 1997.

Manicas, Peter T. *A History and Philosophy of the Social Sciences.* Oxford, 1987.

Monkkonen, Eric H. *Engaging the Past: The Uses of History across the Social Sciences.* Durham, N.C., 1994.

Novick, Peter. *That Noble Dream: The "Objectivity Question" and the American Historical Profession.* Cambridge, U.K., 1988.

Popper, Karl R. *The Poverty of Historicism.* New York, 1961.

Rancière, Jacques. *The Names of History: On the Poetics of Knowledge.* Translated by Hassan Melehy. Minneapolis, Minn., 1994.

Scott, John. *Social Network Analysis: A Handbook.* London, 1991.

Skocpol, Theda. *States and Social Revolutions: A Comparative Analysis of France, Russia and China.* Cambridge, U.K., and New York, 1979.

Steinmetz, George. *Regulating the Social: The Welfare State and Local Politics in Imperial Germany.* Princeton, N.J., 1993.

Tilly, Charles. *Popular Contention in Great Britain, 1758–1834.* Cambridge, Mass., 1995.

Quantification

Gautier, Étienne, and Louis Henry. *La Population de Crulai, paroisse Normande: Étude historique.* Paris, 1958.

Gillis, John R., Louise A. Tilly, and David Levine, eds. *The European Experience of Declining Fertility: The Quiet Revolution 1850–1970.* Oxford, 1992.

Labrousse, Ernest. *Esquisse du mouvement des prix et des revenus en France au XVIIIe siècle.* Paris, 1933.

Laslett, Peter. *The World We Have Lost.* New York, 1965.

Laslett, Peter, ed. *Household and Family in Past Time: Comparative Studies in the Size and Structure of the Domestic Group over the Last Three Centuries in England, France, Serbia, Japan, and Colonial North America, with Further Materials from Western Europe.* Cambridge, U.K., 1972.

Lefebvre, G. *Etudes Orléanaises.* 2 vols. Paris, 1962, 1963.

Lequin, Yves. *Les ouvriers de la région lyonnaise (1848–1914).* 2 vols. Lyon, France, 1977.

Le Roy Ladurie, Emmanuel. *Les paysans de Languedoc.* 2 vols. Paris, 1966.

Markoff, John. *The Abolition of Feudalism: Peasants, Lords, and Legislators in the French Revolution.* University Park, Pa., 1996.

Stone, Lawrence. "The Revival of the Narrative." *Past and Present* 85 (1979).

Wrigley, E. A., and R. S. Schofield. *The Population History of England, 1541–1871: A Reconstruction.* Berkeley, Calif., 1997.

CULTURAL HISTORY AND
NEW CULTURAL HISTORY

Christopher E. Forth

There is little sense in searching for the concrete origins of cultural history, as every apparent intellectual inspiration may be shown to have been in turn inspired by some earlier development. As Peter Burke notes, in some cases the result is a "regress that leads us back to Aristotle, who discussed the internal development of literary genres such as tragedy in his *Poetics,* while his teleological views might entitle him to be called the first recorded Whig historian." (*Varieties,* p. 21). This essay poses for itself a much more modest task, and situates classical and new cultural history within the context of intellectual developments in the western world since the eighteenth century. In light of its relevance in the twenty-first century, new cultural history is taken as the primary focus of the following discussion and attempts are made to articulate its theoretical and methodological ingredients in light of its relationships with cognate approaches and the critical debates that it has inspired.

One of the most obvious differences between these two approaches to the history of culture concerns the rather dramatic expansion of the term itself. As Raymond Williams has shown, the history of this complex idea reveals the interplay of several overlapping meanings, and since the eighteenth century "culture" has denoted: 1) a general process of intellectual, aesthetic, and spiritual development; 2) a specific way of life, be it of a group, a period, or humanity in general; and 3) the works and practices of intellectual and artistic activity. In English the first and third understandings of the term refer to and reinforce one another, thus fueling the assumption that culture is something that certain societies (or at least their social elites) possess while others do not. Matthew Arnold's 1869 definition of culture is often considered exemplary of this view: "a pursuit of our total perfection by means of getting to know, on all the matters which most concern us, the best which has been thought and said in the world" (*Culture and Anarchy,* p. 4). Culture was a moral and exclusivist concept that sketched tacit

distinctions between social and ethnic groups by indicating culturally orthodox works of art and literature as well as the development of a sensibility capable of appreciating them. As we will see below, new cultural historians take as their point of departure the second definition of the word, and by developing it they seek to avoid the elitist and ethnocentric presumptions that inform the other two. This point of departure also brings them into the social historian's field of reference.

The relationship between social and cultural history has been and remains somewhat complex, even with the more anthropological approach to culture. Many social historians were initially impatient with cultural evidence, preferring topics that could be quantified (for example, family structure rather than family values) or looking to non-cultural causes, as in the dominant trends in the history of protest. We will see below that the marxist approach to social history raised some particular issues, though there could be overlap with culture. But a larger shift to cultural issues occurred from the late 1970s onward, often called the cultural "turn," though it to some extent built upon earlier social history traditions. Many social historians turned to cultural factors because they could not otherwise explain change: shifts in birthrates, for example, could be quantified, but their causes were more elusive. Interest in new topics such as gender, where cultural factors loom large, also played a role in the cultural turn. Strong interest in cultural topics and explanations persists in social history, though some social historians worry that quantitative methodologies and more "objective" issues like class structures or power relationships are being unduly downplayed in the process. Whether social history and the "new" cultural history are one and the same, or whether they continue to express different if overlapping orbits, is not yet fully resolved. The "new" cultural history reflects autonomous developments within the cultural field as well as a rebalancing within social history itself.

CLASSICAL CULTURAL HISTORY

Instances of what could be called cultural history have existed throughout the modern era, but most of these have tended to be rather journalistic accounts of day-to-day curiosities that struck the fancy of various amateur historians. There are also many examples of histories of cultural developments like music, art, literature, and ideas, that could be counted as cultural history defined broadly. For instance, Jacob Burckhardt's *Civilization of the Renaissance in Italy* (1860) is often considered a founding work of modern art history. Yet, in its treatment of trends rather than events, this careful study of the art and literature of the sixteenth century also sought to access a broader shift in the European mind during a period of dramatic change. Johan Huizinga's *The Waning of the Middle Ages* (1919) is another famous example of classical cultural history. Yet such concerns were clearly peripheral to the reigning historiographical orthodoxy of the nineteenth century, an ethos traceable to the German historian Leopold von Ranke, who insisted on the careful consideration of documentary evidence with a focus on political leaders and nation states. As academic historical practice became more completely professionalized in the late nineteenth century, with many history departments modeling themselves after German examples, cultural history came to be generally considered the domain of "amateurs" with more of a literary than a "scientific" bent.

Nevertheless, such orthodoxies were increasingly challenged by the end of the nineteenth century by historians in Germany, France, and the United States, with many arguing that the scientific conception of history should meet the demands of modern society. In America, Frederick Jackson Turner's "frontier thesis" directed attention to the role of geography in the creation of national identity, while proponents of the "New History," such as James Harvey Robinson and Charles Beard, called for a shift toward a comparative social and cultural history capable of analyzing broader social processes rather than the agency of prominent individuals. In France, sociologist Émile Durkheim and historian Henri Berr launched a similar critique of conventional historiography, and thus paved the way for the 1929 founding of the journal *Annales: économies, sociétés, civilisations,* a periodical that insisted on a cross-fertilization among the social sciences and that self-consciously refuted the primacy of individuals in history. German historians proved far more resistant to such innovations, however, and responded angrily to Karl Lamprecht's search for laws of social and political development in his multivolume *German History* (1891).

This transitional period suggests that it would be a mistake to draw a sharp break between classical cultural history and late-twentieth-century conceptions of this approach, largely because certain key practitioners of the former were also experimenting with broader definitions of culture. Huizinga himself represented a bridge between old and new cultural history by becoming interested in psychological factors in his later years. In addition, members of the so-called *Annales* school incorporated methodologies from a range of human sciences, from economics and demography to sociology and anthropology. One must also cite the example of Aby Warburg who, in Germany during the 1920s, pioneered a form of interdisciplinary cultural studies called *Kulturwissenschaft* that challenged earlier conceptions of a monolithic cultural tradition with the aid of anthropological models.

NEW CULTURAL HISTORY: INFLUENCES AND ENGAGEMENTS

Not only does the so-called new cultural history represent a more thoroughgoing application of anthropological understandings of cultural life, but it does so in a reflexive manner that problematizes the writing of history itself. Indeed, it calls into question at once the subject and the object of knowledge by asserting how deeply mediated all human life is by signifying systems that vary both from society to society and differ even within societies. For instance, where classical cultural historians like Burckhardt focused on elite culture and emphasized the autonomy of artistic and literary works, today one is likely to encounter treatments of culture that emphasize how such works are invested with significance by critics and audiences whose modes of perception and appreciation are shaped by broader social and cultural developments. Moreover, the broader conception of culture that is employed by new cultural historians often means less of an emphasis on elite culture than on collective structures of perception, emotion, and belief—in short, a consideration into the mental conditions that rendered such things as events and leaders possible.

This section outlines a number of theoretical and methodological precursors to new cultural history. In order to impose some coherence over a body of scholarship that is really quite heterogeneous, it treats new cultural history in terms of one of his most characteristic methodological features: its consideration of the objects of historical study in terms of their place in a wider cultural environment that not only frames them, but that in many respects allows them to exist in a certain way. Sometimes referred to as social or cultural constructionism, for the sake of continuity it refers to this tendency as a new form of "historicism."

Historicism. It is interesting to note that the topical and theoretical innovations of new cultural history were implicit in the same historiographical orthodoxy that marginalized classical cultural history. Traditional or "old" historicism developed in eighteenth-century Germany as a reaction against British and French social contract theories that emphasized the formative role of rational individuals in social life. Utilizing the heuristic fiction of an originary state of nature (wherein men rationally consented to become a society for the mutual protection of life and property), these liberal theories assumed an atomistic view of society in which isolated individuals pursued their own self-interest without the mediation of anything beyond their own minds. Placing a premium on this presocial capacity to reason meant that theorists like John Locke also denigrated the role of "mere custom" as an obstacle to rational thought, and thus in some respects discouraged scholars from taking cultural and social factors seriously.

Many eighteenth-century German thinkers rejected this notion that society was reducible to the sum of its parts, and emphasized instead the emotional nature of the social bond as opposed to the rational calculation of individuals. Johann Gottfried Herder, for instance, emphasized the feelings and traditions that bind a people or *Volk* together, including common customs, common experiences, and most importantly common language. This *Volk* was viewed as a living totality greater than the sum of its parts, thus initiating a rival strand of European social thinking that emphasized organicism and custom. Arguing against "metaphysical" appeals to universal moral standards or assertions of the constancy of human nature over time, Herder proposed that all phenomena be judged only in relation to their historical contexts, and rather than lend his support to widespread assertions of the inherent superiority of western culture, he insisted on the specific and variable nature of cultures across the world and according to various economic and social groups within a single nation. This general historicist standpoint informed Ranke's celebrated claim that historians should not judge the past in moral terms, but should rather "show what really happened," an assertion that has been misunderstood in Anglo-American circles as an affirmation of a simple empirical view of the past. Maurice Mandelbaum's succinct definition of the historicist project is worth quoting: "Historicism is the belief that an adequate understanding of the nature of any phenomenon and

an adequate assessment of its value are to be gained through considering it in terms of the place which it occupied and the role which it played within a process of development" (*History, Man, and Reason,* p. 42).

Although German historicists theoretically validated the study of culture as being worthy of historical interest, in actual practice they narrowed their focus to the study of politics and nation states, thereby restricting themselves to topics supported by voluminous documentary evidence. Informed by more recent theoretical developments in scholarly fields like anthropology, sociology, literary criticism, and feminist theory, new cultural historians have tried to preserve the analytically useful aspects of "old" historicism while jettisoning what they consider its more questionable assumptions. Indeed, in addition to their recognition of the emotional nature of communal bonds and the need to consider all phenomena as the result of historical change, German historicists often glorified the state, insisted on the inherent unity of individual cultures, and envisioned the historical process as being powered by principles that were immanent to that process (and thus not subject to the contingencies of historical flow). While Karl Marx took issue with the idealist tenets of the historicist tradition (chiefly exemplified in the works of G. W. F. Hegel), he nevertheless reproduced many of its metaphysical tendencies in his theory of historical materialism. Looking back on a century that witnessed two world wars, the systematic extermination of millions in Nazi concentration camps, and Stalinist totalitarianism in the Soviet Union, many westerners are understandably skeptical of such overarching historical frameworks and, in the often quoted observation of French philosopher Jean-François Lyotard, often manifest incredulity toward such grand narratives.

Marxism. Among nineteenth-century historicists, Marx was one of the few to observe that economic conditions and social hierarchies contribute to the predominance of certain ideas and institutions, and thus paved the way for many future historiographical innovations. Marxist-oriented social history therefore provided a fertile source for new cultural history, though the relations between these approaches have not always been amicable. Unlike their Soviet counterparts, western marxist social theorists have done much to develop this cultural dimension of Marx's ideas, often by complementing them with insights from Friedrich Nietzsche, Sigmund Freud, and Max Weber. Through his influential concept of "cultural hegemony," for instance, the Italian marxist Antonio Gramsci prompted a rethinking of the power that ideas can exercise over the minds of people, allowing social elites to rule more effectively by securing the consent of the governed. Other notable theorists, especially Theodor Adorno, Max Horkheimer, Herbert Marcuse, and others associated with the so-called Frankfurt School, have proposed viewing mass entertainment as a veritable "culture industry" that neutralizes the potential for dissent in western societies and thus dominates populations through consent. In the hands of many marxist theorists, then, culture is a veritable handmaiden of class domination, and remains firmly tethered to the mode of production.

In addition to these developments in critical social theory, cultural historians have been inspired by the work of British marxist social historians like Eric Hobsbawm, George Rudé, and especially Edward Thompson, who pioneered the notion of a "history from below" partly as a means of restoring to the largely forgotten members of the proletariat a sense of having taken an active role in their own formation. In his epic work *The Making of the English Working Class*, Thompson emphasized the interplay between individual agency and social structure in the case of the proletariat, and thus attempted to reconcile two apparently contradictory aspects of traditional marxist theory. Class consciousness was not something that proletarians blindly attained, but actively cultivated: "the working class was present at its own making." The call to explore "history from below" forms but one part of Thompson's legacy to cultural historians, many of whom have also been inspired by his innovative forays into the world of workers' beliefs and communal values that called into question long-standing understandings of crowd violence as mere irrational outbursts. Taking as his example the so-called "bread riots" of the early modern period, Thompson persuasively argued for the existence of a persistent "moral economy," where grain and other staples were seized during times of hardship in order to be sold at a price considered reasonable to members of the community. In such instances collective outrage at hoarders and speculators were refracted through the cultural traditions already in place.

Despite the undeniable contributions that marxist social history has made to new cultural history, there is significant disagreement on a number of key theoretical points. One point of tension pertains to the status that traditional marxist theory has accorded culture in everyday life. In their treatment of the ideas and institutions that characterize any given society, marxists have generally grounded all such "ideological" phenomena in the dominant mode of production, thus maintaining that the determining role of the economic "base" determines the context of its cultural "superstructure." Marxism therefore usually views culture as an *expression* of underlying forces. Indeed, for all of his attempts to problematize a simple correspondence between consciousness and material life, Thompson too contended that "class experience is largely determined by the productive relations into which men are born—or enter involuntarily" (p. 9). A second point of disagreement concerns the knowledge claims implicit in the marxist practice of ideology critique. As an offshoot of nineteenth-century historicism, marxism too acknowledges that phenomena should be judged in relation to their historical conditions of development. Moreover, in its recognition of the formative role of economic and social conditioning over the world of ideas, marxism comes close to admitting that knowledge is itself contingent and shaped by historical factors. Yet despite these historicist tendencies marxism still tends to view itself as a science that can dispel cultural illusions or "ideology" to reveal the "truth" about economic domination. Whereas all other social actors are supposedly trapped in the web of ideological distortion, the marxist critic implicitly remains capable of perceiving reality in a more or less transparent manner. Finally, both marxism and social theory have often been less concerned with factors of gender and race, and frequently assume that instances of sexual and racial discrimination are ultimately reducible to an economic foundation.

None of this is to suggest that contemporary cultural historians exclude from their analyses a consideration of socioeconomic factors or that they fail to recognize instances of class domination. Rather, they contest the determinist claim that all forms of social control must necessarily be reflections of a material base. Indeed, sexual and racial discrimination have histories that do not rely solely on the means of production for their particular historical manifestations, and thus encourage us to question the marxist insistence on the predominance of economics in all forms of domination. One must also acknowledge that late-twentieth-century marxist theory proved receptive to critiques of the base/superstructure model, and one is now more likely to see more sophisticated analyses of the relationship among economics, culture, gender, and race. The British tradition of "cultural materialism" represents one example of this openness in literary criticism, while the "post-marxist" theories of Ernesto Laclau, Chantal Mouffe, and others also betray an engagement with theoretical developments. In fact, marxist social historians were among the first to apply new linguistic models of culture to the study of the past, though one may wonder to what extent one can do so while remaining marxist.

The* Annales *school. New cultural historians have also been inspired by the "history of mentalities" as practiced by French historians linked to the well-known scholarly journal *Annales*. Opposed to the conventional historical preoccupation with events and seeking to establish productive relationships with other disciplines, founding members Lucien Febvre and Marc Bloch drew upon recent psychological and sociological insights in order to access a hitherto ignored dimension of historical experience. Marc Bloch's classic study *The Royal Touch* demonstrated how popular beliefs in the king's ability to heal scrofula represented a durable mental system that did not die simply because the much sought cure did not always occur. The *Annalistes* nevertheless failed to provide a rigorous theorization of the relationship between *mentalités* and other environmental factors, and some like Pierre Chaunu concluded that it represented a "third level" of historical inquiry more or less determined by developments taking place on the putatively more primary level of social and economic life. Hence, the *Annalistes* contended that culture was at heart an expression of underlying structures, and shared the marxist reluctance to accord it an autonomous status. Fourth-generation *Annalistes* such as Roger Chartier and Jacques Revel proved much more receptive to theoretical developments and conceived of culture as operating independently of social and economic determinants.

Semiotics. Most importantly, new cultural historians generally recognize the centrality of language to the production of cultural forms and human consciousness. By "language" these scholars do not mean individual words or phrases, but language as described by the Swiss linguist Ferdinand de Saussure early in the twentieth century: a signifying system in which individual words acquire meaning through their differential relationships with other words. Concepts such as "white" or "male," for instance, are only arbitrarily connected to their referents in reality, and their meaning is constructed through their *difference* from all other words in the system. Nor is the individual speaker the source of language and the guarantor of its meaning, for shared systems of signification may be shown to precede and mold individual consciousness. Partly inspired by Durkheim's notion of "collective representations," Saussure suggested that our views of the world are always shaped and constrained by the signifying system in which we have been socialized. Contrary to conventional thinking, language does not *express* a pregiven and independent reality, but constructs or *constitutes* it for members of specific linguistic communities.

Saussurean linguistics represented an essential component of the method of semiotic analysis known as structuralism, a manner of systematically studying a wide variety of "signs," from conventional linguistic ones to cultural signs like wrestling matches, cuisine, kinship systems, and bird calls. French structuralists like the anthropologist Claude Lévi-Strauss argued that myths are one example of the sort of "deep structures" of human existence that obey a common "grammar" possessed by all peoples. Such cognitive structures are, for Lévi-Strauss, collective and not reducible to individual consciousness, and illustrate the centrality of binary oppositions for the ordering and categorization of the world. In their extension of Saussurean linguistics into other areas, structuralists performed a double movement that had profound implications for later scholarship: they questioned at once the subject and the object of knowledge—the knower and the known—by showing the extent to which human experience is mediated by cultural or "discursive" structures.

Whereas structuralism focused closely on binary opposites that were considered to be stable and universal characteristics of cultural life, the next generation of French thinkers (dubbed "poststructuralists" by the Anglo-American world) undermined the putative stability of such structures to emphasize the fluidity and "play" that attend all instances of signification. What the philosopher Jacques Derrida termed "deconstruction" is a method of critical reading that demonstrates how all apparent oppositions are not really oppositions at all. Rather, in every instance of an "either/or" opposition, each side of the copula not only depends on the other for its very coherence, but the relationship is always implicitly hierarchical, with one side usually achieving predominance over the other. Some examples of this opposition/hierarchy include "white" and "black," "male" and "female," "center" and "periphery," "healthy" and "diseased," all of which can be deconstructed to reveal the implication of one in the other. The cognitive stability that collective mental structures seemed to ensure was now undermined by the tendency of cultural categories to slide into one another.

One result of this critical attention to language and the double bracketing of the subject and object of knowledge was an increased reflexivity on the part of many historians: if we are able to decipher the internal contradictions and hidden biases of our historical subjects, what then of our own attempts to make the past appear coherent? Although deconstruction is useful for thinking about the ways in which binary oppositions are put together, one is more likely to encounter the deconstructive method in the works of intellectual historians who critically reread classic historical works and theorize the narrative nature of all historical writing. Hayden White is the undisputed pioneer in this field, and was one of the first historians to incorporate the insights of literary criticism in his well-known work *Metahistory: The Historical Imagination in Nineteenth-Century Europe* (1973), which investigates how well-known historians have "emplotted" their works in one of four dominant western narrative styles. Today there are a number of prominent intellectual historians who study the "poetics" of historical writing, including Dominick LaCapra, Hans Keller, F. R. Ankersmit, Allan Megill, and Robert Berkhofer.

Anthropology. While more theoretically inclined and self-reflexive cultural historians have been informed by such insights into language, most seem to have followed the lead of social scientists who have applied such semiotic theories to the study of culture itself. Anthropology has proven an especially influential field for the elaboration of new theories of culture, and many historians have been inspired by Clifford Geertz, who in his approach to culture submitted that "Believing, with Max Weber, that man is an animal suspended in webs of significance he himself has spun, I take culture to be those webs, and the analysis of it to be therefore not an experimental science in search of a law but an interpretive one in search of meaning" (*The Interpretation of Cultures,* p. 5). Unraveling the many layers of significance that inform cultural formations is a hermeneutical operation akin to the interpretation of a literary text, and thus gives rise to what Geertz calls "thick description."

Much new cultural history betrays the influence of semiotic and anthropological theories of culture. British social historians like Gareth Stedman Jones were among the first to experiment with such conceptions, but in so doing they ended up challenging earlier marxist reductions of social consciousness to material reality. Stedman Jones's strong claim that we "cannot therefore decode political language to reach a primal and material expression of interest since it is the discursive structure of political language which conceives and defines interest in the first place" represents a definite departure from conventional marxist theory. Natalie Zemon Davis, an American social historian and former marxist, was also receptive to anthropological models of communal life, and likewise criticized a crude base/superstructure model in her work on peasant customs and rituals in early modern France.

Michel Foucault and historicism. A number of other theorists played a part in the elaboration of new

cultural history, including Pierre Bourdieu, Mikhail Bakhtin, Roland Barthes, and Jacques Lacan, to name but a few. Without a doubt, however, the French philosopher and historian Michel Foucault exercised the most significant and durable impact on this historiographical approach. Inspired by the example of the German philosopher Friedrich Nietzsche, Foucault's "genealogical" method historicizes that which has been considered "natural" or otherwise outside of the reach of historical influences. Where Nietzsche sought the subtle and forgotten beginnings of morality in violence and coercion (rather than in some absolute sense of the good), Foucault turns his attention to topics like sexuality, insanity, criminality, and illness to suggest not only that one can write histories of such phenomena (thus opening up new topics for historical study), but that such phenomena are themselves the effect of historical developments and cannot simply be considered "natural." By refusing to search for the inherent meaning of things in their putatively stable essence or "origin," Foucault insists that such things "must be made to appear as events on the stage of historical process" ("Nietzsche, Genealogy, History," 1977, p. 152).

Foucault advocates a strong version of historicism that questions the pregiven reality of a range of human experiences, from madness and sexuality to criminality and the body. One effect of this historicism is a radical questioning of the metaphysical concept of "Man" that has undergirded the western intellectual tradition. As Foucault asserts in a memorable passage: "Nothing in man—not even his body—is sufficiently stable to serve as the basis for self-recognition or for understanding other men" (1977, p. 153). By challenging the "natural" aspects of human life, Foucault does not recommend that we deny the materiality of the body but, as he explains toward the end of *The History of Sexuality, Volume One,* that we "make it visible through an analysis in which the biological and the historical are not consecutive to one another . . . but are bound together in an increasingly complex fashion." Hence, unlike an *Annaliste* history of mentalities that might consider only how the body has been perceived, Foucault calls for a " 'history of bodies' and the manner in which what is most material and most vital in them has been invested" (pp. 151–152).

Questioning the conventionally understood relationship between knowledge and power was central to Foucault's brand of historicism, and proved especially fruitful for many styles of new cultural history. Traditionally seen as committed only to truth and remaining "disinterested" in the pursuit of social status or professional accolades, knowledge has been often seen not only as distinct from power, but as its veritable antithesis. Eighteenth-century intellectuals set the tone for such an understanding, suggesting that knowledge, reason, and public discussion could be used to unmask the mental domination of religious dogma and to critique the status quo. Although marxist social theory proved instrumental in situating the production of knowledge in its socioeconomic contexts (particularly by showing how accepted ideas frequently mirror the interests of the dominant class), Foucault rejects the marxist assumption that a more judicious use of critical reason may remain free of such constraints. In his thoroughgoing historicism, Foucault contends that knowledge must always been seen as inextricably embedded in its social and institutional context, and therefore denies the possibility that knowledge could ever sever its ties to various forms of power.

Rather in works like *Discipline and Punish* and *The History of Sexuality,* Foucault argues for a much closer relationship between knowledge and power by asking us to reconsider what power means and how it operates. Though acknowledging the conventional understanding of power as a negative force that represses or prohibits (what he calls "juridical" power), Foucault suggests that power also operates in a more productive and subtle manner insofar as it is connected with knowledge. Following Nietzsche, Foucault claims that the will to know is a desire to order the world into categories and hierarchies that seek to effect control as well as create order. Here Foucault breaks with the common assumption that knowledge is the "other" of power. Homosexuality, he argues, shifted in the western imagination from a "sinful" deed that one performed (and for which one could atone) to the expression of one's innermost person, thus chaining an individual to his or her sexual identity. Advances in knowledge about sexuality thus served to create new understandings of the "normal" and the "pathological" by casting nonreproductive desire as deviant and potentially dangerous, thereby classifying those who indulged in it as "sick" and in need of treatment. Foucault argues that the nineteenth-century scientific campaign against sexual vice was at base not so much an attempt to eliminate it altogether (an instance of power as prohibition) as it was a process through which ever-more complex categories of "perversity" were concocted to make it proliferate as the "other" of heterosexual coupling. Knowledge thus discursively constructed "the homosexual" and "the heterosexual" as specific types of persons, thereby defining "normal" desire through the elaboration of a multitude of opposites. In this sense knowledge and power are not opposed to one another but work together creatively.

The interdisciplinary and unconventional style of Foucault's writings have proven to be obstacles to his acceptance among many historians who take exception to his eclectic combination of philosophical reflection, social theory, and historical research. Indeed, Foucault's apt description of his works as "philosophical fragments in historical workshops" has done little to endear them to more conventional historians. Although one must admit the rather incomplete incorporation of his ideas to new cultural history—indeed, much of his radical philosophical agenda has failed to make it into these works—nevertheless Foucault's primary contribution has been to suggest new topics for historical scrutiny along with a method (some say an "antimethod") for analyzing them.

THE PRACTICE OF CULTURAL HISTORY

Some of the earliest and best-known practitioners of new cultural history distinguished themselves through their enthusiastic embrace of anthropological models of culture. A substantial number of such works focus on early modern Europe, thus to some extent extending the preoccupation of the *Annales* tradition with this period. Key early works in this vein include David Sabean's study of the duchy of Württemberg in Germany, *Power in the Blood,* and Carlo Ginzburg's reconstruction of the cosmology of a sixteenth-century Italian miller in *The Cheese and the Worms.* In such matters interpretive history is perhaps best suited, largely because many of the traditional text sources are often not available for, say, everyday life in a peasant village during the Middle Ages. Robert Darnton's *The Great Cat Massacre* is one of the classic examples of this type of scholarship insofar as it applies Geertz's "thick description" to a number of topics, from early modern fairy tales to the tale about the trial and execution of cats told by printers.

Nowadays cultural historians are usually careful to emphasize the performative rather than expressive role of culture. A "performative" statement is one that at once describes and brings about (performs) the very thing it denotes, as in the claim "I now pronounce you husband and wife." Many cultural historians agree with the linguist J. A. Austin's claim that all language is in some sense performative in that it produces an effect as it signifies. In the form of official discourses of, for instance, medicine or criminology, culture plays a mediating role that creates and sustains social practices rather than simply mirroring or expressing them. Roger Chartier has described how this notion of culture must be distinguished from the idea of *mentalité* as a third level of historical experience.

Cultural representations are not dependent upon a pregiven material reality for their existence; rather, Chartier claims that "representations of the social world themselves are the constituents of social reality."

This emphasis on the performative role of culture has encouraged new interpretations of key political events, notably the French Revolution. The contributions of cultural historians like Lynn Hunt, Roger Chartier, Mona Ozouf, and Antoine de Baecque often suggest that a fundamental shift in mind-set had occurred among the French during the eighteenth century that provided the conditions of possibility for radical change. As Chartier has argued in *The Cultural Origins of the French Revolution,* the Revolution became possible because enough changes had taken place in the wider culture to make such a dramatic upheaval conceivable. Moreover, in *Festivals and the French Revolution* Mona Ozouf argues that the highly planned Festival of the Federation (held on 14 July 1790 to commemorate the unity of the nation in the revolutionary moment) was an opportunity to create a sense of national unity where anxieties about division were widespread. That is, such festivals were not so much expressions of a preexisting national unity as they were attempts to create such unity through festivity itself, thus "performing" the very unity whose existence they proclaimed.

The influence of Foucault is palpable in many areas of new cultural history, particularly in works that inquire into the relationship between systems of knowledge, and power relationships in various national contexts. The social history of medicine received a significant boost from the injection of Foucauldian thought, and has encouraged a close examination of the relationships between medical categories of pathology and broader sociopolitical processes whereby a culture constructs a definition of normality through the identification of a range of "others" such as women, criminals, perverts, non-westerners, proletarians, and the insane. Such investigations have also dovetailed with other areas that have been marked by the influence of Foucault, including the history of sexuality and the cultural history of the body, and frequently demonstrate a dialogue among these fields and developments in feminist theory and gender studies. Robert Nye's *Crime, Madness, and Politics in Modern France,* for instance, explores the interconnection between medical discourses on insanity and criminality in the context of a pervasive concern with the decay of the French body politic at the end of the nineteenth century. Although they incorporate a more psychoanalytic framework, works such as Sander Gilman's *Difference and Pathology* and *The Jew's Body* have done much to expand our understanding about

how German-speaking cultures produced concepts of "health" and "normality" through medicalized conceptions of pathological otherness.

Few works in this vein have been as widely cited as Thomas Laqueur's *Making Sex: Body and Gender from the Greeks to Freud,* a book that explores the gender politics behind a rather stunning reorientation in European medical thinking about male and female reproductive physiology. Laqueur argues that for much of the western tradition male and female bodies were viewed as essentially the same, except that the female was seen as an inversion of the male. That is, when doctors examined the womb and ovaries they saw an inverted penis and testicles, and even maintained that both sexes secreted semen. While this "one-sex" medical model hardly guaranteed equality among the sexes, it remained firmly in place until two sexes were discovered in the late eighteenth century. What is most fascinating about this "discovery" is that it was not grounded in new empirical evidence. Rather, the shift to the now prevailing medical belief in sexual dimorphism functioned partly as a means of grounding an emerging ideology of "separate spheres" in the bedrock of incommensurable biological difference. Far from standing apart from the world of interests, the language of science emerges in Laqueur's work as being infused with the rhetoric of gender that marked other discursive fields.

New cultural history and its relations to neighboring fields.

Given the impact of contemporary linguistic theories on most of the humanities and social science disciplines—and the fact that disciplinary boundaries were increasingly and productively blurred in the late twentieth century—it is difficult to argue that new cultural history has simply exercised an "influence" over neighboring fields. It is nevertheless possible to cite certain important intersections between new cultural history and developments in cognate disciplines. Edward Said's influential *Orientalism,* generally considered the founding text of postcolonial studies, reveals many of the same Foucauldian concerns with power, knowledge, and history evident in works of new cultural history. Using a combination of Foucauldian discourse analysis and a Gramscian critique of cultural hegemony, Said powerfully shows how "the Orient" and "Orientals" were constructed as the "other" of the west by French and British intellectuals during the eighteenth and nineteenth centuries. A similar use of contemporary cultural thinking is made by Benedict Anderson, who argues that national identity depends upon a collective imagining. This idea of the nation as an "imagined community" is central to postcolonial studies and also resonated in the Subaltern Studies movement, which in its reconsideration of Indian history combined many of these insights with a more traditional marxist focus on the agency of subaltern groups.

Similar developments may be discerned in feminist scholarship, where a methodologically traditional women's history found itself complemented or challenged (depending upon one's viewpoint) by a new focus on gender as "a useful category of historical analysis," to use Joan Wallach Scott's phrase. Unlike women's history, which generally contributed to the recovery and insertion of women into the historical record without interrogating the bases of their exclusion in the first place, historians such as Scott have shifted the focus from agency to identity to show how gender identities, or one's identification with certain gender roles, are effects of broader cultural schema and practices. Invoking Foucault while pointing out the gender blindness in his work, gender historians contribute to a rethinking of selfhood by revealing the historical nature of a crucial dimension of personal identity. Finally, labor history too has felt the impact of these new ideas, with prominent practitioners like William H. Sewell Jr. and Donald Reid adopting linguistic models of social consciousness that avoid the reductionist tendencies of conventional social history.

These productive interchanges among such new areas of scholarship attest to the difficulty of separating new cultural history from its neighboring fields, and thus in a sense enacts in miniature the broader collapse of disciplinary boundaries in the humanities and social sciences. One may now expect to encounter works of history that are in fact hybridizations of social, cultural, feminist, and postcolonial methodologies, as in the case of Daniel Pick's *Faces of Degeneration,* which revises Edward Said's insights on Orientalism to suggest the simultaneous construction of a sort of "Orient" within European society during the nineteenth century that paralleled the constitution of an external "other" abroad. Pick shows how the conflict between Occident and Orient was not a tension between polar opposites; rather, medicalized discourses of hereditary degeneration and their elaborations in works of fiction and social policy suggest the troubling presence of "atavistic" traits at the heart of the very "civilization" whose achievements were so often counterposed to the "degeneracy" and "effeminacy" of Muslim, Asian, and African cultures. The direction of Pick's argument was modified somewhat by Ann Laura Stoler who, in her study of the unpublished fourth volume of Foucault's *History of Sexuality,* suggests that theoretical and methodological tools for thinking about Europe's inner "others" were first developed for and applied to colonial peoples, thereby

suggesting that "external colonialism provided a template for conceptualizing social inequities in Europe and not solely the other way around" (p. 75). Wherever one situates oneself on this intriguing issue, historicist arguments have contended that discourses of gender, class, and race are in fact "interarticulated"— one cannot construct a discourse of one without employing the terms and metaphors that are present in the others.

The same could be said for the relationship of new cultural history with its fellow-travelers in neighboring fields: insofar as these various approaches are informed by similar theoretical (especially semiotic) frameworks, each articulates its own project with tools that are already present in the other, albeit with different foci and more specific points of application. While it would indeed be an exaggeration to claim that new cultural history has exercised an *influence* over its neighbors, one must admit the current prominence of "the historical" as a widely held contention in the human sciences that one must situate the objects of study within historical frameworks of culture and discourse. In literary studies the so-called New Historicism amply demonstrates a shift away from purely textual analyses to contextual considerations in a manner that parallels the sort of thing many historians have done, while the fields of cultural studies and queer theory have also been marked by this historicizing turn.

CRITICAL DEBATES

Most innovative historical approaches generate some degree of controversy, often stemming as much from professional anxieties, political concerns, and generational tensions as from bona fide intellectual differences. Debates that have arisen around new cultural history have nevertheless been particularly frequent and often rather polemical. Some of the more vitriolic rejections of this approach lump it together with postcolonial studies, feminist theory, multiculturalism, and even marxism as part of a vaguely defined, yet nevertheless menacing, "postmodernism" that threatens to undermine professional historical standards or even basic morality. Some critics have gone so far as to describe proponents of such methodologies as "tenured radicals" who have continued the 1960s assault on western civilization by becoming university professors. Gertrude Himmelfarb, for instance, a high-profile critic of marxist-inspired social history, inveighed against the expansion of "postmodern" ideas in historical circles. Others challenge this approach from a traditional marxist perspective and, in keeping with the old or-

91

thodoxy of the base/superstructure model, accuse its proponents of ignoring the "materiality of the sign" in their focus on culture. Such controversies tend to generate more heat than light, however, and rarely betray much of an engagement with the theories that inform the approaches being condemned.

More careful critics are attentive to the disagreements among those who already profess and employ this approach, and are therefore able to enter into more sophisticated dialogues on key issues. If cultural historians disagree among themselves about the concept of historicism, it is less in regard to the general validity of the method than to the limits of its application. The issue of the physical body has proven a highly charged one for questioning the limits of historicism, and has generated some productive scholarly exchanges. Some historians seem to agree with Bryan Turner, a pioneer in the sociology of the body, that historicist arguments must not be permitted to thoroughly overrun the body's basic materiality. Cultural historian Lyndal Roper echoes this point of view, albeit from a psychoanalytic perspective, and criticizes the overzealous historicism that allows one to make the "real" body disappear behind its various discursive formulations. Roper calls instead for a moderate historicism that facilitates a dialogical relationship between nature and culture without collapsing the former into the latter: "Bodies have materiality, and this too must have its place in history. The capacity of the body to suffer pain, illness, the process of giving birth, the effects on the body of certain kinds of exercise such as hunting or riding—all these are bodily experiences which belong to the history of the body and are more than discourse. . . . Bodies are not merely creations of discourse" (*Oedipus and the Devil,* p. 21).

This question about the limits of historicism also generated political debates about the status of human agency within the cultural networks described by some historians. A brief debate in the journal *Signs* (1990) between two prominent feminist historians, Linda Gordon and Joan Wallach Scott, placed in relief some of the issues that divide practitioners of social and women's history from those who subscribe to arguments drawn from linguistic theories. Scott criticizes Gordon's work about women and welfare agencies, *Heroes of Their Own Lives* (1988), for attributing to its female subjects personal autonomy that did not reflect the complexity of being situated within cultural and discursive networks. In a manner familiar to cultural historians, Scott challenges the idea that one can conceive of agency as existing outside of such frameworks, and recommends viewing it instead as "a discursive effect" in which the ways in which social workers represented the experiences of their clients

helped shape the range of options open to women. Far from denying women the capacity for action in their struggle against domestic violence, Scott claims, such a view recognizes "a complex process that constructs possibilities for and puts limits on specific actions undertaken by individuals and groups." Gordon's response and her subsequent critique of Scott's *Gender and the Politics of History* exemplify the types of criticisms that women's historians have leveled at the poststructuralist theory that informs much new cultural history. She argues that too much of a focus on "discourse" threatens to override agency and personal experience, and undermines women's capacity for concrete political action.

Similar tensions attended the reception of new cultural history among labor historians. Prominent scholars like William H. Sewell Jr., Donald Reid, and Patrick Joyce embraced contemporary theory to challenge a number of tenets of labor history. Contesting the idea that economic factors are inherently "material," for instance, Sewell argues for a "post-materialist labor history" that would consider the symbolic function of money and advertising as well as the intellectual origins of factory construction and the role of worker morale and expertise in production. Social consciousness is not viewed as springing from socioeconomic relationships, but emerges from discourses of social identity and interest that prefigure consciousness. While some labor historians welcomed the new insights such methodologies could bring, they questioned whether the study of culture should eclipse more conventional inquiries into mass movements and political structures. Others contended that discourses of class cannot be thoroughly severed from their extralinguistic referents, and insisted on the primacy of social relationships when it comes to thinking about consciousness.

CONCLUSION

As with any scholarly approach that boasts of being "new" when it bursts onto the scene, new cultural history was fairly well established as one among many ways of thinking about history by the twenty-first century. This is not to say that new cultural historians enjoyed the unanimous esteem of their more traditional colleagues, for the field still managed to draw the fire of critics from the left and the right who believed that after twenty years this approach still represented a mere "trend." One could agree with Peter Novick that this attests to the fragmentation of the historical profession into a plethora of specializations that no longer cohered around shared principles and whose denizens had little common ground for discussion. Yet much has changed in cultural history since its heyday in the 1980s. When new cultural history was actually "new" it provided innovations both in terms of the topics considered worthy of historical attention and in terms of the ways of theorizing such topics within their respective contexts. It is nevertheless apparent that a good portion of what was marketed in 2000 as "cultural history" reflected more of the topical rather than theoretical innovations entailed by this approach. In fact, some of these works even read more like conventional social histories with a few obligatory nods to one of many privileged theorists.

To some extent this state of affairs reflects the success of this approach in the academy and the willingness of historians to combine methodologies in a creative and eclectic manner. On the other hand, though, one might argue that cultural history lost much of its edge by becoming subsumed into a more or less nonreflective historical establishment. Some historians see less fragmentation than the cooptation of erstwhile radical approaches back into a surprisingly resilient mainstream. "Whatever possibilities become evident," notes Patrick Joyce, "something is needed to shake the hold of a history which continually reproduces itself, in the process sucking the erstwhile heterodox into its consensus, in much the way that 'cultural history' is slowly but surely becoming routinized as more methodology, yet one more subdiscipline in the house of history." Joyce's observation is astute, yet one wonders whether a historical approach that could successfully resist such cooptation is possible and, even if it were, whether it would still merit the name "history." It seems evident that what makes history "history" has little to do with methodologies and innovations that are unique to it, and perhaps a more thoroughgoing interdisciplinarity would discourage the domestication of future innovations into mere additions to the mansion of conventional history.

See also other articles in this section.

BIBLIOGRAPHY

Arnold, Matthew. *Culture and Anarchy.* 3d ed. New York, 1882.

Burke, Peter. *The French Historical Revolution: The Annales School, 1929–89.* Stanford, Calif., 1990.

Burke, Peter. *Varieties of Cultural History.* Cambridge, U.K., 1997.

Burckhardt, Jacob. *Civilization of the Renaissance in Italy.* Translated by S. G. C. Middlemore. New York, 1960 (1860).

Chartier, Roger. *The Cultural Origins of the French Revolution.* Translated by Lydia G. Cochrane. Durham, N.C., 1991.

Darnton, Robert. *The Great Cat Massacre and Other Episodes in French Cultural History.* London, 1984.

Derrida, Jacques. *Of Grammatology.* Translated by Gayatri Chakravorty Spivak. Baltimore, 1976 (1967).

Foucault, Michel. *The History of Sexuality, Volume One: An Introduction.* Translated by Robert Hurley. New York, 1978.

Foucault, Michel. "Nietzsche, Genealogy, History." In *Language, Counter-Memory, Practice: Selected Essays and Interviews.* Translated by Donald F. Bouchard and Sherry Simon. Ithaca, N.Y., 1977. Pages 139–164.

Geertz, Clifford. *The Interpretation of Cultures.* New York, 1973.

Gilman, Sander. *Difference and Pathology: Stereotypes of Sexuality, Race, and Madness.* Ithaca, N.Y., 1985.

Gilman, Sander. *The Jew's Body.* New York, 1991.

Hunt, Lynn, ed. *The New Cultural History.* Berkeley, Calif., 1989.

Laqueur, Thomas. *Making Sex: Body and Gender from the Greeks to Freud.* Cambridge, Mass., 1990.

Lyotard, Jean-François. *The Postmodern Condition: A Report on Knowledge.* Translated by Geoff Bennington and Brian Massumi. Minneapolis, Minn., 1984 (1979).

Mandelbaum, Maurice. *History, Man, and Reason: A Study in Nineteenth-Century Thought.* Baltimore, 1971.

Ozouf, Mona. *Festivals and the French Revolution.* Translated by Alan Sheridan. Cambridge, Mass., 1988.

Roper, Lyndal. *Oedipus and the Devil: Witchcraft, Sexuality, and Religion in Early Modern Europe.* New York, 1994.

Sabean, David Warren. *Power in the Blood: Popular Culture and Village Discourse in Early Modern Germany.* Cambridge, U.K., 1984.

Said, Edward. *Orientalism.* New York, 1979.

Saussure, Ferdinand de. *Course in General Linguistics.* Translated by Wade Baskin. New York, 1966.

Scott, Joan Wallach. *Gender and the Politics of History.* New York, 1999.

Stoler, Ann Laura. *Race and the Education of Desire: Foucault's History of Sexuality and the Colonial Order of Things.* Durham, N.C., 1995.

Thompson, E. P. *The Making of the English Working Class.* New York, 1966.

Turner, Bryan. *Regulating Bodies: Essays in Medical Sociology.* London, 1992.

White, Hayden. *Metahistory: The Historical Imagination in Nineteenth-Century Europe.* Baltimore, 1973.

Williams, Raymond. *Keywords: A Vocabulary of Culture and Society.* London, 1983 (1976).

GENDER THEORY

Bonnie G. Smith

Gender theory developed in the academy during the 1970s and 1980s as a set of ideas guiding historical and other scholarship in the West. In social history it particularly thrived in the United States and Great Britain, with far fewer followers on the European continent. Essentially this theory proposed looking at masculinity and femininity as sets of mutually created characteristics shaping the lives of men and women. It replaced or challenged ideas of masculinity and femininity and of men and women as operating in history according to fixed biological determinants. In other words, removing these categories from the realm of biology, it made a history possible. For some, the idea of "gender history" was but another term for women's history, but for others gender theory transformed the ways in which they approached writing and teaching about both men and women. To some extent it may be hypothesized that the major change brought about by gender theory was that it complicated the study of men, making them as well as women gendered historical subjects.

PHILOSOPHICAL AND ANTHROPOLOGICAL SOURCES

Anthropology produced some of the first influential theories using the term "gender" when it began discussing "gender roles." The background to this concept lay in post–World War I research. Margaret Mead, most notably, described non-Western societies where men performed tasks that Westerners might call "feminine" and vice versa. Mead described many variations in men's and women's tasks and sexual roles in her best-selling studies (such as *Coming of Age in Samoa*; 1928), opening one way for scholars to reappraise the seemingly fixed behaviors of men and women and to see stereotypes as contingent rather than determined by nature. Such a reappraisal, however, lay in the wings for much of the 1950s and 1960s.

Another source of gender theory was philosophical and literary. "One is not born, one is made a woman," the French philosopher and novelist Simone de Beauvoir wrote in her 1949 best-seller, *The Second Sex.* This dense and lengthy description of the "making" of womanhood discussed Marxist, Freudian, literary, and anthropological theories that, according to Beauvoir, actually determined women's behavior. In her view women, in contrast to men, acted in accordance with men's view of them and not according to their own lights. This analysis drew on phenomenological and existential philosophy that portrayed the development of the individual subject or self in relationship to an object or "other." Thus, as Beauvoir extrapolated from this theory, a man formed his subjectivity in relationship to "woman" as other or object, spinning his own identity by creating images of someone or something that was not him. Instead of building selves in a parallel way, women accepted male images of them *as* their identity. By this view, femininity as most women lived it was an inauthentic identity determined not inevitably, as a natural condition, but as the result of a misguided choice. This insight had wide-ranging implications for future scholarship, notably in suggesting a voluntaristic aspect to one's sexual role or nature.

A second extrapolation from existentialism in *The Second Sex,* however, did touch on women's biological role as reproducer. For existentialists, living an authentic life entailed escaping the world of necessity or biology and acting in the world of contingency. From this creed Beauvoir posited that women were additionally living an inauthentic life to the extent that they just did nature's bidding by having children and rearing them. They should search for freedom and authenticity through meaningful actions not connected with biological necessity. The assertion that women could escape biological destiny to forge an existence apart from the family also opened the way to gender theory. A group of translators in the Northampton, Massachusetts, area working under the aegis of H. M.

Parshley made *The Second Sex* available to an anglophone audience in the 1950s, and in 1963 Betty Friedan's *Feminine Mystique* further spread Beauvoir's lines of thought to Americans.

Beauvoir's was not the only French doctrine to lay some of the groundwork for gender theory. During that same postwar period Claude Lévi-Strauss, an anthropologist, developed the theory called structuralism. According to structuralist theory, people in societies lived within frameworks of thought that constituted grids for everyday behavior. These frameworks were generally binary, consisting of oppositions such as pure and impure, raw and cooked, or masculine and feminine. Binaries operated with and against one another as relationships. One could draw from structuralism that in the case of masculine and feminine, these concepts or characteristics were mutually definitional because they shared a common border, which, once crossed, tipped feminine behavior into masculine and vice versa. Although Lévi-Strauss saw these binaries as fixed, the ground was laid once again for seeing masculinity and femininity both as interlocking and as a part of culture, even though a more fixed one, as well as a part of biology.

Lévi-Strauss developed these theories in *The Elementary Structures of Kinship* (1949), in which he took kinship, as the fundamental organizing category of all society, to be based on the exchange of women. The American anthropologist Gayle Rubin elaborated on Lévi-Strauss in "The Traffic in Women" (1975), an article that further developed gender theory. Citing Marxist and Freudian deficiencies in thinking about women and men, Rubin essentially underscored the hierarchical character of the relationship between men and women as an ingredient of what anthropologists and sociologists were coming to call gender: "the subordination of women can be seen as a product of the relationships by which sex and gender are organized and produced." The second point Rubin extrapolated from Lévi-Strauss was that the most important taboo in all societies was the sameness of men and women. This "imperative" of sexual difference was what made "all manifest forms of sex and gender," which were thus "a socially imposed division of the sexes." This imposed sexual difference "transform[ed] males and females into 'men' and 'women.'" By 1980 the phrase "social construction of gender" was commonplace among anthropologists, sociologists, and some psychologists. To quote a 1978 textbook: "Our theoretical position is that gender is a social construction, that a world of two 'sexes' is a result of the socially shared, taken-for-granted methods which members use to construct reality" (Suzanne Kessler, *Gender: An Ethnomethodological Approach*, p. vii).

INFLUENCES FROM PSYCHOANALYSIS, FRENCH FEMINISM, AND FOUCAULT

Rubin's article directed scholars to psychoanalysis, and for some, concepts drawn from psychoanalysis also contributed to gender theory, resulting in a limited number of historical applications by the 1990s. Rubin saw the Oedipal moment, as pinpointed first by Sigmund Freud, as being that moment when the societal norm of sexual difference was installed in each psyche. Her article publicized the French psychoanalyst Jacques Lacan, whose writings fused the insights of Lévi-Strauss with an updated Freudianism. Rubin admitted that Freud, Lévi-Strauss, and Lacan could be seen as advocates for the sexism of the psyche and society, yet she also valued them and urged scholars to value them for the descriptions they provided of sexism as a deeply ingrained psychosocial institution. As a result of Rubin's and others' investigations into psychoanalysis and its relevance to scholarship, some gender theory came to absorb this ingredient too.

Freud's publications between 1899 and 1939 touched on questions of women's sexuality and identity formation. His formulations saw a psychosexual development for women that depended on imaginings of the male phallus, and of the female genitalia as in essence lacking one. Privileging the phallus, as did the little boy, the little girl understood her "lack" and that of her mother as somehow a devaluation of femininity. This drove her to appreciate male superiority and to throw herself eagerly into the arms of a man (first her father and then her husband) as part of the development of a normative, heterosexual femininity with marriage and motherhood—not career—as goals. Boys, in contrast, feared that they might become castrated like their mothers, whose genitals they interpreted as deficient, and thus came to fear their fathers, repress their normal, infantile love for their mothers, and construct an ego and sense of morality based on identification with masculinity and accomplishment. In the case of both boys and girls, however, there were many roads to adult identity based on a number of ways of interpreting biology and the parental imago. Thus, in two regards Freudianism became an important ingredient of gender theory: first, it posited an identity that, although related to biology, nonetheless depended on imaginings of biology in relationship to parental identities. Freeing male and female from a strict biological determinism, Freud furthermore saw psychosexual identity as developing relationally. That is, the cultural power of the male phallus was only important in relationship to feminine lack of the phallus or castration. This relativity of masculine and feminine psyches informed gender theory.

The theories of Jacques Lacan nuanced Freudianism and became both influential and contested in gender theory. Lacan described the nature of the split or fragmented subject in even stronger terms. Freud had seen the rational, sexual, and moral regimes within the self as in perpetual contest. In an essay on the "mirror stage" in human development, Lacan claimed a further, different splitting. The baby gained an identity by seeing the self first in terms of an other—the mother—and in a mirror, that is, again, in terms of an other. Both of these images were fragmented ones because the mother disappeared from time to time, as did the image in the mirror. The self was always this fragmented and relational identity. Lacan also posited language as a crucial influence providing the structures of identity and the medium by which that identity was spoken. In speaking, the self first articulated one's "nom" or name—which was the name of one's "father"—and simultaneously and homonymically spoke the "non," the proscriptions or rules of that language, which Lacan characterized as the laws of the "father" or the laws of the phallus. Lacanianism added to gender theory a further sense of the intertwined nature of masculinity and femininity, beginning with identity as based on the maternal imago and fragmented because of it. Second, it highlighted the utterly arbitrary, if superficially regal, power of masculinity as an extension of the phallus, or cultural version of the male organ. Third, the fantasy nature of the gendered self and indeed of all of human identity and drives received an emphasis that became crucial to some practitioners of gender history.

Under the sign of what came to be known as "French feminism," French theorists picked up on Lacanian, structuralist, and other insights to formulate a position that contributed to gender theory. For these theorists, such as Luce Irigaray, masculine universalism utterly obstructed feminine subjectivity. What Simone de Beauvoir called "the Other" had nothing to do with women but amounted to one more version of masculinity—male self-projection. Women thus appeared as erasure, as lack, and, in Irigaray's *This Sex Which Is Not One* (1985), as unrepresentable in ordinary terms. The woman was the divided, nonunitary, fragmented self. The result for the writing of social history were such compendia as Michelle Perrot's *Une histoire des femmes est-elle possible?* (Is a history of women possible?; 1984). The question of how one writes the history of fragments, "decentered subjects," and other characters for whom there are no historical conventions was addressed in some writing derived from French feminism. To some extent, Joan Scott's *Only Paradoxes to Offer* (1996) tried to execute that project by eliminating biography and story from her account of French feminists.

The French philosopher Michel Foucault contested the standard interpretation of social and political power as a palpable force emanating from a single source. Rather, power was almost a Nietzschean life force circulating through society, thus constituting a mesh in which all people operated. The mesh or grid of power produced subjects or, more commonly, people as they articulated its principles. Thus, for instance, in his famous *History of Sexuality* (1977) Foucault maintained that speaking about sex or behaving in some flauntingly sexual way was not in and of itself a liberatory act but rather an articulation of social rules about sex and thus a participation in power and the law. Foucault saw the work of the modern state as an increasingly invisible implication of people in the exercise of power around bodily issues—thus the sense in his work of biopower present in the activities of doctors, the clergy, government officials, and ordinary reformers. Downplaying or even eliminating the traditional sense of human agency, Foucault's work actually fit with some theories current in social history in the 1970s, notably that branch investigating people's behavior as opposed to their subjectivity.

Many aspects of Foucault's theories immediately fed into French social history of women. Arlette Farge, a French social and cultural historian, described the lives of eighteenth-century Parisians in a Foucauldian manner. That is, reading police and legal records, she saw those lives as "produced" and coming into being in this legal encounter (*La vie fragile: Violence, pouvoirs, et solidarités à Paris au XVIIIe siècle*; 1986). In presenting answers to questioners, they gave shape to their lives, as did neighbors and other witnesses. At the same time, they protested and resisted accusations and characterizations. Farge's accounts also showed the production of gender by the law, although this theory had not yet taken on a definite shape in historical work. Similarly Foucauldian, Alain Corbin's *Les filles de noce: Misère sexuelle et prostitution* (1978) interpreted legalized prostitution as arising from the state's ambition to regulate and oversee even these sexual acts. Life in the brothel had its special textures, but these were sex workers' experience of the state.

POSTSTRUCTURALIST GENDER THEORIES

Although many of these theories had more or less influence on the social history of women, in 1986 they came together when the historian Joan Scott issued a stirring manifesto about gender theory in *American*

Historical Review. Scott's "Gender: A Useful Category of Historical Analysis" asked historians to transform social scientific understandings of gender by adding Lacanian psychoanalysis, Jacques Derrida's deconstruction (a philosophical theory showing the difficulties in assigning definite meanings or truth to texts), and Foucauldian-Nietzschean definitions of power. In her view Marxist, anthropological, and psychological moves toward understanding gender had reached a dead end because they tended to see male and female as having essential or enduring characteristics. Marxism always saw women's issues as inexorably subordinate to issues of class, and feminists who believed in Marxism had no convincing way of explaining men's oppression of women. Nor, for that matter, according to Scott, did those feminist scholars who studied patriarchy or sought out "women's voices." Despite great progress, even those who now followed the lead of the "binary oppositions" of structuralist anthropology could not account for them. The rigidity of the male-female categories in any of these systems, especially in the work of those who sought out women's "voices" and "values," kept gender from being as useful as it could be.

As palliative, Scott considered the way the trio of French theorists could overcome the rigidities of gender theory as it had evolved to the mid-1980s. Lacanian psychoanalysis rested in part on the Swiss linguist Ferdinand de Saussure's understanding of language as a system in which words had meaning only in relationship to one another. It coupled this insight with revised Freudian ideas about the psychic acquisition of identity as a process shaped by the supremely high value placed on the phallus, and it was this value that the symbolic system of language expressed. For Scott, Lacanianism and all the psychic variation it involved were one key to understanding gender as an exigent, inescapable relationship. Foucault's theory of power as a field in which all humans operated offered another valuable insight. Scott suggested that using Foucault allowed for the introduction of gender issues into political history, thus overcoming the separation that historians had maintained between women's history and the political foundation on which most historical writing rested.

Scott also explained that gender could be a category or subject of discussion through which power operated. It could operate thus in several ways. For one, because gender meant differentiation, it could be used to distinguish the better from the worse, the more important from the less important. Using the term "feminine" articulated a lower place in a social or political hierarchy. Additionally, gender explained or assigned meaning to any number of phenomena, including work, the body, sexuality, politics, religion, cultural production, and an infinite number of other historical fields. Because many of these were fields where social history had established itself and where Scott herself had done major work as well, gender theory of her variety found a welcoming audience.

The philosopher Judith Butler offered other poststructuralist versions of gender theory that influenced historians. In two highly celebrated books, *Gender Trouble* (1990) and *Bodies That Matter* (1993), Butler argued against talking of femininity in terms of an essential womanhood. Drawing on a range of theories, Butler proposed to discuss human action less in terms of the behavior of a knowing and conscious subject and more as an iteration of social rules. The fact that actions were the iteration of rules should not lead to fatalism, Butler maintained, for such iterations in appropriate settings could have upsetting consequences and even make for social change. *Bodies That Matter* made an important contribution to debates in gender theory that saw gender as "constructed" and sex or the body as somehow more "real" and determined by biology. Butler's response was to deny "sex" as a ground for the "construction of gender." "Sex" was as constructed as gender, especially the construction of "sex" as being more fundamental or real than gender.

By 1990 Scott, Butler, and other scholars had provided two critiques that shaped the use of gender theory in social history. The first was the critique of universalism, meaning the critique of narratives and analyses that took women as having their womanhood in common. Although social historians had been more conscientious than most in assessing class interests, Marxist tendencies in social history tended to see class as a universal too, one that overrode particularities such as race and gender. The critique of universals particularly brought to the fore women of color and women outside the Western framework of social history. Similarly, the critique of essentialism served to encourage more particularist studies because it denied an essence to womanhood. Denise Riley's *"Am I That Name?": Feminism and the Category of "Women" in History* (1988) showed that womanhood as an essential category was constructed in the nineteenth century to represent the "social" and thus a unified essence. The critique of essentialism went even further, however. Joan Scott's "Evidence of Experience" argued that even the claiming of a group identity or essence based on one's own experience that was shared with others was impossible as an authentic or originary entity. Set in an already constructed world of language and culture, no identity could point to an originary and essential moment of self- or group-formation.

CRITIQUES AND NEW DIRECTIONS

While social-scientifically based theories of gender caused less stir, gender theories that incorporated ideas of Foucault, Derrida, and French femininists initially provoked incredible debate and tension among historians. For one thing, the theories raised hackles as elitist and not accessible to everyone. These were "theories," it was charged, with little relevance to real people's problems. In fact, the unabashed elitism associated with difficult theories made some charge that these theories were actually fascistic. Another parallel with fascism appeared in the contempt with which the traditional Left was often viewed by people who had seen the real "light" of postmodernist gender theory. From a variety of perspectives feminist "theorists" became a target; indeed feminist theory associated with this more psychoanalytical and linguistically oriented variant of gender theory attracted some of the heaviest antipostmodern fire.

Although many merely equated gender history with women's history, to some within the profession it looked like a way once again to move women's history to the back burner. Now that historians were dimly acknowledging the legitimacy of women's history, the argument went, why should such progress be thrown aside to do gender history? In this argument gender theory seemed to be working against women's history, and as people rushed to do the history of the more important sex—men—the old paradigms of eliminating women seemed to have been revived by feminist theorists themselves. Another objection focused on a still different aspect of gender history's connections to postmodernism and especially to the theory of deconstruction as it affected women's history. By this view the questioning of subjectivity and agency contained in postmodernist theory undermined one major goal of women's history, namely, to have women figure as subjects and agents of history. The accomplishments and contributions that women's history had taken such pains to accumulate lost their luster. Moreover, in positing a relational or split subjectivity (when such was allowed), gender theory undermined the positive, independent figuration of women. Whereas women's history had struggled to free accounts of women from a history of the family and men, gender theory seemed to relegate them to the "relational" status that historians in general accorded them.

Finally, critics of gender theory interpreted Freudian strains of that theory as draining away the findings of social history that saw women as "rational" actors in, say, devising family strategies of fertility limitation, patterns of work, household management, or

social movements. For these critics the Freudianism in gender theory resexed women and relegated them to those libidinal, irrational, even hypersexual stereotypes that had heretofore characterized their rare appearances in history. The additions of Lacan were equally suspect to these critics, for his theory seemed less to question masculinity than to put it at the unquestionable heart of all power and value. Any attempt to question the power of the phallus or, by extension, of men was a delusion or sickness. Thus, those among the critics who were feminists—and most were—took the Lacanian aspects of gender theory as antifeminist, even misogynist. As cultural icons, Freud and Lacan became further examples of the automatic leadership awarded to misogynists, including most of the male theorists privileged in social thought.

Theorists of postcolonialism, led in particular by Gayatri Spivak, further altered gender theory when they began looking at the colonial-imperial relationship in postmodernist terms. Spivak asked whether the "subaltern" or colonial, dominated subject could "speak." This question could run the gamut of possibilities, from whether a colonized person had the right to speak to whether the person might be so infused with the values of the dominator that she or he had lost the power to be an agent of his or her own culture. The term "subaltern" had special meaning to those who were both women and colonial subjects. From postcolonial theory, social historians began seeing gender as a product of imperial regimes, specifically as produced in the context of Western dominance and non-Western resistance, submission or both.

The sciences bolstered gender theory, most notably as they came to discuss the lives of those born with ambiguously sexed bodies. In "The Five Sexes," the scientist Ann Fausto-Sterling demonstrated that if one determined "sex" by physiological and chromosomal characteristics, there were five sexes. Society, however, often tried by surgery or other means to pare bodily sex down to two—male and female. In addition parents, doctors, psychologists, and teachers reflected society's inability to deal with more than two sexes. As a result they directed the behavior of those of the nontraditional among the five sexes into the well-established behavior of the standard "male" or "female" gender role. This scientific understanding provided still another reinforcement to the gender theory that claimed the arbitrary, social, and invented nature of gender. Exploring sexual behavior and gender identity in the eighteenth century, for instance, Randolph Trumbach has particularly focused on the transvestite male as a "third sex" social actor.

Not suprisingly, historians developed alternatives to gender history and women's history. The German historian Gisela Bock suggested that both were necessary, each having special virtues and contributions to make to history. The medievalist Judith Bennett suggested that the main goal of women historians should be less gender history than a concerted investigation of patriarchy. Motivated to investigate the sources of women's inferior treatment and status in society, Bennett argued that historians needed to chart the historical creation and operation of patriarchy in all its forms. The American historian Gerda Lerner worked along these lines in *The Creation of Patriarchy* (1986). While some historians of race and colonialism welcomed postmodern and gender theory for its commitment to breaking down wholeness and universals, others questioned the emphasis on fragmented and partial visions. People of color and colonized peoples, these critics argued, had already experienced fragmentation and subordination in their actual lives and in their histories. For them, the position of autonomous subject with a universal history would be a refreshing change, even an imperative one.

GENDER THEORY AND SOCIAL HISTORY

The many varieties of gender theory have shaped the writing of European social history. One of the first areas to feel the effects of gender theory was the history of working- and lower-class women. Judith Walkowitz's *Prostitution and Victorian Society: Women, Class, and the State* (1980) demonstrated the ways in which the Victorians had shaped working-class women's recourse to casual prostitution during the off-season into an identity through state policy. Whereas in working-class communities women's seasonal exchange of sex for money or food did not mark them out, the state's policing of prostitution and the imprisonment and coerced medical exams converted these women from workers to outcasts. Instead of being intrinsic, these women's identity was constructed. After the work of Alain Corbin and Walkowitz, the social history of prostitution intersected with an increasingly sophisticated gender theory. Laurie Bernstein's *Sonia's Daughters: Prostitutes and Their Regulation in Imperial Russia* (1995) saw the regulation of prostitution as an enactment of gender by which female inferiority was expounded as disease and as subjection to a patriarchal state in the guise of doctors, police, and other regulators.

At the heart of postwar social history, the history of work has also gained insights from gender theory, as scholars have looked at agricultural, artisanal, industrial, and service work through its prism. Deborah Valenze's *First Industrial Woman* (1995) showed the modernization of work during the transition in the eighteenth and nineteenth centuries as comprised of gender dimorphism. An expert chapter on dairying and gender illustrated this transformation, as women became less valued workers and men became the quintessential and valued ones, whether in agriculture or cottage industries. Taking on one of the staples of social history, Tessie Liu's *Weaver's Knot* (1994) demonstrated that one of the heroes of social history—the male artisan—only survived as an independent worker because of the proletarian labor of his daughters and wife in nearby factories. In a different work arena Francesca de Haan's *Gender and the Politics of Office Work: The Netherlands 1860–1940* (1998) provided a detailed instance of male-female relationships in the Dutch service sector. Highly skilled, hardworking, and in need of money, women office workers were also harassed, underpaid, limited in their job opportunities, and suspect as workers. Meanwhile men were seen as naturally entitled to office work, especially to promotions and managerial positions. The professions have been equally seen as gendered: Christine Ruane's *Gender, Class, and the Professionalization of Russian City Teachers, 1860-1914* (1994) described the special conditions that produced teaching as a gendered profession. Women could only teach in cities, had to remain unmarried, and were said to require extra training in order to be fit for the job.

Because gender theory called attention to language, social history even of the working classes or of ethnic groups took on many aspects of and sometimes merged with cultural history. For instance, worker autobiographies, seen as suspect in the 1970s because of their elite and exceptional nature, had new possibilities with the validation of language as a subject of inquiry. Mary Jo Maynes's *Taking the Hard Road: Life Course in French and German Workers' Autobiographies in the Era of Industrialization* (1995) explored expressions of gender difference in the life course of working women and men and used literary instead of statistical means. Paula E. Hyman's *Gender and Assimilation in Modern Jewish History* (1995) looked at the way Jewish men in Europe and the United States jettisoned their traditional role of publicly promoting Jewish culture. This reaction to anti-Semitism left Jewish womanhood redefined as the exclusive support of that culture, and the household rather than the public sphere as its locus. Such a change in culture reshaped gender and the social role of men and women.

Since E. P. Thompson's *Making of the English Working Class* (1963), religion had earned a place in social history, but gender theory made the religious experience of women as important as that of the men on whom Thompson had focused. Phyllis Mack's *Vi-*

sionary Women: Ecstatic Prophecy in Seventeenth-Century England (1992) and Deborah Valenze's *Prophetic Sons and Daughters* (1985) showed popular Protestantism offering a place where gender roles could mutate somewhat in both the early modern and modern periods. Dagmar Herzog's *Intimacy and Exclusion: Religious Politics in Pre-Revolutionary Baden* (1996) looked at debates over gendered social issues such as mixed marriages, sexuality, priestly celibacy, and Jewish assimilation as central not only to social identity but also to the highest reaches of politics. Gender theory often played a unifying role in connecting social and cultural issues to politics.

Debates over the history of the middle class had started in women's history with scholarship on their daily lives—especially their contributions to philanthropy—religion, and feminism. Gender history opened other narrative and analytical possibilities. For example, Leonore Davidoff's and Catherine Hall's *Family Fortunes: Men and Women of the English Middle Class, 1780–1850* (1987) charted the formation of men's and women's roles, interests, and activities as gender-specific undertakings over the course of almost a century. In contrast, Anne-Charlott Trepp's *Sanfte Männlichkeit und selbständige Weiblichkeit: Frauen und Männer in Hamburger Bürgertum zwischen 1770 und 1840* (1996) claimed that there was less gender dimorphism among the Hamburg upper classes. Men and women shared child rearing, belief in romantic marriages and rational values, and participation in public causes. Such findings raised questions about the relationship among common social practices and legal and economic structures that generated and enforced male privilege and female inferiority.

The social history of women gained much of its early verve from the study of domesticity, child rearing, outwork—that is, paid labor done in the home—and other aspects of the so-called private sphere. However, when gender theory met studies of the public sphere in the guise of coffeehouses, cafés, academies, and other locations of communal life, social history made for a host of new kinds of studies. The work of Sarah Hanley on early modern France detailed the ways in which male privilege in the family shaped the laws of the state, while it also showed women in daily life and on a microlevel contesting these arrangements. Dena Goodman, among others, showed the salon as a gendered social space and thus gendered the "republic of letters." Isabel Hull claimed that civil society and public space in eighteenth-century Germany was essentially male, leading to the gendering of citizenship. Unlike Goodman and Hanley, Hull put her emphasis on male rather than female activism in society.

Studies of World War I attracted intense gender analysis. Equally mixing social, cultural, and political history, Susan Kingsley Kent's *Making Peace: The Reconstruction of Gender in Interwar Britain* (1993) looked at the war as crucial in reshaping the relationships among men and women and thus in producing new forms of gender and of gender politics. For Kent the issue emerging from the war was how to reconstruct gender relationships after men had been away killing for four years, while women had essentially led very different lives, imagining the war from afar for the most part. Depending on whether they had been at the front or stayed home, women had different views of soldiers and thus of gender relations in peacetime. Those who had remained at home implicitly or explicitly saw soldiers as killers, and the feminists among them espoused separate spheres after the war. Those few women who had actually seen maimed, hysterical, and infantilized soldiers had a more sympathetic view of men and of relations among them. The war thus complicated gender, with sexologists and other social experts playing a large role in "making peace."

As gender theory absorbed ingredients of postmodernism, some historians picked up the thread by which gender was seen as a way of addressing issues other than gender, again in the context of World War I scholarship. Mary Louise Roberts's *Civilization without Sexes: Reconstructing Gender in Postwar France, 1917–1927* (1994) showed the way in which battling over the behavior and characteristics of women allowed society as a whole to address the incredible pain suffered by the French in World War I. Gender was speakable, whereas responsibility for the war and unbearable loss were not. So instead of civilization being menaced by war, civilization was menaced by the loss of traditions of femininity. Those following this paradigm in gender theory tipped their accounts of society perceptibly to cultural history, although social history often formed an unspoken background.

The aspects of social history that focused on social movements and protest were affected in various ways by these changes. Early modern protest and riots came to have gendered components and differentials, producing women and men as social actors. The French Revolution (notably in the work of Joan Landes and Lynn Hunt) was seen as mapping familial relationships and fantasies onto the political landscape. *New Voices in the Nation: Women and the Greek Resistance, 1941–1964* (1996) by Jane Hart saw the gendering of national identity in social movements as well. The work of Atina Grossman and Donna Karsch saw the construction of social agency in gendered protests centered on abortion, birth control, and other social rights. Kate Lacey's *Feminine Frequencies: Gender, German Radio, and the Public Sphere, 1923–1945* (1996) explored the relationship between technology, the public sphere, and women's social behavior.

One stream of gender theory has tried to distinguish between gender and sex, and this has coincided with an interest in sexuality and the body as components of both gender and social history. Some of the history of sexuality and the body has used these fields to show the growth of bureaucracy around sex and gender. James Farr's *Authority and Sexuality in Early Modern Burgundy* (1995) described the criminalization of various kinds of sexual behavior as the act of a patriarchal state creating and sustaining both gender order and its own power. Sabine Kienitz's *Sexualität, Macht, und Moral: Prostitution und Geschlechter erziehungen Anfang des 19. Jahrhunderts in Württemburg* (1995) described post-Napoleonic bureaucrats asserting their prerogatives over a new district by criminalizing longstanding sexual and social practices. In the process women's economic use of their bodies, accepted in the particular town as part of social structure, succumbed to state-building.

Gender theory, while operating on the macro-level of social and political history, has also been successful in allowing for micro studies of the body that have large-scale social implications. Barbara Duden's *The Woman beneath the Skin: A Doctor's Patients in Eighteenth-Century Germany* (1991) used the transcribed words of patients to show a very different experience of a gendered body in relationship to the physician than that announced by Foucault for the modern period. Taking issue with the emphasis on discourse, Lyndal Roper's *Oedipus and the Devil: Witchcraft, Sexuality, and Religion in Early Modern Europe* (1994) argued that the body had a palpable and experienced reality that was prelinguistic but nonetheless gendered. On the basis of this individual experience congealing into collective movement, witchcraft, religious reformation, and other forms of social behavior took shape, especially gendered shapes.

A notable accompaniment to gender theory was the study of masculinity as a constructed, social, and not necessarily natural quantity. Among the first to write in this vein, in *Be a Man!: Males in Modern Society* (1979), the historian Peter Stearns detailed the ways in which manhood consisted of a set of unwritten rules backing explicit exhortations to masculinity. Using the case of nineteenth-century France, Robert Nye explored anxieties about normative masculinity. He examined legal and medical records to determine that "honor" was a central feature of this masculinity. However, he also showed that homosexuality had its constructed side as well, serving as a foil to the nor-

mative. By the 1990s the exploration of masculinity added race and colonialism as variables. Gail Bederman's *Manliness and Civilization: The Culture of Gender and Race in the United States, 1870–1917* (1995) looked at turn-of-the-century masculinity in the United States, seeing whiteness and blackness intertwined in its definition and creating a model for studies in European social history. Mrinalini Sinha's *Colonial Masculinity* (1995) investigated British treatment of Bengali men and those men's internalization or questioning of those norms. Both Sinha and Bederman brought in the activism and responses of Bengali and black women. The opening of gender theory, and particularly that related to masculinity, allowed for breakthroughs in the study of fascism and Nazism. Totalitarianism came to be understood as a set of gendered practices and policies operating at the highest levels and affecting everyday life in society. By 2000 a range of masculinities had been charted for many historic places and eras.

Gender theory has been used to question the foundational practices of history itself. Combined with social history, gender theory applied to historiography and the philosophy of history reconsiders the announced objectivity and standards of the profession as it has evolved since the nineteenth century. Using psychoanalytical and anthropological lines of argument, gender theory looks at historical practices in a way that parallels the studies of science from a social point of view and thus finds a niche in social history. In other words, it explores the values of the profession by investigating its actual practices. These practices judged nonwhite people as inferior when it came to thinking objectively and rationally and put women in the same category. The modernizing profession of history, as a social institution, also relegated women to doing much unacknowledged work, even to the extent of writing histories for men who then got the credit. By these practices, the profession was gendered, creating men as a superior category of professionals and women as an inferior one of uninformed copyists, notetakers, and sometimes readers of men's work. Gender theory also allowed for an understanding of the way in which subject matter about men was featured, once the hierarchy of male to female had been established. Because men were important, the history of men was itself more "significant" than the history of women, who were already established as unimportant in the hierarchy of gender. Along with the objectivity and equality of opportunity in the profession came a constitutive gender bias. Gender theory also allows for a reading of why social history is seen as less important than political history, and an analysis of that hierarchization among scholars.

Gender theory is only of interest to a minority of historians. Many social historians also find it of little value, so that histories of social movements, work, religious behavior, crime, education, death, the professions, ethnic groups, sports, and other aspects of social life do not mention gender. Most of these works thus imply either that the male experience is the only important one or that it can stand for everyone's. Others do not discuss gender because they want to focus on class, race, or other issues, and do not see these categories as developed in tandem with gender, as many gender theorists believe. However, all denigrations of gender theory can be read in a gendered way, in which class and race are seen as superior masculine categories, whereas gender is seen as inferior. Not all histories that deal explicitly with women, finally, use gender theory in any self-conscious way. They may proceed empirically, with few wider historical referents. The multiplicity and complexity of gender theories may encourage this gap. But since the mid-1980s use of theory in dealing with women (and sometimes men) in history has increased, providing a richer conceptual framework and a new means of linking specific historical topics to larger issues and comparisons.

See also other articles in this section and the articles in the Gender section in volume 4.

BIBLIOGRAPHY

Beauvoir, Simone de. *The Second Sex.* Translated and edited by H. M. Parshley. New York, 1952.

Bederman, Gail. *Manliness and Civilization: A Cultural History of Gender and Race in the United States, 1870–1917.* Chicago, 1995.

Bernstein, Laurie. *Sonia's Daughters: Prostitutes and Their Regulation in Imperial Russia.* Berkeley, Calif., 1995.

Butler, Judith. *Gender Trouble: Feminism and the Subversion of Identity.* New York, 1990.

Davidoff, Leonore, and Catherine Hall. *Family Fortunes: Men and Women of the English Middle Class, 1780–1850.* Chicago, 1987.

Duden, Barbara. *The Woman beneath the Skin: A Doctor's Patients in Eighteenth-Century Germany.* Translated by Thomas Dunlap. Cambridge, Mass., 1991.

Farge, Arlette. *Fragile Lives: Violence, Power, and Solidarity in Eighteenth-Century Paris.* Translated by Carol Shelton. Cambridge, Mass., 1993.

Foucault, Michel. *History of Sexuality.* Translated by Robert Hurley. New York, 1978.

Haan, Francesca de. *Gender and the Politics of Office Work: The Netherlands 1860–1940.* Amsterdam, 1998.

Herzog, Dagmar. *Intimacy and Exclusion: Religious Politics in Pre-Revolutionary Baden.* Princeton, N.J., 1985.

Hull, Isabel V. *Sexuality, State, and Civil Society in Germany, 1700–1815.* Ithaca, N.Y., 1996.

Hyman, Paula E. *Gender and Assimilation in Modern Jewish History: The Roles and Representation of Women.* Seattle, Wash., 1995.

Irigaray, Luce. *This Sex Which Is Not One.* Translated by Catherine Porter with Carolyn Burke. Ithaca, N.Y., 1985.

Kent, Susan Kingsley. *Making Peace: The Reconstruction of Gender in Interwar Britain.* Princeton, N.J., 1993.

Lacey, Kate. *Feminine Frequencies: Gender, German Radio, and the Public Sphere, 1923–1945.* Ann Arbor, Mich., 1996.

Lévi-Strauss, Claude. *Elementary Structures of Kinship.* Translated by James Harle Bell, John Richard von Sturmes, and Rodney Needham. Boston, 1969.

Liu, Tessie P. *The Weaver's Knot: The Contradictions of Class Struggle and Family Solidarity in Western France, 1750–1914.* Ithaca, N.Y., 1994.

Mack, Phyllis. *Visionary Women: Ecstatic Prophecy in Seventeenth-Century England.* Berkeley, Calif., 1992.

Mead, Margaret. *Coming of Age in Samoa: A Psychological Study of Primitive Youth for Western Civilization.* New York, 1928.

Perrot, Michelle, ed. *Une histoire des femmes est-elle possible?* Paris, 1984.

Riley, Denise. *"Am I That Name?": Feminism and the Category of "Women" in History.* Minneapolis, Minn., 1988.

Roberts, Mary Louise. *Civilization without Sexes: Reconstructing Gender in Postwar France, 1917–1927* Chicago, 1994.

Roper, Lyndal. *Oedipus and the Devil: Witchcraft, Sexuality, and Religion in Early Modern Europe.* London and New York, 1994.

Rubin, Gayle. "The Traffic in Women: Notes on the 'Political Economy' of Sex." In *Feminism and History.* Edited by Joan Wallach Scott. Oxford and New York, 1996. Pages 105–151.

Scott, Joan Wallach. *Gender and the Politics of History.* New York, 1988.

Scott, Joan Wallach. *Only Paradoxes to Offer: French Feminists and the Rights of Man.* Cambridge, Mass., 1996.

Sinha, Mrinalini. *Colonial Masculinity: The "Manly Englishman" and the "Effeminate Bengali" in the Late Nineteenth Century.* New York, 1995.

MICROHISTORY

Karl Appuhn

Microhistory is a historical method that takes as its object of study the interactions of individuals and small groups with the goal of isolating ideas, beliefs, practices, and actions that would otherwise remain unknown by means of more conventional historical strategies. Microhistory emerged, primarily in Italy, in the late 1970s and early 1980s, as a revolt against studies of large social groups and long, gradual historical transformations. The first microhistorians were especially dissatisfied with then predominant social history methods that concentrated on broad subjects over extremely long periods of time, the famous *longue durée*. The microhistorians also objected to the increasingly popular use of quantitative methods inspired by the French *Annales* practitioners, the Cambridge Population Group, and American cliometricians. The source of the microhistorians' frustration was the fact that quantitative approaches tend to reduce the lives of millions to a few economic and demographic data points. The microhistorians' response to these perceived weaknesses in social history, as it was then widely practiced, was to attempt to create a new method that would allow historians to rediscover the lived experience of individuals, with the aim of revealing how those individuals interacted not only with one another, but also with the broader economic, demographic, and social structures that traditional social history had taken as its subject matter.

The term "microhistory" was first coined by a group of Italian historians associated with the journal *Quaderni Storici* and, later, a series of books, *microstorie,* published by Einaudi. The most influential were Carlo Ginzburg, Edoardo Grendi, Giovanni Levi, and Carlo Poni. Together they began to define the theoretical underpinnings of what became known as microhistory. Some French and North American scholars soon followed suit, but their efforts lacked the programmatic dimension of the Italians' work. Thus it was the *Quaderni Storici* group that largely established the terms of debate and the boundaries of the method from an early date, and without them microhistory might not have become a distinct practice.

The Italian microhistorians' interest in the historic variations in people's lived experience of the world was heavily influenced by developments in cultural anthropology in the 1960s and 1970s. The work of Clifford Geertz was particularly important to the emergence of microhistory, even if some of the microhistorians, Giovanni Levi in particular, had reservations about Geertz's method. Geertz had popularized a concept of culture as a system of symbols that permits individuals to relate to and comprehend the external world. In his influential essays, "Thick Description: Toward an Interpretive Theory of Culture," and "Deep Play: Notes on the Balinese Cockfight," Geertz had argued that the key to discovering how these various systems of symbols operated lay not in establishing general rules, but rather in observing the various parts of the system in operation and only then trying to fit them into a larger frame of reference. The rules of social interaction, according to Geertz, could only be reconstructed by inserting the behavior of individual actors into specific social contexts, from which far broader interpretations of a particular cultural group or system could then be derived. Geertz's method, therefore, has two equally important dimensions. On the one hand, the analysis must be grounded in the actions and understandings of individuals. On the other, it must seek to arrive at systemic explanations for group behavior based on rules that are reconstructed by careful analysis of those individual actions.

The quality and nature of the systemic explanations that can be derived from Geertz's method are very different from similar explanations generated by methods based on observing only the larger group. Close observation of individuals in action provides a better description of a particular social system, because it tends to emphasize the unique forces at work instead of relying on universal rules of human behavior to explain individual actions. Geertz was convinced that universal rules, whatever their apparent utility as explanatory tools, were flawed, because every system of social exchange is unique. His method was aimed explicitly at recovering the unique features of different cultures and showing how these provide the foundations for group organization, not some supposedly universal feature of human behavior such as rational choice or self-interest. Geertz's admonishment to anthropologists in the field, therefore, was to studiously avoid starting with a general theory or hypothesis, and instead to allow the accumulated data to suggest the interpretive techniques to be employed in each particular case study. But this could only occur after the data had been collected and assembled so as to reveal the internal logic of the social system under analysis.

Geertz's definition of culture and his approach to fieldwork and ethnographic study were adapted to the needs of history by the microhistorians. Like Geertz, the microhistorians saw culture and social interaction as a complex system of rules and meanings. These rules and meanings were established, in part, by larger social and economic structures, the traditional focus of social history. But the system was also defined by the participants' interactions with each other, and by the particular ways in which they came into contact with broader economic and social structures. It was this experiential dimension of structure that the microhistorians felt social history had largely ignored with its volumes of statistics aimed at creating generalized understandings of historical change.

Like Geertz, the microhistorians were concerned that generalized rules eliminated the cultural distinctiveness of groups, making history the study of people who were, in the end, and in most ways that matter, like us. The microhistorians wanted to avoid this mistake by creating a conceptual and interpretive distance between the historian and the subjects of history. Social history had failed to do this, the microhistorians argued, and thus had often made claims about people in the past that had more to do with our own present conditions than they did with the lives of the people being studied. The microhistorians, therefore, began with the assumption that the past was completely foreign to them. Whatever similarities might appear to exist between the past and the present must be ignored in the interests of discovering the unique features and dimensions of past societies. Carlo Ginzburg summed the process up nicely, describing it as "making the past dead."

PRINCIPLES OF MICROHISTORY

Adapting an anthropological approach to the study of history presented the microhistorians with a number of challenges. The most obvious lay in the difference between ethnographic fieldwork and archival history:

the historian cannot directly observe, interact, or interview the individuals or groups being studied, which creates considerable evidentiary problems. The microhistorians' response was to define new ways of approaching documentary evidence and archival research. The program they developed was aimed at sifting through the evidence looking for traces, however small, of the sorts of social interactions that formed the basis of Geertz's anthropological method. The accumulation of tiny, seemingly trivial bits of evidence would eventually, the microhistorians hoped, enable them to assemble the data into coherent models of specific small-scale social interactions from which they could then, like Geertz, draw much broader conclusions.

The nominative approach. To meet the evidentiary challenge posed by their new method, the *Quaderni Storici* group established a handful of governing principles for microhistory. The most important method involved the reduction of the scale of historical investigation to accurately identifiable individuals. Ginzburg and Poni, in their 1979 *Quaderni Storici* article "Il nome e il come" (translated by Edward Muir as "The Name and the Game") argued that the fundamental unit of analysis for the microhistorian should be people's names, since these may be traced, compared, and confirmed through a wide variety of archival sources, including tax records, birth registers, notarial contracts, and court cases.

Tracing the names of individuals across different documentary sources, Ginzburg and Poni argued, brings into faint relief the outlines of their social world. In the course of an individual's documented lifetime, he or she would come into contact with countless other people as well as official institutions in ways that can be reconstructed by historians. Let us take a single, hypothetical individual as our example. Our subject might appear any number of times in a well-preserved archive, as many significant events in his or her life were formally recorded. Parish records would contain our subject's birth, marriage, and death. A notary's register might contain the terms of the dowry, if any; property transactions of various sorts; business dealings and practices in the form of contracts, partnership agreements, or even bankruptcies; and last, but not least, our subject's testamentary bequests. Tax rolls would provide some notion of our subject's total wealth, and court records would allow us a glimpse of what sorts of disputes, if any, our subject was involved in, as well as how they were resolved. Best of all, the chain of evidence could be picked up at any point along the line, allowing us to work outward to discover the rest.

Taken individually, these scraps of evidence do not seem to amount to much. Yet taken all together, it is possible to trace in broad outline many, if not most, of the important social connections in our subject's life, especially if other identifiable individuals appear often. Once we have assembled the data, we have not only one individual's life, but a significant portion of the social and economic networks within which that person lived. These networks, in turn, ideally reveal both the opportunities and constraints faced by our subject in the course of his or her life, in other words some notion of the person's lived experience.

This hypothetical case also reveals one of the major reasons why microhistory emerged in Italy and not elsewhere. To conduct a study based on the nominative methodology proposed by the microhistorians requires an archive, or in many cases a number of archives, containing many intact sources. Italian archives are by far the richest in Europe in terms of the size and chronological scope of their holdings, and also in terms of the variety of documents they contain, especially the court cases that have provided the most common starting point for microhistorical studies. The Italians had everything from parish birth records to tax rolls to notarial registers available to them in numbers that were often unimaginable elsewhere. Without a similar trove of documents, the nominative approach proposed by the microhistorians would have been inconceivable.

The evidential paradigm. Another microhistorical principle involves a standard of historical proof that Carlo Ginzburg termed the "evidential paradigm," sometimes referred to in English as the "conjectural paradigm." The evidential paradigm suggests that small-scale historical analysis requires not only different techniques of investigation than broader studies, but different standards of evidence and proof as well. The approach has most often been likened to the detective's search for clues at the scene of a crime, in which evidence such as fingerprints rather than the principle of human nature or the larger social conditions that helped create the environment for the crime is used to discover the identity of a particular guilty individual. In a similar fashion the microhistorian uses documentary evidence to uncover the particular motivations, beliefs, ideologies, and worldviews of specific individuals rather than of larger social groups.

As a method, the evidential paradigm is diametrically opposed to the techniques employed by most social historians. In quantitative analyses of historical phenomena the historian looks for statistically significant correlations that provide empirical proof of how most people acted in particular situations. Like

the detective, the microhistorian is hardly interested in how most people behaved. Rather, it is the statistically insignificant deviant who stands out. Ginzburg argued that the traces left behind by exceptional acts and behaviors can reveal previously unknown dimensions of human experience. At the same time, he admitted this necessarily requires a certain amount of conjecture on the part of the historian, because the conclusions that can be drawn from exceptional acts are rarely based on the same types of supposedly verifiable data as broader quantitative studies. Ginzburg posited that the degree to which research concentrated on the individual is inversely proportional to the degree that anything resembling a scientific method can be applied to the study of history. Therefore, the microhistorian must attempt to formulate a hypothesis based on incomplete evidence, rather than use large amounts of data to confirm or disprove some initial theory about past behavior. In essence, microhistory starts from a set of surprising facts and proceeds to seek out a theory that helps explain them. It does not, however, prove the theory, it merely suggests that a particular theory may provide the best available explanation.

CRITICISM AND DEFENSE OF MICROHISTORY

Not surprisingly, the inescapable need for creative conjecture is the feature of microhistorical analysis that has been most often criticized. Historians, especially quantitatively minded ones, have pointed out that the evidential paradigm allows for apparently boundless speculation, precisely because it often rests on conjecture rather than rigorous proof. Moreover, the argument goes, statistically insignificant occurrences are just that. Other Italian historians such as Angelo Venturi were particularly harsh, accusing the microhistorians of, at best, producing trivial history based on the study of trivial data, and, at worst, simply writing historical novels.

Conjecture and relativism. Although the Italian microhistorians defended themselves vigorously from such attacks, they were also quite aware of the dangers inherent in their method. Giovanni Levi advocated caution when employing anthropological techniques for historical research. His major concern centered around the inherent relativism of cultural anthropology. Within the discipline of anthropology a certain type of relativism has the important function of guarding against ethnocentric interpretations and hierarchical rankings of different cultures. Thus for the anthropologist it is crucial to remain open to a wide variety of interpretations of human choices and actions. One effect of this approach that has already been mentioned is the notion that features of human behavior, such as human rationality, that seem to be universal are actually contingent upon the cultural systems that produce them. Such an assertion effectively prevents comparisons between different cultural understandings of the world, providing an effective safeguard against ethnocentric arguments. The obvious danger of such an approach, however, is that the scholar possesses a potentially uncomfortable degree of latitude in deciding what things mean in different situations, and can assign value and meaning to different human behaviors that they may not possess. For anthropologists this freedom is an essential feature of their discipline, which rests in some measure on the scholar's capacity for creative interpretation. For historians, on the other hand, too much interpretive freedom violates the empirical conceits that have been an essential part of historical practice since at least the nineteenth century.

Levi was keenly aware that an unconsidered application of the anthropological methods from which microhistory was derived would open the door to needless relativism. After all, the ability to draw explicit comparisons between different ways of understanding the world is an essential feature of historical practice. Without the ability to draw such comparisons, there would be no way of effectively describing historical differences and changes. Moreover, the type of creative interpretation prized by anthropologists would, if used without reflection by historians, give weight to the criticisms of Venturi and others that the microhistorians were merely in the business of producing historical fiction.

Levi's prescription against this eventuality was to reiterate the microhistorians' commitment to a more traditional historical understanding of human rationality. Levi insisted that while interpretive latitude may be acceptable in anthropology, historians had to employ more formal and restricted notions of social and economic structure, human behavior, and, most importantly, the relative value of rationality. Historians could not, in Levi's view, afford to engage in too much creative interpretation, but had to be constantly mindful that while humans' ways of understanding the world are historically and culturally contingent, they are bounded and restricted by hard realities such as social class and economic power. For example, a creative historical interpretation of raucous sixteenth-century carnival celebrations might see them as a way for peasants and artisans to invert the social hierarchy for a day. The careful historian, however,

would also recognize that this did not mean that the participants thought they were actually changing that hierarchy. In a purely anthropological interpretation based on a highly relative understanding of rationality, the capacity to produce a symbolic language of social inversion and changing the social order might be seen as nearly the same thing. For the historian these two things, thought and belief, or thought and action, had to remain separate. In other words, the symbolic language of culture may be an attempt by individuals to shape reality, but the historian must ultimately recognize that reality usually resists our best efforts to mold it. A restricted level of interpretation that recognizes this fact would, according to Levi, shield the microhistorians from their critics.

The normal exception. Another defense of the method mounted by the *Quaderni Storici* group attacked the critics through the quantitative methods they often favored. Edoardo Grendi suggested a corollary idea to the evidential paradigm based on the statistical concept of the normal exception. Because the individuals whose lives are unearthed by the nominative methods employed by microhistorians are most often exceptional in some way, they should be treated as statistically significant even though they do not appear at first glance to be representative. One of the easiest places in the chain of documents to find likely individuals for microhistorical inquiry has been in trial records, especially the proceedings of the Inquisition. Therefore, the microhistorian often ends up studying individuals whose behavior automatically places them on the social margins. The concept of the normal exception holds that while such statistically insignificant behavior is not representative of the majority of people, it may well be that it is representative of some smaller group whose existence remains hidden to standard data collection techniques.

It has been precisely for such marginal groups that microhistorical methods have proven most fruitful. However, while the most famous microhistories, such as Carlo Ginzburg's *The Cheese and the Worms* or Natalie Zemon Davis's *The Return of Martin Guerre,* have dealt with obviously marginal or exceptional members of society such as heretics and criminals, some lesser-known studies have demonstrated the ability to uncover the existence of invisible groups and activities that might fairly be termed mainstream. For example, Edoardo Grendi, in his study of the small Ligurian town of Cervo, focused on the economic practices of the local elite to show how their decisions were governed by social connections that were almost completely extrinsic to market forces. In a similar vein, Giovanni Levi discovered that the real estate market in a town he was investigating employed a socially established set of rules for fixing property values rather than a market-driven system. In both cases, the findings revealed the existence of elite groups whose business strategies were almost exactly the opposite of what one would normally expect to find based on typical studies of emergent early modern capitalism. In essence, the individuals that Grendi and Levi studied behaved in an apparently irrational fashion, at least if one starts from the hypothesis that the sixteenth century saw the birth of *homo economicus*. But in terms of the everyday social reality of their lives, their lived experience, their decision not to follow the market made perfect sense, for while it may not have been profitable, it helped preserve the social order. This is the promise of the evidential paradigm realized.

To the Italian microhistorians the evidential paradigm with its technique of extrapolating from small bits of evidence to reach broader conclusions constituted the crux of their new method. As individuals, they argued, we relate to the world through the particular, creating understandings of the larger world through the accumulation of small fragmentary pieces of data. The microhistorical method mirrors this aspect of human existence, attempting to reconstruct the sometimes peculiar ways in which individuals have tried to understand the larger world from within the confines of their personal experiences. However, while the Italian microhistorians were revolting against the broad structuralist work of the *Annales* school, they were in no sense antistructuralists. Nearly all of them were dedicated marxists who had brought to microhistory a strong commitment to structuralist analysis in history. In the broadest sense, they were simply trying to re-create the ways in which past people understood and reacted to social and economic structures, which, as the above examples make clear, is not always as obvious as the historian might wish. The microhistorians were particularly interested in the ways in which structure constrained individual choice, and the ways that people shaped their lives in response to those constraints. In other words, they wanted to escape the sometimes simplistic functionalism of the social historians without in any way denying the importance or power of social and economic structure.

The data dictate the method.

One of the best examples of how this movement from individual experience to broader structure, with an eye toward the possibility of the far-reaching conclusion, works in practice remains Carlo Ginzburg's study of the trial of a heretic miller known as Menocchio in sixteenth-century Friuli: *The Cheese and the Worms*. Ginzburg first assembled Menocchio's often conflicting testimony before the inquisition in which he tried to explain to his accusers why he held beliefs that seemed at odds with catholic orthodoxy, including the somewhat odd notion that God had created the world in the same way as peasants made cheese. Ginzburg showed how the relationships between Menocchio's various beliefs revealed how he had constructed a very personal cosmology that drew elements from local beliefs, Catholic doctrine, and a variety of books he had read over a period of many years, not all of which Menocchio could identify by title. Employing philological techniques, Ginzburg spent considerable time and care attempting to reconstruct Menocchio's reading list based on textual clues contained in his testimony before the inquisitors. His most surprising speculation was that Menocchio might have had access to a translated copy of the Koran. From this reconstruction Ginzburg then drew some much larger conclusions about the early spread of print culture to the lower classes and how peasants and other marginally literate people understood the new medium.

Ginzburg's study of Menocchio remains one of the classics of the genre, yet it also points to one of the central problems that historians have faced when attempting to formulate a satisfactory definition for microhistory. It remains very difficult to define, precisely because it is not a coherent set of practices or methods. The philological techniques and cultural model of the spread of print culture employed by Ginzburg bear little resemblance to the economic data and sociological model employed by Grendi in his study of the town of Cervo. Superficially at least, these two studies could easily be seen as belonging to two different genres entirely. Yet they are both microhistory. One might fairly say, therefore, that microhistory is the absence of any specific method, and a recognition that each individual historical case and each set of historical data demands a unique approach. The data dictate the analytical method to be employed, not the other way around.

While the absence of a consistent method has hampered attempts to provide a pat definition of microhistory, it has also allowed for an extremely wide variety of studies to be conducted under its banner. Microhistorical studies have been produced examining everything from legal practices, religious beliefs, and gender roles, to real estate markets, counterfeiting rings, and the economies of entire towns. And while the first microhistorical studies concentrated exclusively on the lives of otherwise obscure individuals or small groups, later studies by Carlo Ginzburg and Pietro Redondi reexamined the lives of famous individuals such as the artist Piero della Francesca and the astronomer Galileo Galilei respectively. But while the fame of the individuals changed, the method did not. Redondi's study of Galileo, for example, used a previously unknown document from his trial to speculate that Galileo's belief in atomism was far more troubling to his accusers than his heliocentric astronomy, because atomism potentially undermined the doctrine of transubstantiation. While Redondi has been criticized for substituting an obscure and complicated explanation for a simple and obvious one, his analysis did reveal a dimension of the infamous proceedings that had not been recognized in any of the scores of previous studies.

DIVERGENCE FROM THE MODEL

Flexibility, as these examples illustrate, is perhaps the greatest strength of microhistory. It has, however, revealed itself to be an impediment as well, especially when it has come to fending off the critics. Because microhistory has few methodological limitations, once the idea had spread beyond the *Quaderni Storici* group, there were very few restrictions on how the new technique would be employed in practice. Indeed, subsequent historians from many different intellectual and methodological backgrounds have often made use of microhistory in ways its founders never intended.

Divergence from the Italian model has been most apparent in the North American context, where microhistory soon began to assume new and different forms. American practitioners of the new cultural history, who were engaged in their own revolt against large-scale social history, latched onto the method as a way of recovering individual agency in history. The differences between this approach and that of the Italians are important. Whereas the Italians were primarily concerned with the limits imposed on individual agency, Americans were concerned with the ways in which people were able to bypass or even subvert structure. In many ways such an approach more closely mimics the anthropological models on which microhistory was based. Many of the microhistorical studies produced in North America tended to ignore the ways in which structure operated to limit the choices of individuals and moved toward interpretations that saw individuals thwarting social structures through the creation of personal visions of reality.

Agency at the expense of structure. The increasing emphasis on agency at the expense of structure was precisely the development that Giovanni Levi had warned against in his discussion of Geertz's method. Indeed, Levi was also outspoken in his criticism of North American works such as Robert Darnton's essay "Workers Revolt: The Great Cat Massacre of the Rue Saint-Séverin," which interpreted a slaughter of cats by a group of Parisian printer's apprentices and journeymen as both a symbolic and real revolt against the existing social and economic order. Levi argued that while such microhistorical studies may be interesting as interpretive exercises, they are of limited use as historical examples because they are ultimately imponderable and meaningless. Concentrating on agency rather than structure serves, in Levi's opinion, only to illuminate the case under scrutiny. In the case of Darnton's cat massacre, the example was revealing only of the dissatisfaction of a few individuals, and did not provide any additional insight into existing understandings of eighteenth-century French society. Agency alone, according to Levi, reveals very little. Only by focusing on structure can the microhistorian hope to formulate hypotheses that have meaning beyond the bounds of a particular moment or incident.

Criticisms of North American microhistory that were already familiar in the Italian context also began to surface. In 1988 the *American Historical Review* published a debate between Robert Finlay and Natalie Zemon Davis concerning her well-known microhistory, *The Return of Martin Guerre,* which analyzed the trial of a sixteenth-century French peasant accused of posing as someone else for the purpose of wrongfully claiming the other man's wife and property. Like Angelo Venturi before him, Finlay accused Davis of writing history that was little more than fiction. Historians, Finlay argued, have a responsibility not to distort the sources they work with. Davis's contention that the accused was in league with the wife was just such a distortion, Finlay claimed, because while he was found guilty, she was cleared of any wrongdoing by the court and her relatives. The documents contained nothing to suggest her complicity, and, therefore, Davis could not responsibly suggest otherwise, or she risked ascribing false motives to real people.

Davis defended herself by pointing out the degree to which she had created a context within which to situate her interpretations through painstaking descriptions of sixteenth-century legal culture and village life. Her conclusions were also justified, she claimed, because the chronicles she had used as her sources already contained significant distortions and interpretations of the events. The only way to discover what happened and what significance it had was to engage in an interpretive exercise aimed at eliminating the distortions contained in the sources. Finlay's overly literal reliance on the source material constituted its own kind of distortion, Davis argued, one that microhistorical methods can at least attempt to rectify.

The debate between Finlay and Davis suggests that despite the best efforts of the microhistorians to guard themselves against the criticisms of empirically minded historians, the problem may ultimately be intractable. While there have certainly been cases of interpretive excess, these have been limited to a few works, and serve more as a reminder of the dangers involved than as a condemnation of the method. Yet the critics remain convinced that any interpretive method such as the evidential paradigm constitutes a distortion of history. The microhistorians also remain convinced that empirical methods distort history by masking variety and difference. There is probably little to be done to reconcile these opposing views.

OTHER LIMITATIONS OF MICROHISTORY

The relentless attention to the interpretive issue has also distracted from other limitations of microhistory for which there may be no immediate solution. Historians are generally faced with the problem of describing phenomena in two, somewhat incompatible, dimensions. In the synchronic dimension most commonly associated with the discipline, the historian must tell a story of change over time. In the diachronic dimension, the historian must offer convincing descriptions of specific moments in time. Microhistory's strengths obviously lie in its ability to provide densely researched diachronic descriptions. This again reflects the use of anthropological methods, which are notoriously unconcerned with change. Likewise, microhistory does not lend itself to effective synchronic narratives. Often, this is the result of practical considerations. The microhistorian is required to spend so much time, effort, and space exploring the implications of a few painstakingly researched events that to expand the boundaries of one case study would be unwieldy.

Microhistory's apparent inability to account for change, however, is also the result of conceptual limitations. The limitation imposed by anthropology on comparative analysis has already been discussed in the context of Giovanni Levi's criticism of Geertz. Levi's proposed solution of employing a restricted interpretive technique, however, has not effectively addressed the issue of synchronic change. In part this is because his arguments were intended as a response to the empirical historians' criticisms of microhistory as much as they were to refining the technique itself. His argument, therefore, focuses on the ways in which culture can be described by the historian, not the mechanisms through which social change eventually occurs.

One potential solution has been suggested by William Sewell, whose analysis of Geertz's technique focuses on the categories employed for analyzing the functions served by culture. Geertz asserts that cultural systems provide "models of" and "models for" reality. The first type of model claims to provide a template for describing and reproducing reality. The second reflects the way that existing social and cultural conditions provide the basis for judging new productions. Scholars who have been influenced by Geertz, including historians, have not recognized, according to Sewell, the extent to which these two functions of culture are different. That is to say, there is often an obvious disjuncture between the reality that is being described in "models of" and the conditions that are being judged and reproduced in "models for." Sewell posits that it is this disjuncture that drives historical change, as people attempt to make the two models coincide in their lived experience.

In terms of microhistory, the original Italian technique may be said to concentrate on the "model of" aspect of culture, while North American practices have concentrated on the "model for" aspect. Sewell's analysis, therefore, not only offers a way of incorporating a mechanism for historical change into microhistorical analysis, but it also provides a way to bridge the gap between the social microhistory of the Italians and the cultural microhistory of the North Americans. There are already signs that this is happening, as Italian scholars employed in American universities have begun to incorporate features of both types of analysis.

Nevertheless, the general lack of synchronic analysis in most microhistories is not damning by itself. After all, the ability to describe change effectively is one of the great strengths of the traditional social history, and therefore need not be a major concern for microhistorians. In this sense it is important to recall that while the Italian microhistorians were critical of social history, they never envisioned their method as a replacement for *Annales* school studies, which they ultimately admired. Rather, the microhistorians wanted to expand the possibilities of social history by adding depth of analysis to the breadth of existing narratives. The synchronic dimension is, therefore, less important than might seem immediately apparent, as traditional social history already tends to provide the larger narrative within which the Italian microhistorians situated their own work. Indeed, microhistory's greatest success has been its ability to reveal the hidden mechanisms at work in social history and provide more subtle interpretations of group behavior. Thus, even if microhistory never manages to reinterpret the process of historical change, it has still provided a meaningful contribution to debates in social history.

See also other articles in this section.

BIBLIOGRAPHY

Brucker, Gene. *Giovanni and Lusanna: Love and Marriage in Renaissance Florence.* Berkeley, Calif., 1986.

Darnton, Robert. "Workers Revolt: The Great Cat Massacre of Rue Saint-Séverin." In his *The Great Cat Massacre and Other Episodes in French Cultural History.* New York, 1984. Pages 75–104.

Davis, Natalie Zemon. *The Return of Martin Guerre.* Cambridge, Mass., 1983.

Davis, Natalie Zemon, and Robert Finlay. "AHR Forum: *The Return of Martin Guerre.* The Refashioning of Martin Guerre." *The American Historical Review* 93 (June 1988): 553–603.

Geertz, Clifford. "Deep Play: Notes on the Balinese Cockfight." In his *The Interpretation of Cultures.* New York, 2000. Pages 412–453.

Geertz, Clifford. "Thick Description: Toward an Interpretive Theory of Culture." In his *The Interpretation of Cultures.* New York, 2000. Pages 3–30.

Ginzburg, Carlo. *The Cheese and the Worms: The Cosmos of a Sixteenth-Century Miller.* Translated by John Tedeschi and Anne Tedeschi. Baltimore, Md., 1980.

Ginzburg, Carlo. "Clues: Roots of an Evidential Paradigm." In his *Clues, Myths, and the Historical Method.* Baltimore, Md., 1989. Pages 96–125.

Ginzburg, Carlo. *The Enigma of Piero: Piero della Francesca: The Baptism, the Arezzo Cycle, the Flagellation.* Translated by Martin Ryle and Kate Soper. London, 1985.

Ginzburg, Carlo, and Carlo Poni. "The Name and the Game: Unequal Exchange and the Historiographical Marketplace." In *Microhistory and the Lost Peoples of Europe.* Edited by Edward Muir and Guido Ruggiero. Baltimore, Md., 1991. Pages 1–10.

Levi, Giovanni. *Inheriting Power: The Story of an Exorcist.* Translated by Lydia G. Cochrane. Chicago, 1988.

Levi, Giovanni. "On Micro-History." In *New Perspectives on Historical Writing.* Edited by Peter Burke. University Park, Pa., 1992. Pages 93–113.

Muir, Edward, and Guido Ruggiero, eds. *Microhistory and the Lost Peoples of Europe.* Translated by Eren Branch. Baltimore, Md., 1991.

Redondi, Pietro. *Galileo Heretic.* Translated by Raymond Rosenthal Princeton, N.J., 1987.

Sewell, William H., Jr. "Geertz, Cultural Systems, and History." In *The Fate of Culture: Geertz and Beyond.* Edited by Sherry B. Ortner. Berkeley, Calif., 1999. Pages 35–55.

COMPARATIVE EUROPEAN SOCIAL HISTORY

Hartmut Kaelble

Since the 1970s comparative European social history has become a growing field of research by European historians. Comparative books crucial for history in general were published by European historians in fields such as family history, the middle class, the lower middle class, workers and labor movements, intellectuals and professionals, private and public bureaucracy, city planning, the welfare state, national consciousness and national ceremonies, religion and denominations, consumption, society at war, and the historical social peculiarities of Europe.

About twenty to thirty books and articles on comparative European history are published each year, with pronounced fluctuations from one year to the next. This may seem a small output, but, in fact, among the subdisciplines of history, works of comparative research in social history comprise a fair number. Comparative social history is built upon a long tradition of comparing societies in history. Notable classical historians and historical sociologists of the first half of the twentieth century, such as Max Weber, Otto Hintze, and Marc Bloch, had published in comparative social history and, in contrast to other historians of the period, were continuously read and discussed by historians. In spite of these encouraging classical texts, however, comparative social history was very rarely explored by historians until the late 1970s.

REASONS FOR THE RISE
OF COMPARATIVE SOCIAL HISTORY

The reasons for the rise of comparative social history have to do not only with the background of the discipline itself but also with social history in general. Without the international rise of social history since about the 1950s and 1960s—as documented by this encyclopedia—comparative social history is unimaginable. Comparative history must draw from a much larger body of historical research; it must ask similar questions concerning different countries. Only a large number of social historians will in the end produce

some comparativists. To be sure, the most influential pioneers of the first generation of European social historians did not produce influential models of comparisons. The first big debates in social history, such as on the living standard during the industrial revolution, on the labor aristocracy, and on the utility of the marxist concept of social class, were sometimes international but almost never comparative. The most widely read and sold books in social history were na-

DEFINING COMPARISON

Historical comparison is usually seen as the explicit contrasting of two or more societies to explore parallels and differences, convergence and divergences. Comparisons are mostly done only for specific themes. Societies as a whole are rarely compared. The main goal of historical comparison is the explanation or the typology of differences and similarities, as well as the better understanding of other societies. Comparisons are mostly international but sometimes also regional or local (in the same country or in different countries) and sometimes between civilizations. Historical comparisons are mostly synchronic but sometimes diachronic, comparing events and structures in different periods. Comparisons usually concentrate on a limited number of countries. Sometimes they might include all countries of one civilization. They almost never intend to explore general rules of human behavior, as the classical sociologists and ethnologists did. Historical comparisons are often limited to the confrontation between societies, but good comparisons should include also transfers, interrelations, and mutual images between the societies under comparison.

tional or local rather than comparative. The rise of social history was a necessary precondition but did not necessarily lead to comparisons.

Hence a second factor, the expansion of international research and scholarly contact since the 1960s, was of crucial importance. The work situation for scholars who wanted to do research in an international perspective clearly improved. Exchange programs for students as well as for researchers became more numerous. Library budgets improved, and history libraries became more international. International workshops, invitations, guest lectures, and visiting professorships increased. International meeting centers in the humanities were established in France, the United States, Britain, Germany, Italy, Sweden, and the Netherlands. Comparative European social historians passed almost without exception through one or several of these institutions and programs, most of which did not exist in the Europe of the 1950s. To be sure, the new comparative social history was not purposely planned by these international meeting centers and exchange programs, but without them comparative social history would not have taken off in Europe, where most history departments lacked systematic regional studies.

However, not all European historians could profit from this new institutional cross-fertilization. For political reasons historians in Eastern Europe were largely excluded until 1989–1991, and for economic reasons historians in southern Europe, especially in Spain, Portugal, and Greece, and to some extent also in Italy, rarely took part. It was mainly historians from the northern part of Europe and the United States who were brought together by these international meeting centers and exchange programs. Hence it comes as no surprise that European comparative social history has been mainly written by French, British, American, West German, Swiss, Austrian, Swedish, Norwegian, and Dutch historians.

Comparative social science was also a major encouragement for comparative social history. In the social sciences, empirical comparative research had a much longer and more solid tradition than in history. That historical social scientists had published major comparative work in a period in which social historians still hesitated to engage in comparison was of great significance. Historians read and discussed intensively the social science work of Europeans such as Stein Rokkan and Jean Fourastié, of Americans such as Charles Tilly and Barrington Moore, and of Americans who were exiled from Europe such as Reinhard Bendix, Seymour M. Lipset, and Karl Deutsch. Even if historians chose other themes and methods, these social science works were major reference points. It is

also clear, however, that social historians could respond to this encouragement more readily than could most other historians because themes in social history are often more transnational than in political history.

The rise of comparative social history is also associated with the general history of the second half of the twentieth century. The end of the traditional, secluded nation-state in Europe and the rise of European supranationalism as a reaction against two nationalistic world wars led to a new open-mindedness and to much greater comparative interest in other European countries and their history. It also led to a type of national consciousness that accepts or even seeks the comparative historical investigation of the dark sides of national history, such as dictatorships and their supporters. Moreover, globalization and the rising economic competition between countries led to more international and historical comparisons between neighboring as well as distant competitors. Finally, several factors—the internationalization of mass culture, consumption, and tourism, the rising knowledge of foreign languages, and the mass immigration by non-Europeans into Europe—render comparison an everyday experience, with changing borders between the domestic and the foreign. In this way international comparison became an attractive dimension of everyday life rather than only the privilege of an elite of scholars and a few international travelers.

DEBATES AND THEMES IN COMPARATIVE INVESTIGATION

Three major debates and motivations among historians have become particularly productive for comparative work. Indeed, it is difficult to imagine the rise of comparative social history without these debates: the debate on different paths of modernization, the debate on national ways or patterns peculiar to individual societies (which might foster the better understanding of other societies), and the debate on the social particularities of Europe. However, not all comparative studies of the social history of Europe are linked to these debates and motivations. The variety of motivations for doing comparative social history is extensive, and some work is focused on much more limited arguments.

The comparative debate about modernization.
The debate on different national paths of modernization was particularly productive for comparative social history, and out of that debate grew many outstanding comparative studies of nineteenth- and twentieth-century social history. The comparative stud-

ies of modernization, such as *European Modernity and Beyond* (1995), by Göran Therborn, and *The Development of Welfare States in Europe and America* (1981), edited by Peter Flora and Arnold J. Heidenheimer, cover a wide range of themes that can only be superficially touched on. Several key themes and topics are at the heart of comparative social history vis-à-vis modernization.

The first of these themes is comparative urban history. Subjects for comparison, in their great variation, include urban growth and the social crisis of the nineteenth-century city, the historical discourse on the modern city, and the rise of modern city planning, modern urban housing, and modern urban transport, especially during the long nineteenth century in Britain, France, the United States, and Germany. The role of the French, American, and German models and the transfers between the European and Atlantic societies were demonstrated by scholars such as Andrew Lees.

A second topic of the debate on modernization is social policy and the rise of the welfare state in Europe. This topic encompasses the reasons for the early and late beginnings of social policy, with Germany, Austria, Britain, and Sweden as pioneers and Switzerland as a latecomer; the reasons for the differences in the rise of the modern welfare state after World War II, with Britain and Sweden as the main models; the contrasts among the institutions of the welfare state within Western Europe and between Western and Eastern Europe from the end of World War II until 1989–1991; and the differences in public social intervention from the perspective of the clients.

The economic and political mentality and performance of elites and upper classes is a third topic in the modernization debate. Various studies were attached to the debate on the German *Sonderweg* (separate path), a subject discussed in detail below. But beyond the *Sonderweg* debate, other aspects of the social history of the elites were investigated comparatively, including the access to higher education and the ranks of the elites, which varied widely between European countries and the United States, among individual professions and schools, and among political systems. A related theme is the social preconditions of economic performance and the quality of schools. Another topic that developed in modernization studies involves professionalization in Europe. It has been shown that professionalization emerged either regulated by autonomous professional corporations, as in Britain, Italy, and sometimes in France, or under greater control by the state, as in Germany and partly also in France, or within an unregulated market of professional services, as in Switzerland. In the comparative history of the intellectuals, one study shows

that the rise of the intellectuals during the second half of the nineteenth century was a Europe-wide process. It was closely linked to the gradual rise of a political public sphere as well as to the rise of a cultural market for the products and services of intellectuals. However, distinct national differences emerged in the dynamics of the cultural market, in the stability of political liberties, and in the models for intellectuals.

An important subject of comparative social history is European revolutions and social conflicts. Several important books, including Jack Goldstone's *Revolution and Rebellion in the Early Modern World* (1991), Barrington Moore's *Social Origins of Dictatorship and Democracy* (1966), Theda Skocpol's *Social Revolutions in the Modern World* (1994), and Charles Tilly's *European Revolution* (1993), compared European and Atlantic revolutions, treating major factors and reasons behind revolutions, such as the social relationships and tensions in the rural societies. The differences among nations in international revolutions, especially in the European revolution of 1848, were also compared. Studies of the 1848 revolution compared the different historical contexts, supporting and opposing milieus, the different goals, and the contrasts in success and failure, but also the European commonalties. The international comparison of strikes and social protest demonstrated how much they depended upon the differing impact of economic modernization, the culture of protest milieus, and the reaction of the governments and employers. The different effects of strikes and social protests on social change were also treated. The international comparison of the social history of labor movements examined the strengths and weaknesses of labor movements, their relation to the state, and their contribution to democracy and social change.

Examining social institutions also entails the comparison of living standards, chances for upward mobility, and social inequalities. National and regional divergences of living standards, real income, real wages, housing, and hygiene standards in Europe were explored less often than one might expect, but some pioneering comparative studies were written. The clear national differences in educational opportunities, from basic learning to access to higher education, as well as national differences in chances of upward social mobility within Europe and in comparison with the United States, were investigated more frequently, leading to diverse interpretations of national differences, to much skepticism about any lasting international divergences or convergence, and to much interest in individual cases of advanced social mobility. The wide national differences in income and wealth distribution were the most frequently investigated aspects of of social inequality. Besides common trends of a mitigation of income and wealth disparities up to the 1970s and the reinforcement of disparities since the 1980s, distinct international differences emerged not only within Europe but also between Europe and other industrial societies, such as the United States and the Southeast Asian countries. These differences were often investigated by economists and sociologists rather than by historians.

International comparative studies of family focus on the regional or local level rather than on the level of national averages because of the large regional and local variations in demographic attitudes and family forms and because of the related rise of anthropological approaches. Studies in this field compare declining birth rates and rates of marriage, illegitimate births, child mortality, and family forms, but they also compare debates on family and family policy.

Several factors have contributed to comparative research in the social history of work and business. These are the debate on the national variations in the rise of the managerial elite in the United States, Europe, and Japan; the debate among sociologists on the impact of the professional training of skilled workers and white-collar workers on business hierarchies and the autonomy of skilled workers, especially in France, Germany, and Britain; and attention to the subject of different systems of communication in business corporations and different concepts of work.

In the 1980s and 1990s, new themes emerged in comparative social history. One new theme was gender history. Historians have investigated the national variations of European gender roles, women in family and kinship systems, the gender division of labor, the history of women's suffrage, and the impact of schooling, work, public administrations and civil law, churches, and the welfare state on gender roles in different societies. Another new theme was the social history of nationalism, which was reexamined through new approaches exploring the invention of identities in history. Scholars such as Heinz-Gerhard Haupt, Charlotte Tacke, and Jakob Vogel have explored the comparative history of national symbols, ceremonies, and monuments, but also the more classical history of the national idea of specific social milieus. A related new theme was the history of immigration within and into Europe. Some sociologists and historians began to explore how immigration gave rise to new ethnic minorities and how historical conceptions of the foreigner and of citizenship have changed in Europe. Scholars have also addressed the great variations among European governments in immigration policy and immigration legislation, even in a period of harmonization of such policy in the European Union.

A further new comparative field examined the social debates and social languages peculiar to each nationality. For example, how might symbols of modernization like the big city or the United States color a society's debate over its own modernity? As new social terms—such as "social question" in the early nineteenth century or "work" and "unemployment" in the late nineteenth and early twentieth centuries—come into use, scholars examine just who invented them and their different national contexts. Studies of this topic by Rainer Koselleck and others also examine the transfers of terminology or concepts from country to country. The comparative history of consumption, in all its national variations, has also become a significant theme, covering the international impact of the American mass consumer society and changes in the American model wrought by other countries; the convergences and fundamental political divergences of consumption in communist and Western countries; the national varieties of consumer goods and pastimes such as cars, books, dining, and sports; and the ways in which consumption highlights national contrasts in social distinctions. Finally, the comparative investigation of the rise of modern social history is often seen as part of the modernization of European historiography. This investigation includes an account of the pioneering role played by French historians such as Lucien Febvre and Marc Bloch in the rise of modern social history, the reasons why historians in other countries lagged behind, and what sort of social history developed in other countries given their particular circumstances.

The comparative debate on specific national patterns. A second type of debate that produced many comparative historical studies is the debate on historical national development patterns. One such national pattern is the German *Sonderweg* (separate path), the contradiction between rapid economic modernization and the persistence of traditional political values and elites, resulting in the peculiar weakness of political liberalism in the German middle class. To be sure, the origins of this debate were political in nature—that is, concerning the long-term preconditions of the rise of Nazism in Germany. Nevertheless, it eventually led to comparative studies to address implicitly comparative arguments. The comparative perspective prompted debates on the comparative distinctiveness of the *Sonderweg* phenomenon and various social explanations of it, such as the aristocratic model in the German middle class, the antimodernist model of the German *Bildungsbürgertum* (professional elites), the strong attachment of the German middle class to the conservative state, middle-class anxieties surrounding the seemingly revolutionary German labor movement, and the limited homogeneity of the German middle class. The comparative explanation was partly reinforced and partly weakened by comparative studies of the middle class in Germany, France, Britain, Sweden, Italy, and Poland.

Another approach to the *Sonderweg* holds that specific social groups such as white-collar employees, the petite bourgeoisie, and peasants had particular difficulties coping with modern industrial society and hence were more inclined to follow extreme right-wing arguments and to vote for Hitler. This argument also led to various comparative studies in the social background of extreme right-wing voting. One comparative study of white-collar employees, Jürgen Kocka's *White Collar Workers in America, 1890–1940* (1980), argues that white-collar workers in Germany were more privileged by governments and employers over blue-collar workers than they were in the United States, Britain, and France. As a consequence, they were more afraid of losing social privileges in the modern market economy and therefore tended to vote for candidates on the extreme right such as the Nazis. Comparative studies of the petite bourgeoisie demonstrated that in spite of similarities in petite bourgeois values, mobility, and economics across Europe, clear differences emerged in the political culture, leading to a more liberal petite bourgeoisie in France or Britain and, gradually, to an extreme right-wing petite bourgeoisie in Germany.

Another controversial comparative argument maintains that the German labor movement was particularly isolated in social and political terms, creating a much weaker social base for a broader left-wing government in Germany than in other European countries such as France, Britain, or the Scandinavian countries. Historians have also argued that military values were supported more frequently and fiercely by Germans than by other Europeans, especially after the late nineteenth century, which paved the way for the German acceptance of Nazi propaganda and of World War II. The military values can be seen not only in the public image of the army, in the debate about war aims and about World War I, and in war monuments, but also in student dueling, German songs, and *Turnervereine* (gymnastics clubs). This argument has been criticized by other historians who maintain that the rise of militarism was a more general process in pre-1914 Europe and that military ceremonies were as frequent and as popular in France as in Germany before 1914. A final approach to the *Sonderweg* argues that family education in Germany was more clearly oriented toward values such as obedience, deference, and militaristic heroism, which weakened liberalism

and resistance against dictatorship more than in other western European countries and the United States.

The comparative study of particular national development patterns in social history is not limited to Germany. It has been argued, for example, that a particular Scandinavian pattern of nonrevolutionary transition toward a liberal, consensus-oriented democracy grew out of the weakness of Scandinavian aristocracy and the strength of independent liberal peasants. It was also argued that the political *exception française*, the continuous split of France into two political camps without much chance of general consensus, had important sources in social history. Similarly, it was argued that the nineteenth-century economic *exception française*, the lack of innovations and export orientation, was linked to the Malthusian mentality of French business—the tendency to see all resources as limited, underestimating the effects of growth and innovation—and to the peculiar immobility of French society up the 1950s. One can expect that studies of distinct Italian, Spanish, and Dutch national patterns will also lead into comparative social history. Studies of Spanish social history have specifically linked developments there to broader European patterns, as against an older insistence on Spanish particularism. A great deal of work on Russian social history is implicitly comparative, on topics ranging from the peasantry to popular reading materials, though full-scale comparative efforts are rare.

The social particularities of Europe. A third debate covers the social particularities of Europe in history. To be sure, this is a long-running debate, starting during European expansion in the early modern period and resuming in the late nineteenth century. The twentieth-century discussion, however, is not simply a continuation of this older debate. It is not based on the assumption of European superiority and deals not only with the very long-term roots of European particularity but also with European social characteristics of the nineteenth and twentieth centuries. It also touches upon social particularities not covered by the older debate, such as the European city, the European active population and work, the European managerial system, European social conflicts, secularization, social inequalities and welfare state institutions, and the European reorientation of values. Such issues have also taken on increasing importance among teachers of world history, a field where the peculiar place of Europe is much debated.

This debate has been most vivid regarding two fundamental themes of social history: the European family and European revolution. In the debate on the "European" family, one school maintains that a particular European family emerged in the early modern period or before, with young families strongly independent from the families of origin, with few households consisting of three generations, with a late age of marriage for both men and women, and with low birth rates and high rates of unmarried people, but also with a specific European family mentality, a strongly protected private family sphere, and strong emotional ties between the members of the core family. Other historians believe that the concept of the European family is not consistent, either because comparisons show distinct divergences within Europe or because the comparison of Europe with Asia shows too many similarities.

The debate on European political revolutions has also gone on for many years. A central issue is determining whether the European revolutions, because they were original, unprecedented revolutions rather than imitations and because they were crucial for the particular role of Europe and the West as a pioneer of modern democratic institutions, were unique events very different from revolutions outside Europe. Historians have also debated whether these revolutions were purely national events or, at least in the case of the revolution of 1848, distinctly European events.

Limitations and omissions. In spite of these three related debates and numerous other studies less strongly related, comparative social history in general is not applied to the study of all countries, periods, and themes in the same way. Individual approaches have their clear virtues and distinct drawbacks. Given the disparate working conditions for research in international history and ongoing debates within the field of comparative historical research, it is natural that no single method is applied to all pursuits.

The clearest limitations to comparative European social history exist in the geographical dimension. European historians have rarely compared Europe with non-Western societies, though it would be highly instructive to do so with Indian, Chinese, Japanese, Arab, or black African societies in history. Jack Goody, who studied family history in Europe and Asia, is one of the few exceptions. Another example of such a fruitful comparison is Roy Bin Wong's work on economic and political development in China and central Europe. Only a few European social historians, such as Eric Hobsbawm and Paul Bairoch, have dared to work on global social history. The comparison of Europe with non-Western societies was more often carried out by a small number of American social historians and historical sociologists, such as Jack Goldstone, Barrington Moore, Theda Skocpol, and

Bernard Silberman. Moreover, even within Western societies, comparisons by European historians of European societies with the United States or Latin American countries are less numerous than one might expect. American historians have published a larger number of intercontinental comparisons of Western societies. Finally, even within Europe comparison in social history has followed distinct preferences. Most comparative research has been done on only three European countries, France, Great Britain, and Germany. Other European countries have been covered much less extensively and compared, if at all, usually with one of these three countries. Hence large parts of eastern and southern Europe, but also small countries in general, have remained almost untouched by historical comparison.

Preferences for certain periods are less distinct. In general, social history comparisons are clearly more numerous for the nineteenth and twentieth centuries than for earlier periods. This emphasis came about because the phenomenon that has been the subject of most comparisons—distinct national societies—appeared in the full sense only during the nineteenth century. But even within the nineteenth and twentieth centuries, a preference for periods characterized by gradual social change rather than by upheavals such as wars and revolutions is characteristic for comparative social history.

It might be surprising that preferences for themes are even less distinct. Although the wide variety of themes in comparative social history has been demonstrated, at the close of the twentieth century three major thematic lacunae remained. The first is the history of work—changes in types of work, in working conditions, and in unemployment. This is an astonishing omission in a period of fundamental changes in work, rising unemployment, and intense debate about a future new era of work. Second, the history of historical discourse itself, and of the historical changes in the social language, social imagery, and social interpretations, is another astonishing omission in what is undeniably a boom time for the analysis of historical discourses. A third area of neglect is the social history of the public sphere, the media, associations, the use of the public sphere by governments as well as by social movements, and the social side of citizenship and civil society.

THE FUTURE OF COMPARISON IN SOCIAL HISTORY

It is difficult to predict the future of the comparative method, which in the end strongly depends upon the content and quality of the published work rather than upon the method itself. So one can present hopes rather than predictions. In the present situation one might hope that five preoccupations will inspire future comparative studies in social history. First, it seems likely that the comparison between civilizations, especially between European and Asian as well as African societies, will become a major interest of historians, including not only comparison with Japan and the other industrialized East Asian countries but also the revival of the classical comparison of Europe with India, China, and the Arab world. The political and economic rise of these societies will reinforce the need for historical comparison. The comparative rise and varying characteristics of civil society will be a major motivation for this comparison between civilizations. A second theme for comparison could be the migration within and into Europe, the rise of new ethnic cultures, and the policies toward these new immigrants—a theme that might lead to comparisons between Western societies, especially, and deal with the large variety of problems and solutions they produced in history. A better understanding of ethnic minorities will be a major task of historical comparison. Third, it seems likely that the transition in central and eastern Europe from communism and a state-controlled economy to democracy and capitalism will become a major theme for historians who compare the different paths of transition and different constructions of history in this area, often in comparative search of long-term historical roots of divergences. A fourth theme might be the comparison of new social problems in the historical context, such as the history of unemployment, social exclusion, rising disparities of income and wealth, and emerging limits of efficiency of the classical modern welfare state. This again will be to a large degree a comparison among Western countries and the different solutions they developed in history. A final theme of comparison might be the making of a European society, its convergences and divergences, and the transfers and mutual images among European countries, especially among the rising number of member states of the European Union. This comparison also has to include the long-term historical perspective, the long roots of divergences and the long history of convergences and commonalities within European civilization. One can hope that comparative

THE DEBATE ON METHODS

Methods of historical comparison have been discussed by a few historians and historical sociologists, most of them with practical experience in historical comparison. The discussion emphasizes two themes. The first is the question of whether historical comparison should mainly cover parallels, commonalities, and convergences, or contrasts, differences, and divergences between the cases under comparison. Since the 1960s contrasts and divergences have received increasing attention, while parallels received declining attention, though there are signs of growing interest in parallels. Moreover, most publications on comparative methods try to show intermediary ways of comparison between the extreme positions of a radically individualizing and a radically universalizing comparison. Charles Tilly describes two additional intermediary approaches: the encompassing comparison of different cases belonging to a system (e.g., an international empire, church, or market) in their relation to the system and the comparison that investigates variations in a global phenomenon which arise from different preconditions. The second question covered in the debate on methods is whether historical comparisons should confront only different historical cases or also cover transfers, mutual images, and relations between the societies under comparison. There is a clear tendency toward including transfers in the debate on methods. So far, the alternative between the analytical-historical comparison that tests arguments and the hermeneutic historical comparison that can lead to a better understanding of other historical societies is not much discussed in this debate.

social history in all these respects will be understood in a broad sense, not only comparing structures and institutions but also mentalities, experiences and emotions, codes and symbols, conversations and debates.

See also **The Industrial Revolutions; Migration; The European Marriage Pattern** *(volume 2);* **Social Mobility; Professionals and Professionalization; Revolutions** *(volume 3); and other articles in this section.*

BIBLIOGRAPHY

Ashford, Douglas E. *The Emergence of the Welfare States.* Oxford, 1987.

Biernacki, Richard. *Fabrication of Labor: Germany and Britain, 1640–1914.* Berkeley, Calif., 1997.

Bock, Gisela, and Pat Thane, eds. *Maternity and Gender Policies: Women and the Rise of the European Welfare States, 1880s–1950s.* London, 1990.

Breuilly, John. *Labour and Liberalism in Nineteenth Century Europe: Essays in Comparative History.* Manchester, U.K., 1991.

Charle, Christophe. *Les intellectuels en Europe au XIXe siècle: Essai d'histoire comparée.* Paris, 1996.

Crossick, Geoffrey, and Heinz-Gerhard Haupt. *The Petite Bourgeoisie in Europe 1780–1914: Enterprise, Family, and Independence.* London, 1995.

Eisenberg, Christiane. *Deutsche und englische Gewerkschaften: Entstehung und Entwicklung bis 1878 im Vergleich.* Göttingen, Germany, 1986.

Flora, Peter, and Arnold J. Heidenheimer, eds. *The Development of Welfare States in Europe and America.* New Brunswick, N.J., 1981.

Frank, Andre Gunder. *ReOrient: Global Economy in the Asian Age.* Berkeley, Calif., 1998.

Geary, Dick. *European Labour Protest, 1848–1939.* London, 1981.

Goldstone, Jack A. *Revolution and Rebellion in the Early Modern World.* Berkeley, Calif., 1991.

Goody, Jack. *The Oriental, the Ancient, and the Primitive: Systems of Marriage and the Family in the Pre-industrial Societies of Eurasia.* Cambridge, U.K., 1990.

Haines, Michael. *Fertility and Occupation: Population Patterns in Industrialization.* New York, 1979.

Hobsbawm, Eric. *Age of Extremes: The Short Twentieth Century, 1914–1991.* London, 1994.

Iggers, Georg G. *Historiography in the Twentieth Century: From Scientific Objectivity to the Postmodern Challenge.* Hanover, N.H., 1997.

Kaelble, Hartmut. *Der historische Vergleich: Eine Einführung zum 19. und 20. Jahrhundert.* Frankfurt, Germany, 1999.

Kaelble, Hartmut. *A Social History of Western Europe, 1880–1980.* Translated by Daniel Bird. Dublin, 1990.

Kocka, Jürgen. *Industrial Culture and Bourgeois Society: Business, Labor, and Bureaucracy in Modern Germany.* Oxford, 1999.

Kocka, Jürgen. *White Collar Workers in America 1890–1940. A Social-Political History in International Perspective.* Translated by Maura Kealey. London, 1980.

Kocka, Jürgen, and Allan Mitchell, eds., *Bourgeois Society in Nineteenth-Century Europe.* Oxford and Providence, R. I., 1993.

Koven, Seth, and Sonya Michel, eds. *Mothers of a New World: Maternalist Politics and the Origins of Welfare States.* New York, 1993.

Laslett, Peter, with the assistance of Richard Wall. *Household and Family in Past Time: Comparative Studies in the Size and Structure of the Domestic Group over the Last Three Centuries in England, France, Serbia, Japan, and Colonial North America, with Further Materials from Western Europe.* Cambridge, U.K., 1972.

Lees, Andrew. *Cities Perceived: Urban Society in European and American Thought, 1820–1940.* Manchester, U.K., 1985.

Locke, Robert R. *The End of the Practical Man: Entrepreneurship and Higher Education in Germany, France, and Great Britain, 1880–1940.* Greenwich, Conn., 1984.

Maynes, Mary Jo. *Taking the Hard Road: Life Course in French and German Workers' Autobiographies in the Era of Industrialization.* Chapel Hill, N.C., 1995.

Miller, Pavla. *Transformations of Patriarchy in the West: 1500–1900.* Bloomington, Ind., 1998.

Mitchell, Allan. *The Divided Path: The German Influence on Social Reform in France after 1870.* Chapel Hill, N.C., 1991.

Moore, Barrington. *Social Origins of Dictatorship and Democracy: Lord and Peasant in the Making of the Modern World.* Boston, 1966.

Palmer, Robert R. *The Age of the Democratic Revolution: A Political History of Europe and America.* 2 vols. Princeton, N.J., 1959–1964.

Ringer, Fritz K. *Education and Society in Modern Europe.* Bloomington, Ind., 1979.

Ringer, Fritz K. *Fields of Knowledge: French Academic Culture in Comparative Perspective, 1890–1920.* Cambridge, U.K., and New York, 1992.

Schmidt, Alexander. *Reisen in die Moderne: Der Amerika-Diskurs des deutschen Bürgertums vor dem Ersten Weltkrieg im europäischen Vergleich.* Berlin, 1997.

Schmidt, Manfred G. *Sozialpolitik: Historische Entwicklung und internationaler Vergleich.* Opladen, Germany, 1988.

Silberman, Bernard S. *Cages of Reason: The Rise of the Rational State in France, Japan, the United States and Great Britain.* Chicago, 1993

Skocpol, Theda. *Social Revolutions in the Modern World.* Cambridge, U.K., 1994.

Stearns, Peter N. *The Revolutions of 1848.* London, 1974.

Sutcliffe, Antony. *Towards the Planned City: Germany, Britain, the United States, and France 1780–1914.* New York, 1981.

Swaan, Abram de. *In Care of the State: Health Care, Education, and Welfare State in Europe and the USA in the Modern Era.* Cambridge, 1988.

Therborn, Göran. *European Modernity and Beyond: The Trajectory of European Societies, 1945–2000.* London, 1995.

Tilly, Charles. *Big Structures, Large Processes, and Huge Comparisons.* New York, 1984.

Tilly, Charles. *European Revolutions, 1492–1992.* Oxford, 1993.

Tilly, Charles, Louise Tilly, and Richard Tilly. *The Rebellious Century, 1830–1930.* Cambridge, Mass., 1975.

Wong, Roy Bin. *China Transformed: Historical Change and the Limits of European Experience.* Ithaca, N.Y., 1997.

Woolf, Stuart. *The Poor in Western Europe in the Eighteenth and Nineteenth Centuries.* London, 1986.

Section 2

THE PERIODS OF SOCIAL HISTORY

PERIODIZATION IN SOCIAL HISTORY

Peter Stearns

Periodization—deciding when one pattern ends and another begins in historical time—is a key component of the historian's conceptual arsenal. Through periodization historians seek to identify coherences and breaks in the past, and therefore to indicate particular points that require causal explanations designed to determine why breaks occur. Not all historians deal with periodization, to be sure, and some who employ a periodization scheme do not justify it explicitly, using conventional labels without serious assessment of them. At best, however, careful use of periodization allows historians to explain why they start their chronology when they do—at the outset of some significant shift in the phenomenon under question—and why they end when they do as well, with possible internal junctures added to the mix. Periods can apply to a particular aspect of a society—the rise and fall of a single institution or idea—or to a whole society.

Changes in direction, that is, the makings of new periods, come in several forms in social history. Researchers on Russian peasants, to take one example, can at points use the new frameworks provided by shifts in the law, like the emancipation of the serfs in 1861 or Soviet collectivization beginning in 1928. Other directional changes, while no less real, do not provide comparable precision. It was around the 1770s, for example, that a dramatic increase in the percentage of all births that were illegitimate suggests a clear break—a new period—in popular sexual behavior in western Europe. (A similar new phase of sexual behavior occurred among Russian peasants in the 1880s.)

Overall, social historians use a variety of periodization schemes, like historians of any stripe. But because their topics are often unfamiliar, they cannot necessarily rely on established markers. Often, indeed, they are compelled to more explicit concern with periodization than are historians dealing with political or intellectual history, precisely because familiar frameworks do not work well. The options explored in European social history are numerous, and no single formula has emerged.

EUROPEAN HISTORY PERIODS

Conventional periodization in modern European history is well known. Of course there can always be debates—when, precisely, the Italian Renaissance began, for example. And familiar periods may overlap in confusing fashion; thus the Northern Renaissance continued, in many ways, even as the Reformation period began. But the list, overall, is unsurprising. Renaissance yields to Reformation. The seventeenth century is often categorized in terms of absolute monarchy. The eighteenth century as the Age of Enlightenment. A period of revolution follows, with an interim conservative reaction between 1815 and about 1830. After 1848 national unifications and then the alliance system may seem to set the tone for several decades. Conventional periodization almost always recognizes the basic importance of World War I. The twentieth century is then further divided by World War II and the rise and fall of the cold war. Some historians have tentatively argued that the end of the cold war marks the beginning of yet another period which will ultimately be seen as the first phase of the twenty-first century.

Periods of this sort are not only well established, but have the merit, usually, of cutting across wide swaths of European geography, because of the European-wide impact of diplomacy, imitation of key political forms like absolutism or the contagion of revolution, and the spread of key intellectual movements like the Enlightenment.

Before the rise of social history, when textbooks or other surveys embraced some social history materials, the periods were set by political or intellectual patterns. Thus the famous Rise of Modern Europe series, edited by William Langer, or the *Peuples et civilisations* series in France, used markers such as the French Revolution, the Napoleonic era, and so on, dealing with phenomena like urban growth or shifts in work patterns in discrete chapters within this framework. Obviously, the dominant assumption was that political or in a few instances intellectual developments set the basic tone for European history, and what social and even economic innovations there were could be fit within the resultant borders.

SOCIAL HISTORY AS ALTERNATIVE

Social history complicates standard periodization in European or any other history. Take a specific example. There is no reason to assume that changes in popular childrearing patterns in England—an obvious social history topic—follow the same rhythm as changes in the political party system, a staple of conventional English history. The key question is whether the causes of change in the two areas are shared. At the very least, this requires explicit determination.

Social historians do not assume that high politics or great ideas necessarily shape the phenomena that interest them. Work on the important contributions of peasants, workers, or women to the historical record deals with groups for whom the state may be a fairly remote force, and on whom Great Ideas may have little direct impact. Research on additional facets of social behavior—demography, or crime, or household functions—similarly must take into account factors beyond politics and intellectual life. The result, in principle at least, opens modern European history to a host of new periodization questions. E. P. Thompson's pathbreaking *The Making of the English Working Class* thus begins toward the middle of the eighteenth century, which few conventional historians would dignify with the inception of much of anything, and ends around the 1830s. Not only this, but key developments within the span, such as the French Revolution and the rise of Napoleon, are not seen as significantly reshaping the phenomena in question. Even a historian dealing with protest itself over a long span of time, like Charles Tilly, may downplay the significance of the French Revolution of 1789, in favor of fitting it into a larger periodization scheme. Or a social history survey may jump over World War I, using a definition of a mature industrial society that begins around the 1870s and ends after 1945, within which the world wars had some impact that fell short of redirecting basic social processes such as class struggle or the domestic emphasis for women.

Social history compounds the periodization problem by rarely focusing primarily on events and specific dates. Events may matter occasionally as causes of social phenomena—thus any history of women's work will pause in each of the two world wars to note some impact in increasing women's employment, and the end of serfdom clearly matters in the chronology of peasant history. Or events may illustrate some larger social trend, but they rarely form clear boundaries for the topics social historians study. Correspondingly, social historians are usually much more comfortable pinning the beginning of a new trend to a decade or so, rather than a specific year, much less a month and day. Thus the dramatic decline of infant mortality that is a key part of demographic transition began in western Europe (and the United States) in the 1880s—not 15 April 1881. The witchcraft furor drew to a close by the 1730s (though here, admittedly, the dates of the last formal trials can add some unwonted precision). The modern European-style family began to take shape in the later fifteenth century, not in 1483. Social history periodization focuses on new directions in collective behaviors, not tidy single occurrences.

In principle the rise of social history opens conventional European history periodization to a host of probing questions. What was long assumed must now be reexamined. The result is no small challenge to historians also busy with new topics, distinctive kinds of source materials, and so on. Challenge, in turn, explains why social history options have been varied, and variously satisfactory.

STICKING CLOSE TO HOME

Two choices minimize social history's disruption to established periodization. One involves using the periods already available; the other involves using no real periods at all.

In the first choice, for reasons both good and bad, many social history topics are placed within familiar chronological boundaries. Very few social history books that get to 1914 do not simply stop there or at least acknowledge a major break. Very few early modernists—people who concentrate on the seventeenth and eighteenth centuries—actually continue their work past 1789 or 1815. There are hosts of French social histories that fit within the framework of 1815 to 1848, a familiar political chunk.

Use of conventional periodization can be explained in several ways, with varying degrees of validity in consequence. Sometimes it simply reflects convenience. Dealing with new topics, it proved too demanding to think through fundamental beginnings and endings, so an acknowledged periodization was tacked on. The result might also help reader-historians who are not specialists in social history make more sense of the novel topic. Even if 1848 saw no major changes in the accelerating pattern of factory work in France, for example, stopping the study in 1848 would hardly be questioned. Archival materials might also be organized according to established dates, which would provide further fuel. All these justifications are perfectly understandable, especially in the early years of the newer social history research, and the resultant periodization could frame exciting studies. But the result involved dates of convenience, not a really thoughtful approach to periodization in terms of basic change and continuity.

Conventional periodization could take on added importance when historians argued more directly that familiar phenomena, and their dates, related directly to social change, either as cause or effect. For example, many social historians use the Reformation as a legitimate beginning point for examination of changes in family life, though in most cases the studies extend well into the seventeenth century to catch the full impact of the developments involved. Studies of European society between the world wars may explicitly establish that the topics involved changed shape as the result of World War I and would change again with the advent of World War II; here, periodization may be conventional but it is explicitly applied. Without question, some conventional periods work better than others for social history topics, because the impact of political or intellectual developments varies.

The second way to minimize periodization issues while dealing innovatively with social historical phenomena is through what might be called postholing—exploring an aspect of the past for its own sake, without caring too much when the phenomena involved began or ended. Thus a social historian might explore mid-seventeenth-century rituals that shed light on marriage or the roles of women. The result might add greatly to the store of knowledge, but the task of fitting into a chronology or of explaining when the phenomena began and why would be left to others. Certain kinds of microhistory have probed exciting specific materials that illuminate the characteristics of a point in the past, but again without worrying about chronological boundary lines. At times, to be sure, this postholing approach is combined with some reference to how different all this is from what would come later—a "world we have lost" approach—but there is no explicit attempt to decide when the changes occurred or even what caused the patterns explored to lose their validity.

LONGUE DURÉE AND BIG CHANGES

At the other extreme, some pioneering social historians have urged a totally different approach, arguing that social history cannot be trapped within conventional periodization at all but also that the need to address periodization questions cannot be evaded simply because topics and materials are unfamiliar.

Following the lead of Fernand Braudel and the French *Annales* school, many social historians argue that certain kinds of social phenomena change very slowly, if at all, across long stretches of time in the European past. Many of the structures of peasant life can be seen through this lens. Methods of work, or land tenure, or popular beliefs and values may long persist, often from the Middle Ages into modern times. There is a beginning to the phenomena, though sometimes shrouded in the mists of a remote past, and there may be an end, but there is no need for a periodization that would identify a few decades, or even a few centuries. Arguments in terms of long duration have been applied less often to the nineteenth and twentieth centuries than to medieval and early modern European history, but survivals are not impossible even into recent times. Thus, without necessarily explicitly invoking *longue durée* (long duration), many historians of European witchcraft have noted important persistence of popular belief into the mid-nineteenth century, even though the formal trials period (dependent as it was on acquiescence of church and state leaders) ended more than a century before.

A *longue durée* approach often allows for identification of key regional patterns within Europe more generally, where persistent structures relate to some combination of geography and cultural tradition. Braudel himself explored particular dynamics in Mediterranean Europe. Others have identified durable structures in eastern Europe or elsewhere, sometimes related to land tenure patterns or other basic rural dynamics.

Periodization based on the *longue durée* framework is also open to criticism. Many social historians have challenged impressions of a stable, even changeless peasantry, noting that persistence sometimes reflects simply a lack of surviving information and that sharp, sudden changes in peasant behaviors and beliefs are common. On the whole, *longue durée* approaches have declined in popularity since the 1980s.

A second approach to social history periodization—not necessarily contradicting *longue durée* arguments about persistence, but offering a different emphasis—focuses on what Charles Tilly has called a quest for "big changes." Here the assumption is that every so often, but not too often, European history tosses up some structural shifts that are so massive that they have a wide array of social consequences. Tilly sees two changes, which he dates back to the sixteenth and seventeenth centuries, as reshaping European society in some senses all the way to the present. Commercialization of the economy, and the attendant formation of a property-less proletariat, is one of his key forces. The growth of the European state through the accumulation of new bureaucracy, new functions, and (gradually) new popular expectations, is his other great force. Tilly argues that the combined effect of his two big changes reshaped popular protest patterns in Europe in ways that can still be traced through the nineteenth century.

Other social historians might dispute Tilly's chronology or his choice of forces. For example, "big changes" in popular culture can also be traced back at least to the later seventeenth and eighteenth centuries. The specific terminology of "big change" is not widely used, but the idea of major turning points gains ground increasingly in the more ambitious social history inquiries. The turning points may bear some relationship to conventional periodization, but they usually require separate definition, dating, and explanation. Thus the protoindustrialization concept, though disputed by some economic and social historians, argues that the spread of commercialized but domestic manufacturing in the late seventeenth and eighteenth centuries ushered in important changes not only in work life, but also in consumption habits, gender relations, sexual behavior, and generational tensions—a kind of "big change," in other words, from which a host of other social shifts directly ushered. Many social historians see the industrial revolution in terms of sweeping social consequences—indeed, they are more comfortable with the industrial revolution concept as marking a whole set of social changes than are their economic historian counterparts, who variously debate the term according to a narrower set of economic indicators. Another big change point—perhaps the overused label "postindustrial" will turn out to apply—may enter in around the 1950s, associated with some familiar developments in the post–World War II state but also changes in family structure and popular values.

SPECIFIC PERIODIZATIONS

Along with long duration and big change, social historians increasingly contribute to periodization by dealing with specific chronological frameworks for specific sociohistorical phenomena. Examples here range as widely as social history itself. One historian, Eric Hobsbawm, sees the first key signs of instrumentalism among British workers in the 1850s; it was at this point, he argues, that some workers stopped viewing work in traditional terms and began to negotiate with employers in the belief that work should be an instrument to a better life off the job. The history of women and work notes the reduction of women's par-

ticipation in the western European labor force during the initial decades of the industrial revolution (while women did gain jobs in factories, they were pushed from domestic manufacturing work in greater numbers still) but then notes the dramatic reentry of married women into the labor force in the 1950s and 1960s. A new concern for slenderness and avoidance of overweight arose in western Europe in the 1890s. It was in the eighteenth century—probably between 1730 and 1770—that women, rather than the aristocracy, began to be seen as the group in European society that should be particularly associated with beauty, and therefore with particular attention to costume. It was also at this time—in a change that has yet to be fully explored—that dominant cultural assumptions began to shift away from traditional assumptions that women were more naturally sinful than men, to an argument that they were in crucial respects, particularly concerning sexuality, more moral. It was in the 1890s that targets for murder in several parts of western Europe began to focus more on family members than on barroom companions—a fascinating if very specific kind of periodization shift. It was in the 1920s that old people began to stop coresiding with younger kin (a pattern that had actually increased in the nineteenth century), a trend that has continued to the present day. It was in the late sixteenth century that modern prisons began to reshape ideas and practices of punishment in western Europe.

The list of specific periodization findings is vast. Some, of course, relate to wider claims; the boundary between specific periodizations and a "big change" argument is not hard and fast. One of the major periodization findings of social historians since 1980 has emphasized the origins of modern consumer society in the eighteenth century. In contradistinction to the older view that consumerism resulted from industrialization, we now realize that in western Europe it preceded it. Demographic historians urge a fairly basic periodization as well, with emphasis on the beginnings of a declining birth rate in the later eighteenth or early nineteenth centuries, measurable population ageing by the early twentieth century, and so on. The work of Norbert Elias, recently revived in several studies, has called attention to the seventeenth and eighteenth centuries as a time of a change in manners and a growing insistence on self-restraint in a variety of aspects of life, from eating to emotion.

Specific periodizations in social history not only vary with particular topics, since clearly not all aspects of human behavior tidily change in concert, but also with regions. Choice of periods and change points for the history of manorialism, for example, obviously vary with each European region, but the same is true for shifts in family structure or sexuality. At times, at least in recent centuries, regional differences in periodization reflect different dates of phenomena such as industrialization, so that the nature of periods is more similar than the specific chronology. Peasant sexuality in Russia, for example, which was beginning to alter in the late nineteenth century as a function of new contacts with cities, enters a new period somewhat similar to that which can be discerned in western Europe in the mid-eighteenth century. But regularities cannot be pressed too far: the regional factor adds further complexity to periodization in European social history.

CONCLUSION

No single periodization scheme currently dominates European social history. Useful approaches range from acceptance of familiar chronologies to a clearly alternative scheme such as long duration or big change, to the array of specific periodizations that have resulted from studies of social classes, gender, and popular behaviors. Add to this the different periodizations necessary for different regions of Europe—such as the decline of manorialism in early modern western Europe even as serfdom intensified in Russia and Poland—and the pattern is unquestionably complex.

And from this welter of approaches, three results stand out. First, while social historians have not fully replaced conventional periodization, they certainly tend to challenge it. Some staples survive better than others. While studies of social history during the Renaissance abound, particularly for Italy, the Renaissance is not usually highlighted as a basic social history period. As a largely elite cultural phenomenon, with some ramifications in politics and commerce, the Renaissance did not have wide enough social resonance to be terribly useful as a social history period overall. As indicated earlier, the Reformation has retained greater utility as a social history period, though only if extended in time. Correspondingly, some developments long linked uncomfortably to political periods, such as the industrial revolution, now gain greater prominence. The concepts are not entirely new, but

their priority shifts once the topics to be accounted for are redefined. Few late-twentieth-century social historians chop up the nineteenth century according to political and diplomatic shifts. Indeed, periodization based on diplomatic developments has survived particularly badly, except when diplomacy breaks down and society-shattering wars ensue. The social history periodization scheme, in sum, looks considerably different from the more conventional markers. The difference includes the need to focus more on transition points for social processes than on precise events and single dates.

Second, no fully agreed periodization has replaced the conventional markers. There are too many aspects of society, too many particular schemes, to yield substantial coherence as yet at least. To some observers or critics, the result is an unfortunate messiness or lack of coherence. One of the motivations behind the "big changes" push was a desire for synthesis, a hope that a few dramatic forces could unite a wide variety of social phenomena. At worst, a separate periodization scheme attaches to every major social history topic, and sometimes even this must be modified depending on the geographic region under examination.

Third, however messy, the ongoing exploration of social history has at its best made the search for appropriate periods more explicit, more open to assessment and debate, than was true for some of the older formulas. Determining when basic changes in direction occur (and what continuities survive them), and what caused them, is much of the stuff of history. Precisely because social history has redefined what the past entails, the need to seek out the appropriate chronology becomes part of the task. Whether some larger unities will emerge in future is anyone's guess, though some clusters of particularly important changes are widely recognized already. For some the need to move into a topic with questions about appropriate chronology make the resultant history more exciting and more usable than when less-examined assumptions predominated. For researchers and history-users alike, the need to think about periodization unquestionably adds to the task of being engaged with social history.

See also other articles in this section.

BIBLIOGRAPHY

Braudel, Fernand. *The Mediterranean and the Mediterranean World in the Age of Philip II.* Translated by Siân Reynolds. New York, 1976. Translation of *La Méditerranée et le monde méditerranéen à l'époque de Philippe II.*

Laslett, Peter. *The World We Have Lost.* New York, 1965.

Stearns, Peter N., and Herrick Chapman. *European Society in Upheaval: Social History Since 1750.* 3d ed. New York, 1992.

Tilly, Charles. *Big Structures, Large Processes, Huge Comparisons.* New York, 1984.

THE MEDIEVAL HERITAGE

Constance B. Bouchard

The European Middle Ages, the millennium now considered to have lasted roughly from 500 to 1500, has long been a difficult period for historians. Ever since the term "Middle Ages" was first coined during the Italian Renaissance, the period has generally been treated as an anomalous gap between antiquity and the birth of the "modern." Renaissance humanists of the fourteenth century rather self-righteously announced that they were reviving the learning and culture of classical Greek and Roman antiquity after centuries of neglect. However, scholars have come to agree that most classical learning and culture would not have been available for the Renaissance to embrace had they not been kept alive during the Middle Ages, and they put the break between the Middle Ages and the early modern period after the Renaissance rather than before it. As turning points, Columbus's voyages to America and the beginnings of the Protestant Reformation, respectively just before and just after the year 1500, are considered more significant than the writings of the humanists a century and a half earlier.

Nonetheless, the humanists' characterization of the medieval period as a time of ignorance and superstition has remained compelling. During the Enlightenment in eighteenth-century France, the church was identified as the source of many of humanity's worst problems, at the same time as Protestant countries feared the plots of Jesuits. It was then but a short step from despising the Catholic Church to assuming that everything one hated about it had also characterized the Middle Ages. America's Founding Fathers, themselves imbued with Enlightenment ideals, looked not to the Middle Ages but rather far earlier, to the Roman Republic (or at least, to the Roman Republic as seen by Renaissance humanists), for the model of what they were creating. Slaveholders who saw the conquest of "inferior" peoples as a desirable goal had no difficulty identifying with Roman society.

The first rehabilitation of the Middle Ages took place during the romantic movement of the nine-teenth century. In France the churches that had been defaced during the Revolution were rebuilt and redecorated; the architect Viollet-le-Duc (1814–1879) in particular created new heads for the kings on the facade of Notre Dame of Paris and added the grotesque gargoyles. In England at the same time, poems and novels, such as *Ivanhoe* (1819) by Sir Walter Scott, were inspired by ruined abbeys and castles, and the Middle Ages were nostalgically depicted as a time of chivalric virtue, pure spirituality, and the birth of sturdy English liberties. This romantic image was so strong that practitioners of scientific history in the early twentieth century felt compelled to debunk it in turn, invoking once again an image of a stagnant and priest-ridden era.

In the late twentieth century, however, medieval scholars managed to go beyond the rather pointless argument as to whether the Middle Ages was a dark age of oppression and ignorance or instead a lost golden era of faith and honor. Instead, they came to a new appreciation of how much of what we take for granted in modern Western society was created by the complex, far from stagnant society that existed in Europe between the sixth and fifteenth centuries.

The significance of the Middle Ages has always been more self-evident to Europeans than to citizens of the United States, a country that from its origins believed that the liberty its people sought was not just freedom from tyranny but freedom from the past's hidebound traditions. In Europe, however, one cannot go about one's business without being constantly reminded of the links between present and past. Shoppers and professionals in the center of cities walk down streets that have had the same layout since the end of the Middle Ages, and people are baptized, married, and buried in churches that date to the twelfth and thirteenth centuries. Most of the villages that dot the countryside of England are mentioned in the great medieval survey, the Domesday Book of 1086, and both in England and on the Continent many hilltops are crowned with grim towers that have stood for over eight hundred years.

But there is more to the importance of Europe's Middle Ages than its physical remains. In antiquity Western civilization was focused on the Mediterranean, the "Roman lake" as it was sometimes termed. The rise of Islam in the seventh century shattered the cultural unity of the Mediterranean basin, and from the time of the emperor Charlemagne (742–814) the center of European civilization was north of the Alps, in France and Germany, which over a thousand years later became the locus of the European Economic Union. Even national boundaries have remained roughly the same since the late Middle Ages, whereas none of the European countries existed as political units at the beginning of the medieval period. Property rights, privileges, and in England the unwritten constitution itself are all still anchored in medieval law.

MEDIEVAL CITIES

Modern Western urban civilization owes its origins not to antiquity, though indeed its great civilizations were city-based, but rather to the twelfth century. During the early Middle Ages, as Roman trade routes broke down and a much colder climate throughout Europe made regular harvests increasingly problematic, cities shrank drastically to little more than administrative centers for the bishops and the counts; most of the population scraped out a living in the countryside. Starting in the eleventh century, however, and picking up speed in the twelfth and thirteenth centuries, cities grew rapidly, even more rapidly than the overall population. In large part this urban growth was made possible by the warmer and drier climate, which meant that crops in the countryside could be harvested much more reliably. Thus overall population could rise, and farms produced enough excess beyond what a farm family or manor required for itself to allow selling to town.

The growth of the cities was due to immigration from the surrounding countryside. Young men especially came to town seeking their fortunes. Although the well-to-do, such as the guild-masters, set up houses for their families, most of the city population was initially male. Women could feel endangered in the rough-and-tumble environment of a rapidly growing city, and everyone agreed that, as chances for disease were much higher there, cities were poor places for small children. Indeed, well-to-do women living in town normally sent their infants out to wet nurses in the countryside. By the late Middle Ages most cities had something closer to a one-to-one sex ratio; nevertheless, there was always well-founded concern that cities were centers of infection—concerns that persisted until the development of modern urban sanitation in the nineteenth century.

In Italy, Spain, and France, the cities of the twelfth century grew out of the administrative units that were all that survived of the Roman capitals of antiquity. Germany, however, had never experienced Roman rule, and thus its cities had to be founded completely anew. In England the Roman cities, along with most other remnants of Roman civilization, had been overwhelmed by Anglo-Saxon settlement starting in the fifth century, and thus the medieval cities grew out of the *burhs,* military centers first established by the Anglo-Saxon kings in the ninth century.

Whatever their origins, medieval cities quickly became centers of trade, commerce, and law. Goods from all over Europe, including wool from England, iron from Germany, leather and horses from Spain, and finely dyed fabric from Italy, were traded in the cities along with produce from the local countryside and silks and spices from fabled Asia. Early forms of capitalist investment flourished: those mounting an expedition to buy luxury goods from the East sold shares so that if disaster struck the loss would be spread out, and if the expedition were hugely successful a great many could share in the wealth. Urban craftsmen made their living not from farming but from creating and selling specialized products, whether shoes or jewelry or weapons. At the turn of the twenty-first century, Europe's major urban centers, with few exceptions, continued to practice trade and commerce in the same locations as those established in the twelfth and thirteenth centuries.

FREEDOM AND SERVITUDE

The cities of the twelfth and thirteenth centuries were also considered centers of freedom, where someone from the countryside could escape the burdens under which he was born and where the city fathers generally obtained a charter of liberties spelling out their right to self-rule. The mayors and elected city councils of these cities especially sought the right to administer justice themselves rather than having to defer to the regional duke or count or to the city's bishop.

The freedom that these cities proclaimed for their citizens highlights one of the curious aspects of medieval history: it was a period in which there was essentially no slavery, even though it was framed at one end by the slave-based society and economy of Rome and on the other by the development of the trans-Atlantic slave trade. Roman slavery had been predicated on the steady acquisition of new prisoners to force into slavery, and once Roman conquests ceased so did the influx of new prisoners. Agricultural slavery,

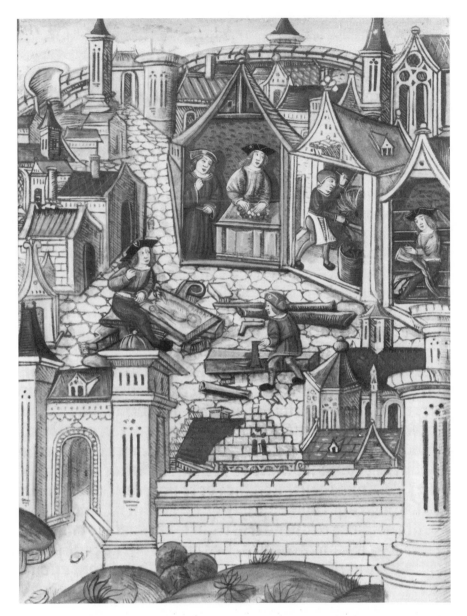

Artisans and Merchants. An illustration from *Book . . . of the Institution and Administration of Public Affairs,* 1520. BIBLIOTHÈQUE NATIONALE, PARIS, RES. VELINS 410

which in antiquity meant working slaves in large gangs, conditions under which they were very unlikely to reproduce themselves, thus became extremely uneconomical by the sixth century. Although Christianity did not condemn slavery per se, it did encourage freeing one's slaves and forbade enslaving a free person who was already a Christian. Thus by the seventh century slavery as an economic arrangement was essentially extinct in western Europe, although for the next two centuries household slaves might still occasionally be found.

With the decline of slavery in the early Middle Ages, the descendants of slaves mostly became serfs.

Although serfs were considered to be born into a state of servitude, and had to gain approval from their masters for their marriages or even to move to another village, they were still substantially better off than slaves. They could not be bought and sold, were not subject to arbitrary commands, and more or less regulated their own lives, having their own families, houses, and plots of land. The rent they paid to their masters for these houses was a combination of money, produce, and the requirement that they work in the lord's fields two or three days a week.

Medieval serfdom has sometimes been termed feudalism by marxist scholars, but among medievalists of the late twentieth century the term has been jettisoned. After all, it is both confusing and misleading to use a single word to designate variously the agricultural practices of peasants in the sixth and seventh centuries; the landholding and ritualized loyalty of knights and lords of castles in the eleventh and twelfth centuries; and the legal privileges such as hereditary judgeships and noble dovecotes abolished in 1789 during the French Revolution, when the revolutionaries announced they were "ending feudalism." Moreover, the serfdom established to replace agricultural slavery at the beginning of the Middle Ages did not persist unchanged throughout the entire period. By the eleventh century many serfs found that the rapidly improving economy of the time provided an opportunity for greater freedom. Some simply slipped off to the city, as suggested above, for a society without good communication or identification methods had no ready way to apprehend them. More frequently, serfs bought their own freedom. In France and Italy serfdom was essentially gone by the twelfth century. Free peasants were still substantially lower on the social and economic ladder than wealthy lords or successful merchants, but no longer were they considered bound by servitude.

In England and Germany, by contrast, serfdom continued in at least some form through the rest of the Middle Ages. In Germany, however, some men who were legally serfs might be much better off than some freemen, especially the *ministeriales,* the "serf-knights" who in many cases actually became the de facto aristocracy of their regions by the late Middle Ages. In England servile status was evoked most commonly in the thirteenth century to argue that one's opponent in a legal case had no standing in court. In the fourteenth century, after the devastation and depopulation by the bubonic plague, many landlords attempted to impose harsh labor dues on any of the surviving peasants who they could claim were serfs. The resulting great peasants' rebellion of 1381, although quickly suppressed, became a model for subsequent peasant rebellions in the following centuries. Fifteenth-century English peasants, in fact, had greater liberty than their grandparents, liberty that was quietly granted them once the worst of the rebellions were put down.

Slavery at this point had been absent from western Europe for more than half a millennium. However, during the Italian Renaissance household slaves began appearing again in small numbers, generally purchased from the eastern Mediterranean. After all, Roman law had had a great deal to say about slavery, and a people who thought of themselves as continuators of Roman culture found the practice perfectly

acceptable. In the sixteenth century, in the great age of exploration, Europeans discovered a number of peoples with whom they had so little in common that they were not even sure these people were entirely human, and began to enslave them with a brutality that medieval people would have found disquieting.

WOMEN AND THE FAMILY

Important developments also took place within the family during the Middle Ages, again creating institutions that we now accept as modern. The basic medieval family was founded on the nuclear unit of husband, wife, and children. Because child mortality was high in an era without modern medicine or infant formula, enough children died in their earliest years to drag down the life expectancy from the sixty or seventy years an adult could anticipate living—unless of course he or she died in war, in childbirth, or in an epidemic—to an average somewhere in the thirties. (An average life expectancy of thirty-five did not, of course, mean that people expected to die in their thirties; the number is the mathematical mean between those who died in infancy and the adults who lived to what the Bible termed a standard "three score years and ten.")

Scholars at one time assumed that parents faced with the deaths of so many young children must have been hardened to the experience, even to the point of not becoming attached to their children. However, scholars studying medieval records have found overwhelming evidence that parents cared deeply for their children and grieved bitterly when they died; indeed, children were not merely the objects of parental affection but potentially an economic advantage, given that Europe was underpopulated for most of the Middle Ages. It should also be noted that high levels of child mortality were not unique to the Middle Ages; infants died at a high rate in Europe and North America until the early twentieth century.

Women played a much more independent role within the medieval family than they had within the family of antiquity. Christianity had always stressed that everyone, men and women alike, were equal in the eyes of God, and a Christian Europe gave women greater scope for action. Beginning in the ninth century, the church argued that a valid marriage could not be arranged solely by the male relatives but required the free consent of both the man and the woman. This argument, initially made on behalf of highborn and visible women, gradually worked its way down the social ladder. By the twelfth century, when marriage had come to be treated as a sacrament, it was clear that the heart of the sacrament was not the words of the priest—whose presence was not required for a marriage to be valid—but rather the free oaths exchanged between the two principals.

Although married women with active husbands would not take the lead in dealing with the outside world, they nonetheless had property rights within marriage that were more extensive in the Middle Ages than they were subsequently in some parts of Europe, even in the nineteenth century. For example, in southern Europe even girls from modest backgrounds brought a certain amount of property, the dowry, to a marriage, and their husbands could not alienate it without their consent. North of the Alps, husbands normally fixed a certain amount of property, the bride-price, on their wives at the time of their wedding and were enjoined not to take it back.

In widowhood, a typical status for women given that men generally chose wives considerably younger than themselves, women had a great deal of autonomy in buying, selling, and even suing in court. Although inheritance of the family patrimony went preferentially to boys, in the absence of brothers girls could and did inherit everything from the family farm even to the Crown, and a girl with many brothers could still expect to receive something from her parents' inheritance. In the urban world of the late Middle Ages, wives and husbands normally worked side by side in guilds, and widows and daughters of guild-masters sometimes became guild-masters themselves.

LANGUAGE AND LITERATURE

Culturally, modern language and literature have their origins in the twelfth century. Those who know modern French, German, Italian, Spanish, and Icelandic can still read, with only some difficulty, literature written in the medieval version of those languages. The language of the poet Dante (1265–1321) is the basis of modern Italian. The English language developed somewhat more slowly than the languages of the Continent, as the Anglo-Saxon of the early Middle Ages and the French of the Normans who conquered England in 1066 did not fuse into a single tongue until the fourteenth century; but with a little practice modern English-speakers can still read the poems of Geoffrey Chaucer (1342–1400).

Vernacular literature first appeared in the twelfth century, initially as stories intended for the entertainment of those who did not know the Latin of the church and the law court, but soon taking on a robust popularity among persons of every level of education, even churchmen. Ancient Greece and Rome of course produced works of entertainment, but the genre had fallen into oblivion for over half a millennium. The epics and romances written in the twelfth century, however, established a long-running tradition. The direct descendant of medieval storytelling is the genre called fantasy—tales of swordfights and magic—which was demoted by the late-twentieth-century literary establishment to marginal status as a subgenre of science fiction. In the Middle Ages, however, fantasy constituted essentially all of literature.

By the thirteenth century, a somewhat rougher form of literature sprang up alongside the courtly literature evoking chivalric deeds and dangerous and honorable battles. Referred to as *fabliaux,* these tales often featured anthropomorphized animal characters and bawdy content. But high literature continued to be a literature of knightly culture, with romances and epics serving both as a critique of that culture and as examples of the kinds of virtue the authors wanted readers to emulate.

By the fourteenth and fifteenth centuries, the most powerful nobles dearly wanted to imagine themselves as chivalric knights. While gunpowder and cannons came to dominate the battles of the final 150 years of the Middle Ages, converting the once formidable armored knight into a hopeless anachronism, leaders dreamed of the glorious days of King Arthur and began to form "orders of knighthood," designed to separate the most courtly and honorable from everyone else. It is ironic that the tournament, which had originally been a way to practice battlefield techniques, had by the end of the Middle Ages become very different from the reality of battle, being instead a ritualized activity in which knights, wearing the heavy plate armor that had recently been developed to withstand musket fire, thrust at each other with wooden lances and were scored on style.

Even after the end of the Middle Ages, the image of a lost but possibly still attainable chivalric golden age lingered. In the sixteenth century all kings owned fine suits of tournament armor, and one French king was killed in a tournament. Dreams of chivalry were still strong enough for Cervantes (1547–1616) simultaneously to ridicule and celebrate them in *Don Quixote.* And of course, as noted above, such images animated the romantic movement of the nineteenth century.

CULTURE: RELIGION AND THE UNIVERSITIES

One of the Middle Ages' greatest contributions to later culture is the creation of the university. Antiquity had nothing similar, but an entity resembling what we call a university (from the medieval Latin *universitas,* meaning something done collectively) does appear in

Working Side by Side. Wife and husband in an apothecary's shop, from an Italian manuscript, *Tacuinum sanitatis,* c. 1385. ÖSTERREICHISCHE NATIONALBIBLIOTHEK, VIENNA

the twelfth century. In France, for example, the schools attached to the various churches of Paris gradually merged into a single entity, its existence given formal recognition by a charter from the king in 1200. The titles still given to university officers, such as dean, chancellor, or provost, were originally the titles given to officers of the cathedral, and academic gowns are in origin priests' robes. The connection between training as a student and training for the priesthood persisted, even though most students never became priests. This connection meant that women, barred from the priesthood, were also barred from university training, a practice that persisted, both in Europe and in the Americas, until well into the nineteenth century.

With recognizable features such as a set curriculum and program of study, degrees granted to show mastery of complex subject matter, professionally qual-

ified teachers, and even students drinking too much, getting into trouble with their landladies, and writing home with plausible stories explaining why they needed even more money for books, the medieval University of Paris seems familiar. Because classes were conducted in Latin, all students had to speak the language; it was also the only easy way for students from all over Europe to communicate. The area of Paris around the university is still called the Latin Quarter.

Universities quickly multiplied, each specializing in a certain subject at the graduate level, although one could receive a B.A. at any. Paris was the preeminent university for both philosophy and theology, where the writings of the ancient Greeks, especially Aristotle, were pored over, debated, and incorporated into such theological treatises as the *Summa theologiae* of Thomas Aquinas (1225–1274). The University of

Bologna in Italy was Europe's preeminent university of law, where students could earn a J.D. in Roman law, in church law, or, most commonly, in both. Medicine was studied at Montpellier (in France) and Salerno (in Italy), while the English universities of Oxford and Cambridge were founded by English teachers and students who preferred not having to cross the Channel to Paris.

It should be stressed that the theologians at the University of Paris did not simply discuss well-accepted "truths" about Christianity. Rather, they argued and debated, often rather heatedly, over exactly what those truths might be. This debate was by its very nature rational and analytic. Theology was considered a vibrant and exciting science, and issues concerning the nature of God and Christian salvation were debated using approaches and ideas borrowed from the pagan thinkers of antiquity, even from Jewish and Muslim philosophers. By the end of the thirteenth century, the bishop of Paris, worried that this openness might lead some undergraduates astray, drew up a list of works that were not to be taught to beginning students, though they were still read and discussed by the professors and advanced students.

These university-centered theological debates are but one of many indications that the medieval church and belief system were far from monolithic. Although by far the majority of the population was made up of baptized Christians, and kings felt that the protection and support of churches were sacred aspects of their rule, for the vast majority of the population no one either knew or cared exactly what they believed. Jews were tolerated, although by the later Middle Ages fairly grudgingly. For the most part, the only people accused of heresy were the learned and preeminent, who it was feared might infect others with their fallacious beliefs, or else those who tried to set up an entire alternative church, complete with its own bishops, as did the Albigensian heretics around the year 1200.

Even from among the most devout in the Middle Ages there emitted a fairly steady low-level criti-

Basis of Modern Italian. Portrait of Dante Alighieri by Domenico di Michelino in the Cathedral of Florence, 1465. DUOMO, FLORENCE/ALINARI/ART RESOURCE, NY

cism of the hierarchical church, on the grounds of lapses from the purity expected of leaders of organized religion. But just as, in the modern United States, those who believe most strongly in democracy may be the biggest critics of a particular government, this medieval criticism of the church should not be seen as a rejection of Christianity. The consensus was that the church hierarchy had become corrupt by the fifteenth century; Martin Luther was preceded by a long line of would-be reformers, though the Reformation he began in 1517 was spectacularly successful in a way previous attempts had not been.

LAWYERS AND GOVERNMENT

Another popular misconception about the Middle Ages is that it was a period when violence was the only law. In fact, some of the most important products of the universities were the lawyers. Law became a trained, well-paid profession for the first time. University-trained lawyers served both at medieval Europe's royal courts and at the court of the papacy. Indeed, from the second half of the twelfth century onward, virtually all the medieval popes themselves were trained at the University of Bologna.

In England, university-trained lawyers were employed as judges as the kings developed their system of common law, with the fundamental understanding that a crime was an offense against the Crown, not merely against the victim, and thus ought to be investigated and punished by the royal courts. Grand juries, so called in contrast to the "petit" juries which might decide a case, assembled both to give and to hear testimony of possible lawbreaking (in a system directly ancestral to that of the United States). In France in the thirteenth century, a somewhat similar function was served by the parlements, courts that might be attached either to the Crown or to a particular region. In all of Europe's countries, the kings assisted by lawyers were not gods as in the empires of antiquity, nor even rulers with the special favor of the Christian God such as ruled Europe in the seventeenth and eighteenth centuries; rather, at least through the thirteenth century, they were men whose authority originated in the consent of the governed.

University-trained lawyers could also serve as bureaucrats and record keepers. No government can function without some sort of record keeping, which was particularly challenging in an age before the printing press. When the Crown wished to keep a record of a grant or privilege made to someone, a clerk wrote out a copy for the records by hand. A government that does not keep good records is bound to find itself embarrassed, unable to account for where money has gone, whether it is owed money, discovering that it has made contradictory rulings or promised the same office to two people. Although some record keeping has existed for as long as humans have used writing, the modern understanding that governments and judicial courts needed permanent staffs of bureaucrats dates to the Middle Ages.

Even operating under severe technical disadvantages, beginning around 1200 medieval courts managed to regularize their records. In France the decisive event was the disastrous Battle of Fréteval in 1194, in which the king lost not only his baggage train but all the royal records, which had customarily followed the king wherever he went. From then on he established a permanent group of administrators who kept the records in Paris. Similar developments took place in England and in the papal court. Even now researchers can peruse the registers that scribes struggled to keep tidy seven or eight centuries ago.

MEDIEVAL INVENTIONS

Economically and socially the final two centuries of the Middle Ages were a difficult time, marked by a cooler climate than that of the twelfth century. The cooling resulted in frequent famines; the bubonic plague broke out in the fourteenth century for the first time in western Europe in eight hundred years; and countries were torn by peasant unrest and governmental tyranny, as seen for example among the men who ruled the city-states of the Italian Renaissance. And yet, alongside the social and institutional innovations already noted, it was also a remarkably inventive period in the material realm.

Eyeglasses, which developed out of experiments with optics, first made their appearance at the end of the thirteenth century. Given that over half the modern Western population wears glasses, the development of this correction for nearsightedness was an important step forward, particularly for the literate. In the fourteenth century the invention of paper, which rapidly replaced parchment for all but the most formal documents, made books and writing substantially cheaper than they had been. The mechanical clock, developed around the same time and often equipped with dials for showing phases of the moon and of the zodiac as well as the hours, made it much easier for someone in business or a profession to plan and schedule his day. But perhaps the single most consequential invention of the fourteenth century was gunpowder. The Chinese had long used gunpowder for fireworks, but it took the West to find a way to use it to kill large numbers of people. As cannons were developed in the second half of the century, the face of war was

Law Lecture. Law lecture at the University of Bologna, fourteenth century. Relief from the tomb of Matteo Gandoni (d. 1330). MUSEO CIVICO, BOLOGNA, ITALY/SCALA/ART RESOURCE, NY

transformed. No longer was fighting glorious and chivalrous, with a few well-aimed cannons capable of bringing down a whole row of charging cavalry. Instead, late medieval wars were increasingly fought by common footsoldiers forced into the army or by mercenaries.

The most significant invention of the fifteenth century was the printing press, developed by Johannes Gutenberg (1400–1468) in Germany. Again, the Chinese had already produced something similar, but they had carved an entire page out of one block of wood, whereas Gutenberg's invention featured movable type. With this type a whole page could quickly be set up using metal letters, and after as many copies as desired were printed, the page could be broken down and the letters reused. As a result of improvements in metallurgy in the preceding century, a by-product of the search for better cannons, this type was crisp and clear. In addition, printing presses lowered the price of books drastically because books could be reproduced far more quickly and easily than had ever before been possible. Whereas earlier every copy of every book had been at least slightly different from the next, all copies were now the same. With cheaper, more widely available books, literacy increased rapidly. From the end of the fifteenth century onward, someone trying to argue a point or to rally public opinion could do so in part through leaflets and booklets.

Finally, the fifteenth century invented much better rigging and shipbuilding techniques. By the end of the century European sailors were sailing hundreds and even thousands of miles down the coast of Africa in an attempt to find a passage to the East. By the time Christopher Columbus set off westward with the same purpose in mind, it was reasonable for him to expect his ships to hold together for weeks on the open ocean. But it was of course unreasonable for him to expect to find "India" as quickly as he did. Those who had mocked Columbus for his goal did so not because they expected him to fall off the edge of a flat Earth—the idea that Columbus's contemporaries thought the world was flat is a myth concocted in the nineteenth century. Both sailors and learned theorists in the fifteenth century knew that the Earth was a globe, as indeed had scholars in ancient Greece. What the naysayers believed, correctly, was that the globe was considerably larger than Columbus estimated, and they therefore feared that an insuperable twelve thousand miles of empty ocean lay before him to cross.

Although Columbus was convinced to the end of his life that he had in fact reached India, despite his frustration at never having found the silk and spices he expected, the Spanish Crown quickly realized he had discovered a hitherto unknown continent and claimed New Spain. The Middle Ages come to an end with Columbus, and with Europe's expansion into new territories a new era begins. But it was an era whose social expectations, government, and intellectual life had been formed in the Middle Ages.

See also other articles in this section.

BIBLIOGRAPHY

Baldwin, John W. *The Government of Philip Augustus: Foundations of French Royal Power in the Middle Ages.* Berkeley, 1986. Details the development of administrative techniques by a medieval monarch.

Bouchard, Constance Brittain. *Life and Society in the West: Antiquity and the Middle Ages.* San Diego, Calif., 1988.

Bouchard, Constance Brittain. *"Strong of Body, Brave and Noble": Chivalry and Society in Medieval France.* Ithaca, N.Y., 1998.

Brown, Elizabeth A. R. "The Tyranny of a Construct: Feudalism and Historians of Medieval Europe." *American Historical Review* 79 (1974): 1063–1088. The article that effectively ended medievalists' use of "feudalism" to characterize their period.

Bumke, Joachim. *Courtly Culture: Literature and Society in the High Middle Ages.* Translated by Thomas Dunlap. Berkeley, 1991. Almost encyclopedic in coverage, with the focus on Germany.

Duby, Georges. *The Chivalrous Society.* Translated by Cynthia Postan. Berkeley, 1977.

Duby, Georges. *The Early Growth of the European Economy: Warriors and Peasants from the Seventh to the Twelfth Century.* Translated by Howard B. Clarke. Ithaca, N.Y., 1974.

Duby, Georges. *Rural Economy and Country Life in the Medieval West.* Translated by Cynthia Postan. Columbia, S.C., 1968. The best introduction to the medieval rural economy.

Evergates, Theodore. *Feudal Society in the Bailliage of Troyes under the Counts of Champagne, 1152–1284.* Baltimore, 1975. Uses a close study of Champagne documents as a base for a clear statement of the nature both of knighthood and of peasantry.

Evergates, Theodore, ed. *Aristocratic Women in Medieval France.* Philadelphia, 1999.

Freed, John B. *Noble Bondsmen: Ministerial Marriages in the Archdiocese of Salzburg, 1100–1343.* Ithaca, N.Y., 1995. Discusses the aristocratic "serf-knights" of the Holy Roman Empire.

Freedman, Paul. *The Origins of Peasant Servitude in Medieval Catalonia.* Cambridge, U.K., and New York, 1991. Includes a good deal of information on the meaning of serfdom outside as well as within Catalonia.

Gimpel, Jean. *The Medieval Machine: The Industrial Revolution of the Middle Ages.* New York, 1976. Discusses agriculture, commerce, industry, and inventions in the late Middle Ages.

Gold, Penny Schine. *The Lady and the Virgin: Image, Attitude, and Experience in Twelfth-Century France.* Chicago, 1985.

Hanawalt, Barbara A. *The Ties that Bound: Peasant Families in Medieval England.* New York, 1986. On family and childhood in the late Middle Ages.

Hilton, Rodney. *Bond Men Made Free: Medieval Peasant Movements and the English Rising of 1381.* New York, 1973.

Hyams, Paul R. *Kings, Lords, and Peasants in Medieval England: The Common Law of Villeinage in the Twelfth and Thirteenth Centuries.* Oxford, 1980.

Jaeger, C. Stephen. *The Envy of Angels: Cathedral Schools and Social Ideals in Medieval Europe, 950–1200.* Philadelphia, 1994.

Murray, Alexander. *Reason and Society in the Middle Ages.* Oxford and New York, 1978.

Pounds, N. J. G. *An Economic History of Medieval Europe.* 2d ed. London and New York, 1994.

Reynolds, Susan. *Fiefs and Vassals: The Medieval Evidence Reinterpreted.* Oxford and New York, 1994.

Rosenwein, Barbara H. *Negotiating Space: Power, Restraint, and Privileges of Immunity in Early Medieval Europe.* Ithaca, N.Y., 1999. Includes a discussion of the medieval roots of modern Anglo-American prohibitions on search and seizure.

Russell, Jeffrey Burton. *Inventing the Flat Earth: Columbus and Modern Historians.* New York, 1991. Disproves the hoary notion that fifteenth-century people thought the world was flat.

Thijssen, J. M. M. H. *Censure and Heresy at the University of Paris, 1200–1400.* Philadelphia, 1998.

Wemple, Suzanne Fonay. *Women in Frankish Society: Marriage and the Cloister, 500 to 900.* Philadelphia, 1981.

Wickham, Chris. "The Other Transition: From the Ancient World to Feudalism." *Past and Present* 103 (1984): 3–36.

THE RENAISSANCE

John Martin

For a hundred years after the appearance of Jacob Burckhardt's *The Civilization of the Renaissance in Italy,* first published in 1860, scholars and their public alike imagined the Renaissance as the first chapter in the history of the modern. According to this view, it was in Italy in the age of Petrarch, the Medici, and Machiavelli that the shift from the medieval to our own world took place. The Italian, Burckhardt noted, "was the first-born among the sons of modern Europe." Historians who embraced this view stressed the importance of the period for the emergence of political, ethical, and cultural ideals that were central to the identities of nineteenth- and twentieth-century elites in Europe and the United States. The Renaissance from this perspective was the cradle of individualism and republicanism, of humanism and realism, of secularism and capitalism; it became a period of study in its own right, reaching from about 1300 to 1530 in Italy, and from about 1500 to 1650 in northern Europe.

Scholars no longer find the origins of the modern in the Renaissance, but they have by no means given up on the idea of a "Renaissance" as an important dimension of not only Italian but European society as a whole. In particular, they locate the Renaissance in a cluster of interrelated practices in which many painters, sculptors, architects, humanists, poets, and publishers, as well as courtiers and other political and economic elites—often with an eye to antiquity as a model for their cultural pursuits—creatively and self-consciously engaged. On a broader level, they associate it with shifts in political organization, family and collective life, the practice of religion, and new notions of the self and community; and they have raised important questions about the relation of nonelite groups (women, artisans, peasants, and the poor) to this larger movement. As a result, the "Renaissance" is less likely to be portrayed as a period in and of itself than as an important aspect of late medieval and early modern social, intellectual, and cultural history. Just as the Earth was no longer seen as the center of the cosmos in the teachings of the sixteenth-century Polish canon and astronomer Nicolaus Copernicus, so the Renaissance—once the central organizing element in the history of Europe—has now been demoted to planetary status.

But no one disputes either the splendor of this satellite or that its own force—like that of other heavenly bodies—inevitably, and certainly by the sixteenth century, exercised some influence over the world it orbited. To be sure, the overwhelming mass of Europeans—the 90 percent that made up the peasantry—was virtually untouched by the Renaissance, but both the humanist's study and the artist's workshop were closely connected to the larger political and cultural life of the city and the court. Moreover, the history of Renaissance humanism and art followed a relatively clear trajectory. First emerging in Florence and Tuscany in the fourteenth century, this new cultural style, which involved not only the arts and literature but also ethical and political thought, spread rapidly throughout Italy in the fifteenth century, and then throughout Europe as a whole in the sixteenth century. In such cities as Florence, Venice, and Rome, these initiatives were pursued by large groups of humanists, artists, and poets. And later, in courts from Urbino and Milan in Italy to those of Francis I in France, Elizabeth I in England, and even Matthias Corvinus in Hungary, a similar pattern emerged. The extraordinary creativity of the period—represented by such emblematic figures as Petrarch, Niccolò Machiavelli, Albrecht Dürer, Desiderius Erasmus, Thomas More, Michelangelo, Michel de Montaigne, William Shakespeare, and Rembrandt—was never a matter of individual achievement alone. It was also a social fact, one closely related not only to the history of the city and the court but also to the whole of European society in the late medieval and early modern periods.

THE CRISIS OF THE FOURTEENTH CENTURY

The social forces that underlay the Renaissance stemmed from a series of transformations that began as early as the eleventh century, when Europe witnessed the revival of commerce and urban life. From the fall of Rome and the barbarian invasions down through the tenth century, European society had ceased by and large to be centered on the city, while commerce had been reduced to relative insignificance. Around the year 1000 this trend reversed. By the twelfth century the increasingly dynamic growth of the population led to the emergence of significant clusters of towns and cities, especially in northern Italy and the Low Countries. The same phase of medieval history was characterized by a robust growth in intellectual and cultural life. The twelfth century saw new initiatives in learning in monastic and cathedral schools; by the thirteenth century universities too had become centers of learning and scholarship. Much of the attention of medieval humanists and scholastics focused on classical writers, especially Cicero and Aristotle. Intellectual historians have correctly stressed the medieval antecedents (the *ars dictaminis*, for example, and other forms of "protohumanism") to many of the cultural interests of Renaissance elites.

Yet a marked cultural shift did occur in the late Middle Ages. In the early fourteenth century, for example, the Tuscan painter Giotto (1266?–1337) invested the human figure with a sense of solidity and three-dimensionality that would become a much-emulated element of Renaissance art. And in the mid-fourteenth century, the Italian humanist Petrarch (1304–1374) demonstrated a new sense of historical distance and a new awareness of personality in the ancient authors (especially Cicero and Saint Augustine) whom he studied. By the early and mid-fifteenth century, these and comparable artistic and intellectual practices had become increasingly fashionable, especially among the urban elite of Italy. From the vantage point of social history, these shifts are of particular interest because they developed not in continuity with the expansionary phase of medieval society that had begun in the eleventh century but rather in the midst of a period of crisis. The fourteenth century began with famine and an evident slowing if not stagnation of demographic growth. In all likelihood, by 1300 if not earlier, Europe was in the grip of a Malthusian dilemma as the continent's population, which was growing in the eleventh, twelfth, and thirteenth centuries, began to outstrip resources. The exploitation of the peasantry within the feudal structures of the medieval economy also contributed to the malnourishment and general weakness of the great mass of Europeans. Then in 1347–1348 Europeans confronted an unprecedented catastrophe, the Black Death—the first strike of bubonic plague (*Yersinia pestis*).

The immediate effect of the Black Death was a precipitous drop in population. From 1348 to 1400, during which time there were several outbreaks of bubonic plague, Europe as a whole (east and west) witnessed a loss of between 22 and 28 million individuals out of a total population of some 73 to 74 million. In short, in a fifty-year period as many as one in three Europeans fell victim to the plague. In Florence the death rate was particularly high; in 1348 alone its population dropped from approximately 120,000 to some 40,000 souls, and losses were even greater in other parts of Tuscany. Italy as a whole probably lost one half its population in the latter half of the fourteenth century. Death became a dominant theme in the art of the period; new religious movements such as that of the flagellants, which placed particular emphasis upon repentance and the physical mortification of the body, attracted large popular followings; and there were outbreaks of hostility toward the poor and the Jews. At the same time, the plague appears to have influenced the direction of intellectual life. New universities—some, in response to the epidemics, with a special emphasis on the study of medicine—were established, certain traditional fields were deemphasized, and new ones, notably rhetoric, came to the fore, at least in Italy. In fact, the plagues may even have played a direct role in intensifying the growing sense that classical Latin was a language that required conscious imitation. Before the Black Death medieval academic Latin was organic, practical, and instilled in students at a very young age—in short, it was a living vernacular. The depletion of the ranks of university and Latin teachers and the disruption of the schools during the ravages of plague changed the equation. Suddenly Latin was a "foreign" language that needed to be mastered through the close study and imitation of ancient texts—a new linguistic attitude that would prove fundamental to the development of the Renaissance.

The social and economic consequences were equally decisive. In the short term, trade and industry were disrupted, family life was strained, and civility was frayed. But over the longer term, especially over the next few generations as recurrent visitations of the plague continued to restrict the population's recovery, the fortunes of the survivors varied. Although the situation differed from one part of Europe to another, the late fourteenth and early fifteenth centuries in general witnessed a fall in rents for traditional landlords (the nobility), new opportunities for merchants and financiers, a rise in wages for urban laborers, the erosion of servile bonds in the countryside, and in general new agricultural regimes that at times benefited and at other times led to the further exploitation of the

Flagellants. Flagellants at Doornik, 1349. Copy of a miniature from *The Chronicle of Aegidius Li Muisis.* PRIVATE COLLECTION/THE BRIDGEMAN ART LIBRARY

peasantry. Cities especially needed new men in the crafts and the professions; this period was, as a result, one of relatively high social mobility. Once the economy began to stabilize under these new terms, the standard of living (at least in the cities) increased— one of the preconditions for the demand for luxury goods and commodities that fostered the material culture of Renaissance Europe.

The emergence of Renaissance culture, however, was far more than a matter of new levels of consumption. To be sure, the postplague prosperity of the urban patriciates and their desire to fashion themselves as deserving elites through the conspicuous display of culture were important factors. But so too were the anxieties inherent in a social structure in which the traditional hierarchies were never fixed and in which the family, especially in the aftermath of the Black Death, underwent profound modifications and adjustments. Urban life itself, given the density of the population, the squalor of the poor, the violent tenor of the night, the constant threat of plague, and of course, the need to maintain peace among so many disparate groups, made politics a major concern. Indeed, each of these facets of urban life inevitably played some role in connecting the artistic and cultural life of the period to the actual issues, problems, and anxieties that men and women confronted in late medieval Italy.

When humanists looked to the ancient world, their interests were rarely purely antiquarian or philological. To the contrary, they found in the writings of such figures as Aristotle and Livy important reflections on the constitutional histories of Greece and Rome—reflections made relevant by the deep analogies between the concerns of citizens in the ancient city-states and those of contemporary Italians, whether they were about political life, civic values, or moral questions. It was in this context that fifteenth-century writers in the Italian cities crafted a "civic humanism," a program that stressed the importance of political and social engagement in the life of the Renaissance city.

Social historians have made it plain, however, that the ideals of the civic humanists were aimed above all at the urban elite. Like other aspects of medieval society, the Renaissance city was a profoundly hierarchical place. To a large degree the social structure of these urban environments had evolved out of earlier social systems. In twelfth-century Italy merchant-artisans had wrested power away from local aristocrats (often bishops) and established communal governments that represented their interests. Although many cities—among them Milan, Mantua, and Ferrara— eventually fell under the control of a single individual or family, in both Florence and Venice—as well as in Lucca, Siena, and Genoa—these new commercial elites established their dominance. In Venice the pa-

145

triciate was almost exclusively based on commercial wealth, whereas in such inland cities as Florence, the patricians included both great feudal families that had begun to invest in urban industries and wealthy merchant families that bought up land in the Florentine *contado,* the agricultural hinterland subject to the city's jurisdiction. In Renaissance republics these groups tended to hold political power. Beneath them in prestige were lesser merchants and skilled artisans (goldsmiths, tailors, silk weavers, masons). Many craftsmen and most workers led humbler lives, though even those who only managed to scrape by in poorly paying trades, either as carders or spinners or stevedores and day laborers, enjoyed a stability that set them off sharply from the very poor—the itinerant beggars and vagabonds who thronged the cities during a famine, and also a large underclass of servants and slaves, prostitutes, common outlaws, and con men. Finally, beyond the city were the peasants whose lives were increasingly linked to those living in urban centers through markets and economic exploitation. By the early fifteenth century in the Tuscan countryside, we know that approximately one quarter of the peasants had come to labor as sharecroppers (*mezzadri*) for landlords, often urban landlords. And it was from their labor that much of the wealth of the Renaissance city derived. The economic underpinnings of the social hierarchies of the period were brutal. In early-fifteenth-century Florence and the vast territories subject to it, there were some 60,000 families, nearly two-thirds of whom labored in the countryside. The richest 100 of these 60,000 households, moreover, controlled one-fifth of the wealth, and more than half of the riches in the region were in the hands of an elite 3,000 families, a mere one-half of 1 percent of the entire population. The hierarchy, therefore, was not merely a cultural construction: it was rooted in an economic system that kept most of the population poor and in debt. As Christiane Klapisch-Zuber observes in her *Women, Family, and Ritual,* "the glory of the Renaissance was built on the heightened exploitation of indigent sharecroppers and provincials short of capital" (1985, p. 13).

What is certain is that it was largely from the urban elites as well as from the nobility that the humanists who staffed the chanceries and the growing bureaucracies of the Renaissance governments were recruited. This is hardly surprising, as the educational program the humanists fostered placed a special emphasis on the liberal arts both at school and in the university, with particular emphasis on the study of Latin and rhetoric, a discipline closely related to the need in republics for leaders trained in public speaking and the art of persuasion. By contrast, painters, sculp-

tors, and architects generally came from slightly more humble though still relatively privileged origins. Their fathers tended to be artisans or shopkeepers, often with a close association to the arts. And indeed throughout much of the fourteenth and fifteenth centuries, artists themselves were viewed primarily as craftsmen who carried out their work according to the stipulations of their patrons. Urban environments such as Venice and Florence and, later on, Paris, London, and Amsterdam, with their relatively high concentration of highly skilled artisans, were especially suited to the development of the painting, sculpture, and architecture that was characteristic of the Renaissance.

Generalizations about the family are difficult for both late medieval and early modern history. What is clear is that the late medieval and early modern family did not follow a simple trajectory of progressive nuclearization, with a large, extended family or household giving way to a smaller conjugal unit. Rather, families varied enormously in structure both within and between regions. In Tuscany at the beginning of the fifteenth century, fewer than one in five households were extended in the technical sense of containing more than one conjugal family, though significantly more than one in five Florentines lived in such extended households at one point or another during their life cycles. In England, by contrast, the nuclear family appears to have been even more the norm, though there, too, many families, especially those at the extremes of the wealth spectrum, tended to be larger, with several couples (brothers and their wives) living under one roof. Among the wealthy the European family was also marked by a strong sense of lineage. The families of artisans and the working poor were more often nuclear, with less likelihood of integration into a larger kin network. Marriages in these strata of society were aimed primarily at economic survival, and women in such households often assisted their husbands in their trade.

Among rich and poor, however, the family played a decisive role in shaping the lives of individuals, regulating the births, marriages, and economic activities of its members. Humanist treatises from the period paint a portrait of a profoundly paternalistic institution, and many of the laws worked to keep the family under the control of a patriarch or at least the male lineage. While the wives of many artisans and workers continued to serve important economic functions in their households, the position of upper-class women deteriorated in the Renaissance city as a bourgeois family structure imposed new limitations on women's social and economic activities. At the same time, women often did find ways to protect themselves and their daughters, whom they often sheltered

The Medici Rulers of Florence. The baptism of Cosimo II de' Medici, son of Grand Duke Ferdinand, 1590. Painting by Ventura Salimbeni (1568–1613) from the *Tavoletta di Biccherna.* ARCHIVO DI STATO, SIENA, ITALY/SCALA/ART RESOURCE, N.Y.

from unhappy marriages or from the convent. Again historians have revealed significant gaps between humanist ideals and social realities. The fifteenth-century Venetian humanist Francesco Barbaro insisted that mothers nurse their own children, but women repeatedly chose to put their infants out to wet nurses, often in the countryside. Finally, about children in this age we know extremely little. To be sure, some sermons and treatises placed a new value on childhood, but infanticide and abandonment remained relatively common practices among the most destitute members of society.

In addition to the family, the lives of many late medieval and early modern men (and some women) were shaped to a large degree by guilds, which, like the city itself, had emerged in the eleventh and twelfth centuries as associations of merchants and craftsmen designed to protect their economic and social interests. In the late Middle Ages the guild had come to play a major role in urban politics as well. In Florence guild membership (especially the more affluent merchant guilds) enfranchised citizens to participate in the city's government. In German and Dutch cities too the guild was often the basis of political power. But even in towns and cities in which guildsmen were excluded from political participation, they often provided a basic framework for social activity and gave their members a

stake in the community, setting them off quite clearly from an underclass of day laborers and unskilled workers who had no such organization to protect their interests. The guild was the institution in which apprentices and journeymen were trained, often eventually becoming master craftsmen themselves. Membership in the guilds was widespread. In fourteenth-century Florence, probably 11,000 to 12,000 men (about 10 percent of the population) belonged to guilds; in sixteenth-century Venice, approximately 30,000 (or nearly 20 percent of the population) were members. Not all work was organized by guild. In Florence most of the workers in the textile industry, which employed as many as one in three adult men in the city, were *sottoposti,* unincorporated laborers who did piecework as carders and combers for local clothiers and drapers. It was these workers who participated in the famous revolt of the *ciompi* (the poorest workers) in 1378. They managed to gain some economic and political concessions (including membership in a guild of their own) from the Florentine government, but these concessions lasted for only a few weeks. At roughly the same time similar uprisings took place in Siena and Perugia.

The Renaissance city was characterized as well by a broad range of associations that extended beyond work and family and involved rich as well as poorer residents. The most salient of these were confraternities, brotherhoods that brought together men (and sometimes women) from similar trades, social backgrounds, or neighborhoods, often around the devotion to a particular saint. Social ties were also forged through godparenting and other less formal forms of friendship. The structure of neighborhoods, too, often functioned to make urban life villagelike, bringing rich and poor face-to-face in the street and the marketplace. We can thus imagine the Renaissance city as a web of social networks in which the social hierarchy based on wealth and status was intersected by a complex of institutions—the family, the neighborhood or parish, the guild, and the confraternity—that both expressed and diffused social tensions in the city. Social tensions were also mitigated by the highly ritualized aspects of the late medieval and early modern city. Cities celebrated their social order and harmony through processions and allowed the lower orders to "let off steam" during such annual festivals as carnival.

Much of the art of the period was also closely related to this complex web of solidarities of Renaissance society. Patrician families, ecclesiastical institutions, guilds, and confraternities were the primary patrons of artistic works. The recurrence of bubonic plague in 1363 appears in particular to have prompted many Italians to attend more deliberately to their salvations and to the preservation of their identities as well as those of their families. They commissioned chapels, funeral monuments, and paintings to ensure the memory of themselves and their families. Such behavior was not limited to the wealthy—even relatively modest artisans and laborers participated in this quest for fame. Thus Renaissance ideas about fame percolated through more than the upper echelons of society, though how far they reached and the ways in which they blended with other aspects of the culture at the time are unclear. What is clear is that large numbers of city dwellers in this period occupied a paradoxical relation to Renaissance ideas. Alongside their interests in antiquity and art, they manifested a continuing fascination with magic and the occult as well as a deep core of piety that expressed itself in a rich array of social and religious beliefs and practices.

THE LONG SIXTEENTH CENTURY

The Renaissance was not an exclusively urban affair. Throughout the fourteenth and fifteenth centuries, several courts—especially in Italy—had also served as the locus for the new cultural pursuits. As centers of political, ecclesiastical, and economic power, the courts were ideally suited to attract some of the outstanding figures of the age; toward the end of the fifteenth and throughout the sixteenth century, the court became increasingly central to Renaissance culture. Throughout the fifteenth century, though in theory Florence remained a republic, the Medici in fact controlled most of the political appointments and policies of the republic before finally establishing themselves as the archdukes of Tuscany in the 1530s. Over the same period the papal court in Rome came to dominate not only much of Italian but also much of European culture. Even Venice, which remained a republic, witnessed a decided aristocratization of culture as its urban elites turned away from commerce, invested increasingly in rural properties, and constructed elaborate villas, a fashion that led to many commissions for the influential architect Andrea Palladio (1508–1580). The early Renaissance may have been a largely urban affair, but the aristocracy had never ceased to play a central role in the shaping of culture. Indeed, by the sixteenth century European nobles, empowered by the rising value of land (in a process that social historians refer to as "refeudalization"), were the major patrons of what is called Renaissance culture.

It was in this period that the Renaissance became an increasingly European movement. Probably the most decisive factor in this Europeanization was the shift of political power away from Italy to the new monarchies of Spain, France, and England. The political elites in these kingdoms were keen on importing Italian culture to their cities and courts; indeed we can see the sixteenth century as a period of translation of Italian art and ideas to northern Europe. Cosmopolitan by their very nature, courts attracted leading figures from the aristocracy and the cultural elite throughout Europe. Popes and princes competed for the most accomplished artists and humanists. The virtuoso painter and engineer Leonardo da Vinci (1452–1519) was active not only in his native Florence, where he was a member of the painter's guild, but also at the Sforza court in Milan, the French court of Francis I, and, though fleetingly, the court of the Medici pope Julius II in Rome. Other factors also contributed to the Europeanization of the Renaissance. By 1500 the printing press, which had been invented in Mainz by Johannes Gutenberg in the 1450s, had led to a diffusion of classical and humanist works on an unprecedented scale. In the early sixteenth century, the Dutch humanist scholar Desiderius Erasmus worked for the printer Aldus Manutius in Venice, for Johann Froben's press in Basel, and for Josse Bade in Paris. Thus the print shop, like the court, served to Europeanize humanist culture.

Social change also underlay this development. From the middle of the fifteenth to the early seventeenth century, with plague now a less frequent occurrence, most of Europe participated in a sustained demographic and economic recovery, a period that historians refer to as the "long sixteenth century." The social consequences of this growth were dramatic. Though the precise chronology varied from one part of Europe to another, land and grain became dear, and the overwhelming majority of peasants saw their living standard erode while their landlords reaped the harvest of higher and higher rents. Also conspicuous was the growth of cities in this period. London, which had some 50,000 to 60,000 inhabitants at the start of the sixteenth century, had doubled in size by mid-century and reached as many as 200,000 in 1600. Other major cities—Paris, Antwerp, and Amsterdam—saw comparable gains, with the result that in the sixteenth century northern Europe underwent a process of urbanization that was in some ways comparable to the earlier phase of urbanization that had taken place in Italy. And as in late medieval Italy, the growth of the city and the development of the new urban elites were closely tied to structural transformations in the rural areas, as more and more land was given to pasturage and as textile production was increasingly put out to peasant households often desperate to increase their incomes.

This process (which historians have variously called the putting-out system, *Verlagssystem,* cottage industry, and protoindustrialization) stemmed from the efforts of drapers and clothiers, who in their efforts to find cheap labor deliberately transferred even weaving to the countryside, bringing peasants and their families more fully into the "industrial economy" and further enriching the entrepreneurs who invested in this industry. The social consequences of such a system were widely felt in Europe, especially in highly urbanized areas. The system produced new social tensions but also created new opportunities. The encroachment of industry on the countryside as well as the increased demand for wool and the decision, especially by English landlords, to enclose their arable lands and turn them over to pasturage led to dislocations in traditional agrarian life, creating a new rural poor and contributing to the quickened pace of immigration to the cities, which quickly filled with impoverished migrants.

The cities were hardly able to absorb them. Both rising prices and the flood of workers on the market made it increasingly difficult for them to work their way up the guild hierarchies and establish shops and families of their own. Women who came in from the countryside often eked out an existence as domestic

Town and Country. Haymaking in June, miniature (early fifteenth century) by the Limbourg brothers from *Tres riches heures du duc de Berry.* VICTORIA AND ALBERT MUSEUM, LONDON/THE BRIDGEMAN LIBRARY ART LIBRARY

servants. Not surprisingly, this very process was the source of much of the prosperity of London as well as such Dutch cities as Amsterdam and Leiden, whose elites based their wealth on both rising incomes from landed investments and from the new patterns of exploitation in early modern industry. To a large degree, it was these wealthy burghers who, alongside the aristocracy, became the patrons and consumers of art, luxury goods, and humanist education.

In northern Europe in this period, as had been the case earlier in Italy, much of the writing by humanists sought to respond to the new social problems of the early modern city. In the early sixteenth century, the Spanish humanist Juan Luis Vives, addressing the problem of the widespread growth of poverty in Bruges, published his treatise *On the Subvention of the Poor* (1526). At roughly the same time in the Burgundian city of Lyon, poor relief was shaped by a

Circulation of Printed Matter. A colporter selling prints carrying the news of the assassination of the duc de Guise, 1563. Sixteenth-century print. BIBLIOTHÈQUE NATIONALE, PARIS, HENNIN T. VI NO. 542

practical humanism that sought to apprentice boys to masters and to dower girls for marriages in ways that would save them from lives of poverty. In England, Thomas More's *Utopia* (1516) was, at least in part, a response to the harsh realities of his day.

The early modern Renaissance differed from the late medieval Renaissance in other respects as well. For one thing, as printing presses spread throughout Europe, the book was a far more important factor in the sixteenth century than it had been earlier, and, along with rising literacy rates, it brought the ideas of humanists and other writers—ancient and modern—into contact with an ever wider readership. The culture of reading (the ubiquity of the bookshop and bookstall, the circulation of books among friends and fellow workers, and so on) meant that in the sixteenth century the diffusion of ideas spread farther, perhaps at times into the countryside. The urban world of craftsman was highly literate, and even illiterate artisans must have often heard their fellow workers read from books and discuss them in the shop or over the loom. The book was not merely a cultural item but was itself an instrument of sociability, creating new solidarities and unexpected friendships. This new intensity of the printed word was made more significant by the religious struggles of the Reformation, and an increasingly literate population was a major force in

shaping the writings of humanists and reformers. Vernacular languages became a popular means of communication, though Latin remained important. Intellectuals competed with one another to shape the ideas of their public.

In addition, the period witnessed a veritable explosion in texts aimed at improving the reader's manners. From Castiglione's *Book of the Courtier* (1518) to Erasmus's *Manners for Children* (1530) and Thomas Elyot's *The Boke Named the Governour* (1531), writers laid down new rules of etiquette and comportment. Their most responsive readers were courtiers, but urban elites too began to internalize the new manners as well. This enterprise was viewed as a crucial one in the increasingly crowded urban spaces of the early modern city, for despite their pockets of prosperity, these urban spaces also overflowed with the poor and seemed to threaten the social order itself. Manners and discipline were therefore part of a perceived social need. Outside the court the new etiquette was not only a language about power, it was also a language about the social order, about *urbanitas* (urbanity) and a new civility. Accordingly, it seems reasonable to see the first part of the early modern period as one in which the ideas of the Renaissance, thanks to such factors as growing literacy, the Reformation, and the revolution in manners, began to have some influence on popular groups, at least in the city. The result of these cultural shifts was that the satellite of the Renaissance exercised a stronger gravitational force on the early modern world than it did on late medieval society.

CONCLUSION

The social history of the Renaissance should be seen as consisting of two phases, defined primarily by the demographic fortunes of the European population rather than by the more traditional designations of the Italian and the northern Renaissance. The first phase was the so-called crisis of the fourteenth century, which lasted from about 1300 to about 1450. This phase appears to have prompted social transformations that intensified, especially in the already highly urbanized environment of northern Italy, cultural practices that would become characteristic of the Renaissance as a movement: a growing interest in antiquity as a cultural model and a new emphasis on artistic consumption or the display of wealth by an urban as well as a courtly elite. The second phase is the long sixteenth century, which lasted from about 1450 to about 1620, and contributed, at least in part, to the consolidation of the new cultural interests and their rapid diffusion throughout the cities and courts of western Europe as a whole. Social history therefore connects the Renaissance to the history of both the late medieval and the early modern periods. At the same time social historians have made it plain that the early Renaissance, which derived in important ways from developments in medieval culture, was primarily urban and Italian, while the later Renaissance, which had become a Europe-wide phenomenon increasingly centered on the court, can be fruitfully examined in relation to longer-term developments in early modern culture (most especially the Reformation and the scientific revolution), even down to the time of the French Revolution.

Despite the centrifugal forces inherent in such a distinction, cultural historians can make a strong case for the unity of the Renaissance as an object of study. It remains true that the new attitudes toward language, education, and the past that developed with particular intensity in Italy in the fourteenth and fifteenth centuries came to exercise an almost hypnotic influence on the elites of Europe as a whole in the sixteenth century. Thus, particularly from the vantage point of cultural history, with its emphasis on representations and practices, the Renaissance continues to bridge the late medieval and the early modern periods. In the end, its fascination lies at least in part in its inability to be reduced to (or explained by) social factors alone.

See also **Protoindustrialization; The Population of Europe: Early Modern Demographic Patterns; Health and Disease; The City: The Early Modern Period** *(volume 2);* **Artists; Artisans** *(volume 3);* **Festivals; The Reformation of Popular Culture; Schools and Schooling; Printing and Publishing; Reading** *(volume 5); and other articles in this section.*

BIBLIOGRAPHY

The Social History of the Renaissance in Italy

Baxandall, Michael. *Painting and Experience in Fifteenth-Century Italy: A Primer in the Social History of Pictorial Style.* New York, 1972. Subtle analysis of the commercial and visual content of Renaissance painting.

Brucker, Gene A. *The Civic World of Early Renaissance Florence.* Princeton, N.J., 1977. Influential and insightful investigation into the social tensions that shaped Florentine civic culture.

Burke, Peter. *Culture and Society in Renaissance Italy, 1420–1540.* London and New York, 1972. Examines the multiple social forces that underlay the emergence of the creative elites of the period.

Cohn, Samuel Kline. *Death and Property in Siena, 1205–1800: Strategies for the Afterlife.* Baltimore, 1988. Explores interplay of inheritance strategies, culture, and demography.

Goldthwaite, Richard A. *The Building of Renaissance Florence: An Economic and Social History.* Baltimore, 1980. Magisterial socioeconomic study that deftly links labor to the history of art and architecture.

Grendler, Paul F. *Schooling in Renaissance Italy: Literacy and Learning, 1300–1600.* Baltimore, 1989. Erudite, thorough analysis of schools and who attended; focuses also on curricular issues and changes.

Herlihy, David, and Christiane Klapisch-Zuber. *Tuscans and Their Families: A Study of the Florentine Catasto of 1427.* New Haven, Conn., 1985. Translation of *Toscans et leurs familles: Une étude du catasto florentin de 1427.* The single most important demographic study of a late medieval population.

Kelly, Joan. "Did Women Have a Renaissance?" In *Becoming Visible: Women in European History.* Edited by Renate Bridenthal and Claudia Koonz. Boston, 1977, pages 137–164. Reprinted in her *Women, History, and Theory: The*

Essays of Joan Kelly. Chicago, 1984. Pages 19–50. Challenged scholars to rethink the position of women in Renaissance society.

Martin, Alfred von. *Sociology of the Renaissance.* London and New York, 1944. Classic statement of the Renaissance as an expression of the bourgeoisie.

Martines, Lauro. *The Social World of the Florentine Humanists, 1390–1460.* Princeton, N.J., 1963. An early successful effort to place Renaissance humanists in their social context.

Rosand, David. *Painting in Cinquecento Venice: Titian, Veronese, Tintoretto.* New Haven, Conn., 1982. Among the best works on the social context of Renaissance art.

Ruggiero, Guido. *The Boundaries of Eros: Sex Crime and Sexuality in Renaissance Venice.* New York, 1985. Pathbreaking work; points to the existence of both an illicit and licit sexual culture in late medieval Venice.

Trexler, Richard C. *Public Life in Renaissance Florence.* New York, 1980. Turgid but brilliant rethinking of Florentine society. A total anthropology of the city.

Wackernagel, Martin. *The World of the Florentine Renaissance Artist: Projects and Patrons, Workshop and Art Market.* Translated by Alison Luchs. Princeton, N.J., 1981. Comprehensive analysis of the social milieu of Renaissance artists.

General Studies of the Social and Cultural History of Europe during the Renaissance

Braudel, Fernand. *The Mediterranean and the Mediterranean World in the Age of Philip II.* 2 vols. Translated by Siân Reynolds. New York, 1972–1973. Examines relations among the environment, structures, social trends, and events in the sixteenth-century Mediterranean.

Davis, Natalie Zemon. *Society and Culture in Early Modern France.* Stanford, Calif., 1975. Pivotal work in early modern studies; opened new avenues of research on the connections between social and cultural history.

Hale, John Rigby. *The Civilization of Europe in the Renaissance.* London and New York, 1994. A magisterial work; opens important perspectives on the field.

King, Margaret L. *Women of the Renaissance.* Chicago, 1991. Superb synthesis of 1980s scholarship.

Le Roy Ladurie, Emmanuel. *The Peasants of Languedoc.* Translated with an introduction by John Day. Urbana, Ill., 1974. Translation of *Paysans de Languedoc.* Annaliste and largely Malthusian treatment of early modern France as a function of demographic cycles.

Sacks, David Harris. *The Widening Gate: Bristol and the Atlantic Economy, 1450–1700.* Berkeley, Calif., 1991. A local history of capitalism; brilliant on the interplay of society, economics, politics, and culture.

THE PROTESTANT REFORMATION AND THE CATHOLIC REFORMATION

Ronnie Po-chia Hsia

Traditionally interpreted as the watershed of western Christianity, the Protestant Reformation, together with the Renaissance, had been seen by many scholars as harbingers of a modern age. This classic paradigm, established on the authority of Karl Marx, Friedrich Engels, R. H. Tawney, and Max Weber in the late nineteenth and early twentieth centuries, held sway until the 1970s. Since then, the social history of the Protestant Reformation and of early modern Catholicism has developed away from this stark contrast between traditional, static Catholicism and innovative, modern-looking Protestantism. Historians in particular are increasingly seeing the period from 1500 to 1750 as forming a long duration of historical change, with similar and common social and cultural impact on both Protestant and Catholic Europe.

THE CLASSIC PARADIGM

In *Capital,* Marx locates the sixteenth century as the period of transition from feudalism to capitalism. The Protestant Reformation, by loosening the "shackles of the medieval Church," contributed in general to progress in history. However, Marx was interested in the Reformation only in connection with his general theory of history; it was Engels who elaborated a paradigm for a more detailed social interpretation of the German Reformation. Relying heavily on a book on the 1525 German Peasants' War by Friedrich Zimmerman, a left-wing Hegelian active in 1848, Engels emphasized that the German Reformation transcended theological and religious reforms. The central action of the Reformation, according to Engels, was the uprising of peasants and townsmen in 1525. They pushed ahead a program of social revolution aimed at the total transformation of feudal society. Providing the ideological support for this social revolution were radical preachers, including Thomas Müntzer, who assumed the role of a prescient revolutionary. In this interpretation, Luther emerged in a relatively negative light, for although he challenged the authority of the Catholic Church, in the end he turned against the social revolution of the plebeian masses and sided with the princes and ruling class in upholding the social and political order.

This socialist interpretation of the Reformation went largely unnoticed among professional historians of the Reformation in Germany for whom the dominant modes of interpretation remained theological and political. In France Marxist views attracted primarily economic historians of the sixteenth century like Henri Hauser, who argued that the Calvinist Reformation in France represented a bourgeois challenge to a Catholic feudal order. In Britain this Marxist view found an echo in the work of the socialist Ernest Belfort Bax, who introduced Engels's study of the Peasants' War and the Anabaptist movement to the English-speaking world.

Max Weber injected another element into the social interpretation of the Reformation. Impressed by the affinities between the asceticism and self-discipline in Calvinist theology and the work discipline manifest in capitalism, Weber postulated, in a now famous essay, the relationship between a Protestant ethic of asceticism and a spirit of denial that allowed for capitalist accumulation. Formulated as part of his grand schema in sketching the relationship between religious cultures and social modalities, Weber's thesis of the Protestant ethic and the spirit of capitalism has a twofold significance: first, it reverses the order of importance between ideology/ideas and social/material structures as argued by Marx; and second, it affirms the centrality of the Protestant Reformation in articulating a modern *Weltanschauung* (worldview)—rational, ordered, disciplined, disenchanted from the religious spirit of the Middle Ages. Weber's thesis met with a spirited critique from the British socialist R. H. Tawney, who argued primarily from English examples that a capitalist spirit of greed and accumulation predated the Reformation, implying that an ideological basis was a preexisting condition for the Reformation. Tawney's contribution extended the scope of the discussion beyond central Europe and suggested the im-

The Peasants' War. Friedrich Engels considered the central action of the Reformation to be the uprising of peasants and townsmen in 1525. Knight surrounded by peasants carrying the banner of the Bundschuh (Peasant League), woodcut by Hans Weiditz, from Petrarch's *Trostspiegel* (Augsburg, 1532). BY PERMISSION OF THE BRITISH LIBRARY, LONDON (C39H/25 43 VERSO)

portance of cross-national comparisons in the social history of the Reformation.

The impact of Marx and Weber was much more evident in the social sciences than in history, especially in the study of historical sociology, an approach heavily Weberian in methodology. Until the 1970s the practice of social theory among historians of the Reformation was largely limited to Marxists. The establishment of the German Democratic Republic created the institutional basis for the further elaboration of the Marx-Engels thesis of the Reformation. Coining the term "early bourgeois revolution," East German historians published a whole series of studies in the 1960s and 1970s on the social character of the Reformation. Collectively, these historians argued for seeing the German Reformation, symbolized by the revolutionary year 1525, as the first stage in a long challenge to feudal society by the bourgeoisie, succeeding eventually in 1789 in overthrowing traditional order. In this vision the German Reformation represented an "early bourgeois revolution," to be succeeded by the more successful examples of the English and Dutch revolutions of the seventeenth and the American and French revolutions of the eighteenth centuries. The failure of the German proletariat-peasant alliance was due to the treason of the bourgeoisie (namely Luther and the conservative forces of reform) and its collaboration with the feudal ruling class in suppressing this revolution.

Rejected on the whole by western historians, and often theoretically heavy-handed, the thesis of an early bourgeois revolution nonetheless made a substantial contribution: by offering a clear periodization and a unified interpretation of the years 1476 to 1535, it draws in diverse topics of research hitherto treated in isolation—peasant revolts, millenarian movements, Martin Luther, the evangelical movement, the rise of Anabaptism, and so forth. The thesis of "early bourgeois revolution" challenged non-Marxist historians to find alternative models to explain the relationship between ideas and social movements in the Reformation. Moreover, by giving the radical reformers and the Anabaptist movement a central place in the interpretation of the Reformation, Marxist scholarship served as a refreshing antidote to the hegemony of Luther-scholarship in Reformation studies, that had tended to relegate dissident reform and sectarian movements to the fringes.

CHALLENGING THE PARADIGM

The dominant mode of interpretation—the Reformation originating in Luther's theology and presaging modernity—came under assault not only from Marxist interpretation. In intellectual history the trend shifted from stressing Luther's modernity to his indebtedness to late medieval scholastic philosophy and mysticism, an interpretive move represented primarily by Heiko Oberman and his students. Thus Luther appeared less "a modern man" than a Christian of his time, steeped in beliefs of the devil and the supernatural. This undermining of Reformation's modernity came also from historians of Catholic background, who have long objected to the unequal treatment of the Protestant and Catholic sides of the religious experience of early modern Europe.

Objecting to the equation of Protestant modernity and Catholic backwardness, isolated voices called for a reinterpretation in the late 1960s. A pioneer historian of Catholic Europe, Henry Outram Evennett objected to "dealing [with] the concept of the Counter-Reformation as essentially 'reactionary' and backward-looking." He and others were dealing with deeply entrenched images of Catholicism propped up by the violence of Spanish arms and the repression of the Inquisition, of a Catholic Church suppressing liberty of conscience and crushing dissent.

By the 1970s there was considerable interest in rewriting the history of Catholicism in the early modern period, a development that paralleled a growing interest in the social history of the Reformation. That latter interest was already sparked by a 1962 landmark essay, "Imperial Cities and the Reformation," by the German Reformation specialist Bernd Moeller. Sensing a fundamental difference between the theology of reformers in south Germany and the Swiss Confederation—such as Martin Bucer and Ulrich Zwingli—and that of Luther, Moeller argues that the experience of communal living in politically autonomous cities (namely, the imperial cities of the Holy Roman Empire) shaped the citizens' response to and adaptation of Luther's message of religious reform. Slowly, Moeller's ideas attracted the attention of historians in Germany and in the English-speaking world. A series of monographs published in the 1970s and 1980s furnished case studies to test his hypothesis in greater detail. This internal development of Reformation scholarship vastly enriched the field, bringing to it a variety of approaches and interpretations after toppling the hegemonic discourse of Protestant modernity. Four distinct approaches in the social and cultural interpretation of Protestantism and Catholicism in early modern Europe have emerged since the 1970s. These approaches may be described by the short-hand labels "communalism," "social discipline," "Catholic modernity," and "dechristianization."

Protestant and Catholic Contrasted. A German broadsheet comments on the restoration of Catholicism in England in the 1550s: the Catholic clergy, portrayed as wolves, kill the sheep under the direction of a devil who holds the inscription "I am the pope." ZENTRALBIBLIOTHEK, ZÜRICH, SWITZERLAND (PAS II 1/4a)

COMMUNAL REFORMATION

The concept of the Reformation as a "communal Reformation" (*Gemeindereformation*) is associated with the German historian Peter Blickle and his students. The fundamental thesis of "communal Reformation" is to argue that the religious reforms of the early sixteenth century originated not only, or perhaps not even primarily, from the top—that is, from reformers and intellectuals—but from the bottom, from the common man—that is, the politically enfranchised peasants and townsmen represented in village and urban communes. One recognizes here an echo of Moeller's thesis of "Imperial Cities and the Reformation," but the origin of "communal Reformation" lies in a long tradition of German social and institutional history. The commune—a juridical, institutional, political, and social construct—shaped the experiences, visions, and actions of the common man, according to this argument. Embedded in oral traditions of rights, rural and urban charters, protest movements, and sometimes political representation in territorial estates, the political rights of commoners were very important in southwest Germany and Switzerland. Used to governing their daily affairs and unafraid to contest the impingement of those rights by feudal lords and territorial officials, the common men shaped the demands of religious reform according to their political and social experiences. Blickle and his students have revealed a high degree of popular participation in religious life prior to the Reformation, in the form of endowment of chantries, charities, and other pious foundations, not only in the numerous towns in this part of the Holy Roman Empire, but also in the village-communes.

It was thus not an accident that the center of unrest in 1525 lay in this region; it was also self-evident that the political, economic, and religious demands of the Revolution of 1525, as Blickle calls the Peasants' War, should be entirely intertwined. What the peasants and townspeople demanded, in the early years of the reform movement, was not less religion, but more; specifically, they wanted a clergy responsive to their spiritual needs and responsible to the communes. Although defeated in 1525, the political power of the common man was not vanquished, for south Germany remained the arena of peasant unrest into the early nineteenth century.

In the Swiss Confederation by contrast, the communal Reformation triumphed. In the Protestant German-speaking cantons religious reforms were enacted not contrary to but in conjunction with popular demands for greater social discipline and moral conformity. Influenced by the thesis of communal Reformation, Heinrich R. Schmidt, a student of Blickle, argues with the example of the moral court (*Sittengericht*) of Bern that a strict disciplinary reform of morals and religious practices was in conformity with the wishes of the common men. The criminalization of sin therefore represented both an act of self-discipline by the politically represented members of communes and an act of repression against the propertyless and unruly elements of rural society.

By arguing for the importance of the common man as an antithesis to the hegemony of the state, Blickle and his students opened up an original and suggestive interpretation for understanding the German Reformation and the development of early modern history in central Europe. The concept of communal Reformation, however, is not without its critics. Some pointed out the exclusion of women, landless cottagers, Jews, youth, and other politically disenfranchised groups in rural society. Others countered that the commune, in certain areas of the Swiss Confederation such as the Grison, had acted as an obstacle to the Protestant Reformation. Above all, the validity of this concept seems limited to a region coterminous with south Germany and Switzerland. One

critic objected that the communal Reformation does not work as a concept to explain the Reformation in northern Germany, where the territorial state played a much more interventionist mode, let alone in France or eastern Europe.

SOCIAL DISCIPLINE

The concept of "social discipline" traces its origins to the 1960s. The German historian Gerhard Oestreich introduced this concept to describe several changes in early modern Europe: namely, the emergence of neostoicism as a life philosophy (for prominent scholars such as Justus Lipsius) and as a philosophy of state (for Calvinist Brandenburg-Prussia and the Netherlands). In these Calvinist territories, neostoicism served to elevate the authority of the prince; military reform, state building, and church discipline went hand-in-hand. According to Oestreich, the rise of absolutism in the late seventeenth and eighteenth centuries, and the creation of powerful military states, such as Prussia, rest upon this foundation of "social disciplining," by which the people became obedient, pious, and diligent subjects of their princes.

Two German historians, Heinz Schilling and Wolfgang Reinhard, later applied this concept, adapted retroactively to the sixteenth century, to the study of confessional societies formed as a result of the Reformation. They speak of the concept of "confessionalization," thus underlining the process of changes that involved the religious, political, cultural, and social structures of early modern Germany. This argument has a threefold implication: first, it points to the structural parallelism between Lutheran, Calvinist, and Catholic societies, with all manifesting "modern" traits of greater state and social coercion and self-disciplining; second, it argues that confessionalization created social groups, "the three confessions," by a variety of means, including the formulation of dogma, confessional propaganda, education, discipline, rituals, and religious language; and third, that confessionalization strengthened political centralization when the early modern state used religion to consolidate its territorial boundary, to incorporate the church into the state bureaucracy, and to impose social control on its subjects.

As a concept, social discipline has an appeal of universality. Developed out of German case studies, it was accepted, modified, and applied to studies in the Netherlands, France, and Italy. Above all, social discipline attempts to unite political history with social history by refocusing attention on the state as a major force that shaped social and religious contours. Its uni-

A Catholic Missionary in Asia. The Jesuit missionary Martino Martini (1614–1661) on his way to visit the emperor of China. Illustration from *Novus atlas sinensis* (Vienna 1653), an atlas of China published by B. Trent, Jesuit missionary and geographer. New York Public Library

versality also stems from its emphasis on structures, almost to the point of effacing the differences between the different Christian confessions, according to some critics. It offers nevertheless a provocative, unified theory in place of the Marxist "early bourgeois revolution" to describe the synchronicity of political, social, and religious changes in early modern Europe.

While the theory of social discipline further refined its argument in the specific cases of Lutheran, Calvinist, and Catholic societies, its initial formulation was modified by a more nuanced dialectic between state intervention and social resistance. Critics of this approach emphasized the ever present importance of popular resistance to confessionalization and social discipline imposed by the state. The debate revived, in some measure, an interest in Max Weber, which seemed to have all but disappeared between the publication of his essay in 1905 and the 1960s. By focusing on the role played by Calvinist states (the Netherlands, Brandenburg-Prussia) in a perhaps enforced modernization, the theory of social discipline influenced late-twentieth-century work in historical sociology as well.

EARLY MODERN CATHOLICISM

The question of modernity, central to Weber's original investigation, also underpins an ongoing reevaluation of the relationship between the Protestant Reforma-

tion and early modern Catholicism. As mentioned above, by the 1970s there was considerable interest in rewriting the history of early modern Catholicism, in recasting the stereotypes of a repressive Counter-Reformation and a modernizing Reformation. A major departure was in chronology. Whereas scholarship on the Reformation concentrates on the period 1517 to 1559, the diversity and multiplicity of historical currents linked to Catholic resurgence clearly cannot be captured within this narrow periodization. Both ends of this time frame were being stretched: while the American historian John C. Olin pushed back the origins of reform within the Catholic Church to late-fifteenth-century Spain and Italy, German and French historians were extending their vision forward to the eighteenth century. The new approach in German Catholic scholarship was not so much to contest the term "Counter-Reformation" as to elevate it to a par with "Reformation." A landmark essay by Wolfgang Reinhard in 1977 rejects the antithesis of "progressive Reformation" and "reactionary Counter-Reformation" and "Catholic Reform" as inadequate concepts in understanding the totality of historical development. Reinhard, in fact, argues for the modernity of Counter-Reformation Catholicism, locating its modern characteristics in its disciplinary and Christianizing measures, its reforms of Church government, its undermining of kinship in favor of social control and a greater individualism, its emphasis on internaliza-

157

tion of values and activism, its extension of European Christianity to the non-European world, and in its creation of a new pedagogic system, new political themes, and a new ethos of political economy.

Other scholars see a similar modernity in early modern Catholicism. The German historian Ernst Walter Zeeden highlights the structural parallels between Calvinism and the Counter-Reformation, while the British historian John Bossy, in a series of studies on Catholic rituals and kinship, demonstrates just how different early modern Catholicism was in comparison with the Christianity of Europe during the Middle Ages. By contrasting a pre-Tridentine Christianity based on the natural allegiances of late medieval society—kinship, friendship, and locality—to one organized theologically and administratively from above by the official, centralizing Church, Bossy's research suggests interesting ways in which the period from 1500 to 1800 witnessed similar and general changes in all of Europe, Protestant and Catholic.

In extending early modern Catholicism beyond the Council of Trent, scholarship of the late 1990s points to the significance of Catholic missions and the encounter between European and non-European civilizations. This shift reflects a greater recognition that any history of Christianization in Europe—the subject matter of popular religion and the social history of Catholicism—would be enriched by a cultural history of Catholic missions. The Catholic world, floating as it were on the seaborne empires of Spain and Portugal, early acquired a world-historical dimension, in contrast to Protestant Europe and its late organization in the mission field.

THE SOCIOLOGY AND MENTALITY OF RELIGION: DECHRISTIANIZATION

The fourth general approach, one that characterized French and Italian scholarship, may be described as the structural investigation into the sociology and mentality of religion. Confessional conflicts between Catholic and Protestant are of less concern for these historians, whose works deal with longer durations. A key figure in this approach to the social history of religion in early modern Europe was the French sociologist Gabriel Le Bras, whose concern with declining rates of church attendance in early-twentieth-century France launched research into what may be called the sociology of ecclesiastical conformity. In studying records of diocesan visits mandated by the Council of Trent, Le Bras and his students began the systematic investigation into the history of all dioceses in early modern France. Producing impressive data on church property, income, and figures of baptisms, communion, confessions, and so forth, this sociological approach provided a far sharper contour of the landscape of piety in early modern France than in any other European country.

The quantitative data provided by parish records and diocesan visitations also yielded interesting material for reconstructing the evolution of religious mentalities. Taking their clue from historians associated with the *Annales,* historians of religion have made interesting excursions into the history of mentalities. Studies of saint cults, attitudes toward death, and particular styles of Catholic piety were undertaken by detailed analyses of wills and donation records at pilgrimage shrines. A major finding in these quantitative studies is that Catholic piety increased in intensity from the second half of the sixteenth century to the beginning of the eighteenth, but was followed by a long and gradual decline in devotional fervor. Particularly striking was the increasing indifference or hostility of elites toward Tridentine and baroque Catholicism during the eighteenth century.

Describing this phenomenon as "dechristianization," Jean Delumeau, a leading French historian of Christianity, saw little long-term structural distinction between Reformation and Catholic resurgence. In his 1977 book, *Catholicism between Luther and Voltaire,* he dismisses the significance of the Counter-Reformation altogether: "The Counter-Reformation existed . . . but it was not essential to the transformation of the Catholic Church from the sixteenth century." Instead, Delumeau establishes a sharp contrast between medieval and early modern Europe: medieval Christianity ("the legend of a Christian Middle Ages" in his words) was magical and pagan; Tridentine Catholicism represented a massive attempt at Christianization, achieved by the training of new clergy, the catechizing of the common people, evangelizing the non-European world, and combating popular beliefs. Weaning the people away from their familiarity with medieval saints and folk beliefs, early modern Catholicism was in contrast a fearful, external, and coercive religion. For Delumeau both the Protestant Reformation and Catholic reform were subordinate to the even longer process of Christianization. But the people, faced with this alien, fearful religion, resisted the "culpabilization" of society, holding on to the familiar rituals and saints that gave them succor and consolation in an age of material want. Dechristianization during the eighteenth century represented, in Delumeau's view, a response to this program of coercive evangelization, and also to the gradual improvement of material life that alleviated fear and anxiety.

Catholic Saints. Title page of *Acta sanctorum* for the month of January edited by Jean de Bolland (Antwerp, 1643), the first volume of a series of lives of the saints published by the Jesuits. BY PERMISSION OF THE BRITISH LIBRARY, LONDON (485.E.1)

The unmistakable implication of Delumeau's work is to demonstrate the distinct character of Catholicism in early modern Europe. Historians no longer see the Counter-Reformation or the Catholic renewal as a revival of pre-Reformation Catholicism. Late-twentieth-century studies of the social history of Catholic Europe between 1500 and 1800 confirm this picture. The French historian Louis Châtellier investigated in turn the elites and the underclasses of early modern Europe. Drawing on sources from France, Spain, Italy, the Low Countries, and central Europe, Châtellier documented the emergence of a distinctly elitist Catholic piety that characterized the supporters of the Jesuits, who comprised nobles and urban elites. At the other end of the social spectrum, the many new Catholic religious orders created after the Reformation targeted the most backward rural inhabitants for evangelization, preaching a message of spiritual consolation

in deference to the state. The creation of a Catholic society of estates was in the making.

REFORMATION, SOCIETY, AND SOCIAL CHANGE

These currents of scholarship challenged received notions of "Counter-Reformation" and "Catholic reform." In the 1990s, works of synthesis spoke of Catholic renewal and early modern Catholicism to denote a distinctly "modern" nature to developments in the Catholic world between the sixteenth and eighteenth centuries. This, taken together with revisionist scholarship on Protestantism that stressed the survival of medieval Christianity in Lutheran rituals and symbols, reveals a remarkable convergence. Whether one speaks of "social discipline," "confessionalization," "Christianization," or other concepts, scholarship on Protestant and Catholic Europe arrived at a general consensus: that the period 1500 to 1800 represents a distinct period in the history of religion, that parallel developments in Protestant and Catholic Europe in the terrain of social and cultural history outweigh the obvious differences in confession, and that the religious transformations of the period cannot be understood without an analysis of the larger trends of global expansion, state centralization, and social revolutions. There remain of course many points of disagreement and controversy; this brief sketch does not do full justice to the rich array of scholarship in the field. Transcending the four general approaches one can also identify clusters of themes that have received the most attention from social historians. These questions all revolve around the nature of religion and society: in other words, the relationships between religious crises and social change in early modern Europe.

Research on confessional societies has focused on two questions: First, how did religion account for differences in Protestant and Catholic societies? And, second, what was the precise relationship between social and religious change?

The first question addresses the notable differences in education, literacy, suicide rates, marital regimes, fertility rates, and social stratification between Catholic and Protestant societies. Two examples must suffice to illustrate the highly interesting research in this area. It has been demonstrated, for example, that in Oppenheim—a small German town on the Rhine with a confessionally mixed population during the early modern era—the Catholic community enjoyed the highest fertility rate and demographic growth, followed at a substantial distance by the Lutheran and Calvinist communities. Other case studies in historical demography seem to confirm this general trend; the general pattern of demographic differences between Protestant and Catholic countries is of course well recognized for the nineteenth and twentieth centuries. Another example is the study of suicide, inspired by Émile Durkheim's classic study that suggested important confessional differences in rates of suicide. Markus Schär's study of the canton of Zurich between 1500 and 1800 demonstrates a remarkable effect of Calvinism: as the Calvinist Reformation took root, first in the city of Zurich and later in its rural hinterland, a successful effort at social discipline vastly reduced the rate of homicide. However this campaign against violence and for self-discipline came at a high price: the decline in the homicide rate reflected almost as a mirror image a sharp rise in suicide rates in the three centuries under study. Particularly telling is that the highest rates of suicide were found among the social and religious elites most responsible for the social disciplining. Until similar studies are undertaken for Lutheran and Catholic areas, it is too soon to draw firm conclusions; but the example of Zurich suggests that Weber's notion of a Protestant (i.e., Calvinist) ethic was connected to more than just the spirit of capitalism.

The second question, on the relationship between social and religious change, is obviously much more complex and ambiguous. Aside from the concept of class struggle, gone out of fashion with the demise of the German Democratic Republic, the term "social class" is still employed by social historians as an imprecise but unavoidable heuristic device. More precise research has instead focused on two social groups: the clergy and the elites.

Although Protestants decried the privileges of the Catholic clergy, the Reformation, particularly in Lutheran Europe, created a self-replenishing Protestant clergy. Recruited primarily from the middling social groups in towns, the Protestant clergy was in terms of social origins markedly different from the Catholic clergy: it was much more homogenous, characterized by endogamy (marriage within the group) and generational succession; it tended to be better educated, with a university training almost a prerequisite ; and its origins were more urban, with the nobility and peasantry heavily underrepresented. Much of the research has focused on Lutheran Germany. Similar social histories of the Catholic clergy are less than abundant.

Study of elites.

The study of elites tries to identify the social groups most responsible for religious change. In spite of numerous monographs, this issue is so complex and conditions differed so much from country to country or even from place to place that valid general conclusions are hard to come by. Nonetheless, research has established some general patterns.

First, it seems that the Reformation movement (in Germany, the Low Countries, France, and England) attracted among its first supporters primarily clerical dissidents, merchants, printers, and artisans; that it found the strongest support in cities, where literacy and modes of communication were the densest; that, aside from the Peasants' War in Germany and other isolated examples, it attracted few followers in rural areas; and that its success was often determined by power politics.

Second, the strongest support for confessionalization and social discipline seems to have been provided by the urban middle and upper classes and by rural elites. These social groups included lawyers, professors, officials, merchants, rich artisans, and village notables—the same social groups that provided most of the clergy for the competing Christian confessions as well. Many urban families apparently underwent a transformation from mercantile to judicial/official pursuits. This transformation seems to have taken place during the course of the entire sixteenth century and corresponded to what Fernand Braudel called "the treason of the bourgeoisie." What seemed clear is that the consolidation of confessional states and the attempt to exercise tighter social and religious control considerably expanded the apparatus of the state (in the form of larger administration, both secular and ecclesiastical) and provided the most significant means of upper social mobility for the urban middle classes. This process was at work in both Catholic and Protestant areas. With the notable exception of the Netherlands and England, service to the state and the church apparently replaced trade as the preferred ladders of social success in early modern Europe.

Women and gender.

Instead of social groups, other researchers chose to analyze women and gender to investigate the relationship between society and religion. Perhaps more than other fields of history, the study of Protestant and Catholic Europe had neglected the role of women, mirroring the marginalization of women in the discourses of Protestant reformers and in Tridentine Catholicism. Research in the 1980s and 1990s filled many gaps: some of the topics include marriage, divorce, the reformers' attitude toward women, Catholic women and the Counter-Reformation, and so forth. Careful rereadings of sources and new research revealed that women were involved in all aspects of religious change, both for and against the Reformation.

The most significant impact of the Protestant Reformation on the family, as recent research argues, was the strengthening of patriarchy. Reformers and magistrates reinforced patriarchal authority and household stability in two ways, by elevating the status of marriage and the family life, and by attacking the elements that threatened the patriarchal household. Along the first line, reformers praised the ethical and Christian status of holy matrimony, arguing that marriage and family provided the optimal institution for Christian instruction and a bulwark against sin. The second strategy aimed at imposing stricter moral discipline for unmarried women, youths, and wayward patriarchs. The keeping of parish records, admonition from pastors, and disciplinary measure from church and state resulted in a stricter disciplinary regime that regulated sexuality and property. While the research on women corrects a long-neglected topic, fewer studies have used gender as a theoretical tool, with the notable exception of works on witchcraft and sexuality.

The study of witchcraft reflects a strong current of interest in religious and social dissent that was rare in Reformation scholarship before the 1960s. This scholarly enthusiasm for popular religion mirrored the political activism of many practitioners, who identified the official church as one of the repressive institutions of society; it also represented a new interest in sources hitherto neglected by historians, namely the rich extant records of the Inquisition in Spain, Portugal, and Italy. While the *longue durée* and quantitative serial sources characterized the practice of the social history of religion in France, a legacy of the *Annales* paradigm, the study of religious dissent found its most interesting practitioners in Italy, in the works of Delio Cantimori and Carlo Ginzburg, among others. Taking Protestant dissent and popular religion as their subjects, these historians of the Left used the documents of the Catholic Church to demonstrate a variety of religious views and practices that were suppressed in the course of the sixteenth and seventeenth centuries. Witchcraft and magic constituted two fulcrums of research.

There have been three important conclusions in this research. First, magical beliefs and practices (the majority of which were associated with healing and medicine) were extremely widespread before the Reformation and persisted, even after concerted efforts at their elimination by the official Church after the sixteenth century. Second, religion and magic often coexisted as complementary systems in popular religion: images of saints, statues of the Virgin Mary, and official prayers were all used for extraliturgical and outright prohibited practices in the rural societies of early modern Europe. It was precisely to draw a sharper line of demarcation that Tridentine Catholicism waged an unrelenting campaign against the cunning men and wise women of the villages. Finally, the battle against magic/witchcraft and the war against heresy merged into one great conflagration. The first examples predate even the Reformation, when Waldensians in the mountainous regions between Switzerland, France, and Italy were hounded as heretics and witches. Images of the witches' sabbath were applied with increasing frequency to charges of heresy; and the ferocity of trials against religious dissidents equaled those conducted against suspects of witchcraft during the course of the sixteenth century. It led to an ineluctible logic at the height of the great witch hunts in the early seventeenth century: the conflation of the heretic and the witch as one and the same.

It is evident from this brief survey that there exist strong national and methodological differences in the social history of Reformation and Catholic Europe in the early modern era. Some of these differences originate in national traditions of historical scholarship; others reflect the different historical sources and legacies of Protestant and Catholic Europe. While social historians of both Protestant and Catholic Europe search parish records and visitation reports to reconstruct histories of piety, specialists on early modern Catholicism have access to the unique documentation of the Inquisition. The fifty thousand dossiers from the Spanish Inquisition and the twenty-three thousand from the Portuguese, in addition to the newly opened records of the Roman Inquisition, have already yielded a rich harvest of scholarship and hold still greater promise for twenty-first-century scholarship.

See also **Witchcraft** *(volume 3);* **Belief and Popular Religion; Catholicism; Church and Society; Protestantism; The Reformation of Popular Culture** *(volume 5).*

BIBLIOGRAPHY

Blickle, Peter. *Communal Reformation: The Quest for Salvation in Sixteenth-Century Germany.* Translated by Thomas Dunlap. Atlantic Heights, N. J., 1992.

Blickle, Peter. *Obedient Germans?: A Rebuttal.* Translated by Thomas A. Brady Jr. Charlottesville, Va., 1997.

Blickle, Peter, *The Revolution of 1525: The German Peasants' War from a New Perspective.* Translated by Thomas A. Brady and H. C. Erik Midelfort. Baltimore, Md., 1981.

Bossy, John. *Christianity in the West 1400–1700.* Oxford, 1985.

Châtellier, Louis. *The Europe of the Devout: The Catholic Reformation and the Formation of a New Society.* Cambridge, U.K., 1989.

Châtellier, Louis. *The Religion of the Poor: Rural Missions in Europe and the Formation of a Modern Catholicism, c. 1500–1800.* Cambridge, U.K., 1997.

Delumeau, Jean. *Catholicism between Luther and Voltaire: A New View of the Counter-Reformation.* London, 1977. Translation of *Le Catholicisme entre Luther et Voltaire.* Paris, 1971.

Delumeau, Jean. *Le péché et la peur: La culpabilisation en Occident (XIIIe–XVIIIe siècles).* Paris, 1983.

Delumeau, Jean. *La peur en Occident, (XIVe–XVIIe siècles): Une cité assiégée.* Paris, 1978.

Evennett, Henry Outram. *The Spirit of the Counter-Reformation.* Cambridge, U.K., 1968.

Friesen, Abraham. *Reformation and Utopia: The Marxist Interpretation of the Reformation and Its Antecedents.* Wiesbaden, Germany, 1974.

Ginzburg, Carlo. *Night Battles: Witchcraft and Agrarian Cults in the Sixteenth and Seventeenth Centuries.* Translated by John and Anne C. Tedeschi. London, 1983.

Gorski, Philip S. "The Protestant Ethic Revisited: Disciplinary Revolution and State Formation in Holland and Prussia." *American Journal of Sociology* 99 (1993): 265–310.

Guggisberg, Hans R., and Gottfried G. Krodel, eds. *The Reformation in Germany and Europe: Interpretations and Issues.* Special volume of the *Archiv für Reformationsgeschichte* (1993).

Hsia, R. Po-chia, *Social Discipline in the Reformation: Central Europe 1550–1750.* London, 1989.

Hsia, R. Po-chia. *The World of Catholic Renewal 1540–1770.* Cambridge, U.K., 1998.

Hsia, R. Po-chia, ed. *The German People and the Reformation.* Ithaca, N. Y., 1988.

Le Bras, Gabriel. *Études de sociologie religieuse.* 2 vols. Paris, 1955.

Moeller, Bernd. *Imperial Cities and the Reformation: Three Essays.* Philadelphia, 1972.

Oestreich, Gerhard. *Neostoicism and the Early Modern State.* Cambridge, U.K., 1982.

Reinhard, Wolfgang. "Gegenreformation als Modernisierung? Prolegomena zu einer Theorie des konfessionellen Zeitalters." *Archiv für Reformationsgeschichte* 68 (1977): 226–252.

Roper, Lyndal. *The Holy Household: Women and Morals in Reformation Augsburg.* Oxford, 1989.

Schär, Markus. *Seelennöte der Untertanen: Selbstmord, Melancholie und Religion im Alten Zürich 1500–1800.* Zurich, Switzerland, 1985.

Schilling, Heinz. *Civic Calvinism in Northwestern Germany and the Netherlands: Sixteenth to Nineteenth Centuries.* Kirksville, Mo., 1991.

Schilling, Heinz, ed. *Kirchenzucht und Sozialdisziplinierung im frühneuzeitlichen Europa.* Berlin, 1994.

Schmidt, Heinrich Richard. *Dorf und Religion: Reformierte Sittenzucht in Berner Landegemeinden der Frühen Neuzeit.* Stuttgart, Germany, 1995.

Scribner, Robert W. "Is There a Social History of the Reformation?" *Social History* 2 (1977): 483–505.

Tawney, R. H. *Religion and the Rise of Capitalism.* London, 1926.

Wiesner, Merry E. *Women and Gender in Early Modern Europe.* Cambridge, U.K., 1993.

Zschunke, Peter. *Konfession und Alltag in Oppenheim: Beiträge zur Geschichte von Bevölkerung und Gesellschaft einer gemischtkonfessionellen Kleinstadt in der frühen Neuzeit.* Wiesbaden, Germany, 1984.

THE EARLY MODERN PERIOD

Jonathan Dewald

Few historical labels conceal so much uncertainty as "early modern Europe." The authors of fifteen late-twentieth-century texts whose titles include the phrase date the beginning of the period variously between 1350 and 1650, with 1500 the plurality choice, and its end between 1559 and 1800. The three-century difference of opinion over when the period begins equals the length of the period itself, as most of these historians understand it; one historian sees the period ending almost a century before another's starting point. The present article defines the period as extending from 1590 to 1720. Thus envisioned, it starts with the last spasms of Europe's religious wars; these opened a period of extreme political violence across the continent, and coincided with a variety of other disruptions of Europeans' daily lives. The early eighteenth century brought this period of instability to a close. By 1720 religion had declined as a factor in European politics, and the Enlightenment's critique of organized religion had begun. The last of Louis XIV's great wars ended in 1713, opening a period of relative peace, and by happy coincidence Europe's most frightening disease, the plague, disappeared from the Continent after 1720. A series of other changes in European social organization added to the sense of relative security that would characterize the eighteenth century. Divergences of this order partly reflect historians' use of "early modern" as a handy catch-all term for a confusing period, whose contours shift according to national and thematic perspectives; but they also result from important interpretive differences.

THE PROBLEM OF PERIODIZATION

Historians' understanding of the early modern period has been affected by their different views of modernity itself, whose foundations are commonly seen to have been established at some point between the Renaissance and the French Revolution; differences of periodization reflect different ideas about the crucial moments in modernity's unfolding. Such uncertainties are the less easily resolved in that seventeenth-century men and women already believed in their own modernity. In 1687 the French writer and architect Charles Perrault launched the "quarrel of the ancients and the moderns" with the claim that recent artists and writers had advanced far beyond anything achieved in the ancient world. His claims with regard to the arts stimulated hot debate, but by that time recent advances had made modernism self-evidently persuasive in the domains of science and philosophy.

Especially since World War II, historians of the early modern period have interested themselves in a second set of interpretive concerns, in some tension with this interest in finding the roots of modernity. Europeans' own experiences of industrialization and their interest in economic development elsewhere encouraged historians to reflect on the break between preindustrial and industrial societies, and to see in industrialization the crucial difference between modern and premodern worlds. Such interpretations set the early modern period within a much larger premodern era, and indeed suggested that the break between medieval and early modern mattered far less than the historical changes of the later eighteenth and early nineteenth centuries, the early phase of the industrial revolution.

During the 1960s and 1970s, European historians working within several independent national traditions offered interpretations of this kind, seeing in the age of industrial and political revolutions around 1800 a break in human history more important than any since the invention of fixed agriculture. In France Emmanuel Le Roy Ladurie used the phrase "immobile history" to suggest that society changed little between the mid-fourteenth and the mid-eighteenth centuries. Stagnant agricultural technology underlay this immobility, for food production set the limits to economic enterprise of all kinds. Population rose in good times, eventually approaching the limit of society's ability to feed itself; since food prices rose with population, discretionary income that might have been spent on industrial products or long-term investments disappeared. Famine, war, and disease (often conjoined) eventually cut population back, freeing resources and according the survivors a temporary prosperity, before the whole cycle of growth and crisis began again. Le Roy Ladurie was concerned mainly with France, but his work coincided with similar ideas that were developed in Germany by such historians as Werner Conze and Reinhart Koselleck. By comparison with the momentous changes around 1800, differences such as that between medieval and early modern periods could have little importance. During the same years, the English historian Peter Laslett likewise developed a vision of the early modern period as sharply set off from modernity, a "world we have lost" (in his famous phrase), governed by specific forms of social and familial organization, and therefore marked by specific worldviews as well.

Although these French, German, and British approaches to the early modern period differ in significant ways, if only because they deal mainly with their own national histories, they share an emphasis on the gap between the early modern period and our own and see that difference as extending to the most fundamental experiences of human life. Another feature common to all three approaches is an interest in the biological constraints on early modern lives. Muscle-power, whether human or animal, set the basic limits to agricultural and industrial production, and people had limited protection against either microbes, which brutally cut back population, or their own reproductive drives, which in good times led to rapid population growth. For these reasons, historical demography was a crucial companion science to the social history written in the 1960s and 1970s, promising insights into the workings of premodern social structures.

In many ways the historiography undertaken by Le Roy Ladurie and his contemporaries still sets the agenda for studies of the early modern period; but since 1975 historians' interpretive stances have again shifted significantly in response to changes in several fields of research. Neither the industrial revolution nor the French Revolution seems so absolute a break as it once did. Economic historians have lowered their estimates of nineteenth-century economic growth, rendering images of economic "take off" inappropriate and drawing attention to the continuing importance of preindustrial modes of production into the twentieth century. Revisionist historians have similarly reevaluated the French Revolution of 1789, which they present as having far less impact on European society than was once believed. While these scholars have downplayed the extent of change at the end of the early modern period, others have found evidence of

more change within the period itself than was once thought to have occurred. Historians have become more aware that even the period's most powerful biological forces were mediated through complex mechanisms of social and cultural organization. As a result, the concept of a technological ceiling on early modern economic development has lost much of its persuasiveness, for early modern society operated far below whatever that ceiling may have been. Revisions and queries like these have made the early modern period seem more complex and much less static than it did to earlier historians.

AN AGE OF CRISIS

To historians of the French school, inspired especially by Le Roy Ladurie, social crisis dominated the period 1590 to 1720. Even historians who question his neo-Malthusian interpretation find crisis an important theme in the period, for early modern Europeans had frequent and horrific experiences of famine, disease, and war. Plague, which had reappeared in Europe in 1348 after several centuries' absence, remained endemic and virulent, producing major epidemics in most regions every generation or so. The Milan epidemic of 1630–1631 killed 60,000 people, 46 percent of the city's population; the London epidemic of 1664–1665 killed 70,000. For reasons that remain mysterious, however, the disease receded after the 1660s, and after a last, terrible epidemic in 1720–1722, centering on the French port city of Marseilles, it disappeared from Europe altogether. The history of famine followed a roughly similar chronology. Food shortages led to actual starvation as late as the mid-seventeenth century in England, and still later in France: the great famine of 1693–1694 is estimated to have reduced French population by 10 percent. Food shortages continued in the eighteenth century, and a last great subsistence crisis came in the mid-nineteenth century; but Europeans' experiences of food shortage after 1710 were essentially different from that of the seventeenth century. Before 1710, for instance, French food prices might triple or quadruple in years of harvest failure; eighteenth-century crises led to a doubling of prices, still a serious burden for consumers, but far less likely to bring outright starvation. Freed from the experience of starvation and plague (though certainly not from many other natural catastrophes), eighteenth-century Europeans could view the world with significantly more confidence than their early modern predecessors.

An abrupt decline in military violence after 1713 meant that eighteenth-century Europeans also

An Age of Crisis. *Massacre of the Innocents,* painting (1565) by Peter Brueghel the Elder (1530–1569). KUNSTHISTORISCHES MUSEUM, GEMÄLDEGALERIE, VIENNA/ERICH LESSING/ART RESOURCE, N.Y.

had a fundamentally different experience of warfare. Organized violence had marked the early modern period to an unprecedented degree, with conflicts extending across the Continent from west to east and south to north. With truce only between 1609 and 1621, Spain and the northern Netherlands fought from 1566 until 1648, a conflict that also touched Spanish Italy (where troops were recruited and organized) and parts of Switzerland (through which they had to march to reach the northern battlefields). Spanish troops also attempted to invade England in 1588, assisted the Catholic side during the French Wars of Religion in 1589–1594, and invaded northern France in 1597; after some skirmishing in the 1620s and 1630s, Spain and France returned to all-out war between 1635 and 1659. Meanwhile the Thirty Years' War (1618–1648) embroiled central Europe in the most destructive of the century's conflicts. The small German states fought one another, their overlord the Austrian Habsburg emperors, and a series of outside powers—Denmark, Sweden, France,

and Spain—that had joined in to secure territorial gain and to defend the European balance of power.

Relative peace prevailed during the mid-seventeenth century, despite the Anglo-Dutch Wars of the 1650s and 1660s and French territorial expansion in the 1660s. But Louis XIV's invasion of the Netherlands in 1672 opened a new round of Europe-wide conflict, which continued with only short breaks until 1713. Louis's armies were larger than any Europe had previously seen, and even the ethics of war seemed to have deteriorated. Under orders from Versailles, French armies systematically devastated the Palatinate in 1689, suggesting to horrified contemporaries that pillaging had become a tool of state policy, rather than a crime of angry soldiers. The financial, demographic, and psychological effects were so exhausting that most of Europe remained at peace for a generation thereafter. Only in 1740 did the principal European powers resume their warlike habits, and then, though armies remained large and destructive, newly effective military discipline protected civilians from their worst ef-

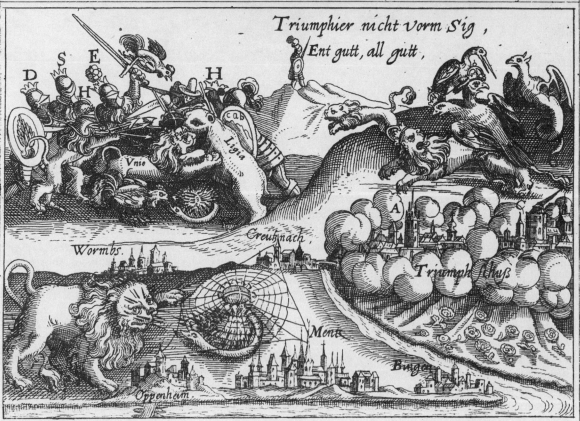

The Thirty Years' War. The Winter King, Frederick V of Bohemia *(top),* declares, "I am not alone," trusting vainly in his allies, S(weden), D(enmark), E(ngland), and H(olland). The Protestant lion *(below)* unsuccessfully battles the bear representing the Catholic League *(upper left),* the double-headed eagle representing Austria *(upper right),* and a snake and spider *(lower left),* representing Spain and the Spanish commander Spinola. German broadsheet, 1620. ASHMOLEAN MUSEUM, OXFORD

fects. Thus 1713 marked a genuine turning point in European social history.

Measuring the social effects of seventeenth-century warfare has proven a complex historical problem. In central Europe the destructiveness was enormous and clearly visible. Over the course of the Thirty Years' War, historians have estimated, the German population dropped by 40 percent in the countryside, and 33 percent in the cities; in some regions the losses were still greater. This war was the century's greatest military disaster, but even local conflicts might have comparable consequences: troop movements around Paris during the Fronde of the Princes in 1652–1653 brought a threefold increase in the region's death rates. Combatants died in great numbers (studies of one Swedish village during the Thirty Years' War show a survival rate after twenty years of 7 percent among conscripted troops); further deaths were caused by the spread of epidemic diseases. But war did much more damage by disrupting already fragile economies, as soldiers took food and livestock for themselves, destroyed farms and other capital, and disrupted trade circuits.

For this very reason, however, the impact of war might vary with the strength of the local economies that it touched. Since the thirteenth century, the Low Countries and northern France had included some of Europe's great battlefields, and—as they formed the border between the Habsburg and Bourbon empires—they witnessed almost continuous war during the early modern period. Yet these regions prospered, despite terrible destruction in specific regions and at specific moments. Even Spanish Flanders, which lost considerable population in the turmoil of the later sixteenth century, recovered amid the warfare of the seventeenth, and the highly vulnerable agriculture of the region continued to develop and innovate. Political organization also played an important role in this resiliency; Dutch garrisons were so well disciplined (in contrast to those of other states) that communities actually welcomed them as an economic resource. Conversely, peace was no guarantee of prosperity. Seventeenth-century Castile had almost no direct experience of war, but its economy stagnated and the region lost even its ability to feed itself. War's effects depended on its social context.

Violence probably also mattered less in the long run than war's secondary, indirect effects, particularly on state organization. The early modern period was the critical point in the process that historians have called "the military revolution," a series of changes that began with the application of gunpowder to warfare in the fourteenth century. The implications of this military technology unfolded slowly and unevenly, but by 1600 they were everywhere apparent. Armies had to be much larger and better trained, fortifications more substantial, military hardware more abundant and more carefully designed and managed. Warfare had to be better organized, with more efficient lines of command and greater subordination of individuals to collective purposes—in short something of a science. Ideally the warrior himself was to become a trained element within a bureaucratic system rather than the autonomous hero of feudal myth. The French peacetime army had numbered 10,000 in 1600; in 1681 it numbered 240,000, and during the last wars of Louis XIV it reached about 395,000.

Changes of this scale, in a period of constant international competition, required heavy governmental expenditures, and taxes rose with the size of armies. In France the nominal tax burden tripled within five years of Louis XIII's entry into the Thirty Years' War, though actual collection rates were much lower. Taxation at these levels was a heavy burden for most economies and an important cause of the economic stagnation that marked the period. After 1672 even the United Provinces, which had prospered amid the violence of the later sixteenth and early seventeenth centuries, found the costs of fighting Louis XIV so overwhelming as to drive their economy into long-term decline. Well before then, Spain's international ambitions had exhausted it. Faced with such pressures, governments tended to reduce some forms of social privilege, notably the protections against taxation enjoyed by most nobles and many commoners. Spain's chief minister Gaspar de Guzmán y Pimental, Count-Duke Olivares (1587–1645) sought to end the fiscal exemptions enjoyed by the outlying provinces of Aragon and Catalonia—with politically disastrous consequences, for the regions rebelled in 1640 and retained their exemptions until the eighteenth century. In France Louis XIV established a form of taxation that hit nobles as hard as commoners. Efforts like these would receive full implementation only by the enlightened despots of the later eighteenth century, when tax immunities were challenged all across Europe, but state challenges to inherited social distinctions had already begun before 1700.

Rapidly rising taxation was the principal cause of a second form of violence that gave the early modern period its air of crisis, the wave of rebellions that extended into the 1670s. Both ordinary people and elites participated in these movements, in ways that historians have found difficult to disentangle. Low levels of popular discontent, producing assaults on tax collectors or other governmental agents, were commonplace, but the period was also marked by much larger movements, with elaborate ideological plans. In

Killing the King. The execution of Charles I, king of England, 30 January 1649. By PERMISSION OF THE EARL OF ROSEBURY/ PHOTO BY NATIONAL GALLERIES OF SCOTLAND

France the Catholic League, a movement dominated by middle-class city dwellers, took over Paris and several other cities between 1589 and 1594 and called for radical social reforms, including an end to hereditary nobility and the institution of parliamentary controls on royal power. The 1640s witnessed rebellions across Europe, most dramatically in England, France, Catalonia, Portugal, and Naples, again mixing popular and upper-class participation and generating widespread calls for significant political change. The example of England, where revolutionaries finally toppled the monarch, tried him in Parliament for political crimes, and publicly executed him, provided an especially frightening example of how far rebellion might lead. Even the Dutch Republic, an apparent oasis of political calm in the seventeenth century, experienced some of the political violence characteristic of the age: in 1618–1619 the overthrow and political execution of the seventy-two-year-old Johan van Oldenbarnevelt, and in 1672 the mob lynching of the brothers Johan and Cornelis de Witt, whose policies were thought to have led to Louis XIV's invasion. Seventeenth-century men and women had a powerful awareness of society's explosiveness. Even the most apparently stable positions might be temporary, and ordinary people might turn savagely on once-respected leaders.

In this regard, too, the late seventeenth and early eighteenth centuries represented a significant break that paralleled the more secure living conditions and international peace that followed Louis XIV's reign: In the late seventeenth century, the wave of great rebellions came to an end. Governments had become much more effective in controlling crowd violence and had begun to treat their subjects somewhat more fairly, for example, by spreading tax burdens more evenly. At the same time, experiences like the English revolution and the Fronde had frightened elites everywhere. They were much more ready to obey governments and more wary of encouraging popular discontent. In the German states governments consciously involved even leading peasants in the powers and profits of government. During the eighteenth century local disorders remained common, especially in moments of food shortage, but contemporaries no longer viewed the social order as constantly subject to violent overturning. When violence returned with the French Revolution of 1789, it came as a devastating surprise to contemporaries.

SIGNS OF STRUCTURAL CHANGE

Alongside its instabilities and sufferings, the seventeenth century also showed signs of important social advances. These begin with the typical European household itself, which at some point in the later sixteenth century appears to have settled definitively into what historians have termed the "European marriage pattern": late marriage for both men and women, nearly equal ages at marriage, limited numbers of children, autonomous households for most married couples, and, outside of marriage, substantial rates of lifelong celibacy. The pattern reached its fullest development in the later seventeenth century, with couples in many regions marrying only in their later twenties, and with about 10 percent of women never marrying. This set early modern Europe apart from most other preindustrial societies, and also from medieval Europe itself, which had been dominated well into the sixteenth century by early marriage and large, multigenerational households. Historians have noted both demographic and social effects of the European marriage pattern. It effectively limited births by reducing the number of childbearing years for many women and by excluding altogether many men and women from reproducing. Controlling natality through the social customs of marriage in turn gave European society an unusual capacity for saving, even during crisis-ridden periods like the seventeenth century, since society was not using all its resources on subsistence. As important, the European marriage pattern accentuated the economic and social freedom of the individual household at the expense of the community and the larger patriarchal family; marrying as mature adults, with the presumption of autonomy from their parents, couples formed highly flexible economic units, far more able than in medieval society to arrange both work and consumption to suit new circumstances.

Closely related to changes in household organization were increasing investments in human capital, especially in formal education. The seventeenth century was among Europe's great eras for school foundation, as Catholic and Protestant churches competed to form educated, articulate believers. The number of Jesuit schools increased from 144 in 1579 to more than 500 by 1626, and more than 800 in 1749; and male literacy reached impressive levels, 70 percent in Amsterdam in the 1670s, 65 percent in the small cities near Paris. In England, the historian Lawrence Stone has estimated, a higher percentage of the male population attended university in the seventeenth century than at any time before World War I. This upsurge in education probably contributed to a change that scholars have noted in several European countries: by the end of the seventeenth century, Europeans of all social classes were becoming more skeptical about magical practices that had long been customary

and more ready to accept the worldviews proposed by physicians and natural philosophers.

A third critical change concerned the organization of space. At varying speeds, seventeenth-century governments succeeded in pacifying their realms, controlling local banditry and civil war, and starting the process of disciplining armies. In this as in many other seventeenth-century changes, the Dutch Republic led the way, establishing in the early seventeenth century forms of social discipline that other regions would still be trying to emulate a century later. England also moved quickly to control brigandage and (in the Puritan armies of the Civil War) to discipline soldiers. Castile had been largely freed of brigandage by the mid-seventeenth century, though other parts of Spain were pacified more slowly.

Such political successes had important social implications, for they allowed people, goods, cash, and information to circulate more freely, cheaply, and predictably, even without improvements in technology. But the technology for dealing with distance did improve in these years as well. Again, the most dramatic example is the Dutch Republic, where by the mid-seventeenth century an elaborate series of canals made movement throughout the country cheap and easy, and a regularly scheduled system of canal boats allowed people and goods to travel freely. Other regions had neither the social resources nor the geographic advantages that allowed the Netherlands this success, but these handicaps make seventeenth-century efforts all the more striking. Significant canals were dug in England and France, and land transport improved there as well. Road-building became a major preoccupation of the French government, starting with the appointment of Maximilien de Béthune, duc de Sully, in 1599 as head of a government road-building service; such projects received further impetus from Jean-Baptiste Colbert's interest in highways. New carriages, with steel springs, allowed people to travel these roads in relative comfort and speed; in the sixteenth century most people had had to travel on horse or mule.

Increased freedom of movement addressed what had been a critical weakness in the European economy, its fragmentation into a collection of nearly autonomous, self-sufficient local societies, dependent mainly on what they themselves produced. Such enclaves might be very small, given the difficulties of transportation and the uncertainties of relying on distant suppliers. Breaking down localism was an important step in economic development, for exchange over large areas allowed specialization and efficiency. The process of economic integration—and consequent gains in specialization—would continue through the eighteenth and nineteenth centuries and include much more dramatic technological advances than the seventeenth century could display. Yet it can be argued that the seventeenth century represented a critical phase in this long process. The economic historian Jan de Vries has demonstrated that Europe first acquired an integrated system of cities in the seventeenth century, with cities for the first time fitting into clear hierarchies of scale according to local, regional, or national functions—functional specialization that reflected the era's increasingly effective networks of communication. Europe's ruling elites also first acquired national rather than regional orientations in these years, as capital cities and courts became the normal sites for at least part of their yearly routines. Yet another indicator of the same process was the seventeenth century's obsession with news. Europe's first daily newspaper, the London *Daily Courant,* appeared only at the end of the period, in 1702, but many other news products, like the weekly Parisian *Gazette,* founded in 1621, had preceded it.

Political stability and improving communications underlay two other critical changes that marked the seventeenth century as a period of decisive social advance. First, nearly everywhere capital cities grew dramatically, approaching modern dimensions that would have been unthinkable in the medieval world. By 1700 both London and Paris had more than 500,000 inhabitants, Amsterdam 200,000. As E. A. Wrigley has argued in regard to London, the very existence of such cities had important effects beyond their boundaries. Many more people had some experience of this urban life than population statistics alone indicate, because these cities were sites of continual population turnover, with rapid in- and out-migration. These very large concentrations of people also focused demand for products of all kinds, encouraging economic activities that expensive transportation rendered impossible in the more scattered, isolated economy of the sixteenth century.

Second, the seventeenth century witnessed the development of new institutions for mobilizing resources, again in ways not previously possible. The Amsterdam stock market opened in 1611, selling shares in the Dutch East India Company. The stock exchange was one of several Dutch institutions that mobilized the wealth of those outside the narrow world of commercial specialists toward economically productive, even adventurous purposes. The Dutch model spread slowly, but by the end of the period similar systems were in place in England and France, allowing both countries to experience stock-market booms and then collapses in 1720, England with the South Sea Bubble, France with the John Law affair.

SOCIAL DIFFERENTIATIONS

The ethics of economic life. The seventeenth century was an especially competitive era that divided winners from losers in fierce, unpredictable ways. The fields of social action had widened, depriving actors of the protections that localism once afforded against distant rivals, while political and social tumults disrupted even the most sensible economic plans, destroying capital and closing markets, but also opening opportunities for the aggressive or lucky. After the mid-seventeenth century, awareness of competition became widespread among European intellectuals, and ethical restraints on it diminished sharply. Changing views of lending money at interest illustrate this shift. During the Middle Ages, theorists taught that fellow economic actors should be treated first as Christians, to whom assistance should be freely offered, without payment of interest. In the seventeenth century both Protestant and Catholic theorists came instead to accept the idea that commercial transactions had their own laws that could not be subject to moral regulation, and condemnation of more basic moral failings was weakening as well. English writers after 1660 regularly argued that pride, greed, self-interest, and vanity formed necessary underpinnings of a successful economy. Still more dramatically, the Anglo-Dutch writer Bernard Mandeville (1670–1733), in his *The Fable of the Bees* (1714), summarized the argument that private vices would produce public prosperity, further eroding moral restraints on individuals' actions in the social realm. On the Continent even the Catholic moralist Pierre Nicole (1625–1695) argued that self-interest rather than altruism formed the basis of public life. Cultural changes conjoined with political and economic circumstances to intensify the era's economic and social competitiveness.

The rural social order. The period from 1590 to 1720 witnessed significant reshufflings of the social order. Peasants experienced these changes most brutally, an important fact given that they constituted the vast majority of seventeenth-century Europe's population, fewer than two-thirds of the total only in the Dutch Republic, at least three-fourths in most other regions. This group experienced a dramatic change in its relations to the most basic means of production, the land itself, essentially amounting to a process of expropriation. The process varied significantly from one region to another because medieval landowning patterns themselves varied. In England, most land belonged to nobles and gentry, but peasants enjoyed relatively secure long-term leases; in France and Germany peasants had direct ownership of most land, subject to loose feudal overlordship. Whatever the initial arrangements, large landowners everywhere took much more direct control of the land during the early modern period, with the crucial change coming at its outset, between about 1570 and 1630. Other changes accompanied and magnified these changes in ownership. Real wages diminished, partly as a result of sixteenth-century population growth, and agricultural leases became more expensive; in central and eastern Europe working conditions deteriorated, with landowners exercising increasing control over peasants' movements and requiring of them several days of unpaid labor each week. The mid-sixteenth-century countryside had been dominated by nearly independent peasants, able more or less to survive from the produce of their own land. By 1650 most regions were dominated instead by large landowners and their economic allies, the large-scale tenant farmers who managed the actual business of farming and marketing. Most peasants had become essentially wage laborers, owning cottages and small amounts of land, but needing to work for others in order to survive.

Both the well-to-do farm managers and the agricultural laborers had been forcibly inserted into a market economy, with enormous attendant insecurities. The laborers now had to purchase their food on the open market and sell their labor, while the large tenant farmers had to market their produce and assemble the cash needed to pay rents and taxes. Indeed, the expropriation of the peasantry tended to advance fastest in regions that were especially open to commercial currents. These facts produced a seeming paradox in some regions of Europe. Precisely where capitalist and modernizing influences were strongest, around cities and in areas (such as east-Elbian Germany) especially open to international trade, peasants were most vulnerable to the era's extraeconomic shocks, notably to its harvest failures. During the seventeenth century starvation was more common in the most advanced regions of France, those nearest Paris, than in regions of poorer land and more backward agricultural technique.

Jan de Vries has drawn attention to a second paradox in this history, the fact that expropriation and declining wages accompanied a steady growth in the number and range of consumer goods that villagers purchased. By 1720 death inventories across Europe reveal villagers' purchases of coffee, tobacco, brightly printed cloths, even books and prints. De Vries explains this paradox by what he calls the "industrious revolution," a readiness to take on (or insist that familial dependents take on) paid work of all kinds so as to orient the household as fully as possible toward the marketplace and its money-making possibilities, thereby diminishing the share of household effort devoted to domestic life. Businessmen responded to this widening of the rural labor pool by bringing some of their manufacturing work to the countryside, especially such easily transportable work as textile manufacturing. By the late seventeenth century, rural manufacturing had become commonplace in France, England, and parts of Germany. Europe remained overwhelmingly a rural society, with about the same percentage of urbanites in 1700 as in 1600, but manufacturing had acquired considerable importance. It counted for about one-fourth of French economic activity in 1700, and much more in England and the United Provinces.

Business and the cities. More intense competition came to characterize the world of urban business as well. Seventeenth-century business was especially vulnerable to the period's instability, for at its highest levels business was inextricably bound up with systems of political power. The connection was most direct in the case of state finance, among the most profitable sectors of early modern business. Governments had been poor credit risks since the early fourteenth century, and as a result soldiers, military suppliers, and other creditors would accept only cash; governments also had difficulty in moving money across long distances (necessary in an era of international warfare) and in assuring the regular flow of money over time (necessary since tax collections did not coincide with expenditures). Businessmen with established credit could meet all these needs, and their indispensability assured them enormous profits. The Dutch banker Louis de Geer (1587–1652) exemplified these possibilities when he took over large sectors of the Swedish economy, in exchange for lending money to Gustavus Adolphus (ruled 1611–1632). But the same governmental untrustworthiness that made the financiers' fortunes regularly unmade them as well, for governments had little hesitation about defaulting on loans as soon as competing bankers offered alternative sources of cash. In France these tacit bankruptcies were often accompanied by show trials in which financiers were prosecuted for their excess profits. After the most famous of these in 1661, the financier and official Nicolas Fouquet barely escaped with his life, and was condemned to lifelong imprisonment in an isolated fortress.

Faced with these risks, the business class could never cut itself off from leading aristocrats and officials, who supplied the political protection and introductions that bankers needed in such tumultuous times. Governments relinquished their reliance on such financiers at very different rates. In the Netherlands reliable state finances were established in the mid-seventeenth century, and the English followed their model. The Bank of England (created in 1694) placed state loans on reliable foundations and diminished the need for the great financiers. France on the other hand continued to need their services until the revolution in 1789.

Power and commerce mixed in other ways during the seventeenth century, most directly in the exploitation of Europe's colonial empires. Already in the sixteenth century Spain and Portugal had organized imperial systems that sustained important mercantile networks. For the rest of Europe, however, profit-making imperialism was essentially a seventeenth-century creation. The first Dutch efforts to trade with the Far East came in 1595; in 1600 the monopoly Dutch East India Company began operations, with permission from the state to undertake such essentially political tasks as establishing a military and diplomatic presence in the regions where it traded. The company used these rights to the fullest, so that by the 1630s it held a string of fortresses and permanent trading centers across the Indian Ocean and had forced Asian rulers into a series of advantageous trade agreements. England attempted to keep up with its own monopoly East India Company, but above all launched concerted efforts to profit from the Americas. Until 1661 French efforts were much less impressive. Thereafter, Jean-Baptiste Colbert channeled state support to imperial ventures as well, financing a large French navy and encouraging French efforts in Canada, India, and the Caribbean.

By the end of the period, colonial products—tobacco, sugar, cotton cloth from India—had become crucial goods of European commerce. In the French case especially, state encouragement of imperial commerce was only part of a larger program of state economic intervention, designed to serve the state's political needs by ensuring success in overseas markets. This mercantilist program involved both state investment in factories and infrastructure like roads and canals and the close regulation of private business. Colbert established a group of commerce inspectors to ensure the quality of French goods, essential, he believed, for sustaining sales. The Dutch East India Company relied much less on state support, its strength lying ultimately in the vitality of Dutch commercial life, but even it owed something to political calculations. Dutch leaders encouraged its development and accorded it extensive powers partly in hopes of undermining Iberian monopolies in Asia and Brazil, an important advantage in the Eighty Years' War with Spain.

The seventeenth century thus offered extraordinary new opportunities to the minority of businessmen who enjoyed governmental connections. Contemporaries believed that they had never seen so much wealth, or wealth so conspicuously displayed, as that of the era's great financiers and merchants. Farther down the commercial hierarchy, however, the business atmosphere of the seventeenth century was much more difficult. Stagnant population and widening competition threatened what had once been comfortable markets, and cities suffered as trades shifted to the countryside, with its relatively cheap labor and freedom from regulation. For shopkeepers and artisans, the result was a contraction of business and a tendency for established families to protect their situations by every available means. In many regions this meant an enthusiastic turn to an institution inherited from the Middle Ages, the guilds. These organizations regulated activity within specific trades, controlling the entry of newcomers, setting prices and wages, and determining standards of training and work. The French government chartered a long series of new guilds in the later seventeenth century, partly for its own fiscal reasons (guild positions could be sold), but also in response to businessmen's eagerness for protection. For ordinary urban workers, this rise of regulation meant a significant worsening in conditions and a widening of class differences within the workshop. The movement of workers into masterships became significantly more difficult, as the guild structure hardened and new masterships were reserved mainly for those who already had familial connections within the trade. Workers who lacked these supports were likely to remain in subordinate positions throughout their lives, forming a permanent and often resentful working class.

The new bourgeoisie and traditional ruling elites.
For embattled businessmen, an appealing response to the difficult times was flight from the marketplace into social realms that promised more stability. Land offered one such option, and the early modern period witnessed a rapid increase in land purchases by the urban rich. The later sixteenth and early seventeenth centuries apparently were the focal point for such purchases, for after 1650 falling rents made landowning much less attractive, and new forms of safe investment had become more readily available. By that point, however, leading bourgeois in most European cities controlled substantial shares of the surrounding territories. A second possibility fitted well with this option, that of acquiring positions in the growing bureaucracies of the period. Civil services expanded everywhere during the early modern period,

giving bourgeois at all levels opportunities to abandon the uncertainties of commerce for the reliable income and social prestige of public office.

France, where public positions were bought and sold, demonstrates in quantitative terms the allure of this mode of life: Between 1600 and 1660, office prices there rose about fivefold, as monied families sought to secure for their sons the tranquil security of officialdom. Though less easily measured, there seems to have been similar enthusiasm for office in the other European states. Most of these new landowners and officials continued to reside in the cities, but they now resembled Europe's traditional elites, its military nobilities, and at their highest levels they began to claim noble status. At the French Estates General of 1614–1615, royal officials had sat with the commoners, but by 1650 the leading judges and officials were generally recognized as nobles, with the full range of noble privileges. In Spain, England, and the German states as well, society generally agreed that such figures counted among the gentlemen, whether the title was formal (as in most of Europe) or informal (as in England).

The accession of new families to noble status was one of several changes affecting Europe's ruling elites during the early modern period. By their very presence, the new nobles brought higher levels of education and urbanity to the nobilities, and in this their impact closely paralleled the growing importance of court life for many nobles. Seventeenth-century monarchs were eager to have their greatest nobles nearby and established elaborate courts for the purpose. Louis XIV's Versailles, to which he moved permanently in 1682, was only the most dramatic example of this policy. By 1700 imitations of Versailles had sprung up all over Europe, and even the court of the Dutch Republic had acquired a new prominence. As a result, the seventeenth-century nobility in general was far more urban than its sixteenth-century predecessors. In Spain and Italy nobles had always played a prominent role in city life, but in the seventeenth century northerners too were drawn to the entertainments and elegance of the city, and urban centers responded to their needs. In the years around 1600, a number of urban development projects were undertaken in London, Paris, Madrid, and other cities so as to make these cities more attractive to this new class of resident.

Nineteenth-century historians tended to view the nobles' urbanization and their increasing focus on the court as signs of weakness, indicative of declining political power and uncertainty about their proper social role. Twentieth-century scholarship, however, has stressed the nobility's continuing vitality despite these changes, and to some extent because of them. New

families of officials brought new wealth to the order and assured that aristocratic values would continue to shape governmental policies. If stronger governments eliminated some political powers that medieval nobles had exercised, they also created new ones. Nobles had numerous new positions available to them in the expanding armies and bureaucracies of the period, and they profited from the development of courts. More fundamentally, governments took their opinions seriously and tailored programs to meet their needs. Until about 1660 even economic circumstances tended to shine for the nobles. Food prices and land rents both remained high, so that nobles' estates remained profitable. There was one exception to this favorable situation, however. For Europe's poorer nobles, the early modern period represented a real social crisis— enough to provoke concerned governments into substantial policy innovations. The benefits of stronger government flowed mainly to nobles able to educate themselves for a public role, whether in the army, at court, or in the civil service. "Mere nobles," who had only their claims to high birth and privilege, could not keep up in this world, and significant numbers left the order.

GEOGRAPHICAL DIFFERENTIATION

By 1720 many Europeans had become aware that the Continent's center of social and economic geography had shifted from the Mediterranean to northwestern countries like England and the United Provinces. The establishment of New World colonies and Atlantic trade do not sufficiently explain the shift. A century after Columbus, Spain remained Europe's dominant political power, partly because of its control of the Atlantic, and Italy remained its leading commercial center. Genoese bankers were among the chief profiteers of the early Atlantic empires. After 1590, however, the United Provinces quickly established themselves as Europe's richest region, with a standard of living unheard of elsewhere. This wealth rested on economic modernity, a situation in which social structures encouraged entrepreneurship and innovation.

With few natural resources, the Dutch established not only the most productive agriculture in Europe—managing to export food even as Mediterranean regions experienced harvest failures—but a variety of novel industries as well. Their example suggested to contemporary observers that wealth derived from social organization, rather than nature, and that such wealth could allow surprising political successes. Despite its population of about only 1.9 million inhabitants, the Dutch Republic defeated the Spanish

Empire at the height of its power and in the 1670s fought Louis XIV to a stand-off. By that point, the Republic's lead over the rest of Europe had begun to diminish, and after 1720 the Dutch fell behind England in economic activity. Yet even then the Republic remained the center of European economic innovation, and its export industries continued to develop. The eighteenth century's great economic success stories, chiefly in England, would reflect the influence of this model.

The Dutch model had social and ethical as well as economic implications, for the United Provinces represented an anomaly among European societies. They formed a republic in which cities had the decisive political voice; they tolerated multiple religions, despite occasional flare-ups of intolerant Calvinist orthodoxy; above all, they accorded higher status to commerce than to warfare or noble birth. Over the years 1590 to 1720, this combination of social arrangements seemed to have been rewarded with ex-

traordinary success, even as Spain sank into economic troubles and French industrial development faltered. In his *Persian Letters* (1721), the French philosopher Charles Louis de Secondat de Montesquieu attributed some of this contrast to Protestantism itself, arguing that their religion encouraged Dutch and English merchants in especially vigorous pursuit of worldly advantage. Late-twentieth-century scholars have been skeptical, but they have suggested that the relative freedom of the United Provinces and England was more conducive to economic enterprise than the growing authoritarianism of seventeenth-century Catholicism. Thus the weakening of religious values during the eighteenth century, following what the French literary historian Paul Hazard termed "the crisis of the European mind," made emulating the Dutch easier for elites throughout Europe. Without renouncing monarchy, nobility, or warfare, European societies would turn in fundamentally different directions after 1720.

See also **The World Economy and Colonial Expansion** *(in this volume);* **Absolutism; Bureaucracy; Capitalism and Commercialization; The European Marriage Pattern; Health and Disease; Land Tenure; The Population of Europe: Early Modern Demographic Patterns; War and Conquest** *(volume 2);* **Moral Economy and Luddism** *(volume 3);* **The Household** *(volume 4);* **Journalism; Schools and Schooling** *(volume 5).*

BIBLIOGRAPHY

Appleby, Joyce Oldham. *Economic Thought and Ideology in Seventeenth-Century England.* Princeton, N.J., 1978.

Aston, Trevor Henry, and C. H. E. Philpin, eds. *The Brenner Debate: Agrarian Class Structure and Economic Development in Pre-Industrial Europe.* Cambridge, U.K., and New York, 1985.

Beik, William. *Urban Protest in Seventeenth-Century France: The Culture of Retribution.* Cambridge, U.K., and New York, 1997.

Bercé, Yves-Marie. *Revolt and Revolution in Early Modern Europe: An Essay on the History of Political Violence.* Translated by Joseph Bergin. Manchester, U.K., 1987.

Cannadine, David N. "The Past and the Present in the Industrial Revolution." *Past and Present* 103 (1984): 131–172.

Cornette, Joël. *Le roi de guerre: Essai sur la souveraineté dans la France du Grand Siècle.* Paris, 1993.

De Vries, Jan. "Between Purchasing Power and the World of Goods: Understanding the Household Economy in Early Modern Europe." In *Consumption and the World of Goods.* Edited by John Brewer and Roy Porter. London and New York, 1993. Pages 85–132.

De Vries, Jan. *The Economy of Europe in an Age of Crisis, 1600–1750.* Cambridge, U.K., and New York, 1976.

De Vries, Jan. *European Urbanization, 1500–1800.* Cambridge, Mass., 1984.

De Vries, Jan. "The Industrial Revolution and the Industrious Revolution." *Journal of Economic History* 54 (1994): 249–270.

De Vries, Jan, and Ad van der Woude. *The First Modern Economy: Success, Failure, and Perseverance of the Dutch Economy, 1500–1815.* Cambridge, U.K., and New York, 1997.

Elliott, John Huxtable. *The Revolt of the Catalans, A Study in the Decline of Spain, 1598–1640.* Cambridge, U.K., 1963.

Flinn, Michael Walter. *The European Demographic System, 1500–1820.* Baltimore, 1981.

Gutmann, Myron P. *Toward the Modern Economy: Early Industry in Europe, 1500–1800.* Philadelphia, 1988.

Hoffman, Philip T. *Growth in a Traditional Society: The French Countryside, 1450–1815.* Princeton, N.J., 1996.

Israel, Jonathan. *The Dutch Republic: Its Rise, Greatness, and Fall, 1477–1806.* Oxford and New York, 1995.

Kriedte, Peter. *Peasants, Landlords, and Merchant Capitalists: Europe and the World Economy, 1500–1800.* Translated by V. R. Bergahn. Leamington Spa, U.K., 1983.

Laslett, Peter. *The World We Have Lost.* New York, 1965.

Le Roy Ladurie, Emmanuel. *The French Peasantry, 1450–1660.* Translated by Alan Sheridan. Berkeley, Calif., 1987.

Le Roy Ladurie, Emmanuel. *The Territory of the Historian.* Translated by Ben Reynolds and Siân Reynolds. Chicago, 1979.

Parker, Geoffrey. *The Military Revolution: Military Innovation and the Rise of the West 1500–1800.* Cambridge, U.K., and New York, 1988.

Scott, Tom, ed. *The Peasantries of Europe from the Fourteenth to the Eighteenth Centuries.* London and New York, 1998.

Stone, Lawrence. *The Crisis of the Aristocracy, 1558–1641.* Oxford, 1965.

Theibault, John. "The Demography of the Thirty Years War Re-visited: Günther Franz and His Critics." *German History* 15 (1997): 1–21.

Wrigley, Edward Anthony. *People, Cities and Wealth: The Transformation of Traditional Society.* Oxford and New York, 1987.

THE ENLIGHTENMENT

Brian Dolan

To refer to *The* Enlightenment, complained the eminent historian of the eighteenth century, J. G. A. Pocock, was to presume inaccurately that one could refer to "a single unitary process, displaying a uniform set of characteristics." Many scholars of the post-Peter Gay world of Enlightenment studies share this grievance, and, at variance to Gay who considered "the Enlightenment" as a fundamentally unified movement involved in the "business of criticism," have preferred to see "Enlightenment" as a dynamic and differentiated "long-eighteenth century" mainly (but not exclusively) European movement. Depending on the historian's preference, "Enlightenment" becomes a period, a process, and/or a product. This article briefly considers how "Enlightenment" has been recently and predominantly defined in each of these frameworks.

Previous conceptions of the Enlightenment have undergone major transformations as a result of the new angles from which historians view the past. At issue is not only the scope of where Enlightenment was considered to have taken place, but accounts of how and through whose contributions as well. Rather than seeing the pursuits of select individuals, for example the editors of the *Encyclopédie*—Denis Diderot or Jean Le Rond d'Alembert—as emblematic of the quest for Enlightenment in a society that worshiped the sovereignty of reason over biblical revelation, recent scholarship has gone much further in altering the canon of central contributors to Enlightenment pursuits. Eighteenth-century gender studies, for example, has refashioned the image of Claudine-Alexandrine Guérin de Tencin as a matron of the Enlightenment, not because she was d'Alembert's mother, but rather because she was bearer of a civilized state, running a highly respected salon on rue Saint-Honoré in Paris and acting as mentor to future salonnières, such as Marie-Thérèse Geoffrin. Madame de Tencin's abandonment of her child, the rejection of the duties of maternity for which she has been so well known, raises uncomfortable questions regarding the Enlightenment's attempt to reconcile the language of individual rights and autonomy with consistent attempts to con-

fine women in domestic settings and reinforce their role as mothers—as, for example, prescribed by Jean-Jacques Rousseau in *Émile*. As an intellectually independent writer and salonnière, Tencin represented a challenge to social values that subsequent thinkers would use as a model to help forge a feminist philosophy. Here late-twentieth-century scholarship has not only illuminated the often contradictory Enlightenment debates about gender, but also the ways that new areas of knowledge were developed that expanded the opportunities for a wider band of people to participate in the pursuits.

But "Enlightenment," as a *process* with which—many believe—we are still engaged in the twenty-first century, is also a pursuit filled with irony and paradox. The psychology of the pursuit—the analysis of what many previous historians preferred to call the "Mind of the Enlightenment"—is complex. This is because Enlightenment thinkers—both men and women—seized upon and then struggled to come to grips with a deep transformation in what were taken as fundamental beliefs and true knowledge about their world. One goal of any history of the Enlightenment—whether the historiography of the 1930s or 1940s, which played on the Enlightenment's intellectual values, or later scholarship which stressed the mechanisms of enlightened practices—has been the attempt to capture some of the wonder and the reflexive pride that enlightened individuals felt when assessing the philosophical and material changes visibly occurring throughout Europe.

Everything was changing, and it seemed—many believed—to be changing for the better. In 1759 a forty-one-year-old d'Alembert leaned back and thought about his times. Putting pen to paper, he wrote his reflections at the beginning of his *Elements of Philosophy*:

> If one examines carefully the mid-point of the century in which we live, the events which excite us or at any rate occupy our minds, our customs, our achievements, and even our diversions, it is difficult not to see that in some respects a very remarkable change in our ideas

An Enlightenment Gathering. A reading of Voltaire's *L'orphelin de Chine* at the salon of Marie-Thérèse Geoffrin in the Hôtel de Rambouillet, Paris. A bust of Voltaire observes the reader. In front of the doorway at the left Jean-Jacques Rousseau leans on his cane. Painting (c. 1814) by Gabriel Lemonnier. MUSÉE DES BEAUX-ARTS, ROUEN, FRANCE/GIRAUDON/ART RESOURCE NY

is taking place, a change whose rapidity seems to promise an even greater transformation to come.

He thought the changes amounted to nothing short than a revolution: "all fields of knowledge have assumed new forms." What was the root of such changes? New developments in natural science which ushered in "a new method of philosophizing," prompting "the kind of enthusiasm which accompanies discoveries, a certain exaltation of ideas which the spectacle of the universe produces in us." What were the consequences? D'Alembert could only wonder, but it was clear that "this general effervescence of minds" would "cast new light on some matters and new shadows on others." Knowledge was shining bright in what his contemporaries were styling the first century of Enlightenment.

What were all these revolutionary changes in knowledge and methods of philosophizing that so impressed d'Alembert? The answer harks back to the activities of some of d'Alembert's intellectual ancestors, whose work in natural philosophy and experimental science culminated in the scientific revolution and helped establish new conceptions of cosmological structure, to readjust (or revolutionize) the foundations of knowledge, and to set the pace for how Enlightened pursuits (with emphasis on empiricism, experimentation, and secular rationalization) began to reshape modern beliefs about the natural world, human nature, and social organization.

CELEBRATING THE "NEW SCIENCE"

The theories, mathematical proofs, and writings of people such as the Polish astronomer (and church administrator) Nicolaus Copernicus (1473–1543), the Danish nobleman and astronomer Tycho Brahe (1546–1601), Galileo Galilei (1564–1642), and Isaac Newton (1642–1727), to name only a select few, were crucial in constructing a new method of establishing facts about nature. Advocates of the "new science" (from the Latin *scientia,* meaning knowledge) emphasized that no traditional knowledge was to be taken for granted. In fact, it was argued that one ought to be downright skeptical of all authority. Rather than rely on what was written in ancient books or what others said about the natural world, the best source of knowledge was to ask nature directly. Personal experience was to be the new arbiter of truth. Why not explore for oneself? Why not rely on one's own experiences, use one's own reason? Natural philosophers (as they were then called; the term "scientist" was not coined until the 1830s) were encouraging others to take seriously the plea by the English statesman and philosopher Francis Bacon (1561–1626) to "unroll the volume of the creation" and learn from the Book of Nature by observing and collecting facts from which one could induce greater knowledge and general truths. As a result, all areas of nature were beginning to be scrutinized through critical eyes, and eighteenth-century philosophers portrayed themselves as the inheritors of the radical changes in what were perceived to be the legitimate means of producing "natural" knowledge.

The seventeenth century ended with a crisis of unbelief. Previously, the Bible was read as the ultimate authority on all matters, metaphysical or moral. But it would be misleading to assume that the new sciences simply subverted the authority of the Bible, or that science was suddenly at war with religion. It was not science versus religion, but rather that natural philosophers defended the Book of Nature as an equally legitimate source of knowledge as the Bible. Why not explore all angles? If your beliefs are worth having, aren't they worth interrogating?

In the ancien régime, social and political organization was modeled on a divine order that enforced a social hierarchy (originally referring to an order of priests; the Greek *hieros* means sacred and is the root of *hiereus,* priest), and authorities attempted to quiet the voices of the new philosophers because of the challenge they presented to the literal truth of the scriptures. But the debates over who had the legitimate authority to speak on matters of divine order and "truth" (were philosophers seeking a status equal to that of priests?) took place among an educated elite. So what effect did the new philosophy have on the broader public? How did the average individual look upon the new science? Who had the knowledge to understand the debates? After all, the preface to Copernicus's *De revolutionibus* declared that mathematics was written for mathematicians, and historians figure that fewer than a hundred contemporaries attempted the whole of Newton's *Principia mathematica,* and only a handful could comprehend the mathematics that he used to prove that the earth's motion could be explained with reference to the same "universal force"—gravity—that moved all other celestial (and terrestrial) bodies.

Here the role of Enlightenment thinkers was particularly effective. The philosophes saw the implications of the new science—its promotion of a new basis of knowledge and its elimination of the traditional hierarchical view of nature—as a platform for revolutionizing the political structures of the ancien régime. The towering genius of Newton was a posthumous construction. He and others such as Copernicus were celebrated not because of what they did, but because of what others thought they did. However few could understand the calculus, hordes could see the implications of having destroyed the distinctions between the terrestrial and heavenly realms.

After his death Newton's achievements were celebrated as a triumph for enlightened inquiry, and later philosophes made him into one of the first heroes of Enlightenment. The famous philosophe François-Marie Arouet de Voltaire (1694–1778), who visited England from 1726 until 1729 (where he befriended Newton's niece and even attended his funeral), was one of his most effulgent admirers. He wrote that Newton had taught philosophers to "examine, weigh, calculate and measure, but never to conjecture." Grounded were the lofty metaphysical theories of the seventeenth century; gone were the dubious tales of saints and miracle workers.

Experiment, observation, and secular reason distinguished an enlightened individual. Newton "saw, and made people see," continued Voltaire. His penetrating insight rendered visible the previously hidden mysteries of nature. His experiment of directing a beam of sunlight through a prism to show that it was actually comprised of a rainbow of colors has often been used to symbolize the pursuit of enlightenment. The message was articulated in the word chosen for this age: *siècle des lumières* (French); *illuminismo* (Italian); *Aufklärung* (German); *Upplysningen* (Swedish; *lyse* means light). Enlightenment signifies the process of coming out from the dark—as in "those times of darkness and ignorance, which we distinguish by the name of the Middle Ages," according to Voltaire. "We are all [Newton's] disciples now," he announced in 1776.

To boldly go . . . Throughout the eighteenth century a growing ensemble of admirers seized upon science as the route to progress and, perhaps, even perfectibility. Unlike Blaise Pascal who became frightened when he contemplated the possibility of an infinite universe, the preeminent German philosopher Immanuel Kant (1724–1804) thought the concept "filled the understanding with wonder."

Kant was not afraid of the challenges presented by the new philosophy. In fact, he was one of the first to sloganize the achievements of the early natural philosophers by popularizing the phrase "Copernican Revolution," albeit to imply that his particular philosophy of knowledge was as radically different from others as the heliocentric from the geocentric model of the universe! But his work is also said to have crowned the philosophy of Enlightenment in Germany. He lived his whole life in Königsberg, where he became professor of logic and metaphysics at its university. His chief works questioned the limits of reason in the advancement of human knowledge—the *Critiques* of pure reason, practical reason, and judgment (published in 1781, 1788, and 1790 respectively). However, it is significant that this leader of the German Enlightenment earlier wrote a work on natural philosophy and the history of the heavens: *General Natural History and Theory of the Heavens* (1755).

But in terms of defining moments in the history of Enlightenment, it is also significant that in 1784 Kant wrote an essay in answer to the question "What is enlightenment?" that was published in a Berlin monthly, *Berlinische Monatsschrift*. His answer was that enlightenment was the attainment of the ability to think rationally for oneself: "Enlightenment is man's release from his self-incurred tutelage. Tutelage is man's inability to make use of his understanding without direction from another." Have no fear, he went on, borrowing a phrase from the Latin poet, Horace: " '*Sapere aude!*' Dare to Know! 'Have courage to use your own reason!'—that is the motto of enlightenment."

However challenging the new philosophy, self-confidence and self-determination would help overcome vanity and foolishness. Kant believed that pursuing Enlightenment was worth the effort since the benefits it brought easily outstripped the perceived dangers. Yes, people would fall a few times before learning to walk alone, but better to do that than to labor in a life of perpetual tutelage. He, like many others, believed that those who learn to think for themselves "will disseminate the spirit of the rational appreciation of both their own worth and every man's vocation." But others remained cautious, fearing the power of authorities who ordered, "Do not argue!" Some of Kant's colleagues lamented the resistance—or the inertia—of the masses to pursue the quest. The Göttingen professor of physics (and seventeenth child of a Protestant pastor) Georg Christoph Lichtenberg (1742–1799) erupted in frustration over humanity's inability to seize its opportunities. "People talk a great deal about Enlightenment and ask for more light. My

God! What good is all this light if people either have no eyes or if those who do have eyes resolutely keep them shut!"

Yet it seemed to others that the greatest irony of enlightenment was that the light it provided illuminated more harsh realities of humanity's condition than havens of happiness. "Has it not always been obvious that the time of highest refinement is precisely the time of the most extreme moral rottenness?" asked the German poet and sardonic critic Christoph Martin Wieland (1733–1813). Was it not obvious "that the epoch of brightest enlightenment is always the very epoch in which all sorts of speculations, madness, and enthusiasm, flourish most?" Was one really to believe that man's perfectibility was an attainable goal—the payoff of Enlightenment pursuits? Could one really overthrow one's inner, savage, corrupting passions? It seemed to Wieland that for every individual who strove to attain enlightened liberty there were many others who were eager to suppress their attempts. "Just think," he wrote, "against one man who actively advances true enlightenment, there are a hundred who work against it with all their might, and ten thousand who neither desire nor miss his services."

Indeed one great paradox of the Enlightenment might be that for all the new meanings of liberty and freedom offered, the same period witnessed the rise of new disciplinary controls over the population and new mechanisms of surveillance. Talk about freedom, but play by the rules. Kant saw this irony when he repeated the words of a prince: "Argue as much as you will, and about what you will, but obey!" "Everywhere there is restriction on freedom," he concluded. And while repression was not as draconian as in the sixteenth or seventeenth centuries, a number of philosophes who voiced their visions of a society liberated from a repressive political regime found themselves meditating over their next messages in prison.

Nevertheless, one of the major achievements of eighteenth-century enlightenment was to spread the word, to popularize the new philosophy through print, in new journals, or the celebrated *Encyclopédie* (published from 1751) and the British answer to it in the form of the *Encyclopaedia Britannica* (which began publication in 1771), through new public libraries and salons, and so forth. They were adept at playing up propaganda. Because of this, philosophes have often been regarded as mere spokespeople for the achievements of the seventeenth century, not sophisticates in their own right, and as a result critics regarded them as shallow. To various degrees either image—the hack writer or the high culture savant—can be defended.

The Victory of Truth. Imagination crowns the the veiled figure of Truth as Reason, Philosophy, Theology, and the arts, crafts, and sciences pay homage. Frontispiece to the volume of illustrations of the *Encyclopédie,* edited by Denis Diderot and Jean Le Rond d'Alembert and published between 1751 and 1776. Engraving (1764) by Benoît-Louis Prévost after a drawing by Claude-Nicolas Chochin II.

RULING AND ORDERING
NATURE AND SOCIETY

The few regularly cited philosophes, who are often criticized as being mere propagandists, represent a minority of those who contributed to Enlightenment pursuits. The term "philosophes" gained currency because it referred to a specifically French membership (a sort of brotherhood, as Voltaire suggested to d'Alembert), and because, unlike references to university or professionally oriented philosophers, philosophes were amateurs, whose society was formed in salons and who wrote for a nonprofessional public. But in common historical usage the term has come to represent far more than a restricted group of French intellectuals (as the term is often translated). Philosophes are no longer only French. Rousseau proudly declared that he was a citizen of Geneva (this before its upright magistrates condemned his philosophy and burned his books). David Hume and Adam Ferguson were Scottish, Thomas Jefferson and Benjamin Franklin were American, Immanuel Kant and Christian Wolff were German, and the Scandinavians Emanuel Swedenborg and Linnaeus's pupil Daniel Solander (among many others) helped spread the Enlightenment in the Baltic. Among those in Italy (where, besides gouty tourists, Enlightenment principles were among the rare imports from the north) were Cesare Beccaria, Pietro Verri (editor of *Il caffè*, organ of the Lombard Enlightenment), and the Neapolitan experimenter Maria Angela Ardinghelli.

This, of course, names only a few, and proportionately fewer still were amateur polemicists—we find academicians, politicians, and other legal or medical professionals filling in the ranks. Perhaps equally variegated were the philosophes' commitments to pursue different Enlightenment goals. As Simon Schama has remarked of the reformers in the Dutch Enlightenment, they rejected "a cosmopolitan, Francophone, universally applicable, rationally discerned set of natural laws, in favor of a highly particular, inward-looking, evangelical, proto-romantic cult of the Fatherland." With regard to the crusade for religious and intellectual toleration, not all European Enlightenment activists rallied around Voltaire's notorious cry to crush the infamous (*écrasez l'infâme*). Enlightenment philosophies of toleration emphasized that rational enquiry necessitated freedom of thought and expression, which usually did not mean abolishing God but recognizing that heterogeneous beliefs might legitimately coexist, something that enlightened Europe, largely through the work of its travelers, anthropologists, and orientalists, was forced to come to terms with.

State responses to this varied around Europe. In England the Toleration Act (1689) permitted freedom of worship for Nonconformists, if at the cost of continuing certain civil disabilities. Elsewhere some monarchs such as Frederick II of Prussia (ruled 1740–1786), Catherine II of Russia (ruled 1762–1796), and Joseph II of Austria (ruled 1764–1790) adopted an enlightened philosophy of conceiving of themselves as the servants, rather than the absolute masters, of their states, leading to the paradoxical way these rulers were referred to by nineteenth-century historians as "enlightened despots." How enlightened and tolerant their rule was in practice is much debated. For example, Charles III of Spain has been described as a minor enlightened despot; nonetheless progressive members of the elite in the Iberian peninsula still faced a tough fight against the Spanish Inquisition.

But a new ruling philosophy was emerging. Social power was increasingly sought by philosophes who seized upon laws of nature as a guide to legitimate governance. One radical philosophy developed was materialism, with John Locke's theory of thinking matter—the material, "corpuscular," sensory origin of ideas—proving an influential model for later clandestine writers who appropriated materialistic arguments to support their theories of an immortal and immaterial soul, of free will, and a naturalistic philosophy of life. In his *Man a Machine* (1747), the French military physician Julien de La Mettrie wrote of how human physiology and behavior could be explained solely in terms of the organization of matter and with reference to the mechanical concepts offered in natural philosophy. La Mettrie, who after the publication of *Man a Machine* settled at the court of Frederick the Great, described the body as a sort of automaton that "winds up its own springs," which physicians, rather than priests, were capable of repairing.

The influence of this philosophy was not, as some critics have emphasized, a matter of an Enlightenment drive to create a "modern paganism" where the so-called Age of Reason was one sustained attack on religious faith. To be sure, deism and natural theology emerged as mediators which postulated that the more rational nature was seen to be—that is, the more law-bound and organized—the more proof this offered of the wisdom and benevolence of God. More germane, perhaps, to Enlightenment pursuits were the ways in which innovators used the man-machine philosophy as a model for their systems of mechanized labor and manufacture.

Enlightened entrepreneurs. Enlightened entrepreneurs translated the concept that nature was mechanical and could be reduced to laws, its powers im-

Enlightened Despots. Meeting of the Holy Roman Emperor Joseph II and the Empress Catherine II of Russia, 18 May 1787. Watercolor by Johann Hieronymus Löschenkohl (d. 1807). ©MUSEEN DER STADT WIEN, VIENNA

itated in machinery and harnessed, into economic advantage. Nature provided not only material resources but sources of power, and the new "mechanics" (referring to people rather than machines) of industry, who became known by the end of the eighteenth century as "engineers," not only used nature's forces to operate their improved windmills, watermills, pumps and other types of machinery, but relied on conceptual tools that became the catchphrases of the Enlightenment: precision measurement, economy of power, environmental management, standardization, interchangeable parts, and so on. We know the ways that this led to the possibilities of mass production and entrepreneurial distribution of products to an expanding consumer market. But what is frequently overlooked is how these products—whether scientific instruments, books, maps, or Wedgwood pottery—encapsulated and distributed the values of the Enlightenment to the bourgeoisie, thus further releasing the Enlightenment from its predominately elite male grip. Consumption by the material culture of the Enlightenment expanded the range of those who were invited to think of themselves as sharing in its accomplishments. But the Enlightenment also commodified philosophic ideas and practices.

Part of the mantra of Enlightenment rationality was the refrain that, like nature which operated under regulated "laws," the human economy—from labor processes to population health—could be reduced to mechanical operations that were rule-bound and controllable. Once this was accomplished, humanity was well on its way to realizing the Enlightenment goal of rendering laborers' techniques visible and allowing entrepreneurs and projectors to assess and reproduce them anywhere. In this protoindustrial and capitalist enterprise, a mechanical, visible workforce was the key to social progress. To the philosophes, as Simon Schaffer has suggested, workers themselves figured as individuals who performed like the machines they managed.

Also accomplished would be the associated benefit of replacing a hereditary social hierarchy with a single strata of enlightened individuals who share knowledge of the mechanical principles that govern nature and society. One popular Enlightenment goal was for careers to be open to the talented, with the intent of introducing a professional meritocracy where status was earned rather than inherited, but proponents first needed to establish rules by which merit could be judged. An illuminating example is the way in which the eighteenth-century French artillery corps—traditionally a second-class branch of the military—obtained new social status when it was recognized that their abilities as technical experts, organized around rigorous discipline and collaboration, could successfully "engineer" the French Revolution. In the Enlightenment, mechanist theories and rule-governed practices were equally as likely to be applied in factories as in prisons, hospitals, or on battlefields.

The links forged during the Enlightenment between manufacturers, entrepreneurs, and natural philosophers became part of the new area where the "business" of Enlightenment expanded, including factories and banks. In addition to the usual locales, such as universities or philosophical academies, late-twentieth-century scholarship has also focused attention on anatomy theaters, various intellectual societies throughout Europe, salons, and even Masonic lodges, whose habitués were allowed to espouse enlightened ideals. All were locales for an effusive Enlightenment rhetoric of liberty, equality, and fraternity. However, the Enlightenment also saw the expansion of areas central to the rapidly expanding and specialized pursuits in natural history—the collection and classification of specimens from the animal, vegetable, and mineral kingdoms.

Spaces of natural history. The founding of the British Museum in 1753 came hot on the heels of the opening of the Luxembourg palace in 1750, the first public art gallery in France. But even earlier, the Enlightenment encyclopedic approach to the acquisition and classification of knowledge was manifest in cabinets of curiosities (such as Peter the Great's in St. Petersburg, which proudly possessed the largest and most famous collection of "monsters"), or the archaeological and artistic collections that generated a thriving commercial economy in Italian cities, where dealers, dilettanti, connoisseurs, aesthetes, and antiquarians busily traded in enlightened taste.

As a descriptive science of forms and categories, natural history complemented mechanical philosophy by merging the living and the nonliving, banishing spirits and metaphysics in favor of empirical methods of classification, often based on external characteristics (such as Linnaeus's use of the sexual organs of plants to classify groups down to the level of species), with the famous exception of Georges-Louis Leclerc de Buffon (1707–1788), who attempted to classify the whole of the natural world in his massive *Histoire naturelle* (1749–1804) using a uniquely historical approach (evidence from the fossil record, for example) and a theory of reproductive relationships to create a biological classification system. In either case, despite their epistemological differences, recognizing patterns

in nature was thought to be the key to understanding not only its operations but its organization, embracing the Enlightenment commitment to render the secrets of nature visible and to display its magisterial order openly to the public.

One Enlightenment pursuit was to set out to catalog nature's diversity, with its contents named and classified accordingly. When Enlightenment pursuits turned to collecting exemplary specimens, the natural history community was vigorously mobilized. And one view of the "geography" of the Enlightenment appears expansive—Russia recruited naturalists particularly from France, Germany, and the Netherlands to help explore its vast natural resources; the Uppsala Royal Society sponsored various expeditions to the polar regions; and Linnaeus gave his pupils specific instructions for collecting specimens and recording information during their worldwide travels, a procedure later imitated by the president of the Royal Society in London, Sir Joseph Banks, when promoting voyages of exploration. Even if everything collected could not be comfortably classified (in an epoch of standardized descriptions, how does one account for "monsters"?), natural historical knowledge was considered useful because it summed up the Adamic process of establishing order from the confusion of the natural world.

Popularizing knowledge. The flip side to collecting and displaying nature's curiosities in particular places was the spread and distribution of Enlightenment knowledge to more distant parts of Europe. Citizens in the eighteenth-century republic of letters followed new codes of sociability and enjoyed a discursive equality where women who participated in Enlightenment debate were seen as a civilizing force, promoting the philosophy of the Enlightenment in the public sphere. Correspondence linked enlightened communities—Voltaire's vast network of correspondents, including Catherine the Great (who eventually bought Diderot's and Voltaire's book collections, which she added to the imperial library), made his estate at Ferney on the Swiss border a crossroads of enlightened Europe. But for many historians of the Enlightenment, the real achievements in spreading Enlightenment knowledge were linked to the production of inexpensive editions of books. As Robert Darnton has shown, "underground" printers, publishers, and booksellers who peddled the philosophes' banned books at great risk were crucial to the popularization of Enlightenment ideas.

Above ground, the translation of scientific and medical tracts played a particularly important role in promoting Enlightenment ideas of utility to a widespread public—the immense success of self-help health-care books such as William Buchan's *Domestic Medicine,* first published in London in 1769 but issued in multiple editions and translated into a number of foreign languages, is testimony to the success of this enterprise. The intended audience for such "useful" works and their wide distribution is a measure of the ambitions of the Enlightenment to include previously marginalized social groups in its goals to educate and improve. In Buchan's case it was the poor, but a similar point has been made about the pedagogic literature written for women, such as the Venetian writer Francesco Algarotti's *Newtonianism for Ladies* (1737), or by women, such as the Bolognese *filosofesse* and critic of Cartesian thought Laura Bassi or the French translator of Newton, Émilie Du Châtelet.

Enlightenment advocates stressed that science served moral as well as utilitarian ends, which was a message most effectively presented to the public in the form of "popular" writing. But the rhetoric of Enlightenment "public science" was also crucial to establishing the natural philosophers' social legitimacy by demonstrating that the improvements they were arguing for would serve the interests of the public. Therefore, "science" is often seen as the centerpiece to Enlightenment thought because, when placed alongside a number of other important implications of Enlightenment thought on society, science was considered the embodiment of reason and rationality, it spearheaded the assault on superstition and priestcraft, and it promised human progress and social improvement. These latter utopian dreams were a leitmotiv of the Enlightenment. Acquiring knowledge through enlightened pursuits, some believed, would conquer fear, perfect humanity, and even eliminate death. At least that is what Benjamin Franklin imagined, while lamenting that he was born a century too early to benefit. "It is impossible to imagine the heights to which may be carried in a hundred years, the power of man over matter," he wrote to the English chemist and Presbyterian minister Joseph Priestley. "All diseases may by sure means be prevented or cured, not excepting even that of old age, and our lives lengthened at pleasure even beyond the antediluvian standard."

THE HEALTH OF NATIONS

Progress was perhaps the key term of Enlightenment thought, the most celebrated, if also the most contentious, term. It embodies the tensions and paradoxes of Enlightenment thought, and an exploration of how the idea of progress was promoted and criticized reveals no consensus among philosophes. However, it does reveal the degree to which Enlightenment philosophes were "conductors" (in both senses) of debate between science and politics.

One point of disagreement among writers was how progress was related to the morally charged optimistic or pessimistic visions of future society. Rousseau wasn't very optimistic. He argued that the more civilization progressed, the farther humanity was from happiness. The savage, he wrote, "breathes only peace and liberty," while "civilized man, on the other hand, is always moving, sweating, toiling, and racking his brains to find still more laborious occupations: he goes on in drudgery to his last moment . . . and, proud of his slavery, he speaks with disdain of those, who have not the honor of sharing it." This is from his *Discourse on the Origin of Inequality,* which, in various ways, was an evolutionary tract explaining how the natural and social attributes of man affect *perfectibilité,* or the capacity for self-improvement. As was more forcefully stated in his direct attack on the notion of progress in *Discourse on the Arts and Sciences,* this capacity could be misdirected, and lead humanity down the road of self-destruction.

The Enlightenment analysis of "wealth" elaborated on its dangers. European economics, it has been widely noted, are future-oriented, a perspective rooted in Enlightenment theories of progress. In the eighteenth century, European economic thought asserted that the purpose of an economy was to increase national wealth—to "grow." For the French physiocrats, this meant that economic and political administration should be based on the scientific, secular management of public welfare. They maintained that the distribution of goods and services operated under the same Newtonian "natural laws" as the rest of the universe. For them, wealth was dependent on free trade in agricultural products. Freedom from government interference (laissez-faire economics) would lead to greater profits, which would result in greater agricultural productivity, upon which "the success of all parts of the administration of the kingdom" depended, according to François Quesnay (a French physician and leader of the physiocrats). Anne-Robert-Jacques Turgot, a disciple of Quesnay, used physiocracy to attack mercantilism and its economic isolationism, which, he said, only "nourishes among nations a germ of hatred and wars," destroying the wealth and happiness of the whole population.

But not all agreed with the physiocrats' view of economic progress. Some eighteenth-century critics thought that too much wealth was far from "progressive" in the sense of improvement, but instead was a symptom of the "diseases of civilization." Primitivists

Dinner at Sans Souci. Frederick the Great, king of Prussia (1740–1786) *(at the head of the table, center)*, entertains the writers Voltaire *(leaning across the table at left)*, J.-B. de Boyer, marquis d'Argens *(in the foreground, leaning to the right)*, Francesco Algarotti *(leaning forward, third from right)*, and Julien Offroy de La Mettrie *(far right)* at the royal palace of Sans Souci at Potsdam, outside Berlin. Voltaire resided at the Prussian court from 1750 to 1755. Painting (1850) by Adolph von Menzel (1815–1905). NATIONAL GALLERY, BERLIN/AKG LONDON

such as Rousseau or physicians such as George Cheyne or Thomas Trotter argued that in the early stages of human development, "noble savages" had pursued healthy lifestyles—hunting and gathering, exercising in the open air—which were very different from modern, congested urban squalor. "The strength and vigor of body are found under the coarse homely coverings of the laboring peasant, not under the courtier's embroidery," wrote Rousseau.

Even though many eighteenth-century Enlightenment thinkers aspired to write "universal histories" of civilization that emphasized progressive "stages" of

social refinement, leading eventually to societies where even luxurious desires are catered to, others perceived in the accumulation of wealth (associated with overindulgence in luxury, idleness, and inequality) a dissolution of morals. In various ways wealth did not lead to health.

Wealth, according to Adam Smith, was not merely the same as money. Wealth required new moral responsibilities. Smith wondered just how far prescriptions for individual responsibility to maintain public health would be implemented, believing that certain refinements of wealthy society made people less interested in the welfare of strangers. The Enlightenment invention of the social sciences proposed new forms of collective organization to guarantee the health and wealth of populations. Since medical theory saw the health of individuals as bound to environmental concerns, civic environmentalism proved a profitable trade, spawning a host of commercial enterprises addressing problems of drainage, sanitation, and ventilation that were deployed in the eighteenth-century campaign to lessen disease.

In England the Enlightenment pursuit of environmental health was haphazardly implemented through philanthropic programs, while elsewhere in Europe the drive to quantify the size and strength of the state in terms of the health of its citizens was given more—if at the same time uneven—state support, such as through the efforts of the *Physici,* the state-salaried physicians in Protestant northern Germany. While statistical enquiries into population trends and patterns of epidemic disease were undertaken at least in Italy and Spain since the sixteenth century, the Enlightenment quantifying spirit is best represented in the state census bureaus set up earliest in Sweden (1749) and followed elsewhere, such as with France's bureaus of statistical investigation instituted during the Napoleonic era. As Dorothy Porter has pointed out, the Enlightenment pursuit of medical statistics and state accounting used the data it acquired either to prescribe preventative health measures to avoid epidemic disease or to introduce efficient state regulation of medical practice and the standardization of pharmaceutical preparations and sales, depending on which state is being examined.

Attitudes toward progress were often burdened with ambivalent feelings, oscillating between optimism and pessimism, with underlying uncertainties over humanity's new social and moral responsibilities. For every attempt made in the Enlightenment to reduce the natural and social world to a formulaic equation or neatly catalog all knowledge, a catastrophe seemed to threaten the entire enterprise. This led to further anxiety and a paradox of the Enlightenment. If nature was rational and law-bound, then why did earthquakes and floods occur? If government was best placed democratically in the hands of its citizens, then why the Reign of Terror?

Every pigeonholed piece of knowledge seemed to add to a mosaic of larger questions. Was nature really a mechanical entity that could be controlled? Was rationality the best guide to human happiness? Was the emphasis on scientific knowledge and rational pursuits really the key to unbounded progress? What were the limits to humanity's intellectual horizon? What were the limits of enlightenment?

LIMITS OF THE ENLIGHTENMENT

This sketch can only point to a few of the major "long eighteenth-century" trends that characterize Enlightenment pursuits. There have been many attempts to present a working definition of the Enlightenment—from its chronology to its geography as well as its intellectual and material representations. Some believe that the Enlightenment has not ended, that the attitudes of enquiry that probe the potential powers of human achievement, social improvement, and political reform continue to characterize even the early twenty-first century—spreading throughout the world. Other scholars have been far less sanguine in the analysis of the legacy of the Enlightenment. For Theodor Adorno and Max Horkheimer, writing their *Dialectic of Enlightenment* in wartime exile in New York, Enlightenment worship of reason gave man sovereignty not only over nature but over humanity itself, creating a new totalitarian regime that ultimately led to fascism and new levels of human barbarism. Still others have argued that the Enlightenment ended with the withdrawal of confidence in the authoritarian regime of Napoleon Bonaparte. But late-twentieth-century scholarship also questioned the geographical limits of the Enlightenment.

The Enlightenment was obsessed with geography, at once seeking to identify others who were thought to share Enlightenment values, searching for the boundaries of where rational, enlightened civilization ended and the yet unenlightened, savage world began. But precisely because the Enlightenment concerned itself with its own propagation under the banner of the "civilizing process," precise boundaries can never be located. However, debates over who best embodied and applied the principles of the Enlightenment to civil duty and social improvement began to refine the general category of "European" to a narrower, national level. The Enlightenment vocabulary that gave birth to "civilization" also invented Eurocentrism, which by the end of the eighteenth century had turned into "enlightened nationalism." This increasing fragmentation within Enlightenment geography has multiplied the number of sites that must be investigated in local context rather than by presuming a unified "European" Enlightenment, which is reflected in late-twentieth-century scholarship's attempt to analyze the Enlightenment in context and within a comparative framework (as pioneered, for example, by Roy Porter and Mikulás Teich).

Virtually all assessments of the Enlightenment have received their fair share of criticism, mainly because any attempt to delimit or define the results or pursuits of the Enlightenment appear to impose sta-

PURSUING THE MOOD OF THE ENLIGHTENMENT

Here are a few sources that can help capture some of the spirit of the Enlightenment.

Music
Wolfgang Amadeus Mozart. *The Magic Flute.*
Franz Joseph Haydn. Quartets
Christoph Willibald Gluck. *Iphigénie en Tauride*

Museums
A visit to any museum is worthwhile, as Enlightenment pursuits often ended with the public display of all manner of "curiosities." For background, read:
Yveline Cantarel-Besson, *La naissance du musée du Louvre,* 2 vols (Paris, 1981)
Edward Miller. *That Noble Cabinet: A History of the British Museum* (London, 1973)

Poetry and Drama
Isobel Armstrong and Virginia Blain. *Women's Poetry in the Enlightenment: The Making of a Canon, 1730–1820* (Basingstoke, U.K., 1999)
Robert Marcellus Browning. *German Poetry in the Age of the Enlightenment: From Brockes to Klopstock* (University Park, Pa., 1978)
Alan Bewell. *Wordsworth and the Enlightenment: Nature, Man, and Society in the Experimental Poetry* (New Haven, Conn., 1989)
Denis Diderot. *Le fils naturel* (1757, various editions and translations)
Carlo Goldoni. *Pamela nubile* (1751, a dramatization of Samuel Richardson's famous novel)

Fiction
Jean-Jacques Rousseau. *Émile* (1762, various translations)
Voltaire. *Candide* (1759, various translations)

Travel Writing
Voltaire. *Lettres anglaises et philosophiques* (1734, various translations)
Denis Diderot. *Supplément au Voyage de Bougainville* (1772)
Lady Mary Wortley Montagu. *Letters Written during Her Travels in Europe, Asia, and Africa* (1763; reprinted 1790 and in various modern editions)

Painting
Johann Georg Sulzer, *Allgemeine Theorie der schönen Künste* (1771–1774), for contemporary art theory and commentary on the German Enlightenment
Charles Coulston Gillispie (ed.). *A Diderot Pictorial Encyclopedia of Trades and Industry: Manufacturing and the Technical Arts. . . .* (New York, 1959)
On CD-ROM, *History through Art: The Enlightenment* (1994)

Contemporary reactions
Cyril O'Keefe. *Contemporary Reactions to the Enlightenment (1728–1762): A Study of Three Critical Journals, the Jesuit* Journal de Trévoux, *the Jansenist* Nouvelles ecclésiastiques, *and the Secular* Journal des savants (Geneva, Switzerland, 1974)

---

bility on what was, by most accounts, a dynamic movement. Hence defining the Enlightenment is yet another paradox scholars continue to confront.

THE ENLIGHTENMENT AND SOCIAL HISTORY

While scholars most often approach the Enlightenment as a chapter in European intellectual history, there are many important questions to be examined from a social history standpoint. Enlightenment thinkers came from a variety of social backgrounds. They advanced and promoted technology and science, theorized about education and social change, and advocated ideas with great potential social impact. To what extent their ideas actually played a causal role in changing society remains open to debate. How much, for instance, did Enlightenment thinking contribute to the motivations and tactics of the budding entrepreneurs who would soon trigger an industrial revolution? How did Enlightenment thinking affect gender, if thinkers tended to downplay women while at the same time expounding ideas that could inspire women to demand equal rights?

The links between the Enlightenment and the French Revolution have prompted particularly heated debate among historians. There is no question that Enlightenment ideas challenged the ancien régime and served to guide the revolutionaries. But historiography has shifted repeatedly in evaluating the importance of these ideas; while at one point social tensions—including unrest among peasants and artisans—prevailed over abstract ideas in historical accounts of the Revolution, in the 1990s the balance shifted back toward intellectual developments.

The Enlightenment had an impact on European societies insofar as its ideas were popularized. It was through the sale of books and pamphlets or through coffeehouse and tavern discussions that the thought of Jean-Jacques Rousseau or Immanuel Kant managed to reach a wider public. For the first time in European history, some writers—such as Voltaire—were able to support themselves from the sale of their works. But just how deeply Enlightenment ideas penetrated society and how widely they spread has sparked much debate and inspired much imaginative historical research. The Enlightenment was most effectively popularized in western Europe. Even here, though, its forces faced competition, not only from traditional religions, but also from new faiths like Methodism in Britain and from popular writers who attacked Enlightenment rationalism, emphasizing a new, Romantic cultural approach. Finally, while the Enlightenment was an eighteenth-century movement, its impact continues well into nineteenth-century social history, where it may be traced both in politics and in popular scientific outlook.

See also other articles in this section.

BIBLIOGRAPHY

Adler, Ken. *Engineering the Revolution: Arms and Enlightenment in France, 1763–1815.* Princeton, N.J., 1997.

Berg, Maxine. *The Age of Manufactures, 1700–1820: Industry, Innovation, and Work in Britain.* Oxford and New York, 1994.

Carpanetto, Dino, and Giuseppe Ricuperati. *Italy in the Age of Reason, 1685–1789.* Translated by Caroline Higgitt. Longman History of Italy, vol. 5. London, 1987.

Clark, William, Jan Golinski, and Simon Schaffer, eds. *The Sciences in Enlightened Europe.* Chicago, 1999.

Crocker, Lester G. *An Age of Crisis: Man and World in Eighteenth Century French Thought.* Baltimore, 1959.

Darnton, Robert. *The Business of the Enlightenment: A Publishing History of the Encyclopédie, 1775–1800.* Cambridge, Mass., 1979.

Darnton, Robert. *The Literary Underground of the Old Regime.* Cambridge, Mass., 1982.

Dolan, Brian. *Exploring European Frontiers: British Travellers in the Age of Enlightenment.* Basingstoke, U.K., and New York, 2000.

Findlen, Paula. "Translating the New Science: Women and the Circulation of Knowledge in Enlightenment Italy." *Configurations* 2 (1995): 167–206.

Frängsmyr, Tore. "The Enlightenment in Sweden." In *The Enlightenment in National Context.* Edited by Roy Porter and Mikulás Teich. Cambridge, U.K., 1981. Pages 164–175.

Gascoigne, John. *Joseph Banks and the English Enlightenment: Useful Knowledge and Polite Culture.* Cambridge, U.K., 1994.

Geras, Norman, and Robert Wokler, eds. *The Enlightenment and Modernity.* Basingstoke, U.K., 2000.

Golinski, Jan. *Science as Public Culture: Chemistry and Enlightenment in Britain, 1760–1820.* Cambridge, U.K., and New York, 1992.

Goodman, Dena. *The Republic of Letters: A Cultural History of the French Enlightenment.* Ithaca, N.Y., 1994.

Grell, Ole Peter, and Roy Porter, eds. *Toleration in Enlightenment Europe.* Cambridge, U.K., and New York, 2000.

Hankins, Thomas. *Science and the Enlightenment.* Cambridge, U.K., 1985.

Hoffmann, Paul. *La femme dans la pensée des lumières.* Paris, 1977.

Jacob, Margaret C. *Living the Enlightenment: Freemasonry and Politics in Eighteenth-Century Europe.* New York and Oxford, 1991.

Jardine, Nicholas, J. A. Secord, and Emma Spary, eds. *Cultures of Natural History.* Cambridge, U.K., and New York, 1996.

Jordanova, Ludmilla. "The Authoritarian Response." In *The Enlightenment and Its Shadows.* Edited by Peter Hulme and Ludmilla Jordanova. London and New York, 1990.

Kramnick, Isaac, ed. *The Portable Enlightenment Reader.* London and New York, 1995.

Lindemann, Mary. "The Enlightenment Encountered: The German Physicus and His World, 1750–1820." In *Medicine in the Enlightenment.* Edited by Roy Porter. Amsterdam and Atlanta, Ga., 1995. Pages 181–197.

Oppenheim, Walter. *Europe and the Enlightened Despots.* London, 1990.

Outram, Dorinda. *The Enlightenment.* Cambridge, U.K., 1995.

Pomian, Krzysztof. *Collectors and Curiosities: Paris and Venice, 1500–1800.* Translated by Elizabeth Wiles-Portier. Cambridge, U.K., 1990. Translation of *Collectionneurs, amateurs et curieux.*

Porter, Dorothy. "Enlightenment and Industrial Ideology." In *Health Care Provision and Poor Relief in Enlightenment and Nineteenth Century Northern Europe.* Edited by Andrew Cunningham, Ole Peter Grell, and Robert Jütte. London, 2000.

Porter, Roy. *Enlightenment: Britain and the Creation of the Modern World.* London and New York, 2000.

Porter, Roy, and Mikulás Teich, eds. *The Enlightenment in National Context.* Cambridge, U.K., 1981.

Porter, Roy. "Science, Provincial Culture, and Public Opinion in Enlightenment England." *British Journal for Eighteenth-Century Studies* 3 (1980): 20–46.

Schama, Simon. "The Enlightenment in the Netherlands." In *The Enlightenment in National Context.* Edited by Roy Porter and Mikulás Teich. Cambridge, U.K., 1981. Pages 54–71.

Schofield, Robert E. *Mechanism and Materialism: British Natural Philosophy in an Age of Reason.* Princeton, N.J., 1970.

Spencer, Samia I., ed. *French Women and the Age of Enlightenment.* Bloomington, Ind., 1984.

Venturi, Franco. *Italy and the Enlightenment.* London, 1972.

Williams, David, ed. *The Enlightenment.* Cambridge Readings in the History of Political Thought. Cambridge, U.K., and New York, 1999.

THE FRENCH REVOLUTION AND THE EMPIRE

Isser Woloch

THE RISE AND FALL OF THE SOCIAL INTERPRETATION

To most liberal writers looking back from the nineteenth century, the French Revolution seemed a historically ordained landmark on humankind's long, arduous, and honorable road to freedom. Its excesses were deplorable and gave serious pause but in the final analysis were incidental. In their view, agency in the French Revolution resided essentially in the middle classes, history's anointed avatars of freedom.

As marxist ideology ripened and spread at the end of the century, this emphasis on class received a new and powerful inflection. To Karl Marx and his followers the French Revolution was rooted in class struggle, its major protagonists a rising bourgeoisie (the hero in the liberal saga) and a declining but still powerful aristocracy. A subplot in the marxist drama offered a glimpse of the class struggle to come: the complex relationship during the revolutionary decade of the dominant bourgeois revolutionaries with and against the common people.

Liberal historians such as Louis-Adolphe Thiers and François-Auguste-Marie Mignet shared with the Marxists an assumption that the French Revolution had positive results of world-historic importance and had not originated from mere contingent circumstances, from mistakes of judgment, for example, by the royal court in the crisis of 1787–1789. Both perspectives saw it as a bourgeois revolution in its origins, course, outcomes, and significance. Both, in other words, provided a social interpretation of the French Revolution.

The anatomy of social class in the Old Regime.
During the first half of the twentieth century this social interpretation crystallized into a dominant historical paradigm, exemplified in the work of Georges Lefebvre, the respected dean of French revolutionary historians until his death in 1959. While the nobility of late-eighteenth-century France still maintained the highest rank and positions in society along with the aristocratic upper clergy, Lefebvre wrote, "in reality economic power, personal abilities and confidence in the future had passed largely to the bourgeoisie. Such a discrepancy never lasts forever. The Revolution of 1789 restored the harmony between fact and law."

This classic paradigm or orthodoxy later eroded. A growing body of research required new assessments of both the nobility and the middle classes. The stark line once presumed to have divided those social groups blurred, while internal divisions within each became more apparent. With its two traditional protagonists thus dissolving into a more complex and less tidy social landscape, the social interpretation of the revolution's origins lost its sway.

In the so-called revisionist view, one sees intra-elite jostling and conflict where once two armies of bourgeois and noble were girding for their titanic clash in 1789. Instead of a bourgeoisie we see various parochial groups at the top of the old third estate (the commoners). Merchants of course formed an important subculture; at their most dynamic they did indeed represent "money in motion," the strategy of high risk in quest of high return, as against the minimal risk and secure if low return that funneled most people's capital into land or annuities. But such dynamic merchants were scarcely typical of the middle classes. Moreover, they often distrusted outsiders, and their "culture of the counting-house" must have seemed esoteric and arcane to others. The same was true of lawyers (barristers), attorneys, doctors, and other professionals. Meanwhile among the numerous middle-class rentiers, some identified their *état* (social status) as "bourgeois living nobly"—perhaps the most suggestive piece of social nomenclature in Old Regime society.

On the other side of the divide, the nobility formed a complex pyramid, with an enormously wealthy plutocracy at the apex whose sources of income and investments differed little from those of the wealthiest bourgeois. Nor can one legitimately see the Enlightenment as a bourgeois ideology, since many of its patrons, not to mention some of its leading writers,

Patriot Deputies. *The Oath of the Tennis Court,* painting after a drawing by Jacques-Louis David. On 20 June 1789, the deputies of the Third Estate (nonclergy and nonnobles) to the Estates General, met in the tennis court at Versailles and swore not to disperse until the king agreed to a constitution. MUSÉE CARNAVALET, PARIS/BULLOZ/THE BRIDGEMAN ART LIBRARY

came from the second estate (the nobility). Indeed, a convincing case can be made that the elites of both the second and the third estate were growing closer and more homogeneous even as their parochial rivalries and jealousies increased. While nobles assuredly retained a keener and more exclusive notion of honor, most of the elite respected the role of wealth, talent, and public service in society. Together they might well have constituted an incipient class of *notables* that would eventually render obsolete the constricting framework of first, second, and third estates. But we will never know, because the Revolution erupted in 1789.

Cultural origins? In a narrow sense, the monarchy's impending financial bankruptcy and political ineptitude in the period 1788–1789 opened the door to the French Revolution. But what deeper causes explain the explosive outcome in the summer of 1789? In the revisionist view the generative force for the French Revolution lies less in class conflict than in cultural ferment. The elites of late-eighteenth-century France constituted a cultural class. The growth of a civil society less tied to the state or to official hierarchies, the concomitant expansion of a public sphere of discourse and criticism, an expanding reading public, a publishing industry vigorously entrepreneurial

and skilled at the distribution of officially banned works—these were perhaps the incubators of revolutionary sentiment. A growing public consciousness might have eroded or "desanctified" traditional social values and political authority. Contributing to such ferment were barristers who published widely selling briefs (not subject to royal censorship) in which the private lawsuits and scandals of high aristocrats became public causes célèbres. Acrimonious controversies within and around the clergy did not help the cause of traditional orthodoxy. And in the best-selling underground books and pamphlets, the world of high royal politics was ridiculed as a sink of incompetence and corruption.

Elite elements from all three estates shared this consciousness and in 1789 constituted a self-styled "patriot party" that led the struggle first against absolutism and then against hereditary privilege. At that point the more traditional elements of the nobility balked and dug in their heels to defend the status quo. They fought to halt the transformation from its inception and at every point forward. By so doing, they set themselves apart as much-reviled "aristocrats" who stood against the interests of a virtuous people and a regenerated France. The early experience of patriot deputies to the Estates General in confronting this opposition is what made them "revolutionaries."

194

SOCIETY, INDIVIDUALS, AND THE STATE

The French Revolution called into question and largely destroyed the juridical and institutional framework of traditional society. Social position and political influence would no longer correspond to divisions between the three estates. The first estate of the clergy lost its corporate standing, privileges, and special consideration, while the noble second estate lost its formal identity altogether. The nobles' fiscal and juridical privileges disappeared in 1789, and in the following year the National Assembly abolished their titles. Thereafter their situation deteriorated, as nobles became the most exposed aristocrats in an increasingly hostile environment. Their ranks were thinned by the executions of the Terror, while many who escaped by emigrating from France had their property confiscated and sold off as national properties *(biens nationaux)*. In one sense this change was permanent. Nobles would never regain their full material or (except for a brief interlude between 1815 and 1830) political preeminence. Yet their aura of social superiority could not be entirely extinguished. The prestige of the Faubourg Saint-Germain (the neighborhood par excellence of the nobility) not only revived but flourished in the nineteenth century, as the most eminent noble families nurtured an almost racial sense of pride in their "houses," whether or not they still served the state. In this sense the Old Regime lived on in postrevolutionary France.

Revolutionary individualism.

The traditional concept of liberty, however, expired almost completely. Before 1789 liberties had been understood as a series of customs, arrangements, and perquisites that conferred privileges on social groups, some corporations, and localities such as towns or provinces. In 1789 this tradition of liberty as privilege gave way to a universalized concept of liberty common to all citizens. In the economic domain this concept dictated the abolition of institutions that restricted individual initiative, such as guilds, chambers of commerce, and workers' associations. Revolutionary ideology extolled the notion of individual opportunity and competition *(émulation)*. Even regulatory restrictions over the professions were reduced to a minimum or eliminated altogether to facilitate *émulation*. Instead, the competitive examination *(concours)* became a favored vehicle for achieving meritocratic selection in certain professions and branches of the armed forces.

Individualist thinking extended into family relations as well. Marriage, for example, came to be viewed as a contract between two free, consenting individuals rather than an arrangement between families sanctified by the Catholic clergy. As a logical corollary, an unsatisfactory marriage could now be dissolved either by mutual consent or for cause, and after 1792 divorce became an option. Revolutionary legislatures lowered the age of minority while granting women greater rights in regard to property and to contracts. In the crucial matter of inheritance, regional customs and traditions favoring eldest sons gave way (at least in law) to an egalitarian individualism that required equal shares for each child, regardless of age or sex.

National integration.

Lest French society be entirely atomized by such liberal individualism, however, revolutionary ideology simultaneously advanced extremely strong claims for the national state, continuing in a different register the centralizing work of the absolute monarchy. But where once the king had played both a substantive and a symbolic role in representing his people, the National Assembly stripped him of any claim to sovereignty and reduced him to a mere executive head of state with real but limited powers. The power to make laws devolved (on behalf of the sovereign people) to an elected legislature.

The National Assembly's first constitution achieved a subtle fusion of centralization and decentralization. On the one hand, it sought to establish uniformity across the variegated mosaic of French provinces and *pays,* so that French citizens, no matter where they lived, would have the same rights, powers, responsibilities, and obligations. The pyramidal and almost geometric structure of departments, districts, cantons, and communes became a blueprint for integrating villages into a new civic order, with the intention of bridging the mental and behavioral chasm between town and countryside. While this could be interpreted in the villages as an attempt by towns to impose their own interests on rural France and to dominate the countryside, it arguably inaugurated a modernizing process that proved beneficial to everyone, even if it took more than a century to complete. At the same time the revolutionaries provided for self-government—that is, for local administrative powers—so long as national law reigned supreme everywhere. As French political life grew increasingly polarized during the revolutionary decade, however, that supremacy was repeatedly challenged. Rebellion against Paris became commonplace, especially in areas hostile to the Revolution because of its religious policies or because of the imperious ways of urban revolutionaries in their departments and districts. But in the long run the design implanted by the National Assembly established a supple civic infrastructure for public services in France—an empowering framework for the collective life of the French people of town and country.

Gradually a set of normative provisions and public responsibilities entered the fabric of French collective life: the upkeep of local roads; the hiring of a rural constable *(garde champêtre)* in every village; a quasi-public poor-relief agency in every town; and (briefly in 1793–1794) a remarkable system of public-assistance entitlements paid by the national treasury. Arguably the most important public service that any state could provide to its people was primary education. Here the French Revolution made a precocious commitment to free, universal public primary education for boys and girls. The National Convention's Lakanal Law of 1794, calling for salaried male and female teachers in every commune above a certain population, was implemented in the districts for about a year before hyperinflation and a changing political climate aborted the effort. But universal public education remained a benchmark for subsequent regimes, all of which kept alive the commitment in some normative fashion.

War on the Châteaus. Peasants attack a château during rural protests in summer and autumn 1789. Anonymous engraving, 1789. MUSÉE CARNAVALET, PARIS/ THEARTARCHIVE

THE REVOLUTION AND RURAL SOCIETY

If a social interpretation of the Revolution's origins has been undermined by modern research, does it still illuminate the course and consequences of the Revolution? For Marx, of course, it was all that really mattered: the Revolution marked the definitive transition from feudalism to capitalism, from the reign of the nobility to the era of the bourgeoisie. By implication at least, that interpretation grossly overestimates the role of capitalists in forwarding the Revolution; most merchants were reluctant revolutionaries who were left far behind by more aggressive lawyers, former royal officials, and the like. Similarly, the effects of the Revolution in stimulating, enabling, or advancing industrial capitalism are dubious. To be sure, the liberal ideology of 1789 and its legislative record are not inconsistent with that outcome. The revolutionaries abolished almost all privileged corporations; formalized the Old Regime's prohibitions against trade unions and strikes; abolished most forms of state intervention in the economy; and on paper at least, granted to individuals maximal freedom to pursue their economic interests. But for the most part the era of the Revolution and empire was an ordeal rather than a golden age for maritime commerce, capitalist innovation, and industrial entrepreneurs.

On the other hand, a strong case can be made for the impact of the Revolution on landed society. "The National Assembly hereby completely abolishes the feudal system": thus began the historic decree of 4 August 1789 that forever destroyed several key underpinnings of the Old Regime social order. Technically, feudalism as a sociopolitical system of vassalage had long since disappeared in France, so the term "feudalism" is wildly misleading. But insofar as the word stigmatized France's pervasive skein of social, corporate, and regional privileges (and that was its most common contemporary usage), feudalism was very much alive in 1789. This was especially true of seigneurialism in the French countryside. The 4 August decree dissected seigneurialism, abolishing on the spot certain seigneurial prerogatives while leaving others to an uncertain fate, which popular mobilization eventually resolved.

The abolition of seigneurialism. Thus the Assembly without hesitation abolished seigneurial hunting rights. Previously, local lords *(seigneurs)* were free to hunt over any land in their jurisdiction, no matter who farmed it and without regard to the depredations they might cause; the right to hunt was more or less reserved exclusively to them. The Revolution's affirmation of a right to hunt on one's property in 1789 in fact led to an orgy of hunting and an ecologically dubious slaughter of game. (Later this right to hunt would be restricted by the imposition of steep gun-licensing fees.) Similarly, the Assembly suppressed seigneurial courts, previously the lowest tier of both criminal and civil justice in the French countryside.

196

Judges appointed by the lords had often used their powers in this system to further the interests of their employers in disputes with their peasants. The Revolution replaced these generally unpopular and incompetent officials with locally elected justices of the peace who brought a far more accessible, honest, expeditious, and inexpensive form of conflict resolution to the French countryside—a reform that endured through every subsequent political upheaval.

The Assembly also abolished other elements of seigneurialism that it stigmatized as personal or servile obligations, such as demeaning labor or transport services owed by peasants to their lords, and seigneurial monopolies over ovens, winepresses, and olive presses. But property dues and rights that the Assembly considered legitimate—deriving from concessions to peasants of land held originally by lords in exchange for payment of various kinds—were not abolished. True, the Assembly considered such obligations outmoded and regressive, in contrast to a straightforward contractual obligation to pay rent. It hoped ultimately to disentangle land from considerations of social status and thus to commodify land completely. The Assembly ultimately expected these seigneurial rights—quitrents *(cens)*, harvest dues *(champarts, tasques)*, and heavy transfer fees *(lods et ventes)*—to disappear. But it would promote that goal only by making such dues redeemable (at great cost) by the peasants subject to them, so as not to trample the legitimate property rights of the lords. (The Assembly approached the question of venal offices somewhat differently. Stigmatizing the purchase of public offices as obsolete and objectionable, it recognized existing offices as a form of property. In this case, however, the state simply abolished all such venal offices but generously indemnified their owners for the losses.)

The distinction between illegitimate "servile" seigneurial rights and legitimate if obsolete seigneurial dues as property made eminent sense to the learned jurists who framed this legislation. But their blueprint left an onerous burden on peasants who might hope to buy their way out of those obligations. In fact, the vast majority of peasants considered the distinction meaningless, condemned the seigneurial system, and were determined to demolish it—by lawsuits, by passive resistance (not paying any of these dues), and in many parts of France by direct action (specifically, resuming the "war on the châteaus" that had first erupted in the summer of 1789 and had provoked the 4 August decree). After France went to war in 1792 and the government in Paris needed to rally popular support, it finally bowed to this popular pressure and in 1793 abolished all seigneurial obligations without any compensation.

Agrarian innovation? The abolition of seigneurialism did not in itself modify the ownership of France's arable land. Land owned by the lords, whether as part of their direct domain (demesne) or as parcels that they rented to peasants, remained their property, and the rents or crop shares continued to be paid. Whether the abolition of seigneurialism opened the way to a more capitalist agrarian system is another question. Some historians have argued that seigneurialism itself—by virtue of the lord's enormous power over land and families—had permitted market-driven innovation in regions such as Burgundy. Hence, by strengthening the small peasant's position, the abolition of seigneurialism retarded capitalist innovation, since most peasant smallholders sought security in habit and tended to resist the risk-reward enticements of serious innovation. A different kind of argument supports the same net conclusion. Many lords in France's more backward regions (and even in places like Burgundy) had been content to extract income from their tenants without any interest in productive methods or innovation. After 1789 they simply continued to rent out their parcels of land under short-term leases that discouraged innovation, often under sharecropping *(métayage)* arrangements. In this respect the abolition of seigneurialism would have done little to stimulate agrarian capitalism.

But an alternative perspective would suggest that the Revolution brought a turning point in French agrarian history by favoring the large peasant-proprietors. Such men indisputably gained a more advantageous position in rural society after the abolition of seigneurialism. Operating with less constraint and more income at their disposal, they could better capitalize on market opportunities and in due course increase production by way of innovation. The other major agrarian change brought by the Revolution might have reinforced this effect.

Revolutionary land transfers. A great quantity of land changed hands as a direct result of the French Revolution. The church collectively owned approximately 10 percent of the land in France. The rental income from this land constituted one of the church's two main sources of revenue abolished in the 4 August decree, the other being the tithe. The Assembly proceeded to nationalize the church's property—to put its land "at the disposition of the nation." The state would now take responsibility for maintaining the church and paying the clergy's salaries. Meanwhile, it would gradually sell off the land and use the income to pay down the enormous state debt that had precipitated the crisis of the royal government and the calling of the Estates General.

197

DISTRIBUTION OF
NATIONAL PROPERTY

The historian Georges Lefebvre tracked the sale of the *biens nationaux* in one department in the north of France, where the church had owned 20 percent of the land (an unusually large amount) before 1789. Altogether, 20,300 peasants purchased 52 percent of this property (totaling 71,500 hectares), while 7,500 bourgeois purchased 48 percent (65,700 hectares). But those raw totals do not tell the whole story. Lefebvre looked in detail at the land that ended up in peasant hands and found that the lion's share went to a very small number of already-wealthy peasants. During a brief interval when land was being sold in smaller plots or to syndicates of peasants, 90 percent of the peasant purchasers came onto the scene and acquired about 40 percent of the land that ultimately went to peasants. But another 9 percent of peasant purchasers bought up 39 percent of the total peasant acquisitions in parcels ranging from 5 to 40 hectares, while a mere 1 percent (or about 200 peasants) came away with 21 percent of the total, usually in lots greater than 40 hectares.

France had long possessed an active and complex land market—with ownership distributed across the social order: nobility, church, urban middle class, and peasants. This complexity resulted in great competitiveness for land—by far the dominant source of wealth and status as well as subsistence. Now up to a tenth of France's land was to come on the market. While some believed that this could be used to turn landless peasants into proprietors—that it could support a social policy of redistribution—most insisted that since the purpose of nationalization was financial, the terms of transfer had to maximize the inflow of revenue to the state treasury. Hence the *biens nationaux* (national properties), as this land was now called, were sold off in large rather than small plots and at auction in the district capitals rather than in the localities. Therefore, most of the former church land ended up in the hands of the wealthy urban middle class and the large peasants, while first-time peasant owners acquired relatively little. The same was true of a second component of the *biens nationaux,* the land of the émigrés confiscated by the state after they were banned from returning to France on pain of death in 1793.

Although the *biens nationaux* were generally sold in large plots beyond the reach of small peasants, some of this land came back on the market when the original purchasers subdivided their acquisitions and resold them. In Alsace it would appear that the proportion of peasant purchasers thereby ultimately reached as high as 80 percent. Nonetheless, the typical purchaser was a wealthy middle-class person or a large-scale peasant. These purchasers, among other things, now had the most tangible interest in the success of the Revolution and in resisting counter-revolution, whose triumph would jeopardize their acquisitions.

The peasant community. Before the Revolution many regions of France sustained a strong peasant communalism. Peasant interdependence revolved around shared routines of husbandry and use of common land for grazing (when such property was not leased out to produce income for common village expenses). In open-field regions in the north and center all cultivators followed similar agrarian practices, including the right of "vacant pasture," which opened fields to grazing by the livestock of all citizens in a village right after the harvest. Progressive thinking generally condemned such practices as a drag on individual initiative, innovation, and productivity. French agrarian reformers *(agronomes)* advocated changes comparable to the English model of agrarian modernization: the rearrangement of small scattered plots into large compact farms, the enclosure of those farms, and the division of common land so that it could be cleared and incorporated into the arable. The inertia of landlords and peasants, misgivings among some provincial royal authorities, and occasional resistance by peasants had defeated most efforts to introduce such changes before 1789.

With its ideology of liberal individualism, the Revolution promised new departures in this area. The National Assembly proclaimed that individuals should be free to use their land as they saw fit, without communal constraints. But it proved impossible to legislate such a notion. Communalism, vacant pasture, and the like were too deeply ingrained. The common lands *(biens communaux),* however, presented an especially inviting and tangible target. Considered by most political economists an unproductive, regressive use of resources, the common lands were also eyed by small or landless peasants in certain regions as a way of finally coming into possession of their own land. On the other side, wealthy peasants who maintained large flocks of livestock might favor the status quo in which the common land helped support their sub-

198

stantial grazing needs. The interests at play were complex and difficult to predict. In any case, in the same radical climate that abolished seigneurial rights, the National Convention passed a law in June 1793 authorizing the division of common land if one-third of a village's households voted to do so. Such a division would provide each household with an equal share of land, which could not be immediately resold. Some common land was duly divided under this policy, but local contention and indecision limited its effect. In 1795 the Convention suspended the law, which was annulled in 1797. The status quo of village communalism survived largely intact, perhaps above all because it provided security to most peasants.

THE SANSCULOTTES

After centuries of oligarchic rule under the sway of the monarchy, France's cities and towns vaulted toward democracy in 1789. In Paris and in twenty-six of the thirty largest cities, municipal revolutions ousted royal officials or traditional ruling cliques and installed broader-based local governments reflecting "patriot" sentiment. National legislation soon normalized this transformation, providing for the popular election of mayors and town councils in all towns and villages. Middle-class groups dominated the scene at first, but gradually the sansculottes—local businessmen, master artisans, journeymen, shopkeepers, white-collar employees, and wage earners—invaded the political arena as well.

Revolutionary crowds. Revolutionary crowds first appeared during the historic mass protests *(journées)* of 1789 in Paris, when spontaneous mobilizations saved an imperiled National Assembly by storming the Bastille in July and forcibly returned the royal family to Paris from Versailles in October. Subsequent mobilizations were less spontaneous but equally large and momentous: the Parisian insurrection of 10 August 1792 that drove Louis XVI from the throne; the armed demonstration of 2 June 1793 that forced the National Convention to purge the Girondins; and the menacing mass demonstration of 5 September 1793 that led the convention "to place terror on the order of the day." The Parisian crowd was arguably the most tangible force propelling the Revolution forward. At the least these crowds are remembered as the Revolution's most visible social phenomenon—the symbol or embodiment, at least in its own eyes, of popular will and the power of an aroused people. The last *journée* of the revolutionary decade came in the spring of 1795, at the height of the Thermidorian reaction, when embittered and desperate Parisian sansculottes stormed the Convention to demand food and to resuscitate the moribund democratic constitution of 1793. The repression that followed, coupled with an increasingly vigilant policing of the capital, put an end to the revolutionary crowd but not to its memory. In July 1830 and in 1848—not only in Paris but in several European capitals—revolutionary crowds, conscious of their historic antecedents, again made history.

Revolutionary Journée. March of the women from Paris to Versailles, 5 October 1789.
MUSÉE CARNAVALET, PARIS/BULLOZ/THE BRIDGEMAN ART LIBRARY

"Terror on the Order of the Day." Engraving of the first execution by guillotine, in the Place du Carrousel, Paris, 13 August 1792. MUSÉE DE LA VILLE DE PARIS, MUSÉE CARNAVALET, PARIS/LAUROS-GIRAUDON/ART RESOURCE, NY

The Paris sections.   The sansculottes did not appear on the revolutionary stage solely in this spasmodic, episodic guise. In remarkable fashion they established an ongoing presence in municipal life, especially in the forty-eight sections, or neighborhood wards, of Paris. From the bottom up, and outside the prescribed framework of local government, the Parisian sansculottes built an unprecedented participatory infrastructure. Each section had a general assembly (much like a New England town meeting), an executive committee, a revolutionary committee to deal with "suspects," a welfare committee, a force of national guardsmen, and an elected police commissioner and justice of the peace. Thus the sections resembled forty-eight small Rousseauesque republics where direct democracy seemed to be operative.

In reality, that image is deceptive. In each section small and shifting local oligarchies dominated. In social terms these leadership cadres have been aptly described as a "sansculotte bourgeoisie"—not the oxymoron it may seem. Many men who thought of themselves as sansculottes were property owners, often employers of artisanal labor, shopkeepers, or local entrepreneurs. Deeply rooted in their communities, they were advocates for their proletarian neighbors, whom they could mobilize for action. These cadres of sectional militants numbered no more than five or six thousand in a city of about 600,000, but they formed a new kind of socially heterogeneous and populist elite. Intensely preoccupied if not obsessed with the issue of subsistence supplies and bread prices, ferociously antiaristocratic, and sentimentally egalitarian, they were pedagogues to their more plebeian neighbors in the revolutionary ideology of fraternity and civic equality. Believers in as much direct democracy as possible, they distrusted the National Convention even while serving as its fiercest partisans. They backed the war effort to the hilt on the home front and advocated redistributive Jacobin social policies, such as national pension entitlements for needy working families with children.

Provincial militants.   While never as dominant or as well organized as in Paris, sansculottes could be found in many other towns, filling local Jacobinic clubs *(sociétés populaires)*, staffing revolutionary committees, and manning ad hoc paramilitary battalions formed to provide "force behind the laws" of the Terror. Wary like their Parisian counterparts of the motivation and behavior of rural citizens, the provincial sansculottes were obsessed with the requisitioning of food supplies (on which urban consumers as well as the armed forces depended) and the imposition of price controls. They were also the staunchest partisans of the Terror and of the most radical "de-Christianization" initiatives of 1793–1794—harassment of constitutional priests, rituals of blasphemy in church buildings, and the conversion of churches to "temples of reason."

It has been easy to demonize the sansculottes for their fanaticism, violence, populist intolerance, and philistinism. But it has also been tempting to romanticize them, as Richard Cobb has done. As the historian of the sansculottes' paramilitary battalions *(armées révolutionnaires),* a key instrument of the Terror, Cobb admired their spontaneous revolutionary enthusiasm. He defined them less by their mixed and largely popular social composition than by their temperament—imprudent, naive, dogmatic, fervent. In his mind they were the opposite of the "possiblists" and the calculating "revolutionary bureaucrats" (chief among them Maximilien Robespierre). While this is an interesting way to see the sansculottes, their significance is perhaps greater in more conventional social terms. In the sansculottes the chasm between elites and popular masses was briefly bridged. Their leaders may have been men of property, but that did not prevent them from fraternizing with ordinary workers, fulminating against aristocrats and *les gros,* and propagating egalitarian values.

The social amalgam of sansculottes would have been unthinkable before 1789, when men who worked with their hands had scarcely anything in common with the educated, propertied elites. And in 1848 scant possibility remained of resuscitating that amalgam. By then the social mix had disaggregated, notably by way of the national guard in the 1815–1848 period. Far more than the notorious plutocrats of those decades, the national guard drew a stark line through the social order between the working man who could not afford the uniform necessary for membership and the lower-middle-class master artisan or shopkeeper who could. Thus, the June days of 1848 provided the final epitaph for the remarkable phenomenon of sansculottism in the French Revolution.

THE NAPOLEONIC REGIME AND FRENCH SOCIETY

On 18 Brumaire Year VIII (9 November 1799) a group of disillusioned republican moderates joined forces with General Napoleon Bonaparte to overthrow the Directory. While the politicians did not desire or foresee the emergence of an untrammeled dictatorship in France or a French empire stretching across Europe, they did envisage the pacification of a society fractured by a decade of revolution. First they eliminated the unpredictable annual elections and the governmental instability that ensued. While maintaining the republic in name, they put in place a strong centralized

government headed by General Bonaparte and a legislature that was little more than a co-optive oligarchy. Within two or three years the Napoleonic regime forged the outlines of a social settlement. Civil equality and the abolition of seigneurialism would stand as the fundamental social gains of the Revolution. The transfer of the *biens nationaux* would be irrevocable. Émigrés would be allowed to return and the Vendée rebels pardoned as long as they submitted to the laws. Social peace would be promoted by a reinstatement of the Catholic Church by a concordat negotiated with Rome in 1801.

The self-constituted governing oligarchy of Brumaire largely comprised moderate parliamentary veterans of the revolutionary regimes. Most moved directly from the defunct legislative houses of the Directory era into the new institutions created after Brumaire: a Senate; a bicameral, rubber-stamp parliament; an apolitical Council of State to draft laws at the behest of first consul Bonaparte; and a corps of appointed prefects who would replace the locally elected departmental administrations of the revolutionary decade. Continuity and consolidation brought an unprecedented degree of security, both political and financial, for these men of the Revolution. The vast majority of his collaborators proved so grateful to Napoleon that they readily supported him in his most extravagant ambitions.

Elite formation: Notables and nobles. What of provincial society under the Napoleonic regime? The government assembled lists of the six hundred largest taxpayers in each of the ninety-odd departments. The regime thereby identified the important local people who were likely to have networks of clients under their influence. Informally, at least, these men became the new *notables* of France and later of the non-French areas of the empire. The regime could confer tangible recognition on these *notables* in various ways, such as appointing them to honorific posts in departmental electoral colleges or local advisory councils.

This process of regime-sponsored elite formation reached a climax with the creation of a Napoleonic nobility in 1808. An emperor, after all, needs a nobility and courtiers to refract his own pretensions. But this was to be a nobility based on state service, military and civil, and solid wealth. ("Such titles will henceforth serve only to mark for public recognition those who are already noted for their services, for their devotion to the prince and the fatherland.") The first cohorts were filled with the generals, senators, and counselors of state intimately associated with the regime. Later, however, Napoleon cultivated prominent Old Regime nobles by conferring new titles on them.

The Revolution Commemorated. *Departure of the Volunteers in 1792, or The Marseillaise,* sculpture by François Rude (1784–1855) on the Arc de Triomphe, Paris, 1833–1836. PETER WILLI/BRIDGEMAN ART LIBRARY

Thus the Napoleonic nobility was a novel amalgam reflecting the emperor's eclectic ideas about the basis for high status. By 1814, 3,263 citizens of the empire had received titles, with 59 percent bestowed on military officers and 22 percent on high state functionaries; over a fifth of the Napoleonic nobility came from noble families of the Old Regime.

While Napoleon's permanent legacies to modern France were institutional—the corps of prefects, the Council of State, the centralized university, the Bank of France, the civil and criminal codes—his concept of *notables* also proved durable. When the Old Regime nobility regained its titles and recovered its prestige after the Restoration, the Bourbon also recognized the titles of the Napoleonic nobility, perhaps giving the whole idea of a French nobility greater credibility. More important, the idea of provincial *notables* identifiable by their superior level of property and land taxes regardless of birth endured through much of the nineteenth century. Napoleon thereby helped realize the vision in progressive thought before 1789 of an amalgam of wealth and talent from across the three estates—a true elite in which birth alone would not be decisive.

Conscription. Another practice of the Napoleonic regime proved equally durable and of far greater consequence: the claim of the state on young men for military service. Initiated as a one-time emergency measure in 1793—the *levée en masse* in which all single, able-bodied young men were drafted into the army—military conscription was enacted on a formal basis by the Directory in 1798, but it was only under Napoleon that it was consolidated, rendered permanent, and integrated into the normative fabric of social life. At first the draft evasion that had plagued the troop levies of the Convention and the Directory continued under Napoleon. But gradually by persistence, intense commitments at every level, improved administrative methods, and sheer coercion, the Napoleonic state broke the back of this endemic resistance and made conscription a routine obligation throughout the empire. By winning this battle Napoleon assured a steady flow of manpower into his increasingly large and far-flung armies. But perhaps more important, by decisively establishing this power of the state over society, the Napoleonic regime created the prototype for the mass conscript armies and reserve forces that nearly destroyed European society a century later.

See also **France** *(in this volume);* **Land Tenure; The Liberal State; Military Service; Peasant and Farming Villages; Serfdom: Western Europe** *(volume 2);* **The Aristocracy and Gentry; Collective Action; Revolutions; Urban Crowds** *(volume 3);* **Patriarchy** *(volume 4);* **Journalism** *(volume 5).*

BIBLIOGRAPHY

General Works

Furet, François. *Revolutionary France, 1770–1880.* Translated by Antonia Nevill. Oxford, 1992.

McManners, John. *The French Revolution and the Church.* New York, 1969.

Sutherland, Donald. *France, 1789–1815: Revolution and Counter-Revolution.* New York, 1986.

Woloch, Isser. *The New Regime: Transformations of the French Civic Order, 1789–1820s.* New York, 1994.

Origins of the Revolution

Chartier, Roger. *The Cultural Origins of the French Revolution.* Durham, N.C., 1991.

Doyle, William. *Origins of the French Revolution.* 2d ed., Oxford, 1988.

Lefebvre, Georges. *The Coming of the French Revolution, 1789.* Translated by R. R. Palmer. Princeton, N.J., 1947.

Tackett, Timothy. *Becoming a Revolutionary: The Deputies of the French National Assembly and the Emergence of a Revolutionary Culture (1789–1790).* Princeton, N.J., 1996.

Rural Society

Jones, Peter. *The Peasantry in the French Revolution.* Cambridge, U.K., 1988.

Lefebvre, Georges. *The Great Fear of 1789: Rural Panic in Revolutionary France.* Translated by Joan White. New York, 1973.

Markoff, John. *The Abolition of Feudalism: Peasants, Lords, and Legislators in the French Revolution.* University Park, Pa., 1996.

Tilly, Charles. *The Vendée: A Sociological Analysis of the Counter-revolution of 1793.* Cambridge, Mass., 1967.

Social Issues

Bertaud, Jean-Paul. *The Army of the French Revolution: From Citizen Soldiers to Instrument of Power.* Translated by R. R. Palmer. Princeton, N.J., 1988.

Forrest, Alan. *The French Revolution and the Poor.* Oxford, 1981.

Gross, Jean-Pierre. *Fair Shares for All: Jacobin Egalitarianism in Practice.* Cambridge, U.K., 1997.

Jones, Colin. *Charity and Bienfaisance: The Treatment of the Poor in the Montpellier Region, 1740–1815.* Cambridge, U.K., 1982.

Phillips, Roderick. *Family Breakdown in Late-Eighteenth-Century France: Divorce in Rouen, 1792–1803.* Oxford, 1980.

Traer, James. *Marriage and the Family in Eighteenth-Century France.* Ithaca N.Y., 1980.

The Sansculottes

Cobb, Richard. *The People's Armies.* Translated by Marianne Elliott. New Haven, Conn., 1987.

Godineau, Dominique. *The Women of Paris and Their French Revolution.* Translated by Katherine Streip. Berkeley, Calif., 1998.

Rudé, George. *The Crowd in the French Revolution.* Oxford, 1959.

Soboul, Albert. *The Parisian Sans-Culottes and the French Revolution, 1793–4.* Translated by Gwynne Lewis. Oxford, 1964.

The Napoleonic Regime

(See also the books by Sutherland and Woloch under General Works)

Bergeron, Louis. *France under Napoleon.* Translated by R. R. Palmer. Princeton, N.J., 1981.

Broers, Michael. *Europe under Napoleon, 1799–1815.* London, 1996.

Lyons, Martyn. *Napoleon Bonaparte and the Legacy of the French Revolution.* New York, 1994.

THE NINETEENTH CENTURY

Timothy B. Smith

Many historians, including Theodore Hamerow, argue that the period 1815 to 1914 marks a distinct epoch in human history—an age dominated by the spirit of industry and commerce, the rise of democracy, the triumph of science, and the emergence of an almost religious faith in the idea of progress. As Hamerow stresses, no comparable change in the way of life had occurred since the prehistoric era, when humans made the leap from nomadism to farming, permanent settlements, and animal husbandry.

In 1800, Europe was closer to the old world of enlightened despotism, monarchy, and preindustrial modes of production than it was to the modern world. Europe was overwhelmingly rural and, with the exception of England, identities revolved around the local community, not the nation. By 1914, much of Europe had industrialized, become urban, and embraced democracy, the ideology and practice of individualism, consumerism, and the ideal (if not practice) of social mobility. The state had been transformed from a provider of basic security to a provider of social welfare, at least in parts of Europe (Germany and Britain in particular). Social welfare legislation had been introduced by the 1880s, and by 1914 many European nations had crude forms of welfare states. Legal privilege was gone or under intense attack. Societies organized around birth and divided according to estates or orders gave way by 1900 to class-divided societies, in which the main fault lines were economic, not based on birth.

During the nineteenth century, Europe prospered as never before. From a population of just under 200 million in 1800, the continent grew to 401 million in 1900, at which point there were also 100 million North Americans and 40 million Latin Americans of European descent. Europeans constituted 25 percent of the world's population but produced more than 60 percent of the world's manufactured goods. (At the end of the twentieth century Europe represented less than 10 percent of the world's population and produced less than 30 percent of all manufactured goods.) Reliable food supplies, better diet, stricter housing and public health regulations, and a period of prolonged peace and economic prosperity had conspired to lift many parts of Europe out of the age-old Malthusian trap. During the nineteenth century, the crop cycle was finally tamed even if the business cycle was not. A sign of Europe's prosperity was the sudden and dramatic drop in the birthrate in the two decades before World War I. The rate of death by infectious diseases—another sign of the relative health of European society—was also on the decline in the period 1880–1914. As people became richer and more children survived into adulthood, families became smaller and expectations of material comfort rose, as did hope for the future.

By 1900, no continent, no region of the world had been left untouched by Europe, for better or for worse. Each year between 1871 and 1914, the European imperialist powers added an area the size of France to their empires. European superiority in technology—weaponry, steamships, battleships, industrial production, and military organization—made this possible, backed by Europe's belief in its inherent superiority. This confidence was grounded in a faith that European science and rationalism were necessarily superior to superstition. Machines, Michael Adas writes, were seen as the measure of men. The imbalance between Europe (and its settlements in North America) and the rest of the world in scientific knowledge and industrial capacity is one of the most important developments in world history since 1800.

Having said this, Europe was by no means a monolithic bloc in 1900. Much of the European peasantry was still mired in poverty, superstition, and tradition. Typhus and tuberculosis still stalked the poor. Approximately one-third of the population of London was considered poor. More than half of the French population still lived in small rural villages and towns. Tens of thousands of Russian peasants starved in the 1890s and 1900s. More than half of all Italians were illiterate in 1900. As a whole, and in relation to the rest of the world, the continent was indeed very rich, having accumulated layers of wealth and knowledge

A Century of Technological Change. Searchlights at the top of the Eiffel Tower illuminate the monuments of Paris during the Paris Exposition, 1900. CIVICA RACCOLTA DELLE STEMPE, ACHILLE BERTARELLI

over the centuries in its urban banks, corporations, academies, and universities. But, generally speaking, in the countryside (and in several regions) things were often quite different.

The popular image of the nineteenth century, however, is dominated by two major themes: 1) this was the age of the industrial revolution across Europe and North America; 2) this was also the age of political revolution, the century that witnessed the rise of democracy. It is not difficult to find convincing evidence to support these obvious facts. But this image of the nineteenth century may be colored excessively by the English, French, and American experiences, which were anything but typical. In fact, a good case could be made that continental European countries, whose economic, political, and social development was slower, represented the norm. In other words, it was the English, in particular, who deviated from the European norm.

In the case of the industrial revolution there is a common view that it began in England in the last quarter of the eighteenth century and by the nineteenth century (and certainly by 1914) Europeans had moved to the mines, the mills, and the factories, or to the city. In fact, as Maxine Berg and others remind us, this was not even true for most English workers as late as the 1850s. Most Russians, Portuguese, Spaniards, and Italians were still peasants in the 1890s, and half of France was still engaged in agriculture. By 1850, there were still only 400,000 factory workers in

all of France—one tenth of the entire manufacturing labor force. In England, they constituted one-half of the manufacturing labor force. Not until the last two decades of the century did the French and Italian economies really take off and become more urban-industrial. But as late as 1900, some 60 percent of French workers still worked in units of under ten employees. Industrial change and urbanization was rapid where it occurred (especially in England, Belgium, and Germany) but in many nations, including France, Italy, and Russia, urban-industrial society was concentrated in only a few places.

The nineteenth century was thus a time of great social change, but not for all people and all places. Pockets of misery, traditionalism, and inertia persisted into the twentieth century, escaping the winds of industrial, political, and social change. This is as true for Sicily and Spain as it is for large regions of central Europe, Russia, the Balkans, and even parts of France. There is a danger, however, in overemphasizing what did not change. Viewed through the lens of social history, the picture can become nuanced to the point where one loses a sense of the greater whole. Even as we distinguish between the varying rates of social change in different parts of Europe, and as we distinguish between the period 1815–1870 and the period 1870–1914 (the age of the second industrial revolution and the age of rapid urban growth), the general argument holds true: the nineteenth century in Europe witnessed more important social, economic, scientific, and industrial changes than all previous eras of history combined.

THE BOURGEOIS CENTURY?

For many scholars who have written general histories of the century, including Roger Magraw, Harold Perkin, William Reddy, and Geoff Eley and David Blackbourn, the nineteenth century was the "bourgeois century," the age of the middle class, the age of commerce and the pursuit of wealth. The idea that the middling classes took over European society during the nineteenth century has a long pedigree. In *The Communist Manifesto* (1848), Karl Marx and Friedrich Engels wrote these famous words:

> the bourgeoisie has . . . since the establishment of Modern Industry and of the world market, conquered for itself, in the modern representative state, exclusive political sway. The executive of the modern State is but a committee for managing the common affairs of the whole bourgeoisie. . . . [which] during its rule of scarce one hundred years, has created more massive and more colossal productive forces than have all preceding generations together.

Marx and Engels had a tendency to overstate their case. But certainly at some point in the nineteenth century the middle class exerted considerable influence on politics and in the realm of culture. In some nations, this occurred later in the century; in Britain, much earlier. Some of the key achievements of the century were: freedom of commerce, freedom of association, freedom of profession, an end to the key legal privileges of the aristocracy, free trade, freedom of religion, and written constitutions. Through the spread of such civic or cultural institutions as museums, the opera, zoos, and a flourishing press, the middling ranks set the tone for society.

Not everyone would agree with this argument. Some, like the historian Arno Mayer, would argue that in fact the aristocracy continued to dominate political and civil society right up to World War I. Others, such as Peter Gay, view the notion of a rising bourgeoisie as a "folktale" begun by Marx. In his influential study of the European and American middle classes during the nineteenth century, *The Bourgeois Experience*, Gay emphasizes the anxiety that permeated the middle classes: they knew they were not of the aristocracy above them, and they feared the workers beneath them. Everywhere the bourgeoisie attempted to reshape values, polities, and institutions in their image, all the while remaining a distinct minority of the population. In nineteenth-century Bochum and Barmen (Germany), only 10 to 12 percent of the population could claim bourgeois status. In Paris, perhaps 15 percent could. The bourgeoisie had universal pretensions but not powers. Like Theodore Zeldin, Gay emphasizes the various fractured group identities within the middling ranks.

If the nineteenth century was indeed the bourgeois century, it nevertheless cannot be understood without reference to the continuing social, economic, and above all political power of the nobility. This is as true for England as it is for France, Germany, and Austria-Hungary. The old French nobility still owned one-fifth of the land in 1815. They continued to wield their social and political influence in rural France, especially in the poorer areas of the center and the west. Patronage was dispensed and political influence flowed from it. The church also retained its strong social and political influence into the twentieth century in many parts of rural France. Politics took a turn toward social inclusiveness beginning only in the 1870s, when the *nouvelles couches sociales* (new social types, or layers) were finally admitted to the political nation. At precisely this time, in the three decades before World War I, the European nobility lost economic power as agriculture prices plummeted (due to overproduction and North American competition). The new middling ranks born of commerce and industry were only too happy to nudge aside the nobility and seize the reins of government. Arguably, they succeeded only at the local level.

This process was gradual: the aristocracy still dominated the upper houses of most European legislatures, as well as the military and foreign service. Likewise, the peasantry remained the dominant social group right up until 1900. The survival of a large traditionalist and semiliterate peasant sector engaged in subsistence agriculture was the key obstacle to faster economic growth. The peasantry owned nearly half the land in nineteenth-century France, and it retarded economic growth, as it did in Spain, Italy, and eastern Europe. This basic fact explains the general economic backwardness of several areas in 1914, compared with Europe's two most dynamic economies of the time: Germany and Britain.

And yet, even as we accept these caveats, as well as Gay's nuanced portrayal of a complicated situation, it cannot be denied that there was a segment of the population—the middle classes—that managed to have the entire legal and economic framework of society recast in its favor by 1914. One of the many merits of Gay's work is his emphasis on the movement and uncertainty of a century that called myriad accepted truths to question.

Gay emphasizes that during the nineteenth century, everything was called into question: from the very foundations of religious principles to political princi-

Effervescence of Urban Culture. The Opernring, Vienna, part of the circle of wide boulevards that replaced the walls of the old city in the nineteenth century. The Hofoper (court opera house, now the Vienna Staatsoper) is at the left. Halftone engraving after a watercolor by Wilhelm Gause (1853–1916). ARCHIV FÜR KUNST UND GESCHICHTE, BERLIN/AKG LONDON

ples, social ideals, and sexual morality. The century witnessed the rise of the worker's movement, the feminist movement, evolutionary biology, universal male suffrage, the end of slavery, and so on. The late nineteenth century, Stephen Kern reminds us, broke down the age-old barriers of distance, as fast steamships, the railroad, and the telegraph helped to link rural Europe to its capital cities and Europe to the world.

A CONTINENT ON THE MOVE

Between the 1820s and 1920s, over 60 million Europeans left for the New World. Globalization began in the nineteenth century, as Europeans carved up the world amongst themselves, linking it together with the "Victorian Internet" (the telegraph) and the steamship. Most European emigrants settled in North America, but several million headed for South America and Australia. Several hundred thousand French colonized Algeria. Within Europe, migration was equally important, as the countryside emptied into the cities. Paris had a population of fewer than 600,000 in 1800; by 1900, it had grown to well over 2.5 million. Most of this increase came from migration from the countryside. Similarly, Berlin grew from 170,000 in 1800 to 420,000 in 1850 to 2 million in 1900 and then 4 million in 1925. In Germany, the number of cities with a population of over 100,000 increased from 2 to 48 between 1830 and 1914. Most of this growth

occurred after 1870. Although the European population doubled between 1800 and 1900, its urban population increased by an unprecedented 600 percent. This created great strains on resources, but it also led to an effervescence of urban culture. Museums, public libraries, sports arenas, gardens, concert halls, and new parliamentary houses were erected across urban Europe. Rapid urban growth magnified social problems and brought them into sharper focus; collectivist remedies resulted.

The social impact of these movements of people was enormous. In 1830 the German town of Bochum was a sleepy town of 4,000. By 1900, it was a city of 65,000, and when neighboring industrial suburbs are included, an area with a population of 120,000 and an industrial labor force of 50,000. The vast majority of this population increase was due to immigration into the city. Nothing like this had ever happened before in history—to be sure, large cities had witnessed rapid growth (London in the eighteenth century, for instance), but never before had small towns been transformed into industrial cities in the span of one or two generations.

THE FRENCH REVOLUTION AND THE NEW POLITICAL ECONOMY

The French Revolution is traditionally designated as the turning point between "early modern" European history and "modern Europe," or Europe of the nineteenth and twentieth centuries. More and more, however, there is a tendency among historians to downplay the social impact of the French Revolution. It is still common to portray it as a political and legal revolution of the greatest magnitude, but it is less common to stress its immediate social impact. Similarly, far from being a shot in the arm for capitalism, as Marxist historians used to claim, the Revolution probably retarded capital accumulation, (at least in France), by confirming the division of the nation's rural property into millions of smallholding plots. But in the long term, there is no doubt that the Revolution reconfigured the basic legal and political structures of France (and of parts of Germany, Italy, Belgium, and other parts touched by Napoleon's armies) in a way conducive to the development of a more commercially vibrant and socially fluid society.

The impact of the Revolution was not necessarily immediate, but over the course of the nineteenth century, dozens of ideals and goals proclaimed during the 1790s came to fruition in France and across western Europe. After the Revolution, most major western European states introduced some form of semidemocratic forum or parliament, with some form of limited suffrage (voting rights) for men of property. The Revolution gave rise to the concept of "human rights," and over the course of the nineteenth century political, civil, and human rights were gradually extended to all men (and to some women). Chief among these was the principle of equality before the law, the end of legal privilege for the aristocracy. Some feminist scholarship stresses the idea that political equality between the sexes, while proclaimed during the Revolution, was in fact set back several decades, and that, on the contrary, the nineteenth century witnessed the legal codification of *in*equality between the sexes, as in the Napoleonic Code. The lynchpin in the Napoleonic system, where male-female relations were concerned, was the concept of the *chef du famille*. Upon marriage, women became the property of their husbands. Formerly, of course, they were the property of their father or their brothers. The concept of the *chef du famille* forbade women to own property in their names, to make decisions concerning their children, where the family would live, and so on. Women could not serve on juries in many countries or even testify in court. If the Revolution created a more rigidly gendered legal system, it also provided for uniformity of other laws: henceforth there would be one legal system for one country.

During the nineteenth century, the old corporate order was demolished in nation after nation. A more absolute conception of private property rights (that is, the end of feudal dues and obligations, and the end of the seigneurial system of property) was codified in the law. The ownership of property became the fundamental basis of the new bourgeois political order. In France between 1791 and 1848, holders of property generally had greater political rights than the propertyless. Property rather than privilege became, as Sewell says, "the symbolic and practical hinge of the new political order" (p. 138).

The economic ramifications of the abolition of legal and commercial privilege, and above all the abolition of the guild system, were significant. After the French Revolution (and by the 1850s in most of western Europe), relations between employer and employee were free conventions between individuals. There were no barriers keeping a journeyman from becoming a master craftsman; he could go into business by himself, for himself, as soon as his savings enabled him to do so. This was a great boost to competition, trade, and capitalism. Employers and em-

Rights of Women. "Woman is equal to man." Commemorative print of a demonstration sponsored by the Rights of Women group and *La Citoyenne* (a newspaper founded by Hubertine Auclert) at Place de la Bastille, Paris, on 14 July 1881. BIBLIOTHEQUE MARGUERITE DURAND, PARIS

ployees were no longer superiors and subordinates, operating according to the traditional rules of a guild. Now they were either individual proprietors or propertyless proletarians, linked only through the free market, through the cash nexus. If the Revolution did not lead, overnight, to the modern industrial society of the late nineteenth century, it certainly cleared France (and its principles soon cleared most of western Europe) of what Marx called the "medieval rubbish" standing in the way of dynamic capitalism.

THE RISE OF THE WORKING CLASS

The rise of working-class consciousness is another key development in nineteenth-century social history, and it is directly related to the emergence of a more liberal-individualistic political order discussed above. The worker question dominated European politics until the 1950s, when the brightest flames of labor radicalism were finally extinguished by prosperity. In 1900, labor conflict was threatening to tear European society apart—or so many people thought at the time.

In 1800, most European workers had very few rights beyond a few paper, or legal, ones, which really had little impact on their economic well-being. Mistreatment by bosses was expected; there was no notion of workplace safety or worker's rights (a rudimentary form of worker's compensation emerged in France and Italy in 1898). When the century began, horizontal, cross-occupational class consciousness was in its infancy. Things changed in the 1830s as the urban artisanate was threatened by mechanization and de-skilling, and by 1900 parts of Europe (especially Germany and northern Italy) were polarized into easily identifiable, hostile social classes. Scholars such as E. P. Thompson, Gareth Stedman Jones, Louise Tilly, William Reddy, and William Sewell have provided us with detailed studies of this topic. Urban uprisings and revolutions in 1830, 1848, and 1871 (the Paris Commune); 1905 (in Russia and Poland); and 1914 (Red Week in Italy) pit workers against the bourgeois state.

What were workers' grievances? During the nineteenth century the law of supply and demand assaulted the traditional rights of labor, and displaced the traditional concept of "just" prices (for bread or wages). Liberal political economy replaced an older, apparently more humane (at least to many scholars) "moral economy." New "time-discipline" techniques were introduced in factories; "Saint-Monday" was eliminated as workers were pressed into a new, more rigid mold. By 1900, traditional communal usage rights over the land—to glean the stubble of the harvest, to forage, to squat, to collect wood in the forest, to traverse properties—were eroded by the developing civil codes of central states. Property was increasingly protected by a thick layer of laws, to the benefit of owners.

By the middle of the nineteenth century, the old webs of paternalism were unraveling at the local level or were simply broken as a matter of central-state policy, and peasants and workers were increasingly left to fend for themselves. The law was unabashedly biased in favor of property and sometimes in favor of birth (as with the three-tiered voting system in Prussia), but nowhere was it resolutely on the side of the common person. In France, labor law was blatantly biased in favor of bosses, against the interests of workers. The Napoleonic Code, copied in Italy, Belgium, and parts of southern Germany, declared that in disputes between bosses and employees, the bosses were to be taken at their word. Until 1890, French industrial workers were required to carry a sort of internal passport as a means of social control.

If the middle classes increasingly set the tone of civil and political life, the emerging working class increasingly resented this tone. By the late nineteenth century, the battle lines had been drawn clearly between the new classes called forth by industrialization. The old guard, the aristocracy, tried to hold the dyke. It was challenged by the middling ranks, who in turn were challenged by the growing ranks of the working classes. Charles Tilly has estimated that the number of urban proletarians in Europe increased from 10 million in 1800 to 75 million in 1900 (Tilly, in Merriman, 1979). Some industrial cities might be 80 to 90 percent proletarian. These new, "dangerous classes" stirred fear in the hearts of European elites. Henri Mendras and Alistair Cole argue that in nineteenth-century France a clear class structure emerged, which today has become blurred beyond recognition. Prior to 1914, France was clearly divided between the peasantry, the working class, the middle class, and the leisured upper-middle class (and remnants of the nobility) at the top. Class divisions and resentments were ingrained and a very real part of people's lives.

FROM THE FAMILY ECONOMY TO THE FACTORY

The process was not linear and it did not occur overnight, but ultimately, in nation after nation, by World War I, the industrial revolution 1) removed most manufacturing work from the home; 2) segregated it by gender; 3) organized it into twelve-hour shifts (or some rigid length of time); 4) brought a new, less

Defending Workers' Rights. "Attack" from *The Weavers' Uprising,* a series of prints by Käthe Kollwitz (1867–1945). Kupferstuckkabinett, Staatliche Kunstsammlungen, Dresden, Germany ©ARTISTS RIGHTS SOCIETY (ARS), NEW YORK/VG BILD-KUNST, BONN

rooted population to the city; and 5) eroded, to varying degrees, the old craft-based economy.

As Elinor Accampo argues in her detailed study of Saint-Chamond (France), the early-nineteenth-century urban economy was small-scale, cohesive, and artisanal. Work and family were inextricably linked. Wives and children often participated in the "family economy." Fathers and mothers often passed on skills to sons and daughters. The family economic unit was characterized by relative stability, in that the ribbon maker's son grew up knowing that he would most likely do what his father had done—and his father and mother would train him. In this system of domestic production, skills themselves became a sort of property. This shaped children's worldviews, expectations, and determined whom they might marry. Few outside forces (schools, nationally disseminated cultural norms) competed with the authority and influ-

ence of the family and the neighborhood. Mechanization threatened this balance. From the 1830s and 40s, nail making and ribbon weaving declined. Domestic industry in general declined and eventually disappeared. Work once done at home either left the city or became mechanized. By the 1860s, then, most workers had to leave the home to work in factories for wages.

Much recent work stresses the ability of families to adapt to new urban and work conditions. Scholarship by Ellen Ross and others, for example, emphasizes the mutual-support networks established by the laboring poor in the eighteenth and nineteenth centuries. Their work, however, is centered on large, semi-artisanal cities. Accampo makes a good case for the sudden disruption to family life brought on by the factories in smaller industrial towns. With the division of home and work, women could no longer easily

Work Moves from Home to Factory. Silkweavers in Lyon, France. Engraving in the *London Illustrated News,* 1862. THE ILLUSTRATED LONDON NEWS PICTURE LIBRARY

coordinate productive and reproductive capacities (worker-mother roles). Many married women had no choice but to leave the home for work since their husbands' wages were indadequate. Men were also affected by this shift to the factory. Their presence in the home was reduced. Their moral authority over children suffered. The parent-child training process was destroyed or weakened.

Mechanization not only led to de-skilling: it also eroded paternal power. In Saint-Chamond in the 1820s, 50 percent of sons took up their father's occupation. By 1870, only 25 percent did. Workers became less and less able to choose their line of work. The bonds of shared experience, between parents, sons, and daughters, were more or less gone by 1900 in heavy-industry towns like Saint-Chamond. Slowly but surely the generation gap was widening in western Europe on the eve of World War I. Families were dispersing at a faster rate than before, through migration, and through the gender segregation of the new factory economy. New everyday work rhythms dictated by the factory whistle replaced the older, more flexible family-centered work routines.

The mechanization process is illustrated well by the case of Limoges, whose history has been told by John Merriman. Limoges was the capital of the European porcelain industry. In 1892, there were 5,246 porcelain workers in 32 factories; by 1905, 13,000 workers in 35 factories. The standardization of production meant that plates began to be decorated by impression, not by hand. Female workers increased as the porcelain industry de-skilled: women workers increased from 24 to 35 percent of the industry's workforce between 1884 and 1901. Improvements in machines, like the Faure plate machine, meant that a worker could put out some 8,000 saucers in 15 days, compared to 1,500 earlier. A number of factors, including the concentration of capital, standardization, mechanization, larger factories, larger kilns, more workers, and above all more industrial discipline, transformed the work place.

SOCIAL MOBILITY AND EDUCATION

One of the key promises of the nineteenth century was self-advancement, the opening of careers to talent. Significant social mobility, from the working class or the peasantry to the upper-middle class, however, was still very rare in the nineteenth century, although more and more exceptional individual cases could be found. Universities were reserved for the upper 1 percent of society until World War I. There were only 77,000 university students in Germany (population

65 million) in 1913. As late as 1938, there were still only 150,000 university students in Britain, France, and Germany combined. In the nineteenth century, higher education was a closed, male club. But at long last the idea of social mobility could no longer be seen as a myth, for there were enough prominent cases in the business world to give the ideal a basis in reality. Perhaps the twentieth century began, from a historian of social mobility's point of view, with the rise to power of a Welsh coal miner's son, David Lloyd George, to the position of chancellor of the exchequer in 1906.

Lloyd George's rise to prominence was made possible, to a certain extent, by a slow but significant expansion of the middling ranks and the lower-middle class in the three decades before the war. During the period 1870–1914, the lower-middle class, composed of clerks and modestly (but regularly) paid civil servants, mushroomed. People of modest birth were given more and more responsibilities, and gained more and more power in government, especially at the local level.

Social mobility was usually limited to the movement from the (poorly paid sector of) the working class up to the lower-middle class, or from the lower-middle class to the middle class. Scarcely was it possible to make the jump from peasant or proletarian status to respectable middle class. A significant barrier existed between manual and nonmanual labor. By 1890 only 7.7 percent of all manual workers in Bochum (Germany) had been able to cross into the non-manual world. By 1907 the figure was still only 18 percent. By contrast, in the United States, in late-nineteenth-century Birmingham, 50 percent of manual workers crossed the barrier into the world of nonmanual work. In Atlanta, after one decade 20 percent, or 1 in 5, had crossed the line; in Bochum, only 1 in 13. The primary purpose of Bochum's gymnasium, and of secondary education in Europe in general, seems to have been to ensure status continuity of the middle class and professional class, not to aid social mobility. In France on the eve of World War I, only 5 percent of students went on to secondary education, to what we call high school (lycée). Less than 1 percent of European men went to university at this time. In Germany, 0.1 percent of the population went on to university in 1909.

Although the aristocracy continued to dominate the highest ranks of the army and the foreign service in most European countries, the nineteenth century did indeed witness the gradual spread of (official) civil and political equality. By the 1870s common people were entering the political arena, at least in local assemblies. In the period 1870–1890, western European society and politics opened up to new social groups. Politics became more inclusive; traditional social elites and the landed aristocracy saw their local influence wane. Peasants became active in local politics, and new job opportunities arose for those with a modicum of education: clerical positions, jobs in expanding municipal governments, nursing jobs, and teaching jobs (particularly for young women).

In the late nineteenth century major structural changes in the economy of Europe had widespread repercussions in the world of work and social relations. Beginning in the 1860s and 1870s, as the railroad began to create national markets and as the second industrial revolution boosted output and created massive new institutions, the world of work became more bureaucratized. A new army of white-collar clerks was spawned by the rise of the service sector and government bureaucracies. Schools, post offices, railroads, department stores, large companies, and burgeoning municipal governments required a new type of employee: semieducated, respectable, but modestly paid. Many of these new workers were young single women. In Britain in the 1870s, there were 7,000 female employees in local and central government; by 1911, there were 76,000. A new (but uncertain) class was born: the white-collar lower-middle class, situated uneasily between workers and the middle classes. To many social critics, this was a disturbing trend. But it signaled the emergence of a more fluid society; with a sort of passage between the working class and the middle class. Gradually, the social ladder was gaining more rungs.

Urban, economic, and social change was particularly intense and rapid in Germany. Industrial progress achieved over the course of two or three generations in England and France was achieved in one generation in Germany. No other nation was so thoroughly transformed by industry and cities: in 1907, only half of all Germans lived in their place of birth, and 40 percent of Germans worked in industry. Many historians would argue that there was a tragic lag between political change and social-economic change. Old elites clung to power at the expense of a more democratic and open society.

In general, however, across Europe the political world expanded, admitting more and more to the game. Accordingly, the tone of politics changed, and nationalism became a way to bind the nation together. Popular nationalism was not simply an elite conspiracy—it must have touched a receptive nerve with the general population. This was helped in no small part by the education and welfare systems, and mass-circulation newspapers (all of which date to the 1870s and 1880s), which made people see that they be-

longed to a larger whole. Educational and social welfare services were expanded in most major nations in the two decades before the war. One of German chancellor Bismarck's key goals in introducing social welfare legislation in the 1880s was to provide workers with a reason to support the newly forged German empire; the Liberals in Britain passed social legislation in the 1900s in order to steal the rising Labour Party's thunder; and in France radical republicans attempted to forge national "solidarity" and to ease class tensions with social legislation in the 1890s and 1900s.

Protective labor legislation, workday reduction legislation, and worker's accident insurance were introduced (the 1890s were particularly active). Some would argue that the advent of male suffrage was a political and social development of the utmost importance; others would argue that conservatives managed to contain the potentially revolutionary implications of universal male suffrage by rigging electoral districts, retaining property or wealth requirements for office, maintaining a multitiered electoral system (Prussia), literacy requirements (Italy), and so on. But in the decade before World War I, most of these restrictions were lifted. A slow democratization of political life and indeed of civic life in general was taking place on the eve of the war, particularly at the local level, where expanding municipal services necessitated greater input from people who had hitherto been excluded from power.

Rising living standards late in the century helped integrate workers into society. At precisely the moment when workers were uniting behind national parties of the left, the capitalist system was beginning to put more bread on their tables. Railroads created national markets for standardized goods, and prices of everyday staples dropped. Nominal wages increased in France by 50 percent between 1871 and 1913. In Britain, real wages rose by a third between 1850 and 1875 and again by 45 percent between 1870 and 1900. In Sweden, they rose by 75 percent in the last quarter of the nineteenth century; in Germany, by 30 percent. Diet became more diversified, with workers consuming more meat, vegetables, fruit, and wine. In the 1830s, bread alone consumed some 30 percent of a French worker's budget; by 1913, it required only 11 percent of monthly income to put bread on the table. By 1900, fewer children died before they reached the age of 5. Department stores tempted workers with new goods, although most were consumed by the expanding middling ranks. Cheap railroad tickets made it possible for the skilled working class to escape the city for a brief, modest annual vacation. In Britain, seaside resorts had become affordable for the members of the "labor aristocracy" by 1900. Workers now had a bit of disposable income to spend at the pub, the tavern, the racetrack, or the soccer match when they were not toiling away at their 50–60 hour per week jobs. Thus, by 1900, for the first time in history, a society (western Europe as a whole) had managed to provide a regular and decent living for up to two-thirds of its citizens (in 1800, perhaps only one-third of Europeans lived in comfort).

THE DISTRIBUTION OF WEALTH

Despite the immense social changes of the late nineteenth century, Europe remained a highly unequal place in 1900. Roughly speaking, the rich accounted for around 5 percent of any given nation; the middle class comprised perhaps 15 percent; the lower-middle class, the working class, and the poor comprised the remaining 80 percent of the population. In England in 1913, 10 percent of the population owned 92 percent of the nation's wealth.

Nowhere were the persisting class inequalities more evident than in death. The life expectancy of the wealthy was as much as ten years greater than that of the average manual laborer in England in 1900. The infant mortality rate in two London districts in 1901–1903 tells the story: in rich Hampstead it was 92 deaths per 1,000 live births; in poor Shoreditch, 186 deaths per 1,000 live births. In southern Europe (Spain and Italy) and eastern Europe (present-day Poland, Russia, etc.), life was much as it was in the feudal era. Serfdom was abolished in Russia in 1861 but the economic conditions associated with it remained for decades. In 1900 in the southern Spanish province of Andalusia, 2 percent of the population owned 67 percent of the land. One Hungarian family, the Esterhazys, owned 750,000 acres of land in Hungary. In parts of eastern and southern Europe, 5 percent of the population owned 90 percent of the land in 1900.

Yet the glass was half-full. By 1900, poor harvests no longer spelled disaster for most of Europe. A bad crop in Germany could be offset by imported grain from France or even Canada. By 1900 food supplies were stable around the western world. Beef and wheat from Canada, the U.S., Australia, and Argentina were shipped to Europe by steamship. Beef consumption among European workers doubled between 1880 and 1900. Tea, coffee, sugar, butter, chocolate, and half-decent wine were now within the reach of the common person.

Despite their relative prosperity, western workers were still haunted by the threat of illness or unemployment. Only in Germany did a significant portion of the population have guaranteed access to health care, and sickness and accident insurance (four million Germans were covered by 1914). Working-class life was still fraught with risk and stalked by debt. As Ellen Ross recounts in her history of working-class London women, the local pawn shop was a sort of lifeline, without which many people would have had to seek charity.

Framed by political and industrial change in the nineteenth century, complex patterns emerged for women and gender relations. On the one hand, with the general separation of work from home, economic roles for women declined, particularly after marriage, and women came to depend on marriage for their economic well-being more than before (or since). Patriarchal assumptions in law and culture deepened this dependency. But women did gain ground in education. Among the middle classes, a powerful ideology arose emphasizing women's domestic virtue and their crucial role in the moral regulation of sexuality. With regard to morals, proper women were considered superior to men. The decline in the birthrate also affected women's opportunities, again particularly among the middle classes. And new political ideas spurred politically active women, and even some men, to push for voting rights and an end to legal inequality.

CONCLUSION

The vast political, social, and economic impact of World War I prompts most social historians to end consideration of nineteenth-century themes with 1914. On the eve of World War I, a powerful women's movement was threatening to overturn the sexual and political status quo. Some social historians would argue that this constituted one of the greatest threats to the stability of European society. Workers, who launched an unprecedented number of strikes in France and Britain in the 1890s and 1900s, and organized women were campaigning to overturn the cornerstones of nineteenth-century bourgeois society (or so it seemed). The Italian political system was in a state of crisis on the eve of the war, as were the Russian and Austro-Hungarian empires. Britain was divided over the Irish question, France was deadlocked due to labor unrest, political stalemate over military spending issues, and the income tax. Germany seemed to be under siege from the socialist party. Beneath military and diplomatic rivalries, social tensions unnerved European aristocratic and big-business leadership.

As the genie of mass democracy was let out of the bottle, Europe's outdated political class (especially in Austria and Germany) feared for their futures, and they may have decided that a Europe-wide war to distract the population was preferable to facing the necessity of domestic reform. Some historians argue that the social origins of World War I are just as important as the diplomatic origins. Others dismiss this as too simplistic, and impossible to prove. Most historians would probably agree that the desire to avert difficult domestic reform played *some* small part, if not the overriding part, in the decision to risk a Europe-wide war. Political change in several nations had not kept pace with economic growth; Europe was divided by the labor question, ethnic tensions, and tensions between the sexes. After the war, these issues would be addressed, one way or another.

See also **Capitalism and Commercialization; Civil Society; The Industrial Revolutions; The Liberal State; Nationalism; The Population of Europe: The Demographic Transition and After; Urbanization** *(volume 2);* **The Middle Classes; Social Class; Social Mobility; Working Classes** *(volume 3); and other articles in this section.*

BIBLIOGRAPHY

Accampo, Elinor. *Industrialization, Family Life, and Class Relations: Saint Chamond, 1815–1914.* Berkeley, Calif., 1989.

Adas, Michael. *Machines as the Measure of Men: Science, Technology, and Ideologies of Western Dominance.* Ithaca, N.Y., 1989.

Berg, Maxine. *The Age of Manufactures, 1700–1820: Industry, Innovation, and Work in Britain.* 2d ed. London, 1994.

Blackbourn, David, and Geoff Eley. *The Peculiarities of German History: Bourgeois Society and Politics in Nineteenth-Century Germany.* Oxford, 1984.

Charle, Christophe. *A Social History of France in the Nineteenth Century.* Translated by Miriam Kochan. Oxford, 1994.

Cohen, William B., ed. *The Transformation of Modern France.* Boston, 1997. Useful collection of essays on large themes.

Craig, Gordon A. *Germany, 1866–1945.* New York, 1978. A classic.

Crew, David F. *Town in the Ruhr: A Social History of Bochum, 1860–1914.* New York, 1979.

Frader, Laura Levine. "Women in the Industrial Capitalist Economy." In *Becoming Visible: Women in European History.* Edited by Renate Bridenthal, Claudia Koonz, and Susan Stuard. 2d ed. Boston, 1987.

Fuchs, Rachel G. *Poor and Pregnant in Paris: Strategies for Survival in the Nineteenth Century.* New Brunswick, N.J., 1992.

Gay, Peter. *The Bourgeois Experience: Victoria to Freud* 5 vols. New York, 1984–1998.

Gillis, John R., Louise Tilly, and David Levine, eds. *The European Experience of Declining Fertility, 1850–1970.* Cambridge, Mass., 1992.

Green, David R. *From Artisans to Paupers: Economic Change and Poverty in London, 1790–1870.* Aldershot, UK, 1995.

Hamerow, Theodore. *The Birth of a New Europe: State and Society in the Nineteenth Century.* Chapel Hill, N.C., 1983. An important but underused survey.

Harris, José. *Private Lives, Public Spirit: A Social History of Britain, 1870–1914.* Oxford, 1993.

Hobsbawm, Eric J., and Terence Ranger, eds. *The Invention of Tradition.* New York, 1983.

Hobsbawm, Eric J. *The Age of Empire, 1875–1914*. New York, 1987. The best volume in his series on the nineteenth century.

Hughes, Michael. *Nationalism and Society: Germany, 1800–1945*. London, 1988.

Kern, Stephen. *The Culture of Time and Space: 1880–1918*. Cambridge, Mass., 1983.

Landes, David S. *The Unbound Prometheus: Technological Change and Industrial Development in Western Europe from 1750 to the Present*. Cambridge, U.K., 1969. A seminal work.

Lehning, James R. *Peasant and French: Cultural Contact in Rural France during the Nineteenth Century*. New York, 1995.

Lewis, Jane, ed. *Labour and Love: Women's Experience of Home and Family, 1850–1940*. Oxford, 1986.

Loubère, Leo. *Nineteenth-Century Europe: The Revolution in Life*. Englewood Cliffs, N.J., 1994.

Magraw, Roger. *France 1815–1914: The Bourgeois Century*. London, 1983.

Mason, Michael. *The Making of Victorian Sexuality*. Oxford, 1995.

Mayer, Arno J. *The Persistence of the Old Regime: Europe to the Great War*. New York, 1981. A contrarian piece.

McKeown, Thomas. *The Modern Rise of Population*. London, 1976.

Mendras, Henri, and Alistair Cole. *Social Change in Modern France: Towards a Cultural Anthropology of the Fifth Republic*. Cambridge, U.K., 1991.

Merriman, John M., ed. *Consciousness and Class Experience in Nineteenth-Century Europe*. New York, 1979. Important articles.

Merriman, John M. *The Red City: Limoges and the French Nineteenth Century*. New York, 1985.

Miller, Michael B. *The Bon Marché: Bourgeois Culture and the Department Store, 1869–1920*. Princeton, N.J., 1981.

Mosse, George L. *The Culture of Western Europe: The Nineteenth and Twentieth Centuries*. 3d ed. Boulder, Colo., 1988. Still useful.

Perkin, Harold. *Origins of Modern English Society*. London, 1969.

Perrot, Michelle, ed. *A History of Private Life*. Vol. 4: *From the Fires of Revolution to the Great War*. Cambridge, Mass., 1987. Important essays on the nineteenth century.

Popkin, Jeremy. *A History of Modern France*. Englewood Cliffs., N.J., 1994.

Price, Roger. *A Social History of Nineteenth-Century France*. London, 1987.

Reddy, William M. *Money and Liberty in Modern Europe*. New York, 1987.

Ross, Ellen. *Love and Toil: Motherhood in Outcast London, 1870–1918*. New York, 1993.

Sewell, William. *Work and Revolution in France*. New York, 1980.

Stearns, Peter N., and Herrick Chapman. *European Society in Upheaval: Social History since 1750*. 3d ed. New York, 1992.

Thompson, E. P. *The Making of the English Working Class*. New York, 1963.

Thompson, F. M. L. *The Rise of Respectable Society: A Social History of Victorian Britain, 1830–1900*. Cambridge, Mass., 1988.

Thompson, F. M. L., ed. *The Cambridge Social History of Britain, 1750–1950*. 3 vols. Cambridge, U.K., 1990. Essential reading.

Valenze, Deborah. *The First Industrial Woman*. New York, 1995.

Weber, Eugen. *Peasants into Frenchmen: The Modernization of Rural France, 1870–1914.* Stanford, Calif., 1976.

Wehler, Hans-Ulrich. *The German Empire, 1871–1918.* Leamington Spa, U.K., 1985.

Zeldin, Theodore. *France 1848–1945.* 5 vols. Oxford, 1973–1979. A masterpiece.

THE WORLD WARS AND THE DEPRESSION

Jay Winter

The treatment and interpretation of major questions in the social history of Europe between 1914 and 1918 have been transformed since 1980. One way to characterize the shift of research interest and publication in this field is to summarize (and caricature) social history as the history of defiance and cultural history as the history of consent. This is a wild oversimplification, but like most, it has a grain of truth in it. Another formulation distinguishes social history as the study of social stratification, civil society, family life, and social movements; and cultural history as the study of language, idiom, representations, and images. However this distinction is nuanced, these two overlapping areas of study have increasingly diverged.

Divergence is not divorce, and it is critical to recognize the extent to which the social history of cultural life and the cultural history of social stratification overlap. It is probably best in a survey of relevant literature to mark out the terrain as described in the form of intersecting concentric circles of scholarship in which the mix of social and cultural history has become irreversible.

WORLD WAR I

Labor militancy: Social history as history of defiance.
In World War I studies, the transition from an emphasis on social history to an emphasis on cultural history occurred between the 1960s and the 1980s. In the 1960s and 1970s, labor militancy was a subject of central importance to European historians of all periods. World War I was a terrain on which new forms of industrial militancy were played out because the war undermined the legitimacy of traditional political and economic structures. In Britain, James Hinton's *The First Shop Stewards' Movement* (1973) clearly anticipated a second movement—financial and electoral domination of the party—which, alas, never materialized. Ross McKibbin's *The Evolution of the Labor Party* (1974) showed what trade-union muscle meant, although he was careful to distance himself from claims made by others that clause

4 of the 1918 Labor Party constitution was a real statement of political will and aspirations rather than an electoral ploy to graft middle-class socialist sprouts to a pragmatic trade union tree. Clause 4 committed the party to work to secure the public ownership of industry. But this wartime commitment in principle did not bind the party to postwar action.

On the Continent, much seminal work in the history of labor militancy in wartime appeared at this time. Jean-Louis Robert began his path-breaking study of militancy among Parisian metalworkers. Leopold Haimson gathered together a wide group of historians interested in tracing the upsurge of agitation and protest during the war years. The study of the reemergence of revolutionary movements in central Europe grew in parallel, at times taking biographical form or, as in the case of Jürgen Kocka's powerful study of increasingly bitter class conflict in Germany, the form of an analysis of the compression of the class pyramid. Here the crucial issues were the emiseration of the lower middle class and the growing confidence and anger of workers about wartime inequalities in provision and entitlement. Barrington Moore made an important intervention in this field in a book entitled *Injustice* (1978).

"The dignity of defiance" is a phrase used to try to capture the essence of what these scholars were after (Winter, 1986). In their search, they provided us with powerful scholarship on the complex fissures in societies led by governments proclaiming national unity. But the emphasis on the history of labor militancy has not weathered well. The reasons for this are complex. Among them is the linkage between such scholarship and the more general, theoretical debate on Marxism that occurred at this time. Many historians doubted the validity of a model that "read" political militancy directly off data on social stratification and inequality.

The language of soldier writers.
Marxist approaches to the history of World War I were still visible, but in their place there emerged a set of concerns the origins of which are elsewhere. Whereas diplo-

World War I. In the trenches at Verdun. POPPERFOTO/ARCHIVE PHOTOS

macy, strategy, political conflict, military mobilization, and war industry had long been staples of historical presentations of the war, these aspects of World War I had rarely been presented to the profession or to the general public as cultural phenomena, as having been encoded within rich and complex images, languages, and cultural forms. Now was the time for this kind of history to be told.

There was another set of reasons for the emergence of this kind of scholarship. By the late 1970s many scholars came to the subject of the cultural history of the 1914–1918 war through their reflections on the Vietnam War. For a number of American scholars, the debacle of Vietnam entailed a trajectory from innocence to experience, from anticipation to an outcome very remote from expectations. Where had this happened before? The question drew them to the battlefields of the Somme and Verdun and Passchendaele.

The bitter taste of war was a personal matter to some of these scholars, men who had served in World War II. It is no accident that two of the most important works in this field, Paul Fussell's massively influential *The Great War and Modern Memory* (1975) and Samuel Hynes's *A War Imagined* (1991), were produced by an infantry officer wounded in Alsace in 1945 and an airman who served in the Pacific War, both of whom also wrote powerful autobiographies about their war service.

Fussell and Hynes helped transform the social history of the 1914–1918 war. Fussell in particular set in motion an avalanche of studies, which gained momentum in the twenty-five years following the publication of his study. Fussell claims that the language of prose and poetry dominant in prewar Britain was unable to accommodate the experience of the trenches. A number of writers therefore turned older forms around and produced a language of ironic force that not only described the landscape of the 1914–1918 war, but also came to serve as the grammar of later literary imaginings of war. In effect, the way we saw war at the end of the twentieth century was through the prism provided by the soldier-writers of the 1914–1918 conflict.

War literature, Fussell posited, was located on the knife edge between the realistic mode of writing, in which the hero's freedom of action is the same as the readers', and the ironic mode of writing, in which the hero's freedom of action is less than the readers' and in which the hero is trapped in a world of unreason and mass death. Frequently, these ironic writers turned to myth to inscribe their view of betrayal, disenchantment, and loss.

Hynes spoke of the anger that soldier-writers directed at the older generation who had sent them out to a war they, the elders, never had to see. By spreading the range of cultural reference well beyond the small canon of war poets and writers discussed by

Fussell, he analyzed the power of memorials and anti-memorials to galvanize opinion about the conflict. Above all, his emphasis was on soldiers' language, bearing with it the authority of the witness, of the man who had been there, the authenticity of direct experience.

Women and gender, family, and commemoration.

One facet of the achievement of these scholars was a direct departure from earlier writings on World War I. Fussell and Hynes wrote masculine history: the history of men at war and the language they developed to try to ascribe meaning to their world. Women rarely inhabited that world. Consequently, the power of this cultural history tended to move scholarly discussion away from a centerpiece of the earlier social history of war, namely, the history of women and gender.

A shift of emphasis did take place, but it should not obscure the development of robust and powerful scholarship on the history of women and war. Mary Louise Roberts's *Civilization Without Sexes* (1994) and Susan Kent's *Making Peace: The Reconstruction of Gender in Interwar Britain* (1992) showed the cultural and political consequences of the war. The fluidity of gender roles was hard to deny: witness the critical part women played in agricultural work and the new positions they occupied in heavy industry. But as the Higgonets and others argued in *No Man's Land: Gender and the Two World Wars* (1987), a shift in women's roles rarely led to an increase in women's power, since war entailed a heightened sense of the significance of what were seen as "masculine" values. Thus the "double helix" of gender preserved the prewar distance between the degrees of freedom men and women enjoyed.

For no intrinsic reason these approaches tended to become antagonistic. Many studies of women at war concentrated on the munitions industries and the new array of tasks women had to accomplish under the pressure of war. They were responsible for the house or farm and employed in war-related production or as substitutes for male farm laborers. In central and eastern Europe, they had to cope with scarcity of a kind not registered in Britain or France that meant standing in endless lines for rations they might never see or scavenging in the countryside for food or fuel. In addition historians of the family contributed to our knowledge of the reconfiguring of gender roles in such a way as to preserve the patriarchal family the soldiers left behind.

What a different story there was to tell when the family in question was the brotherhood in the trenches. Important studies of trench newspapers, produced by ordinary soldiers and speaking their own language about the war were produced for Italy, Britain, and France. This kind of fictive kinship—based on love and suffering, to be sure—endured in the interwar years and spread into the fields of veterans affairs and politics. George Mosse and Antoine Prost contributed seminal works on the ways in which what Mosse called "the myth of the war experience"—or soldiers' tales about their war—encapsulated prewar cultural and political traditions and came to fashion much of postwar representations of what had happened between 1914 and 1918.

One unsettled dispute about the nature of the soldiers' war concerns the degree of control they exercised over the conditions of their lives. Tony Ashworth, in an early study, *Trench Warfare: The Live and Let Live System* (1966), asserted that the war of position involved tacit truces and informal arrangement whereby both sides avoided shelling latrines or disturbing breakfast time. In an extension of this argument, Len Smith's *Between Mutiny and Obedience* (1994) showed how French infantrymen engaged in informal negotiations with their officers about what kind of gains in an offensive justified what level of losses. A sense of "proportionality" determined the extent and limits of soldiers' tolerance of orders. Thus the French mutiny of 1917 was an explicit statement of what had been implicit throughout the war. An entirely different approach is that of Eric Leed, whose *No Man's Land* (1979) documents soldiers' impotence in the face of a new kind of industrial warfare. The truth probably lies in a blend of these two interpretations.

The overlap between social history and cultural history in late-twentieth-century writing on World War I is perhaps most explicit in the discussion of commemoration, where comparative work dominated the field. Discussions of local forms of social agency and pilgrimage paralleled work on secularized religious language in rhetoric and sculpture. Most research moved away from national generalizations about commemoration as political manipulation and toward the decoding of messages frequently fashioned in de-centered ways that ascribed some kind of meaning to the disaster of the war.

THE INTERWAR YEARS

The capacity of social history to withstand the incursions of cultural historians is more evident in studies of the interwar period than in the case of the two world wars. Three areas of scholarly debate produced much of substance in the social history of interwar Europe. The first concerns the sources of the political

Armaments Workers. Women workers polishing high-explosive shell casings at Vickers Ltd., 1915. ©HULTON GETTY/LIAISON AGENCY

defeat of organized labor in the 1920s and 1930s; the second concerns the social consequences and costs of the interwar depression; and the third concerns the nature of family life and domesticity in this period. While all three subjects entail explorations of cultural issues, older paradigms relating to class structure and class struggle are still evident in the literature.

Labor in retreat. The spirit of the old Second International—the prewar Socialist confederation created by Marx and Engels—was smashed on the outbreak of war in 1914. After the armistice, some of the idealism at the heart of the European labor movement was reborn. But in the following two decades, caught between Stalinism on the one hand and Nazism on the other, that political and moral configuration of aspirations clustered under the heading of "labor movement" was defeated time and again. First came the counterrevolutionary movements in central Europe in 1919 and 1920; then came the eclipse of labor in Italy followed by the fascist seizure of power. Then came a host of struggles in the democratic countries to defend workers' living standards and jobs in a period of chronic depression before 1929 and of acute depression between 1929 and 1933. The latter year saw the Nazis in power in Germany. Labor, and ultimately democracy itself, was defeated in Austria, in Czechoslovakia, and after a brutal three-year civil war, in Spain.

The question is, why so many defeats and so many setbacks? One set of answers relates to the evolution of communism and the relation between European communist parties and the Soviet Union. This is the domain of conventional labor history, which has replicated in scholarship many of the ideological conflicts of the period under review. Some scholars argued that defeat was built into faulty leadership; others countered that a vanguard became separated from the rest of the working class.

A second debate concentrated not on the organization of labor but on the social structure of the working class it purported to represent. Here considerable attention was paid to the decline of the old staple industries out of which much of the militant leadership of labor came. But it was not only the demise of the older industrial sectors that weakened labor, it was also the growth of the service sector, and of white-collar employment as a whole. Clerical workers did not have the same outlook as did manual laborers; it was very difficult to link up their grievances or to make common cause when one set of workers was threatened with job losses. The failure of the British General Strike of 1926 exposed these fissures in the world of labor; they remained exposed throughout the interwar years.

The costs of the Great Depression. The question of the effects of the onset of mass and sustained unemployment has drawn much scholarly attention. Most of such work concentrates on urban poverty, despite the fact that a decline in the price of primary products devastated rural economies, in particular in eastern and southern Europe.

In the West, industrial decline was the key problem. Social policy initiatives were launched throughout Europe to try to soften the blow of unemployment. Their effects are disputed. One area of controversy is that of public health. There is a paradox to be resolved here. On the one hand, millions of working people lived on inadequate wages and social transfer payments. Deprivation was unmistakable in every European capital city. And yet some measurements of well-being that relate to health—infant mortality rates and life expectancy at birth—seem to have declined in a period of aggravated poverty and widespread distress. How was this possible? Some scholars have pointed to the difference between long-term economic trends, leading to higher survival rates especially at the earliest years of life, and short-term trends of grinding poverty. This position suggests that the onset of mass unemployment in the interwar years did not undermine fully the long-term trend toward better nutrition and better health in many parts of Europe.

Other scholars disagree. They point out that aggregate statistics rarely reflect lived experience. Furthermore, it is probable that some groups lived longer but with chronic illness as their fate. Populations can have deteriorating health conditions and increases in life expectancy at the same time.

When different age groups are analyzed, a possible resolution of these different interpretations emerges. Unemployment is not one phenomenon but many. There is considerable evidence that it damages the health of pregnant women and the unborn, who bring their deprivation with them, as it were, throughout their later lives. The capacity of adults to resist and survive deprivation is greater. For the elderly, unemployment brings increased vulnerability, since it diminishes the resources of the support systems—social agencies, family members, and other elderly people—on which they rely.

The effect of mass unemployment on the unemployed themselves is an area less well researched. Some scholars have followed the spiral of despair into crime and prostitution. Others have considered the possibility that a cycle of deprivation kept the less well educated and the less well nourished people trapped within areas of heavy joblessness. The better educated and fitter therefore were able to leave and find a better life elsewhere. Who was left in the old urban industrial belts? Only those with few chances and fewer hopes.

They intermarried and perpetuated the disadvantages of poverty.

Here is a possible resolution of another puzzle: why were there aggregate improvements yet no reduction of inequality? While overall survival chances increased in the population as a whole, the demographic disadvantage of being born into a manual working-class household as opposed to a professional household was maintained. Perhaps out-migration of the better educated and healthier helped maintain the demographic disadvantages of working-class life.

This position does not lack its critics either. Some have pointed out that there are undertones of eugenics in this form of reasoning. It suggests that there was a kind of propagation of disadvantage through selective migration and marriage patterns. The unfit stayed behind; the fitter and brighter got out of the old working-class ghetto. What was called "the residuum" before 1914—the bottom 10 percent of the population—appeared to be a self-perpetuating community. Blaming the poor for their own poverty is an old conservative gambit, critics say, and the explanation for persistent levels of inequality are located in the indifference of ruling elites to the fate of those most vulnerable to the swings in the labor market that

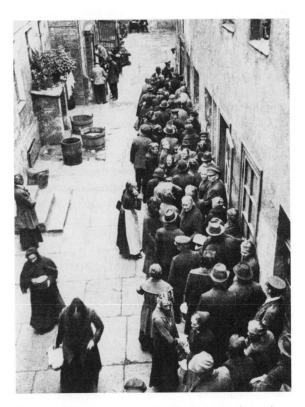

Queuing for Food. Line at a soup kitchen in Berlin, early 1920s. MARY EVANS PICTURE LIBRARY

produced unemployment rates of between 50 and 90 percent in some depressed regions.

Family, marriage, migration, and gender.   In interwar Europe, fertility rates dropped to record lows. Many commentators voiced fears of "race suicide"; some injudicious prophets posited that in the year 2030 there would be four people left in Britain. Even when we brush aside such panicked reasoning, there is still much left to explain. Why was it that family size was at an all-time low, and given the appearance in the mid to late 1930s of some resurgence in birth rates, why was the decline in fertility at an end?

At this point we enter a field in the history of the family and the history of gender in which cultural norms are crucial. Family life was not egalitarian in this period. If we want to know why fertility went down, we need to interrogate the evidence about the attitudes and behavior of men and women differently.

Here there are many unknowns. One of the most glaring is the propensity of women to resort to abortion. Illegality precludes accurate estimates of the practice, but throughout Europe, it must have been an important way in which women kept their family size at manageable levels. A second unknown is the range of contraceptive practices and the ways different sectors of the population resorted to them. We simply cannot conclude that there were national uniformities in contraception.

Patterns of nuptiality are also difficult to specify with any degree of certainty. It may be the case that with the closing of the gates to unrestricted immigration to the United States and with it the end of the vast movement of European out-migration of the period 1880–1920, millions of young marriageable men were "trapped" in Europe, thereby preserving marriage rates. The upheavals of the labor market and the downturn in world trade also made non-European receiver states less likely to welcome newcomers. Some minimal relief was offered to victims of persecution in the later 1930s, but most of those who wanted to get out of Europe were trapped there at the end of the interwar years.

There remains the question of a notable upward inflection of birth rates in the mid to late 1930s. Some argue that these changes were a reflection of the end of the world economic crisis. Others consider that they were responses to the appearance of population policies favoring families and a rising birth rate, in particular in Fascist Italy and Germany. The problem is that the period of slightly increasing fertility was too brief to reach any firm conclusions. It is perhaps safest to conclude that it is unlikely that the "baby boom" of the post-1945 period began before World War II.

WORLD WAR II

The social history of World War II is not as well developed professionally as is the social history of World War I. This difference may reflect the relative nearness of Hitler's war. Time may rectify this imbalance.

The range of subjects central to the social history of the 1939–1945 war overlaps only in part with work done on World War I. There are similar studies of military and civilian mobilization. The activity of women in all corners of the war economy has been investigated too. Social policy in wartime has been the subject of extensive research, drawing on parallels and divergences with World War I literature.

But there are two features of the social history of the Second World War that break new ground. First is the issue of resistance and collaboration. Second is the matter of the social history of the Holocaust as seen through the eyes and lives of its victims. Both entail complex problems of interpretation and of commemoration.

Mobilization for total war.   The social history of mass mobilization after 1939 describes terrain similar to that of the 1914–1918 war, but in Hitler's war, everything was heightened and deepened. Both coercion and consent brought populations to a level of participation in war industry never before realized. The numbers mobilized and the numbers killed were higher than ever before. Aerial bombardment brought cities into the front lines. The occupation of virtually the entire European continent created administrative networks linking the German war effort and its requirements to the resources of conquered states.

Within wartime Germany, a remarkable degree of mobilization was maintained despite intensive Allied bombardment of German cities. Nutritional levels were higher for German citizens in the 1939–1945 war than in the 1914–1918 conflict, and many studies have pointed to the success of the regime in keeping together a society under increasing pressure the longer the war went on. Clearly, the regime operated through terror. But it also commanded respect and, among a part of the population, a degree of legitimacy that commanded consent.

Women at war.   The mobilization of women on the land and in the factories was even more marked after 1939 than it had been after 1914. There is some dispute, though, as to the effect of women's activities in wartime on their long-term status as citizens. To be sure, women did get the vote in France in 1946, and the role of women in the resistance was part of the background to this long-overdue development.

World War II Bombing. Air-raid wardens inspect damage after a German bombing raid, London, 1940. ©HULTON-DEUTSCH COLLECTION/CORBIS

But the arduous effort required of women to balance child rearing, housework, and extradomestic employment may have impelled them back toward a more singularly domestic definition of their lives and aspirations. Thus a kind of "inner migration" toward family life and away from economic and political independence may describe women's trajectories in the period during and after World War II.

Social policy in wartime. War entailed the invasion of the household by the state. Partly this was a reflection of the air war. When whole city blocks were flattened, emergency services had to rehouse and rehabilitate as best they could. In addition, the medical services had to be centrally organized and distributed, diminishing significantly the independence of medical practitioners. In the case of Britain, prewar anticipation of civilian casualties in air raids produced the first full survey of medical services in the country. This was a prelude to the creation of a National Health Service after the war.

Similar steps were taken in every wartime country. The state expanded to include areas of activity previously in private hands. Historians call this the "concentration effect" of war. Its consequence was a "threshold effect," whereby the costs of social services rose to a levei entailing permanent financial commit-

ments. In turn a threshold was passed in the tolerable level of personal taxation, a threshold that was maintained in the postwar years. Many local studies provide much of value on this theme.

Collaboration and resistance. These issues describe the social history of World War II as a continuation and intensification of the social history of World War I. But in two respects World War II was terra incognita for historians. The first was in the dialectic between collaboration and resistance within occupied countries. The second was in the social history of the extermination of the Jews.

The social history of collaboration with the Nazis has developed roughly along three lines. The first is the arrival at the center of social and political life of those who had been outcasts in the interwar years. Extreme right-wing groups flourished under the aegis of the Nazis in a way they could never have done on their own. The second is the study of how administrators, both high and low, tended to carry on running affairs within the framework of what was called the "new order." Some of this activity was harmless, or even beneficial. Consider for instance, the ongoing work of the socialist Henri Sellier as mayor of the Paris suburb of Suresnes. Other administrators actively or tacitly aided the Nazis in the deportation of Jews. The

225

work of Maurice Papon in Bordeaux is in this category; he helped in the roundup of Jewish children and consequently has been condemned as a war criminal. The third area of inquiry is in the "normalization" of occupation and the degree of consent given by ordinary people to the new order.

Here we overlap with the social history of the resistance, for the vast majority of the population in occupied Europe lived in conditions that produced a mixture of resignation and submission, on the one hand, and rejection and resistance on the other. The life of François Mitterrand, later president of France, is a good instance of the blurring of distinctions between collaboration and resistance in wartime. He had a foot in both camps, as did many others.

Mythmaking after the war inflated the numbers of those who joined resistance organizations. We must discount much of the oral history gathered after the war about the heroism of the occupied. Heroism there was, but it was the exception and not the rule. This third area of research aims to explain why this was so.

There are moral problems in formulating the question of why resistance was so weak. Historians today have the moral luck to avoid such choices and risks, although some at the time, like the great medievalist Marc Bloch, paid with their lives for their work in the resistance. Can we judge those who did not follow the path Bloch chose? There is little consensus on an answer to this question.

The Holocaust.
The same issues plague the social history of the victims of the Nazi plan to exterminate the Jews. Ever since Hannah Arendt provided a stinging indictment of Jewish submission to and (in some cases) complicity in their own demise in her account of the Eichmann trial, the analysis of Jewish responses to the Holocaust has been trapped in the culs-de-sac of justification, accusation, and vilification. Again, we are dealing with excruciating choices that careful scholars can treat only with diffidence.

The social history of the perpetrators has also produced a firestorm of debate. The problem is that some scholars, following Daniel Goldhagen's approach in *Hitler's Willing Executioners: Ordinary Germans and the Holocaust* (1996), use categories of national character or national traditions as if they were immutable features of historical processes. Blaming everyone who was German for the Holocaust is historical nonsense. But what are the alternatives? Here we return to the question of collaboration, since many of the killers were not German at all. Many of those who committed atrocities were what Christopher Browning in his 1992 study called "ordinary men." The police battalion he studied was composed of men

who, when sent to the east, became murderers in no time at all. Jonathan Steinberg's *All or Nothing: The Axis and the Holocaust, 1941–1943* (1991) showed that this mutation was not universal; Italian soldiers in Yugoslavia behaved quite differently from German units posted to the same areas. Why the difference? Evil retains its mysteries, still to be unraveled.

Commemoration.
The eighth of May is celebrated in most parts of Europe as V-E Day—the end of the war against Hitler. The social history of this commemoration follows in most respects the scholarship surrounding public remembrance of the 1914–1918 war. Soviet war memorials are grandiose and romantic, a throwback to nineteenth-century representations of war, which had already been discarded in western Europe.

National rebuilding after World War II required myths of heroism and resistance. Many of these narratives have a kernel of truth, but little more than that. The need for stories of great achievements had one particularly negative consequence: until the 1960s and 1970s, the story of the extermination of the Jewish people was eclipsed by tales of uprisings and espionage elsewhere in Europe. It is as if the crime of the century was simply too horrible to contemplate. Other stories were easier to swallow, even when they entailed treason. But the problem with Auschwitz was that it could not be treated as if it were just another historical site. Something so monstrous happened there and at the network of camps it has come to represent that ordinary language falls away.

That silence, while understandable, could not be sustained indefinitely, for it threatened to bury the victims once again under a mound of historical indifference. But scholars have yet to formulate a consensus as to how to approach the problem of writing the social history of the enormity of this unique event. Similarly, political and social leaders risk a hail of criticism whenever they offer an idea as to how to commemorate the Holocaust. Debates during the 1990s on a national Holocaust memorial in reunified Berlin are cases in point. Silence will not do; but representations of an allegorical or metaphoric kind are inadequate as well. Since the subject itself brings us to the limits of representation, it is unlikely that any way out of this dilemma will appear in the foreseeable future.

CONCLUSION

By 1945 the outlines of a new Europe could be discerned beyond the rubble of war. It was a Europe drastically different from that which went to war in

Victims of War. Russian civilians in the ruins of their home following the German invasion of the Soviet Union, 1941. SOVFOTO/EASTFOTO

1914. First, it was imprinted with the experience of mass death. Bereavement was a nearly universal experience, as families were torn apart by war. There were gaps in the age structure. Missing were men of military ages and the children they would have fathered; these lost cohorts would take seventy years to work their way through the age structure.

By 1945 Europe was a continent without a substantial Jewish community, leveled throughout Europe and wiped out in large parts of eastern Europe. Other population movements changed the face of the continent. Families of German origin were forced west by the millions. Other refugees found homes in other continents, where another element was added to the European diaspora.

As a result of the war, gender boundaries had been blurred and then reconfigured. The restoration of family life was of the highest priority after 1945, not primarily to politicians but to ordinary people. Given rapid economic recovery after 1945, the baby boom was the result.

The discrediting of the radical right gave a new lease on life to the European labor movement. Hardened by war and essential to the organization of reconstruction, moderate labor leaders moved to the center of the political spectrum. The Communists entered the political mainstream too, largely on the record of resistance in wartime, but, except in countries occupied by the Red Army, they were blocked in their bid for power.

These developments were entangled in the cold war, but some developments superseded it. By the late 1950s there emerged a Franco-German power bloc in which a French political structure—later called the European Community—controlled and harnessed the economic strength of German industry. The aim was to put an end to the threat of war among European states. This it has done, though armed conflict in the Balkans, where war broke out in 1914, returned at the century's end.

The major nightmares of the social history of Europe from 1914 to 1945, war and economic collapse, slowly faded from the European landscape. But in bodies and minds, the scars and traumas of the earlier catastrophes lingered, some of them never to heal.

See also **Marxism and Radical History; The Jews and Anti-Semitism** *(in this volume);* **Health and Disease; War and Conquest; Migration; Fascism and Nazism;**

The Welfare State *(volume 2);* **Labor History: Strikes and Unions** *(volume 3);* **Gender and Work** *(volume 4).*

BIBLIOGRAPHY

Arendt, Hannah. *Eichmann in Jerusalem: A Report on the Banality of Evil.* New York, 1964. Rev. enl. ed. 1994.

Barber, John, and Mark Harrison. *The Soviet Home Front, 1941–1945: A Social and Economic History of the USSR in World War II.* London and New York, 1991.

Briggs, Asa, and John Saville, eds. *Essays in Labor History: 1918–1939.* London, 1977.

Fussell, Paul. *The Great War and Modern Memory.* New York, 1975.

Geary, Dick. *European Labor Protest, 1848–1939.* London, 1981.

Gillis, John R., ed. *Commemorations: The Politics of National Identity.* Princeton, N.J., 1994.

Goldhagen, Daniel Jonah. *Hitler's Willing Executioners: Ordinary Germans and the Holocaust.* New York, 1996.

Haimson, Leopold, and Charles Tilly, eds. *Strikes, Wars, and Revolutions in an International Perspective: Strike Waves in the Late Nineteenth and Early Twentieth Centuries.* Cambridge, U.K., and New York, 1989.

Hinton, James. *The First Shop Stewards' Movement.* London, 1973.

Hynes, Samuel. *A War Imagined: The First World War and English Culture.* London, 1990.

Kocka, Jürgen. *Facing Total War: German Society, 1914–1918.* Translated by Barbara Weinberger. Leamington Spa, U.K., 1984.

McKibbin, Ross. *The Evolution of the Labor Party 1910–1924.* Oxford, 1974.

Moore, Barrington. *Injustice: The Social Bases of Obedience and Revolt.* White Plains, N.Y., 1978.

Mosse, George L. *Fallen Soldiers: Reshaping the Memory of the World Wars.* New York, 1990.

Poirot-Delpech, Bertrand. *Papon: Un crime de bureau.* Paris, 1998.

Robert, Jean-Louis. *La scission syndicale de 1921: Essai de reconnaissance des formes.* Paris, 1980.

Sellier, Henri. *Une cité pour tous.* Paris, 1998.

Smith, Harold L. *Britain in the Second World War: A Social History.* Manchester, U.K., and New York, 1996.

Winter, J. M. "The Dignity of Defiance: Some Recent Writing on British Labor History." *Journal of Modern History* 68 (1986): 225–231.

SINCE WORLD WAR II

Donna Harsch

How have historians applied the methods and perspectives of modern social history to the postwar era, the historical period from whence the discipline itself sprang? The five and half decades that followed the war have, in fact, remained relatively understudied, if only because social historians, like historians in general, prefer to investigate the bona fide past rather than what has just passed. Moreover, it may seem that a foreshortened perspective does not do justice to social-historical subjects such as class formation, family structure, or mentality that tend to change only over a substantial stretch of time. In consequence, studies of the decades since 1945 do not fill bookshelves quite as lengthy as those occupied by the voluminous specialized literature on, say, the industrial revolution. Historical attention has also been distracted by prewar interpretive issues, such as the causes, social and otherwise, of the rise of Nazism, rather than centered on postwar historical issues or broader studies that would embrace postwar developments in a larger social history of the twentieth century. The resultant paucity of work makes it at once simple and difficult to assess the historiography of social history after World War II. The discipline can be easily overseen, yet a sparse field offers a thin selection of the detailed empirical research that, hard to synthesize as it may be, constitutes the raw material of historiographical trends. Nonetheless, enough literature exists to allow not only a summary of social historians' major conclusions about the era but also a characterization of the field itself. Furthermore, the pace of sociohistorical inquiry is speeding up, as the time elapsed since the war lengthens and as the urgent need to explain it diminishes. Some findings call into question the notion that the war itself was as complete a watershed, in social history terms, has been supposed. In some areas, such as gender, important changes and breaks may have occurred a bit later.

The social-science corner of the field of postwar social history has been, this essay argues, quite well-tended. Because the period is so contemporary, social historians of the postwar era have been particularly influenced by the questions and quantitative research pursued by political scientists, sociologists, and economic historians. The social-science bent has also been fostered, no doubt, by the central place in all discussions of postwar Europe accorded the economic boom. Whatever the reason, scholars have produced a number of national and pan-European analyses of big social processes, including demographic, social-structural, educational, employment, consumption, and leisure trends. Working on this broad canvas, those in the field have arrived at an impressively wide consensus not only about the defining tendencies but about which ones represent continuity and which a break with the past. Historians also agree on periodization of the era, though, not surprisingly, their perceptions of the main dividing lines have shifted from the 1960s to the 1990s as new trends have been revealed or older ones reversed. The consensus on social trends even crosses deep political divides, especially those between authoritarian southern Europe and democratic northwest Europe.

Strong as it is on national and comparative syntheses of complex processes, trend-tracking, and periodization, the field has not agreed on a comprehensive theoretical construct for the era, hence the discussion here of the weaknesses and lacunae in the social history of postwar Europe. Having charted and labeled the key developments, historians have found it difficult to wrap them up as a single package. Certainly the period has earned several epithets, most of which append the prefix "post-" to a concept that characterizes the preceding era. Thus, scholars have bandied about "postindustrial," "postmodern," "post-Fordist," even "postcapitalist." Social historians, as well as other social scientists and humanists working on the period, have grown uncomfortable with their inability to confer an overarching identity on the era. Like historians in general, most have distanced themselves from modernization theory and so are left without an organizing principle that draws together the disparate and indisputably enormous changes that have occurred since 1945.

If it has not settled on a conceptual framework, the historiography of the era has at least grappled with this issue. Postwar social history remains weakest not at the high plane of theory but on the ground level of human experience. Not until the later 1990s did there appear a critical mass of historical studies that deconstruct general trends into their local variations or that examine social relations from the "bottom up" in this town or that industry. Social historians started only in the 1990s to mine qualitative, as opposed to statistical, archival collections to ascertain how individuals, villages, youth groups, women's associations, male choruses, soccer clubs, and so on adapted to political, economic, and social change. Typical social-historical topics—organized protest, industrial relations, interactions between state officials and citizens—have remained, by and large, the stuff of good reporting or, sometimes, bad sociology, rather than becoming the object of in-depth historical investigation. Few historians have exploited the abundant opportunities for oral history that the recency of the era affords. The field has also not made the "anthropological turn," that is, the shift away from a focus on social causes and effects and toward the interpretation of cultural practices and mentalities. Insofar as mentalities and their particular contexts have been explored, anthropologists themselves have done the work.

The historiography of the postwar era has not (yet) been etched with the distinctive methodological profile of either the "new" new social history of the 1970s or the sociocultural history that permeated the historiography in the 1980s. This essay ends with a brief consideration of why postwar social history has thus evolved. Like social history as a whole and indeed all historiography, postwar social history has been characterized by national differences in topic, method, and perspective. Thus the literature on each country has been shaped by the discipline's particular style in, for example, Great Britain, France, or Germany. The nature of the field has in turn interacted with a structural "recency effect" and the meaning of "1945" in each country to produce a social historiography that was more or less developed by the 1980s. However, at least until the mid-1990s, it everywhere tended to focus on impersonal social change writ large rather than on human agency and the history of everyday life.

DEFINING THE MAJOR SOCIAL PATTERNS

Like many social historians, those who study Europe in the second half of the twentieth century have been especially interested in the relationship between social change and economic development. In this case, they have asked about the impact of the extraordinarily steep, broad, and long economic boom of the 1950s and 1960s on living patterns, social structures, and class relations. Alongside other social scientists, they have explored, for example, the links between consumption patterns and rising incomes, social mobility and rising levels of education, or family organization and rising employment of married women. To address these issues, they have turned above all to the huge quantity, if not always unblemished quality, of statistics gathered on many aspects of life by every European regime since 1945. Their answers can be summarized in several categories that, taken together, constitute what are seen to be the main attributes of (Western) Europe's "new society" as it emerged in the 1950s and 1960s: high rates of urbanization and the demise of a distinctly rural style of life; the attenuation of class antagonism and acceleration of social mobility; the extraordinary expansion of vocational, secondary, and higher education; the fall in the birth rate, rise of divorce, and semisocialization of child rearing; the emergence of a full-blown welfare state and its accompanying new relationship between government and citizen; and the triumph of "American-style" consumerism.

The postwar era, social historians have argued, witnessed not only the continuation of centuries-old European urbanization but, more significantly, the end of the sharp opposition between city and country that characterized large stretches of Europe in 1945. Rural areas, occupations, and people persisted; but after 1945 the lines between village and city blurred and the lives of villagers and city dwellers grew increasingly similar, thus blunting ancient mutual resentments. Historians and social scientists have written of the "death of a separate peasant culture" (Eric J. Hobsbawm) and the "end of the peasantry" (Henri Mendras), attributing its collapse to technological advances, urban migration, and the extension of consumer society into the countryside. The peasantry's demise has been of particular interest to historians of France, presumably because peasant culture persisted so robustly there through the 1940s, only to decline precipitously by 1970. The peasant way of life virtually disappeared, however, in every Western European country—even in authoritarian Spain, where the regime was invested in its preservation—and, though not for all the same reasons, in Eastern Europe as well. Farmers continued to form a strong bloc in European politics, yet even their protests mimicked the tactics of urban dissident movements.

If the gap between rural and urban narrowed dramatically as prosperity, tractors, and television penetrated the village, income disparities—another promi- nent topic in the historiography—remained wide in most Western European countries. However, inequal- ity produced social and political consequences differ- ent from those that occurred before 1945. Class an- tagonism did not disappear but became milder and, when expressed, less likely to take violent, organized, or political forms. Social historians have associated this change with others: First, the gap between top and bottom did narrow to some extent. Moreover, mobility was rapid enough to assuage workers' sense of grievance. Full employment and, later, unemploy- ment compensation also contributed to a change in workers' consciousness, as the social historian Eric Hobsbawm has argued. Workers were now linked to the bourgeoisie, as were farmers to city folk, by com- monalities of consumption. Everyone shopped at chain stores and supermarkets and ever-increasing numbers of people owned expensive private goods such as a car, even if some drove a luxury vehicle and others a jalopy.

Expanding prosperity contributed to the decline of a distinct proletarian milieu. Even though workers continued to compose a plurality of most European populations, they were much less visible than before. Workers were ever less likely to hang out in pubs, cafés, or bars, not to mention union or political halls, and much more likely to go to the movies or watch television with their families. As working-class pur- suits became more private, workers' lives became more like those of the middle classes. The decline of a sepa- rate, and politicized, proletarian milieu has particu- larly occupied the interest of historians of the Federal Republic of Germany (West Germany), presumably because of the huge size, extraordinary network, and political significance of social democratic and com- munist organizations in Germany before 1933.

As the working-class way of life became less cul- turally distinct, bourgeois culture too grew less socially definable. Again, most authors contend that real changes underlay the decline of older social, cultural, and political distinctions. A different social structure emerged with the final disappearance of the aristoc- racy and the transformation of industrial barons into economic managers. The old middle class—shop- keepers, artisans, and other self-employed—shrank to a tiny minority of the European population and be- came, after a few last gasps, incapable of effective, usually reactionary, activity in defense of its interests. Social class was ever less defined by ownership of tra- ditional kinds of property and ever more based on education and one's position within a bureaucratic hi- erarchy, whether corporate or governmental.

The social effects of economic changes were has- tened, most analysts have argued, by the spread of mass culture via the electronic media. As Peter Stearns observed in *European Society in Upheaval: Social His- tory since 1750* (1975), tastes were converging across the urban-rural boundary, class divides, and national borders as ever greater numbers of Europeans enjoyed more leisure, participated in similar leisure activities and vacations, and labored in the increasingly indis- tinguishable environments of the large, automated of- fice and big, mechanized factory. In *An Economic and Social History of Europe from 1939 to the Present* (1987), Frank Tipton and Robert Aldrich pointed to the high television ratings of the 1955 World Cup series, broadcast over all Western Europe, as a water- shed event that revealed both the expansion of leisure in postwar Europe and the shared ways Europeans spent their free time.

Whether because the social gap narrowed slightly or because dress, demeanor, and possessions no longer blatantly expressed "class," the meaning of that social division faded. Social historians not only agree that this process occurred but rank it as one of the most significant changes in European society since World War II. They do not, however, see the attenuation of class antagonism as linear, much less absolute. Each country followed its own path, and nowhere did class distinctions disappear. If the class struggle was no longer a central theme of social relations, tensions still flared, especially during periods of recession or infla- tion, such as in France and Italy in the late 1960s and in Great Britain in the 1970s and early 1980s. In fact, the topic of class and its continuing significance has especially engaged historians of postwar Britain, pre- sumably because the distinctions between "upstairs" and "downstairs" were understood to be especially sharp there before 1945. Surveying not only the Brit- ish Isles but all Europe, Stearns and Herrick Chapman (1992) found class still to be a vibrant category of popular perceptions of society and criticized the "rosy view of homogenization" found in assessments of the "new Europe" from the 1960s.

Since the 1970s social historians have also be- come interested in the mass migration of workers be- tween and into European countries as simultaneously a new source of social tension and a siphon of class antagonism. Initially that migration consisted mostly of southern Europeans going north; later, Europe re- ceived an influx of immigrants from former colonies and other countries. Although racism, not to mention chauvinistic nationalism, has an old, terrible history in Europe, largely new is its tendency to divide work- ers along ethnic lines in the factory and in the neigh- borhood. As a result, it has contributed, social histo- rians have argued, to the decline of class-based politics and an increase in racial tension. In this way, as in so many others, Europe has become more like the United States. Social historians have in fact manifested considerable interest in the Americanization of Europe as well as in Europeans' love-hate relationship with the United States.

Clearly, one path of European and American convergence has been the rising educational levels on both sides of the Atlantic. From a continent starkly divided between a mass of elementary-school graduates and a thin layer of academics, Europe—west and east, north and south—has become a society of high-school and college graduates, a change that has greatly interested social-science historians. A dramatic improvement in vocational training inaugurated the educational reforms of the postwar era, allowing the majority of working-class boys to enter skilled occupations and also providing many proletarian daughters access to a vocation. The expansion of secondary schooling and universities, for its part, provided a new means of recruitment into social elites. Social historians have argued that this second stage of the educational boom reversed the order of class and gender effects achieved by the first phase. The expansion of higher education functioned less well as a lever to lift workers' children into the middle class than as a formidable leveler of young women's historic educational disadvantages.

The historiography has generally associated the education boom with two other developments: first, the emergence of a youth culture that crossed national boundaries in its tastes, styles, and mores and, second, the rise of new social movements, often peopled by students or graduates who discovered their political cause while at university. As one might expect, social historians have attributed social significance to the explosion and spread across Italy, Spain, France, Belgium, and Germany of the student movement for university reform and against consumer capitalism. When it comes to actual research, however, they have tended to leave the investigation of the mass strikes of the 1960s and the terrorism of the 1970s to political scientists and sociologists such as, most famously, Alain Touraine. Though the feminist movement emerged later in Europe and never attained the same strength as in the United States, the struggles for women's rights and, especially, for reproductive rights have since the late 1970s inspired more social-historical research than has the student revolt.

Interest in the women's movement was heightened by the recognition that this social movement was associated with a major social change: the demise of patriarchal power and the rise of the two-earner family. As measured by social historians, changes in the European family were many and varied. After the baby boom of the 1950s, the birth rate fell, reaching historic lows in virtually every country and approaching zero population growth in several by the 1970s. The institutionalization of a smaller nuclear family occurred along with changes in domestic gender relations. Wives' level of education rose, companionate marriage based on friendship and joint decision making spread, and both men and women expected sexual fulfillment in marriage; as a result of these tendencies, standards of marital happiness rose. As legal barriers to divorce fell in country after country, the divorce rate accelerated, accompanied by an increase in the percentage of single-parent families and of single-person households. Ever more married women entered the workforce, leaving only briefly to bear and raise children, although precise rates varied widely between countries like Spain and Portugal on the one hand and the Scandinavian countries on the other. The offspring of these women entered (usually public) daycare and kindergartens. Thus, the family declined as the primary institution for the socialization of young children.

The state increased its influence not only on the early-childhood development of Europeans but on every phase of their lives. Needy individuals, in particular, came to rely much less on family and much more on state intervention in periods of crisis. The European welfare states socialized many services and at least some industries, manipulated economic measures in order to create full employment, redistributed wealth via taxes and state programs, and provided health and other social insurance. After the flush days of the 1960s, state budgets were hard hit by the oil shocks of the 1970s and the aging of populations. A wave of privatization occurred in the 1980s, especially in Great Britain; but nowhere was the welfare state dismantled. Social historians concluded that people might grumble about taxes and bureaucracies but would not countenance a return to a society whose state did not guarantee at least social security, health insurance, and unemployment compensation.

One European postwar trend was of particular fascination to social critics and historians from the 1950s to the turn of the century: the triumph of consumer society in Western Europe and, after 1989, the extension of mass consumerism into Eastern Europe. Historians have attributed the breakthrough of mass, American-style consumerism, like other social changes, to the unprecedented prosperity generated by the long postwar boom. The boom, several historians have been at pains to point out, was founded on the continued and indeed rapid industrialization of European economies in the 1950s and 1960s. So, for example, industrial work relations spread quite dramatically among some subpopulations, such as women or southern Europeans. Yet social historians have not scrutinized their experiences, presumably because they did not constitute a break with the kind of work patterns already established in Europe. Rejecting the productionist bias of nineteenth-century studies, social historians have defined the "New Europe" instead by how, what, and how much it consumed—that is, by the market's new status as the main means by which people satisfied their bodily, emotional, and even spiritual needs. In dubbing the era the "Age of the Automobile," Hobsbawm referred not to "Fordism" and its mass-production methods but to mass accessibility to commodities on the one hand and to an individualistic, liberated, mobile style of life on the other.

WHAT'S NEW, WHAT'S NOT, AND WHY

The triumph of consumer society, then, stands at the heart of what is really different about the new age—and has, in turn, influenced the historiography of the era. Or does it—and has it? It is difficult, as Stearns and Chapman noted, to assess continuity and change in the postwar era because most of its major trends—including the spread of consumerism—continued prewar social tendencies. It is even more difficult to judge the nature of change because there occurred not a true recasting of the class structure, as in nineteenth-century western Europe, but a reformation of the occupational framework. Many historians maintain, nonetheless, that postwar changes, while neither new nor revolutionary, were so dramatic, profound, and transnational that their very quantity adds up to a qualitative shift toward a more open and dynamic society.

Hartmut Kaelble has taken the argument about the significance of a cross-national pattern of change one step further. In his *A Social History of Western Europe, 1880–1980* (1989), he argued that Western European societies have converged substantially since 1945. Pointing to the trends outlined above, he maintained, first, that this convergence was multifaceted. Second, it stood in contrast to a tendency toward political and even social divergence through the 1930s. Third, it occurred without turning Europe into a version of the United States but preserved distinctively European urban patterns and styles of life. Finally, Kaelble posited, the social integration of Europe since 1950 contributed appreciably to the new peacefulness of European relations and to the political and economic integration that is still under way. Rather than look at Kaelble's converging metatrends, other historians have focused instead on differences in particular

tendencies or on different rates of change within a similar trend. Thus, historians of women have shown an interest in why the rate of women's employment in Great Britain and especially the Federal Republic of Germany has lagged behind that in France and Sweden. They have pointed to the less advanced development of public child-care systems in the former two countries as one reason for the difference. Obviously, whether they support Kaelble's convergence theory or not, social historians of the postwar era share a trait that is pronounced in the social historiography of postwar Europe: a strong proclivity toward the comparative analyses of social trends.

Social, along with political, historians of the postwar era have long been interested in why the effects of World War II were so profoundly different from those of World War I. Whereas the unprecedented carnage of 1939–1945 ushered in an age of greater (Western) European unity, peace, and prosperity, in the wake of World War I followed discordance, crises, and, finally, an even more terrible war. Social historians have not denied the significance of the political lessons learned from the interwar crises or, certainly, the division of Europe between the superpowers as spurs to solidarity within each camp; but in their view the major generator of the New Europe is the economic boom. Like political historians and experts in international relations, they attribute the boom in part to international conditions (fostered, again, by the cold war) that helped jump-start Western European industry in the 1950s. But social historians, especially of the Federal Republic of Germany, also point to certain social effects of the war and immediate postwar years that were internally generated and peculiar to Europe. They cite, for example, the destruction of aristocratic and landed elites and the migration westward of young populations with considerable skills as difficult transitions that eventually contributed both to the more liberal and conciliatory political climate and to the economic dynamism of the 1950s. As for the authoritarian southern nations, economic dynamism followed by liberalization came later.

PERIODIZATION

Social historians have constructed their periodization of the postwar era in Western Europe above all around its economic phases. The first period, from 1945 to 1950–1951, was one of dearth, social crisis, and mass migrations. The boom ushered in two decades of rising prosperity that was punctuated at the end (1966–1971) by a sudden and cross-European rise in social unrest associated with the explosion in the student and working-class populations. The years from 1973 through the late 1980s are grouped together as a time of economic malaise, characterized by inflation, budget crises, stagnation, and high levels of long-term unemployment, although this was also a period of significant democratization. Finally, the 1990s are seen as a decade of partial economic recovery that was also distinguished by striking political developments. Social historians highlight, first and foremost, the end of communism in Eastern Europe, but also emphasize the rapid steps toward, on the positive side, European unity and, on the negative side, the resurgence of nationalism and instability, particularly in the Balkans.

This periodization, by attributing as much significance to the postwar economic boom as to the wars and political upheavals of the first half of the century, challenges the utility of the conventional periodization of twentieth-century history. It also diverges from perceptions of the postwar era that cast the 1950s as socially dull, conformist, conservative, and even retrograde rather than as a decade that harbored new social tendencies and so prepared the way for changes in the family, the position of women, and generational relationships in the 1960s and 1970s. Although at any given point scholarly definitions of both the intervals and the meaning of the periodization have tended to intersect, definitions have varied according to when the appraisals were written. Commentaries on the "golden years" of the 1950s and 1960s that appeared during those years were not mindlessly optimistic, but they did tend to overestimate the transformative impact of mass consumption and changes in class structures. Overviews of postwar development written in the late 1970s were not all retrospective gloom and doom, though their sense of postwar development—and emphasis on what had *not* changed—was clearly colored by the mood of crisis that gripped Europe during the decade's oil crises and wave of terrorism. Their authors were more likely, for example, to highlight the devastating effects on certain regions of the decline of old industries such as textiles and mining than to trumpet, as had earlier writers, the rise of new industries such as petrochemicals and electronics.

THEORIZING CONSUMER SOCIETY

In *The Age of Extremes: A History of the World, 1914–1991* (1994), Hobsbawm held that the postwar world had undergone a great social transformation. Yet simultaneously, he acknowledged the difficulty of characterizing this new world of constant change. Hobs-

bawm, as had Stearns and Kaelble in their own surveys of the era, rejected the term "postindustrial," coined in 1959 by the American sociologist Daniel Bell (first appearing in his *The Coming of Post-Industrial Society: A Venture in Social Forecasting*), as a misnomer, at least for Europe. After all, the continent experienced not only greater industrialization into the 1970s but also the continuation of other classic trends of the industrial age. Other historians, though, have found the term useful. If not postindustrial or, in a subsequent variation, post-Fordist, they have often appended "postmodern" to at least the period after the 1970s. The sociological economist Amitai Etzioni in 1968 first applied this term to the radical transformation of the technologies of communication and knowledge after 1945. Recognizing that the social-structural effects of the technological revolution remain unclear, historians use the concept to refer to a vaguer, though palpable, shift in social mentality that has accompanied the movement toward a Europe dominated by the production of services of all kinds.

Other versions of "post-" mania have been less controversial. On the one hand, it is accepted that Eastern Europe became "postcommunist." On the other hand, virtually no historian has embraced the term "post-capitalist," put forward in the 1960s by the sociologist Ralf Dahrendorf as a label for Western Europe, if only because in the 1990s the market organization of the economy experienced a resurgence throughout Europe and, of course, in Eastern Europe in particular. Even the social democratic parties that came to power in Spain, France, Germany, Italy, and Britain in the 1980s and 1990s pursued economic policies more neoliberal than socialist.

Historians who have refused to see the world since 1945 as a postscript are at the same time increasingly reluctant to encompass it within the long-term and universalizing pattern of development encapsulated in the theory of modernization. Historians and other scholars have questioned the usefulness of the concept on several grounds. First, its normative and teleological assumptions have come under attack by historians who point out that, in the twentieth century, modernity's dissonances tended to drown out the harmonious strains of its progressive march. Works on the postwar era that appeared after the 1970s highlighted the troubles in paradise such as environmental degradation, loss of regional diversity, and erosion of traditional culture. Second, ever more scholars have come to doubt the theory's ability to describe social facts. Historians of the postwar era have argued that modernization theory cannot encompass the fragmentary and contradictory currents of social and cultural "progress" and "regression"—such as the renascence of regionalism and racist nationalism in Western and Eastern Europe—that characterize change in even the most highly industrialized and, indeed, postindustrial European societies. Thus one might say that social-historical interpretations often adopt a "postmodern" viewpoint insofar as they stand judgment on modernity, counting not its blessings but its costs. Yet this critical perspective cannot be assimilated to the postindustrial, postmodern camp, for its adherents see postwar European society as shaped by modern developments taken to their extreme, if not necessarily logical, ends.

A SOCIAL, BUT NOT YET A PEOPLE'S, HISTORY

The historiography of postwar Europe, distancing itself from modernization theory with its underpinnings in social-science methodologies, has also been moving away from its fascination with big social trends. An outline of a social history that is new to the study of postwar Europe has begun to take shape. This emergent history rests, like the familiar social histories of industrialization, on painstaking archival reconstructions of the evolution of one region, town, or industry across periods of economic expansion and contraction. Alternatively, its practitioners track the history of one social group's occupations, education, and living patterns, such as those of women or workers. Or they trace the development of a particular social activity, such as radio listening, or organization, such as sports leagues. Social-historical publications cover topics of interest including urban planning; nuclear power; tourism, radio, and other leisure pursuits; women's integration into the industrial labor force; and the assimilation of refugees after the mass migrations of the mid-1940s. Articles and books in the field offer social-historical versions of discourse analysis: they plumb the daily press, official records and decrees, written memoirs, and interviewees' memories to trace, to take two disparate examples, popular perceptions of American culture and GI's or the gendered construction of shopping in the new consumer economy. Findings have suggested that, just as national surveys and comparative syntheses of social change established, by the 1960s Europeans were already living tremendously different lives from those twenty years earlier. Yet these studies have also uncovered the persistence of the old within, around, and against the new—documenting, for example, continuities in male attitudes about the proper gender of industrial labor or in the socializing patterns and cultural beliefs of refugees. The goal of such research is to obtain a rich picture of how Europeans actually used and interpreted their prosperity, greater social mobility, higher education, and more egalitarian family structures.

The attention to popular experience and local processes has not yet touched all the big issues. The decline of peasant culture, for example, needs to be addressed. The anthropologists Lawrence Wylie and Julian Pitt-Rivers produced classic treatments of villages after the war, but these date to the 1950s. The shrinking of the old middle classes and their demise as a sociopolitical force also remain understudied topics, with the exception of the 1956 book on the Poujadist movement, a right-wing French protest movement in the 1950s, by the political scientist Stanley Hoffmann. The social experiences and cultural adjustments of immigrants from Africa and southern Europe into Europe's northwestern nations since the 1960s also deserve greater attention. The social history of Eastern Europe is in general underresearched, including not just the fate of its peasant and lower-middle-class cultures but also the experience of workers during the Stalinist-style industrialization there in the 1950s. The opening of the archives in Eastern European countries in the early 1990s allowed graduate students from every European nation, the United States, and Canada to conduct research into myriad important social-historical topics. The emerging dissertations and books based on these researches mark an important stage in the social history of the period.

NATIONAL TRENDS IN HISTORIOGRAPHY

The country whose postwar social history has received the most attention is Germany, especially its western part (although comparative German history has become a growth field). German historians have, not surprisingly, played the prominent role in this research, but they have been joined by both Americans and Britons in the field. Several factors explain the preeminence of the German wing of postwar social history and the great interest in understanding German social development. Of all Western European countries, the political break across the 1945 divide was most dramatic in what became the Federal Republic of Germany. German historians have been eager to determine what exactly distinguishes, and why, the second postwar era from the first. Social historians, for their part, have a special interest in Germany's postwar evolution. Central causes of the character, popular appeal, and political-military course of National Socialism must be sought, they have argued, in German society and culture from 1900 to 1945—in short, the "German question." Similarly, they attribute German political stability since 1945 to the nation's new social dynamics. To understand what changed in German political culture and whether it has become more like that of its western neighbors, they have been determined to establish the exact nature of social change and continuity after the war. Interest in social history was also motivated by the massive transfer and flight of Germans from the east after 1945, a topic that is probably better researched than any other social question in Germany.

The concentration on German social history in the postwar era derives, too, from the character of historiography in the Federal Republic. The German historians who inaugurated modern social history—called the Young Turks because of the challenge they posed to the conventional methods—in the late 1960s, such as Hans Ulrich Wehler, Jürgen Kocka, and Hans Mommsen, listed toward the social-science corner of the field and showed a keen interest in the comparative social development of Germany, western European nations, and the United States in the nineteenth and early twentieth centuries. They drew a sharp line between their comparative, structural perspective and the dominant tradition of national political history for which the German academy was once famous and, after 1945, infamous. Though Wehler and others directed their critical sights on Germany before 1945, some of their students chose to apply their training in sociological methods and issues to contemporary history.

German social history's own history has been subjected, ironically, to the same critical questions about continuities with the pre-1945 and especially National Socialist past as those it posed concerning German society and traditional German historiography. In the late 1990s several scholars established that the deceased historians Werner Conze and Theodor Schieder, whose students in the 1950s developed into the 1960s generation of Young Turks, had written position papers during the war on the right of Germans to settle eastern Europe. These papers promoted a chauvinistic agenda and were suffused with National Socialist assumptions about ethnic hierarchies. The discovery unleashed a controversy about why their students, now famous historians in senior university posts, had failed to question them or other older social historians about their activity during the Third Reich. It also ignited a continuing debate about what came to be called the "brown roots of social history" in Germany (brown being the color associated with the Nazis because of their uniforms). Both Conze and Schieder conducted research on the postwar era. Schieder, in fact, directed the huge government-financed project of the 1950s that gathered statistics

and qualitative evidence on what happened to the German refugees and expellees from Eastern Europe. This controversy touched, if far from tainted, the history of postwar social history.

Into the early 1990s the social history of France in the 1950s and 1960s consisted of a relatively small number of syntheses of social, economic, and policy trends. Overviews of French development that appeared in the 1980s argued that 1950s policymakers had taken the country through a planned leap into modern life after the crisis of the Third Republic and the shock of German occupation. The results, they believed, clearly broke with decades of social and economic stagnation. Only in the late 1990s did there appear a specialized social-historical literature, mainly written by young American scholars, on particular aspects and local versions of French social change. Several reasons underlie the lagging development of postwar social history in France. First, 1945, dramatic though it was, did not, as in Germany, constitute the so-called zero hour, much less the end of an aggressive, murderous regime. Compared to German historians' anxious scanning of their nation's recent history, the French did not feel the need to establish exactly what was different about the New France in order to assure themselves and their readers that the Old France would not reemerge. In fact, the French were more invested in denying the French roots of the country's own wartime regime. Second, modern social history in France was the child of the *Annales* school, famous for its interest in the *longue durée* of historical evolution and its contempt for short-term trends; in continuity rather than breaks; in slow-brewing popular mentalities rather then elite-driven "events"; and, finally, in medieval and early modern history. French social historians have, as a result, been inclined to shy away from contemporary history.

In Great Britain, too, the meaning of "1945" there and the character of the historiography conspired to reduce the interest of social historians in the postwar era. Whether looked at from a political or social angle, the break there was less dramatic than in any other major European combatant. The country was already highly urbanized and industrialized in 1945; changes in class relations were not very noticeable there until the 1980s, following the onset of rapid deindustrialization. Moreover, the economic boom was considerably weaker and shorter in the United Kingdom than in Germany, France, or Italy. Early postwar governments followed an assertive socialization policy and created a well-developed welfare state, but the social effects of these policies emerged only over several decades. Finally, British social historians have generally concentrated on the industrial revolution as the most important era of social change in modern British history. Thus, the British historiography, even more than the French, has been characterized by synthetic treatments of national social development over the entire postwar era or the twentieth century as a whole.

As the postwar era in Europe—defined by political scientists and historians as having ended with the fall of communism—recedes in time, research into the social and sociocultural aspects of its history will most certainly flourish, as has the field's knowledge of earlier historical periods.

See also **Immigrants** *(in this volume);* **Modernization; Migration; Birth, Contraception, and Abortion; The Welfare State** *(volume 2);* **Social Class; Social Mobility; Student Movements** *(volume 3);* **Consumerism; Schools and Schooling; Standards of Living** *(volume 5); and other articles in this section.*

BIBLIOGRAPHY

Comparative and Pan-European Literature

Ambrosius, Gerold, and William H. Hubbard. *A Social and Economic History of Twentieth-Century Europe.* Cambridge, Mass., 1989.

Hobsbawm, Eric. *The Age of Extremes: A History of the World, 1914–1991.* New York, 1994.

Kaelble, Hartmut. "Boom und gesellschaftlicher Wandel 1948–1973: Frankreich und die Bundesrepublik, Deutschland im Vergleich." In *Der Boom 1948–1973: Gesellschaftliche und wirtschaftliche Folgen in der Bundesrepublik Deutschland und in Europa.* Edited by Hartmut Kaelble. Opladen, Germany, 1992.

Kaelble, Hartmut. *A Social History of Western Europe, 1880–1980.* Translated by Daniel Bird. Dublin and New York, 1989.

"Looking for Europe." *Daedalus* 108 (winter 1979). Special issue.

"A New Europe?" *Daedalus* 93, no. 1 (1964). Special issue.

Siegrist, Hannes, Hartmut Kaelble, and Jürgen Kocka, eds. *Europäische Konsumgeschichte: zur Gesellschafts- und Kulturgeschichte des Konsums (18. bis 20. Jahrhundert).* Frankfurt and New York, 1997.

Siegrist, Hannes, Hartmut Kaelble, and Jürgen Kocka, eds. "Sozialgeschichte in Frankreich und der Bundesrepublik: Annales gegen historische Wissenschaften?" *Geschichte und Gesellschaft* 13 (1978): 77–93.

Sampson, Anthony. *Anatomy of Europe: A Guide to the Workings, Institutions, and Character of Contemporary Western Europe.* New York, 1968.

Stearns, Peter. *European Society in Upheaval: Social History since 1750.* 2d ed. New York, 1975.

Stearns, Peter, and Herrick Chapman. *European Society in Upheaval: Social History since 1750.* 3d ed. New York and Toronto, 1992.

Tipton, Frank B., and Robert Aldrich. *An Economic and Social History of Europe from 1939 to the Present.* Baltimore, 1987.

Works on France

Ardagh, John. *The New French Revolution. A Social and Economic Survey of France, 1945–1967.* London, 1968.

Bloch-Lainé, François, and Jean Bouvier. *La France restaurée, 1944–1954: Dialogues sur les choix d'une modernisation.* Paris, 1986.

Fourastié, Jean. *Les trente glorieuses; Ou, La revolution invisible de 1946 à 1975.* Paris, 1979.

Hecht, Gabrielle. *The Radiance of France: Nuclear Power and National Identity after World War II.* Cambridge, Mass., 1998.

Hoffmann, Stanley. *Le mouvement poujade.* Paris, 1956.

Larkin, Maurice. *France since the Popular Front: Government and People, 1936–1986.* Oxford and New York, 1988.

McMillan, James F. *Twentieth-Century France: Politics and Society, 1898–1991.* London, 1992.

Mendras, Henri, with Laurence Duboys Fresney. *La seconde révolution française, 1965–1984.* Paris, 1988.

Ross, George. *Workers and Communists in France: From the Popular Front to Eurocommunism.* Berkeley, Calif., 1982.

Wakeman, Rosemary. *Modernizing the Provincial City: Toulouse, 1945–1975.* Cambridge, Mass., 1997.

Works on Germany

Conze, Werner, and M. Rainer Lepsius, eds. *Sozialgeschichte der Bundesrepublik Deutschland: Beiträge zum Kontinuitätsproblem.* Stuttgart, 1983.

Erker, Paul. *Ernährungskrise und Nachkriegsgesellschaft: Bauern und Arbeiterschaft in Bayern 1943–1953.* Stuttgart, 1990.

Kaschuba, Wolfgang, Gottfried Korff, and Bernd Jürgen Warneken, eds. *Arbeiterkultur seit 1945: Ende oder Veränderung?* Tübingen, 1991.

Klessmann, Christoph. *Zwei Staaten, eine Nation: Deutsche Geschichte 1955–1970.* Bonn, 1997.

Münz, Rainer, Wolfgang Seifert, and Ralf Ulrich, eds. *Zuwanderung nach Deutschland: Strukturen, Wirkungen, Perspektiven.* Frankfurt, 1999.

Niethammer, Lutz, Alexander von Plato, and Dorothee Wierling. *Die volkseigene Erfahrung. Eine Archäologie des Lebens in der Industrieprovinz der DDR: 30 biografische Eröffnungen.* Berlin, 1991.

Schildt, Axel. *Moderne Zeiten: Freizeit, Massenmedien, und "Zeitgeist" in der Bundesrepublik der 50er Jahre.* Hamburg, 1995.

Schildt, Axel, and Arnold Sywottek, eds. *Modernisierung im Wiederaufbau: Die westdeutsche Gesellschaft der 50er Jahre.* Bonn, 1993.

"Sozialgeschichte der Bundesrepublik Deutschland." *Archiv für Sozialgeschichte* 35 (1995). Special issue.

Works on Great Britain

Cannadine, David. *The Rise and Fall of Class in Britain.* New York, 1999.

Gillis, John R. *For Better, for Worse: British Marriages, 1600 to the Present.* New York, 1985.

Marwick, Arthur. *Class: Image and Reality in Britain, France, and the USA since 1930.* 2d ed. Houndmills, Basingstoke, Hampshire, U.K., 1990.

Marwick, Arthur. *The Penguin Social History of Britain: British Society since 1945.* London, 1995.

McKibbin, Ross. *Classes and Cultures: England 1918–1951.* Oxford and New York, 1998.

Perkin, Harold. *The Rise of Professional Society: England since 1880.* London and New York, 1989.

Pugh, Martin. *State and Society: British Political and Social History, 1870–1997.* 2d ed. London, 1999.

Topical Literature: Women

Brookes, Barbara. *Abortion in England, 1900–1967.* London and New York, 1988.

Budde, Gunilla-Friederike, ed. *Frauen arbeiten: Weibliche Erwerbstätigkeit in Ost- und Westdeutschland nach 1945.* Göttingen, Germany, 1997.

Duchen, Claire. *Feminism in France from May '68 to Mitterrand.* London and Boston, 1986.

Heitlinger, Alena. *Reproduction, Medicine, and the Socialist State.* New York, 1987.

Katzenstein, Mary F., and Carol M. Mueller, eds. *The Women's Movements of the United States and Western Europe: Consciousness, Political Opportunity, and Public Policy.* Philadelphia, 1987.

Morcillo, Aurora G. *True Catholic Womanhood: Gender Ideology in Franco's Spain.* DeKalb, Ill., 2000.

Saraceno, Chiara. "Constructing Families, Shaping Women's Lives: The Making of Italian Families between Market Economy and State Interventions." In *The European Experience of Declining Fertility, 1850–1970: The Quiet Revolution.* Edited by John R. Gillis, Louise A. Tilly, and David Levine. Cambridge, Mass., 1992. Pages 251–269.

Topical Literature: Peasants

Mendras, Henri. *The Vanishing Peasant.* Cambridge, Mass., 1970.

Pitt-Rivers, Julian A. *The People of the Sierra.* 2d ed. Chicago, 1971.

Wright, Gordon. *Rural Revolution in France: The Peasantry in the Twentieth Century.* Stanford, Calif., 1964.

Wylie, Laurence. *Village in the Vaucluse.* Cambridge, Mass., 1957.

Topical Literature: New Social Movements

Bauss, Gerhard. *Die Studentenbewegung der sechziger Jahre in der Bundesrepublik und Westberlin.* 2d ed. Cologne, 1983.

Lumley, Robert. *States of Emergency: Cultures of Revolt in Italy from 1968 to 1978.* London and New York, 1990.

Touraine, Alain. *The May Movement; Revolt and Reform: May 1968.* New York, 1971.

Section 3

REGIONS, NATIONS, AND PEOPLES

PRINCIPLES OF REGIONALISM

John A. Agnew

The nation-state as the fundamental geographical unit of account has been at the heart of the social sciences as a whole since the late nineteenth century. The origins of fields oriented to the "solution" of such public problems as wealth creation (economics), state management (political science), and social order (sociology) lay in providing services to the nation-state. Yet the "view from below," or that of social groups marginalized in orthodox political history and often associated with social history as a field of study, rests on the premise that the national scale typically represents the privileging of attention to the institutions associated with the interests and outlooks of modern political elites more than the reality of a homogeneous and enclosed society conforming to the political boundaries imposed by the modern system of territorial states. Moreover, not only have Europe's political boundaries been unstable over even relatively short periods of time, the geographical patterning of social life is by no means successfully captured by a singular focus on the national scale.

Of course, this is not to say that national processes of political and economic regulation are without substance in European social history. One study shows how a coherent rural region in the Pyrenees divided into separate Spanish and French national areas with the growth of effective monarchies as early as the seventeenth century. And, since the nineteenth century in particular, nation-states have played influential roles both in reinforcing and in changing various social phenomena. Rather, it is to suggest that the national is only one geographical scale among several in terms of relevance to understanding the long-term structuring of such phenomena as household and family organization, literacy, social protest, social-class formation, and political ideologies. Consequently, depending on the phenomenon in question, regions at a subnational level and regions at a supranational level are often invoked by social historians to provide more appropriate territorial units than the putative nation-state upon which to base social-historical investigation. As Otto Dann expresses it in *Gli spazi del potere:*

With the region, social history, liberated for some time from the weight of the national state, finally has found a more adequate concept of space. The region is the territory of the social historian, varying in its size and structure depending on the object of research. (p. 117)

The term "region" is often used without much conscious motivation other than either to group together nations that are apparently similar and thus to simplify complexity or to ground local studies within a larger geographical field of reference. The drawing of regional differences above and below the national scale also frequently involves deploying such familiar, and often theoretically unexamined, conceptual oppositions as modern-backward, commercial-feudal, and core-periphery, depending upon the theoretical orientation of the social history in question. The region, whatever its precise geographical and social parameters, seemingly cannot be avoided in social history, even when it is not rigorously defined as an inherent feature of a particular study. In the 1990s, however, there was a resurgence of studies explicitly engaging with subnational regions, not least because of the regional-ethnic revivals going on around Europe, from Spain and the British Isles to the former Yugoslavia and the Soviet Union. Regions as geographical units with which to define the contexts of study of a wide range of social structures and processes are therefore important both implicitly and explicitly in European social history.

Some "schools" of social history, particularly that associated with the *Annales* in interwar and immediate postwar France, have been explicitly devoted to avoiding the privileging of the state as the primary unit of geographical context. Perhaps the close link between geography and history in France led to a greater recognition by social and economic historians of the importance of assumptions about the spatial units used in research—recognition that is largely missing in the English-speaking world where an abstract sounding but usually nationally oriented sociology has tended to be more influential than geography among historians. Fernand Braudel's classic study,

La Méditerranée (1949), is an excellent example of the use of a geographical frame of reference, in this case an ocean basin, as an alternative to the nation-states that had dominated historical research during the nineteenth and much of the twentieth century. For Braudel's long-term total history the relatively short histories of European states posed a significant barrier to the historical understanding that only a larger regional entity, such as the Mediterranean world, could adequately convey. Of course, even Braudel eventually succumbed to the allure of national history in his *L'identité de la France* (1986), though this work remains more sensitive than the typical national history to the physical geography and regional distinctions of the territory that later became France as we know it today. In addition, according to Lynn Hunt:

> Despite the enormous prestige of *La Méditerranée*, Braudel's example did not elicit many works within the French historical community on cross-national networks of commercial exchange. Rather, French historians of the third *Annales* generation focused largely on France, and usually on one region of France. The best known of these great *thèses* were *Les Paysans de Languedoc* (1966) by Emmanuel Le Roy Ladurie and *Beauvais et le Beauvaisis* (1960) by Pierre Goubert. (p. 212)

Since the 1960s, world-systems frameworks such as that of Immanuel Wallerstein, based on distinguishing dynamic economic-geographical core macroregions, such as northwest Europe after 1700, from relatively peripheral or exploited ones, such as eastern and southern Europe; theoretical frameworks such as that of Edward W. Fox (*History in Geographic Perspective*, 1971), posing an opposition between "commercial" and "feudal" regions within countries such as France; and internal-colonial or mode of production arguments such as those of Michael Hechter (*Internal Colonialism*, 1976) and William Brustein (*Social Origins of Political Regionalism*, 1988), identifying different types of regions within states with respect to political and social characteristics, represent different ways of explicitly incorporating regions into social-historical analysis. Even greater emphasis on the role of regions as contexts for social invention and political affiliation can be found in the work of the economic historians Sidney Pollard (*Peaceful Conquest*, 1981) and Gary Herrigel (*Industrial Constructions*, 1996), and in that of economic sociologists such as Arnaldo Bagnasco on local economic development and the social construction of the market (*Tre Italie*, 1977). Demographers like Peter Laslett have found regional principles in typologies of family structure, such as East European extended families versus West European nuclear families. Much research, however, tends to operate on an implicit rather than an explicit conception of region. Even as they adopt regional frameworks in their research, social historians are not necessarily very aware of the nature of the geographical divisions that they use.

Europe, of course, is itself a region in the most macro-scale sense of the term. It serves to define the territorial space with respect to which European social history is practiced. Yet, analyses of Europe as a whole in social history are relatively recent, notwithstanding the tendency to make generalizations about "Europe" on the basis of studies of only small parts of it. The principles of regionalism must take this wider context into account so as to identify the various and sundry geographical divisions of the continent. Such principles, or rules, for defining the geographical basis to European social-historical variation must also pay attention to intellectual disputes about the nature of regions and to how regions have been used by social historians. The four sections of this article present, first, a discussion of Europe as a world region; second, a recounting of disputes over the character of regions as meaningful entities in social-historical research; third, a survey of some ways in which regions have been used in European social history; and, fourth, a review of the principles upon which a geographical division must rest, drawing from both the practice of social history and recent work by geographers interested in the ways in which Europe can be thought about in terms of its internal geographical divisions.

EUROPE AS A REGION

"Europe" can be thought of in geographical, historical, and institutional terms, if in practice its various meanings are often conflated. With respect to physical geography, the ancient Greeks used the term "Europe" to denote the lands to their west and north as part of a threefold division of the world that distinguished Europe from Asia to the east and Libya (Africa) to the south. Writers such as Herodotus and Strabo regarded these terms as conventional or arbitrary ones, open to systematic questioning. But, for most of the two millennia or more since they wrote, the continental scheme has been largely taken for granted as betraying some sort of essential geographical division of the world (Lewis and Wigen, 1997). Controversy has flared up over the precise delimitation of Europe from its continental neighbors, with the Ural Mountains replacing the Don River and the Sea of Azov as its eastern border by the early twentieth century, and religious, racial, and civilizational criteria increasingly substituting for physical criteria as the basis for identifying Europe in opposition to other world regions. However, Europe is still largely seen as a self-evident unit whose history has a unity too as a result of a collective destiny created by its global location and the physical attributes (physiographic range, temperate climates, location relative to oceanic wind belts, internal environmental diversity, and so forth) associated with it. One effect of this reasoning, seen in so many global histories (for example, Paul Kennedy's *Rise and Fall of the Great Powers,* 1987; and David Landes's *Wealth and Poverty of Nations,* 1998), has been to exempt Europe from the rule of absolute environmental determinism, seeing it as distinctive among the continents in offering the environmental possibilities out of which European "inventiveness," "inquisitiveness," and, finally, justifiable domination of the rest of the world, including the identification and naming of world regions, are seen as arising. Nevertheless, the logic underpinning Europe's claim to distinctiveness is still a physical-geographical one.

To most social historians, however, it is not the physical character of the continent that lies behind the appropriate use of the term. Rather, Europe's existence is understood as that of a geographical entity with a set of common or overlapping historical experiences (Wilson and van der Dussen, 1993). Thus, much of southern and western Europe was a part of the Roman Empire for at least several centuries. After the collapse of the empire, a much larger part of Europe became the global stronghold of Christianity, if with increasing sectarian divisions creating geographical ones (such as that of the tenth century A.D. between the western Catholic and eastern Orthodox traditions and the later-fifteenth-century division between Catholic and Protestant Christianity). The growth of merchant capitalism beginning in the eleventh century reintroduced city trading networks into the fabric of European society after the long retreat of trade during feudalism. With the decline of royal dynastic authority, the rise of city- and then territorial states as the premier and totalistic means of organizing political sovereignty was initially peculiar to Europe and led to political competition that then spilled out into the rest of the world and brought about the various European-based world empires.

Among other forces at work in producing a common European experience must be included the geographically differential impact of the French Revolution's (1789) call to overthrow the established aristocratic political order, the explosion of industrial urbanism from the mid-eighteenth century on, the spread of nationalist and socialist ideologies in the nineteenth century, and, above all, the slow secularization of society from the singular hold of religious authority in the nineteenth and twentieth centuries that created a Europe-wide experience of competing social allegiances and political ideologies that then distinguished the region as a whole from all others. As a result, according to the historical demographer Emmanuel Todd in *L'invention d'Europe* (1990), and with respect to political ideologies:

> European religious and ideological passions are written in space. Each nation, each region [within Europe] adheres either to the Reformation or to the Revolution, to social democracy or to anarchism, liberalism, communism, fascism, or nazism. Each confronts its neighbors in the name of values equally absolute and undemonstrable. (p. 9)

The menu of political choices, therefore, is determined by experiences particular to the space labeled "Europe." The same goes for all manner of other phenomena that have been influenced by the common social, political, and economic experience of the region. As social history has turned more to cultural sources, a few efforts have attempted to describe how popular myths and beliefs have originated and spread across Europe.

Finally, today Europe is increasingly thought of in institutional terms, reflecting the rising importance within segments of the geographical and historical Europe of such entities as the European Union and its affiliated organizations such as the European Court of Justice and the European Parliament (Lévy, 1997). With the removal of the Iron Curtain, the ideological frontier within Europe established after World War II, the project of European unification, initiated by the Treaties of Rome in 1957 between the original six members of the post-1993 European Union, is potentially available to a large number of countries both to the east of the original core members and around the Mediterranean. The Maastricht Accord of 1992 offered a calendar for European political and monetary unification. The introduction in 1999 of the new currency, the euro, by eleven of the fifteen member countries of the European Union represents an important step in the institutional construction of a Europe with a common citizenship, political economy, and policymaking apparatus. The term Europe has become the basis for deciding which countries can be eligible for membership. Rather than singularly geographical or historical, however, the criteria are largely economic and political. Above all, conformity to a neoliberal political economy and to the practices of electoral democracy are now necessary prerequisites for joining the European Union. The project of creating a "common European home," therefore, represents a break with preexisting ways of defining Europe. Now it is a set of common values arising out of the European past but without precise geographical limits that defines who can be "inside" and who is left "outside" the European "project." Neither the physical barrier provided by the Urals nor the influence of common European experiences, such as that of Christianity, can tell who is inside and who is outside of Europe. From the institutional perspective, therefore, Europe now has a culturally virtual rather than a geographically actual existence.

WHAT ARE REGIONS?

The term "region" typically conjures up the idea of a homogeneous block of space that has a persisting distinctiveness due to its physical and/or cultural characteristics. Yet, many regions are more networks of connections between concentrations of populations and places than simply uniform spatial units. An allied claim is often that regions exist "out there" in the world, notwithstanding the prior necessity on the part of an observer of thinking that the world is in fact divided up into regions. Over the years, six disputes about regions have episodically flared up both to challenge and enliven the generally consensus view in the social sciences of regions as homogeneous, self-evident blocks of terrestrial space.

The first controversy has been about the ways in which the areas designated as regions are integrated and/or exhibit homogeneous characteristics. Typically, regions are thought of as areas exhibiting uniformity with respect to one or more characteristics. This view has been challenged by scholars who claim that such regions are often purely formal, in the sense that they are the result of aggregating smaller geographical units (census districts, municipalities, provinces, and so forth) according to statistical similarity without attending to what it is that binds the region together with respect to functional ties. Functional ties include the network or circulation linkages (transport, migration, trade, and capital flows) and central-place (settlement hierarchy) links that create distinctive regions and from which their other characteristics are derived (as described, for example, in Paul Hohenberg and Lynn H. Lees, *The Making of Urban Europe,* 1995). Of course, regions are often politically defined by governments (Patriarca, 1994) and political movements (such as separatist ones). They can also have affective meaning for local populations (Applegate, 1999). In such cases, the absolute formal-functional opposition fails to account for the subjective identifications that people can have with formal regions, even if it continues to serve a useful analytic purpose more generally.

Another dispute concerns the belief that regions are real in the sense of marking off truly distinctive bits of the earth's surface versus the view that they are the product solely of political and social conventions that impose regions on a much more geographically variegated world. There is a visceral tension between the idea that something is real and that is constructed. But are these ideas indeed as mutually exclusive as the dispute suggests? On the one hand, the real is like the body in philosophy's mind-body problem. It is tangible, touchable, and empirically visible. On the other hand, the constructed is like the mind making sense of itself and the body. Each of these positions rests on the same confusion between an object (a region) and an idea about that object (regional schemes). Regions reflect both differences in the world and ideas about the geography of such differences. They cannot be reduced to simply one or the other (Agnew, 1999).

A third controversy has focused on the tendency to see regions as fixed for long time periods rather than as mutable and subject to reformulation, even over relatively short periods. Leading figures in the *Annales* school, such as Marc Bloch and Fernand Braudel; world-systems theorists; and demographic historians have been particularly drawn to the idea of macroregions as the settings for long-term structural history. At the same time others, particularly local historians and regional geographers, have invested heavily in the idea of fixed regional divisions and unique regional entities within countries, owing their uniqueness to "internal" characteristics. However, with the increased sense of a world subject to time-space compression, following the opening of national borders to increased trade, capital, and labor mobility and the shrinkage of global communication and transportation costs, regions are increasingly seen as contingent on the changing character of the larger contexts in which they are embedded rather than dependent on unique features of a more-or-less permanent nature (Johnston, Hauer, and Hoekveld, 1990; Gupta and Ferguson, 1997).

Less noted but perhaps more important with respect to the meaning of regions for social history, a debate has periodically erupted over regions as fundamental contexts for social life as opposed to mere accounting devices or case study settings taken as examples of national or Europe-wide norms and standards. With respect to industrialization, for example, Sidney Pollard has argued that regions are the relevant entities for considering the processes whereby different industries developed. Each region has different combinations of attributes crucial to the establishment of specific industries. In like manner, social and political processes relating to household structures, class formation, and political movements can all be thought of as embedded in regional and local contexts, "the physical arenas in which human interaction takes place" (Weitz, 1995, p. 291), rather than as abstract or national-level processes only manifesting themselves regionally, as presumed by the idea of the regional case study.

A fifth controversy has involved the tendency to represent the character of regions by locating them along a temporal continuum from the backward, or traditional, at one end and the advanced, or modern, at the other. This conversion of time into space has been particularly important in historicizing certain subnational regions (such as the Italian south, the Scottish Highlands, and Andalusia) and countries as a whole (such as Italy or Ireland) into a schema representing the historical trajectory of Europe as a whole (Agnew, 1996). Thus, presumably isolated and remote regions with lower levels of economic growth than more central regions are viewed as lagging behind the more advanced ones, notwithstanding the long-term ties that bind such regions into their particular nation-states. This tendency has given rise to a contending view that poorer regions are poor because the richer ones have become rich at their expense (as in Hechter, 1976, on the British Isles)—in other words, it is not a temporal lag but rather spatial exploitation that lies behind regional differences in economic development and social change.

Finally, perhaps the dominant sense of social historians about regions, particularly regions at the subnational level, has been of entities destined to fade in significance with the creation of national markets, the emergence of national political parties with more or less uniform support across all regions, and the spread of national cultures robbing local and regional identities of their specificity. This nationalization or modernization thesis, articulated in works ranging from Eugen Weber's general study of late-nineteenth-century France, *Peasants into Frenchmen* (1976), to Susan Cotts Watkins's survey of demographic indicators (fertility rates, women's age at marriage, and so forth) across western Europe between 1870 and 1960, *From Provinces into Nations* (1991), relies on the premise that social organization in Europe has undergone a fundamental shift from local and regional levels to the national scale. This premise is a shaky one, however. Some of the data in a study such as that of Watkins can be interpreted to indicate reprovincialization after a period of nationalization, and nationalization of demographic indicators need not indicate the substitution of regional sources of social influence by national ones. Rather, demographic behavior may still be mediated through the regionally specific routines and institutions of everyday life yet yield increasing similarity of behavioral outcomes across regions. The same goes for religious affiliations, voting, consumption, and other types of social behavior (Agnew, 1987; Cartocci, 1994).

REGIONS IN EUROPEAN SOCIAL HISTORY

Four modes of usage of regions dominate social histories of Europe. The first consists of macroregions as units for the pursuit of total history. The locus classicus of this approach is Fernand Braudel's *La Méditerranée* (1949). The claim is that over long periods of time regions emerge based on functional linkages that then continue to distinguish one from the other. Such regions need not be ocean basins such as the Black Sea, the Indian Ocean, or the Mediterranean. They can be units determined by their relative orientations toward certain modes of production and exchange. Edward W. Fox's *History in Geographic Perspective: The Other France* (1971) may be used to illustrate this case briefly, as the logic of the argument need not be restricted to a single national setting.

The second and perhaps most common mode of use is that of dividing up Europe into functional regions to examine specific phenomena such as class transitions and transformations of rule, the nature of landholding and manorialism, industrialization, urbanization, and trade. Sometimes these regions are at a macro scale, as with the divisions between western and eastern Europe (or between western, central or middle, and eastern Europe) in such works as Barrington Moore Jr.'s *Social Origins of Dictatorship and Democracy* (1966; although this study extends in scope well beyond Europe per se), Perry Anderson's *Lineages of the Absolutist State* (1974), and William McNeill's *The Shape of European History* (1974). Sometimes the regions are more fine-grained and subnational, as in Gary Herrigel's study of German industrialization, *Industrial Constructions* (1996), Charles Tilly's work (for example, *Coercion, Capital, and European States, A.D. 990–1992,* 1992) on the logics of coercion and capital in European urbanization and state formation, and work on regional differences in artistic production as in Enrico Castelnuovo and Carlo Ginzburg, "Centre and Periphery" (1994), on Italy. Stein Rokkan's geographical template for Europe as a whole with respect to rates and degrees of state formation (for example, Rokkan and Urwin, *Economy, Territory, Identity,* 1983) serves as an example of work that brings together the main west-east division of the continent with the center-periphery differences that have developed within the emerging states.

The third use is to aggregate together lower-level units (counties, departments, and so forth) without much regard for national boundaries to identify persisting patterns of demographic, social, and political behavior. Regions are thus geographical areas of similarity extending across space and time. This inductive approach to regionalization is most common in studies of demography, literacy, land tenure, economic growth, and the development of political ideologies. Emmanuel Todd's *L'invention d'Europe* (1990) is an example of this genre of usage.

Finally, the explosion of regionalist and separatist movements in Europe has stimulated considerable interest in the emergence and roots of regional identities in relation to national ones. Charlotte Tacke's comparison of the regional bases to German and French national identities, "The Nation in the Region" (1994), serves as an example drawn from a now vast and diverse literature because of its emphasis on regionality as a source of political identities.

Macroregions. Struck by a France that seemed to repeatedly divide itself since the Revolution of 1789 into two sociopolitical divisions around "order" and "movement," Edward W. Fox writes, "For an American, it was natural to begin by seeking to identify these societies in sectional terms" (p. 13). Unlike the United States, however, France has had nothing like a regional-sectional civil war since at least the medieval Albigensian Crusade. Fox finds the regional division in the different communications orbits that have emerged down the years between a Paris-oriented interior France and an externally oriented commercial France along the coasts. He gives the argument a transcendental appeal by claiming that the opposition between an agricultural-military society, on the one hand, and a commercial-seagoing society, on the other, can be found in ancient Greece and in medieval Europe as much as in the modern world. Fox is distinguishing between a subsistence society dependent on control of territory and a waterborne commercial society dependent on access to flows of goods and capital. The two "types" of society achieved their most characteristic forms during the "long" century between the revolutions of the sixteenth century and the French Revolution. The social commentators of the time, such as Montesquieu, clearly recognized them. Fox uses the dichotomous model as a framework for exploring the course of French social history since 1789, but accepts that by the Fifth Republic the opposition between two societies had largely run its material course, even if the legacy of the two Frances still "left its imprint upon the political preferences of their members" (Fox-Genovese and Genovese, 1989, p. 237).

Fox's regionalization rests on what can be called a fixed spatial division of labor between two different modes of production which though present within the boundaries of the same state nevertheless have both fractured that state and led to distinctive social orders (class struggles, inheritance systems, religious and political affiliations, and so on) within it. Thus, the history of France (and, Fox suggests, many other states) cannot be understood satisfactorily as a singular whole but only in terms of the opposition and interaction between "two Frances" based upon competing principles of social and economic organization. Though articulated in the setting of a specific (perhaps the quintessential) nation-state, Fox's argument is similar to other macroregional ones in pointing to the persistence of regional patterns of social and political behavior as the foundation for interpreting other social phenomena. Whether such phenomena can be invariably reduced to the opposition is, of course, another thing entirely.

Functional regions. The late Stein Rokkan's research enterprise was oriented to understanding the varying character (unitary versus federal, democratic versus authoritarian, and so forth) of Europe's modern states (see Rokkan and Urwin, *Economy, Territory, Identity*, 1983). Among other things, he noted that adjacent states tended to develop similar forms of government and that there was a fairly systematic north-south and east-west dimensionality to this variation. He represented spatial variation between states in a series of schematic diagrams transforming Europe into an abstract space by drawing on crucial periods and processes in European socio-political history. Three periods or processes are seen as crucial. The first is the pattern of the peopling and vernacularization of language in the aftermath of the Roman Empire. This produces a geo-ethnic map of Europe based on the south-north influence of the Romans and a west-east physical geography—ethnic geography of the settlement of new groups and their differentiation from one another. The second is the pattern of economic development and urbanization in medieval to early modern Europe, distinguishing a south-north axis drawn largely with reference to the impact of the Protestant Reformation and the Catholic Counter-Reformation and an east-west axis with strong seaward states to the west, a belt of city-states in the center, and a set of weak landward states to the east. The third is the way in which democratization has produced different responses in different regions with smaller unitary states in the extreme west, larger unitary states flanking them to the east, a belt of federal and consociational states in the center, and a set of "retrenched empires" and successor authoritarian states yet further to the east.

This geographical template draws attention to systematic geographic variation in the forms of European states and how they arose out of different combinations of social and economic processes. It is particularly original in pointing out the distinctiveness of a long-established urbanized region running from Italy in the south to Flanders in the north. But this use of regionalization neglects the ways in which the social divisions to which Rokkan refers (ethnic identities, city-states versus territorial states and empires, religious affiliations) are translated into political power and how this in turn affects the character of state formation. An entire stage in the process of creating the political map of Europe is missing. As Charles Tilly puts it, perhaps a little too forcefully: "It is hard to see how Rokkan could have gotten much farther without laying aside his maps and concentrating on the analysis of the mechanisms of state formation" (Tilly, 1992, p. 13).

Supranational regions. A very different approach to the use of regions is to use local government areas in different countries as the basis for identifying clusters of units that can cross national boundaries and that define formal regions sharing particular attributes to one degree or another. Maps can be made of such phenomena as family types, fertility and mortality rates, rates of suicide, types of landholding, modes of agrarian organization (sharecropping, peasant proprietorship, capitalist agriculture, and so forth), literacy, religious practice (for example, attendance at Catholic mass), levels of industrial employment, civic culture, and levels of support for ideological parties of the right and the left (see, for example, Goody et al., 1976; Le Bras, 1979; Graff, 1981; and Putnam, 1993). These maps can also be correlated to see to what extent the various phenomena covary spatially with one another. For example, high suicide rates do correlate highly in some places with high rates of illegitimate births and high female autonomy (for instance, much of Sweden and Finland), but elsewhere, as in southern Portugal, they seem to correlate more with something absent in the rest of Europe, perhaps going back to the recovery of the region from Islamic conquest, matrilineal inheritance of names, equal relations in families between parents, and a nuclear ideal of family (Todd, 1990, pp. 56–61).

Various hypotheses about secularization of European society, the impact of industrialization, and the persisting effects on politics and social life of historic forms of household and family organization have been investigated by Emmanuel Todd and others taking this approach. Todd is perhaps the most forceful in his claim for basing the incidence of a wide range of social phenomena on the prior spatial distribution of family types. He shows quite convincingly that family

types (communal, nuclear, stem, and so on), inheritance customs, parent-child relations, and certain features of fertility in Europe do not conform to national-level patterns. Rather, there are both localized clusters within countries and regional groupings that crisscross national boundaries. What is less convincing is the degree to which other social phenomena are truly the outcome of the "underlying" demographic and familial characteristics rather than mediated regionally by a range of economic and social pressures that have extraregional rather than historically accrued local sources. The tendency is to rigidly interpret regional patterns of "higher-level" phenomena (such as political ideologies or civic cultures) as arising from long-term regional patterns of familial and demographic features (see Sabetti, 1996).

Subnational regions. Finally, subnational regional identities have become the focus for social historians and others concerned with the history and restructuring of European political identities (for example, Applegate, 1999). Nations and regions are typically understood as categories of practice that are reified or given separate existence by people struggling to define themselves as members of this or that group. Much work seeks to identify the diversity of group identities in contemporary Europe and how they have arisen. A distinctive current, however, tries to relate regional to national identities as they have arisen over the past several hundred years. The basic premise is that regional and national identities are often intertwined rather than necessarily oppositional. In comparing the historical construction of French and German national identities, Charlotte Tacke claims that "the individual's identification with the nation . . . rests on a large variety of social ties, which simultaneously forge the links between the individual and the nation" (Tacke, 1994, pp. 691–692). The most important ties are those constituted in regions, which serve as "cultural and social space" for "civic communication" (p. 694). Local bourgeoisies in both countries created renewed regional identities at precisely the same time that the symbols they selected (honoring ancient heroes in statues, for example) were made available for appropriation by nation-building elites. In these cases, therefore, regional identities fed into the national ones and were thus lost from sight.

Elsewhere in Europe, however, regional identities appear more as acts of opposition than of accommodation to national ones. This is the message not only of the internal-colonial and mode of production approaches but also of constructivist approaches that emphasize the tendency of region and nation to become synonymous in some social-cultural contexts.

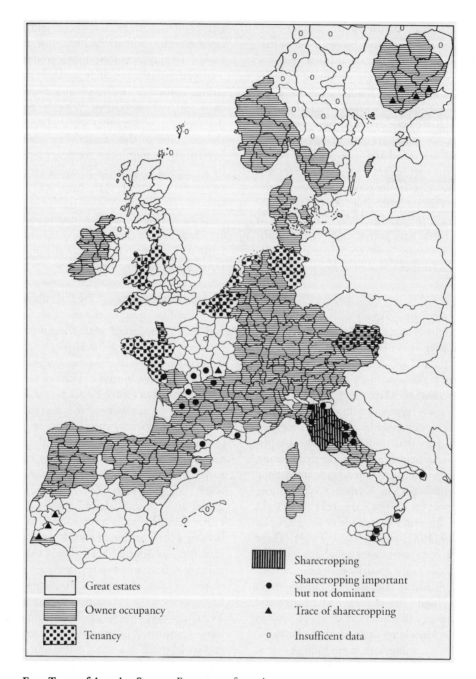

Four Types of Agrarian Systems Four types of agrarian systems: great estates, owner-occupancy, tenancy, and share-cropping. There is little or no conformity to national boundaries. The map suggests that socioeconomic regions have persisted over time regardless of the imposition of political boundaries. From Emmanuel Todd, *L'invention de l'Europe* (Paris: Seuil, 1990), map 16, p. 78. © IN *L'INVENTION DE L'EUROPE* BY EMMANUEL TODD, ÉDITIONS DU SEUIL, 1990

Resistant regional identities, such as the Irish and Basque ones, have taken shape around claims to nationhood. Unlike the French and German cases, they have tried to develop spatial mythologies alternative to the dominant nations within their respective states (the English and the Castilian, respectively) but are often forced into terms of debate and the use of institutional forms that signify the inevitability of at least a degree of accommodation to the territorial status quo. Of course, the resistant regional identities suggest that the word "region" in political usage is itself dependent on the prior existence of nation-states

250

of which the regions are presently part but from which they could possibly separate to become their own nations in the future. One lesson is clear. If all of the other meanings of the term discussed previously are neglected in pursuit of the currently fashionable interest in political regionalism, then we are left with thin intellectual gruel indeed: regions are only potential nations-in-the-making. The attempt to find an alternative regional accounting system to that of the dominant national one would then have come full circle.

PRINCIPLES OF REGIONALISM

The division or partition of Europe into regions cannot be reduced to one best way or a single overarching parameter. Usage is so diverse and disputes over the substance and philosophy of regions are too contentious to allow for application of a single principle of division. This being the case, it makes more sense to tailor usage to specific needs. In this spirit, I want to explore four principles of regionalism that can be applied to the analysis of different research problems based on current practice among social historians and geographers.

The first principle is that of distinctive regional communities that can share identities as well as other sociopolitical characteristics. This principle is most useful for those focusing on the vagaries of subnational political regionalism as well as the persistence of sociopolitical traits from the past. Europe has long been divided in complex ways with respect to language, religion, urbanization, the persistence or reinstatement of feudalism, agrarian systems, and the experience of industrialization. These are all symptomatic of the patchwork of social and place identities and interests that define Europe's varied communities. Nomadic and immigrant groups, most importantly, Roma (or Gypsies), Jews, and non-European immigrants, have had to fit themselves into this kaleidoscope of local and regional communities. With nation-state formation from the eighteenth century on, such groups have had to cope with the tension, and sometimes the conflict, arising between regional identities (known as *Heimat* in German) and national ones (represented in German by the word *Vaterland*). In different countries the tension has resolved itself, at least temporarily, in different ways. If in Germany identification with a *Heimat* has not proved inimical to the growth of a *Vaterland* identity, elsewhere the "resolution" has been to the advantage of one or the other.

The second principle is that of geopolitical territories under construction and challenge, often on the peripheries of states. Apparently less relevant to the interests of many social historians, this one is useful for those concerned with the tensions and conflicts associated with state formation and disintegration. As authors such as Stein Rokkan and Charles Tilly have suggested, historically based lines of geographical fracture both between and within states have emerged due to differences in state organization and the divergent histories of capitalism in different parts of Europe. Such fractures, typically involving center-periphery cleavages across the political map of Europe, have been reinforced by the popular memory of wars and the territorial claims these have entailed (such as Alsace-Lorraine in the Germany-France conflicts from 1870 to 1945). Within-state regional divisions were dampened by the growth, uneven and partial, of redistributive mechanisms associated with the growth of the European welfare state. With the advent of potentially Europe-wide organizations, such as the European Union, the fractures between states have receded somewhat as the ones within states, largely because of the perception that power now flows increasingly from Brussels as the site of the governing European Commission, have become increasingly important.

The third principle is that of geographical networks that tie together regions through hierarchies of cities and their hinterlands. This is most relevant to studies of industrialization, urbanization, and trade. The European settlement hierarchy has long been one of the most important integrative factors in the continent's history. Linking cities and their hinterlands into a network of centers organized by size and specialization, the European urban system has always worked against a singular territorial organization of Europe into national-state territories. Of course, this system has waxed and waned relative to the significance of national boundaries in channeling flows of goods, capital, and people. In the late twentieth century it was once again in ascendancy after a long period of relative subservience to the regulatory activities of Europe's states. Its recognition led to an emphasis on Europe as a set of connected functional regions rather than the tendency of the other principles to highlight the role of adjacency in creating formal regions homogeneous with respect to one or more social characteristic.

The fourth and final principle is that of regional societies that share a wide range of social and cultural characteristics. This fits the needs of those interested in associating social indicators to examine hypotheses about trends in social phenomena such as classes, family types, secularization, and political activities by identifying formal regions. With industrialization and urbanization since the nineteenth century, the more or less settled dimensions of social life, associated pri-

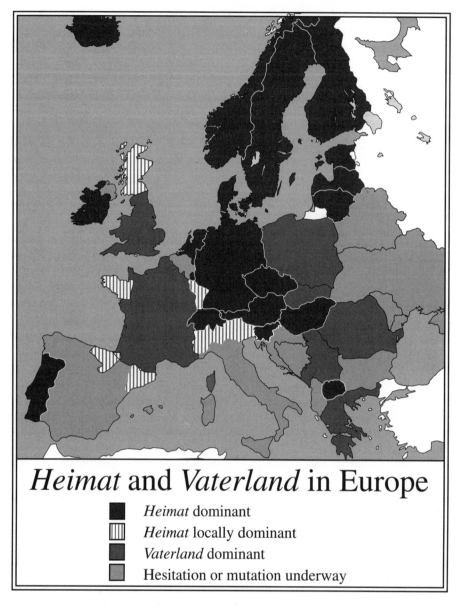

Heimat and *Vaterland* in Europe

- ■ *Heimat* dominant
- ▥ *Heimat* locally dominant
- ■ *Vaterland* dominant
- ■ Hesitation or mutation underway

***Heimat* and *Vaterland* in Europe** The map suggests the complexities associated with the political regionalism of Europe in the late twentieth century. Previous eras would make different classifications, putting Italy and Germany in the 1930s in the *Vaterland* or mutation categories. From Jacques Lévy, *Europe: Une géographie* (Paris: Hachette, 1997), fig. 7, p. 77.

marily with the relative social stability of rural life, have been disrupted in major ways. Initially the growth of the industrial working class was the most significant development. How this happened differed between different subnational regions, the primary geographical scale at which industrialization took place in Europe. Important social trends, also differing regionally, include the relative decline of social class as a marker of identities, the rise of so-called postmaterialist values

(environmentalism and the like), growing secularization, and the development of new social identities as women and immigrant minorities acquire distinctive social imaginations. Above all is the increasing tension between established commitments to larger groups, on the one hand, such as families, occupational groups, or religious sects, and the growth of consumer and personal values that celebrate the choices of the individual, on the other. Given their divergent histories, regions, both sub- and cross-national, can be expected to differ with respect to how they cope with such social change.

Each of the four principles is recognizably related to the existing main categories of the research agenda of European social history. The first focuses mostly on the regional social inheritance from the past whereas the second is concerned with the mutual roles of regions and states in creating social and political identities. The third principle of regionalism identifies the functional regions of European urbanization as lying at the heart of the geographical organization of European economic development, notwithstanding the historically important roles in economic policy conducted by national-state governments. The fourth and final principle is directed at understanding the regional impacts of social change by means of how regions provide the contexts of everyday lives, on the one hand, in which the effects of larger-scale changes are mediated, on the other.

CONCLUSION

The point of thinking about European social history in terms of regions is not to use them, whether supra- or subnational, as a totalizing alternative to the geographical template provided by Europe's national-state boundaries. This is missed by commentators who wrongly think that nations and regions are simply opposite ways of dividing up Europe and, typically, that the former invariably, at least since the nineteenth century, trump the latter (for example, Hobsbawm, 1989). Of course, "nations" are in fact a type of region, albeit of a highly institutionalized variety. Rather, the purpose of regions is to consider the geography of Europe in a more complex way than that usually adopted: the simple coloring in of a map of Europe on the basis of its national boundaries, as in Émile Durkheim's now infamous use of national boundaries to represent a much more variegated pattern of the incidence of suicide. These national boundaries have been both too unstable over the medium term and too unimportant for representing the incidence of a wide range of phenomena (family types and agrarian systems, for example) to justify their dominating the practice of social history.

Regions are themselves obviously contestable. Hence the need to carefully adumbrate the principles upon which a given exercise in regionalizing should rest. That said, the emplacement of social phenomena is inevitably fraught when the phenomena themselves elude placement, as is increasingly the case in a world characterized by flow more than by territorial stasis. Increasingly, "social identities, geographical locations, and national allegiances all tend to be out of sync, at least more so now than in the recent past" (Rafael, 1999, p. 1210). This does not license abandoning regionalism, only attending to the potential dislocations of existing schemes of regions in a world in which a global field of forces is increasingly disrupting the territorial status quo in Europe.

See also other articles in this section.

BIBLIOGRAPHY

Europe As a Region

Foucher, Michel. *Fragments d'Europe: Atlas de l'Europe médiane et orientale.* Paris, 1993.

Hay, Denys. *Europe: The Emergence of an Idea.* New York, 1966.

Kennedy, Paul. *The Rise and Fall of the Great Powers: Economic Change and Military Conflict from 1500 to 2000.* New York, 1987.

Landes, David S. *The Wealth and Poverty of Nations: Why Some Are So Rich and Some So Poor.* New York, 1998.

Lévy, Jacques. *Europe: Une géographie.* Paris, 1997.

Lewis, Martin, and Kären Wigen. *The Myth of Continents: A Critique of Metageography.* Berkeley, Calif., 1997.

Todd, Emmanuel. *L'invention d'Europe.* Paris, 1990.

Wilson, Kevin, Jan van der Dussen et al, eds. *The History of the Idea of Europe.* Rev. ed. London, 1995.

What Are Regions?

Agnew, John A. *Place and Politics: The Geographical Mediation of State and Society.* London, 1987.

Agnew, John A. "Regions on the Mind Does Not Equal Regions of the Mind." *Progress in Human Geography* 23 (1999): 91–96.

Agnew, John A. "Time into Space: The Myth of 'Backward' Italy in Modern Europe." *Time and Society* 5 (1996): 27–45.

Applegate, Celia. "A Europe of Regions: Reflections on the Historiography of Sub-National Places in Modern Times." *American Historical Review* 104 (1999): 1157–1182.

Cartocci, Roberto. *Fra lega e chiesa: L'Italia in cerca di integrazione.* Bologna, Italy, 1994.

Dann, Otto. "La regione: Una cornice elastica per la nuova storia sociale." In *Gli spazi del potere.* Edited by Franco Andreucci and Alessandra Pescarolo. Florence, Italy, 1989. Pages 115–118.

Gupta, Akhil, and James Ferguson, eds. *Culture, Power, and Place: Explorations in Critical Anthropology.* Durham, N.C., 1997.

Hechter, Michael. *Internal Colonialism: The Celtic Fringe in British National Development.* Berkeley, Calif., 1976.

Hohenberg, Paul, and Lynn Hollen Lees. *The Making of Urban Europe, 1000–1994.* Cambridge, Mass., 1995.

Johnston, R. J., J. Hauer, and G. A. Hoekveld, eds. *Regional Geography: Current Developments and Future Prospects.* London, 1990.

Patriarca, Silvana. "Statistical Nation Building and the Consolidation of Regions in Italy." *Social Science History* 18 (1994): 359–376.

Pollard, Sidney. *Peaceful Conquest: The Industrialization of Europe, 1760–1970.* New York, 1981.

Watkins, Susan Cotts. *From Provinces into Nations: Demographic Integration in Western Europe, 1870–1960.* Princeton, N. J., 1991.

Weber, Eugen. *Peasants into Frenchmen: The Modernization of Rural France, 1870–1914.* Stanford, Calif., 1976.

Weitz, Eric D. "The Realms of Identities: A Comment on Class and Politics in Milan." *Social Science History* 19 (1995): 289–294.

Regions in European Social History

Anderson, Perry. *Lineages of the Absolutist State.* London, 1974.

Bagnasco, Arnaldo. *Tre Italie: La probematica territoriale dello sviluppo italiano.* Bologna, Italy, 1977.

Braudel, Fernand. *L'identité de la France.* Paris, 1986. English translation by Siân Reynolds. *The Identity of France.* Vol. 1: *History and Environment.* New York, 1989.

Braudel, Fernand. *La Méditerranée et le monde Méditerranéen à l'époque de Philippe II.* Paris, 1949. English translation by Siân Reynolds. *The Mediterranean and the Mediterranean World in the Age of Philip II.* New York, 1972.

Brustein, William. *The Social Origins of Political Regionalism: France, 1849–1981.* Berkeley, Calif., 1988.

Castelnuovo, Enrico, and Carlo Ginzberg. "Centre and Periphery." In *History of Italian Art.* Vol. 1 Edited by Peter Burke. Cambridge, U.K. 1994. Pages 29–112.

Fox, Edward Whiting. *History in Geographic Perspective: The Other France.* New York, 1971.

Fox-Genovese, Elizabeth, and Eugene D. Genovese. "Social Classes and Class Struggles in Geographic Perspective." In Eugene D. Genovese and Leonard Hochberg, eds. *Geographic Perspectives in History.* Oxford, 1989. Pages 235–255.

Goody, Jack, Joan Thirsk, and E. P. Thompson. *Family and Inheritance: Rural Society in Western Europe.* Cambridge, U.K., 1976.

Graff, Harvey J., ed. *Literacy and Social Development in the West.* Cambridge, U.K., 1981.

Hechter, Michael. *Internal Colonialism: The Celtic Fringe in British National Development.* Berkeley, Calif. 1976.

Herrigel, Gary. *Industrial Constructions: The Sources of German Industrial Power.* New York, 1996.

Hunt, Lynn. "French History in the Last Twenty Years: The Rise and Fall of the *Annales* Paradigm." *Journal of Contemporary History* 21 (1986): 209–224.

Le Bras, Hervé. *L'enfant et la famille dans les pays de l'OCDE.* Paris, 1979.

McNeill, William. *The Shape of European History.* New York, 1974.

Moore, Barrington, Jr. *Social Origins of Dictatorship and Democracy: Lord and Peasant in the Making of the Modern World.* Boston, 1966.

Pollard, Sidney. *Peaceful Conquest: The Industrialization of Europe, 1760-1970.* New York, 1981.

Putnam, Robert. *Making Democracy Work: Civic Traditions in Modern Italy.* Princeton, N.J., 1993.

Rokkan, Stein, and Derek W. Urwin. *Economy, Territory, Identity: Politics of West European Peripheries.* London, 1983.

Sabetti, Filippo. "Path Dependency and Civic Culture: Some Lessons from Italy about Interpreting Social Experiments." *Politics and Society* 24 (1996): 19–44.

Tacke, Charlotte. "The Nation in the Region: National Movements in Germany and France in the Nineteenth Century." In *Nationalism in Europe: Past and Present.* 2 vols. Edited by Justo G. Beramendi, Ramon Maiz, and Xosé M. Nunez. Vol. 2. Santiago de Compostela, Spain, 1994. Pages 658–675.

Tilly, Charles. *Coercion, Capital, and European States, A.D. 990–1992.* Oxford, 1992.

Wallerstein, Immanuel. *The Modern World-System.* Vol. 1: *Capitalist Agriculture and the Origins of the European World-Economy in the Sixteenth Century.* New York, 1974.

Conclusion

Hobsbawm, Eric. "La dimensione statale come fondamento delle articolazioni regionali." In *Gli spazi del potere.* Edited by Franco Andreucci and Alessandro Pescarolo. Florence, Italy, 1989. Pages 230–237.

Rafael, Vicente L. "Regionalism, Area Studies, and the Accidents of Agency." *American Historical Review* 104 (1999): 1208–1220.

BRITAIN

Brian Lewis

NATION BUILDING

Britain was neither a state nor a nation during the Renaissance period, and the histories of the English, the Welsh, and the Scots need to be considered separately. The medieval English state was notable for its precocious cohesion. Monarchs might be insecure tenants of the throne, and rival claimants might do battle for it, as the Norman Conquest of 1066, the Anarchy of Stephen of the mid-twelfth century, and the Wars of the Roses of the fifteenth century amply demonstrated. But once each monarch was firmly ensconced, the ruler's writ traveled to the borders of the kingdom uninterrupted by regional jurisdictions or powerful localist forces. The expanding administration and the monarch's itinerant judges extended across the realm, while counties and boroughs from all parts sent representatives to Parliament to consent to royal taxes.

Linguistic cohesion was also established at an early date. The languages of church and state after the Norman Conquest were French and Latin, but these made little impact on the bulk of the population except for foreign words spicing the vernacular English. Intermarriage, the loss of Normandy in the early thirteenth century, the tendency of the church to use English in prayers and sermons, and a patriotic distaste for all things French during the Hundred Years' War (1337–1453) gradually encouraged the use of English even at the highest levels of society. "Standard English," the English of London and the southeast, owes much to the decision of William Caxton, who introduced the printing press to England around 1476, to print in that dialect. While spoken English remained strikingly diverse, written standard English, the English gloriously embellished by William Shakespeare over a century later and disseminated to the population in the austerely beautiful prose of the King James Bible (1611), has had no real rivals.

Wales was divided politically into three major regions. The principality of Wales, conquered by Edward I of England toward the end of the thirteenth century, was subjected to a substantial measure of English-style administration and was held in check by an impressive series of castles. Some of the great Norman barons established the Marcher lordships along the border with England, and some independent lordships remained, chiefly in the south. Resentment at misgovernment found an outlet in the rebellion led by Owain Glyndwr from 1400, the most formidable manifestation of the chronically troubled relationship between the English crown and the Welsh. Henry VIII sought to overcome the division of powers and jurisdictions by pushing through the Acts of Union between 1536 and 1543. These incorporated the whole of Wales into the English system of government and law, making it barely distinguishable from any of the regions of England. Its towns remained tiny until the nineteenth century. Its population was only 200,000 in 1500; its regional markets were the English towns of Bristol, Shrewsbury, and Chester; and its gentry thoroughly intermarried with the neighboring English gentry. Only one thing marked Wales as a potential nation, its language. By ordering the translation of the Bible and Prayer Book into Welsh in 1563, Elizabeth I helped ensure the survival of the language, and as late as 1800 over 80 percent of the Welsh still used it as their first language. They tended to regard the English, the *saison* (Saxons), as a different people.

Scotland was divided into three main cultures: a Scandinavian fringe in the north and in the Orkney and Shetland Islands; the Gaelic-speaking Highlands of the west, where the clan system predominated and which had close cultural ties with Gaelic Ireland; and the Lowlands of the south and east, the area mostly strongly influenced by the Anglo-Normans. Here the Gaelic language lost out to Scots, a cognate to English that survives in the poetry of Robert Burns. In contrast to Wales, Scotland was an independent state that successfully resisted the attempts by Edward I and Edward II to claim the Scottish crown as the thirteenth turned into the fourteenth century. During the Hundred Years' War and in later Anglo-French confron-

This hurtlesse beast with meeke moode yelds his woll
And kin. to cloth our naked clotte of claye
He giues his flesh to feede our bellies full
Nought for him selfe he bringe but for our staye

June
Cancer

mayd milke cleane

Shepherds. Tending sheep, a drawing from the *Book of Divers Devices,* sixteenth century. BY PERMISSION OF THE FOLGER SHAKESPEARE LIBRARY

standards of northern Italy or the Low Countries. But London, as the funnel for the wool and other trades to the Continent, was an exception, and its leading merchants were already establishing themselves as men of considerable wealth and power. Their role was enhanced by the most important change in the English economy in the late Middle Ages, the development of cloth manufacturing for the domestic and foreign markets. England was emerging as a manufacturing nation. It is worth emphasizing that for many centuries most manufacturing was domestic and rural and that women and children fully participated in it.

Lower down the social scale, demographic shifts proved crucial. The population reached an unsustainable high of maybe 5 million in the early fourteenth century, but the impact of the Black Death (1348–1349) and successive plagues scythed that figure down to a half or less by the 1440s. Such a severe population contraction had its beneficial side for the peasantry in lowered food prices, cheaper rents, and increased wages. Landowners bore the brunt, but the mightier magnates sought to compensate through the pursuit of heiresses, patronage at court, and the profits of war. Certainly the visual evidence of fifteenth-century England—the nobility's fortified houses with a new emphasis on domestic comforts, rebuilt towns and villages with impressive parish churches in the perpendicular style, and the increasing number of peasants' stone houses—suggests a considerable amount of surplus wealth.

The population figures began to recover from the late fifteenth century and surged back to over 5 million by 1640. The rise had been the product above all of younger and more frequent marriages. These were rough years of soaring prices, tumbling wages, underemployment, and land hunger for the common people, many of whom eked out a marginal living through pawning and borrowing, poaching and pilfering, gleaning corn, and reliance on poor relief. The perception and fears of greater lawlessness in the late sixteenth and early seventeenth centuries generated a two-fold response: the construction of "houses of correction" across the country and the codification of the Elizabethan Poor Laws (1598 and 1601), which aimed to prevent the "deserving poor" from starving by a modest redistribution of income through local taxation. More positively for some, population growth stimulated demand and increased available labor, encouraging the expansion of commercialized agriculture to an unusual degree by contemporary standards. Not only did major landowners, capitalistic farmers, and urban mercantile elites prosper during these years, but improved agricultural productivity was sufficient to stave off a recurrence of catastrophic subsistence

tations, the Scottish crown looked to the French to guarantee independence from England, and the English-Scottish border became a subsidiary theater of war. The crown's reliance on the nobility to raise sufficient troops enhanced noble power in parliament, the church, and the boroughs, while the focus on the border allowed Highlanders considerable latitude. The Protestant Reformation in the sixteenth century intertwined with the Anglo-French dynastic struggles, noble ambitions, and stark regional variation in explosive ways. A critical moment came in 1567, when a noble faction forced Mary, Queen of Scots, a French-backed Catholic, to abdicate in favor of her son James VI. He was brought up as a staunch Protestant and succeeded to the English throne in 1603 on the death of the childless Elizabeth I. This was a union of crowns under the House of Stuart, nothing more.

Economically, the island's principal wealth derived from farming, especially the production of wool. Socially, the large landowners—the crown, the church, the monasteries, and above all the lay magnates—predominated. Towns, serving as markets for their rural hinterlands, remained small and unimpressive by the

crises. Plague, pestilence, and famine diminished in intensity in England and Wales during the seventeenth century, again to an unusual extent by the standards of the rest of Europe and even of Scotland, where a substantial number perished in the dearth of 1695–1698.

The Protestant Reformation played out against this socioeconomic backdrop. It was the product of a political compromise in the 1530s to overturn the authority of the pope so Henry VIII could divorce his first wife. The consequent dissolution of the monasteries amounted to a huge land grab by the crown. But Henry and his successors squandered their opportunities, selling off much of the land to pay for continental wars and thus handing a significantly larger share of the ownership of the country to the nobility and gentry. The Reformation did not have broad appeal outside intellectual elites. The Church of England that emerged under Elizabeth was a hybrid of reformed theology and episcopal authority. Its appeal was above all to the literate, and its bibliocentrism helped stimulate literacy in turn. Its godliness and awareness of omnipresent sin rubbed uncomfortably against popular pastimes, rituals, and beliefs, and it required the rest of the century to become firmly established across the country as the common religion of the people. Even then plenty of scope remained for those who preferred a more rigorous set of beliefs or alternative forms of church governance. The tumult of events in the 1640s and 1650s, when parliamentary forces took up arms against Charles I, executed him, and established a republic, gave an opportunity to those English and Scots who favored Presbyterian or Independent forms of godly worship. The breakdown of established authority allowed a voice to a rich profusion of socially modest religious and political radicals, including Quakers, Baptists, Ranters, Levellers, Diggers, Muggletonians, and Fifth Monarchy Men. The Restoration of Charles II in 1660 saw the world turned the right way up again, reestablishing the authority of the gentry and the episcopal Church. The English Revolution's social impact was therefore modest, but it undermined belief in the Church's pretensions to uniformity, ensuring a future significant role for Protestant Dissent. It also left a memory of antiestablishment rhetoric for later radicals to exploit and transform.

GREAT TRANSFORMATION

Between the late seventeenth century and the end of the Napoleonic Wars in 1815 Britain was transformed from a second-rate state on the fringes of European power politics into the leading colonial, economic, and military great power of the age. It achieved this

The Scots' Petition. A Scot presents a petition to a Roundhead (supporter of the English Commonwealth in the 1650s). From "The Humble Petition of Jock of Braid," mid-seventeenth century. MANSELL COLLECTION/TIME PIX

through warfare, mainly against the French, who had a clear advantage on paper in terms of resources and manpower. The British proved more effective at mobilizing the sinews of war, but without a massive increase in direct governmental power and with rights and liberties still comparatively intact, contrary to the typical continental pattern. The Glorious Revolution of 1688, which displaced the Catholic James II in favor of the Protestant William of Orange, locked the country into a struggle against Louis XIV of France. The political nation in Parliament, committed both to the Protestant succession and to bettering the nation's commercial interests by picking off neighbors' colonies, supported an unprecedented level of taxation, the underwriting and servicing of a national debt, and the building of a small but efficient bureaucracy. This parliamentary consent, tempered by a vigorous tradition of "Country" opposition to Court intrigue, was a key means of keeping a check on executive authority. A second critical factor was that Britain's "island moat" and its policy of maritime colonial expansion meant that it could pour its resources into the Royal Navy, "the wooden walls of Old England," and subsidize allies and mercenaries where necessary rather than rely on a large, potentially oppressive standing army.

The ability to mobilize sufficient resources depended on a rise in national prosperity after the Restoration. A traditional interpretation posited a landlord-led "agricultural revolution" from the mid–eighteenth century, in which improved breeds, better crop rotation, and greater field enclosure produced more food with fewer people. This enabled the country to survive the population increase of the late eighteenth century without demographic crisis and also released workers for rural industry and the towns. This fed into a traditional interpretation of an "industrial revolution" from the late eighteenth century, a takeoff into self-sustained growth due to widespread application of steam power in proliferating factories.

Most historians have rejected this chronology. The transition from an agrarian to an industrial world of unimagined wealth for ordinary citizens is not in doubt and is revolutionary by any standards, but the nature and timing of key changes have been controversial. Late-twentieth-century scholars placed more emphasis on the period between 1660 and 1740, when the burgeoning London market demanded and received more and better grains and animal products. These came increasingly from arable regions, where temporary pastures had become the normal way to feed crop, beast, and soil, allowing a virtuous spiral of improvement. Many historians call the expansion of

trade before steam a "commercial revolution." Certainly the rise in real incomes after 1660 stimulated demand both for foreign imports and domestic industry. The Navigation Acts of the 1650s and 1660s, which stipulated that trade with the colonies must be in English ships, rapidly turned the merchant fleet into the largest in Europe and English ports, above all London, into entrepôts for the import, export, and re-export trades. The development of the Atlantic economy and trade with India and the Far East, as Europeans acquired a taste for luxury commodities and the British exported textiles and metalware to the colonies in return, gradually eclipsed the long-standing export leader, textiles to Europe. Many merchants in Liverpool and Bristol made fortunes from the "triangular trade." The first leg took manufactured goods to West Africa to be exchanged for slaves; the second, the notorious and deadly "middle passage," transported the slaves to be sold in the Americas and the West Indies; and the third shipped tobacco, sugar, rum, and molasses back to England.

But the expansion of domestic trade may well have been even more important. Small, permanent shops began to dot the country, competing with fairs, village markets, and itinerant peddlers. The threading of a network of turnpike roads across the island from the late seventeenth century, improvements in river navigations, the construction of canals from the 1750s, and better harbor and dock facilities for coastal shipping reduced transaction costs and gradually integrated the nation's markets. This encouraged regional specialization in handicraft manufacture and the development of a new economic geography, including pottery in Staffordshire, metalware in the West Midlands and South Yorkshire, worsted manufacture in the West Riding of Yorkshire, and toward the end of the eighteenth century, cotton in Lancashire. The growth of towns reflected this vibrant commercial economy, and London's dominance was extraordinary. It had a population of 575,000 in 1700, 10 percent of the people of England. Norwich, the second biggest city, had a mere 30,000. London handled the lion's share of the country's foreign trade, provided an enormous economic stimulus for a market in provisions, services, and manufactured goods, and was the site of the court, the political life, and the fashionable world of the ruling elite. As London's population rocketed to 900,000 by 1800, making it by far the largest city in Europe, other cities had overtaken Norwich and were making inroads. These included the mercantile towns of Bristol, Liverpool, and Newcastle, which supplied coal by sea to London from northeastern mines; Royal Navy dockyard towns, like Portsmouth and Plymouth; and the manufacing towns of Birmingham, Sheffield, Leeds, and Manchester.

Why did Britain undergo such rapid economic change in comparison with the western European continent? Britain's role in colonial trade, based in turn on its advantageous geographical position, was surely an element in its success. So was its relative speed in expanding consumer outlets and expectations in the eighteenth century, which both reflected economic change and promoted further expansion. The British aristocracy was less hostile to trade than its continental counterparts, and the guild system was looser, so that there was less resistance to the adoption of new technologies. The economic position of the lower classes may have deteriorated more markedly than elsewhere, creating a source of unusually cheap labor. Child labor, for instance, was exploited in early industrial Britain to an extent never matched on the continent. There were other factors, environmental and political. Exhaustion of forests made it harder to supply charcoal for traditional metallurgy, promoting the use of coal. Both coal and iron were in abundant supply, and Britain's waterways facilitated access and transport for industry. Limited religious tolerance allowed numerous minority Protestant groups to flourish but denied them political participation, leading them to emphasize business success as an alternative means of advancement. Success in India taught the British the advantages of cotton textiles early on, and Britain soon limited Indian industry to the advantage of its own manufacturing. Through the convergence of these various factors, Britain for a considerable time led the world in economic development.

Throughout the eighteenth century the landed elite—the aristocrats and gentry who owned most of the country—remained socially, economically, and politically preeminent, their income swollen by agricultural improvements, extraction of minerals, and urban expansion on their property. Their extravagant country houses, surrounded by landscaped gardens and parkland, were emphatic declarations of wealth and power, as were the desirable urban areas this amphibious ruling class developed for their town sojourns. But nonlanded wealth was increasingly important as well. The leading London merchants rubbed shoulders with aristocrats and especially their younger sons. Provincial merchants and professional men, especially physicians, barristers, and clergymen, intermarried with the lesser gentry and mingled with them socially in the "polite society" of the assembly rooms and the theaters in the county towns. Lower down, the "middling sort," the master craftsmen in the towns and the yeomen and husbandmen in the countryside, enjoyed a modest if precarious prosperity

in these years and could hope to spend their surplus disposable income on better food or household furnishings. But bankruptcy always lurked close at hand, and solvency often depended on the goodwill of relatives and other creditors.

For those at the bottom of the social pyramid, the relative improvements earlier in the eighteenth century seem to have retreated toward the end. Population expanded rapidly after 1740, as female marriage ages fell again. Adam Smith in *An Inquiry into the Nature and Causes of the Wealth of Nations* (1776), T. R. Malthus in *An Essay on the Principle of Population* (1798), and even later classical economists believed that the economy had almost exhausted its potential for expansion. The landed elite, to maintain their rental incomes, compounded the demographic pressures and consequent immiseration by moving to the piecemeal dismantling of a "moral economy" of communal and customary rights in favor of the freer operation of the "laws" of the market. Local elites throughout the eighteenth century had tolerated the occasional riot and the boisterousness of the crowd at elections, patriotic celebrations, and the rituals of public punishment since this was a way of legitimizing their rule without recourse to wholesale repression. Better that, they argued, than a French-style absolutism or a repetition of Oliver Cromwell's regime of the 1650s, both of which would undermine local elite power. But from the 1770s, as the gap widened between the patricians and the plebeians, the authorities relied more on troops to control rioters, used spies to curb the contagion of revolutionary ideas from France in the 1790s, and clamped greater restrictions on freedom of expression. The space between polite, refined, literate culture and rough, popular, oral culture seemed to increase as well. Only the "vulgar" still believed in witches, magic, and malign forces. A movement of evangelical renewal, which found its first expression in the late 1730s in John Wesley's Methodist movement, targeted not only upper-class self-indulgence and the complacency of the Church of England but also campaigned against popular pastimes, such as drinking, cockfighting, and wife "sales," in favor of prayer, sobriety, and hymn singing.

Whatever the socioeconomic divisions, the constituent parts of the island became more integrated. The Scots joined in a parliamentary union with England in 1707 from a variety of economic, security, and corrupt motives but only on condition that the new Great Britain should be a union, not a unitary state. Scotland would retain its Presbyterian Established Church and its distinctive legal, local government, and educational institutions. Since only a dwindling number, clustered in the western Highlands and islands, still spoke Gaelic, these institutional concessions were important in keeping Scotland distinct. But the overall tendency in the following decades, in spite of persistent hostile caricaturing on both sides, was toward convergence of identity. The defeat of the Jacobite insurrections of 1715 and 1745, when the Catholic, Stuart descendants of James II attempted to reclaim the throne from the Hanoverians by recruiting the support of Catholic and Episcopalian Highland clan chiefs, gave the government the opportunity to begin taming the Highlands by building military roads and dismantling the symbols and substance of the clan system. The persistent wars against the Catholic French helped forge a joint sense of Britishness against a foreign "other." Scottish troops and administrators joined enthusiastically in empire building, and the spread of transportation and market networks aided in the blending of the British nation. The intellectual elites in Edinburgh and Glasgow who led the "Scottish Enlightenment" from the 1760s, people like Smith and the philosopher David Hume, saw themselves as part of the greater entity of Britain and Scottishness as backward and conservative. When the novelist Sir Walter Scott helped invent and popularize a "cult of tartanry" in the early nineteenth century, it was in a safe and sanitized form, devoid of political content. It seemed to suggest that a Scot could be a committed Briton as well as a proud Scot. George IV gave this interpretation the royal imprimatur when he visited Edinburgh in 1822 and wore tartan, kilt, and tights.

SHOCK CITIES

Malthus and the other pessimistic political economists failed to predict the transition from an organic to an inorganic economy. In other words, they did not foresee what would happen once a highly commercialized, market-integrated country turned to coal-fueled steam power. The steam engine, from unpretentious beginnings mostly in the cotton industry, transformed the industrial landscape and introduced railway locomotion in the second quarter of the nineteenth century. Urban populations exploded at a staggering rate as they absorbed surrounding rural labor. The collapse of domestic arable farming from the 1870s accelerated the pace still more. Twenty percent of people lived in urban areas in 1800, and by 1900 it was 80 percent. London ballooned sevenfold to 6.5 million, and in 1900 Britain boasted five out of the ten largest cities in Europe: London, Manchester, Birmingham, Glasgow, and Liverpool.

The dislocating effects of the French Revolutionary and Napoleonic Wars (1793–1815), the rate of population increase, and recurrent economic crises in rural communities, manufacturing villages, and factory towns made the period up to midcentury particularly traumatic. The lower orders hurled a succession of overt and covert, radical and revolutionary, peaceful and violent challenges at employers and governments, who responded by sending in troops and building permanent barracks next to the manufacturing districts. Part of the lower-class anger was economic, for example, the 1811–1812 protests of the Luddites, the framework knitters and handloom weavers who wrecked new machinery to protect their livelihoods. Part of it was political, the beliefs that the old notion of a just price and a fair wage had been demolished by rapacious and corrupt elites supported by a repressive state apparatus and that the only recourse was political reform to get workingmen into Parliament.

Scholars once saw in these repeated encounters the making of a working class whose class consciousness found full expression in the Chartist movement of the 1830s and 1840s, a nationwide campaign for political change based on the six points of the People's Charter. By the late twentieth century few historians set much store by the class interpretation of history, preferring to stress multiple forms of identity and oppression, none of which can automatically or ultimately be reduced to class. Class of course remains important as a category of description, self-understanding, and political mobilization. Some Chartists made use of class terminology of capitalists against workers, but more deployed a language of "productive classes" against "idle aristocrats," of political liberties and "the rights of freeborn Englishmen," reaching back to the rhetoric of the 1790s and even beyond to the English Revolution of the mid-seventeenth century.

The radical threat was one part of the famous "Condition of England" question of the 1830s and 1840s; another was the deterioration of the towns. To keep pace with the influx of migrants and at a time of high land prices and rising building costs in the early decades of the century, speculative builders had hastily crammed shoddy housing into every available space. Observers like Friedrich Engels, a mill owner turned communist, described in horrified detail the wretched dwellings, the overcrowding, the lack of sanitation, and the open-sewer rivers of cities like Manchester. Statistics demonstrated that in a typical cotton mill town like Blackburn, Lancashire, the average working-class life expectancy was under twenty years. Partly because of such woeful figures and the all too visible signs of grime and squalor and partly because of a fear that the masses' festering resentment would break out in revolutionary upheaval, ruling elites, local and national, began to see towns as pressing problems requiring solutions.

The bluntest instrument for dealing with popular unrest was the military. But this was only a temporary expedient, its use infrequent and low-key in comparison with continental Europe and Ireland. Britain had a long history of suspicion of a standing army. The "Peterloo Massacre" of 1819, when the local yeomanry waded into a peaceful crowd in Manchester and killed eleven people, turning them into radical martyrs, showed that its actions could be counterproductive. It was no help at all in dealing with crime. The new vogue for collecting statistics produced figures for lawlessness and larceny that seemed to indicate an alarmingly disorderly society. Sir Robert Peel introduced the Metropolitan Police Force in London in 1829, marking the beginnings of a policed society, a significant step beyond the previous rudimentary assortment of parish constables and night watchmen. Borough police followed in 1835 and county forces in 1839. The police were initially widely unpopular—too much like the French gendarmerie, deemed to be inconsistent with British liberties—and from the start they were unarmed as a sop to libertarian fears. But slowly they established a permanent presence and proved their worth to the propertied majority, threatening the liberty only of the unruly in the streets and those the law held to be criminal. People at the receiving end of policing might seethe with resentment, but it is a remarkable fact that a flattering image of the British police constable—the bobby on the beat, flat-footed and rather slow but resolutely impartial and incorruptible, an honest upholder of the rights and values of decent, respectable citizens—came to be widely admired, almost a national icon.

More thorough policing accompanied new methods of imprisonment, which replaced both transportation to convict colonies and the "Bloody Code," the two hundred hanging crimes on the statute book. Humanely intentioned but chilling experiments with the "separate" and "silent" systems of incarceration, loose interpretations of the "panopticon" model suggested by the utilitarian philosopher Jeremy Bentham, generally failed to reform the inmates, many of whom were less the hardened criminals of middle-class lore than the simply desperate who turned to petty theft as a perfectly logical means of survival. As the initial optimism about rehabilitation waned, hard labor and harsher conditions became the staples of the late-nineteenth-century prison regime.

These were the coercive aspects of the state. Another such feature was the New Poor Law of 1834, which attempted to replace the relatively generous

Nineteenth-Century Housing. A slum in Staithes, Yorkshire, late nineteenth century. MARY EVANS PICTURE LIBRARY

provision of poor relief with a system designed to reduce costs and improve labor discipline. In a more benign fashion, government enquiries into hours worked in factories and into the governance and sanitary states of towns resulted in piecemeal legislation that, in the face of much opposition, began to improve working and health conditions and to increase central oversight of local affairs. Around midcentury most towns began to coordinate their fractured forms of local government and to acquire some of the necessary powers to lay down adequate sewerage systems and provide sufficient potable water; to regulate the construction of the row houses characteristic of late-nineteenth-century England and Wales; and to open municipal parks, town halls, libraries, and market halls in a flowering of civic pride.

Still Britain remained a lightly governed society until the twentieth century, and much of the work of social cohesion depended on other agencies. In response to the demographic boom, the religious denominations launched the last major crusade in British history to reclaim the kingdom for Christ. The Protestant Dissenters led the way, expanding rapidly

The Peterloo Massacre. The yeomanry charges a crowd protesting high food prices and calling for parliamentary reform, 16 August 1819, in St. Peter's Fields, Manchester, England. The attack, likened to the Battle of Waterloo four years before, left eleven dead and about five hundred injured. ©HULTON GETTY/LIAISON AGENCY

with unpretentious chapels to keep pace with the population shifts; the different sects of Unitarians, Quakers, Independents, Presbyterians, Baptists, and Methodists appealed to different social strata. Catholicism found new strength in the 1830s, mainly because of Irish immigration and in spite of the vociferous anti-Catholicism that helped define British national identity. The Church of England was hampered by its inflexible parochial structure, but it too began to reform and launched an energetic church-building spree after 1815. With the spread of churches and chapels came the spread of denominational schools, the primary means by which the bulk of the population learned reading, writing, arithmetic, and the social values of their superiors. This missionary zeal helped postpone the secularization and dechristianization typical of the western European urban experience.

British towns developed a rich associational culture. The middle-class voluntary association was a self-governing organization funded by the subscriptions of its members. Its main function was to mobilize support and resources for collective action, often across divisions of sect and party. Some of these associations were cultural, ranging from literary and philosophical societies to cricket clubs, designed to provide leisure activities for ladies and gentlemen of the middling ranks or to enhance the aesthetic image

of dingy towns. Others were charitable and philanthropic, intended to distribute resources to the "deserving poor" in times of economic distress. Still others, such as mechanics institutes, set out to teach bourgeois morals to the lower ranks of society. The working classes had a vibrant self-help and associational culture of their own in the form of friendly societies, labor unions, and cooperative societies worked out and refined over the protracted period of British industrialization and providing a basic safety net of support to tide individuals and families over the bad times of unemployment and sickness.

All of these state-led, local governmental, and associational initiatives help explain how the British created a relative stability and learned to cope with city growth. For some families, taking an individual approach, the flight to suburbia was the solution to urban ills. The suburb was one of the most notable features of the developing English city. Most continental European cities retained the well-off in their cores in desirable, high-rise apartment buildings. Scottish cities such as Edinburgh, Glasgow, and Aberdeen, which have a strikingly different look from English cities, followed the continental pattern. In England the process of suburbanization began first in London in the early eighteenth century, spread to larger towns by 1800, and increased dramatically from the second half of the nineteenth century with the development of the omnibus, the suburban railway line, and then the car. First the wealthy middle classes then the armies of lower middle classes in the expanding service sector escaped from the city center workplace to detached and semidetached suburban homes with small patches of garden, strung out along winding avenues or crescents.

One of the explanations for the English drive toward suburbanization dwells on a pervasive ideology of domesticity inspired chiefly by evangelical Christianity. Suburbia ideally suited notions of the "naturally" separate spheres of gender with men in the sordid public world of business and politics and women confined to the private, domestic world as "angels of the house." It is clear that the overlap between public and private was greater than moralists would have liked. Nevertheless, women were shut out of the important arenas of power, and respectable middle-class ladies did not work except in charitable endeavors or maybe as writers, safely in the home. The celebrated radical writer Mary Wollstonecraft in the 1790s and the gender-egalitarian commune movement of the 1820s to 1840s inspired by the mill owner Robert Owen challenged this. But the early labor and trade union movement, aware that poorly paid women could undermine male earnings, reinforced the separate-

spheres ideal by campaigning for a decent family wage for the husband so the wife need not work. A number of higher-class women from the mid-nineteenth century fought for and secured important gains, including the greater possibility of escape from an abusive marriage, the right to retain their property within marriage, entry into the medical profession, the establishment of women's colleges of higher education, and in 1918, after a long campaign led by moderate and militant "suffragettes," the right to vote. Britain was one of the sites where organized feminism developed particular strength and importance in the decades around 1900.

WELFARE STATE

While Britain was helping carve up Africa and creating the biggest empire the world had ever seen, it experienced an atmosphere of crisis at home. The mid-Victorian economic boom faltered. Social investigators in the 1880s rediscovered poverty, especially in London, speaking in aghast tones of "darkest England," the cramped courtyards and "rookeries" of the East End, a concentration of 2 million working-class people who were as unknown to the respectable classes

James Keir Hardie. James Keir Hardie (1856–1915), one of the founders of the Scottish Labor Party in 1888 and of the Independent Labor Party in 1893, addresses the Suffragettes Free Speech meeting in Trafalgar Square, London, May 1913. ©HULTON GETTY/LIAISON AGENCY

and as uncivilized as the natives of "darkest Africa." Slum housing seemed to have worsened over vast acres in large cities as more people, often displaced by slum clearance or the construction of buildings and railways elsewhere, crowded into deteriorating housing stock. A gulf grew between the better-off working classes in regular jobs, living in bylaw housing, furnishing their homes moderately well, spending money on soccer matches, the music hall, and a couple of weeks each summer in seaside resorts like Blackpool and Southend, and the physically stunted, badly nourished, casually employed slum dweller. Anxieties about national weakness in an increasingly competitive international climate found expression in fashionable languages of social Darwinism and of racial and sexual degeneration.

One answer to poor living conditions was for the central government to take more vigorous measures. Mindful of the establishment of small socialist parties and of the stirrings of the union-backed Labour Party, which aimed to attract working-class votes on the left, progressive thinkers in the Liberal Party began advocating a more interventionist strategy. Some of their ideas found expression in the famous 1909 and 1911 budgets of David Lloyd George, Liberal chancellor of the exchequer, that introduced old-age pensions and social insurance schemes. In simultaneously attacking unearned, landed wealth, the Liberal measures gave an extra push to the sociopolitical decline of the aristocracy and gentry. Aristocratic social, economic, and political power during the twentieth century remained too substantial for radical tastes, but it was a mere shadow of its former self.

Both world wars boosted the living standards of the poor even at a time of intense rationing because full employment enhanced lower-class purchasing power, thereby improving nutritional intake. Equally significantly, total mobilization during World War I habituated the public to an unprecedented degree of government intervention in social and economic affairs and brought the labor movement into the heart of government. Lloyd George, wartime coalition prime minister, combining his earlier progressivism with wartime state interventionism and a rhetorical appeal to the men fighting in the trenches of Flanders, promised to build "a land fit for heroes."

For many this did not come to pass. The war did serious damage to Britain's place as the top trading nation, and the interwar decades were years of severe contraction for the staples of the British economy, the textile industry, shipbuilding, and coal mining. Persistently high unemployment, exacerbated by the worldwide slump after the Wall Street crash in 1929, had a devastating impact on the old industrial regions

of the country. Nonetheless, beginning in 1919 governments made serious commitments to slum clearance and to building new public, subsidized rental housing for the working classes. This council housing, built by local authorities with subventions from the central government, was largely semidetached, "cottage"-style dwellings on suburban estates, unadorned variations on the middle-class suburban ideal. They were not always well built or easy to maintain and were often far from jobs and amenities. It was difficult to recreate the alleged neighborliness and community values of the old streets. But for many families this generously proportioned public housing with indoor plumbing provided unprecedented amounts of space, light, privacy, and hygiene.

World War II unleashed in government circles a passion for planning. Once again a coalition government coordinated the entire country for total war, with a remarkable degree of efficiency. Civil servants, economists, and academics, in drawing up bold plans for postwar reconstruction and the rebuilding of blitzed cities, were determined not to repeat the failures after 1918 and the misery of high unemployment. After 1945 Clement Attlee's Labour government introduced the sweeping nationalization of public utilities and major industries, the taxpayer-funded National Health Service, and the comprehensive scheme of social insurance "from cradle to grave" advocated in the famous report drawn up in 1942 by a Liberal intellectual, William Beveridge. Subsequent governments, Labour and Conservative, held steady to a commitment to the welfare state, to full employment, to massive defense spending, and to other variations on the interventionist economic-management ideas of John Maynard Keynes.

Rebuilt town centers not only repaired the damage done by the Luftwaffe but also replaced much of the despised legacy of Victorian industrialization with a predominantly concrete landscape of modern, functional, clean, well-lit buildings, shopping precincts, internal road networks, and pedestrian underpasses. Labour and Conservative governments competed with each other in encouraging council housing, which accounted for almost 60 percent of the new housing in Britain between 1945 and 1970, a percentage closer to the Soviet bloc countries of Eastern Europe than to the Western European norm. More local authorities heeded the call of modernist architects to economize on space and to avoid the unsightly errors of the past by building light, airy tower blocks, a significant departure in English architectural history.

The Conservative prime minister Harold Macmillan's statement in a speech in 1957, "Most of our people have never had it so good," was more than political hyperbole. Full employment, a generous social safety net, universal access to health care, and affordable public housing went hand in hand with a consumer spending boom. More working-class families could afford washing machines, televisions, and cars. Teenagers had sufficient disposable income to buy the clothing and records suitable to a succession of exotic youth cultures. This was in retrospect a golden age of capitalism and of social stability. The 1960s added a "permissive moment," a number of liberal social measures, to the picture. The abolition of capital punishment (1965) confirmed a trend toward a more humane criminal justice system. The introduction of the contraceptive pill and the legalization of abortion (1967) gave women much greater reproductive freedom, and with the help of the new feminist movement women advanced significantly toward equality by the end of the century. The decriminalization of sex between consenting men (1967) overturned sixteenth-century statutes against sodomy and an amendment of 1885 that outlawed all homosexual acts. Gays and lesbians made enormous advances over the next three decades in perhaps the most important civil rights crusade of the era, galvanized rather than set back by the AIDS epidemic and backlashes from self-described family-values moralists. Governments rapidly granted independence to most of the colonies, and the arrival after 1948 of sizable black and Asian immigration from the Caribbean, Africa, and the Indian Subcontinent presaged a much more thoroughly multicultural society.

In spite of these advances, all was not well. Economists repeatedly pointed out that the British economy was underperforming in comparison to other advanced economies. Their checklist of reasons for slower growth ranged from the price of sustaining imperial and world-power pretensions to blaming too-powerful trade unions or an antibusiness ethic in elite circles or a too-expensive welfare state. Some on the political left were frustrated that this era of social democracy and public ownership had given little control to ordinary people. Workers had no say in running nationalized industries, and tenants played small roles in decision making regarding their flats and houses. Residual poverty, racial tensions, the rapid decline of some of the new housing, the destruction of much of the architectural legacy of towns, and the alleged inadequacies of new forms of comprehensive state education drew sharp critiques.

The "stop-go" rhythm of the economy, the oscillation between growth spurts, balance of payments crises, and slowdowns, entered a new phase in 1973 with the Middle Eastern oil crisis. The 1970s proved to be a troubled decade of high inflation, rising un-

employment, and repeated confrontations between governments and trade unions, culminating in the "winter of discontent" of 1978–1979, when public sector unions created havoc in their pursuit of higher wages and acted as inadvertent midwives for the Thatcher government. Margaret Thatcher, a self-styled "conviction" politician, abandoned what was left of the postwar consensus. During the next decade the Conservative government sold most of the nationalized industries and public utilities; allowed council tenants to buy their houses in a bid to increase individual responsibility; humbled the trade unions, most spectacularly in the miners' strike of 1984–1985; and attempted to tame public institutions and to roll back public expenditure. The commitment to full employment, already crumbling, vanished during the recession of the early 1980s. The service and white-collar sectors rose rapidly, and U.S. business and policy models exerted strong influence. The jobless totals climbed to over 12 percent, and once again in the older industrial areas of the country a bleakness descended similar to that of the 1930s. For those in secure jobs these were relatively prosperous years of rising real wages, low inflation, and maybe the opportunity to buy a council house at a bargain price along with cheap shares in the formerly nationalized companies. But a growing underclass was left behind. Some of the resulting anger found expression in race riots in the large cities in the early 1980s, some in white, male, racist soccer hooliganism, and some in the larger crime statistics, to which the government's response was more police and prisons, one of the few favored areas of public expenditure.

The United Kingdom was a casualty of these years. Since the onset of industrialization, the Welsh and the Scots had proved adept at reinventing their cultural identities, even as the national economy became more integrated and the original cultural markers, such as the Welsh language, declined. But separatist, nationalist parties made little headway before the 1960s. With many of the symbols of Britishness like the empire being dismembered, the economy on a roller coaster, and the rise of the European Economic Community questioning the notion of national sovereignty, more Scots and Welsh began to question the usefulness of the union with England or at least to suggest a greater degree of self-government. The Thatcher government, in charge in Scotland and Wales but with little support outside England, made a powerful but unintentional case for devolution. The Labour government of Tony Blair introduced a Scottish parliament with strong Scottish endorsement and a Welsh assembly with lukewarm Welsh support in 1999. In many respects the mood of the country was more buoyant, tolerant, and optimistic than in the recent past, and the impact of these far-reaching constitutional changes on English and British national identity remained to be seen. Few as yet seemed unduly worried about how much longer Britain would be a nation or a state.

See also other articles in this section.

BIBLIOGRAPHY

Borsay, Peter, ed. *The Eighteenth-Century Town: A Reader in English Urban History, 1688–1820.* London and New York, 1990.

Brewer, John. *The Sinews of Power: War, Money, and the English State, 1688–1783.* Cambridge, Mass., 1990.

Briggs, Asa. *A Social History of England.* London, 1983.

Cannadine, David. *The Rise and Fall of Class in Britain.* New York, 1999.

Clarke, Peter. *Hope and Glory: Britain 1900–1990.* London, 1996.

Colley, Linda. *Britons: Forging the Nation, 1707–1837.* New Haven, Conn., 1992.

Daunton, M. J. *Progress and Poverty: An Economic and Social History of Britain, 1700–1850.* Oxford, 1995.

Davidoff, Leonore, and Catherine Hall. *Family Fortunes: Men and Women of the English Middle Class, 1780–1850.* Chicago, 1987.

Davies, John. *A History of Wales.* London, 1993.

Devine, T. M. *The Scottish Nation, 1700–2000.* London, 1999.

Devine, T. M., and Rosalind Mitchison, eds. *People and Society in Scotland: A Social History of Modern Scotland.* 3 vols. Edinburgh, 1988–.

Evans, Eric J. *The Forging of the Modern State: Early Industrial Britain, 1783–1870.* 2d ed. London and New York, 1996.

Floud, Roderick. *The People and the British Economy, 1830–1914.* Oxford and New York, 1997.

Gilbert, Alan D. *Religion and Society in Industrial England: Church, Chapel, and Social Change, 1740–1914.* London and New York, 1976.

Harris, José. *Private Lives, Public Spirit: Britain, 1870–1914.* London, 1993.

Hay, Douglas, and Nicholas Rogers. *Eighteenth-Century English Society: Shuttles and Swords.* Oxford and New York, 1997.

Hill, Christopher. *The World Turned Upside Down: Radical Ideas during the English Revolution.* London, 1975.

Holmes, Geoffrey. *The Making of a Great Power: Late Stuart and Early Georgian Britain, 1660–1722.* London and New York, 1993.

Holmes, Geoffrey, and Daniel Szechi. *The Age of Oligarchy: Pre-Industrial Britain, 1722–1783.* London and New York, 1993.

Jenkins, Philip. *A History of Modern Wales, 1536–1990.* London and New York, 1992.

Jones, Gareth Elwyn. *Modern Wales: A Concise History.* 2d ed. Cambridge, U.K., 1994.

Jones, Gareth Stedman. *Languages of Class: Studies in English Working Class History, 1832–1982.* Cambridge, U.K., 1983.

Kearney, Hugh. *The British Isles: A History of Four Nations.* Canto ed. Cambridge, U.K., 1995.

Keen, Maurice. *English Society in the Later Middle Ages, 1348–1500.* London, 1990.

Kent, Susan Kingsley. *Gender and Power in Britain, 1640–1990.* London and New York, 1999.

Langford, Paul. *A Polite and Commercial People: England 1727–1783.* Oxford, 1989.

Lynch, Michael. *Scotland: A New History.* London, 1992.

Marwick, Arthur. *British Society since 1945.* 3d ed. London, 1996.

McCrum, Robert, William Cran, and Robert MacNeil. *The Story of English.* revised ed. London and Boston, 1992.

McKibbin, Ross. *Classes and Cultures: England 1918–1951.* Oxford, 1998.

Morgan, Kenneth O. *The People's Peace: British History, 1945–1989.* Oxford, 1990.

Morgan, Kenneth O., ed. *The Oxford History of Britain.* Oxford and New York, 1993.

Morris, R. J., and Richard Rodger, eds. *The Victorian City: A Reader in British Urban History, 1820–1914.* London and New York, 1993.

O'Brien, Patrick K., and Roland Quinault, eds. *The Industrial Revolution and British Society.* Cambridge, U.K., 1993.

Porter, Roy. *English Society in the Eighteenth Century.* London, 1982.

Porter, Roy. *London: A Social History.* London, 1994.

Prest, Wilfrid. *Albion Ascendant: English History, 1660–1815.* Oxford, 1998.

Robbins, Keith. *The Eclipse of a Great Power: Modern Britain, 1870–1992.* 2d ed. London and New York, 1994.

Rowley, Trevor. *The High Middle Ages, 1200–1550.* London and New York, 1986.

Royle, Edward. *Modern Britain: A Social History, 1750–1997.* 2d ed. London and New York, 1997.

Rule, John. *Albion's People: English Society, 1714–1815.* London and New York, 1992.

Rule, John. *The Vital Century: England's Developing Economy, 1714–1815.* London and New York, 1992.

Sharpe, J. A. *Early Modern England: A Social History, 1550–1760.* 2d ed. London and New York, 1997.

Smith, Alan G. R. *The Emergence of a Nation State: The Commonwealth of England 1529–1660.* London and New York, 1997.

Smout, T. C. *A Century of the Scottish People, 1830–1950.* London, 1986.

Smout, T. C. *A History of the Scottish People, 1560–1830.* Glasgow, Scotland, 1977.

Stevenson, John. *British Society, 1914–45.* London, 1984.

Thomas, Keith. *Religion and the Decline of Magic: Studies in Popular Beliefs in Sixteenth and Seventeenth Century England.* Harmondsworth, U.K., 1973.

Thompson, E. P. *The Making of the English Working Class.* Revised ed. Harmondsworth, U.K., 1968.

Thompson, F. M. L. *The Rise of Respectable Society: A Social History of Victorian Britain, 1830–1900.* London, 1988.

Thompson, F. M. L., ed. *The Cambridge Social History of Britain, 1750–1950.* 3 vols. Cambridge, U.K., 1990.

Thomson, John A. F. *The Transformation of Medieval England, 1370–1529.* London, 1983.

Waller, P. J. *Town, City, and Nation: England, 1850–1914.* Oxford, 1983.

Weeks, Jeffrey. *Sex, Politics, and Society: The Regulation of Sexuality since 1800.* 2d ed. London and New York, 1989.

Wrigley, E. A., and R. S. Schofield. *The Population History of England, 1541–1871: A Reconstruction.* London, 1981.

Youings, Joyce. *Sixteenth-Century England.* Harmondsworth, U.K., 1984.

IRELAND

David W. Miller

Although recent students of modern Irish social history have concentrated on topics which reflect the country's peripheral position vis-à-vis England, their conclusions have highlighted the differences within the Irish experience as often as the contrasts between Ireland and its powerful neighbor. This essay uses spatial differentiation within Ireland to explicate both continuity and change since the Middle Ages.

LAND, SOCIAL STRUCTURE, AND THE STATE

At the end of the Middle Ages Ireland was divided into two zones with different social systems, each dominated by overmighty subjects able to frustrate the ambitions of the centralizing English monarchy. In the south and east of the country much of the English lordship (see map 1) had been organized on the pattern of feudalism since the Norman invasion of the twelfth century, and a small portion of this zone (the "Pale") was actually governed by an English administration based in Dublin. The remainder of the country, including most of the north and west, retained the lineage-based Gaelic social system. That system was distinguished from feudalism by, for example, rules which might allow a number of kinsmen to contend for succession to a chieftaincy and which sometimes provided for periodic redistribution of landholdings. It was better adapted to the lifestyle of transhumance—the seasonal movement of livestock between upland and lowland pastures, which still prevailed in some parts of the Gaelic zone—than to the settled agriculture which underlay classic feudalism.

The differences between the two social systems and the geographic boundary separating them had become blurred by more than three centuries of contact. The distribution on map 1 of sites occupied for at least some part of that period by Anglo-Norman settlers, however, reflects the latter's preference for the well-drained, fertile soils of the south and east over the more oceanic north and west. Some such division

between those two areas remained a feature of the social landscape even after both the systems which it demarcated had disappeared.

Military conquest of Gaelic territory by the Crown was sometimes followed by "surrender and regrant," the process by which a defeated chieftain might surrender the lands under his jurisdiction and receive them back from the Crown as a fief in which his rights and duties as an English-style nobleman would be clearly spelled out. Another mechanism for getting rid of the old order was plantation, the process of inducing English (and, after 1603, Scottish) gentry to settle on confiscated lands with British tenants. Both mechanisms often led to disappointing results, but in one spectacular instance of surrender and regrant the former chieftains inexplicably abandoned their new fiefs, and the government seized upon their default to launch the most ambitious and successful of its plantations. The resulting settlement in Ulster left another enduring mark upon the social landscape, which can be seen in map 2.

When the English state became Protestant in the sixteenth century, the state church in Ireland followed suit, but virtually the entire native-born population, including most members of both the English and Gaelic elites, remained Catholic. As politics in the three kingdoms became increasingly polarized along religious lines, both Gaelic and "Old English" Catholic landowners in Ireland became especially vulnerable to confiscations of their property for disloyalty. The political upheavals throughout the British Isles in 1638–1660 and in 1688–1692 resulted in huge transfers of property to "New English" Protestants. Although in 1641 Catholics still owned about 59 percent of the land, by 1688 their share had been reduced to 22 percent and by 1703 to 14 percent. Except in parts of Ulster, the class division between landlord and tenant corresponded to an ethnoreligious distinction between English Protestant and Irish Catholic. Even in Protestant districts of Ulster, Scottish Presbyterian tenants usually had members of the (Anglican) established church for landlords.

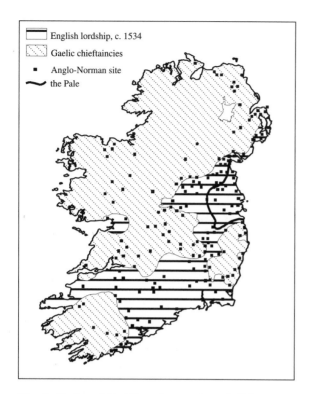

Map 1. Gaelic and English territory at the end of the Middle Ages.

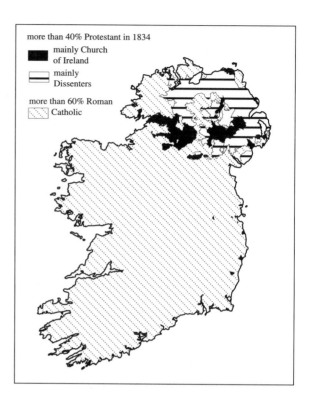

Map 2. The Ulster planation (area of settlement) of the seventeenth century as reflected in a nineteenth-century religious census.

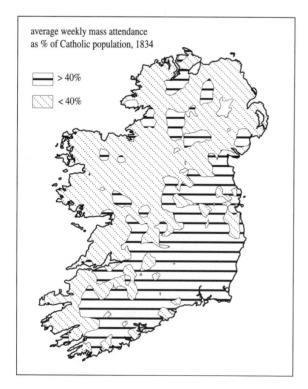

Map 3. Attendance at Mass in 1834.

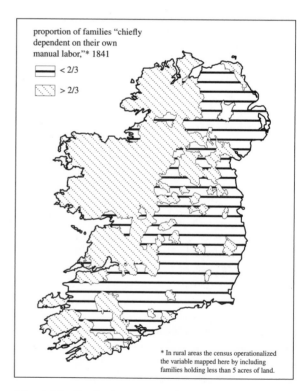

Map 4. The "underclass": proportion of families "chiefly dependent on their own manual labor," 1841.

In the years following the defeat of Jacobite forces in 1691, the "Ascendancy," as the Protestant landed class came to be known, consolidated its position by anti-Catholic legislation in the Irish parliament known as the "Penal Laws." If strictly enforced, the Penal Laws might theoretically have stamped out the Catholic religion entirely. The conversion of the Catholic population, however, was not a serious objective in the enforcement of these laws. Rather, they were used to exclude the Catholic elite from the polity by denying them access to military resources and the franchise and by preventing them from increasing their much-diminished landed property. Students of the period have been impressed by the extent to which members of the Catholic elite managed to retain status and power by husbanding their resources, by winning assistance from well-disposed Protestants (including relatives who had at least nominally converted), and by entering mercantile careers in the major towns.

Whether eighteenth-century Ireland should be treated as an example of colonialism or as a European ancien régime is a subject of debate. Proponents of the colonialism model are impressed by similarities between the dominance of a settler elite in Ireland and power relationships in modern colonialist societies. Certainly the confiscations contributed to the relatively early modernization of agrarian economic rela-

tionships. Nearly everywhere land was owned by landlords under clear modern titles and held by tenants for cash rents. (Indeed, one of the difficulties in making the plantations work as planned had been the willingness of native occupiers to pay higher rents to be left undisturbed than potential immigrants from Britain would offer.) There were relatively few feudal anachronisms left to be swept away in Ireland compared, for example, with the country from which the concept "ancien régime" was borrowed.

Advocates of the ancien régime model, notably S. J. Connolly in *Religion, Law, and Power*, point to evidence of vertical ties of patronage between landlord and tenant despite differences of both religion and ethnicity. Although the decades after 1760 were marked by recurring waves of rural violence, the perpetrators—who adopted such names as Whiteboys and Rightboys—were usually reacting to innovations such as the enclosure of common pasture and were appealing to the landed class to restore their traditional rights. As the use of force by both the rioters and the authorities seems to have been markedly less lethal than in England, one can reasonably speak of a "moral economy" until the 1790s, when, as Thomas Bartlett argues, the panicked response of the governing class to widespread disturbances generally severed reciprocal ties of patronage and deference between Protestant landlords and Catholic tenants.

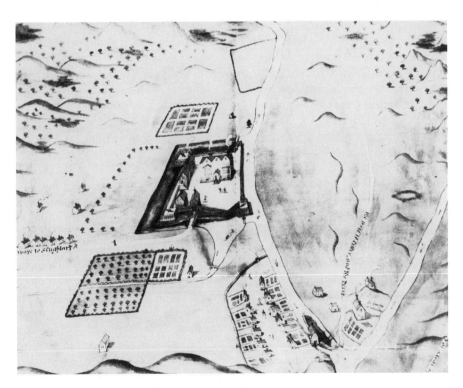

Irish Village. Omagh, county Tyrone, seventeenth century.

Cork. Panorama of Cork in 1750. NATIONAL LIBRARY OF IRELAND

Indeed, during the last two decades of the eighteenth century the exclusion of various nonlanded and/or non-Protestant groups from the Irish polity was being actively challenged. The culmination of these excitements in a 1798 rebellion backed by France persuaded the British government to abolish the separate Irish polity by the Act of Union (1801), which created a new polity with a parliament in London for the entire British Isles. The delay of full membership for respectable Catholics in the new polity until 1829, when they were finally permitted to hold parliamentary seats, no doubt contributed to the rise of Irish nationalism, but ironically the landed Protestant class were the long-term losers from the union. After the famine of the 1840s, the Irish land tenure system was blamed by British elite opinion for many of Ireland's ills, although economic historians now doubt various components of that diagnosis. Irish landlords were unable to prevent a series of land reforms which ultimately made Irish land such an unattractive investment that they welcomed land purchase legislation in 1903 which converted Irish farmers from tenants into owner-occupiers.

The fact that land agitation was closely connected to nationalist politics in the late nineteenth century has tended to obscure stratification and even conflict within the agricultural labor force. Agrarian "outrages," especially common during the decades immediately prior to the famine, were often committed against Catholic farmers by Catholic agricultural laborers. The sharp contraction of this "underclass" from the time of the famine no doubt facilitated the mobilization of farmers in disciplined and effective nationwide agitation for land reform from the late 1870s. The holders of substantial farms—say fifty acres or more—together with Catholic tradesmen in provincial towns emerged as the main political elite which overthrew the old landlord class and dominated the politics of the southern Irish state for more than a generation after its formation in 1922.

SETTLEMENT, POPULATION, AND THE FAMILY

To the extent that the sixteenth- and seventeenth-century shift in land ownership had led to market-oriented agriculture, it tended to promote dispersed settlement in isolated farmsteads with individual tenancy of farms. However, the large-scale Ordnance Survey maps of 1824–1846 reveal that nucleated settlement was common, especially in the area where Gaelic social structures had been dominant in the late Middle Ages (map 1). Early students of these settlement clusters saw them as a direct survival of Gaelic communal practices of tillage and pasturing. Further research suggests that many of the particular settlement clusters extant in the early nineteenth century are postenclosure outcomes of population pressure rather than relics of continuous practice in situ of rundale (a system of joint tenancy under which each landholder cultivates a collection of noncontiguous strips) dating back to medieval times. Such spatial discontinuity, however, may well be consistent with substantial temporal continuity in the mentalities associated with collective agrarian decision making. An important task confronting Irish social historians, as Robert Scally suggests in *The End of Hidden Ireland,* is to tease out the mentalities which this settlement pattern may have sustained in a huge underclass whose creation and destruction were the primary social consequences of modern Ireland's peculiar demographic experience.

Ireland's population rose from perhaps 1 million in the mid-sixteenth century to something over 2 million in the early eighteenth, with especially high rates of growth in the latter part of this period compensating for the devastations of mid-seventeenth-century conflicts. Growth slowed during the second quarter of the eighteenth century, but from mid-century the population increased at extraordinary rates which outpaced even those of England until the decade or so prior to the great famine of the 1840s. Unlike England, however, Ireland experienced far too little industrialization to provide new sources of employment for its increased population. The potato, which had hitherto been used mainly to supplement a cereal diet, could be grown in sufficient quantities on a very small plot of land to meet the caloric requirements of a family. The smallholder might subdivide a modest farm to provide subsistence for several heirs and the more substantial farmer carve out several subtenancies, each consisting of a cottage and a garden, to accommodate agricultural laborers (cotters), all of whom depended for nutrition almost exclusively on the potatoes they could grow. The result was the emergence of an agrarian underclass.

Earlier demographers' reliance on high fertility resulting from extraordinarily low marriage ages to explain the pre-famine rise in population has generally been rejected (though differences in nuptuality between the underclass and better-off farmers remain an important area for investigation). Current explanations rely on relatively low mortality rates made possible by the nutritionally complete, if dull, regimen of a diet composed almost solely of potatoes and dairy products. Mortality was driven even lower by the fact that such a small proportion of the population was subject to the bacteriological hazards of urban life. Until around 1830 rates of emigration remained low among Catholics, though not among Protestants, for whom migration to a frontier was already an option validated by tradition. The slowing of population growth after 1830 raises the possibility that Irish society was beginning to respond to the dysfunctions of rapid population growth unsupported by new sources of employment. Whether a less traumatic transition to a new demographic regime was possible must remain conjectural, however, for the 1845, 1846, and 1848 potato harvests were virtually destroyed by *Phytophthora infestans*. The 1851 census reported a total population of 6,552,385, nearly a 20 percent decline from the 1841 population of 8,175,124, and 2 million fewer than would have occurred if the previous decade's growth rate had continued. Deaths in excess of normal mortality probably totaled about 1 million.

Much famine research has focused on British government policy. In 1838 an Irish Poor Law had been enacted on the model of the new English Poor Law. A board of guardians in each of 130 districts would levy local taxes to support the destitute in workhouses under principles of "less eligibility"—conditions sufficiently severe to ensure that no pauper would prefer workhouse life to the least attractive employment available. The new system failed its first serious test, for when the famine struck the number of starving soon far exceeded the total capacity of all the workhouses. Sir Robert Peel's Conservative government had prepared "outdoor" relief plans before it fell in the summer of 1846. The new Liberal government of Lord John Russell was so wedded to classic liberal ideology reinforced by a providentialist evangelicalism that, despite a second harvest failure, it initially refused to take actions which political economy might condemn as incentives to indolence or as interference with a divinely ordained free market.

Within a few months officials realized that their policy was having catastrophic consequences, and they began to implement outdoor relief and other departures from liberal orthodoxy. It was too late, however, to prevent massive mortality in the terrible winter of 1846–1847. The popular belief that the government had deliberately sought to exterminate the Irish people was generally dismissed, along with many other nationalist verities, by "revisionist" historians beginning in the 1950s. In the 1990s the sesquicentennial observances called forth "postrevisionist" accounts, which document official thinking that certainly seems callous to modern sensibilities. There is no serious challenge to the argument that official policy was wrongheaded. Postrevisionists, however, have failed to persuade many of their colleagues that policymakers were motivated by such malice as would justify the term "genocide" or "holocaust."

The continued decline of population for another century had two principal components. First, emigration became a routine part of Irish life; between 1851 and 1920 an average of more than sixty thousand persons left for overseas destinations each year, in addition to substantial migration to Britain. The fact that males and females went in approximately equal numbers distinguished Irish emigration sharply from the male-dominated emigrant streams of various other European countries. What was left of the underclass after the calamity of the 1840s was steadily depleted by emigration. Second, although age at marriage rose only slowly, the proportion who never married doubled between 1851 and 1911, at which time more than one quarter of those aged 46 to 55 had never been married. In consequence, despite quite high levels of marital fertility, overall birth rates were moderate.

Since urban growth remained sluggish, these two factors—emigration and permanent celibacy—should be understood in the context of the rural economy. Throughout much of the country in the aftermath of the famine, the tiny subsistence holdings of the agrarian underclass were eliminated, farms were consolidated into commercially viable units, and the practice of subdivision was permanently abandoned. In some northern and western areas of marginal ag-

Irish Emigration. *Between Decks on an Emigrant Ship,* engraving by A. B. Houghton, 1870.
THE METROPOLITAN MUSEUM OF ART, HARRIS BRISBANE DICK FUND, 1928

riculture, however, seasonal migration of agricultural laborers to Britain and to more prosperous parts of Ireland enabled some families to retain possession of otherwise unviable holdings and thus resist for a time the trend toward population decline.

Generally the standard of living of country people rose over the two generations after the famine. A demographic regime which had probably governed the behavior of better-off tenants before the famine became the norm for most of rural society. Since the farm was to be maintained intact at all costs, all but one son and probably all but one daughter would typically face a choice between migration and staying at home as an unmarried member of the farm's labor force. Timothy Guinnane, in *The Vanishing Irish,* argues that we should understand the workings of this regime not as a set of inflexible rules but as a framework within which the individual negotiated and made choices in accordance with his or her preferences and personal circumstances. Thus, for example, it could happen that the son favored with succession to the family farm was not the eldest but the one left after more ambitious and adventurous brothers had chosen other alternatives. Even substantial rates of celibacy among those males who did inherit holdings can be explained as rational choices in a culture which construed marriage much less as an opportunity for sexual expression than as an economic transaction. Joanna Bourke documents in *Husbandry to Housewifery* the resourcefulness with which women carved out a distinctive economic role, for example in poultry rearing, within this domestic regime.

TRADE, COMMUNICATION, AND INDUSTRY

In the late Middle Ages, towns were confined mostly to the English lordship. There was an arc of ports around the southern half of the island: Drogheda and Dublin on the east coast facing Britain; New Ross, Waterford, and Cork on the south coast; and Limerick and Galway at the head of great western harbors facing the open Atlantic. As the New World was colonized by Europeans, these towns, several of them Norse foundations from about the tenth century, were well positioned to participate in the resulting long-distance trade.

The existing urban system was less well suited to the commercialization of the countryside. Within the English lordship some local markets did exist, but only in the southeast—where there was one inland town, Kilkenny, comparable to the major ports—was a classic central-place hierarchy beginning to develop. In Gaelic areas most exchange consisted of goods extracted by chieftains from their subjects in return for such services as military protection and redistributive rituals of feasting. To the extent that a chieftain participated in the global market, it was mainly through barter with the occasional captain who sailed into a coastal haven in his territory. The transformation of the Gaelic peasantry from tribute-rendering "freeholders" to rent-paying tenants in a cash economy in consequence of the sixteenth- and seventeenth-century confiscations was an important step toward a fully monetized market economy in the countryside.

Towns were Anglophone islands in a sea of Irish (Gaelic) speakers. There was a significant body of literature in the Irish language; indeed, the old Gaelic social system had well-established roles for the learned classes. Hereditary jurists (*breithiúna,* brehons) arbitrated disputes under Gaelic law. The poets (*filid*) not only sang the praises of their patrons but also had the shamanlike role of issuing curses against enemies. Readers of this volume will be pleased to learn that even historians (*seanchaithe*) enjoyed special status. The literate elite, however, were generally the first to acquire English in a given locality. By the end of the eighteenth century, therefore, only a minuscule number of Irish speakers were literate, even though about half the population still spoke Irish. Most country folk who acquired literacy did so in English, though whether literacy was acquired in the same generation as the spoken language varied according to local conditions. The spread of literacy was greatly accelerated by the establishment of the national education system, which provided state-funded primary education starting in the 1830s, four decades earlier than the comparable innovation in England. The movement to revive the Irish language beginning in the 1890s was primarily composed of townsfolk whose families had been monoglot English speakers for some time.

The erection of a network of planned towns as part of the Ulster plantation not only accelerated commercial development in that region but also provided the marketing infrastructure for protoindustrialization. Partly because of mercantilist legislation to exclude Irish woolens from the English market, a vigorous domestic linen industry developed during the eighteenth century in various parts of Ireland. Only in Ulster, however, did protoindustrialism evolve into successful factory-based industry. A catalyst of this process was the importation of cotton, which began in the late 1770s. Between 1800 and 1830 cotton-spinning mills in Belfast attracted many handloom weavers from the countryside to continue plying their craft in an urban, but still domestic, setting. After 1825, when the invention of the wet-spinning process made machine spinning of linen possible, the Belfast textile industry abandoned cotton for the region's traditional fabric.

In the absence, prior to the 1850s, of a satisfactory power loom to produce the fine linens in which Ulster specialized, weaving continued to be done on handlooms in workers' homes both in the Belfast area and in the countryside. Very low wage rates prevailed and country weavers still spent part of their time cultivating their tiny agricultural holdings. These weavers were nearly as vulnerable as the potato-dependent underclass in other parts of Ireland at the time of the famine of the 1840s. Indeed, a sharp rise in wages, resulting from scarcity of weavers after the calamity, prompted rapid investment in power looms, which completed the transition to factory-based production.

Throughout most of its domestic phase, linen manufacture had been a highly gendered process—women spun and men wove—though a "Rosie the weaver" phenomenon did emerge during the Napoleonic Wars. At least in Belfast itself, most of the linen mill workers were female, but this gender imbalance was complemented by a predominantly male labor force in the engineering and shipbuilding industries, which grew rapidly during the second half of the nineteenth century. Belfast was transformed from a commercial center of about 20,000 in 1800 to the only industrial city in Ireland. By the turn of the century its population (about 350,000) was comparable to that of Dublin and its suburbs, though Dublin remained the commercial and cultural capital of the country even after partition.

Industrial development has been an important priority of the southern Irish state since its formation in the 1920s, but until the 1960s its efforts had disappointing results. Analysts disagree over whether those results were due to structural factors such as the heritage of colonial dependency or to cultural factors reflected, for example, in the antimaterialist values which President Eamon de Valera expounded. Since 1960 the agricultural sector has become relatively less dominant in the overall economy of the state. Some of this change resulted from manufacturing growth, but as in much of Europe, the service sector has grown even faster. Although Dublin and its immediate hinterland has experienced much of the service-driven growth, many new industrial enterprises, in response to government incentives, have located in less developed western districts. A striking feature of the manufacturing labor force is its recruitment of many small farmers who continue part-time agricultural work and retain possession of their holdings as a hedge against job insecurity.

RELIGION, ETHNICITY, AND IDENTITY

In the early Middle Ages the Irish church was notorious for its noncompliance with Roman norms of morality and organization, and indeed a papal commission to redress the situation was the pretext for Henry II's assumption of the title "lord of Ireland" in the twelfth century. Especially within Gaelic territory (map 1) the situation was still quite unsatisfactory in the early sixteenth century. Neglect of sacraments, lack of preaching, and failure even to conduct regular

Linen Workers. A bleach mill. One of twelve prints (1739) relating to the manufacture of linen by William Hincks. VICTORIA & ALBERT MUSEUM, LONDON/ART RESOURCE, NY

religious services were all common. Vocations had decreased and the requirement of clerical celibacy was widely disregarded. At least among the Gaelic elite, Celtic secular marriage—which permitted divorce—was much more common than Christian marriage.

Thus the failure of the new state church to gain the adherence of any significant group living in Ireland in the mid-sixteenth century was not the result of extraordinary Irish devotion to Rome. Indeed, in its early years the Reformation did gain some adherents, at least among those members of the Old English elite who were in contact with government officials. It is clear, however, that by the early seventeenth century the state church had lost whatever opportunity it may have had to convert either the Gaelic or the English elite, not to mention the general population. The established "Church of Ireland" would draw its constituency essentially from New English officials and from the beneficiaries of the land confiscations and the settlers whom they brought with them from England. A third religious system, Presbyterianism, emerged among the Scottish settlers in the north and assumed permanent institutional form after the Restoration.

Outside the elite, three ethnic groups—English, Scottish, and Irish—distinguishable by such factors as speech, diet, and dress, became the constituencies of three religious systems—Anglican, Presbyterian, and Catholic. For most of the eighteenth century each of the three churches was content to

minister to its ethno-religious community and made little serious effort to win converts from the other two. Internally, each of the three religious systems, as Raymond Gillespie argues in *Devoted People,* was shaped by a dialogue between elite theological ideas and popular supernatural beliefs which had evolved to meet the needs of ordinary folk.

To the extent that the resulting syntheses helped validate and sustain popular magical and providentialist beliefs, they contributed to the forms of eighteenth-century collective action. In *Aisling Ghéar* (Bitter Vision), Breandán Ó Buachalla documents the rich messianic, millenarian, and prophetic traditions through which Catholic country folk made sense of their past and future. Such traditions informed the Whiteboys and other agrarian movements which flourished from 1760 as well as, significantly, the Defenders—the rural Catholic component of the rebel coalition of the 1790s. I. R. McBride, in *Scripture Politics,* provides a complementary analysis of the rural Presbyterian mind. He demonstrates how an active expectation of providential action, together with the obvious millennial implications of the downfall of the Catholic Church in revolutionary France, might lead country Presbyterians into alliance with those very Catholics in Ireland whom the Almighty, in his inscrutable wisdom, had invited to lend a hand in laying low the Antichrist.

The excitements of the 1790s could not have risen to the revolutionary level, however, without the leadership which came from critical groups within or at least on the margins of the polity: members of the Belfast Presbyterian elite, certain wealthy Dublin Catholics, and some descendants of the dispossessed Catholic elite (notably in the extreme southeast of Ireland), together with a few radicalized members of the Ascendancy. These elements created the initially reformist but ultimately revolutionary societies of United Irishmen. The abortive nature of the United Irish rebellion in 1798 reflected harsh repression during the preceding year, but the geography of the principal outbreaks is nevertheless significant. Major insurrection under local leadership occurred only in the northeastern and the southeastern corners of the country. In the northeast a sophisticated, enlightened Presbyterian elite successfully mobilized at least some of their country cousins. The rising in the southeast used to be depicted as a spontaneous peasant *jacquerie,* but L. M. Cullen and Kevin Whelan have established that it benefited from crucial leadership by relatively well-off local Catholics. The only important 1798 insurrectionary activity in the Gaelic zone (map 1) occurred not in response to indigenous leadership, but as a result of a belated landing in County Mayo by a small French expeditionary force.

These events of the late eighteenth century are central to all interpretations of identity formation in modern Ireland. In traditional nationalist history the participation of northern Presbyterians on the same side as Catholics in 1798 demonstrated their membership in the Irish nation, and their stubborn refusal in the twentieth century to accept the consequences of their own nationality was treated as a kind of false consciousness induced by the British. Many professional Irish historians in recent decades, in keeping with the view widely held by social scientists that every nationality is a social construction, have doubted the supposed continuity between the "colonial nationalism" of late eighteenth-century Protestants and late nineteenth-century Irish nationalism, which had an almost totally Catholic constituency. These revisionist interpretations are challenged by postrevisionist authors who stress, for example, the "politicization" of elite Catholics concurrently with the flowering of colonial nationalism.

Pre-famine peasants were seen by revisionist authors as identifying more strongly with local communities than with an imagined national community. Postrevisionist accounts have attended to expressions of national consciousness in Gaelic popular literature prior to the nineteenth century and to the politicizing role of the Defenders and of a successor secret society, the Ribbonmen, in the early nineteenth-century countryside. What gave Irish Catholics their standing with respect to nationalism, however, was not rebellion but electoral politics. Although the land question was useful in mobilizing the Catholic electorate for nationalism, the settlement of that question

Religion in Ireland. Donegal parishioners at the dedication of a holy well, c. 1885. PHOTO COURTESY OF MILWAUKEE COUNTY HISTORICAL SOCIETY

did not diminish the remarkable electoral solidarity among Catholics for the claim to national autonomy. Although the political process which led to that outcome is beyond the scope of this article, its social origins are to be found in demographic, class, and religious change.

On the eve of the famine the Catholic Church was still struggling to attain the standard of canonical practice prescribed by the Council of Trent nearly three centuries earlier. As map 3 illustrates, compliance with the requirement of weekly Mass attendance was substantially higher in the area which had been within the English lordship at the end of the Middle Ages than in the north and west. During the nineteenth century Catholic Ireland underwent changes which Emmet Larkin has called a "devotional revolution" and associated with reforms of discipline and devotional practice initiated by Paul Cardinal Cullen between 1850 and 1878. Population decline no doubt facilitated the process, not only by relieving the strain on the church's resources for providing pastoral services, but perhaps also by virtually eliminating the underclass, whose members may well have been the least observant stratum of Catholics (see maps 3 and 4).

From the late nineteenth century until the 1960s there seems to have been virtually universal observance of Tridentine norms within the Catholic ethnoreligious community. In recent decades this pattern has been significantly eroded, to the point where one journalist has entitled a book *Goodbye to Catholic Ireland*—though she was unaware that the "Catholic Ireland" to which her generation has been saying "Goodbye" had said "Hello" only slightly more than a century earlier. As Lawrence Taylor has argued in *Occasions of Faith,* the religious consequences of the devotional revolution are closely intertwined with the consolidation of Irish nationalism as a fundamentally Catholic identity. The direction of any causal arrow which might relate extremely observant Catholicism to nationalism (like that of one which might relate it to the unusual nuptuality patterns of the same period) is difficult to determine. Such relationships, however, were no doubt mediated by the formation of a respectable class of Catholic farmers and townfolk in the wake of the departed underclass.

The obverse of the rise of an essentially Catholic Irish national consciousness (which liberal-minded Protestants were welcome to adopt, but not to challenge) was the development of a Protestant identity which replaced the separate—indeed, mutually hostile—identities of Church of Ireland members and Dissenters which were so evident in the 1790s. The Loyal Orange Order, which now reflects a pan-Protestant identity, originated between 1795 and 1798 in the Anglican zone south of Lough Neagh (map 2). The shift among Presbyterians to emphasis on their Protestantism rather than their Dissent has usually been explained as a reaction to the better-understood rise of nationalism on the Catholic side during the nineteenth century. An explanation grounded in the social realities of the Protestant communities themselves would be more satisfying. In "Irish Presbyterians and the Great Famine" David Miller suggests the beginnings of such an explanation in the transformation of Presbyterianism in the nineteenth century from a communal to a (middle) class church which by mid-century had already lost much of its own underclass of handloom weavers. The origins of the system of ethnoreligious identities so central to the Northern Ireland conflict of the past generation, however, remain poorly understood.

CONCLUSION

Casual observers of Irish affairs often surmise that nothing much ever changes in Irish history. In fact, despite many continuities largely dictated by the country's peripheral position, Irish society has experienced sharp discontinuities in several important domains of social history during the period since the end of the Middle Ages. Will the late twentieth century come to be seen as a new moment of fundamental discontinuity in Irish social history? Certainly the striking and rapid secularization occurring among the Catholic majority will not easily be reversed. But will the end of the devotional regime which began in the nineteenth century erode the nationalism which that regime did so much to foster? Net population decline has ended, but there is still significant emigration, notably among skilled professionals. Nonagricultural employment has been growing briskly, but risk-averse agrarian mentalities continue to shape work patterns. Enthusiasm for the European Union remains high, but whether EU membership will ultimately transform Irish society or lead to a new form of peripherality remains uncertain.

See also other articles in this section.

BIBLIOGRAPHY

Bartlett, Thomas, and Keith Jeffery, eds. *A Military History of Ireland*. Cambridge, U.K., 1996.

Bourke, Joanna. *Husbandry to Housewifery: Women, Economic Change, and Housework in Ireland, 1890–1914*. Oxford, 1993.

Clark, Samuel, and James S. Donnelly Jr., eds. *Irish Peasants: Violence and Political Unrest, 1780–1914*. Madison, Wis., 1983.

Connolly, S. J. *Religion, Law, and Power: The Making of Protestant Ireland, 1660–1760*. Oxford, 1992.

Cullen, L. M. *The Emergence of Modern Ireland, 1600–1900*. London, 1981.

Curtin, Nancy J. *The United Irishmen: Popular Politics in Ulster and Dublin, 1791–1798*. Oxford, 1994

Gillespie, Raymond. *Devoted People: Belief and Religion in Early Modern Ireland*. Manchester, U.K., 1997.

Graham, B. J., and L. J. Proudfoot, eds. *An Historical Geography of Ireland*. London, 1993.

Guinnane, Timothy. *The Vanishing Irish: Households, Migration, and the Rural Economy in Ireland, 1850–1914*. Princeton, N.J., 1997.

Larkin, Emmet. "The Devotional Revolution in Ireland, 1850–75." *American Historical Review* 77 (1972): 625–652.

McBride, I. R. *Scripture Politics: Ulster Presbyterians and Irish Radicalism in the Late Eighteenth Century*. Oxford, 1998.

MacCurtain, Margaret, and Mary O'Dowd, eds. *Women in Early Modern Ireland*. Edinburgh, 1991.

McKernan, Ann. "War, Gender, and Industrial Innovation: Recruiting Women Weavers in Early Nineteenth-Century Ireland." *Journal of Social History* 28 (1994): 109–124.

Miller, David W. "Mass Attendance in Ireland in 1834." In *Piety and Power in Ireland, 1760–1960: Essays in Honour of Emmet Larkin*. Edited by S. J. Brown and D. W. Miller. Belfast, 1999.

Moody, T. W., and F. X. Martin, eds. *The Course of Irish History*. Rev. ed. Boulder, Colo., 1994. Still the best general introduction to Irish history.

Moody, T. W., F. X. Martin, and F. J. Byrne, eds. *A New History of Ireland*. Oxford, 1976–. The standard multivolume reference work. Publication still in progress.

Ó Buachalla, Breandán. *Aisling Ghéar: Na Stíobhartaigh agus an tAos Léinn, 1603–1788*. Dublin, 1996.

Ó Gráda, Cormac. *Ireland: A New Economic History, 1780–1939*. Oxford, 1994.

Scally, Robert James. *The End of Hidden Ireland: Rebellion, Famine, and Emigration*. New York, 1995.

Taylor, Lawrence. *Occasions of Faith: An Anthropology of Irish Catholics*. Philadelphia, 1995.

Vaughan, W. E. *Landlords and Tenants in Mid-Victorian Ireland*. Oxford, 1994.

Whelan, Kevin. *The Tree of Liberty: Radicalism, Catholicism, and the Construction of Irish Identity, 1760–1830*. Notre Dame, Ind., 1996.

FRANCE

Jeremy D. Popkin

From 1500 to 2000 the societies of France and its European neighbors evolved in the same general direction. Populations that had been overwhelmingly composed of peasants dominated by a class of noble landowners became predominantly urban, made up of workers and members of the middle classes. Societies characterized by an elaborate hierarchy were replaced by ones in which all citizens theoretically enjoyed equal rights. France's path to modernity had many unique features, however, of which the most important was the Revolution of 1789, the most sweeping attempt deliberately to change social relations undertaken in any European country up to that time. The Revolution had long-lasting effects on all levels of French society; but, paradoxically, it did not make France a leader in the transition to the social patterns that have come to characterize Europe at the beginning of the twenty-first century. France provided the paradigm case of modern social revolution and yet experienced a slow, evolutionary pattern of social change from 1800 to the mid-twentieth century, a paradox that makes the country's modern social history a challenge to investigation.

FRENCH SOCIAL HISTORY UNDER THE OLD REGIME (1500–1789)

Drawing on documentary sources—parish registers, long series of grain prices, and royal tax and judicial records—unmatched in Europe, the French historians of *Annales* school social history, beginning with Marc Bloch and Lucien Febvre in the 1920s, made this period their special focus. In contrast to social historians inspired by the marxist tradition, the *Annales* scholars deemphasized class conflict and the teleological notion that the history of the early modern period could be summed up as "the transition from feudalism to capitalism." Borrowing freely from other social-science disciplines—demography, geography, economics, and anthropology—the Annalistes tried above all to understand how the population of the

past supported itself without the benefit of modern technology and medicine. Bloch's classic *French Rural History* (1930; English translation, 1966) depicted the farming arrangements of the period, such as the two- and three-field crop rotation systems and collective constraints on individual owners, not as evidence of backwardness but as a coherent system functioning to provide a dependable food supply without exhausting natural resources. Thanks to the *Annales* school historians, a clear picture emerged of the period's remarkably stable demographic system. Its key feature was an unusually late average age of marriage for both men and women: first marriages normally involved partners in their mid- to late twenties. Only at that age were the partners likely to have inherited a farm that would enable them to set up an economically independent household. Coupled with strict regulation of premarital sexuality, late marriage reduced the number of children a woman was likely to bear and thus limited the overall growth of the population. The high infant mortality rates characteristic of premodern societies were an additional drag on population growth.

France's population growth during the Old Regime was also held down by periodic demographic crises. At least once a generation, a major epidemic, famine, or other disaster devastated major parts of the kingdom, creating a dismal peak in the death statistics. The seventeenth century especially was marked by a succession of such catastrophes. In the aftermath of each crisis, marriage rates and birthrates rose above normal levels and the population eventually recovered; but these periodic setbacks ensured that the country's overall population, which was probably around 19 million in the mid-1500s, did not grow steadily thereafter but instead fluctuated with only a slight tendency toward growth until after 1700.

In the early modern period, France was among the largest of European states. Farming patterns, family structures and inheritance systems, dialects, and cultural practices varied from region to region, making generalization risky. Nevertheless, it is clear that by 1500 most French peasants had the legal status of freedmen, able to own and bequeath property and to migrate in search of new opportunities. New patterns of trade and the steadily growing power of the French monarchy fostered the growth of a bourgeois elite, whose richest members, like the court banker Jacques Coeur, had wealth and influence to rival those of the greatest nobles. The social structure of the country was still heavily influenced by the seigneurial system, however. Even free peasants still owed their landlord—usually a noble, though the seigneur might also be the church or a bourgeois from a nearby town— a variety of dues, obligations, and marks of honor that reinforced a sense of hierarchical inequality.

Peasants, nobility, and clergy.

After 1500, French society settled into a fairly stable pattern whose main features would endure until the second half of the eighteenth century. Labeled by the revolutionaries of 1789 *ancien régimen,* it was an overwhelmingly rural and agricultural society: the percentage of the population living in towns of two thousand or more was about 15 percent in 1600, and still under 20 percent in 1750. Peasants lived in village communities of five hundred to fifteen hundred persons. Households typically consisted of nuclear families, although extended-family households were common in some regions of the center and south. French peasants usually owned some land but not enough to support themselves fully. They supplemented the produce of their own plots by leasing additional land from a local seigneur or working as hired laborers. All members of the peasant household contributed to the family economy, although tasks were divided by gender and age. Peasant houses usually had only one room, which served for shelter, indoor work, meals, and sleep. The peasant diet was simple and monotonous, based on bread or gruel made from one or another of the cheaper grain crops—rye, barley, buckwheat, or millet—so as to save the more valuable wheat for sale. Meager as French peasants' existence was, their standard of living was still better than that of villagers in most other regions of Europe.

Most Old Regime peasants' horizons were bounded by their village and its local region. Villagers chose marriage partners from their own community or a neighboring one. Although individual families farmed their own land, the village community dictated crop rotation patterns and set dates for sowing and harvesting. The village council, usually dominated by the wealthier families, allocated taxes and looked after other community concerns. Few peasants received any formal education. The local curé was often the only educated person in the village, and the post-Reformation church accommodated the peas-

antry by translating basic religious texts into their dialects. Those peasants who could read served as cultural intermediaries for their communities, often by reading aloud from almanacs and chapbooks carried by traveling peddlers.

Although peasants formed the majority of France's population under the Old Regime, other groups also played an important part in the country's life. The hereditary nobility was a small minority— some estimates suggest they numbered less than 1 percent of the population—but they loomed large in its affairs. Nobility was in principle a hereditary status characterized by the possession of certain legal privileges, particularly exemption from many of the most important taxes. In practice noble status was almost always accompanied by ownership of a seigneury or landed estate. Not only were seigneurs' landholdings usually considerably larger than those of even wealthy peasants, but they also enjoyed the right to maintain a court, to collect dues and labor services from tenants, and to compel peasants to use the seigneur's oven and mill; they also enjoyed a variety of honorific privileges, such as special seating in church.

In the early modern period, most French nobles were the descendants of commoner families that had enriched themselves and elevated their status over a period of several generations. Starting in the 1500s the French monarchy institutionalized this process through the sale of venal offices; these were administrative and judicial positions whose exercise conferred noble status, either on the purchaser or on his heirs if the post stayed in the family for a specified number of generations. The possibility of buying noble status meant that the group was never a closed caste but instead regularly absorbed the descendants of the most successful and ambitious commoners. This wealthy and educated office-holding *noblesse du robe* (nobility of the robe) often looked down on poorer members of the *noblesse d'épée* (nobility of the sword), whose status depended on military service. During the sixteenth century, and especially during the disorders resulting from the country's long religious civil war (1562–1598), local nobles often exercised considerable autonomy. As the kings of the Bourbon dynasty, established by Henri IV in 1594, consolidated their authority in the course of the seventeenth century, ambitious nobles increasingly realized that the road to individual and family preferment ran through clientage ties with powerful figures at the royal court, and ultimately with the king himself. The court, permanently established at Versailles under Louis XIV, became a magnet for the wealthier and more influential nobles, as well as a center for the propagation of new models of aristocratic behavior.

Peasants, Nobility, and Clergy. French society in the ancien régime comprised three estates: the clergy, the nobility, and the third estate, or everyone else, most of them peasants. "It Won't Last Forever," French print, late eighteenth century. BIBLIOTHÈQUE NATIONALE, PARIS

Like the nobility, the Catholic clergy enjoyed a number of special privileges, including tax exemptions and the right to be judged in special courts. The Protestant Reformation of the sixteenth century had challenged the church's position in French society. Henri IV's Edict of Nantes (1598) granted the Protestant Huguenots the status of a protected minority, but also ended any real threat to Catholic predominance; the gradual implementation in France after 1600 of the reform program laid down earlier by the Council of Trent consolidated the church's position. Parish clergy received better training and tightened their control over the laity's behavior. The period's religious enthusiasm fueled the spread of new religious orders, many of them created by women, such as the Filles de la Charité and the Ursulines. Louis XIV's revocation of the Edict of Nantes in 1685 marked the triumph of this Catholic revival. A substantial number of Huguenots emigrated—the one significant instance of emigration from France during the early modern period—while those who remained were driven into clandestinity.

Urban and rural social structures. France's cities grew slowly during this period. The Paris population reached 400,000 during the reign of Louis XIV, but regional metropolises such as Lyon, Bordeaux, Marseille, and Rouen had fewer than 100,000 inhabitants until the end of the eighteenth century. Cities served as administrative centers for the monarchy and the church, as market and cultural centers, and as homes to specialized artisans and professionals such as lawyers and doctors. The dense crowding of urban habitats and the lack of sanitation facilitated the spread of disease. Death rates in cities were higher than in most rural areas, and city populations were sustained only by a steady flow of immigrants. In France more than in any other European country, the custom of entrusting newborns to wet nurses became widespread, both among artisan families, to whose economy the wife's labor was essential, and among elites, whose female members did not want to be burdened with childrearing. Because wet nurses often neglected their charges, this practice led to very high rates of infant death.

Urban social structures were more complex and hierarchical than those found in rural areas. Urban society was usually dominated by wealthy commoners, especially merchants. In smaller towns, prosperous artisans, organized in guilds, played a significant role. By the early sixteenth century, city governments had usually taken over from the church such functions as providing aid to the poor and running schools. Local elites struggled to maintain their autonomy from the

285

encroaching royal government. Louis XIV perfected a system of exploiting cities by converting municipal positions into venal offices and forcing towns to buy back the right to name their own leaders. At the same time, urban elites imitated the nobility in waging protracted struggles over matters of honor and prestige. Urban leaders spent much time and energy dealing with the poor, who made up the vast majority of every city's population. Below the level of the skilled artisans was a mass of apprentices and journeymen, casual laborers, beggars, criminals, prostitutes, and groups in need of assistance, such as orphans, the aged, the sick, the insane. City governments tried to maintain the authority of guild masters over their workers. Knowing that high food prices provoked disorder, they worried incessantly about supplies and sought to regulate market procedures. They also sought to control and sometimes confine the unemployed, the sick, the insane, and criminals.

Tensions and instability. Social tensions were always present in Old Regime France, and collective violence was no rarity. The religiously inspired violence of the second half of the sixteenth century often had social overtones. Protestantism found a following among some nobles and among artisans and educated elites in urban areas; it was less successful in the countryside, outside of a few specific regions, and among the urban lower classes. The seventeenth century saw a number of important regional uprisings by peasants, who often turned to local seigneurs for leadership. These uprisings were directed primarily against the royal government's relentless drive to collect ever more tax revenue to pay for the wars that marked the reigns of Louis XIII and Louis XIV. These movements were significant signs of the social cost imposed by the growth of the absolutist state, but their impact was limited by their focus on local issues. Considerable social disorder also accompanied the series of revolts against royal authority known as the Fronde (1648–1653), but these movements, too, failed to coalesce into a coherent challenge to the existing social order and collapsed when their elite leaders made peace with the king. The centralized administration developed under Louis XIV and perfected over the course of the eighteenth century was more effective both in preventing conditions from degenerating to the point where revolts were likely and in repressing protests before they could spread.

From 1500 to around 1750, the social system of the French Old Regime thus maintained itself largely intact. The slow pace of technological and economic change and the absence of an alternative to the traditional hierarchical order ruled out any radical alterations. Around the middle of the eighteenth century, changes that undermined this social order began to occur. One of the most significant of these, although contemporaries were only dimly aware of it, was the beginning of a sustained growth in population. By 1740 the population had risen to an unprecedented level of over 24 million; after a brief setback in the following decade, it grew even more rapidly over the next four decades, reaching a figure of about 28 million by 1789. The causes of this marked increase are unclear. Population growth was well under way before any significant changes in agriculture occurred. Changes in medical practices had at best a marginal effect; infant mortality remained high. A shift in climate—the "little ice age," with its many cold, wet summers and bitter winters and a cycle of warmer weather that resulted in good harvests—may have been one factor; the cumulative effect of slight improvements in farming methods, birthing practices, and sanitary arrangements may also have contributed.

The eighteenth-century population increase—which, although substantial, was more gradual than that in other European countries—had important social effects. With more peasants competing for opportunities to farm, landlords were able to raise rents, and the larger number of mouths to feed meant more demand for their marketable surplus. The gulf between rich and poor thus tended to grow. Some developments, however, slowed the growth of discontent. Although fewer peasants had enough land to maintain themselves, the gradual spread of rural manufacturing industries organized on the putting-out system provided many peasant families with a second source of income. Since most of the increased income from agriculture ended up in the hands of urban landowners—nobles and bourgeois—who spent it on fancier homes, additional servants, and other forms of consumption, France's cities absorbed some of the surplus rural population.

The rising tension between rich and poor was one important aspect of the growing instability in eighteenth-century France; changing relations among the country's elites was another. The country's growing economy benefited especially members of the urban bourgeoisie. Merchants in port cities grew rich off the booming colonial trade, which flourished after the end of Louis XIV's wars; manufacturers profited from the growth of the textile industry and other enterprises. As they enriched themselves, members of the bourgeoisie adopted a lifestyle that increasingly resembled that of the privileged nobility. Nobles, for their part, found ways around the traditional restrictions that prevented them from engaging in commerce;

through their investments, they increasingly shared the same economic interests as the bourgeoisie. As the real differences between the two groups diminished, the special privileges that set nobles off from bourgeois commoners came to seem unjustified. The spread of the rationalist ideas of the Enlightenment, adopted both by many nobles who saw themselves as cosmopolitans above petty class prejudices and by educated members of the bourgeoisie, provided an ideological rationale for criticism of traditional social arrangements.

THE FRENCH REVOLUTION, 1789–1815

The social history of the Old Regime poses the question of how a highly inegalitarian society managed to maintain itself intact over a long period. The period of the French Revolution, the broadest social upheaval European society had witnessed in many centuries, raises very different questions: what forces led to the sudden overthrow of the earlier system, and which social groups gained and lost from the new order? The social history of the Revolution, in contrast to that of the Old Regime, was long dominated by scholars working in the marxist tradition, who emphasized the "bourgeois" character of 1789 and the importance of socioeconomic conflicts in determining its outcome. The last two decades of the twentieth century saw a strong revisionist reaction against this social interpretation of the Revolution. Even historians who retained an interest in social history radically redefined its content. Historians of women challenged a definition of the social that ignored gender, and cultural historians looked at forms of symbolic behavior rather than trying to identify distinct social classes.

The social tensions that had been building up in the second half of the eighteenth century exploded when the threat of insolvency forced the king to summon the Estates-General, a representative assembly that had last met in 1614. The Estates-General was traditionally divided into separate chambers for the nobility, clergy, and commoners, or third estate; its convocation immediately posed the question of the privileged orders' special rights. Bourgeois deputies such as the abbé Sieyès called for the elimination of all social privileges that divided the "nation" and the restructuring of the Estates-General as a single body, the National Constituent Assembly. To ensure their triumph over the king and the privileged orders, the deputies needed the support of a popular insurrection. The storming of the Bastille on 14 July 1789 and the subsequent wave of antiseigneurial peasant violence known as the Great Fear guaranteed the Revolution's success.

The National Constituent Assembly now had a unique opportunity to legislate sweeping social changes. Its declared intent was to eliminate all group privileges and all vestiges of the feudal regime, leaving a society composed of equal individuals who would be rewarded on the basis of merit. At the same time, the revolutionaries guaranteed the right of property and accepted the economic inequality that this was bound to perpetuate. In its first, or liberal, phase (1789–1792), the Revolution abolished noble status and the clergy's special privileges, as well as those of guilds, towns, and provinces, and gave minority groups such as Protestants and Jews full rights. Obstacles to market capitalism, such as internal customs barriers and guild restrictions, were wiped out. The 1791 Le Chapelier law forbidding workers' organizations consecrated the triumph of employers. Nobles retained their land, however, and when the church's extensive holdings were put up for sale, the procedures favored wealthy bidders over peasants. The new constitution enacted in 1791 restricted voting rights to wealthier taxpayers. This favoritism toward the wealthy produced a reaction, as the popular classes realized that the new order offered them few tangible benefits. Confronted also with a domestic counter-revolutionary movement and, after April 1792, with a foreign war, the largely bourgeois revolutionaries split. Their more radical, or Jacobin, wing turned to the urban populace.

The most militant members of that group, the famous Parisian sansculottes, a mixture of shopkeepers, artisans, and workers, led the crowd that stormed the royal palace on 10 August 1792, setting off a "second," or "radical," revolution. Their actions forced the summoning of a new assembly, the National Convention, elected on the basis of universal manhood suffrage. Still composed primarily of bourgeois deputies, the Convention nevertheless enacted measures designed to eliminate the last vestiges of class privilege and distribute wealth more widely. It also bowed to popular pressure for drastic action against enemies of the Revolution, resulting in the Reign of Terror. The alliance between the radical bourgeois Jacobins and the popular classes disintegrated as external threats to the new regime receded. Under the leadership of Robespierre, the Convention brought the sansculottes under control. This alienated the Jacobins' poorer supporters, however, and when Robespierre himself was overthrown by more conservative bourgeois politicians on 27 July 1794—in the revolutionary calendar, 9 thermidor, year II—the masses abandoned him. The result was the "thermidorian reaction" and the installation of the Directory, a regime dedicated to the narrow defense of bourgeois interests.

The Revolution. The National Guard attacks the palace of the Tuileries, Paris, 10 August 1792. Painting by Jean Duplessi-Bertaux. CHÂTEAU DE VERSAILLES, FRANCE/GIRAUDON/ART RESOURCE, NY

Social effects. The changes in property distribution and social conditions brought about by the Revolution were less dramatic than its rhetoric suggested, but they were still substantial. Noble families were often surprisingly successful in restoring their landholdings in the years after the Terror, but nobles as a group never regained their privileged status. The Revolution opened many new opportunities to educated commoners, thereby creating a self-conscious bourgeoisie who would never again allow themselves to be reduced to subordinate status and a landowning peasantry that fiercely defended its interests and prevented an English-style enclosure movement. The Revolution did not immediately put France on the road to a modern capitalist industrial economy—in fact, the disorder it caused set economic development back considerably—but revolutionary legal reforms, codified in 1804 in the Napoleonic Code, eliminated restrictions on the use of property inherited from the seigneurial system and cleared the way for further changes in the nineteenth century. By selling off church lands and confiscated noble properties, the Revolution caused a significant redistribution of wealth. The numerous landholding peasants became a distinctive component of France's social structure into the mid-twentieth century.

One of the Revolution's major social effects was a redefinition of gender roles. Men enjoyed many legal advantages over women in the Old Regime, starting with French law's prohibiting a woman from inheriting the throne; but the complex nature of privilege before 1789 allowed some women considerable prerogatives. Noblewomen had greater rights than male commoners', guild masters' widows could inherit and run their enterprises, and some women's guilds did exist. The Revolution's assault on the notion of special privilege raised the question of gender privileges, and some radicals, both female and male, argued that true equality between the sexes was a necessary consequence of the movement's principles. Women participated in revolutionary uprisings, and legislation such as the egalitarian divorce law passed in 1792 gave them increased rights. Other revolutionaries contended, however, that the equality of all males necessarily implied the subordination of all women. In 1793 the National Convention put itself firmly on the side of those who claimed that "nature" militated against any female participation in public affairs. In

288

the Jacobin republic, women were to tend the home and raise patriotic children.

The Napoleonic period (1799–1815) was marked by a return to a more hierarchical social order, particularly with respect to gender. The Napoleonic Code deprived women of the right to own property in their own name and gave full control over the family to its male head. Poorer male citizens lost ground, too. Workers had to carry a *livret*, or work book, and could not change jobs without a favorable report from their previous employer; wealthy men could buy exemption from military service. Napoleon claimed that the Legion of Honor he created in 1802 did not mark a return to aristocracy, since any citizen could theoretically earn admission by outstanding service to the state and membership was not hereditary; but in 1808 he established a new nobility, rewarding his most loyal supporters with titles and landed estates. A highly centralized system of specialized national schools, begun during the revolutionary decade, was consolidated as a mechanism for training an educated elite for state service. The "Napoleonic settlement" guaranteed the land purchases made during the Revolution, but returned unsold noble properties to their original owners. Although he encouraged the growth of some industries, Napoleon still envisaged France as an essentially agricultural society, with the peasantry as the reservoir from which he would fill his army's ranks; the populations of some major cities actually fell during his reign. At the time of Napoleon's final defeat in 1815, it was not yet evident that France was launched on the processes of urbanization and industrialization that were to mark the nineteenth century.

URBANIZATION AND INDUSTRIALIZATION (1815–1968)

The first half of the nineteenth century saw the beginnings of the changes that would eventually transform France from a rural, agricultural society to an urban, industrial one. The rural population peaked in the 1830s; after that date population growth shifted to the cities. New forms of wealth derived from industry and commerce displaced landownership. Compared with most other European countries, France experienced these changes slowly: on the eve of the 1914 war, 40 percent of the population still lived in the countryside, versus 6 percent in England. Thus it may be misleading to talk about an "industrial revolution" in France. Historians have actively discussed causes for the French lag, ranging from resource disadvantages (in coal, for example) to a conservative business culture to the slow population growth, which limited

consumer demand and the available labor force. But change did occur, as even artisanal sectors became more commercial. And by the 1830s and 1840s, the introduction of power-driven machinery and the building of the first French railroads were making an impact. There was an acute consciousness that the country faced a critical "social problem" in its major cities. Middle-class writers described the poverty, overcrowding, disease, and social breakdown that characterized slum neighborhoods in Paris and in provincial manufacturing centers such as Lille and Lyon. Early socialist theorists—Henri de Saint-Simon and his followers, Charles Fourier, Étienne Cabet, and Louis Blanc—identified capitalism and individualism as the causes of these ills and offered various prescriptions for healing them. The Saint-Simonians were especially sensitive to the fact that the growth of industry depended heavily on the exploitation of female labor, and that overcoming the challenges of modernity required reexamining established gender roles.

In 1830, after several years of economic distress and political confrontation, opposition to the conservative Restoration regime set up after Napoleon's defeat boiled over into another revolution. Although the urban crowd played a major role in the insurrection, rural protests were minor compared with those in 1789, and middle-class liberals were able to keep control of the country's institutions. Proclaimed as a "citizen king," Louis-Philippe, duc d'Orléans, a relative of the deposed Restoration king, took the throne. His period of rule, from 1830 to 1848, was categorized even at the time as a "bourgeois monarchy." This reflected in part the king's deliberate policy of adopting the lifestyle of a wealthy bourgeois in contrast with his predecessors' efforts to revive aristocratic court practices. The label also reflected, however, the sense that the new regime was dominated by bourgeois interests. The right to vote was extended, giving more members of the middle classes a voice, and government policies such as subsidies for railroads promoted industrialization.

The bourgeois social order that took shape after 1830 was often depicted, in the novels of Honoré de Balzac and Gustave Flaubert and the biting caricatures by the artist Honoré Daumier, as one in which money was the measure of all things. In fact the French bourgeoisie also put a high value on honor and reputation, sometimes adopting what had been aristocratic practices, such as dueling. One hallmark of bourgeois life was the withdrawal of women from economic activities. Although working-class and peasant women had to contribute directly to family income, the bourgeois "lady" increasingly restricted herself to the household, overseeing servants who did the actual domestic chores.

The bourgeois July Monarchy initiated public elementary schooling for boys, but religiously inspired conservatism prevented the creation of public schools for girls until the early 1880s. Secondary education remained a privilege of the wealthy; the school system was one of the main means by which France's bourgeois social hierarchy perpetuated itself.

Although a social order dominated by bourgeois values was firmly in place after 1830, political stability remained elusive. A severe economic crisis in 1845–1847 alienated much of the population from Louis-Philippe's regime, which was overthrown in February 1848. As in 1830, the Paris crowd played the leading role in the movement, and the provisional government that took power made important gestures to the working classes, including the creation of the Luxembourg Commission to hold public hearings on their problems. The February revolution set off an unprecedented outburst of popular demonstrations and political activity; socialist and feminist groups actively spread radical ideas. The entire male population was allowed to vote in elections for a constituent assembly. Peasant voters generally backed conservative candidates, however, and the Assembly took a confrontational attitude toward urban workers. The result was the bloody June Days uprising in 1848 in the working-class neighborhoods of Paris, put down at a cost of perhaps some two thousand lives. Its defeat strengthened the conservatives' hold on the assembly, which later passed the Falloux law allowing religious education in public schools for the first time and an electoral law disenfranchising much of the urban population.

The Assembly's conservatism worked in favor of the country's elected president, Napoleon I's nephew Louis-Napoleon Bonaparte, who ousted the deputies in December 1851 and restored the Napoleonic empire in 1852. Resistance to his takeover in parts of rural southern France showed that the brief republican interlude had convinced many members of the lower classes that they deserved political rights. Taking the title Napoleon III, the new ruler initially followed a conservative social policy. His regime benefited from a renewed surge of industrial activity in the 1850s; general prosperity and an authoritarian police quelled unrest. As economic growth slowed in the 1860s, however, social protest resurfaced. Napoleon III sought to broaden the base of his regime by making some concessions to the labor movement. Self-proclaimed working-class candidates ran in Paris municipal elections in 1864, and unions were legalized. The period also saw an important resurgence of feminist activity. Napoleon III's faith that rational social engineering, firmly directed from above, could produce improved living conditions for all classes was exemplified by the remodeling of Paris under Baron Georges Haussmann, prefect of the Seine. Slum neighborhoods were cleared away, modern water and sewer systems built, and broad new boulevards eased traffic problems. As a result, however, the city's poor were increasingly forced out to the suburbs: the elegant new spaces of the city center were largely reserved for the well-to-do.

That social tensions still ran high became obvious when Napoleon III's regime collapsed after defeat by Bismarck's Prussia in 1870. In March 1871 the Parisians revolted against the conservative assembly that had replaced the emperor. They set up a directly elected council, the Commune. During the two months of its existence, the Commune launched numerous social experiments. Women played a major role in the movement. Conservative reaction against the Paris "reds" was violent. Some 20,000 to 25,000 were killed when government troops retook the capital in the "bloody week" of fighting in May 1871. The Commune uprising generated long-lasting myths on both sides: to bourgeois conservatives, it showed the danger from the unruly masses; to workers, it demonstrated the possessing classes' implacable enmity. Ironically, however, the real victors after 1871 proved to be the moderate republican representatives of France's middle classes. Led by Leon Gambetta, the republicans appealed to the "new social strata," the lower middle class and a now republicanized peasantry. These groups became the social basis of the Third Republic (1875–1940). This regime proved remarkably stable, suggesting that it satisfied the wishes of a strong majority of the population that wanted a regime respectful of property but willing to take some steps to benefit the poor.

The Third Republic. With the consolidation of the Third Republic's institutions in the early 1880s, the social program elaborated in 1789 seemed at last to have been accomplished. The new regime guaranteed the civil equality of all male citizens, provided a uniform (but gender-specific) elementary education for all children, and protected property and order. The century between the French Revolution and the definitive installation of the republic had seen important social changes, however. The industrial working class's place in French society remained a controversial issue. An 1884 law legalized strikes, and a general trade union federation, the Confédération Générale du Travail (CGT), was created in 1895. The socialist movement, damaged by the defeat of 1871, recovered in the 1880s and attracted the support of many workers; working-class families also provided the base for a flourishing network of consumer cooperatives. French

290

The Second Empire. Prosperous Parisians promenade on the Avenue de l'Impératrice (today the Avenue Foch), c. 1865.
© LL-VIOLLET

socialism was weakened by its division into several competing parties, but all expressed workers' dissatisfaction with a society in which they remained largely marginalized. The growth of large industry and of new forms of commerce, such as department stores, put pressure on artisans and shopkeepers, who looked to the government for protection. As in other European countries, a "new middle class" of salaried clerks, teachers, and professionals developed; some of them embraced trade unionism to defend their interests.

The place of women in French society was another major social issue in the Third Republic. Women were still denied voting rights, but their civil rights expanded. Divorce, banned since 1816, was legalized in 1884, and single women gained control of their own income and property. By the 1880s France had become the first country to experience the demographic transition to low birthrates. Fearing that a stagnant population endangered the country's future, even social conservatives supported "maternalist" welfare measures designed to encourage women to have children and to improve the health of the babies they

did have. France was thus in some respects a pioneer in the development of the modern welfare state. The low birthrate meant a demand for labor that gave France the highest rate of female participation in the labor force of any industrialized country. Partly as a result, the country was also in the lead in providing daycare through a system of public nursery schools (*écoles maternelles*) founded in 1886. The late nineteenth century also saw the beginnings of women's entry into the educated professions. In 1870 a medical degree was granted to a woman for the first time. The creation of public schools for girls in the 1880s created a demand for trained schoolteachers, and women were also hired as inspectors under many of the welfare laws created during the period. The emergence of these "new women" provoked a vocal conservative backlash, and many women themselves, particularly those loyal to the Catholic Church, denounced these developments.

The world wars. In France, as in all combatant countries, World War I caused profound social

291

changes. Because of the country's low birthrate, the staggering casualties—1.3 million men—had a lasting effect on its demographic structure, leaving a population disproportionately elderly and female. The needs of war production dramatized industrial workers' role in the country and gave them an increased sense of their importance. Inflation devalued the savings and investments that undergirded middle-class families' status. Women moved into many jobs that had formerly been reserved for men, causing further tension over gender roles; but France did not follow Britain, the United States, and Germany in giving women the vote. A conservative backlash followed the war, marked by a law banning contraceptives. Immigration, already significant before the war, continued afterward as employers and the government systematically recruited workers from Poland and Italy to fill the ranks of the country's depleted labor force. French industries followed American models in rationalizing their workplaces and trying to establish paternalist discipline over employees, whose militance diminished after the defeat of a widespread wave of strikes in 1919–1920. Industrial workers' living conditions continued to be worse than those of other population groups, especially in the desolate suburbs of Paris's "red belt" of communist-dominated suburbs and other urban areas.

Compared with more industrialized countries, France was not hit as hard by the world economic depression that started in 1929; but its effects were still significant. Together with fear of fascism, protest against economic conditions fueled a mass movement that swept the Popular Front coalition of Socialist, Communist, and middle-class Radical parties to power in 1936. Immediately after the elections, workers staged the largest wave of strikes the country had ever experienced, occupying factories to demand better pay and working conditions. The most long-lasting of the Popular Front's responses was France's first law on paid vacations, generalizing to the entire population what had been a bourgeois privilege. The Popular Front era allowed the Communist Party to implant itself solidly in working-class neighborhoods. The reunification of the French union movement in 1936 extended Communist influence. The party would dominate French labor politics until the 1970s. Some middle-class groups responded to the surge of left-wing radicalism in the 1930s by backing France's numerous quasi-fascist movements.

The military defeat of 1940 ended the Third Republic and brought to power the Vichy government of the authoritarian, conservative World War I hero Philippe Pétain. Under Pétain's aegis, conservative and fascist ideologues tried to remodel French society, often in contradictory ways. Vichy glorified the peasant and artisan traditions of the past but also accelerated industrial modernization to meet the production demands of the occupying Germans. Vichy propaganda talked of replacing the unregulated capitalist economy and its conflicts with a corporatist system, but the organizations it created heavily favored employers. Vichy's paternalist tendencies led to the continuation of prewar trends toward a more comprehensive welfare state: it was Pétain's government that implemented the system of family allowances passed just before the war. Hostility to foreign immigrants, already heightened by the depression, played a role in Vichy's decision to pass anti-Semitic legislation and to turn many of France's Jewish residents over to the Germans.

Opposition to Vichy and the Germans grew steadily as the war progressed. Discredited in 1939 by its support for the Hitler-Stalin Pact, the Communist Party recovered once the Germans invaded Russia in 1941; its working-class base became a stronghold of resistance. Other resistance movements brought together trade unionists, intellectuals, feminist activists, Catholics, and a cross-section of patriots from other social groups. From exile, General Charles de Gaulle established himself as the leader of this opposition, but the government he established at the moment of the Liberation in 1944 had a strong left-wing slant. The constitution of the new Fourth Republic, adopted in 1946, included a long list of social rights that laid the basis for a comprehensive welfare state, embodied in the creation of a comprehensive social security system. Although the Communist Party was ousted from the post-Liberation government in 1947, its strong support among workers, especially those in the greatly expanded government-owned sector of the economy, gave it considerable influence. World War II did not cause as many changes in the position of women as had the previous war, but they finally received the right to vote in 1944.

Postwar developments. Economic reconstruction was high on the national agenda after the war, spurred by a centralized planning system and by generous American aid. France's version of the baby boom, evident in statistics as early as 1942, continued into the early 1960s and also stimulated growth. During the "thirty glorious years" from 1945 to the early 1970s, France became a consumer society. Urban centers grew rapidly; the more technocratic government of the Fifth Republic, established in 1958, deliberately encouraged the conversion of small farms into more efficient units and a shift of population from country to city. Increasing prosperity did not end social ten-

Les Événements de Mai 1968. Members of the Confédération Générale du Travail (trade union) demonstrate in Paris, May 1968. MARC RIBOUD/MAGNUM PHOTOS

sions, however. Workers continued to feel excluded from French society, and the large cohorts of young people born after the war chafed at its rigidity and conservatism. The marked decline in birthrates that followed the introduction of the birth control pill in 1965 was a sign of a widespread shift in social values. Even more spectacular were *les événements de mai* (the events of May) in 1968, a nationwide wave of strikes by students and workers that completely paralyzed the country. Although this movement did not result in any institutional changes, it profoundly changed the social climate. After 1968 France would become more individualistic, more concerned with consumption than production, and less respectful of hierarchical authority structures.

In retrospect it also became clear that 1968 marked France's move into the era of postindustrial society. The 39 percent of the workforce employed in industry that year was an all-time high. The international economic slowdown that began in the early 1970s hit the country's traditional heavy industries hard and led to a decline of the classic factory proletariat that had been the basis for Communist support. Unemployment, almost unknown during the postwar decades, became a major issue, remaining above 10 percent from the early 1980s to the end of the century. The economic slowdown of the 1970s, like the Great Depression of the 1930s, led voters to turn to the left. The Socialist François Mitterrand, elected as the country's president in 1981, initially took measures

similar to those put through by the Popular Front and the Liberation. The minimum wage was raised sharply, workers' rights were increased, and the government promised a break with the world capitalist system. When this policy proved impossible to reconcile with France's increasing integration into the European Community and the world economy, however, Mitterrand changed course. His subsequent policies, often damned by critics as neoliberal, reduced inflation and favored economic growth, but at the cost of high unemployment and the disappearance of many traditional industries.

The most prosperous sectors of the workforce in France, as elsewhere in the developed world, became those in white-collar managerial and bureaucratic jobs, the educated cadres whose consumer-oriented lifestyle has increasingly become the country's social model. Women have succeeded in moving into this group, but only with difficulty; France has lagged behind other industrialized countries on gender issues. Another social problem highlighted once economic growth slowed was the increasing population of non-European immigrants, often from France's former colonies. Many immigrants successfully assimilated into French society, but the poorest found themselves confined to ghettos in the suburbs of large cities, where riots have broke out on several occasions after 1980. As unemployment rose, so did resentment against these groups, particularly those from North Africa; in elections in the late 1980s and 1990s, the vociferously anti-immigrant National Front party regularly claimed up to 15 percent of the vote.

French society at the turn of the century has increasingly come to resemble those of the other nations of western Europe. Like them, France came to be characterized by a very low birthrate, an aging population, a high average per capita income, and an overwhelmingly urban society. The rising costs of France's extensive welfare system have posed major problems, as have the integration of postcolonial immigrants and the achievement of greater equality for women. Some traditional social problems have persisted: neither poverty nor substantial inequality between social groups has been banished from French life. Nevertheless, France's problems can unmistakably be seen as those of a prosperous society protected from the hunger and disease that dominated its life in earlier eras. France's history shows that there has been more than one route to modernity in western Europe. Increasingly ready to merge into a larger European community, the French can take pride especially in having been the first to articulate the principles of individual freedom and social equality that have become the bases of modern European social life.

See also other articles in this section.

BIBLIOGRAPHY

The literature on modern French social history is so extensive that a short bibliography can provide only a suggestion of the richness of the literature and the multiplicity of approaches the subject has inspired.

Synthetic Overviews

Braudel, Fernand, and Ernest Labrousse, eds. *Histoire économique et sociale de la France.* Paris, 1970–1982. A comprehensive survey of the country's social and economic development.

Duby, Georges, and Armand Wallon, eds. *Histoire de la France rurale.* Paris, 1975–1976.

Dupâquier, Jacques, ed. *Histoire de la population française.* Paris, 1988. Stresses demographic developments.

Specialized Monographs

Auslander, Leora. *Taste and Power: Furnishing Modern France.* Berkeley, 1996. An example of newer cultural-history approaches to social history.

Becker, Jean-Jacques. *The Great War and the French People.* Translated by Arnold Pomerans. New York, 1986.

Bloch, Marc. *French Rural History: An Essay on Its Basic Characteristics.* Translated by Janet Sondheimer. Berkeley, 1966. Classic founding text of the *Annales* social-history tradition.

Burrin, Philippe. *France under the Germans: Collaboration and Compromise.* Translated by Janet Lloyd. New York, 1996. Summary of research on the Vichy period.

Evenson, Norma. *Paris: A Century of Change, 1878–1978.* New Haven, Conn., 1979.

Gaspard, Françoise. *A Small City in France.* Translated by Arthur Goldhammer. Cambridge, Mass., 1995. Case study of tensions caused by non-European immigration in late-twentieth-century France.

Godineau, Dominique. *The Women of Paris and Their French Revolution.* Translated by Katherine Streip. Berkeley, 1998. Women's revolutionary experience from a social-history perspective.

Goubert, Pierre. *The French Peasantry in the Seventeenth Century.* Translated by Ian Patterson. Cambridge, U.K., and New York, 1986.

Guillaumin, Emile. *The Life of a Simple Man.* Translated by Margaret Crosland. Edited by Eugen Weber. Hanover, N.H., 1983. Invaluable first-person account of nineteenth-century rural life.

Jackson, Julian. *The Popular Front in France: Defending Democracy, 1934–38.* Cambridge, U.K., and New York, 1988. The great social movement of the 1930s.

Liu, Tessie P. *The Weaver's Knot: The Contradictions of Class Struggle and Family Solidary in Western France, 1750–1914.* Ithaca, N.Y., 1994. A regional study of industrialization, offering an exemplary combination of economic and women's history.

Markoff, John. *The Abolition of Feudalism: Peasants, Lords, and Legislators in the French Revolution.* University Park, Penn., 1996. Exhaustive quantitative study of rural protest in the French revolutionary era.

Ménétra, Jacques-Louis. *Journal of My Life.* Translated by Arthur Goldhammer. With commentary by Daniel Roche. New York, 1986. A unique first-person account of an eighteenth-century historian's life, with a leading historian's commentary.

Merriman, John. *The Red City: Limoges and the French Nineteenth Century.* New York, 1985. A fascinating study of change in this city.

Miller, Michael B. *The Bon Marché: Bourgeois Culture and the Department Store, 1869–1920.* Princeton, N.J., 1981. The rise of a new commercial culture and its social effects.

Noiriel, Gérard. *Workers in French Society in the 19th and 20th Centuries.* Translated by Helen McPhail. New York, 1990.

Rudé, George. *The Crowd in the French Revolution.* Oxford, 1959. A monument of modern social history.

Sewell, William H., Jr. *Work and Revolution in France: The Language of Labor from the Old Regime to 1848.* Cambridge, U.K., and New York, 1980. Traces continuities and changes in working-class culture.

Smith, Bonnie G. *Ladies of the Leisure Class: The Bourgeoises of Northern France in the Nineteenth Century.* Princeton, N.J., 1981.

Wylie, Laurence. *Village in the Vaucluse.* 3d ed. Cambridge, Mass., 1974. Classic anthropological study of small-town life in mid-century France.

THE LOW COUNTRIES

W. P. Blockmans

THE POLITICAL AND GEOGRAPHICAL FRAMEWORK

During the fifteenth and sixteenth centuries the Low Countries were gradually united into a dynastic union. In 1548–1549, Emperor Charles V secured the autonomy of the so-called Seventeen Provinces as the Burgundian Circle within the Holy Roman Empire. Only his son Philip II profited from the concession that this union should remain under one ruler, because the Dutch Revolt, which started in 1566, led to a definitive split between the northern and southern Netherlands—roughly, present-day Netherlands and Belgium—formalized in the Treaty of Westphalia in 1648. However, the principalities that constituted the former Seventeen Provinces cherished their centuries-old institutional traditions and identities. Two of them, the counties of Flanders and Artois, had belonged to the kingdom of France until 1529, while the others had formed part of the Holy Roman Empire. Neither of these sovereign powers had been able to impose its authority effectively on this peripheral and relatively prosperous region. Until the end of the eighteenth century, regional autonomies prevailed over the sovereignty of the Dutch Republic in the north, and of the Habsburg dynasty in the south. After the revolutionary movements of the 1780s and the French occupation, the Congress of Vienna in 1815 created the kingdom of the Netherlands, reuniting most of the territory of the former Seventeen Provinces, with Artois and parts of Flanders lost to France but including the previously independent prince-bishopric of Liège. The Belgian Revolution of 1830 divided the region again, forming the kingdom of Belgium, formally recognized in 1839. In the opinion of Belgian historians, the very progressive, liberal character of the new Belgian constitution of 1831 gave the secession a revolutionary character; Dutch historiography sees the 1830 events only as a "Belgian uprising."

There has been a lot of discussion about the factors uniting and dividing the Low Countries. The absence of natural external borders, the decentralized political structure, and the relative prosperity made the region an easy and tempting target of invasion throughout the centuries. Political integration was slow, and resistance against centralization was one of the issues in the revolt against Philip II. In the Dutch Republic, local and provincial magistracies enjoyed the same sovereign power as the States General. In the Spanish (later Austrian) Netherlands, the Habsburgs had learned to respect the local and provincial privileges and did not impose centralization until the last decades of the eighteenth century. The kingdoms of the nineteenth century insisted on the formation of national identities, but in Belgium the imposition of nationhood as defined by the French-speaking bourgeoisie provoked a reaction from the majority of the population, who spoke various Dutch dialects. They slowly saw their cultural and political rights confirmed constitutionally, culminating in the transformation of Belgium into a federal state in 1993. The linguistic border, which cut through all the southern principalities of the ancien régime (Flanders, Hainaut, Brabant, Liège), had not caused serious problems until it became a divisive factor in the development of the nation-state.

If there are no external natural borders to the Low Countries, there are internal ones—large rivers separate provinces—and they formed a frontier Spanish troops were unable to cross reliably during the Dutch Revolt (1568–1648). As a consequence, south of the rivers, the Spaniards maintained control and continued to impose Catholicism. When the Spanish withdrew in 1648, the Dutch Republic respected freedom of religion but did not grant the newly acquired territories the same sovereign rights as the seven United Provinces north of the great rivers. Therefore, the Catholic regions in the south developed a distinct cultural pattern, including the perception of being second-rate citizens. Only in the second half of the nineteenth century did Catholics in the Netherlands obtain rights fully equivalent to those of Protestants.

The river delta was also a unifying factor. In preindustrial economies, ships were the easiest means of transport for bulk cargos. The dense network of river-mouths, including the Rhine, Meuse, and Scheldt, created opportunities for commercial linkages with distant regions in northern France and western Germany. Along these rivers larger cities developed earlier than in landlocked regions. Thus, rivers facilitated the development of the transport-oriented economy that typified the region from the early Middle Ages to the late twentieth century.

The decentralized political structure, distant sovereigns (and, until 1559, distant bishops, except in Utrecht), an economy oriented toward long-distance trade over rivers and seas, and a high level of urbanization: these factors gave the Low Countries their special character through the centuries, and help us to understand the strength of local and regional power, especially that of citizens. With the exception of northern and central Italy, before 1800 no other region in Europe was so highly urbanized and commercialized; this concentration of men and capital was the source of an extraordinary degree of freedom for citizens and of political rights for artisans.

During the last eight centuries, the southern and northern areas of the Low Countries have alternately spearheaded the European economy. From around 1200 to around 1600, the southern Low Countries formed the core of the northwestern economy, with Bruges and, from 1480 onward, Antwerp as its metropolises. The former, a city of around 45,000 inhabitants at its zenith, served as the economic center of northwestern Europe, while the latter, with around 100,000 inhabitants in the 1560s, integrated markets throughout the continent and Europe's overseas colonies. At the end of the sixteenth century, the locus shifted to Amsterdam, which attained yet another level of integration as a world market. From the late eighteenth century onward, the innovative role shifted again to the south, thanks to the early industrialization in Wallony, intensive husbandry and the textile industries in Flanders, and the growth of the Antwerp harbor. After World War II, the harbors of Amsterdam and especially Rotterdam took the lead, with rapidly developing chemical industries. Dutch companies grew into important multinationals and their financial sector proved exceptionally dynamic. This remarkable continuity of core functions is directly related to the natural infrastructure of coasts and rivers.

PROTOINDUSTRIAL DEMOGRAPHY

Around 1500, the Low Countries counted some 2.3 million inhabitants, of whom 32 percent lived in cities. The population density reached 72 per square kilometer in the county of Flanders and 63 in the county of Holland. In Spain, repression provoked the emigration to the Dutch Republic of some 150,000 persons, mainly Protestants, two-thirds of whom settled in the north; others fled to Germany and England. Most of the migrants belonged to an elite of entrepreneurs, skilled artisans, artists, and intellectuals, who greatly stimulated the boom of the Dutch Republic, which counted 1.5 million inhabitants in 1625 and 1.9 million from 1650 to 1750. The province of Holland was by far the most populated and the most urbanized of the Seven Provinces. In 1625, 675,000 lived there, and by 1680, 61 percent of its population was urban, while in the rest of the republic it was below 25 percent, though still far higher than the European average. Amsterdam had 220,000 inhabitants, Leiden 80,000. Religious tolerance attracted those persecuted in other countries, such as French Huguenots after 1685 and Portuguese Sephardic Jews. In 1675, the latter formed a community of 4,000, mostly wealthy merchants, in Amsterdam. Later, crowds of poor Ashkenasi from central Europe found a safe haven there as well. In 1797, the Jewish community in Amsterdam counted 20,000 persons, who had their synagogue but were restricted in their intercourse with Christians. Amsterdam also attracted numerous landless laborers from rural regions in the southern Netherlands and western Germany, who found employment mainly as sailors. Given the high mortality on the ships making intercontinental journeys, Dutch people voluntarily left these jobs to these *Gastarbeiter,* whom they labeled *Moffen,* a discourteous expression used for Germans in later times as well.

The strong immigration during the seventeenth century probably brought about a relative overrepresentation of younger age groups and, as a consequence, lowered the death rate. At any rate, a series of death- and birthrates for Rotterdam shows a birthrate increase until 1700. Between 1700 and 1730 there was a sharp decline in the birthrate, which afterward stabilized at 3 to 4 percent. In 1626–1627, brides at first marriage in Amsterdam were on average 24.5 years old, with 60.9 percent marrying at an age below 25 and another 28.2 percent from 25 to 30. In 1676–1677, the average age climbed to 26.5, and one century later it was 27.8. Bridegrooms were 25.7 in 1626–1627, 27.7 in 1676–1677, and 28.6 in 1776–1777. This pattern demonstrates clearly the demographic stagnation from the middle of the seventeenth century onward. The household composition in Gouda, a city of 15,000 to 20,000 inhabitants, confirms the break in the secular trend around 1650. In 1622, the average number of household members was 4.25, while in 1674 it had decreased to 3.55 as a consequence of the reduction of the number of children (2.07 to 1.71) and of other people living in (0.28 to 0.06). In 1749, households in Delft and Leiden counted 3.47 and 3.62 persons, with even fewer children (1.27 and 1.42, respectively) but more servants and others living in. The figures for the countryside are only slightly higher: 4.68 in 1622 Rhineland (the region between Haarlem and The Hague) and 4.9 in 1775 northwestern Brabant.

The dominance of the nuclear household in the preindustrial Netherlands has been explained by the high level of urbanization as well as by the high number of nonagrarian activities in the countryside. In the early sixteenth century, a great variety of artisanal activities were located in villages. Small households could combine fishery with the cultivation of tiny plots of land. More often, linen bleaching, weaving, shipbuilding, hunting of waterbirds, ground work for the upkeep of the drainage system, and many other crafts provided wage incomes that allowed small households to survive as long as they observed a controlled reproduction pattern.

GUILDS

One of the most particular features of the social history of the Low Countries is the early emergence of class struggle in large Flemish cities. The earliest date from around 1250 in cities like Douai, and from the 1280s onward in Ypres, Bruges, and Ghent. These cities numbered at least 30,000 inhabitants, the latter two even more, up to two-thirds of whom were artisans in the textile industry. Flemish cloth, produced mainly from English wool, was exported to all parts of the continent and to the Near East. Merchant-entrepreneurs introduced a putting-out system that threw the risks of the international trade on the workers. The social tensions of the later thirteenth century arose as a consequence of major shifts in the international division of labor, which provoked large-scale unemployment in traditional industrial cities.

In Flanders, social antagonism was heightened by a political conflict between the urban political elites (merchant-entrepreneurs), the count of Flanders, and his suzerain, the king of France. When the latter occupied the county in 1297 and 1300, the count's relatives mobilized as many craftsmen and peasants as they could. Together with a relatively small army of mounted noblemen, they destroyed the French mounted knights in 1302. This battle marked the breakthrough of the infantry on European battlefields; it also implied that the count had to recognize the social and political rights of the artisans. In all the major cities of the county of Flanders, dozens of craft guilds were organized; they were awarded autonomy in the regulation and control of their trade and given rights of participation in the new political structure. In the larger crafts in the textile sector, with thousands of workers, the journeymen—salaried artisans working for a master who owned his shop and his tools—could vote in the election of the dean and the board, and could even be elected themselves. The deans of all the crafts formed, together with the delegation of the bourgeoisie, a large council, which voted on taxes and other main issues of the city.

The Flemish guild revolution was an exceptionally early and radical breakthrough made possible by the huge scale of the industry, its vulnerability to international business cycles, and the confluence of economic problems with a major political conflict. In the main cities of other principalities, similar guild revolutions took place, but they were mostly beaten back by more coherent elites. Only in Liège, Dordrecht, and Utrecht did the guild organizations last until the early modern period. The reality of the new power structures differed from one town to another as a consequence of local conditions. The most extreme case was that of Ghent, the largest industrial city of its time, with about 65,000 inhabitants around 1350. After protracted and bloody struggles between the largest crafts of weavers and fullers, the latter were excluded from political power and guild autonomy in 1360. Twenty of the twenty-six seats of aldermen were earmarked for particular crafts, the six others, including the two chairmen, were reserved for members of the bourgeoisie. All delegations of the city, as well as the whole of the city's personnel, were neatly proportioned to reflect each of the sociopolitical sections of the community. This extreme case illustrates the harshness of the class conflicts, even among the small entrepreneurs in the textile sector itself who held the rank of guild masters. At the same time it shows how pacification could be installed through a complicated system of power sharing, which functioned until its abolition after another revolt in 1540. In other cities, more moderate forms of participation and autonomy survived until the French occupation of 1794.

STANDARD OF LIVING AND IDEOLOGY

Guild power helped shelter the employment and income of urban artisans from the effects of depressions. Its aim was purely protectionist: solidarity never reached further than one's own guild or one's own city. Labor mobility was considerable, thanks to the relatively high wages paid in cities. During the prosperous years from 1400 to 1450, the Bruges building industry recruited high numbers of laborers from outside the city; 75 to 80 percent of the outsiders even came

Market in Antwerp. Market day on the Place de Meir in Antwerp, seventeenth century.
ROYAL MUSEUM OF FINE ARTS, BRUSSELS/A.C.L. BRUSSELS

from outside the county of Flanders. After 1450, the economy of Bruges stagnated, which led to a shift in labor migration toward fast-growing Antwerp, and later toward Amsterdam. Considerable differences in real wages continued to exist between town and countryside and between cities. Further, a laborer's income fluctuated heavily depending on variations in employment, since most were paid on piece rates, or were engaged for a number of days only. Because the purchasing power of nominal wages depended on fluctuations in the price of bread, which was the primary household expenditure, real wages can best be expressed in liters of rye, which allows comparisons. In Bruges, in the bumper years 1463 to 1468, a master craftsman could purchase with his theoretical maximal income some sixty-four liters of rye, while his counterpart in Leiden could purchase only thirty-eight liters, or 40 percent less. Real wages in the 1460s in Bruges were the highest of the preindustrial period. During the sixteenth century, real wages declined generally. In Bruges, they were at twenty-seven liters of rye from 1500 to 1505 (still more than the 23 in Ghent and 21 in Antwerp), but in the crisis years 1548 to 1557 they reached only 44 percent of that level in Bruges, while in buoyant Antwerp they were at 81 percent.

Generally, artisan households needed more than one salary to survive, and even then they suffered in the periods of high food prices, which occurred either as a consequence of weather conditions, political blockades, or a combination of both. In any case, the Low Countries were so highly populated that they could

not feed their inhabitants and needed the constant import of grains. Until the mid-sixteenth century, most grain came from Picardy and Artois; later Prussia became the main rye supplier. During the sixteenth to eighteenth centuries Amsterdam built its position as a staple market entirely on this so-called mother trade, from which all other trades in the Baltic were derived. Blockades of the Sund Strait created serious problems for the grain supply of the Low Countries. Riots resulted, for example, in 1530 and 1565–1566. Poor relief normally helped up to 25 percent of the population through the most difficult months, but it remained insufficient when grain prices tripled, as they did in 1565–1566. In this so-called hunger year, the iconoclast movement, which spread in three weeks in August 1566 from western Flanders to Leiden, Amsterdam, and Utrecht, made clear the relationship between living conditions and the propensity for Protestantism.

Lutheran ideas had been spread in word and print through Antwerp since the early 1520s. The first victims of the persecution of Protestants were two Augustinian monks from Antwerp, who died at the stake in 1523. Anabaptism also found supporters in Antwerp, as well as in Amsterdam. From the 1540s onward, a new wave of Protestantism spread through the Low Countries. The rural textile industries in southwestern Flanders had created a proletariat, which gave the impetus to the iconoclast movement in 1566. Most Calvinists were found among the middle classes in the major cities, including some French-speaking ones such as Tournai and Valenciennes. Calvinist republics took over local government in Bruges, Ghent, Mechelen, Brussels, and Antwerp in the late 1570s and early 1580s until Spanish troops subdued each of these after sieges. In 1585, the largest city, Antwerp, fell; one-third of the population had declared itself in favor of Protestantism, and only one-third was said still to be Catholic.

The massive emigration of Protestants, combined with the reconversion of those who stayed under the Spanish repression, explains how the Spanish Netherlands became exclusively Catholic again. The Spaniards introduced there all the tools of the Counter-Reformation, including Jesuit schools, episcopal visiting of parishes, and new charitable institutions. Society was disciplined back into its former pattern. This rapid shift all too often makes people forget that, before the massive military repression of the 1580s, Protestantism had been disseminated predominantly in the more urbanized and more commercialized south, including rural regions with a high level of industrialization. In Holland, it had until then mainly been an elitist movement, and the outlying provinces remained entirely Catholic. In 1650, half of the population of the Dutch Republic was Catholic, and it was only around 1700 that the Reformed Church became the largest among the official churches. It never was, however, a monopolistic state church. Religious tolerance had been one of the main motives for the Dutch Revolt, and it remained embedded in the society of the Dutch Republic. As long as services were not held publicly, they were tolerated, and even Catholic and Anabaptist churches continued to function, albeit it hidden behind discrete facades.

A BOURGEOIS OLIGARCHY

In the Dutch Republic (the United Provinces) sovereignty was dispersed among three levels: the local community, the province, and the confederation. For example, nineteen cities had a vote in the assembly of the local estates of Holland. Each of the Seven Provinces also had sovereign rights; a majority could not impose its decisions against the will of a minority. The confederal representative system made intensive consultations necessary to seek consensus wherever possible, especially on the third level of sovereignty, that of the States General. Nevertheless, the fact that the province of Holland alone paid for 58 percent of the expenditure of the national government had some consequences. Informal pressure, patronage and clientage, the sale of offices, and corruption were widespread practices. The whole governmental system recruited its personnel exclusively among the wealthy regents, who directly served their class interests as

merchants, bankers, and rentiers. Although the absence of a monarchy prevented the creation of new nobility, while the old noble families died out, the regents developed an aristocratic lifestyle, which combined luxurious houses along the prestigious canals in Amsterdam with lordship and a country residence.

One may wonder why this obviously oligarchic government provoked relatively little social unrest. One reason is that ordinary people in the Dutch Republic were generally better off than in other countries. There was full employment, wages were relatively high, and upward mobility was possible. Second, the guild organization helped to defuse social tensions. Artisans had a place in the political culture of the public sphere, even if they had no direct impact in the daily government, as had been the case in medieval Flanders. Third, the churches, private persons, and public authorities competed in the foundation of charitable institutions, which by the late eighteenth century sustained about one-quarter of the population of the major cities. Fourth, the preachers in the Protestant churches were very good at moralizing. Churches exercised control over their members and promoted the acceptance of the social order as divinely ordained. In a probably less intensive way, public authorities also used symbolic means to convey their message of an ideal orderly state.

Guilds are usually viewed as antithetical to commercial capitalism and as obstacles against all kinds of modernization. Recent research has stressed instead that, already in the Middle Ages, the putting-out system prevailed not only between great merchants and artisans, but also between master artisans themselves. Some masters employed other craftsmen, provided them with credit in the form of raw material, and made them dependent on piece-rate salaries. Entrepreneurs reduced both costs for fixed capital goods and marketing risks by employing artisans. Already in the middle of the sixteenth century, some brewers and building entrepreneurs used their capital accumulation in combination with political power to establish de facto monopolies. Therefore, the guild system continued to function as a means to absorb social tensions, but it did not prevent the full development of commercial capitalism nor the steady modernization of production techniques.

DRAINAGE DEMOCRACY

One of the most striking features of the history of the Netherlands is that about half of its territory is situated a few meters below sea level. This is because marsh soils sank as they were drained for cultivation. This process has been going on for centuries, and so-

Polders. Reclaimed land near Enkhuizen, Netherlands. Anonymous painting, c. 1600, in the town hall. ZUIDERZEE MUSEUM, ENKHUIZEN, NETHERLANDS/©GEMEENTE

lutions have been incremental. To keep the river waters out of the land dikes were built beginning in the eleventh century. Canals were dug in a systematic rectilinear way to evacuate the water from the land into the same rivers. Sluices were needed to take advantage of the tides. By around 1400, the soil in Holland had sunk to a level below the lowest tide. Evacuation of the superfluous water could therefore only be done by mechanical means, that is, by pumping it up to the level of the river behind the dike. By 1408, the first windmill for this purpose had been built near Alkmaar. The system was then generalized and elaborated: in the deepest marshes, a series of windmills pumped the water up step by step. In the seventeenth century, new polders were created using these devices. In the middle of the nineteenth century, the lake south of Haarlem was drained by a major steam engine. In the 1970s, a new province, Flevoland, was created by draining a large section of the interior sea, the IJsselmeer.

This drainage system had a social dimension because it required collaboration. Local communities took the first protective measures; when these interfered with opposing interests of neighbors, cooperation had to be negotiated or higher authorities had to intervene. Large drainage authorities were officially recognized by the count of Holland in the thirteenth century, and a number of small authorities continue to coexist in the north of Holland. The construction, control, and steady upkeep of the system of canals, dikes, sluices, and windmills could work effectively only with the full participation of all people having an interest in the protected area. Not only their funds

were needed, but also their labor and continuous vigilance. Only a public system that granted rights of protection in strict proportion to duties could foster the solidarity on which the life and property of all depended.

The public authority developed for this purpose is unique, as it combined direct participation in decision making with responsibility. Residents and owners of the land were charged with the execution of the common decisions in proportion to the size of their plots. Every inhabitant was obliged to comply with the decisions commonly taken. The authority had the power to tax and even to prosecute negligence. The land still reflects its systematic clearance; fields are rectangular, divided by the straight canals. A particular political culture grew from the constant concern surrounding this man-made environment. Its elements were solidarity, working toward the common interest, the rational evaluation of purposes and means, freedom of speech during the discussion of a project, and strict adherence to agreed actions. Many of these features are still typical of Dutch political culture.

The nineteenth century saw relatively little economic change in the Dutch Republic. Indeed, this slowness to industrialize is an important topic in the Republic's social history. Although it had sufficient capital for industrialization, the Republic lacked other components—including natural resources (in contrast to coal-rich Belgium)—and fell into a rentier mentality. The hold of religion also intensified, counter to the trend in most other parts of western Europe. Not all areas of the Dutch economy, however, were immune to innovation: for instance, some Dutch farmers actively converted to market agriculture, especially after 1850, producing vegetables and milk products for Europe's growing urban markets.

BELGIAN INDUSTRIALIZATION

The situation in Belgium was more dynamic. In the 1780s, the population of the southern Low Countries was between 2.4 and 2.6 million, considerably more than the 2.1 million in the Dutch Republic. Agricultural innovations had increased the profits of the landowners and stimulated population growth. Various traditional crafts had been transformed. Linen weaving and especially cotton processing flourished in new manufactures in Ghent, while coal mining and iron industries prospered in Liège and Hainaut. The combination of accumulated capital, artisanal traditions, transport facilities on the rivers, the availability of raw materials, sympathetic authorities, and daring entrepreneurship made Belgium the first industrial nation in Europe. Before 1843 railways were constructed connecting all major cities of the country; later, the network became the world's most dense. In the 1846 census, only 23 percent of the population in the provinces of Liège and Hainaut were still active in agriculture. A very unequal income distribution resulted from the industrial boom: by 1880, the business class, 10 percent of the population, possessed two-thirds of the country's real income. Predominantly agrarian Flanders suffered greatly in the potato crises of 1846–1849. Many smallholders starved and had to seek employment in the coal mines in the region of Douai or in Wallony. The first industrial survey of 1846 revealed that the average yearly income of a cotton worker was only 88 percent of the official minimum cost of living. Working time was eighty hours a week. Underpaid female and child labor was widespread in the factories and mines. These observations stimulated the young Karl Marx, who lived as an émigré in Brussels from 1845 to 1848, to write his *Communist Manifesto*. Only after mid-century did economic growth bring a 49 percent increase in real wages (between 1853 and 1875).

The first labor organizations arose around 1850; they were strongly reminiscent of medieval and early-modern guilds. Ghent textile workers established a union in 1857; under the prohibition of unionization, which was lifted only in 1867, they presented themselves as associations for mutual aid. In the Walloon industrial centers, a more activist revolutionary socialism was popular, and a syndicalistic form of organization developed. The formation of the Belgian Socialist Workers' Party in 1885 made universal manhood suffrage the main goal of the movement. In Wallony, strikes underscored this aim; when they escalated into a general strike and the police shot some demonstrators, Parliament accepted general male suffrage in 1893, albeit with extra votes for rich and educated men. In 1896, the number of workers in the industrial sector had grown to 934,000, and in 1910 to 1,176,000.

The effect of universal manhood suffrage was not that socialists won a parliamentary majority, but that the liberals, of whom many favored social reforms, were reduced to a tiny minority. The Catholic party held power for thirty years. During this period, labor productivity increased dramatically, but real wages increased by a poor 4 percent between 1896 and 1910. The Catholic party was firmly led by conservatives, although it claimed to include all "orders." As the workers' movement gained importance, the Catholic Church, inspired by the encyclical *Rerum Novarum,* tried to recuperate it by organizing Catholic unions, newspapers, health insurance, and other parallel institutions. While in Wallony the rapid urbanization had led to massive secularization because the Church could not expand adequately, in Flanders the majority of the workers was attracted by the moderate Catholic workers' movement. The contrast between the two regions remained until the general strike of 1960–1961; even then, Wallony was near revolution, while the Flemish socialists remained loyal to parliamentarism. The Belgian workers' movement was thus divided between a reformist tendency prevailing in Flanders and Brussels and a revolutionary tendency with strongholds in Hainaut and Liège; further, Catholic unionism functioned to moderate the working class as a whole. In this it was most successful in Flanders, where Catholicism remained strong until the 1970s and where industrialization triumphed only after World War II.

WOMEN AT WORK: A COMPARISON

Early industrialization required the participation of women, which reduced their fertility. The declining birthrate perpetuated the need for more female workers. The greater demand for women to be available for factory work helped to spread bottle-feeding of babies much earlier in Belgium than in the Netherlands. Institutional arrangements were created earlier in Belgium for child care in crèches, kindergartens, and primary schools with day care after the class hours. The participation of the Belgian Workers' Party in the government since 1919 favored the early introduction of such measures, which became generally accepted and valued. In the Netherlands, industrialization was generalized only after 1945, when the new industries demanded fewer workers. Until then, the Social Democratic Party had been relatively small and very moderate. As a new participant in coalition governments from 1945 onward, it saw no reason to insist on measures to change the role of women, who happily stayed at home, where especially the dominant Christian parties had always wanted to keep them.

Female participation in higher education lagged far behind in the Netherlands until the 1970s, because both institutional arrangements and cultural prejudices worked against professional activity by women outside the home. Also, while the Netherlands remained neutral during World War I, in Belgium women had to take over tasks of the absent soldiers. The early introduction of female labor, and its generalization during the war, helped its continuation under new conditions. The growth of the service sector (which already counted 784,000 employees in 1910) and the emergence of the welfare state after the World War I required more female work in offices, schools, and hospitals. In most countries, female suffrage logically followed shortly after the war. Paradoxically, this happened in the Netherlands, but not in Belgium, where female suffrage was granted only in 1949. The reason is mainly political: the socialists opposed it because of their fear of conservative (that is, Catholic) voting by women. Indeed, a Catholic majority was elected in 1949, albeit only for one parliamentary term.

PILLARIZATION

The institutional buildup of Catholic organizations to keep the sheep within the herd was long successful. Not only workers, but also peasants, entrepreneurs, housewives, shopkeepers, youth, and many other categories were labeled as "orders," which in a harmonious vision of society were supposed to collaborate under the aegis of Mother Church. Catholic power was widespread, especially in Flanders, where it was dominant until late in the 1990s. Most of the hospitals and charitable institutions, education, the press and private mass media, health insurance, the largest trade union, important banks, insurance companies, the Peasants' League, middle-class organizations, and many other institutions belonged to the Catholic "pillar," which cooperated with the Catholic Party, which governed the country for all but four years between 1884 and 1999. All sectors had to be kept in balance in order to secure continuity of power in as many sectors of society as possible. Secularization could be slowed down and the labor movement kept under control by dividing it. The socialist movement reacted by employing similar measures: it erected cooperatives, unions, health insurance companies, newspapers, a youth movement, and so on. The idea was to offer an ideological haven from cradle to grave. However, socialists lacked almost per definition the support of capital, and therefore they needed the state to provide the resources for their action.

In Wallony, the socialist pillar dominated society, in Flanders the Catholic. The two pillars needed to collaborate in order to govern the country smoothly. They did so by privileging their own organizations in performing numerous public tasks at the expense of the state budget. Their grip on society was so tight that it was difficult, after the 1950s, to obtain any appointment to an office in the public sector or any public service without the intervention of one of the pillars. A system of clientage was established in which citizens had to pass through pillar organizations to obtain public employment. The most successful politicians were those who managed to do a maximum of favors for people who would in return vote for them. Electors had become clients, and politicians became brokers of state power and fiscal resources.

The pillarized system in the Netherlands was analyzed first by the political scientists Arend Lijphart and Hans Daalder. They argued that the emancipation of the Catholics in the second half of the nineteenth century, and the Protestant organization in reaction to that, plus the demands of the workers' movement tended together to form a system aiming at the pacification of these claimants on the state. Protestants and Catholics wanted to control their own hospitals, charitable institutions, schools, and universities, but also wanted the state to pay for them. The liberals were the least interested in these organizations, but they were pushed by the competition for public funds to participate in some way. Thus, Dutch society became pillarized in four columns. The differences with Belgium are immediately clear and significant: only in the southern Catholic provinces—the "generality lands" from the time of the Republic—was one pillar, the Catholic, dominant; elsewhere, each of the pillars had to collaborate. The absence of a tradition of violent political or social action, and the tradition of consensus seeking, helped the elaboration of a political culture in which power was shared in deals between the leaders of the four pillars, who aimed at "sovereignty in their own circle" and proclaimed in their public rhetoric to be essentially different from all the others. As in Belgium, the pillars used public funds to finance their private organizations. At variance with Belgium, no one of the pillars was regionally dominant—not even in the southern provinces, where all the others jointly kept an eye on the Catholics. So, none was able, as the Belgian pillars were, to act as the corrupt gatekeepers of the public domain.

DEPILLARIZATION AND MODERNIZATION

During the late 1960s and 1970s, a rapid depillarization occurred in the Netherlands, while the pillars remained strong in Belgium until the 1990s. Why the difference? In 1945, both countries had around 8 million inhabitants. In 2000, the Netherlands counted more than 15 million, Belgium 10 million. Population growth was much higher in the north as a consequence of the continued high natality in Catholic and Protestant communities, at least until c. 1970, and the strong intercontinental immigration of people with a high fertility (Portuguese, Spaniards, and Turks), numbering up to about two million in 2000. On the other hand, the political culture and society had remained very traditional since industrialization had remained geographically and socially a marginal phenomenon. Only the fast postwar growth of the harbor economy, the third wave of industrialization, had a great impact, especially in the regions of Rotterdam and Amsterdam. The old pattern of extremely high population density in Holland continued, but now the concentration of various ethnic groups raised new tensions.

In the sixties, international examples provided new models of social protest, propagated by the new mass media. In Belgium, these tensions were much smoother, since the population pressure was much less and since modernization had taken place gradually in many sectors. Moreover, the particularity of the linguistic problems focused the tensions on that issue. In the Netherlands, however, the new generation, led by young journalists and academics, demonstratively broke away from the traditional norms and values imposed by the pillar organizations. The media proclaimed their independence and encouraged further criticism of the old order. New forms of democracy were legally introduced in the universities and in many other public organizations. The most dramatic breakdown occurred in the Catholic pillar, which faced massive desertion of the Church after conservative reactions from the hierarchy to demands for modernization. The Catholic Party, which had been very influential, disappeared in a fusion with two Protestant parties. This may all be more apparent than real in the sense that in the late 1990s institutions still bore names referring to one or the other pillar, and still handled public money under the control of their private boards. Still, hardly any of them could claim exclusivity since only a small minority of the population strictly observed a "pillar" ideology. Secularization was certainly the main underlying factor in this process. The first so-called "purple" cabinet (a combination of socialist red and liberal blue) in 1995 was followed by a second in 1999, demonstrating the effects of massive secularization and depillarization in the public sphere. The "social market economy" fit extremely well with the buoyant economic opportunities the country enjoyed.

In Belgium, the two major pillars, with their regional dominance, were stronger. They managed to divert most of the dissatisfactions to linguistic tensions, which they certainly exacerbated for short-term political purposes. They could even strengthen their positions in the federalized state structure, which was gradually elaborated between 1963 and 1993. However, the "end of ideologies" came to Belgium as well. Church attendance sank to 13 percent in Flanders and 11 percent in Wallony in 1998, and the Catholic Party lost votes in each successive election. The socialist party lost credibility in a series of corruption scandals. A "purple plus green" cabinet governed beginning in 1999 and launched a new political and social climate free of political clientage.

See also **Revolutions** *(volume 3) and other articles in this section.*

BIBLIOGRAPHY

Blockmans, Willem, and Walter Prevenier. *The Promised Lands: The Low Countries under Burgundian Rule, 1369-1530.* Philadelphia, 1999.

Blom, J. C. H., and E. Lamberts, eds. *History of the Low Countries.* New York, 1998.

de Vries, Jan, and Ad van der Woude. *The First Modern Economy: Success, Failure, and Perseverance of the Dutch Economy, 1500–1815.* Cambridge, U.K., 1997.

Israel, Jonathan I. *The Dutch Republic: Its Rise, Greatness, and Fall 1477–1806.* Oxford, 1995.

Schama, Simon. *Embarrassment of Riches: An Interpretation of Dutch Culture in the Golden Age.* New York, 1997.

Schama, Simon. *Patriots and Liberators: Revolution in the Netherlands, 1780–1813.* New York, 1992.

THE IBERIAN PENINSULA

Montserrat Miller

The Iberian Peninsula is a landmass situated at the mouth of the Mediterranean Sea in southwestern Europe. Its southern tip represents Europe's nearest approximation to Africa and borders on the only western entrance into the sea, known in Roman times as the *mare nostrum.* Constituting roughly 230,000 square miles of territory, the Iberian peninsula is marked by important regional differences in culture, history, and socioeconomic structure. The area is characterized as well by a significant degree of linguistic variety. Currently comprised of the nation-states of Portugal and Spain, the Peninsula also includes the Basque Country and Catalonia as subject nationalities with autonomous statutes that offer a modicum of home rule within Spain.

The Iberian Peninsula has generated considerable social history scholarship. Even though in Spain through the 1960s and 1970s open discussion of the legitimacy of Francisco Franco's (1892–1975) regime was not permitted, studies of nineteenth- and twentieth-century Spanish economic and social patterns, and of regional processes, especially those pertaining to Catalonia, contributed to a corpus of social history work before the dictator's death in 1975. Since the transition to democracy and increased exposure to historiographical developments outside Spain, the social history work on Spain has expanded its chronological and thematic foci and grown in methodological complexity.

Portugal, too, spent much of the twentieth century under an authoritarian dictatorship that limited full and open inquiry of its social and political past. Since the 1974 revolution that ended the Antonio de Oliveira Salazar (1889–1970) regime, however, social history work on Portugal has flourished. As in the case of Spain, much of this work is explicitly comparative in its orientation.

The Iberian Peninsula has long been treated by historians as exceptional within a larger European framework; much of the recent scholarship, however, stresses the degree to which the region adheres at least in broad outline to the social, cultural, economic, and political patterns found north of the Pyrenees Mountains. Attention to deeply rooted ideological and social conflict and regional agricultural problems notwithstanding, the newest interpretations argue that Spain's economy from 1700 on was characterized by a long-term vitality which, though interrupted at various points, has born fruit in the second half of the twentieth century's industrial growth and democratization.

MEDIEVAL STATE-BUILDING AND CONSOLIDATION OF TERRITORIES

When the Carolingians began their push southward across the Pyrenees into Islamic territory in the 770s, the Iberian Peninsula had already experienced more than a millennium of invasion and settlement by outside peoples. Phoenicians, Celts, Greeks, Romans, Visigoths, and Muslims had all contributed to shaping the culture and economy of the peninsula. No group was more influential than the Romans. Having colonized Iberia for more than six hundred years, they left a firm linguistic imprint. Of the numerous languages spoken on the Peninsula before Roman conquest, only Basque survived. Elsewhere dialects of *latin vulgar* remained deeply entrenched, and even the Muslim invasion of 711 did not permanently eradicate the linguistic and religious patterns established under Roman rule. Over the course of the Middle Ages, three distinct languages developed on the Peninsula: Castilian, Portuguese, and Catalan.

Frankish overlordship in northeastern Spain during the early middle ages led to the establishment of three historic kingdoms: Navarre, Aragon, and Catalonia. Navarre, located on the western half of the Pyrenees and eastern Cantabrian Mountains, included Basque territories and remained deeply entrenched in French power struggles until the early sixteenth century. Aragon and Catalonia were joined in the late twelfth century by a dynastic union that permitted a considerable degree of autonomy for both. The Catalan-Aragonese kingdom grew quickly into a regional powerhouse. By the thirteenth century, Catalan-Aragonese society featured an emerging commercial stratum of colonizers and merchants who enjoyed broad privileges set forth in a series of charters.

In the northwestern region of the Peninsula, a second state-building process had gotten underway in the ninth century. Largely free of Frankish influence and shaped by Visigothic ideals, Christian kingdoms emerged in Asturias and León, which further dashed Muslim aspirations to control the Peninsula. The Kingdom of Asturias-León scored a series of military victories over the forces of Al-Andalus and then repopulated the Duero River tableland with Christian peasant farmers in the tenth century. Still, Asturias-León was not fully capable of carrying out the Reconquista on its own. It was rather the emerging Kingdom of Castile that seized the initiative and spread its control over the interior *meseta*. Then in the first half of the thirteenth century both León and Asturias were definitively joined to Castile under the rule of Ferdinand III (c. 1201–1252), and with the aid of the Crown of Aragon succeeded in driving the recently established Almohad authorities out of Andalusia and eliminating Muslim rule from all of the Peninsula save Granada.

Also taking shape on the Iberian Peninsula during the medieval period was the Kingdom of Portugal. Rebelling against the feudal overlordship of León and Castile in the twelfth century, Portugal achieved independence in 1140. Initially consisting of the northern half of the contemporary state of Portugal, the kingdom extended its boundaries to the south by driving out Muslim forces in 1297. By the end of the thirteenth century, the Iberian Peninsula consisted of three powerful kingdoms: Castile-León, Aragon-Catalonia, and Portugal.

SOCIAL AND ECONOMIC DEVELOPMENTS IN MEDIEVAL IBERIA

In the wake of the victories against Islamic forces, Castile extended administrative control over Andalusia in a manner that would have profound social and economic consequences for Spain's historical development into the twentieth century. The Castilian crown distributed large tracts of land to the aristocracy and thus left intact the latifundia system that had developed under Islamic rule. Out of this landholding system arose a social system comprising a minority of large landowners and a majority of landless laborers, or *braceros,* which survived well into the twentieth century and which contrasted with the small peasant holdings of northern Spain. The emerging bourgeoisie of Castile,

concentrated in the northern cities of the kingdom, was unable to exert a counterbalancing role. With a reliance on livestock rather than commerce or productive agriculture, and without access to merchant fleets that linked the region to the markets of Europe, the economy of Andalusia collapsed under Castilian rule.

This stood in sharp contrast to the Catalan-Aragonese administration of the newly conquered region of Valencia. There, nobles were given only mountainous land near Aragon and the rest was distributed among Catalan knights and farmers who adopted the productive Muslim agricultural techniques and enjoyed broad freedoms through royal charters and semi-autonomous governance. Valencia flourished economically under Christian rule, and it developed as Spain's most prosperous commercial agricultural region into the modern period. These distinctive patterns of administration thus contributed to a growing economic and social differentiation between the periphery and hinterland of the Peninsula.

Castilian society was transformed by the efforts to repopulate Andalusia. The lack of manufacturing coupled with high levels of demand for luxury goods on the part of an aristocracy led the Castilians toward a dependence on the sale of wool. The *mesta* emerged as a powerful influence within the Castilian state. The *mesta* was an association of sheep and cattle owners whose council taxed the whole wool industry on behalf of the crown and whose political influence grew as the economy stagnated. With a population that was stretched thin, the northern part of Castile lost much of its earlier character of social egalitarianism, and in the fourteenth century town councils came under the influence of knights. Rounds of inflation and debasement of the coinage contributed to the weakness of the Castilian economy as it extended over the new territories of the peninsula. This socioeconomic stagnation contrasted sharply with well-known periods of cultural brilliance during which the intellectual fruits of the "School of Translators" in Toledo disseminated the classics of antiquity and of Islamic science to the rest of Europe.

Still, the contrast between the Kingdom of Castile and the Kingdom of Aragon in the High Middle Ages was a sharp one that was reflected in the nature and extent of each realm's relationship to larger European trade networks. The Crown of Aragon, with its dynamic Catalan economic base that rested on the production of woolen textiles, cast iron, and leather for export, experienced the consolidation of an urban patriciate whose membership was open to successful manufacturers, merchants, and bankers of humble birth. But the strain resulting from the effort to repopulate new areas also contributed to social tensions within Aragon. In the oldest part of Catalonia, the peasantry, which had historically held land under limited seigniorial obligations, increasingly suffered legal servitude by the thirteenth century under what came to be known as the remança system. Uprisings began in the countryside in 1388 and laid the groundwork for rupture.

Aragonese social and economic development followed the general western European pattern much more closely than did Castile. Whereas Castile was industrially stagnant, aristocratic, and pastoralist, Aragon-Catalan society featured an urban middle class that dominated the politics of privileged towns and an expanding trade network in the Mediterranean. Portugal lay somewhere between the two. The Portuguese solution to the economic challenge of absorbing new Muslim territories had been to turn toward the sea. Lisbon emerged as an important port and fueling station for maritime traffic between the Mediterranean and the Atlantic, and Portugal developed early commercial links to west Africa. Still, there was less manufacturing there than in Aragon and southern areas of Portugal remained largely unproductive.

In the fifteenth century the Iberian Peninsula experienced a crisis similar to that which took place in other areas of Europe. Many of the problems were the direct result of the Black Death, which depleted the labor force. In Castille, the aristocracy used the economic contraction to secure greater privileges from the crown. In Catalonia, the remança peasants rose up against landlords; artisans came into direct conflict with the urban patriciate; and the patriciate itself rebelled against the authority of the crown. Particularly noteworthy is the outcome of the peasant uprisings and war that extended from 1388 to 1486. Nowhere else in Europe did peasants so successfully achieve relief from seignorial obligations through royal intervention on behalf of their cause (Freedman).

Popular unrest in the fifteenth century also manifested itself in the first intense wave of pogroms against the Jews. Beginning in the south, they spread to the north and led to the looting of Jewish neighborhoods in major cities. Fueled by clerics and the Castilian aristocracy, this wave of violence set the stage for the more concerted effort to impose religious orthodoxy that began under Isabella I (1474–1504).

forged in the late fifteenth century. Economic and social dislocation coupled with conflicts over succession in Castile and revolution in Catalonia served as a backdrop for the emergence of a new Spanish polity under the rule of Ferdinand of Aragon (1452–1516) and Isabella of Castile. From 1479 to 1504 these monarchs pursued a coordinated policy of foreign and domestic affairs. Though the historic charters of the Crown of Aragon were held as inviolable in this union, the administration of the conjoined kingdoms was increasingly carried out from, and in the broad interests of, Castile. The larger territory and population of Castile, along with the limited constitutional restrictions on monarchical rule there, contributed to this shift in the epicenter of political power away from the periphery of the peninsula.

At the close of the fifteenth century, the Iberian Peninsula's role in European and global politics and economics expanded dramatically. The newly broadened powers of the Catholic monarchs led to a series of important military victories and effective diplomatic strategies vastly increasing the territories under their domain. In 1492 Spanish forces conquered Granada. Not long afterward, Ferdinand was able to annex Navarre and thus curtail French power in the Pyrenees altogether, though the historic charters or *fueros* were, as in the Crown of Aragon, held as legal limitations on expanding royal power. In Italy, the Spanish were able to retake Naples and then use it as a strategic military and political outpost. By negotiating crucial marriage alliances, the Catholic kings produced a grandson, Charles (1500–1558), who was heir to these territories and to the Hapsburg royal line as well.

By 1550, the new Spanish state's holdings in Europe were enormous and included the Low Countries, Austria, Hungary, and most of Italy. In 1580 Philip II (1527–1598) seized Portugal, and Hapsburg control of the Peninsula was completed. Added to all these holdings were new territories in the Americas and the impressive riches and prestige derived from colonial domination and being the first colonial power. Indeed, with the rise of the Hapsburg monarchy, the kingdoms of the Iberian Peninsula entered into a new period marked by an intensification of demands for religious orthodoxy and Castilian aspirations for political hegemony.

EMPIRE BUILDING IN THE SIXTEENTH CENTURY: CASTILE'S PATH TO POLITICAL HEGEMONY

These were the circumstances under which the dynastic union of the crowns of Aragon and Castile was

THE POLITICS OF RELIGION IN "GOLDEN AGE" SPAIN

The drive toward the imposition of religious orthodoxy in this period had its roots in the Christian fervor that accompanied the political aims of the Reconquest

The Iberian Peninsula. Sixteenth-century map. BY PERMISSION OF THE BRITISH LIBRARY

and was particularly potent in Castile. Though Christians, Muslims, and Jews had coexisted through most of the period of Islamic rule and much of that of Castilian, Portuguese, and Aragonese, Isabella secured papal authorization for the establishment of a state rather than an ecclesiastically based Inquisition. The persecution of heresy began in 1478. The first targets of the Inquisition were the converted Jews or *conversos,* many of whom had advanced socially and economically and were suspected of being insincere in their Christian beliefs. Then in 1492, the persecution intensified when the Jewish population was ordered en masse by the Crown to convert or leave Spain; some fifty thousand became *conversos* while another one hundred thousand departed. In 1502, the Catholic kings issued a similar order regarding the Muslims of Castile. As a consequence, large numbers of Muslim peasants left the Peninsula, though three hundred thousand stayed and converted to Christianity, becoming known as *moriscos.* As the Spanish Crown worked itself into position as defender of the Catholic faith in Europe, popular support for the imposition of religious orthodoxy grew. In 1609 under Philip III

(1578–1621), the *moriscos* were expelled altogether. Over the course of three centuries the Inquisition brought about the execution of some three thousand persons suspected of various forms of religious heresy. Still, the inquisition was by no means a wholly centralized program. Regional courts carried out their repression in varying ways. In some areas, such as Aragon, there was shifting popular support and opposition to the Inquisition, and acts of sexual transgression were punished just as harshly as spiritual heresy (Monter, p. xi).

ECONOMIC DECLINE IN THE SEVENTEENTH CENTURY

This pattern of religious persecution involving expulsion, forced conversion, trial, and torture, though modest in its scale in comparison to the deaths resulting in the religious wars of France and Germany, had a considerable impact on the economy of Castile. Most of the confiscated wealth ended up in the hands of the nobility and government officials who put the policies into effect. While the short-term benefit was the financing of some of the Catholic kings' and Habsburgs' foreign policies, the long-term effect was to stifle the economic development of many Castilian towns by depleting the very population whose commercial and manufacturing activity was greatest. The impact of *morisco* expulsion, however, was greatest in the countryside of Aragon, Valencia, and Andalusia, where a vital force of productive agricultural workers could not easily be replaced; rural economies foundered as a result. Though wealth poured into Castile from the Americas, and the cities of Seville and Madrid emerged as major urban centers, old weaknesses in the agricultural base and problems resulting from the aristocratic dominance of the social and economic structures counterbalanced the modest gains made in manufacturing and market development through the sixteenth century.

Ultimately Castile under Habsburg rule did not succeed in effectively exploiting the wealth from the Americas and in using that wealth to invigorate the domestic economy. The well-known bankruptcies and ultimate collapse of the Spanish economy in the seventeenth century resulted from a number of causes. The balance of state policies continued to favor the aristocracy, whose real economic privileges had barely been touched by the consolidation of royal power. The influence of the *mesta* in this period grew, and so too did the quantity of uncultivated land and the threat of famine. The enormous financial burdens that the Hapsburgs assumed in fighting Protestantism on the Continent coupled with poor fiscal policies further undermined the interests of the middle classes.

Also a factor in the intensification of the financial collapse that set in after 1600 was the rise of Madrid itself. Growing from 35,000 inhabitants in 1560 to 175,000 in 1630, Madrid's rapid development further upset the Castilian economy by accelerating the demand for and prices of subsistence goods needed to feed its vast population of poor residents (Ringrose, p. 67). Without a viable middle class to bolster demand from regionally produced manufactured goods and wine, the bulk of the city's discretionary income remained in the hands of the aristocracy, whose preference in consumption leaned toward luxuries produced abroad. Many of the specialized economies of towns surrounding Madrid fell into ruin in the seventeenth century as a result (Ringrose, pp. 71–73).

While Castile under Habsburg rule faced tremendous economic challenges, it was certainly not entirely rigid in its social character. The renowned seventeenth-century Spanish accomplishments in elite culture included elements, such as popular theater, that were accessible to those of modest means in the towns and cities of the realm. The theater of the *siglo de oro,* though produced largely for and subsidized by the dominant social elements, did not unilaterally reinforce existing hierarchies: many of the comedies, in fact, ridiculed aristocratic values and some even portrayed female assertiveness in a sympathetic light (McKentrick, pp. 196–201). Saints Day feasts, festivals, and *autos de fe* (religious pageants) provided more broadly shared leisure for the rural population.

POLITICAL CENTRALIZATION AND "ENLIGHTENED" REFORM

In terms of political centralization and bureaucratization, the Iberian Peninsula in the early modern period followed many general western European patterns. The Catholic kings and then the Hapsburgs put into place a system of royal councils to govern the state and a new civil service began funneling university-educated administrators into government for the first time. Still, the move toward a modern centralized state was thwarted by the continued insistence by Catalonia, Navarre, and the Basque Country that their ancient *fuero* liberties be respected by the Crown. Questioning the practicality of their union to an increasingly bankrupt Castilian Kingdom, both the Catalans and the Portuguese in 1640 rebelled against Spanish rule. While Portugal achieved independence, Catalonia was forced to settle for the Crown's renewed recognition of the region's historic liberties.

By the time that the Spanish Hapsburg line came to an end at the close of the seventeenth century, Portugal's independence was firmly established and Catalonia made another attempt to free herself. The Bourbon Philip V's (1683–1746) triumph in the War of Spanish Succession (1701–1714) resulted in a dramatic advance in the project of political centralization. Catalonia lost her medieval liberties and was severely punished for having opposed the Bourbon ascendency to the throne. The final battles preceding Barcelona's surrender in 1714 remain among the most commemorated episodes in Catalan historical consciousness today. In the Basque Country the *fueros* remained intact as a reward for having supported the Bourbons in the war. The Bourbon Kings completed the process of politically integrating Aragon into the Castilian state by suspending the latter's *cortes* and drafting a new constitution that included none of the Aragonese-Catalan liberties.

Equipped with greater centralized powers, the new Bourbon rulers of Spain implemented policies engendering economic revitalization and middle-class growth. During the reign of Charles III from 1759 to

Marketplace. *Holiday in Madrid* in the plaza de la Cebada, painting (c. 1800) by Manuel de la Cruz. MUSEO MUNICIPAL, MADRID/LAURIE PLATT WINFREY

1788, reform endeavors were undertaken in agriculture, the church, education, and the finances of the state. The long-term problems of Andalusian agriculture were addressed through measures to control peasant rents, state-sponsored irrigation projects, and efforts to repopulate uncultivated lands. The *mesta* was disbanded as well. The Crown also made some progress in limiting the power of the church and in increasing the educational preparation of the priesthood. The government encouraged the development of secondary schools and established new academies for the training of engineers and surveyors, and implemented fiscal reforms, including the establishment of a national bank, standardization of coinage, and the introduction of paper money. Bourbon Spain in the eighteenth century clearly reflected the currents of enlightened despotism that moved through much of the continent, despite tendencies in earlier historiography to discount the influence of the Enlightenment in Spain.

Among the most important triggers of economic growth in the eighteenth century was the opening of ports throughout Spain to trade with the Americas. In the first decade of the new policy, trade increased

tenfold. The process of industrialization in northeastern Spain gained full force in the eighteenth century. In Catalonia the agricultural economy underwent increasing conversion to viticulture, and the profits from the export of brandy were re-invested in the mechanization of cotton cloth production. Barcelona's expanding commercial activities placed it at the head of a western Mediterranean urban trade network that extended from Málaga to Marseilles (Ringrose, p. 44). Other trading networks also expanded on the Peninsula in this period and laid the foundation for two centuries of economic growth. With Bilbao as the dominant city, a northern Spanish urban network consolidated from Vigo near the Portuguese border to San Sebastián. In the interior of the Peninsula, a third urban network emerged with Madrid at its center. Composed of trade with specialized market towns and seaports, and fueled by the demand generated by the government administration and the military, luxury goods continued to figure as an important component of Madrid's overall commerce. A fourth network in the south included two economically powerful urban centers in Seville and Cádiz (Ringrose, pp. 46–50).

THE NINETEENTH CENTURY: LIBERAL REVOLUTION

The French Revolution (1789) and then Napoleon's (1769–1821) invasion (1808) disrupted the economic and demographic expansion of the first century of Bourbon rule in most of the peninsula. Between 1790 and 1820, Spain lost population, and trade and manufacturing dropped off sharply, partly as a result of the loss of the bulk of her American colonies. The conflict was complicated, with diverse factions opposing and supporting France for different reasons. Still, the subsequent portrayal by political and cultural elites of the War of Independence (1821) as a moment of Spanish unity contributed to the War's use as a rallying point of nationalism in the second half of the nineteenth century and remained viable in the decades leading up to the Spanish Civil War (1936–1939) (Alvarez Junco).

The nineteenth century was politically and socially tumultuous, and was defined by a liberal revolution that transformed political, property, and church-state relations. Inspired by a range of liberal ideas emanating from France, the forces favoring sweeping change coalesced in Cádiz to produce a constitution in 1812 that limited monarchical power more extensively than anywhere else on the Continent. When the Bourbon Ferdinand VII (1784–1833) re-assumed the throne in 1814, these precepts, and indeed the constitution itself, were cast aside in favor of monarchical privilege. Through the reign of Ferdinand VII the polarized political factions adamantly favoring and opposing the ancien regime gained momentum. At one extreme were liberals who supported the 1812 constitution and significant limitations on monarchical power; on the other were traditionalists who viewed Ferdinand as the epitome of all that was wrong with the vacilating monarchs of the modern world. One traditionalist faction supported Ferdinand's more pious brother Charles over the succession of the King's daughter Isabel. This Carlist movement was centered in the rural mountainous regions of Navarre, the Basque Country, Aragon, and Catalonia. Carlists launched several protracted uprisings in the nineteenth century and remained a force of reaction emanating from the north of the peninsula up to and during the Spanish Civil War. However, by the 1840s the liberals had gained control of the political system.

The rest of Spain's nineteenth-century political history reflected the struggle of contesting liberal visions of the constitutional terms that would govern the relationships between state and society. Certainly a broad consensus in favor of the concept of constitutional limitations on the power of the monarchy had spread widely through the Peninsula over the course of the century.

As in France, Germany, and elsewhere in Europe, Spain in the nineteenth century was also involved in a contested social struggle to democratize the emerging liberal order. New groups entering the political arena included army officers adhering to shades of liberal ideology and intervening in government through the use of a tool known as the *pronunciamiento* (military coup) and urban mobs who variously supported and opposed the military officers' leads. Added to these were Catalan factory workers who had organized collectively by the 1850s and Andalusian peasants, who, as a result of population pressure and the underpinning of the *latifundista* system that resulted from the 1837 nationalization and sale of church lands, were experiencing worsening living conditions. The liberal revolution in property relations had failed to create a new nation of stable farmers along French lines. It instead reinforced existing landholding patterns.

The Portuguese state, too, underwent dramatic change in the century that followed the Napoleonic invasion. After a long period of economic decline that had set in over the course of the sixteenth century, Portugal's colonial empire shrank, and in 1822, even Brazil was lost. Liberal ideologies had gained ground and experiments with constitutional limitation of monarchic rule eventually gave way to authoritarianism. A resurgence of liberalism ushered in a sixteen-year Republic that collapsed in 1926 and was replaced with what would become Europe's longest dictatorship.

The struggle to democratize the liberal order, 1876–1939.

After a tumultuous six years of revolution (1868–1874), the period in Spanish history known as the Restoration (1876–1931) featured a modicum of political stability alongside economic growth and social polarization. Though the 1876 Constitution called for universal manhood suffrage, in fact the commitment to democracy was an empty one. Elections were quite openly subverted through the use of political bosses in the countryside who collaborated in the Liberal and Conservative parties' agreement to simply take turns in power. The loss of Cuba in 1898 as a result of the Spanish-American War (April–August 1898) came as a painful blow to Spanish confidence, setting off an intellectual movement that sought to define the essence of Spain and the best future path for the recovery of her grandeur. Ironically, the Generation of 98's reflections coincided with the assertion of regional political aspirations, which questioned the viability of Castilian dominance of the Spanish polity.

Regional nationalism. In both Catalonia and the Basque country, modern political nationalism took shape in the late nineteenth century. Emerging somewhat earlier, and serving as a model for the Basques, Catalan nationalism had its roots in the linguistic continuities of everyday life, but also in a varied number of other factors and circumstances. The Catalan language, though sharing much with Spanish and other Romance tongues, was distinct and remained the dominant if not exclusive language in the majority of households in every social stratum of the region through the nineteenth century. Catalan predominated especially among the popular classes, which responded favorably to the elite-driven romantic cultural movement of nationalist rediscovery that began in the 1830s and was known as the *Catalan Renaixança*. By the end of the nineteenth century a series of explicitly Catalanist groups emerged, but none as powerful as the *Lliga Regionalista* that was founded in 1901. At first representing a broad coalition, it was soon reduced to its core of support among the upper ranks of the industrial and commercial bourgeoisie and Catalan Carlists. Still, Catalan nationalism was broad based and its forms varied along the political spectrum from radical to reactionary.

Basque nationalism also had its roots in historical experience. The three Basque provinces, Álava, Vizcaya, and Guipúzcoa, along with Navarre, retained their *fueros* as they were incorporated into the Spanish state. It was the formal abolition of the fueros in 1876 followed by the Spanish state's attempt to raise tax quotas in 1893 that set off Basque nationalism and led to the creation of the *Partido Nacionalista Vasco*, the PNV. Much more explicitly Catholic in its orientation than the Catalan variant, Basque nationalism was also distinct in its emphasis on the construct of race over the much more linguistically oriented identification of Catalanism. The growth and intensification of collective identities based upon social class and ideology fueled the emergence of these nationalist identities in the periphery of the peninsula during the Restoration.

ECONOMIC CHANGE AND WORKING-CLASS PROTEST

Modern working class protest took shape in Spain over the course of the nineteenth century in response to industrialization and the commercialization of agriculture and as an outgrowth of the larger European movement. Since industrialization developed in distinct regional centers, working-class organization began as a local and regional phenomenon. Thus, the first trade unions appeared among textile workers in Catalonia in the 1830s and contributed to a broad-based labor movement in the 1850s. In 1879, the Spanish Socialist Party (P.S.O.E.) was founded in Madrid. Though the Socialist federation of trade unions (General Union of Workers) was formed in 1888, in Valencia, Murcia, and Andalusia, the labor movement that developed was much more explicitly anarchist in its orientation. This was especially the case among the landless peasants of Andalusia, where the ideas of Mikhail Bakunin (1814–1876) spread widely. While Spain remained behind the leading nations of Europe in its agricultural productivity, considerable increases in the output of the rural economy accompanied industrial growth and the urbanization of the nation's most important cities. Migration from rural Andalusia to industrialized Catalonia added to the fervent mix of ideological currents among the working classes. By the turn of the century, Spain was embroiled in class warfare, especially in the industrial centers of Vizcaya and Asturias, where industry was based on mining and metallurgy, in the textile region of Catalonia, and in the latifundia areas of the south. Some of the most bitter battles were fought, as in 1909, on the streets of Barcelona where anarchism mixed with violent strains of anticlericalism. In 1910, the anarchosyndicalist trade union, the CNT, was formed and began quickly to gain widespread support among workers.

Through the second decade of the twentieth century, especially as World War I inflation far outstripped wages in Spanish cities and Andalusia, labor unrest intensified. The dictatorship of General Miguel Primo de Rivera y Orbaneja (1870–1930) from 1923 to 1931 temporarily forestalled further conflict by suspending the constitution, repressing labor organizations, and reversing the very limited Catalan regional autonomy that had been achieved over the course of the previous two decades. Still, the Primo regime's political repression only resulted in further ideological polarization between left and right. When municipal elections in 1931 swept Republicans into office, King Alfonso XIII (1883–1941) abdicated and the Spanish Second Republic was born.

Reflecting the profound shifts in political culture that had taken shape over the course of the previous century, the Second Republic moved to contain spreading anticlericalist violence and worker unrest by implementing policies of secularization and reform. The Second Republic instituted freedom of religion and the church was separated from the state. Other efforts included a modest restructuring of the Spanish army and a program of land reform to address the problems of the Andulsian peasantry. The Second Republic also granted womens' suffrage and instituted

Spanish Civil War. Troops loyal to Francisco Franco search government prisoners at Torrejou, near Madrid. ©BETTMAN/CORBIS

civil marriage laws and the right to divorce. Though essentially moderate, these reforms failed to go far enough to satisfy the left, while they were perceived by the right as extreme and dangerous to the future of the Spanish state. The election of a Popular Front government that included communists coalesced the disparate forces positioned against the regime. The church, the army, large landowners, and a host of rightist groups, including the Spanish Fascist Party, threw their lot together to overthrow the democratically elected government. The conflict was heightened by the European context of fascist victories and democratic decay.

The Nationalist uprising of July 1936 led by General Francisco Franco marked the beginning of a protracted and complex struggle. The Spanish Civil War involved considerable fragmentation on the Republican side and desperate struggles on the part of Spain's *de jure* government to maintain control of a social revolution set off by military revolt. Competing militias formed around trade union groups, and anticlerical violence pulsated through major cities. In Barcelona in May of 1937, a smaller civil war broke

out behind Republican lines between anarchosyndicalist and communist militias. The conflict was a bloody one that ended in anarchosyndicalist defeat. The Spanish Fascist Party, the *Falange,* took a leadership role in the uprising against the Republic, and General Franco's forces were aided by Benito Mussolini (1883–1945) and Adolf Hitler (1889–1945) in the struggle. The Republicans, internally divided and aided by Joseph Stalin (1879–1953) and by the volunteer International Brigades, were outmatched, and met defeat in 1939 after three long years of war. The struggle to democratize the liberal order had ended in defeat.

THE FRANCO REGIME: DICTATORSHIP AND ECONOMIC MODERNIZATION

The Spanish Civil War brought the Franco Regime to power and an abrupt change, through repressive dictatorship, to Spanish society. A single-party state, featuring a fascist-inspired system of vertical syndicates, was designed by Franco as an "organic" alternative to supposed "inorganic" marxist and liberal-capitalist political models. Under Franco, all power rested in the dictator's hands and a program of ideological mobilization was effected through propaganda organizations that targeted youth, university students, and women. All of the rights accorded women under the Republic were rescinded and pronatalist policies were promulgated. Trade union activities outside the vertical syndicates were extinguished, strict press censorship was instituted, and autonomous regional structures of the Republic dismantled. The regime also outlawed the public use of Catalan in the professions, in education, and in the arts. Expressions of Basque nationalism and culture were likewise forbidden.

In the first ten years of the Franco regime, real wages and Gross Domestic Product (GDP) fell to levels as low as 50 percent of those obtained before the war. Everywhere economic misery was the order of the day with rationing remaining in effect throughout the 1940s. The Franco regime's policy of economic autarky sharply limited the prospects of recovery. Only after the defeat of the Axis powers in 1945 did the regime begin to distance itself from fascist rhetoric. It was not until 1957 that Franco embraced an alternative to the fascist ideal of national economic independence and replaced Falangist advisors with neoliberal technocrats committed to economic modernization. The technocrats' 1959 Stabilization Plan, after an initial recessionary period, bore fruit in a spectacular economic recovery extending from 1961 to 1973, the so-called "economic miracle." During those years Spain's

Forbidden to Strike. Spanish workers, forbidden to strike under the Franco regime, find a way to make their point. Madrid, May 1968. ©HULTON DEUTSCH COLLECTION/CORBIS

industrial sector grew dramatically and the Gross National Product (GNP) per capita more than doubled (Maxwell and Speigal, p. 7), partly funded by a booming tourist industry that brought cultural revolution as well as hard currency. Spain moved quickly in the 1960s to participate in the general expansion of consumer society that was taking place across western Europe. Moreover, the economic boom led to broad social changes, from the transformation of peasant into farmer in the north to the exodus of landless laborers from the rural south.

Such changes had not come about without pressure on the regime. Though Franco normalized relations with the west in the 1950s by playing its anticommunist Cold War card, the Catholic church began to distance itself from the regime and even defend the Catalans and Basques against linguistic and more generalized cultural repression. Censorship was eased somewhat in the early 1960s and proconsumerist policies were designed to dampen student and worker unrest. Still, opposition to the regime built, and clandestine political and trade unionist activities spread widely. Political imprisonment and violations of human rights in Spain remained common throughout the final decades of the dictatorship.

The Catalans and the Basques mounted some of the strongest movements in opposition to the Franco regime in its final years. The regime's policies of cultural and linguistic oppression had unintentionally strengthened the collective identities of Basque, Catalan, and other regional groups within the Spanish polity. Regionalist nationalist symbolism served as a potent rallying point for demonstrations of opposition to the dictatorship. Regionalism's mass appeal played an important role in the formulation of a consensus among Spaniards that Spain after Franco should become a pluralist state. Still, an important exception to the overwhelmingly peaceful and federalist aims of regional nationalist movements in late-twentieth-century Spain was the appearance in this period of the Basque separatist terrorist movement, ETA, which began a campaign of assassination designed to de-stabilize the regime. Several other terrorist groups emerging in the final years of the regime contributed to an atmosphere of political and social tension.

POLITICAL TRANSITION AND DEMOCRATIZATION

The transition to democracy after the death of Franco in 1975 was facilitated by his successor, King Juan Carlos I (1938–) who favored liberal reform. In 1978, the Spanish Cortes ratified a new constitution that

316

created a parliamentary monarchy featuring broad freedoms and a guarantee of autonomy to historic subnationalities and regions. Apart from a failed military coup attempt in 1981, Spanish political culture since the transition has exhibited respect for pluralism and the rule of law.

In 1982, a moderate European-style social democratic party, the P.S.O.E., won an overwhelming majority in Spanish parliamentary elections. Under the leadership of Prime Minister Felipe González, a process of political decentralization took place as autonomy was granted to a series of Spanish regions, including Catalonia and the Basque Country, and military reform placed the armed forces under civilian control. Spain joined the European Community (now part of the European Union) in 1986 and became a leader of the poorer nations of western Europe within that structure. Dramatic economic growth in the late 1980s brought the further spread of consumerist values, the growth of the middle class, and the rapid expansion of the tertiary sector of the economy.

The European-wide economic recession of the early 1990s led to a sharp rise in business failures and unemployment. Under investigation for financial cor-

ruption, the P.S.O.E. lost the parliamentary elections of 1997 to the center-right *Partido Popular* (PP), which formed coalition government with the Catalan nationalist *Convergencia i Unió* (CiU) Party, creating an alliance that cut across the divides of the Civil War and early Franco periods. Still, significant problems persisted, especially with respect to the achievement of European Union fiscal goals and the definition of the constitutional limits of regional autonomy. In addition, the profound disagreement between the Spanish state and those who supported the ETA terrorist movement remained a particularly violent and unresolved problem.

Portugal's history has in many ways paralleled Spain's in the twentieth century. The Portuguese First Republic, established in 1916, was never fully democratic and depended on the support of liberal army officers. In 1926 a military coup that drew simultaneously upon ideas of regeneration and millenarianism brought the Republic to an end. From 1932 to 1969 Antonio de Oliveira Salazar ruled as an authoritarian premier. Salazar, like Franco, sought above all else to preserve traditional Catholic values and began his rule by pursuing policies of economic autarky. By

Holiday Destination. Sunbathers along the beach at San Sebastian, Spain, c. 1987. GALEN ROWELL/©CORBIS

the late 1950s, though, Salazar had begun to accept foreign capital as a means to accelerate industrial growth. Yet the economy continued to lag behind that of Spain and Europe. Significant waves of outmigration in the 1970s contributed to slow demographic growth in a nation that was still largely agricultural.

In Portugal, too, by the time of the dictator's death, the transition to democracy occurred with relative ease. The 1974 "Revolution of Flowers" brought a parliamentary democracy to power, though one that included a continued role for the military in government. Since the establishment of democracy, centrist and rightist parties have dominated national politics.

CONCLUSION

The social history of the Iberian Peninsula has followed a course that in a great number of ways mirrors that of western Europe. Participating in the urbanization processes and vibrant Mediterranean commercial capitalism of the Middle Ages, the peninsula played a leading role in the creation of the transatlantic world economy. The financial and imperial collapse of the early modern period, previously used to mark the start of Spain's long decline, did not in fact forestall the emergence of powerful regional economic networks and the beginnings of industrialization in the second half of the eighteenth century. Middle-class growth and the spread of liberalism in the nineteenth century roughly paralleled the social and political course followed by a number of western European nations, though some differences, of course, remain.

Much of the Iberian Peninsula's twentieth-century history has featured more variation from the western European pattern, at least in political terms. Remaining neutral in both World Wars and experiencing a much longer period of right-wing dictatorship, economic recovery and the growth of postwar European consumer society came later to the Peninsula than to those regions of Europe participating in the Marshall Plan (1948–1952). The liberalization of social and sexual mores was delayed until the transition to democracy in both Spain and Portugal in the mid-1970s. Though in the last quarter of the twentieth century the Iberian Peninsula came to share in all of the main characteristics of western Europe's economic, social, political, and cultural structures, the region continues to adhere to more specific Mediterranean patters of leisure, public sociability, and culinary practice.

See also **The World Economy and Colonial Expansion** *(in this volume);* **Fascism and Nazism** *(volume 2);* **Catholicism** *(volume 5); and other articles in this section.*

BIBLIOGRAPHY

Alvarez Junco, José, and Adrian Shubert, eds. *Spanish History since 1808.* London and New York, 2000.

Alvarez Junco, José. "La invencion de la guerra de la independencia." *Studia Historica. Historia Contemporánea* 1994 (12): 75–99.

Amelang, James S. *Honored Citizens of Barcelona: Patrician Culture and Class Relations, 1490–1714.* Princeton, N.J., 1986

Bilinkoff, Jodi. *The Avila of Saint Teresa: Religious Reform in a Sixteenth-Century City.* Ithaca, N.Y., 1989.

Carr, Raymond. *Spain: 1808–1939.* Oxford, 1970.

Carr, Raymond, ed. *Spain: A History.* New York, 2000.

Carr, Raymond, and Juan Pablo Fusi Aizpurua. *Spain: Dictatorship to Democracy.* London and Boston, 1979.

Cruz, Jesus. *Gentlemen, Bourgeois, and Revolutionaries: Political Change and Cultural Persistence among the Spanish Dominant Groups, 1750–1850.* Cambridge, U.K., 1996.

Ellwood, Sheelagh M. *Spanish Fascism in the Franco Era: Falange Española de las Jons, 1936–76.* Basingstoke, U.K., and New York, 1987.

Enders, Victoria Lorée, and Pamela Beth Radcliff. *Constructing Spanish Womanhood: Female Identity in Modern Spain.* Albany, N.Y., 1999.

Fontana, Josep, ed. *España bajo el Franquismo.* Barcelona, 1986.

Freedman, Paul H. *The Origins of Peasant Servitude in Medieval Catalonia.* Cambridge, U.K., and New York, 1991.

Graham, Helen, and Jo Labanyi, eds. *Spanish Cultural Studies: An Introduction: The Struggle for Modernity.* Oxford and New York, 1995.

Kaplan, Temma. *Red City, Blue Period: Social Movements in Picasso's Barcelona.* Berkeley, Calif., 1992.

Kurlansky, Mark. *The Basque History of the World.* New York, 1999.

Johnston, Hank. *Tales of Nationalism: Catalonia, 1939–1979.* New Brunswick, N.J., 1991.

McDonogh, Gary Wray. *Good Families of Barcelona: A Social History of Power in the Industrial Era.* Princeton, N.J., 1986.

McKendrick, Melveena. *Theatre in Spain, 1490–1700.* Cambridge, U.K., and New York, 1990.

Maddox, Richard. *El Castillo: The Politics of Tradition in an Andalusian Town.* Urbana, Ill., 1993.

Maxwell, Kenneth, and Steven Spiegel. *The New Spain: From Isolation to Influence.* New York, 1994.

Molinero, Carme, and Pere Ysas. *El regim franquista: Feixisme, modernitzacio, i consens.* Vic, Spain, 1992.

Monter, William. *Frontiers of Heresy: The Spanish Inquisition from the Basque Lands to Sicily.* Cambridge, U.K., and New York, 1990.

Nader, Helen. *Liberty in Absolutist Spain: The Hapsburg Sale of Towns, 1516–1700.* Baltimore, 1990.

Nalle, Sara T. *God in La Mancha: Religious Reform and the People of Cuenca, 1500–1650.* Baltimore, 1992.

Nash, Mary. *Defying Male Civilization: Women in the Spanish Civil War.* Denver, Colo., 1995.

Ortiz, David, Jr. *Paper Liberals: Press and Politics in Restoration Spain.* Westport, Conn., 2000.

Payne, Stanley G. *Falange: A History of Spanish Fascism.* Stanford, Calif., 1961.

Preston, Paul. *The Politics of Revenge: Fascism and the Military in Twentieth-Century Spain.* London and Boston, 1990.

Radcliff, Pamela Beth. *From Mobilization to Civil War: The Politics of Polarization in the Spanish City of Gijon, 1900–1937.* Cambridge, U.K., and New York, 1996.

Reher, David Sven. *Perspectives on the Family in Spain: Past and Present.* Oxford and New York, 1997.

Ringrose, David R. *Spain, Europe, and the "Spanish Miracle," 1700–1900.* Cambridge, U.K., and New York, 1996.

Shubert, Adrian. *A Social History of Modern Spain.* London and Boston, 1990.

Vicens Vives, Jaime. *Approaches to the History of Spain.* Translated by Joan Connelly Ullman. Berkeley, Calif., 1967.

Ullman, Joan Connelly. *The Tragic Week: A Study of Anti-clericalism in Spain, 1875–1912.* Cambridge, Mass., 1968.

Woolard, Kathryn A. *Double Talk: Bilingualism and the Politics of Ethnicity in Catalonia.* Stanford, Calif., 1989.

ITALY

Lucy Riall

Diversity is possibly the most enduring feature of Italy's history from the Renaissance to the end of the twentieth century. Variations in geographical regions, each with its own distinctive system of agriculture; in climate, depending on latitude and altitude; and in peoples and societies, with a gamut of cultural and linguistic forms, contribute to a remarkable array of competing and overlapping identities and economic and social structures. These variations, moreover, do not always conform to the established patterns of historical analysis, as they occur at times within regions and localities and within families and ruling elites; some differences disappear or are altered, only to be reestablished over time.

For the social historian, such diversity can be frustrating, as it works against meaningful generalizations. Yet it also makes Italy a fascinating subject for the study of social behavior and interaction. The social history of Italy offers particular examples of broader trends such as the structure of family life, the emergence of middle classes and the decline of the nobility, the crumbling of feudal jurisdictions, the process of refeudalization, and the road to modernity. Its complexities have consistently challenged historians' assumptions and forced them to reformulate both their explanations and the models on which these explanations are based.

To the reality of social diversity must be added the unevenness of scholarly attention: Italian social history has long been overshadowed by the country's cultural and political past. Thus Italy's social structures in the early modern period have tended to be neglected in favor of Renaissance art and learning; in the nineteenth and twentieth centuries, historians have traditionally focused on the Risorgimento or Mussolini's Fascism, or have concentrated on the emerging sense of "Italianness" (*italianità*) in the same period, rather than examine underlying social change. The popularity of the Renaissance, Risorgimento, and Fascism as subjects for study has meant that the almost two hundred years between the end of the Renaissance and the beginning of the eighteenth-century Enlight-enment—the "forgotten" centuries of so-called baroque Italy—remain relatively understudied.

FROM THE RENAISSANCE TO THE RISORGIMENTO (c.1250–1860)

The perception of early modern Italy as a "dreary interlude" (in Benedetto Croce's memorable phrase) between the Renaissance and the Risorgimento is itself the product of nation-building during the nineteenth century. At the time of national unification in 1860–1861, Italian political leaders appealed to and spoke about the nation's resurgence (*risorgimento*) after centuries of decline. Academics presented Italy's recent past as an experience of unremitting decay and backwardness. According to this interpretation, the high point of the Renaissance in the fourteenth and fifteenth centuries—when Italy led Europe in economic and cultural achievements—had given way to foreign invasion and internal divisions, with Italy succumbing to Spanish and, later, Austrian despots and the influence of a Counter-Reformation clergy. Languishing in the cultural, political, and economic doldrums of European life, Italian patriots saw it as their duty to rescue Italy and restore it to its former status. This view of Italian history as a frustrated nation persists in political rhetoric; but it is almost entirely useless for understanding the course, chronology, and rhythms of the peninsula's social development between the fifteenth and nineteenth centuries.

Environment and populations.   From the late Renaissance to the nineteenth century, Italy's cities and countryside attracted wealthy outsiders in search of beauty, art, or sheer escape. Yet northern Europeans seem rarely to have taken note of the lives and activities of the Italian people themselves, and they failed to see the landscape as the product of an interaction between Italians and their environment. The empty, open grainfields of southern Italy and Sicily were largely the product of deforestation in the sixteenth and seventeenth centuries—itself a response to rapid rises in the price of wheat. The physical appearance of the Lombardy plain, an intensively cultivated land of corn, rice, and animal husbandry, was the result of vigorous land reclamation, of irrigation and drainage, during the same period. Italians had fled to the hilltop towns of the southern Italian interiors and drained the marshlands largely to avoid malaria ("marsh fever"). Thus behind the beauty that visitors enjoyed lay Italians' responses to the difficulties of everyday life.

Malaria proved, until the mid-twentieth century at least, the deadliest scourge of the Mediterranean plains. But it was only one of several factors, including war and environmental change, behind the dramatic fluctuations in the population of the Italian peninsula between the fourteenth and seventeenth centuries. From an estimated 7.3 million in 1150, the population rose to 11 million by 1300 and then fell dramatically with the so-called calamities of the fourteenth century—the Hundred Years' War, the Black Death of 1348, and four famines between 1339 and 1375—to about 8 million. In contemporary accounts the Black Death alone was said to have killed some 70 percent of Venetians and Genoans, and while historians have revised these figures to an estimated third of the total population, its impact on urban centers—emptying cities like Florence and leading to the disappearance of smaller towns and villages—was devastating. Although after 1400 Italy's population gradually increased again, reaching 11.6 million by the mid-sixteenth century, this trend was frequently interrupted by wars (Rome, Brescia, Pavia, Ravenna, Prato, and Genoa were all sacked by invaders between 1510 and 1530), by the return of major outbreaks of the plague in the 1520s, and by the arrival of syphilis from the New World. Affected by these pressures, the population of, for example, Verona fell from 47,000 in 1501 to 26,000 in 1518, and that of Pavia from 16,000 in 1500 to under 5,000 in 1535. Interestingly, however, the halt to Italy's population growth was only temporary. It continued to increase steadily until the two great demographic crises of the late sixteenth century: the plague of 1575–1576 and the crop failures of 1590–1592. By the beginning of the seventeenth century, Italy had become one of the most densely populated regions in Europe. Then, during the seventeenth century, the pace of population growth slackened once more, affected as it was by famines and by the outbreak of bubonic plague in northern Italy in 1630 and in southern Italy in 1656, which caused mortality rates of 30 to 40 percent in the affected areas.

These fluctuations in population affected the cities and countryside differently; they also varied from one part of Italy to another and were sometimes accompanied by a process of internal migration. In the eighteenth century, however, emerged the entirely new demographic trend of sustained population growth. In approximate figures, from 13 million at the beginning of the eighteenth century, Italy's population increased to 18 million at its end, reached 24 million by 1850, and stood at just under 26 million in 1861. The huge population increases in eighteenth- and nineteenth-century Italy correspond to, although lag behind, the more general European trend, attributable to a decline in the mortality rate probably caused by changes in diet and improvements in hygiene, which in turn halted the spread of disease.

Nevertheless, the decline in the mortality rate did not signal the end of demographic crises. Outbreaks of plague recurred until the early nineteenth century (notably in Messina and Reggio Calabria in 1743), malaria increased along with the rural population, and tuberculosis accompanied the process of urbanization. The peninsula was affected by famine and subsistence crises in the eighteenth and nineteenth centuries. Improvements in diet were not all they seemed. Pellagra, a disease of malnutrition caused by a diet based exclusively on corn, became endemic to much of the Lombardy plain. Indeed, differences in diet and nutrition among the poor may explain why in this period population growth in the southern half of the peninsula, where the diet waas varied, consistently outstripped that of the center-north, where diet was almost exclusively polenta and potatoes. Finally, cholera, a new and deadly epidemic disease, swept through the cities of Italy in the mid-nineteenth century. An estimated one-sixth of the population of Palermo died in 1837. A widespread popular panic led to the temporary abandonment of cities, disrupting economic activity. Encouraged by antigovernment conspirators, the poor came to believe that cholera was a poison deliberately spread by their rulers, so that the epidemics also sparked off waves of political disorder and popular revolt.

City and countryside. During the Renaissance cities dominated the countryside, as is suggested by the formation of powerful city-states in northern and central Italy and by the centrality of urban areas to cultural, religious, and economic life. Hence Italian cities, especially those of the center-north, have long been associated with Italian civilization and with the banking, trade, and manufacturing activities for which Italy became famous during the thirteenth, fourteenth, and fifteenth centuries. Not surprisingly given this perspective, Italy's supposed economic, political, and cultural decline thereafter is allied to the process of ruralization and to the increasingly agrarian character

The Plague in Rome. Anonymous engraving, 1617. ©THE BRITISH MUSEUM, DEPARTMENT OF PRINTS AND DRAWINGS

of Italian society, a characteristic that did not alter substantially until well into the nineteenth century. Whereas much of Europe outside Italy became increasingly urbanized during the sixteenth and seventeenth centuries, in Italy the proportion of those living in towns of 100,000 or more fell to just 13 percent of the total population, while some medium-size towns like Pavia and Cremona lost between 20 and 40 percent of their inhabitants.

However, this juxtaposition between urban and rural life is a false one. Renaissance society was not in fact urban but largely rural: the rural population greatly outnumbered that of cities, many of which incorporated fields and orchards within their territory. Renaissance elites developed a taste for rural retreats and the rural aesthetic even as they mocked the crudeness of rural life. An idealized vision of the countryside as a place of escape and respite from the rigors of urban life persisted into the eighteenth and nineteenth centuries (and, of course, beyond). Furthermore, the economy of the countryside (*contado*) was closely integrated into urban life in Renaissance Italy. The countryside was a source of food, raw materials, revenue, and manpower for the towns; especially after the population decline of the fourteenth century, urban dwellers invested heavily in land, for example through sharecropping contracts in Tuscany and elsewhere. Moreover, the ruralization of the sixteenth century was accompanied by considerable prosperity, investment in agriculture, land reclamation, and the growth of textile production in parts of southern Italy. In the north the economic bust of the seventeenth century was also followed by a rural boom: by the recovery of agriculture, rural industrialization, and a further round of investment and innovation by energetic and innovative landowners.

In much of southern Italy and the islands in the early modern period, the relationship between city and countryside developed differently. Apparently unaffected by the demographic problems of the sixteenth century, the city of Naples grew rapidly from 100,000 in 1500 to an astonishing 245,000 less than fifty years later to become the largest city in Europe. By the mid-eighteenth century its population numbered 337,000. Although the growth of Naples was unusual, the result in part of incorporating the economic and political privileges of an administrative capital with the advantages of a Mediterranean port, it was not unique. Seventeenth-century Palermo grew substantially too, and for similar reasons.

The pattern of settlement within southern Italy shows considerable variation, notably a strong contrast between the market-oriented coastal areas and the more isolated interiors. In general, however, urban settlements in the south were fewer and much larger. Particularly in the remote and often mountainous interior, people tended to live concentrated in substantial nucleated centers occupying the high ground; they rarely took up residence permanently in the countryside. The lack of integration between city and countryside—indeed, the economic and cultural rift between them—was striking. This pattern of settlement in the south was partly a response, as has been noted, to the flight from the malarial plains. It was also the result of the deliberate "colonization" of the interior in the sixteenth and seventeenth centuries for the purposes of grain cultivation: many of the towns were newly created and their inhabitants originally migrant labor. Hence, the separateness of city and countryside in southern Italy reflects social and economic relations, specifically, the concentration of a great deal of farmland in the hands of relatively few, powerful landowners. In these southern grain-estates (*latifondo*), rural life was far from idealized; hardly bent on improvements and innovations, many landowners tended to be absentee rentiers. Unlike Lombard agriculture, the southern grain-estates were not subjected to the process of modernization that took place in the late seventeenth century.

Throughout the Italian peninsula, population growth in the eighteenth and nineteenth centuries was accompanied by a renewed process of urbanization, initially in the administrative centers and the ports and subsequently in areas of early industrialization.

Once again, however, this pattern was uneven. Turin, the capital of Piedmont, grew rapidly in the course of the eighteenth century, from 44,000 in 1702 to 92,000 by the 1790s and 138,000 by 1850. Milan grew from 123,000 in 1750 to 193,000 in 1850, by which year the population of Naples reached 416,000. Some cities grew much more slowly: from 1750 to 1850 Rome increased its population by only 13,000 (from 157,000 to 170,000), while the population of Venice stalled at about 138,000.

At around the same time, politics and economic change disrupted the traditional balance between city and countryside and between different cities. The modernizing and reforming rulers of eighteenth- and early-nineteenth-century Italy began to dismantle some of the financial and political prerogatives, such as trade guilds, tax concessions, and industrial and administrative monopolies, with which cities had traditionally dominated the countryside and on the basis of which some cities did better than others. One major nineteenth-century victim was the city of Palermo, the administrative capital of Sicily; after the Bourbon monarchy's restoration in 1814–1815, the city saw its economic and political privileges eroded so that, by the time of national unification, its status had been reduced to that of a provincial town. Other Sicilian towns benefited from the administrative changes, while some ports profited considerably both from the increase in the volume of trade and the decline of Palermo. The societies of eighteenth- and early-nineteenth-century Italy remained predominantly agrarian. In 1800 less than 5 percent of the country's population lived in cities of over 100,00 inhabitants; in England and Wales the figure was 10 percent, in the Netherlands 11.5 percent.

Social orders and social classes. Before the mid-nineteenth century, Italy's system of social stratification is best described as one of orders. The hierarchy was defined in terms of reputation, honor, and birth. A class system, in which the role played in the process of production or, more simply, income and wealth determined an individual or family's position, did not exist. Nevertheless, it would be foolish to assert that money played no role in deciding collective alignments and identities.

Even during the most stable periods, this society of orders was never entirely static. An important distinction must be drawn between the feudal nobility, associated especially with the southern kingdoms, and the urban ruling class, or patriciate, which, triumphant after the struggles of communal Italy, emerged in cities like Florence, Siena, Venice, and Genoa. Yet the status and internal composition of both groups

was often quite confused; by the sixteenth century the distinctions between them had become blurred by intermarriage and by the pursuit of common economic interests. Relations beween urban and rural nobility, on the one hand, and the ruler, on the other, and between both and the church, also varied considerably over time, enhancing or undermining the predominance of the nobility. In the countryside feudal privilege persisted almost everywhere. Moreover, if at the apex of the social hierarchy stood the nobility, jealously controlling entrance to their ranks, their status, and their privileges, there was also more than one way to become ennobled—through service to the ruler, through professional qualifications, or, in a simpler and increasingly popular route, through money. In addition, access to power for the non-nobles was provided by vertical networks of friendship and patronage, and further avenues of influence were provided by guilds, religious confraternities, and community organizations.

On the whole, the Italian nobilities were remarkable for their success. Although scholarly opinion is divided on the long-term impact of this success, the defense of noble privilege, from the Renaissance to the eighteenth century, is uniformly regarded as no small achievement. Many historians of the Renaissance have pointed to the persistence of feudal jurisdictions long after the end of the Middle Ages, even in the more "capitalist" north; they argue that such persistence was often the result of an enduring legitimacy, popular loyalty, and "good lordship" rather than merely of coercion and exploitation. Feudal privileges and feudal lords survived, in other words, as an integrated part of a changing and progressive Renaissance society. Other historians write more negatively of a process of refeudalization during the sixteenth and seventeenth centuries, of the reappearance at this time of feudal prerogatives, enabling the nobility to reassert both its political position "above the law" and its economic control of the countryside. The baroque seventeenth century also saw the strengthening of an ideology of nobility, of the growth of a cult of genealogies and a code of chivalry pursued sometimes obsessively for its own sake. The increasing tendency of urban patriciates, previously involved in trade and manufacturing, to invest in land and engage in agriculture as an occupation more fitted to their noble status, seems further proof of the (re)consolidation of feudal power.

This refeudalization thesis seems to explain both the relative industrial decline of Italy in the baroque period and the apparent capacity of the nobility, especially in the south, to smother the progressive middle class and exploit the rural poor. However, this

Aristocratic Family. *Banquet after the Hunt,* painting by Carlo Cane (1618–1688). Castello Sforzesco, Milan/Scala/Art Resource, NY

thesis is perhaps too simple. In the crucial area of relations with the ruler, some nobilities were more successful than others. During the expansion of state power in the seventeenth and eighteenth centuries, some nobilities, most obviously where there was a preexising tradition of state service among the urban patriciate, adapted relatively easily to the growth of the state; they negotiated a new and profitable status quo whereby they cooperated with the ruler as administrators or tax collectors and were allowed to exercise considerable autonomy in local affairs. This pattern can be observed in cities like Florence and Milan. By contrast, the feudal nobility, which enjoyed extensive political and economic power in the countryside, was much more threatened by the process of state formation. Attempts to make the nobility accept the sovereignty of the state in fiscal affairs and in matters of law and order, and to push through a program of land reform and commercialization in the countryside, led to open confrontation with the state.

Resistance to reform was especially strong in Sicily and the kingdom of Naples, where in the late eighteenth century reformers attempted a direct assault on baronial privileges, and in the Papal States. In all these states the nobility successfully frustrated most of the major reforms. Yet the price of their success was a more or less permanent breach with the state and hence both the breakdown of the old status quo and the failure to arrange a new one. The consequences of this breach became all too clear in the first half of the nineteenth century, when the Bourbon monarchy in Naples made a renewed and more fortunate attempt to dismantle noble privileges and undermine the noble monopoly of landholdings. This second round of reforms had particularly devastating effects on the Sicilian nobility, who by the time of unification in 1860–1861 had lost a great deal of their economic and political power.

The extent to which the middle orders, or middle classes, were effectively smothered by the nobility is also open to question. The middle orders were a remarkably mixed group—merchants, professionals, bureaucrats, and magistrates—often internally divided and varying considerably in composition from region to region and from city to city. Before the industrialization of the late nineteenth century, it is probably more accurate to think of the middle orders in "humanistic" terms, as a group whose social formation was determined by participation in public institutions rather than by economic activity. From the Renaissance onward they seem to have been especially keen to acquire titles and other trappings of noble status and to ape the cultural styles and social habits of the nobility, despite attempts by the nobility to maintain their political and cultural distance. When they acquired spare capital, they tended to invest it in land rather than in industry or commerce, and, as the nobility's wealth and economic privileges were eroded in the course of the eighteenth and nineteenth centuries, they also tended to intermarry with the nobility. Does this evidence suggest, therefore, that the "middling orders" were never a distinct social grouping with a separate identity, value system, and ideology and were largely incapable of challenging the aristocratic domination of society and the state?

First, it must be remembered that mingling with the nobility was far from unusual, and such behavior can be found equally among German or British counterparts. Second, the attitudes and habits mentioned above can be somewhat misleading, and may mask entrepreneurial skills and a process of accumulation and upward mobility in which land ownership and even marriage were the most appropriate outlets. Considerable evidence also points to the emergence of a bourgeois identity and a separate bourgeois sphere in the late eighteenth and early nineteenth centuries: clubs formed theaters and cafés proliferated where middle-class men (but not women) could mingle and associate. These circles of sociability were a particularly prominent feature of Milan, Florence, and, to a lesser extent, Turin; they seem to have been less common in the cities of the south, although the scarcity of research makes it difficult to reach definitive conclusions. In other words, the reforms of the eighteenth century, the upheavals of the French Revolution and the Napoleonic period, and the economic and political changes of the Restoration era (1815–1860) contributed to the formation of a vigorous new elite, composed roughly of rich middle orders and the (perhaps less wealthy) nobility, an elite that was neither wholly aristocratic nor wholly bourgeois.

At the other end of the social spectrum were the urban and rural poor. The political, cultural, and economic gulf that divided the elites from the rest in Renaissance, baroque, and Risorgimento Italy was immense: it was the poor who were undernourished and more prone to disease and who, being close to destitution even in the best of times, suffered and died in times of war and famine. Yet research into the lives and conditions of the poor in early modern Italy has revealed that the poor too were divided by an internal hierarchy. Rural communities show considerable social differentiation among well-to-do farmers, tenants, sharecroppers, and landless laborers, just as in urban areas an acutely felt rift between a "labor aristocracy" of artisans, organized into and protected by guilds, and dependent wage earners caused friction and conflict.

The internal composition and definition of the poor was also affected by the political reforms and economic developments of the eighteenth and early nineteenth centuries. For example, the transformation of agriculture in the Po Valley and Lombard plain, and the development there of capitalist relations of production, led to a diminution in the number of sharecroppers and independent farmers and a corresponding increase in landless wage earners, or *braccianti*. In the large grain-estates of the south, where the peasant economy had always been precarious, many peasant families were rendered destitute by changes in the system of land tenure. In particular, government attempts to convert feudal domains to private property, in part by abolishing common-use rights and common land, resulted in what Emilio Sereni in *History of the Italian Agricultural Landscape* has called "a true and proper mass expropriation of the rights of those who farmed the fiefs" (Sereni, 1997, p. 283). Elsewhere, for example on the Po Delta and in the Tuscan Maremma (marshlands), land reclamation programs deprived traditional farmers of their means of subsistence and way of life.

For rural people, an obvious response to such expropriation was to migrate to the towns. Rural migration partly explains the increasing numbers of urban poor in cities like Milan, Turin, and Naples during the eighteenth century and afterward; once in town, rural men, women, and children came to form a hungry, underemployed mass of casual and easily exploitable labor. Indications of the mounting strain this placed on urban areas include the greater visibility of vagrants and prostitutes, the rising numbers of illegitimate births and abandoned infants in cities throughout Italy, and perhaps most tellingly, the increasing anxiety among urban elites about a tide of criminals and the threat from "dangerous classes." Especially in traditional urban centers, this situation also brought the rural poor into conflict with artisans and craftsmen, whose own status, skills, and earnings was threatened by imports of cheap, foreign-made goods and by government attempts to dismantle barriers to trade and the labor market. Thus, it is possible, to write about a certain proletarianization of the labor force in the first decades of the nineteenth century— that is, the loss of economic independence, the perceived erosion (if not the disappearance) of internal differentiations, and in some cases a deterioration in their material conditions. One direct consequence was a rapid escalation of social tensions.

Stability and conflict. The family played a crucial role in early modern Italian societies. Patrician families, such as the Gonzaga of Mantua and the Medici of Florence, could dominate a city's political and ecclesiastical life from generation to generation. The structures of family life also served as a safeguard and transmitter of wealth, and marriage served to increase

326

Land Use

Northern Italy

- ▨ Alpine zone
- ▤ Pre-Alpine zone of family farms
- ▨ Intensive capitalistic farming
- ▨ New land of Lower Po Valley
- ▲ Natural gas deposit

Southern Italy

- ▨ *Mezzadria*
- ▨ Extensive capitalistic farming
- ▨ Peasant mixed-farming
- ▥ Peasant *latifondo*
- ▤ Intensive farming

ONE HUNDRED MILES

Land Use in Italy. Adapted from Muriel Grindrod, *Italy* (London: Ernest Benn, 1968), p. 195.

wealth and cement personal alliances. There is also some evidence that the value placed on family life gave women a status and role not afforded them in public: the central role played by women within the family in Renaissance Italy, and especially their role in the upbringing of children, may have given them an economic and even spiritual leverage within society as a whole. For poorer families, kinship ties could offer both economic protection and security in hard times and a ready source of labor in others.

Yet for all the recognition of the family's persistent importance in Italian societies, there was little permanency about its internal structure. The historian of Renaissance Italy, for example, is struck above all by the enormous variety of family structures, by the coexistence of conjugal and multiple households, by the possibility of frequent change in family structures over time and of fluctuations according to economic circumstance, as well as by the distinctions between noble and non-noble families. In the course of the eighteenth and nineteenth centuries, following a general European trend, the number of conjugal households seems to have increased; this trend can be linked both to urbanization and to the proletarianization of the rural workforce, as wage laborers tended to live in nuclear families. Nevertheless, rural families in the center-north bucked this trend (and did so not merely where sharecropping and tenant farming survived); extended families of three generations and of several conjugal units living under one roof remained a common occurrence.

Arguably, the prominent role played by the family in Italian societies also left its mark on the public sphere of politics and the economy. On the one hand, both the affective ties of love and friendship and the emphasis within the family on hierarchy and obedience gave stability and sometimes legitimacy to the prevailing social and political order. On the other hand, the family remained a world apart, an alternative source of loyalty and identity to that of the increasingly powerful state. For example, as new forms of social stratification emerged in the course of the nineteenth century, and especially as the new middle orders began to merge with the old nobility, the family could become a means of retaining a sense of distinctiveness, a way for the nobility to maintain their cultural and ideological distance, if only on a personal level.

Of course, the family was not the only alternative source of stability and loyalty. Another central pillar of the social order in early modern Italy was the Catholic Church. During the Counter-Reformation of the late sixteenth and early seventeenth centuries, the confused and self-promoting systems of the Catholic Church were reformed. In their place emerged a much more absolutist and monolithic hierarchy, claiming for itself the sole right to decide doctrinal truth and define religious discussion and maintaining itself as rigidly separate from and superior to lay society. Repression of heresy and persecution of minorities (the virtual elimination of Protestantism and the expulsion or marginalization of Jews) also followed. In terms of its social impact, however, this change is perhaps less significant than what accompanied it—that is, a new commitment by the church to spreading the message of reform and an engagement with feelings of popular religiosity. This new mission manifested itself in the proliferation of cults, sanctuaries, and pilgrimages. It was so successful that by the eighteenth century religious fervor and the use of religious symbolism had become one of the most striking, and indeed persistent, features of Italian popular culture.

Family, church, and state, the pillars of the social and political order in early modern Italy, came increasingly into conflict with each other in the eighteenth and nineteenth centuries, as secular rulers sought to establish absolute power through a series of administrative and economic reforms. A main target of this reform program was, as has been noted, the privileges and prerogatives of the nobility; but the church's economic and political powers were similarly challenged (and it should be remembered that the church hierarchy was made up largely of the nobility). Like the nobility, the church resisted this attack on its position in many ways. Two of the most important were by mobilizing popular religiosity and by posing as the defenders of the rural poor, whose livelihood was threatened by land reform. In the Jacobin period (1798–1799), the church actively encouraged and organized popular discontent against the new revolutionary order, notably in the violent counterrevolutionary movements in Tuscany, the Papal States, and in the bloody Sanfedist rising of Cardinal Ruffo in Calabria. Earlier agitation over land issues and the later revolts against the Napoleonic regimes in Italy (1801–1814), were also partly the result of church attempts to direct peasant unrest for conservative purposes.

Given the extent of political and economic upheaval, foreign wars, famines, and epidemic diseases affecting the Italian peninsula between the sack of Rome in 1527 and national unification in 1860–1861, the number of rebellions during this period is surprisingly limited. In fact, popular unrest did become a mark of Italian society, but not until the mid-to late nineteenth century. Before then, banditry was a fairly widespread, even infamous, feature of the Italian countryside. There were only two periods of urban revolt that resonated beyond their immediate areas: the first occurred during the seventeenth century, above all in southern Italy (Naples in 1647, Messina in 1671); the second occured during the European revolutions of 1848–1849, affecting all the states of the Italian peninsula. The 1647 revolt in Naples, preceded by revolt in Palermo and followed by one in Messina, was a popular revolt with a strong religious dimension, led by a charismatic fisherman known as Masaniello (Tomasso Aniello), against taxation and against the Spanish government. It spread rapidly to the countryside and to provincial towns and, in the struggle between peasants and nobility, acquired something of a class character. The 1848–1849 revolutions followed a prolonged period of economic deprivation and were led mostly by artisans and craftsmen in the cities demanding democratic rights of suffrage and association. Like the revolt in Naples, the later revolutions were undermined and eventually defeated by internal divisions, by the gulf between the

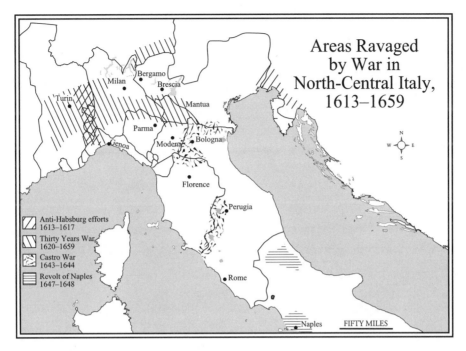

Areas Ravaged by War in North-Central Italy, 1613–1659. Adapted from Gregory Hanlon, *The Twilight of a Military Tradition: Italian Aristocrats and European Conflicts, 1560–1800* (London: UCL Press, 1998).

elite and the masses, and by huge differences separating the city from the countryside. The 1848–1849 revolutions also revealed the mounting health, housing, and employment crisis within Italian cities, a crisis that neither the welfare systems nor the police proved able to control or withstand.

FROM NATIONAL UNIFICATION TO THE REPUBLIC (1861–c.1990)

It is a truism of historical research that Italy in 1860–1861 was united in name only. Geography, culture, economic activity, and regional and local loyalties continued to separate Italians after national unification as before. National unification was nevertheless a climactic moment in the long transition from a traditional to a modern society, a process that extended from the mid-eighteenth to the mid-twentieth centuries throughout the Italian peninsula and that affected different areas and different groups in different ways. Yet perhaps the greatest social changes took place only after 1945, during the "economic miracle" of the 1950s and 1960s and as a result of the "cultural revolution" of the 1970s.

The transformation of landscape and populations. Between 1861 and 1981 the Italian popula-

tion more than doubled, from just under 26 million to 56.5 million. At the time of unification, Italy's birth and mortality rates (38 percent and 30.9 percent respectively) were high relative to Britain and France, and life expectancy, at 30.5 years, was more than ten years shorter. By 1981, however, these trends had been completely reversed. Compared with figures for Britain and France, Italy's birthrate (10.1 percent) and mortality rate (9.5 percent) were lower, and its life expectancy (77.3 years) was higher. Particularly noteworthy is the decline in the birthrate, which in 2000 was the lowest in the world.

The link between these demographic shifts and rising living standards is hard to pinpoint. Between 1870 and 1900, because of overpopulation leading to unemployment, the standard of living in rural Italy probably worsened, and many wage laborers fell below subsistence level. Population increase also led to the spread of endemic disease (pellagra in the north, malaria in the south). The Fascist years (1922–1943) saw a stagnation in wages and consumption. In reality the real transformation of living standards and lifestyles took place after the end of World War II, when real per capita income increased by a factor of 4.4. The number of cars, telephones, and televisions increased hugely between 1951 and 1987, as did the number of hospital beds, university students, and airline passengers. Housing and diet improved dramatically, the

Italy since 1919. Adapted from Christopher Duggan, *A Concise History of Italy* (Cambridge, U.K.: Cambridge University Press, 1994).

average height of Italians shot up (an Italian born in 1949 reached an average height of 1.69 meters; one born in 1955 reached 1.71 meters), and malaria was wiped out. The old-age pensioner became a common figure in Italian society. Yet an estimated one-seventh of Italians still lived below the poverty line in the 1980s, although income distribution in Italy was rather less unequal than in the other advanced European economies.

Hence, the transformation of Italian society took place at an uneven pace, reflecting in part the irregular rhythms of economic development. Undoubtedly the most striking and well-known aspect of Italy's uneven transformation is its regional imbalance, in particular, the gap between north and south. Notions of a north-south divide are, in social and economic terms, an oversimplification (economic historians refer to three Italies—northwest, center and northeast, south), and perceptions of southern backwardness tend to under-estimate both the economic dynamism and the extent of social diversity within the south; nevertheless, one constant of Italian history since 1861 has been the south's lower living standards, lower per capita income, lower per capita GDP (gross domestic product), higher unemployment, and higher rates of illiteracy as compared with the north. The process of industrialization—after unification in the triangle of Piedmont, Liguria, and Lombardy, and after World War II in central and northeastern Italy—together with the partial shift to a service economy after 1945, has led to marked changes in the composition of the Italian labor force. The percentage of those employed in agriculture fell from 52 percent in 1936 to 11 percent in 1981 and in industry rose from 25.6 to 41.5 percent during the same period. But the number of those employed in agriculture in the south has remained far greater than in the north (in 1981, 28 percent in Basilicata versus 3.8 percent in Lombardy), reflecting a weaker process of industrialization. The modernization of agriculture, moreover, has proceeded at a much slower pace in the south.

Another feature of the transformation of Italy's population was the acceleration of both internal migration and emigration. Emigration came first, reaching a peak in the decades between 1880 and 1910, when roughly 14 million applied to the government to leave. The majority of those who left were young men, often illiterate peasants, and while initially they came from the north, after the 1880s huge numbers left from the south. Interestingly, Italians dispersed more widely than other European migrants, arriving in the United States and Canada, Argentina and Brazil, Africa, Australia, and northern Europe. Although a significant proportion of migrants returned (an estimated 50 percent from the Americas between 1905 and 1920) and peasant households and whole villages could be enriched by emigrants' remittances, emigration also caused social upheaval, perhaps especially for the women who waited behind.

After 1945 came a further wave of emigration, notably to Argentina and Australia, but the 1960s and 1970s saw an unprecedented migration within Italy. The migration from the south to the northern cities was probably helped by the rapid improvement in communications and the construction of motorways, but it also reflected the rejection of a rural way of life by many southerners. The huge population influx placed the cities of the north under a terrible strain—the proliferation of squalid housing on city peripheries dates from this time—and led often to the bitter resentment and bad treatment of southern migrants (called *terroni,* bumpkins). It also emptied southern

The Emigrant's Guide. An aid to learning English published in San Francisco in 1860.

towns and villages of young men and, later, young women. Another demographic trend emerged after the 1980s, that of Italy as "receiving nation." Migrants to Italy, often from north and east Africa, some of them illegal (that is, without residence or work permits), have tended to concentrate in the larger Italian cities and in Palermo and Naples almost as much as in the north.

The challenge of a changing society. Perceptions of the Italian middle class as economically and politically backward relative to their counterparts in northern Europe, and as subordinate to the nobility, pervade the historiography of modern Italy. This analysis of middle-class weakness, particularly as applied to the social structures of southern Italy, is used to explain the so-called peculiarities of Italy's political development, above all the collapse of parliamentary government and the rise of Fascism after World War I. However, a subsequent analysis that has replaced the older one stresses the vitality of the Italian middle class, the rapid pace of social change, and the marginalization of the nobility from the mainstream of Italian life.

Research has shown that considerable social mobility, whether through education, public employ-

Sicily. *Occupation of Uncultivated Land in Sicily,* painting (1949–1950) by Renato Guttuso (1912–1987). DEUTSCHE AKADEMIE DER KUNSTE, BERLIN

ment, or commercial and entrepreneurial activity, produced an increasing number of middle-class Italians in the decades after national unification. A distinct bourgeois identity was defined through sociability, marriage, and political activity. In many regions of Italy, the process of amalgamation with the old nobility—in terms of politics and economics if not always culture—also continued. One unusual feature was the tendency of this new elite to keep to their immediate regions and cities, to marry those from nearby, to form clubs confined to their own area, and to maintain a strictly local focus on national politics. However, this too was to change, if only gradually, beginning in the years before 1914 but especially occurring during the Fascist period and above all in the postwar decades. Yet notwithstanding the growth of a national identity among the middle classes, that identity has continued to coexist with a strong sense of local or regional loyalty.

Some of the greatest changes affecting Italian society after 1861 were felt by the poor in urban and rural areas, but their impact varied greatly. A major spurt of industrial development took place after 1896, concentrated in the engineering and automobile sectors, but only in the provinces of Lombardy, Piedmont, and Liguria. Milan in particular saw the pioneering of methods of the "second industrial revolution," and its inhabitants experienced the first developments of

mass consumption and leisure. Still, older industries, notably textiles, continued to be important, and they continued as in the past to employ unskilled, often underpaid female workers. Although real wages in industry rose by 40 percent from 1900 to 1913, it was mainly the "labor aristocracy" of skilled workers whose lifestyles perceptibly improved.

The industrial cities also became a focus of political and social radicalism and remained so throughout most of the twentieth century. There were violent riots in Milan in 1898, and Milan and Turin were the focus of much strike activity in the years before 1914 and in the *biennio rosso* (two red years) of 1919 and 1920. The unexpected labor radicalism of the late 1960s and early 1970s were also partly centered on Milan. Indeed, radical and socialist movements tended to concentrate their organizational activities in the north and were disinclined, especially in the 1890s and in 1919–1920, to take an interest in peasant unrest in the southern half of the peninsula.

The Italian peasant world changed in fits and starts. In truth it was never as unchanging or unvaried as outsiders liked to think, but in the late nineteenth and twentieth centuries, it was subject to unprecedented commercial pressures and to greater government intervention. Peasants in the south, already a rural proletariat at the time of unification, continued to suffer badly as a result of the privatization of common and church land in the 1860s. Popular revolt first erupted in southern Italy in the decades preceding unification, and it expressed the anger and desperation of peasant families excluded from land and the means of subsistence. This situation reached a climax after 1860 in the "brigands' war" on the mainland and in the spread of unrest and general lawlessness through the western provinces of Sicily. Demands for land redistribution and for the negotiation of new, less unequal contracts between landlord and peasant resurfaced again in Sicily during the 1890s, and this time peasants formed agricultural unions (*fasci siciliani*) to press their case. Like the protests of the 1860s, however, these movements were repressed by the state. Arguably, greater benefits may have been gained from emigration which, starting in the 1890s, caused a scarcity of labor and may have resulted in higher wages being paid to rural workers.

The situation in the north was equally complex. The agricultural revolution of the 1890s in Lombardy, Venetia, and Emilia-Romagna was spearheaded by large tenant farmers and limited companies employing day laborers; the system of sharecropping further declined. Great wealth was in other words achieved through the proletarianization of the labor force, which bore the brunt of seasonal unemployment; huge disparities in wealth became a dominant feature of northern agriculture. It was also in this area, the Po Valley, that rural strikes spread during the turbulent early years of the century and after World War I. Throughout the Fascist period peasant landownership continued to decline in the north and made little headway in the south. Despite efforts by Benito Mussolini, the Fascist dictator, to encourage both rural smallholdings and extol the virtues of a rural way of life, a process of deruralization (migration to industry and the towns) was under way. Some steps were taken to establish a rural society peopled by small peasant farmers in the huge land reform of 1950, aimed mainly at the southern grain-estates, and in the local seizures of land led by communist activists, which took place in central Italy. However, as mentioned above, the flight from the land accelerated during the 1950s and 1960s, and, in the south at least, many peasants lacked the money or skills to farm their newly acquired plots. Southern peasants also found that in the setting up of state agencies to administer the reform, they had merely swapped one landowner for another, equally powerful one.

Nationalization and politicization.

The eighty or so years between national unification and the establishment of the first Italian Republic were years of immense political upheaval. The elitist parliamentary structures of the first decades, when less than 2 per-

cent of the population had the vote, gave way reluctantly to a broader-based, but arguably more corrupt, system prior to World War I. After 1922 came the years of the Fascist dictatorship, which in its turn collapsed into the turmoil of 1943–1948. This period also marks the emergence, often contested and sometimes reversed, of mass participation in politics in Italy and accompanied by successive waves of popular and political protest.

To what extent does this process of mass politicization point to the creation of a national culture in Italy? After unification the task of *fare gli italiani* (making Italians) was seen as one of the most pressing facing Italy's rulers, not simply because of the huge cultural and social disparities within the peninsula but also because the only truly national institution at the time, the Catholic Church, had declared itself openly hostile to the new political order. The aim to make Italians from Sicilians, Calabrians, Neapolitans, Florentines, and Venetians lay behind the educational and infrastructural programs of liberal Italy (1861–

The New Italy. Assembly line at a Ferrari automobile factory, 2000. GEORGE STEINMETZ

1922). It also produced statues and monuments in every Italian city, the organization of festivals and demonstrations, and, under Mussolini, more explicit attempts at social control through cinema, radio, and the organization of mass leisure. The extent to which these efforts were crowned with success is open to question. Especially in the liberal period, efforts at nation building were compromised by political resistance, by the opposition of the Catholic Church, and by the glaring gap between the myth of national unity and the reality of *campanilismo* (localism). Although the importance of nationalist sentiment among the elite should not be underestimated, local loyalties and identities continued to predominate.

Postwar trends seem to point in another direction entirely. The 1960s saw the rise of a mass or consumer society, in part the result of the "economic miracle" and of migration to the cities. The rising tide of cinema, television, and pop music, of automobile travel and mass publishing, among other expressions of modern life, led to a decline in local peasant cultures, traditions, and dialects; this trend continued during the 1980s and 1990s with the creation of national newspapers like *La Repubblica* and the concentration of ownership in the mass media. A number of countertrends should also be noted. The creation of a national culture was accompanied by its Americanization, especially in cinema and music, while at the same time Italy began to export its own distinctive lifestyle—cars and scooters, coffee and Chianti, women's shoes and men's suits. The creation of a consumer society was opposed by a vigorous counterculture, which found its fullest expression in the protest movements of the late 1960s and 1970s. And despite the secularization of Italian culture, a striking feature of the postwar period, religious symbols and icons did not disappear. All in all, the creation of a national culture from the different regions, cities, and localities of the Italian peninsula has been one of the slowest and most compromised processes of social change in the modern period. But it has also been one of the most remarkable. It has helped to produce a culture that is as varied as it is vibrant, and this not least because of its open-ended character.

See also **Emigration and Colonies** *(in this volume);* **Fascism and Nazism** *(volume 2);* **Banditry** *(volume 3);* **Catholicism** *(volume 5); and other articles in this section.*

BIBLIOGRAPHY

General Works

Braudel, Fernand. *The Mediterranean and the Mediterranean World in the Age of Philip II.* 2 vols. Translated by Siân Reynolds. Berkeley, Calif., 1995. Seminal work by celebrated *Annales* historian.

Carpanetto, Dino, and Giuseppe Ricuperati. *Italy in the Age of Reason, 1685–1789.* Translated by Caroline Higgitt. London and New York, 1987.

Clark, Martin. *Modern Italy, 1871–1995.* London and New York, 1996.

Cochrane, Eric. *Italy, 1530–1630.* Edited by Julius Kirshner. London and New York, 1988.

Duggan, Christopher, and Christopher Wagstaff, eds. *Italy in the Cold War: Politics, Culture, and Society, 1948–1958,* Oxford and Washington, D.C., 1995.

Ginsborg, Paul. *A History of Contemporary Italy: Society and Politics, 1943–1988.* London and New York, 1990.

Hay, Denys, and John Law. *Italy in the Age of the Renaissance, 1380–1530.* London and New York, 1989.

Hearder, Harry. *Italy in the Age of the Risorgimento, 1790–1870.* London and New York, 1983.

Holmes, George, ed. *The Oxford History of Italy.* Oxford and New York, 1997.

Riall, Lucy. *The Italian Risorgimento: State, Society, and National Unification.* London and New York, 1994.

Sella, Domenico. *Italy in the Seventeenth Century.* London and New York, 1997.

Woolf, Stuart. *A History of Italy, 1700–1860: The Social Constraints of Political Change*. London and New York, 1979.

Zamagni, Vera. *The Economic History of Italy, 1860–1990*. Oxford and New York, 1993.

Rural and Urban Life

Cochrane, Eric. *Florence in the Forgotten Centuries, 1527–1800: A History of Florence and the Florentines in the Age of the Grand Dukes*. Chicago, 1973.

Marino, John A. *Pastoral Economics in the Kingdom of Naples*. Baltimore, 1988.

Petrusewicz, Marta. *Latifundium: Moral Economy and Material Life in a European Periphery*. Translated by Judith C. Green. Ann Arbor, Mich., 1996. Revisionist account that challenges the view that southern grain-estates were uniformly backward.

Sella, Domenico. *Crisis and Continuity: The Economy of Spanish Lombardy in the Seventeenth Century*. Cambridge, Mass., 1979.

Sereni, Emilio. *History of the Italian Agricultural Landscape*. Translated by R. Burr Litchfield. Princeton, N.J., 1997. Pathbreaking study by Marxist historian using interdisciplinary methodology.

Waley, Daniel. *The Italian City-Republics*. 3d ed. London and New York, 1988.

Demography, Disease, Migration

Cipolla, Carlo M. *Fighting the Plague in Seventeenth-Century Italy*. Madison, Wis., 1981.

Gabaccia, Donna R. *Italy's Many Diasporas*. Seattle, Wash., 2000.

Snowden, Frank. *Naples in the Time of Cholera, 1884–1911*. Cambridge, U.K., and New York, 1995.

Religion, Family, Culture

Burke, Peter. *The Historical Anthropology of Early Modern Italy: Essays on Perception and Communication*. Cambridge, U.K., and New York, 1987.

Forgacs, David. *Italian Culture in the Industrial Era, 1880–1980: Cultural Industries, Politics, and the Public*. Manchester, U.K., and New York, 1990.

Forgacs, David, and Robert Lumley, eds. *Italian Cultural Studies: An Introduction*. Oxford and New York, 1996.

Gentilcore, David. *From Bishop to Witch: The System of the Sacred in Early Modern Terra d'Otranto*. Manchester, U.K., and New York, 1992. On the Counter-Reformation in southern Italy.

Ginzburg, Carlo. *The Cheese and the Worms: The Cosmos of a Sixteenth-Century Miller*. Translated by John and Anne Tedeschi. New York, 1982. On heresy.

Hay, Denys. *The Church in Italy in the Fifteenth Century*. Cambridge, U.K., and New York, 1977.

Herlihy, David, and Christiane Klapisch-Zuber. *Tuscans and Their Families: A Study of the Florentine Catasto of 1427*. New Haven, Conn., 1985.

Kertzer, David I., and Richard P. Saller. eds. *The Family in Italy from Antiquity to the Present*. New Haven, Conn., 1991.

Klapisch-Zuber, Christiane. *Women, Family, and Ritual in Renaissance Italy*. Translated by Lydia Cochrane. Chicago, 1985.

Social Classes and Social Conflict

Cardoza, Anthony L. *Aristocrats in Bourgeois Italy: The Piedmontese Nobility, 1861– 1930.* Cambridge, U.K., and New York, 1997.

Davis, John A. *Conflict and Control: Law and Order in Nineteenth-Century Italy.* Atlantic Highlands, N.J., 1988.

Davis, John A., and Paul Ginsborg, eds. *Society and Politics in the Age of the Risorgimento: Essays in Honour of Denis Mack Smith.* Cambridge, U.K., and New York, 1991. Contains a useful collection of essays on the Italian middle classes, crime, poverty, the family, and women.

Pullan, Brian. *Rich and Poor in Renaissance Venice: The Social Institutions of a Catholic State, to 1620.* Oxford and Cambridge, Mass., 1971. On the problems of welfare.

Riall, Lucy. " 'Ill-contrived, badly executed [and] . . . of no avail'? Reform and Its Impact in the Sicilian *Latifondo* (c.1770–c.1910)." In *The American South and the Italian Mezzogiorno: Essays in Comparative History.* Edited by Rick Halpern and Enrico dal Lago. New York, forthcoming. An analysis of the changing social structure of Sicilian rural society.

Villari, Rosario. *The Revolt of Naples.* Translated by James Newell and John A. Marino. Cambridge, U.K., and Cambridge, Mass., 1993. The classic account of the famous revolt.

CENTRAL EUROPE

Mary Jo Maynes and Eric D. Weitz

Central European social historians can never "leave the politics out." From the sixteenth century through the twentieth, and to a degree uncommon elsewhere in Europe, the role of the state has loomed large in shaping key social-historical developments. In such realms of social history as class formation, the evolution of the public sphere, family life, gender relations, religious and educational institutions, migration, urbanization, and communications, the state has played a constitutive, at times determining, role.

Complexities of scale, related to a persistent regional pattern of decentralized state building, have also been significant. Central Europeans have retained local loyalties because of both localized state building and other localizing institutions such as craft and merchant guilds, splintered dialect and religious communities, and land tenure patterns. At the same time, links to other parts of Europe and the wider world have also played a historical role. Commercial ties and shared culture linked the central European bourgeoisie with counterparts in England, France, and elsewhere. Catholics of course retained loyalties to a church with universal claims. The notably large number of central European socialists and communists claimed that loyalties should be class-based and international in scope. Jews, also numerous in this part of Europe, had far-flung religious, family, business, and social ties. Over the course of several hundred years, nationalist ideology and the nation-state became superimposed upon the local, regional, and transnational, but these other levels of social relations nevertheless persisted.

CENTRAL EUROPE: THE REGION AND ITS DIVERSITY

"Central Europe" denotes the lands bordered on the west by the Rhine River basin and in the east by a topographically unmarked line running roughly from just west of Warsaw to Budapest and then, swinging further west, to Trieste. In the north, the Baltic and North Seas mark its bounds; in the south, the south-

ern descent of the Alps. Central Europe is a region marked by a high level of diversity—political, religious, and regional—as well as by the more common European divisions by class and gender.

Linguistically, German speakers have dominated central Europe; even in those parts of central Europe where German was a minority language it was usually the language of commerce, governance, and high culture. But German speakers often lived among speakers of Polish, Czech, Danish, Yiddish, French, and other languages or dialects. Significantly, for its entire modern history, central Europe has been politically decentralized, and borders have shifted frequently. In the early modern era there were several hundred virtually sovereign states in the region (over two thousand if the tiny enclaves ruled by Imperial Knights are added). Napoleonic consolidation and national unification in the nineteenth century reduced this number dramatically. Yet political consolidation has never been a one-way street; as empires collapsed in the twentieth century, smaller political units reemerged—an Austria shorn of its possessions further east, an East Germany, a Czech Republic.

Central Europe has also been divided along religious lines. Since the Reformation, the Main River has marked the border between a largely Protestant north and a Catholic south. Jews were once present in communities all across central Europe, in greater numbers as one moved further eastward. But even in some small villages in the rural southwest, one could find significant Jewish communities until the 1940s.

Still another divide has persistently marked central European history—an economic one. Here the Elbe River border has played a persistent role. To its east lay large estates worked by a peasant labor force subject to the "second serfdom"—that is, a system of labor control established around 1500 in conjunction with the rise of export agriculture. This newer form of servitude appeared even as medieval serfdom was waning to the west, where small-scale peasant farms predominated. With industrialization the east-west divide reemerged in a new form when industry de-

The Reformation. *Luther Preaching,* detail from a triptych (1547) by Lucas Cranach the Elder (1472–1553). CHURCH OF ST. MARTIN, WITTENBERG, GERMANY/THE BRIDGEMAN ART LIBRARY

veloped earliest in the Ruhr and Saar basins and in Saxony, southern Germany, and Switzerland, leaving eastern Prussia and Austria relatively underdeveloped. Patterns of social-class formation and political divisions reflected this economic divide. East of the Elbe, the Prussian landed nobility, the Junkers, secured local autonomy in return for their loyalty to the Prussian Hohenzollern dynasty. A few reformers emerged from their ranks in the eighteenth and nineteenth centuries, but for the most part, the Junkers remained firmly committed to an authoritarian and aristocratic order. In the west, a more developed middle class, broader commercial and industrial activity, and substantial influence from France created more fertile ground for the emergence of liberalism in the nineteenth century.

EARLY MODERN SOCIAL HISTORY AND THE CONFESSIONAL STATE

The heavy hand of the state in central European society dates back to the early modern era. The Treaty of Westphalia in 1648 marked the end of the Thirty Years' War (1618–1648), the last of a series of wars launched by the Lutheran Reformation. The treaty reaffirmed the distinctive central European pattern of decentralized state building in the Holy Roman Empire. "Dual power" was confirmed. That is, political authority remained divided between the Holy Roman Emperor ruling from the Habsburg capital in Vienna and the nearly four hundred fairly autonomous "estates of the empire," including princes of the huge *Länder* of Brandenburg-Prussia and Bavaria, representatives of city-states like Frankfurt and Hamburg, and prince-bishops like those of Cologne and Mainz. In addition,

roughly two thousand Imperial Knights lorded over tiny territories of a few acres or square miles. The settlement at Westphalia was a definitive acknowledgment that the Holy Roman Emperor would continue to exist as the highest level of authority in the region, but with few effective powers. Real governance, the settlement confirmed, was based in the capitals of the territorial rulers.

This particular pattern of political development was enormously significant in social-historical terms. Social-historical development—religious life, of course, but also economic growth in agricultural, industrial, and commercial sectors; family and gender relations and demographic growth; bureaucratization, education, and literacy; migration and urbanization—was penetrated and to some extent organized by the territorial states. Moreover, the intensity of governmentality—the particularly elaborated mechanisms of political authority—meant more state intervention into and more record keeping about the activities of everyday life.

Confessionalization. "Confessionalization"—the establishment of an official territorial religion based on a creed and binding on all subjects—became characteristic of post-Reformation state building throughout the Holy Roman Empire. Beginning in the early sixteenth century, confessionalization dramatically extended the reach of the state. The threat to social order manifested not only in Luther's revolt against Rome but also in the widespread rebellions of peasants and urban underclasses between the 1480s and the 1520s gave territorial rulers the impulse to discipline. The Reformation offered the vehicle. Starting first in the

Lutheran territories—where the lure of a state take-over of Catholic Church properties usually figured along with religious ideals into the conversion strategies of princes and city-states—the confessional state eventually was established to some extent even in territories such as Bavaria where the ruling dynasty remained Catholic.

Henceforward, state bureaucracies supervised religious matters. Branches of this bureaucratic structure expanded beyond the administration of church buildings, properties, and staff to include the teaching of religious doctrine, parish visitation, the establishment of primary schools, the supervision of some aspects of secondary and higher education, the regulation of marriage, the enforcement of morality through church consistory courts, and the oversight of charity. In other words, through confessionalization, state-church bureaucracies not only took over many of the functions previously performed by the Catholic Church but also brought state authority into many more aspects of everyday life. Historians have pointed to the ways in which these innovations served to subject the population of central Europe to unprecedented state discipline.

Historians have also argued that confessionalization exacerbated aspects of patriarchal domination. Under the slogan "Gottesvater, Landesvater, Hausvater," the Christian God, the territorial prince, and the male household head were linked in a hierarchical and explicitly patriarchal order. Arguably the Lutheran critique of clerical celibacy and Catholic views of marriage opened a new approach to gender relations. In contrast with Catholic teachings, Lutheran writings exalted marriage as superior to celibacy; marital sexuality was seen as natural and not sinful. But the abolition of female religious orders also removed an honorable alternative to marriage for women. Moreover, the disappearance of female saints as objects of veneration masculinized religious vision and practice. According to the Protestant gender order, adult women belonged in male-headed households under the supervision of a husband whose authority reflected divine and princely authority. Ironically, even where the Protestant Reformation did not come to dominate, women were also brought under tighter male authority. In the wake of the Catholic Reform, nuns had to be cloistered and their convents supervised by male spiritual authorities. The intensification of witchcraft persecutions that were particularly virulent in central Europe in the centuries after Reform was another mark of the epoch's misogynism and need to control women.

It is worth noting that this new discipline, though generalized, did not operate identically in all territories, nor was it as effective as proponents had hoped. Certainly there were differences between the oligarchic governments of the city-states and the more autocratic monarchies like Prussia. Size also mattered; it was in many respects easier to administer smaller

The Thirty Years' War. Siege of Magdeburg, May 1631. Engraving by Matthaeus Merian the Elder from J. P. Abelin, *Theatrum Europaeum* (1643). ©BRITISH MUSEUM, LONDON

than more sprawling and divided territories. More-over, state authority was more complete over Protestant Germans than over the Catholics and Jews of Central Europe. Catholics continued to hold both international and local religious allegiances, and they took more seriously the tie to the Catholic Habsburg emperor. German Jews continued to reside on sufferance, mostly in cities, where they paid annual *Schutzgeld* (literally, "protection money") for residence rights but maintained ties with kin and business associates all over the map of central and eastern Europe. The so-called *Hofjuden* (literally, "court Jews") played a special role in central European state building by putting their wide credit networks and commercial ties to the service of territorial overlords in the hopes of gaining protection and profit for themselves and their communities. While individual Jewish financiers were often immensely powerful, the legal status of Jews was little improved before the nineteenth century; moreover, their association with moneylending and the aggressive fiscal policies of the courts reinforced anti-Semitism.

Fiscal planning. State fiscal planning, with bankers and financiers playing a key role, was crucial to success in the competitive and belligerent arena of central Europe. The Treaty of Westphalia ended one phase of civil war, but European dynastic wars and the new wars of global commerce and colonization continued to involve many central European states. Standing armies became the pattern after the Prussian rulers decided not to disband the armies they had raised during the Thirty Years' War. The Prussian army, the largest in the region, grew from 8,000 troops in 1648 to 200,000 by the mid-eighteenth century. Less ambitious princes satisfied themselves with fewer troops; the duke of Weimar had an army of only thirty-three guards in the eighteenth century! But nearly all of the states of the region invested heavily in armies and armaments throughout the early modern period, and the costs involved drove state governments toward further bureaucratic expansion, fiscal planning, and tax increases.

Beyond the realm of religion and morality, then, states also intervened strongly in the economy of central Europe beginning in the seventeenth century. Arguably, the princely state builders of the Holy Roman Empire created the modern notion of "the economy" as a specific terrain of state activity. Standing armies, courts, and bureaucracies required funds in excess of the income from the ruling family's estates and from secularized church properties. Permanent tax levies, along with policies designed to increase population and taxable wealth, became hallmarks of effective governance. By the eighteenth century, most German universities had newly established chairs in *Cameralwissenschaften*—university-based studies in the legal, political, and economic sciences of managing the state's population and administration with the goals of rationalizing governance and enhancing tax revenues.

Agriculture and early industry. In the early modern era, most of this wealth still came from agrarian pursuits. In the western and southern parts of the empire (including the Rhineland, Württemberg, Baden, and parts of Bavaria) peasant tenure was fairly secure; holdings were often quite small because of generations of division among heirs. Landlords—sometimes aristocrats, but sometimes towns or merchants or religious establishments—typically relied on rents for their income rather than farming their lands directly. Dense settlement patterns and large numbers of towns and cities in these areas supported small-peasant agriculture as well. Population growth toward the end of the eighteenth century put pressure on land. In some villages, new crops and more intensive farming methods brought marked increases in productivity by the century's end.

But these regions, along with parts of Switzerland, also emerged as classic zones of protoindustry or "putting out"—a form of industrial organization whereby merchants advanced raw materials such as wool to rural households whose members would then work them up into finished products for sale by the merchant. State authorities were interested in increasing farm productivity and in tapping into the newer sources of wealth. They drew on the advice of men of academic education to found "industry schools" that taught rural children work discipline and handicrafts. Model farms disseminated new agricultural techniques. States granted monopoly concessions to entrepreneurs to establish and regulate rural putting-out industries, and they also established state "manufactories"—large-scale handicraft workshops—for the production of luxury goods such as porcelain, tobacco, and silk. Growth in the agricultural and industrial sectors brought wealth visible in new consumption habits documented, for example, by Hans Medick's research on the Württemberg weaving village of Laichingen. But these changes brought new problems as well. The intensification of agricultural labor and the introduction of putting-out work disrupted traditional gender and generational divisions of labor and brought increasing conflict to overcrowded households and communities. Even though some peasants, artisans, and putting-out workers prospered during the economic expansion of the late eighteenth century, the social costs of growth were manifested in rising rates of infant mortality, divorce, and pilfering of firewood and fodder.

Further east, especially in the eastern provinces of Brandenburg-Prussia, the pattern was different. A much larger proportion of the land was farmed by large estate owners who had been shipping grain north through Baltic ports to the cities of western Europe since the sixteenth century. On these large estates, labor supply was the landlord's main concern. The political compromise struck here allowed the Junker landowners a relatively free hand on their own estates in exchange for their loyalty and military service to the Prussian state. There were few nearby cities to lure them or their peasants off the land or to provide an alternative marketing strategy. To be sure, there were attempts in the eighteenth century to reform peasant-landlord relations or at least to reduce the worst abuses. Peasant smallholders fared better on Crown lands than on the typical Junker estate. Labor resistance in a few regions pushed wages higher. But the generally proaristocratic tenor of the state, the practice of filling the upper echelons of the military and civilian administration with Junkers, meant relatively little change in agrarian social relations until the twentieth century.

Cities. The urban economy of early modern central Europe grew around commerce. Urban locations recalled the medieval trade routes along which cities had been founded. Many medieval cities survived into the early modern era, although they had been economically and politically weakened by centuries of warfare and by shifting patterns of global trade that favored Atlantic over northern European ports. The Baltic port cities belonged to the Hanseatic League, whose power in the Middle Ages had been built upon the trade linking eastern Germany and Russia with western ports. Buildings in the proud town of Lübeck recalled its fourteenth-century centrality to the Hanseatic network. Its city hall, like those of other commercial cities, served as the site of both city-state government and commercial transactions, so closely intertwined were the fates of merchants and towns. Urban social and political visions challenged those prevailing in the countryside. By way of illustration, in the city hall of the North Sea port of Hamburg, a painting of the Day of Judgment showed knights and princes being tossed into hell, while merchants were raised to God's right hand.

Other cities were sited on the overland routes that linked the Mediterranean with northern Europe. Leipzig, the largest of these, flourished as a reshipment point. The Leipzig fairs had become the most active in central Europe by the end of the Middle Ages.

Local residents even called their city "eine kleine Paris" (a little Paris). Because its merchants had persuaded the town's overlord, the elector of Saxony, that toleration was good for business, the city was open to foreigners of all kinds at fair time. (However, Glückel of Hameln, the wife of a Jewish merchant, did report being fearful for her husband's safety when he traveled to the Leipzig fair.) Leipzig was famous for its inns and coffeehouses—coffee and cocoa were both relatively new products in Europe, first imported in the early sixteenth century—and most of all, for its flourishing book trade.

Despite originally democratic impulses in the constitutions of the cities, by the early 1600s most central European cities were oligarchies ruled by men from the town's wealthiest families. The older egalitarian spirit diminished as evolving social and political structure sharpened distinctions among the urban citizenry. By 1500 most towns had several legally defined citizenship classifications, usually distinguishing among patrician families whose male members qualified for election to the council, citizens with full civic rights, resident noncitizens, and protected residents without guaranteed residence rights. Women were active in gender-specific sectors of the urban economy, but they (along with children) held civic status only by way of their relationship to male citizens; among women only widows and licensed female retailers could operate with a degree of freedom from male legal authority.

Moreover, cities that princely territories had absorbed, or that were founded as capitals, had little basis for democratic institutions. These cities—such as Berlin, first a garrison town and later the Prussian capital, or Karlsruhe, the baroque capital of Baden designed so that the grand duke could see every street in town from his palace windows—were policed by state governments desiring order and revenue. Princes generally suppressed the traditional liberties of towns with a medieval heritage of freedom. For example, in Munich, the capital of the Bavaria, residents lost their rights to trade freely, to elect representatives to the town council, and to grant citizenship.

THE BOURGEOISIE AND THE EMERGENT PUBLIC SPHERE

Still, the cities of early modern central Europe were important as sites of formation of middle-classes and a bourgeois public sphere. As was true elsewhere in Europe, the new institutions of communications and sociability associated with the "the public" were dominated by urban, educated, middle-class men. Such men were attracted to Enlightenment notions of free

341

and rational inquiry, self-cultivation, and social and scientific progress. Historians have argued that German Enlightenment writers, in comparison with British or French, tended to put more faith in reformist princes than in representative governments as the engine of social improvement, although this was a contested notion throughout the "republic of letters." Participants in the emergent public sphere of central European cities met in scientific societies, agricultural reform organizations, reading groups, theaters, cafés, and literary salons. They made their living as bureaucrats, rentiers, pastors or university professors, in a few cases from their literary or artistic works, and from trade and commerce. They were more likely than in other parts of Europe to be in state employ. The newspapers, journals, and books through which they communicated were published at rates that increased exponentially in the eighteenth century.

They were a group particularly defined both by *Bildung*, education and self-cultivation, and by *Besitz*, the possession of wealth. The education on which they based their expertise and participation in public discussion was a highly masculine enterprise. Although literary salons and a few of the reading and other clubs did include a few bourgeois and aristocratic women, the gender ideals that characterized this urban middle-class milieu restricted women's access to formal education and to the public sphere. According to Marion Gray's analysis of German economic treatises and manuals, the change was apparent by the mid-eighteenth century. Whereas in earlier epochs household enterprises had rested on the specific economic contributions of the *Hausmutter* as well as the *Hausvater*, the modern economic experts, academically trained in the *Cameralwissenschaften*, relegated women and their tasks to the margins of the economy. Moreover, the female domestic realm was increasingly separated conceptually, legally, and in practice from the masculine world of the economy and politics. This gender dichotomy was most exaggerated in milieus first built around the male career pattern—namely, professionals and civil servants. University education was advocated for sons as a means toward broad cultivation rather than merely narrow professional training. Nevertheless it also came to be a prerequisite for the practice of the professions and for many state administrative offices. The exclusion of women and most lower-class men from access to *Bildung* was one of the many unacknowledged limits upon the supposedly open public sphere.

The political upheavals brought by the French Revolution and Napoleonic rule in central Europe had a decisive influence on middle-class formation and political culture. Liberals who were the product of the German Enlightenment initially welcomed the Revolution. Its promise of progressive reform, its admiration for the world of antiquity, and its hostility to repressive monarchical and religious institutions echoed their commitments. Later, in reaction to the more radical turn of the Revolution and the conquest of large swaths of central Europe by French revolutionary armies, many came to oppose developments in France, but at the same time remained influenced by revolutionary ideals.

During the Vormärz era (1815–1848, so named by historians because it preceded the March 1848 revolts), a liberal political culture matured. Throughout the German Confederation, established in 1815 by the reactionary Congress of Vienna, repressive laws precluded outright party formation. Still, liberal ideas circulated in the associations of bourgeois civil society—singing clubs, gymnastic societies, Monday clubs, literary groups, and student fraternities. These were mostly local organizations, reflecting the character of urban bourgeois sociability, but they were replicated in cities throughout central Europe. The growth of commercial capitalism and the first glimmers of industrialization provided a new basis for middle-class fortunes and careers built more on *Besitz* than *Bildung*. Liberalism and the articulation of middle-class political perspectives were most at home in city governments and parliamentary bodies in those few states where constitutional rights to representation existed—most notably in the southwestern grand duchy of Baden.

In the lower house of Baden, elected by limited male franchise, an increasingly outspoken group of liberal deputies played a key role in the articulation of German liberalism. As Dagmar Herzog has demonstrated, however, their political vision was limited by the social and cultural context in which they operated. Their parliamentary battles with the neoorthodox Catholics who came to power in Baden in reaction against the French Revolution were fueled as much by views on marriage and sexuality as they were by constitutional ideals. The liberals' attacks on clerical celibacy as "unnatural" and antipathetic to the emergent bourgeois gender order were crucial to liberals' notions of manhood and citizenship. Reawakened religious conflict linked liberals with anti-Catholic hostilities that would persist throughout the nineteenth century. Moreover, it was their hostility to orthodox Catholicism rather than an embrace of pluralism that pushed reluctant Badenese liberals toward advocating Jewish emancipation as well. In short, the implicitly Protestant, masculine, and middle-class character of early German liberalism resulted in tacit exclusions (of women, Jews, men without property) that contradicted universal ideals.

Revolution of 1848. Entry of the imperial regent John of Austria into Frankfurt, after having been offered the regency by the national assembly, or parliament, that met there in 1848. In March 1849 the parliament adopted a constitution for a German empire and offered the crown to Frederick William IV of Prussia. He refused to accept the crown from a popularly elected assembly, and the parliament broke up in April. HISTORISCHES MUSEUM, FRANKFURT AM MAIN, GERMANY

THE 1848 REVOLUTIONS

The contradictions of liberalism came to the fore in the revolution of 1848. Paralleling the French Revolution, the revolts that began during the "March Days" of 1848 resulted from the convergence of political challenges and socioeconomic crises.

The political challenge involved clamor for reform on several fronts. Since the 1820s student fraternities and other bourgeois associations had called for a single German state. At the same time treaties creating a Zollverein, or customs union, among many central European states, had also promoted unification. The nation-state became the focus of liberals' hopes as well; by the late 1840s, liberals from the smaller states in the south and west were increasingly speaking to allies throughout central Europe. A unified German state based on principles of constitution-alism, representation, and civil liberties would end divisiveness and princely autocracy. This challenge was coming to a head by late 1847, when liberals issued a call for a convention to make plans for a national constitution.

Meanwhile, social and economic hardships intensified among peasants and artisans throughout central Europe. Rising population growth put pressure on land prices. Peasants had been emancipated from serfdom in Austria in the late eighteenth century and in Germany during the Napoleonic era. But emancipation was costly; often it required reimbursing landlords with substantial parcels of land or cash outlays. By the 1820s, many peasants were heavily indebted and land-poor. The golden era of protoindustry was also waning as overproduction and falling prices impoverished putting-out workers. The worst hit were the linen weavers of Silesia, who rose up

343

against their employers in 1844, only to be crushed by armed intervention. Urban artisans also suffered with the increased competition brought by open markets and the first entry of factory goods into the region. The final straw came at the end of the decade of the "Hungry Forties," when crop failures drove food prices upward. The poor were hardest hit; potatoes, upon which their diet increasingly depended, were hit by blight in 1846 and 1847. Food riots ensued and supplies were low at the end of the winter of 1847–1848. The actual rebellion was sparked by peasant revolts; peasants attacked landlords' castles or burnt the books that held their records of debt. Liberal reformers were quick to seize the opportunity to forward their cause. Alarmed princes began to incorporate reformers into their cabinets and to grant constitutions. Plans for unification moved into full gear; deputies from all over central Europe were elected to the Frankfurt Assembly, which convened in May 1848, to write a constitution for a united Germany.

But of course liberal visions and the aims of peasants and handicraft workers were quite divergent. Some of the very reforms sought by parliamentarians—for example open markets—undermined the livelihood of artisans. The peasants' attacks on landlords' property violated the interests of bourgeois property owners as well. The Assembly proceeded apace and indeed wrote a constitution, but as it deliberated the revolutionary forces collapsed or were defeated around it. The princes still commanded armies, and once they realized the weaknesses of the revolutionary coalition, they were able simply to quash the revolutionary governments and assemblies—in Vienna in October 1848, in Berlin in November, and in Frankfurt in May 1849. The strongest army, that of Prussia, played a key role in the repression not only in Berlin but also in Frankfurt and in the last revolutionary holdouts in Baden and Saxony. Military courts-martial sentenced and executed rebels. The lucky ones fled abroad, joining the growing streams of emigrants who had been leaving central Europe since the 1830s in search of better economic conditions in North America and elsewhere.

CREATING THE NATIONAL SCALE, BROADENING THE PUBLIC SPHERE

National unification was created in the end with help from these same Prussian armies. The Second German Empire was forged under the leadership of the Prussian state, led by the conservative chancellor Otto von Bismarck. Social, economic, and political trends favoring unification had been developing for decades (including communications networks, the Zollverein market region, and nationalist organizations). Bismarck had been a reactionary in 1848, but by the 1860s he had come to recognize the powerful potential of the nation-state. Industrialization (already advanced in Prussia's western provinces), nationalism, and a limited form of popular sovereignty could be harnessed by the Prussian state in the service of the monarchy and the Junkers. Bismarck, the classic "revolutionary from above," recognized that to preserve the existing social and political hierarchies, Prussia needed to adapt. Through three short wars between 1864 and 1871, he defeated Austria and rallied the remaining German states behind Prussia as the architect of national unification. Many Germans rallied behind Bismarck and Prussia, including liberals who were joyous that their goal of national unity had been realized, even if in a politically awkward form.

The new German Empire that emerged was a strange hybrid of liberal and conservative elements. The government and the army were responsible to the Crown, not to the Parliament. The inner circle of the emperor (also the king of Prussia) wielded immense powers. As part of the unification compromise individual states retained substantial political autonomy; they even had their own armies and, in some instances, their own foreign ministries. The federalist solution was, in many ways, a persistent central European pattern, one that also characterized Switzerland and the Austrian Empire. The German system was distinctive in its dualism: Prussia, the largest and most conservative state, exercised inordinate powers in the empire. Prussia's authoritarian and aristocratic traditions were carried into the new Germany.

At the same time, the German constitution did not simply reflect the authoritarian proclivities of the Prussian aristocracy. Importantly, the constitution provided for universal manhood suffrage and an elected, if weak, national parliament. The imperial political structure encouraged the development of a national public sphere because it mandated periodic parliamentary elections. Because of the broad suffrage, political parties had to move beyond their practice of "notable politics," whereby community elites controlled party affairs. By 1900 Germany presented the curious spectacle of an authoritarian state with actively contested elections and the most highly mobilized voters anywhere in Europe. Moreover, Bismarck's constitution had established equality under the law, rights of association, and other liberties. Despite periodic and serious harassment of socialists and Catholics, the constitutional prerequisites for a national public sphere did exist.

In terms of religion, the unified nation was very much a Protestant one. Although the southern Catholic states had agreed to unification in 1871, Catholics still had reservations. These suspicions were confirmed when Bismarck, joined by liberal reformers in localities throughout Prussia, launched an attack on Catholic schools and other institutions in the so-called Kulturkampf of the 1870s. These efforts to weaken German Catholicism ultimately failed; the persecution of Catholics helped fuel the expansion of the Catholic Center Party and of educational, social, and welfare organizations that provided the institutional basis of a persistently strong German Catholic social and political identity. For Jews, the new nation offered great promise. The constitution accorded Jews full equal rights under the law. Social discrimination remained immense. The army and bureaucracy proved largely impregnable, the professorate only slightly less so. But in the rapidly growing professions of law, medicine, journalism, and the arts, Jews were able to find places and to advance significantly. Jews invested their hopes in the nation since the end of legal discrimination and economic subordination accompanied unification. Later, these hopes would be tragically disappointed.

In terms of social historical development, the unification process allowed for the survival of powerful nobles, the Prussian Junkers in particular, who continued to predominate in sectors of the bureaucracy and the army. The idealization of Crown and army, conveyed through court ceremonies, military parades, and in schools and the press, contributed an authoritarian and militaristic strain to German society. German employers mimicked the military hierarchy by adopting military discipline over their workers. Even the forceful role of the father in the family was sustained, in part, by the larger culture of authoritarianism. Nevertheless, the German Empire arguably reflected the interests of the professional and entrepreneurial middle classes as well. In the economic sphere, the constitution provided the legal framework for the full development of a capitalist market economy, measures that had been long demanded by businessmen and liberals. The German Empire created a vast market with a single currency, a single system of weights and measures, and eventually a coordinated system of transportation and communications.

Moreover, political unification and the new institutions of the empire contributed to an unprecedented phase of economic growth that despite intermittent recessions lasted until 1914, creating new patterns of wealth. In one generation, Germany became an urban, industrial society and an economic powerhouse. The total value of industrial and crafts production increased more than fivefold between 1871 and 1913, the export of finished products, fourfold. Germany soon became the world leader in the production of coal, steel, and chemicals, and later in electro-technical manufacturing and electrical power generation. German industrialization was distinctive for more than its speed. Military needs and available resources produced an emphasis on heavy industry and a prevalence of large corporations and cartels. Moreover, the state played a broad role in promoting industrial development and forged links with big industrialists. Finally, industrial advancement in some ways outstripped other kinds of social and cultural change, leaving Germany somewhat disjointed and also prompting, from various quarters, resistance to modern developments. Some historians have designated this as part of a special German pattern— termed *Sonderweg*, or separate path—in modern social history.

Nevertheless, with industrialization, the social structure shifted dramatically, and many changes resembled those in other parts of industrial Europe. Germans became more urban and their livelihood was very much more dependent upon industry. Overseas migration slowed dramatically as employment opportunities expanded within Germany. Instead of sending land-starved emigrants abroad to the United States and elsewhere, regions like the Ruhr attracted eastern Germans and Poles to mine coal and tend blast furnaces. In 1881, 4.89 percent of the German population emigrated abroad. In 1910, only 0.39 percent did so. In 1871, only 4.8 percent of the population lived in cities with a population of over 100,000. In 1910, 21.3 percent of the population did so. The proportion of the population that worked in agriculture declined between 1882 and 1907 from 41.6 percent to 28.4 percent; that which worked in industry increased from 34.8 percent to 42.2 percent.

Social developments fed back into politics. The society of the empire—urban, industrial, mass— proved deeply unsettling to state officials, priests and pastors, middle-class reformers, and ordinary citizens. While migrants to the cities usually found or established networks based upon extended family, village, and religious communities, the very fact that so many Germans were uprooted accentuated fears of urban anomie. The immiseration of a substantial segment of the population living in shanties or crowded tenements, working fourteen-hour shifts, and lacking clean water and sanitation, conditions publicized by investigative journalists and reformers, seemed to threaten the very survival of the German people. The expansion of female factory labor aroused fears that gender proprieties and the family itself were being subverted.

German Industry. *Iron Rolling Mill,* painting (1875) by Adolf von Menzel (1815–1905). NATIONAL GALLERY, BERLIN/AKG LONDON

The "social question," the general label for these responses, charged politics in the new empire, leading to new forms of state intervention. In the 1880s Germans pioneered the modern welfare state with three key programs: old-age pensions, accident insurance for work-related injuries, and health insurance. Bismarck had viewed these programs as a way of binding workers to the state and undermining the appeal of socialism. He was right on the first count, wrong on the second. By and large, German workers came to appreciate the benefits they received, however minimal at first. The programs did little to undermine the appeal of socialism, but they did help convince leaders of the German labor movement that improvements for workers would have to come from the state. Moreover, these programs were geared toward male industrial workers and their dependents. As such they helped constitute workers as a class structured by gender, since women workers were either barred totally from the programs or received reduced benefits. Social-welfare programs normalized the patriarchal male breadwinner, even when very few working-class families could subsist solely on one male wage. At the same time, working women were subject to ever increasing supervision by employers and state officials, who sought to ensure that workplace and living conditions would not detract from their roles as housewives and mothers.

The rise of socialism marked another major response to the crisis of industrialization and a new form of the politicization of social conflicts. Never solely political, German socialism grew out of the networks of sociability that workers created in pubs, courtyards, and street corners of working-class neighborhoods and in the factories and mines in which they labored. The close links, spatial and social, between work and community created the substratum for successful socialist organizing. The German Social Democratic Party (SPD) helped accentuate a consciousness of class among people who already shared similar working and living conditions. While most of the SPD's specific activities were local—demonstrations at the market square, voting, paying dues—they were replicated all over Germany and reported in the nationally circulated socialist newspapers.

Mass political organizing was facilitated by new technologies of transportation and communications. A newspaper culture had also emerged throughout central Europe; dailies espousing varying perspectives competed for readership in the big cities. The pace of travel quickened. In Germany, Austria, and Switzerland, it was possible to travel easily by rail. Train stations in all of the major cities of central Europe were simultaneously symbols of a modernized local civic pride and links to the national and international realms. The Leipzig train station, the busiest in Europe, was the major connector between east and west and north and south. It was a magnificent soaring steel skeleton framed by glass panels and boasting over thirty platforms.

By around 1890, these social and economic transformations together allowed for the full-blown emergence of a public sphere on a national scale.

Moreover, the public broadened as virtually all segments of society, from workers to women, businessmen to peasants, became more vocal and organized; the public sphere was far more multidimensional, far less exclusively liberal, bourgeois, and male than it had been in the first half of the nineteenth century. For the most part in Germany, the national scale became accepted as the locus of effective political organization. To win support for their interests, groups could no longer operate solely on the local or regional level. In contrast, in the Austro-Hungarian Empire, where ethnically based nation building countered centralizing impulses, the construction of a national public sphere was more uneven.

Central European socialists pioneered many of the techniques of modern political mobilization, but their opponents used these techniques as well. The 1890s also saw the emergence of a populist right, evident especially in the founding and expansion of a large number of nationalist pressure groups like the Naval League, the Colonial Society, the Agrarian League, and others. Typically, these were organized by people from the middle and upper classes, who sought to influence workers, employees, and peasants. They lobbied, sponsored leafleting campaigns, demonstrations, and petition drives, and engaged in electoral politics. These groups espoused an ideology of extreme nationalism and anti-Semitism; they promoted military expansion and the acquisition of colonies, and they supported an authoritarian political system.

Through their appeals to antifeminism and racism they radicalized conservatism and moved the right, including traditional conservatives of the Protestant middle and upper classes, toward a rhetoric and politics of nationalism that emphasized race and biology.

This tendency was exacerbated as well by international developments. By the 1890s, Germany had joined the European rush to establish colonies in Africa and the Pacific. The hunger for raw materials like cotton and the competition for markets were among the lures that led German businessmen to join with naval proponents and argue for global empire. A hungry public lapped up imperial exotica that became part of a new, commercial culture: African people were put on display at carnivals; Asian dance groups performed in Berlin. Karl Peters's memoir, *New Light on Dark Africa,* was an 1890s bestseller that described Peters's use of guns, whips, and fire to teach Africans "what the Germans are." The notion of *Bildung* was now supplemented by an imperialist and racialized understanding of the cultural order; German civilization contrasted with the primitive world encountered in overseas empire.

THE RENEGOTIATION OF STATE-SOCIETY RELATIONS: WORLD WAR I AND THE 1920s

The next stage of renegotiation of state-society boundaries came in World War I, which required an un-

German Workers. Meeting of a workers' cultural association, 1868. AKG LONDON

Hyperinflation. Thousand-mark banknote overprinted to increase its value to 1 billion marks. AKG LONDON

precedented mobilization of society. The army drafted men and reoriented resources, human and material, into the war economy. Beyond its intensified control over the economy, the wartime government found it necessary to maintain morale at home and at the front, a task fraught with contradictions. The state moved into even the most intimate spheres of life. While the army provided soldiers with prostitutes, women at home came under increasing moral scrutiny. Since the state provided soldiers' wives with allowances, it also claimed the right to supervise their conduct.

But increased state intervention into the economy and everyday life also politicized these spheres. As conditions deteriorated drastically by 1916, both at home and the front, unrest grew exponentially. The workplace became an extension of the public sphere. Workers in munitions plants, including women drawn from other industrial sectors or the countryside, talked among themselves about the difficulties of work and the loss of loved ones. Leaflets composed by more radical socialist workers circulated surreptitiously. They demanded adequate food supplies, less onerous working conditions, and, most defiantly, an end to the war and the establishment of democracy. By 1917 there was shoptalk about the Russian Revolution, or of gains to be won by a strike. Strikes for food, pay, and peace multiplied in the summer of 1917. Another site of public debate, a primarily female one, emerged in the course of the war. In marketplaces and city squares and in the nearby countryside, women demonstrated and rioted against merchants whom they accused of charging exorbitant prices for food; together they foraged and stole from the fields.

All these actions—food riots and strikes, demonstrations, and foraging trips—were directed not just at employers and merchants but ultimately at the state itself. The massive popular upsurge against desperate wartime conditions contributed to the state's collapse in the face of military defeat. Some of the wartime innovations in the public sphere became institutionalized in the local workers' and soldiers' councils that seized power throughout Germany in the fall of 1918. In these councils, trade unionists, workers, officials, and employers attempted to lay the groundwork for a new social order to arise out of the revolutionary situation. The councils—as their name indicated—gave political authority to associates from military units and workplaces, especially in the heavy industries of coal and steel. They were thus overwhelmingly masculine in character. The visionaries could not so easily incorporate the new female forms of activity. Under the interim government and in the Weimar regime established in 1919, the marketplace with its mainly female consumers was a sphere to be regulated, not a site for the exercise of power.

During the Weimar Republic (1919–1933), the state became more interventionist, though its activities were increasingly subject to critique. Industrial development reached a certain plateau, but not stability, as labor and management battled for control over the workplace. Gender and the family became highly politicized sites as women's rights, sexuality, and reproduction were opened to discussion, experimentation, and contest.

In many ways, Weimar fulfilled the liberal promise; it was a parliamentary nation-state. But more open political contention made social and cultural rifts even more apparent. The unending round of elections provided focal points of political activism, as did mass campaigns like the one to repeal restrictive abortion laws. Strikes were a frequent occurrence in the first half of the decade. The socialist movement fractured, resulting in two leftist parties, Social Democratic and Communist. In their competition for workers' loyalties, these two parties recruited a higher percentage of the working class than ever before, and organized more deeply in workplaces and working-class communities. Hundreds of thousands of workers participated in choirs, theaters, sports clubs, hiking groups, and other associations sponsored by the labor parties.

On the far right a plethora of groups emerged— extreme nationalist, racist, and anti-Semitic. They foisted the problems of the 1920s onto Jews and socialists, who were portrayed as betrayers of the nation. The right gave a highly charged, violent tenor to social and political life in the 1920s. But the communists and, less consistently, the socialists also contributed to this trend. Both the right and the communists extolled violence as the path to the future and built paramilitary groups. The style of both political groups drew upon the long-standing idealization of the military in German culture, but took on a new, mass form in the 1920s, legitimizing everyday political violence.

Economically, the 1920s demonstrated the perils of both autarky and international linkages. Germany's territorial losses had disrupted the steel industry; subsequent domestic reorientation, designed to foster German self-reliance in coal and steel, brought only limited success. The chemical industry lost its monopoly of the world synthetic dyes market. Agricultural producers were battered by deflated prices caused by worldwide overproduction. Following American leadership, "rationalization" of the labor process became a slogan of the 1920s and was applied to everything from factory to farm to household. Its success in strict economic terms is much debated; socially, it led to speedup, further diminution of workers' control over their own labor, and substantial unemployment.

Hyperinflation in 1923, rooted in war debt and government efforts to undermine reparations, undermined security. In the autumn of 1923, one dollar could purchase almost 14 billion marks. The middle class suffered as savings became worthless, while workers again experienced the misery of wildly escalating prices, shortages, and unemployment. The agreements that ended the inflation tied Germany more firmly to the international, largely American, economy. At first, the benefits were substantial, as American capital flowed into Germany. But when the American economy crashed, American banks called in their loans, spreading the depression rapidly and forcefully to Germany. Like the hyperinflation, the depression beginning in 1929 caused intense political disorientation, which ultimately redounded to the benefit of the radical right.

Cultural innovations, many of them building on prewar precedents, also added to political polarization. The cinema came fully of age in the 1920s, and movie palaces were built all over central Europe. This cheap entertainment brought the world of film stars and glamour to even small-town audiences. By the end of the decade, the radio brought news, sporting events, and music into homes. Cultural modernists among the communists deployed the new media. The brilliant Willie Münzenberg adapted the bourgeois medium of illustrated magazines for working-class audiences with the highly successful *Arbeiter-Illustrierte-Zeitung* (Workers' Illustrated Magazine).

Among the cultural icons of the 1920s, the "new woman" was of particular political significance. Slender, active, sexually emancipated, employed, and childless, she was touted in popular magazines, posters, and films. She was also a focal point of intense political conflicts, especially as it became possible for

real women to claim aspects of the emancipated life the cultural images promised. Not only were young women going to dance halls and wearing short skirts, they also sought birth control. Left-wing health care professionals and social workers even provided sex counseling and contraceptives to working-class women in clinics that were subsidized by the municipalities. To more conservative elements, the new woman was the symbol of everything that was wrong in German society. In the 1920s the hostility aroused by the new woman fed into radical nationalism, as women's supposed lack of devotion to family and fatherland were seen as the root of social conflicts. Sexuality became a major topic of public discussion. Sexual politics became one of the right's major weapons against the Republic, and in both Germany and Austria antifeminist crusades facilitated the transition of conservatives from nationalist political parties to the fascist right.

Weimar also brought real social change and new opportunities for women. Granted the vote in 1919, women were initially courted by all the political parties, and a substantial number held office. In city councils and social-welfare agencies professional women played prominent roles. More women attended universities than ever before. In other social arenas, cities under social democratic leadership made great gains in building new housing for workers and expanding access to health care. One of the great milestones of social-welfare legislation, a national unemployment insurance program, was created in 1927. These mea-

Women in Politics. Klara Zetkin (1857–1933; *center*), deputy in the Reichstag for the German Communist Party, 1920. AKG LONDON

sures undoubtedly improved the quality of life. They were, however, accompanied by enhanced supervision of daily life. In the Frankfurt housing developments, for example, models visited by municipal leaders from all over Europe, each apartment had a speaker wired to the director's office, from which he delivered announcements and speeches to residents. The legacy of the Weimar period was thus ambiguous. The state's interventionist tendencies remained, but Weimar's liberal constitution protected civil liberties and the autonomy of institutions like the family, churches, and the associations of civil society. The Nazi state would overthrow these limitations.

STATE OVER SOCIETY IN NAZI GERMANY

The Nazis assumed power in 1933 with the backing of a substantial segment of the German population (they had won 37 percent of the vote in 1932), but they were not voted into power by an electoral majority. Instead, the Nazis were brought into government by a camarilla of powerful individuals around President von Hindenburg. These army officers, nobles, big businessmen, and state officials made Hitler chancellor not because they were enthralled with him and his party but rather because they had exhausted the other political possibilities acceptable to them and the interests they represented. No chancellor or government had been able to fulfill their program to move Germany out of the depression, restore its great-power status, repress socialism and communism, and establish an authoritarian order in place of Weimar democracy. They agreed with Hitler's extreme nationalism and anticommunism; they either agreed with his anti-Semitism or found it unworthy of concern. The roughly one-third of the electorate that supported the Nazis had similar views. Some radical anti-Semites supported the Nazis for this reason. But most Germans were not mobilized by Nazi anti-Semitism. Compared to other European nations, Germans were not remarkably anti-Semitic in 1933. All that would change drastically in the ensuing twelve years.

There are certainly lines of continuity that connect the Third Reich to earlier German regimes. But the central reality of the Third Reich is that a radical right-wing political party assumed power and adapted the resources and techniques of a highly modern state and society to a new end: the creation and advancement of a racially pure German nation. In so doing, the Nazis broke radically with previous patterns of state and society in German history. The "racial state" threw overboard all previously existing limitations—ethical, religious, legal, and constitutional—on state power. The Nazi state banned political opposition, sought to diminish and ultimately eliminate the Christian churches, abolished the traditional lawfulness of state bureaucracy, radically limited the powers of businessmen and managers, and subjected the army to Hitler's personal command. The fact that so many people—pastors, industrialists, army officers, and state officials—supported or acquiesced to Nazi policy does not in any way undermine the contention that they departed from historical precedent to do so. The racial state offered visions of greater glory; on a more mundane level, it offered collaborators, professionals in particular, career advancement and wealth; most simply took advantage of the opportunities. The racial state was also a "total state," at least in ambition. In return for the advantages and benefits bestowed upon them, Nazi supporters acquiesced to the Nazi state's assertion of its right to intervene and regulate every aspect of life.

Racial politics constituted the core of the Nazi program. Its aim was a *Volksgemeinschaft*, an organically unified and racially select community. Nazism always envisaged a society of domination and subordination, with the inferior races allowed to survive to provide menial labor for Aryans, the racially elect Germans. This racial utopia could only be established by struggle. Jews constituted the preeminent enemy, the people who threatened the very existence of Aryans. Nazi rhetoric was infused with biological and sexual metaphors; Jews were the "cancer" or the "bacillus" that threatened the healthy Aryan body and had to be eliminated. The physical annihilation of Jews was certainly not planned at the outset of Nazi rule; the initial plans usually called for elimination through deportation. The exigencies of war—itself a manifestation of racial politics—and the internal dynamics of the Nazi system radicalized the solution, leading to the physical extermination of close to 6 million European Jews.

While the Holocaust was the ultimate and most radical manifestation of Nazi racial politics, an array of other racialist measures laid the groundwork. The Nazis implemented programs of compulsory sterilization and killing of the mentally and physically handicapped. They isolated, interned, sterilized, and executed large numbers of Roma and Sinti (Gypsies). "Asocials," a highly elastic category that could include everyone from political opponents to alcoholics, the work-shy, promiscuous women, jazz fans, and homosexuals, were packed off to concentration camps. In all of these programs, the Nazis moved the management of society and everyday life to the epicenter of state policies in the most radically interventionist state program ever seen.

But for the vast majority of Germans, the experience of Nazi society was very different. By promoting war-related industries, the Nazis revived the economy, eliminating the burden of unemployment. By 1936 full employment returned. While wages were kept at a low level, more family members were working, so household income increased. The Nazis honored workers and Aryan mothers, enhancing their status in society. The German Labor Front offered workers social amenities that few had enjoyed before, like Rhine cruises and vacations in the Alps. The Hitler Youth and the League of German Girls provided youth with the pleasures of peer-group companionship, and an escape from church and parents. All of these developments of the Nazi "social revolution" helped the regime win the loyalty of the German population. There were, of course, opponents, but Gestapo repression was largely successful in eliminating organized communist and socialist resistance. Discontent was rife when food shortages appeared, or when Nazi officials received preference from the local butcher or baker. By the late 1930s, workers were complaining about low wages. But none of this grumbling gelled into active resistance. Overall, the Nazis had largely succeeded in destroying the old solidarities of class, replacing them with the solidarity of race and the promise of national and racial aggrandizement.

POSTWAR RESTRUCTURING

At the end of World War II, Germany lay devastated, the country divided and occupied by the victorious Allied powers. Ultimately the national scale would survive, but in altered form. Two distinct German nation-states, the Federal Republic of Germany (FRG) and the German Democratic Republic (GDR), joined Austria and Switzerland, whose prewar borders were preserved. Both German states and Austria were subordinated in an international system marked by the rivalry of the two superpowers, the United States and the Soviet Union. In the postwar political order of central Europe, the international scale took on a new significance.

In the FRG (developments were similar in Austria), the basic structures of the liberal state and the market economy were firmly in place by 1949. The Allies, especially the Americans, repressed any radical plans for either social restructuring or widespread de-Nazification. Indeed, many old elites, businessmen, army officers, and state officials made an easy accommodation so long as they abandoned overt affection for Nazism. Through international monetary arrangements, the Marshall Plan and others, West Germany's

"social market economy" became firmly integrated into the U.S.-led international system. The benefits of the ensuing economic boom trickled down by the late 1950s. West Germans largely retreated into the private realm, experienced as a refuge after the incessant claims of the Nazi state and the economic hardships from 1943 to 1949. West Germans worked hard, saved, and spent on consumer goods. The automobile became the symbol of the age, the icon for which they worked and which enabled them to vacation all over Europe. Probably more than anyplace else in Europe, Germany was becoming "Americanized," even while many traditional features of German society remained strong. Social historians are devoting increasing attention to postwar Germany, finding some surprising continuities in social and gender structure into the 1950s, but afterward, in West Germany, more substantial change.

The West German postwar system, liberal and capitalist in its essentials, was marked by a higher quotient of welfare measures and more active labor union participation than many other Western societies. Social-welfare programs had survived through all the regime changes of the twentieth century, and benefits became more generous. The strictures of the programs continued to reinforce the gender hierarchy, as they had in the nineteenth century, with women disadvantaged and sometimes completely excluded from benefits. Despite the large number of households headed by single women, the nuclear family with the male breadwinner quickly reemerged as the norm. The formal labor participation rate of women remained low in comparison to other European countries, although it crept up throughout the 1950s.

A very different pattern developed in the GDR. While the Western Allies sought to reestablish elements of the pre-Nazi social structure in their area of influence, the Soviets pursued a radical transformation. Controlling the region of Junker estate agriculture, they quickly collectivized land, finally eliminating the social basis of noble power. State control of industry eliminated the powers of entrepreneurial and managerial classes. With an entirely new governmental and security apparatus in the East, the leading members were anything but old elites. As a self-proclaimed "workers' and peasants' state," the GDR actively promoted social mobility. Thousands of citizens from lower-class backgrounds were given opportunities for advanced training and education, enabling them to move up the occupational ladder. Yet a kind of retreat to the private developed in the GDR as well, as many lives were structured by a determination to get ahead coupled with a feeling that the intimate world of

Devastation. Germany at its nadir: the ruins of Cologne, 1945. ARCHIVE PHOTOS/POPPERFOTO

New Currency. Berliners in the American sector of the city line up to exchange old marks for the new Deutsche Mark, June 1948. ©BETTMAN/CORBIS

family and friends was the only safe place, a refuge from the unceasing claims of the state.

As a Soviet-style state, the GDR tightly controlled its citizenry. The Ministry for State Security became a vast apparatus that spied on the population. Tied to the Soviet rather than the American economy—and subject to Soviet reparations into the 1950s—living conditions were quite straitened well into the 1960s. The GDR had the highest labor force participation of women in the world. While women were accorded formal equality with men, the labor market remained segmented, with women largely con-fined to low-paying jobs. Women also managed the vast bulk of household labor even while they worked full-time jobs. At the same time, they did have broad educational opportunities. Beginning in the 1970s, when state and party leader Erich Honecker proclaimed the "unity of economic and social policies," women were granted important social benefits, like extensive maternity leave.

In the aggressive international economy of the 1980s, the GDR fell further and further behind. When Mikhail Gorbachev introduced economic and political reforms in the Soviet Union, the communist world quickly crumbled. In the GDR, discontent had been on the rise through the 1980s; dissident groups founded a protest movement that demanded democratic socialism. In the context of the international changes initiated in Moscow, the public sphere re-emerged in East Germany. Moreover, by summer 1989 East Germans crowded into the Federal Republic's embassies in Prague and Budapest, demanding the right to settle in the West. In the fall of 1989, the combined force of protest demonstrations and exodus led to the collapse of the government, an exhilarating moment for people until then resigned to a heavy-handed state.

The exhilaration did not last long. The moment was dominated, and ultimately limited, by West German visions of state and society, which promised East Germans instant prosperity in return for reunification.

The transition has proven difficult. Germans, indeed all central Europeans, now live in a world of intense economic competition, regional disparities, and multiculturalism. The region's population is increasingly diverse. Some communities, like the Turks, are seen as immigrants despite three generations of residence. In Germany, Austria, and Switzerland, the definition of the nation and the relation between state and society continue to be debated. The nation-state remains significant, though borders altered once again in 1990. Since then the international scale has become ever more important. Negotiating the relationship between state and society, a persistent problem of central European history, will become more complex in the new century as international economic developments, international migration streams, and international organizations have an ever greater impact on social life.

See also other articles in this section.

BIBLIOGRAPHY

Barclay, David E., and Eric D. Weitz, eds. *Between Reform and Revolution: Studies in German Socialism and Communism from 1840 to 1990.* New York, 1998.

Blackbourn, David, and Geoff Eley. *The Peculiarities of German History: Bourgeois Society and Politics in Nineteenth-Century Germany.* New York, 1984.

Blickle, Peter. *From the Communal Reformation to the Revolution of the Common Man.* Translated by Beat Kümin. Leiden, Netherlands, and Boston, 1998.

Bridenthal, Renate, Atina Grossmann, and Marion Kaplan, eds. *When Biology Became Destiny: Women in Weimar and Nazi Germany.* New York, 1984.

Bruford, Walter. *Germany in the Eighteenth Century: The Social Background of the Literary Revival.* Cambridge, U.K., 1952.

Burleigh, Michael, and Wolfgang Wippermann. *The Racial State: Germany, 1933–1945.* Cambridge, U.K., 1991.

Canning, Kathleen. *Languages of Labor and Gender: Female Factory Work in Germany, 1850–1914.* Ithaca, N.Y., 1996.

Crew, David F. *Germans on Welfare: From Weimar to Hitler.* New York, 1998.

Daniel, Ute. *The War From Within: German Working-Class Women in the First World War.* Translated by Margaret Ries. Oxford, 1997.

Davis, Belinda. *Home Fires Burning: Food, Politics, and Everyday Life in World War I Berlin.* Chapel Hill, N.C., 2000.

Eley, Geoff, ed. *Society, Culture, and the State in Germany, 1870–1930.* Ann Arbor, Mich., 1996.

Evans, Richard J., and W. R. Lee, eds. *The German Family.* London, 1981.

Evans, Richard J., and W. R. Lee, eds. *The German Peasantry: Conflict and Community in Rural Society from the Eighteenth to the Twentieth Centuries.* New York, N.Y., 1986.

Feldman, Gerald D. *The Great Disorder: Politics, Economics, and Society in the German Inflation, 1914–1924.* New York, 1993.

Frevert, Ute. *Women in German History: From Bourgeois Emancipation to Sexual Liberation.* Translated by Stuart McKinnon-Evans. New York, 1989.

Friedrichs, Christopher R. *Urban Society in an Age of War: Nördlingen, 1580–1720.* Princeton, N.J., 1979.

Gehmacher, Johanna. *Jugend ohne Zukunft: Hitler-Jugend und Bund Deutscher Mädel in Österreich vor 1938.* Vienna, 1994.

Gehmacher, Johanna. *Völkische Frauenbewegung: deutschnationale und nationalsozialistische Geschlechterpolitik in Österreich.* Vienna, 1998.

Glückel of Hameln. *The Memoirs of Glückel of Hameln.* Translated by Marvin Lowenthal. New York and London, 1932.

Gray, Marion. *Productive Men, Reproductive Women: The Agrarian Household and the Emergence of Separate Spheres during the German Enlightenment.* New York, 2000.

Grossmann, Atina. *Reforming Sex: The German Movement for Birth Control and Abortion Reform, 1920–1950.* New York, 1995.

Hamerow, Theodore. *Restoration, Revolution, Reaction: Economics and Politics in Germany, 1815–1871.* Princeton, N.J., 1958.

Hausen, Karin, and Heide Wunder, eds. *Frauengeschichte—Geschlechtergeschichte.* Frankfurt and New York, 1992.

Herzog, Dagmar. *Intimacy and Exclusion: Religious Politics in Prerevolutionary Baden.* Princeton, N.J., 1996.

Hohorst, Gerd, Jürgen Kocka, and Gerhard A. Ritter, eds. *Sozialgeschichtliches Arbeitsbuch, Bd. II: Materialien zur Statistik des Kaiserreichs 1870–1914.* Munich, 1975.

Hull, Isabel. *Sexuality, State, and Civil Society in Germany, 1700–1815.* Ithaca, N.Y., 1996.

Kocka, Jürgen. *Facing Total War: German Society, 1914–1918.* Cambridge, U.K., 1984.

Kriedte, Peter, Hans Medick, and Jürgen Schlumbohm. *Industrialization before Industrialization: Rural Industry in the Genesis of Capitalism.* With contributions from Herbert Kisch and Franklin F. Mendels. Translated by Beate Schempp. Cambridge, U.K., 1981.

Lamberti, Marjorie. *State, Society, and the Elementary School in Imperial Germany.* New York, 1989.

Lidtke, Vernon. *The Alternative Culture: Socialist Labor in Imperial Germany.* New York, 1985.

Mason, Tim. *Nazism, Fascism, and the Working Class: Essays by Tim Mason.* Edited by Jane Caplan. Cambridge, U.K., 1995.

Maynes, Mary Jo. *Taking the Hard Road: Life Course in French and German Workers' Autobiographies in the Era of Industrialization.* Chapel Hill, N.C., 1995.

Medick, Hans. *Weben und Überleben in Laichingen 1650–1900: Lokalgeschichte als Allgemeine Geschichte.* Göttingen, Germany, 1996.

Midelfort, H. C. Erik. *Witch Hunting in Southwestern Germany, 1562–1684: The Social and Intellectual Foundations.* Stanford, Calif., 1972.

Moeller, Robert. *Protecting Motherhood: Women and the Family in the Politics of Postwar West Germany.* Berkeley, Calif., 1993.

Peters, Karl. *New Light on Dark Africa: Being the Narrative of the German Emin Pasha Expedition.* London, New York, and Melbourne, 1891.

Planert, Ute. *Antifeminismus im Kaiserreich: Diskurs, soziale Formation und politische Mentalität.* Göttingen, Germany, 1998.

Roper, Lyndal. *Oedipus and the Devil: Witchcraft, Sexuality, and Religion in Early Modern Europe.* London and New York, 1990.

Rosenberg, Hans. *Bureaucracy, Aristocracy, and Autocracy: The Prussian Experience, 1660–1815.* Cambridge, Mass., 1958.

Sabean, David Warren. *Property, Production, and Family in Neckarhausen, 1700–1870.* Cambridge, U.K., and New York, 1990.

Scribner, R. W. *The German Reformation.* Atlantic Highlands, N.J., 1986.

Walker, Mack. *German Home Towns: Community, State, and General Estate, 1648–1871.* Ithaca, N.Y., 1971.

Wehler, Hans-Ulrich. *Deutsche Gesellschaftsgeschichte.* 4 vols. Munich, 1987–1997.

Weitz, Eric D. *Creating German Communism, 1890–1990: From Popular Protests to Socialist State.* Princeton, N.J., 1997.

Wiesner, Merry E. *Working Women in Renaissance Germany.* New Brunswick, N.J., 1986.

Wunder, Heide. *He is the Sun, She is the Moon: Women in Early Modern Germany.* Translated by Thomas Dunlap. Cambridge, Mass., 1998.

THE NORDIC COUNTRIES

Panu Pulma

The principalities of Sweden and Denmark-Norway took their shape in the sixteenth century. Gustavus Vasa of Sweden ascended to the throne in 1523, while Christian III became king of Denmark in 1534, bringing the independent kingdom of Norway to an end. The consolidation of monarchy gained further momentum from the incipient Lutheran reformation, but a centralized state power did not, however, come about swiftly or suddenly in either kingdom nor were its consequences similar. Sweden (including the Finnish provinces) became a unitary state with a unitary legislation and a fairly uniform administration. Exceptions to the rule were the conquered lands south of the Baltic Sea (such as Swedish Pomerania), but Swedish law and administration were imposed on another conquered land, Scania, immediately after it was won from Denmark in 1658. The Scanian peasantry was integrated into the state system as one of the four estates—the Swedish diet was an assembly for the nobility, clergy, burgesses, and peasants—and given power at the local parish level.

In contrast, the kingdom of Denmark-Norway was a typical European conglomerate state. The sovereignty of the Danish king covered areas with different systems of administration and legislature: Norway applied its own law, also in use in the Faroe Islands, whereas Iceland was ruled centrally from Copenhagen, but as a separate legislative unit. The duchies of Schleswig and Holstein, too, were entities of their own. The Scandinavian kings ruled over large and sparsely populated areas with heterogeneous economies and social structures.

Seventeenth-century European history was about war and state-building. The two were linked, and the Scandinavian countries did not escape either. Sweden and Denmark-Norway fought over supremacy in the Baltic, and Sweden became embroiled in a struggle against Russia's growing influence. To succeed in the contest, the Scandinavian countries, mainly dependent on agrarian production, needed resources that could only be produced through a reliable military and bureaucratic machinery. The creation of this machinery—the centralized state power—was key in molding the Scandinavian social order.

While important variations exist in the social histories of the individual regions in Scandinavia, there are some unifying themes. Scandinavian society in the early modern centuries was distinguished from other parts of western Europe by its highly agrarian character, as well as by the extent of the government's impact on society. Aided by pervasive Lutheranism, government efforts led to high literacy rates beginning in the early modern period. In many cases, this resulted in exceptionally good record-keeping, which has allowed social historians to undertake detailed studies of such topics as demography.

The nineteenth century in Scandinavia was marked by rapid population growth and high rates of emigration. Industrialization brought many familiar features, but by the late nineteenth century Scandinavia began in some ways to set itself apart from most of industrialized western Europe, particularly with its rapid development of a reformist welfare state and with changes in women's rights and, later, family forms. In these areas many Scandinavian countries anticipated trends that subsequently played themselves out in the rest of Europe, and they took these trends farther than most countries. As a result, foreign attention repeatedly turned to Scandinavian social history—whether as a model or as a target for criticism.

PEASANT SOCIETY UNDER PRESSURE

The population of the Nordic countries was small and unevenly distributed, estimated to have risen from 1.6 million to 2.6 million in the course of the sixteenth century. The population concentrated in the heartlands, but the fastest growth took place on the fringes: there were three times more Danes than Norwegians in the early sixteenth century, but three hundred years later the Danes outnumbered the Norwegians by only 10 to 20 percent. The population of 1.9 million in Denmark-Norway in 1800 included a million Danes,

The Nordic Countries. Map commissioned by King Gustavus Adolphus II (1611–1632). Drawn by Anders Bure de Boo (Buraeus) and published by Willem and Johan Blaeu, c. 1635. DEPARTMENT OF MAPS, BRITISH LIBRARY, LONDON

just under 900,000 Norwegians, and 50,000 inhabitants in Iceland and the Faroe Islands. Among the subjects of the Swedish crown, there were three times more Swedes than Finns in the sixteenth century, five times more in the early eighteenth century but only two and a half times more in the year 1800 (2.3 million in Sweden; 830,000 in Finland). The population and economic importance of Norway and Finland grew considerably in the eighteenth century in particular.

Scandinavia was predominantly rural throughout the early modern era. Only the capitals, Stockholm and Copenhagen, stood out in European terms: the population of Copenhagen grew from 70,000 to almost 100,000 in the eighteenth century, while Stockholm's population almost doubled from more than 40,000 to more than 70,000 people. Except for the busy trading port of Bergen in Norway, other Scandinavian towns remained commercially stunted and under close state control. The principalities relied on the countryside instead.

The core agricultural lands in Denmark (including Scania), mid-Sweden, and southwestern Finland had mostly passed to the hands of the nobility as early as the Middle Ages. However, the countryside took different routes of development. Noble estates

and a peasantry tied to their lords became common in southern Scandinavia. Burdened with strict labor services, peasants were forbidden to leave the estates without permission. Where 15–20 percent of Danish peasants had been independent at the beginning of the sixteenth century, only 2 percent retained their independence in the 1680s. Until the late eighteenth century, the conditions of serfdom in Denmark and the duchies of Schleswig and Holstein were similar to those found east of the river Elbe. The economic, social, ecological, and political pressures of the eighteenth century finally spurred an agrarian reform that gave birth to an independent peasantry also in Denmark. The transition from *Gutherrschaft* (in which the landlord's economy is based on the work of dependent peasants on the manorial lands) to *Grundherrschaft* (in which the landlord receives rent or other revenue from peasant landholdings) is a peculiar and much-debated process, which nevertheless made the social structure of the Danish countryside more typically Nordic. Manorial estates were few in Norway and nonexistent in Iceland.

Swedish peasantry could be divided into three categories: freehold tax-paying peasants (*skattebönder*); peasants on crown land (*kronobönder*); and peasants

358

on noble estates (*frälsebönder*), whose owners enjoyed tax-free status in return for services rendered to the crown. Lacking all political rights, the *frälsebönder* were in the weakest position, but they never lost their personal freedom and, in contrast to Denmark, the Swedish lords of the manor did not have the right to administer justice over their peasants.

The nobility in seventeenth-century Scandinavia grew stronger, as the state needed ever more revenue to maintain growing armies. At first, the crown allowed for an expansion of tax-free *frälse* land, thus gaining much-wanted manpower in the army. In the eastern parts of the Swedish realm, and in Finland, the number of *frälsebönder* tripled as early as the end of the sixteenth century. In 1655, the nobility held 65 and 58 percent of the arable land in Sweden and Finland, respectively. However, in the seventeenth century the crown counteracted its previous policy, because the large-scale transfer of crown land to the noble estates was eating away at the tax base. When royal absolutism was introduced in Denmark (1660), it became possible for any man of wealth to own a manorial demesne, irrespective of his birth. In Sweden, the Crown carried out a large-scale cancellation of donations to the nobility in the late seventeenth century, transferring great numbers of peasants from the category of *frälsebönder* to that of crown peasants. Out of the Finnish peasant holdings, as many as 70 percent were crown estates. By the mid-eighteenth

century, a third of the Swedish farms, but only 7 percent in Finland, were on tax-free *frälse* land owned by the nobility.

The need for officials in the much-expanded state machinery shifted the emphasis from a landed nobility to a service nobility, whose economic interests were not as immediately tied to the land as they had been in the early seventeenth century. In Denmark, the large estates began to be transferred into the hands of the nonnobility in the 1600s, in Sweden a century later. Norway and Sweden underwent an even bigger change: crown estates and church tenant estates were increasingly being bought as independent tax-paying estates. In the course of the eighteenth century, this strengthened the economic, social, and political status of the peasantry, although land was obviously ceded to other groups in the society as well. The absolutist Swedish king Gustavus III was forced to buy the support of the lower estates in 1789 by granting them the right to own tax-free land and by improving the state of the crown peasants. At the time, the transfer of tax-free land from the nobility, often badly in debt, to the clergy and the burgesses, but also to wealthy peasants, was in full swing in Sweden, too. In Iceland, where agriculture was possible only on a narrow coastal strip, the biggest landowner was the church, but the clergy and officials also owned estates in large numbers, occupied by tenant farmers.

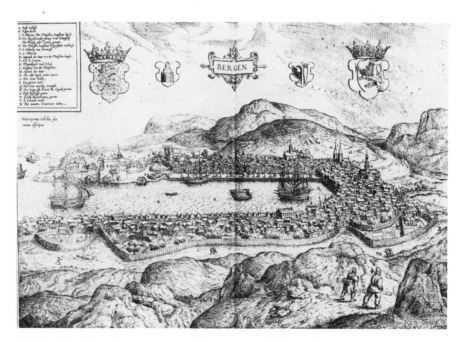

A Norwegian City. Bergen, print (1581) by Frans Hogenberg and Hieronymus Scholeus.
DEPARTMENT OF MAPS, BRITISH LIBRARY, LONDON

Peasant households. Whether Scandinavian agriculture was based on manorial estates or (semi)independent peasant farms, farming nevertheless relied on peasant families, whose lives were bound by restrictions on farm ownership and the demands imposed by coping with increasing responsibilities. As in northwest Europe, the typical Scandinavian family type was the three-generational stem family. One of the sons would inherit the estate or tenure to it, but the old farmer and his wife would still live on the farm. Normally, the peasant household also had one or more maids or farmhands. Because the transfer of farm ownership was governed by many administrative restrictions (permission from the lord of the manor or crown official), the son would get to his inheritance fairly late in life, which in turn raised the average marriage age. The families therefore remained fairly small: three to four persons made for an average Danish peasant household in the eighteenth century, while the average size in Norway and Iceland—where peasants were free from such restrictions and thus could marry earlier—was seven persons, and households there often included more distant relatives.

As a rule, the family structure and size in the old Scandinavian rural society reflected the economic and social status of the family. The households of the nobility and clergy could be very large indeed, making room even for unmarried relatives, whereas the landless families were typically nuclear. This is evident in the development of the Åland archipelago, part of the heartland of the Swedish realm: in the seventeenth century, when most of the population were peasants with their own land, the number of extended families could rise to more than 30 percent of households. With the rapid rise in the number of landless households in the eighteenth century, the family structure became simpler and the share of large extended families decreased to less than 10 percent.

Family size was also affected by the system of production. Before their landless population grew in the eighteenth century, the Åland islanders, living off fishing and the sea, and the tar-burning inhabitants of Finnish Ostrobothnia could live well in complex family systems. In eastern and southeastern Finland, where labor-intensive slash-and-burn agriculture and haulage of goods to St. Petersburg were increasingly important, the extended family was the common family type. The different partnership-type households typical of the region ensured an adequate workforce on the farms, which functioned like conglomerate companies. Each family was allotted certain responsibilities, which were outlined in a legally binding document; disputes between families were often resolved in court. People married earlier than elsewhere in the Nordic countries, because marriage was not tied to land tenure or to the division of the inheritance. The old farmer or his widow was head of the farm until his or her death. Likewise, there were fewer landless people and births outside wedlock than in the rest of the Nordic area. Even if the prevalence of the large and complex households in these eastern and northern parts is easiest explained in socioeconomic terms, we cannot completely overlook cultural factors. Complex families were also common in Russia, the Baltic countries, and eastern central Europe as far as the Balkans.

Loose population and other vagrants. People relegated to the margins for one reason or another were an integral part of the old society. In an estate society, "official" status was only granted to those unable to work and to the infirm and poor, who ended up being the responsibility of parish poor relief. Among the marginalized were also different travelers' groups, vagrants, prostitutes, and people engaged in despised trades. The state resorted to ever-tightening vagrant restrictions and forced labor for the Crown to control the marginal population.

In the seventeenth century, when life was burdened with continuous wars and army recruitments, vagrants able to work had little chance to escape the control machinery of the state, even if estate owners and peasants facing labor shortages were willing to employ them and could to a certain extent protect them. A new category emerged in vagrant restrictions as early as the sixteenth century—the "Egyptians," who were beginning to be known as *zigenare* or *tattare* in the seventeenth century. The Roma (or Gypsies) were kept under close surveillance because of their foreign origin and traveling way of life. Apparently, in the other Nordic countries, the Roma started to mix with other marginal vagrant groups in the eighteenth century. In the nineteenth and twentieth centuries, they called themselves the "travelers." In Finland, however, where the wilderness was out of reach of state control and where there was a demand for the services of the traveling Roma among the sparse population, no such mixing took place. When Finland was annexed as an autonomous region to the Russian empire in 1809, the Finnish Roma population joined that of Russia and the Baltic area.

Birth of the rural proletariat. The need to secure an adequate workforce led to the birth of a new type of worker. Tenant farmers on manorial estates could not increase their daily workload indefinitely, so the lords of the manors started to set aside land in order to establish small crofts. In Denmark, the crofters were called *husmaend,* in Norway *husmann,* and in Sweden they were known as *torpare.* Where new settlements could be established, the peasants, too, increased their cultivation by setting up crofts. The Danish *husmaend* already outnumbered the peasants in places at the end of the seventeenth century, while elsewhere in the Nordic countries the crofter class started to grow vigorously in the mid-1700s. This coincided with the rapidly increasing population growth in general. Many peasant farms resorted to setting up crofts to settle the sons' inheritance.

The *husmaend/husmann/torpare* were an intermediate category of sorts between the landowners and the landless population. Their social status varied dramatically according to whether the croft was part of a manorial demesne, established to alleviate a labor shortage; a new settlement on a peasant holding; or part of an inheritance settlement, in which case the croft could have significant cultivation of its own.

Underneath the crofters there grew even more vigorously a heterogeneous landless class. This new proletariat was separate from the servant population, who were hired for a year at a time and whose time in service usually finished with their getting married. The new proletariat were often already married and lived in their own cottages on somebody else's farm or on the village common land. They paid their rent mainly in work and had no cultivation of their own, at most only a small vegetable plot and a couple of livestock, grazing on common village grounds. Members of this class went by several names: *inderster* and *indsittere* in Denmark; *gadehusmand* in Denmark and Scania; *arbeidhusmann* and *strandsittere* in Norway; *backstugusittare* and *inhysing* in Sweden; and *itsellinen, loinen,* and *kesti* in Finland. The poorest among them did not even have a cottage of their own, but would live under other people's feet, in the drying-houses and saunas of the peasantry.

Rather than hiring a large workforce year round, the peasant household needed a reliably available seasonal workforce. This is where the landless population, reasonably stationary, proved vital. It was also this section of the population that grew quickest from the late eighteenth century onward.

The rapid population increase, the growth of the rural proletariat, and the agricultural reforms changed the social structure of the countryside. The peasantry started to form an intermediate group in society, a rural middle class that, together with the clergy, civil servants, and other burgesses, was in charge of local administration. Ever more conscious of its own estate and status, the peasantry demanded a say in the political processes either through the po-litical system (Sweden and Finland) or through protest and rebellion (Norway).

Sami regions squeezed by population growth.

The Sami people, also known as Lapps, differ from the Scandinavians both genetically and linguistically. The Sami region, known as Sameätnam, consisted of different ecological environments that left their mark on Sami sources of livelihood, ways of life, and culture. The Skolt and Kola Peninsula Sami relied on hunting and trading for their livelihood. Their life was inextricably tied to the Russian Orthodox cultural sphere. The sea Sami of the North Atlantic and Arctic Sea coasts lived off hunting, fishing, and trade. The fell (pelt) Sami used to occupy areas in both Norway and Sweden, and in Sweden in particular they adapted their way of life to the annual reindeer migrations between the Swedish woods and the Norwegian coast. The forest Sami of Sweden and Finland drew their livelihood from the wilderness, living in a more confined area than did the nomadic fell Sami. It was the forest Sami who came to bear the brunt of the population growth, as there was a persistent migration of Finns from the southern parts of Finland to the north. The slash-and-burn farming, fishing, and hunting Finns pushed the forest Sami ever farther north. With the colonizing push, the Sami increasingly started to settle down, tending the reindeer and farming their small farms. Communication and intermarriage with the colonists was common.

State-building processes at first interfered little with the Samis' largely nomadic way of life, although their taxation began already in the Middle Ages. When the consolidation of centralized states began, however, there emerged a need to draw the borders more clearly. This proved especially harmful to the fell Samis. The states were primarily concerned with tax collection, and the Lapp Codicil enclosed in the border agreement between Sweden and Denmark in 1751 regulated this matter. The agreement also guaranteed the Sami right to their traditional livelihoods and free passage across the borders, and even made provision for Sami officials to supervise the passage. However, the agreement that the Sami have called their Magna Carta failed to protect them against the pressure later caused by the migration of Norwegian, Swedish, and Finnish populations to traditional Sami regions. The Sami in Finland found it especially hard that Russia, of which Finland was then part, canceled the Lapp Codicil in 1852. This stopped the free passage of Finnish Sami over to Sweden and Norway. At the same time, nationalistic policies all over the Nordic countries were starting to make ever more significant inroads into the Sami language, culture, and way of life.

Advertisements for Emigrants. "Golden Belt Country" in Kansas proclaims a Union Pacific pamphlet in Swedish. UNION PACIFIC HISTORICAL COLLECTION

BREAKUP OF THE SOCIETY OF ESTATES

Population growth was rapid in the eighteenth and nineteenth centuries as mortality rates, and infant mortality in particular, kept falling and birthrates remained high. The Nordic countries went through a "revolution of life," followed by decreasing birthrates from the late nineteenth century onward, first in towns and central areas, and then, in the early years of the twentieth century, on the peripheries, too. The populations of Denmark and Finland almost tripled in 1814–1914, and the populations of Sweden and Norway doubled despite the fact that almost three million Scandinavians emigrated before 1920, mainly to North America. Some of the emigrants did return, but the emigration from Norway, in particular, was truly large-scale. In relative terms, the only countries to see off more emigrants than Norway were Ireland and Italy. There was also sizeable immigration to the New World from Sweden, but less from Denmark, Finland, and Iceland. Emigration from these countries also started later than from Norway and Sweden, where the massive emigration of young men left its mark in the demographic and labor force structure.

The rapid population growth in the country and the beginning of the massive migrations of the nineteenth century were part of a fundamental change in society. Urbanization, emigration, and internal colonization all took place at the same time. Toward the latter part of the nineteenth century, the wood and paper industry also gave rise to new growth centers in previously sparsely populated areas. Still, industrialization did not cause the breakup of the society of estates, although it did speed up the process.

The Nordic society based on the hierarchy of four estates had begun to crumble while still at its peak. Outside the stilted estate structure, there was a power base of nonnoble officials and entrepreneurs known in Sweden as *ofrälse ståndspersoner,* people of wealth, position, and "quality." As tax-free land was increasingly granted to nonnobility, the traditional landed gentry found its status weakened. The various elite groups began to mix, and their financial discrepancies evened out.

An even bigger change took place among the rural laborers. The peasantry grew stronger economically, socially, and politically, first in Sweden and Norway, and then also in Denmark, in the nineteenth century. In Norway it was only in the 1800s that the number of peasant farms grew substantially, but there was a rapid increase in all other Nordic countries in the number of crofters and landless peasants. By mid-century, the rural proletariat was the biggest population group in the Nordic countries. The social gap between them and the peasants, who were decreasing in relative terms and getting richer in absolute terms, opened up in more ways than one. The peasantry closed the doors of upward mobility to the landless population, but sought their own ways of moving up the social ladder through education and political involvement.

The change in the peasants' social status was also seen in the powerful religious awakenings of the eighteenth and nineteenth centuries. These movements drew part of their strength from a self-pedagogical and educational strain in evidence throughout Scandinavia (Grundtvigianism in Denmark, Haugeanism in Norway, free-churchism in Sweden, Laestadionism in the north of Sweden and Finland) and shared a critical attitude toward the elite and the Lutheran state church.

Economy, industrialization, and urbanization. Scandinavian economic and social development were influenced by the changes in European economic structures and international trade. Industrialization in Europe opened up expanding markets to agriculture in western Scandinavia in particular. Agriculture in Denmark and fishing in Norway and Iceland underwent a boom, while forestry in Norway, Sweden, and Finland benefited from a growing demand in Britain and Germany. The Nordic home market remained undeveloped, leaving economic expansion mainly dependent on export production. This led Nordic industrialization in different directions: the industrial development in Denmark served dairy and cattle farming, while the forest resources in Norway, Sweden, and Finland found their utilization first in sawmills, then in the pulp and paper industry. The Swedes had long made use of their iron ore supplies, which gave them a head start in metal industries and technical engineering, whereas Danes and Norwegians rose to be important seafarers with a shipbuilding industry that also opened up markets for other branches of industry.

Export-led and boosted by industrialization, economic growth leaned on overseas demand and extensive indigenous labor force reserves. The migration from the country to the towns gathered speed, and the social structures of the Nordic countries were shaped by urbanization and industrialization from the 1840s onward. The share of the rural population was already under 60 percent in Denmark in 1840, and in 1870 agriculture employed 44, 54, and 72 percent of the population in Denmark, Norway, and Sweden, respectively. In Finland, urbanization had speeded up but did not yet affect the population distribution, because the growth in rural population continued to exceed the urban growth rate as late as the end of the nineteenth century. Nor did migration to the New World or St. Petersburg, large as it was at times and in places, decrease the growth of the rural proletariat. In Iceland, too, the share of the rural population remained high until the early twentieth century, when the "industrialization" of fishing finally pushed for a change in the economic structure.

Industrial development in Scandinavia gained momentum in the latter half of the nineteenth century. Before World War I, industry employed more than 30 percent of the employable population in Sweden, just under 30 percent in Denmark and Norway, but only 10 percent in Finland. Danish industries were typically small in size, while in the other Nordic countries economic development was led by large-scale industries such as metal and wood processing.

Rise of the urban population. The urban population boom was the result of growth in trade, crafts, industry, construction, and administration and services for the expanding middle class. In 1914, one in every four Swedes and two-fifths of the Danes were town-dwellers. Even in agrarian Finland the urban population made up almost 15 percent of the popu-

Peasants. Peasants near Bergen, Sweden (now Norway). Painting by Johan Christian Dahl. BERGEN BILLEDGALLERI, BERGEN, NORWAY/ARCHIVO ICONGRAFICO, SA/©CORBIS

lation, and there were tens of thousands of Finns living in St. Petersburg. The capitals were the seats of the most rapid growth: at the beginning of the twentieth century, Copenhagen already had more than half a million inhabitants, while Stockholm had a population of 380,000; Christiania (Oslo) a quarter of a million people; and Helsinki more than 100,000 inhabitants. The trade centers of Gothenburg and Bergen also grew significantly. The development of inland towns and the building of railroads typically went together. The railroads also gave rise to a new type of population center.

Rapid urbanization left the towns heavily segregated. Those who had left the countryside settled on the outskirts of the towns or outside and beyond the town administrative boundaries, in areas that grew into slums. Housing policy turned into an object of speculation: housing costs were high, housing standards poor. The new working-class areas were densely populated, with poor hygienic conditions and a high infant-mortality rate. The situation swiftly improved, however, with the introduction of municipal waterworks and public health care at the turn of the twentieth century. The administration of the urban centers had been rationalized, though not democratized, in the nineteenth-century local government reforms, but national legislation was often used as a stick—and state subsidies as carrots—to make the local bodies carry out effective reforms. Little by little, local self-government was beginning to be controlled more closely by national government.

Urban life and restructuring of the society.
What the urban middle and working classes found in common was the growing separation of work and home. Those who had moved to town from the country were often young and about to be married. In towns, the nuclear family became the norm, even if the middle class kept their servants, and the working class often shared their homes with others. The increasing mass production of consumer goods began to take over from the production of homemade goods, which decreased the need for servants. The middle-class husband worked outside the home, while the wife devoted her life to looking after home and children. The ideal of a family wage was kept alive in working-class families, too: the husband was supposed to provide for his family, but practice usually proved otherwise. The wife and children had to supplement the husband's earnings by working outside the home or by taking in work such as sewing, laundry, and child minding.

The growing social problems in towns—the "dangerous liberty" of working-class children and the high extramarital birthrates in particular—had been cause for concern to the middle classes and the elites ever since the early nineteenth century. One of the first manifestations of civil society were the philanthropic organizations. Charitable work, teaching, and poor relief were considered suitable areas of social engagement for middle-class women.

Women's organizations and the fact that single women from the upper classes increasingly took up white-collar positions fostered a wider debate about women's status, duties, and rights from the 1840s onward. At the core of practical charitable work and of the social and national debate was the significance of the family, particularly of the mother as the backbone of social and moral upbringing. In societies geared around family farms it was difficult to justify the tradition of male supremacy with a peripheral female status. The man might be the head of the farm, but the wife still held the keys to the larder. The status of boys and girls as inheritors was brought into line without much opposition. Women had started their march toward a public role. The universities opened their doors to them in the 1870s and 1880s. The 1906 parliamentary reform in Finland—enacted in a euphoria of national self-defense against Russian inroads against Finnish autonomy—earned women equal and universal suffrage and the right to stand as candidates in national elections. Other Nordic countries followed suit later.

There were many ways to get involved in civic organizations. National and cultural associations, voluntary fire brigades, savings associations, and agrarian organizations grew more popular in all the Nordic countries from the 1830s onward, and political organization was boosted by the crises that stirred political life and reforms throughout the Nordic countries. The reorganizing and consolidation of the civil society tied in with the diminishing significance of the monarchy, the expansion of political participation, the growing importance of public debate, and the bureaucratization of the state.

The birth of the labor movement was part of this social mobilization. The basis of working-class organization lay in the old trade guilds, extinct in all the Nordic countries by the mid-nineteenth century. Run by middle-class liberals, the first phase of the labor associations was mostly pedagogical in nature, aimed at educating and civilizing the masses. Socialist doctrine began to be widely debated in the press in the 1840s, and the ideas were examined by both middle-class and working-class organizations, although workers' associations did not adopt the socialist line until much later—in the 1870s in Denmark, the 1880s in Sweden and Norway, the 1890s in Finland,

and only in the 1910s in Iceland. Behind the decision to adopt a socialist line lay the reorganization of labor relations, the breakup of patriarchal ties, and the increased frequency of industrial action such as strikes. It was not surprising that trade unions should grow into strong national organizations in early-nineteenth-century Scandinavia. In a limited democracy, the trade unions became even stronger than the political (Social Democratic) movement. In Finland, however, where all political forces were united in national self-defense against Russia, the position of the political labor movement was stronger by far than that of the trade unions.

In the Nordic countries, the agrarian population and the workers typically organized at the same time. This was especially well demonstrated in the breakthrough of the cooperative movement. The Danish peasant movement and production cooperatives gained a prominent status both economically and politically. The working class and in part the rural and urban middle classes, too, favored the consumers' cooperatives, which tied political movements to economic and business life. The cooperative movement grew to be a significant economic power base.

BASIS OF THE WELFARE STATE

The course of nineteenth-century Nordic societies was determined by urbanization and the political involvement of the proletariat. At the local level, the changes meant higher taxes, because one of the core duties of autonomous municipal administrations was to look after the ever-increasing poor relief costs. Attempts to reduce these costs had failed: neither the efforts to create British-style workhouses nor the classically liberal poor relief laws of the 1860s and 1870s, which stressed individual responsibility, had succeeded in bringing down the costs. A crucial factor in the widening economic and social gap between the middle classes and the lower classes was the tightening grip on power at the local level by the middle class. Local government was practiced—and its autonomy boosted by reforms—in all Nordic countries in the nineteenth century. But the rural and urban middle classes did not content themselves with wielding increasing power locally; they wanted their share in national politics as well.

Health insurance and pension reforms in Denmark in the 1890s and Sweden in the 1910s relied on state funding. Rather than stemming from abstract egalitarian ideals, they were born out of the struggle between agrarian parties, the urban middle class, and the conservative elites who had traditionally ruled the

state. The competition was about power, customs duties, and taxation. The labor movement had little initial impact on the reforms, although the status of the working class was an important political argument. When the Nordic countries adopted social security systems, ideals of solidarity and egalitarianism took second place to the old statist traditions. The state-centered nature of politics fostered the aim to create large political coalitions—a politics of consensus—which further reinforced the legitimacy of national politics. With the rise of the labor movement in the twentieth century as a political player of the first degree through reformist Social Democratic Parties, it was natural to continue the egalitarian and universalistic social policy, usually supported by the strong agrarian movements and the middle class. The depression of the 1930s further spurred welfare measures, amid lower levels of political polarization than occurred elsewhere in Europe.

The Nordic countries grew to be important industrial states, albeit at varying dates and rates. Relying on metal and engineering industries, Sweden changed quickest, whereas Finland retained an agrarian character until the 1960s. Agriculture employed 20 percent of the Swedish workforce in 1950, some 25 percent in Denmark and Norway, and almost 50 percent in Finland. The difference was less marked in industry: 40 percent of the Swedish workforce was employed in manufacturing, 35–37 percent in Denmark and Norway, and 28 percent in Finland. The biggest differences in 1950 were in the service sector, which accounted for as much as 47 percent of the workforce in Norway, around 40 percent in Sweden and Denmark, and only 25 percent in Finland. The differences evened out in the years following World War II, which saw the birth of the "Nordic welfare state" as we know it. In 1970, the service sector employed a little more than 50 percent of the workforce in the Scandinavian countries, and 46 percent in Finland.

WELL-ORGANIZED SOCIETY

Twentieth-century Nordic societies were characterized by the high organization rates of the occupational groups. Blue- and white-collar workers' trade union membership and the extent of organization among farmers were among the highest in the world. This corresponded with intense class loyalty in political involvement, which is explained by the ethnic and religious homogeneity of the Nordic countries. National politics has built on a hegemonic tradition guided by prevailing ideological conceptions of the common good or the interest of the nation, and starting from the 1930s, on coalitions between the labor movement and the agrarian parties in particular.

Another important component of Nordic social policy is the politics of consensus, institutionalized in many ways. The collaboration between labor market organizations and interest groups was elevated to an official policy, particularly in times of crisis and war. After World War II, a special form of consensual politics was seen in so-called social corporatism: social, employment, and tax aims and resolutions were jointly settled by the trade-union movement, employees, and the government. Political settlements were made in conjunction with collective-bargaining agreements.

There are of course differences between the countries, but the fact remains that ever since the 1950s the social conditions in the Nordic countries have been brought into line by joint institutionalized state policies. These helped create a joint labor market for the Nordic countries and a broadly uniform social policy at an early stage. Nordic cooperation also shaped common principles into more or less official "national programs." These principles include universal social rights; government responsibility in ensuring general welfare; equal opportunities for both sexes and in income distribution (including redistribution through taxation); and (in varying degrees in different countries) the target of full employment and high employment participation.

NORDIC GENDER SYSTEM

Women have gained a prominent position in the Nordic societies, both at work and in public life. This was possible because industrialization came late and because the countryside was dominated by family farms. The wife's role was determined by the division of labor in family farms and would change according to whether the household was dependent on jobs, such as fishing and logging, that necessitated the husband's being away. In these cases, it was the women who bore the main responsibility for agriculture and animal husbandry. The division of labor between the sexes was ecologically determined and flexible, but it was socially determined as well, because the low wages of the landless population and urban working classes meant that both sexes and even their children had to earn their share of the family's living. These structural terms become especially evident, if we compare Finland, where industrialization came last, to the Scandinavian countries. The Finnish level of industrialization was the lowest in the Nordic countries between 1860–1970, the pay rates were two-thirds of those in

Sweden, but the women's employment rates were the highest.

The sovereignty of single women and their right to dispose of their property became established between the 1840s and 1880s. This was especially important to the growing urban middle classes, whose ranks were swelling with single women to be recruited as teachers, nurses, and office workers in the expanding service sector. These urban middle-class single women were also the basis of the women's charitable organizations and the women's movement that kept the flag flying for women's issues. What came into being in the Nordic countries was a singular concept of bipartite female citizenship: the fact that she was expected to raise the future generation determined the woman's role within the family and in the society at large. Voting rights for women were granted earlier in the Nordic countries than in any other European region.

The family mother fulfilled her social responsibility in raising the children and in promoting rational housekeeping, whereas a single woman's duties were done in civic organizations, in schools and various childcare institutions. Education was a prerequisite for women to be able to optimally fulfill their parenting and housekeeping roles. Because the married woman's dependency on her husband was considered a problem, the marriage law reforms of the 1920s and 1930s defined paid employment outside the home and work within the home as equal functions for the benefit of the family. Women were released from needing a man to speak and act for them.

The gender bias in the welfare systems goes back to how welfare services were developed. Charity and child rearing were considered women's jobs. This view became entrenched when the state expanded its services. A case in point is the statutory municipal daycare system, the expansion of which helped women work outside home toward the latter part of the twentieth century and also provided tens of thousands of jobs. The public sector employed between 25 and 34 percent of the Nordic workforce in 1975, and 52–62 percent of public-sector employees were women.

The development of wide-ranging social service systems in the latter half of the twentieth century was based on the aims of high employment rates and equality. The high employment rate was a necessary condition for taxation and social security contributions, which laid the basis for the development of the service systems. These were justified both in terms of equal opportunities and labor policy. Women's integration in the labor market was linked to the individual nature of the rights of both sexes. In the individual model, both spouses were seen as equal providers and caregivers. Social security benefits applied to all citizens as individuals, irrespective of their family status. The fact that spouses were taxed independently was also an incentive for women to work outside home.

There are both differences and similarities among Nordic countries in the women's employment participation. Part-time work in Scandinavia was clearly more common than in Finland, where women traditionally worked full-time. The similarity lies in a persistent difference between men and women: in 1960, women in industry were paid less than 70 percent of men's wages; in the 1980s, women received 90 percent of the men's earnings in Sweden, 85 percent in Denmark and Norway, and 77 percent in Finland. These were much higher figures than in Germany or Britain at the time. In sectors dominated by women (such as textile industries and public services) the pay rates are usually lower than in male-dominated sectors. In the public sector, however, the internal sex hierarchy, or glass ceiling, has grown more fragile. Women have been employed in senior positions more often than before.

The twentieth century saw the consolidation of female participation in public life. That the Nordic welfare model has helped to improve the lot of women is a widely accepted political truth, which has also slowed down the tendency to erode the welfare state. Changes in women's status, along with a steady decline in religious influence, accounted also for significant shifts in family forms in the later twentieth century, including a rapid growth of sexuality outside of marriage and, particularly in Sweden, a decline in the marriage rate altogether.

Old and new minorities. Social and political development in the Nordic countries has been determined to a great extent by the extraordinary ethnic and religious homogeneity. There are, however, endogenous minorities, both nation-specific and multinational minorities. The more than 300,000 Swedish speakers in Finland gained linguistic equality in the 1920s and 1930s, and they see themselves not as a national or ethnic minority but as a linguistic minority only. The status of the German-speaking population (some 15,000 of them) in southern Denmark was also established in the twentieth century. A little more complicated is the status of the Finnish-speaking minorities in Sweden and Norway. The Finnish-speaking minority in northern Sweden (some 50,000 people) is part of the indigenous population, whereas the Norwegian Finns, known as *kveenit* (totaling around 7,000) moved to the area in the nineteenth century. Both groups were the targets of nationalistic

pressure, and their linguistic rights were given due consideration only at the end of the twentieth century.

The biggest endogenous multinational minorities include the Sami (totaling some 45,000), the Roma (some 10,000), and the Jews (around 25,000). The Sami came into conflict with the majority population and the state apparatus when traditional reindeer herding became harder in the structural economic changes. Sami status has been granted on the basis of varying criteria: in Finland, with a population of 4,000 Sami, they were classified on ethnic-linguistic grounds, whereas in Norway and Sweden, with a Sami population of 25,000 and 15,000, respectively, only reindeer herders qualified, even if most Sami were engaged in other trades altogether. Ever since the 1960s, the Sami have applied for a special linguistic, cultural, and economic status. Their efforts have been rewarded by the granting of the status of an indigenous people, ratified by the United Nations. Sami-language schools, political bodies for self-rule, and cultural institutions were granted official status on a pan-Nordic level and in each individual country in the 1990s. The struggle for the privilege of utilizing certain natural resources in Sami areas goes on.

Among the minorities in the Nordic countries, those in the weakest position are the Roma. Assimilation attempts have been overpowering, but Roma resistance has proved stubborn. The largest Roma population is in Finland, which has more than half of all the Roma in the Nordic countries. There was little official discrimination, but unofficial discrimination and pressures were tangible until the 1960s. It was then that the Roma became organized and made themselves heard as part of the international racial discrimination debate. Officially, the discrimination of Roma, as of all other minorities, was banned throughout the Nordic countries, but there was little positive action to improve their social status. A similar awakening as an "ethnic minority" took place toward the end of the 1990s among the "travelers" of Sweden and Norway. They have demanded that the sterilization policies and the many incidents in which their children were forcibly taken into care be reexamined and that they be compensated. Since the Roma were granted minority status, ratified by the European Union, the "travelers" have started to identify themselves as Roma, something they still refused to do in the 1970s.

Attempts at assimilating the Roma to the majority population may have come to nothing, but the opposite is true in the case of the Jews. They were tolerated between the seventeenth and nineteenth centuries, but their position grew more secure in the twentieth century. Also, neither the Nordic governments nor their peoples went along with the anti-

Semitic Nazi agenda, even when Denmark and Norway were under German occupation. The most recent additions to the Jewish population in Sweden (numbering some 15,000) came from those escaping the Nazis and Stalinist terror after World War II, but in the other Nordic countries the Jewish population is so small that their being assimilated out of existence was a real threat until the final decades of the twentieth century.

While the Nordic countries learned to accept their endogenous minorities and even safeguarded their position in many ways in the twentieth century, the composition of the societies was at the same time changed by new minorities who arrived as immigrants. In Sweden in particular the rapid economic growth and labor shortages in the 1960s led to a widespread recruitment of labor from abroad. Finland was at the time in the throes of an economic upheaval, and as many as 400,000 Finns moved to Sweden. The Finnish immigrants still numbered some 300,000 by the mid-1970s. Sweden also got its share of the *Gastarbeiter* ("guest workers"), typical of the west European labor market after World War II. A particularly large number came from Yugoslavia, Greece, and Turkey, some 50,000 people altogether.

The labor migrations slowed down in the 1970s but, instead, growing numbers of refugees flowed to the Nordic countries from Eastern Europe, Asia, Africa, and Latin America. The biggest cities in Sweden and Denmark in particular but also in Norway became multicultural communities. Official policies and public practices were antiracist and adhered to international regulations. There have been no serious political demands to weaken the minority rights and status. However, the tensions between minority groups and parts of the majority population had grown by the end of the twentieth century.

The relatively high degree of internal homogeneity in the Nordic countries has been tested in the face of expanding international integration, but the responses to these challenges have changed. Sweden would not let the Roma settle in the country between 1914 and 1954, and by refusing to let the Norwegian Roma return to their homes via Danish territory in the 1930s, Denmark sent them to the Nazi concentration camps. In contrast, the Nordic countries in the era of the European Union deal with immigrants and minority groups in accordance with common European norms. What used to be a historical European periphery has become part of the Western European core in economic, social, political, and ideological terms.

Translated from Finnish by Pirkko Hirvonen.

See also other articles in this section.

BIBLIOGRAPHY

Åkerman, Sune, et al, eds. *Chance and Change: Social and Economic Studies in Historical Demography in the Baltic Area.* Odense, Denmark, 1978.

Alapuro, Risto. *State and Revolution in Finland.* Berkeley, Calif., 1988.

Allardt, Erik, et al, eds. *Nordic Democracy: Ideas, Issues, and Institutions in Politics, Economy, Education, Social and Cultural Affairs of Denmark, Finland, Iceland, Norway, and Sweden.* Copenhagen, Denmark, 1981.

Baldwin, Peter. *The Politics of Social Solidarity: Class Bases of the European Welfare State, 1875–1975.* Cambridge, U.K., 1990.

Barton, H. Arnold. *Scandinavia in the Revolutionary Era, 1760–1815.* Minneapolis, Minn., 1986.

Battail, Jean Francois, Régis Bouyer, and Vincent Fournier. *Les sociétés scandinaves de la Réforme à nos jours.* Paris, 1992.

De Coninck-Smith, Ning, Bengt Sandin, and Ellen Schrumpf, eds. *Industrious Children: Work and Childhood in the Nordic Countries 1850–1990.* Odense, Denmark, 1997.

Derry, T. K. *A History of Scandinavia: Norway, Sweden, Denmark, Finland, and Iceland.* Minneapolis, Minn., 1979.

Engman, Max, and David Kirby, eds. *Finland: People, Nation, State.* London, 1989.

Flora, Peter, ed. *Growth to Limits: The Western European Welfare States since World War II,* vol. 1. Berlin, 1986.

Gissel, Svend, et al. *Desertation and Land Colonization in the Nordic Countries c. 1300–1600.* Stockholm, Sweden, 1981.

Grell, Ole Peter, and Andrew Cunningham. *Health Care and Poor Relief in Protestant Europe 1500–1700.* London and New York, 1997.

Gustafsson, Harald. *Political Interaction in the Old Regime: Central Power and Local Society in the Eighteenth-Century Nordic States.* Lund, Sweden, 1994.

Häkkinen, Antti, ed. *Just a Sack of Potatoes? Crisis Experiences in European Societies, Past and Present.* Helsinki, Finland, 1992.

Heikkinen, Sakari. *Labour and the Market: Workers, Wages, and Living Standards in Finland, 1850–1913.* Helsinki, Finland, 1997.

Hietala, Marjatta. *Services and Urbanization at the Turn of the Century: The Diffusion of Innovations.* Helsinki and Jyväskylä, Finland, 1987.

Jessop, Bob, et al, eds. *Flexibilization and the Alternatives of the Nordic Welfare States: Restructuring State and Industry in Britain, Germany and Scandinavia.* Aldershot, U.K., 1991.

Jörberg, Lennart. *The Industrial Revolution in Scandinavia, 1850–1914.* London, 1970.

Kirby, David. *The Baltic World, 1772–1993: Europe's Northern Periphery in an Age of Change.* London and New York, 1995.

Kirby, David. *Northern Europe in the Early Modern Period: The Baltic World, 1492–1772.* London and New York, 1990.

Kosonen, Pekka. "The Scandinavian Welfare Model in the New Europe." In *Scandinavia in a New Europe.* Edited by Thomas B. Boje and Olsson Hort Sven S. Oslo, Norway, 1993. Pages 39–70.

Lappalainen, Mirkka, and Pekka Hirvonen, eds. *Crime and Control in Europe from the Past to the Present.* Helsinki, Finland, 1999.

Norman, Hans, and Harald Runblom. *Transatlantic Connections: Nordic Migration to the New World after 1800.* Oslo, Norway, 1988.

Riis, Tomas, ed. *Aspects of Poverty in Early Modern Europe.* Vol. 3: *La pauvreté dans les pays nordiques 1500–1800.* Odense, Denmark, 1990.

Tägil, Sven, ed. *Ethnicity and Nation Building in the Nordic World.* London, 1995.

West, John F. *Faroe: The Emergence of a Nation.* London, 1972.

THE BALTIC NATIONS

Alfred Erich Senn

In the course of European history, the term "Baltic" has had various meanings. To a philologist, it refers to the language family that includes Latvian and Lithuanian. In nineteenth-century Imperial Russia, the Baltic Provinces included only the territory now called Latvia and Estonia. At the same time the term "Balt" referred to the German nobility in the region. Only in the nineteenth century did the masses of Latvians, Lithuanians, and Estonians become a factor in the politics of the region, and only in the twentieth century, when the independent states of Estonia, Latvia, and Lithuania appeared on the European scene, did observers link them together as the Baltic States.

The eastern shore of the Baltic Sea constituted a major crossroads of military, mercantile, and cultural currents. Although Latvians and Lithuanians speak related languages, the history of the Latvians is more closely tied to that of the Estonians, who speak a non-Indo-European language akin to Finnish and, more distantly, to Hungarian. First Germans and then Swedes dominated the northern part of the eastern Baltic littoral until the Russian Empire incorporated the territory in 1721. The Lithuanians, on the other hand, lived in close union with Poland until their incorporation into the Russian Empire at the end of the eighteenth century.

Between World War I and II, independent statehood allowed all three nationalities to consolidate their distinct identities, which then carried them through half a century of Soviet rule until they again emerged as independent states in the 1990s.

THE MIDDLE AGES

In the historic division of Europe between Latin Christianity and Eastern Orthodoxy, the Baltic region lay on the eastern frontier of western Europe. Crusading Teutonic knights brought Latin Christianity in the thirteenth century, when they conquered the lands inhabited by the ancestors of the Estonians and Latvians. The ancestors of the modern Lithuanians resisted, establishing the Grand Duchy of Lithuania. The Lithuanian grand duke Mindaugas accepted Latin Christianity in 1251, but the Lithuanians soon reverted to their pagan practices. Between 1386 and 1387, the Lithuanians officially returned to the Catholic Church as the result of a political union with Poland.

The Teutonic conquerors drew the northern part of the region into the Hanseatic League, imported the Magdeburg Law for the cities, and established a ruling German upper class. The Lithuanian Grand Duchy, on the other hand, moved into the void created by Mongol invasions of the thirteenth century and incorporated territories that eventually became Belarus and Ukraine, where the population was Slavic in language and Eastern Orthodox in religion. On its western frontier, however, the Grand Duchy of Lithuania controlled only what became known as Lithuania Major, including the cities of Kaunas and Vilnius. Lithuania Minor, the seacoast of present-day Lithuania, including the city of Klaipėda (Memel), lay under German rule until the twentieth century.

In the fourteenth century Jews began to immigrate into the region, primarily coming from Germany, and their numbers grew rapidly. Winning the right to maintain their own traditions and ways, Jews found that they could establish stronger communities in the eastern, less-developed lands of the grand duchy, which in 1386 became part of the Polish-Lithuanian Commonwealth, and therefore they sank particularly deep roots in Lithuania. Vilnius (or Vilna), the capital of Lithuania, became a major Jewish cultural center.

On the eve of the modern era, the indigenous people of the region lived and worked primarily as peasants. As such they were caught up in the process of intensifying enserfment and were excluded from any political or economic power. In the north the landowning nobility was mainly German, and German merchants together with some Germanized locals dominated urban affairs. In Lithuania, Polish or Polonized nobility, church officials, and merchants dominated the cities and towns, but a significant portion of commerce and banking came into the hands of the growing Jewish population. In the sixteenth century all three native peoples—Estonians, Lithuanians, and Latvians—developed their own written literature, largely as a result of the religious controversies arising from the Reformation.

THE EARLY MODERN PERIOD

In the sixteenth century the Reformation drastically changed the nature of the region's cultural development, and the emergence of the Grand Duchy of Moscow as an eastern European power radically changed the course of the area's political and economic history. By the end of the eighteenth century the region had fallen under the control of the Russian Empire.

In 1525 the Livonian Order of the Teutonic Knights secularized its landholdings and formed the state of Livonia with Lutheranism as the official religion. In the middle of the century the Lithuanian nobility, which over time accepted Polish language and customs, showed considerable sympathy for Calvinist teachings. But the Catholic Counter-Reformation, led by the newly formed Jesuit order, restored the grand duchy and Poland to the dominion of Rome.

In 1558 Tsar Ivan IV of Moscow attacked Livonia to extend his realm to the Baltic Sea. Moscow had already begun driving the Lithuanians back from Belarusian and Ukrainian territories. The so-called Livonian War lasted twenty-five years. Although Ivan failed to reach the Baltic, the conflict radically changed the political face of the Baltic region. The Livonian state collapsed. Sweden occupied the northern part of the Livonian lands, while Poland-Lithuania took in the southern part.

The social structure of the Baltic changed little as a result of this conflict. In occupying the northern part of the former Livonian lands, the Swedish government guaranteed the rights of the German nobility. While most Estonians came under Swedish rule, Latvians found themselves split between Sweden and Poland-Lithuania. In the eastern section, Inflanty, or Latgallia, Polish nobility and Catholic influences dominated. In the western section, the Duchy of Courland, the dukes were nominally vassals of the Polish Crown, but they maintained considerable autonomy, adhering to the Lutheran Church and even briefly establishing colonial holdings in Africa. In Lithuania, Polish influences intensified, especially after the Union of Lublin in 1569, which tightened the administrative bonds between the two states. By the terms of this agreement, Poland took over the Ukrainian territories that had previously been a part of the grand duchy.

Estonian Peasants. In the 1600s most Estonians were living on the farming estates of rich landowners. MANSELL COLLECTION/TIMEPIX

In the seventeenth century the population suffered grievous losses as warring Swedish, Polish, and Russian troops marched through the territory. These losses culminated in the devastation wrought by plague from 1708 to 1711. Lithuanian historians estimate that the plague reduced the Lithuanian population by one-third. Estonian and Latvian historians calculate that by 1721 the population count was at most 150,000 to 170,000 Estonians and some 220,000 Latvians. The original population of Prussia, which spoke a language akin to modern Latvian and Lithuanian, died out almost completely, and an influx of German and Swiss settlers gave this region, centered on the city of Königsberg, its historic German character.

At the beginning of the eighteenth century Tsar Peter I of Moscow drove the Swedes from the region. He crowned his efforts to expand the Muscovite state by proclaiming it the Russian Empire. As provided by the terms of the Treaty of Nystadt (1721), the Baltic German nobility maintained their privileges. Constituting a privileged caste, they obtained ever greater authority over their peasants, who at times mounted violent resistance to the landlords.

In the eighteenth century Russian influences in Lithuania grew. The tsarist court established control over the Duchy of Courland, which it formally incorporated in 1795. In the first partition of the Polish-Lithuanian state in 1772, the Russian Empire incorporated Inflanty (Latgallia), and in the second and third partitions it incorporated most of Lithuania. Prussia took the Lithuanian region of Suvalkai/Suwałki in the partitions. Napoleon subsequently incorporated it into the Duchy of Warsaw, then at the Congress of Vienna (1814–1815) Russia took the territory as part of the Kingdom of Poland.

At the time that the Russian Empire occupied this territory, the indigenous population had yet to express any voice in its public affairs or in its future. In the middle of the eighteenth century German romantics, to be sure, discovered these peoples, and the German writer Johann Gottfried von Herder paid special note to the particular genius of all national cultures as he wrote about his discovery of the Latvian peasantry. Baltic intellectuals later cherished these thoughts, but they objected that their German visitors often seemed to want to preserve the past as a collection of relics rather than to contribute to the future development of these cultures. It was by no means clear that these local peasant cultures would ever emerge from foreign domination and develop to the level of national statehood.

THE NINETEENTH CENTURY

After the conclusion of the Napoleonic Wars in 1814–1815, the Baltic region, for the first time together under one government, experienced a century without foreign invasions. Under the Russian administration, Estonians and Latvians lived in the Baltic Provinces of Kurland (Courland), Livland, and Estland, while most Lithuanians lived in the Northwest Province centered around the city of Vilnius/Vilna. Under these relatively stable conditions, the population recovered, and according to the Russian census of 1897, the population of the Estonian region stood at about 1 million and the population of the Latvian region at almost 2 million. Calculating the geographic and demographic dimensions of Lithuania is more difficult for reasons explained below.

The major social and economic change the nineteenth century brought to life in the three Baltic peoples was the emancipation of the peasants. In the Baltic Provinces between 1816 and 1819 the peasants were freed from serfdom without land. They gained new rights as individuals, but delays in the implementation of the new order and legal restrictions on their right to migrate meant that remnants of the serf system lingered until the middle of the century. In the Lithuanian lands and Latgallia emancipation came in 1861. Since the Russian government wanted to weaken the Polish nobility in the Northwest Province, the peasants received relatively favorable terms in obtaining land. Even so, the population did not feel the full economic and social impact of the emancipation until the 1880s.

Freed from the bonds of serfdom and emerging from their history as the peasants in a region dominated by landowners who represented strong neighbors, all three peoples entered new phases of their national development. Latvians and Estonians enjoyed a more diversified economic life and a more active political life than did the Lithuanians. Riga, an important entrepôt for the Russian Empire, drew migrants from the countryside, and by the end of the nineteenth century Latvians were important participants in Russian Socialist politics. Lithuanians lagged behind for several reasons. The Russian government limited economic development in the region because it lay on the border with Germany, and the local Russian authorities, seeking to weaken Polish influences on Lithuanian culture, banned the use of Latin characters in printing Lithuanian texts—in effect a ban on the Lithuanian press. (The Russian authorities lifted the ban in 1904.) Latvians and Estonians developed a lively public press, discussing social issues at a time when Lithuanians had to publish materials abroad, mostly in East Prussia and later in the United States, and smuggle them into the empire at great risk.

Toward the end of the nineteenth century, as a result of the peculiar economic and political conditions, Lithuanians emigrated from the region in much greater numbers than did Latvians or Estonians. Lithuanians wanting to leave rural life for jobs in cities could not expect to find work in Vilnius, which, restricted by Russian government policy, had little industry and remained predominantly a city of artisans. Lithuanians looking for urban work had to think of Riga, St. Petersburg, or other Russian cities, and in growing numbers they chose to go abroad. Those seeking only seasonal work might settle for jobs in Germany or the Scandinavian countries, but those seeking long-term prospects set off in growing numbers for North America. As a result Vilnius, which the Lithuanians claimed as their capital, looked like a Polish city, and according to the Russian census of 1897, Jews constituted a plurality of the city's population (39 percent).

Lithuanian emigration to the United States had far-reaching repercussions on Lithuanian development. Many émigrés, who were mostly young men, nurtured the idea of returning home after they had accrued a sufficient nest egg, usually thought of as perhaps $500. But in America, working primarily in industry and in mining, they found a completely new life that both confused and absorbed them. Upton Sinclair's novel *The Jungle* (1906) focused on one such Lithuanian immigrant to Chicago. The majority of these young men in fact did not return to Lithuania but sent considerable amounts of money back to their relatives at home. Lithuanian nationalist leaders despaired of this emigration, believing that the nation was losing its hope for the future.

By the beginning of the twentieth century nationalist leaders in the Baltic had to define their national existence against a complicated background of circumstances. Although they lived under Russian rule, leaders of all three nationalities saw the greatest threat to their national identities in their own landowners, Poles and Germans. Latvians and Estonians, who could not claim to have had a historic state, talked of the right of national self-determination, but they had to free themselves of the historically entrenched power of the German nobility, who had provided many military figures and diplomats in the Russian government. For both Estonians and Latvians, language was the major factor in their national identities. The Estonians were mainly Lutheran, as were the Germans. But the Latvians found their religious preferences split between the Lutherans in the west and the Catholics in the east.

The Lithuanians faced a different set of circumstances in defining their national identity. They claimed to be the heirs of the historic Lithuanian Grand Duchy, but the heritage of that state was confusing. The ancestors of the modern Lithuanians had constituted only a minority of that state's population. The Poles had dominated the culture of the state, and a person Polish in culture might well use "Lithuanian" as a designation of the territory in which he or she lived. As a result, even the name "Lithuanian" was subject to confusing interpretations. Lithuanian nationalists nevertheless insisted on their historic right to national self-determination, founding their identity on their language and the Roman Catholic religion. Historically, however, the Roman Catholic Church had been a vehicle for the Polonization of Lithuania, and therefore some Lithuanian freethinkers objected to idealizing the role of the church in Lithuanian culture.

On the eve of World War I, despite the obvious growth of national consciousness among all three Bal-

tic peoples, none of them occupied a significant place in the tsarist Russian government's consideration of "national questions" in its empire. Poles, Finns, Armenians, and Jews posed much more visible problems. The particular circumstances of the military conflict from 1914 to 1918 created a situation that suddenly allowed these three peoples to create their own political systems and to emerge as independent states.

INDEPENDENCE

World War I brought the opportunity for independence but at a high price. In the course of the conflict, German forces occupied most of the Baltic region. The Bolshevik government, which took power in Russia in 1917, announced that it had no claim to the territory, but Moscow nevertheless attempted to impose Communist governments on the three Baltic peoples. By 1920 Estonia, Latvia, and Lithuania had established three national republics, and in turn their independence contributed greatly to the development of national societies and cultures in each.

All three newly independent Baltic States considered the strengthening of their respective national cultures as imperative for their new governments. This in turn necessitated consideration of the interests of national minorities. In Latvia minorities constituted 20 to 25 percent of its almost 2 million inhabitants, of which Russians, including Belorussians, represented the largest group (about 12 percent). Estonians made up two-thirds of the 1 million inhabitants of Estonia.

Because of Lithuania's boundary conflicts, calculating the republic's minorities was more difficult. The 1923 census did not include Vilnius, which Poland had seized in 1920, and Memel/Klaipėda, which the Lithuanians occupied from 1923 to 1939. That census reported that minorities constituted 16 percent of Lithuania's reported 2.5 million inhabitants and that Jews made up almost half of the minorities (7.6 percent). Jewish leaders had almost idealized the Lithuanian state at its creation, expecting to play a major role in its affairs, therefore they resented the government's efforts to strengthen the Lithuanian role in society while restricting Jewish participation in public affairs. During the period that Lithuania controlled Memel, the republic had a larger minority population because of the number of Germans living in that region. In 1939 the Soviet Union, after occupying eastern Poland, turned the Vilnius region over to Lithuania, greatly increasing both the Jewish and the Polish minorities in that state. The uncertainty of Lithuania's borders was a troublesome consideration in relations between the three republics.

The majority of the population in all three republics was peasants, and the first concern of the new governments was land reform. In Estonia 86 percent of the expropriated land had belonged to Baltic Germans, who were not permitted to keep any land. The Latvians and the Lithuanians permitted the expropriated landowners to keep small estates. In Latvia the landowners affected were mostly German, Russian, and Polish, and in Lithuania they were Polish and Russian. Expropriated Latvian Germans appealed to the League of Nations in protest, but in 1925 the League Council declared that the reforms constituted acceptable agrarian reform and not national discrimination. In all three republics authorities encouraged agricultural cooperatives as a means of relieving the disruption to production efficiency resulting from the breakup of large estates. All three republics reported population increases but declining birth rates during the period between the two world wars.

Throughout the period between the two world wars, the economies of all three republics were primarily agricultural. As of 1934, 60.2 percent of the Estonian workforce was engaged in agriculture, 17.8 percent in industry, and 5.1 percent in commerce. Latvia in 1930 reported 66.2 percent of its workforce in agriculture, 13.5 percent in industry, and 5.2 percent in commerce. Lithuania in 1936 estimated that 76.7 percent of its workforce was in agriculture, 6.4 percent in industry, and 2.5 percent in commerce. Lithuania was self-sufficient in grain production, while Estonia and Latvia normally had to import grain. Lithuania was an important exporter of flax. All three republics significantly expanded their output of dairy products in this period.

The era of independence gave the people of each society the opportunity to develop their national culture to new dimensions. Besides creating new educational institutions and broadening economic life, this involved standardizing and modernizing the native language to meet the new demands of business and technology and building a broader and stronger national self-consciousness as a nation. Although the democratic institutions in each republic gave way to authoritarian rule—Lithuania in 1926, Latvia and Estonia in 1934—by 1939 the society in each of the republics had a clearer collective identity than it had in 1918 and 1919. This sense of identity played a vital role in each nation's survival during the half-century of Soviet rule.

THE SOVIET PERIOD

In 1939 the Soviet Union signed agreements with Nazi Germany whereby the Germans recognized the

End of German Occupation. The German army retreating from Latvia, 1944. FPG

Baltic region as part of the Soviet sphere. In 1940 Soviet troops overran the three republics, and the USSR annexed them as constituent republics. Soviet historians called the process a simultaneous social revolution in each republic. In reality envoys from Moscow restructured institutions to mirror the Soviet system. Although the authorities did not at first collectivize agriculture, they carried out extensive land reforms.

Soviet authorities also struck at the bases of the national self-consciousness by closing national institutions and religious organizations. Some individuals of the old order joined the new, but the authorities, aiming at discrediting the period of independence, put greater effort into winning the support of previously dissatisfied groups, particularly among the minorities. At the same time, through an agreement between Moscow and Berlin, the German population of the Baltic could emigrate to Germany, thereby essentially ending the historic role of local Germans in the lives of the Estonians and the Latvians.

Just a week before Nazi Germany invaded the Soviet Union in June 1941, Soviet authorities carried out massive arrests and deportations in all three Baltic republics. As Soviet forces retreated, Lithuanian activists proclaimed the reestablishment of the Lithuanian state, and in many areas Lithuanians indiscriminately attacked and killed Jews, who, they declared, had served the Soviet regime. German forces suppressed the provisional Lithuanian government and then carried out their own systematic campaign of arresting and executing Jews. By the end of 1941 the Jewish population constituted only a small portion of what it had been at the beginning of the year, and only some 5 percent survived the war.

The Baltic region remained under German occupation until 1944. Partisan resistance, first organized by Communists, developed and helped prepare the way for the return of Soviet troops. The Soviet Red Army brought the Soviet system back, and this time Moscow tolerated even fewer local peculiarities than it had in 1940. The local populations faced the choices of complying, resisting, or fleeing. A great many city dwellers chose flight. Since the Western powers, led by the United States, had not recognized the Soviet annexation of the Baltic States in 1940, Baltic refugees in Western Europe were considered "displaced persons" (DPs). As émigrés they struggled to construct a new diaspora to keep their national cultures alive. The resistance in the Baltic, supported mainly by the peasantry, continued into the early 1950s.

Under Soviet rule the population of the Baltic republics underwent considerable social change. In the late 1940s the authorities collectivized agriculture, doing away with the private farming that had prevailed up to that time. They deported hundreds of thousands of locals. They introduced new industries, which in turn brought in workers from other parts of the Soviet Union, especially to Latvia and Estonia. In contrast, the Lithuanians limited the influx of workers from other regions and even established Lithuanian majorities in the populations of both Vilnius and Klaipėda (Memel). By agreement with Warsaw, Poles in Lithuania could leave the republic for Poland.

Latvians, Lithuanians, and Estonians participated actively in the scientific and intellectual lives of the Soviet Union. Whenever Soviet authorities considered reforms aimed at improving the general welfare, the Baltic republics joined in enthusiastically, and at the time of the collapse of the Soviet system, the Baltic peoples enjoyed a higher standard of living than other parts of the Soviet Union. In the late 1970s, as part of a plan to "merge" the nationalities of the USSR, Soviet educators introduced a new policy called "bilingualism," in accordance with which local children began studying Russian in school before they received any instruction in their native languages. Many Western observers expected rapid assimilation of the Baltic populations into the great mass of the Soviet population.

Mikhail Gorbachev's policies of perestroika (restructuring) and glasnost (openness) opened the way for new developments. Given the opportunity to raise social and cultural concerns, Latvians, Lithuanians, and Estonians reacted quickly. Gorbachev responded by encouraging the non-Baltic minorities—Russians, Belorussians, and Poles—against the eponymous nationality in each republic. Baltic national leaders nevertheless persisted. The Baltic example gave focus to considerable national discontent throughout the rest of the Soviet Union and ultimately constituted a major factor in the collapse of the USSR. Latvia, Lithuania, and Estonia won general recognition as independent states in the fall of 1991.

THE POST-SOVIET PERIOD

The post-Soviet societies in the Baltic nations were very different from those of the 1920s. In 1989 only 12 or 13 percent of the workforce in the three republics was engaged in agriculture, 32 to 41 percent in industry. The metalworking industries obviously depended on Soviet supplies and markets, while food and timber enterprises used local resources. Institutions of the 1930s could not be revived easily. The countries faced difficult decisions on returning socialized property to former owners and on privatizing enterprises established in Soviet times. Behind these general questions lay even more difficult ones concerning guilt, atonement, and punishment of individuals and groups for collaboration with the Soviet authorities. In any given dispute, all of these factors interlocked in varying ways, both rational and emotional.

The question of minorities arose in new dimensions. Russians, who had been part of the majority in the large Soviet state, now resented being a minority in a much smaller state. In Lithuania, where the eponymous nationality constituted 80 percent of the 3.6 million inhabitants, the government accepted the socalled "zero-option," granting citizenship to any persons living in Lithuania on a given date. Latvians, only 52 percent of the 2.5 million inhabitants in their state, and Estonians, 60 percent of the 1.5 million inhabitants of their country, adopted more restrictive laws, thereby evoking strong protests from Moscow. That the three Baltic republics continued to enjoy higher living standards than Russia mitigated the complications of this continuing problem.

Another aspect of citizenship laws concerned the rights of émigrés to return to their homelands. A number of those who had settled in the West wanted to return and to participate in public life. Some nationals who had not previously returned from Siberian exile came back. Many émigré institutions and publications moved to the homelands. At the same time it became obvious that the various branches of the national culture had grown apart, carrying differing and even conflicting intellectual baggage with them. In addition, to limit the potential problems posed by their Russian inhabitants, the states hesitated to make every émigré a citizen automatically, and they forbade their citizens from holding citizenship in another state.

Lithuanian Demonstration. Vilnius, 7 April 1990. ©Vladamir Vyatkin/Lehtikuva/SABA

The social history of the Baltic nations has been heavily dependent on the kaleidoscope of its political history. The original inhabitants of the region fell prey to the ambitions of neighbors. In the first phase, the upper classes of the native peoples assimilated into the predominant foreign cultures, German in the north and Polish in the south. The three Baltic nations began to emerge as political factors in the region during the Russian Empire. They enjoyed a brief period of independence between the two world wars, when they developed their national cultures with the support of their administrations. The half-century of Soviet rule, extending from the 1940s to the 1990s, threatened their continued existence as ethnic-territorial units. But with the collapse of the Soviet Union, they received the opportunity to start again, this time with considerably stronger foundations than they had commanded in the 1920s.

See also other articles in this section.

BIBLIOGRAPHY

Atamukas, Solomonas. *Lietuvos žydų kelias* (The path of the Jews of Lithuania). Vilnius, Lithuania, 1998.

Baltic States, The: A Reference Book. Tallinn, Estonia, 1991.

Levin, Dov. *Baltic Jews under the Soviets, 1940–1946.* Jerusalem, 1994.

Lieven, Anatol. *The Baltic Revolution: Estonia, Latvia, Lithuania, and the Path to Independence.* New Haven, Conn., 1993.

Misiunas, Romuald J., and Rein Taagepera. *The Baltic States: Years of Dependence, 1940–1990.* Expanded and updated ed. Berkeley, Calif., 1993.

Pinchuk, Ben-Cion. *Shtetl Jews under Soviet Rule.* Oxford, 1991.

Plakans, Andrejs. *The Latvians: A Short History.* Stanford, Calif., 1995.

Rauch, Georg von. *The Baltic States: The Years of Independence, Estonia, Latvia, Lithuania, 1917–1940.* Berkeley, Calif., 1974.

Raun, Toivo U. *Estonia and the Estonians.* 2d ed. Stanford, Calif., 1991.

Royal Institute of International Affairs. *The Baltic States: Estonia, Latvia, Lithuania.* London, 1938.

Senn, Alfred Erich. *Gorbachev's Failure in Lithuania.* New York, 1995.

Sinclair, Upton. *The Jungle.* New York, 1981.

Smith, Graham, ed. *The Baltic States: The National Self-Determination of Estonia, Latvia, and Lithuania.* New York, 1994.

Thaden, Edward C., ed. *Russification in the Baltic Provinces and Finland, 1855–1914.* Princeton, N.J., 1981.

Urban, William. *The Baltic Crusade.* De Kalb, Ill., 1975.

Vardys, V. Stanley, and Romuald Misiunas, eds. *The Baltic States in Peace and War, 1917–1945.* University Park, Pa., 1978.

EAST CENTRAL EUROPE

Steven Béla Várdy and Emil Niederhauser

The four states that make up East Central Europe appeared in their current form only in the twentieth century, but the political history of three of them—Poland, the Czech Republic, and Hungary—reaches back to the tenth century. The fourth state—Slovakia—had no separate identity until 1918, and even then only as part of Czechoslovakia until the end of 1992. It had been part of Hungary from the tenth century until after World War I. Thus, Slovakia's social development has to be discussed within Hungary's and Czechoslovakia's historical evolution. This essay uses the term Czechia (*Česky* in Czech) to refer to the Czech state.

East Central Europe was for centuries a transitional region between western Christendom and the Orthodox Christian world (Russia, Ukraine, and the Balkans), although because it was Christianized by Rome (not by Constantinople), its countries always constituted what the Polish historian Oscar Halecki called the "borderlands of Western civilization." As such, its political, constitutional, and social development had much more in common with western than with eastern Europe and the Balkans. At the same time, from the western European point of view the region represented the "eastern frontier," beyond which lay the lands of "invisible Barbary."

The region's most important characteristics that distinguished it from both western and eastern Europe included:

1. its relative backwardness as compared to western Europe and its relatively advanced development as compared to eastern Europe and the Balkans
2. its persistent agrarian socioeconomic structure, and the resulting preponderance of the peasantry, which did not really change until the nineteenth century
3. the large size of its nobility (5 percent in Hungary and perhaps 10 percent in Poland), compared to less than 1 percent in many of the western countries, which had an impact even upon developments in the age of nationalism and

4. its highly mixed ethnic composition, wherein ethnic differences often manifested themselves as class distinctions, and vice versa (e.g., Polish nobility versus Lithuanian and Ruthenian peasantry, and Hungarian nobility versus Slovak, Romanian, and Serbian peasantry)

EAST CENTRAL EUROPEAN SOCIETY AROUND 1500

The social structures of the region's three longstanding states—Poland, Czechia, and Hungary—were similar. This was the result of a number of factors that affected them simultaneously. All three emerged from tribal federation into feudal statehood simultaneously, accepted Christianity in its western form about the same time, and fell under German socioeconomic influences. As a result, most of the local peasantry acquired their own plots of land and moved from collective to individual cultivation. Following this transformation, only the meadows, grasslands, and forests were held in common.

The landowning classes came from the nobility divided into two categories: the higher, or titled, nobility (usually called barons, magnates, or *pans*) and the lower nontitled nobility. The relationship between these two subclasses resembled western feudal relations, the lower nobility serving the magnates in various civil or military capacities.

By the end of the fifteenth century, the nobility's political organization had been fully formed in all three countries. Poland and Hungary were divided into smaller administrative units called *comitat*s (counties) or voivodships, each having considerable autonomy. The members of the nobility were represented in their respective feudal diets, which had evolved in the course of the thirteenth through the fifteenth centuries. The representatives of the clergy were likewise present. In all three countries Catholicism was the established state religion, but Poland's eastern provinces (modern Ukraine and Belarus) were populated mostly by Orthodox Christians. To a lesser degree, this was also true

EAST CENTRAL EUROPE'S POLITICAL MAP AROUND 1500

At the end of the fifteenth century Poland was part of the Polish-Lithuanian Commonwealth formed by the Union of Krewo of 1385 and consolidated fully by the Union of Lublin of 1569. It was a federated dual state of about 315,000 square miles, whose territory also included what in the twentieth century became Belarus and Ukraine. Only one-third of this vast country was Poland proper, but it held 60 percent of the country's population of six million.

The Czech Kingdom, or Czechia, was the smallest of the three states of East Central Europe. Its territory was only one-seventh and its population only about one-third of that of Poland-Lithuania. It consisted of the core provinces of Bohemia and Moravia (30,000 square miles) and, since the mid-fourteenth century, also of Silesia (15,000 square miles). In contrast to Poland and Hungary, however, the Czech Kingdom was part of the Holy Roman Empire, and its rulers were among the seven electors of the Holy Roman Emperors. Its membership in the Empire had placed limitations upon Czech sovereignty, but it also held certain advantages. By virtue of being

part of the Germanic world, Czechia became the most urbanized, most industrialized, and most advanced of the three states, although much of this urbanization and industrialization was in the hands of German settlers.

With a territory of about 130,000 square miles, Hungary was two-fifths the size of Poland-Lithuania but almost three times the size of Czechia. Around A.D. 1500 its population was between 3.5 and 4 million. It had two autonomous regions, Croatia and Transylvania, as well as a few frontier *banats* (provinces) in the northern Balkans. Croatia was an associated kingdom in personal union with Hungary. Transylvania was a province with minimal autonomy under an appointed governor called *vajda* or *voievod*. The small defensive *banats* in the northern Balkans were buffers in Hungary's struggle against the Byzantines, the Venetians, and later the Ottoman Turks. Today's Slovakia was also part of Hungary, but it had no separate identity. This also holds true for Carpatho-Ruthenia (now part of Ukraine) and Voivodina (now part of Serbia).

for Hungary's eastern provinces, particularly among the ancestors of present-day Rusyns and Romanians.

At the end of the fifteenth century, all three countries had a significant number of cities and towns. In Poland-Lithuania their number reached five hundred, while in Czechia and in Hungary they numbered about half as many. The majority of the walled cities had been established by western (mostly German) settlers, who had migrated during the twelfth through the fourteenth centuries. Originally these cities were regarded as royal property and were classified as "royal free cities." Their founders had acquired directly from the king privileges that included city autonomy, the right to live under their own laws, and the right of taxation. These privileges had been incorporated into their founding charters. Only a minority of the inhabitants held full citizenship rights, and only "citizens" had the right to vote. Even fewer were the number of those who could run for office, a right usually reserved for affluent citizens.

The royal free cities were free from all feudal control, and at times they could also send represen-

tatives to the feudal diets. Not so the "agricultural towns" *(oppidum,* pl. *oppida),* whose inhabitants, well-to-do peasants, had been given limited autonomy by their lords. They paid their feudal obligations collectively in money. In appearance they were more like overgrown villages. Most of the royal free cities, and occasionally even the *oppida,* controlled a number of villages in their vicinity. Serving in effect as their feudal lords. The city of Prague, for example, controlled over one hundred villages beyond its walls. Prague in those days was the largest city in East Central Europe, and at times also the capital of the Holy Roman Empire.

None of the countries was ethnically homogeneous, and each was inhabited by a number of nationalities. The citizens of the most important royal free cities were mostly Germans. In the Czech Kingdom, the inhabitants of many of the mountainous mining regions were also Germans—the ancestors of the Sudeten Germans. In the case of Poland, the most numerous of the non-Polish nationalities were the Lithuanians and the east Slavs (ancestors of the Ukrainians and Belorussians). Hungary also had a significant non-Hungarian population. In addition to the Croats, who had their own associated kingdom, these included the ancestors of the Slovaks in the north, the Rusyns in the northeast, the Vlach (the ancestors of the Romanians) in the east, and various south Slavic elements.

EAST CENTRAL EUROPEAN SOCIETY IN THE EARLY MODERN PERIOD

The sixteenth and seventeenth centuries brought many political and territorial changes to East Central Europe. The Union of Lublin of 1569 merged Poland and the grand duchy of Lithuania into a single state, the Czech Kingdom became an autonomous part of the Habsburg Empire, while Hungary fell victim to Ottoman Turkish expansion and was divided between the Turks and the Habsburgs.

The late fifteenth and the sixteenth century witnessed a major economic transformation of East Central Europe. It became an exporter of agricultural

EAST CENTRAL EUROPEAN CITIES AROUND 1500

In addition to Prague (Praha) in Bohemia and Breslau (Wroclaw) in Silesia, whose population may have been close to 100,000, East Central Europe's largest cities around 1500 included Cracow, Buda (later part of Budapest), Brünn (Brno), Pozsony (Pressburg, Bratislava), and Kassa (Kaschau, Košice), with populations ranging between 7,000 and 25,000. Most of the other cities with urban characteristics and urban governments had populations of 3,000 to 5,000. Among the villagelike *oppida* it was not uncommon to find some with a population of over 8,000. The best example of this is Szeged in southern Hungary, which—although one of the country's largest settlements—retained its rural appearance right into the late nineteenth century.

LAND OWNERSHIP IN POLAND-LITHUANIA, THE CZECH KINGDOM, AND HUNGARY AROUND 1500

Around 1500, the average peasant plot in the Polish-Lithuanian Commonwealth was about fifteen hectares, while in Czechia and Hungary it was only slightly smaller. The serfs paid their feudal obligations both in kind and in money. In the Czech Kingdom, many of the serfs held their lands in perpetuity, which was not the case in Poland-Lithuania and Hungary. Agricultural lands were divided into two categories: dominical lands *(terra dominicalis)* and rustical lands *(terra rusticalis)*. The former were held by the lords and the latter by the serfs. In practice, however, many of the dominical lands had also been parceled out to the peasants. The legal differences in ownership rights, however, had no significance until serf emancipation in the mid-nineteenth century. Originally, all peasant families had enough land to supply their needs, but the growth of population soon necessitated the division of the original plots into smaller entities, which gave rise to the category of increasingly impoverished half-plot-peasants and quarter-plot-peasants.

products to western Europe, a role that profoundly altered the region's economic life and social relations. This situation was the direct result of Europe's expansion into the Americas and Southeast Asia, which also increased western Europe's needs for agricultural products. This need was filled with Polish-Lithuanian grain and Hungarian cattle.

The resulting economic boom was more beneficial to the lords than the peasants. The former took direct control over most of the lands and extended their power over the peasants. The latter's right of free movement was terminated and their work obligations *(robot)* increased. Obligatory *robot* varied from region to region and from time to time. Most commonly, however, it amounted to three days per week for a full peasant lot (the total area allocated to the peasant family by the lord), two days per week for a half lot, and somewhat less for a fragment lot. Laws binding the peasants to the land were passed in the Czech Kingdom in 1487, in Poland in 1498, and in Hungary in 1514. The latter came in the wake of the region's most violent peasant war under the leadership of György Dózsa (c. 1470–1514), himself a member of the Hungarian lower nobility. Known as the "second serfdom," this bonded serfdom survived until the mid-nineteenth century.

East Central Europe, Fifteenth Century. Adapted from Paul Robert Magocsi, *Historical Atlas of East Central Europe* (Toronto: University of Toronto Press, 1993).

East Central Europe, 1570. Adapted from Paul Robert Magocsi, *Historical Atlas of East Central Europe* (Toronto: University of Toronto Press, 1993).

Ottoman Expansion into Hungary. Single combat between Turks and Hungarians before the Battle of Mohács, August 1526, at which the Ottomans decisively defeated the Hungarian monarchy. Miniature from manuscript H.1517, fol. 200r. TOPKAPI PALACE MUSEUM, ISTANBUL

The nobility and the burghers. The nobility became increasingly polarized, as the higher nobility acquired more land at the expense of the lower nobility. In early-seventeenth-century Bohemia about 150 families (fifty aristocratic and one hundred noble families) owned most of the large estates. In Moravia eighty aristocrats owned half of the land and 58 percent of the serfs. After the Battle of White Mountain secured both Habsburg domination and the victory of the Counter-Reformation in the Czech lands in 1620, however, the old Czech aristocracy and nobility disappeared. Those who did not fall in the battle left the country permanently. Their estates were appropriated by the Habsburgs and then distributed to a new pro-Habsburg nobility, recruited from the empire's multinational armies. At this time the title "count" became commonly used by the aristocracy.

The role of the higher nobility remained unchanged in seventeenth-century Poland and Hungary. Their numbers also remained small. In Hungary the number of aristocratic families varied between forty-nine and sixty-four. In contrast to the aristocracy, the lower nobility increased significantly. This was the result of perpetual warfare on the southern frontiers and the consequent growth of military forces. A significant number of these fighting men were ennobled, although only a few of them received grants of land. In Hungary these newly ennobled landless elements were known as the armalists *(armalisták),* and their numbers soon reached 4 to 5 percent of the population. By 1840 they numbered 680,000 out of a population of 13 million. They were even more numerous in Poland, where they constituted 8 to 10 percent of the population.

In addition to these ennobled servicemen, there were also various freebooters, who reached a seminoble status. Among them were the Cossacks of the Polish-Lithuanian state and the *hajdú*s of Hungary. The former were escaped serfs, who constituted themselves into Cossack hosts, and then entered the services of the Polish-Lithuanian state. Later, many of them were acknowledged, as of a seminoble rank. This was also true for the *hajdú*s, who were given collective nobility and then settled on the Great Hungarian Plain by Prince István Bocskay of Transylvania (ruled 1605–1606).

Changes also took place in the ethnic composition of these countries after the Battle of White Mountain. Poland saw the influx of many Ashkenazi Jews from the Holy Roman Empire. In the Czech lands, the population of Germans increased markedly, both in the cities and in the mining regions. Turkish Hungary saw a progressive influx of South Slavic elements, and Transylvania witnessed a similar influx of Vlachs from the Balkans. This process continued into the eighteenth century, ultimately altering Hungary's ethnic composition.

The Protestant Reformation had a significant impact on all three countries. The urban centers, with their large German population, gravitated toward Lutheranism, while the nobility favored Calvinism. In Poland, anti-Trinitarianism (known as Arianism) became popular, as it did in Transylvania under the leadership of Ferenc Dávid (c. 1510–1579), the founder of Unitarianism.

Led by the Jesuits, the Counter-Reformation was able to reconquer much of the population for Catholicism. In the Czech Kingdom the Counter-Reformation triumphed after the defeat of the Hussite nobility in 1620. In Hungary, it was somewhat less successful. Among the ethnic Hungarians in the country's eastern regions, Calvinism remained the dominant religion.

The Reformation had a positive impact on education in all of East Central Europe. Its emphasis on literacy in the vernacular languages necessitated the establishment of a great number of primary schools headed by the clergy. In Poland, the number of parish schools rose to four thousand. The number of secondary schools, usually under the control of the Jesuits, also increased. A number of new institutions of higher learning were also established.

AGRARIAN RELATIONS AND ECONOMIC CHANGES IN THE EIGHTEENTH CENTURY

Through much of the eighteenth century the Habsburgs engaged in settling southern Hungary with German, Dutch, and French peasants of the Catholic faith. These western settlers—whose numbers reached 200,000 by the end of the century—were enticed by grants of land, houses, draft animals, agricultural implements, and temporary exemption from taxation. At

POLITICAL DEVELOPMENTS IN POLAND-LITHUANIA, THE CZECH KINGDOM, AND HUNGARY IN THE SIXTEENTH AND SEVENTEENTH CENTURIES

The Union of Lublin of 1569 merged the Kingdom of Poland and the Grand Duchy of Lithuania into a single state. This restructured Polish-Lithuanian Commonwealth (commonly referred to simply as Poland) became a significant regional power. From the mid-sixteenth to the mid-seventeenth century it was a powerful rival of the rising Muscovite state. Although weakened in the 1650s, it survived in this form until the late eighteenth century, when is was partitioned by Russia, Prussia, and Austria (1772–1795), and then wiped off the map of Europe until 1918.

The fortunes of the Czech Kingdom and Hungary were somewhat different. Following the Battle of Mohács in 1526—which witnessed Hungary's defeat by the Ottoman Turks and the death of Hungary and Bohemia-Moravia's common ruler, King Louis II (ruled 1616–1526)—both of these states lost some of their full sovereignty. By electing Ferdinand of Habsburg (ruled 1626–1564), the Czech and the Hungarian kingdoms became component units of the ever-expanding Habsburg Empire. In 1547 the Czech nobility was forced to give up its right of free election, and had to accept the Habsburg dynasty's hereditary right to the Czech throne. They rebelled against this in 1618, but after their defeat at the Battle of White Mountain in 1620, they lost even more of their sovereignty. The Czech nobility was decimated, expelled, and replaced by a new pro-Habsburg nobility, and the Czech state was relegated to the position of autonomous province of the Habsburg Empire. It remained in that position right up to the end of the nineteenth century.

The case of Hungary was complicated by the Turkish conquest of the country's central regions and the election of John Zápolya (ruled 1526–1540) as a rival to King Ferdinand. The result of this situation was the country's fragmentation into three parts, which lasted until the early eighteenth century. Hungary's eastern third developed into the principality of Transylvania, nominally under Ottoman suzerainty, but actually headed by Hungarian princes, who were elected to their post by the principality's three recognized nations: the Hungarians, the Székelys (another tribe of the Hungarians), and the Saxons (Germans who had settled there in the thirteenth century). The Vlachs (later called Romanians) did not have a role in this selection process, because, lacking a nobility, they had no political elite to represent their cause.

Hungary's central section, including the capital city of Buda, was conquered by the Turks and then integrated into the administrative system of the Ottoman Empire. Its western and northern sections developed into Habsburg-controlled "Royal Hungary," where the city of Pozsony (Pressburg) served as the kingdom's temporary capital until the mid-nineteenth century. Only the expulsion of the Turks in the late seventeenth and early eighteenth centuries brought about the reestablishment of the country's unity, but even then only as a component state of the Habsburg Empire. Hungary retained that autonomous position until 1867, when it became a partner in the Dual Monarchy of Austria-Hungary (1867–1918).

EDUCATION AND LITERACY IN EAST CENTRAL EUROPE
(FOURTEENTH TO EIGHTEENTH CENTURIES)

Up to the early sixteenth century—when the Protestant Reformation altered the situation completely—education in East Central Europe was controlled by the Catholic Church. On the lower and the middle levels, teaching was in the hands of religious orders and larger parishes, many of which had their own schools. By the end of the fifteenth century Poland had over three thousand parish schools. The number in the Czech Kingdom and Hungary was somewhat smaller.

Several universities had also been established before the end of the fifteenth century—usually at the initiative of the ruling monarchs. The earliest of these institutions of higher learning were founded in the middle of the fourteenth century in Prague (1348) and Cracow (1364) as well as in Pécs (1367) and Óbuda (1388/95) in Hungary.

In the sixteenth century they were followed by numerous other institutions of higher learning, largely in consequence of the spread of Protestantism and the resulting Catholic Reformation. These include the famed Calvinist colleges of Sárospatak (1531), Pápa (1531), Debrecen (1538), and Gyulafehérvár (1629) in Hungary, as well as a few new universities. Among the latter were those of Vilna (Vilnius; 1578) in the Polish-Lithuanian Commonwealth, Olmütz (Olomouc; 1576) in Moravia, and Nagyszombat (Tyrnau; 1635) in Hungary. The latter eventually evolved into the University of Budapest.

It should be noted here that in the Middle Ages and early modern period all universities used Latin as their language of instruction. This makes it difficult to classify them by their language, and makes it possible for the University of Prague to be claimed by both the Czechs and the Germans. In contrast to the universities, Hungarian Calvinist colleges functioned only in Hungarian from the very start.

By the end of the seventeenth century, about 70 percent of the nobility and 60 percent of the burghers of East Central Europe were able to read and write.

Progress in education also continued in the eighteenth century. In Poland a college for the training of noble military officers was founded in 1740 (*Collegium Nobilium*); and in 1773 a National Educational Commission was established as Europe's first Ministry of Education. At the same time the Jesuits began to revive their schools first established in the sixteenth century.

In Hungary, Maria Theresa promulgated the *Ratio Educationis* in 1777. This law called for the establishment of a series of basic schools for the teaching of the *trivium* (reading, writing, and arithmetic) and several normal schools for the training of teachers. In light of the absence of the needed funds and teaching personnel, however, compulsory mass education had to wait for another century.

the same time the Habsburgs also encouraged a large number of Serbs to settle in the Hungarian territories freed from Turkish control, thereby changing the ethnic composition of the area later called Voivodina. A similar population change also took place in Transylvania with the rapid influx of Vlach peasants and shepherds from the Balkans, who came because of better economic opportunities. There were also population shifts within Hungary itself, manifested by the movement of many Slovaks down to the Great Hungarian Plain. In 1781 the population of the Czech lands was about 4 million (2.5 in Bohemia and 1.5 in Moravia). At the same time, according to the census of 1784–1787, the population of the kingdom of Hungary was 9.3 million (6.5 million in Hungary

proper, 1.45 million in Transylvania, 650,000 in Croatia, and 710,000 in the Military Frontier District).

During the second half of the eighteenth century, the position of the serfs generally improved as a result of reforms instituted in the spirit of enlightened absolutism under Maria Theresa (ruled 1740–1780) and Joseph II (ruled 1780–1790). These reforms, most of which followed peasant uprisings in Hungary (1735, 1767), Silesia (1771), and the Czech lands (1775), gave the state a basis for intervention into the relationship between lord and peasant. Initially, the state separated the rustical lands (the lord's own lands, sometimes parcelled out among the serfs) from the dominical lands (the lands allotted by the lord to peasant families for their own use), defined the serfs' specific obligations, and adjusted these obligations to the size of the peasants' plots. The work obligations of serfs with full plots was set at three days per week; a landless serf with a houses had to work twenty-six days per year, and those without houses only thirteen days. Moreover, if the stipulated *robot* was not sufficient to complete the needed labor, the serfs were also obliged to work for wages, which amounted to seven to fifteen *kreutzers* per day. Previously, they had often been obliged to work with no compensation. The next step in this process of improvement of the peasants' lot was Joseph II's peasant reforms, promulgated in 1781 and then gradually implemented throughout the Habsburg Empire. The serfs became personally free and could also hire themselves out for wages. Joseph II was planning additional reforms that would have abolished work obligations altogether, but he died before he could implement these reforms.

After the Jesuit Order was dissolved in 1773, their lands in the Czech kingdom were parceled out among the peasants, who, it was hoped, would eventually purchase them. This experiment resulted in a significant increase in the productivity of the former Jesuit estates. The government hoped that this experiment would serve as a model for the noble landowners.

In Poland-Lithuania agricultural conditions changed very little during the eighteenth century. At the beginning of the century a new wave of western settlers arrived from the Low Countries called *holender* (Holländer). They brought with them the newest methods of land cultivation, but their impact on Polish society was minimal. In 1768 there was a major peasant rebellion in the country's Ukrainian-inhabited eastern provinces. At the end of the century, about 70 percent of the country's population was still engaged in agriculture. Only 20 percent of the serfs possessed full plots, while nearly one-third of them were completely landless.

The most significant event in eighteenth-century Polish history was the partitioning of Poland by Russia, Prussia, and the Habsburg Empire. While the first partition of 1772 still left the Poles with a sizable state with nine million inhabitants, the second and third partitions of 1793 and 1795 wiped the country off the map of Europe. The three sections of Poland became part of three different socioeconomic systems. The northwestern section came under the influence of advanced German socioeconomic developments. Habsburg-controlled Galicia remained backward until the very end of the empire. The largest and least developed eastern part of Poland was integrated into the even more backward Russian Empire.

During the late eighteenth century the Czech lands experienced a government-inspired industrialization drive. The loss of most of Silesia in the War of Austrian Succession (1740–1748) prompted the Habsburgs to develop Bohemia-Moravia as the new center of their manufacturing industry. Many of the factories were established by Habsburg aristocrats, who recruited their workers from the ranks of the landless peasantry.

SERF EMANCIPATION AND SOCIAL TRANSFORMATION

The nineteenth century saw the transformation of a feudal society into a civil society in East Central Europe. In light of the region's fundamental agrarian nature, this transformation affected most of all the peasants. In the Grand Duchy of Warsaw (1807–1815) the emancipation of the serfs occurred in 1807. The serfs received their personal freedom, but the lands remained in the hands of the nobility, and the peas-

MILITARY FRONTIER DISTRICTS IN THE HABSBURG EMPIRE

The Military Frontier District *(Militärgrenze, Határrvidék)* was an anti-Ottoman defensive belt established by the Habsburgs between 1699 and the 1760s. Its inhabitants consisted of free peasants, who, in return for their plots, were obliged to perform military service. Most of these peasant soldiers were south Slavs, but in the mid-eighteenth century a number of Hungarian and Romanian Vlach districts were also established in southern and eastern Transylvania. Those who were settled there or who remained in these military districts received free lands. Their tax obligations were also reduced by two-thirds, and in times of war they were free from all taxes. In return for this, all healthy adult males were obliged to participate in military training on a regular basis. In case of a war, they were the first to be mobilized. With the decline of the Ottoman Empire and the Turkish danger, the military districts lost their usefulness. Those in Transylvania were disbanded in 1851, while those in Croatia-Slavonia and southern Hungary were liquidated between 1871 and 1885. Following their dissolution, all of the military districts were integrated into the regular civil administration system of the Kingdom of Hungary.

TRIPARTITIONED POLAND
IN THE NINETEENTH CENTURY

Only twelve years after the final partitioning of Poland in 1795, Napoleon established the Grand Duchy of Warsaw, which survived for less than a decade (1807–1815). After Napoleon's defeat, the Congress of Vienna (1815) partitioned Poland again, with most of its territories of about 227,000 square miles going to Russia. This included the autonomous Congress Kingdom, with about 49,000 square miles and a population of 4 million. Habsburg Austria received 30,000 square miles of Galicia with a population of 4.2 million, while Prussia received 11,000 square miles of Pomerania with 776,000 inhabitants. The city of Cracow and its vicinity was made into a free city of 444 square miles and 88,000 people until 1846, when it was attached to the Austrian Empire. The autonomy of the Congress Kingdom was cut down after the anti-Russian uprising of 1830–1831 and then completely eliminated—creating the Warsaw Province—after the second anti-Russian uprising of 1863–1864.

ants were obliged to pay for their use with money and agricultural produce.

At the Congress of Vienna (1815) Poland was partitioned again, with most of its territories (including the autonomous "Congress Kingdom") going to Russia and the rest to Prussia and Habsburg Austria. Of these three sections, Prussian Poland had the most progressive social structure. Serf emancipation was begun there in 1823 and completed in 1850. All serfs received their personal freedom, and the landlords were compensated for the lost services with government bonds. In the Austrian Empire, including Czechia but excluding Hungary, serf emancipation was carried out by the Act of the Imperial Council on 7 September 1848. The serfs were personally freed and received the plots they had been cultivating. In the Czech lands, one-third of the compensation was paid for by the peasants, one-third by the government, and one-third was abolished in lieu of the termination of the lords' obligations to the serfs.

Serf emancipation in Russian Poland came after the anti-Russian Polish Revolution of 1863–1864. The Russians wished to turn the peasants against their Polish lords, so they carried out this emancipation un-

der generous terms. In addition to personal freedom, the peasants also received the lands under their cultivation, plus an additional one million hectares taken from the nobility. Redemption payments made by peasants to the Russian government, which in turn paid the lords in government lands, were extended through many decades, and then abolished in 1905.

Hungary had a much broader autonomy within the Austrian Empire, wherefore the serf question was solved internally. The emancipation decree was passed by the last feudal diet and made part of the so-called April Laws of 11 April 1848. The serfs received their personal freedom and all the rustical lands in their possession. The lords were compensated by the government. But, as many of the serfs held dominical lands—which legally belonged to the lords—two-thirds of the Hungarian peasantry became landless. The outbreak of the Hungarian Revolution of 1848–1849 intervened, and much of the emancipation was carried out by the imperial government in 1853.

Serf emancipation was the most important development in the birth of a modern civil society, going hand in hand with industrialization and the rise of the factory system. This was particularly true for Prussian Poland and the Czech lands, both of which developed a large textile industry. The textile workers of Prague were in the forefront of collective action when they protested against the lowering of their wages in 1844.

The modernization process produced two new classes: the bureaucracy and the proletariat. Bureaucracy was a necessary byproduct of the administrative efficiency and centralization aspired to by enlightened absolutism. The growth of bureaucracy was paralleled by the rise of a new intelligentsia, consisting of the clergy, educators, lawyers, physicians, and engineers. The last of these professions was particularly present in Hungary, where it was needed for large public projects, such as the regulation of rivers, land reclamations, and the construction of dams, dikes, and railroad lines. The latter activities also gave birth to the category of ditchdiggers *(kubikusok)*, whose number reached 100,000 by the end of the century.

SOCIAL DEVELOPMENTS
IN THE SECOND HALF
OF THE NINETEENTH CENTURY

From the mid-nineteenth century to the end of World War I, the borders of the East Central European states did not change, but in 1867 the Austrian Empire was transformed into Austria-Hungary, with an additional dualistic arrangement between Hungary and Croatia in 1868. Transylvania was fully reintegrated into Hungary, but the future Slovakia and Carpatho-Ruthenia still had no separate identity. Lands of the Czech Crown (Bohemia, Moravia, and portions of Silesia) remained autonomous within the Austrian half of the dual monarchy. After 1864, the Congress kingdom of Poland was reduced into the Warsaw Province of the Russian Empire.

If national borders did not change during this period, population did grow markedly. In 1870 about 10 million Poles lived on the territories of the tripartitioned Polish state. By 1914 their numbers had increased to 18 million, with nearly 16 million of them living within the Russian Empire. During the same period, the population of the lands of the Czech crown increased from 7.6 million people to 10.3 million. Of these, however, close to one-third were Germans. During the same period, Hungary's population increased from 13.3 million to 21.5 million, but of these only sightly over half were Hungarians. The rest were Slovaks, Romanians, Croats, Serbs, Rusyns, and Germans.

During the same period ethnic conditions changed only slightly. The most important change was the migration of Yiddish-speaking Jews from Galicia to Hungary. In the period between between 1780 and 1840, their number increased from 78,000 to 250,000, and by World War I it reached 911,000. The Jews gradually replaced the Greeks and the Armenians in commerce, industry, and the development of the market economy. They were able to do so partially because they filled a void that the peasants were unable, and the nobility unwilling, to fill.

Migration within the region had been going on for many centuries, but intercontinental migration was a new phenomenon. It was the result of new economic developments connected with the rise of capitalism. In the period between 1870 and 1914, 3.5 million Poles, 2 million Austrian citizens (among them 50,000 Czechs), and 1.8 million Hungarian citizens emigrated to America. Of this 1.8 million over one-third were Hungarians, under one-third were Slovaks, and the remaining one-third was divided among the Rusyns, Romanians, Croats, Serbs, and Germans.

The region's growing population was divided into several social classes: The peasantry, the new industrial working class (proletariat), the growing professional middle class, and the still prominent nobility. Numerically the largest social class was the peasantry, but it was not evenly divided among the various countries and provinces. In 1870 peasants made up 65 percent of the population of Russian Poland and 42 percent in Prussian Poland. The peasant population of the Czech and the Hungarian lands was somewhere between these two extremes. Population growth compelled peasants to divide their lands, until many holdings were not large enough to support a family. These peasants were forced to supplement their income by becoming seasonal workers in the better-endowed provinces (e.g. Prussian Poland), by turning into industrial workers (in Prussian Poland, Bohemia, and Hungary), or by emigrating to America. The Hungarian scene was slightly different. There, two-thirds of the serfs (those on dominical lands) were emanci-

The Polish Uprising of 1863. Polish insurgents intercepting a Russian train. Mary Evans Picture Library

Austria-Hungary after 1867.

pated without land. From their ranks came the above-mentioned ditchdiggers and agricultural laborers. Some of the latter were seasonal workers *(napszámosok)*, while others became attached to large estates *(cselédek)*.

One of the most significant developments in the second half of the nineteenth century was the appearance of the modern industrial working class. Small-scale industry and handicrafts continued to survive, but their place was increasingly taken by large-scale industry. By World War I, the number of factory workers in Prussian Poland reached 350,000. In the Czech lands, they and their families numbered around 3.1 million, or about 600,000 workers. In Hungary their number was 1.4 million, of whom 500,000 worked in large-scale industry.

The new industrial working class derived its membership from two sources: the peasantry and the lower urban classes. Among the latter were those artisans who had lost their traditional livelihood in consequence of industrialization. In the Polish territories,

they were joined by the lower members of the rural nobility, who were simply too numerous to maintain their noble status.

Working conditions in industry were harsh and dangerous. But the social welfare measures introduced by Bismarck in Germany also affected conditions in East Central Europe. Thus, in the western half of Austria-Hungary a number of protective laws were introduced after 1884, including a ten-hour work day and obligatory health insurance.

The coming of capitalism signaled not only the birth of the proletariat, but also the genesis of labor movements and political parties, often divided along ethnic lines and over the complex relationship between socialist and nationalist politics. Polish socialists in the last decade of the nineteenth century founded two separate Marxist parties, one placing social revolution before national independence. Both were legalized only after the Russian Revolution of 1905. In the Austrian half of Austria-Hungary, the Social Democratic Party, founded in 1888–1889, soon splintered into several "national" parties, although outwardly retaining its unity. After the introduction of universal manhood suffrage in 1907, it was represented in the imperial Parliament. The Socialist Party of Hungary was founded in 1890 and immediately established several nationality divisions, although officially it favored unity and assimilation. As Hungary did not introduce universal manhood suffrage until 1919, the Socialist Party failed to become a parliamentary party. But it did direct labor activism and was also involved in the great labor strike of 1912. The turn of the century also saw the rise of several peasant parties in all of the countries under consideration. These parties were more traditional and closer to established religions than the socialists.

At the pinnacle of East Central European society stood the members of the landed aristocracy. Following serf emancipation, most of them retained their estates, and controlled about one-third of the land in each of the three countries. In the Czech lands and Hungary, the members of the traditional aristocracy were joined by newly titled industrial magnates, many of them with the rank of baron.

Under them was a middle layer. In Russian Poland, the members of this class came almost exclusively from the ranks of urban merchants and artisans, and perhaps a few were well-to-do farmers. In the Czech lands, this middle layer was made up of civil servants and white-collar workers in private enterprises. In Hungary, it comprised rich merchants and artisans. By the turn of the century they and their families numbered about 100,000. They were joined by an equal number of professional intelligentsia, and also by about 30,000 to 35,000 nontitled middle nobles who owned moderate size estates (200–1,000 *holds* = 284–1,420 acres). These sublayers collectively made up the Hungarian gentry class. Their mentality and attitude displayed many features of the bygone feudal age. As such, notwithstanding their middle-class status, in mentality they were close to the Polish nobility.

National consciousness and national assimilation.
The rise of national consciousness in East Central Europe was the direct result of the impact of the Enlightenment and the Napoleonic wars that spread this ideology far and wide. National revival began among the region's "historic" nations—the Poles, Hungarians, and Czechs—in the second half of the eighteenth century. It gradually spread in the nineteenth century to such nationalities as the Slovaks, Romanians, and various southern and eastern Slavic peoples.

At the start, these national revivals were elitist movements, for only the intelligentsia were involved. Among the Poles and the Hungarians this intelligentsia came from the ranks of the nobility, among the Czechs from the ranks of the burgher class, and among the rest of the nationalities from the ranks of the clergy, with peasant roots. Historians of East Central Europe tend to distinguish between "aristocratic nationalism," "middle-class nationalism," and "peasant nationalism."

In general, these national revival movements remained confined to the literate classes until the late nineteenth and early twentieth century. Then they were spread by mass education and mass journalism to the ranks of the peasantry. In the case of the Hungarians, Czechs, and Poles, however, the mid-nineteenth-century revolutions (1848–1849 and 1863–1864) had already aroused national consciousness in a sizable segment of the rural classes.

RELIGIOUS DIVISIONS IN EAST CENTRAL EUROPE

Most ethnic Poles were Catholic, but historical Poland also contained large Orthodox Christian and Jewish populations. The Czechs were 95 percent Catholic, although they were much more lax in their beliefs and practices than the Poles, as many of them perpetuated certain Hussite traditions.

The population of historical Hungary was about 50 percent Catholic, 14 percent Calvinist, 13 percent Orthodox Christian, 11 percent Greek Catholic (Uniate), 7 percent Lutheran, 5 percent Jewish, and 0.4 percent Unitarian. The ethnic Hungarians themselves were two-thirds Catholic, and the remaining third Calvinist, Lutheran, Jewish, and Unitarian. The Slovaks were about 80 percent Catholic and 20 percent Lutheran. The Rusyns and the Romanians were evenly divided between Orthodox Christianity and Greek Catholicism (Uniates). The Serbs were all Orthodox Christians, while the Germans were two-thirds Catholic and one-third Lutheran.

The situation in Hungary changed significantly after World War I, when the country, reduced in size by the peace settlements, lost all of its Orthodox Christian population. Two-thirds of the remaining citizens were now Catholic, 20 percent Calvinist, and the remaining 14 percent divided evenly between Jews and Lutherans.

As national consciousness spread, late-nineteenth and early-twentieth-century East Central European society also underwent a process of national assimilation. This occurred throughout the whole region, although there were individual differences, which depended on the historical past and the social makeup of a particular nationality, as well as on its position within the hierarchy of nations. For example, the Slovaks lacked traditions of independent statehood, and most of them were peasants, with only a smattering of artisans and merchants. They also lacked an aristocracy, nobility, and even upper-level urban elements. A number of Slovaks had been ennobled in the sixteenth through the eighteenth centuries by the Habsburg kings of Hungary, but by this act they immediately joined the ranks of the *Natio Hungarica* (in effect, the Hungarian nobility). They thereby lost touch with their own ethnic group, and following the rise of modern nationalism, virtually all members of the *Natio Hungarica* opted to become members of the Magyar-speaking modern Hungarian nation.

When the Austrian Empire was transformed into Austria-Hungary, the successive Hungarian governments engaged in various levels of Magyarization through administrative means. This was done in violation of the progressive laws passed during the early years of the Dual Monarchy (e.g., Law of Nationalities and the Education Law of 1868). Much of the success of Magyarization, however, was not due to administrative pressures. Rather, it was the result of rapid urbanization and industrialization affecting primarily the country's inner regions. Slovak peasants, turned into construction workers, were heavily involved in turning Buda and Pest into the modern metropolis of Budapest. But once they settled in the interior, they remained there and became assimilated into the Hungarian majority. By 1914, as many as 100,000 had changed their nationality.

During the same period, the Russian imperial government also pursued a policy of Russification in Russian Poland. In contrast to Hungary, however, where thousands of primary schools functioned in several languages, the Russians did not tolerate the existence of Polish schools. This extreme policy produced a widespread reaction, which ultimately undermined Russification. Assimilation was much more successful in Prussian Poland, in spite of the constant influx of Polish Peasants in search of better working conditions. This success was due to the improved quality of life in German society.

In contrast to the other governments, the Austrian Imperial Government did not pursue a policy of Germanization in the Czech lands. For this reason, and because of the spread of Czech nationalism, in many of the Bohemian and Moravian towns it was the German burghers who became assimilated into the Czech nation. At the beginning of the nineteenth century, Prague was virtually a German city. By the end of the century, however, it already had a Czech-speaking majority. A similar process occurred in Hungary, where in the course of the nineteenth century, the city of Budapest (until 1872 Buda and Pest) was transformed from a German into a Hungarian city.

The process of modernization also produced a new intelligentsia, many of whose members had non-noble roots. In Russian Poland, a Polish intelligentsia hardly existed. Most of them were concentrated in Austrian Galicia, where two Polish universities (Cracow and Lemberg/Lwów) and a Polish Academy of Sciences functioned, as well as a whole series of Polish primary and secondary schools. Moreover, in the province's eastern section, there were also Ukrainian schools. As a result, Galicia became the main breeding ground for Polish and Ukrainian nationalism.

The birth of modern society also sped up the spread of literacy. During the first half of the nineteenth century, literacy was still limited in the region. Progress was made only by the Polish and Hungarian nobility, and the Czech burghers. The situation changed in the second half of the century, when in Bohemia and Moravia education in Czech and German was made available at all levels. True, until 1882 the University of Prague functioned only in German. But in that year a Czech-language university was also established. A number of specialized colleges were likewise founded, which after World War II developed into full-scale universities.

The situation was similar in Hungary. The Education Law of 1868 introduced compulsory universal education, and by 1912 there were 16,861 elementary schools, of which 3,408 functioned in Romanian, German, Slovak, Serbian, Rusyn, and Italian. Secondary schools were more elitist and fewer in number. In 1879, the study of Hungarian was made mandatory in all non-Hungarian secondary schools, and then in 1907 in all primary schools. The non-Hungarian nationalities resented this, leading to increased nationality squabbles. In contrast to Bohemia-Moravia, higher education in Hungary was available only in Hungarian. In addition to the University of Budapest (1635), three new universities were established: Kolozsvár (1872), Pozsony (1912) and Debrecen (1912).

WORLD WAR I AND ITS CONSEQUENCES

World War I had a very disruptive impact upon the region, breaking up old empires and creating several new and small states. Although established in the

East Central Europe, 1930

East Central Europe, 1930. Adapted from Paul Robert Magocsi, *Historical Atlas of East Central Europe* (Toronto: University of Toronto Press, 1993).

name of national self-determination, with the exception of the rump Austrian and Hungarian states, all of the new states were multinational. Poland was reestablished after 123 years, put together from Russian, Prussian, and Austrian-held territories. It became a state of 150,000 square miles, with a population of 27 million, of which nearly one-third were Ukrainians, Jews, Lithuanians, and Germans. Czechoslovakia was formed from the three Czech provinces (Bohemia, Moravia, and Silesia) plus the Slovak- and Rusyn-inhabited regions of Hungary. It became a state of 54,000 square miles, with a population of 13.6 million. It had no majority nationality, for the Czechs and the Slovaks together made up only 64 percent of the population. The remaining 36 percent included Germans, Hungarians, and Rusyns.

Hungary suffered the most in this new arrangement, losing 71 percent of its territory and 63 percent of its population. It became a small state of 36,000 square miles with a population of only 8 million. At the same time 3.5 million Hungarians were left on the other side of the new borders, creating unending conflicts with its new neighbors.

In addition to nationality conflicts, the most pressing issue faced by the new or reestablished states was their outdated agrarian structure. Czechoslovakia introduced the most comprehensive land reform, but it was motivated partially by the desire to undermine the German and Hungarian landed nobility. About 4 million hectares were nationalized, of which 1.2 million were divided among 634,000 peasants. After Slovakia's separation in 1939, all lands in Jewish ownership were likewise nationalized and distributed, but only to former Slovak legionnaires and bureaucrats.

Polish land reform was less drastic because it was directed against Polish landlords. All landholdings above three hundred hectares in western Poland, or five hundred hectares in eastern Poland were nationalized and distributed. But implementation was so slow that it was still in process when World War II broke out.

Land reform in Hungary was first initiated by the Hungarian Socialist Republic in 1919, but the regime's rapid collapse ended these plans. On the basis of the new land reform law of 1920, 640,000 hectares were nationalized and 400,000 hectares were distributed among 427,000 peasants. Completed in 1929, this reform altered very little about Hungary's traditional social structure.

There were many similarities and dissimilarities in the social makeup of these states. In the early 1920s, 63.8 percent of Poland's population worked in agriculture, in contrast to Hungary's 55.7 percent and Czechoslovakia's 37.2 percent. But in the two northern states there were major regional differences: the agricultural sector in eastern Poland engaged 87 percent of the workforce, and in eastern Czechoslovakia (Slovakia and Carpatho-Ruthenia) 58.5 percent.

The Czech provinces of Czechoslovakia had the most advanced social structure. In 1921, the industrial sector in the country as a whole was 34 percent, the commercial sector 5.5 percent, transportation 3.7 percent, and the bureaucracy and professionals 4.3 percent. Naturally, the situation was much worse in the eastern provinces.

Czechoslovakia was followed by Hungary, where in 1920 the industrial sector embraced 19.1 percent of the population, and the bureaucracy and professionals 4.6 percent. The nonagricultural economy was less developed in Poland, where the industrial sector was 16.5 percent, and the heavy industry only 4 percent. By the end of the interwar years, however, these ratios had risen significantly.

The upper middle class constituted a relatively small portion of the population of these countries. In 1930 it was about 1 percent in Poland, 5.8 percent in Czechoslovakia, and 8 percent in Hungary. This higher percentage is derived from the fact that many of Hungary's lower nobility became integrated into the gentry-dominated bureaucracy. But of this middle layer only about 2,200 families belonged to the "historic middle class" that consisted of well-to-do noble families. Above them were the landed aristocracy (745 families) and the nouveaux riches leaseholders (350 families), who had acquired their wealth from various commercial and industrial activities.

Jews in interwar East Central Europe. The Jews occupied a special position in interwar East Central Europe, although there were considerable differences in their position in these three countries. Whereas in Hungary and in Czechoslovakia they were considered Hungarians or Czechoslovaks of the Jewish faith, in Poland they were treated as a distinct nationality. For this reason, in Hungary it is not even possible to tell the exact number of Jews. In the period between 1867 and 1938 (from the Law of Jewish Emancipation to the First Jewish Law) census takers counted practicing Jews as Hungarians of the Jewish faith. Their number in 1925 was 477,000. Along with the converts and the nonpracticing Jews, however, their numbers may have been as high as 600,000, or close to 8 percent of the population. After the the territorial revisions of 1938–1940 their numbers grew to nearly 800,000.

After Poland's reestablishment as an independent state, its Jewish population numbered over two million, or about 8 percent of the population of twenty-seven million. At the same time they numbered around 250,000 in Czechoslovakia, half of whom were former Hungarian Jews who had been attached to the new state after World War I.

A significant portion of the Jews in these states were involved in business activities and thus made up a major portion of the commercial middle classes. This was more true in Hungary and in Czechoslovakia than in Poland. In each of these states Jews also made up a major portion—perhaps as much as one-third—of the intelligentsia, including physicians, lawyers, journalists, and literary and cultural figures. Their role was even more pronounced in Hungary, where in some professions they constituted half or more of the practitioners. Not even the quota law (numerus clausus) of 1920, which limited their number at the nation's colleges and universities to their ratio in the population, altered the picture. Thereafter, many Hungarian Jews simply went abroad to study and returned with highly rated western European degrees to join the Hungarian labor force.

In contrast to the Jews of Hungary and of the Czech lands, those in Carpatho-Ruthenia (within Czechoslovakia) and Galicia (within Poland) were much poorer and much less educated. They were generally engaged in handicrafts, small-scale industry, shopkeeping, and peddling.

Just before and during World War II, Jews were singled out for persecution in all three (after 1939, in all four) of these countries. In German Poland, Bohemia-Moravia, and Slovakia they were liquidated during the early phase of the war. In Hungary—although their rights had been curtailed by three separate laws in 1938, 1939, and 1941—they were able to survive until after the country's German occupation on 19 March 1944. Among them were also many Polish, Czech, and Slovak Jews who had fled to Hungary's relative safety in 1939. Following the German occupation, however, most of the Jews were collected and taken to German death camps.

According to recent estimates—which vary significantly—the Jewish population of Poland was completely annihilated. Those killed in Czechoslovakia numbered between 233,000 and 260,000 (90,000 Slovakia), those in Romania between 215,000 and

INTERWAR POLITICAL PROCESS IN EAST CENTRAL EUROPE

As in industrialization and modernization, so in the development of democracy, Czechoslovakia was the most advanced among the states of East Central Europe. Universal suffrage for those twenty-four years of age or over was introduced after the establishment of the state. In Poland and in Hungary the right to vote was limited not only by age, but also by property and educational qualifications. Whereas in Czechoslovakia even the Communist Party was permitted to function until October 1938, it was outlawed both in Poland and in Hungary. Moreover, whereas in Czechoslovakia the Social Democratic Party was a member of the ruling coalition, in Poland and in Hungary it remained permanently in opposition.

As beneficiaries of post–World War I territorial changes, Poland and Czechoslovakia wished to preserve the status quo. Hungary, on the other hand, had lost territories inhabited by Hungarians and therefore advocated revisionism. Thus, while the first two states became victims of German expansionist agression in 1938 and 1939, Hungary was a temporary beneficiary of those territorial changes. In return for its gains, how-

ever, it was bound to Germany in a master-vassal relationship.

In September 1939, Poland was again partitioned between Germany and the Soviet Union. Both conquerors aspired to eradicate the Polish military and political elite to prevent the resurgence of the Polish state. Under German rule even Polish secondary schools were disbanded, and university personnel were interned. Under Russian rule Polish elites suffered persecution, incarceration, and extermination—as was the case with the thousands of Polish military officers who were massacred at Katyń. The eastern segment of the interwar Polish state remained under Soviet rule even after World War II, and Poland was compensated with eastern German territories.

Like Poland, Czechoslovakia was also dismembered in 1938 and 1939. German-inhabited Sudetenland was annexed to Germany, and the remaining Czech lands were made into the German protectorate of Bohemia-Moravia. Slovakia emerged as a German vassal state, while Carpatho-Ruthenia was returned to Hungary.

The Jews of Warsaw. Street scene in the Warsaw ghetto, 1906. Ullstein Bilderdienst, Berlin

530,000, those in Hungary between 220,000 and 450,000. In all probability, the higher figures are closer to the truth.

WORLD WAR II
AND ITS CONSEQUENCES

World War II produced significant changes in all three countries. Hungary lost all the territories it had regained in the course of 1938–1941, plus three additional Hungarian villages in the vicinity of Bratislava. Czechoslovakia was reestablished, but had to relinquish Carpatho-Ruthenia to the Soviet Union. Poland was shifted westward at the expense of Germany. This resulted in massive population shifts, with many millions of Germans expelled from the ceded territories. Their place was taken by Poles who left the eastern territories given to the Ukrainian and Byelorussian republics of the Soviet Union. Germans were also removed from Czechoslovakia, which expelled about 3.5 million of them. Czechoslovakia also wished to expel its nearly one million Hungarians, but the victors agreed only to a voluntary exchange of population. About 70,000 Slovaks left Hungary and 100,000 Hungarians left Czechoslovakia—a third of the latter having been evicted.

In consequence of these massive population shifts, all of these countries had lost much of their multinational character. Poland, the Czech Republic, and Hungary remained with 3 to 4 percent minori-

ties, and Slovakia with about 14 percent—most of them Hungarians. These calculations do not take into consideration the special case of the Gypsies (Roma), who were never counted as national minorities until after the collapse of communism.

The war's impact on the region's population was harsh and all-embracing. It made no difference whether the individual countries were victims (Poland and the Czech Republic) or "unwilling satellites" of Nazi Germany (Hungary, Slovakia, Croatia, and Romania). Poland and Hungary, in particular, became major battlegrounds for the German and Soviet armies during the latter phase of the war. Most of the cities, towns, industrial establishments, livestock, and rollingstock were destroyed and the population terrorized and decimated by both combatants. The two capitals were nearly totally annihilated during the Warsaw uprising (1 August–2 October 1944) and the siege of Budapest (25 December 1944–13 February 1945). A large percentage of the women were raped (according to one source, 600,000 in Hungary alone), and a sizable percentage of the male population was taken to the Soviet Union. Many of them never returned. Others did so after several years of slave labor in Siberia.

East Central Europe under communist rule. Next to the territorial changes and population displacements, the most significant factor in the region's post–World War II history was that all three countries became part of the Soviet bloc. For about three years all of them had coalition governments and nurtured the hope for democracy, but by 1948 they had all become communist-dominated Soviet satellites. The parliamentary system and some of the elements of democracy (including universal suffrage above age eighteen) were preserved, but these turned out to be meaningless trappings in these one-party states.

The initial steps of postwar social transformation included the elimination of the former elite and upper-middle classes. Through radical land reforms, landed estates and later even small farms were nationalized. These were distributed among the peasantry or made into state farms. Peasant lands were later collectivized. In Czechoslovakia and in Hungary, this collectivization began soon after the communist takeover. In Hungary, the Revolution of 1956 reversed this process temporarily, but in the 1960s collectivization was resumed. By 1970, 82.9 percent of Hungary's agricultural lands were either collectives or state farms. In Czechoslovakia this figure was 85.1 percent. Poland followed a different path. In 1970 only 15.6 percent of the Polish lands were collectives or state farms.

As a consequence of the economic liberalization (New Economic Mechanism) initiated in 1968, Hungary introduced private ownership of household plots. These plots constituted less than 10 percent of the agricultural lands yet produced one-third of all agricultural goods and one-half of all the produce going to foreign markets.

Land reform was paralleled by the nationalization of all financial institutions, industrial establishments, and commercial concerns. By 1948 even small-scale industry, handicrafts, and retail were nationalized. This process was most thorough in Czechoslovakia. Initially, Poland and Hungary also moved in that direction, but later they gradually restored the autonomy of the small craftsmen and shopkeepers.

With the disappearance of the old elite (whose surviving members either emigrated or were declassed), the communist-controlled governments began to reshape society. They emphasized social egalitarianism and industrial development. The former resulted in a thorough social transformation, while the latter brought about the artificial development of heavy industry at the expense of consumer goods and agriculture. The consumers were simply forgotten, and the agricultural sector declined to the point where by the 1980s it encompassed only about 10 to 15 percent of the population (higher in Poland than in Hungary or Czechoslovakia). The majority of the peasantry was transformed into the industrial proletariat.

In light of the need for an expanded bureaucracy, the number of white-collar workers also increased significantly, but their overall quality declined. Traditional elitist education was rapidly transformed into mass education. Literacy increased radically, more in quantity than in quality.

By 1948, Marxism-Leninism became the only acceptable ideology in communist-dominated East

After World War II. A Warsaw shop in ruins in 1947 with the "Three Times Yes" slogan of the June 1946 referendum. ©HULTON GETTY/LIAISON AGENCY

EDUCATION ON THE SOVIET MODEL

Following the communist takeover, the educational system of East Central Europe was transformed in accordance with the Soviet model. The German-influenced gymnasium system, which emphasized classical studies, languages, and the natural sciences through eight years of study (ages ten through eighteen), was abandoned. It was replaced by a four-year high school type of education that rejected cultural elitism and geared the curriculum more to the needs of modern socialist society. The new secondary schools concentrated on specific practical fields and became so specialized that they began to approximate the trade schools of the interwar years. The goal of producing well-rounded, cultured individuals was replaced by the goal of teaching useful practical skills.

This also applied to a large degree to institutions of higher learning. Their number and size increased significantly, due in part to new foundations and in part to the dismemberment of comprehensive universities into numerous specialized institutions. Students gained a thorough knowledge of certain limited fields, but they acquired less general knowledge. Progress in education was more quantitative than qualitative. In point of fact, the introduction of mass education, without making some universities into intellectually exclusive institutions on the American model, lowered the overall quality of education. This applied both to secondary schools and to institutions of higher learning. Moreover, in spite of this mass education, functional illiteracy remained a major problem in the increasingly industrialized societies of East Central Europe.

Following the collapse of communism, some of the Soviet-inspired experiments ended, while others continued. There was a partial return to precommunist models, but at the same time there were also borrowings from the West, especially from the United States. At the end of the twentieth century, the educational infrastructure of East Central Europe was in a state of flux.

Central Europe. This destroyed the position and influence of the established churches. In Czechoslovakia and Hungary the majority of the population was alienated from mainstream denominations and became skeptics or even atheists, but few of them became dedicated marxists. The situation was different in Poland, where the majority of the people remained faithful Catholics; the Catholic Church there retained its influence over society and played an important role in the opposition movement.

The communist regimes were more successful in popularizing social welfarism than communist ideology. In point of fact the most positive feature of communist rule was the creation of the welfare state, where a citizen was taken care of by the omnipotent state from birth until death. Initially, the most important social welfare measures affected only industrial workers. By the early 1970s, however, this system was also extended to the rural population. By that time, education, health care, social care, and all the other social welfare measures (including the right to a job, the right to an apartment, and the right to a state pension) were free and available to all, although their quality was increasingly questionable. Even so, both literacy and average age increased significantly, while the retirement age was kept low (55 for women, 60 for men). This policy brought many benefits, but also resulted in an inactive aging population. Moreover, full employment (the right of every adult to a job) resulted in hidden unemployment and much inefficiency in the industrial, commercial, and agricultural sectors, as well as in the burgeoning bureaucracy. In consequence of rapid and massive industrialization, the number of unskilled and semiskilled workers increased markedly. The full employment policy worked for a while, but by the 1970s it began to fail. Rapid technological innovations and automatization made the unskilled and semiskilled workers increasingly superfluous.

The size of the state and party bureaucracy also increased manifold. Along with the administrators of large industrial establishments, party and state officials made up the highest level of the *nomenklatura* that had replaced the old elite and came to constitute what the Yugoslav dissident Milovan Djilas called the "new class."

Quality of life began to improve during the 1960s, but per capita gross domestic product (GDP) and living standards were still far below those of the West. This, of course, did not apply to the members of the *nomenklatura,* who enjoyed much higher incomes and many privileges, including the right to buy in special stores and to travel abroad.

The Polish and Hungarian Revolutions of 1956—although suppressed—ultimately had an ameliorative effect upon conditions in those two countries. Political control and ideological rigor eased and life generally improved. Eventually even Western travel became easier. At the same time, the population was firm in its belief that Soviet control was there to stay. Thus, while paying lip service to the Soviet Union and to communist ideals, they concentrated on improving their personal lives. This was particularly true for Hungary under the Kádár regime, but less so in Poland, where the late 1970s and the 1980s witnessed a clash between the Solidarity labor movement (led by Lech Wałęsa) and a political regime, led by General Wojciech Jaruzelski, that feared Soviet intervention.

The situation was different in Czechoslovakia, where strict political control and ideological orthodoxy continued. The Prague Spring of 1968, only a momentary break in this orthodoxy, was followed by a more severe regime in which all dissent was stifled. Progressive party leaders, such as Alexander Dubček, and liberal intellectuals, such as Václav Havel, who had been leaders in the events of 1968 and in the dissident movements that followed, were barred from public life and often forced to make their livings through physical labor.

The collapse of communism and the transition to capitalism.
Convinced of the indestructibility of Soviet communist control, the people of East Central Europe were not prepared for the radical changes of 1989–1990. Nor were they ready to deal with the intricacies and challenges of true democracy. Conse-

quently, the euphoria that accompanied the collapse of communism and the dissolution of the Soviet Union in 1991 was followed by a short period of great expectations followed by a longer period of disenchantment. By the mid-1990s, this disenchantment had reached the point where people began to vote the restructured and renamed communist parties back into power.

The change of political regimes was followed in all three (since 1993, when Slovakia became an independent state, all four) countries by a massive privatization of state assets. In Poland and Czechoslovakia, this was done by giving the population shares in the former state-owned enterprises. In Hungary, however, state-owned companies were sold off to private investors—many of them Westerners with little appreciation for the social problems faced by the population. By virtue of their social connections, the members of the former party elite were able to seize the lion's share in this privatization process. Many of them transferred themselves from the political elite to the new financial elite. At the same time they also avoided being called to account for their past deeds.

This fact alone would have been enough to produce mass disillusionment. But even greater was the disenchantment with the economic and social developments. The formerly all-encompassing social wel-

Prague Spring Remembered. Alexander Dubček, first secretary of the Czechoslovak Communist Party in 1968 during a brief period of reform that ended when the Soviet Union invaded Czechoslovakia in August 1968. During the Velvet Revolution of 1989 Dubček became chairman of the federal assembly. ©PETER TURNLEY/CORBIS

East Central Europe, 1992

East Central Europe, 1992. Adapted from Paul Robert Magocsi, *Historical Atlas of East Central Europe* (Toronto: University of Toronto Press, 1993).

fare network collapsed. This was accompanied by mass layoffs, growing unemployment, pressure to produce more, and also an end to the notion that having a job is everyone's natural right.

The coming of capitalism also produced an increasingly visible social and economic polarization. By the late 1990s, this process had reached the point where the average income of the lowest tenth of the population was only one-sixth of that of the highest tenth. Those who were able to take advantage of the opportunities offered by raw capitalism became wealthy and openly flouted their newly won social and economic positions. At the same time, the standard of living for the population declined. This was particularly true for the large number of pensioners and fixed-income employees, who became pauperized and dreamed about the "good old days" of socialism.

These changes were most drastic in Poland, whose postcommunist leaders adopted policies of rapid transition to a free market economy, or "shock treatment." The result was temporary despair, but the promise of a more rapid solution. This path may have paid off, because at the end of the second millennium, the Polish economy appeared to be healthiest. At the same time, however, Western assessments judged Hungary's economy to be the most promising.

Privatization of industry, banking, and trade was accompanied by the privatization of agriculture. This affected Hungary and Czechoslovakia more than it did Poland. In the first two, one-third of the agricultural lands remained in the hands of the restructured cooperatives, one-third went into the hands of private owners (peasants or speculators), and one-third was acquired by agricultural corporations.

The collapse of communism also affected the region's educational system. During the 1990s, much of the Soviet system was dismantled. There was a partial return to the precommunist system, and a partial adjustment to the American educational system. This applied both to the universities and to the secondary schools. Many of the former religious schools were restored to the churches or religious orders, and several new institutions of higher learning were also established. These included a number of Catholic and Protestant universities, as well as private institutions. Among them were a few business schools and the Central European University, based in Budapest and Prague (1991). Sponsored by the Hungarian-American billionaire George Soros, this English-language postgraduate institution espoused the principles of "open society."

The emergence of the English language as the region's dominant international language was another important byproduct of the collapse of communism. English replaced Russian almost immediately, and several secondary schools and universities created programs in English, and in a few cases also in German. As an example, by the late 1990s, one could acquire an M.D. degree in English at all four of Hungary's traditional universities (Budapest, Debrecen, Pécs, and Szeged).

Soon after the collapse of communism, Czechoslovakia fell apart, giving birth to two distinct states: the Czech Republic and Slovakia (1 January 1993). Following their divorce, the difference between these two parts of former Czechoslovakia became immediately apparent. The Czech Republic emerged as a more uniform and balanced country, with a strong industrial base, and a cadre of skilled workers and bureaucrats. Slovakia, on the other hand, sank back into the position of an agricultural-industrial state. Of the four countries in today's East Central Europe, Slovakia is the most multiethnic, with a minority population of 14 percent, of whom most are Hungarians who live next to the Hungarian borders, with all the problems which that entails.

In 1999 Hungary, Poland, and the Czech Republic became members of NATO, with the hope that they soon would also be admitted into the European Union. Slovakia trailed significantly behind them. With the strong support of the other three, however, it may also make it into NATO and the European Union during the first decade of the twenty-first century.

See also other articles in this section.

BIBLIOGRAPHY

Bak, János M., and Béla K. Király, eds. *From Hunyadi to Rákóczi: War and Society in Late Medieval and Early Modern Hungary.* New York, 1982.

Berend, T. Iván, and György Ránki. *Economic Development in East-Central Europe in the 19th and 20th Centuries.* New York, 1974.

Berend, T. Iván, and György Ránki. *The European Periphery and Industrialization, 1780–1914.* Cambridge, U.K., 1982.

Deák, István. *Beyond Nationalism: A Social and Political History of the Habsburg Officer Corps, 1848–1918.* New York and Oxford, 1992. An excellent study of the role of the military elite.

Dillon, Kenneth J. *Kings and Estates in the Bohemian Lands, 1526–1564.* Brussels, 1976. A detailed study of the relationship between the Czech estates and their first Habsburg ruler, Ferdinand I.

Fél, Edit, and Tamás Hofer. *Proper Peasants: Traditional Life in a Hungarian Village.* Chicago, 1969. A synthesis of peasant life by two noted scholars.

Fischer-Galati, Stephen, ed. *Man, State, and Society in East European History.* New York, 1970. Includes primary sources, as well as short selections from synthetic works.

Fügedi, Erik. *Kings, Bishops, Nobles, and Burghers in Medieval Hungary.* Edited by János M. Bak. London, 1986. A collection of path-breaking essays on early Hungarian society.

Glatz, Ferenc, ed. *Ethnicity and Society in Hungary.* Vol. 2 of *Etudes historiques hongroises.* 7 vols. Budapest, 1990. Essays on national and ethnic minorities in modern Hungary.

Jędruch, Jacek. *Constitutions, Elections, and Legislatures of Poland, 1493–1977: A Guide to Their History.* Washington, D.C., 1982. A useful guide to Polish constitutional history.

Kann, Robert A. *A History of the Habsburg Empire, 1526–1918.* Berkeley and Los Angeles, 1974. A standard political history that can serve as a good background.

Kerner, Robert Joseph. *Bohemia in the Eighteenth Century: A Study in Political, Economic, and Social History, with Special Reference to the Reign of Leopold II, 1790–1792.* 2d. ed. Orono, Maine, 1969. A classic and still very useful study of eighteenth-century Czech developments.

Király, Béla K., and András Bozóki, eds. *Lawful Revolution in Hungary, 1989–94.* New York, 1995. Contains some very useful studies on the social implications of the collapse of the communist regime.

Komlós, John. *Nutrition and Economic Development in the Eighteenth-Century Habsburg Monarchy: An Anthropometric History.* Princeton, N.J., 1989. Examines the relationship between the availability of food, physical stature, and population health.

Kosáry, Domokos G. *Culture and Society in Eighteenth-Century Hungary.* Budapest, 1987. An abridged English version of a comprehensive survey of eighteenth-century Hungarian society.

Landau, Zbigniew, and Jerzy Tomaszewski. *The Polish Economy in the Twentieth Century.* London, 1985. A competent and clear survey of modern Polish economic developments.

Lukács, John. *Budapest 1900: A Historical Portrait of a City and Its Culture.* New York and London, 1988. A brilliant portrait of an emerging capital city.

Magocsi, Paul R. *The Shaping of a National Identity: Subcarpathian Rus', 1848–1948.* Cambridge, Mass., 1978. A good treatment of the Rusyns of former northeastern Hungary.

Marczali, Henrik. *Hungary in the Eighteenth Century.* Cambridge, U.K., 1910. Reprint, New York, 1971. A still-useful survey of Hungary's society and institutions.

Mazsu, János. *The Social History of the Hungarian Intelligentsia, 1825–1914.* New York, 1997. A pioneering study.

McCagg, William O. *A History of the Habsburg Jews, 1670–1918.* Bloomington, Ind., 1989. A very readable and useful survey.

Macartney, C. A. *The Habsburg Empire, 1790–1918.* New York, 1969. The most comprehensive treatment in English of nineteenth-century developments.

Marcus, Joseph. *Social and Political History of the Jews in Poland, 1919–1939.* Berlin, 1983. A comprehensive, but somewhat opinionated account.

Myant, Martin R. *The Czechoslovak Economy, 1948–1988: The Battle for Economic Reform.* Cambridge, U.K., 1989. A comprehensive survey of economic developments under communism, as well as some of the attempts at reform.

Niederhauser, Emil. *A jobbágyfelszabadítás Kelet-Európában* (Serf Emancipation in Eastern Europe). Budapest, 1962. Still the most comprehensive treatment of serf emancipation.

Niederhauser, Emil. *The Rise of Nationality in Eastern Europe.* Budapest, 1981. Treats all the nationalities from the Baltic down to the Balkans.

Rothschild, Joseph. *Return to Diversity: A Political History of East Central Europe since World War II.* 3d. ed. New York and Oxford, 2000. The most popular synthesis of the recent history of East Central Europe.

Subtelny, Orest. *Domination of Eastern Europe: Native Nobilities and Foreign Absolutism, 1500–1715.* Kingston, Ontario, 1986. Discusses the role of the nobility in Poland-Lithuania, Hungary, Ukraine, and Moldavia.

Taylor, Jack. *The Economic Development of Poland, 1919–1950.* Westport, Conn., 1970. Particularly useful for interwar economic developments.

Várdy, Steven Béla. *The Hungarian-Americans.* Boston, 1985. Discusses the social and economic causes of emigration and the immigrants' fate in the United States.

Várdy, Steven Béla, and Agnes Huszár Várdy. *The Austro-Hungarian Mind: At Home and Abroad.* New York, 1989. A collection of two dozen essays on social and cultural developments in the nineteenth and early twentieth centuries.

Várdy, Steven Béla, and Agnes Huszár Várdy, eds. *Triumph in Adversity: Studies in Hungarian Civilization.* New York, 1989. A collection essays by over two dozen scholars on Hungarian social, cultural, and intellectual developments.

Wandycz, Piotr S. *The Lands of Partitioned Poland, 1795–1818.* Seattle, Wash., 1974. An exhaustive survey of Polish development during the period of partitions.

Wright, William E. *Serf, Seigneur, and Sovereign: Agrarian Reform in Eighteenth-Century Bohemia.* Minneapolis, 1966. Discusses attempts at agrarian reform under Maria Theresa and Joseph II, and the reasons for the failure of some of these reforms.

403

RUSSIA AND THE EAST SLAVS

Rex A. Wade

The East Slavs comprise three closely related peoples, who between the thirteenth and the sixteenth centuries emerged as distinguishable linguistic-cultural groups: the Great Russians (usually called Russians), the Ukrainians (in earlier times often called Little Russians), and the Belorussians (Byelorussians, Bielorussians, White Russians). The Great Russians (hereafter simply Russians) are numerically the largest and have been politically and culturally dominant. Occupying the area around Moscow, they are the people around whom the state of Russia (and the Soviet Union) was built, and most histories of the area focus on them and their political, social, and cultural patterns. The Ukrainians and Belorussians followed a separate historical course from the thirteenth to seventeenth or eighteenth centuries, during which time they were under the political domination of the Grand Principality of Lithuania or the Kingdom of Poland; these groups, western Ukrainians especially, drew some special cultural and social traits from that association. In the seventeenth and eighteenth centuries, the Belorussian and most of the Ukrainian lands and peoples were incorporated into Russia as the latter defeated Poland in a series of wars.

As the Russian empire expanded beyond the ethnically Russian homeland over the course of the sixteenth to nineteenth centuries, it went from having a largely homogeneous population of Great Russians (who themselves probably resulted from the intermingling of early East Slavs and Finnic peoples) to being an enormous multiethnic empire comprising over twenty major ethnicities and about a hundred smaller ones. By the last census of Imperial Russia in 1897, when the state was perhaps at its most extensive and diverse, people who identified themselves as Russian (by native language) constituted only 44.3 percent, Ukrainians 17.8 percent, and Belorussians 4.3 percent of the population, so that East Slavs were 68.4 percent of the total. In the former Soviet Union, Russians were about half the population and East Slavs collectively nearly 70 percent. Although tsarist Russia generally tolerated the continuation of local customs, some minorities and especially their elites and educated population underwent full or partial cultural "Russification," a process that accelerated with the spread of education in the Soviet era. The following discussion focuses primarily on the social classes and traits of the Russians, the dominant group within a diverse social universe.

Russian and East Slavic society of the sixteenth to eighteenth centuries, and to a significant degree even the nineteenth century, was based on agriculture and military activity. It is therefore easy to view its social structure as a simple dichotomy of peasant and noble landlord, with only insignificant other classes. While these certainly were the two most important classes, such a view obscures what was in fact a much more diverse society divided into a large number of recognized groups by social-economic functions, legal classifications, wealth, geography, gender, and ethnicity. In Russia all belonged to legally defined social estates (*sosloviia*): nobles, serfs, state peasants, clergy, various and changing urban classifications, slaves, Cossacks, and many others. At the same time almost all fit into one of two larger categories, the privileged and the tax-paying. The latter were subject to the head tax, to military and labor conscription, and to corporal punishment, whereas the former were exempted from the head tax and corporal punishment and, in return for personal military or civil service to the state, received various privileges, most notably land and the right to own serfs. Despite important divisions within these categories, the distinction between privileged and nonprivileged (tax-paying) divided society in a fundamental way and continued to influence social attitudes and realities into the twentieth century. At the same time, the state's military and economic needs shaped many social features and changes.

THE NOBILITY

Nobility was defined by heredity and service to the ruler. The function of the nobility through the seventeenth century was to provide the cavalry army that was the mainstay of battle on the east European plain; in the eighteenth century military service still predominated as a defining function of the class, but nobles served as officers in a new type of army. The nobility also provided most of the officialdom of the state. It was a highly diverse group, ranging from extremely wealthy and powerful aristocrats to impoverished noblemen who held little or no land and struggled to keep from losing their status altogether.

At the top of Russian society (apart from the royal dynasty) stood the small number of elite noble families originally termed "boyars," who resided in or near Moscow and provided the tsars' major advisors and top government officeholders and army commanders. Below them were another group of families who held important, but lesser, state and military offices. Both of these descended mostly from either the old princely families or the personal military retinues of the early Moscow princes. Below them came the great majority of nobles, who made up the bulk of the army and who held modest estates. Originally the nobility held their land as *votchina,* or pure inheritance without service obligations, but in the fifteenth and sixteenth centuries the Moscow rulers managed to convert landholding to *pomestie* or land held on condition of service, although it still tended to be hereditary in practice.

The Russian nobility had several special features. First, except for a few titles such as prince and, later, count and baron, individual nobles did not carry titles but were simply registered as noblemen. Second, all sons and daughters inherited noble status, including any titles. Third, the elaborate *mestnichestvo* system served to register and accord precedence to noble families according to the time of their entry into Moscow's service and their status at that time. This system allowed families and individuals to claim offices and military command by right of family precedence and to refuse service under a person of a lower place. The *mestnichestvo* practices were an important part of a complex social system, lasting until 1682, that stressed family honor and status. Yet another special feature of the nobility was the large number of Tatar, Ukrainian, Baltic German, Georgian, Polish, and other nobilities that were absorbed as the Muscovite-Russian state expanded territorially from the fifteenth to the nineteenth centuries.

The nature, structure, and role of the nobility changed during the eighteenth century, the result of the state's changing military and service needs combined with Peter the Great's measures to make service more regular and to tie it more closely to status. Changing military practices made the traditional noble cavalry obsolete while requiring a new type of army and new government apparatus. To address these needs, Peter created a new army and in 1722 instituted the Table of Ranks, which created fourteen parallel ranks of military and civil officers. All nobles now had to serve in a regular, bureaucratized system of duties and ranks. The new system also provided a mechanism whereby men of non-noble status could enter state service and, by advancement in rank, acquire personal and even hereditary nobility, a practice that increased in importance and frequency over time. Moreover, social status came to be defined in significant part by acquired service rank, so that even when the requirement of noble service was abolished in 1762, it was so ingrained that entering service and acquiring a respectable rank remained an important part of noble life, identity, and social status through most of the nineteenth century. At the same time, the abolition of the requirement for state service by nobles severed the traditional link between service and rights on which the Muscovite social-political system had been based. Previously, all subjects served in various capacities, and some, especially nobility, received privileges in return for their service. After 1762 the nobles retained their privileges but no longer were required to serve in return. This created an elite distinguished primarily by its legally defined privileges rather than by functions or service. Moreover, as the constantly reiterated justification for serfdom was that the serf served the noble so that the noble could serve the state, serfdom itself was cast into question; the essential link between noble and serf was now broken.

The Ukrainian and Belorussian nobility under the Polish-Lithuanian state shared many of the general characteristics of the Russian nobility: in a hereditary system based on traditions of military service, the great noble families were of princely descent, with the wealth of the broader nobility varying widely. In the sixteenth century, however, the Polish nobility gained greater political authority at the expense of the monarchs—the opposite of the situation in Russia—and Ukrainian nobles shared in that gain. Among other things the Ukrainian nobles successfully reduced their military obligations while increasing their control over the land and peasantry earlier than did nobles within Muscovite territory. After the Russian acquisition of almost all of the Ukrainian and Belorussian territories in the seventeenth and eighteenth centuries, the Russian service and social characteristics applied to almost all East Slavic nobles, who functioned within a largely homogeneous noble system, including the Table of Ranks. Indeed, the Ukrainian and Belorussian elites, primarily nobles, had been largely Russianized during the eighteenth century, so that to be Ukrainian or

Belorussian came to be associated with being peasant. The Russianization of the elites also meant that Ukrainians and Belorussians were deprived of a natural national leadership, which presented problems in terms of nation-building in the nineteenth and early twentieth centuries.

Wealth remained a significant divider among the nobility. The truly rich, with more than a thousand male serfs, composed only about 1 percent of the hereditary nobility (and less of the total nobility), while 17 percent owned a hundred to a thousand serfs, four-fifths owned less than a hundred, and most of these had fewer than twenty, if any. By the nineteenth century many nobles did not own any serfs, either for economic reasons or because as "personal nobles" they did not have the right. State service and its salary were essential for the poorer nobles, who in each generation were continually threatened with impoverishment because the system of equal inheritance meant that property was constantly divided into smaller holdings and thus smaller income.

PEASANTRY

The peasantry collectively made up 85 to 90 percent of the population of the sixteenth to mid-nineteenth centuries and was the core of the tax-paying population. Within the peasantry, the largest group of the population by the end of the sixteenth century was the serfs, peasants who lived in bondage to private landowners and whose personal freedoms were curtailed. Until the fifteenth century most of the agricultural population had been "black peasants," free men living in small villages, paying taxes to the rulers, but increasingly also paying dues—cash, crop shares, labor—to noble and church landowners. They were, however, legally free, with the right to change residences. During the fifteenth and sixteenth centuries they were driven into bondage by economic factors and the state's military requirements. Economic need (resulting from bad harvests, wars, disease, or other factors) caused peasants to borrow from landlords; they were then prohibited from moving as long as the debt was unpaid. That debt often became hereditary and permanent, tying the peasant to the land and the master. The needs of the state formed an even more powerful force in establishing serfdom. Constant warfare meant that the state needed military servitors, whom it compensated by grants of land. That land was of value to nobles only if it had peasants to work it; because peasants could leave and seek other land, the nobles appealed to the state for help to curtail their movement. The Muscovite state responded by re-

stricting the right of peasants to move, originally during a period around St. George's Day (November 25), then during certain years, and finally prohibited it entirely. The peasantry was permanently tied to the land and could not move. The final fixing of serfdom in Russia is usually dated to the law code of 1649, which abolished time limits on recapture of runaway serfs, imposed penalties on those who received runaway serfs, and generally considered as serfs all peasants living on private landholdings.

Serfdom among Ukrainian and Belorussian peasants, carried out under Polish and Lithuanian political authority, was similar to the Russian. Although they paid dues to noble landlords, the peasants originally controlled their own land. In the sixteenth century the nobles asserted their ownership of the land and the right to restrict peasant movement, reducing peasants to serfdom, especially in the western Ukranian and Belonissian regions nearer Poland. In the sparsely settled southern and eastern areas, especially the area east of the Dnieper River known as Left Bank Ukraine, peasants managed to evade serfdom longer and were fully subjugated to it only in the eighteenth century, when the area became more settled and came under Russian control. On a comparative note, serfdom developed in Russia and the East Slavic lands just as it was disappearing in western and central Europe.

Serf owners held extensive power over serfs. Through their judicial and other state-granted authority they could beat and punish serfs, banish them to Siberia, order them into the army (a twenty-five year obligation), pressure them through increased dues and fees, force arranged marriages, use women serfs sexually, and in other ways abuse them. Serfs could leave the village area only with the lord's permission. Their condition generally worsened in the eighteenth century, as nobles for a time acquired the right to move them about and to sell them. Serfs came close to being slaves, which probably facilitated the melting of the slave category into the peasantry in the eighteenth century. Nobles, however, had a vested interest in not abusing their serfs, for they required their cooperation for tilling the land, but many did nonetheless, and the threat of maltreatment always hung over the heads of peasants (as the threat of peasant rebellion hung over the nobility). On the other hand, the serfs retained traditional practices of communal self-government and action and a sense that they had "rights," often defined in economic terms (what rents they owed, use of woodlands, and so on), that the landowner could not rightfully or morally infringe. They also retained three characteristics of "free" men but not of slaves: they paid taxes, were subject to military conscription, and could go to court (sue and be

Wagering Souls. An engraving by Gustave Doré satirizes Russian landowners who wager their serfs at poker. From *Histoire pittoresque, dramatique, et caricaturale de la Sainte Russie* by Doré (1832–1883). PRINT COLLECTION, MIRIAM AND IRA D. WALLACH DIVISION OF ART, PRINTS AND PHOTOGRAPHS, NEW YORK PUBLIC LIBRARY, ASTOR, LENOX AND TILDEN FOUNDATIONS

sued). Serfs differed from slaves also in that, through the communal system, serfs organized their own labor rather than working under an overseer.

The second largest part of the population, making up most of the rest of rural society, were the state peasants, agriculturalists on land owned or administered by the government. This category grew dramatically as miscellaneous groups of peasants and other rural elements were so classified, and especially with the addition of most of what had been church and monastic peasants after those lands were secularized in the eighteenth century. In the eighteenth and nineteenth centuries they collectively made up about half of the peasantry. State peasants were bonded to the land and their position but in the service of the state rather than a private landlord. Their condition generally was slightly better than that of serfs, but they otherwise shared the same general characteristics. They could be transformed into serfs when the ruler gave the land on which they lived to a noble as reward for his service. Other small categories included the crown peasants, those on land belonging to the royal family.

Russian peasant society was characterized by its communal structure and periodic land repartition, important features that many historians have deemed peculiarly Russian developments. By the communal system, the peasants as a group (village, several small villages, part of a large village) were organized for certain administrative functions, with elders elected by household heads. The commune's collective respon-

sibility was to make tax payments, provide military conscripts, deal with state officials and landlords, exercise limited self-government functions, organize cooperative labor, and oversee land repartition. Repartition, the system by which the land available to a peasant community was periodically redivided among its members for use, was strongest in central Russian areas around Moscow and along the Volga and weakest in Ukraine and Belorussia.

Peasant society and families were patriarchal and hierarchical—that is, all members had a right to share in the common resources (of the village or family), but not equally. Senior males dominated in both, while "stronger" families, measured in wealth or manpower, dominated "weaker" ones. The authority of the senior males was reinforced by the role of the heads of households in electing the communal officials and participating in the key communal decisions. While agriculture was the main activity of most peasants, especially serfs, many engaged in other work. During the winter handicraft activity was common. Many hired themselves out as seasonal labor, rural or urban, and some engaged in seasonal trade, while others took to trading activity or urban labor on a full-time basis. They remained, however, bonded to the noble landowner or the state and paid cash dues on their labor accordingly. Some were household servants. A special category of possessionary serfs applied to serfs attached to factories as a permanent, hereditary workforce. In the central and northern regions, population density on poor land induced increasing numbeers of peasants to work away from the land. In the more fertile lands of the south and Ukraine, peasants remained more fully engaged in agriculture and were less inclined to seek seasonal or other employment outside of the village.

CITIES AND URBAN POPULATIONS

In the East Slavic, especially Russian, lands of the sixteenth to eighteenth centuries, urban dwellers constituted only about 4 to 6 percent of the population and, excepting the ruler and his chief officials, were relatively unimportant. Russian towns were characterized primarily by their administrative-military functions, with commercial activity playing a lesser role than in Western towns and cities. Among Russian cities only Moscow was truly a large city: in 1689 the population of Moscow was 150,000 to 200,000, a significantly smaller number than that of such cities as Paris, London, or Rome at the time.

In the towns, as elsewhere, the population was divided into legally defined estates. The law code of 1649 defined townsmen as those employed in trade and artisan activities within the town. At the top were the elite merchants (*gosti*), important personages who received some privileges and thus were in some ways part of the privileged element. Below them were categories of lesser merchants, artisans, and the lower class of miscellaneous laborers. During the early eighteenth century the townsmen were redefined into three groups according to capital resources: a higher "guild" of important merchants and other upper-economic urban dwellers; artisans, minor merchants, and others of middling property; and the urban poor. In the late eighteenth century the state redefined urban estates again, this time into six categories. These urban classes, especially the merchants and artisans, were often organized as communes with collective responsibility for payment of taxes and management of city services. In return the town estates received the right to engage in certain trades and, at the upper levels, some privileges such as exemption from corporal punishment and the right to ride in carriages. In addition to the legally defined townsmen estates, there resided in the cities and towns various numbers of people of other social estates, including nobles, government employees, clergy, peasants, and slaves, who in fact made up the majority of town dwellers.

In the eighteenth and early nineteenth centuries, towns grew in number and size, and the new capital, St. Petersburg, joined Moscow as a genuinely large city (the capital was moved to St. Petersburg in

1712–1713 and was returned to Moscow in 1918). In the Ukrainian and Belorussian lands the towns were influenced by Germanic and Polish traditions, especially in the western regions, and had more corporate autonomy from Polish and Lithuanian rulers in the sixteenth and seventeenth centuries. This was lost after incorporation into Russia. A notable feature of Ukrainian and Belorussian towns was that they were populated primarily by non-Ukrainians and non-Belorussians (Jews, Poles, Russians, others); this was true into the twentieth century, as Ukrainians and Belonissians remained even more rural than the Russians.

OTHER SOCIAL GROUPS

Although the noble-peasant dichotomy was predominant, Russian society was diverse. The clergy was a special category. The white (parish) clergy was required to marry before taking up posts, and in practice they became a mostly hereditary estate, with sons following in their fathers' steps. The village clergy was quite poor, living at about the same level as their peasant parishioners. Higher church officials came almost entirely from the black (monastic) clergy, including nobles who had entered monastic life. In the eighteenth and nineteenth centuries, because of their access to seminary education (however limited), members of the clerical estate became an important source of the new professional, bureaucratic and middle-class population.

Until the eighteenth century slaves were a significant social category (perhaps 10 percent of the population as late as 1649). Slavery in the East Slavic lands reached far back into antiquity. Slaves derived from a variety of sources, primarily war prisoners, descendants of slaves, and people who, faced with economic or other catastrophe, sold themselves (and their families) into slavery in return for food, shelter, and protection. Slaves performed a variety of functions as agricultural labor, household servants, artisans, merchants, estate managers, and even as soldiers. The state's constant search for tax revenues eventually led it to forbid people to sell themselves into slavery, a practice that represented a loss of taxpayers. Thus over the course of the eighteenth century slaves as a category disappeared into the serf population.

A few other examples illustrate the social diversity. Two rural social categories occupied a space between peasants and nobles. In the sixteenth and seventeenth centuries the Cossacks, people of primarily Russian and Ukrainian origins who had fled from serfdom and other troubles into the wild frontiers between the Muscovite, Polish, and Tatar states, emerged as self-governing military communities. They were incorporated into Russia as a special military caste that, although tax-paying, retained limited privileges of land-ownership, self-government, and exemption from some taxes in return for military service. Another special group was the *odnodvortsy,* literally "one-householders" but perhaps better called "homesteaders," who were descendants of minor service people who claimed noble status because they had provided personal military service. The state sometimes subjected them to the head tax, like state peasants, into which most eventually were folded. In the towns, the term *raznochintsy,* "people of diverse ranks," emerged in the eighteenth century to refer to a variety of low-ranking government officials of non-noble and nonmerchant estate origins, retired soldiers, soldiers' children, and others. This category acquired importance in the nineteenth century as a pool from which the new, non-noble educated elements were drawn. There also were wandering minstrels (*skomorokhi*), against whom the church railed, vagrants, fishermen, and others, both inside and outside the estate (*soslovie*) system. The expanding Russian state also contained an ever-growing number of minority ethnic groups with their own unique social patterns, such as Lutheran Latvian peasants, Armenian merchants, nomadic herdsmen of both the frozen north and desert south, large Muslim populations, and tribal groups of the Caucasus and Siberia, to name only a few examples of the increasingly diverse ethnic population.

Reshaping Society by Decree. An Old Believer protests as the barber, perhaps Peter the Great, cuts his beard. PRINT COLLECTION, MIRIAM AND IRA D. WALLACH DIVISION OF ART, PRINTS AND PHOTOGRAPHS, NEW YORK PUBLIC LIBRARY, ASTOR, LENOX AND TILDEN FOUNDATIONS

THE STATE AND SOCIETY

In the East Slavic world, and Russia in particular, the state had a powerful impact on shaping and reshaping the social structure, more so than in western Europe. It created and abolished social categories, redefining people's legal identities, functions, status, obligations to the state, privileges, property, economic activity, and lives in general. Decrees affected who could live in towns and what they could do there. It turned peasants into serfs and later emancipated them, defined and then ended slavery, and redefined groups of minor servicemen in or out of the nobility. Through its decrees and tax demands the state affected such diverse social features as the size and generational shape of households (a response to tax policies), the communal system (which it enforced in some areas), and alcoholism; vodka being a state monopoly, the state encouraged alcohol consumption to boost receipts, a practice that continued into the Soviet era. Rulers, especially after Peter the Great in the early eighteenth century, held that they had the right and ability to

reshape society by decree. The most conspicuous of many examples of government's consciously altering social behavior and structures were the Table of Ranks and the decrees calling for Western styles of dress. Moreover, the system of legally defined estates profoundly affected people's self-identity; indeed, one's estate was one of the identification entries on the internal passports used in Imperial Russia.

WESTERNIZATION

Western influences also shaped Russian society in fundamental ways, beginning haphazardly in the seventeenth century and accelerating in the eighteenth, when Westernization became government policy under Peter the Great as part of his attempt to restructure society so that it could better serve the state, especially militarily. The new military methods required education and new values and attitudes as well as new weapons and organization. Such external actions as forcing nobles to shave their beards and wear Western-style clothing and ending the seclusion of elite women were part of a campaign to change social behavior and mentalities. The new capital in St. Petersburg was consciously built to resemble a western European city, as were the palaces that soon surrounded it. Despite some resistance, Westernization of the nobility and most of the urban classes was remarkably successful within only a generation or two. Before the end of the eighteenth century, the elites were speaking French or other Western languages and as a result of formal schooling were beginning to absorb Western intellectual and cultural values as well, including the new rationalist attitudes of the eighteenth-century Enlightenment. The peasantry, however, was left alone, thus creating a growing cultural division between a Westernized upper stratum and the mass of traditional peasantry.

THE GREAT REFORMS, INDUSTRIALIZATION, AND SOCIAL CHANGE

Dramatic social and economic changes took place during the last half-century of Imperial Russia, from 1861 to 1917. Emancipation of the serfs in 1861 shook the social system to its roots. Emancipation made serfs "free rural inhabitants," although much of the landlord's control over property rights, economic activities, movement, and so on was simply transferred to the commune rather than to individual peasants, who were still subject to restrictions on movement, special taxes, and corporal punishment. Peasants collectively, through the commune, now jointly owned the land and were responsible for taxes and many obligations and self-government activities. The Stolypin reforms of 1906–1914, initiated by Pyotr Stolypin, premier of Russia, attempted to break down the communal system in favor of individual, consolidated farmsteads held in full title by individual peasant families; but these reforms were short-lived, and after 1917 the peasant villages reverted to their traditional communal structures and practices.

This did not mean that peasant life remained entirely unchanged. Expanding industry, coupled with rural overcrowding, led growing numbers of peasants to take up seasonal, temporary, or permanent work in the cities, while retaining their ties to the villages in most cases (most urban workers were still legally classified as peasants). This introduced a new awareness of the outside world into the village, as did the army reform of 1874, which subjected peasants to universal military service and thus exposed most males to life outside the village and its traditional values. Schooling began to produce a growing literacy rate in the village, especially among younger males. At the same time growing trade affected the villages, introducing factory made textiles and other goods, including books. Slowly the village was changing.

The nobility was also undergoing change. Landowners lost about half of the land during emancipation and had to deal differently with the peasants to obtain labor for the land they retained (while the peasants resented having to rent land or do sharecropping labor on it). Although some noble landlords sought to introduce machinery and other modern agricultural practices on their remaining land, most were forced, by habit or circumstance, to continue with traditional peasant agricultural practices. The nobility remained highly diverse in wealth, education, and function, even as its importance slipped. Some remained landowners in terms of self-identity and ethos, others became professional bureaucrats (the government bureaucracy increased fourfold after mid-century), and some entered the newly flourishing professions. At the same time sons of the nobility found themselves in competition for both state and private positions with the offspring of the new, educated middle classes. State efforts to aid the nobility and preserve them as a viable class had mixed results, although the extent of that before 1917 is much disputed.

The beginnings of an industrial revolution and urbanization in the nineteenth century started a fundamental social transformation that continued to the turn of the twenty-first century. This industrialization grew in part out of government policy—the imperial regime confronted the need to industrialize to ensure that Russia would maintain its great-power ambitions in a world where military power and industrialization were ever more closely linked—and in part out of the steady movement eastward across Europe of the industrial revolution. Russia averaged an annual industrial growth rate of over 5 percent between 1885 and 1914, with even faster growth rates in the 1890s. Trade, both domestic and foreign, grew significantly. The new economy changed Russian society fundamentally and permanently, creating two largely new urban classes while reducing the significance of some old ones. The old legally defined estate classifications, still used by the government and still an important part of self-identity, became increasingly irrelevant to the actual social-economic class structure.

Industrialization produced, for the first time, a significant urban and industrial working class. This was a deeply discontented class. The factories demanded long hours at low pay amid unsafe conditions, a harsh and degrading system of industrial discipline, and a total absence of employment security or care if a worker became ill or injured. Housing was overcrowded, unsanitary, and lacked privacy. Families often shared single rooms with other families or single workers. The conditions of industry not only left workers poor but robbed them of personal dignity.

Russian Industry. Workers in the Ivanovo textile mill, late nineteenth century. SOVFOTO/EASTFOTO

Labor unions, strikes, and similar ways of banding together for mutual improvement were prohibited or strictly limited by the government, which usually supported employers in labor disputes. Government-sponsored improvements in the decade before 1914 only slightly mitigated conditions. All this made the industrial workers a fertile ground for revolutionary agitation, which grew with the new century. Moreover, although industrial workers were not more than 2.5 percent of the population in 1913, their concentration in large cities—especially the "two capitals," St. Petersburg and Moscow—and their organization by the factory process put them in a position to play a role in any revolutionary upheaval far out of proportion to their numbers (as they in fact did in the revolutions of 1905 and 1917). Moreover, once revolutionary disturbances began, they usually could draw support from the much larger laboring class of railwaymen, longshoremen and boatmen, construction workers, day laborers, and others, who together made up about 10 percent of the total population and a much larger percent of the urban population.

The industrial revolution accelerated the growth and increased the importance of the new educated "middle classes" of professionals and commercial-industrial white-collar employees—doctors, lawyers, teachers, engineers, entrepreneurs, managers, office workers, accountants, and others—that had arisen after the Great Reforms of the 1860s and 1870s. They initially found employment in the growing government bureaucracy and in the new organs of limited local self-government, the *zemstva,* which employed large numbers of doctors, teachers, agronomists, and other professionals. The judicial reforms of the 1860s created a new demand for lawyers, and the expanding educational infrastructure opened opportunities for teachers. These and other professions flourished in the growing commercial and industrial sectors, as did the increasing urban population of merchants, shopkeepers, salaried employees, and artisans. Although by the early twentieth century they made up only a small part of the total population, the new middle classes were a large part of the major cities. Moreover, their education and concentration in the major cities, especially

412

the capitals, gave them an importance beyond their numbers. They had for the first time become a significant element in society.

Along with some of the old nobility, the new middle classes made up an "educated society" that provided the basis for a liberal political movement focused on changing the political system through reform. This educated society produced the important, and at the time specifically Russian, phenomenon of the intelligentsia. This primarily intellectual element had evolved out of small circles of mid-nineteenth-century nobles discussing public issues to encompass the most politically involved portion of educated society. The intelligentsia was generally characterized by opposition to the existing order in Russia and a strong desire to change it; out of its radical wing emerged the revolutionary parties, and out of its more moderate wing came the political reformers and liberal parties.

WOMEN

What of the status of women within this society? Traditional Russian and East Slavic society in the sixteenth and seventeenth centuries had a complex, even contradictory attitude toward women, seeing in them the image of both Mary (Mother of God) and Eve (temptress), of good and sin. The Orthodox Church looked upon the sexuality of women with suspicion and regarded sexual activity, even within marriage, as impure. Both descriptive literature and folk sayings denigrated women and emphasized male domination, suggesting that a woman be regularly beaten for her own and the family's good, while she was enjoined to obey her husband silently and in all matters. At the same time, however, especially among the upper classes, women did have legal rights, including the ability to sue in court to defend their property rights and honor and to divorce their husbands for adultery or other sins. By the sixteenth century upper-class women in Moscow were largely secluded, living in the women's quarters (*terem*), for reasons debated by scholars but most probably having to do with maintaining family honor and prospects for desirable marriage alliances. Seclusion was impractical among the provincial nobility, as wives managed estates while their husbands were away on military campaigns, and among peasants, as women labored in the fields. Seclusion was not practiced in Ukrainian and Belorussian areas. Marriages were arranged by the families among all classes. Pregnancy and child-rearing consumed much of the energy of women of all classes.

The situation of upper-class women changed dramatically in the eighteenth century because of Western influences. Peter the Great abolished seclusion as part of his overall Westernizing policies and ordered women of the elite to participate in mixed social gatherings and to wear Western-style gowns to match the Western clothing styles imposed on men. Elite and then noble and urban women generally became much more Westernized, at least in fashion, a process facilitated by the series of women rulers who dominated the eighteenth-century throne after 1725. Nonetheless, Russia remained a highly patriarchal society. Both folk sayings and law emphasized the husband or father's authority, including the right to inflict corporal punishment, and commanded the woman to "unlimited obedience." Although during the nineteenth century Western ideas about the wife as companion and cultured person changed gender relations and softened patriarchy among the upper classes, among the lower classes, the great bulk of the population, gender relations changed little.

Among the peasantry it remained common for two and three generational households to live together in a single small hut. In such situations younger women, daughters and daughters-in-law, were subject to the authority of the patriarch of the family and to senior women as well as husbands, and often were seen primarily as a source of labor. Peasant women's low status was reflected in numerous folk sayings, such as, "a hen is not a bird and a woman is not a person." Nonetheless, peasant women wielded significant authority. They not only managed the house and performed essential economic activities such as animal care, crafts, and some fieldwork but collectively maintained the essential social rituals of the village: matchmaking, birth and upbringing, community morals and behavior.

During the nineteenth century the situation of upper-class women continued to diverge from that of their lower-class sisters. Increasing numbers gained an education and some began to enter certain professions, such as teaching and medicine, although they were still excluded from most professions and from state service. Educated women also became more involved in civic affairs, including the revolutionary movement. In turn, equal rights for women was a central part of the programs of all revolutionary movements and parties, although socialist parties generally emphasized that "women's issues" could be resolved only after the overthrow of autocracy and a sweeping social revolution. A feminist movement patterned on Western feminism appeared among educated women late in the century and pressed for a variety of legal rights and educational opportunities. The All-Russia Union for Women's Equality added the franchise to feminist demands after men received the vote following the Revolution of 1905. Still, only a minority of women worked outside the home, the management of which was their responsibility, and often a taxing one.

Among lower-class women a different evolution took place. As industrialization took men off to the factories, women took more responsibility in the village. Some joined the migrations to the cities to work as domestics, shop clerks, menials, and factory labor. For most this led only to miserable conditions and a degraded life, but a minority managed to use their newfound economic independence to expand their horizons and forge a new identity. For most women, however, whether peasant or urban working class, life remained harsh, traditional, and patriarchal.

REVOLUTIONARY RUSSIA AND THE SOVIET ERA

Russia at the opening of the twentieth century was a rapidly changing society. In addition to industrialization, urbanization, and the growth of new social classes, the era saw a rapid expansion of education and literacy, new directions in art and literature, the appearance of social, economic, and professional clubs and associations, the emergence of a feminist movement, nationalist stirrings among some of the non-Russian half of the population, a broader contact with the Western world, and many other changes. The percentage of nonhereditary nobles and commoners increased at all levels of both the army officer corps and the government bureaucracy except the very highest. Children of the clergy, the merchant class, and the new professional classes increasingly held these government and military positions, which formerly had been the preserve of the nobility. At the same time there was a dramatic population growth, from about 73 million in 1855 to around 168 million in 1913, the result of improved medical care, food, and other factors that produced a longer life expectancy, especially fewer deaths in infancy and childbirth. During the same period urban population grew from 10 to 18 percent of the population, and the largest cities grew extremely fast, tripling or quadrupling their size. Political and social-economic discontent was also growing, producing a potentially revolutionary situation that erupted first in 1905 and then, more profoundly and successfully, in 1917.

The February Revolution of 1917 that overthrew the Russian monarchy also initiated a far-reaching social upheaval. In the new political freedom all classes of society were able to assert themselves as never before and to organize to fulfill their varied aspirations. Thousands of public organizations, reflecting class,

occupation, gender, ethnicity, residence, beliefs, and other human characteristics, emerged and competed in the marketplace of ideas and in the political arena. Swiftly, those representing the interests of industrial workers (and urban lower classes generally) and peasants asserted their dominance, displacing the old middle and upper classes in control of effective power. The October Revolution was, in an important sense, only a confirmation of this successful social inversion, with the Bolshevik Party providing its political articulation and leadership.

After the Bolsheviks took over in the October Revolution, the civil war of 1918–1921 extended the social upheaval even further. The peasants by mid-1918 successfully expropriated noble and other non-peasant lands in the countryside. The nobility as a class disappeared in the maelstrom of 1918–1921, a remarkable social transformation, far exceeding what had happened in the French and English revolutions. The rest of the educated and propertied classes were not so extensively destroyed as identifiable social elements, but they lost their status in society and much of their property (such as houses or apartments). Even the civil war's "victors" were profoundly affected. In 1921, with the devastated industrial economy at only about 13 percent of prewar levels, factories were largely closed, major cities half emptied, and industrial workers scattered. The peasants achieved their main aspiration, possession of all the land, but the famine of 1921–1923 claimed about five million of them and left millions more permanently impaired in health; even their control of the land proved short-lived. Overall, nine years (1914–1923) of war, revolution, civil war, and famine had killed about 25–30 million people and uprooted millions more, who roamed the countryside or squatted in towns and villages. An estimated seven million children were homeless. Two to three million people, mostly of the best educated classes, fled the country permanently. The social upheaval, and its impact, beggars the imagination.

This was, however, only the beginning. The new political rulers were not content to take the society they found but were determined to transform it even further according to their own socialist vision. Central to this was the so-called Stalin revolution. Begun about 1929, it was a dual program to industrialize the Soviet Union at an extraordinary speed while also creating a socialist society, all under the direction and control of the Communist Party. In this process society was to be reshaped on a scale matching or exceeding Peter the Great's Westernizing effort two centuries earlier.

The new industrialization drive accelerated the social revolution that had begun with the earlier industrialization of the 1890s. Cities grew at a tremendous rate as millions of peasants poured off the land and into the new industrial world. The Soviet Union shifted from being less than 20 percent urban in 1914 to about half urban at Stalin's death in 1953 to about two-thirds by 1989 (higher in the Russian areas). By the 1980s the Soviet Union had twenty-three cities with populations exceeding 1 million (mostly in the Russian and Ukrainian areas), and Moscow exceeded 8 million. Along with urbanization came horrendous problems, as had accompanied such changes in other societies, of overcrowded housing, inadequate sanitation, and the psychological and social traumas accompanying the shift from rural to urban, agricultural to industrial. The family changed from extended to nuclear, and the number of children per family dropped among the newly urban. Industrial workers became the symbol of the new society, as the Communist government declared itself based on a "proletarian revolution" and to be building a "workers' state." At the same time, the traditional tie of industrial workers to the village was broken, not only because of generational change but because the traditional village, and with it the old peasant culture and safety net, was simultaneously being destroyed.

The peasants, who had appeared to be the most successful of all social groups in achieving their aspirations (land and control of their lives) out of the revolution, became the great losers in the new Stalinist social upheaval. Beginning in 1929, collectivization of agriculture took the land and destroyed the ancient patterns of village relationships and life. The peasants resisted—about ten million lost their lives in collectivization and in the famine that followed—but by the mid-1930s they had become collective farmers. Peasants saw the collective farms as the new serfdom, and indeed heavy taxation, restrictions on movement, and subordination to party and state officials (the new "lords"), gave it that essence. The peasants' condition declined by almost every social and economic measurement, even more so than for other parts of the population, and recovered slowest when things got better after the death of Stalin in 1953. At the same time their numbers dropped: by the 1980s only about a fifth of the population made a living in agriculture, although that figure was still high by Western standards.

The new Soviet class system evolved in unexpected ways. Stalin declared in 1936 that the "exploiting classes" had been liquidated and that there now existed only three classes in society: workers, peasants (collective farm members), and intelligentsia. This obscured a more complex social reality. Although the old upper and middle classes were gone, a new class of factory and other managers assumed many of the functions and status of the old commercial and managerial class. The professions also quickly reassembled, in altered form, within the new society. Assorted white-collar elements grew in number and diversity. At the same time the Soviet Union abandoned its early egalitarian theories, introducing significant wage differentials as well as differential access to the scarce food and consumer goods. It allowed de facto class stratification to evolve based on education, occupation, income, and access to goods, as well as the new factor of Communist Party membership.

A new elite quickly developed, made up of Communist Party officials and high-ranking government, military, economic, and even artistic and cultural figures. This elite was marked both by power and by access to material goods. The latter was the special feature of the new political-social system in that many goods and services were not available for money but only by regime allocation: large private apartments, dachas (summer houses in the countryside), access to special food and other merchandise stores, use of special medical clinics, choice vacation spots, differential access to news and information, use (and later ownership) of automobiles, and other privileges. This new elite was able to ensure preferential admission to the best schools (and then jobs) for their children, thus handing down its advantages. A new, partially inherited class system of privileged and unprivileged evolved. The Soviet regime initially made an effort to conceal social stratification and the elite's privileges, but during the era Leonid Brezhnev's rule (1964–1982) it was much more open about them. The social hierarchy took on more formal characteristics, some reminiscent of the old legally defined estates of tsarist Russia. Probably the most significant of these was placement on the *nomenklatura* list, the list of important positions the filling of which was controlled by a party official, central or local; assignment to these positions made one by definition a part of the elite and participant in its own graduated schedules of privileges and access rights. Other signs of regime-designated hierarchy appeared, such as enterprises (usually defense-related) authorized to give their workers special benefits and the residency permits required to live in certain cities (such as Moscow), which carried with them better access to goods and other opportunities.

The Soviet system introduced other changes in the life of the population as well. One of the more important was the broad range of social welfare and public services—free universal medical care, guaranteed employment, old-age pensions, cheap public transportation—which softened the impact of the new social stratification on citizens. Education expanded dramatically, producing a generally well-educated population. On the other hand, state-sponsored terror and lawlessness, reaching its height in the Great Terror of the 1930s but continuing at varying levels of intensity throughout the entire Soviet era, had an enormous and traumatic impact on society. Even at its mildest, in the 1960s to 1980s, it fostered a distrust in interpersonal relations and artificial public behavior that affected all social relationships. Organized religion, which formerly played a central role in both public and private life, was mercilessly attacked and largely disappeared from the East Slavic scene until the 1990s. Adding to the complex social picture was a new problem, the immense environmental damage done by decades of industrial policies indifferent to ecological concerns, and an old one, heavy drinking and alcoholism, which became ever more of a major social problem.

Overall the standard of living declined after 1928 and then began to improve again in the late 1950s, with increases in available food, clothing, consumer goods, and appliances. Even the traditionally wretched housing situation improved, although in the 1980s a fifth of the population still resided in communal lodgings (dormitories or apartments with multifamily shared kitchen and bath). Because of the regime's control over allocation of the scarce consumer goods, the quality of life tended to be much better in the cities than in the countryside and to differ significantly among cities (Moscow had more of everything than other cities, Leningrad, formerly St. Petersburg, and republic capitals more than other cities). There is no doubt but that the standard of living improved in Russia, especially from the late 1950s to the 1980s; but whether that offset the terrible losses and traumas inflicted by the regime, or even if living standards were higher than would have occurred under a different kind of regime (they went up, after all, everywhere in Europe during the period from 1918 to the 1980s), remains debatable. The standard of living, in any case, still lagged well behind Western countries (the measurement used by both government and people) and even behind Eastern European bloc countries. Moreover, by the late 1970s there was a growing popular belief that conditions were getting no better, as well as an increasing sense of relative poverty.

Elements both of continuity and of change affected the condition of women in the Soviet era. In 1917, before the Bolshevik Revolution, women received the vote and also entered public life in unprecedented numbers. The Bolsheviks, however, came to power with a vision of a transformed society in which women would become fully equal by becoming fully employed wage earners. Indeed, despite sometimes utopian debates about transformed social and familial relationships, and some social legislation, perhaps the most important impact on women's condition was the massive industrialization and urbanization. The need for workers drew millions of women into factories and other employment, and the need for technical and professional skills opened up educational opportunities. Women entered the professions and managerial ranks in unprecedented numbers. At the same time, however, traditional Russian patriarchal values continued to apply. Women generally held lower-paying jobs, continued to carry the burden of household work and family care alongside full-time employment, had few modern conveniences with which to ease that burden, and suffered especially from the housing and other shortages. Men held most supervisory and higher-ranking positions, even in professions (such as medicine and teaching) and factories that were numerically predominantly female. Indeed, some scholars have suggested that the Soviet regime emphasized the "proletarian" and public aspects of life, areas traditionally considered "masculine," whereas the traditional "female" spheres of life—family, private life, housing, food and consumer goods—were downgraded and under funded.

POST-SOVIET SOCIETY

After the breakup of the Soviet Union in 1991, Russia, Ukraine, and Belorussia struggled with the problems of simultaneously creating new states, new market economies, new political systems, and new pluralistic and open societies. The result was renewed social upheaval for all three East Slavic peoples. Privatization on top of an already collapsing economy led to massive unemployment, declining real income, and hardship for large parts of the society, even as a minority thrived in the new conditions. Conspicuous and extravagant wealth contrasted harshly with new depths of poverty and hardship, creating sharp social tensions. Salaried people (most of the population), went for long periods without being paid. The elderly, women, and children suffered especially, while the younger urban population and those already part of the old elite prospered the most. Health and public services declined precipitously. The death rate exceeded the birthrate, while life expectancy dropped sharply, falling from a high of about 67 to 58 years for men in 1995 (women's expectancy was higher but also fell). Crime rose dramatically, creating insecurity in a population unaccustomed to it. Education opened up intellectually but suffered loss of economic support. Personal freedoms, including literary, artistic, political, religious, and others, expanded dramatically. Creating new national identities has proved more difficult than expected for all three peoples and states.

Clearly, the East Slavic peoples have embarked on yet another period of social turmoil and dramatic change, the outcome of which remains uncertain.

See also **Collectivization; Communism; The Industrial Service; Serfdom: Eastern Europe; The Welfare State** *(volume 2);* **Aristocracy and Gentry; Peasants and Rural Laborers; Revolutions; Slaves; Working Classes** *(volume 3);* **Patriarchy** *(volume 4);* **Eastern Orthodoxy** *(volume 5); and other articles in this section.*

BIBLIOGRAPHY

Andrle, Vladimir. *A Social History of Twentieth-Century Russia.* London and New York, 1995.

Bailes, Kendall. *Technology and Society under Lenin and Stalin: Origins of the Soviet Technical Intelligentsia, 1917–1941.* Princeton, N.J., 1978.

Bartlett, Roger, ed. *Land Commune and Peasant Community in Russia: Communal Forms in Imperial and Early Soviet Society.* New York, 1990.

Bater, James H. *St. Petersburg: Industrialization and Change.* Montreal, 1976.

Becker, Seymour. *Nobility and Privilege in Late Imperial Russia.* De Kalb, Ill., 1985.

Blum, J. *Lord and Peasant in Russia, from the Ninth to the Nineteenth Century.* Princeton, N.J., 1961.

Bradley, Joseph. *Muzhik and Muscovite: Urbanization in Late Imperial Russia.* Berkeley, Calif., 1985.

Brooks, Jeffrey. *When Russia Learned to Read: Literacy and Popular Literature,* 1861–1917. Princeton, N.J., 1985.

Brower, Daniel R. *The Russian City between Tradition and Modernity, 1850–1900.* Berkeley, Calif., 1990.

Bushkovitch, Paul. *The Merchants of Moscow, 1580–1650.* Cambridge, U.K., and New York, 1980.

Bushkovitch, Paul. *Religion and Society in Russia: The Sixteenth and Seventeenth Centuries.* New York, 1992.

Chase, William J. *Workers, Society, and the Soviet State: Labor and Life in Moscow, 1918–1929.* Urbana, Ill., 1990.

Clements, Barbara Evans, Barbara Alpern Engel, and Christine D. Worobec, eds. *Russia's Women: Accommodation, Resistance, Transformation.* Berkeley, Calif., 1991.

Clowes, Edith W., Samuel D. Kassow, and James L. West, eds. *Between Tsar and People: Educated Society and the Quest for Public Identity in Late Imperial Russia.* Princeton, N.J., 1991.

Edmondson, Linda, ed. *Women and Society in Russia and the Soviet Union.* Cambridge, U.K., and New York, 1992.

Engel, Barbara Alpern. *Between the Fields and the City: Women, Work, and Family in Russia, 1861–1914.* Cambridge, U.K., and New York, 1994.

Engel, Barbara Alpern. *Women in Imperial, Soviet, and Post-Soviet Russia.* Washington, D.C., 1999.

Engelstein, Laura. *The Keys to Happiness: Sex and the Search for Modernity in Fin-de-Siècle Russia.* Ithaca, N.Y., 1992.

Fitzpatrick, Sheila. *Education and Social Mobility in the Soviet Union, 1921–1934.* Cambridge, U.K., 1979.

Fitzpatrick, Sheila. *Stalin's Peasants: Resistance and Survival in the Russian Village after Collectivization.* New York, 1994.

Fitzpatrick, Sheila, Alexander Rabinowitch, and Richard Stites, eds. *Russia in the Era of NEP: Explorations in Soviet Society and Culture.* Bloomington, Ind., 1991.

Freeze, Gregory. "The *Soslovie* (Estate) Paradigm and Russian Social History." *American Historical Review* 91 (1986): 11–36.

Gleason, Abbott, Peter Kenez, and Richard Stites, eds. *Bolshevik Culture: Experiment and Order in the Russian Revolution.* Bloomington, Ind., 1985.

Glickman, Rose L. *Russian Factory Women: Workplace and Society, 1880–1914.* Berkeley, Calif., 1984.

Hamm, Michael F., ed. *The City in Russian History.* Lexington, Ky., 1976.

Hartley, Janet. *A Social History of the Russian Empire 1650–1825.* New York, 1998.

Hellie, Richard. *Enserfment and Military Change in Muscovy.* Chicago, 1971.

Hellie, Richard. *Slavery in Russia, 1450–1725.* Chicago, 1982.

Hittle, J. Michael. *The Service City: State and Townsmen in Russia, 1600–1800.* Cambridge, Mass., 1979.

Hoch, Steven L. *Serfdom and Social Control in Russia: Petrovskoe, a Village in Tambov.* Chicago, 1986.

Inkeles, Alex, and Raymond A. Bauer. *The Soviet Citizen: Daily Life in a Totalitarian Society.* Cambridge, Mass., 1959.

Johnson, Robert Eugene. *Peasant and Proletarian: The Working Class of Moscow in the Late Nineteenth Century.* New Brunswick, N.J., 1979.

Kingston-Mann, Esther, and Timothy Mixter, eds. *Peasant Economy, Culture, and Politics of European Russia, 1800–1921.* Princeton, N.J., 1991.

Koenker, Diane. *Moscow Workers and the 1917 Revolution.* Princeton, N.J., 1981.

Lewin, Moshe. *The Making of the Soviet System: Essays in the Social History of Interwar Russia.* New York, 1985.

McAuley, Alastair. *Women's Work and Wages in the Soviet Union.* London, 1981.

Millar, James R., ed. *Politics, Work, and Daily Life in the USSR: A Survey of Former Soviet Citizens.* Cambridge, U.K., and New York, 1987.

Mironov, Boris. *The Social History of Imperial Russia, 1700–1917.* Vol 1. Boulder, Colo., 2000.

Owen, Thomas C. *Capitalism and Politics in Russia: A Social History of the Moscow Merchants, 1855–1905.* Cambridge, U.K., and New York, 1981.

Piirainen, Timo. *Towards a New Social Order in Russia: Transforming Structures and Everyday Life.* Aldershot, U.K., and Brookfield, Vt., 1997.

Pethybridge, Roger. *One Step Backwards, Two Steps Forward: Soviet Society and Politics in the New Economic Policy.* Oxford and New York, 1990.

Raeff, Marc. *Understanding Imperial Russia: State and Society in the Old Regime.* Translated by Arthur Goldhammer. New York, 1984.

Ransel, David L., ed. *The Family in Imperial Russia: New Lines of Historical Research.* Urbana, Ill., 1978.

Rieber, Alfred J. *Merchants and Entrepreneurs in Imperial Russia.* Chapel Hill, N.C., 1982.

Riordan, Jim, ed. *Soviet Youth Culture.* Bloomington, Ind., 1989.

Rosenberg, William G., and Lewis H. Siegelbaum, eds. *Social Dimensions of Soviet Industrialization.* Bloomington, Ind., 1993.

Smith, Hedrick. *The Russians.* New York, 1976.

Smith, Hedrick. *The New Russians.* New York, 1990.

Smith, R. E. F., and David Christian. *Bread and Salt: A Social and Economic History of Food and Drink in Russia.* Cambridge, U.K., and New York, 1984.

Stites, Richard. *Russian Popular Culture: Entertainment and Society since 1900.* Cambridge, U.K., and New York, 1992.

Stites, Richard. *The Women's Liberation Movement in Russia: Feminism, Nihilism, and Bolshevism, 1860–1930.* Princeton, N.J., 1978.

Subtelny, Orest. *Ukraine: A History.* 2d ed. Toronto, 1994.

Thompson, Terry L, and Richard Sheldon, eds. *Soviet Society and Culture: Essays in Honor of Vera S. Dunham.* Boulder, Colo., 1988.

Wade, Rex A. *The Russian Revolution, 1917.* Cambridge, U.K., and New York, 2000.

Wirtschafter, Elise Kimerling. *Social Identity in Imperial Russia.* De Kalb, Ill., 1997.

Worobec, Christine D. *Peasant Russia: Family and Community in the Post-Emancipation Period.* Princeton, N.J., 1991, and De Kalb, Ill., 1995.

THE BALKANS

Maria Bucur

Definitions of the Balkans employ a variety of criteria. Geographically, the Balkans occupy the lands south of the Danube and Sava Rivers to Istanbul, encompassing the peninsula bordered by the Black, Aegean, and Adriatic Seas. Current political definitions include Romania, located north of the Danube, but often leave out Slovenia and sometimes Turkey. Historically, the Balkans have been identified with the expanse of the Byzantine and later the Ottoman Empire in Europe. However, parts of the western Balkans (Croatia, Slovenia) never came under the control of the two empires. Therefore, any single definition according to geography, political frontiers, or even cultural influences falls short of encompassing all the lands and people within the area. If anything, the staggering variety of languages, religions, social customs, and cultures in this area, and their ability to coexist for hundreds of years, seems the one unifying feature of the Balkans. Though many similarities exist between this area and east-central Europe, the following discussion is limited to the lands currently within the borders of Romania, Yugoslavia, Croatia, Slovenia, Bosnia, Macedonia, Bulgaria, Albania, Greece, and the small European portion of Turkey.

BALKAN SOCIETY BEFORE THE OTTOMAN CONQUEST (1453)

Between 1345 and 1453 the Ottoman Empire advanced steadily into the Balkans, finally to control most of the peninsula after the fall of Constantinople in 1453. During this period Balkan society was marked by a few important characteristics. Over the previous thousand years the Eastern Roman Empire, Byzantium, had been the most important political-administrative state structure in the area. The Byzantine Empire developed its own form of Christianity that eventually led to the creation of Orthodox Christianity. In the western Balkans, incursions by various Catholic missionaries during the late Middle Ages led to a battle over religious allegiance. The territories of what today are Slovenia, Croatia, and parts of Bosnia

were converted to Catholicism. Along with these two main churches, other smaller religious sects developed regionally, some considered heretical, like the Bogumils, and others tolerated by the main churches. By and large, however, most inhabitants of the Balkans considered themselves Orthodox Christian.

Religious institutions had an important position in Balkan society, both in terms of spirituality, morality, and customs and in terms of economic and political power. The Orthodox Church, especially its monastic orders, acquired large estates because of the custom among the aristocracy and rulers of making large donations to the church as a sign of social prestige and a means to salvation. By 1453 the clergy was one of the two privileged estates in Balkan society, alongside the nobility, but it was far more secure than the latter in its social prestige and economic power.

An important difference between the development of religious institutions in the West and the Balkans was the greater dependence of the Orthodox Church on secular authority. In the Byzantine Empire the Orthodox Church had evolved as fundamentally a state religion, and the higher clergy had for a long time the status of employees of the emperor. But even the Catholic Church was more dependent on the generosity of secular rulers in the western Balkans than in the rest of Europe.

Another important element of Balkan society before 1453 was its ethnic diversity. During the Middle Ages, the Balkans had been a territory crossed and occupied by many successive nomadic tribes. The Slavs and the Bulgars were the most important ones, as they settled and transformed not only the linguistic map of the Balkans but also the material culture and traditions of these lands.

By the fifteenth century, these populations were predominantly settled, rural, and engaged in agriculture. The geography of the Balkans, mostly broken up by mountains and small rivers crossing it both north-south and east-west, generally did not favor the development of large areas for cultivation. Small holdings dominated much of the territory. The landholding system varied in the area, with larger estates more prevalent in areas like the Albanian plains and Thrace. The Orthodox Church controlled a great portion of the larger landholdings, while a class of semihereditary nobility controlled the rest of the large estates. But no elaborate and centralized system of vassalage and feudalism comparable to western Europe developed in the Balkans. In fact, while some forms of serfdom existed on large estates, there were many areas, such as the mountainous zones of Albania and Bosnia and the Rhodope Mountains, where peasants lived in free communities, as taxpaying subjects of the local and central authorities.

Life even for free peasants was increasingly difficult during the fourteenth century. The political disarray of the Byzantine Empire facilitated the emergence of local warlords, who threatened the stability of the local population, increasingly subject to both higher taxes and irregular violence that threatened their livelihood. Thus, some of the areas that had been more densely populated, especially where large estates existed (in the plains and large valleys), became partially depopulated as the rural population sought refuge in more protected areas, such as mountains. There was already a long tradition of transhumance in the area. Many shepherds had long lived isolated on top of the mountains in the summer, descending to the lowlands in the winter and then returning to their isolated abodes after selling their products to the seasonal spring and summer markets. Now a larger population was retreating into the isolation of the transhumant lifestyle in order to save themselves from the larger taxes and mounting disarray.

In other areas larger family units organized as clans and, through strong kinship links, remained relatively stable during this period of disintegration. Generally patriarchal, these clans existed in parts of Serbia, Bosnia, Albania, and Bulgaria, especially where animal husbandry was more widespread than crop agriculture. Such extended families usually included male siblings, their children, and often their parents. Female siblings married into another clan and lost any rights in their birth family. They could, however, acquire power in the clan of their husband, especially if they married the eldest brother. Sometimes these extended families included four generations of one clan, but more often it was two generations.

The function of these extended families was both to secure the social status and welfare of the individual members and to consolidate and help increase the economic power of the clan. Such arrangements were clearly patriarchal and nondemocratic even with respect to the male members. Age hierarchy was very important in internal decision making. This struc-

ture had great strengths in withstanding economic hardship and other challenges that came from the outside, such as war, but was also vulnerable to weaknesses from within. The power that came with being the oldest brother was easy to abuse, creating discontent among the other siblings. The quarrel between two brothers could precipitate the breakup of the family, bringing misfortune for all its members. Yet the primary victims of this patriarchal family structure were most often the wives and daughters in the clan, who could only exercise power through their husbands. They were otherwise open to sexual and physical abuse from all the elders in the family, both men and women. This type of family structure survived in the Balkans with some minor modifications into the nineteenth century, and in some isolated areas, such as the mountains of Albania and Macedonia, into the twentieth century.

Though most people lived in rural communities, the Balkans also had a small urban population. The largest city in the area was Constantinople, while Athens and Belgrade were rather small towns. Most historians consider the Balkans as increasingly ruralized over the last century before the Ottoman conquest, partly because of the political disarray and partly because of the accompanying economic disarray. The two elements that had brought about the development of cities—local administration and commerce—were in decline. During the Middle Ages, Byzantine cities had developed not only as places of commerce between Europe and Asia but also as centers of artisanship. A guild system to protect and regulate such enterprises had developed, not unlike those in the rest of Europe. In fact, the increasing control of Venice over commerce in some of the important coastal cities also translated into influence over the occupational and social makeup of these ports. Yet Balkan cities did not follow the trend toward self-government that became an important element of urban development in west and central Europe during the same period. They were dependent on the local landowning aristocracy and the administrative interests of the Byzantine Empire.

THE BALKANS UNDER THE OTTOMAN EMPIRE, 1453–1804

By 1453, when they finally took Constantinople and turned it into the capital of their empire, the Ottomans already controlled much of the Balkans. However, the occupation, settlement, and thorough transformation of an enemy land into a *dar al-Islam* (house of Islam) territory took several centuries.

Constantinople. Procession of Süleyman the Magnificent (ruled 1520–1566) through the Atmeidan (Hippodrome). Woodcut after Pieter Coecke van Aelst from *Ces moeurs et Fachons de faire de Turez*, 1553. THE METROPOLITAN MUSEUM OF ART, HARRIS BRISBANE DICK FUND, 1928

Social and religious organization. Several important theological, institutional, and geopolitical factors helped this process, but the most important element was the *millet* system of social organization. Since the Qur'an already recognized the "people of the book" as a privilged category of infidels, with whom Muslims were allowed to coexist without being constantly at war, the Ottomans created a system that divided the population of the empire into four basic religious categories: Muslims, Orthodox Christians, Armenian Christians, and Jews. Populations in each of these categories would be allowed to live basically according to the precepts of their religion, and their welfare would be the responsibility of their respective religious heads.

This was a unique arrangement in Europe and had far-reaching consequences for the social development of the Balkans over the next four centuries. To begin with, the *millet* system institutionalized religion as the most important element of individual and social identification, surpassing regional, ethnic, occupational, or linguistic criteria. In the eyes of the Ottoman authorities, a peasant from Serbia had the same status as a patrician urban dweller from Athens if they were both Christian Orthodox. However, two Bosnians, speaking the same language, living in the same village, and sometimes with kinship ties, would be treated as two distinct types of subjects of the sultan if one were Muslim and the other Orthodox. This was a very common situation in the Balkans. No other state in Europe made religion as essential to defining its subjects as the Ottoman.

The *millet* system was relatively tolerant toward each of the recognized religions. The sultan generally did not interfere in the administrative affairs of the Orthodox Church (at least in the first centuries), in quarrels between Orthodox subjects, over whom the church had jurisdiction, in the development of church-based education, or in the social networks that developed around local parishes. However, the Muslim *millet* was clearly superior to the others in terms of the possibilities for social advancement in the service of the sultan. Members of the other *millets* were clearly second-class citizens, a fact that was inscribed into public life, among other ways, through the clothing codes imposed by the Ottomans and by the interdiction against any non-Muslim and *reaya* (anyone who was not in the service of the sultan) to ride a horse.

The *millet* system allowed a great deal of continuity in the social and cultural practices in most of the Balkans after the Ottoman conquest. In the first centuries of Ottoman rule, the rural peasant population was left largely undisturbed by the changes in the system, especially with regard to family structure, occupations, and daily life. This situation contrasts greatly with the general worsening of the rural population's lot during the same period in central and western Europe, which saw the height of feudalism and several religious wars that were particularly disastrous for the peasantry.

Land tenure. Until the end of the sixteenth century, the main form of land tenure was the *timar* system. The military servants (spahis) of the sultan received the right to draw income from agricultural areas in the form of various taxes regulated by the state. The spahis were thus administrators and had a temporary right over some of the products of those lands, but could not keep them in the family. A much smaller percentage of the land was part of a different type of tenure system, which allowed the right of inheritance. A more important category was the *vakifs,* which were lands granted in perpetuity to servants of the sultan (e.g., spahis and the ulema) for the purpose of almsgiving. These lands could not be taxed by the state, but a tax was levied on agricultural production in order to fund specific public works such as a hospital or inn. These lands could be inherited and used to sustain the family who donated the land.

Overall, peasants living on any of these estates initially had an easier time than before the Ottoman arrival because taxes were relatively fixed, based on a census, and the *timarlis* were not entitled to exploit the peasants for profit. This was even more the case on *vakif* property. Instead of generating an economy based on the incentive for profit or wealth, as was the case under the feudal system in western Europe, the *timar* system encouraged stability and the status quo, which was socially less disruptive for the rural population. But it also became generally deleterious to the economic well-being of the empire once population grew and external market forces began to create an increasing gap between the empire and the outside world.

Starting in the late sixteenth century, this system changed under the pressure of demographic and external economic factors, corruption of the system, and the desire of the civil servants to have right of inheritance over the lands they were granted for use. More lands were turned from *timars* to *vakifs,* and a new form of land tenure emerged, the *çiftlik,* a hereditary private estate. *Çiftliks* were a semi-illegal form of land tenure because during this period they extended far beyond what was accepted under the law—a plot small enough to feed the family of the peasant living on the land. But the Ottomans tolerated this illegality because of the rising corruption among *timarlis.* The *çiftlik* system seemed to provide more reliability in terms of actually collecting the taxes needed for the state and enabling more social stability at the local level. For the peasants living on these lands, however, the system allowed greater abuses and a form of sharecropping that in practice, though not by law, turned a large portion of the population into serfs.

The worsening of peasants' socioeconomic standing was paralleled in the lands outside of direct Ottoman control. In the vassal states of Walachia and Moldavia, the local aristocracy began to exercise more control over the rural population and to impose taxes and labor obligations that amounted to a form of serfdom. This process is often identified as the "second serfdom," though it was not preceded by any similar

practices in the Balkans and eastern Europe at large. It was, in fact, a form of "late" serfdom, in response to demographic regional changes and external economic forces such as trade. Thus, as central and western Europe was slowly emerging from the feudal system, the Balkans were starting to implement it. Serfdom was not legally abolished until the mid-nineteenth century and continued in some areas of the Balkans in the form of sharecropping practices until the twentieth century.

Social changes. Alongside continuities, Ottoman occupation brought about some important social changes. The Ottomans not only controlled the Balkans militarily and politically but also viewed this area as a land that could be colonized by Muslims. Overall, the Ottomans did not seek to convert the Orthodox, Jewish, or Catholic populations, but there were some important exceptions in this regard, in Albania and Bosnia. Because of the religious diversity in these two areas, where Orthodox, Catholic, and other Christians often coexisted in the same family, religious affiliation was not as strong an element of identification here as in the rest of the Balkans. The socioeconomic advantages presented by conversion to Islam, given the already well-recognized military qualities of the Albanians and Bosnians, led to a campaign by the Ottomans to recruit many of the local nobles or chiefs as members of Islam and the Ottoman army. Thus, by the eighteenth century, these areas became some of the mainstays of Islam in the Balkans.

Another important change introduced by the Ottomans was a different set of criteria for vertical social divisions, in accordance to the state's fundamentally religious nature. The subjects of the sultan were divided into those who served him—the military/administrative servants and the clergy, the *askeri,* who were the privileged estates—and the rest of his realm, the *reaya,* or taxpaying subjects. In some ways, this social division was similar to the three estates that existed in western Europe under the old regime—clergy, nobility, and the rest of the population. But the roles of the two privileged estates were different and linked much more closely to the sultan's personal power than in western Europe. The clergy were the interpreters and administrators of justice, which was by and large based on the teachings of the Qur'an, while the nobility were exclusively an aristocracy of the sword, the spahis. Unlike France or England, the Ottoman Empire did not have a hereditary nobility. The spahis gained and maintained their power through military prowess on the battlefield and sometimes by serving as administrators of various imperial functions at the local level, such as levying taxes.

Ottoman Territories in Europe. Adapted from *An Economic and Social History of the Ottoman Empire,* edited by Halil İnalcik with Donald Quataert, volume 2: *1600–1914* (Cambridge, U.K.: Cambridge University Press, 1994), map 5.

The *reaya* encompassed the whole non-Muslim population and a large portion of the Muslims as well, including the peasants but also much of the urban population, such as artisans, entrepreneurs, or urban workers. These populations served the sultan by paying taxes and in exchange received some forms of protection against the abuses of local administrators, at least in principle. By and large, abuses were greater against the Christian population, especially since in quarrels between Muslims and non-Muslims the law always placed the word of a Muslim above that of an infidel.

Another form of abuse against the Christian population was the practice of *devshirme,* a blood tribute of young Christian boys, which was levied by the Ottomans between the last half of the fourteenth century and the end of the seventeenth century. Every year the Ottomans collected young Christian boys, who became the sultan's personal slaves and had to renounce their parents and religion. However, these boys also gained access to the empire's highest positions. They received a superior education and military training. Later they often joined the infantry (janissaries) or the spahis. Some of the most prominent military men and administrators of the empire, even grand vezirs (de facto administrators of the whole empire), had been *devshirme* children. It was a way for the sultan to refresh the ranks of his army and ensure the loyalty of his closest servants. Yet in Balkan folklore this practice remains depicted as barbaric.

The practice of slavery continued in the Ottoman Empire until the nineteenth century. Trade in white slaves was abolished in 1854, while the practice of trading black slaves continued until 1895, having been legally abolished in 1857. There were great variations in the status and actual socioeconomic position of different categories of slaves. Born Muslims could not be slaves, and the offspring of slaves converted to Islam were automatically born free. Some slaves rose to positions of great status and economic power. Many others, however, were confined to a very low position in Ottoman society, performing menial tasks with little if any hope for a decent lifestyle. The situation of male and female slaves was similar, though women's roles were overwhelmingly confined to domestic duties. A racial hierarchy also existed among slaves, with white Circassians ranked as the most "noble" and black Africans as the most "barbaric." After the end of the seventeenth century, the practice of slavery did not involve the Balkan population itself, even though many slaves lived in this area, especially in cities. One should also keep in mind that the definition and function of slavery were qualitatively different from that of slavery in North America, as Ottoman slaves did not have the same essential economic function.

The Ottomans did not utilize slaves in the type of labor-intensive capitalist economy that developed in the American South. The land tenure system makes that self-evident. Slaves were utilized more in household chores and their presence in a Muslim house was a matter of social status. There were also far fewer slaves present in the Ottoman Empire than in the United States. By 1800 there were at most twenty thousand slaves in the whole empire and only a small fraction of them in the Balkans.

Cities. Aside from reshaping the religious landscape and social hierarchy of the Balkans, the Ottomans also brought about important changes in urban development. Balkan cities saw a revival during this period, but as a particular hybrid between Muslim cities and European administrative and commercial centers. In fact, cities were one of the most important sites for Muslim settlement in the Balkans, so much so that the 3 to 1 ratio between Christians and Muslims in the fifteenth century was 1 to 2 by the end of the sixteenth century.

Overall, the Ottomans built upon the already existing urban centers in the Balkans and did not have an active policy of displacing non-Muslim populations to introduce Muslims. In fact, Sephardic Jews found a haven in Thessaloniki under Ottoman rule after their expulsion from Spain in 1492. Yet the architecture and structure of cities did change dramatically during this period. Balkan cities reflected in many ways the general divisions in Ottoman society. The living quarters were divided into *mahalles* (boroughs), each representing a particular *millet.* Thus Jews lived together but separate from Muslims. The Muslim *mahalles* were easy to identify in any city because they were dominated by the presence of tall minarets and mosques, and overall had the right to build higher walls and buildings. They were also located more centrally than other *millets'* quarters. Christians were not able to build towers for their churches, but they developed a distinct style of ecclesiastical architecture, which enabled both inhabitants and visitors to easily identify a Christian *mahalla.* The presence of synagogues and their own unique architecture was often the marker of Jewish *mahalles.* Each *millet* was relatively self-governed, and though non-Muslims paid an additional head tax as *zimmis* (tolerated infidels), all urban inhabitants were taxpayers.

Another important new feature of Balkan cities was the public institutions created by various Muslim philanthropists as part of following one of the five pillars of Islam, almsgiving. Many wealthy subjects created *vakifs* to build and maintain at no public cost hospitals, inns, schools, bathhouses, and public fountains, all to the benefit of the general population. These were located mostly in the commercial center of town, which also contained the government buildings and famous *bazaars* (markets).

Though people lived in quarters divided along religious lines, they most often worked together in the central commercial *mahalles.* For instance, all silversmiths had shops on the same street, and all carpet weavers had their workshops in the same district. Ottoman cities had a strong guild system that adapted to already existing practices in the Balkans and accepted as members individuals from all *millets.* It was similar in many ways to the associations that were developing during the same period in the rest of Europe. Yet some important differences exist between western European and Ottoman guilds in their long-term social and economic role. While in western Europe guilds became an engine of growth in terms of economic production, technological innovation, and capital accumulation, to the point where the guild system was rendered obsolete, in the Ottoman Empire guilds contributed to stagnation.

Sarajevo. Muslim quarter and bazaar in Sarajevo. Watercolor (1851) by Alois Schön.
GRAPHISCHE SAMMLUNG ALBERTINA, VIENNA

As in many other areas of economic and social life, the Ottoman Empire instituted strict guild regulations that would enable the state's splendor to remain unspoiled by greed, rapid growth, or corruption. Yet those regulations rendered the state unable to deal with important external pressures on Ottoman society. Guilds were closed and were not allowed to grow in any significant fashion. In a period of increased consumption and commerce, unofficial artisan associations were formed and helped corrupt the system in place. In addition, the Ottomans placed a ceiling of 10 percent profit for almost all artisans, which certainly hampered their transformation into a powerful social group. Artisans remained numerically small and their economic power less significant than their counterparts in western Europe.

One group that was able to take advantage of these strict regulations and the growing markets were commercial entrepreneurs, the middlemen, who had far fewer restrictions placed on their markups. Thus, by the eighteenth century, Balkan cities had an urban patrician class, still officially *reaya,* many of them non-Muslims, especially from among Greeks, Jews, Armenians, and Serbs. Many of these Greeks and Serbs were able to transfer their economic power into land-holding, though officially all territories controlled by the Ottoman state were the property of the sultan. Thus important avenues developed for the empow-

erment and social advancement of certain members of all *millets,* many of them tolerated by the Ottoman Empire because these subjects were still taxpayers whose activities benefited the state, and others went unpenalized because of the increasing corruption of local administration.

Family structure. Non-Muslim families retained the structure they had before the Ottoman conquest, with virtually no interference from the Ottoman authorities. Muslim families, both those of the colonizers and of the converts, followed practices already existing under Islam. Polygamy was widespread, especially among servants of the state. Also, because the military obligations of the spahis forced them to be absent for prolonged periods of time from their families, women often assumed more authority in managing the household, though the presence of several wives sometimes created tensions absent from most Christian homes. Muslim rural families were generally smaller than urban families and much more similar to those of Christian peasants. One important effect of polygamy, birth-control practices and related sexual customs of the Islamic population, and the spread of venereal diseases was the gradual slowing down of the birthrate by comparison with the Christian population. For instance, though at the end of the sixteenth century Muslims made up the great majority of the

427

urban population, the ratio shifted back in favor of the Christian population by the beginning of the nineteenth century.

THE BALKANS BETWEEN 1804 AND 1948

While the industrial revolution and the political aftereffects of the French Revolution helped bring about a dramatic change in western European societies, Balkan societies remained only indirectly and somewhat marginally affected by these developments. During the nineteenth century, changes in the Balkans were largely political, military, and administrative. One cannot speak, for instance, about the development of a civil society here, as one can in the case of France or Germany. Still, the rise of nationalism as the most important ideological movement of the century was the product of intellectual movements and social shifts that occurred in the Balkans, and it helped in turn to introduce some broader social changes in the area.

The nationalist movements in the Balkans arose out of the interaction of a small but active intelligentsia with the ideas of the French Revolution and the "springtime of nations" in 1848. This group was a relatively recently developed social cluster of either merchants (especially in Greece and Serbia) or entrepreneurial young landowners (in Romania), who had made their fortunes through the Ottoman system but perceived it as decaying and fundamentally anachronistic. Another important characteristic of many of these individuals was their critical view of the Orthodox Church. Though most of the young intellectuals were churchgoing Christians, many viewed the practices of the church hierarchy as compromised and antiquated. Although this was a small group of individuals, their activities proved influential beyond their numbers.

To begin with, they conceptualized for the first time for their own conationals the concept of national identity based on a common language, religion, and cultural traditions. Initially, such ideas reached an insignificant portion of the population, but over the course of the nineteenth century, with the creation of more educational institutions, cultural nationalism became one of the founding principles of education. By the end of the century, the gospel of nationalism was internalized by the educated population, still a minority but now a sizable portion of Balkan society.

The intelligentsia also introduced new concepts of social justice into their discussion about national rights and the oppression of their conationals by the ruling empire (the Ottomans in most of the Balkans and the Habsburgs in Transylvania and the northwestern Balkans). They defined the poor conditions in the countryside and the persistence of serfdom less as the result of class exploitation at the hands of the aristocracy than as the inevitable outcome of imperialism. Their call for justice found a limited echo among the peasantry (most prominently in the Habsburg lands) until the end of the nineteenth century. But it did lead to the abolishing of serfdom.

Otherwise, life in the rural areas changed very little. The structure of families remained relatively unchanged, while the size of families decreased somewhat because of both lower mortality rates and new birth-control practices among both Muslims and non-Muslims. There was also minimal migration to urban areas, unlike western Europe, where the relationship between urban and rural areas changed dramatically.

Still, some notable changes took place in most Balkan cities. To begin with, the ratio between the Muslim and non-Muslim population continued to shift toward the non-Muslims, with Orthodox Christians making up the overwhelming majority of urban inhabitants by 1914. This change was a function both of different natality rates among Muslim versus non-Muslim populations and of political developments. Most prominently, with the retreat of Ottoman authority from Greece (1833) and Serbia (1829), and with the end of Phanariot rule in Romania (1829), the Ottoman administrative apparatus and its representatives gradually left the capitals of the emerging new states. Athens, Thessaloniki, Belgrade, and Bucharest became important administrative centers. The leadership that emerged in the second half of the nineteenth century focused on rebuilding them as European cities and creating a native bureaucracy as the backbone of the new nations.

With the emergence of national educational, cultural, and administrative institutions by 1914, the new national bureaucracies in the Balkans produced an important social class, generally well educated, with ambitions to a middle-class lifestyle comparable to that of their counterparts in western Europe, and at the same time entirely dependent on the state for their employment and social status. This development somewhat resembled the rise of the educated middle class in Germany. But it was not accompanied by the development of a significant native entrepreneurial middle class.

The interwar period saw a continuation of trends already described. The Ottoman and Habsburg presence disappeared, and the new states operated under the principle of national sovereignty, though they all had significant ethnic minorities. Greece alone tried to solve this issue by the resettlement of massive numbers of Greeks and Turks. Elsewhere, minorities were legally protected, though they were everywhere at a

The Greek Revolution. *Greece Expiring on the Ruins of Missolonghi,* painting (1826) by
Eugène Delacroix (1798–1863), commemorating the Greeks who died when they blew up
their town on 23 April 1826 rather than surrender it to the Turks. MUSÉE DE BEAUX ARTS,
BORDEAUX/ART RESOURCE, NY

disadvantage in terms of access to the economic, political, educational, and other cultural resources provided by the state. Nationalism in fact became a
stronger force in Balkan society, with more aggressive
populist, exclusivist overtones. The outcomes of this
trend were dramatic during World War II and continued through the communist period: Great human
losses during the war and Stalinist years and a continued splintering (though mostly muted) of Balkan societies due to ethnic-nationalist animosities.

The most significant change in Balkan societies
brought about by World War II was in the realm of

demography. The ethnic map of the Balkans was drastically altered through the elimination of most Jews, either victims of internal anti-Semitic movements or as a result of the German occupation. Likewise, the Turkish population suffered at the hands of the Bulgarians and Greeks. The Croat *ustase* (a fascist movement) and Serbian partisans (a communist group) were merciless in their decimation of each other. By and large, the human losses in the war were tremendous, especially in Yugoslavia. Likewise, both the German occupation and the Soviet "liberation" greatly damaged the existing economic base.

THE BALKANS DURING THE COMMUNIST PERIOD (1948–1989)

The most important period of change in Balkan societies during the modern era took place after World War II. Because most of the developments described here are the result of the communist takeover that was accomplished by 1948, they are more specific to the communist bloc, in the south and north of the Balkans, than to the Balkans as a whole.

The communist regimes transformed the overwhelmingly rural, peasant societies in the area into much more urbanized, industrial ones. The structural transformations that accompanied industrialization in western Europe happened over more than a century, but in the communist bloc this was accomplished in two generations. By the 1970s, most people in the Balkans were urban workers and lived in cities.

By the same token, rural life changed dramatically with the collectivization of much of the agricultural land (accomplished less thoroughly in some parts of Yugoslavia than elsewhere). The peasants became a rural proletariat, many seeking seasonal employment in urban industries. Thus a pattern of seasonal migrant labor developed in the entire region, as well as a permanent movement of rural population to urban areas. As a result of the quick and large-scale transplantation of peasants to the cities, one can speak of a process of ruralization of Balkan cities, where peasants tried to replicate their rural lifestyle in the new high-rises. Many new urban dwellers tried to preserve family and kinship relations in the new environment through various living arrangements and by preserving various symbolic links. For instance, many families chose to live in multigenerational living arrangements (grandparents, parents, and children together), although this practice was sometimes also motivated by economic constraints. Some of these families often returned to their countryside residence for any important rites of passage events, such as baptisms, weddings, and funerals.

In addition to the newly created proletariat, another important new class emerged as a result of the new regime—the *nomenklatura*. In order to generate the kind of economic growth required by the five-year plans, the new state bureaucracies had to educate increasing numbers of technical specialists and managers. Though nominally also workers, these specialists soon developed a sense of their authority and became the new elite of the communist regime, more entrenched in their statist loyalties than the bureaucracies under the pre-1948 regimes.

The communist regimes also transformed the state into a welfare state, albeit with rather poor performance on most of the services provided, but still a paternalist form of state that came to replace the traditional safety nets in Balkan societies. Now that women were emancipated in order to become full members of the proletariat, the role of nursing, socializing, and educating children fell on the shoulders of the child-care system. The young could no longer take care of the elderly, as they were engaged in working and generally unable to provide for more than the immediate family. A system of state pensions was to take care of the elderly.

The development of these and other social programs resembled many of the projects of the postwar welfare states in western Europe. The major difference, however, was that in the Balkans these services were constructed and implemented entirely in a top-down fashion, as a gift from the paternalist state. All inhabitants came both to expect these services and to depend on them heavily, to the point where, after 1989, when some of this safety net disappeared, a wave of nostalgia for the communist regime grew strong among many sectors of society.

Overall, what the communist regimes accomplished was equalization of standards of living and of expectations among most inhabitants. The members of the *nomenklatura* lived marginally above this level, and a handful among the party elite had a truly extravagant lifestyle. Yet most people's expectations of professional success, comfort, and pleasure were made to fit a strict standard. This equalization was supposed to represent social justice. Thus members of all different ethnic groups became equal, men and women were treated equally, and young and old had the same expectations. At the same time, this procrustean measure of social satisfaction hid important injustices, such as the discrimination against national minorities by the welfare state and the saddling of women with the double burden of home and professional responsibilities. In this regard, the faults of the egalitarian socialist system resembled the weaknesses of the western welfare states.

Turkish Refugees. Bulgaria's policy of forced assimilation of the Turkish minority in 1989 led to the expulsions of Turks. REUTERS/©CORBIS

An important result of this equalization of society was the growing emigration of people from this area to western Europe, Israel, and the United States. Aside from Yugoslavia, where many people had a chance to work as guest workers in the west and then return, a sizable portion of the educated professionals found ways to leave their countries behind, leading to a damaging brain drain. By 1989 this exodus had produced serious holes in many of the industries and professions essential for the economic performance of their countries. This exodus has not stopped or reversed significantly since 1989.

POSTCOMMUNIST DEVELOPMENTS

During the period of postcommunist transition, one can speak of very little improvement in the standard of living or level of satisfaction in Balkan societies. In areas that have not been plagued by war, the impoverishment of the general population, the disappearance of social services considered essential by the population, and the appearance of other social problems such as crime, prostitution, and various diseases have been the somber legacy of postcommunism. Still, though there is some nostalgia for the communist period among the older population, most people are simply interested in becoming more like Greece, with political and economic standards closer to those of western Europe. One important development in the area has been the revival of religious institutions and the growth of the Orthodox Church, which has again become an important center of authority in society.

Another important development since 1989 has been the explosion of nationalist violence that brought about the dismemberment of Yugoslavia. All ethnic groups of that country have been hurt tremendously in terms of personal human losses, economic losses, and prospects for social advancement in the future. The young are fleeing from Yugoslavia, desperate and cynical about the possibilities for peace and prosperity in their country. It is difficult to estimate today the long-term impact of the decade-long conflict in Yugoslavia, but one can be certain that the ethnic map will remain forcibly redrawn to keep the different groups separate, with virtually no hope for reconciliation.

See also **Serfdom: Eastern Europe; Welfare State; Nationalism; Communism; Military Service** *(volume 2);* **Slaves** *(volume 3);* **Kinship; The Household** *(volume 4);* **Eastern Orthodoxy** *(volume 5); and other articles in this section.*

BIBLIOGRAPHY

Barany, Zoltan, and Ivan Volgyes, eds. *The Legacies of Communism in Eastern Europe.* Baltimore, 1995.

Chirot, Daniel, ed. *The Origins of Backwardness in Eastern Europe: Economics and Politics from the Middle Ages until the Early Twentieth Century.* Berkeley, Calif., 1989.

Clogg, Richard, ed. *Balkan Society in the Age of Greek Independence.* London, 1981.

Einhorn, Barbara. *Cinderella Goes to Market: Citizenship, Gender, and Women's Movement in East Central Europe.* New York, 1993.

Inalcik, Halil. *Studies in Ottoman Social and Economic History.* London, 1985.

Inalcik, Halil, and Donald Quataert, eds. *An Economic and Social History of the Ottoman Empire, 1300–1914.* 2 vols. New York, 1994.

Jelavich, Charles, and Barbara Jelavich, eds. *The Balkans in Transition: Essays on the Development of Balkan Life and Politics since the Eighteenth Century.* Hamden, Conn., 1974.

Lampe, John R. *Balkan Economic History, 1550–1950: From Imperial Borderlands to Developing Nations.* Bloomington, Ind., 1982.

Levin, Eve. *Sex and Society in the World of the Orthodox Slavs, 900–1700.* Ithaca, N.Y., 1989.

Ramet, Sabrina, ed. *Eastern Europe: Politics, Cultures, and Society since 1939.* Bloomington, Ind., 1999.

Stavrianos, Leften Stavros. *The Balkans since 1453.* Hinsdale, Ill., and New York, 1958.

Stoianovich, Traian. *Balkan Worlds: The First and Last Europe.* Armonk, N.Y., 1994.

Stoianovich, Traian. *Between East and West: The Balkan and Mediterranean Worlds.* 4 vols. New Rochelle, N.Y., 1992–1994.

Sugar, Peter F., ed. *Nationalism and Religion in the Balkans since the 19th Century.* Seattle, Wash., 1996.

Sugar, Peter F. *Southeastern Europe under Ottoman Rule, 1354–1804.* Seattle, Wash., 1977.

Todorov, Nikolai. *The Balkan City, 1400–1900.* Seattle, Wash., 1983.

Todorova, Maria. *Balkan Family Structure and the European Pattern: Demographic Developments in Ottoman Bulgaria.* Washington, D.C., 1993.

THE JEWS AND ANTI-SEMITISM

Michael C. Hickey

INTRODUCTION: DISTINCTIVE CHARACTERISTICS OF EUROPEAN JEWISH SOCIAL HISTORY

The Jews' status as a diasporic people has shaped their social history. Expulsions from western and central Europe, settlement in Poland and the Ottoman Empire, then later resettlements in the West reinforced transnational characteristics of Jewish life. Common faith, languages (Hebrew, Yiddish, and Ladino), culture, and kinship networks linked distant communities and allowed the transmission of ideas, people, and trade. This held for both linguistic-cultural branches of European Jewry, the Sephardi (Hebrew for Spain) and the Ashkenazi (Hebrew for Germany), at once fostering Jews' integration and reinforcing their segregation.

The problems of integration and segregation are central to Jewish social history. Some Jewish communities remained segregated from Christian society into the nineteenth century. Segregation both constrained and nurtured the internal development of Jewish society. Jewish communal associations (*kehillot*) negotiated relations with Christian society and regulated Jewish community, family, and devotional life. Communal authority, although under constant strain, remained a feature of Jewish life into the twentieth century. Segregation meant Jews were enmeshed in and apart from European social history. Jewish social history intertwined, for instance, with the rise of the nation-state, modern commerce and capitalism, professionalism, urbanization, individuality, and mass politics. Yet it often followed a different chronology or revealed different characteristics. Jewish emancipation strained but did not dissolve communal institutions, opened paths of acculturation, and threw the nature of Jewish identity into question. Yet even where acculturation was most pronounced, the question of Jews' "otherness" remained, particularly in the form of anti-Semitism.

State-imposed repression and anti-Jewish popular violence punctuate Jewish social history. The nature of popular anti-Semitism is a matter of scholarly contention. Some elements of popular anti-Semitism transcend historical periods, such as the hatred of Jews as alleged enemies of Christianity and as dangerous economic competitors or exploiters. Increased Jewish population and economic integration often precipitated popular violence. But the emergence of modern nationalist and racial consciousness and, in particular, mass politics, grafted onto traditional anti-Semitism the specter of Jews as malignant aliens, which lay at the core of Nazi racial doctrine.

EXODUS WITHIN THE DIASPORA (1450–1570)

In the century before 1450, Jewish populations across Europe collapsed, Jewish economic activity severely contracted, and anti-Jewish violence was widespread and frequent. Jewish life in Europe reached a nadir in the late fifteenth century and the early sixteenth century with expulsions from the Iberian Peninsula and most of central Europe. Jewish communities already had been forced from England (in 1290), France (1306 and 1394), and many Germanic cities (in the mid-1400s). Jews remaining in Germany were restricted to ghettos or dispersed to small villages. In the late 1400s Jews in Spain, home to Europe's largest Jewish community, were subjected to state extortion and forced conversion to Catholicism. Conversion offered little protection, as the Spanish Inquisition made Conversos its special target. Expulsions from Spain in 1492, from Portugal in 1497, and from Italian and German principalities forced the massive resettlement of Jews and "new Christians" on Europe's eastern periphery in the Polish-Lithuanian Commonwealth and the Ottoman Empire.

Expulsion transformed Jewish economic life, reversed demographic trends, and reinforced transnational characteristics. Polish magnates encouraged Jewish settlement in underdeveloped territories, where Jews became intermediaries between landlords and peasants (managing estates and collecting taxes) and facilitated East-West trade. Jews in Poland-Lithuania engaged in artisanal crafts, from which they had been excluded in the West. Similarly the Ottomans encouraged Jews to engage in a range of economic activities, and Jewish communities quickly dominated critical trade routes through the Balkans. Resettlement had profound demographic consequences. Large Sephardic communities arose in the Ottoman Empire. For instance, the community in Salonika grew from a few families in 1492 to more than fifteen thousand people by 1520. In contrast to the West, the relatively secure standard of living and minimal restrictions placed on Jews in the East facilitated population growth. Diffusion to hundreds of small settlements in Poland set the stage for Jewish demographic recovery in the next century, which far exceeded the growth of the general population. In 1500 Jews accounted for some 30,000 of Poland's roughly 5 million inhabitants. By 1600 the Jewish population had increased by almost 500 percent and the population as a whole by only 50 percent. Expulsion also isolated Jewish communities linguistically from their neighbors. But Ashkenazic and Sephardic communities developed cultural and kinship ties that spanned the East, facilitated an impressive degree of cultural exchange, and built trade networks that transformed European commerce.

Expulsions added a racial dimension to religious charges against Jews. Conversion, inquisitors argued, did not cure Jews' "bad blood." While religious and racial charges emanated from clergymen, anti-Jewish violence and demands for expulsions also came from guilds in German and Italian towns, that is, from merchants and tradespeople who saw Jews as an economic threat. The social ferment of the Reformation and the Counter-Reformation accentuated these antagonisms.

During the Reformation and the Counter-Reformation, ecclesiastic authorities became a principle force behind expulsions and anti-Jewish agitation. In the 1530s Martin Luther, having failed in his efforts to win Jews over to Christ, called on Christians to expel them. Vehement anti-Jewish sermons fomented anti-Jewish riots and expulsions across Protestant Germany from the 1530s to the 1570s. The Counter-Reformation proved no less dangerous. Papal policy toward Jews was inconsistent, but from 1553 on it favored pressuring them into conversion and quarantining them from Christian society. In Italy, as in Protestant Germany, the clergy sometimes encouraged anti-Jewish violence involving guilds that feared Jewish competition. The Papal States, employing the model of Venice, confined Jews in ghettos to segregate them from the general population. While the ghetto has been a symbol of oppression and its overcrowding

has been linked with poverty and disease, in Italian and German cities Jewish numbers increased at a far greater rate than did the general population. The Jewish population of Prague doubled from 600 to 1,200 between 1522 and 1541. Like expulsion, ghetto life reinforced the importance of Jewish communal associations.

State and ecclesiastic authorities strictly limited the size of Jewish communities and circumscribed Jews' occupations, movement, and contact with Christians through Jewish communal associations. *Kehillot* collected taxes, sustained the ghetto infrastructure, and regulated Jewish social, economic, and devotional life. Elected boards of elders maintained cemeteries, synagogues and prayer rooms, slaughterhouses, schools and talmudic academies, charitable societies, and rabbinical courts. They also hired and supported rabbis, teachers, and doctors to treat the poor. To raise funds they levied taxes and fines. *Kehillot* oversaw markets and business practices and ensured proper attention to devotional activities. They regulated personal behavior and family functions, from granting permissions for marriage to supervising forms of dress and public deportment, and were particularly concerned with sexual conduct, especially that of women, who as a rule were secluded. The authority of rabbis declined in central Europe beginning in the mid-1500s with the emergence of a professional rabbinate, often appointed by state authorities to circumscribe community autonomy. Like communal boards, state rabbis coordinated the collection of taxes in the form of fines, which generated hostilities among the laity.

Ghetto overcrowding created social tensions. Divorce increased in German and Italian communities, and complaints of fraying sexual morality were common. Many communities responded by lowering the marriage age while mandating the deferment of childbearing, simultaneously protecting public morality and limiting population growth. Economic stratification increased, and along with an elite of wealthy merchants, a poor stratum of domestics and menial laborers who lived outside the formal legal and tax ordinances emerged. As class differentiation increased, fraternal societies and voluntary associations dominated by the economic elite subsumed charitable activities, burials, and other community functions. As in Christian communities, debate over the function of the laity accompanied social change. Lay officials displaced rabbinical authority on communal boards, and in several cities lay courts began hearing civil cases. Other aspects of Jewish community life paralleled broader social phenomena despite Jews' segregation. The printing of Hebrew books increased, popular as well as religious literature flourished, and

In an Amsterdam Synagogue. Jews processing with palms during the Hoshana Rabba festival in the Portuguese Synagogue in Amsterdam. Engraving by Bernard Picart from *Cérémonies et coutumes religieuses de tous les peuples du monde* (1725). NEW YORK PUBLIC LIBRARY

secular concerns became more integrated into intellectual life.

REINTEGRATION AND SEGREGATION (1570–1750)

In the 1570s Jewish life recovered rapidly across western and central Europe. The readmission of Jews to western and central Europe and the growth of their communities were tied to political and cultural phenomena in Christian society and to the strategic networks Jews had formed in the East. Secular statecraft, mercantilism, and radical skepticism justified princely and imperial reversals of the previous century's expulsions. Because Jewish trade networks made resettlement a tool of economic development, the revival of Jewish communities was intertwined with the rise of nation-states, the growth of modern commerce, and preindustrial urbanization. This revival integrated Jews into European economic life, and new social strata emerged in Jewish communities, which contin-

ued to experience demographic expansion until the early 1700s.

Readmission of Jews, expansion of Jewish economic life, and growth of Jewish communities occurred simultaneously across western and central Europe. In 1577, for instance, the Holy Roman emperor Rudolf II allowed Prague's Jews to practice trades previously denied them, like gold and silver work. Jewish artisans, shopkeepers, and merchants prospered, and Prague's Jewish community grew to three thousand by 1600. Relaxed restrictions fostered economic and demographic expansion in Frankfurt, where the Jewish population grew from 419 to 3,000 between 1540 and 1615. Official toleration was extended also to smaller settlements; the majority of German Jews, as many as 90 percent, lived in small towns. In Italian cities dependent on the Levantine trade, readmitted Jews formed thriving communities. The population of the Venice ghetto grew from 900 in 1552 to 2,500 in 1600 as Jews came to dominate trade with the Balkans.

Jewish demographic recovery outstripped that of Christian communities throughout the seventeenth century, even during the Thirty Years' War (1618–1648). Both Protestant and Catholic forces relied on Jews for loans and services, and Jewish victuallers supplied both the Habsburg and the Swedish armies. In return both sides granted concessions to Jews, reduced economic restrictions, and permitted new Jewish settlements. During the war Jewish populations generally remained stable or even grew, while the general population declined. A similar dynamic held for the Jewish communities in Alsace, the Dutch Republic, and Italian cities like Livorno, where the war enhanced Jewish trade and the ghetto escaped the ravages of the great plague of 1630–1631. Jewish population growth and economic expansion extended into eastern Europe. When Poland pushed eastward into Belorussia and Ukraine, Polish magnates encouraged Jewish colonization. In these territories Jews played a variety of economic roles, from artisans to estate managers, and Jewish numbers grew more rapidly than did those of the native populations.

Jewish population growth and economic integration produced violent backlashes. With the end of the Thirty Years' War, the clergy and guilds in German towns demanded expulsion of the Jews, and anti-Jewish violence erupted in several Austrian settlements. Resentment against Jewish economic encroachments was a common theme. The worst violence occurred in Polish territory when Ukrainian peasants and Crimean Tartars led by Bohdan Khmelnytsky rebelled against Polish rule between 1648 and 1651. Besides attacking Polish nobles and Catholic clergy, Khmelnytsky's followers slaughtered thousands of Jews. Religious hatreds blended with economic grievances, and Jews were attacked as the intermediaries between nobles and peasants and as instruments of Polish domination. The massacres sent streams of Jewish refugees to the West.

The violence of the mid-1600s did not deter Jewish demographic growth or economic integration, which actually accelerated. Jewish birthrates exceeded those of Christians. With notable exceptions, like Prague, where three thousand Jews died in an epidemic in 1680, the Jewish population increased, while the general population stagnated. In Amsterdam the economically influential Jewish population grew from three thousand in 1650 to over six thousand in 1700. Similar statistics exist for German, Austrian, and Italian communities, and Jewish population growth was even greater in eastern Europe.

Demographic success followed economic integration. By 1700 Jews were prominent in international and colonial trade, and they were active in industry across most of the Continent. Again, ties between communities helped facilitate this trade. Jews exercised great geographic mobility, and merchants and tradespeople moved across international and continental borders. A new elite, "court Jews," provided loans and other services to royal houses. In rural districts in central and eastern Europe, Jewish peddlers linked peasants to urban commerce. Jewish crafts thrived in places where Jews suffered few restrictions on artisanal activities or where Christian guilds were weak.

Economic integration had strict limits. Jews were still banned from landownership in most states. Craftspeople could not compete for Christian customers, and new restrictions arose when they threatened Christian guilds, as in the Dutch silk-weaving industry. Moreover changing state policies undermined Jewish economic life. In eighteenth-century Prussia export prohibitions and high tariffs crippled Jewish trade and produced widespread poverty. Despite economic integration, Jews remained segregated. State authorities circumscribed their settlements, controlled their contacts with Christians, and denied them the legal status afforded Christians. From the early 1700s state control over Jewish communal life increased, as did internal tensions. Enlightenment absolutist principles dictated that states weaken Jewish self-government, and economic thought de-emphasized Jewish-dominated areas of international commerce. States attacked the autonomy of *kehillot* and Jewish regional associations, and most German states limited the power of Jewish courts in the eighteenth century. For example, in Hamburg a 1710 regulation gave Christian courts power over Jewish divorce cases. The Polish Commonwealth also weakened Jewish communal autonomy in the 1740s.

The assault on communal autonomy coincided with the deterioration of Jews' economic and demographic positions. Beginning in 1713 Jewish populations grew more slowly than the general population in all of Europe except Poland, where Jewish numbers continued to soar. Most estimates set the number of Jews in Poland in 1700 at 350,000, whereas by 1750 the Jewish population there neared 750,000. Population growth in Poland was accompanied, however, by a wave of anti-Jewish violence and accusations of ritual murder, peaking in the 1740s to the 1760s. In some places, such as the Balkans and Holland, the reversal of demographic trends was linked to the contraction of trade. Elsewhere, such as Prussia and other German states, it stemmed from changes in governmental economic policies and the new restrictions on the size of Jewish communities. Simultaneously, Jewish communities in western and central Europe faced accelerated economic stratification and rising rates of poverty and indigence. More than half of all German Jews lived in poverty by the mid-1700s, and 10 percent were vagrants. The situations in Italian, Dutch, Bohemian, and Moravian communities were no better. Social problems like crime worsened, and communal and voluntary associations had difficulty raising revenues for charitable and other institutions. Jews responded by dispersing to smaller communities. In this social context and in light of the growing number of Jews conversant with the secular culture of the Enlightenment, rabbinical and communal authority declined.

THE QUESTION OF EMANCIPATION (1750–1815)

The partitioning of Poland carried out between 1772 and 1795 had a great impact on Jewish social history. The partitions divided Europe's largest Jewish population among three states that would follow very different Jewish policies. Around 1 million Polish Jews became subjects of the Russian Empire, which had banned Jewish settlement. Russia granted Jewish communal institutions limited autonomy but imposed new civil disabilities. Over 200,000 Galician Jews came under Austrian rule, joining the 70,000 Bohemian and 80,000 Hungarian Jews in the Habsburg Empire. In 1781 Emperor Joseph II reduced legal disabilities but left residency restrictions in place. Jews in western Poland were put under the authority of Prussia, where a debate had arisen over transforming Jews into useful members of civil society by ending legal disabilities. But the question of emancipation was put most forcefully in France, which had only a small Jewish population.

In December 1789 the French national assembly considered the question of Jewish emancipation. Debate over the civil status of France's forty thousand Jews ended in September 1791 with recognition of their equal rights, and emancipation forced the problems of integration and Jewish identity to the foreground. Were Jews a separate nation or simply adherents of a different religion? Now that law no longer required segregation, would Jews assimilate or remain ghettoized?

Emancipation relaxed external constraints, but reactions varied. France's two principle Jewish communities, the Sephardim in Bordeaux and Bayonne and the Ashkenazim in Alsace, had developed along different lines. Sephardim had resident status and had formed a prosperous merchant community with close ties to Amsterdam and London. In Alsace, Jews lived in small ghettoized communities of poor tradespeople.

JEWISH MESSIANISM

One transnational response to violence in the sixteenth century was the strengthening of mystical currents in Jewish life. The mystical teachings of Rabbi Isaac Luria in the late 1500s, for instance, spread quickly from Safed (in Galilee) to the ghettos of Vienna, Amsterdam, and other centers of European Jewish life, as did the teachings of Rabbi Judah Loew of Prague. Messianism promising redemption and justice—a common current of seventeenth-century European popular religious culture—reflected growing social tensions in the ghetto and the constant threat of violence. Anti-Jewish violence contributed to Jewish messianism, which found its greatest popular expression in the Sabbatian movement. Shabbetai Tzevi of Smyrna was one of several self-proclaimed messiahs to appear in the sixteenth and seventeenth centuries. Shabbetai declared himself the Messiah in 1648, but his movement had little impact in Europe. In 1665, though, news of the Messiah's arrival spread from Salonica, the epicenter of Sabbatianism, through Jewish communities across Europe. The movement had broad appeal, and popular messianic fervor lasted for nearly a year, triggering anti-Jewish riots in several cities in Poland and Germany. Arrested in Constantinople by the sultan in 1666, Shabbetai's subsequent conversion to Islam halted the movement but did not destroy the underlying basis of popular Jewish mysticism, which reemerged, for instance, in Hasidism in eastern Europe.

During the French Revolution prosperous Jews in Bordeaux defined themselves as French citizens of the Jewish faith and identified with the new national state. Alsatian Jews, in contrast, retained communal associations and traditions and identified with their own communities. Emancipation introduced many individual and community responses, from assimilation (exiting the community) to radical assertion of Jewish differences.

SOCIAL UPHEAVALS IN THE LONG NINETEENTH CENTURY (1789–1914)

During the nineteenth century the movement of people and ideas across borders still contributed to cultural homogeneity among Jews, even as they integrated

HASKALAH AND HASIDISM

The Jewish encounter with modernity produced complex social tendencies toward both acculturation and the renegotiation of community and identity. These tendencies were evident even before 1789 in two social phenomena born of the late eighteenth century, the *Haskalah* (Enlightenment) and Hasidism (the doctrine of piety).

The Enlightenment spread to Jewish society only in the late 1700s in the form of the *Haskalah*. In Berlin a circle of scholars around Moses Mendelssohn embraced the scientific and universalistic worldview of the German Enlightenment and rejected religious obscurantism but not Judaism. A second, independent center of Jewish Enlightenment developed in Prague. Enlightened Jews (*maskilim*) argued for Jewish renewal through reform and integration into European society. In the 1780s *maskilim* began calling for an end to Jewish legal disabilities. The *Haskalah* emphasized self-understanding and the cultivation of individuality, which like its universalism deemphasized communal identity. These principles, particularly attractive to elites, spread primarily through literature and the founding of new Jewish schools. The *Haskalah* penetrated a broader strata of German Jewish society only after the French Revolution.

Hasidism posed a more immediate threat to traditional authority though from a different theological, sociological, and geographical position. With roots in seventeenth-century mystical currents, Hasidism emerged in the mid-1700s in southern Poland. Its progenitor, Israel Bacal Shem Tov (the Teacher of the Good Word), merged cabalism with the elevation of wholehearted devotion over talmudic scholarship. In practice Hasidism combined this doctrine with the veneration of charismatic rabbis in dynastic "master-disciple" communities. The movement spread far more rapidly than did the *Haskalah*, had great currency with poor Jews, and was enormously successful in rural districts of eastern Europe. Its penetration into Lithuania and Belorussia and into urban areas created conflicts with *kehillot*, as Hasidim rejected communal oligarchs and established their own separate courts and schools. This challenge coincided with the Polish assault on Jewish autonomy and the partitions of Poland.

into European life. A greater proportion of Jews than non-Jews rose into the middle class, and resentment of Jewish social mobility and the public's association of them with the dislocations of capitalism blended with anti-Semitism. Embourgeoisement, though, was more typical of communities of western and central Europe than of the larger populations in eastern Europe, where the majority clung to petty bourgeois status or hovered between the working class and abject poverty. Political contexts shaped the differing paths open to Jews, and divergent social trends manifested themselves along an east-west axis. Demographic stagnation held in western and central Europe, while the Jewish population continued to rise more rapidly than the general population in eastern Europe. Overpopulation and poverty fueled an exodus westward in the late 1800s, creating new tensions within communities and feeding popular anti-Semitism

Prior to the late twentieth century historians juxtaposed Jewish assimilation in western and central Europe against Jewish traditionalism in the East. According to this paradigm, emancipation destroyed communal authority, assimilated Jews, and either redefined Jewishness as a solely religious attribute or rejected it. Historians of the late twentieth century distinguished between assimilation and acculturation and recognized that communal structures proved tenacious. In Britain communal associations actually strengthened. By 1860 thirty-five thousand publicly acculturated Sephardic and Ashkenazic British citizens privately supported Jewish communal institutions, synagogues, schools, and welfare agencies; lived on predominantly Jewish streets; and maintained Jewish homes, the significance of which differed between Orthodox and Reform Jews. Debates over communal authority, Jewish identity, and integration intensified in the late 1800s as a consequence of immigration from the East. French Jews did not routinely abandon their Jewish identity when affiliating with the French nation. Some wealthy Jews broke ties with communal institutions, which were then voluntary, but most Jews did not. Acculturation began to affect rural Jewish life only when the village economy declined and state educational institutions penetrated the Alsatian countryside in the late 1800s.

In Germany and Italy the piecemeal process of emancipation culminated with national unification. Individual German states granted partial Jewish legal and economic integration, which sped acculturation. One of the most significant measures was the inclusion of Jewish children in compulsory state schooling. Although acceptance into the German middle class required assimilation, in the 1840s most Jews remained at least partially segregated and practiced endogamy. Legislation in the 1860s eliminated legal disabilities, and the unified state abolished compulsory membership in *kehillot* in 1876. Emancipation and Germany's rapid economic growth accelerated embourgeoisement and acculturation but did not eradicate Jewish identity. Middle-class Jews, while subscribing to the German emphasis on moral education and self-cultivation, formed new Jewish mutual aid, reading, and insurance societies, clubs, and associations. The renegotiated German Jewish identity united an otherwise religiously and socially fragmented community, and politicized hostility toward Jews reinforced this sense of identity. While tensions between German, Czech, and Magyar cultural loyalties complicated acculturation in the Habsburg Empire, Austrian and Hungarian cities underwent similar processes.

Although Jews could be found at all levels of the nineteenth-century economy, from wealthy bankers like the Rothschilds to laborers at the margins of poverty, most Jews in western and central Europe rose into the middle classes. Relatively few, though, entered the industrial bourgeoisie, instead benefiting from the expansion of commerce and the professions. In Germany, where over half of all Jews had lived in poverty in the mid-1700s, tax records indicate that nearly 80 percent were bourgeois by 1870. Germany's 470,000 Jews constituted only 1 percent of the country's population but accounted for nearly a quarter of its bankers and 10 percent of its merchants. Jews in Britain, France, Italy, and the cities of Austria-Hungary also rose into the middle class. In Budapest, Jews dominated the liberal professions, journalism, and the arts and occupied a disproportionate number of places in the secondary schools and universities.

Rapid urbanization and declining birthrates accompanied embourgeoisement in most of western and central Europe. As states lifted residency restrictions and education and economic opportunities opened, Jews gravitated toward cities. Jewish urban populations rose most dramatically in Austria-Hungary. Only 290 Jews lived in Vienna in 1806, but 146,926 Jews lived there in 1900 (9 percent of the population). In Budapest between 1870 and 1900 the number of Jews rose from 44,747 to 166,198 (24 percent of the population). But like the middle class in general, western and central European Jews had begun limiting family sizes, and their birthrates and death rates remained lower than those of the general population. The nineteenth century's massive Jewish population expansion, from approximately 2.7 million in 1825 to 8.7 million in 1900, resulted entirely from demographic trends in eastern and southeastern Europe.

By the late nineteenth century most Jews lived in the Russian Empire, where government policies re-

WOMEN AND ACCULTURATION

Public acculturation into the dominant culture and private renegotiation of Jewish identity were manifest in women's roles. Bourgeois Jewish women in Germany, for example, ensured that their children dressed, spoke, and carried themselves as Germans. They insisted that Jewish communities recognize the shifts in gender roles taking place in German society as a whole. Yet they still participated in exclusively Jewish women's organizations; transmitted Jewish cultural traditions to their children, although not always by observing Jewish rituals; maintained Jewish family networks; associated Jewishness with a respectable family life; and socialized primarily with other Jews.

stricted them to western provinces known as the Pale of Settlement. The state initially recognized *kehillot* but also required that Jews, like all other subjects, enroll in a social estate. Most Jews belonged to the town-dwellers' estate, although a few were registered as peasants, merchants, honorary citizens, and even nobles. Until 1880 most restrictions placed on Jews applied to all nonnoble subjects, who were denied freedom of movement and, as town-dwellers, could not reside in rural districts. In the Pale, though, Jews provided the trade nexus between town and country. The state periodically expelled them from rural districts, then subsequently relaxed restrictions out of economic necessity.

Early-nineteenth-century Russian-Jewish social history reached its nadir under Nicholas I, who in 1827 rescinded Jews' exemption from the military and began conscripting Jewish boys, who were removed from their homes and pressured into conversion. Between 1827 and 1854 about seventy thousand Jews were conscripted, of whom nearly fifty thousand were minors. Consequently conflicts within the Jewish community amplified as resentment grew against the privileged elite, who dominated communal boards and arranged for their own sons' exemptions. State policies and economic differentiation accentuated these tensions. In 1844 the state weakened the *kehillot* by abolishing communal boards but did not abolish the communal association itself. Communal associations still governed most aspects of Jewish social and devotional life, although under stricter state supervision, but antagonisms against communal leaders festered as communities were torn between acculturation and the reassertion of tradition.

Historical generalizations about the traditionalism of eastern European Jews require qualification. In the mid-nineteenth century a minority of Russian Jews followed a path of embourgeoisement and acculturation similar to that occurring in the West. This process accelerated in the 1850s through the 1870s as industry and trade expanded and the state liberalized its Jewish policies. In the 1860s child conscription ended, and the state permitted Jews in professions and in state schools to live beyond the Pale. By 1880 Jews accounted for less than 4 percent of the empire's total population but 12 percent of its students and 14 percent of its university students. Growing numbers of Jews entered the professions, where they were disproportionately represented in law, medicine, and banking, and a handful of Jewish entrepreneurs amassed large fortunes. By 1897 nearly a quarter of the empire's Jews could read Russian, and the percentage was higher in cities. Embourgoisement and acculturation increased conflicts between *maskilim* (enlightened Jews) and traditional rabbis, both of whom claimed to speak for the community.

But in the 1880s state policies constrained Jewish embourgeoisement in Russia. In the wake of pogroms, the government in 1882 issued laws banning new Jewish settlements outside of towns and cities, which debilitated the already declining Jewish trade in the countryside and contributed to urbanization. The state also imposed quotas on Jews' access to higher education. In 1887 Jews could constitute only 10 percent of students in state schools in the Pale, 5 percent outside the Pale, and 3 percent in Moscow and St. Petersburg. In 1889 Jews were banned from legal practice.

Most eastern European Jews remained poor. In 1897 about a third of Russia's Jewish males were petty traders with small shops or stores or were peddlers. At least 300,000 Jews, including several thousand women, worked in small plants concentrated in the consumer sector, and a much greater number toiled in artisanal shops. Another 10 percent of adult Jews were day laborers or domestics, while nearly a tenth had no regular employment. Fewer than 3 percent of Jews farmed. Population growth, restrictions on movement and occupations, and changes in transport and trade that undermined traditional Jewish rural occupations contributed to growing poverty. By 1900 nearly 20 percent of all Jews in the Pale relied on charity from either the commune or Jewish philanthropic associations.

Jewish demographic patterns in eastern Europe resembled those of western and central Europe in two regards. The Jewish population became increasingly urban as people migrated in search of economic and social opportunities, and Jewish death rates fell below those of the general population. But unlike western and central Europe, the Jewish population in eastern Europe rose more rapidly than the general population. Between 1772 and 1897 the Jewish population of the Pale grew from 1 million to over 5 million people, and Jews constituted 11 percent of the Pale's population and over half the population of many urban districts. Similarly, between 1825 and 1900 the Jewish population grew in Galicia from 275,000 to over 800,000 (11 percent of the total population) and in Hungary from 200,000 to 852,000 (5 percent of the total population). Overpopulation, poverty, government repression, and anti-Jewish violence prompted mass emigration, and between 1880 and 1914 over 3 million Jews left eastern Europe. While the majority resettled in the Americas, nearly a million moved to western and central Europe.

This exodus changed Jewish communities, creating new internal tensions and feeding popular anti-Semitism. In Germany, in 1880 foreign-born Jews accounted for 3 percent of the Jewish population, but immigrants constituted 13 percent of all Jews there by 1910. In Britain immigration brought a surge in Jewish residents, from 60,000 in 1880 to 300,000 by 1914. Bourgeois Jews generally considered poor, Yiddish-speaking immigrants to be backward, excessively traditional, a burden on the community, and a threat to acculturation and acceptance. Anti-Semites cited the immigrants as evidence of Jewish racial inferiority. The alleged threat posed by poor Jews competing for low-paying jobs and cheap housing became a staple of anti-Semitic rhetoric and thereby contributed to popular anti-Semitism, especially in Britain.

Modern, political anti-Semitism arose later in the century, built on religious and economic hatreds, resentment of Jews' upward mobility, fear that Jewish influence corroded the national culture, and new racial theories. Political anti-Semitism was also based on traditional views, of course, but they involved new arguments, groups, and manifestations, though historians debate how much change occurred. Following the 1873 stock market crash, mass politics, particularly but not exclusively on the right, commonly identified the Jewish middle class with corporate capitalism and charged that Jews exercised undue influence. Scapegoating blamed Jews for a variety of ills, from department stores and banks to socialism. Political anti-Semitism was a complex social phenomenon that drew support from those who felt threatened by economic and cultural change, including elements of the middle classes, the working class, the aristocracy, and the peasantry. As a force in German politics, it reached its apogee in the 1880s, supported by several popular intellectuals as well as a political party. But in Austrian cities, where the Jewish middle class was most prominent, anti-Semitism based on resentment of Jewish social mobility remained a mass political movement through 1912. In Britain the influx of cheap Jewish labor, the identification of Jews with big business, and the political influence of Jewish grandees fostered political anti-Semitism in the 1890s. In France those same factors plus the rise of Jews into state service contributed to political anti-Semitism at the end of the century. False accusations of spying charged against a Jewish army officer brought the surprisingly strong Dreyfus movement to a head in the 1890s. But in nineteenth-century western and central Europe political anti-Semitism rarely translated into anti-Jewish violence.

Popular anti-Semitism was more intense and more violent in eastern Europe. In 1882 pogroms broke out in Hungary, where resentment of Jews' social mobility was compounded by their association with the Magyar elite. Anti-Jewish violence was recurrent in Romania, where virulent anti-Semitism cut across the political and social spectrum. To peasants Jews were parasitic agents of the landlords, the weak Romanian middle class considered Jews dangerous economic rivals, and intellectuals argued that immigrant Galician and Russian Jews threatened Romanian nationhood. Russia experienced waves of pogroms in 1881–1882, 1903, and 1905. Government policies and anti-Semitic instigation fomented violence, but savage attacks on Jews, like that in Kishinev in 1903, were complex social events. Peasants who associated Jews with economic exploitation participated in attacks, but so did members of the middle class, who saw Jews as competition, and workers, for whom Jews represented both the class enemy and rivals for work and housing. Workers perpetrated most of the violence in Odessa, for instance, where more than three hundred Jews were killed in 1905.

Jews actively participated in mass social movements and mass politics. They enrolled in national parties across the political spectrum. Jewish intellectuals, often assimilated, were heavily represented in leftist movements. Specifically Jewish mass movements developed as well, as emancipation and acculturation failed to end discrimination and anti-Jewish violence. The General Jewish Workers' Bund, a social democratic party promoting Jewish cultural autonomy, attracted broad support among Jewish factory workers and artisans in the Russian Empire. Political Zionism proved even more important as a trans-European movement. Jewish nationalism united a diverse range of Zionists, from secular liberal members of Theodor

Herzl's World Zionist Organization, to Zionist socialists, to Orthodox supporters of the religious party *Mizrachi*. Zionists argued that antagonisms against Jews would not disappear and Jews must therefore emancipate themselves by creating their own national state or territory. The events of 1914 through 1945 seemed to prove the Zionists' point.

EUROPE'S JEWS IN THE AGE OF TOTAL WAR (1914–1945)

World War I severely disrupted Jewish life. In every country charges proliferated that Jews profited off the war and lacked loyalty to their homelands. Yet Jews volunteered and were conscripted for service, often in percentages higher than the general population. In Britain 14 percent of the Jewish population served, compared with 11 percent of the total population. Nearly 18 percent of Germany's Jews served, as did 20 percent of France's Jews and 11 percent of the Jews in Austria-Hungary. Some 300,000 Jews served in the Russian army. Jews accounted for roughly 1 percent of the total population of the countries engaged in the war but made up 2 percent of all conscripted soldiers.

The majority of Europe's Jews lived within major war zones in the East and suffered deprivations along with the general population, including devastation, hunger, and epidemics. Some 400,000 Galician Jews fled to western Austria during the war, creating a refugee crisis in cities like Vienna, where largely acculturated local communities swelled with waves of traditional Orthodox and Hasidic Jews. In Russia popular anti-Jewish sentiment was matched by the government's fear that Jews would sympathize with Germany. In 1915 the Russian military expelled more than 600,000 Jews from the Pale into the country's interior, creating another mass refugee crisis. As the war dragged on economic hardships increased, and so did anti-Semitic agitation and outbreaks of anti-Jewish violence, particularly in central and eastern Europe. This was especially true in regions devastated by fighting and occupation, such as Galicia and western Ukraine. But popular anti-Semitism raged in Germany and Austria as well. The collapse of old regimes in central and eastern Europe in 1917 and 1918 then loosed mass anti-Jewish violence.

Revolutions in Russia, Germany, and Hungary resulted in greater civil equality for Jews, but the association of Jews with leftist upheavals added another dimension to political and popular anti-Semitism. In Russia the provisional government formed in March 1917 recognized Jewish civil equality, ushering in a brief but fruitful period of Jewish political and social organization. But deteriorating economic conditions again heightened resentment toward Jews, whom nationalist parties charged with profiteering and promoting Bolshevism. Charges that Jews controlled the Bolshevik (Communist) Party became a rightist commonplace after the October 1917 Revolution, but anti-Jewish violence knew no political boundaries during Russia's civil war, from 1918 to 1921. Communist and anti-Communist forces both carried out atrocities in Russia and Ukraine. Ukraine alone experienced more than two thousand pogroms at a cost of as many as forty thousand lives. Most Jewish communities eventually sought accommodation in Vladimir Ilich Lenin's government, which proved less hostile than its military opponents. Because of that relationship and the number of assimilated Jews in the Bolshevik leadership, political anti-Semites equated the Communist regime with Jews. Similarly Jewish participation in and support for the Social Democrats in the 1918 German revolution and during the Weimar Republic fed into political anti-Semitism, as did the prominence of Jews in Béla Kun's short-lived Communist regime in Hungary in 1919.

In the wake of the war, declining Jewish birthrates, which characterized demographic trends in western and central Europe, extended to the ravaged communities of eastern Europe. The birthrate among Polish Jews, for instance, dropped by nearly 50 percent between 1900 and 1934. Most social patterns prevailing before the war continued, often at an accelerated rate. Intermarriage became increasingly common across Europe, especially among working-class Jews and in urban districts. In Germany more than half of all Jews who married between 1926 and 1929 chose non-Jewish spouses. The pace of urbanization accelerated, so by 1925 more than a quarter of Europe's Jews lived in cities with populations of 1 million or more. In Germany, where some 550,000 Jews accounted for less than 1 percent of the population, two-thirds of the Jewish population lived in six large cities. Acculturation remained complex. Increases in out-marriage and declining religious observance came with expanded Jewish political, social, and cultural activity and a revived interest in Jewish culture and history in the 1920s. This continuing renegotiation of Jewish identity took place not only in major centers for Jewish learning, like Berlin and Vilna, but also in the USSR, where the state tried to detach Jewish cultural identity from its religious foundations and encouraged Jews to take up "useful labor."

Jewish acculturation, though, did not prevent the rise of anti-Semitism during the interwar period of instability and cultural change. In most of Europe in the 1920s, Jewish social mobility and influence in politics, the economy, and cultural life escalated pop-

ular resentments. The 1929 stock market crash and the Great Depression spurred mass mobilization of popular anti-Semitism. In Romania the Iron Guard, which called for the destruction of Romanian Jewry, emerged as the third largest political party. But the Nazi movement in Germany most effectively mobilized anti-Jewish sentiment and transformed anti-Semitism into a central aspect of state policy.

From 1933 to 1937, Nazi Jewish policy reversed the achievements of Jewish emancipation and integration in Germany. Historians debate the extent to which Nazi racial theories resonated with the general public, but it is generally agreed that Nazi anti-Semitism tapped into the popular association of Jews with social disruption. While prohibitions on marriage or even intercourse between Jews and non-Jews elicited little enthusiasm, laws stripping Jews of citizenship rights, removing them from government service and educational institutions, attacking their participation in the media and cultural activities, and circumscribing their economic activities were popular. The 1935 Nürnberg Laws establishing strict racial classifications of Jews similarly elicited virtually no public opposition. By 1937, though, only 130,000 of Germany's 540,000 "racial Jews" had emigrated. Restrictions in the West deterred the flow of refugees, and many acculturated Jews preferred to remain in their homeland. Nazi disruption of Jewish public and economic life in a sense strengthened Jewish communal institutions and structures. Jewish welfare and educational institutions became essential as the Nazis isolated Jews from public life, and new forms of communal representation took shape.

From 1938 until 1941, the stated goals of Nazi Jewish policy were the removal of all Jews from greater Germany and, pending that outcome, their complete isolation and segregation. Historians debate whether the Nazis followed a deliberate program (the "intentionalist" perspective) or whether the "Final Solution to the Jewish Problem" developed piecemeal (the "functionalist" view). Nazi policy clearly became radicalized in 1938, as the regime faced flagging popular support and embarked on an expansionist foreign policy. Annexation of Austria and Czechoslovakia in 1938 and 1939 brought more than 400,000 Jews into the Nazi orbit. In 1938 the Nazis openly encouraged pogroms; repealed the legal status of *kehillot* and dissolved most Jewish public organizations; stripped Jews of property and the rights to engage in labor, trade, or professional activities; and imposed other punitive and restrictive measures. Still, previous to 1939 public expectation that the state would maintain law and order constrained the regime's use of overt violence against Jews. In the meantime the Nazis endorsed the creation of a national Jewish communal organization. The organization facilitated the emigration of another 100,000 Jews, created a network of Jewish schools, and provided welfare for the masses of Jews impoverished by Nazi policies, in part by taxing those who still had property. The extent of Jewish poverty in the prewar Nazi realm is illustrated by conditions in Austria, where 32,000 of 58,000 Jews relied on communal welfare in fall 1939.

The September 1939 German invasion of Poland and the onset of war initiated a new stage in Nazi policy. The regime began deporting Jews from greater Germany to occupied Poland, where it concentrated Jews in ghettos. It also began using Polish Jews as slave laborers and in 1940 established the first concentration camps in Poland. The overcrowded ghetto populations of Warsaw, Łódź, and other cities suffered from hunger, disease, and grinding poverty. Once again communal councils bore the responsibility for social welfare, education, and the conduct of ghetto residents, and mediated relations with Nazi officials. Research emphasizes the variety of Jewish responses to ghettoization and divisions in the ghetto community, and there is controversy among historians particularly over the extent and significance of collaboration with the Nazis by communal councils struggling to create a modicum of social stability in desperate conditions. In occupied western Europe the Nazis imposed discriminatory laws on Jews in 1940, but a number of factors, including Nazi administrative difficulties, manpower shortages, and the high level of integration of Jews into society, prevented them from implementing reconcentrations, or roundups, for forced labor until 1942.

Nazi policy toward Jews became openly genocidal with the June 1941 invasion of eastern Poland and the USSR. Mobile killing units slaughtered well over a million Jews, often in mass actions, like the murder of 33,000 people at Babi Yar outside Kiev in September 1941. In December Nazi forces began using gas to kill Jews at extermination camps like Chełmno. By spring 1942 the Nazis had murdered some 1.5 million Jews. As the 1942 offensive in the east bogged down, the genocide escalated. Mass exterminations began at Auschwitz, Majdanek, and other labor camps, and the Nazis began mass deportations of Jews to camps and began killing Jews in ghettos. German military and police units, together with local collaborators, killed masses of Jews in smaller eastern European cities and towns. In summer 1942 the Nazis and collaborating local officials began relocating western European Jews to ghettos and concentration camps in the East. In the camps those incapable of work, in particular children and the elderly, were murdered directly; those who could work starved or were worked to death. By February 1943 the Jewish death toll had risen to over 4 million. As the war on the eastern front turned against Germany in 1943, the Nazis "liquidated" most remaining eastern European ghettos, killing residents outright or sending them to camps, while deportations to the camps continued in occupied territories across Europe. The last mass deportations, commenced in April 1944, removed the Hungarian Jews. In November 1944 gassing in the camps ended, but mass deaths in the camps continued as the Nazi war effort collapsed. Tens of thousands of Jews died of starvation and disease in the war's final weeks. By the end of the war the Holocaust had claimed the lives of between 5,596,000 and 5,860,000 Jews, approximately 60 percent of Europe's Jewish population. The death tolls were highest in eastern Europe—in Poland, the USSR, Hungary, Romania, and Lithuania.

No general social-historical interpretation of the Holocaust has emerged, although social-history methods have been applied to questions ranging from the social order in the ghettos and concentration camps to the brutalizing effects of war on the eastern front. Three issues reveal the difficulty of generalization: the social basis of support for genocidal policies in Germany, the social basis of collaboration with Nazi extermination policy in occupied territories, and the nature of Jewish resistance. Although it has been argued that the German populace as a whole shared "eliminationist" anti-Semitic attitudes, most Germans welcomed the exclusion of Jews but remained passive and silent in the face of Nazi genocide. Policemen and soldiers involved in mass killings relied on anti-Semitism to rationalize their atrocities, but the brutality and dehumanization of war on the eastern front and the pressures toward conformity were equally important factors in their actions. In much of western Europe, Nazi sympathizers and local officials collaborated in the deportation of Jews. Even in France and Holland, though, where collaboration was greatest, local officials were more willing to deport foreign Jews than natives. In both western and eastern Europe collaboration in Nazi atrocities transcended social categories. Peasant cooperation was especially common in eastern Europe, the product of long-standing anti-Semitism and antipathy toward Jewish middlemen in the countryside, accentuated by wartime hardships. Finally, the lack of widespread, armed Jewish resistance to the Nazis was a function not simply of passivity but also of the difficulty of obtaining arms and mounting resistance in the ghettos and camps. Even though few ghetto councils prepared for resistance and armed rebellion meant annihilation, revolts occurred in the Warsaw ghetto (April–May 1943) and

Nazi Genocide. Residents of the Warsaw ghetto being rounded up, April 1943. ©ROGER-VIOLLET

at the camps at Sobibor (October 1943) and Auschwitz (October 1944). Moreover thousands of escaped Jews joined armed resistance movements, and an armed underground formed in several ghettos.

A VANISHING DIASPORA? (1945–2000)

In the first few years following the war, at least a third of Europe's surviving Jews lived in displaced-persons camps, where they struggled to rebuild shattered families and community structures. The experience of the Holocaust cast a shadow over all aspects of Jewish life, in particular survivors' family lives. In general, though, the dominant patterns in post-1945 Jewish social history continued or elaborated pre-Holocaust dynamics.

Demographic trends in postwar Europe continued patterns established in the late 1800s. The first and most dramatic trend was mass emigration. The main destinations of emigrants were the Americas and Israel, established in 1948. By 1967 nearly a million Jews, a quarter of Europe's surviving Jewish population, had emigrated. Emigration increased after the period 1989–1991, as Jews fled eastern Europe and the former USSR. A second trend was continued declining birthrates among Europe's aging Jewish population, though the birthrates were no longer lower than those of the general populations. Between emigration and declining birthrates, Europe's Jewish population declined steadily. In 1946 Europe's surviving Jewish population was just under 4 million. By 1967

that number had fallen to just over 3 million with declines of over 300,000 in Romania, 200,000 in Poland, and 120,000 in Germany. By 1994 fewer than 2 million Jews remained, and the number in the former USSR fell by a million between 1967 and the end of the century. Only in Spain and France did Jewish populations rise. At the close of the twentieth century France's Jewish community numbered over 500,000, nearly a third of Europe's Jews. Many were immigrants from North Africa. Two other nineteenth-century social patterns, the paired processes of acculturation and embourgeoisement, also continued, and the meanings of Jewish identity and community remained contested.

Anti-Semitism, too, remained a factor in postwar Jewish life regardless of the decline in Jewish populations. Jews in Eastern Europe faced waves of state-sanctioned anti-Semitism in the first decade after the war, especially in Poland and the USSR. In periods of political or social tension, communist regimes sought to manipulate popular anti-Semitism. Ironically, one of the major elements of Eastern European popular anti-Semitism was the belief that Jews controlled the Communist parties. While a high percentage of Jews participated in several Eastern European Communist parties, most were later purged, as in Poland in 1967 and 1968. The most overt anti-Jewish violence was in Poland, where pogroms took the lives of as many as 1,500 Jews between 1945 and 1947. During the postcommunist social disruption of the 1990s, nationalist

444

HOLOCAUST DEATHS

Country	Prewar Jewish Population	Low Estimate of Jewish Deaths	High Estimate of Jewish Deaths
Austria	185,000	50,000	50,000
Belgium	65,700	28,900	28,900
Bohemia and Moravia	118,310	78,150	78,150
Bulgaria	61,000	11,000	11,000
Denmark	7,800	60	60
Estonia	4,500	1,500	2,000
Finland	2,000	7	7
France	350,000	77,320	77,320
Germany	185,000	134,500	141,500
Greece	66,380	49,000	56,000
Hungary	825,000	550,000	569,000
Italy	44,500	7,680	7,680
Latvia	91,500	70,000	71,500
Lithuania	168,000	140,000	143,000
Luxembourg	3,500	1,950	1,950
Netherlands	140,000	100,000	100,000
Norway	1,700	762	762
Poland	3,300,000	2,900,000	3,000,000
Romania	609,000	271,000	287,000
Slovakia	88,950	68,000	71,000
USSR	3,020,000	1,000,000	1,100,000
Yugoslavia	78,000	56,200	63,300
Total	9,415,840	5,596,029	5,860,129

Source: Vital, 1999, p. 897.

movements in eastern Europe and Russia sought to manipulate popular anti-Semitism by associating Jews with both communism and rapacious capitalism. In western and central Europe ultranationalist movements played on the established themes of popular anti-Semitism. In France and Germany expressions of political and popular anti-Semitism were most common during periods of economic stagnation. Still, popular anti-Semitism remained a complex social phenomenon.

See also **Judaism** *(volume 5); and other articles in this section.*

BIBLIOGRAPHY

Abramson, Henry. *A Prayer for the Government: Ukrainians and Jews in Revolutionary Times, 1917–1920.* Cambridge, Mass., 1999.

Baron, Salo Wittmayer. *A Social and Religious History of the Jews.* 2d ed. 18 vols. New York, 1983.

Bauer, Yehuda. *The Jewish Emergence from Powerlessness.* Toronto, 1979.

Birnbaum, Pierre. *Anti-Semitism in France: A Political History from Leon Blum to the Present.* Oxford, 1992.

Birnbaum, Pierre. *The Jews of the Republic: A Political History of State Jews in France from Gambetta to Vichy.* Translated by Jane Marie Todd. Stanford, Calif., 1996.

Birnbaum, Pierre, and Ira Katznelson, eds. *Paths of Emancipation: Jews, States, and Citizenship.* Princeton, N.J., 1995.

Browning, Christopher R. *Ordinary Men: Reserve Police Battalion 101 and the Final Solution in Poland.* New York, 1992.

Dawidowicz, Lucy S. *The War against the Jews, 1933–1945.* New York, 1975.

Dubnov, S. M. *History of the Jews in Russia and Poland, from the Earliest Times until the Present Day.* Translated from the Russian by Israel Friedlaender. 3 vols. Philadelphia, 1916.

Engelman, Uriah Zevi. *The Rise of the Jew in the Western World: A Social and Economic History of the Jewish People of Europe.* New York, 1973.

Frankel, Jonathan, ed. *Studies in Contemporary Jewry.* Vol. 4: *The Jews and the European Crisis, 1914–21.* New York, 1988.

Frankel, Jonathan, and Steven J. Zipperstein, eds. *Assimilation and Community: The Jews in Nineteenth-Century Europe.* Cambridge, U.K., 1992.

Gay, Ruth. *The Jews of Germany: A Historical Portrait.* New Haven, Conn., 1992.

Gerber, Jane S. *The Jews of Spain: A History of the Sephardic Experience.* New York, 1992.

Gilman, Sander L., and Steven T. Katz, eds. *Anti-Semitism in Times of Crisis.* New York, 1991.

Gitelman, Zvi. *A Century of Ambivalence: The Jews of Russia and the Soviet Union, 1881 to the Present.* New York, 1988.

Gitelman, Zvi, ed. *Bitter Legacy: Confronting the Holocaust in the USSR.* Bloomington, Ind., 1997.

Goldhagen, Daniel Jonah. *Hitler's Willing Executioners: Ordinary Germans and the Holocaust.* New York, 1996.

Gordon, Sarah. *Hitler, Germans, and the "Jewish Question."* Princeton, N.J., 1984.

Gow, Andrew Colin. *The Red Jews: Antisemitism in an Apocalyptic Age, 1200–1600.* Leiden, Netherlands, 1995.

Graetz, Michael. *The Jews in Nineteenth-Century France: From the French Revolution to the Alliance Israélite Universelle.* Translated by Jane Marie Todd. Stanford, Calif., 1996.

Hertzberg, Arthur. *The French Enlightenment and the Jews.* New York, 1968.

Israel, Jonathan I. *European Jewry in the Age of Mercantilism, 1550–1750.* 3d ed. London, 1998.

Kahan, Arcadius. *Essays in Jewish Social and Economic History.* Chicago, 1986.

Katz, Jacob. *Out of the Ghetto: The Social Background of Jewish Emancipation, 1770–1870.* New York, 1978.

Kershaw, Ian. *Popular Opinion and Popular Dissent in the Third Reich, Bavaria 1933–45.* Oxford, 1983.

Langer, Lawrence L. *Holocaust Testimonies: The Ruins of Memory.* New Haven, Conn., 1991.

Langmuir, Gavin I. *History, Religion, and Antisemitism*. Berkeley, Calif., 1990.

Langmuir, Gavin. *Toward a Definition of Antisemitism*. Berkeley, Calif., 1990.

Lindemann, Albert S. *Esau's Tears: Modern Anti-Semitism and the Rise of the Jews*. Cambridge, U.K., 1997.

Lindemann, Albert S. *The Jew Accused: Three Anti-Semitic Affairs (Dreyfus, Beilis, Frank), 1894–1915*. Cambridge, U.K., 1991.

MacDonald, Kevin. *Separation and Its Discontents: Toward an Evolutionary Theory of Anti-Semitism*. Westport, Conn., 1998.

Magnus, Shulamit S. *Jewish Emancipation in a German City: Cologne, 1789–1871*. Stanford, Calif., 1997.

Marrus, Michael R. *The Holocaust in History*. Hanover, N.H., 1987.

Mayer, Arno J. *Why Did the Heavens Not Darken?: The "Final Solution" in History*. New York, 1990.

McCagg, William O., Jr. *A History of Habsburg Jews, 1670–1918*. Bloomington, Ind., 1989.

Meyer, Michael A., ed. *German-Jewish History in Modern Times*. 4 vols. New York, 1996–1998.

Pinkus, Benjamin. *The Jews of the Soviet Union: The History of a National Minority*. Cambridge, U.K., 1988.

Rogger, Hans. *Jewish Policies and Right-Wing Politics in Imperial Russia*. Berkeley, Calif., 1986.

Ro'i, Yaacov, and Avi Beker, eds. *Jewish Culture and Identity in the Soviet Union*. New York, 1991.

Rose, Paul Lawrence. *German Question/Jewish Question: Revolutionary Antisemitism from Kant to Wagner*. Princeton, N.J., 1992.

Roth, Norman. *Conversos, Inquisition, and the Expulsion of the Jews from Spain*. Madison, Wis., 1995.

Scholem, Gershom. *Sabbetai Sevi: The Mystical Messiah, 1626–1676*. Princeton, N.J., 1973.

Stow, Kenneth R. *Alienated Minority: The Jews of Medieval Latin Europe*. Cambridge, Mass., 1992.

Vital, David. *A People Apart: The Jews in Europe, 1789–1939*. Oxford, 1999.

Waddington, Raymond B., and Arthur H. Williamson, eds. *The Expulsion of the Jews: 1492 and After*. New York, 1994.

Wasserstein, Bernard. *Vanishing Diaspora: The Jews in Europe since 1945*. Cambridge, Mass., 1996.

Weinberg, Robert. *Stalin's Forgotten Zion: Birobidzhan and the Making of a Soviet Jewish Homeland: An Illustrated History, 1928–1996*. Berkeley, Calif., 1998.

Wistrich, Robert S. *Antisemitism: The Longest Hatred*. New York, 1991.

Zipperstein, Steven J. *Imagining Russian Jewry: Memory, History, Identity*. Seattle, Wash., 1999.

ROMA: THE GYPSIES

David M. Crowe

The Roma, or as they are more commonly known in the English-speaking world, the Gypsies, entered Europe in the late Middle Ages from India. Many early chronicles referred to the Roma as "Egyptians," which is the basis for the term "Gypsy." In the non-English-speaking parts of Europe, the Roma are known as *cigán, cigány, tsiganes, Zigeuner,* and similar terms. These words come from the Byzantine Greek word *Atsínganoi,* which means itinerant wanderers and soothsayers. The Roma prefer a name of their own choosing, since "Gypsy" and derivatives of *cigán* are riddled with negative stereotypical meanings. In the Roma language, Romani (Romany) or Romanes, *rom* means man or husband and is singular; *romni* is singular for a female. *Roma* is plural and is used to refer to the group as a whole. The term "Romani" can also be used as an adjective to refer to someone who is a Rom or Romni.

ORIGINS AND STATUS IN EUROPE

Three different phenomena have dramatically affected the Roma since they entered Europe from India: nomadism; non-Roma (*gadźé* or *gadje*; singular, *gadźo*) mistreatment and prejudice; and enslavement in Romania's historic provinces, Walachia and Moldavia. The Roma entered Europe in the late Middle Ages after a long, slow journey from India that began several centuries earlier. Ian Hancock uses linguistic evidence to argue that the Roma are descendants of India's Rajput warrior caste. Other Roma specialists are skeptical of these roots, though most agree that the Roma originally came from India. Regardless of their origin, the Roma picked up characteristics of a number of peoples as they migrated from India to the Balkans, which gave them the unique cultural and social traits that remain a very important aspect of Roma ethnic identity.

Nomadism has probably had the greatest impact on the Roma. Nomadism was a very common practice among peoples in the Ottoman Empire and the Balkans. What made Roma nomadism unique was its link to Roma skills and crafts. From the time that the Roma entered the Balkans, they traveled seasonally, plying their skills as metalsmiths, gunsmiths, equine specialists, and musicians. Roma women and children also played an important role in Roma economic life. Children were taught food-gathering skills, which meant occasional begging, while Roma women practiced fortune telling and small trade. Given the tenuous nature of this nomadic lifestyle, particularly after post-Reformation European states began severely to restrict Roma movement and settlement patterns, Roma women and children came to play an important role in any family's basic survival.

The Balkans were the first area in Europe that the Roma entered; they soon moved into central and eastern Europe. Most of Europe's Roma still live in these regions. Initially, the Roma were highly valued for their skills. Towns and villages looked forward to the seasonal arrival of Roma craftsmen and women fortune tellers. However, with the gradual Turkish move into the Balkans and parts of central Europe in the late fourteenth and fifteenth centuries, attitudes toward the Roma began to change. In the early sixteenth century, local and regional officials in the non-Ottoman parts of the Balkans and central Europe implemented laws that placed severe restrictions on Roma movement and settlement patterns. Increasingly, the dark-skinned, impoverished, nomadic Roma came to be viewed as something of a Turkish fifth column. And while it was true that some Roma did work for the hated Muslims and even converted to Islam, most Roma in the Balkans were Christians. Roma tradition was to adopt the religion and language of the majority ethnic group in the region where they lived while remaining close to their own ethnic traditions within the Roma family and clan. In Bulgaria, for example, Turkish census and tax records indicate that many Roma converted to Islam because it meant they would be taxed at a lower rate than Bulgarian Christians. In multiethnic areas such as Bosnia and Herzegovina,

Bulgaria, and Serbia, there were Muslim and Christian Roma.

The increasing linkage of the Roma to the Turks, particularly when combined with the upheavals triggered by the Protestant Reformation, saw the Roma pushed to the edge of Balkan and central European society. The new legal restrictions locked the Roma into a nomadic way of life that kept them marginalized and deeply impoverished. Because the nomadic Roma were almost completely illiterate, there is little information about their life and social customs from the Roma themselves at this time. The first written evidence of Romani surfaced in England in 1547. These early writings were little more than scraps of spoken Romani. It would not be until the eighteenth and nineteenth centuries that serious efforts were made by non-Roma linguists to transcribe the rich, diverse Romani dialects scattered across Europe. Since there was no body of Roma writings to detail their almost seven centuries in Europe, much of what we know about Roma life in Europe during most of this period is drawn from non-Roma sources.

Unfortunately, some of these sources are riddled with many of the negative stereotypes that have haunted the Roma. They do, though, give us a glimpse into Roma life and society. The Hungarian Slovak *Book of the Execution of the Lords of Rozmberk* (1399) notes that one Rom worked as a groom for a nobleman, Andrew. Travel documents given to Roma nomads by King Sigismud of Hungary and the Holy Roman Empire several decades later indicate that the monarch awarded these privileges to the Roma *voivode* (Romanian; prince or lord) Ladislaus because he felt the Roma had important military information on the Turks and could work as metalsmiths and musicians. Hungarian rulers so valued the Roma that in the sixteenth century the Hungarian Crown appointed a chief of the Roma to oversee a number of Roma *voivodes* in counties throughout Hungary. The Roma *voivodes* served as judges for their respective clans.

Habsburg rulers continued this tradition of appointing a Roma chief, known as a chief provisor, well into the eighteenth and nineteenth centuries. Polish kings followed similar practices, though by the eighteenth century non-Roma assumed these roles. Zoltán Zsupos describes a similar arrangement for eighteenth-century Hungarian Aurári or "gold-washing" Roma in Transylvania:

Many of our rivers and brooks carry smaller or greater amounts of gold, which are usually a grain of sand in size. . . . The collection of this gold dust has always been a concern of our country: the closer we come to the childhood of mining, the more prosperous this branch of mining seems to be. In our old books, all

the Gypsy folks are described as people making a living by washing gold. It is unambiguously proven by the data on the gold-washing Gypsies living legally in a separate voivodeship between 1747 and 1832, without any overlord.

Not only single Gypsy families, but also whole villages or settlements depended on this thankless job. . . . By the way, gold-washing does not need much expertise. The gold-washer goes to the riverbank especially after floods, placing his long table so that one end is high above ground, the other almost lying on it. He places a blanket on this table, takes his hoe, puts sand in his basket, pours it on the tables, then pours water on it until all sand is washed away. He goes on with this Sisyphian work all day. When he feels like checking on his luck, he washes his blanket, which gives him sand with iron, copper and gold dust. This he puts in a separating bowl with an opening in front. He keeps shaking it until first the sand, then the iron and the copper get out, leaving a few gold dust grains behind. These he unites with aqua fortis and takes to his exchanger, because they must deliver it officially. (Zsupos, p. 25)

Records from the fourteenth- and fifteenth-century Republic of Ragusa in what is now Croatia provide us with another view of Roma life. In 1362 a local judge ordered a jeweler in Dubrovnik to return a number of silver coins to two "Egyptians," Vlachus and Vitanus. Most of the Roma referred to in this Venetian-controlled kingdom over the next century had Slavic surnames, indicating that they came to Ragusa from other parts of the Balkans. Ragusan records also show that though the Roma were free, they rested at the lowest rung of the republic's socioeconomic ladder. Most Roma lived on the outskirts of towns and cities and worked as servants, musicians, and craftsmen.

Deep impoverishment became the hallmark of Roma existence throughout Europe. In an early seventeenth-century account, Gyorgy Thurzó, the royal governor of Hungary, described the desperate lifestyle of a Roma clan that passed through his kingdom. According to Reimer Gilsenbach, Thurzó, who had granted the Roma chieftain Franciscus and his clan a travel permit in 1616, was less driven by sympathy toward the Roma than the desire to exploit their considerable skills as arms craftsmen.

While the birds of the sky have their nests, foxes their earths, wolves their lairs, and lions and bears their dens, and all animals have their own place of habitation, the truly wretched Egyptian race, which we call *Czingaros*, is assuredly to be pitied, although it is not known whether this was caused by the tyranny of the cruel Pharaoh or the dictate of fate. In accordance with their ancient custom they are used to leading a very hard life, in fields and meadows outside the towns, under ragged tents. Thus have old and young, boys and children of this race learned, unprotected by walls, to bear with rain, cold and intense heat; they have no inherited goods on this earth, they do not seek cities, strong-

Gypsy Encampment. After an etching by Jacques Callot (c. 1592–1635). CORBIS/BETTMANN

holds, towns or princely dwellings, but wander constantly with no sure resting place, knowing no riches or ambitions, but, day by day and hour by hour, looking in the open air only for food and clothing by the labour of their hands, using anvils, bellows, hammers and tongs. (Crowe, p. 72)

These observations, particularly when combined with the practice of Roma slavery in Walachia and Moldavia, underscore the desperate plight of the Roma throughout much of their history in Europe. The first concrete evidence of Roma slavery dates from 1385, when the *voivode* Dan I confirmed an earlier gift of forty Roma families to the Monastery of St. Anthony at Vodita. Most of the early Roma slaves or *robi* were captives of war. Over time, their skills became so valuable to Romania's nobility that the institution became widespread. Roma slaves provided the nobility or boyars and monasteries with skilled labor that the serfs and free peasants could not provide. In most instances, the Romanian nobility treated their Roma slaves like cattle. In fact, it was growing embarrassment in Walachia and Moldavia over their harsh treatment that led to the emancipation of Romania's *robi* in 1864.

CLANS AND FAMILIES

Since Romania remains the home to the world's largest Roma population, it should come as no surprise that the names of many Roma slave occupations became the names of Roma clans throughout Europe. Among the groups who trace their origins to these occupations are the Aurári (gold washers), the Rudari (miners), the Ursari (bear leaders), and the Lingurari (spoon makers). Roma Lăieśi (members of a horde)

were multitalented and gave their names to a number of modern Roma clans such as the Vlach or Vlax (Walachian or Danubian), the Kirpači (basket makers), the Kovači (blacksmiths), the Čurari (sieve makers), and others. These occupations of enslavement became valued professions to the Roma that were passed from family to family and modernized over time.

These groups or tribes, which the Lovara (horse dealers) call a *rása* (race) and the Kalderása (English Kalderash, coppersmiths) a *natsia* (nation), are subdivided into *vítsi* (clans; singular, *vitsa*) or *tsérba* (Lovara for tent). Very often clan names come from the name of an ancestor, an animal, or another object of respect. Relations within the *vitsa* are familial, and marriages are encouraged as a way to strengthen these relationships. Ideally, a male should marry a cousin from within the *vitsa,* though there are occasional marriages outside of the clan. Marriages are arranged by the two fathers, and traditionally the father of the groom had to pay a significant bride-price to secure the marriage.

Below the clan is the *familia* or extended family. Individual family units are known as *tséra.* Separate from these categories is the *kumpánia* (company), which can be made up of Roma from a number of clans and families who have joined together for a common economic or other purpose. The *kumpánia* is led by a *rom báro* (big man) who deals with the *gadźé.* Disputes within the *kumpánia* are usually resolved by the *kris,* a Roma court made up of male leaders from various clans. The *kris* is headed by one or more judges, and its decision is binding on all involved in the dispute.

Although many Roma social, linguistic, and cultural traditions would remain rooted in their Romanian and Balkan past, the adaptive Roma took on new social and cultural traditions as they migrated westward and northward to other parts of Europe. There were Roma in France by the early fifteenth century, and over the next hundred years Roma groups appeared in England, Scotland, Wales, the German states, and Scandinavia. The bulk of European Roma, though, remained in the Balkans and central Europe. Some of the most important migratory groups were the Vlach Roma, who were known through the end of the twentieth century for their close adherence to traditional Roma practices such as the *kris;* the Kalderása; the Lovara; and the Čurari. The Kalderása moved to Russia, Greece, Serbia, and Bulgaria. Over time, other Roma groups settled across western Europe: the self-styled Romanichaals settled in Britain, where they are called Travellers; the Calé in southern France and Spain, where they are known as Gitanos; the Kaale in Finland; and the Sinti and Lalleri in Germany and Austria.

SOCIAL BOUNDARIES AND FORCED ASSIMILATION

As the Roma moved out of the Balkans to escape persecution, enslavement, war, and hunger, they faced prejudice and official abuse that deeply affected Roma social values and culture. To the Roma, the *gadžé* became an object of defilement and disgust. In discussing Roma fear of pollution and contamination, it is important to emphasize that the Roma are not a monolithic group. What is a common practice for one Roma group is not necessarily true for another. Many Roma groups, though, do have strong practices concerning pollution and contamination. According to Angus Fraser, these codes tend to define and set boundaries for the Roma in their relations with non-Roma. Many Balkan Roma use the term *marimé* or *marimo* (unclean), while those in western and central Europe have similar terms that define relations between males and females and between Roma and *gadžé*. According to Fraser, the worst fate to befall a Roma male is to be declared polluted. This means "social death" for the Roma male and his family. Such codes apply not only to individuals but to language, parts of the body, inanimate objects, and food. *Marimé* codes automatically make *gadžé* unclean because of their ignorance of such codes and enforce Roma distrust of the *gadžé*.

The ongoing discrimination and mistreatment of the Roma tended to fortify such practices. From the sixteenth through the eighteenth centuries, the Roma became so despised that their very survival was in question. In some of the German states and the Habsburg empire, officials threatened the Roma with branding, torture, and death for moving through their kingdoms.

Official policies toward the Roma began to change during the Enlightenment. The Habsburg rulers Maria Theresa (1740–1780) and her son Joseph II (1780–1790) tried to halt Roma nomadism and forced the Roma in their vast domains to adopt the lifestyle of sedentary Catholic peasants. Maria Theresa, who worked hand-in-hand with the future Joseph II during the second half of her reign, also tried to destroy the traditional Roma family by forcing Roma children into foster Catholic homes. Other decrees struck out against traditional Roma professions such as metalworking and music. A detailed series of censuses were taken on the Habsburg Roma in Hungary and Croatia-Slavonia from 1780 to 1783, which provided the Crown with a unique glimpse of Roma life. The censuses indicated that though a growing number of Roma fit into the new category of *Neubauern* (new peasants) or settled Roma, they did not accept their new status very well. Many Roma found ways around Habsburg policies. Some left their settlements to avoid paying taxes, while most of the Roma children in foster homes soon ran away and returned to their families. Moreover, many Hungarian noblemen resented the high costs of trying to assimilate the Roma into their local communities. Consequently, by the time that Joseph II died in 1790, many Roma were already beginning to return to their nomadic way of life. Yet Roma censuses in Hungary and Transylvania a century later indicate a much higher degree of Roma assimilation and settlement than in any other part of Europe.

ROMA MUSIC

At the very time that Maria Theresa and Joseph II were trying to force the Roma to assimilate, in some parts of Europe a new appreciation of Roma contributions to European society began to develop, particularly in the field of music. In Russia, for example, a court favorite of Catherine the Great (1762–1796), Count Aleksei Orlov, organized a Roma chapel choir on his estate that became the rave of St. Petersburg, the Russian capital. Soon no respectable nobleman of any consequence was without his private Roma choir. Over the next century, Roma themes became a constant fixture in Russian literature, drama, and music.

Aleksandr Pushkin, Russia's Shakespeare, did the most to promote the romantic image of the Roma in his lyric poem and play "The Gypsies." In certain sections of his poem, Pushkin captures the romantic image that many Russians had of the nomadic Roma.

> The Gypsies Bessarabia roam
> In noisy crowds . . . Above a river
> In tattered tents they make their home,
> From night's cool breeze seeking cover.
> In open air calm is their sleep;
> Like freedom glad their rest is . . . Under
> The rug-hung caravans there leap
> A fire's bright flames whose shadows wander
> And lick the wheels; close to the blaze,
> A family for supper gathered,
> Prepare their meal; a tame bear lies
> Behind the tent; nearby, untethered,
> The horses graze . . . The steppe all round
> Is full of life . . .
>
> "Go, proud one, leave us! We are led
> By different laws and want among us
> No murderer . . . Go where you will!
> By your black deeds and foul you wrong us
> Who do not like to wound or kill.
> Your love of freedom—how you flaunt it!
> Yet for yourself alone you want it,
> This freedom, and a stranger dwell
> Here in our midst. We're kind and humble;
> You're hard; where you dare tread, we stumble—
> So go in peace and fare you well."
> (Pushkin, "The Gypsies," pp. 65, 82)

The great Russian writer, Lev Tolstoy, the author of *War and Peace,* was fascinated by Roma music and women. His brother, Sergei, was married to a former member of a Roma chorus. Three distinct types of Roma Russian music emerged during the nineteenth century. The first was the *polevuiye tsiganskiye peisny* (Gypsy songs of the fields), which were quite simple and could be performed by a group or an individual. Another type of Roma music, the "Road House" music, was only for choral groups. The third type, the "Gypsy romances," was not Roma music at all, but music composed by Russians who copied Roma musical traditions. This type of Russian "Gypsy" music was commonly found in the home of most educated Russians.

The influence of Roma music extended beyond the confines of tsarist Russia. Franz Liszt, who once delayed a concert at the famed Bolshoi Theatre in Moscow because he was visiting with some local Roma, laid the soul of Hungarian music at the feet of the Roma. Two other Hungarian musical giants, Béla Bartók and Zoltan Kodály, strongly disagreed with Liszt's claim. In his 1924 study of Hungarian peasant music, *Magyar népdal* (The Hungarian folk song), Bartók concluded that Roma music was shallow and had a limited repertoire; in his view Roma music was not innovative and simply adapted to the musical currents of a particular period.

Roma Music. A group of four gypsy men play stringed instruments on the streets of Vienna, 1920s. ARCHIVE PHOTOS

Yet what Bartók and other non-Roma musicologists have missed in their analysis of Roma music are the private songs and tunes of the non-*gadźé* world. As Michael Stewart and Isabel Fonseca have both pointed out, music is the traditional form of expression of the Roma, and embedded in that music, whether it be instrumental or choral, are all of the deeper Roma traditions of a traditionally nomadic people. The "Gypsy" music heard in a Russian café, in a Budapest restaurant, or in the Flamenco *cafés cantantes* in Seville was quite different from that performed by Vlach Roma in their *mulatšago* (celebration) or by other Roma groups. According to Stewart, Roma music performed at the *mulatšago* was the principle vehicle for the expression of Roma feelings and personal associations. Strong traditions of gender segregation, hospitality, and respect for one another were the central themes of the music performed at the Vlach *mulatšago*. Most important, this music was sung in Romani, the purest means of Roma self-expression.

THE "GYPSY PROBLEM"

Unfortunately, the fact that Roma music fascinated European *gadźé* did little to temper the prejudice that haunted the Roma. Deep hatred toward the Roma thrived not only in the Balkans throughout the nineteenth century but also in other parts of Europe. A new wave of Roma migrations westward began in the second half of the nineteenth century as Balkan Roma fled the region to escape upheavals caused by war, revolution, and the emancipation of Romania's Roma slaves in 1864. In 1868, for example, officials in the Netherlands initiated policies designed to stop Roma from settling there. Soon after the creation of Germany three years later, the state's first chancellor, Otto von Bismarck, encouraged local officials to do everything possible to force non-German Roma out of his new Second Reich. Those allowed to remain in Germany were forced to give up their nomadic way of life.

In 1899 the Bavarian police formed a special anti-Roma squad, headed by Alfred Dillman. Six years later, Dillman published the infamous *Zigeuner Buch* (Gypsy book), which centered around the investigation of five thousand Roma, who Dillman felt were innately criminals and a societal disease. In 1906 the Prussian minister of the interior issued a directive, *Bekämpfung des Zigeunerunwesens* (Combating the Gypsy nuisance), that linked anti-Roma agreements with a number of countries throughout Europe with domestic Prussian efforts to stop Roma from continuing their nomadic way of life. In 1911 the Bavarian police sponsored a conference in Munich with delegates from other German states that discussed the "Gypsy problem." The conferees agreed to work more closely together on this matter and to add information to the *Zigeuner Buch*.

In 1922 the German state of Baden ordered that all Roma be photographed, fingerprinted, and required to carry travel permits at all times. Four years later a Bavarian law required that all Roma adopt a sedentary way of life. Those who refused could spend up to two years in a state work camp. Other German states passed similar legislation, and in 1928 a new German law placed all Roma under police surveillance. The following year the German government transformed Bavaria's special Roma bureau into the Zentralstelle zur Bekämpfung des Zigeunerunwesens (Central office for the fighting of the Gypsy nuisance), headquartered in Munich. This bureau established ties with an international police organization in Vienna to share information on the Roma throughout Europe. In 1938 the Nazis moved this office to Berlin and renamed it the Reichszentrale zur Bekämpfung des Zigeunerunwesens (Reich central office for combating the Gypsy nuisance).

When the Nazis came to power in Germany in early 1933, they considered the anti-Roma legislation and the Zentralstelle sufficient to deal with the Third Reich's thirty to thirty-five thousand Roma. The Germans also used other laws that were not Roma-specific to force foreign Roma out of the country or to sterilize those that remained in the Third Reich. However, by 1935 local pressure prompted German officials to begin to force Roma into special camps known as *Zigeunerlager* (Gypsy concentration camps). They also did a special roundup of Roma before the 1936 Berlin Olympics to hide them from international visitors.

Nazi officials also strengthened the 1935 Nuremberg Laws, which outlawed sexual relations and marriages between German Aryans and Jews, to include Roma, who they felt had *artfremdes Blut* (alien blood). The Roma were seen as a threat to German society, an asocial criminal element. Yet the Germans were not satisfied with such general designations. Robert Ritter, a German child psychologist, became the Third Reich's principle Roma expert. Ritter headed several Nazi research institutes and spent much of his time doing genealogical surveys of thirty thousand German and Austrian Roma. He and his assistant, Eva Justin, developed categories for Roma based on ancestry. These five categories ranged from *Vollzigeuner* (full-blooded Gypsy) to four different categories of *Zigeunermischling* and finally a non-Gypsy category for someone who exhibited stereotypical Gypsy "traits."

Though German officials struggled with efforts legally to deal with the Third Reich's "Gypsy problem," their solution came not through any specific law but through their dealings with the Jewish population of the countries they conquered from 1938 onward. Once the General Government was created out of what remained of the Polish state in 1939, this area became a dumping ground not only for Jews but also for Roma. Yet as late as 1941, the German failure legally to come to grips with the "Gypsy problem" meant that there were still some German and Austrian Roma (the Sinti and the Lalleri) registered for the draft, married to non-Roma, or attending public schools. As German forces swept into the Soviet Union in the summer of 1941, Nazi leaders began to lay the foundations for the Final Solution, the plan to exterminate the Jews of Europe. New anti-Roma restrictions were also put in place. At the end of 1942, Heinrich Himmler, the head of the SS and the architect of the Final Solution, ordered that all Roma in the Greater Reich (Germany, Austria, the Protectorate of Bohemia and Moravia, and parts of western Poland) be deported to Auschwitz. Himmler tried to protect pure Sinti and Lalleri Roma, whom he felt were original Aryans, though Martin Bormann, Hitler's private secretary, tried to stop this. Although Himmler convinced Hitler to side with him, few German Roma survived the Holocaust. Estimates vary, but it is reasonable to assume that between 250,000 and 500,000 European Roma were killed during the Holocaust.

STATUS SINCE WORLD WAR II

Like many other people in Europe, the Roma were devastated by the horrors and dislocations of World

DEATHS AND PERSECUTION OF ROMA DURING THE HOLOCAUST

	Prewar Roma Population	*Roma Deaths/Persecuted Roma*
### The Greater Reich		
Germany	20,000	15,000/5,000
Austria	11,200	6,500/4,700
Bohemia & Moravia	13,000	6,500/6,500
Poland	44,400–50,000	28,200–35,000/9,400–21,800
Slovenia	No figures available	
### German or German Satellite Occupation		
Albania	No figures available	
Belgium	500–600	500/100
Bosnia & Herzegovina	Figures included in Croatian deaths and persecutions	
Denmark	No figures available	
Estonia	1,000	1,000/
France	40,000	15,000–18,000/22,000–25,000
Greece	No figures available	50/
Latvia	5,000	2,500/2,500
Lithuania	1,000	1,000/
Luxembourg	200	200/
Macedonia	Included in Serbian figures	
Moldova	Included in Romanian figures	
The Netherlands	500	500/
Norway	60	60/
USSR (Russia)	200,000	30,000/170,000
Belarus & Ukraine	42,000	30,000/12,000
### German Satellite States		
Bulgaria	100,000	5,000/95,000
Croatia	28,500	26,000–28,000/500–2,500
Finland	No figures available	
Hungary	100,000	28,000/72,000
Italy	25,000	1,000/24,000
Romania	300,000	36,000/264,000
Serbia	60,000	12,000/48,000
Slovakia	80,000	1,000–6,500/73,500–79,000
Totals	*1,072,360–1,078,160*	*246,010–263,310/809,200–832,100*

War II. In central and eastern Europe, they seemed to disappear. In the regions' first postwar communist censuses, few Roma identified themselves as such. But by the mid-1950s, leaders throughout the Soviet bloc began to see dramatic increases in Roma population statistics. As usual, the Roma rested at the lowest rung of central and eastern Europe's socioeconomic ladder. Many still lived a life of nomadism, poverty, and illiteracy. Over the next three decades, states across both regions mounted major campaigns designed to improve Roma literacy, job skills, and living conditions. Governments from Prague to Moscow outlawed Roma nomadism and began to force Roma children into the public schools without any concern about their ability to speak the language of instruction. Administrators usually regarded Roma children without such skills as retarded and put them into special schools for the mentally challenged. Roma settlements were often destroyed without any regard for replacement housing. When Roma were given precious housing, little was done to help them adjust to a new, urbanized lifestyle away from the traditional Roma nomadic camps.

Over time, people in central and eastern Europe came to view the Roma as a privileged group that lived off special funds not available to the average citizen. These new stereotypes blended with the traditional prejudices toward the Roma and help explain the tremendous outpouring of anti-Roma sentiment in the region after communism collapsed in 1989. With democratization came a proliferation of anti-Roma prejudice that saw gangs of miners in Romania and skinheads in Hungary, Czechoslovakia (after 1 January 1993, the separate Czech and Slovak republics), Bulgaria, and elsewhere devastate Roma settlements and beat or murder individual Rom. The Roma became scapegoats in both central and eastern Europe for all societal problems. Efforts by groups such as the International Romani Union, Human Rights Watch, Helsinki Watch, Amnesty International, the Gypsy Research Centre, the European Community, the United Nations, and other organizations to publicize the mistreatment of the Roma helped ease their plight. The Roma themselves also began to take advantage of the new democratic rights in some of the countries in both regions to form political, cultural, and other organizations to help enhance the quality of Roma life and draw national and international attention to their problems.

The Roma in post-1948 noncommunist Europe suffered from some of the same economic and social problems, though government efforts to deal with them have been a little more enlightened and humane. The largest Roma populations outside the former Soviet bloc were in Spain, France, Greece, Italy,

ESTIMATES OF THE ROMA POPULATION
(1999)

Country	Population
Romania	1.35 million–2.5 million
Bulgaria	500,000–750,000
Spain	650,000–800,000
Hungary	550,000–800,000
Slovakia	458,000–520,000
Rump Yugoslavia (Serbia and Montenegro)	400,000–600,000
Turkey	300,000–500,000
Russia	220,000–400,000
France	280,000–340,000
Czech Republic	150,000–300,000
Greece	160,000–200,000
Italy	90,000–110,000
United Kingdom	90,000–120,000
Albania	90,000–100,000
Macedonia	110,000–260,000
Portugal	40,000–105,000
Ukraine	50,000–60,000
Bosnia and Herzegovina	35,000–80,000
Poland	15,000–50,000
The Netherlands	35,000–40,000
Croatia	30,000–40,000
Switzerland	30,000–35,000
Germany	110,000–130,000
Ireland	22,000–28,000
Austria	20,000–25,000
Moldova	20,000–25,000
Sweden	15,000–20,000
Belgium	10,000–15,000
Belarus	10,000–15,000
Slovenia	7,000–10,000
Finland	7,000–9,000
Lithuania	3,000–4,000
Denmark	1,500–3,000
Latvia	2,000–3,500
Norway	500–2,500
Estonia	1,000–1,500

and the United Kingdom. Nomadism was the biggest issue for officials in these countries. Most of Europe's non-Soviet states put laws in place that made Roma nomadism difficult, though never specifically illegal. In Great Britain the government created special camp-sites for the officially designated Travellers, though the number of sites, which were the responsibility of local officials, was never adequate for the thousands of Roma caravans that traveled throughout the country. Many of Germany's states fell back on legislation from the 1920s to deal with the Roma. French officials used an old system created in 1912 that required all no-mads to carry a *carnet anthropométrique,* an identity card with personal information and fingerprints. Lo-cal French communities also put up signs that read *interdit aux nomades* (nomads prohibited) that were specifically aimed at Roma nomads. These regulations remained in force until 1969, when officials replaced the 1912 *carnet* with a *carnet de circulation,* which police review monthly. France has created some sites for nomadic Roma, though they do not meet Roma needs. The same is true in Italy.

Most governments in western Europe have given significant lip service to educating Roma children, though the implementation of such programs, which often falls on the shoulders of local officials, has been far from successful. There have been few centralized national efforts to enhance the educational opportu-nities for Roma children, which vary from region to region and country to country. According to Jean-Pierre Liégeois, who used 1988 statistics, only 30 to 40 percent of the children in the ten European Com-munity nations attended school regularly. Another 50 percent never went to school. Very few of the Roma children who did attend school got beyond the pri-mary level. According to Liégeois, over half of the

Travellers in Great Britain. Hungarian Roma women and children take morning tea outside a caravan parked in a field near Epsom Downs racetrack, May 1937. ©HULTON-DEUTCH COLLECTION/CORBIS

European Community's Roma were illiterate, and in some places Roma illiteracy was as high as 80 to 100 percent. When combined with similar figures from central and eastern Europe, the resulting picture is of a large, growing, impoverished, illiterate people that remains at the edge of European society.

The fact that over half of Europe's Roma be-came sedentary does not seem to have dramatically improved their quality of life. What Roma leaders throughout Europe call for are opportunities for in-tegration that open doors for the Roma while respect-ing their unique history and culture. Many oppose assimilation, which some Roma leaders feel forces the Roma to give up these age-old traditions.

See also **Racism** *(in this volume);* **Migration** *(volume 2).*

BIBLIOGRAPHY

Acton, Thomas, ed. *Gypsy Politics and Traveller Identity.* Hatfield, U.K., 1997.

Acton, Thomas, and Gary Mundy, eds. *Romani Culture and Gypsy Identity.* Hatfield, U.K., 1997.

Commission on the Security and Cooperation in Europe. *Romani Human Rights in Europe.* Washington, D.C., 1998.

Crowe, David M. *A History of the Gypsies of Eastern Europe and Russia.* New York, 1995.

Crowe, David M., and John Kolsti, eds. *The Gypsies of Eastern Europe.* Armonk, N.Y., 1991.

Druker, Jeremy. "Present but Unaccounted For." *Transition* 4, no. 4 (September 1997): 22–23.

Feher, Gyorgy. *Struggling for Ethnic Identity: The Gypsies of Hungary.* New York, 1993.

Fonseca, Isabel. *Bury Me Standing: The Gypsies and Their Journey.* London, 1996.

Fraser, Angus. *The Gypsies.* Oxford, 1992.

Friedlander, Henry. *The Origins of Nazi Genocide: From Euthanasia to the Final Solution.* Chapel Hill, N.C., 1995.

Hancock, Ian. *The Pariah Syndrome.* Ann Arbor, Mich., 1987.

Hubert, Marie-Christine. "The Internment of Gypsies in France." In *In the Shadow of the Swastika: The Gypsies in the Second World War.* Edited by Donald Kenrick. Vol. 2. Hatfield, Hertfordshire, U.K, 1983.

Human Rights Watch. *Destroying Ethnic Identity: The Persecution of the Gypsies in Romania.* New York, 1991.

Human Rights Watch. *Rights Denied: The Roma of Hungary.* New York, 1996.

Kenrick, Donald, and Grattan Puxon. *The Destiny of Europe's Gypsies.* New York, 1972.

Kenrick, Donald, and Grattan Puxon. *Gypsies under the Swastika.* Hertfordshire, U.K., 1995.

Lewy, Guenther. *The Nazi Persecution of the Gypsies.* Oxford, 2000.

Liégeois, Jean-Pierre. *Roma, Gypsies, Travellers.* Strasbourg, France, 1994.

Lutz, Brenda Davis, and James M. Lutz. "Gypsies as Victims of the Holocaust." *Holocaust and Genocide Studies.* 9 (winter 1995): 346–359.

Office of the United Nations High Commissioner for Refugees. *The State of the World's Refugees: A Humanitarian Agenda.* Translated by Don Bloch. London, 1997.

Open Society Institute. *Roma and Forced Migration: An Annotated Bibliography.* 2d Ed. New York, 1998.

Pushkin, Alexander. "The Gypsies." In *Alexander Pushkin: Selected Works.* Translated by Irina Zhelezovna. 2 vols. Moscow, 1974.

Puxon, Grattan. *Rom: Europe's Gypsies.* London, 1973, 1975.

Puxon, Grattan. *Roma: Europe's Gypsies.* London, 1980, 1987.

Rummel, R. J. *Democide: Nazi Genocide and Mass Murder.* New Brunswick, N.J., 1992.

Sparing, Frank. "The Gypsy Camps: The Creation, Character, and Meaning of an Instrument for the Persecution of Sinti and Romanies under National Socialism." In *From "Race Science" to the Camps: The Gypsies during the Second World War.* Edited by Karola Fings, Herbert Heuss, and Frank Sparing. Translated by Donald Kenrick. Vol. 1. Hatfield, Hertfordshire, U.K., 1997.

Stewart, Michael. *The Time of the Gypsies.* Boulder, Colo., 1997.

Tong, Diane. *Gypsies: A Multidisciplinary Annotated Bibliography.* New York, 1998.

Tritt, Rachel. *Struggling for Ethnic Identity: Czechoslovakia's Endangered Gypsies.* New York, 1992.

Willems, Wim. *In Search of the True Gypsy: From Enlightenment to the Final Solution.* London, 1997.

Zang, Ted. *Destroying Ethnic Identity: The Gypsies of Bulgaria.* New York, 1991.

Zsupos, Zoltán. *Az erdélyi sátoros taxás és aranymosó fiskális cigányok a 18. században* (Nomadic tax-paying and gold-washing Gypsies in Transylvania in the eighteenth century). Budapest, Hungary, 1996.

EUROPE AND THE WORLD

THE WORLD ECONOMY AND COLONIAL EXPANSION

Gayle K. Brunelle

The integration of Europe into the world economy, following a period of insularity between the disappearance of the Roman Empire after about 500 and the beginning of the Crusades in the eleventh century, took place in three stages. In the early Middle Ages, under the pressure of repeated waves of barbarian incursions, European population, cities, and trade declined precipitously. Even during the recovery of the High Middle Ages, European contacts with the world were circumscribed compared with the expansion after 1500. Despite some limited colonial ventures—the Mediterranean Balearic Islands (Majorca, Minorca, Ibiza, and Formentera), Genoese colonies on the coast of the Black Sea, the crusader kingdoms, and the Spanish colonization of the Canary Islands—Europeans focused primarily on intra-European trade. Their meager knowledge of the world beyond Europe, and of the currents and prevailing winds of the Atlantic Ocean, confined them mostly to the world familiar to the Romans, the Mediterranean basin. The caravan trade across central Asia along the famous Silk Road flowered in the thirteenth century under the Mongol Yuan dynasty, but despite the fame of Marco Polo, the actual quantity of goods and travelers that made the overland journey to China was quite small. Only after 1450 did the Portuguese successfully round the Cape of Good Hope and enter the complex, monsoon-driven commercial world of the Indian Ocean, initiating what J. H. Parry called "the age of reconnaissance."

The second and third phases of European expansion are more controversial than the first. Sometime between 1492 and 1900, Europe moved from the edge of the world economy to its center. In the process it was transformed from a relatively backward, underpopulated region in which at least 90 percent of the population worked in agriculture, to a highly industrialized, urbanized society that controlled much of the world, either directly through colonies or indirectly through economic and military hegemony.

Historians disagree as to when Europe moved from being a backwater to the dominant economic

and military power of the world. There is likewise great debate about the causes of that metamorphosis. Traditionally historians of the "age of discovery" emphasized the continuity and heroic nature of European expansion. They traced the beginnings of European ascendancy almost to the moment when Europeans arrived in Asia, Africa, and the New World, and discerned the roots of this phenomenal success largely in the internal development of the European economy and society beginning in the Renaissance—what has generally been termed the "rise of Europe." In their judgment, European society during the Renaissance rejected the stagnation of the Middle Ages. Instead it developed qualities such as individualism, faith in reason, and curiosity about the natural world that other cultures lacked. Europeans also had the good fortune to inhabit the most favorable climate in the world, which, unlike the tropics, fostered good health, energy, and action rather than torpor and disease. As a result, the expansion of European economic and military might was inevitable, and positive, in that Europeans through colonization spread worldwide the benefits of their superior civilization. In developing this interpretation, European historians were deeply influenced by Europe's relatively early and easy conquest of the New World, and by the success of the second wave of colonization and "gunboat diplomacy" of the nineteenth century.

Most historians today reject this highly Eurocentric interpretation. They discern two stages in European expansion after 1450. Between the fifteenth and the eighteenth centuries, Europe managed to insert itself into preexisting trade networks in Asia and Africa, although its success relied heavily on the use of force. Scholars recognize that the influence of European culture on most non-European societies was quite limited before 1800. In regions outside of Africa and the Eurasian landmass, notably the New World, European diseases decimated the vulnerable native populations. In these areas Europeans established colonies in which voluntary and forced migration from Europe and Africa provided labor to supplement or

461

replace the diminished indigenous supply of workers. The first confirmed European landing on the coast of Australia, that of Abel Tasman (for whom Tasmania is named) took place in 1644. The first European settlement in Australia was established still later, in 1788, after the North American colonies had become independent. Even so, the history of European colonization in Australia and New Zealand closely resembles the patterns established in North and South America, especially in the devastating impact of European diseases upon the native populations. In Asia and Africa, by contrast, where the inhabitants possessed societies and immune systems more capable of resisting European microbes and weapons, Europeans were obliged to content themselves with wresting trading privileges and fortified enclaves from the local authorities. The European impact on these societies before 1800 was thus much more limited than on those of the New World and Australia.

After 1800, however, Europe's rapid industrialization afforded it the wealth and military might with which to expand its political and economic control over large swaths of Africa and Asia, even as some of its older colonies in North and South America began to slip from its grasp. The second half of the nineteenth century saw a veritable orgy of colonization as Europeans and now the United States as well, used gunboat diplomacy to carve up Africa and Asia and open China forcibly to outside trade and missionaries. The British in India used the "country trade," or intra-Asian exchanges, to generate capital with which to acquire Asian products in demand in Europe. The advent of the steamboat and treatment for yellow fever and malaria permitted Europeans to explore deeper into Africa than in the past and to establish colonies designed to produce commodities for export. Although most of the later colonies in Africa and Asia lasted less than a century, as decolonization commenced in earnest after World War II, they profoundly affected the development of Europe and the rest of the world.

THE EARLY MODERN PERIOD, 1415–1800

New worlds: Africa. The expansion of Europe began as part of the Iberian *reconquista* (reconquest), which in turn was one front in the larger European contest with Islam known as the Crusades. Although we associate the Crusades primarily with the Holy Land, in fact Europeans saw in the Crusades a worldwide struggle against an aggressive, heretical Muslim enemy. The contest had not ended with the Muslim overthrow of the last crusader kingdom in the Holy Land in the thirteenth century. In 1453 Constantinople fell to the Ottoman Turks, generating shock waves of fear that reverberated throughout Europe. The advance of Christianity down the Iberian Peninsula culminated in 1492 with the fall of Granada, the last Muslim caliphate on Iberian soil. The Spanish and the Portugese in the fifteenth century carried the war against Islam into North Africa, where ports, such as Algiers, offered havens for Muslim pirates who preyed upon shipping in the Mediterranean. That is why the first step in Portuguese expansion was across the Strait of Gibraltar to the wealthy Moroccan city of Ceuta in 1415. Safety for European merchants at sea, as well as a desire to spread Christianity, were the main inspirations of the fifteenth-century Portuguese explorers and of their famous patron Infante Dom Henrique (Henry the Navigator, 1394–1460), brother of the Portuguese king. A prince without a kingdom of his own and an official of the crusading Order of Christ, Henrique hoped that the voyages he sponsored would bring him both fame and fortune, the former as a crusading defender of Catholicism, the latter in the form of access to the sub-Saharan goldfields.

He failed in both regards, in that he neither gained a reputation as a great crusader nor alleviated his chronic poverty with African gold, but the voyages around the bulge of Africa that took place under his aegis opened up the Atlantic world to Europe. In 1434, the Portuguese sailor Gil Eannes became the first European to round Cape Bojador on the Saharan coast. He subsequently discovered the Madeira Islands on the return voyage to Portugal. The Canaries had been known since the fourteenth century and the Azores since 1431. Europeans stumbled upon the Cape Verde Islands in 1456. Bartolomeu Dias explored the full length of the Atlantic African coast and rounded the Cape of Good Hope in 1487, and in 1497 Vasco da Gama finally entered the Indian Ocean and sailed up the East African coast. After visiting the trading ports of Mozambique, Mombassa, and Malindi, where he was disappointed to find a significant Arab merchant community already present, he located a native pilot familiar with the Indian Ocean who was willing to guide him to India, which he reached in 1498. In 1500 the Portuguese sailor Pedro Álvares Cabral reached the coast of Brazil, largely by accident. The strong southerly Canary Current flowing down the coast of Africa required mariners to swing west into the Atlantic both in order to return to Europe from the Gold Coast and as the easiest means to catch the southern trade winds and then the westerlies that most efficiently conduct ships around Africa and into the Indian Ocean.

The names of the three coasts in tropical Africa where the Portuguese concentrated their attention, the Ivory Coast, the Gold Coast, and the Slave Coast, as well as the name of their principal outpost, Elmina (the mine), reveal the primary commodities that attracted the Portuguese. At first they concentrated on gold and ivory. But with the growth of the Atlantic plantation economy in the sixteenth century, the demand for slaves, and the profitability of the slave trade, expanded enormously. Nor did the Portuguese have Africa to themselves for long. The Castilians had shadowed them down the African coast, and by the seventeenth century the Dutch and the English were challenging Portuguese domination of both the African and Indian Ocean trades.

In this period Portugal possessed neither the population nor the military capability to overwhelm and colonize large swaths of tropical Atlantic territory. In the Niger River delta and the Congo River basin, as well as the Swahili cities of East Africa, the Portuguese encountered wealthy, populous kingdoms that were willing to trade with them but were also quite capable of defending themselves against Portuguese aggression. By the same token, the Portuguese were less interested in settlement than in commerce in Africa, especially as they lacked immunities to yellow fever, sleeping sickness, and a form of malaria endemic to the continent.

Trade with Europeans gradually distorted the African political economy over the sixteenth, seventeenth, and eighteenth centuries. African demand for European products, especially weapons, and European craving for slaves, led to an expansion of slave raiding that destabilized many weaker African polities and disrupted normal trade patterns. The European impact on African society was even greater in the nineteenth century, when with the aid of steamboats, mosquito nets, and quinine they were able to travel deep into the African interior and carve out colonies there. Still, in the early modern period Africans, rather than Europeans, controlled the production, accumulation, and transport to the coast of the merchandise Europeans purchased, including slaves.

Sugar, however, more than any other commodity, was the engine driving the economy of the Portuguese empire in the Atlantic basin. Portuguese, Castilians, and Catalans had already experimented successfully with sugar cultivation on the Balearic Islands, the Canaries, Madeira, and the Cape Verde Islands, where they were able to enserf or enslave the native populations. These early conquests and plantation-style settlements became the prototype for later plantations in the tropical Americas, from South Carolina to Brazil. In 1549 the Portuguese began to plant sugar in

Brazil. Ecological conditions proved favorable, and soon it became apparent that the only real obstacle to the expansion of sugar cultivation was the absence of a reliable workforce, especially as the growing European taste for sugar ensured an expanding market for it in Europe. Sugar production was extremely labor intensive and physically demanding. European diseases ravaged the indigenous Tupinambá of Brazil, and the survivors either melted into the rainforest or died under the harsh conditions of plantation labor. Overwork and ill treatment killed many of the African slaves brought to the sugar plantations to replace the Tupinambá. By the end of the sixteenth century, the Portuguese were importing growing numbers of slaves from both East and West Africa, not only for use in their own colony in Brazil but also to supply the Caribbean islands, where sugar production also was spreading. Already by the beginning of the seventeenth century, almost 300,000 African slaves had been shipped from Africa to the New World. By the end of the next century the number rose to about 1.5 million. Sugar production, including the refining process, brought enormous wealth to European investors as sugar became widely available to the European masses rather than a rare luxury of the wealthy.

In 1580 the Portuguese royal line died out when the heir to the throne was killed in an ill-advised crusade in North Africa. From 1580 until 1640, the crowns of Spain and Portugal were merged, and Castilian merchants began to compete with the Portuguese in the African trade, although Brazil itself remained Portuguese. Nor were the Iberians able to monopolize the slave trade. The Dutch and French attempted to carve out enclaves in Brazil, seeking brazilwood, which yielded a red dye useful for tinting cloth, and to establish sugar plantations and trade with the Portuguese colonies. Although the Portuguese and the Spanish eventually drove the interlopers out of the South American mainland, they were unable to close the Caribbean to English, Dutch, and French pirates and colonists, who alternately traded with and raided the Spanish colonies. The fleets carrying American silver to Spain were especially tempting targets for marauders, but much of the illicit trade was in slaves. The licit slave trade to Spanish colonies took place almost entirely under *asientos* (licenses) issued to foreign firms. The Portuguese dominated in the sixteenth century, the Dutch for much of the seventeenth, and the French and English in the eighteenth. Ironically, it was the British who squelched the slave trade in the nineteenth century. Their chief opponent in this trade was the Portuguese, who continued to supply slaves to the Americas, including Brazil, where demand remained high. In 1856 the British,

African Slaves in Spanish America. African slaves searching for gold in Varaguas. Drawing from *Histoire naturelle des Indes,* a French manuscript of the late sixteenth century known as the Drake Manuscript. THE PIERPONT MORGAN LIBRARY/ART RESOURCE, NY

finding themselves unable to rein in the Portuguese slavers, who eluded them on the high seas, threatened to turn the British navy loose against Brazil. This ended the trade, although slavery itself remained legal in Brazil until 1888.

The Americas and Australia. Two momentous events took place in Spain in 1492: the fall of the kingdom of Granada, the last Muslim polity on Iberian soil, and the voyage of Christopher Columbus. At the time, it was the former far more than the latter that seemed most significant to Europeans. Rediscovery of the past—the classical golden age of Greco-Roman culture and the spiritual purity of the early Christian church—inspired European intellectuals during the Renaissance and Reformation. Like the Portuguese adventurers, the Spanish conquistadores (conquerors) were driven by a crusading spirit and tales of medieval heroism. Above all, however, Europeans dreamed that their forays into the Atlantic

would reveal a new passage to the riches of Asia, one that was free of Muslim domination.

The Portuguese achieved such a route in 1498 when Vasco da Gama sailed around the Cape of Good Hope and entered the Indian Ocean. The trip around Africa was highly lucrative but also long and arduous, and in East Africa and the Indian Ocean the Portuguese again had to contend with Arab-dominated trade networks. When Columbus arrived at the royal court in Lisbon seeking funds for his venture, he failed to elicit much interest, especially as the scholars and mariners advising the Crown were justifiably skeptical about his low estimate of the distance between Europe and Asia. Isabella of Castile, on the other hand, was willing to take a chance on the Genoese mariner. Her decision had profound consequences for the development of Spanish civilization. As queen of Castile, she bestowed the right to trade with and colonize the New World exclusively to Castilians, which meant that Castile, and especially the Castilian cities of Seville and Cadiz, reaped the benefits of New World trade and plunder, whereas Aragon, which was focused on the Mediterranean and traditionally the more urbanized, wealthy, and commercial of the two kingdoms of Spain, languished. The balance of power between Aragon and Castile, and between the Mediterranean and the Atlantic regions of Europe, was altered irrevocably as the economic and, eventually, cultural center of Europe migrated north and west toward the Atlantic littoral.

The first civilizations the Spanish encountered in the New World, the Aztecs of the central Mexican highlands and the Inca of the Peruvian Andes, were highly sophisticated, populous, wealthy, and urban cultures. The Aztecs built their capital, Tenochtitlán, in the middle of Lake Texcoco. An intricate hydraulic system, which the Spanish subsequently destroyed, provided the city's 400,000 inhabitants with water for their famous *chinampas,* or floating gardens, and with a means of transportation and sanitation superior to that of European cities. The Incas had a well-developed system of communications based on roads crisscrossing the Andes. Both societies possessed all the conventional hallmarks of civilization, including religion, science, monumental architecture, and trade networks. Even so, several factors rendered them vulnerable to the tiny invading Spanish forces (Cortés had fewer than five hundred Spanish soldiers with him when he reached Tenochtitlán).

The most useful allies of the Europeans in their conquest of the New world were diseases such as smallpox, measles, and tuberculosis to which the native Americans lacked immunities. Europe ecologically belonged to a vast Eurasian disease pool that also included Africa to a lesser extent. Trade, migration, and military invasion led to frequent movement of human beings and their livestock, which constituted a significant reservoir of disease, among the geographically contiguous continents of Europe, Asia, and Africa. Although the Sahara acted as a limited barrier and thus disease filter, enough caravans crossed the desert to ensure that Africans were exposed to at least some Eurasian microbes. At the same time, Africans harbored unique pathogens of their own, such as yellow fever, which inhibited Europeans from advancing very far into the African interior until the nineteenth century.

An infectious disease attacking a new host population quickly becomes virulent. Mortality rates as high as 90 percent often result. Over time, either the disease kills so many people that there are no new hosts available, in which case it dies out itself, or it evolves into a weakened form that becomes endemic in the population. In that form it preys mostly upon the feeble, the very young, and the old, whereas survivors of childhood infections are partially or fully immunized as adults. Smallpox and measles, both endemic illnesses in Europe by the Renaissance, ravaged the native American population. Europeans also transferred influenza and typhus to the New World, the latter new and highly lethal to them as well, and through the slave trade brought to the New World from Africa yellow fever and malaria. Other indigenous populations unexposed to the Eurasian disease pool suffered similarly, including the Aborigines of Australia and the Maoris of New Zealand. Historians once thought that North and South America had been relatively sparsely populated upon the arrival of Europeans, except for the obviously densely peopled Aztec and Inca empires. Now scholars believe that the New World may have supported as many as 100 million inhabitants in 1492, and that as many as 90 percent of them may have died during the following century, mostly from disease.

Ecology and evolution aided Europeans in another respect as well. As part of the Eurasian cultural pool, Europeans had learned by Greek and Roman times to domesticate large mammals as food sources and beasts of burden. Horses, cattle, pigs, goats, and sheep all did well in the European climate, which produced adequate fodder and was free of parasites, such as the tsetse flies of Africa; these flies carry sleeping sickness and thus greatly limit the range of horses and cattle on that continent. Aside from the llama and alpaca of the Andes, the native populations of North and South America lacked large beasts of burden. Some sizable game animals existed: the buffalo of the Great Plains and the tapirs of South America, as well as kangaroos, ostriches, and emus in Australia. But neither in the Americas nor in Australia did herds of animals able to support a significant pastoral economy exist. Moreover, unlike Europeans, many peoples around the world do not have the gene that permits humans to digest nonhuman milk and milk products after weaning. Thus Europeans were able to benefit doubly from the cattle they brought to the New World because they were able to consume highly nutritious milk and cheese as well as beef. Cheese kept well on voyages and supplied a significant source of portable protein and calcium. Many of the animals the Europeans introduced to the New World and Australia quickly adapted to their new environment and became feral, thus providing successive waves of explorers and conquerors with an abundant and familiar food supply.

Europeans also possessed weapons and horses new to the native Americans and Australian Aborigines. It is important to note that throughout North

Aztecs and Spanish at Tenochtitlán. Massacre of the Aztec rulers at Tenochtitlán in 1521. From the codex of Diego Duran, 1579. The Spanish built Mexico City on the site of Tenochtitlán. BIBLIOTECA NACIONAL, MADRID

and South America indigenous peoples eventually adapted their societies to both horses and guns and even turned them against European colonists. The peoples of the Great Plains made the horse, which proved an invaluable tool in hunting buffalo, a new pillar of their culture. Contemporary Spanish accounts no doubt exaggerate the awe and fear that the mounted Spanish soldiers and their guns inspired. After their initial confusion the Aztecs and Incas fought bravely against Cortés's men on a number of occasions. Still, guns and horses greatly enhanced the effectiveness of each of the Spanish soldiers, helping to compensate for their enormous numerical inferiority. Also important was the Spanish style of warfare. The goal of much Aztec combat was to capture prisoners for ritual sacrifices, which demoralized the enemy while pleasing the gods, rather than to indulge in wholesale slaughter. The Spanish, many of them battle-tested veterans, fought according to different rules and did not shrink from using ruses and guile and inflicting significant casualties, often through very brutal means, such as setting ferocious dogs upon unarmed civilians. The Aztecs and the Incas were thus in many ways unprepared for what soon became a life and death struggle with the European invaders.

The Spanish were also supremely fortunate in timing. The Aztecs were a relatively young empire; it was only in 1325 that they had settled on Lake Texcoco, and they had consolidated their empire less than one hundred years before the arrival of Cortés. The Aztecs were not well liked by many of their subject peoples, and as a result Cortés was able to cultivate numerous, invaluable native allies, among them La Malinche, his interpreter and lover; without the aid of these indigenous allies he would not have succeeded in his war against the Aztecs. Similarly, the Incas had barely ended a bloody civil war when in 1531 Francisco Pizarro arrived in Peru, and he too was able to take advantage of their internal divisions and augment his forces greatly with fighters drawn from the native population. Wherever Europeans established commercial or colonial empires, in Spanish America, Africa, Southeast Asia, and the British Raj in India, they consistently profited from divisions within indigenous societies, among whose members they found allies willing for a variety of reasons to aid them. Non-Europeans experienced contacts with Europeans in a variety of ways and were actors in creating their own destinies rather than passive victims of European aggression.

European contacts with the New World and Australia had profound effects on both European and indigenous native American and Aboriginal societies. The ecological impact alone was enormous. In what Alfred Crosby has termed the "Columbian exchange," Europeans were able to bring much useful flora and fauna from other parts of the world to the Americas. Like the disease microbes, most of these plants and animals were able to flourish in the more isolated and thus less biologically diverse and competitive New World. A similar process took place in Australia and New Zealand. Many of the animals became feral and often overwhelmed native species. Pigs, goats, and rabbits, for example, have taken a serious toll on Australian wildlife, despite efforts to introduce natural predators to reduce their numbers. Wild horses, called "brumbies," throve in the Australian bush. The Argentine pampas and the American West also became home to vast herds of wild horses, donkeys, and cattle. Such transfers had of course happened before in the peripatetic human past. Aborigines most likely brought the dingo, a kind of dog, to Australia thousands of years ago. Still, the Columbian exchange witnessed more massive introductions of new species over greater geographical ranges and on a shorter time scale than ever before, with much greater consequences for ecology and human history.

The migration of plant species around the world, both in the form of planned cultivation and accidental dispersion, was even more significant than that of animals. The clover and grass ubiquitous in North American lawns and meadows came from Europe. Europeans brought wheat, sugar, and coffee, all originally from the Middle East, cotton from India, and a host of other edible grains, fruits, and vegetables to the New World and Australia, many of which became valuable export crops in these regions and, along with the tobacco indigenous to the New World, the main-

stay of plantation economies. They also carried with them a plethora of less useful or even harmful plants that, like the animals, tended in the absence of natural predators to occupy ecological niches that native species once held. Such weed species are still being introduced today and threaten the biodiversity of the Americas, New Zealand, and Australia. Of equal importance were New World plants that Europeans introduced to Europe, Africa, and Asia. Corn, tubers such as the Andean potato and sweet potatoes, tomatoes, and squashes have all become central to the diets of many Europeans, Africans, and Asians.

The economic impact of interaction between Europe and the New World was similarly of great consequence. On the one hand, Europeans disrupted native societies and economies, the highly structured Aztec and Inca civilizations being the earliest and most deeply affected. Massive depopulation alone destroyed Mexican and Peruvian trade networks and agriculture, markets collapsed, and fields remained untilled. The conquistadores enslaved many of the natives for use as labor in the mines and on their *encomiendas,* the large estates in the New World granted them by the Crown. Forced labor, such as the *mita* in Peru, which took men away for their homes for months at a time, weakened traditional village life and kinship ties.

Native Peoples. Aborigines at Oyster Cove, Tasmania, Australia, c. 1860. BEATTIE COLLECTION, NATIONAL LIBRARY OF AUSTRALIA, ALBUM 229

The popularity of the "Black Legend"—the belief that Spain's cruelty to subject peoples exceeded that of other colonial powers—notwithstanding, the native Americans had defenders within Spanish society. The Dominican Bartolomé de Las Casas greatly publicized their plight and petitioned the Crown to rein in the Spanish settlers who insisted on enslaving them and working them to death. Missionaries attempted to gather as many natives as possible in the missions, where they were proselytized in the Christian religion and protected from exploitation. The Crown sympathized with these efforts and decreed repeatedly that the natives were not to be enslaved except under very specific circumstances, such as open rebellion or religious backsliding. Determined to prevent the haughty conquistadores and their descendants from carving out semi-independent feudal domains in the New World, the Crown established an elaborate hierarchy of royal officials, centered on Madrid and charged with the responsibility of governing the new colonies in accord with Crown policies. Unfortunately, although the royal officials were able to reduce the power of the *encomenderos* (holders of royal land grants), they frequently were unable to carry out their mandate to protect native Americans. The Habsburg Crown was embroiled in almost constant warfare in Europe during the sixteenth and seventeenth centuries. Charles V (Charles I of Spain, 1516–1556) ruled an empire that stretched from Spain to Austria, and from Italy to the Low Countries. He and his son, Philip II (1555–1598), needed every ounce of silver they could extract from the American mines to finance their armies. Their thirst for silver often outweighed their moral scruples regarding the treatment of the native Americans who worked in the mines and payed tribute to the Crown.

The European economy gained enormous wealth from the Americas. The vast quantities of precious metals, especially silver, flowing from Mexico and Peru to Spain played an essential role in the expansion of Europe's economic and political power throughout the world after the fifteenth century. Historians have always recognized the importance of American silver in the development of the European economy. Formerly, however, they emphasized the negative consequences of that flow of silver over the positive. Europe during the sixteenth century suffered from significant price inflation, which had serious economic and social consequences, especially for people whose incomes were fixed, such as nobles living off rents and artisans and peasants whose wages rose more slowly than the cost of living. By the same token, Spain, in whose American territory the silver mines lay, failed to invest in manufactures and infrastructure, relying instead on the seemingly endless flow of wealth from the New World to pay for products imported from more industrialized societies, such as the Netherlands. This condemned Spain to stagnation and decline, scholars asserted, once the silver began to run out in the seventeenth century and as other nations forged industrialized economies.

More nuanced views of the role of American silver in the evolution of the European economy prevail today. The prime engine of sixteenth-century inflation appears to have been population growth and a concomitant rise in the price of grain and other essentials, rather than the influx of silver. Likewise, American silver was only one of many factors in the underdeveloped economy of Spain, although there is no doubt that silver from the New World flowed through Spain like water through a sieve. Most of it ended up in the hands of the Dutch, English, and French merchants who supplied Spain with manufactures. Still, the chronic European military contests in which Spain's Habsburg rulers were embroiled drained capital that could have been invested in Spanish manufacturing and trade. Much of this wealth ended up in the hands of Dutch merchants who, ironically, sold the Spanish many of the weapons they later used against Dutch Protestant armies. The Dutch, in turn, exported the silver to Asia. European merchants had little else that the Asians were willing to accept in exchange for the luxury products so much in demand in Europe. Thus Europeans financed their growing importance in Asian trade networks with precious metals from their colonies in the New World. In this respect, historians are in agreement that American silver was the linchpin of Europe's ability to compete in Asian trade. Only after 1850 did European industrial superiority usher in the age of "gunboat diplomacy," during which force and opium replaced silver as the key to Europe's expanding role in Asia.

Asia and East Africa. The history of Europe's interaction with Asia and Africa was quite different from the history of the conquest and colonization of the New World and Australia. Asian and African societies were populous and urbanized. Complex maritime trade routes based on the seasonal monsoons of the Indian Ocean connected China, Southeast Asia, and the Spice Islands with the ports of India, the Persian Gulf and Red Sea, and East Africa. This trade, much of it in Arab hands, had existed for centuries before the arrival of the Europeans. Although Europeans succeeded, largely through the threat of force, in abrogating a portion of it to themselves, they did not dominate it or supplant native merchants until the nineteenth century.

As in the case of Africa, the Portuguese were the first Europeans to enter the Indian Ocean. Like the Spanish in the New World, the Portuguese were uncannily lucky in timing. During much of the Middle Ages, the Chinese under the Sung and Yuan dynasties were the dominant maritime power in Asia. They sent out a series of enormous flotillas designed to collect tribute and emphasize China's world hegemony. Some historians have posited that if these Chinese expeditions had continued, the Portuguese, despite their superior armaments, would have found themselves faced with an adversary too formidable for them to dominate. In 1433 the Ming dynasty, preoccupied with a renewed Mongol threat, abandoned the voyages, leaving a vacuum of power in the Indian Ocean that the Portuguese subsequently occupied. In the Indian Ocean trade tended to be conducted far more peacefully than in the North Atlantic and the Mediterranean and most commercial vessels were only lightly armed. Outsiders in the established Asian trade networks, the Portuguese found few willing trading partners. Without the powerful Chinese navy to hinder them, however, they were free to use force to pry open the Indian Ocean markets that otherwise would have been closed to them.

At first, the Portuguese ran a maritime "protection racket." They used their superior firepower to conquer Goa on the west coast of India in 1510. Subsequently they occupied Malacca in the Malay straits (1511) and Hormuz in the Persian Gulf (1514), and constructed a fort at Colombo, all key points in the Indian Ocean trade. From these outposts as well as from a series of fortified trading posts from East Africa to Nagasaki in Japan, they were able not only to conduct their own trade but to oblige merchants of other countries to buy permits from them in order to sail without fear of Portuguese attack. Eventually, the Portuguese, like the British and the Dutch, were obliged to adapt to Indian Ocean trading patterns by entering the "country trade." They generated the wealth with which they acquired exports for Europe by participating in the preexisting trade between India and East Africa, exchanging Indian cloth for African gold, slaves, and ivory.

Despite the breadth of the Portuguese Asian empire, and the stunning speed (less than seventy years) in which it was created, tiny Portugal's limited resources always circumscribed its power. The Portuguese soon found themselves hard pressed to defend their overseas empire from European interlopers. Their most aggressive and dangerous competitors were the English and Dutch, each of whom in the seventeenth century carved out their own spheres of influence. The Dutch dominion, like that of the Portuguese, was a trading empire, consisting of strategically located territorial enclaves embedded within larger indigenous kingdoms and a series of fortified and unfortified "factories" (trading posts). By 1670 the Dutch had established a vast empire in the Indian Ocean, stretching from Nagasaki in Japan and Fort Zeelandia on Taiwan to Ceylon. Although the Portuguese demonstrated remarkable staying power, retaining Goa as well as strengthening their hold on Brazil, the Dutch dominated most of coastal India. Spanish and Chinese merchants competed in the Philippines and the Portuguese held Macao, but the Dutch had the Moluccas (Spice Islands) all to themselves.

The English finally crushed Dutch naval power in the late seventeenth century through a series of commercial wars fought in Asia and the New World (1652–1654, 1665–1667, 1672–1674). The wars of the late seventeenth century, the first in which Europeans fought as much outside of Europe as at home, helped to shift the balance of power away from trading-post empires to colonial empires, in which control of territory, the generation of colonial markets for European goods, and access to raw materials to fuel European industrial expansion mattered more than the exportation of precious metals, spices, and luxury items to Europe.

THE NEW IMPERIALISM: 1800 TO THE PRESENT

Several factors distinguish the "new imperialism" of the nineteenth and early twentieth centuries from the early modern European commercial and colonial empires. Like the explorers and conquerors of the preceding centuries, European imperialists of the modern era sought wealth, converts to Christianity, prestige for themselves and their fellow countrymen, and strategic advantage in the competition among European states. The nature of that competition, however, and of the economic role that Europeans expected colonies to play in the enrichment of the mother country had changed. Europeans now sought primarily raw materials from the colonies to feed Europe's growing industries. The growth of consumerism in Europe reinforced the need for inexpensive raw materials that European workers could transform into manufactured goods for European consumers. Dynastic rivalries had become geopolitical struggles among nation states waged on a worldwide stage as Europeans maneuvered to build and protect empires made up of colonies spread around the world. The British, for example, acquired Egypt in 1882 because they were determined to safeguard the Suez Canal, completed in 1869,

India, the "Jewel in the Crown." Calcutta Harbor, c. 1880. ©BBC HULTON/LIAISON AGENCY

which they regarded as the key to safe and easy transport to and from India, the "jewel in the crown" of their empire. The economic power of mechanized industry, superior weaponry (which the 1884 invention of the first machine gun symbolized), and the steamship and the railroad, which greatly improved the speed and reliability of transportation, led to an accelerated pace of European conquest and colonization in the nineteenth century. Likewise, during this period the first real "world economy" came into being, with industrialized Europe at its center and all the continents linked in a vast network of unequal exchange of raw materials and manufactured products. Finally, many scholars also argue that it was only during the new imperialism that European political and cultural influence significantly penetrated indigenous societies and affected the everyday lives of ordinary non-Europeans.

Another significant shift had taken place during the eighteenth and nineteenth centuries. Due in part to limited means for disseminating information and in part to the limited impact of overseas conquests on the lives of ordinary people, most Europeans before the eighteenth century knew very little about European overseas conquests and trade. Fantastic fictions about strange overseas lands tended to be mingled with accurate information in most maps and publications about the non-European world. Only during the modern period did the rise of nationalism fuel a ground swell of support in Europe for the creation of national empires. As late as the eighteenth century,

the setbacks of the South Sea Bubble, which bankrupted scores of investors, and the American Revolution fed the doubts of many Europeans about the utility of empires. By the nineteenth century, however, Europeans of all social classes not only had come to see overseas empires as lucrative investments vital to the growth of European capitalism, but had also come to share the view of their rulers that empires were powerful symbols of national glory.

The primary goals of European imperialism in the early modern era had been twofold: to obtain Asian goods for export to Europe through a series of fortified trading bases and to establish colonies containing a substantial population of settlers from the mother country that would export commodities in demand at home. Luxury goods, such as precious metals, silks, beaver pelts, and the products of plantation agriculture (sugar, spices, and tobacco), tended to make up the most valued portion of these early cargoes from Asia, Africa, and the Americas. Only over the course of the eighteenth century did the advantage of colonies as markets for European manufactured products become a central factor in colonial policy. Thus Britain's desire to restrict the growth of manufacturing in its North American colonies, in order to eliminate competition with British industry, played an important role in the American Revolutionary War and the War of 1812. During the nineteenth century the British suppressed cotton cloth manufacturing in India in order to prop up the market throughout their empire, including India, for British-made cloth, often woven from raw cotton imported from the plantations of the southeastern United States and from India itself. This shift made the fortune of the cloth industry in northern England, but at the expense of Indian cloth manufacturing, which was ravaged. Many political and economic struggles in the underdeveloped economies of Asia and Africa in the present stem from their peripheral role in the world economy Europeans forged in the eighteenth and nineteenth centuries.

The spread of plantation agriculture in Africa and Asia—facilitated by the steamboat, harbor-dredging capability, railroad construction, mechanization in agriculture, and such improved treatments for disease as quinine—assured a steady supply of commodities for European industry, but only at great cost to indigenous peoples. Europeans often subdued uprisings with force: the soldiers of Leopold II of Belgium in the Congo Free State slaughtered thousands between 1876 and 1909 to protect the goldfields and rubber plantations. Further, plantations tended to disrupt the ecological balance where they were located by encouraging monoculture at the expense of native agricultural systems that had evolved in closer harmony with local climate and topography. Small-scale village and family agriculture gave way to export farming, which in turn made the population dependent on imports of food and manufactured goods from outside. European merchants profited from this situation, which through lower prices fostered rising consumerism in Europe but often led to weakened social structures and economic impoverishment among colonized peoples.

The Opium War (1839–1842) between Great Britain and China in many ways exemplifies the world economy that the new imperialism created. Because England during the sixteenth and seventeenth centuries lagged behind the Portuguese and the Dutch in establishing itself in the Indian Ocean, it lacked access to the richest sources of spices. Nor did England possess New World colonies rich in silver and gold with which to pay for the Asian merchandise it wanted. Forced to make the best of a bad situation, English merchants generated capital with which to buy goods for export to Europe by taking part in intraregional Asian trade, called the "country trade." This necessity had two important consequences. It drew the English East India Company, and eventually the British government, ever deeper into the direct rule of India, culminating in the 1861 appointment of the first British viceroy of India and the 1877 proclamation of Queen Victoria as empress of India. It also led the British to develop a complex commercial web linking its colonies, in which political control, through either direct rule or indirect hegemony, of other places such

as China and Egypt was necessary to ensure that the system functioned without disruption.

Already by the 1830s, the British found that they could no longer pay for their Chinese tea and silk with English wool and Indian cotton. They had, however, identified another commodity, opium, that was in demand in China. Opium had two other advantages. It was produced in India, a territory already under British control, and it was addictive, which meant that once it was introduced into a market, demand was likely to grow indefinitely. The Chinese, naturally, did not share the British enthusiasm for opium. The social problems that widespread opium addiction fostered alarmed Chinese authorities. Worse, they were humiliated because the economic tables were now turned: Chinese importers paid for the opium with silver, thus shifting China for the first time from a net importer of silver to a net exporter. The Chinese government reacted by destroying a store of British opium in Canton in 1839, opening the Opium War, which ended three years later in Chinese defeat. The war exposed Chinese military weakness in the face of European gunboat diplomacy. Soon the European colonial powers and the United States jostled with each other to carve out their own spheres of influence and treaty ports in China where their commerce would be free of interference.

A similar frenzy marked the scramble for Africa, which Leopold II initiated in 1876 with the creation of the African International Association to exploit the Congo goldfields. The Berlin Congress of 1884 confirmed Leopold's hold on the Congo and set the standards by which European occupation of African territory was hence recognized as legitimate. Within three decades all of Africa except Ethiopia and Liberia was under direct European rule. Even the Germans, who sat out the early modern wave of colonization, carved out four African colonies for themselves in the nineteenth century. Especially rapacious was Cecil Rhodes, whose British South Africa Company ruthlessly suppressed an uprising of the Ndebele and Shona peoples of Zimbabwe and initiated the Boer War (1899–1902). Although European racism obviously played a significant role in both modern and early modern imperialism, the treatment of Boers, who were white Dutch Calvinists, demonstrates that race was by no means the only factor behind the ruthless logic of nineteenth-century European colonial expansion. Ironically, during the eighteenth and nineteenth centuries most of Europe's older colonies in the New World had become independent. By 1914 Europe controlled a new colonial empire; the end of World War II ushered in a new process of decolonization.

CONCLUSION: THE "RISE OF EUROPE" AND WORLD HISTORY FROM A SOCIAL HISTORY PERSPECTIVE

Since 1960 social historians, drawing on the work of anthropologists, have profoundly altered our understanding of Europe's interactions with and influence on the rest of the world since the Renaissance. The triumph and sense of inevitability that surround the phrase the "rise of Europe," so ubiquitous in Western civilization textbooks, and the heavy reliance on modernization theory have gradually ceded influence to a much less Eurocentric perspective. Although European civilization changed profoundly after the Middle Ages in ways that clearly enhanced the quantity and profitability of its contacts with the rest of the world, historians studying European expansion have reduced their emphasis on the unique nature of European culture and society. They are less likely to follow Max Weber and ascribe Europe's rise to dominance in the modern world to innate moral qualities lacking in other peoples. They have also, for the most part, rejected environmental determinism, or the belief that Europe's uniquely favorable climate shaped European culture, economy, society, and even its human biology in such a manner as to afford Europeans a decisive edge in a worldwide competition for wealth and power.

By the same token, following the anthropologist Eric Wolf, they now recognize that non-Western peoples, whom Wolf ironically called "the people without history," at least from the perspective of European scholars, indeed did have a history. The evolution of European contacts with non-Western peoples is a history of interaction, in which each side deeply influenced the other and non-Europeans devised creative ways to cope with, adapt to, and even profit from the European exploitation of their societies.

See also **Modernization; Health and Disease** *(volume 2); and other articles in this section.*

BIBLIOGRAPHY

World History

Abu-Lughod, Janet L. *Before European Hegemony: The World System* A.D. 1250–1350. Oxford and New York, 1989.

Blaut, J. M. *The Colonizer's Model of the World: Geographical Diffusionism and Eurocentric History.* New York, 1993.

Braudel, Fernand. *Civilization and Capitalism, 15th–18th Century.* Translated by Siân Reynolds. 3 vols. New York, 1981–1984.

Fernández-Armesto, Felipe. *Millennium: A History of the Last Thousand Years.* New York, 1995.

Lewis, Martin W., and Kären E. Wigen. *The Myth of Continents: A Critique of Metageography.* Berkeley, Calif., 1997.

McNeill, William H. *Plagues and Peoples.* New York, 1989.

European Exploration and Empires

Anderson, Benedict. *Imagined Communities: Reflections on the Origin and Spread of Nationalism.* Rev. ed. London, 1991.

Andrews, Kenneth R. *Trade, Plunder and Settlement: Maritime Enterprise and the Genesis of the British Empire, 1480–1630.* Cambridge, U.K., 1984.

Bentley, Jerry H. *Old World Encounters: Cross Cultural Contacts and Exchanges in Pre-Modern Times.* Oxford and New York, 1993.

Conklin, Alice L., and Ian Christopher Fletcher, eds. *European Imperialism, 1830–1930.* New York, 1999.

Crosby, Alfred W. *Ecological Imperialism: The Biological Expansion of Europe, 900–1900.* Cambridge, U.K., 1986. Discusses in depth the Columbian exchange.

Curtin, Philip D. *Cross Cultural Trade in World History.* Cambridge, U.K., 1984. Especially important for trading post empires and the concept of cross-cultural brokerage.

Fernández-Armesto, Felipe. *Before Columbus: Exploration and Colonization from the Mediterranean to the Atlantic, 1229–1492.* Philadelphia, 1987. Shows the connection between medieval expansion, especially in the Canary Islands, and the patterns of conquest and colonization in the New World.

Israel, Jonathan I. *Dutch Primacy in World Trade, 1585–1740.* Oxford, 1990.

Phillips, J. R. S. *The Medieval Expansion of Europe.* 2d ed. Oxford, 1998.

Russell-Wood, A. J. R. *A World on the Move: The Portuguese in Africa, Asia, and America, 1415–1808.* Manchester, U.K., 1992.

Scammell, G. V. *The First Imperial Age: European Overseas Expansion c. 1400–1715.* London and Boston, 1989. An excellent, up-to-date overview of European expansion in the early modern era.

Subrahmanyam, Sanjay, ed. *Merchant Networks in the Early Modern World.* Aldershot, U.K., and Brookfield, Vt., 1996.

Tracy, James D., ed. *The Political Economy of Merchant Empires.* Cambridge, U.K., 1991.

Tracy, James D., ed. *The Rise of Merchant Empires: Long Distance Trade in the Early Modern World.* Cambridge, U.K., 1990.

Wolf, Eric R. *Europe and the People without History.* Berkeley, Calif., 1997. One of the most significant books since World War II. Wolf, an anthropologist, obliged historians to see native peoples as actors rather than mere victims in the interaction between Europeans and non-Europeans.

Atlantic World and Australia

Altman, Ida. *Emigrants and Society: Extremadura and Spanish America in the Sixteenth Century.* Berkeley, Calif., 1989.

Brunelle, Gayle K. *The New World Merchants of Rouen, 1559–1630.* Kirksville, Mo., 1991.

Cervantes, Fernando. *The Devil in the New World: The Impact of Diabolism in New Spain.* New Haven, Conn., 1994.

Curtin, Philip D. *The Rise and Fall of the Plantation Complex: Essays in Atlantic History.* Cambridge, U.K., 1990.

Davidson, Basil. *Africa in History.* London, 1991.

Eccles, W. J. *The French in North America, 1500–1783.* Rev. ed. East Lansing, Mich., 1998.

Hughes, Robert. *The Fatal Shore.* New York, 1987.

Karttunen, Frances E. *Between Worlds: Interpreters, Guides, and Survivors.* New Brunswick, N.J., 1994. Karttunen is especially good on La Malinche, Cortés's native American mistress and interpreter.

Padden, R. C. *The Hummingbird and the Hawk: Conquest and Exploration in the Valley of Mexico, 1503–1541.* Columbus, Ohio, 1967.

Postma, Johannes Menne. *The Dutch in the Atlantic Slave Trade, 1600–1815.* Cambridge, U.K., 1990.

Seed, Patricia. *Ceremonies of Possession in Europe's Conquest of the New World, 1492–1640.* Cambridge, U.K., 1995. Seed points out effectively the immense cultural gap between the Europeans' world view and that of the native peoples they encountered in the New World.

Thornton, John. *Africa and Africans in the Making of the Atlantic World, 1400–1800.* 2d ed. Cambridge, U.K., 1998.

Trigger, Bruce G. *Natives and Newcomers: Canada's "Heroic Age" Reconsidered.* Kingston, Ontario, and Manchester, U.K., 1985.

Wightman, Ann M. *Indigenous Migration and Social Change: The Forasteros of Cuzco, 1520–1720.* Durham, N.C., 1990.

The Middle East, Asia, and the Indian Ocean Trade

Adas, Michael, ed. *Islamic and European Expansion: The Forging of a Global Order.* Philadelphia, 1993.

Ames, Glenn J. *Colbert, Mercantilism, and the French Quest for Asian Trade.* DeKalb, Ill., 1996.

Chaudhuri, K. N. *Asia before Europe: Economy and Civilisation of the Indian Ocean from the Rise of Islam to 1750.* Cambridge, U.K., 1990.

Frank, Andre Gunder. *ReOrient: Global Economy in the Asian Age.* Berkeley, Calif., 1998.

Lach, Donald F. *The Century of Discovery.* Vol. 1 of *Asia in the Making of Europe.* Chicago, 1965.

Lach, Donald F., and Edwin J. Van Kley. *A Century of Advance.* Vol. 3 of *Asia in the Making of Europe.* Chicago, 1993.

Pearson, Michael N. *Port Cities and Intruders: The Swahili Coast, India, and Portugal in the Early Modern Era.* Baltimore, 1998.

Prakash, Om, ed. *European Commercial Expansion in Early Modern Asia.* Aldershot, U.K., and Brookfield, Vt., 1997.

Rafael, Vicente L. *Contracting Colonialism: Translation and Christian Conversion in Tagalog Society under Early Spanish Rule.* Ithaca, N.Y., 1988.

Reid, Anthony. *Southeast Asia in the Age of Commerce 1450–1680.* Vol 2, *Expansion and Crisis.* New Haven, Conn., and London, 1993.

European Conceptions of the World

Campbell, Mary B. *The Witness and the Other World: Exotic European Travel Writing, 400–1600.* Ithaca, N.Y., 1988.

Elliot, J. H. *The Old World and the New, 1492–1650.* Cambridge, U.K., 1970.

Fausett, David. *Writing the New World: Imaginary Voyages and Utopias of the Great Southern Land.* Syracuse, N.Y., 1993.

Greenblatt, Stephen. *Marvelous Possessions: The Wonder of the New World.* Chicago, 1991.

Pagden, Anthony. *Lords of All the World: Ideologies of Empire in Spain, Britain, and France, c. 1500–c. 1800.* New Haven, 1995.

Schlesinger, Roger. *In the Wake of Columbus: The Impact of the New World on Europe, 1492–1650.* Wheeling, Ill., 1996.

EXPLORERS, MISSIONARIES, TRADERS

Steven S. Maughan

European trade, cultural contact, and colonization, following the geographical discoveries and maritime innovations of the fifteenth century, profoundly altered non-European societies throughout the world. European exploration was inevitably followed by penetration of markets by traders and the establishment of Christian missions, if not always by formal imperial control and colonization. Aggressive venturers, seeking personal, national, and religious advantage, were at the forefront of new encounters with non-European peoples. Explorers, traders, and missionaries were thus crucial to the construction of European systems of commercial and cultural exchange as they negotiated and interpreted European contacts with other world cultures. From the sixteenth century Europeans engaged the world in increasing numbers, motivated by variously mixed ambitions for wealth, fame, honor, and the advancement of Christian spirituality, authority, and philanthropy. European society was itself significantly altered by these material and cultural exchanges as it acted in every region of the world as an aggressive force for the transformation of economies and societies.

Exploration, trade, and proselytizing often shaded into each other, and were frequently entangled with the use of military force and the establishment of colonial rule. Traders carried European technologies of warfare and production as well as goods, while missionaries often advocated European social organization and education as well as religious beliefs. All had the power to profoundly alter traditional patterns of non-European society. In Europe itself, new wealth generated through seaborne trade contributed to increasing urban cosmopolitanism, while access to colonial markets significantly shifted patterns of consumption. Visions of the world abroad, filtered through Christian belief, supported assumptions of European spiritual and cultural ascendancy that were eroded only in the twentieth-century era of decolonization.

However, explorers, traders, settlers, soldiers, and government officials often came in conflict with missionaries over European "vices" and the mistreatment of non-Europeans. Additionally, competition from the mid-sixteenth century between Roman Catholics and Protestants, as well as between traders and other agents of emerging European nation-states, generated considerable friction between Europeans of differing national and religious identities. Thus the history of European trading and proselytizing in the world since the Renaissance has been characterized by complex and rapidly changing patterns of coercion, resistance, opportunism, collaboration, cooperation, and competition between many European and non-European groups.

Both trading and missionary activity are inherently transcultural with objectives that are advanced by an understanding of, if not always an empathy with, their target societies. Militant belief in the universal import of their religious message drove missionaries to surprisingly persistent activity in the midst of foreign, and often hostile, cultures. Missionaries frequently operated at the forefront of the production of knowledge for and about foreign societies as influential educators, social reformers, language scholars, and medical providers. While missionaries often sought to strip their message of salvation from European cultural trappings, just as traders often adopted the guise of the cultures in which they operated, both nevertheless carried the ideological, political, and social baggage of their particular cultures.

THE "FIRST" EUROPEAN IMPERIAL AGE: THE IBERIAN POWERS AND THEIR EMULATORS

European overseas expansion grew out of fifteenth-century Iberian crown-sponsored expeditions of discovery designed to open ocean trading routes to Africa and the East. In the "first" age of European expansion, spanning the sixteenth and seventeenth centuries, the Portuguese and Spanish were the pioneers, although they were effectively challenged within a century by the Dutch, English, and French. Portuguese (and later

Dutch) commercial domination of the Indian Ocean trading economy, and Spanish, Portuguese, French, and English exploitation of resources and colonization in the "New World" of the western hemisphere were the hallmarks of this era. Iberian exploration shattered the cultural isolation that characterized past ages by inaugurating an intercontinental world trading economy.

The growth of European overseas trading was dependent upon earlier European developments: with the late-medieval emergence of a cash economy based on expanding internal trade, the growth of cities and population, and the emergence of an aggressive class of investors increasingly experienced in organizing trading ventures, the social and financial resources to support commercial ambition were in place. Additionally, continuing conflict with Islam—expressed from the eleventh century in crusading in the Holy Land and on other frontiers—when combined with the emergence of popular mendicant religious orders committed to Christian education and evangelism, most notably the Franciscans and Dominicans—produced both strong military and moral stimuli to Christian expansion. Thus, when in the fifteenth century waning Mongol rule in central Asia and waxing Ottoman power in the eastern Mediterranean disrupted trade routes carrying eastern luxury goods and spices, Europeans had both the incentives and means to seek new lines of commerce.

The relative poverty and peripheral location of Europe limited knowledge of Asia and Africa to the geographies of the ancients, notably Ptolemy (c. 100 C.E.), and the travelers' accounts of moderns, notably the Venetian trader Marco Polo (1254–1324). Many reports of the East, including those of missionary embassies sent by the papacy to China and India from the twelfth to fourteenth centuries, provided glimpses of lands containing gold, silks, and spices, and reputed to hold mysterious realms, such as the legendary Christian kingdom of Prester John.

Early exploration. Iberian exploration vastly enlarged this knowledge. Iberians, utilizing their advantageous geographical position on the Atlantic seaboard, sought to circumvent Mediterranean commerce dominated by Italians and Arabs by employing the martial skills of a crusading aristocracy and gentry seasoned in the conquest of Iberia from Moorish Muslims while drawing on the experience of both local and Italian (particularly Genoese) seamen and pilots.

The Portuguese and Spanish crowns, confident in their possession of the true religion, received papal sanction to establish monopolies in overseas trade and missions, and promoted ecclesiastical expansion as official state ideology. By the sixteenth century, Portuguese trading networks and Spanish territorial conquests provided poorly connected men, often from the tough, ambitious lower gentry, opportunities to escape the limitations of hierarchy and poverty. Increasingly independent private traders grew rich. Missionary orders—including by the mid-1500s the newly founded Jesuits, who operated as specialists in expansion as part of a larger commitment to oppose the "heresies" of northern European Protestantism—offered overseas challenges to the piously devoted. The Portuguese and early Spanish empires absorbed thousands of men, and in both, partially because Iberian society included substantial numbers of female slaves, miscegenation was common. These practices resulted in large mixed-blood communities, from which new generations of powerful local traders and ambitious priests were drawn.

From the 1420s the Portuguese royal dynasty systematically supported exploration of the western African coast, encouraging innovations in ship design and navigation to support the search for Christian allies, slaves, gold, and spices. A large Portuguese seafaring population and an Atlantic seaboard commercial class that included many aristocratic shipowners aided exploration that by the early 1500s revealed a rich network of ancient seaborne trade lanes in the Indian Ocean. Through piracy, interdiction, and licensing of existing trades, control of the critical Spice Islands (Indonesia and Sri Lanka), and seizure of most of the important trading entrepôts from Arabia to India, the Portuguese crown and its trading servants wrested control of the seas from ubiquitous Arab and Asian traders. These latter were too ethnically, religiously, and regionally diverse to effectively oppose a heavily armed and single-minded opponent. Dynastic rivalry also led the Spanish crown to sanction exploration to open an eastern trade; its servants arrived in the Caribbean in the 1490s to discover a continent and a range of societies, from simple and nomadic to sophisticated and urban, hitherto unknown in any records available to Europeans. Portuguese and Spanish explorers were essentially predatory, seizing what trade and territory they could. That lightly populated Portugal encountered sophisticated, militarily powerful, and populous Asian societies where Europeans suffered high mortality from endemic fevers meant that, after limited initial conquests, the crown focused on creating a trading monopoly in spices (pepper, cloves, cinnamon, nutmeg, and others), drugs, and dyes for the European market. That more heavily populated Spain, recently unified as a kingdom and just entering a period of European imperial ascendancy, encoun-

476

tered societies lacking military technology based on iron and the horse and resistance to European epidemic disease meant Spanish rule in the New World was characterized by widespread territorial conquest and Christianization.

Trade drove the Portuguese empire: royal officials and trading agents dominated a system theoretically controlled from Lisbon, but in which government agents, sailors, ex-soldiers, priests, and even proscribed foreign traders like Spanish-speaking Jews (expelled from Spain in 1492) enriched themselves through private trade in Asian textiles, porcelain, gems, and bulk commodities. Europeans profitably inserted themselves into preexisting Asian trading networks, expanding trade from fortified trading enclaves known as factories and aiding the rapid diffusion of European knowledge and technology in gunnery, shipbuilding, astronomy, and navigation.

The impact of early encounters: populations, material goods, and trade.

Where the Portuguese seized territory, as at Goa, they created Christian communities of Europeans, indigenous people, and their Eurasian offspring from which an aggressive, independent, and increasingly indigenized class of traders developed. Similar racial mixing occurred in Portuguese Brazil (discovered in 1500 and developed as Portugal's only major settlement colony) where extensive slave holding and contact with Amerindians produced large multiracial populations of mulattos and mestiços that grew into an officially Portuguese, yet multiethnic, polyglot civilization, from which farmers, clerks, and traders were drawn. In a more rigidly controlled Spanish empire, where administration and extensive landholding was vigorously reserved for those of European blood, large mestizo populations were relegated to poverty and living off of Amerindians, many adopting trade as the best route to social advancement.

The shape of the Spanish empire largely resulted from the profound and extensive consequences of the "Columbian exchange" between the old and new worlds of previously separated diseases, plants, and animals. When amplified in effect by relentless Spanish warfare and brutal forced labor, Old World diseases (smallpox, measles, and influenza among others) devastated Amerindian populations, which declined from perhaps 80 to 8 million within a century of European contact. Throughout the western hemisphere, those who would resist European aggression were depopulated and demoralized while European assumptions of the superiority of European culture, religion, and socioeconomic models were reinforced.

Old World animals (horses, cattle, pigs, sheep) revolutionized American food production by introducing carting and heavy plowing, widespread herding and ranching, and equestrian mobility to nomadic frontier cultures. Old World plants (sugar, coffee, wheat, barley, and others) provided export commodities, often produced on Mediterranean-patterned slave plantations, and food crops able to sustain European settlement. New World crops like tobacco, chocolate, and dyes made from brazilwood and cochineal, could also be effectively developed for trade to Europe, but of greater impact was the introduction of New World food crops like potatoes, beans, and maize, which had a powerful, stimulating effect on European population growth, especially among the lower social classes. New World wealth, in the form of thousands of tons of looted and mined gold and silver, flowed to Europe, fueling economic growth (and inflation) already underway in Europe as Spain, resource poor and lacking manufacturing capacity, spent freely on essential supplies in northern European ports. Similarly, as trade to Asia grew, gold and silver flowed eastward, accelerating the use of currency, and the pace of commercial activity, thus creating new, mostly urban, centers of power in Asian societies.

In the New World, as early exploration quickly gave way to plunder, warfare, and the seizure of indigenous peoples as slaves and peons—processes that overtook the Aztec, Maya, and Inca empires—a trading economy grew fueled by emerging European markets for New World agricultural goods. Crucial to this emerging order, rationalized, export-oriented agriculture, especially of sugar cane, spread rapidly throughout the Caribbean. Worked increasingly by African slaves, the sugar economy stimulated a transatlantic trade that transformed European habits and nutrition while enriching Atlantic seaboard ports and their merchant elites. With traders working furiously throughout the Iberian empires to supply products demanded by colonial settlements and the populations that surrounded them with household goods, food, wines, luxury items, and slaves, the range and volume of European trade expanded as never before.

This trade began to shift the centuries-old center of European economic weight from the Mediterranean to the Atlantic, as northern European port cities rose to economic preeminence. And with demand for sugar came a parallel demand for slaves, largely supplied by Portuguese slave traders, operating out of Guinea and Angola under crown-licensed contractors and subcontracting independent traders. Here alliances with African tribes and an emerging Afro-Portuguese community that took grain, cloth, beads, iron goods, and horses in exchange for slaves supplied a market that grew rapidly after 1550, inaugurating the forced migration, over three and a half centuries, of approximately 10 million African slaves, mostly male, to the Americas.

Missionaries and their impact in the East. Missions spread rapidly along the routes of Iberian trade and conquest, as priests and friars frequently accompanied exploration and trading voyages. The nature of missionary practice was strongly determined by its relationship to colonial power, with coercive methods employed more frequently in areas of strong political control. In the East centers like Goa, Macao, and Nagasaki rose rapidly as missionary as well as trading hubs, but only in strongly controlled port enclaves like Goa could religion and governance be melded in crusading style through forced conversions.

Outside these enclaves missionaries in the eastern empires—many recruited from urban and cosmopolitan Italy as well as Portugal—adopted accommodationist strategies; notably, Jesuit missionaries embraced indigenous dress and customs, allowed converts local rituals, and developed indigenized Christian rites and sympathetic responses to eastern religious beliefs. In China Jesuits were able to exchange knowledge in western science at the imperial court for the opportunity to convert, by the seventeenth century, approximately thirty thousand followers; in southern India missions more successfully drew perhaps a quarter million converts, many from lower castes seeking Portuguese protection; and even more spectacularly in Japan, some 300,000 were converted in a period of internal Japanese turmoil.

Many converts appear to have been attracted by the ethical content of Christianity; however, inducements to conversion, including commercial favoritism and bribery, and extensive missionary trading generated vigorous criticism among priests and friars of different nationalities and orders, as well as from Asian elites. State persecutions in China and Japan largely extinguished missionary influence in these regions by the eighteenth century. Despite the problems of penetrating eastern societies, however, Catholic missions secured as many as a million converts (from populations of tens of millions) in the lands surrounding the Indian Ocean, many linked to trading communities associated with Eurasians and the Portuguese. In the process of contact, excellent, detailed missionary reports of China, Japan, the Pacific, and other areas (including pioneering studies of eastern languages like Chinese and Vietnamese) generated a much greater knowledge of the East.

Spanish missions in the Americas. Spanish missions faced similar problems in the Americas: in frontier regions accommodationist measures were attempted, while in heavily settled areas, coercion and social advantages to conversion aided missions. The Spanish secular church was rapidly swept up in trade and exploitation of the Americas, sharing the contempt and impatience with unfamiliar foreign cultures of Spanish colonists intent on re-creating an essentially feudal social hierarchy of noble landowning rulers commanding dependent agricultural laborers. Expectations of social hierarchy, including widespread acceptance of slavery for black Africans, also characterized the ideas of most missionaries, who were recruited from a culturally confident Spanish population.

Nevertheless, it was primarily missionaries who condemned the brutal results of the virtual enslavement of Amerindians and, however imperfectly, cooperated with the Crown (which was interested in ordering colonial society) to protect them. Often finding themselves at odds with settler communities that habitually defied royal authority to violently conscript indigenous labor, missionary policy developed, as in Mexico, for example, on the logic of separating Amerindians into town communities, where protective mission institutions (church, school, orphanage, hospital), prohibitions on European contact, and Christianization were mixed with attempts to re-create traditional agricultural and artisanal self-sufficiency. In mission compounds, proselytes were taught Christianity and Latin, and often compelled to adopt European customs such as domestic architecture and manners, western dress, and monogamy.

Missionary reservations were the most developed form of this latter policy. The first was established by the Franciscans in Guatemala in the 1540s, and later Jesuits favored this strategy, most famously applied in the nearly autonomous Jesuit state that arose in Paraguay. In one Asian Pacific area, the Philippines, Spanish colonization (following territorial claims made in 1521 by the explorer Magellan in his circumnavigation of the globe) also led to widespread conversions. In hostile and economically unproductive regions, however, like California and many rugged inland South American areas, while mission communities were established with a zeal that produced martyrs, few conversions resulted owing to the absence of widespread Spanish social power.

As culturally aggressive institutions allied to state power, Spanish missions offered social structure and economic opportunity in return for at least the outward forms of Christian practice. The ritual of Catholic worship was often readily syncretized with previous beliefs, especially in the Aztec and Incan lands where subject populations already accustomed to paternalistic priestly religion and inured to docile agri-

Missionaries and Settlers. Portrait of settler nobility and Jesuit saints in the Casimiento de Loyola de Campanía at Cuzco, Peru, seventeenth century. The couple in the left foreground are Martin de Loyola, governor and captain general of Chile, and his wife, Beatris Clara Coya Inga, a descendant of Inca royalty. At the right are their daughter, Ana Maria Coya de Loyola Inga, and her husband, Juan Enrique Borja. In the middle are St. Ignatius Loyola, the founder of the Society of Jesus, and St. Francis Borgia (Borja), the third superior general of the Society. COURTESY THE LATIN AMERICAN LIBRARY, HARTH-TERRE COLLECTION, TULANE UNIVERSITY

cultural toil came rapidly under control of the Church. Because missions baptized freely and parishes were often enormous in their extent, missionaries in reality contributed to the creation of a set of local cultures that were wide-ranging amalgams of Christianity and the cultural forms—music, dance, and iconography—of ancient religions.

European religious zeal produced a population of around 5,500 missionaries in the Americas by 1600, nearly 75 percent of them Franciscans and Dominicans. Early idealism faded as missions became routinized and adopted European monastic practices, including heavy involvement in trade and the management of indigenous labor (especially in agriculture and textiles). Widespread criticism of apparent greed resulted as missionary trading extended to virtually every form of colonial product and missions acquired enormous land holdings. The Church and its missions also succumbed to the growing racial consciousness of colonial society, ordaining few indigenous bishops

(and none at all in its first century), and increasingly denying European education to converts. Thus, while missionaries could be important preservers of indigenous languages and certain cultural forms, the effective spread of Roman Catholicism and Spanish and Portuguese as dominant languages must be considered the single greatest unifying influence in the creation of cultural identities throughout Latin America.

Spanish and Portuguese experience in the New World and the East commanded educated attention throughout Europe. The accounts of explorers, traders, travelers, and missionaries—Columbus, Bartolomé de Las Casas, Amerigo Vespucci, Bernal Díaz del Castillo, Gonzalo Fernández de Oviedo, Matteo Ricci, Jean de Léry, and others—were repeatedly published throughout Europe and stirred wonder at lands and peoples unknown to the ancients and productive of abundant wealth. With rare exceptions, Europeans, with their technological power in ships, warfare, and writing, strongly expressed their sense of superiority

BARTOLOMÉ DE LAS CASAS

Spanish missionaries in the New World faced the enormous challenge of converting entirely unknown cultures of people that had been immediately and brutally exploited by conquistadors for tribute and labor. The most famous and influential of the early Spanish churchmen and missionaries advocating more enlightened treatment of the Amerindians was Bartolomé de Las Casas (1474–1566).

Born in Seville to a minor merchant family, Las Casas sailed to Hispaniola in 1502, and as a conquistador participated in numerous expeditions, for which he was granted an *encomienda* (a royal grant of land and Indian laborers). Following the colonial pattern, Las Casas established a large estate, worked many of his Indian serfs in local mines, and participated (as a priest, having been ordained in 1512) in the bloody subjugation of Cuba, for which he received additional *encomienda*. Evangelistic work among ''his'' Indians led to a radical change in his outlook; relinquishing his *encomienda,* he became a champion of the rights of Amerindians and leader of a small but vocal group of churchmen crusading for the general improvement of Indian conditions.

When he returned to Spain, Las Casas advocated the natural rights of Amerindians in the Barcelona Parliament and received royal support for a utopian plan to build towns where free Indians and carefully selected Spanish farmers would create harmonious mixed Christian communities. The failure of a model South American settlement in 1522, in the face of opposition from *encomenderos* and violent resistance from local indigenous inhabitants, led Las Casas to join the Dominican order and begin writing the first of several historical and prophetic exposés on the oppression and injustice of Spanish colonialism. He also expressed the growing uncertainty in church and government circles concerning the enormous human costs of Spanish colonization, yet royal attempts to regulate abuses largely failed in the face of fierce resistance from *encomenderos* in the distant, expansive empire. The weight of reforming opinion led the papacy in 1537 to declare all humans deserving of freedom, property, and true religion. A successful peaceful mission led by Las Casas and several Dominicans in the still-unconquered region of Tuzutlan (in present-day Costa Rica) induced Las Casas to again return to Spain in 1540 to condemn worldly lust for wealth as an indefensible basis for Spanish expansion.

Rejecting the views of contemporaries that all native Americans were ''naturally lazy and vicious, melancholic, cowardly, and in general a lying shiftless people,'' Las Casas instead characterized Amerindians as ''a simple

The Black Legend. Spanish massacre natives in America. From *Narratio regionum indicarum* (1614) by Bartolomé de Las Casas (1474–1566), missionary and bishop who advocated laws protecting the native peoples of the Western Hemisphere. NEW YORK PUBLIC LIBRARY

people without evil and without guile . . . most submissive, patient, peaceful and virtuous,'' lacking only true religion. His arguments induced the Spanish crown in 1542 to pass the New Laws, outlawing the *encomienda* system, yet when Las Casas returned to the Americas as bishop of Chiapas in Guatemala, his uncompromising application of these laws and the attempt to again create model mission villages brought widespread and violent Spanish resistance, including that of governing officials and his brother bishops.

Armed attacks forced Las Casas to return to Spain in 1547 where as an influential courtier he sought to defeat popular Aristotelian arguments that Amerindians were naturally inferior and thus could be justly conquered and enslaved. Arguing from classical texts that Indians, as rational and charitable peoples, did not fit the category of slaves ''by nature,'' he characterized Spaniards as the true barbarians in the colonial encounter. Nevertheless, the practice of slavery continued in Spanish America, although waning slowly over the eighteenth century. The wide publication of Las Casas' works in translation throughout Europe, however, brought him to notice in northern nations where his view that the Spaniards brought destruction, not salvation, and that their methods of colonization were fundamentally unjust armed Protestant propagandists to justify aggressive opposition to Spanish control in the New World.

and a confidence that their religious truths and established social hierarchies should and would be universally adopted. The wonderful strangeness of the New World in particular led first generations of observers to fall back on traditional allusions, envisioning the Americas as an Arcadia or Eden, abounding in simplicity, innocence, and abundance. Strongly influenced by millenarianism and Erasmian humanism, many mystical Catholic friars believed an evangelized America could answer the moral corruptions of Europe. However, because Catholic missions were carried out as state policy by specialized orders, missionary perspectives had little popular resonance or impact among the laity and clergy of Europe.

The first northern European encounters: the logic of trade. Iberian overseas successes drew north Atlantic nations into maritime exploration. Failing the discovery of northern passages to the East or lands of abundant gold, northern Europeans, including Swedes and Danes but dominated by the Dutch, English, and French, engaged first in parasitic activities against Iberian trade. Early smuggling and privateering, however, quickly gave way to competitive trade, settlement, and agricultural production. Religious passions arising from the conflicts of the Protestant Reformation and the rise of mercantilist economic attitudes, with their stress on acquiring bullion and enhancing exports, led to new exploration, trading ventures, and settlement. The French, for example, after widespread privateering against Iberians (often launched from Protestant Huguenot Atlantic ports) established backwoods traders at widely dispersed trading posts reaching into the North American Great Lakes region. From these they established contacts with the fiercely independent North American Indian tribes to exchange blankets, brandy, steel weapons, and other manufactured goods for beaver and otter skins for the European luxury market. As traders from other nations entered the field, the growing trade and availability of weapons led to increased indigenous warfare, making missionary work treacherous. Following the pattern of Catholic Iberian powers, French Canada was dominated by a monopolistic church that in 1636 gave the Jesuits control of missionary activity and sent hundreds of "Black Robes" inland. Their efforts resulted primarily in stirring accounts of missionary courage and martyrdom, but few conversions.

From the late sixteenth century, Protestant Dutch traders with more efficient ships and single-minded commercial intensity successfully seized the bulk of Spanish Caribbean trade while simultaneously stripping Portugal of most of its Indian Ocean empire. Organizing themselves under speculative joint-stock trading companies that were given monopolies and rights to act with diplomatic and military authority, the Dutch established traders as quasi-governmental agents pursuing profitable trade at minimal cost in the name of religious and commercial war. In the Indian Ocean and the Atlantic the Dutch displaced the Portuguese from their most important factories, ruthlessly seizing the high-profit trade in spices and slaves. The Dutch pushed the English and French into the less profitable Indian trade in pepper and cotton textiles and into settlement colonies on islands like Barbados (1627) and Martinique (1635) where sugar was produced by Dutch-supplied slaves. In India, operating at the sufferance of the powerful Mogul empire, English and French company traders established factories, hoping to survive high mortality from disease long enough to amass fortunes. In the Caribbean significantly expanded production of sugar brought forth a flourishing economy in which European adventurers, half-castes, and escaped slaves engaged in opportunistic trading and piracy in a roiling, underpoliced area of multiple colonial frontiers.

The Dutch and the English combined strongly anti-Catholic religious attitudes with a secular profit motive. However, because Protestant religion rejected religious orders, lacked central leadership, and possessed a theology emphasizing predestination, they produced few foreign missionaries. Instead, the logic of trade and the society of the trader defined northern European contact with the outside world, reflecting the strength of the urban commercial classes in Amsterdam and London. The result of northern European entry into international trade was a rapidly expanding Atlantic economy in which imperial consumption patterns—driven by a growing emulation of elite fashion—fed an emerging consumer revolution. As Britain, following a series of successful wars with the Dutch and French, established itself by the 1760s as Europe's most powerful trading nation, rapidly rising demand throughout western Europe for sugar, tobacco, Indian fabrics, coffee, and tea meant increasing standards of material and social existence, even for ordinary western Europeans.

At the center of this economy was an expanding slave trade shared by traders from the Dutch Republic, Portugal, France, Prussia, and Denmark, but dominated in the eighteenth century by the British, that expanded from an average of seven thousand to sixty thousand slaves per year between 1650 and 1760. Individual traders, trading dynasties, and absentee plantation owners made fortunes out of slaving. Accelerating internal demographic and economic pressures in Africa supported the growth of warrior states, which fed and were supported by the trade.

THE "SECOND" EUROPEAN IMPERIAL AGE: THE NORTHERN EUROPEAN POWERS

In the eighteenth century Europe slowly entered the era of its "second" empires, dominated at first by the English and French, joined later in the nineteenth century most prominently by the Germans, Belgians, and Italians, as European hegemony was extended into Africa, Asia, and the Pacific. Cultural frontiers were eroded in these centuries of intimate and sustained contact with Old World societies. European traders penetrated more deeply into regions opened by treaty or direct rule (as in China and India) and exploration (as in the Pacific Islands and Africa). Of profound importance to Christian missions, Protestant churches, under the influence of German pietism and English evangelicalism, launched a second wave of proselytizing that had deep impact in these areas.

The often independent activities of traders could have substantial impact in this environment. In India, which became a crucial possession in the second British empire, the first bridgehead was seized in Bengal, where success was due in part to the effective infiltration of Indian states by rival English and French company traders acting to capitalize on local rivalries in an era of declining Mogul power. Led by a company trader turned soldier, Robert Clive, the British East India Company emerged in the 1770s as the dominant Indian power, able to plunder Bengali government revenue. Fantastic enrichment of company traders generated debate in Britain over how a "legitimate" empire should be administered and the inauguration of more strictly controlled imperial governance. A similar process also led to the opening of China to western trade in the 1840s when independent traders built a flourishing market for smuggled opium in China, and convinced the British government to bombard Chinese ports in the name of "free trade" when Chinese authorities seized their illegal stocks from Guangzhou (Canton) trading factories. The Opium Wars (1839–1842; 1856–1860) forced open more ports to western traders and missionaries from France, Germany, and North America, as well as Britain, while the humiliations suffered by the Chinese government helped initiate the catastrophic civil war known as the Taiping Rebellion.

"Scientific" exploration and imperial systems of knowledge. Continuing European rivalries, particularly between the French and English, ushered in an era of state-sponsored "scientific" exploration designed to establish geographical knowledge in the service of imperial ambition. Louis-Antoine de Bougainville's 1766–1769 exploratory surveys of the South Pacific were a model followed by Captain James Cook's 1768 voyage to the South Pacific where he discovered and claimed the eastern coast of Australia and several islands, including New Zealand, for Britain. Rationalized programs to compile economic and strategic inventories of geographical, botanical, and anthropological information were sponsored by learned societies—most notably the Royal Society in London—which not only pressed for exploration of the South Pacific, but also the Arctic and Africa. Despite the high casualty rate of early African explorers owing to disease, from the 1790s African exploration engaged many British, French, and German adventurers. Exploration spurred new interest among secular intellectuals to examine the nature of humanity. Prominent philosophes in France, like Denis Diderot and Jean-Jacques Rousseau, as well as Scottish realist philosophers, employed visions of the "savage" that were gleaned from reports of South Seas explorations and the rediscovery of the writings of many earlier Spaniards to criticize European social and political structures.

Additionally, attempts were made to identify attributes that distinguished "civilized" social organization. These invariably favored Mediterranean cultures, followed by the Chinese, Indians and Arabs, pastoral peoples such as Mongols and Turks, and the hunter-gatherers of North America, Africa, and Australia. By the late eighteenth century these classifications were increasingly associated with presumed biological differences of race; by the mid-nineteenth century, the catalog of races was largely fixed along a color line, with the capacity for civilization descending through white, yellow, brown, red, and black. This catalog remained contested, however, particularly by missionaries, who, despite tendencies to ethnocentrism, were disposed to argue that all peoples could be raised to a common level of civilization. One important arena for the contest lay in the widely publicized exploration of Africa where the paternalistic evangelical argument for development articulated by missionary and explorer David Livingstone was implicitly pitted against the "scientific" racism characteristic of many secular explorers, like the scholar and adventurer Richard Burton, though all European travelers constructed African exploration as a narrative of "manly" European actions and "native" inferiority.

By the nineteenth century many European explorers and missionaries, although profoundly convinced of the superiority of Western civilization, were also deeply influenced by anxieties connected to emerging industrial and urban conditions at home. The growth of the factory system, crowded cities, the social challenges of poverty and class, and new standards of

Western Traders in China. Western factories in Guangzhou (Canton). Oil painting on glass, after 1780. MARK SEXTON/PEABODY ESSEX MUSEUM, SALEM, MASSACHUSETTS

"respectable" conformity could all encourage individuals to seek independence and a sense of usefulness or adventure in colonial exploits. Over the course of the century increasing numbers of missionaries found contact with "primitivism" and the challenge of native conversion preferable to growing secularism in Europe itself.

Protestant missionaries and colonialism. The expansion of traders into Asian and African interiors brought rapid, often disruptive, changes to indigenous societies, not least because the staples of those trades were often guns, cash, and drugs like liquor and opium. Increasingly, traders came under the intense criticism of burgeoning numbers of Protestant missionaries. By the end of the eighteenth century the rise of evangelicalism unleashed a religious emotionalism that stressed freely chosen conversion, spiritual equality, and activism. Protestant missionary societies emerged suddenly in Britain, led by the Baptists (1792), Congregationalists (1795), and evangelical Anglicans (1799), to be followed by other denominations and in other nations like Switzerland and Germany. As part of a larger evangelical humanitarianism, missionary activity and the campaign to abolish slavery both emerged most strongly in northwestern Europe, especially Great Britain, and the northern American states—urbanizing and industrializing regions characterized by free contract labor and growing na-

tional identities emphasizing the legal rights of free citizens. Conservative reactions to the French Revolution helped direct evangelical attention away from domestic populations and into distant areas of exploration and European expansion: the South Seas and the recently seized Indian territories were the first places to receive missionaries.

Protestant missionary societies, operating predominantly from nations where the state had ceased enforcing religious conformity, were organized as voluntary associations that while often willing to accept state aid, rejected state control. William Carey (1761–1834), the pioneer Baptist missionary to India, was the most important theorist to the Anglo-American missionary movement. He urged that missionary organizations embrace "the spread of civil and religious liberty" as a reality and opportunity that among the western churches necessitated new methods of organization to secure mass lay and clerical support.

By the mid-nineteenth century, public meetings and rallies, often featuring returned missionaries, and the mass publication of books and periodicals (disseminated in Britain by the millions through a national network of local parish and chapel associations) emphasized the violence, subjugation, and ignorance purportedly bred of "heathen" religions, and the desperate need of non-Christians for European tutelage. Support for missions crossed class lines but was strongest, as was the recruitment of missionaries, among

Western Missionary in Africa. "The Main Stream Came Up to Susi's Mouth" from David Livingstone, *Livingtone's Travels and Researches in South Africa* (Philadelphia, 1858), p. 33. NORTH WIND PICTURE ARCHIVES

artisans, tradesmen, clerks, manufacturers, professionals, and other "respectable" classes. Leadership came from the educated middle classes (many university trained by century's end) and societies relied heavily on activist women both as organizers and financial supporters. By the first decade of the twentieth century approximately ten thousand voluntarily supported European Protestant missionaries (about 80 percent British, 15 percent German, 5 percent Scandinavian, French, Dutch, and Swiss, supplemented by a rapidly increasing American force of about four thousand) were concentrating their efforts in Africa, China, and India; a parallel revival of Catholic missions, strongly French and newly aided by voluntary organizations, fielded some eight thousand missionary priests.

European missions continued to have an ambivalent relationship with colonialism. Often operating in conjunction with imperial power, as in the founding of French missions in the Congo and Tahiti or British missions in New Zealand and Uganda, missions nevertheless often had strained relations with colonial authorities, while many missionaries expressed doubts about the value of western culture to evangelization. However, the continuing problem of communication meant considerable effort was spent on linguistic work that produced pioneering grammars and dictionaries for virtually every world language. Educational work resulted in the founding of over twenty thousand mission schools by century's end.

While such efforts did support colonial administration, as in India, missionaries were often highly critical of the religious neutrality practiced by their governors. Major social problems, especially those associated with slavery and "destructive" western trades in weapons and drugs, elicited missionary condemnations of imperial policy. Early in the century British missionaries encouraged trade in "legitimate" goods—especially cotton—envisioned as supporting working and trading communities of indigenous Christians. The failure of attempts to create such missionary communities in the West Indies (following Parliamentary abolition of British slavery in 1833) and both West and East Africa—and reinforced by the shock of colonial rebellions in India (1857) and Jamaica (1865)—caused some missionaries, especially charismatic evangelicals like those of the China Inland Mission (1865), to reject westernization strategies in favor of itinerant evangelization and the adoption of indigenous dress and manners. Many others reaffirmed commitments to strategies that had been designed to "leaven" indigenous societies in preparation for widespread conversion: the creation of orphanages, schools, and colleges (higher education being especially emphasized in India and China) was supplemented with the tutoring of women by women and medical work in dispensaries and hospitals.

As professionalized strategies increased, so did a "social work" emphasis in missions, to which women, and especially after 1885 unmarried women, were of growing importance; by 1899 women accounted for at least 56 percent of all British missionaries in the field, while as many as forty thousand Catholic sisters worked in charitable and educational missions. Overall, the variety of missionary responses to trade, colonial governance, and non-western cultures produced variable results. But as the century progressed, missionaries displayed an increased willingness to lobby for standard colonial governmental protections to safeguard their converts and institutions.

The impact of Christian missionaries in the modern world.
The Christian message, with its strong egalitarian strains, had the potential to fundamentally subvert hierarchies and authority built on ethnic, historical, or racial arguments. Yet paternalistic missionary attitudes, which frequently assumed the superiority of Western economic and social organization, often supported colonial dependency. Indigenous responses varied widely. In India, for example, churches grew with late-century converts from the lowest castes, but more importantly both Hinduism and Islam were spurred to major reform movements and revivals by the religious and ethical challenges presented by Christianity and Western power. Africa, by contrast, saw missions evolve into flourishing African churches, but only after separatist African-led churches split from missions or charismatic leaders founded syncretic Christian sects that embraced traditional African beliefs. In

every field, missions and their resources were used for local purposes, as in South Africa where in Methodist and Congregationalist missions indigenous chiefs retained considerable powers over local life while adopting market agriculture and accepting imperial protections lobbied for by missionaries. In these ways the self-supporting churches that had been the stated goal of missionary policy throughout the nineteenth century were achieved over the misgivings of white missionaries.

European missionaries were largely ineffective in responding to anti-imperialist critiques in the twentieth century. Missionary education served to shape educated elites and produced nationalist leaders in India, China, and Africa. However, the many real and imagined connections of missions to white power were emphasized by nationalists. In some areas missions met with disaster—in China, missionaries were expelled after the 1949 communist seizure of power. In others, like India, missions produced small minority communities, but failed at any meaningful dialogue with organized majority religions. In yet others missions could be succeeded by large indigenized churches, as in Africa, Korea, and Indonesia. European missionary societies remained active in the late twentieth century, but had little of the public profile

European Tutelage. Portraits of Kaiser William II and Kaiserin Augusta Victoria dominate a classroom in a German missionary school in Dar es Salaam, German East Africa, 1903.
ULLSTEIN BILDERDIENST, BERLIN

485

MARY KINGSLEY

Nineteenth-century European empires provided increasing opportunities for women in travel and professional pursuits. In missions women worked as educators and nurses, but outside of these religious institutions, because imperial structures excluded women, their primary roles were as writers and social observers, capable of delivering powerful commentaries on foreign peoples to a wide readership. European exploration from the eighteenth century onward became an increasingly publicized endeavor, and in the nineteenth century narratives of exploration, like those of David Livingstone, sold impressive numbers of books and spawned a growing market for travel writing. In this market women were increasingly able to compete, providing narratives of vicarious female intrepidity. From the 1870s onward, larger numbers of women journeyed abroad to ever more remote destinations: some few, like Florence Baker, were married to famous explorers, but most were single women freed financially and socially for travel by the deaths of male relatives.

Perhaps the most influential and extraordinary of these was the British traveler Mary Kingsley (1862–1900). After a life of duty to the care of her ailing parents, Mary Kingsley—self-educated (in the sciences and anthropology) and following the interests of her widely traveled father—embarked in 1892 upon a series of journeys in West Africa as "a beetle and fetish hunter." Her widely read *Travels in West Africa* (1897) and *West African Studies* (1899) were reinforced in their impact by her extensive and popular public lecturing.

Kingsley adopted the identity of pragmatic scientist—naturalist and anthropologist—but also embodied the profound ambivalence about gender roles that female travel evoked in her insistence on maintaining respectable Victorian attire throughout her African journeys. In a further elucidation of gender difference, she relinquished the vigorously domineering voice of the self-actualized male

travel writer for self-deprecation, humor, and a willingness to credit the assistance received in her travels from traders and Africans alike. Coming to see the central conflict in West Africa as lying between missionaries and traders, Kingsley sided with the traders, decrying the attempts of missionaries to transform Africans, whom she saw as different in kind from Europeans, as naive and ignorant.

Supporting herself by trading with Africans in rubber and palm oil, and relying on the assistance of various trading "agents," Kingsley supported the imperial endeavor but lobbied the Colonial Office to leave the governance of West Africa to traders, who supplied Africans with necessary goods while allowing their "development" along more autonomous lines. Her expression of sympathy for the efforts of traders—such as her comment on the "terrible . . . life of a man in one of these out-of-the-way factories, with no white society, and with nothing to look at . . . but the one set of objects—the forest, the river, and the beach"—reinforced notions of the stoic European persevering in primitive environs. Yet her equal sympathy for Africans, their "remarkable mental acuteness and large share of common sense" and serious interest in their lives reinforced the exhortations from professional anthropologists that a clearer understanding of the integrated structure of indigenous societies was necessary. Her view that racial and cultural differences were to be appreciated rather than decried was set against common missionary assumptions that Europeanization and reform of "childlike" indigenous manners were an essential part of the "civilizing" colonial process.

Thus, despite antipathy to missionaries, Kingsley and late-century anthropologists advanced a general European change in attitudes that also brought increasing numbers of missionaries to more sophisticated and sympathetic attitudes to indigenous cultures.

and support or sense of cultural mission that characterized the nineteenth century. Instead, they evolved a philosophy of partnership and outreach, partially as a result of the postcolonial rise of independent churches throughout the world and the decline of activist European religiosity, partially through the growth of

theological liberalism that spawned an ecumenical movement of world Christian cooperation. In the twentieth century, the educational, developmental, and humanitarian activities carried out by missions were extended by transnational nonprofit charitable corporations. However, the primary effect of the missionary movement from the Renaissance on has been the transformation of Christianity from an almost exclusively European faith to a far more eclectic world religion, with hundreds of millions of adherents in Africa, Asia, and Latin America.

The twentieth century, then, largely brought to an end the era of exploration, independent trading, and missionary activity as European pursuits carried out with almost complete cultural self-assurance. With the exploration of the polar caps in the first decades of the twentieth century, few frontiers remained that did not require the resources of a modern nation-state to explore. At the same time, the rise of modern multinational corporations and the creation of major communication and transport networks allowing retail marketing throughout the globe largely ended the age of the independent freebooting trader. Though the era of European world dominance has passed, the modern world has been significantly shaped by the economic, social, and cultural forces transmitted through the activities of exploration, trade, and proselytizing.

See also other articles in this section.

BIBLIOGRAPHY

Bickers, Robert A., and Rosemary Seton. *Missionary Encounters: Sources and Issues.* Richmond, Surrey, U.K., 1996. Selection of articles dealing with domestic organization of missionary societies, female medical missionaries, anthropological use of missionary archives, and other relevant topics.

Cox, Jeffrey. "The Missionary Movement." In *Nineteenth-Century English Religious Traditions: Retrospect and Prospect.* Edited by D. G. Paz. Westport, Conn., 1995. Pages 197–220. Provides an excellent overview of scholarly historiography of missions and underlying social and organizational themes in their development.

Crosby, Alfred. *The Columbian Exchange; Biological and Cultural Consequences of 1492.* Westport, Conn., 1972. A clear and detailed account of the impact of Old and New World contact.

Elliot, John Huxtable. *The Old World and the New, 1492–1650.* Cambridge, U.K., 1970. A concise synthesis of the impact of New World discoveries on European politics, economics, and culture.

Grafton, Anthony. *New Worlds, Ancient Texts: The Power of Tradition and the Shock of Discovery.* Cambridge, Mass., 1992. An illuminating and readable assessment of the challenges to tradition and strategies of interpretation used by Europeans to comprehend the information generated by the Age of Discovery.

Greenblatt, Stephen. *Marvelous Possessions: The Wonder of the New World.* Chicago, 1991. An intriguing analysis of the rhetorical strategies used by the first generations of Europeans in their attempt to comprehend the New World.

Hall, Catherine. *White, Male, and Middle-Class: Explorations in Feminism and History.* New York, 1992. Two key chapters provide a clear exposition of how British domestic models and class assumptions were inscribed in the abolition movement and missionary programs to reorder ex-slave societies in the West Indies, and how racial prejudice intensified at mid-century.

Marshall, Peter James, and Glyndwr Williams. *The Great Map of Mankind: British Perceptions of the World in the Age of Enlightenment.* Cambridge, Mass., 1982. Provides an excellent overview of changing conceptions of human societies and nature in the eighteenth century.

McNeill, William Hardy. *Plagues and Peoples.* Garden City, N.Y., 1976. A classic analysis of the impact of epidemic disease throughout history.

Neill, Stephen. *A History of Christian Missions.* 2d ed. Revised by Owen Chadwick. Harmondsworth, U.K., 1986. A comprehensive account of Christian missionaries, heavily narrational and sympathetic to the missionary enterprise.

Porter, Andrew. "Religion and Empire: British Expansion in the Long Nineteenth Century, 1780–1914." *Journal of Imperial and Commonwealth History* 20, no. 3 (1992): 370–390. An important assessment of the changing relationship between imperial government and missions stressing the importance of the interplay between missionary experience and theology.

Scammell, Geoffrey Vaughn. *The World Encompassed: The First European Maritime Empires, c. 800–1650.* Berkeley and Los Angeles, 1981. An excellent series of brief and accessible histories of different national imperial experiences. Weaves exploration, trade, and missionary activity together with an eye to social and economic background and consequences.

Stanley, Brian. *The Bible and the Flag: Protestant Missions and British Imperialism in the Nineteenth and Twentieth Centuries.* Leicester, U.K., 1990. A detailed and critical analysis that emphasizes the unique imperial perspective of missionaries. The only comparative account available of British missions throughout the empire.

EMIGRATION AND COLONIES

Kenneth J. Orosz

Shortly after the first European voyages of discovery brought news of the New World back to the Old, settlers and conquerors began flocking out to the newly claimed territories to begin the process of extracting colonial wealth for the benefit of the metropole. Although the desire for profit remained a constant for the duration of the European colonial endeavor, as the various imperial powers expanded their holdings beyond the Americas, the process of colonial emigration took on new forms and led to the creation of profoundly different social structures in each of the colonial regions. It is these differences that provide the groundwork for a social history of colonial settlement by European emigrants. This essay will address four major regional cases in which colonization was accompanied by significant European settlement: South America, North America, the antipodes, and Africa.

In the Americas different economic imperatives resulted in the transportation of racially homogenous settler populations to the British and French holdings in the north while their Iberian counterparts in the south created colonies comprised of relatively small settler groups ruling over much larger populations of Amerindians, imported African slaves, and mixed-race groups. The eventual loss of its American colonies in the late eighteenth century forced Britain to open up new settlement colonies in the antipodes as a means of divesting itself of growing numbers of convicts. Despite its origins as a penal settlement, over the next several decades growing numbers of free settlers from northern Europe flocked to the region to set up farms and ranches in Australia and New Zealand. Subsequent efforts to shed the region's violent and brutal convict past in favor of middle-class Victorian respectability were complicated by the existence and poor treatment of aboriginal populations, who stood in the way of European-style economic progress. No such problems affected the European settlement colonies in Africa. As the final region of colonial emigration, most of which occurred in the nineteenth century, Africa enjoyed the least complicated colonial society. The advent of social Darwinism and visions of the "white man's burden" necessitated the creation of racially segregated colonial societies in which white settlers unabashedly enriched themselves by systematically divesting Africans of land, wealth, and political independence. Despite the different social structures, in all cases European emigration created new forms of social hierarchy in which Europeans displaced existing ruling elites.

COLONIAL EMIGRATION IN SOUTH AND CENTRAL AMERICA

The completion of the Reconquista in 1492 and the end of hostilities in Spain and Portugal eliminated the prospects for the accumulation of loot and social advancement in the Iberian Peninsula via service on the battlefield for a whole generation of Iberians. The Muslim presence had, however, exposed the Spanish and Portuguese to tales of African gold fields and the lucrative Asian trade. In an effort to profit from and possibly control these resources, both powers began equipping a series of merchant vessels for voyages of trade and discovery. Central to these voyages was the search for faster, more lucrative trade routes that would propel the mother country to the forefront of European commerce. These efforts, which focused primarily on attempts to discover shortcuts to Asia, quickly led explorers and conquistadors to the Americas, where a limited number soon found wealth beyond their wildest dreams in the form of plantations and gold mines.

The bulk of these activities fell to Spain, which took an early lead in conquering and exploiting the New World. As news of Inca and Aztec wealth reached Spain in the early sixteenth century, scores of individual conquistadors, including some who lacked royal authorization or approval, flocked to the Americas. Aided by firearms and disease, these small bands of European soldiers quickly defeated the indigenous peoples and began looting their treasures of gold, silver, and gemstones. As they conquered Inca and Aztec

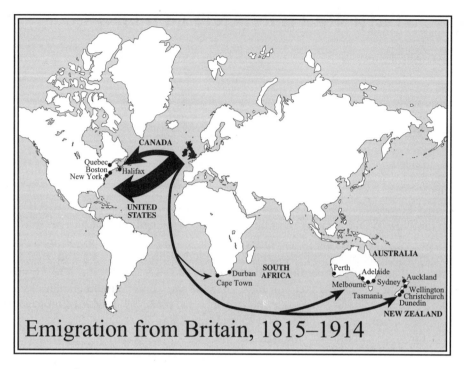

Emigration from Britain, 1815–1914. Adapted from A. N. Porter, ed., *Atlas of British Overseas Expansion,* London, Routledge, 1991.

villages in pursuit of profit, the conquistadors also turned their attention to reopening local gold and silver mines. This process was greatly facilitated by the creation of the *encomienda* system. Eager to both reward conquistadors and to secure larger shares of tax and tribute, the Spanish crown granted soldiers serving in the New World an *encomienda,* or license that allowed the holder to direct and exploit the labor of all native peoples living within the borders of his grant. While some of these forced laborers were put to work growing food on haciendas, the vast majority found themselves performing backbreaking work in mines and coastal plantations for the benefit of their Spanish overlords.

Social hierarchies in Spanish America.

The earliest of these overlords were the conquistadors themselves, most of whom stayed on in the colony to oversee their land grants. As a result they formed a new landed colonial aristocracy that quickly came to dominate local politics and economics. Over the next three centuries the conquistadors were joined by an average of twenty-six hundred new emigrants every year. Since labor in the form of Amerindians, African slaves, and mixed-race populations was so readily available in Spanish colonies, there was no need to import a white proletariat. Consequently, the vast majority of the 750,000 Spaniards who eventually emigrated to the

colonies were lower-middle-class young men in search of social mobility and economic opportunity. On arrival, these emigrants took up support roles as artisans, clerics, merchants, and civil servants. Since they came from a largely urban environment, the new arrivals tended to join the conquistadors in newly built colonial towns, thereby recreating the social hierarchy of Castile in which an urban upper class lived off the profits of landed estates worked by peasants.

Although this upper-class settler community presented a largely uniform facade, it was actually beset with a wide variety of internal social divisions. Within the settler community of Spanish America, social order was highly stratified according to class, occupation, birthplace, and race. Settlers born and raised in the colonies, known as Creoles, were generally looked down upon as ignorant, backcountry yokels by more recent arrivals who were better versed in current metropolitan culture. Offensive as this was, the Creole population was even more bitter about the Crown's tendency to ignore them, despite their obvious wealth, knowledge, and experience, in favor of candidates from the metropole when it came time to fill the upper echelons of colonial administration. This situation was further compounded by the tendency of royal appointees, most of whom arrived in the colony knowing little of local affairs, to retire to Spain once they had served out their term of office. As a result, tensions between the two groups grew steadily throughout the colonial period and eventually helped contribute to the Creole population's declaration of independence in the early nineteenth century.

As important as geographical origin was to the social hierarchy in the colonies, Spanish settlers were even more interested in the racial background of community members. The dearth of white women, who made up 6.2 percent of sixteenth-century emigrants before peaking at 28.5 percent a century later, made miscegenation common. Despite the prevalence of this practice, children born of such unions (known as mestizos) represented the lowest levels of settler society and faced significant social discrimination. Efforts to avoid this stigma led settlers to carefully document their racial origins via elaborate genealogies based on marriage and baptism records. While this suggests a fairly rigid color bar within Creole society, in practice things were much looser, particularly for richer community members. Wealth not only bought greater social acceptance, it also enabled individuals to bribe priests and government clerks in an effort to alter official records to hide Indian or, eventually, African bloodlines.

Social hierarchies in Portuguese America.
As the Spanish presence in the Americas solidified, Portugal began pressing its own claims to the region and set up a rival settlement colony in Brazil. Although some aspects of Portuguese emigration patterns mirrored those of their Spanish counterparts, colonial society in Brazil contained some notable differences, particularly in regard to racial issues. Part of the reason for this was economic. While Brazil lacked readily accessible mineral resources, its climate lent itself to the creation of sugar plantations, something that the Portuguese had already experienced in the Azores. Despite the lucrative nature of sugar plantations, Portugal's chronic lack of resources and the brutal tropical climate in Brazil meant that emigration to the colony was destined to lag far behind that to Spanish America. This in turn meant that Portuguese settlers were more accustomed to interacting with Amerindians and, eventually, African slaves than were their Spanish counterparts.

Mirroring Spanish colonial emigration, most Portuguese settlers were young men in search of economic opportunity in the New World. While a lucky few created large landed estates and plantations hacked out of the countryside at the expense of native peoples, the majority of Portuguese settlers became small ranchers and farmers concentrated along the coast. This remained true even after the brief population boom generated by the discovery of gold and dia-

monds in the 1690s. Disturbed by the slow population growth within the largely male settler society, the Portuguese crown began openly encouraging intermarriage with the indigenous peoples. Consequently, and in stark contrast to the Spanish colonies, the Portuguese welcomed the arrival of mixed-race children and easily assimilated them into the larger settler community. As color lines faded, Brazilian colonial society found itself split more by socioeconomics and Creole-metropolitan rivalries than by physical appearance.

Amerindians and African slaves in colonial society.
As conscious of their own internal hierarchies as the settlers and mestizos in both Spanish and Portuguese America were, they all agreed that the Amerindian population ranked still lower on the social scale. From the very beginnings of the European presence in the Americas the indigenous peoples were exploited for land, treasure, and, most importantly, manual labor. Amerindians, however, quickly discovered that work on Spanish and Portuguese plantations, haciendas, and mines was harsh and had a high death toll due to poor conditions, exhaustion, mistreatment, and disease. Consequently, many resisted European

Racial Background. A wealthy Spaniard with his Amerindian wife and mestiza daughter, eighteenth century.
PRIVATE COLLECTION/PHOTO BY CAMILO GARZA

demands for labor by staging uprisings, fleeing into the bush, and engaging in sabotage. To their extreme frustration, both the Spanish and the Portuguese discovered that the combination of these factors led to chronic labor shortages and delayed the all-important process of extracting wealth from their colonial holdings.

This situation was further compounded by the presence of missionaries and the creation of official native policies. Although all missionaries focused their efforts on converting the masses to Christianity, the missionary presence in the Iberian colonies changed over time. Like their settler counterparts, the first generation of missionaries in Latin America tended to destroy and denigrate indigenous culture, customs, and society. As colonial society took root, however, the missionaries came to believe that the only way to truly root out pagan beliefs and win converts over to Christianity was to study and fully understand the indigenous peoples. As a result of these efforts, missionaries became better informed and often sympathetic about the plight of the indigenous peoples. This in turn gave birth to a running debate in both the Spanish and Portuguese holdings about the nature and extent of Amerindian rights. According to the conquistadors and large landowners, the indigenous peoples were not only uncivilized heathens who had lost the right to govern themselves, they had to be tamed and transformed into useful members of society by the settlers for the good of all concerned. Such lofty goals, so the argument went, justified any and all means, including the brutal slavelike working conditions in the mines and plantations. Missionaries sympathetic to the plight of the indigenous peoples argued instead that they were childlike innocents that could be converted if shown the right behaviors and values. Consequently, in both the Spanish and Portuguese holdings, missionaries set themselves up as protectors and defenders of Amerindian rights, exerting constant pressure on the crowns back in Europe to follow their lead.

In the Spanish case this led Charles V (1500–1558) to finally abolish Indian slavery in 1542. Although the Portuguese rulers were generally sympathetic to the missionary point of view, pressure from wealthy plantation owners and their lobbyists at court delayed them from taking similar action until the mid-1700s. In both cases, however, abolition was in name only. While Indians were transformed from slaves into wage laborers, they were crushed by heavy taxes, demands for tribute, poor wages, and work conditions. These pressures collectively forced the indigenous peoples into debt peonage—they took on the role of serfs. Consequently, despite the change in their legal status, Amerindians enjoyed no corresponding changes in their socioeconomic position for the duration of the colonial period.

When the Spanish and Portuguese discovered shortly after their arrival in the New World that the indigenous peoples were incapable of and unwilling to provide sufficient labor for the process of extracting wealth from the colonies, both powers resorted to the importation of large numbers of African slaves. While insufficient records make it impossible to determine exactly how many Africans suffered this fate, by 1810 some 10 million had been enslaved and shipped to the New World. Most were sent to South America where they were expected to spend their lives toiling in European-owned economic enterprises. Treatment of slaves, while better than that meted out during transatlantic journies, was still poor. In addition to the loss of their liberty, harsh working conditions, and mistreatment, slaves faced brutal punishments and short life expectancies. Since few women were brought to the New World as slaves, and since those who did make the journey were often the victims of unwanted sexual advances from their white owners, most blacks either lacked family lives or found them by intermarrying with the Amerindian population. The result was the creation of a mulatto community, which, along with slaves and free blacks, made up the lowest echelons of colonial society and faced constant discrimination and exploitation.

COLONIAL EMIGRATION IN NORTH AMERICA

While both France and England also relied to some extent on slave labor in their American possessions, they encountered far fewer racial problems and were able to construct more homogenous settlement colonies built primarily around small farmers. France and England were relative newcomers to colonization; this in part explains why they created colonial societies so different from those of their Iberian counterparts. When news of the wealth pouring into Spain and Portugal from their American holdings finally roused the British and French into action, the most lucrative pieces of the New World had already been claimed. The remaining pieces of North America lacked readily accessible mineral wealth, easily exploitable supplies of Amerindian labor, and, with the exception of the Carribean and the southernmost portions of the mainland, climates suitable for plantations. Britain and France therefore contented themselves with piracy and occasional forays into North America for furs, timber, and fish.

This situation swiftly changed in the early seventeenth century due to changing conditions at home in Europe. The resumption of steady population growth as the religious wars of the Reformation wound to a close made land increasingly scarce. At the same time the rise of political and religious dissenters presented intolerable challenges to increasingly absolute central governments. Political leaders in both France and England quickly came to see the creation of colonies in the remaining portions of North America as simple solutions to both problems. The wide-open spaces and temperate climate of North America not only provided ample opportunity for quenching the masses' thirst for land, but they could also serve as dumping grounds for religious and political opponents. Moreover, once established, these resident populations could further serve the state by providing the metropole with markets and raw materials.

French versus British settlements. France began the process of colonization in 1609 when Louis XVI (1754–1793) shipped four thousand peasants from western France to Quebec at crown expense. Over the next century and a half, they were joined by an additional six thousand men and women, including soldiers, convicts, orphans, and free settlers. Although the French hoped that emigration to Canada would take off and lead to the creation of a large colony capable of serving as both a guaranteed market for metropolitan manufactured goods and a supplier of cheap timber, furs, and other colonial commodities, the region's cold climate and the existence of more lucrative Caribbean colonies discouraged many potential emigrants from making the journey. The bulk of those who did emigrate were landless young men who signed on for three-year contracts as indentured servants working to clear land, cut timber, farm, and trap animals for their furs. Most saw their time in the colony as temporary and tried to return home as soon as their period of service ended. When coupled with the small number of women present in Quebec, this trend ensured that the French colony remained small and widely dispersed.

Although similar motives lay behind the creation of Britain's North American colonies, local climatic conditions ensured that the resultant settler societies were much more complex than their French counterparts. Like its scattered Caribbean holdings, Britain's southern colonies possessed climates suitable for the creation of a plantation economy. Instead of sugarcane, however, the southern colonies focused their efforts on harvesting cotton and tobacco with the help of indentured servants shipped out from the metropole in large numbers. Indentured servants were similarly responsible for helping the middle colonies of the Chesapeake region produce timber, grain, and other farm products. Unlike their French counterparts, British indentured servants included both craftsmen and landless farmers. Moreover, most chose to stay on in the colonies after their service was up in hopes of attaining social mobility and access to cheap land. Nevertheless, population growth in the early years of colonial development was slow due to high death rates and the relative lack of female emigrants. Reductions in the number of emigrants after 1680, caused by changing economic conditions back in Britain, also took their toll on population growth. As the supply of labor began to dry up, the southern plantation colonies turned to the use of imported African slaves to make up the difference. Although large, the size of this slave population never approached that of either the Carribean or Iberian colonies in South America.

The final pieces of Britain's colonial puzzle in the Americas were New England and Canada. While emigration to other colonies was spaced out over a century and a half and frequently was composed of young male indentured servants, the Puritan migration to New England was limited to 1629–1642 and consisted of whole families fleeing religious persecution and economic hardship in England. On arrival, the Puritans created small, religiously based independent farming communities mirroring those they left behind in England. Canada, on the other hand, was more diverse, particularly since it was acquired as the result of Britain's ongoing wars with France. After seizing the last vestiges of French Canada during the Seven Years' War (1756–1763), the British decided that they had spent too much time and money just to give it all back. While most French settlers chose to emigrate to other colonies in the New World rather than fall under permanent British political control, a sizeable portion remained, thereby presenting their new rulers with the difficult and delicate task of absorbing them into Britain's American Empire. Early efforts to buy the loyalty of these French settlers by granting them local autonomy and accommodating their cultural, linguistic, and legal differences quickly broke down, particularly after loyalists flocked northward into Canada in the wake of the American Revolution. The resultant Anglo-French tensions gradually intensified over the course of the nineteenth century as Britain opened the rest of Canada to settlement by emigrants eager to flee land shortages and poverty in Europe.

Despite their different origins, the British and French settlement colonies in the Americas shared a number of important similarities. In each case, the nature of the climate and the resultant colonial economy meant that the slave population remained small and was confined largely to the Carribean and southern colonies. When coupled with the small and widely dispersed Amerindian population in North America, this presented very few opportunities for either miscegenation or the creation of racially stratified colonial societies. Instead, the British and French settlement colonies in the Americas were composed almost exclusively of European emigrants bent on recreating metropolitan style communities of yeoman farmers. As a result, colonial communities imported European social hierarchies in which social status depended almost exclusively on the accumulation of landed wealth. Those who managed to acquire this wealth were accorded deference, respect, and quickly came to dominate both local politics and society. As in the Iberian colonies of South America, however, these Creole gentlemen farmers were denied representation in Parliament and had to submit to governors sent out from the metropole.

Although Canada proved to be an exception, by the end of the eighteenth century settlers in the British and Iberian colonies were chafing under the economic restrictions of mercantilism and the lack of political representation. Tensions eventually rose to the breaking point, triggering a series of successful political revolutions. Despite new-found independence, the emigration and basic social patterns of each former colony remained largely unchanged throughout the nineteenth century.

EMIGRATION AND SETTLEMENT IN AUSTRALIA AND NEW ZEALAND

The winning of independence by the American colonies presented Britain with a major social problem. Prior to the revolution Britain had sold convicts to its American colonies as cheap sources of labor. When the newly independent United States made it clear that it would no longer accept shipments of convicts, Parliament began contemplating the creation of a penal colony as a means of coping with Britain's dangerously overcrowded prison system. After toying with several potential sites in Africa, the British finally settled on Australia, possibly in hopes that it would yield a wide variety of colonial spin-offs, ranging from timber and lucrative cash crops to strategic military and trading bases.

Settlement in Australia. Britain's first shipment of 750 convicts arrived in New South Wales in January of 1788 and immediately fell on hard times. Although they were expected to create a self-sustaining farming community shortly after arriving in the an-

tipodes, most convicts were urban dwellers with no farming or construction experience. Worse still, they were ignorant of the southern hemisphere's seasons and rain patterns. As a result, the colony faced disease and chronic shortages until subsequent fleets arrived bearing more convicts, supplies, and the first in a growing wave of free settlers.

As the new colony took shape, it quickly assumed a highly stratified social structure. At the apex were the free settlers, colonial administrators, and soldiers sent to guard the convict population. These figures not only regarded themselves as paragons of civilized society and looked down upon all other social groups, but they also took advantage of their position to acquire and develop the largest and most lucrative land grants, which they worked with convict labor. After serving out their sentences, former convicts took on the title of emancipists and occupied the middle level of Australia's settler society. Although many became quite wealthy and eventually acquired large land grants and positions of authority within the community, their social mobility was generally restricted by their convict past. Finally, Australia's large convict population naturally occupied the lowest level of white society where they faced extensive discrimination, hard labor, and brutal punishment for any additional offenses committed in the penal colony. Paranoid personal feuds, drunkenness, brawls, floggings, and public hangings were all common features of early colonial life and served to create an atmosphere of violence and social division. Further divisions came in the form of Anglo-Irish and Protestant-Catholic rivalries imported from the metropole.

The aboriginal population, a group that received the worst treatment meted out to any indigenous people in the entire British empire, constituted the very bottom of Australia's social hierarchy. While Lachlan Macquarie (1761–1824), who served as governor of New South Wales (1810–1821), made some early efforts to assimilate the aborigines and transform them into European-style farmers, the bulk of settlers concentrated on dispossessing the aborigines of their land as quickly as possible. Resistance was met with military reprisals and forced relocations. As settlers expanded deeper and deeper into Australia's interior, they initiated a campaign of genocide in which the aborigines were denied access to water holes, shot, driven off their land, given poisoned food, and deliberately infected with smallpox. While most survivors retreated even further into the interior, some drifted into the newly created towns to beg or take jobs as prostitutes or menial laborers.

By the early 1840s the influx of free settlers, which had risen to fifteen thousand 15,000 per year,

Conditions in Canada. "The Emigrants Welcome to Canada" (c.1820). PUBLIC ARCHIVES OF CANADA, OTTAWA

and the introduction of sheep and cattle changed the nature of Australian society. The impatience and intense land hunger of most new arrivals led many to bypass the colonial administration's land-grant system, preferring instead to raise sheep and cattle on illegally occupied crown lands. Government efforts to halt the proliferation of squatters led to the abolition of land grants in favor of leases and land auctions. Proceeds from these auctions and leases were then put toward assisted emigration in the hopes that subsidized tickets to Australia would enable the administration to exert some control over who was permitted to emigrate to the colony. While well intentioned, this effort proved to be a dismal failure. Most new arrivals lacked the necessary funds to purchase or lease crown land and chose instead to squat illegally. In the process they deprived the colonial administration of both income and the ability to control the nature and pace of colonial emigration.

In addition to creating squatters, the settlers' intense land hunger drove many of them into other regions of the Australian continent where they set up independent and autonomous colonies alongside New South Wales. Although some of the new colonies were founded exclusively by free settlers, the chronic shortage of labor forced some of them to begin accepting shipments of convicts. Others turned instead to the policies of the English colonist Edward Gibbon Wakefield (1796–1862), who in 1829 proposed colonization by the sale of small farms to ordinary citizens.

According to Wakefield, the solution to Australia's labor shortage was to make land prices so high that new arrivals had no choice but to obtain paying jobs in order to earn the necessary funds to buy land. As in the government's assisted emigration schemes, the proceeds from these land sales were to be used to pay for the passage of the next wave of emigrants. In theory this would not only ensure a constant labor supply, it would also allow the settlers to choose a better, more suitable class of migrants. Although the preponderance of squatting and the general lack of funds rendered Wakefield's schemes a failure, they did help to attract increasing numbers of lower-middle-class farmers and ranchers. As they grew in number, these free settlers increasingly sought to shed the region's jailhouse image and to create more respectable colonial societies.

Settlement in New Zealand. While Australia's free settlers began to struggle with the continent's convict past, a few chose instead to move to nearby New Zealand. From the beginning the growing European presence disrupted the lifestyle of New Zealand's indigenous Maori population. Settlers and merchants from Australia not only brought their arrogance, brutality, and lawlessness with them, they also alienated the Maori by cheating them in trade negotiations. The presence of rival missionary societies and denominations further confused and alienated Maori converts. Finally, and of even greater importance, was the decision of early settlers and merchants—motivated by the pursuit of profit and the desire to support those Maori seen as potential allies—to provide their Maori neighbors with firearms, leading to the eruption of a series of deadly and highly destructive civil wars among the Maori.

News of these events scandalized the British public and led to calls for immediate government intervention to protect the Maori from further brutality and exploitation. Intervention was also justified on the grounds that it was necessary to protect Europeans from possible massacre at the hands of alienated and enraged Maori warriors. These calls for action eventually led Britain to formally annex New Zealand in February 1840 via the Treaty of Waitangi with some of the Maori tribes of North Island. According to the terms of the treaty, Britain assumed full administrative control and acquired a monopoly on land purchases in exchange for granting the Maori full citizenship and recognition of their land rights.

Shortly after the treaty was signed, settlers began flocking to North Island, site of the largest Maori settlements. In addition to land grants and travel subsidies provided by the Crown, settlers were also assisted by private ventures. As the Crown was in the process of negotiating the Treaty of Waitangi, Wakefield and his followers established the New Zealand Land Company to promote emigration of free settlers to North Island. Within a decade he convinced the Anglican and Presbyterian churches to follow suit and found denominational settlements in South Island. As in Australia the idea behind each of these private ventures was to sell land bought from the government at high prices so that the proceeds could be used to subsidize the travel of respectable lower-middle-class settlers eager to recreate an English-style farming and sheepherding community in the South Seas. Although Wakefield's schemes failed just as dismally in New Zealand as they had in Australia, they did help to attract large numbers of educated lower-middle-class settlers to the colony. Thus, unlike Australia with its convict population and propensity for violence and brutality, New Zealand's settler community tended to be more peaceful and "civilized." This image not only affected their relations with the Maori, it also enabled the settlers to obtain local self-government in 1852.

The position of the Maori within New Zealand's colonial society was ambiguous at best. Thanks to the protection of the Crown, their status as full citizens, and their reputation as fierce warriors, they avoided becoming the victims of genocide. Nonetheless they were still regarded by most settlers as "noble savages" to be civilized and as common laborers to be exploited. As a result, the Maori became the targets of ongoing assimilation campaigns as early as the mid-1840s. These campaigns, which attempted to teach the Maori to become farmers and adopt British culture, instead left them hostile and bitter about the growing European colonial presence. While the Maori were also upset about settler violations of Maori law and customs and the high property qualifications that denied them a voice in New Zealand's new governmental structures, their greatest complaint by far stemmed from the issue of land ownership and sales. The Maori argued that the Treaty of Waitangi confirmed their ownership of all the land and consequently felt betrayed when the British disagreed. According to the British, the Maori owned only the land that they physically occupied. All remaining lands were considered unoccupied and hence under governmental control. The Maori also came to resent the government's monopoly on land purchases and the poor prices that it paid for undeveloped Maori land.

The last straw came in the 1860s when the government, responding to settler demands that Maori land be seized and sold, sent teams of surveyors to map out all land plots. Feeling that they had been pushed too far, the Maori rose up in open revolts known as the New Zealand Wars, which raged intermittently for the next decade. During the course of this conflict the colonial government punished Maori rebels by seizing and selling their land. The government also abolished its monopoly on land purchases and established Native Land Courts to resolve disputes arising from land sales. Over the next few decades, the bulk of Maori land fell into European hands as the result of sales or legal action, or as payment for taxes and other fees.

Colonial society after the gold rush. While the basic structure of British colonial society in the antipodes seemed to have been set by the mid-nineteenth century, the discovery of gold in both Australia (1851) and New Zealand (1861) had profound effects on both colonies. News of the discoveries triggered a massive influx of settlers eager to try their luck in the gold fields. Among these settlers was a contingent of foreign laborers, many of whom were Chinese, imported by mining companies. As miners began competing for lucrative claims, xenophobia and racism rose dramatically, resulting in violent pogroms against foreign laborers and calls for immigration quotas. In Australia the gold rush was further compounded by an upsurge in violence, vigilantism, and chaos that amounted to a class war between squatters and land prospectors eager to invest their gold profits and secure access to new potential claim sites. Observation of the effects of the Californian and Australian gold rushes prompted the colonial administration in New Zealand to take prompt regulatory action that enabled it to avoid a similar bout of lawlessness.

Overall the gold rushes created wealth, urbanization, limited industrialization, and furthered the impulse to create respectable Victorian societies in both colonies. In Australia this included both the end of its status as a penal colony and new efforts to protect the aborigines from possible conflicts with the growing settler population. The result was an official ideology of protection, segregation, and control that reflected contemporary social Darwinism and its vision of the "white man's burden." Central to this new campaign were efforts to force aborigines onto reservations, ostensibly to provide them with a safe haven free from European interference. In reality the reservation movement, which peaked in the 1890s, pushed the aborigines even further onto the margins of Australian society. Poor conditions on the reservations increasingly forced aborigines to hire themselves out as wage laborers; as such, they faced constant discrimination and had no control over their working conditions.

In New Zealand the gold rush sparked a new population boom as European emigrants flocked to the colony in the hopes of striking it rich. The land hunger of the European population intensified as the new arrivals settled in. Having learned from the New Zealand Wars that armed force only made their plight worse, many Maori chose to retreat into the interior. Others turned toward assimilation and accommodation with the settlers, reasoning that cooperation would give them some protection from loss of their land and rights. This policy quickly paid off in the form of four seats in New Zealand's parliament that were reserved for Maori candidates. The Maori used this parliamentary representation in conjunction with an ongoing series of lawsuits to try to prevent further land seizures and loss of their rights. While they still faced discrimination and hostility at the hands of settlers, who perceived the Maori as annoying obstacles to land development, overall the Maori emerged from the nineteenth century much more independent, affluent, and politically powerful than the Australian aborigines.

In addition to affecting the treatment of the indigenous peoples, the wealth and population booms triggered by the gold rushes enabled both Australia and New Zealand to demand increasing degrees of independence from Britain. In Australia this process occurred gradually, with each of the independent colonies gaining local autonomy in the 1850s. This was followed in the 1890s by calls for federation, resulting in the end of British imperial rule in January of 1901.

These events were mirrored in New Zealand, which gained its independence in 1907. Although emigration to both former colonies continued throughout the first half of the twentieth century, little changed in their social makeup until the end of World War II.

EMIGRATION AND SETTLEMENT IN AFRICA

European settlement in southern Africa dates from the mid-seventeenth century, when the Dutch decided to establish a permanent base at the Cape of Good Hope in order to resupply passing ships with food and water. While the original settlement consisted of only a few hundred whites, by the 1680s the Dutch were actively recruiting settler families. Within a hundred years these Dutch settlers, also known as Boers (a Dutch term meaning "farmers"), had grown in number to almost twenty thousand. Since the best farmland around the Cape had long since been claimed by their predecessors, most new arrivals moved into the interior where they seized cattle and land from the indigenous peoples to create small European-owned farms and ranches. As the Boers pressed deeper and deeper inland, they not only aroused increasing waves of hostility among the displaced native peoples, they also developed a reputation as highly individualistic and quarrelsome people.

Boers versus English in South Africa. By the dawn of the nineteenth century, the Napoleonic wars caused control over Cape Colony to shift from the Dutch to the British. Eager to exploit the colony's strategic location, Britain quickly dispatched five thousand settlers to the Cape to bolster their ownership claims. The Boer population viewed these arrivals with some alarm. In addition to being forced to adopt a new language, customs, and legal system, the largely pastoralist Boer population was suspicious of the British settlers' predominantly urban background. The biggest source of tension between the two settler groups was, however, their different approaches to native relations. The Boers had long held the view that Africans were not only inferior, but were ordained by God to serve South Africa's white population as poorly paid manual laborers. As allegedly inferior competitors for pasture land and cattle stocks, Africans were also subject to repeated Boer seizures of their land and livestock. While the British were tainted by their own racism and belief in social Darwinism, they were uncomfortable with the naked exploitation of the African masses perpetuated by the Boers and worried that it might erupt into racial violence. These fears became particularly apparent when the migrating Boers came into contact with the fierce and expanding Xhosa and Zulu peoples.

British attempts to legislate better treatment for Africans in the 1830s and 1840s infuriated the resident Boer community and unleashed the Great Trek in which some ten thousand Boers gathered their belongings and migrated into the interior of the African veld in search of pasture land. After taking up residence in Natal, the Transvaal, and the Orange Free State, the Boer migrants declared these areas independent republics. While Boer expansion and independence ran contrary to British aims for the development of the colony, official responses repeatedly vacillated between accommodation and demands for immediate annexation of the self-styled republics. In particular, the British demonstrated their conciliatory attitude toward the Boers when the Boers' chronic demand for land and labor provoked the indigenous peoples into further armed insurrections. Fearful that the resultant conflicts might spread and engulf the entire tip of southern Africa, the British repeatedly stepped in militarily to aid their fellow Europeans. For their trouble, the British met with renewed colonial expansion by the Boers, who fled even deeper into the African interior.

While the Boers were moving inland during the Great Trek, the Cape itself was becoming increasingly prosperous, urbanized, and populous. As in other settlement colonies, rising prosperity led to the creation of local self-government and desires for social respectability. This in turn helped give rise to the position termed Cape liberalism, which sought to educate and gradually integrate Africans into colonial society. This provided a stark contrast to the treatment that Africans received in Boer-controlled areas, where they were second-class citizens with no prospect of ever acquiring the right to vote or to hold political power. Worse still, in Boer-run areas, Africans continued to be treated as a labor force to be exploited and stripped of its land. Clear though these goals were, the relatively low density of the resident African population resulted in chronic labor shortages that were only partly relieved by importing indentured servants from India. This naturally served to further complicate the racial landscape by adding a new "colored" group to the mix.

Indians were brought into South Africa in the 1860s. Most were sent to Natal, which, although officially annexed by the British, was dominated by Boer settlers. The Indians were brought in for five-year terms during which they were supposed to work in "industrial" sectors. This included railroad construction, coal mining, and other forms of heavy labor. When their term of service was up, Indians were free to sign contracts with any employer for a further five years. After a total of ten years in South Africa they were entitled to free passage back to India or a land grant worth an equivalent amount. Most chose to stay despite the fact that they were routinely given the poorest land, forcing many to find work as tenant farmers or domestic servants. At the same time, growing numbers of Indian businessmen paid their own passage to South Africa and set up shop as merchants, small traders, and low-level government clerks.

The discovery of diamonds in the latter half of the nineteenth century compounded South Africa's increasingly complex racial hierarchy by bringing in large numbers of European prospectors and shifting the financial balance of power to the Boer Republics. The need for increased agricultural output to feed this growing settler population led to new rounds of land seizures in the 1880s and 1890s. While the Boer farmers and ranchers prospered, Africans were progressively impoverished as they lost land and were forced into poorly paid positions as manual laborers on Boer farms. Similar scenes unfolded in the newly discovered gold and diamond fields, where Africans toiled as diggers and unskilled laborers on white-owned claims. As monopolies were created in the mining industry, Africans' wages plummeted still further, causing them to spend even more time away from their families in a desperate bid to make ends meet. The resultant labor patterns, which kept men out of the villages and prevented them from practicing or passing on their local traditions and ancestral way of life, eventually had a catastrophic effect on the structure of South African family life, culture, and society.

Eager to continue and expand the gold rush, settlers in southern Africa began migrating ever deeper into the interior in the hopes of finding even richer veins of ore. Led by agents of the great financial titan Cecil Rhodes (1853–1902), these settlers found their way blocked by the increasingly restrictive Boer Republics, which sought to limit the financial and civil rights of all non-Boer inhabitants. Frustrated, Rhodes eventually tried to topple the Republics in the ill-fated Jameson Raid (1895), which ruined his own political career and finally convinced the Boers that the British would stop at nothing short of permanent annexation. The resultant Anglo-Boer tensions eventually erupted into the short but brutal Boer War (1899–1902). A scant eight years after the war's end, all of South Africa's settler communities were finally united in an independent, albeit Boer dominated, Union of South Africa. Once free of London's control and oversight, the new Union's government began passing a series of discriminatory laws to force Africans and mixed-race populations into clearly defined professions, relocate them onto reservations, and restrict their movements via the creation of internal passports. The restrictive nature of these policies enabled the settler community to continue their exploitation of African laborers and greatly facilitated South Africa's ongong industrialization campaign. In the process, however, they sowed the seeds of the post–World War II apartheid regime.

French settlement in Algeria.

While the British were solidifying their hold on South Africa, France was busy promoting emigration to its new settlement colony in Algeria. Initially invaded by Charles X (reigned 1824–1830) in 1830 in an effort to divert the Parisian masses from his bid to restore absolutist power, Algeria quickly came to be regarded by both the Second and Third Republics as a potential breadbasket, a source of labor, and a dumping ground for the more radical elements of French society, where it was hoped their revolutionary zeal would be blunted by the availability of cheap land. As settlers moved in, however, their plans to assimilate the local Arab-Berber population met with resistance, which quickly took on the form of an anticolonial jihad (holy war). Over the next half century the French army, convinced that its honor was at stake, insisted on pushing ever deeper into the Algerian interior in hopes of defeating the indigenous rebels. The result was a costly and bloody guerilla war, which the French met with scorched-earth tactics and systematic terrorism.

Despite the hostilities that continued to rage on the frontier, thousands of French settlers, known as *pieds-noirs* (black feet), began pouring into Algeria, eventually constituting 10 percent of the colony's total population. They were soon joined by equally large numbers of foreigners who migrated into the new colony from all over Europe. As they arrived in Algeria these settlers, including the newly assimilated foreigners, forcibly evicted the Algerians from the fertile coastal region and relocated them in poorer lands deeper in the interior. Within a few years, however, most settlers moved from their purloined farmlands into urban coastal communities where they set about recreating metropolitan French society. These efforts were ultimately paid for by the labor of displaced and impoverished Algerian farmers, who worked the otherwise empty landed estates for their absentee French landlords.

France's official revolutionary doctrine of assimilation assured that the settler community, although composed of diverse elements, was transformed into a homogeneously French one that saw itself as a distant French province. To this end, Algeria was subject to the same parliamentary decrees formed in Paris as the rest of France. It also enjoyed parliamentary representation in the form of deputies elected by all those holding French citizenship. While citizenship was theoretically open to the colonized Algerians, few acquired it despite official efforts to "uplift" the indigenous people. These efforts included compulsory French language education and official discrimination against natives who failed to assimilate in the form of heavy taxes, forced labor, and the *indigénat,* an arbitrary legal code that allowed colonial officials to impose nonjudicial fines and short prison terms on colonial subjects for a host of minor offenses. The only escape from these oppressive measures was to abandon Islam, traditional Algerian customs, and the Arabic language in favor of assimilation into French culture and society. While some tried, most Algerians preferred instead to resist, both passively and militarily.

By the turn of the century the French, responding to social Darwinism and the racist atmosphere prevalent throughout late-nineteenth-century Europe, abandoned the colonial policy of assimilation in favor of accommodation. While the distinction between the two policies was frequently blurred in practice, in theory accomodation was geared toward the economic development and exploitation of colonial areas, while leaving their indigenous populations free to operate within their own cultural and social patterns. While this may seem a benevolent effort to safeguard indigenous cultures and traditions in the face of European cultural imperialism, it was in fact motivated at least as much by the desire to insulate French culture from foreign and allegedly inferior influences. In Algeria this shift in colonial ideology manifested itself by 1918 in the decision to allow native rulers in the southern sections of the colony to exercise complete local autonomy, provided that they followed the general outlines of official French policy. This decision granted long-simmering Algerian nationalism what appeared to be a harmless political outlet. In practice, however, it spelled doom for French colonial rule in north Africa.

The collapse of France and its occupation by the Nazis in World War II sent shockwaves through both the metropole and the colonial empire. When the war finally ended, nationalist leaders all over the French Empire began to claim that the war had proved France's weakness and unsuitability to rule any foreign possessions. For their part, the French just as loudly demanded the retention of their colonial empire as a means of reviving their shattered economy and retrieving their national honor. By the mid-1950s these conflicting impulses finally erupted into a nasty and brutal war for independence in which both sides frequently resorted to torture and terror. The war weariness of the French, coupled with the realization

Immigrants to Argentina. European immigrants awaiting processing upon arrival in Argentina, late nineteenth century. LIBRARY OF CONGRESS

that they could not win, finally forced them to give in and grant Algeria its independence on 3 July 1962. Although they felt betrayed by the French decision, most settlers seized the opportunity to flee back to France, leaving behind an enormous economic and political vacuum from which Algeria has yet to fully recover.

CONCLUSION

From the beginning of the European colonial endeavor, settlers migrated to the colonies in pursuit of new economic opportunities and social mobility. Ef-

forts to realize these dreams invariably entailed interaction with racially diverse groups of indigenous peoples, imported slaves, and other foreign laborers, resulting in varying degrees of accomodation and exploitation. In the process, settlers created highly complex colonial societies that were curious and unique mixtures of rigid social stratification and upward mobility. These trends, while best demonstrated in the Iberian colonies of the Americas, are also evident in subsequent settlement efforts by Europeans in Africa, Australia, and New Zealand, thus proving that the more colonization and emigration changed, the more it remained the same.

See also **War and Conquest Migration** *(volume 2);* **Social Mobility;** *(volume 3); and other articles in this section.*

BIBLIOGRAPHY

Aldrich, Robert. *Greater France: A History of French Overseas Expansion.* New York, 1996.

Anderson, Benedict. *Imagined Communities.* 2d ed. London, 1991.

Baines, Dudley. *Emigration from Europe 1815–1930.* Cambridge, U.K., 1991.

Cain, P. J., and A. G. Hopkins. *British Imperialism: Innovation and Expansion, 1688–1914.* New York, 1993.

Canny, Nicholas P. *Europeans on the Move: Studies on European Migration, 1500–1800.* Oxford, 1994.

Day, David. *Claiming a Continent: A New History of Australia.* Sydney, 1997.

Elliot, John Huxtable. *Spain and Its World, 1500–1700.* New Haven, Conn., 1989.

Emmer, P. C., and M. Mörner, eds. *European Expansion and Migration: Essays on the Intercontinental Migration from Africa, Asia, and Europe.* New York, 1992.

Fieldhouse, D. K. *The Colonial Empires: A Comparative Survey from the Eighteenth Century.* 2d ed. London, 1982.

Hughes, Robert. *The Fatal Shore: A History of the Transportation of Convicts to Australia, 1787–1868.* New York, 1987.

James, Lawrence. *The Rise and Fall of the British Empire.* London, 1994.

Judd, Denis. *Empire: The British Imperial Experience from 1765 to the Present.* London, 1996.

Keen, Benjamin, and Mark Wasserman. *A History of Latin America.* 3d ed. Boston, 1988.

Lloyd, T. O. *The British Empire, 1558–1995.* 2d ed. Oxford and New York, 1996.

Lorcin, Patricia M. E. *Imperial Identities: Stereotyping, Prejudice, and Race in Colonial Algeria.* New York, 1995.

Martin, Ged, and Benjamin E. Kline. "British Emigration and New Identities." In *The Cambridge Illustrated History of the British Empire.* Edited by P. J. Marshall. New York, 1996. Pages 254–279.

Moorehead, Alan. *The Fatal Impact: An Account of the Invasion of the South Pacific, 1767–1840.* London, 1966.

Pagden, Anthony. *European Encounters with the New World from Renaissance to Romaticism.* New Haven, Conn., 1993.

Prochaska, David. *Making Algeria French: Colonialism in Bône, 1870–1920.* Cambridge, U.K., 1990.

Sinclair, Keith. *A History of New Zealand.* London, 1984.

Williamson, Edwin. *The Penguin History of Latin America.* London, 1992.

IMPERIALISM AND DOMESTIC SOCIETY

Laura Tabili

A persistent feature of the historiography of Europe has been a bifurcation between European histories and identities and imperial ones. Yet in fact imperialism has been intrinsic to European expansion, European identity, and European history.

SOURCES OF IMPERIAL CULTURE

Scholars have traced the origins of European imperialism at least as far back as the Middle Ages. Through the expansion of Latin Christendom, doubling European territory between 950 and 1350, Europe became "a colonizing society and the product of one" (Bartlett, p. 314). Frankish, Germanic, and English territorial conquests secured institutional hegemony over a periphery then as now encompassing the Celtic lands, the Baltic and Scandinavia, eastern Europe, and the Mediterranean. Institutional mechanisms and ideological predispositions that prefigured later imperialisms took shape on these European frontiers through the often violent and seldom complete imposition of cultural, ethnic, racial, linguistic, and legal hierarchies, patriarchy and primogeniture, social stratification, militarization, feudalism and tributary agriculture, urbanization, standardized educational and religious practice, and, with the Cistercian monastic order, international organization. European identity itself was constructed through these processes, among them the abortive Crusades, based not on cultural homogeneity or affinities but imposed through conquest and terror. The Catholic Church participated in these colonizing processes, its universalistic professions masking territorial and ethnic agendas. Thus European societies were readied, institutionally and culturally, for the period of exploration and colonization beyond Europe that began in the fifteenth century.

Ideological justification for this new expansion was provided by Orientalism, the dialectical unity of ideas and institutionally reinforced practices subordinating the colonized and depicting them as inferior to and polar opposites of Europeans. In European literary artifacts from the Renaissance onward, colonized "Others" were viewed and constructed so as to maintain the illusion of European superiority. Even anti-Semitism toward European Jews has been interpreted as the projection inward of imperialistic impulses first directed outward in the form of the Crusades. The demonization of Islam, a product of binary thinking that may be uniquely European, thus became the "strange secret sharer" (Ballard, p. 27) of European anti-Semitism. Anti-Islamic Orientalism helped to define European identity by defining what Europe was not. "The Orient" itself was arguably a construction of the Western imagination, its deficiencies demanding political and economic domination. It originated and was sustained, therefore, in Europe rather than in the colonized world.

Continuities from the Crusades through the Christian reconquest of Spain to European overseas exploration suggest that the mechanisms and practices of colonization, including aggression and exploitation, were intrinsic to European social formation and economic and political development. It follows that imperialism was inherent in domestic societies even before overseas colonization, an artifact of European patterns rather than of these new worlds. Yet imperialism assumed new forms in response to indigenous resistance. The European predisposition was to frame human attributes and cultural processes in terms of dichotomies and hierarchies, thereby justifying relations of dominance and subordination. This predisposition then interacted with colonizing processes: colonial racial discourses, for example, were dialectically and mutually constitutive of European class and gendered discourses. Empire and colonization gave Europeans a vocabulary in which to express and legitimize domestic class and gender relations. Dichotomies such as home/empire, colonizer/colonized, white/black, familiar/foreign, and civilized/savage were explicitly developed out of the colonial experience. They helped to shape and were in turn shaped by other dichotomies that structured ruling class males' consciousness and actions, including man/woman, lady/woman,

The Orient in Western Imagination. *The Turkish Bath,* painting (1862) by J.-A.-D. Ingres (1780–1867). Musée du Louvre, Paris/Giraudon/Art Resource, N.Y.

middle class/working class, control/chaos, purity/pollution, clean/dirty, culture/nature, intellect/emotion, rationality/sensuality, self/Other, and subject/object. These in turn were assigned unequal value as good/evil, superiority/inferiority (Davidoff, 1979).

European aristocratic notions of blood infused developing colonial definitions of racial hierarchy and practices of racial exclusion with overtones of rank, status, and class. These in turn were reimported to Europe. Representations of the colonized mirrored, as they helped to reinforce and justify, European cultural processes and social hierarchies such as gender and class. In concrete terms, many attitudes and practices developed in the colonial setting were reimported to European societies and applied to socially marginal populations. Poor people and their neighborhoods, for example the East End of London, were portrayed and treated as an unruly and primitive "dark continent," in need of pacification and even "colonization," in the words of Judith Walkowitz (p. 194). "Urban explorers" or *flaneurs* satisfied their taste for the

exotic and prurient with forays into working class neighborhoods. Certain categories of domestic populations were "racialized"—portrayed as inferior based on apparent physical attributes. That prostitutes, for example, were born to their profession rather than driven to it by poverty was allegedly detectable in overdeveloped secondary sex characteristics such as large buttocks. Dirt, darkness, degradation, physicality, sexuality, and immorality were multiply and symbolically conflated to portray poor people, like colonized people, as morally wayward and in need of discipline and uplift. Homeless or unsupervised children were called "street Arabs" in apparent reference to their peripatetic existence. On the other hand, lower class as well as colonized men were "feminized"—portrayed as less than men to justify ruling class measures of coercion and control. Intensified social class stratification in mid-nineteenth-century Britain, for example, coincided with enhanced racialization of social inequalities in British colonies. In the Darwinian discourses of the end of the century, inequalities were viewed through the lens of biology and nature so as to justify them.

Europeans projected a variety of fears and fantasies onto disparate colonized Others that originated in their own minds, rather than any place in the colonized world. Orientalists purveyed spurious privileged "knowledge" of the colonized to bolster their cultural authority while justifying colonial rule. Nineteenth-century European literature reproduced as it simultaneously enlisted popular collaboration in what Edward Said called "paternalistic arrogance" toward colonized people. Although this focus on empire at home provides a valuable perspective, it can degenerate into a sort of historiographical navel-gazing, enabling scholars of Europe to continue their longstanding neglect of colonized people and overseas empires while claiming to support the more challenging historiographical task of integrating empire back into the history of the metropole.

IMPACT OF THE COLONIAL ENCOUNTER

Overseas colonization and colonized people's agency and resistance had dramatic effects on European societies. Contacts with the world beyond Europe not only reproduced imperialist patterns of aggression, subordination, and exploitation but introduced Europeans to new and disturbing ideas and practices. The encounter with the Americas helped to destabilize the hegemony and credibility of the Christian church, indeed of the European worldview, speeding secularization by introducing knowledge unforeseen in biblical or classical texts. The European way of life was transformed and its burgeoning population simultaneously sustained and menaced by the introduction of new foods such as maize, tomatoes, squashes, tapioca, peanuts, and especially cacao and potatoes; new crops such as tobacco and rubber; new animals such as llamas, buffalo, jaguars, and other beasts real and mythical; and new diseases such as syphilis.

The inflow of New World bullion produced the massive European inflation and resultant economic and social dislocations of the sixteenth and seventeenth centuries. Europe's commercial bourgeoisie gained wealth and power at the expense of the aristocracy, and a stronger bargaining position globally: Mexican silver offered European merchants something the Chinese would accept in exchange for their coveted silks and porcelain. Indigo, annatto, and fustic supplied the textile industries until the development of aniline dyes in the late nineteenth century, and sisal supplied the maritime industries sustaining northwest Europe's global power. The related evolution of a global capitalist system with Europe at its financial and geographical core had profound effects on Europe as well as on the non-European world.

By the eighteenth century, colonial products such as furs and sugar warmed the backs and graced the tables of the well-to-do, becoming symbols of privilege and social distance. Ginger, allspice, nutmeg, mace, coffee, chocolate, sugar, rum, arrowroot, and sago became staples of the middle-class larder. Elite women's participation in shaping demand for colonial products such as Indian cotton, coffee and tea from Asia and South America, Caribbean sugar, Chinese and Japanese porcelain and lacquer goods, and objects made from exotic woods implicated them in projects of empire and of slavery.

European identities themselves were forged in the process of overseas colonization: Scottish merchants, for example, came in the colonial context to recognize the profit to be derived from being British. The Enlightened superiority of eighteenth-century Europe was constructed not only in relation to the imputed barbarism of the Middle Ages but also to the innocence of the Amerindian "noble savage" and the alleged brutishness of the African.

CAPITALISM AND SLAVERY

The slave trade that supplied labor to the New World colonies contributed in many ways to Europe's social transformations. Enslaved Africans, replaced after 1834 by indentured or otherwise coerced colonized workers, provided the cheap labor that brought erstwhile luxuries such as sugar, tea, coffee, and tobacco within reach of middle-class consumers. Slaves produced the cheap raw materials such as cotton that fueled the industrial system by keeping its products affordable and its profits high. West African slave traders accounted for a high proportion of the demand for early British industrial goods such as textiles—"shirts for Black men" (Williams, p. 133)—and for iron ingots, used as currency. Colonies were virtually captive markets for European and colonial products, including slaves themselves.

Profits from this "triangular trade" flowed mainly to Holland, France, and Britain, contributing to the rapid capital formation that made them commercial and industrial leaders. Wealth derived from slavery and colonialism financed infrastructure such as roads, canals, factories, and warehouses throughout Europe. In *Capitalism and Slavery* (1944), Eric Williams showed how slave trade profits were used in Britain to capitalize James Watt's steam engine, Isambard Kingdom Brunel's Great Western Railway, Britain's metallurgical industries, the Welsh slate industry, numerous banks, notably Barclay's, and the marine insurer Lloyd's of London. Thus industry and empire went hand in hand. Yet deep involvement in the trade in human beings shook Enlightenment thinkers' confidence in the superiority and rationality through which they distinguished their societies from those of the past or of the non-European world.

British high politics were preoccupied with slavery and emancipation for decades during the eighteenth and nineteenth centuries. Wealthy Caribbean planters, "the West India interest," purchased parliamentary seats, further threatening and displacing the landed aristocracy. One of these, the owner of plantations in Guiana, was the father of William Gladstone, Liberal prime minister in the Victorian era. Gladstone's maiden speech was in defense of slavery. On the other hand, antislavery was a defining issue in reform, Chartist, and socialist politics in Britain as well as in French republican and revolutionary movements.

Africans and other colonized people were not found only in the colonies, however; many were found in European metropoles and were commonly depicted in the works of such artists as William Hogarth and Joshua Reynolds. Their widespread appearance in domestic painting of the period suggests the prevalence of black house servants and slaves in eighteenth-century western European societies, and estimates place between ten thousand and thirty thousand in London alone. In the nineteenth century an Indian ayah or nanny became an upper-class status symbol. Some slaves or former slaves, such as Ignatius Sancho, Olaudah Equiano, and Francis Barber, became prominent in public life as spokesmen for emancipation. Like nineteenth-century elite travelers from India, such as Pandita Ramabai, Cornelia Sorabji, and Behramji Malabari, they brought empire home, embodied in their persons, while contributing dissenting voices to metropolitan conversations about empire.

SOCIAL AND CLASS RELATIONS: THE STRUCTURE OF POWER

The bulk of scholarship on the domestic effects of imperialism has concerned the nineteenth and twentieth centuries, the period climaxing in the "new imperialism." Much of the literature focuses on Britain, the most powerful empire of the industrial period. The focus on the nineteenth and twentieth centuries may be a result of the preponderance of scholars working in the modern period. Until 1953, when Ronald Robinson and John Gallagher traced the continuities between "old" and "new" imperialism, scholars such

as Joseph Schumpeter viewed the apparent reemergence of imperialism in the 1880s as an alarming atavism from Europe's barbaric past. Framed as a problem demanding explanation, it thus generated a substantial literature. This "new imperialism" was so called because it followed an apparent hiatus in the formal acquisition of overseas possessions. It was an effect of renewed competition among European powers, as continental industrial systems expanded to challenge Britain. That the hiatus was more apparent than real was exposed by Robinson and Gallagher, who found that British "free trade imperialism" involved exerting control "informally if possible"—that is, in the absence of competition, as was the case in the period between the "old" and "new" imperialism—but "formally if necessary" (p. 13).

John Hobson and Vladimir Ilich Lenin put imperialism at the center of their critiques of industrial societies at home. Although they have been much maligned, it was they who initiated the discussion of the dialectical relationship between overseas expansion and domestic economic, political, social, and cultural relations. Hobson argued that imperialism was an irrational strategy that stood in the way of domestic social reform. Lenin, conversely, saw imperialism as a rational strategy for a system that was not reformable but inexorably doomed. In 1916, in *Imperialism: The Highest Stage of Capitalism,* Lenin argued that the monopoly stage of capitalism, which corresponded with and stimulated the new imperialism, had undermined the allegedly progressive characteristics of industrial capitalism, such as individual ownership, independent, autonomous producers, consumer choice, and the decentralization of power: "private property based on the labour of the small proprietor, free competition, democracy, *i.e.,* all the catchwords with which the capitalists and their press deceive the workers and the peasants—are things of the past" (Lenin, 1939, p. 10). The late nineteenth-century renewal of aggressive overseas territorial expansion corresponded to, because it flowed from, the restoration of domestic economic and political oligarchy. Both Lenin and Hobson agreed that the profit-making agendas of finance capital drove overseas expansion to the detriment of the European majority, both middle and working class. As Hobson put it in 1902 in his *Imperialism: A Study* "While the manufacturing and trading classes make little out of their new markets, paying . . . more in taxation than they get out of them in trade, it is quite otherwise with the investor" (p. 53). Hobson denounced these rentier elements for using "public policy, the public purse, and the public force to extend the field of their private investments" (Hobson, 1965, p. 53).

506

Subsequent investigation seems to support these conclusions. Although efforts to calibrate precisely the rhythms of "old" and "new" imperialism to the "phases" of industrial capitalism failed, the connection of domestic economic and political agendas with imperial expansion has endured. Making much of evidence that British imperialism "did not pay" overall, extensive economic and statistical analysis reinforces the more damning conclusion: as Hobson argued in 1902, the imperial system was a vast money-laundering mechanism lining the pockets of private investors at public expense, transferring wealth from middle-class taxpayers to the superrich, thus enhancing class disparities and entrenching a financial oligarchy.

This conclusion is consistent with a broader revision minimizing industrialization's destabilization of British class stratification. Scholars have further argued that while the self-made upwardly mobile captains of British industry may have benefitted from imperialism, old and new, they did not control it. Imperial expansion was directed by an entirely different social group, a cultural, political, and financial oligarchy of "gentlemanly capitalists," who maintained their control over the empire from 1688 through 1945. Personal contacts and information exchanges among networks of such men, formed in the public schools and Oxford and Cambridge and continued via London club life, sustained the hegemony of a limited ruling-class fragment over several generations of dramatic political, economic, and social change.

The important shift in British domestic politics, and thus overseas expansion, was therefore not from the dominance of the landed aristocracy to the industrial bourgeoisie in the middle decades of the nineteenth century, but from one group of gentlemanly capitalists, the commercially progressive landed interest, to another: the financiers in the City of London. Financial and by extension political power resided not with the moneygrubbing merchants and factory owners of the eighteenth and nineteenth centuries but with this infinitely adaptable upper-class stratum. Whoever was "on top" politically—whether the landed aristocracy or public school-educated bankers—had the power to influence both politics and the investment of national wealth. Thus imperial expansion was "rational" for those who possessed the wherewithal to influence Parliament and stood to gain financially from it.

This analysis seeks to detach industry from empire in British historiography, arguing for continuity rather than abrupt change in British economic development, in political institutions, and in ongoing processes of overseas expansion. Formal and informal imperialisms appear as merely pragmatic responses to

new global demands rather than the outcomes of dramatic shifts in ideology or changes in economic structure or political culture. The continuity argument is consistent with revisions of the Whiggish or progressive view of the industrial bourgeoisie, which envisions a more complete, uniquely British, transformation of social structure. It also contests the Marxian view of the industrial bourgeoisie as the gravediggers of feudalism, and of industrialization as the primary motor of modern history.

Yet this interpretation, stressing persistence over change in the identity of a flexible, pragmatic imperialist class, does not challenge the view that overseas expansion was an extension of domestic politics and economic arrangements. In fact the continuity argument corroborates other scholars' emphasis on continuities between the personnel and practices of informal and formal imperialism, old and new imperialism, protection versus free trade, commerce versus industry, and home versus empire. It also deflates assumptions about British exceptionalism relative to European class systems, industrialization processes, and imperialist projects—the view that British precocity stemmed from an early and decisive bourgeois triumph. While perhaps slighting the degree of upheaval industrialization inflicted on the lower end of the social formation, this interpretation also appears to corroborate the view that empire's impact on domestic populations was deleterious, draining wealth away to pay for colonial infrastructures from which a handful of financial insiders reaped massive profits. It was these elites, operating as a manipulative oligarchy outside of popular control or awareness, who had the political and economic wherewithal to affect outcomes. A historiography that emphasizes the role of the oligarchy—whatever "attitudes" might have been prevalent at the time—asserts a conceptual and perceptual chasm between colonies and metropoles marked by popular indifference and ignorance toward empire. It also absolves metropolitan populations from responsibility for imperialist abuses.

Such an explanation challenges the fundamental premises undergirding social history: the emphasis on class struggle as the engine of history; on the efficacy of mass action, resistance, and agency "from the bottom up"; and on popular participation as a precondition for historical change. Social historians' contribution to the analysis of empire at home has been to explore how metropolitan populations as well as colonized people participated in, negotiated, and contested imperial projects, albeit on varying terms and with competing agendas. This is a necessary corrective both to the longstanding historiographical compartmentalization between empire and metropole, and to

Kashmir Shawl. The marquise de Sorcy de Thélusson wearing a kashmir shawl. Portrait (1790) by Jacques-Louis David. BAYERISCHE STAATSGEMÄLDESAMMLUNGEN, MUNICH

the stress in later scholarship on imperialism as a top-down imposition on credulous or passively receptive domestic populations.

POPULAR PARTICIPATION

Scholars seem to agree that the burdens and benefits of empire were unequally distributed among metropolitan populations according to class, gender, region, culture, and other social dynamics. Middle-class consumers appear to have benefited more than the poor from overseas colonization. Middle-class women created demand for colonial products, thus integrating colonial artifacts and cultural practices into metropolitan societies. European matrons in India spurned colonial foods and home furnishings, but once back in Europe they imported these goods, presenting them as gifts and creating demand for them. Evidence from cookbooks, advice columns, newspaper articles, and ladies' magazines indicates that Kashmir shawls valued at up to a hundred pounds and Rampore (Rampur) chuddars (a type of shawl) were highly prized status symbols among the well-to-do ladies of early nineteenth-century Britain. These fashion leaders stimulated upper-middle-class demand for affordable domestic imitations from Paisley, Norwich, Edinburgh, and Lyon, establishing shawls as women's wardrobe staples for the balance of the century. Indian shawls and dresses, lushly draping muslins and silks, cloaks, scarves, peacock feathers, jewelry, and artifacts such as carved wood and ivory figured in trousseaux and inheritances. They embodied a form of capital that a returning memsahib or a soldier's widow could barter for necessities in the metropole. Similarly, returnees from the colonies introduced Indian cuisine into the drab British diet, importing and creating demand for turmeric and curry powders and proffering recipes for curries, kedgeree, mulligatawny soup, dal, chapatis, and pickles. In the absence of mangoes, a hybrid emerged—gooseberry chutney.

In contrast, European working classes survived in spite of rather than because of the impact of empire at home. By the late nineteenth century, the prevalence of colonial products such as tea and sugar, cheap jams and treacle in the northern European working-class diet linked even the poorest to the colonized world, to the detriment of nutritional standards and the despair of their social "betters." Sidney Mintz has argued that, although considered temperance beverages, colonial drug foods or food substitutes such as heavily sugared tea, coffee, and cocoa—like tobacco, another colonial product—served sinister purposes: as convenience foods freeing housewives for industrial labor; to "provide a respite from reality, and deaden hunger pangs" of workers, who might imbibe the illusion that "one could become different by consuming differently" (Mintz, 1985, pp. 186, 185). As John Burnett observes, "a cup of tea converted a cold meal into something like a hot one, and gave comfort and cheer besides" (Mintz, 1985, p. 129). Arguably, refined cane sugar, a colonial product and what Mintz calls "an artifact of intraclass struggles for profit," became and remains a symbol of quintessentially European modernity. (Mintz, 1985, p. 186). Increases in these colonial products coincided with a decline in consumption of dairy products and other fresh foods. Deterioration in the stature and general health of populations introduced to these products in the course of the eighteenth and nineteenth centuries echoes the physical deterioration that accompanied the shift toward cereals in agriculture, and thus diet, on the medieval frontier.

SOCIAL IMPERIALISM

The rubric of social imperialism has described a number of competing interpretations, agendas, and practices. The advent of social imperialism was originally understood as the moment in the late nineteenth century when socialists and the working-class movement became collaborators in imperialism. Its origin has been linked to the depression of the 1870s and 1880s and efforts by governments to recuperate economic losses while simultaneously frustrating socialist and labor agitation. Advocates of imperialism such as Jules Ferry and Joseph Chamberlain justified it by arguing that the fruits of empire would subsidize social reform, remedy the stagnation and instability of late-nineteenth-century European economies, and ameliorate the plight of the poor—"the cry of our industrial population," in Ferry's words—by affording steady employment producing goods for captive colonial markets. Hobson debunked such arguments: overseas investment, whether in formal colonies or informal spheres of influence, he argued, drained resources from European domestic economies. More cynical politicians such as Otto von Bismarck merely invoked imperial "crisis ideology," using overseas military adventures and a focus on external enemies to divert popular attention from the deficiencies of domestic political and economic arrangements. Privileging the pursuit of empire enabled the German state to postpone the democratization of political power and evade redistribution of wealth.

Perhaps because, unlike Britain, France lacked a substantial informal empire in the mid-nineteenth century, French imperial gains in the "scramble for Af-

Colonial Product. Parisians in front of a candy store. Consumption of sugar, a colonial product, by people of modest means rose during the French Second Empire (1851–1870). Drawing by Alfonse Leduc. BIBLIOTHÈQUE DES ARTS DECORATIFS, PARIS

Enlisting Popular Support. "An Ideal Lord Mayor's Show," engraving by W. Corpe after W. Kelly, nineteenth century. The floats represent the colonies of the British Empire. CORAM FOUNDATION, LONDON/THE BRIDGEMAN ART LIBRARY

rica" late in the century did succeed in generating markets and profits unavailable in the domestic economy. This success afforded France economic parity with Germany, the Ottomans, and Russia. But in the course of the twentieth century the importance of these economic resources diminished.

WHO SUPPORTED IMPERIALISM?

Scholars continue to debate the degree to which various social groups supported or opposed imperialism. The culture of imperialism, many have argued, was not only ethnocentric and racist but narrowly class-based in origin and profoundly gendered and misogynist. The construction of the Manichaean or polar dichotomy undergirding imperialist and Orientalist discourses involved fabricating historical, cultural, and national identities for hegemonic ends. Almost invariably, the effort by elites to retain power and influence in changing structural contexts entailed representing themselves as arbiters of imagined or invented collective interests. All of this suggests that European populations' alleged innocence of participation in empire-building is a myth, for they were continually exposed to imperialist propaganda.

Yet scholars have differed as to the effectiveness of state or ruling-class strategies to enlist popular support for imperialism. Abundant artifactual and documentary evidence has been produced to illustrate employers', social workers', and military men's propagandistic efforts to recruit lower-class people into support for empire, jingoism, and other nationalist projects, especially through implicit promises of economic reform and political participation. Artifacts from schoolbooks to cigarette cards, biscuit tins, and boys' magazines, as well as performances in music halls, on radio, in cinemas and via imperial exhibitions, show that popular culture was saturated with triumphalist images of empire and its benefits to colonizers and colonized alike. Jam pots and tea packets adorned with fantasies of the tropics—palm trees, elephants, and odalisques—allegedly constructed popular perceptions along Orientalist lines.

Literary and cultural artifacts of empire articulated ideals of "imperial masculinity"; effeminacy was seen as a danger to empire, and women were held responsible for imperial decline and dissolution. Public schoolmasters promoted a shrill ruling-class ideology in which "warrior patriots" were encouraged to heroic physical sacrifice on behalf of a nation invariably feminized in popular song and verse as Britannia, or "she." The Boy Scouts mobilized the lower middle class for imperialism in a specifically masculine form. There was nothing covert about the link between scouting and Edwardian imperialism: they were both explicitly promoted as vehicles of class conciliation, patriotism, citizenship, and militarism, vehicles that encouraged nonruling groups to identify with the imperial state.

Feminist scholars were among the first to address metropolitan women's involvement and culpability in imperial projects. British "feminist Orientalists" have been criticized for participating in and reproducing imperialist discourses and practices as a means of challenging gender hierarchies within their own class. In striving for equal participation with European men, European women reproduced class and racial hierarchies by representing themselves as spokeswomen for allegedly downtrodden indigenous or colonized women, perpetuating the women's marginalization, silencing, and erasure, while at the same time deepening the stigma of colonized societies as barbaric and backward.

Perhaps because of the minimal benefit working people actually derived from imperialism, there is little unequivocal evidence to suggest that the bulk of working people were successfully coopted into supporting imperialism. Popular support for displays of jingoism such as "mafficking" appears to have come instead from the lower middle class, which, threatened with proletarianization, bargained desperately for status and inclusion by identifying with the state through jingoism.

Although scholarship about popular resistance to empire is not copious, critics of empire were never absent from the metropole. European critics included the theosophist Annie Besant and the socialists Karl Marx and James Keir Hardie. Colonial subjects living in Europe for educational or professional reasons also formed vocal if numerically small networks of opposition to empire and imperial abuses. C. L. R. James, a West Indian-born activist, was prominent in the Pan-Africa movement; a series of Pan-African Conferences brought well-articulated anti-imperial agendas to the heart of empire. Figures such as Olaudah Equiano, Dr. John Alcindor, and Ho Chi Minh spent substantial time in Europe and intervened in debates about empire.

GENDER AND RACE

Metropolitan class and gender relations were infused with imperialist agendas. When the near loss of the Boer War prompted belated scrutiny of the physical

debility of Britain's poor, working-class mothers became subjects of surveillance and pronatalist regimentation. Sexism, classism, and racism were combined in the eugenic effort to rehabilitate an "imperial race" without modifying class relations or material inequalities. The first steps toward assisting poor and unmarried mothers in France were taken, similarly, in the name of invigorating the French nation for its imperial strivings. Fears of physical unfitness and deterioration in metropolitan populations interacted with definitions of racial qualities formulated in colonial contexts. The origin of European welfare states was thus deeply implicated in imperial projects.

If the Nazi drive for *Lebensraum* (living space) in eastern Europe may be considered a dimension of imperialism, then Nazi racial engineering and eugenics must also be considered in assessing the impact of imperialism on domestic populations. The impact of measures to breed a "master race" by bribing or manipulating ordinary Germans—with marriage bonuses,

Empire as Commercial Image. An 1887 advertisement for Pears' Soap assures the British consumer "Even if our invasion of the Soudan has done nothing else it has at any rate left the Arab something to puzzle his fuzzy head over." The British governor general of the Sudan, Charles George Gordon, was killed in the fall of Khartoum in 1885. ©THE FOTOMAS INDEX

mothers' medals and mothers' pensions, as well as surveillance, coercion, eugenic sterilization and forced motherhood—was of a profoundly classed and gendered character. In light of Nazi expansionist and colonialist aims, the massive displacement of and genocide against central and eastern European populations in the course of World War II must also be traced to European imperialism. Programs of eugenic sterilization, coerced breeding, and ethnic cleansing, under the aegis of what Foucault called "the biopolitical state," illustrate the racial dimensions of empire as they operated within and between European societies.

AFTER EMPIRE

While some scholars have argued that a popular cultural "retreat" from empire occurred in the 1920s and 1930s, structural interdependence continued and even intensified. Although Europe's formal empires all but disappeared after 1945, informal imperialism continues to shape the world European empires made; European societies and landscapes are ineluctably marked by the imperial past and the postcolonial present.

Economic and cultural interdependence between former colonies and metropoles persists in spite of formal autonomy. Through the extraction of raw materials and food by means of cheap labor, European industrial economies in effect remain parasites, benefiting at the expense of postcolonial ones. Colonialism's destabilization of colonized societies has produced an unforeseen legacy: empires have come home in the form of migrants and guest workers from former colonies, disrupting Orientalist and imperial dichotomies between "home and away." As in the colonial period, the metropolitan economy benefits from a labor force reproduced "offshore" at minimal cost and denied many social benefits. European states invoke national boundaries, redefinitions of citizenship, and other legal and state structures to keep this industrial workforce vulnerable, subordinated, and on the verge of exclusion.

The culture of imperialism has survived in new guises, betrayed in contemporary xenophobic notions of "fortress Europe" (Pieterse, p. 5) and "Western civilization." Renewed embrace of Christendom and the Enlightenment embodies continued Eurocentric arrogance, elitism, and chauvinism. Contemporary emphasis on a common European culture, increasingly reinforced institutionally by the European Union, excludes the non-European world in an implicitly hierarchical and Manichaean dichotomy. Simultaneously it obscures internal diversity and lingering internal marginalizations, such as the Celtic fringe. Continued Franco-German domination of the European Union reproduces imperial relations within Europe that are a millennium old.

Islam has reemerged as an immediate and visible threat in the form of migrants from the colonies and of the collective power of Middle Eastern oil producers. The collapse of one "evil empire" in the East has demanded a new Oriental adversary in Islam. Consistent with a thousand years of Orientalism, immigration controls have sought to repulse the enemy at the gates, while prurience about Muslim gender relations—a horrified fascination with "those poor downtrodden women"—remains a projection of Western sexual fantasies that simultaneously reassures Westerners of their cultural superiority, and the depiction of Muslims as a whole as violent and fanatical "fundamentalists" supports the discursive construction of a European self that is free of these qualities.

European landscapes and cultures remain imprinted with imperial aspirations and attainments. From the West India Docks and Jamaica Bridges that mark British commercial estuaries to the Mafeking Streets (named for the siege put down in Mafeking, South Africa, in 1900) and imperial monuments, to the rhododendrons adorning European gardens and the elephants and golliwogs decorating the jam pots and tea packets on European tables, the iconography of empire continues to saturate the physical geography of the metropole. Yet European societies are being transformed and enriched by African, Asian, and Caribbean people and cultures. In 1996 curry surpassed roast beef and Yorkshire pudding as the meal most frequently prepared in British households. The historical experience of empire has thus left Europeans with a common history shared with much of the globe.

See also other articles in this section.

BIBLIOGRAPHY

Ballard, Roger. "Islam and the Construction of Europe." In *Muslims in the Margin: Political Responses to the Presence of Islam in Western Europe.* Edited by W. A. R. Shadid and P. S. Van Koningsveld. Kampen, The Netherlands, 1996.

Bartlett, Robert. *The Making of Europe: Conquest, Colonization and Cultural Change, 950–1350.* Princeton, 1993.

Bock, Gisela. "Racism and Sexism in Nazi Germany: Motherhood, Compulsory Sterilization, and the State." *When Biology Became Destiny: Women in Weimar and Nazi Germany.* Edited by Renate Bridenthal, Atina Grossman, and Marion Kaplan. New York, 1984. Pages 271–296.

Cain, P. J., and A. G. Hopkins. "Gentlemanly Capitalism and British Expansion Overseas I: The Old Colonial System, 1688–1850." *Economic History Review,* 2d ser., 39 (1986): 501–525.

Cain, P. J., and A. G. Hopkins, "Gentlemanly Capitalism and British Expansion Overseas II: New Imperialism: 1850–1945." *Economic History Review,* 2d ser., 40 (1987): 1–26.

Cooper, Frederick, and Ann L. Stoler. "Tensions of Empire: Colonial Control and Visions of Rule." *American Ethnologist* 16 (November 1989): 609–621.

Crosby, Alfred W. *The Columbian Exchange: Biological and Cultural Consequences of 1492.* Westport, Conn., 1972.

Davidoff, Leonore. "Class and Gender in Victorian England: The Diaries of Arthur J. Munby and Hannah Cullwick." *Feminist Studies* 5 (spring 1979): 87–141.

Davin, Anna. "Imperialism and Motherhood." *History Workshop Journal* 5 (1978): 9–65.

De Groot, Joanna. " 'Sex' and 'Race': The Construction of Language and Image in the Nineteenth Century." In *Sexuality and Subordination: Interdisciplinary Studies of Gender in the Nineteenth Century.* Edited by Susan Mendus and Jane Rendall. London, 1989. Pages 89–128.

Gallagher, John and Ronald Robinson. "The Imperialism of Free Trade." *Economic History Review* 6 (1953): 1–15.

Hobson, J. A. *Imperialism: A Study.* Ann Arbor, Mich., 1965.

Huttenback, Robert, and Lance E. Davis. *Mammon and the Pursuit of Empire: The Political Economy of British Imperialism, 1860–1912.* New York, 1986.

Lenin, V. I. *Imperialism: The Highest Stage of Capitalism.* New York, 1939.

Mackenzie, John M. *Propaganda and Empire: The Manipulation of British Public Opinion, 1880–1960.* Manchester, U.K., 1984.

Mintz, Sidney W. *Sweetness and Power: The Place of Sugar in Modern History.* New York, 1985.

Noiriel, Gérard. *The French Melting Pot: Immigration, Citizenship, and National Identity.* Translated by Geoffroy de Laforcade. Minneapolis, Minn., 1996.

Pieterse, Jan Nederveen. "Fictions of Europe." *Race and Class* 32 (1991): 3–10.

Said, Edward. *Orientalism.* New York, Vintage, 1979.

Stoler, Ann Laura. *Race and the Education of Desire: Foucault's History of Sexuality and the Colonial Order of Things.* Durham, N.C., and London, Duke University Press, 1995.

Walkowitz, Judith R., and Daniel Walkowitz. " 'We are Not Beasts of the Field.' Prostitution and the Poor in Plymouth and Southampton under the Contagious Diseases Acts." In *Clio's Consciousness Raised: New Perspectives on the History of Women.* Edited by Mary S. Hartmann and Lois Banner. New York, 1974. Pages 192–225.

Williams, Eric. *Capitalism and Slavery: The Caribbean.* London, 1964.

IMPERIALISM AND GENDER

Nupur Chaudhuri

In European imperial discourses, scholars usually discuss colonizers' foreign or economic policies. Some scholars have shown that the lasting images of the latter half of the nineteenth century are those associated with the achievements of empire and colonizing societies. While such studies shed light on the public roles of the colonizers and consequently on the most obvious aspects of colonial domination, this public sphere constitutes only part of the Western colonial experience.

Among all the European imperialist nations, Great Britain controlled the largest colonial empire until the end of World War II. Imperialism, as many scholars argue, became the foundation of British national identity after the mid-nineteenth century, and India became the jewel in the crown of the British Empire. With its long history, India was the empire's most important possession and the major component of Britain's political and economic prominence in the world. The contours of colonial construction in India provide a model shape of the inner and outer dynamics of British colonialism and of colonial rule more generally. Thus this essay focuses on the specific example of British imperialism in India to raise general questions about gender and imperialism.

Scholars of British imperialism followed the general trend of neglecting the social history of imperialism. With few exceptions, systematic studies of the social history of British imperialism were not produced before the mid-1960s. Only a handful of historians after that time focused solely on women's history. Much work has yet to be done on the private sphere and on the intersection of public and private spheres in a colonial setting. As gender is key to the construction of imperial hierarchies, the experiences of women offer especially important insights. Gender is essential to an understanding of the social impacts of colonialism on the rulers as much as on the ruled and thus to the social history of empire.

The British imperial system in India functioned by means of direct and indirect rule. Direct rule was created to maximize imperial interests by abolishing indigenous administrative institutions and establishing others that were maintained by a small number of salaried British at higher echelons along with selected indigenous men hired at the lower echelons. Indirect rule let some traditional political or administrative units and social practices remain intact, subject to treaties or agreements with the traditional rulers and resident agents whose aim was to accomplish colonial objectives through the façade of indigenous leadership. The British government gradually expanded direct rule, as it proved impractical to work first through existing traditional agents and institutions and then increasingly through chartered British East India company agents. It is important to keep in mind that neither the colonizers nor the colonized were homogeneous groups, as both were bound by inherent hierarchies of class, gender, and status.

BRITISH WOMEN AND THE EMPIRE

Since the dawn of European imperialism, the "masculine" element, emphasizing the cardinal features of authority and rule and entailing structures of unequal power, remained ever present in all social and political organs of colonialism. One of the prevailing ideologies of imperialism was that colonies were "no place for a white woman." But women had an undeniable role in the empire. British women were the guardians of spiritual and moral values for the families in the colony, where they embroidered ideas of motherhood, homemaking, and spirituality on the tapestry of imperialistic ideology. In the second half of the nineteenth century, the swelling impetus of the imperial mission began to draw women in great numbers—for instance, over one thousand arrived in 1875, and over sixteen hundred in 1895. Their colonial experiences increasingly became sources of fascination for people at home, and indeed those experiences helped redefine the contours of British women's public and private lives. The views of British women in India made their way into contemporary domestic discourses within Britain, helping to fashion a gendered legitimation of British rule in India. British women in colonial India, by enabling the widespread dissemination of an imperial identity of superior race, had a visible impact on British political, social, and cultural life.

The nineteenth-century British empire in India provided unique opportunities for British women to compare their social positions to those of the indigenous population of the subcontinent. Victorian feminists viewed Indian women both as passive subjects and as examples against which to gauge their own progress. Although Indian women of the period were pursuing their own paths of social reform and feminist causes many British feminists insisted on devising alternate causes. They portrayed Indian women as passive colonial subjects partly so as to imagine and to realize their own feminist objectives within the context of the imperial nation into which they sought admission. The empire, far from being outside the sphere of women, was central to it. In insisting upon their right to citizenship, suffragettes not only claimed their right to be part of the political nation but also demanded to take their part in the political empire.

India provided British men not only with career opportunities; in metropolitan society men gained influence and prestige because the British government viewed them as contributing to Britain's international eminence and power. Imperialism, as has become clear, was also beneficial to British women. In India they were able to go out freely, to assert greater independence, to shape and control their life situation, to increase their personal power, and to become socially more mobile than they were in Britain. However, it was only in the 1990s that feminist scholars acknowledged the contradictory positions of British women—subordinate at home yet wielding the power of their imperial position to subordinate the colonial "other." White women as homemakers and mothers maintained and promoted the domestic sphere of the empire in India. By writing about both domestic and public lives in India, British women also adopted an identity of specialists on Indian life and in the process participated in the British imperial ethos. They assumed the role of the authors of Indians and the Indian world, thus contributing to the ideological reproduction of the empire.

British women frequently shared the ethnocentrism of their male counterparts and acted in condescending and maternalistic ways. Many British women felt that Indian women were not like English ladies. In England ladies had some degree of rank, wealth, and education; as British women saw it, that rank implied either personal achievement or inherited refinement and a place in civilized society. During a short stay in India to visit missionary friends, one British woman, who signed her book *Overland, Inland, and Upland: A Lady's Notes of Personal Observation and Adventure* (London, 1873) with the initials A.U., recorded that, despite having many opportunities to adorn themselves with jewelry and fragrance, Indian women seemed powerless to elevate their minds or to bridge the enormous gulf that separated the mere female from the lady. In India, as A.U. noted, only very poor women moved around freely while the movements of women from higher classes were restricted, a situation contrary to the one at home. A.U. observed that wealth provided opportunities for British women to gain education, to travel in foreign countries, and to cultivate tastes for everything beautiful and refined in nature and art. To British women the faceless, nameless Indian women blended into the landscape, thus further distinguishing British women's own identity in the imperial scene.

British women's contacts with Indian domestics further shaped their construction of images of indigenous people. For British women the negative connotations of dark-skinned people were embedded in their social consciousness. They therefore found the new experience of employing dark-skinned domestics unsettling. The religious and social customs of both the Hindus and Muslims confused them, and they felt that India was a conglomerate of different cultures without a stable center. To avoid dealings with Indian servants, some memsahibs (the wives of British officials) chose Indian Christian domestics with at least partial European heritage. But Christian servants also posed problems. For one thing, being descendants of the Portuguese settlers and Indians, a substantial number of the Christian servants were Roman Catholics rather than members of the Anglican, Scottish, or Evangelical sects, to which most British colonists belonged. But above all many British women felt that the common ground of Christianity might set the masters and servants on similar footings, blurring the class and social distinctions between them.

Motherhood and the family. A new dimension of British familial relations arose in the colonial setting. British parents in India felt a unique psychological stress when faced with an inescapable choice: the health and educational needs of children compelled many British families to send their children to Britain by the time they were about seven. The departure and long separation of children from their parents in the colony caused a major disruption in familial happiness. British mothers in India had to make a painfully difficult choice between their duties as wives and as mothers by either staying with their husbands in India or returning to Britain with their children. Although separation of British children from their parents was not uncommon, as many upper-class or upper-middle-class Victorian parents sent their children away to boarding school, what was unusual for the British wives in India was that they were unable to see their children for periods extending over many years. It was a very long and expensive journey from India to Britain, and in some instances parents saw their children only after an interval of nine or ten years. (And some very unfortunate mothers and fathers who sent children home died without ever seeing them again.) Separation of parents and children created psychological tension for the families. The family disunions that were so common among British families in India clashed with the Victorian emphasis on a stable home and family. A British woman went to colonial India as a wife, her aim and duty to establish a British home for her husband and children in the subcontinent. But when in fact she became a mother, her roles as wife and mother came into conflict.

REFORM

It was women more than men who pushed for reforms in the situation of Indian women out of a commitment to improving the lot of women generally. Given that male foreign missionaries had little access to indigenous women, female British missionaries played a special role in Indian societies, offering education to Indian women in the homes of prominent upper-caste families and providing public school lessons for lower-caste women. Christian teachings and handicrafts dominated the content of early women's education.

Despite their central role in the missions, British women operated under certain constraints within the patriarchal structure of the churches and missionary societies that oversaw their work. For example, the Ladies Association for the Promotion of Female Education Among the Heathen, established in 1866, had to convince its male colleagues that Zenana Education—education of small groups of girls at home (in the women's quarters or zenana) by missionary women—was important and that women themselves could organize it, teach it, and pay for it.

Other prominent British Victorian women in India also took active interests in improving the social conditions of Indian women. Lady Harriot Dufferin, wife of the Indian viceroy, established the Fund for Female Medical Aid in August 1885. The Dufferin Fund was closely associated with the National Indian Association, originally founded by Mary Carpenter to promote Indian female education in the 1870s. The Dufferin Fund was created specifically to provide female medical aid to Indian women because social custom prevented them from being treated by male doctors.

In the 1890s British female missionary doctors began to arrive in India. Having been sent to India as part of the Zenana Mission Movement, they added medical education to the curriculum. Dr. Edith Brown, who stayed for more than thirty years, founded the North Indian School of Medicine for Christian Women to train Christian women as nurses and assistants. Dr. Ellen Farer established a hospital near Delhi. But this charitable work had other consequences. In nineteenth-century India European women, especially British women, displaced educated indigenous women and men in employment. While colonialism induced some Indians to seek Western medical treatment, purdah, the seclusion of women by Muslims and some Hindus, created a demand for female physicians. Some Westernized middle-class Indians responded by educating their daughters to become doctors. But priority was given to female British doctors, who often came to India to avoid discrimination at home. Thus the arrival of British female doctors to India caused a loss of medical employment for indigenous female doctors.

British women tended to have more social interaction with Indian men than with Indian women. Nineteenth-century British feminists frequently formed working relationships with Indian male reformers. Yet they varied considerably in the extent to which they responded to Indian values and life. Unusual among British feminists, Margaret Noble, also known as Sister Nivedita, adopted Indian culture, in part to teach Hindu women more effectively. Noble, who established a school for Hindu girls in 1898, joined the neotraditional monastic community of Swami Vivekananda. Active in a wide range of religious and welfare work, she also participated in Indian nationalist politics in India and Britain, to which she returned in 1907 to escape arrest in India. At times the feminism of these British reformers collided with indigenous culture. Annette Ackroyd Beveridge came to India in 1872, drawn by the personality and teaching of Keshub Chandra Sen, the leader of the Brahmo Samaj, a progressive Hindu reform movement. Breaking with Sen because of his rather conventionally Victorian notions of education for women, she founded a girls' school in Calcutta in 1873. The curriculum of the school slanted heavily toward British culture. Although Beveridge knew the language, she had little knowledge of Bengali culture, and because of that insensitivity her attempts to educate Bengali girls were unsuccessful.

British society, in its prismatic view of the positions of women, always saw Indian women as oppressed and as having an inferior position compared to that of Western women. This view seemed to many to be a justifiable moral ground for British imperial policies and rules. In an effort to lift the oppression of Indian women, educated Indian male social reformers, many of whom were Western-educated, joined in with the reform efforts of Christian missionaries and British officials. Education for girls, later marriages, prohibitions on sati, or widow burning, and on female infanticide, and relaxation of purdah restrictions, allowing intra- and intersocial mobilities for women became the major goals of the reform movement driven by this emerging collective force. Educated Bengali middle-class men, led by many with Western education, conceived of an Indian domestic ideology of modesty, humility, and self-sacrifice, influenced by British Victorian ideas about the roles of women. The reformers emphasized secular education for girls, designed to prepare them to be good wives (especially to Western-educated men) and mothers and to have some voice in public life. Reform of marriage practices, reflecting Victorian beliefs about marriage, was also an important component in implementing this new ideology. The Civil Procedure Code of 1859 asserted that, contrary to the Hindu tradition permitting a woman to leave her husband—at great cost to her reputation—and to return to her natal family, a husband could sue his wife for restitution of conjugal rights. Widow remarriage, another tenet of the domestic ideology promoted by Indian reformers, was intended to give widowed women the opportunity to continue their lives as wives and to avoid becoming financial burdens to their families or those of their deceased husbands.

During the last decades of the nineteenth century, British and Indian women began to be noticeably visible in the social reform movement on behalf of Indian women. A contemporary notion was that British women played a key altruistic role in shaping the women's movement in India. But later scholarship has been more ambivalent about that altruism, implying that British women were maternal imperialists who, so as to enhance their own social and professional positions, presented a picture of the pitiable plight of Indian women in need of liberation from social, political, and economic oppression.

The imperial power in India attempted to create a legislative framework for the social improvement of Indian women, but forces opposed to such reform prevented full implementation of the laws. In 1856 the Widow Remarriage Act, which allowed Hindu widows to remarry by forfeiting their rights to their deceased husbands' estates, was enacted, but its impact was at best limited and in some cases negative. Lower-caste widows who by customary law had previously been able to remarry without loss of property would now, according to the terms of the Act, lose their rights to their deceased husbands' property upon remarriage. The British selectively upheld customary law, such as that practiced by the Hindi-speaking population in Haryana in Punjab. This practice permitted a widow to marry a close relative (often a younger brother) of her deceased husband to prevent the division or loss of landed property. In these instances, the British sought to regulate and formalize customary law in order to reinforce their political control. Indian women themselves, including those in the reform movement, had little to do with the implementation of the Widow Remarriage Act and other reform legislation, in part because Indian reformers failed to mobilize them. And since the British failed to actively enforce their legislation, the reform had minimal effect on the lives of Indian women.

The Age of Consent Act of 1891, which raised the age of consent to sexual relations for married and unmarried girls from ten to twelve and thereby provided a statutory foundation for later marriage, was also ineffectual. British officials and Indian nationalists, both reformers and traditionalists, joined forces to limit the terms of the Act and its implementation. Although a marital rape clause had been included in the Act, it was never enforced. Male control over female sexuality prevailed, as Indian men opposed to changes in women's status were successful in drawing British officials to their side; as a result, reforms enacted by the British had little impact. The imperial power failed to substantially affect Indian gender relations, its reform impulses—never wholehearted or unequivocal—losing their force in the face of indigenous anti-reform pressures. Attempts to improve their lot through legislation under the British empire left Indian women themselves in the position of objects rather than initiators and active participants.

EUROPEAN GENDER STANDARDS IN THE MAINTENANCE OF EMPIRE

It is not only the impact of British women abroad that made gender relevant to empire. Gender distinctions operated on a more metaphorical level to define the relationship between ruler and ruled. Casting the ruled into a feminine image and identifying the ruler with masculine power became a path of imperial ethos. Nourishing a masculine ethos, British men and women had long held a view of Indian men as weak or effeminate. The masculinity-femininity contrasts were often painted in sociocultural contexts. Aesthetic judgments of Indian and colonial clothing styles, for instance, often served as the basis for judging Indian society. The clothing of Indian women, for instance, was seen as slovenly and revealing to a degree inappropriate for ladies, and was thus, in British eyes, indicative of Indians' lack of the refinements of civilized society. The British author A.U. remarked after visiting a middle-class Indian home: "The *ladies* [A.U.'s italics], naked to the waist, or with only a loose piece of muslin thrown over their shoulders, stood or sat on the floor. . . . I could rather have fancied myself in some spot beyond the limits of civilization than among members of the respectable middle class of a great capital." British women saw Indian men as effeminate, and this view began to have a widespread effect through remarks about India made in articles in popular women's periodicals of the mid-nineteenth century. For example, the *Englishwoman's Domestic Magazine* in 1854–1855 created an effeminate image of Hyder Ali by describing his vest being fashioned much like the gown of a European lady. Hyder Ali was a ruler of Mysore State in southern India in the second half of the eighteenth century and a formidable opponent of the British, and as such would have been a familiar figure to many of the readers of this article. The article further enhanced the image of effeminacy by noting that in India men and women devoted much time to embroidery and that it was not unusual to see several men engaged in such work, seated cross-legged on a mat—a position and an activity that in Europe would be considered quite below the dignity of any man.

The profile of the people of India as effeminate dates back to the early days of British colonialism. One Richard Orme wrote in the 1760s that all natives displayed effeminacy, a quality especially evident among the Bengalis, who lacked firmness in character and physical strength. Time and again over a hundred years, British rulers and elites projected this notion of the absence of integrity in the traits of the Indian people. In the 1820s Reginald Heber, bishop of Calcutta, found the Bengalis to be cowards. The Scottish philosopher James Mill echoed that view with his characterization of Bengali Hindus as passive and effeminate. The English writer Thomas Babington Macaulay, member of the Supreme Council of India in the 1830s, called Bengalis feeble.

The British used the same terminology to discredit anticolonial activists, who emerged in the late nineteenth century. Among the Indian intellectuals who surfaced to dispute the legitimacy of the grounds of colonialism, many were Western-educated and a large majority were Bengalis. The British now began to derogate the babus, the term for Indians with education in English, as "effeminate babu," a term later used against all middle-class Indians.

CONCLUSION

While the British interaction with India has been particularly well studied from the social history standpoint, other cases have been examined as well. In Africa, for example, as in India, Europeans tended to portray indigenous men as effeminate. Images of African women differed somewhat from those of Indian women, with more emphasis on potentially dangerous sexuality. But here, too, colonial experiences interacted with gender standards back home.

Many points remain open to further analysis. The social and cultural backgrounds of colonial administrators and missionaries suggest that there was some degree of divergence from social norms back home. Many aristocrats and Christian leaders were uncomfortable with social trends in Europe and therefore sought status and adventure elsewhere—even though they asserted European superiority wherever they went.

The impact of imperial experiences on Europe itself is another complex topic. In the years of the empire, particularly around 1900, individual women gained a sense of independence. But what effects did this have on the larger development of feminism? The hypermasculinity displayed in the colonies reverberated in European sports culture and in the enthusiastic embrace of military causes by an ever-widening segment of the male population in Europe. But the importance of empire for ordinary Europeans, its role in daily life in the home country, has yet to be established. For some, surely, the latest news of imperial victory would bring a brief surge, quickly forgotten in the routine of industrial life.

What is clear, however, is that the story of European empire is not just an account of military actions and diplomatic decisions. The imperial experience related closely, if in complex ways, to developments at home and may have affected these developments in turn.

See also **Feminisms, Gender and Education, Gender History, History of the Family, The Household** *(volume 4); and other articles in this section.*

BIBLIOGRAPHY

Ballhatchet, Kenneth. *Race, Sex, and Class under the Raj: Imperial Attitudes and Policies and Their Critics, 1793–1905.* London, 1980.

Barr, Pat. *The Memsahibs: The Women of Victorian India.* London, 1976.

Borthwick, Meredith. *The Changing Role of Women in Bengal, 1849–1905.* Princeton, N.J., 1984.

Brantlinger, Patrick. *Rule of Darkness: British Literature and Imperialism, 1830–1914.* Ithaca, N.Y., 1988.

Bratton, J. S., et al. *Acts of Supremacy: The British Empire and the Stage, 1790–1930.* Manchester, U.K., and New York, 1991.

Burton, Antoinette. *Burdens of History: British Feminists, Indian Women, and Imperial Culture, 1865–1915.* Chapel Hill, N.C., 1994.

Burton, Antoinette. *At the Heart of the Empire: Indians and the Colonial Encounter in Late-Victorian Britain.* Berkeley, Calif., 1998.

The Englishwoman's Domestic Magazine, 1850–1876.

Chatterjee, Partha. "Colonialism, Nationalism and the Colonized Woman: The Contest in India." *American Ethnologist* 16 (1989): 622–633.

Chaudhuri, Nupur. "Nationalism and Feminism in the Writings of Santa Devi and Sita Devi." In *Interventions: Feminist Dialogues on Third World Women's Literature and Film.* Edited by Bishnupriya Ghosh and Brinda Bose. New York, 1997. Pages 31–41.

Chaudhuri, Nupur. "The Memsahibs and Motherhood in Nineteenth-Century Colonial India." *Victorian Studies* 31 (summer 1988): 517–535.

Chaudhuri, Nupur, and Margaret Strobel, eds. *Western Women and Imperialism: Complicity and Resistance.* Bloomington, Ind., 1992.

Cox, Jeffery. "Independent Englishwomen in Delhi and Lahore, 1860–1947." In *Religion and Irreligion in Victorian England: Essays in Honor of R. K. Webb.* Edited by R. W. Davis and R. J. Helmstadter. London and New York, 1992. Pages 164–184.

Forbes, Geraldine. "In Search of the 'Pure Heathen': Missionary Women in Nineteenth-Century India." *Economic and Political Weekly,* 26 April 1986, pp. 1–7.

Forbes, Geraldine. "Women and Modernity: The Issue of Child Marriage in India." *Women's Studies International Quarterly* 2 (1979): 407–419.

Hyam, Ronald. *Britain's Imperial Century, 1815–1914: A Study of Empire and Expansion.* New York, 1976.

Hyam, Ronald. *Empire and Sexuality: The British Experience.* Manchester, U.K., and New York, 1990.

Jayawardana, Kumari. *The White Woman's Burden: Western Women and South Asia during British Rule.* London, Routledge, 1995.

Kennedy, Dane. *The Magic Mountains: Hill Stations and the British Raj.* Berkeley, Calif., 1996.

Mackenzie, John M. *Propaganda and Empire: The Manipulation of British Public Opinion, 1880–1960.* Manchester, U.K., and Dover, N.H., 1984.

Mackenzie, John M., ed. *Imperialism and Popular Culture.* Manchester, U. K., and Dover, N. H., 1986.

Pierson, Ruth Roach, and Nupur Chaudhuri, eds. *Nation, Empire, Colony: Historicizing Gender and Race.* Bloomington, Ind., 1998.

The Queen: A Ladies Weekly Magazine, 1870–1900.

Ramusack, Barbara, and Sharon Sievers. *Women in Asia: Restoring Women to History.* Bloomington, Ind., 1999.

Sinha, Mrinalini. *Colonial Masculinity: The "Manly Englishman" and the "Effeminate Bengali" in the Late Nineteenth Century.* Manchester, U.K., and New York, 1995.

Strobel, Margaret. *European Women and the Second British Empire.* Bloomington, Ind., 1991.

AMERICA, AMERICANIZATION, AND ANTI-AMERICANISM

Rob Kroes

What kind of "ism" is anti-Americanism? Like any "ism" it refers to a set of attitudes that help people to structure their worldview and to guide their actions. It also implies a measure of exaggeration, a feverish overconcentration on one particular object of attention and action. Yet what is the object in the case of anti-Americanism? The word suggests two different readings. It could refer to anti-American feelings taken to the heights of an "ism," representing a general rejection of things American. Yet it can also be seen as a set of feelings against (anti) something called Americanism. In the latter case, we need to explore the nature of the Americanism that people oppose. As we shall see, the word has historically been used in more than one sense.

Yet whatever its precise meaning, Americanism—as an "ism" in its own right—has always been a matter of the concise and exaggerated reading of some characteristic features of an imagined America, as a country and a culture crucially different from places elsewhere in the world. In that sense Americanism can usefully be compared to nationalism. In much the same way that nationalism implies the construction of the nation, usually one's own, in a typically inspirational vein, causing people to rally around the flag and other such emblems of national unity, Americanism helped an anxious American nation to define itself in the face of the millions of immigrants who aspired to citizenship status. Particularly at the time following World War I it became known as the "one hundred percent Americanism" movement, confronting immigrants with a demanding list of criteria for inclusion. Americanism in that form represented the American equivalent of the more general concept of nationalism. It was carried by those Americans who saw themselves as the guardians of the integrity and purity of the American nation.

There is, however, yet another historical relationship of Americanism to nationalism. This time it is not Americans who are the agents of definition, but others in their respective national settings. Time and time again other peoples' nationalism not only cast their own nation in a particular inspirational light, it also used America as a counterpoint, a yardstick that other nations might either hope to emulate or reject. Foreigners, as much as Americans themselves, therefore, have produced readings of America, condensed into the ideological contours of an "ism." Of course, this is likely to happen only in those cases where America has become a presence in other peoples' lives, as a political force, as an economic power, or through its cultural influence. Again the years following World War I were one such watershed. Through America's intervention in the war and the role it played in ordering the postwar world, through the physical presence of its military forces in Europe, and through the burst of its mass culture onto the European scene, Europeans were forced in their collective self-reflection to try to make sense of America and to come to terms with its impact on their lives. Many forms of Americanism were then conceived by Europeans, sometimes admiringly, sometimes in a more rejectionist mood, often in a tenuous combination of the two. The following exploration will look at some such moments in European history, high points in the American presence in Europe, and at the complex response of Europeans.

To be sure, certain European attitudes toward the United States formed before 1918. Various European travelers commented admiringly on American democracy and religious freedom, or else they voiced distress about American commercialism or the absence of an appropriate hierarchy in American family life. The United States was widely seen as a land of prosperity and economic opportunity, aspirations to which spurred many European emigrants. But larger reactions to Americanism awaited the growth of global influence of the United States in the twentieth century, though some earlier themes (particularly on the more critical side) continued.

Statue of Liberty. The Statue of Liberty under construction in a Paris courtyard before being shipped to New York in 1886. ©BETTMAN/CORBIS

AMERICANISM AND ANTI-AMERICANISM

"Why I Reject 'America.' " Such was the provocative title of a piece published in 1928 by Memo ter Braak, a young Dutch author who was to become a leading intellectual light in the Netherlands during the 1930s. The title is not a question but an answer, assessing his position toward an America in quotation marks, a construct of the mind, a composite image based on the perception of current dismal trends that ter Braak then links to America as the country and the culture characteristically—but not uniquely—displaying them. It is not, however, uniquely for outsiders to be struck by such trends and to reject them. Indeed, as ter Braak himself admits, anyone sharing his particular sensibility and intellectual detachment he is willing to acknowledge as a European, "even if he happens to live on Main Street." It is an attitude for which he offers us the striking parable of a young newspaper vendor whom he saw one day standing on the balcony of one of those pre–World War II Amsterdam streetcars,

surrounded by the pandemonium of traffic noise yet enclosed in a private sphere of silence. Amid the pointless energy and meaningless noise the boy stood immersed in the reading of a musical score, deciphering the secret code that admitted entrance to a world of the mind. This immersion, this loyal devotion to the probing of meaning and sense, to a heritage of signs and significance, are for ter Braak the ingredients of Europeanism. It constitutes for him the quintessentially European reflex of survival against the onslaught of a world increasingly geared toward the tenets of rationality, utility, mechanization, and instrumentality, yet utterly devoid of meaning and prey to the forces of entropy. The European reaction is one that pays tribute to what is useless, unproductive, defending a quasi-monastic sphere of silence and reflexiveness amid the whirl of secular motion. Here was a combination characteristic of European anti-Americanism: a real concern about new levels of American influence plus a rejection of real or imagined Americanism as symbolic of developments in contemporary social and economic life.

This reflex of survival through self-assertion was of course a current mood in Europe during the interwar years, a Europe in ruins not only materially but spiritually as well. Amid the aimless drift of society's disorganization and the cacophony of demands accompanying the advent of the masses onto the political agora, Americanism as a concept had come to serve the purpose of focusing the diagnosis of Europe's plight. The impulse toward reassertion—toward the concentrated retrieval of meaning from the fragmented score of European history—was therefore mainly cultural and conservative, much as it was an act of protest and defiance at the same time. Many are the names of the conservative apologists we tend to associate with this mood. There is Johan Huizinga, the Dutch historian, who upon his return from his only visit to the United States at about the time that ter Braak wrote his apologia, expressed himself thus: "Among us Europeans who were traveling together in America . . . there rose up repeatedly this pharisaical feeling: we all have something that you lack; we admire your strength but do not envy you. Your instrument of civilization and progress, your big cities and your perfect organization, only made us nostalgic for what is old and quiet, and sometimes your life seems hardly to be worth living, not to speak of your future"—a statement in which we hear resonating the ominous foreboding that "your future" might well read as "our [European] future." For indeed, what was only implied here would come out more clearly in Huizinga's more pessimistic writings of the late 1930s and early 1940s, when America became a mere piece of evidence in Huizinga's case against contemporary history losing form.

Although the attitude involved is one of a rejection of "America" and Americanism, what should strike a detached observer is the uncanny resemblance with critical positions that Americans had reached independently. Henry Adams of course is the perfect example, a prefiguration of ter Braak's "man on the balcony," transcending the disparate signs of aimlessness, drift, and entropy in a desperate search for a "useless" and highly private world of meaning. But of course his urgent quest, his cultural soul-searching, was much more common in America, was much more of a constant in the American psyche, than Europeans may have been willing to admit. Cultural exhortation and self-reflection, under genteel or not-so-genteel auspices, were then as they are now a recurring feature of the American cultural scene. During one such episode, briefly centered on the cultural magazine *The Seven Arts,* James Oppenheim, its editor, pointed out that "for some time we have seen our own shallowness, our complacency, our commercialism, our thin self-indulgent kindliness, our lack of purpose, our fads and advertising and empty politics." In this brief period, on the eve of America's intervention in World War I, there was an acute awareness of America's barren landscape, especially when measured by European standards. Van Wyck Brooks, one of the leading spokesmen of this group of cultural critics, pointed out that "for two generations the most sensitive minds in Europe—Renan, Ruskin, Nietzsche, to name none more recent—have summed up their mistrust of the future in that one word—Americanism." He went on to say "And it is because, altogether externalized ourselves, we have typified the universally externalizing influences of modern industrialism." Here, in the words of an American cultural critic, we have a crisp, early version of ter Braak's and Huizinga's later case against Americanism, against an America in quotation marks. American culture no more than "typified" what universal forces of industrialism threatened to bring elsewhere.

One further example may serve to illustrate the sometimes verbal parallels between European and American cultural comment. In a piece written in honor of Alfred Stieglitz, entitled "The Metropolitan Milieu," Lewis Mumford spoke of the mechanical philosophy and the new routine of industry and the dilemmas this posed to the artist whose calling it was "to become a force in his own right once more, as confident of his mission as the scientist or the engineer," yet, unlike them, immune to the lure of mindless conquest. "In a world where practical success canceled every other aspiration, this meant a redoubled interest in the goods and methods that challenged the canons of pecuniary success—contemplation and idle reverie" (it is almost as if we hear ter Braak), "high craftsmanship and patient manipulation, . . . an emphasis on the ecstacy of being rather than a concentration on the pragmatic strain of 'getting there.' "

Yet, in spite of these similarities, the European cultural critics may seem to argue a different case and to act on different existential cues: theirs is a highly defensive position in the face of a threat which is exteriorized, perceived as coming from outside, much as in fact it was immanent to the drift of European culture. What we see occurring is a retreat toward cultural bastions in the face of an experience of a loss of power and control; it is the psychological equivalent of the defense of a national currency through protectionism. It is, so to speak, a manipulation of the terms of psychological trade. A clear example is Oswald Spengler's statement in his *Jahre der Entscheidung* (Years of Decision): "Life in America is exclusively economic in its structure and lacks depth, the more so because it lacks the element of true historical tragedy, of a fate that for centuries has deepened and informed the soul of European peoples." Huizinga made much the same point in his 1941 essay on the formlessness of history, typified by America. Yet Spengler's choice of words is more revealing. In his elevation of such cultural staples as "depth" and "soul," he typifies the perennial response to an experience of inferiority and backwardness of a society compared to its more potent rivals.

Such was the reaction, as Norbert Elias has pointed out in his magisterial study of the process of civilization in European history, on the part of an emerging German bourgeoisie vis-à-vis the pervasive influence of French civilization. Against French *civilisation* as a mere skin-deep veneer it elevated German *Kultur* as more deeply felt, warm, and authentic. It was a proclamation of emancipation through a declaration of cultural superiority. A similar stress on feeling, soul, and depth vis-à-vis the cold rationality of an overbearing foreign civilization can be seen in an essay entitled *Ariel,* written in 1900 by the Urugayan author José Ednrique Rodó. He opposed the "alma" (the soul) of the weak Spanish-American countries to the utilitarianism of the United States (although, tellingly, he at the same time admired America's democratic form of government). In his critique, once again cultural sublimation was the answer; in what would become known as the Arielista ideology, Rodó's ideas would inspire several generations of Latin-American intellectuals.

Americanism, then, is the twentieth-century equivalent of French eighteenth-century *civilisation* as perceived by those who rose up in defense against it. It serves as the negative mirror image in the quest for a national identity through cultural self-assertion. Americanism in that sense is therefore a component of the wider structure of anti-Americanism, paradoxical as this may sound.

AMERICANISM, UN-AMERICANISM, ANTI-AMERICANISM

Let us dwell briefly on the conceptual intricacies of such related terms as Americanism, un-Americanism, and anti-Americanism. Apparently, as we have seen, Americanism as a concept can stand for a body of cultural characteristics deemed repugnant. Yet the same word, in a different context, can have a highly positive meaning, denoting the central tenets of the American creed. Both, however, duly deserve their status of "isms": both are emotionally charged code words in the defense of an endangered national identity. In the United States, as "one hundred percent Americanism," it raised a demanding standard before the hordes of aliens aspiring to full membership in the American community while threatening the excommunication of those it defined as un-American. Americanism in its negative guise fulfilled much the same function in Europe, serving as a counterpoint to true Europeanism. In both senses, either positive or negative, the concept is a gate-keeping device, a rhetorical figure, rallying the initiates in rituals of self-affirmation.

Compared to these varieties of Americanism, relatively clear-cut both historically and sociologically, anti-Americanism appears as a strangely ambiguous hybrid. It never appears to imply—as the word suggests—a rejection across the board of America, of its society, its culture, its power. Huizinga and ter Braak may have inveighed against Americanism, against an America in quotation marks, but neither can be considered a spokesman of anti-Americanism in a broad sense. Both were much too subtle minds for that, in constant awareness of contrary evidence and redeeming features, much too open and inquiring about the real America, as a historical entity, to give up the mental reserve of the quotation mark. After all, ter Braak's closing lines are: " 'America' I reject. Now we can turn to the problem of America." And the Huizinga quotation above, already full of ambivalence, continues thus: "And yet in this case it must be we who are the Pharisees, for theirs is the love and the confidence. Things must be different than we think."

Now where does that leave us? Both authors were against an Americanism as they negatively constructed it. Yet it does not meaningfully make their position one of anti-Americanism. There was simply too much intellectual puzzlement and, particularly in Huizinga's case, too much admiration and real affection, too much appreciation of an Americanism that had inspired American history. Anti-Americanism, then, if we choose to retain the term at all, should be seen as a weak and ambivalent complex of anti-feelings. It only applies selectively, never extending to a total rejection of both Americanisms. Thus we can have either of two separate outcomes: an anti-Americanism rejecting cultural trends which are seen as typically American, while allowing of admiration for America's energy, innovation, prowess, and optimism, or an anti-Americanism in reverse, rejecting an American creed that for all its missionary zeal is perceived as imperialist and oppressive, while admiring American culture, from its high-brow to its pop varieties. These opposed directions in the critical thrust of anti-Americanism often go hand in hand with opposed positions on the political spectrum. The cultural anti-Americanism of the interwar years typically was a conservative position, whereas the political anti-Americanism of the Cold War and the war in Vietnam typically occurred on the left wing. Undoubtedly the drastic change in America's position on the world stage since World War II has contributed to this double somersault. Ever since this war America has appeared in a radically different guise, as a much more potent force in everyday life in Europe than ever before. This leads us to explore one further nexus among the various concepts.

The late 1940s and 1950s may have been a honeymoon in the Atlantic relationship, yet throughout the period there were groups on the left loath to adopt the unfolding Cold War view of the world; they were the nostalgics of the anti-Nazi war alliance with the Soviet Union, a motley array of fellow travelers, third roaders, Christian pacifists, and others. Their early critical stance toward the United States showed up yet another ambivalent breed of anti-Americanism. In their relative political isolation domestically, they tended to identify with precisely those who in America were being victimized as un-American in the emerging Cold War hysteria of loyalty programs, House Un-American Activities Committee (HUAC) inquiries, and MacCarthyite persecution. In their anti-Americanism they were the ones to rally to the support of Alger Hiss and of Ethel and Julius Rosenberg. Affiliating with dissenters in America, their anti-Americanism combined with un-Americanism in the United States to form a sort of shadow Atlantic partnership. It is a combination that would again occur in the late sixties when the political anti-Americanism in Europe, occasioned by the Vietnam War, felt in unison with a

Anti-Vietnam War Demonstration. French communists demonstrate against American involvement in Vietnam, 1969. ©HULTON-DEUTSCH COLLECTION/CORBIS

generation in the United States engaged in antiwar protest and the counterculture of the time, burning American flags along with their draft cards as demonstrations of their un-Americanism. As bumper stickers at the time reminded them: America, Love It or Leave It.

The disaffection from America during the Vietnam War, the un-American activities in America, and the anti-Americanism in Europe at the time may have appeared to stand for a more lasting value shift on both sides of the Atlantic. The alienation and disaffection of this emerging adversary culture proved much more short-lived in America, however, than it did in Europe. The vigorous return to traditional concerns in America since the end of the Vietnam War never occurred in any comparable form in countries in Europe. There indeed the disaffection from America had become part of a much more general disaffection from the complexities and contradictions of modern society. A psychological disengagement had occurred that no single event, such as the end of the Vietnam War, was able to undo. The squatters' movement in countries such as Germany, Denmark, or the Netherlands, the ecological (or Green) movement, the pacifist movement (particularly in the 1980s during the cruise missile debate), had all become the safe havens of a dissenting culture, highly apocalyptic in its view of the threat that technological society posed to the survival of mankind. And despite the number and variety of anti-feelings of these adversary groups, America to each and all of them could once again serve as a symbolic focus. Thus, in this more recent stage, it appears that anti-Americanism can not only be too broad a concept, as pointed out before—a configuration of anti-feelings that never extends to all things American—it can also be too narrow, in that the "America" which one now rejects is really a code

word, a symbol, for a much wider rejection of contemporary society and culture. The more diffuse and anomic these feelings are, the more readily they seem to find a cause to blame. Whether or not America is involved in an objectionable event—and given its position in the world it often is—there is always a nearby MacDonald's to bear the brunt of anger and protest, and to have its windows smashed. If this is anti-Americanism, it is of a highly inarticulate, if not irrational, kind.

The oscillations and changes in focus of anti-Americanism have social as well as political dimensions, though the social history has yet to be fully explored. Most commentary between the wars was not only conservative but elitist. It was not clear that the attacks on American cultural and commercial influence resonated with ordinary people. But the discussion could have social effects, as in debates over whether French retail shops should imitate American "dime stores" or have a more distinctively French devotion to style over mass marketing. Political attacks on American diplomacy in the Cold War enlisted large working-class followings, but the older cultural criticisms persisted as well, often (particularly in France and communist countries) with some government backing against American commercial inroads.

GLOBALIZATION, AMERICANIZATION, AND ANTI-AMERICANISM

As American culture spreads around the world, American emblems, from Marlboro Country ads to MacDonald's franchises, tend to be found more places. They testify to Americanization while at the same time providing the targets for protest and resistance against Americanization. Many are the explanations of the worldwide dissemination of American mass culture. There are those who see it as a case of cultural imperialism, as a consequence of America's worldwide projection of political, economic, and military power. Others, broadly within the same critical frame of mind, see it as a tool rather than a consequence of this imperial expansion. Behind the globalization of American culture they see an orchestrating hand, whetting foreign appetites for the pleasures of a culture of consumption. Undeniably, though, part of the explanation of the worldwide appeal of American mass culture will have to be sought in its intrinsic qualities, in its blend of democratic and commercial vigor. In individual cases the particular mix of these two elements may differ. At one extreme the commercial component may be well-nigh absent, as in the worldwide dissemination of jazz and blues music. At the other extreme the commercial rationale may be the central carrying force, as in American advertisements. While trying to make a sales pitch for particular products, advertising envelops these in cultural messages that draw on repertoires of American myths and symbols that find recognition across the globe.

In a series of posters made by a Dutch advertising agency solely for the Dutch market, a particular brand of cigarette produced by a large Anglo-American tobacco company is being promoted. The posters combine visual and linguistic messages without apparent coherence, each a disjoint marker of larger semiotic repertoires. The only direct reference to the product being advertised is the picture of a packet of cigarettes, its flip-top open, with two cigarettes protruding as if offered to the viewer. Otherwise, there are no signs of a hard sell in the classic manner, no references to taste, to tar content, or other qualities of the product. The jumble of other messages on the poster all serve to illustrate its central slogan: "There are no borders." Remarkably, although the market addressed is Dutch, the slogan is in English, as if to illustrate its message of internationalism. That message, apparently, is the subtext of the entire poster. It is meant to evoke a world culture of leisure and pleasure, mentioning the names of places and hotels where the jet set congregates, and graphically showing the sensual pleasures they indulge in.

Yet this is only one way to read the slogan. It does evoke a global culture of consumption, assembling its attractions for the creation of an image attached to this particular brand of cigarette. A second way to read the message is in terms of the echoes it contains of more narrowly American dreams and images. In spite of the relative absence of patently American markers that, for example, characterize the worldwide advertising campaign for Marlboro cigarettes, the Stuyvesant posters do evoke repertoires of American images, known the world over, where "America," and more particularly the American West, symbolizes a world without borders. The established imagery of America as open space, a land that knows no limits, sets no constraints, allowing all individuals to break free and be the agents of their own destinies, has a venerable pedigree as an ingredient for the construction of commercial images.

Some of the oldest traceable examples go back to the early 1860s. Two tobacco brands, the Washoe brand and a brand called "Westward Ho," already used images of the West, in addition to more general American imagery, embodied in representations of the Goddess Columbia. We see vast stretches of open country, a pot of gold brimming over, an American eagle, a bare-breasted Columbia, loosely enveloped in an American flag, galloping forth on elk-back. Westward Ho, indeed. This is not Europa being abducted by Jupiter; this is a modern mythology of Columbia riding her American elk. At the time, clearly, an abundance of mythical markers was needed to tie Virginia tobacco to the beckoning call of the West. Today we no longer need such explicit reference to trigger our store of images concerning America as a dream and a fantasy. A simple slogan, "There are no borders," is all it takes. It is no longer the cryptic message it may seem at first glance. We know the code and have learned how to crack it.

In its dual reading, then, the Stuyvesant slogan illustrates two things. It evokes a world increasingly permeated by a culture of consumption, geared toward leisure and pleasure. At the same time it illustrates the implicit Americanness of much of this emerging global mass culture. It is a point to bear in mind when we engage in discussions concerning the globalization of culture taking place in our day and age. Too often in these debates the point seems to be missed when people try to separate the problems of an alleged Americanization of the world from the problems of the globalization of culture. A closer reading will reveal that in many cases it is a matter of American cultural codes being picked up and recycled for the production of meaningful statements elsewhere.

Students of Americanization broadly agree that semantic transformations attend the dissemination of American cultural messages across the world. Depending on their precise angle and perspective, some tend to emphasize the cultural strategies and auspices behind the transmission of American culture. Whether they study Buffalo Bill's Wild West Show when it traveled in Europe, Hollywood movies, or world's fairs, to name just a few carriers for the transmission of American culture, their focus is on the motifs and organizing views that the producers were trying to convey rather than on the analysis of what the spectators and visitors did with the messages they were exposed to. All such cultural productions taken as representations of organizing worldviews do tend to lead researchers to focus on senders rather than receivers of messages. Yet, given such a focus, it hardly ever leads these researchers to look at the process of reception as anything more than a passive imbibing. Whatever the words one uses to describe what happens at the point of reception, words such as hybridization or creolization, current views agree on a freedom of reception, a freedom to resemanticize and recontextualize meaningful messages reaching audiences across national and cultural borders. Much creativity and inventiveness go into the process of reception, much joy and exhilaration spring from it. Yet making this the

whole story would be as fallacious as a focus centered solely on the schemes and designs of the senders of messages. Whatever their precise angle, researchers agree on the need to preserve balance in their approach to problems of Americanization.

Furthermore, some researchers tend to conceive of Americanization as tied to an American economic expansionism early on and then, more recently, to an emerging global economy structured by the organizing logic of corporate capitalism, still very much proceeding under American auspices. The main area in which they see Americanization at work is in the commodification of culture that colonizes the leisure time of people worldwide. World's fairs and other transmitters of America's commercial culture conjure up a veritable "dream world" of mass consumption, a simulation through spectacle of the good life afforded by the technological advances associated with modernization. One could go on to contrast this simulacrum of the good life with the ravages wrought by corporate capitalism in many parts of the globe. It would be one good reason to keep the concept of Americanization in our critical lexicon as a useful reminder of what American economic expansionism has meant in terms of advancing the interests of American corporate culture overseas.

It is important to note also that the American influence in many ways continues to expand. This is true in consumer culture, as witness the success of Euro-Disney (near Paris) in the 1990s after some initial resistance and necessary adjustments to the preferences of European visitors. It is also true in terms of business practices, where, again in the 1990s, consulting firms of American origin, American management texts translated from English and specific American fads such as Total Quality Management gained unprecedented attention and prestige.

Yet others take a different tack. They would argue that one should not look at the autonomous rise of global corporate capitalism as due to American agency. It is a common fallacy in much of the critique of Americanization to blame America for trends and developments that would have occurred anyway, even in the absence of America. From Karl Marx, via John Hobson and V. I. Lenin, all the way to the work of the Frankfurt School, a long line of critical analysis of capitalism and imperialism highlights their inner expansionist logic. Surely, in the twentieth century, much of this expansion proceeded under American auspices, receiving an American imprint, in much the same way that a century ago, the imprint was British. The imprint has often confused critics into arguing that the havoc wreaked by an overarching process of modernization, ranging from the impact of capitalism to pro-

Euro-Disney. Fifth anniversary celebration of the opening of the amusement park (later renamed Disneyland Paris), 1997. REUTERS/ARCHIVE PHOTOS

cesses of democratization of the political arena, was truly the dismal effect of America upon their various countries. From this perspective the critique of Americanization is too broad, exaggerating America's role in areas where in fact it was caught up in historic transformations much like other countries were.

From a different perspective, though, this view of Americanization is too narrow. It ignores those vast areas where America, as a construct, an image, a phantasma, did play a role in the intellectual and cultural life of people outside its national borders. There is a repertoire of fantasies about America that even predates its discovery. Ever since, the repertoire has been fed in numerous ways, through many media of transmission. Americans and non-Americans have all contributed to this collective endeavor, making sense of the new country and its evolving culture. Especially in the twentieth century America became ever more present in the minds of non-Americans, as a point of reference, a yardstick, a counterpoint. In intellectual reflections on the course and destiny of non-American countries and cultures, America became part of a process of triangulation, serving as a model for rejection or emulation, providing views of a future seen in either a negative or a positive light. America has become a *tertium comparationis* in culture wars elsewhere, centering on control of the discourse concerning the national identity and the national culture. When America was rejected by one party in such contests, the other party saw it as a liberating alternative. Writing the history of such receptions of America is as much American studies as it is an endeavor in the intellectual history of countries other than the United States. It also should form part of a larger reflection upon processes summarily described as Americanization.

Undeniably, though, in the course of the allegedly "American Century" America assumed a centrality that one might rightly call imperial. Like Rome in the days of the Roman Empire, it has become the center of webs of control and communication that span the world. Its cultural products reach the far corners of the world, communicating American ways and views to people elsewhere, while America itself remains relatively unaware of cultural products originating outside its national borders. If for such reasons we might call America's reach imperial, it is so in a number of ways. It is imperial in the economic sphere, in the political sphere, and in the cultural sphere. If it is still possible to use the word in a relatively neutral way, describing a factual configuration rather than the outcome of concerted effort and motive, we might speak of an American imperialism, of its economic imperialism, political imperialism, and cultural imperialism. Trying to accommodate themselves to their diminished role and place in the world, European countries have at times opted to resist particular forms of America's imperial presence. Thus, in the most telling case, France chose to resist political imperialism by ordering NATO out of the country, it warned against America's economic imperialism through Jean Jacques Servan-Schreiber's *Le défi américain,* (which nonetheless urged imitation of management styles), and it briefly considered preventing *Jurassic Park* from being released in France, seeing it as a case of American cultural imperialism and a threat to the French cultural identity.

Yet, suggestive as the terms are of neat partition and distinction, the three forms of imperialism do in fact overlap to a large extent. Thus America, in its role as the new political hegemon in the Western world, could restructure markets and patterns of trade through the Marshall Plan, which guaranteed access to the European markets for American products. Political imperialism could thus promote economic imperialism. Opening European markets for American commerce also meant preserving access for American cultural exports, such as Hollywood movies. Economic imperialism thus translated into cul-

tural imperialism. Conversely, as carriers of an American version of the "good life," American products, from cars to movies, from clothing styles to kitchen apparel, all actively doubled as agents of American cultural diplomacy. Thus trade translated back into political imperialism and so on, in endless feedback loops.

Many observers in recent years have chosen to focus on the cultural dimension in all these various forms of an American imperial presence. American culture, seen as a configuration of ways and means that Americans use for expressing their collective sense of themselves—their Americanness—is mediated through every form of American presence abroad. From the high rhetoric of its political ideals to the golden glow of McDonald's arches, from Bruce Springsteen to the Marlboro Man, American culture washes across the globe. It does so mostly in disentangled bits and pieces, for others to recognize, pick up, and rearrange into a setting expressive of their own individual identities, or identities they share with peer groups. Thus teenagers may have adorned their bedrooms with the iconic faces of Hollywood or rock music stars in order to provide themselves with a most private place for reverie and games of identification, but they have also been engaged in a construction of private worlds that they share with countless others. In the process they recontextualize and resemanticize American culture to make it function within expressive settings entirely of their own making.

W. T. Stead, an early British observer of Americanization, saw it as "the trend of the twentieth century." He saw Americanization mostly as the worldwide dissemination of material goods, as so many signs of an American technical and entrepreneurial prowess. It would be for later observers to look at these consumer goods as cultural signifiers as well, as carriers of an American way of life. An early example of an observer of the American scene with precisely this ability to read cultural significance into the products of a technical civilization was Johan Huizinga. In his collection of travel observations, published after his only trip to the United States in 1926, he showed an uncanny awareness of the recycling of the American dream into strategies of commercial persuasion, linking a fictitious world of self-fulfillment—a world where every dream would come true—to goods sold in the market. High-minded aesthete though he was, forever longing for the lost world of late-medieval Europe, he could walk the streets of the great American cities with an open eye for the doubling of American reality into a seductive simulacrum. He was inquisitive enough to ask the right questions, questions that still echo in current research concerning the reception of mass culture in general and of commercial exhortations in particular. He wondered what the effect would be on everyday people of the constant barrage of commercial constructions of the good life. "The public constantly sees a model of refinement far beyond their purse, ken and heart. Does it imitate this? Does it adapt itself to this?" Apposite questions indeed. Huizinga was aware of the problem of reception of the virtual worlds constantly spewed forth by a relentless commercial mass culture. More generally, in these musings, Huizinga touched on the problem of the effect that media of cultural transmission, like film and advertising, would have on audiences not just in America but elsewhere as well. In these more general terms, the problem then becomes one of the ways in which non-American audiences would read the fantasy worlds that an American imagination had produced and that showed all the characteristics of an American way with culture so vehemently indicted by European critics.

See also other articles in this section.

BIBLIOGRAPHY

Barber, Benjamin, R. *Jihad vs McWorld.* New York, 1995.

Braak, Menno ter. "Waarom ik 'Amerika' afwijs." In *Verzameld Werk.* Amsterdam, 1949–51. Pages 255–265.

Cowan, Paul. *The Making of an Un-American: A Dialogue with Experience.* New York, 1970.

Friedman, Thomas. *The Lexus and the Olive Tree.* New York, 1999.

Herman, Edward S. *The Global Media: The New Missionaries of Corporate Capitalism.* London and Washington, D.C., 1997.

Hollander, Paul. *Anti-Americanism: Critiques at Home and Abroad, 1965–1990.* New York, 1992.

Huizinga, J. *Amerika levend en denkend: Losse opmerkingen.* Haarlem, The Netherlands, 1926.

Joseph, Franz M. *As Others See Us: The United States Through Foreign Eyes.* Princeton, N.J., 1959.

Kroes, Rob, and Maarten van Rossem, eds. *Anti-Americanism in Europe.* Amsterdam, 1986.

Kroes, Rob. *If You've Seen One, You've Seen the Mall: Europeans and American Mass Culture.* Urbana, Ill., 1996.

Kroes, Rob. *Them and Us: Questions of Citizenship in a Globalizing World.* Urbana, Ill., 2000.

Kuisel, Richard. *Seducing the French: The Dilemma of Americanization.* Berkeley and Los Angeles, 1993.

Lacorne, Denis, Jacques Rupnik, and Marie-France Toinet, eds. *L'Amérique dans les têtes: Un siècle de fascinations et d'aversions.* Paris, 1986.

Lutz, Friedrich A., ed. *Amerika-Europa: Freund und Rivale.* Stuttgart, Germany, 1970.

Visson, André. *As Others See Us.* Garden City, N.Y., 1948.

Maase, Kaspar. *BRAVO Amerika: Erkundungen zur Jugendkultur der Bundev republik in denfünfziger Jahren.* Hamburg, 1992.

Maltby, Richard, ed. *Passing Parade: A History of Popular Culture in the Twentieth Century.* Oxford and New York, 1989.

Morgan, Thomas B. *The Anti-Americans.* London, 1967.

Mumford, Lewis. "The Metropolitan Milieu." In *America and Alfred Stieglitz: A Collective Portrait*. Edited by Waldo Frank et al. Millerton, N.Y. 1979.

Pells, Richard. *Not Like Us: How Europeans Have Loved, Hated, and Transformed American Culture Since World War II*. New York, 1997.

Spengler, Oswald. *Jahre der Entscheidung*. Munich, 1933.

Stead, W. T. *The Americanization of the World; or, the Trend of the Twentieth Century*. New York, 1902.

Tomlinson, John. *Cultural Imperialism: A Critical Introduction*. London, 1991.

Wagnleitner, Reinhold. *Cocacolonization and the Cold War: The Cultural Mission of the United States in Austria after the Second World War*. Translated by Diana M. Wolf. Chapel Hill, N.C., 1994.

Wagnleitner, Reinhold, and Elaine Tyler May, eds. *Here, There, and Everywhere: The Foreign Politics of American Popular Culture*. Hanover, N.H., 2000.

Watson, James L., ed. *Golden Arches East: McDonald's in East Asia*. Stanford, Calif., 1997.

IMMIGRANTS

Panikos Panayi

The movement of people to Europe from beyond its shores does not represent a new phenomenon. Indeed, an attempt to trace the history of the peoples which now form the dominant ethnic population of individual nation-states would reveal that they all have origins outside the boundaries of the territories in which they currently live. For some nations, such as the English, who originated in north Germany, the original settlers did not have to travel far. Other groups, including the Hungarians and Finns, migrated over vast distances from their homeland in central Asia. Many of the peoples who now control European countries originally migrated one or more millennia ago.

MIGRATION TO EUROPE SINCE THE MIDDLE AGES

With the emergence of settled societies and monarchical states during the Middle Ages, migration into Europe from further east became highly problematic, as the Roma (Gypsies) discovered. Arriving in the Balkans in the thirteenth century, by the end of the sixteenth they lived throughout Europe. They faced intense hostility wherever they settled, resulting in deportation, murder, and enslavement. In contrast, the Turks, who arrived in the Balkans at about the same time as the Roma, did so as conquerors, which meant that they did not face the persecution endured by the Roma. By the sixteenth century they had settled throughout the Balkans, although not as immigrants in the contemporary understanding of the term.

From the close of the Middle Ages until the end of World War II, migration into Europe did not take place on any significant scale. This does not mean that people from beyond European shores did not settle on the continent. One of the main influxes consisted of African slaves, who differed from subsequent immigrants because the latter had some degree of choice in their decision to move. Significant numbers of Africans appeared in Britain during the eighteenth century because of Britain's centrality in the slave trade, although they had assimilated by the beginning of the nineteenth.

Imperial expansion after 1800, especially involving Britain and France, brought non-Europeans to these two states. In the case of Britain the numbers remained small, so that it is unlikely that the total of ethnic Chinese, Africans, Afro-Caribbeans, and Indians ever exceeded 20,000 before World War II. In contrast, by 1931 102,000 North Africans were living in France, which had a higher proportion of aliens within its population than any other nation in the world. The vast majority of the immigrants in France consisted of other Europeans, pointing to the dramatic increase of migration within the continent during the nineteenth century, as a result of industrialization and population growth.

More immigrants have made their way to Europe since the end of the World War II than all previous immigrants since about 1500, due to a combination of reasons which have transformed modern Europe and its relationship with the rest of the world. Demographic factors have played a central role in this development. Population growth beyond Europe's shores has created pressure on shrinking land resources, resulting in rural and urban unemployment. For instance, Turkey, one of the main sources of labor supply for western Europe from the late 1950s, sending over 2 million workers abroad, has had one of the highest birthrates in the world since 1945, peaking at forty-four per thousand in 1960. In 1972 the country had a population of 36,500,000, which had increased to 55,000,000 by the end of the 1980s, when it was growing by 1 million a year. Economic development did not keep pace with the population explosion, which meant that the country may have counted 5 million unemployed by the early 1970s.

Overpopulation and underemployment beyond Europe has combined with the continuing economic growth of the continent, creating a demand for foreign labor for much of the postwar period. Most states made use of workers from their immediate periphery: for instance, over a million Irish people moved to Brit-

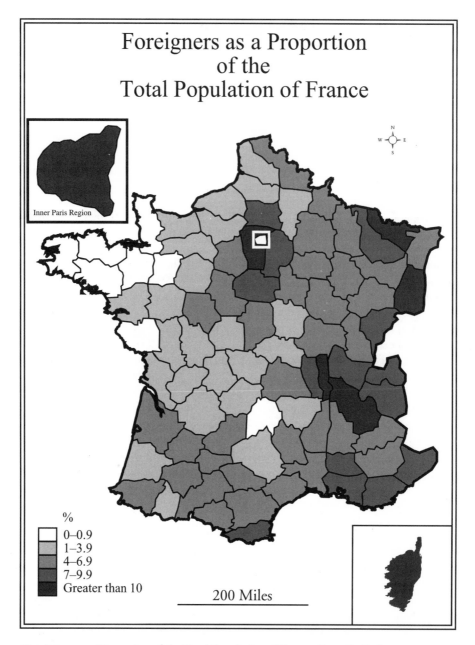

Foreigners as a Proportion of the Total Population of France

%
0–0.9
1–3.9
4–6.9
7–9.9
Greater than 10

200 Miles

Inner Paris Region

Foreigners as a Proportion of the Total Population of France. From P. Ogden, "International Migration in the Nineteenth and Twentieth Centuries" in *Migration in Modern France,* edited by P. Ogden and P. White (London: Unwin Hyman, 1989).

ain, while the main origins of newcomers to France have included Spain, Portugal, and Italy. But as these southern European states became wealthier, they needed to retain their own labor power, which necessitated the search for workers from beyond European borders. Colonial states such as France, Britain, and the Netherlands simply allowed the entry of people from the areas of the world which they currently on formerly controlled, which generally had much lower living standards. In 1967 the per capita gross national product was 125 dollars in Pakistan, 250 dollars in Jamaica, but 1,977 dollars in the United Kingdom. Those countries which did not have foreign possessions had to turn to other sources of labor. The Federal Republic of Germany, for instance, tapped the exploding Turkish population. By the middle of the 1970s, western Europe had stopped the relatively free admission of people from overseas. This has meant that Africans and Asians in particular started making their way to the Mediterranean. While those who moved to western Europe during the 1950s and 1960s generally did so with the full knowledge of the states to which they moved, a large percentage of immigrants to southern Europe have entered states such as Greece, Spain, Italy, Portugal, and Cyprus illegally, without the knowledge of the government. Relatively little immigration took place into the Soviet bloc before 1989, although East Germany did import people from other Soviet-backed regimes both within and beyond Europe, the latter including Vietnam, Cuba, and Mozambique.

Technology, more specifically its application to transport, has also made population movement easier. Before the advent of canals, modern road-building technology, railways, and steamships, movement of people over any sort of distance proved a hazardous process. Trains, ships, and, during the twentieth century, cars and airplanes have meant that human beings can travel over distances of all ranges extremely quickly.

Since the 1960s political factors have increasingly pushed people out of Africa, South America, Asia, and Turkey to European states, which have obligations toward refugees under the 1951 United Nations Geneva Convention. Consequently, despite increasingly tight immigration controls, people migrating from repressive regimes grew in numbers, including Kurds, Vietnamese, Iranians, Iraqis, Chileans, Afghans, Ni-

gerians, Ethiopians, and Sri Lankan Tamils. While European policymakers have increasingly tried to distinguish economic migrants from political refugees, in reality most population movements have always occurred due to some combination of economic and political reasons in the homeland.

The concept of the immigrant and immigration has increasingly become an issue in industrial Europe as state power has grown. Just as the modern nation-state controls all aspects of the lives of those who live within its borders, so it also displays concern about the people it allows to enter its borders. "Immigration" (as a formal phenomenon) only exists where states become organized and, through the use of passports and nationality and immigration laws, can admit or exclude people. Since World War II, and especially since the 1970s, European states have increasingly tried to control and, more recently, keep out people from beyond the continent, especially as the European Union allows free movement of all citizens within its territories, therefore lessening the need for workers from other parts of the world. This reflects an increasing tendency to divide Europeans from other peoples and demonstrates a racial exclusion of people with black and brown skins. Before 1945 such implicitly or explicitly racist policies had not been necessary because few Africans and Asians wanted to move to Europe.

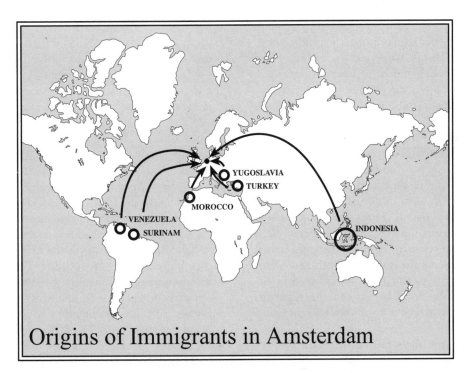

Origins of Immigrants in Amsterdam. Adapted from A. Segal, *An Atlas of International Migration* (London: Hans Zell, 1993), p. 72.

Refugees. Albanian refugees on the ship *Lirija,* sailing to Brindisi harbor in southern Italy, 7 March 1991. ©REUTERS/CORBIS

IMMIGRANTS IN EUROPEAN SOCIETY

With few exceptions, immigrants who have made their way to Europe since the Renaissance have remained, in the short run at least, distinct from the dominant populations. While their physical difference has played a large role in this process, their place in European society has also confirmed their differences. Newcomers to Europe have, initially at least, lived separately from the dominant populations, usually in worse accommodations, carrying out jobs which members of the dominant ethnic groupings shun, especially after 1945.

Immigrants in any European society have usually become ghettoized, largely because of their occupational patterns but also because of the hostility of members of the dominant society toward them. The Chinese community in nineteenth-century Britain, which evolved mainly from sailors, concentrated in London, Liverpool, and Cardiff. Similarly, black people, who also consisted largely of seamen, settled in Cardiff, Liverpool, Bristol, and North and South Shields. These groups remained concentrated in enclaves within these locations, as did the Algerians who settled in French cities from the late nineteenth century.

Such patterns intensified further in the postwar period. In the case of some states, including both West and East Germany, the housing policies of employers and the state made concentration inevitable. In both of these countries, many immigrants from all parts of the world found themselves initially accommodated in company barracks, in mostly all-male surroundings, with virtually no space or privacy. In France the lack of housing meant that shantytowns (*bidonvilles*) sprang up on the outskirts of many cities. One official inquiry from 1966 counted 225 of these concentrations of foreign workers, 119 of them in Paris. Altogether they housed seventy-five thousand people. In the British case immigrants from the West Indies and the Indian subcontinent initially found accommodation in some of the worst inner-city areas, but many have subsequently made their way into wealthier suburban locations. The Japanese offer an exception to the above picture of immigrants confined to the poorest parts of cities. Arriving as professionals, they have settled in wealthy parts of European cities, as the example of the Japanese in Düsseldorf indicates.

Immigrants have tended to move to urban areas. Only 8.1 percent of foreigners in France lived in rural areas in 1981, compared with the 27.3 percent of the French population living outside towns. Immigrants often gravitate to capital cities. In 1982 Paris housed 39 percent of France's Tunisians, 37 percent of its Algerians, and 28 percent of its Moroccans. North Africans have also moved to many of the other large French cities, including Marseille, where they made up 6.9 percent of the population in 1982. Surinamese immigrants to Amsterdam have concentrated in two particular areas of that city. South Asian and West

Indian immigrants to Britain have focused exclusively in urban areas, especially inner London but also many of the largest cities, notably Birmingham and Manchester, together with smaller cities such as Bradford and Leicester. In the latter, Asians form over a quarter of the population.

Immigrants from beyond Europe have clearly changed the demography of many European states, both because of the number of arrivals and, in the short run at least, their higher fertility. In this sense a vast difference exists between the few individuals who made their way to Europe before 1945 and the communities who arrived subsequently. By 1995 ethnic minorities in Britain totaled 3.2 million people, or 5.7 percent of the population. Most European states have a foreign population of between 5 and 10 percent, although in many of these the bulk of the minorities consist of other Europeans.

Most people who have moved to Europe from beyond its borders have been men. This was certainly true of colonials in Britain and France before 1945. This pattern continued after 1945, especially in the early postwar decades, because labor importation involved the exploitation of people to carry out some of the most unpleasant physical tasks, which also meant that mainly young people entered European states. In the longer run these patterns changed because many men who had migrated for the purpose of earning money to send back to their families eventually decided to bring over their wives and children instead. Thus the proportion of Turkish women to men in Germany increased from 6.8 percent in 1960 to 65.8 percent by 1981. Turks in Germany have certainly had a younger age structure than natives. In 1976 Berlin contained just 211 Turks over the age of sixty-five among the total population for this minority in the city of 84,415. In the short run immigrants had much higher fertility rates than natives, although these have evened out over time. Thus, while Algerian women in France produced an average of 8.5 children during

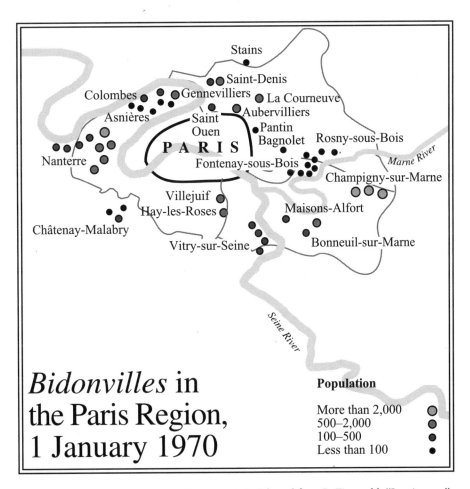

Bidonvilles in the Paris Region, 1 January 1970. Adapted from B. Fitzgerald, "Immigrants." In *France Today,* 7th ed., edited by J. E. Flower (London: Hodder and Stoughton, 1993).

North Africans in France. Immigrants arriving in Marseille, France, 1974. ©BETTMANN/
CORBIS

the early 1960s, this figure had declined to 3.2 by
1990, although this was still higher than the figure of
1.8 for French women.

The majority of immigrants into Europe since
1945 have found themselves working in manual occupations, reflecting European countries' reasons for
encouraging immigration and the racism expressed
against immigrants. Many of the West Indians who
made their way to Britain during the 1950s had qualifications of some sort, but these usually proved useless
because racism forced them into employment such as
factory work and bus driving. The same applied to
immigrants from South Asia. A similar situation has
existed in France and West Germany. In 1976 a total
of 89.2 percent of foreigners in France worked in unskilled, semiskilled, or skilled manual employment. In
the Federal Republic of Germany the majority of
Turks worked in metal and textile manufacture and
construction. Similarly, those who have immigrated
to southern Europe since the 1960s have worked in
manual occupations. In 1981, for instance, 47.6 percent of Tunisians in Italy labored in seasonal occupations connected with fishing, while 14.3 percent
were employed in agriculture. In Greece immigrants
from Egypt and the Philippines have worked in domestic service, cleaning, tourism, construction, and
harvesting.

Some changes have taken place in the employment patterns of those who moved to western Europe
in the decades directly after World War II. In the first
place, many have seen a deterioration in their position
due to the rise in unemployment caused by the oil
crisis of 1974 and subsequent increasing mechanization. Racism has also ensured that their offspring have
had more difficulties in securing employment than
natives. Thus, in 1985, while the unemployment rate
for Bangladeshi and Pakistani males between the ages
of sixteen and twenty-five in Britain stood at 39 percent in 1985, the figure for whites was 18 percent. In
1990, when the total unemployment rate in France
stood at 10.9 percent, the rate for Africans in France
stood at more than a quarter.

While most immigrants in postwar Europe have
experienced working conditions worse than those of
natives, opportunities have presented themselves for
social mobility in two areas in particular. The first of
these is sport, especially for those who have grown up
in Britain, France, and Holland. The most obvious
illustration of this is the French soccer team that won
the World Cup in 1998, which included many people
of African origins. On a more mundane level, immigrants throughout Europe have opened their own,
usually small, businesses. These often simply cater to
people of their own community, where ethnic econ-

omies develop. In addition, foreign restaurants have also taken off, including those serving Indian food in Britain, Turkish establishments in Germany, and Chinese restaurants throughout the continent.

ETHNICITY

Most non-European immigrants who have moved to the continent have differed from the more established populations in terms of their appearance, language, or religion. While these three factors naturally distinguish foreigners from natives, ethnic leaders have used them to create communities since the Second World War. Those overseas migrants who moved to the continent before 1945 would have been marked by the same differences, but small numbers, as well as a less politicized climate and the absence of omnipresent and omnipotent states, meant that ethnic minorities did not organize themselves to the same degree as their successors.

During the past five hundred years, appearance has distinguished most overseas immigrants from the more long-term populations of the European continent. In terms of skin color, those who have arrived in Europe from Asia, Africa, and the West Indies are clearly darker than Europeans. Newcomers to Europe have also worn different clothing, at least at first. Islamic women, in particular, who have moved to all western European states since World War II, have introduced their distinctive dress into these countries. Similarly, many Sikh men and women, as well as Hindus, have continued to wear their traditional clothing. Furthermore, newcomers to Europe since World War II have brought their own food with them, which also marks their difference from the dominant groups. This applies especially to Muslims with dietary restrictions, but also to groups such as vegetarian Hindus. The development of ethnic concentrations has meant that such minorities can continue their dietary practices.

Language has also played a large role in distinguishing immigrant communities from dominant groups in modern European history. A large percentage of newcomers to Europe have little or no command of the language of the state in which they settle. In the early 1970s only 7 percent of Turks in West Germany described their command of German as very good. Ten years later over 50 percent of Turks still reported speaking bad German. The percentages had changed partly because, in the intervening years, Turkish children had gone through the German education system. But because so few immigrants have command of the language of the state in which they settle, they naturally bring their own form of discourse with them, which they can use when large communities develop. This has meant the introduction of all man-

West Indians in Britain. Arrival of West Indian immigrants in Customs Hall, Southampton, England, 1951. ©HULTON-DEUTSCH/CORBIS

ner of languages into Europe since World War II. Among Asians in Britain, for instance, these have included Gujarati, Punjabi, Urdu, and Hindi.

Postwar immigrants have brought new religions to Europe, to which many of them have turned even more than before because of the trauma involved in residing in a foreign land. During the nineteenth century the few colonial sailors living in British ports had great difficulties in practicing their religion due to their numbers, the temporary nature of their stay, and the activities of local Christian missionaries interested in converting them. Since 1945 larger numbers, more permanent settlement, and greater toleration from established Christian churches have helped immigrants to establish sophisticated systems of worship.

While religions such as Hinduism and Buddhism have made their first significant appearance in Europe since 1945, the faith which has really stood out in much of western Europe for the first time is Islam. In Britain, where the first mosque opened in the southern town of Woking in 1889, the number of mosques had reached 5 in 1966 and 452 by 1990. By 1991 Britain counted 1,133,000 Muslims, including 476,000 Pakistanis, 160,000 Bangladeshis, and 134,000 Indians. These Muslims, who do not form a homogeneous group, had established their own schools, which began receiving state support in 1998. By the middle of the 1980s France contained 3 million Muslims. A total of 1.7 million Muslims lived in Germany a decade later, 75 percent of whom were Turks. Mosques began to appear during the 1950s, often in flats, although minarets have subsequently been constructed. The Netherlands counted 450,000 Muslims in 1991, mostly Turks, Moroccans, and Surinamese. The Dutch government had actually constructed the first mosque in 1953. By 1989 the Netherlands contained about three hundred mosques and prayer halls spread over about a hundred urban locations throughout the country.

Immigrants to Europe have established their own politicized ethnicities which have gone beyond the religious basis of their distinctiveness. These developments largely represent a reaction against the all-embracing nationalism in the states in which immigrants settle, to which the newcomers cannot relate. Consequently they develop their own cultures and even form their own political organizations.

Early West Indian settlers in Brixton set up associations devoted to cricket, drinking, and dancing, as well as informal groups focusing upon unlicensed drinking, gambling, and ganja smoking. The size of the Turkish community in Germany has facilitated a wide range of cultural developments. Eleven newspapers existed by the early 1990s; the oldest of these,

Hürriyet, had a circulation of 110,000, followed by *Türkiye,* with 35,000, and *Milliyet,* with 25,000. Since 1964 the German regional radio station WDR, based in Cologne, has broadcast radio programs in Turkish, which, in 1990, attracted an audience of 52 percent of Turks in the city on a daily basis. Turks also watched television programs provided for them by the regional broadcasting companies, and, with the development of satellite television, many tuned in to TRT-International, a station broadcasting from Turkey for Turks settled abroad, which made a third of its programs in Germany.

Immigrants into Europe have also become politically active. Before 1945 both African and Indian nationalists in Britain established all manner of associations. One of the most significant of these was the Pan-African Association, established in London in 1900. After 1945 some West Indians became involved in antiracist organizations. Asians established a variety of groups, according to their ethnic identification. Thus the Indian Workers Association, founded in Coventry in 1938, essentially represents a Punjabi working-class group. Meanwhile, a Supreme Council of British Muslims came into existence in 1991. North African immigrants in France have also become involved in a variety of organizations. In the first place, their homeland governments established associations for the immigrants. The Algerian state set up the Amicale des Algériens en Europe, with the aim of preventing the assimilation of those of its citizens who had gone overseas. The Moroccan government founded a group called the Amicale des Commerçants Marocains en France, with the aim of maintaining the loyalty of emigrants. More recently, a series of Islamic organizations aimed at North African immigrants have developed in France, including the National Federation of French Muslims and the Union of Islamic Organizations in France. Latin American refugees who moved to France during the course of the 1970s continued the activities which had caused their expulsion from their native lands. The political bodies which they established also had *peñas,* or social clubs, attached to them, where friends could meet and listen to music. In Germany Turkish immigrants have organized themselves across the entire political spectrum. One of the best-known organizations, formed by ethnic Kurds in Turkey, is the Kurdistan Workers Party (PKK) which may have counted up to fifty thousand members in Germany by the middle of the 1990s.

While many immigrants in Europe have turned to formal methods of political activism, others, especially younger people, have resorted to street protest, including violence, in order to make themselves heard.

This happened in Britain during the 1980s when West Indians combined with other groups to protest against inner-city poverty. In the same decade SOS-Racisme organized huge marches in France. After racist violence took off in Germany during the early 1990s and skinheads targeted the Turkish community, Turks participated in civil disobedience.

RACISM

All immigrants to Europe have faced hostility from the dominant community, although the interaction between natives and newcomers does not simply manifest itself in a negative manner. Overall the relationship largely consists of indifference, which, however, historians have difficulty in measuring. Fewer difficulties exist in documenting hostility toward immigrants, largely due to the attention which scholars have devoted to this subject. The development of European racism during the course of the nineteenth century has shaped attitudes toward non-European people. Negative views of non-European peoples had existed from the Renaissance, evidenced, for instance, by the destruction of indigenous civilizations by conquering Spaniards in Central America and the organization of the black slave trade by the British. Such hostility became ideologically racist from the middle of the nineteenth century in connection with two major developments. First, the transformation of Charles Darwin's theories of evolution into social Darwinism applied his ideas of natural selection among species of animals into natural selection among races of human beings, developing a hierarchy of different races. The other development which helped this process was the first major encounter of Europeans with Africa and its inhabitants as a consequence of imperial expansion, which reinforced ideas of a hierarchy of races.

Consequently, those people with darker skins who have moved to western Europe have faced a native population with preconceived opinions about them, even after the decline of overt ideological racism following World War II. In Britain, for instance, nineteenth-century popular literature presented negative stereotypes of Chinese, African, and Asian people. More seriously, anti-Chinese violence broke out in south Wales in 1911, while riots against black people occurred in nine locations at the end of World War I.

Since 1945 immigrants from beyond Europe have faced hostility in virtually all of the states in which they have settled. Responsibility for this situation lies largely with the nationalistic, xenophobic, and racist ideologies which continue to exist in European states. While overt racism has become unfashionable since the Nazi period, the actions of European nation-states toward immigrants and their offspring point to the centrality of an exclusionary ideology toward foreigners. Indeed, the very concept of a nation-state, with borders delimiting a "nation" as well as a "state," reinforces the will and ability of those within the boundaries to keep people out. As the twentieth century progressed, immigration laws became increasingly racialized, with the aim of excluding groups from the developing world. Nationality laws supported immigration controls, especially in states such as Switzerland and Germany, where people inherited their citizenship, which meant that individuals born of foreign parents on Swiss or German soil remained outsiders.

Throughout western Europe, immigrants have also been victimized by the police and judiciary. In Britain these issues reached the national stage in the early 1980s following the inner-city riots, while the murder of the black teenager Stephen Lawrence also brought the issue to the fore in the following decade. In Denmark during the late 1980s and early 1990s many blacks in Copenhagen were warned to stay away from public places because of a suspicion, common throughout western Europe, that they were involved in drug smuggling. In Germany during the 1990s some police officers participated in acts of violence against minorities already facing attack from the population as a whole. Similarly, in France police officers have mistreated people whom they perceived as foreign. In fact, one of the worst instances of racism toward non-European immigrants occurred in 1961, when, in the context of the Algerian War of Independence, the Paris police murdered at least two hundred Algerians protesting against the implementation of a curfew against them.

Not surprisingly, European natives have followed the lead of their governments, especially as a racist press has also legitimized their actions. During the late 1950s and early 1960s newspapers in Britain regularly carried stories claiming that too many immigrants from Asia and the Caribbean had entered the country. In these decades immigrants faced regular hostility in their search for employment and accommodation. This hostility continues to exist in Britain and elsewhere.

The development of extreme right-wing political parties throughout Europe has given further credibility to racist attitudes. One of the most enduring of these groups is the Front National, a seemingly permanent fixture on the French political spectrum during the last two decades of the twentieth century. Its central aim consisted of keeping France free from foreign, especially African, influences. Similarly, the most successful of the German postwar racist groups, the National Democratic Party and the Republikaner,

Pro-Immigrant Demonstration. Protest against bill restricting immigration to Britain, London, 21 March 1971 ©BETTMANN/CORBIS

devoted much attention to Turks. In 2000 the anti-immigrant Freiheitliche Partei Österreichs (Freedom Party of Austria) became part of a coalition government in Austria, a development that provoked concern and protest within Austria and abroad.

Racist violence has become endemic in postwar Europe. The 1958 Notting Hill riots against West Indians were the largest such incident in Britain, but since that time murders of members of ethnic minorities, taking place on a regular basis, have replaced rioting. The worst incident in France occurred in 1973, following the murder of a bus driver by a mentally disturbed Arab and resulting in death or serious injury to fifty-two people. The reunited Germany experienced an explosion of racist violence just after the new state came into existence in the early 1990s. More recently, murders of Africans have taken place in Spain and Italy.

MULTIRACIALIZATION

Immigrants and their offspring in postwar Europe have remained outsiders, whether because of social status or legal exclusion. But their position is not all negative, as most European states have made efforts to deal with overt racism, even if they continue to practice it. At the same time, immigrants have had a deep impact upon European life.

Most European states have signed the various international guarantees which protect the rights of minorities, including the United Nations-sponsored International Convention for the Elimination of All Forms of Racial Discrimination, ratified in 1965. Some states have their own antiracist legislation. Britain, for instance, introduced a series of acts during the 1960s, superseded by the Race Relations Act of 1976. Other states, such as Germany, have constitutional guarantees protecting everyone within their borders from discrimination. Such legislation does not eliminate prejudice, but it does make members of the dominant group conscious of their actions and therefore lessens animosity toward minorities.

Evidence of positive attitudes toward minorities is more difficult to trace than negative manifestations. Nevertheless, positive attitudes clearly exist. Mixed marriages represent one indication of acceptance. In Germany, for instance, 9.6 percent of marriages in 1990, 38,784 out of 414,475, involved a German and a foreigner. Similarly, while racist organizations have come into existence, so have associations to help newcomers. In Britain, for instance, virtually all of the refugee groups which entered the country during the nineteenth and twentieth centuries have received some degree of assistance from natives.

Since World War II immigrants have had a profound impact upon European life. In Britain they have transformed culinary practices, dress codes, and popular culture. At the end of the twentieth century, virtually every high street in Britain had an Indian and a Chinese restaurant. At the same time, big supermarket chains and brand labels have jumped onto the bandwagon of ethnic food. Similarly, the presence of Turkish immigrants in Germany has meant that their cuisine has become widespread throughout the country. Furthermore, European women have taken up some aspects of the dress of the immigrant minorities, although this multiracialization of clothing is largely inspired by the international fashion industry. In Britain Afro-Caribbeans, taking their lead from America, have profoundly influenced the music and club scene.

CONCLUSION

Any overall assessment of the relationship between native white Europeans and overseas immigrants would have to note that newcomers have always retained an unenviable position in comparison with more established populations. The experience of many immigrants before the twentieth century does not offer very much hope to those who entered the continent after 1945, especially if the Roma are used as an example. In other cases, such as that of black people in Britain, they have either faced assimilation or deportation. Increasing multiracialization certainly suggests growing acceptance, although the greater influence of the state means that people from beyond Europe's shores have increasingly had problems entering the continent.

Ultimately, the relationship of European states with people from outside the continent's borders remains similar whether Asians, Africans, West Indians, and South Americans reside in Europe or remain in their homeland. Part of the problem lies in the legacy of imperialism—the underdevelopment and exploitation of many areas of the globe that had been controlled by Europeans. Once the colonial states left, many of the areas they ruled faced almost insurmountable political and economic problems. At the same time the racist mentality and ideology of imperialism has continued to affect the states and peoples of Europe and determines their attitudes toward foreigners moving to the Continent. The exclusion of black and brown people from European shores simply reflects the desire of European states to fix world markets in their own favor by controlling the world's resources. Allowing such people into Europe would, in the eyes of European policymakers, threaten the well-being of their own citizens.

How long this policy of exclusion will continue seems questionable for two reasons in particular. First,

Violence against Immigrants. Burned home of Turkish immigrants in Solingen, Germany, 2 June 1993. ©Peter Turnley/Corbis

the continuing poverty of much of Africa and Asia compared with Europe makes the continent attractive as a destination for immigrants. In 1990 the developed world had a per capita gross national product twenty-four times greater than that of poor countries. Unequal birthrates also make future migration likely. On the one hand the faster growth of non-European peoples creates land pressure and consequent unemployment and poverty in the countries in which they originate. At the same time the increasingly aging and infertile population of Europe will need people to work and care for them, which, however, means that foreigners will continue to move to the Continent as a disadvantaged manual work minority. In this sense the unequal relationship between Europe and the rest of the world will continue.

See also **Migration** *(volume 2);* **Labor Markets** *(volume 4); and other articles in this section.*

BIBLIOGRAPHY

Books

Castles, Stephen, with Heather Booth and Tina Wallace. *Here for Good: Western Europe's New Ethnic Minorities.* London, 1987.

Castles, Stephen, and Godula Kosack. *Immigrant Workers and Class Structure in Western Europe.* 2d ed. London, 1985.

Fryer, Peter. *Staying Power: The History of Black People in Britain.* London, 1984.

Hargreaves, Alec G. *Immigration, 'Race,' and Ethnicity in Contemporary France.* London, 1995.

Herbert, Ulrich. *A History of Foreign Labour in Germany, 1880–1980: Seasonal Workers, Forced Laborers, Guest Workers.* Translated by William Templer. Ann Arbor, Mich., 1990.

Holmes, Colin. *John Bull's Island: Immigration and British Society, 1871–1971.* Basingstoke, U.K., 1988.

MacMaster, Neil. *Colonial Migrants and Racism: Algerians in France, 1900–62.* London, 1997.

Nielsen, Jürgen S. *Muslims in Western Europe.* 2d ed. Edinburgh, 1995.

Panayi, Panikos. *An Ethnic History of Europe since 1945: Nations, States, and Minorities.* London, 2000.

Panayi, Panikos. *Outsiders: A History of European Minorities.* London, 1999.

Ramdin, Ron. *The Making of the Black Working Class in Britain.* Aldershot, U.K., 1987.

Shaikh, Farzana. *Islam and Islamic Groups: A Worldwide Reference Guide.* Harlow, U.K., 1992.

Solomos, John. *Race and Racism in Britain.* 2d ed. London. 1993.

Visram, Rozina. *Ayahs, Lascars and Princes: Indians in Britain, 1700–1947.* London, 1986.

Walvin, James. *Black and White: The Negro and English Society, 1555–1945.* London, 1973.

Edited Collections

Abadan-Unat, Nermin, ed. *Turkish Workers in Europe, 1960–1975: A Socio-Economic Reappraisal.* Leiden, Netherlands, 1976.

Cross, Malcolm, and Hans Entzinger, eds. *Lost Illusions: Caribbean Minorities in Britain and the Netherlands.* London, 1988.

Brock, Colin, ed. *The Caribbean in Europe: Aspects of West Indian Experiences in Britain, France, and the Netherlands.* London, 1986.

Gerholm, Tomas, and Yngve Georg Lithman, eds. *The New Islamic Presence in Western Europe.* London, 1988.

King, Russell, and Richard Black, eds. *Southern Europe and the New Immigration.* Brighton, U.K., 1997.

Ogden, Philip E., and Paul E. White, eds. *Migrants in Modern France.* London, 1989.

Wrench, John, and John Solomos, eds. *Racism and Migration in Western Europe.* Oxford, 1993.

Articles

McDonald, J. R. "Labour Immigration in France, 1946–1965." *Annals of the Association of American Geographers* 59 (1969): 116–134.

RACISM

Gisela Kaplan

Racism is a specific form of discrimination within civil society. Such discrimination, although it still occurred, was outlawed in Western societies in the twentieth century, signaling that no one should be disadvantaged on grounds of cultural background or skin color. Modern racism evolved in the Renaissance amid claims that some specific peoples were worth less than others. Europeans cultivated the art of supremacy and, in the process, looked upon most other cultures and their people as "inferior."

Although racism in one form or another may have existed as long as recorded human history, accurate accounts of it have not always survived. Another term may have been used for what came to be called racism. Moreover acts of racism or racist attitudes were often not in themselves historical events. Social history and the history of ideas reveal whether actions were "racist" according to twentieth-century criteria. For instance, slavery of modern times was a strong manifestation of racism because slavery was tied to skin color and origin, but this was not always so. Greeks and Romans knew slavery as an integral part of their societies, based on class and property but not on racial differences. A conquered people could become slaves in the spoils of war, as the Greeks became slaves of the Romans, or members of the lower classes were slaves. In Rome slavery was also one of the severe forms of punishment, along with exile and banishment, and as part of the criminal code it was used against Roman citizens. That changed in the Renaissance. This article outlines some of the chief moments in the evolution of racism and how it was politically, culturally, and socially founded.

SLAVERY AND THE DEVELOPMENT OF MODERN RACISM

The arrival in the Americas of Christopher Columbus in 1492 inaugurated "the age of discovery." The Renaissance was as much a discovery of classic Greece and Rome as it was of new lands and oceans. One might ask why the flurry of voyages and exploration occurred at that time. An obvious reason for travel beyond the charted world was the fall of Constantinople in 1453. The Turks wrested Constantinople, once the seat of the Christian emperors of the East, from Christians, and this symbolized Islam's challenge to Christian Europe. The Ottoman Empire, already vast in size, was acquiring more territory on European soil, in the Balkans and even some Italian territories. By doing so the Turks suddenly cut off the well-established land trade routes to the East, that is, to India and to China. The victory had a tremendous impact on how European history and world history developed subsequently. The clash of ideologies and religious beliefs led to concerted efforts by Europeans to restore their strength and renew their fight against "infidels." Accordingly, the first substantial defeat of the Turks in 1571 was heralded as a victory of "united Christendom." Within this period, between 1453 and 1571, the foundations were laid for the modern slave trade, for transatlantic commerce, and for colonialism. Within Europe events and discoveries in this period also laid the foundation for the shift in hegemony of power and money from the Mediterranean to the Atlantic coastal nations, that is, from Italy and Greece to Spain, Portugal, France, the Dutch provinces, and England.

Portugal and the Spanish empire, in particular, had a renewed purpose for expanding naval expeditions. These expeditions often had dual aims, commercial and military: to find a new route to the East by literally circumnavigating the Islamic world and to detect weaknesses in the defenses of Islam. Portugal and Spain expanded their naval activities, sailing along the West African coast, and they formed basic naval support units that became vital in the development of a transatlantic slave trade. Their quest to reach the East via the sea was a search for gold, ivory, spices, and any other valuables. The demand for slaves rose almost immediately after the discovery of the Americas and particularly after the discovery of Brazil in 1500. The Spanish and the Portuguese wanted to supply labor to the territories. Marauding the coastlines, the Portuguese started building "slave factories" at their trading posts on the west coast of Africa, bypassing Arab territories and hence pocketing vast profits. The first official slave cargo sailed to Hispaniola in 1505. The economic gains first made by the Spaniards and the Portuguese then by the Dutch, French, and English were secured at the expense of everyone else. Europeans seized upon economic opportunities with a mixture of ingenuity, exceptional recklessness, exploitation, and unofficially condoned piracy. Little or no qualitative difference existed between the Spanish extortion of the Americas and the Dutch expansion of the East Indies or South American trade. One of the tragedies of sixteenth- and seventeenth-century history is that nothing was learned from the discoveries of the Americas and the new cultures. The Europeans came as executioners and looters and often utterly destroyed what they found.

The slave trade assumed large-scale enterprise proportions after 1650. Europe was used to serfdom and forms of slavery or indentured labor, so its involvement in the slave trade was, in some ways, a familiar extension of former practices. The new slave trade, however, captured free people and sold them in large numbers. Increasingly color and slavery were seen as one and the same. Eighteenth-century Europeans thought that blacks wore the sign of Cain, and their enslavement was therefore legitimate.

The instigation of the slave trade in conjunction with the establishment of plantations served economic and ideological interests of European nations well. For Europe these presented opportunities for untold riches, and they were fiercely contested by all Atlantic European nations. A triangle traffic developed, a trail leading from Europe to Africa and from Africa to the transatlantic plantations. A small trickle also went back to Europe with a ready supply of slaves. From the Americas produce was shipped to local European markets for high profits. In England the main slaver ports were Bristol, Liverpool, and London. In France, Nantes became important in the eighteenth century. Some slaves stayed in Europe and were at times freed after a period of servitude. France in 1571 was the first slave-trading country that forbade the presence of black slaves on its soil. This declaration was not enforced well, and by the eighteenth century France had its share of black former slaves. In 1777, just twelve years before the French Revolution, France prohibited importations of blacks in fear of "mixing blood" and teaching them wrong ideas about freedom. In England, where the number of blacks had risen to about 20,000 in London, people expressed concerns that blacks would "pollute" English society.

Economic interests focused on the growing markets for tobacco, sugar, and coffee. In the mid–seventeenth century the West Indies leaped into enormous productivity. In 1640 sugar planting was introduced to Barbados, and sugar quickly became the main crop of the entire Caribbean. The British took Jamaica from Spain and developed sugar there. By 1650 the sudden increase in demand for labor was associated with a sharp drop in sugar prices in Europe, making sugar accessible to wider sections of western European populations. As the demand for tobacco increased after 1713, so did the demand for labor. By 1700 some 1.5 million blacks had been shipped forcibly to the West Indies. By the eighteenth century the number of blacks deported to the West Indies alone had quadrupled. By 1890 Jamaica was the world's largest sugar producer with some 200,000 black slaves from Africa's shores. The same patterns were repeated in most of the Caribbean, in other Central and South American countries, and in North America. In North America slavery became an institution, setting expectations that servitude was for blacks only, was for life, and included the children of slaves. This black chattel slavery regarded black human life as mere property. Eventually, by the eighteenth century at the latest, any traces of the human status of black slaves had vanished.

British slave trade was formally abolished in 1807, but illegal activities continued for some time thereafter. In Brazil tobacco and coffee continued to draw cargoes of black slaves into the middle of the nineteenth century. By 1872 Brazil had over 5 million blacks. Slave trading diminished slowly through the second half of the nineteenth century.

MISSIONARIES, BIBLE SOCIETIES, AND THE WHITE MAN'S BURDEN

In many ways a resurgence in religious interests and missionary endeavors to Christianize cultures subscribing to pantheistic or animistic beliefs supported colonialism. In the early nineteenth century a Bible society movement formed in European countries. Between 1804 and 1815 most European countries, including Russia, Estonia, and Poland, founded their own Bible societies. Northern and central Europe expressed a new religious fervor for scripture, and German principalities, the Dutch Lowlands, and Scandinavia took the lead. Some were encouraged by pecuniary assistance from the British and the Foreign Bible Society.

From this strong, new Bible network grew another movement, the missionary movement. It is important to note that the Bible societies formed the organizational and financial basis for the new missionary movement. They collected money through charity, actively and successfully catapulting entire communities into believing that they had to donate money for missionary activities abroad, to do good works. The English Parliament had an interest in fulfilling "the mission of the Anglo-Saxon race, in spreading intelligence, freedom, and Christian faith wherever Providence gives us the dominion of the soil" (Banton, 1977, p. 26). Many missionaries, especially Protestants, worked in India, China, and Africa in the seventeenth and eighteenth centuries. But as a movement with substantial funds collected as charity by the Bible societies at home, the nineteenth-century missionary endeavors were on a different scale than earlier attempts and were propelled by a new urgency. Since African tribes were regarded as lacking any of the visible ingredients of civilization, they were considered not just savages but also children, who could not be trusted to conduct their own affairs. Hence racism was the moral underpinning of imperialism. Rudyard Kipling's 1899 poem "The White Man's Burden" captured the contemporary European sentiment.

The pioneer period of the new missionary movement, 1856–1885, was followed by European occupation of the targeted countries. The beginnings of the Bible societies followed hard on the heels of the abolition of slavery. Moreover the strong missionary period coincided with the disappearance of the last slave ships from the oceans of the world. One form of control of native populations replaced another. Slavery bled the countries dry by taking away the healthiest and youngest of the adult population. The missionary and colonial zeal undermined cultures from within, working in the countries from which the slaves were formerly drawn. The English explorer and missionary David Livingstone set in motion the missionary invasion of East Africa. His follower Henry M. Stanley argued after Livingstone's death in 1873 that "the work of England for Africa must henceforth begin in earnest," and it did. The zenith of missionary zeal coincided entirely with the zenith of colonialism and its ideological underpinning of imperialism. Colonialists found a well-prepared infrastructure when they moved in and annexed territories to their European nations. In general they perceived no conflict of interest between the activities.

COLONIALISM AND IMPERIALISM

The terms "colonialism" and "imperialism" sometimes are used interchangeably. Although they have a good deal in common, historically they are different.

Both systems rely on the colonization and exploitation of other peoples. Imperialism, however, was an integrated system, a set of beliefs far more coherent and pernicious than early colonialism ever had been. European imperialism, defined as the period between 1885 and 1918, pursued aggressive world political goals and systematically annexed other nations not just for economic gain, as colonialism always had, but to increase its power base abroad, no longer just at home. Some European countries, such as Spain, Portugal, Britain, France, and the Netherlands, began to take colonial possessions early in the sixteenth and seventeenth centuries. By the end of the nineteenth century vast territories of the world were parceled up among Europeans.

To justify the systematic, political annexation of other countries, the ground needed to be prepared in a number of ways and directions. The spoils were at once harnessed to remain in bourgeois and aristocratic hands. The flourishing bourgeoisie was more likely to side with the aristocracy than with the emerging working classes. Neither at home nor abroad could anyone who was less fortunate than they were hope for mercy. For instance, Adam Smith's economic theory of laissez-faire and Thomas Malthus's population theory of letting the poor die because they represent human surplus gave the industrialization in England and France of the early nineteenth century perfect vehicles to legitimize human misery.

Some, however, had concerns about the poor at home. The French Revolution of 1789 had taught that political systems could be toppled by beliefs in equality. An imperialist solution, advocated by men like Cecil Rhodes (1853–1902), one of the chief players in British imperialism, was to ship these wretched souls to the colonies and let them expand and multiply there. The British had a long history of doing precisely that. For example, they shipped convicts and other undesirables, such as Irish or Scottish rebels or Jewish inhabitants of England, to the far coasts of Australia almost from the moment Britain claimed ownership of that continent in 1788.

Another solution opted for biosocial explanations at home. Because, some believed, inferior status was not socially and willfully ascribed by those in power but rather was a consequence of the individuals' inherent inferiority, the poor had no recourse for complaint. Biosocial explanations were applied to the working classes, women, and the "inferior races." In those European countries where industrialization first took off, imperialism and racism took root almost immediately. In a sense racism publicly legitimized the European capitalist bourgeoisie of the nineteenth century. World War I (1914–1918) represented, in a way, the culmination of imperialism, but after its end the force of imperialism was spent.

ARYAN IDEAS AND SOCIAL DARWINISM

To hardened colonialists the perceived differences in races justified attributing lower status to some groups on the basis of skin color or culture alone. This thinking led to the rise of national racism in the waves of nationalism that swept across Europe in the second half of the nineteenth century. Among the most respected proponents of racist imperialist ideas were Joseph-Arthur de Gobineau (1816–1882) and Houston Stewart Chamberlain (1855–1927). In 1854 and 1855 Gobineau published his popular work *Essai sur l'inégalité des races humaines* (Essay on the inequality of human races), in which he used a simple and dangerous weapon. He praised the superiority of the white race, claiming that civilization had progressed only when "Aryans" had been involved, and he invoked fear. Gobineau's message took hold in France and Britain. In Germany, which had entered the race for colonial possessions late by acquiring African colonies in 1884 and a Chinese holding in 1897, his message fueled the Pan-German movement by "reawakening the Aryan Germanic soul," and it became a powerful weapon in the hands of anti-Semites. In the absence of the "yellow and black perils," Germans identified Jews as their "polluting race." Chamberlain introduced his views of race to the Nazi theoretician Alfred Rosenberg (1893–1946). In 1899 Chamberlain published a widely influential book, *The Foundations of the Nineteenth Century.* Chamberlain's and Gobineau's theories were acclaimed internationally.

Racist views gained new impetus and respectability with Darwin's theory of evolution and Herbert Spencer's interpretation of Darwin's idea of the "survival of the fittest" (1910). This new model, the so-called "scientific" model that signified the shift from theology to science, had lasting importance.

In Germany social Darwinism obtained a new twist in a new branch of eugenics. Independently of Gobineau and Chamberlain, Ernst Haeckel (1834–1919) came to the conclusion that "lower races," such as "the Vedahs or Australian Negroes," were psychologically nearer to animals, especially apes, than to civilized Europeans and "therefore [we must] assign a totally different value to their lives" (quoted in Stein, 1988, p. 55). For Haeckel the only morality lay in the process of natural selection. According to him, this "morality" of natural selection in human society required positive intervention to correct the errors humans had already brought upon themselves. Haeckel's

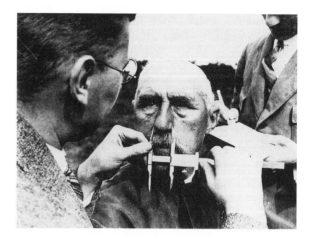

Measuring the Face. A researcher from the Anthropological Institute of the University of Kiel, Germany, measures the face of a north German villager, 1932. ULLSTEIN BILDERDIENST, BERLIN

most successful work, *The Riddle of the Universe at the Close of the Nineteenth Century* (1900), was translated into twenty-five languages and by 1933 had sold more than 1 million copies in Germany alone.

The reason for Haeckel's success lay partly in the history of black slavery and partly in Jewish emancipation. Freed black slaves had intermarried with the English and the French throughout the eighteenth and nineteenth centuries. Jewish emancipation laws in German territories after the reforms of 1813 had allowed Jews to leave ghettos and mingle with the local population. The anthropologists of the time and the Society for Racial Hygiene supported Haeckel and pronounced similar views.

Hand in hand with the idea of racial superiority came the idea of racial purity and the fear of "miscegenation" or "mixing blood." Gobineau had already warned that "blood impurities" were the beginning of the downfall of even the best race. The fear and horror of "miscegenation" made its way into popular novels and propagated racist fears and views on the lowest possible denominator. Artur Dinter (1876–1948), a German fascist writer, sold over 250,000 copies of his novel *Sins against the Blood* (1918). In the nineteenth century and early twentieth century the concept of pollution was carried to great extremes. An obsessive thought at the time of the rise of fascist ideology after World War I, it became a centerpiece of Nazi propaganda. With something to fear, the Nazis had to find solutions, even a "final" solution.

Imperialism ended, but in its stead arose in the early 1920s fascism, which lasted as a major political and ideological force until the end of World War II (1939–1945). Fascism's political program was intentionally racist, and the intellectual elite of western Europe largely supported such a program. By the 1920s supposedly respectable scholars proposed concrete programs of euthanasia, sterilization, and other methods of artificial selection to "revitalize the gene pool." In 1935 H. F. K. Günther was awarded the prestigious Prize for Science for his less than scientific work on such problems as the "racial knowledge" of the German people. In this cultural context Hitler's race laws of 1935 appeared almost as a rational consequence of the pseudoscientific racism that had influenced public opinion for decades (see the entry "Fascism and Nazism" in volume 2).

World War II was fought with an unsurpassed level of civilian involvement. Fifty million people, civilians and soldiers, were killed during the war. Among the dead were groups and individuals, including 6 million Jews, who died solely because of racist and eugenicist policies. The war also ended European hegemony over the rest of the world. Europe was weakened and Germany had to capitulate unconditionally. European countries were forced to retreat from the soil of other continents; however, they let go of overseas dominions reluctantly and gradually. Not until the close of the twentieth century had most colonies been returned to their rightful owners, and the transitions were often accompanied by prolonged wars, uprisings, and bloodshed. In the 1990s France and Great Britain still had overseas possessions they considered part of the mother country, some with various degrees of self-government. The end of imperialism (1918) and of active European colonialism (1950s–1980s) finally brought to a close a five-hundred-year trail of blood and greed that had started in 1492. The scars of colonialism and imperialism were deep and ugly, and remained into the twenty-first century, as many countries struggled to overcome the effects of imposed European foreign rule, exploitation, racism, and zealous coercion toward Christianity. Some, mostly island nations, were still under foreign rule at the start of that century.

RACISM AFTER WORLD WAR II

Globally racism was unacceptable after 1945, largely because of the Holocaust. International opinion, arguing that no person must be discriminated against on the grounds of origin and skin color, successfully prevailed in the postwar period. The fall of the apartheid regime in South Africa marked the end of a period of formal institutional racism in the capitalist world. Subsequently, explicitly racist positions were shunned by all major parties in Europe.

However, extreme right-wing groups, whether informal or politically inclined, existed in Europe after World War II despite the defeat of the Fascists, the Nazis, and the Axis pact. Most of those groups were regarded as marginal oddities in the cultural, social, and political landscape of Europe. In the 1970s the emergence and strengthening of the New Left drowned out much of the New Right and therefore obscured the existence of networks with specifically racist agendas. In the 1980s, especially late in the decade, the tide turned. The developments of the 1980s were emphasized by populism in the mainstream political arena. Margaret Thatcher of England, for instance, was one of the most powerful populist political leaders in the 1980s, and Jacques Chirac of France was regarded by some as her equivalent in the 1990s.

NEW RACISM AS ANTIPLURALIST TRENDS

Internationally the world had seen a trend toward ethnic homogeneity from the nineteenth century to the twentieth century. Peace settlements following World War I redrew boundaries in favor of homogeneity. In 1910 about 26 percent of homogeneous groups were still without self-government, that number dropped to 7 percent in 1930. After World War II the percentage of ethnic minorities without autonomy dropped to a mere 3 percent. The Holocaust had added substantially to these developments, based on the premise that, if Jews had been granted their own homeland, the Holocaust never would have happened. Because they lacked a state, Jews were the refugees of modern times. Although movement toward self-government, in support of the modern European nation-state, was considered liberating at the time, an inevitable consequence was a sustained antipluralist stance unlike the inherent pluralism of New World countries, such as the United States, Australia, and Canada. Antipluralism in turn was capable of feeding and renewing racism should "foreigners" arrive in these European nations.

In European countries before the 1960s foreigners accounted for about 1 to 2 percent or, at the most, 4 to 5 percent of the population. Most of these foreigners were recruited from neighboring European countries, for example, the Finns in Sweden, Hungarians in Austria, and Poles in East Germany. The minute remainder of foreigners was largely derived from the colonies or former colonies of individual countries, for instance, Algerians in France, Indonesians in the Netherlands, and Indians in the United Kingdom; from international students; and rarely from displaced people. The one exception was the Lapps, whose "nation" remained divided between Norway, Sweden, and Finland.

In the 1950s and 1960s, however, widespread labor shortages set into motion the most far-reaching labor recruitment program ever conceived. Some western European countries sought to fill their labor shortages with refugees from the East, but when this source dried up, they recruited "guest workers" from the southern European countries (Italy, Greece, Portugal, and Spain) and from as far afield as Turkey. They invited labor on short contracts but found that people came with their families, ready to settle rather than to disappear after the initial contract period ended. Their children learned the local language, and many grew up within the guest country, knowing very little about their countries of origin and their parents' languages and cultures. Hence one pool of foreigners was created at the host countries' own behest. Hate campaigns, especially against Turks, were directed against people that had come by invitation but had apparently overstayed their welcome.

Another pool was foreigners who asked to be admitted to the wealthy nations of Europe. These were the asylum seekers and economic and political refugees from wars or former colonies. In the 1970s people began to criticize asylum seekers and refugees, and the new racism asserted itself aggressively across western Europe on that issue. The first significant steps in the unification of Europe and the 1992 Maastricht Treaty shifted the definition of "foreigner" from neighbors, such as Italians in Germany or Spaniards in Switzerland, to those who came from outside Europe. In the early 1980s European social scientists spoke of a new racism, expressed not in terms of biology so much as in a fear of the alleged impossibility of assimilation of ethnically different groups. People from Vietnam, from black and Islamic Africa, and from Turkey were singled out as targets of racial violence. Deaths resulted from clubbings, bombings, and burnings. A politics of resentment was supplemented by a politics of fear, scapegoating asylum seekers for all the ills of national identity and national crises.

Surprisingly, especially in countries with a low per capita number of refugees, public discourse sounded as if millions had arrived. In France public agitation against immigration was run by extreme right groups outside Parliament. One particularly suggestive poster that appeared in Paris demanded a stop to immigration with the slogan *Halte à l'immigration sauvage*" (stop savage immigration). *Sauvage* translates as "uncontrolled" or "unchecked," but in this context it can also mean "savage" or "uncivilized." Both clusters of meanings set the parameters for the induction of fear, bigoted nationalism, and a supremacy discourse without necessarily claiming any affinity with racism.

Noisy antiforeigner campaigns, often constituted as nonaffiliated citizen initiatives, lobbied about the increasing threat of "overforeignization" (*Überfremdung*), a favorite term in German-speaking countries. This was a gross exaggeration. In the United Kingdom, Spain, France, Italy, and Belgium the number of asylum seekers admitted was usually less than 2 percent of the applications. The foreigner presence, including that of former guest workers, for those countries and the rest of the European Union remained solidly under 4 percent. In some capital cities clusters in excess of this collected; however, at the time of the campaigns in the 1980s and early 1990s, no European country's population was over 10 percent foreigners in any of its regions. Europe received only about 5 percent of the world's refugees. Some went to New World countries, but by far the majority of the world's refugees were accommodated in Third World countries.

Some writers distinguished three phases of postwar development of the extreme right. Phase one was a refoundation or reconstitution of fascist groups immediately after 1945. These groups changed little of the ideological package of fascism and nazism but added the denial of Jewish persecution referred to as "the lie of Auschwitz" to deny that the Holocaust ever happened. In the second phase, the late 1960s and 1970s, organizations such as the National Front in the United Kingdom (1967) and the Front National in France (1972) were founded. The equally well-known Republikaner in Germany was founded relatively late (1983).

The third phase occurred in the 1990s, when extremist organizations mushroomed in western Europe and in the former eastern bloc countries. Russia alone had over eighty such organizations by 1994. In 1994, 308 extremist organizations were documented in western Europe, and of them only a minority were political parties with electoral success. A number of small parties mustered considerable clout in local areas, such as the Italian extreme right-wing movement, the so-called Lega Lombarda, and the extreme right groups in the Scandinavian countries. Although they denied it, many extremist parties paraded their wares on a platform of racism. On the intellectual right, the words "race" and "racism" generally did not appear. The arguments were not presented as if racist notions were defining them but as if their objections to immigration, asylum seekers, and foreigners in general were all a matter of cultural difference.

LEVELS OF RACIST ACTIVITIES

It is difficult to place the epicenter of racist-inspired activities and even more difficult to describe the racist movements as political, social, or cultural. The new racism of the post–World War II era was not as politically powerful as scientific racism was. However, as some have argued, the new racism was not just a transitional epiphenomenon. One reason was that its hold in political parties emerged from a fringe in the European political landscape. Another and perhaps more important reason was that the new intellectual elite found the arguments attractive, and they opened think tanks and other cultural venues to support their interests.

A third powerful reason for the establishment and maintenance of racism was the large group of youth subcultures. Racist arguments, expressed as antipluralism, a rejection of foreigners, and a gospel of hatred, attracted widespread support among the disillusioned youth. Most of these subcultures were also simplistically masculinist, antiwoman, anti-intellectual, antigay, and antisocial. Skinheads, hooligans, and rock bands of this persuasion, such as Skrewdriver in the United Kingdom, imbibed the messages of neo-Nazi propaganda. The modern "skinheads" and "boneheads" were linked internationally via music or, more precisely, "white power rock." They had no political program and no identifiable discourse, but they created a subculture with a set of rituals and codes that, in their manifestations, were not at odds with right-wing extremism. Through these subcultures a new phenomenon evolved, apolitical street-level activists, extremely young, dangerous, brutal, and unpredictable. The social and educational profiles of the loose gangs suggested that they cut across most strata, from unemployed to university student. Although they were usually not motivated by clearly articulated ideological positions, gangs played a rather significant part in creating the overall climate.

A culture of hatred was not confined to young people. It formed a blanket across all groups, political or social, embraced any age and either sex, and spread through the entire occupational and educational spectrum. The reasons for that widespread attraction to authoritarian ideas and tacit support for violence have never been fully understood, although numerous analyses have attempted to explain the phenomena. In the early and mid-1990s the network of groups dedicated to nationalistic ideals, which were antiforeigner, racist, and almost always anti-Semitic, widened. Racism in Europe at the close of the twentieth century bore dimensions similar to that in the 1930s: based largely on color and on varying degrees of ethnicity perceived as alien to the host culture. The goal of new racism was largely exclusion rather than exploitation, as was the old racism, because of the presence of non-European cultures within the European fortress, exposing the absence of clearly defined pluralist strategies and frameworks.

CONCLUSION

Europe has had a legacy of revolutions and authoritarian traditions. Europe was among the first polities to proclaim human dignity and human rights by declaring, during the French Revolution, that all human beings were equal. Many forces before and after World War II condemned racism of any kind. In the United Kingdom a substantial dialogue on racial questions, cynically referred to as the race-relations industry, began in the 1970s. Antiracist strategists optimistically thought in the 1970s that reasoned argument and education, equitable social policies, and the creation of equal opportunities would curb racism of any shade or intensity. It did not. In Germany, millions of people marched against racist murders and bomb attacks in the so-called candle marches to indicate their outrage. This action signaled to the world but did not diminish the incidence of hate crimes and racist activities.

Although Europeans expressed genuine outrage, racism was inherent in European thinking and tradition. Europe, acting like a fortress in the world, fought back the Muslims from Spain, Turks from the Ottoman Empire, Slavs from the East, Jews from within, and in the late twentieth century asylum seekers and refugees from without. Resentment against invasion by non-Europeans was deep-seated and profound. European history has shown a remarkable zest to conquer territory outside Europe and an equally remarkable resilience and hostility to outsiders.

The historian Jacques Barzun said in his 1937 book, *Race: A Study in Modern Superstition,* that race thinking was largely a "habit." Part of the racist habit was feeling superior. The new racism in Europe structurally built on the soil of the old racisms because racism was firmly linked to national identity. Racism never vanished from the stage. As one writer put it, "At best the props have changed" (Balibar and Wallerstein, 1990, p. 262).

The symbols of oppression create a lasting irony. The skinheads, hooligans, and boneheads, shunned by most, adorned themselves with tattoos and shaved heads. In the Roman Empire slaves were dehumanized and stigmatized with tattoos on their faces and arms and with shaved heads. At the end of the twentieth century powerful symbols of oppression were worn by the bullies, the looters, and the burners. Ironically, over the two thousand years of European history, the symbols of a victim turned into symbols of force, moving from oppression to the oppressor, from slavery to an ideology of enslaving.

See also **The Jews and Anti-Semitism** *(volume 1);* **Slaves** *(volume 3);* **Anthropometry** *(volume 4).*

BIBLIOGRAPHY

Apostle, Richard A., C. Y. Glock, T. Piazza, and M. Suelzle. *The Anatomy of Racial Attitudes.* Berkeley, Calif., 1983.

Arendt, Hannah. "We Refugees." In *The Jew as Pariah: Jewish Identity and Politics in the Modern Age.* Edited by Ron H. Feldman. New York, 1978. Pages 55–66.

Balibar, Étienne, and Immanuel Wallerstein. *Rassismus und Krise.* Hamburg, Germany, 1990.

Banton, Michael. *The Idea of Race.* London, 1977.

Barkan, Elazar. *The Retreat of Scientific Racism.* Cambridge, U.K., 1992.

Cheles, Luciano, Ronnie Ferguson, and Michalina Vaughan, eds. *Neo-Fascism in Europe.* London, 1991.

Cohen, Robin. *Frontiers of Identity: The British and the Others.* London, 1994.

Chorover, Stephan L. *From Genesis to Genocide: The Meaning of Human Nature and the Power of Behavior Control.* Cambridge, Mass., 1979.

Drescher, Seymour. *Econocide: British Slavery in the Era of Abolition.* Pittsburgh, Pa., 1977.

Hainsworth, Paul, ed. *The Extreme Right in Europe and the USA.* London, 1992.

Harris, Geoffrey. *The Dark Side of Europe: The Extreme Right Today.* Edinburgh, 1990.

Hastings, Adrian. *The Church in Africa: 1450–1950.* Oxford, 1994.

Inikori, Joseph E., and Stanley L. Engerman, eds. *The Atlantic Slave Trade: Effects on Economies, Societies, and Peoples in Africa, the Americas, and Europe.* Durham, N.C., 1992.

Institute of Jewish Affairs. *Political Extremism and the Threat to Democracy in Europe.* London, 1994.

Jalali, Rita, and Seymour Martin Lipset. "Racial and Ethnic Conflicts: A Global Perspective." *Political Science Quarterly* 107, no. 4 (1992–1993): 585–606.

Kaplan, Gisela, and Lesley J. Rogers. "Race and Gender Fallacies: The Paucity of Biological Determinist Explanations of Difference." In *Challenging Racism and Sexism: Alternatives to Genetic Explanations.* Edited by Ethel Tobach and Betty Rosoff. New York, 1994. Pages 66–92.

Mosse, George L. *Toward the Final Solution: A History of European Racism.* New York, 1978.

Münch, Ursula. *Asylpolitik in der Bundesrepublik Deutschland.* Opladen, Germany, 1992.

Oliver, Roland Anthony. *The Missionary Factor in East Africa.* London, 1952.

Owen, John. *The History of the Origin and First Ten Years of the British and Foreign Bible Society.* New York, 1817.

Rich, Paul B. *Race and Empire in British Politics.* Cambridge, U.K., and New York, 1986.

Silverman, Maxim, ed. *Race, Discourse, and Power in France.* Aldershot, U.K., 1991.

Stein, G. J. "Biological Science and the Roots of Nazism." *American Scientist* (1988): 50–57.

Walvin, James. *Black Ivory: A History of British Slavery.* London, 1992.

Winks, Robin W., ed. *Slavery: A Comparative Perspective: Readings on Slavery from Ancient Times to the Present.* New York, 1972.

Young, Robert. *Modern Missions: Their Trials and Triumphs.* 2d ed. Freeport, N.Y., 1972. First published in 1882.